CONSTITUTIONAL LAW
OF CANADA

Volume 1 - 9th Edition

FEDERALISM

ABORIGINAL PEOPLES

CONSTITUTIONAL LAW
OF CANADA

Volume 1 - 9th Edition

FEDERALISM

ABORIGINAL PEOPLES

Joseph Eliot Magnet, F.R.S.C.

B.A., L.L.B., L.L.M., Ph.D.
of the Ontario Bar
Professor of Law, University of Ottawa

Juriliber

Library and Archives Canada Cataloguing in Publication

Magnet, Joseph Eliot.
 Constitutional law of Canada / Joseph Eliot Magnet. -- 9th ed.

Contents: v. 1. Federalism, Aboriginal Peoples.
ISBN 978-0-919311-60-2 (v. 1).

1. Constitutional law--Canada. 2. Constitutional law--Canada-Cases.
I. Title.

KE4218.5.M328 2007   342.71   C2007-903250-8
KF4482.A1M328 2007

*The cover picture by contemporary Canadian artist, John Abrams.
<http://www.johnabramsartist.com>.(Group Portrait /Repatriation 1982) is a detail from Canadian Trilogy (1999) series; oil on canvas, 66 X 96" collection for the National Gallery of Canada.*

Published in Edmonton, Canada
by Juriliber Limited

Printed in Canada

For Arielle Suzannah

"God has brought me laughter;
everyone who hears will laugh with me."

Gen. 21:6

"Our constitution does not copy the laws of neighboring states; we are rather a pattern to others than imitators ourselves. Its administration favours the many instead of the few; this is why it is called a democracy....we do not feel called upon to be angry with our neighbour for doing what he likes ... We cultivate refinement without extravagance and knowledge without effeminacy; wealth we employ more for use than for show, and place the real disgrace of poverty not in owning to the fact but in declining the struggle against it."

Pericles, "Funeral Oration"
Thucydides, *The Peloponnesian War*, Bk. II, ch. vi, §§ 37-40)

"A good constitution is like a good poem, both are concerned with the spirit of man."

F. R. Scott

Thank you to the friends and colleagues
who helped this book come into existence.

It is a pleasure to record how grateful I am to my friend and research assistant, Kirsten Odynski, who provided thoughtful, imaginative and energetic research for the preparation of this ninth edition, and to my friends and former research assistants, Clare Crummey, Jay Holsten, Marc Cousineau, Leslie Kelleher, Cheryl Emberly, Deborah Glendinning, Todd White, Mark Ertel, Karen Lovell, Andrew Lokan, Howard Rosenoff, Nancy Thomson, Annick Demers, Derek Bell, Barry Segal, Jula Hughes, Andrea Ormiston, Vanessa Gruben, Michael Robb, Wendy Montgomery, Heidi Rubin, and Sina Muscati, for all their help and support on previous editions of this book; to Walter Mis, Joan Mis and Deborah Lewis of Juriliber, for their hard work, encouragement, fortitude and good cheer in the daunting labours that go into a project of this size and scope.

Joseph Eliot Magnet

2007

TABLE OF CONTENTS

VOLUME I

PART I - STRUCTURE OF CANADIAN GOVERNMENT

PART II – TECHNIQUES OF FEDERALISM REVIEW

PART III – DIVISION OF LEGISLATIVE POWERS

TABLE OF CASES

TABLE OF CASES

BOOKS BY JOSEPH ELIOT MAGNET

ESSAYS ON OFFICIAL LANGUAGES (Toronto: Butterworths, 2007 forthcoming)

LITIGATING ABORIGINAL CULTURE (Edmonton: Juriliber, 2005)

LEGAL ASPECTS OF ABORIGINAL BUSINESS DEVELOPMENT (Toronto: Butterworths, 2004) (with D. Dorey)

MODERN CONSTITUTIONALISM: IDENTITY, EQUALITY AND DEMOCRACY (Toronto: Butterworths, 2004)

ABORIGINAL RIGHTS LITIGATION (Toronto: Butterworths, 2003) (with D. Dorey)

THE CANADIAN CHARTER OF RIGHTS AND FREEDOMS: REFLECTIONS ON THE CHARTER AFTER TWENTY YEARS (Toronto: Butterworths, 2003) (with G.A. Beaudoin, et. al.)

FEDERALISM FOR THE FUTURE: ESSENTIAL REFORMS (Montreal: Wilson & LaFleur, 1998) (with G.A. Beaudoin, Gordon Robertson, et. al.)

OFFICIAL LANGUAGES OF CANADA: PERSPECTIVES FROM LAW, POLICY AND THE FUTURE (Montreal: Editions Blais, 1995)

WITHHOLDING TREATMENT FROM DEFECTIVE NEWBORN CHILDREN (Montreal: Editions Blais, 1985)

IMPLEMENTING OFFICIAL BILINGUALISM IN MANITOBA: A CASE STUDY (Winnipeg: SFM, 1982)

CONSTITUTIONAL LAW OF CANADA (8th edition), Vol. I, Federalism, Aboriginal Peoples, Procedure and Remedies. (Edmonton: Juriliber, 2001), 7th edition Juriliber, 1998, 6th edition QL systems online, 1997, 5th edition Blais 1993, 4th edition Blais, 1989, 3rd edition Carswell, 1987, 2nd edition Carswell, 1985, 1st edition, Carswell, 1983

CONSTITUTIONAL LAW OF CANADA (8th edition), Vol. II, Canadian Charter of Rights and Freedom. (Edmonton: Juriliber, 2001), 7th edition Juriliber, 1998, 6th edition QL systems online, 1997, 5th edition Blais 1993, 4th edition Blais, 1989, 3rd edition Carswell, 1987, 2nd edition Carswell, 1985, 1st edition, Carswell, 1983

CONSTITUTIONAL LAW OF CANADA (9th edition), Vol. I, is available on QL Systems.

ACKNOWLEDGMENTS

This book, like others of this nature, contains extracts from published materials. The author has attempted to request permission from and to acknowledge as instructed all sources of such material. Specific reference is made here to the authors, publishers, journals and institutions that have been generous in giving their permission to reproduce earlier works in this text. If any acknowledgment has inadvertently been overlooked, the publisher will gladly undertake to rectify the omission in subsequent editions.

R. Beehler, "Waiting for the Rule of Law". Reprinted by permission of © University of Toronto Press Incorporated (www.utpjournals.com) 1988. All rights reserved.

L. Bouchard, "Why We Are Sovereigntists". Reprinted by permission of the Canadian Parliamentary Review.

Albert Breton, *Federations of the World: Distribution of Powers and Functions in Federal Systems*, pages 18-20, 1991. Reproduced courtesy of The Privy Council Office, with the permission of the Minister of Public Works and Government Services, 2007.

Comité national du oui, "To Build a Quebec Society: Our Hearts Into Work". Reprinted by permission of the Parti Québécois.

D.J. Elazar, "Federalism and the Way to Peace". Reprinted by permission of the Institute of Intergovernmental Relations, Queen's University.

T.M. Franck, *Why Federations Fail*. Reprinted by permission of New York University Press.

Herperger, *Federations of the World: Distribution of Powers and Functions in Federal Systems*, pages 18-20, 1991. Reproduced courtesy of The Privy Council Office, with permission of the Minister of Public Works and Government Services, 2007.

Indian and Northern Affairs Canada, *First Nations in Canada*. Reproduced with the permission of the Minister of Public Works and Government Services Canada, 2000.

Elizabeth F. Judge, "The Internet and the Division of Powers". Original contribution to this text.

G.V. La Forest, "Delegation of Legislative Power in Canada". Reprinted by permission of G.V. La Forest and the McGill Law Journal.

W.R. Lederman, "The Balanced Interpretation of the Federal Distribution of Legislative Powers in Canada", in W.R. Lederman, *Continuing Canadian Constitutional Dilemmas*. Reprinted by permission of L. Lederman.

W.R. Lederman, "The Concurrent Operation of Federal and Provincial Laws in Canada". Reprinted by permission of L. Lederman and the McGill Law Journal.

P. Leslie, "The Maastricht Model: A Canadian Perspective on the European Union". Reprinted by permission of the Institute of Intergovernmental Relations, Queen's University.

K.M. Lysyk, "The Canadian Charter of Rights and Freedoms: General Principles". Reprinted by permission of Patricia Lysyk.

ACKNOWLEDGMENTS

Kenneth Lysyk, "Constitutional Reform and the Introductory Clause of Section 91: Residual and Emergency Law-Making Authority". Reprinted by permission of Patricia Lysyk and the Canadian Bar Review.

John A. Macdonald, Parliamentary debates on the subject of the confederation of the British North American provinces, 3rd session, 8th Provincial Parliament of Canada - Quebec: Hunter, Rose & Co., Parliamentary Printers, 1865. pp. 29-45. Reprinted by permission of the Office of the Law Clerk and Parliamentary Counsel, House of Commons.

J. Magnet, "The Constitutional Distribution of Taxation Powers in Canada". Reprinted by permission of the Ottawa Law Review.

Melanie Mallet, "A Primer on Treaty Making and Treaty Implementation in Canada". Original contribution to this text (2007).

W.H. McConnell, *Commentary on the British North America Act*. Reprinted by permission of W.H. McConnell.

B. McLachlin, *Unwritten Constitutional Principles: What is Going On?* Reprinted by permission of B. McLachlin.

B. McLachlin, *Rules and Discretion in the Governance of Canada*. Reprinted by permission of B. McLachlin and the Saskatchewan Law Review.

B. Morgan, "The Trade and Commerce Power". Original contribution to this text.

A. Pape, "The Section 35 Justification Test: The Developing Jurisprudence". Original contribution to this text (2007).

Position of the Parti Québécois on the Separatist Movement Today . Reprinted by permission of the Parti Québécois.

Royal Commission on the Economic Union and Development Prospects for Canada Report, Vol 3: Supplementary Statement, Pg 487-512, 1983. Notes omitted. Reproduced courtesy of The Privy Council Office, with the permission of the Minister of Public Works and Government Services, 2007.

K.S. Rosenn, "Federalism in the Americas in Comparative Perspective". Reprinted by permission of University of Miami Inter-American Law Review.

Shetreet, *Judicial Independence: New Conceptual Dimensions and Contemporary Challenges*, in Shetreet and Deschênes, eds., *Judicial Independence*. Reprinted by permission of Martinus Nijhoff Publishers, © MNP, and with the kind permission of Kluwer Law International.

R.E. Simeon, "Criteria for Choice in Federal Systems". Reprinted by permission of the Queen's Law Journal and R.E. Simeon.

D.V. Smiley, *The Federal Condition in Canada*. Reprinted by permission of G.R. Smiley.

B.L. Strayer, *The Canadian Constitution and the Courts*. Reprinted by permission of B.L. Strayer and LexisNexis Canada Inc.

K. Swinton, "Courting Our Way to Economic Integration: Judicial Review and the Canadian Economic Union". Reprinted by permission of K. Swinton and the Canadian Business Law Journal.

R.L. Watts, *Comparing Federal Systems*. Reprinted by permission of R.L. Watts and the Institute of Intergovernmental Relations, Queen's University.

PHOTOGRAPHIC ACKNOWLEDGMENTS

PHOTOGRAPHIC ACKNOWLEDGMENTS

PHOTOGRAPHIC ACKNOWLEDGMENTS

During periods of existential moments in national life we can see harmonization occur, and in some cases witness it being explained by constitutional actors. The most frequent mechanism of harmonization is elaboration of and adherence to "constitutional principle."

An example may again serve to clarify. The *Charter of Rights* invests Canadian courts with authority to consider the relevance of equality guarantees to benefit schemes designed by the legislature. The legislature may itself have studied this problem, and designed its scheme to further equality rights specifically. How should the court interrelate with the legislature's work? Deferentially? Suspiciously? Not at all? Is it relevant that the legislature may have devised its scheme to respond to previous rulings of the Court? And how should the legislature interrelate with the court's work when the two institutions differ about the relevance of equality guarantees? Deferentially? Suspiciously? Creatively? By quick resort to constitutional overrides where these are available, as in Canada?

These are difficult questions. Important answers are to be found in constitutional principles. The principle that the court and legislature are engaged in a constitutional dialogue is relevant to the benefit scheme example. The principle of constitutional dialogue imbues each institution with a sense of respect for the work of the other on the understanding that both institutions, fulfilling their separate constitutional mandates, are engaged in a process of imbuing reason and justice into the marketplace of public expectations (see *Vriend v. Alberta* and *R. v. Mills*, infra.).

A second example: In the early 1980s, the Government of Canada proposed extensive renovation of Canada's constitution. The process, which Canada led, was contentious. Some, using hyperbole, conceived the process as analogous to a *coup d'état*. In the *Patriation Reference*, the Supreme Court reached deep into the sources of constitutional law to explain that the Constitution of Canada includes "the global system of rules and principles which govern the exercise of constitutional authority in the whole and in every part of the Canadian state." By resort to constitutional principle the Court was able to elaborate how the process led by the Government of Canada was occurring within Canada's constitutional framework, and was valid at constitutional law (although departing

Prime Minister Pierre Elliot Trudeau whispering to Jean Chrétien, Minister of Justice, during the 1981 Constitutional Conference.

from 'constitutional conventions'). When, a generation later, the Legislature of Quebec proceeded on a unilateral march towards secession from the Canadian Federation, without involving any other constitutional institutions, the Supreme

Court again delved deep into the sources of constitutional law. In the *Secession Reference*, the Court explained that "the supporting principles and rules [...] are a necessary part of our Constitution because problems or situations may arise which are not expressly dealt with by the text of the Constitution." The Court continued:

> In order to endure over time, a constitution must contain a comprehensive set of rules and principles which are capable of providing an exhaustive legal framework for our system of government. Such principles and rules emerge from an understanding of the constitutional text itself, the historical context, and previous judicial interpretations of constitutional meaning.

In the earlier *Reference Re Provincial Judges*, [1997] 3 S.C.R. 3 the Court explained how constitutional principles "have important legal effects" in two ways: by providing a key to construing the express provisions of the *Constitution Acts*; and also by filling in gaps in the written text (para. 95). The Court then explained how the unwritten constitutional principle of judicial independence could supplement the judicature provisions (s. 96 -101) of the *Constitution Act, 1867* and s. 11(d) of the *Charter of Rights* by providing guarantees of judicial independence for the provincial judiciary in the exercise of their civil jurisdiction.

The Court confirmed this approach in the *Secession Reference*. Underlying constitutional principles, the Court stated, "assist in the interpretation of the text." The Court extended this point to make constitutional principles relevant to "the delineation of spheres of jurisdiction, the scope of rights and obligations and the role of our political institutions;" (para 52). Underlying constitutional principles also fill in gaps in the written constitutional text (para 53). This is why constitutional principles "give rise to substantive legal obligations ... which constitute substantive limitations upon government action ... and are binding upon both courts and governments;" (para 54). The court then identified "four fundamental and organizing principles of the Constitution" relevant to the question of secession — "federalism, democracy, constitutionalism and the rule of law, and respect for minorities." The Court noted that the enumeration was not exhaustive. By means of these principles, the Court was able to show how unilateral secession by the Legislature of Quebec, without the involvement of other constitutional institutions, was unconstitutional.

Constitutional theory, constitutional principle, constitutional law: the progressive hardening of one into the other takes place in the daily work of a nation's political institutions, especially under conditions of stress. Constitutional theory is the collection of grand abstract ideas about how people should be governed, irrespective of local history or national particularity. Constitutional principle is the adaptation of these grand ideas to the individual circumstances of particular polities. The examples discussed above shed light on the process by which, as constitutional actors operate the political institutions of society, constitutional theory solidifies and takes on a national character. As so formed, constitutional principle secretes itself into the gaps that separate constitutional institutions, reveals the purposes of those institutions and indicates how their diverse mandates may be harmonized.

Constitutional Law

Constitutional law is the law that establishes the State and creates its basic institutions. Constitutional law endows the State's institutions with political power, specifies the procedures through which political power may be exercised and provides for limits to official uses of power.

In modern times most constitutions are written, although this is not invariably so, and some major constitutions – that of the United Kingdom, for example – remain unwritten. Canada's Constitution is somewhat unique. It is partly written, although the writings are in several rather than one statute; and partly unwritten, consisting of the traditions to which political actors are expected to conform in exercising the power invested in them by the written constitution.

The written part of Canada's Constitution consists of statutes of the Imperial (that is, the United Kingdom) Parliament, the Parliament of Canada and the legislatures of the Canadian Provinces. The major constitutional document is the *British North America Act, 1867*, later renamed the *Constitution Act, 1867*. This statute was first enacted by the United Kingdom Parliament in 1867; it brought the Dominion of Canada into being as a federal state. (A collection of Canada's constitutional statutes is available on the web at http://www.constitutional-law.ne t/docs.html and http://www.solon.org/Constitutions/Canada/English/index.html.)

Written constitutions, unlike most ordinary statutes, tend to be phrased in broad general language in many areas. Canada's written Constitution provides for institutions, like the Canadian House of Commons or Canada's Superior Courts, but leaves them incompletely manufactured or subject to renovation. The written Constitution foresees that the institutions will be completed and from time to time renovated by statutes of Parliament or the legislatures. Such statutes are called 'organic' enactments — statutes whose object is to fill in the detail of constitutional institutions left somewhat vague in the formal Constitutional text.

The *Constitution Act, 1867* also expresses the federal distribution of legislative powers in quite general terms. This creates the possibility for much flexibility in interpretation. Over time, it is the work of the Courts in interpreting the written Constitution that has given more precise meaning to the language of the *Constitution Act, 1867*. It has been remarked that each decision of the Supreme Court of Canada which interprets the *Constitution Act, 1867*, as far as it goes, is tantamount to an amendment of the Constitution. This is not wholly untrue; as a metaphor, the thought does convey colorfully the importance of judicial decision for delimiting the powers of the organs of governance ordained by the Constitution. Without an understanding of the judicial decisions elaborating the written constitution, the written text would seem very strange as compared to the actual distribution of power observed by governments in practice.

There are other parts of the *Constitution of Canada* that derive from the work of the courts. For example, the law of Parliamentary privilege (the implied powers necessary for operating the Parliamentary institution) or the prerogatives of the Crown (the powers inherent in the Crown and so far unextinguished) are to be found in judicial decisions. Some of these areas result from judicial glosses on written constitutional texts (the law of Parliamentary privilege, for example, is referred to in s. 18 of the *Constitution Act, 1867*). Other constitutional areas, as with the law of Crown prerogative, may result from court decisions only, without any basis in the written constitutional text.

Constitutional Convention

As stated, parts of Canada's Constitution are unwritten. In an important sense these are the most important parts. The written Constitution provides the formal establishment of the institutions of public power. Over time, daily political life develops expectations as to how the institutions of governance should be operated. Constitutional writers call these expectations the 'usages, practices, customs and conventions' of the constitution. The institutions of the Prime Minister and Leader of the Opposition, for example, indeed the entire system of responsible government, are nowhere mentioned in the written constitution. Yet, without understanding the usages, practices and conventions established in these institutions, Canada's written Constitution would make no sense. A person reading the written Constitution would think that Judges are appointed by the Governor General. A person familiar with the constitutional conventions relevant to judicial selection would understand that the Minister of Justice and Prime Minister follow a procedure which results in a name being forwarded to the Governor General for her rubber stamp. If the Governor General were to ignore this process and appoint a person on her own, her act would be 'unconstitutional' in the conventional sense. The consequences of such 'unconstitutional' action are discussed in two cases that follow (*Patriation Reference* and *Osborne v. Canada*). These cases also discuss how constitutional conventions may be identified and their overall significance.

Constitutional Amendment

Oddly, the *British North America Act, 1867* provided no formula for its general amendment. The record of conference proceedings leading to enactment does not disclose the reason why, but the result is that as the *British North America Act, 1867* was a statute of the United Kingdom Parliament, constitutional amendment in Canada took place through enactments of the United Kingdom Parliament. Some of these enactments are detailed as a schedule to the *Constitution Act, 1982* (the schedule also includes certain 'organic' and other enactments of the Canadian Parliament). Section 52(2) of the *Constitution Act, 1982* states that the Constitution of Canada 'includes' the *Acts* listed in the Schedule. The use of the word 'includes' signifies that other *Acts* also form part of the Constitution of Canada.

British responsibility for constitutional amendment in Canada continued until 1982, when the *Canada Act* terminated British involvement, and set out in Part V of the *Constitution Act, 1982* a domestic constitutional amending formula for use by the Canadian authorities. Since that time, the Canadian authorities have used the Part V amending formula on several occasions to modify the Constitution of Canada. The result is that until 1982 Imperial statutes continued to be added to the Constitution of Canada. After 1982, Canada's Constitution has only been modified pursuant to the amending formula at Part V of the *Constitution Act, 1982*.

Summary

As we have observed, written constitutions are typically very sketchy as compared with the detail found in taxing statutes or technical regulatory regimes. Constitutional language overflows with broad concepts like 'freedom of expression' or incompletely manufactured institutional relationships such as those between the judicial and legislative powers. For that reason, the work of the courts in the taxation and regulatory areas tends to be more or less straight forward rule application. By contrast, the work of the courts in the constitutional area tends to be more rule creation and rule definition, and therefore correspondingly more difficult. The broad language and incomplete manufacture which characterizes constitutions explain why constitutional theory and constitutional principle remain crucially important guides to the judiciary. The broad language and incomplete manufacture also explains why the elaboration of constitutional theory and constitutional principle is such a lively activity for modern legal writers.

REFERENCE RE PROVINCIAL JUDGES
[1997] 3 S.C.R. 3

[P.E.I., as part of its budget deficit reduction plan, enacted the *Public Sector Pay Reduction Act* and reduced the salaries of Provincial Court judges and others paid from the public purse in the province. Following the pay reduction, numerous accused challenged the constitutionality of their proceedings in the Provincial Court, alleging that as a result of the salary reductions, the court had lost its status as an independent and impartial tribunal under s. 11(d) of the *Charter*. The Lieutenant Governor in Council referred constitutional questions to the Appeal Division of the P.E.I Supreme Court to *determine* whether the Provincial Court judges still enjoyed a sufficient degree of financial security for the purposes of s. 11(d). In a second Reference the Lieutenant Governor in Council questioned all three elements of the judicial independence of the Provincial Court: financial security, security of tenure, and administrative independence.

In Alberta, three accused challenged the constitutionality of their Provincial Court trials by motion before the Court of Queen's Bench. They argued that the Provincial Court was not an independent and impartial tribunal for the purposes of s. 11(d) because the Provincial Court judges' salaries were reduced by 5% pursuant to the *Payment to Provincial Judges Amendment Regulation* and s. 17(1) of the *Provincial Court Judges Act*. The 5% reduction was accomplished by a 3.1 percent direct salary reduction, and by 5 unpaid days leave of absence. The respondents also attacked the constitutionality of changes to the judges' pension plan which reduced the base salary for calculating pension benefits, and limited cost of living increases to 60 percent of the Consumer Price Index. In addition, the respondents challenged the constitutionality of the power of the Attorney General to designate the court's sitting days and judges' place of residence. McDonald J., on the motions, also put at issue the process for disciplining Provincial Court judges and the grounds for removal of judges of the Provincial Court.

Manitoba's *Public Sector Reduced Work Week and Compensation Management Act* ("Bill 22") reduced the salary of Provincial Court judges and of a large number of public sector employees as part of a plan to reduce the province's deficit. The Provincial Court judges through their Association launched a constitutional challenge to the salary cut, alleging that it infringed their judicial independence as protected by s. 11(d) of the *Charter*. They also argued that the salary reduction was unconstitutional because it effectively suspended the operation of the Judicial Compensation Committee ("JCC"), a body created by *The Provincial Court Act* whose task it is to issue reports on judges' salaries to the legislature. They alleged that the government had interfered with judicial independence by ordering the withdrawal of court staff and personnel on unpaid days of leave, which in effect shut down the Provincial Court on those days. Finally, they claimed that the government had exerted improper pressure on the Association in the course of salary discussions to desist from launching this constitutional challenge, which also allegedly infringed their judicial independence.]

The judgment of Lamer C.J. and L'Heureux-Dubé, Sopinka, Gonthier, Cory and Iacobucci JJ. was delivered by

THE CHIEF JUSTICE: —

¶ 6 [...] I feel compelled to comment on the unprecedented situation which these appeals represent. The independence of provincial court judges is now a live legal issue in no fewer than four of the ten provinces in the federation. These appeals [...] demonstrate that the proper constitutional relationship between the executive and the provincial court judges in those provinces has come under serious strain. Litigation [...] is a very serious business. In these cases, it is even more serious because litigation has ensued between two primary organs of our constitutional system — the executive and the judiciary — which both serve important and interdependent roles in the administration of justice. [...]

¶ 8 The task of the Court in these appeals is to explain the proper constitutional relationship between provincial court judges and provincial executives, and thereby assist in removing the strain on this relationship. The failure to do so would undermine "the web of institutional relationships [...] which continue to form the backbone of our constitutional system" (*Cooper v. Canada (Human Rights Commission)*, [1996] 3 S.C.R. 854, at para. 3).

[...]

A. Introduction: The Unwritten Basis of Judicial Independence

¶ 82 These appeals were all argued on the basis of s. 11(d), the *Charter's* guarantee of judicial independence and impartiality. From its express terms, s. 11(d) is a right of limited application — it only applies to persons accused of offences. Despite s. 11(d)'s limited scope, there is no doubt that the appeals can and should be resolved on the basis of that provision. To a large extent, the Court is the prisoner of the case which the parties and interveners have presented to us, and the arguments that have been raised, and the evidence that we have before us, have largely been directed at s. 11(d). In particular, the two references from P.E.I. are explicitly framed in terms of s. 11(d), and if we are to answer the questions contained therein, we must direct ourselves to that section of the Constitution.

¶ 83 [W]hile the thrust of the [parties'] submissions was directed at s. 11(*d*), [certain parties] addressed the larger question of where the constitutional home of judicial independence lies, to which I now turn. Notwithstanding the presence of s. 11(*d*) of the *Charter*, and ss. 96-100 of the *Constitution Act, 1867*, I am of the view that judicial independence is at root an <u>unwritten</u> constitutional principle, in the sense that it is exterior to the particular sections of the *Constitution Acts*. The existence of that principle, whose origins can be traced to the *Act of Settlement* of

1701, is recognized and affirmed by the preamble to the *Constitution Act, 1867*. The specific provisions of the *Constitution Acts, 1867 to 1982*, merely "elaborate that principle in the institutional apparatus which they create or contemplate": *Switzman v. Elbling*, [1957] S.C.R. 285, at p. 306, *per* Rand J.

¶ 84 I arrive at this conclusion, in part, by considering the tenability of the opposite position — that the Canadian Constitution already contains explicit provisions which are directed at the protection of judicial independence, and that those provisions are exhaustive of the matter. Section 11(*d*) of the *Charter*, as I have mentioned above, protects the independence of a wide range of courts and tribunals which exercise jurisdiction over offences. Moreover, since well before the enactment of the *Charter*, ss. 96-100 of the *Constitution Act, 1867*, separately and in combination, have protected and continue to protect the independence of provincial superior courts: *Cooper*, [1996] 3 S.C.R. 854 at para. 11; *MacMillan Bloedel Ltd. v. Simpson*, [1995] 4 S.C.R. 725, at para. 10. More specifically, s. 99 guarantees the security of tenure of superior court judges; s. 100 guarantees the financial security of judges of the superior, district, and county courts; and s. 96 has come to guarantee the core jurisdiction of superior, district, and county courts against legislative encroachment, which I also take to be a guarantee of judicial independence.

¶ 85 However, upon closer examination, there are serious limitations to the view that the express provisions of the Constitution comprise an exhaustive and definitive code for the protection of judicial independence. The first and most serious problem is that the range of courts whose independence is protected by the written provisions of the Constitution contains large gaps. Sections 96-100, for example, only protect the independence of judges of the superior, district, and county courts, and even then, not in a uniform or consistent manner. Thus, while ss. 96 and 100 protect the core jurisdiction and the financial security, respectively, of all three types of courts (superior, district, and county), s. 99, on its terms, only protects the security of tenure of superior court judges. Moreover, ss. 96-100 do not apply to provincially appointed inferior courts, otherwise known as provincial courts.

¶ 86 To some extent, the gaps in the scope of protection provided by ss. 96-100 are offset by the application of s. 11(*d*), which applies to a range of tribunals and courts, including provincial courts. However, by its express terms, s. 11(*d*) is limited in scope as well — it only extends the envelope of constitutional protection to bodies which exercise <u>jurisdiction over offences</u>. As a result, when those courts exercise civil jurisdiction, their independence would not seem to be guaranteed. The independence of provincial courts adjudicating in family law matters, for example, would not be constitutionally protected. The independence of superior courts, by contrast, when hearing exactly the same cases, would be constitutionally guaranteed.

¶ 87 The second problem with reading s. 11(*d*) of the *Charter* and ss. 96-100 of the *Constitution Act, 1867* as an exhaustive code of judicial independence is that some of those provisions, by their terms, do not appear to speak to this objective. Section 100, for example, provides that Parliament shall fix and provide the salaries of superior, district, and county court judges. It is therefore, in an important sense, a subtraction from provincial jurisdiction over the administration of justice under s. 92(14). Moreover, read in the light of the *Act of Settlement of 1701*, it is a partial guarantee of financial security, inasmuch as it vests responsibility for setting judicial remuneration with Parliament, which must act through the public means of legislative enactment, not the executive. However, on its plain language, it only places Parliament under the obligation to provide salaries to the judges covered by that provision, which would in itself not safeguard the judiciary against political interference through economic manipulation. Nevertheless, as I develop in these reasons, with reference to *Beauregard*, s. 100 also requires that Parliament must provide salaries that are adequate, and that changes or freezes to judicial remuneration be made only after recourse to a constitutionally mandated procedure.

¶ 88 A perusal of the language of s. 96 reveals the same difficulty:

> 96. The Governor General shall appoint the Judges of the Superior, District, and County Courts in each Province, except those of the Courts of Probate in Nova Scotia and New Brunswick.

Section 96 seems to do no more than confer the power to appoint judges of the superior, district, and county courts. It is a staffing provision, and is once again a subtraction from the power of the provinces under s. 92(14). However, through a process of judicial interpretation, s. 96 has come to guarantee the core jurisdiction of the courts which come within the scope of that provision. In the past, this development has often been expressed as a logical inference from the express terms of s. 96. Assuming that the goal of s. 96 was the creation of "a unitary judicial system", that goal would have been undermined "if a province could pass legislation creating a tribunal, appoint members thereto, and then confer on the tribunal the jurisdiction of the superior courts": *Re Residential Tenancies Act, 1979*, [1981] 1 S.C.R. 714, at p. 728. However, as I recently confirmed, s. 96 restricts not only the legislative competence of provincial legislatures, but of Parliament as well: *MacMillan Bloedel*, supra. The rationale for the provision has also shifted, away from the protection of national unity, to the maintenance of the rule of law through the protection of the judicial role.

¶ 89 The point which emerges from this brief discussion is that the interpretation of ss. 96 and 100 has come a long way from what those provisions actually say. This jurisprudential evolution undermines the force of the argument that the written text of the Constitution is comprehensive and definitive in its protection of judicial independence. The only way to explain the interpretation of ss. 96 and 100, in fact, is by reference to a deeper set of underscore{unwritten} understandings which are not found on the face of the document itself.

¶ 90 The proposition that the Canadian Constitution embraces unwritten norms was recently confirmed by this Court in *New Brunswick Broadcasting Co. v. Nova Scotia (Speaker of the House of Assembly)*, [1993] 1 S.C.R. 319. In that case, the Court found it constitutional for the Nova Scotia House of Assembly to refuse the media the right to record and broadcast legislative proceedings. The media advanced a claim based on s. 2(*b*) of the *Charter*, which protects, *inter alia*, "freedom of the press and other media of communication". McLachlin J., speaking for a majority of the Court, found that the refusal of the Assembly was an exercise of that Assembly's unwritten legislative privileges, that the Constitution of Canada constitutionalized those privileges, and that the constitutional status of those privileges therefore precluded the application of the *Charter*.

¶ 91 The relevant part of her judgment concerns the interpretation of s. 52(2) of the *Constitution Act, 1982*, which defines the "Constitution of Canada" in the following terms:

> 52. [...]
>
> (2) The Constitution of Canada <u>includes</u>
>   (*a*) the *Canada Act 1982*, including this *Act*;
>   (*b*) the *Acts* and orders referred to in the schedule; and
>   (*c*) any amendment to any *Act* or order referred to in
>   paragraph (*a*) or
>   (*b*) (emphasis added.)

The media argued that parliamentary privileges did not enjoy constitutional status, and hence, were subject to *Charter* scrutiny like any other decision of a legislature, because they were not included within the list of documents found in, or referred to by, s. 52(2). McLachlin J. rejected this argument, in part on the basis of the wording of s. 52(2). She held that the use of the word "includes" indicated that the list of constitutional documents in s. 52(2) was not exhaustive.

¶ 92 Although I concurred on different grounds, and still doubt whether the privileges of provincial assemblies form part of the Constitution (*Harvey v. New Brunswick (Attorney General)*, [1996] 2 S.C.R. 876, at para. 2), I agree with the general principle that the Constitution embraces unwritten, as well as written rules, largely on the basis of the wording of s. 52(2). Indeed, given that ours is a Constitution that has emerged from a constitutional order whose fundamental rules are not authoritatively set down in a single document, or a set of documents, it is of no surprise that our Constitution should retain some aspect of this legacy.

¶ 93 However, I do wish to add a note of caution. As I said in *New Brunswick Broadcasting*, supra, at p. 355, the constitutional history of Canada can be understood, in part, as a process of evolution "which [has] culminated in the supremacy of a definitive written constitution." There are many important reasons for the preference for a written Constitution over an unwritten one, not the least of which is the promotion of legal certainty and through it the legitimacy of constitutional judicial review. Given these concerns, which go to the heart of the project of constitutionalism, it is of the utmost importance to articulate what the source of those unwritten norms is.

¶ 94 In my opinion, the existence of many of the unwritten rules of the Canadian Constitution can be explained by reference to the preamble of the *Constitution Act, 1867*. The relevant paragraph states in full:

> Whereas the Provinces of Canada, Nova Scotia, and New Brunswick have expressed their Desire to be federally united into One Dominion under the Crown of the United Kingdom of Great Britain and Ireland, with a Constitution similar in Principle to that of the United Kingdom:

Although the preamble has been cited by this Court on many occasions, its legal effect has never been fully explained. On the one hand, although the preamble is clearly part of the Constitution, it is equally clear that it "has no enacting force". *Reference Re Resolution to Amend the Constitution*, [1981] 1 S.C.R. 753, at p. 805 (joint majority reasons). In other words, strictly speaking, it is not a source of positive law, in contrast to the provisions which follow it.

¶ 95 But the preamble does have important legal effects. Under normal circumstances, preambles can be used to identify the purpose of a statute, and also as an aid to construing ambiguous statutory language: *Driedger on the Construction of Statutes* (3rd ed. 1994), by R. Sullivan, at p. 261. The preamble to the *Constitution Act, 1867*, certainly operates in this fashion. However, in my view, it goes even further. In the words of Rand J., the preamble articulates "the political theory which the *Act* embodies": *Switzman*, supra, at p. 306. It recognizes and affirms the basic principles which are the very source of the substantive provisions of the *Constitution Act, 1867*. As I have said above, those provisions merely elaborate those organizing principles in the institutional apparatus they create or contemplate. As such, the preamble is not only a key to construing the express provisions of the *Constitution Act, 1867*, but also invites the use of those organizing principles to fill out gaps in the express terms of the constitutional scheme. It is the means by which the underlying logic of the *Act* can be given the force of law.

¶ 96 What are the organizing principles of the *Constitution Act, 1867*, as expressed in the preamble? The preamble speaks of the desire of the founding provinces "to be federally united into One Dominion", and thus, addresses the structure of the division of powers. Moreover, by its reference to "a Constitution similar in Principle to that of the United Kingdom", the preamble indicates that the legal and institutional structure of constitutional democracy in Canada should be similar to that of the legal regime out of which the Canadian Constitution emerged. To my mind, both of these aspects of the preamble explain many of the cases in which the Court has, through the normal process of constitutional interpretation, stated some fundamental rules of Canadian constitutional law which are not found in the express terms of the *Constitution Act, 1867*.

¶ 97 I turn first to the jurisprudence under the division of powers, to illustrate how the process of gap-filling has occurred and how it can be understood by reference to the preamble. One example where the Court has inferred a fundamental constitutional rule which is not found in express terms in the Constitution is the doctrine of full faith and credit. Under this doctrine, the courts of one province are under a constitutional obligation to recognize the decisions of the courts of another province: *Hunt v. T & N PLC*, [1993] 4 S.C.R. 289. The justification for this rule has been aptly put by Professor Hogg (*Constitutional Law of Canada* (3rd ed. 1992 (loose-leaf)), vol. 1, at p. 13-18):

> Within a federal state, it seems obvious that, if a provincial court takes jurisdiction over a defendant who is resident in another province, and if the court observes constitutional standards [...], the resulting judgment should be recognized by the courts of the defendant's province.

Speaking for the Court in *Hunt*, La Forest J. identified a number of sources for reading the doctrine of full faith and credit into the scheme of the Constitution: a common citizenship, interprovincial mobility of citizens, the common market created by the union, and the essentially unitary structure of our judicial system. At root, these factors combined to evince "the obvious intention of the Constitution to create a single country": *Morguard Investments Ltd. v. De Savoye*, [1990] 3 S.C.R. 1077, at p. 1099. An alternative explanation of the decision, however, is that the Court was merely giving effect to the "[d]esire" of the founding provinces "to be federally united into One Dominion", an organizing principle of the Constitution that was recognized and affirmed in the preamble, and which was given express form in the provisions identified by La Forest J.

Doctrine of Paramountcy

¶ 98 Another example where the Court has inferred a basic rule of Canadian constitutional law despite the silence of the constitutional text is the doctrine of paramountcy. Simply stated, the doctrine asserts that where both the Parliament of Canada and one or more of the provincial legislatures have enacted legislation which comes into conflict, the federal law shall prevail. The doctrine of paramountcy is of fundamental importance in a legal system with more than one source of legislative authority, because it provides a guide to courts and ultimately to citizens on how to reconcile seemingly inconsistent legal obligations. However, it is nowhere to be found in the *Constitution Act, 1867*. The doctrinal origins of paramountcy are obscure, although it has been said that it "is necessarily implied in our constitutional act": *Huson v. Township of South Norwich* (1895), 24 S.C.R. 145, at p. 149. I would venture that the doctrine of paramountcy follows from the desire of the confederating provinces "to be federally united into One Dominion". Relying on the preamble explains, for example, why federal laws are paramount over provincial laws, not the other way around.

¶ 99 The preamble, by its reference to "a Constitution similar in Principle to that of the United Kingdom", points to the nature of the legal order that envelops and sustains Canadian society. That order, as this Court held in *Reference Re Manitoba Language Rights*, [1985] 1 S.C.R. 721, at p. 749, is "an actual order of positive laws", an idea that is embraced by the notion of the rule of law. In that case, the Court explicitly relied on the preamble to the *Constitution Act, 1867*, as one basis for holding that the rule of law was a fundamental principle of the Canadian Constitution. The rule of law led the Court to confer temporary validity on the laws of Manitoba which were unconstitutional because they had been enacted only in English, in contravention of the *Manitoba Act, 1870*. The Court developed this remedial innovation notwithstanding the express terms of s. 52(1) of the *Constitution Act, 1982*, that unconstitutional laws are "of no force or effect", a provision that suggests that declarations of invalidity can only be given immediate effect. The Court did so in order to not "deprive Manitoba of its legal order and cause a transgression of the rule of law" (p. 753). *Reference Re Manitoba Language Rights* therefore stands as another example of how the fundamental principles articulated by preamble have been given legal effect by this Court.

Constitutional Democracy

¶ 100 Finally, the preamble also speaks to the kind of constitutional democracy that our Constitution comprehends. One aspect of our system of governance is the importance of "parliamentary institutions, including popular assemblies elected by the people at large in both provinces and Dominion": *Saumur v. City of Quebec*,

[1953] 2 S.C.R. 299, at p. 330, *per* Rand J. Again, the desire for Parliamentary government through representative institutions is not expressly found in the *Constitution Act, 1867*; there is no reference in that document, for example, to any requirement that members of Parliament or provincial legislatures be elected. Nevertheless, members of the Court, correctly in my opinion, have been able to infer this general principle from the preamble's reference to "a Constitution similar in Principle to that of the United Kingdom."

¶ 101 One implication of the preamble's recognition and affirmation of Parliamentary democracy is the constitutionalization of legislative privileges for provincial legislatures, and most likely, for Parliament as well. These privileges are necessary to ensure that legislatures can perform their functions, free from interference by the Crown and the courts. Given that legislatures are representative and deliberative institutions, those privileges ultimately serve to protect the democratic nature of those bodies. The Constitution, once again, is silent on this point. Nevertheless, and notwithstanding the reservations I have expressed above, the majority of this Court grounded the privileges of the Nova Scotia Legislative Assembly in the preamble's reference to "a Constitution similar in Principle to that of the United Kingdom": *New Brunswick Broadcasting*, supra. It argued that since those privileges inhered in the Parliament in Westminster, the preamble indicated that the intention of the *Constitution Act, 1867* was that "the legislative bodies of the new Dominion would possess similar, although not necessarily identical, powers" (p. 375). Similarly, in discussing the jurisdiction of courts in relation to the exercise of privileges of the Senate or one of its committees, Iacobucci C.J. (as he then was) considered the significance of the preamble's reference to "a Constitution similar in Principle to that of the United Kingdom" in *Southam Inc. v. Canada (Attorney General)*, [1990] 3 F.C. 465 (C.A.), at pp. 485-86:

> Strayer J. was of the opinion that courts had such a jurisdiction and found, in particular, that the adoption of the *Charter* fundamentally altered the nature of the Canadian Constitution such that it is no longer "similar in Principle to that of the United Kingdom" as is stated in the preamble to the *Constitution Act, 1867*. Accepting as we must that the adoption of the *Charter* transformed to a considerable extent our former system of Parliamentary supremacy into our current one of constitutional supremacy, as former Chief Justice Dickson described it, the sweep of Strayer J.'s comment that our Constitution is no longer similar in principle to that of the United Kingdom is rather wide. Granted much has changed in the new constitutional world of the *Charter*. But just as purists of federalism have learned to live with the federalist Constitution that Canada adopted in 1867 based on principles of parliamentary government in a unitary state such that the United Kingdom was and continues to be, so it seems to me that the British system of constitutional government will continue to co-exist alongside the *Charter* if not entirely, which it never did, but certainly in many important respects. The nature of [sic] scope of this co-existence will depend naturally on the jurisprudence that results from the questions brought before the courts.

¶ 102 Another implication of the preamble's recognition of Parliamentary democracy has been an appreciation of the interdependence between democratic governance and freedom of political speech. Thus, members of the Court have reasoned that Parliamentary democracy brought with it "all its social implications" (*Switzman*, supra, at p. 306, *per* Rand J.), including the implication that these institutions would

> wor[k] under the influence of public opinion and public discussion [...] [because] such institutions derive their efficacy from the free public discussion of affairs, from criticism and answer and counter-criticism, from attack upon policy and administration and defence and counter-attack, from the freest and fullest analysis and examination from every point of view of political proposals.

> (*Reference Re Alberta Statutes*, [1938] S.C.R. 100, at p. 133, *per* Duff C.J.)

Political freedoms, such as the right to freedom of expression, are not enumerated heads of jurisdiction under ss. 91 and 92 of the *Constitution Act, 1867*; the document is silent on their very existence. However, given the importance of political expression to national political life, combined with the intention to create one country, members of the Court have taken the position that the limitation of that expression is solely a matter for Parliament, not the provincial legislatures: *Reference Re Alberta Statutes*, supra, at p. 134, *per* Duff C.J., and at p. 146, *per* Cannon J.; *Saumur*, supra, at pp. 330-31, *per* Rand J., and at pp. 354-56, *per* Kellock J.; *Switzman*, supra, at p. 307, *per* Rand J., and at p. 328, *per* Abbott J.

¶ 103 The logic of this argument, however, compels a much more dramatic conclusion. Denying jurisdiction over political speech to the provincial legislatures does not limit Parliament's ability to do what the provinces cannot. However, given the interdependence between national political institutions and free speech, members of the Court have suggested that Parliament itself is incompetent to "abrogate this right of discussion and debate": *Switzman*, supra, at p. 328, *per* Abbott J.; also see Rand J. at p. 307; *Saumur*, supra, at p. 354, *per* Kellock J.; *OPSEU v. Ontario (Attorney General)*, [1987] 2 S.C.R. 2, at p. 57, *per* Beetz J. In this way, the preamble's recognition of the democratic nature of Parliamentary governance has been used by some members of the Court to fashion an implied bill of rights, in the absence of any express indication to this effect in the constitutional text. This has been done, in my opinion, out of a recognition that political institutions are fundamental to the "basic structure of our Constitution" (*OPSEU*, supra, at p. 57) and for that reason governments cannot undermine the mechanisms of political accountability which give those institutions definition, direction and legitimacy.

¶ 104 These examples — the doctrines of full faith and credit and paramountcy, the remedial innovation of suspended declarations of invalidity, the recognition of the constitutional status of the privileges of provincial legislatures, the vesting of the power to regulate political speech within federal jurisdiction, and the inferral of implied limits on legislative sovereignty with respect to political speech — illustrate the special legal effect of the preamble. The preamble identifies the organizing principles of the *Constitution Act, 1867*, and invites the courts to turn those principles into the premises of a constitutional argument that culminates in the filling of gaps in the express terms of the constitutional text.

Protection of Judicial Independence

¶ 105 The same approach applies to the protection of judicial independence. In fact, this point was already decided in *Beauregard*, and, unless and until it is reversed, we are governed by that decision today. In that case (at p. 72), a unanimous Court held that the preamble of the *Constitution Act, 1867*, and in particular, its reference to "a Constitution similar in Principle to that of the United Kingdom", was "textual recognition" of the principle of judicial independence. Although in that case, it fell to us to interpret s. 100 of the *Constitution Act, 1867*, the comments I have just reiterated were not limited by reference to that provision, and the courts which it protects.

¶ 106 The historical origins of the protection of judicial independence in the United Kingdom, and thus in the Canadian Constitution, can be traced to the *Act of Settlement* of 1701. As we said in *Valente*, infra, at p. 693, that *Act* was the "historical inspiration" for the judicature provisions of the *Constitution Act, 1867*. Admittedly, the *Act* only extends protection to judges of the English superior courts. However, our Constitution has evolved over time. In the same way that our understanding of rights and freedoms has grown, such that they have now been expressly entrenched through the enactment of the *Constitution Act, 1982*, so too has judicial independence grown into a principle that now extends to all courts, not just the superior courts of this country.

¶ 107 I also support this conclusion on the basis of the presence of s. 11(*d*) of the *Charter*, an express provision which protects the independence of provincial court judges only when those courts exercise jurisdiction in relation to offences. As I said earlier, the express provisions of the Constitution should be understood as elaborations of the underlying, unwritten, and organizing principles found in the preamble to the *Constitution Act, 1867*. Even though s. 11(*d*) is found in the newer part of our Constitution, the *Charter*, it can be understood in this way, since the Constitution is to be read as a unified whole: *Reference Re Bill 30, An Act to amend the Education Act (Ont.)*, [1987] 1 S.C.R. 1148, at p. 1206. An analogy can be drawn between the express reference in the preamble of the *Constitution Act, 1982* to the rule of law and the implicit inclusion of that principle in the *Constitution Act, 1867*: *Reference Re Manitoba Language Rights*, supra, at p. 750. Section 11(*d*), far from indicating that judicial independence is constitutionally enshrined for provincial courts only when those courts exercise jurisdiction over offences, is proof of the existence of a general principle of judicial independence that applies to all courts no matter what kind of cases they hear.

¶ 108 I reinforce this conclusion by reference to the central place that courts hold within the Canadian system of government. In *OPSEU*, as I have mentioned above, Beetz J. linked limitations on legislative sovereignty over political speech with "the existence of certain political institutions" as part of the "basic structure of our Constitution" (p. 57). However, political institutions are only one part of the basic structure of the Canadian Constitution. As this Court has said before, there are three branches of government — the legislature, the executive, and the judiciary: *Fraser v. Public Service Staff Relations Board*, [1985] 2 S.C.R. 455, at p. 469;

R. v. Power, [1994] 1 S.C.R. 601, at p. 620. Courts, in other words, are equally "definitional to the Canadian understanding of constitutionalism" (*Cooper*, supra, at para. 11) as are political institutions. It follows that the same constitutional imperative — the preservation of the basic structure — which led Beetz J. to limit the power of legislatures to affect the operation of political institutions, also extends protection to the judicial institutions of our constitutional system. By implication, the jurisdiction of the provinces over "courts", as that term is used in s. 92(14) of the *Constitution Act, 1867*, contains within it an implied limitation that the independence of those courts cannot be undermined.

¶ 109 In conclusion, the express provisions of the *Constitution Act, 1867* and the *Charter* are not an exhaustive written code for the protection of judicial independence in Canada. Judicial independence is an unwritten norm, recognized and affirmed by the preamble to the *Constitution Act, 1867*. In fact, it is in that preamble, which serves as the grand entrance hall to the castle of the Constitution, that the true source of our commitment to this foundational principle is located. However, since the parties and interveners have grounded their arguments in s. 11(*d*), I will resolve these appeals by reference to that provision. [...]

[After analysis of the governing constitutional law the Court established these principles:

1. governments may reduce, increase, or freeze the salaries of provincial court judges, either as part of an overall economic measure aimed at persons remunerated from public funds, or aimed at provincial court judges only;

2. provinces must establish independent, effective, and objective commissions which must review proposed changes to judicial remuneration in advance;

3. these commissions must consider the adequacy of judges' salaries in light of the cost of living and other relevant factors regularly, i.e. every three to five years;

4. the commission recommendations are non-binding, but government must justify decisions to depart from those recommendations according to a standard of simple rationality, if need be, in a court of law;

5. the judiciary may never negotiate with the executive or the legislature over remuneration. However, the judiciary may express concerns or make representations to governments regarding judicial remuneration.

In light of these principles the majority held that P.E.I.'s and Alberta's salary reductions of Provincial Court Judges infringed s. 11(d) of the *Charter* because the reductions were made without being considered first by a commission (no such commission existed in PEI or in Alberta). P.E.I. and Alberta made no attempt to justify the s. 11(d) violation under s. 1. The court commented that if, after P.E.I. and Alberta established commissions, the commissions issue reports which the governments decline to follow, the salary reductions (in P.E.I., from $106,123 to 98,243; in Alberta, from $113,964 to 108,266 in 1994) would probably be *prima facie* rational and justified because they were part of an overall measure reducing the salaries of all persons remunerated from public funds. In Manitoba the government effectively suspended operation of its Judicial Compensation Commission. Accordingly, the salary reductions infringed s. 11(d) and, Manitoba offering no s. 1 evidence, the infringement was not justified.]

La FOREST J. (dissenting in part): —

¶ 301 [I do not agree with the Chief Justice's] broad assertion concerning the protection provincially appointed judges exercising functions other than criminal jurisdiction are afforded by virtue of the preamble to the *Constitution Act, 1867*. Indeed I have grave reservations about the Court entering into a discussion of the matter in the present appeals. Only minimal reference was made to it by counsel who essentially argued the issues on the basis of s. 11(*d*) of the *Charter* [...]

¶ 302 I am all the more troubled since the question involves the proper relationship between the political branches of government and the judicial branch, an issue on which judges can hardly be seen to be indifferent, especially as it concerns their own remuneration. In such circumstances, it is absolutely critical for the Court to tread carefully and avoid making far-reaching conclusions that are not necessary to decide the case before it. If the Chief Justice's discussion was of a merely marginal character — a side-wind so to speak — I would abstain from commenting on it. After all, it is technically only *obiter dicta*. Nevertheless, in light of the importance that will necessarily be attached to his lengthy and sustained exegesis, I feel compelled to express my view.

II. <u>The Effect of the Preamble to the *Constitution Act, 1867*</u>

¶ 303 I emphasize at the outset that it is not my position that s. 11(*d*) of the *Charter* and ss. 96-100 of the *Constitution Act, 1867* comprise an exhaustive code of judicial independence. As I discuss briefly later, additional protection for judicial independence may inhere in other provisions of the Constitution. Nor do I deny that the Constitution embraces unwritten rules, including rules that find expression in the preamble of the *Constitution Act, 1867*; see *New Brunswick Broadcasting Co. v. Nova Scotia (Speaker of the House of Assembly)*, [1993] 1 S.C.R. 319. I hasten to add that these rules really find their origin in specific provisions of the Constitution viewed in light of our constitutional heritage. In other words, what we are concerned with is the meaning to be attached to an expression used in a constitutional provision.

¶ 304 I take issue, however, with the Chief Justice's view that the preamble to the *Constitution Act, 1867* is a source of constitutional limitations on the power of legislatures to interfere with judicial independence. In *New Brunswick Broadcasting*, supra, this Court held that the privileges of the Nova Scotia legislature had constitutional status by virtue of the statement in the preamble expressing the desire to have "a Constitution similar in Principle to that of the United Kingdom". In reaching this conclusion, the Court examined the historical basis for the privileges of the British Parliament. That analysis established that the power of Parliament to exclude strangers was absolute, constitutional and immune from regulation by the courts. The effect of the preamble, the Court held, is to recognize and confirm that this long-standing principle of British constitutional law was continued or established in post-Confederation Canada.

¶ 305 There is no similar historical basis, in contrast, for the idea that Parliament cannot interfere with judicial independence. At the time of Confederation (and indeed to this day), the British Constitution did not contemplate the notion that Parliament was limited in its ability to deal with judges [ ]

¶ 307 Professor Lederman writes, for example, that it would be "unconstitutional" for the British Parliament to cut the salary of an individual superior court judge during his or her commission or to reduce the salaries of judges as a class to the extent that it threatened their independence (supra, at p. 795). It has thus been suggested that the preamble to the *Constitution Act, 1867*, which expresses a desire to have a Constitution "similar in Principle to that of the United Kingdom" is a source of judicial independence in Canada: *Beauregard v. Canada*, [1986] 2 S.C.R. 56, at p. 72.

¶ 308 Even if it is accepted that judicial independence had become a "constitutional" principle in Britain by 1867, it is important to understand the precise meaning of that term in British law. Unlike Canada, Great Britain does not have a written constitution. Under accepted British legal theory, Parliament is supreme. By this I mean that there are no limitations upon its legislative competence. As Dicey explains, Parliament has "under the English constitution, the right to make or unmake any law whatever; and, further, that no person or body is recognised by the law of England as having a right to override or set aside the legislation of Parliament" (A. V. Dicey, *Introduction to the Study of the Law of the Constitution* (10th ed. 1959), at pp. 39-40). This principle has been modified somewhat in recent decades to take into account the effect of Great Britain's membership in the European Community, but ultimately, the British Parliament remains supreme; see E. C. S. Wade and A. W. Bradley, *Constitutional and Administrative Law* (11th ed. 1993), by A. W. Bradley and K. D. Ewing, at pp. 68-87; Colin Turpin, *British Government and the Constitution* (3rd ed. 1995), at pp. 298-99.

¶ 309 The consequence of parliamentary supremacy is that judicial review of legislation is not possible. The courts have no power to hold an Act of Parliament invalid or unconstitutional. When it is said that a certain principle or convention is "constitutional", this does not mean that a statute violating that principle can be found to be *ultra vires* Parliament. As Lord Reid stated in *Madzimbamuto v. Lardner-Burke*, [1969] 1 A.C. 645 (P.C.), at p. 723:

> It is often said that it would be unconstitutional for the United Kingdom Parliament to do certain things, meaning that the moral, political or other reasons against doing them are so strong that most people would regard it as highly improper if Parliament did these things. But that does not mean that it is beyond the power of Parliament to do such things. If Parliament chose to do any of them the courts could not hold the Act of Parliament invalid.

See also: *Manuel v. Attorney-General*, [1983] Ch. 77 (C.A.).

¶ 310 This fundamental principle is illustrated by the debate that occurred when members of the English judiciary complained to the Prime Minister in the early 1930s about legislation which reduced the salaries of judges, along with those of civil servants, by 20 percent as an emergency response to a financial crisis. Viscount Buckmaster, who vigorously resisted the notion that judges' salaries could be diminished during their term of office, admitted that Parliament was supreme and could repeal the *Act of Settlement* if it chose to do so. He only objected that it was not permissible to effectively repeal the Act by order in council; see U.K., H.L. *Parliamentary Debates*, vol. 90, cols. 67-68 (November 23, 1933). It seems that the judges themselves also conceded this point; see R. F. V. Heuston, *Lives of the Lord Chancellors 1885-1940* (1964), at p. 514.

¶ 311 The idea that there were enforceable limits on the power of the British Parliament to interfere with the judiciary at the time of Confederation, then, is an historical fallacy. By expressing a desire to have a Constitution "similar in Principle to that of the United Kingdom", the framers of the *Constitution Act, 1867* did not give courts the power to strike down legislation violating the principle of judicial independence. The framers did, however, entrench the fundamental components of judicial independence set out in the *Act of Settlement* such that violations could be struck down by the courts. This was accomplished, however, by ss. 99-100 of the *Constitution Act, 1867*, not the preamble.

¶ 312 It might be asserted that the argument presented above is merely a technical quibble. After all, in Canada the Constitution is supreme, not the legislatures. Courts have had the power to invalidate unconstitutional legislation in this country since 1867. If judicial independence was a "constitutional" principle in the broad sense in nineteenth-century Britain, and that principle was continued or established in Canada as a result of the preamble to the *Constitution Act, 1867*, why should Canadian courts resile from enforcing this principle by striking down incompatible legislation?

¶ 313 One answer to this question is the ambit of the *Act of Settlement*. The protection it accorded was limited to superior courts, specifically the central courts of common law; see Lederman, supra, at p. 782. It did not apply to inferior courts. While subsequent legislation did provide limited protection for the independence of the judges of certain statutory courts, such as the county courts, the courts there were not regarded as within the ambit of the "constitutional" protection in the British sense. Generally the independence and impartiality of these courts were ensured to litigants through the superintendence exercised over them by the superior courts by way of prerogative writs and other extraordinary remedies. The overall task of protection sought to be created for inferior courts in the present appeals seems to me to be made of insubstantial cloth, and certainly in no way similar to anything to be found in the United Kingdom.

¶ 314 A more general answer to the question lies in the nature of the power of judicial review. The ability to nullify the laws of democratically elected representatives derives its legitimacy from a super-legislative source: the text of the Constitution. This foundational document (in Canada, a series of documents) expresses the desire of the people to limit the power of legislatures in certain specified ways. Because our Constitution is entrenched, those limitations cannot be changed by recourse to the usual democratic process. They are not cast in stone, however, and can be modified in accordance with a further expression of democratic will: constitutional amendment.

¶ 315 Judicial review, therefore, is politically legitimate only insofar as it involves the interpretation of an authoritative constitutional instrument. In this sense, it is akin to statutory interpretation. In each case, the court's role is to divine the intent or purpose of the text as it has been expressed by the people through the mechanism of the democratic process. Of course, many (but not all) constitutional provisions are cast in broad and abstract language. Courts have the often arduous task of explicating the effect of this language in a myriad of factual circumstances, many of which may not have been contemplated by the framers of the Constitution. While there are inevitable disputes about the manner in which courts should perform this duty, for example by according more or less deference to legislative decisions, there is general agreement that the task itself is legitimate.

¶ 316 This legitimacy is imperiled, however, when courts attempt to limit the power of legislatures without recourse to express textual authority. From time to time, members of this Court have suggested that our Constitution comprehends implied rights that circumscribe legislative competence. On the theory that the efficacy of parliamentary democracy requires free political expression, it has been asserted that the curtailment of such expression is *ultra vires* both provincial legislatures and the federal Parliament: *Switzman v. Elbling*, [1957] S.C.R. 285, at p. 328 (*per* Abbott J.); *OPSEU v. Ontario (Attorney General)*, [1987] 2 S.C.R. 2, at p. 57 (*per* Beetz J.); see also: *Reference Re Alberta Statutes*, [1938] S.C.R. 100, at pp. 132-35 (*per* Duff C.J.), and at pp. 145-46 (*per* Cannon J.); *Switzman*, supra, at pp. 306-7 (*per* Rand J.); *OPSEU*, supra, at p. 25 (*per* Dickson C.J.); *Fraser v. Public Service Staff Relations Board*, [1985] 2 S.C.R. 455, at pp. 462-63 (*per* Dickson C.J.); *RWDSU v. Dolphin Delivery Ltd.*, [1986] 2 S.C.R. 573, at p. 584 (*per* McIntyre J.).

¶ 317 This theory, which is not so much an "implied bill of rights", as it has so often been called, but rather a more limited guarantee of those communicative freedoms necessary for the existence of parliamentary democracy, is not without appeal. An argument can be made that, even under a constitutional structure that deems Parliament to be supreme, certain rights, including freedom of political speech, should be enforced by the courts in order to safeguard the democratic accountability of Parliament. Without this limitation of its powers, the argument runs, Parliament could subvert the very process by which it acquired its legitimacy as a representative, democratic institution (cites omitted). It should be noted, however, that the idea that the Constitution contemplates implied protection for democratic rights has been rejected by a number of eminent jurists as being incompatible with the structure and history of the Constitution (cites omitted).

¶ 318 Whatever attraction this theory may hold, and I do not wish to be understood as either endorsing or rejecting it, it is clear in my view that it may not be used to justify the notion that the preamble to the *Constitution Act, 1867* contains implicit protection for judicial independence. Although it has been suggested that guarantees of political freedom flow from the preamble, as I have discussed in relation to judicial independence, this position is untenable. The better view is that if these guarantees exist, they are implicit in s. 17 of the *Constitution Act, 1867*, which provides for the establishment of Parliament; see Gibson, supra, at p. 498. More important, the justification for implied political freedoms is that they are supportive, and not subversive, of legislative supremacy.

That doctrine holds that democratically constituted legislatures, and not the courts, are the ultimate guarantors of civil liberties, including the right to an independent judiciary. Implying protection for judicial independence from the preambular commitment to a British-style constitution, therefore, entirely misapprehends the fundamental nature of that constitution.

¶ 319 This brings us back to the central point: to the extent that courts in Canada have the power to enforce the principle of judicial independence, this power derives from the structure of <u>Canadian</u>, and not British, constitutionalism. Our Constitution expressly contemplates both the power of judicial review (in s. 52 of the *Constitution Act, 1982*) and guarantees of judicial independence (in ss. 96-100 of the *Constitution Act, 1867* and s. 11(*d*) of the *Charter*). While these provisions have been interpreted to provide guarantees of independence that are not immediately manifest in their language, this has been accomplished through the usual mechanisms of constitutional interpretation, not through recourse to the preamble. The legitimacy of this interpretive exercise stems from its grounding in an expression of democratic will, not from a dubious theory of an implicit constitutional structure. The express provisions of the Constitution are not, as the Chief Justice contends, "elaborations of the underlying, unwritten, and organizing principles found in the preamble to the *Constitution Act, 1867*" (para. 107). On the contrary, they <u>are</u> the Constitution. To assert otherwise is to subvert the democratic foundation of judicial review.

¶ 320 In other words, the approach adopted by the Chief Justice, in my view, misapprehends the nature of the *Constitution Act, 1867*. The Act was not intended as an abstract document on the nature of government. The philosophical underpinnings of government in a British colony were a given, and find expression in the preamble. The Act was intended to create governmental and judicial structures for the maintenance of a British system of government in a federation of former British colonies. Insofar as there were limits to legislative power in Canada, they flowed from the terms of the Act (it being a British statute) that created them and *vis-à-vis* Great Britain the condition of dependency that prevailed in 1867. In considering the nature of the structures created, it was relevant to look at the principles underlying their British counterparts as the preamble invites the courts to do.

¶ 321 In considering the nature of the Canadian judicial system in light of its British counterpart, one should observe that only the superior courts' independence and impartiality were regarded as "constitutional". The independence and impartiality of inferior courts were, in turn, protected through the superintending functions of the superior courts. They were not protected directly under the relevant British "constitutional" principles.

¶ 322 This was the judicial organization that was adopted for this country, with adaptations suitable to Canadian conditions, in the judicature provisions of the *Constitution Act, 1867*. In reviewing these provisions, it is worth observing that the courts given constitutional protection are expressly named. The existing provincial inferior courts are not mentioned, and, indeed, the Probate Courts of some provinces were expressly excluded. Given that the express provisions dealing with constitutional protection for judicial independence have specifically spelled out their application, it seems strained to extend the ambit of this protection by reference to a general preambular statement. As the majority stated in *McVey (Re)*, [1992] 3 S.C.R. 475, at p. 525, "it would seem odd if general words in a preamble were to be given more weight than the specific provisions that deal with the matter".

¶ 323 This is a matter of no little significance for other reasons. If one is to give constitutional protection to courts generally, one must be able to determine with some precision what the term "court" encompasses. It is clear both under the *Constitution Act, 1867* as well as under s. 11(*d*) of the *Charter* what courts are covered, those under the *Constitution Act, 1867* arising under historic events in British constitutional history, those in s. 11(*d*) for the compelling reasons already given, namely protection for persons accused of an offence. But what are we to make of a general protection for courts such as that proposed by the Chief Justice? The word "court" is a broad term and can encompass a wide variety of tribunals. In the province of Quebec, for example, the term is legislatively used in respect of any number of administrative tribunals. Are we to include only those inferior courts applying ordinary jurisdiction in civil matters, or should we include all sorts of administrative tribunals, some of which are of far greater importance than ordinary civil courts? And if we do, is a distinction to be drawn between different tribunals and on the basis of what principles is this to be done?

¶ 324 These are some of the issues that have persuaded me that this Court should not precipitously, and without the benefit of argument of any real relevance to the case before us, venture forth on this uncharted sea. It is not as if the law as it stands is devoid of devices to ensure independent and impartial courts and tribunals. Quite the contrary, I would emphasize that the express protections for judicial independence set out in the Constitution are broad and powerful. They apply to all superior court and other judges specified in s. 96 of the *Constitution Act, 1867* as well as to inferior (provincial) courts exercising criminal jurisdiction. Nothing presented in these appeals suggests that these guarantees are not sufficient to ensure the independence of the judiciary as a whole. The superior courts have significant appellate and supervisory jurisdiction over inferior courts. If the impartiality of decisions from inferior courts is threatened by a lack of independence, any ensuing injustice may be rectified by the superior courts.

¶ 325 Should the foregoing provisions be found wanting, the *Charter* may conceivably be brought into play. Thus it is possible that protection for the independence for courts charged with determining the constitutionality of government action inheres in s. 24(1) of the *Charter* and s. 52 of the *Constitution Act, 1982*. It could be argued that the efficacy of those provisions, which empower courts to grant remedies for *Charter* violations and strike down unconstitutional laws, respectively, depends upon the existence of an independent and impartial adjudicator. The same may possibly be said in certain cases involving the applicability of the guarantees of liberty and security of the person arising in a non-penal setting. I add that these various possibilities may be seen to be abetted by the commitment to the rule of law expressed in the preamble to the *Charter*. These, however, are issues I would prefer to explore when they are brought before us for decision. [...]

[La Forest J. dissented from the principle established by the majority that judicial compensation commissions were required by s. 11(d), and that the commissions must review proposed changes to judicial remuneration in advance. La Forest J. would have established a reasonable perception test to distinguish between changes to judicial compensation made for a valid public purpose and changes designed to influence judicial decisions. Changes to judicial salaries that applied equally to substantially all persons paid from public funds would almost invariably be held constitutionally valid. Differential increases to judicial salaries would warrant a higher degree of scrutiny, and differential decreases would invite the highest level of review.

La Forest J. also disagreed with the principle that the judiciary could not engage in direct consultations with government over salaries. If the government used salary discussions to manipulate or influence the judiciary, the government's actions, in His Justice's opinion, would be reviewed to the same reasonable perception test applicable to salary discussions.

Since P.E.I. and Alberta were not required to have recourse to a salary commission, La Forest J. ruled that the salary reductions they imposed as part of an overall public economic measure were consistent with s. 11(d). The Manitoba government placed economic pressure on the judiciary so that they would concede the constitutionality of the planned salary changes. La Forest J. ruled that this action violated judicial independence.]

REFERENCE RE SECESSION OF QUEBEC
[1998] 2 S.C.R. 217.

THE COURT: —

¶ 1 This Reference requires us to consider momentous questions that go to the heart of our system of constitutional government. The observation we made more than a decade ago in *Reference Re Manitoba Language Rights*, [1985] 1 S.C.R. 721 (*Manitoba Language Rights Reference*), at p. 728, applies with equal force here: as in that case, the present one "combines legal and constitutional questions of the utmost subtlety and complexity with political questions of great sensitivity". In our view, it is not possible to answer the questions that have been put to us without a consideration of a number of underlying principles. An exploration of the meaning and nature of these underlying principles is not merely of academic interest. On the contrary, such an exploration is of immense practical utility. Only once those underlying principles have been examined and delineated may a considered response to the questions we are required to answer emerge.

[...] Question 1

Under the Constitution of Canada, can the National Assembly, legislature or government of Quebec effect the secession of Quebec from Canada unilaterally?

(1) Introduction

¶ 32 [...] The "Constitution of Canada" [...] includes the constitutional texts enumerated in s. 52(2) of the *Constitution Act, 1982*. Although these texts have a primary place in determining constitutional rules, they are not exhaustive. The Constitution also "embraces unwritten, as well as written rules", as we recently observed in the *Provincial Judges Reference*, supra, at para. 92. Finally, as was said in the *Patriation Reference*, supra, at p. 874, the Constitution of Canada includes

> the global system of rules and principles which govern the exercise of constitutional authority in the whole and in every part of the Canadian state.

These supporting principles and rules, which include constitutional conventions and the workings of Parliament, are a necessary part of our Constitution because problems or situations may arise which are not expressly dealt with by the text of the Constitution. In order to endure over time, a Constitution must contain a comprehensive set of rules and principles which are capable of providing an exhaustive legal framework for our system of government. Such principles and rules emerge from an understanding of the constitutional text itself, the historical context, and previous judicial interpretations of constitutional meaning. In our view, there are four fundamental and organizing principles of the Constitution which are relevant to addressing the question before us (although this enumeration is by no means exhaustive): federalism; democracy; constitutionalism and the rule of law; and respect for minorities. The foundation and substance of these principles are addressed in the following paragraphs. We will then turn to their specific application to the first reference question before us.

(2) Historical Context: The Significance of Confederation

¶ [...] 35 Confederation was an initiative of elected representatives of the people then living in the colonies scattered across part of what is now Canada. It was not initiated by Imperial fiat. In March 1864, a select committee of the Legislative Assembly of the Province of Canada, chaired by George Brown, began to explore prospects for constitutional reform. The committee's report, released in June 1864, recommended that a federal union encompassing Canada East and Canada West, and perhaps the other British North American colonies, be pursued. A group of Reformers from Canada West, led by Brown, joined with Etienne P. Taché and John A. Macdonald in a coalition government for the purpose of engaging in constitutional reform along the lines of the federal model proposed by the committee's report.

¶ 36 An opening to pursue federal union soon arose. The leaders of the maritime colonies had planned to meet at Charlottetown in the fall to discuss the perennial topic of maritime union. The Province of Canada secured invitations to send a Canadian delegation. On September 1, 1864, 23 delegates (five from New Brunswick, five from Nova Scotia, five from Prince Edward Island, and eight from the Province of Canada) met in Charlottetown. After five days of discussion, the delegates reached agreement on a plan for federal union.

¶ 37 The salient aspects of the agreement may be briefly outlined. There was to be a federal union featuring a bicameral central legislature. Representation in the Lower House was to be based on population, whereas in the Upper House it was to be based on regional equality, the regions comprising Canada East, Canada West and the Maritimes. The significance of the adoption of a federal form of government cannot be exaggerated. Without it, neither the agreement of the delegates from Canada East nor that of the delegates from the maritime colonies could have been obtained.

¶ 38 Several matters remained to be resolved, and so the Charlottetown delegates agreed to meet again at Quebec in October, and to invite Newfoundland to send a delegation to join them. The Quebec Conference began on October 10, 1864. Thirty-three delegates (two from Newfoundland, seven from New Brunswick, five from Nova Scotia, seven from Prince Edward Island, and twelve from the Province of Canada) met over a two and a half week period. Precise consideration of each aspect of the federal structure preoccupied the political agenda. The delegates approved 72 resolutions, addressing almost all of what subsequently made its way into the final text of the *Constitution Act, 1867*. These included guarantees to protect French language and culture, both directly (by making French an official language in Quebec and Canada as a whole) and indirectly (by allocating jurisdiction over education and "Property and Civil Rights in the Province" to the provinces). The protection of minorities was thus reaffirmed.

¶ 39 Legally, there remained only the requirement to have the Quebec Resolutions put into proper form and passed by the Imperial Parliament in London. However, politically, it was thought that more was required. Indeed, Resolution 70 provided that "The Sanction of the Imperial and Local Parliaments shall be sought for the Union of the Provinces on the principles adopted by the Conference." (Cited in J. Pope, ed., *Confederation: Being a Series of Hitherto Unpublished Documents Bearing on the British North America Act (1895)*, at p. 52 (emphasis added).)

¶ 40 Confirmation of the Quebec Resolutions was achieved more smoothly in central Canada than in the Maritimes. In February and March 1865, the Quebec Resolutions were the subject of almost six weeks of sustained debate in both houses of the Canadian legislature. The Canadian Legislative Assembly approved the Quebec Resolutions in March 1865 with the support of a majority of members from both Canada East and Canada West. The governments of both Prince Edward Island and Newfoundland chose, in accordance with popular sentiment in both colonies, not to accede to the Quebec Resolutions. In New Brunswick, a general election was required before Premier Tilley's pro-Confederation party prevailed. In Nova Scotia, Premier Tupper ultimately obtained a resolution from the House of Assembly favouring Confederation.

¶ 41 Sixteen delegates (five from New Brunswick, five from Nova Scotia, and six from the Province of Canada) met in London in December 1866 to finalize the plan for Confederation. To this end, they agreed to some slight modifications and additions to the Quebec Resolutions. Minor changes were made to the distribution of powers, provision was made for the appointment of extra senators in the event of a deadlock between the House of Commons and the Senate, and certain religious minorities were given the right to appeal to the federal government where their denominational school rights were adversely affected by provincial legislation. The British North America Bill was drafted after the London Conference with the assistance of the Colonial Office, and was introduced into the House of Lords in February 1867. The Act passed third reading in the House of Commons on March 8, received royal assent on March 29, and was proclaimed on July 1, 1867. The Dominion of Canada thus became a reality.

¶ 42 There was an early attempt at secession. In the first Dominion election in September 1867, Premier Tupper's forces were decimated: members opposed to Confederation won 18 of Nova Scotia's 19 federal seats, and in the simultaneous provincial election, 36 of the 38 seats in the provincial legislature. Newly-elected Premier Joseph Howe led a delegation to the Imperial Parliament in London in an effort to undo the new constitutional arrangements, but it was too late. The Colonial Office rejected Premier Howe's plea to permit Nova Scotia to withdraw from Confederation. As the Colonial Secretary wrote in 1868:

> The neighbouring province of New Brunswick has entered into the union in reliance on having with it the sister province of Nova Scotia; and vast obligations, political and commercial, have already been contracted on the faith of a measure so long discussed and so solemnly adopted. [...] I trust that the Assembly and the people of Nova Scotia will not be surprised that the Queen's government feel that they would not be warranted in advising the reversal of a great measure of state, attended by so many extensive consequences already in operation.

> (Quoted in H. Wade MacLauchlan, "Accounting for Democracy and the Rule of Law in the Quebec Secession Reference" (1997), 76 Can. Bar Rev. 155, at p. 168.)

The interdependence characterized by "vast obligations, political and commercial", referred to by the Colonial Secretary in 1868, has, of course, multiplied immeasurably in the last 130 years.

¶ 43 Federalism was a legal response to the underlying political and cultural realities that existed at Confederation and continue to exist today. At Confederation, political leaders told their respective communities that the Canadian union would be able to reconcile diversity with unity. It is pertinent, in the context of the present Reference, to mention the words of George-Etienne Cartier (cited in J. C. Bonenfant, "Les Canadiens français et la naissance de la Confédération", [1952] C.H.A.R. 39, at p. 42):

> [translation] When we are united, he said, we shall form a political nationality independent of the national origin or the religion of any individual. There are some who regretted that there was diversity of races and who expressed the hope that this distinctive character would disappear. The idea of unity of races is a utopia; it is an impossibility. A distinction of this nature will always exist, just as dissimilarity seems to be in the order of the physical, moral and political worlds. As to the objection based on this fact, that a large nation cannot be formed because Lower Canada is largely French and Catholic and Upper Canada is English and Protestant and the interior provinces are mixed, it constitutes, in my view, reasoning that is futile in the extreme. [...] In our own federation, we will have Catholics and Protestants, English, French, Irish and Scots and everyone, through his efforts and successes, will add to the prosperity and glory of the new confederation. We are of different races, not so that we can wage war on one another, but in order to work together for our well-being.

The federal-provincial division of powers was a legal recognition of the diversity that existed among the initial members of Confederation, and manifested a concern to accommodate that diversity within a single nation by granting significant powers to provincial governments. The *Constitution Act, 1867* was an act of nation-building. It was the first step in the transition from colonies separately dependent on the Imperial Parliament for their governance to a unified and independent political state in which different peoples could resolve their disagreements and work together toward common goals and a common interest. Federalism was the political mechanism by which diversity could be reconciled with unity.

¶ 44 A federal-provincial division of powers necessitated a written Constitution which circumscribed the powers of the new Dominion and Provinces of Canada. Despite its federal structure, the new Dominion was to have "a Constitution similar in Principle to that of the United Kingdom" (*Constitution Act, 1867,* preamble). Allowing for the obvious differences between the governance of Canada and the United Kingdom, it was nevertheless thought important to thus emphasize the continuity of constitutional principles, including democratic institutions and the rule of law; and the continuity of the exercise of sovereign power transferred from Westminster to the federal and provincial capitals of Canada.

¶ 45 After 1867, the Canadian federation continued to evolve both territorially and politically. New territories were admitted to the union and new provinces were formed. In 1870, Rupert's Land and the Northwest Territories were admitted and Manitoba was formed as a province. British Columbia was admitted in 1871, Prince Edward Island in 1873, and the Arctic Islands were added in 1880. In 1898, the Yukon Territory and in 1905, the provinces of Alberta and Saskatchewan were formed from the Northwest Territories. Newfoundland was admitted in 1949 by an amendment to the *Constitution Act, 1867.* The new territory of Nunavut was carved out of the Northwest Territories in 1993 with the partition to become effective in April 1999.

¶ 46 Canada's evolution from colony to fully independent state was gradual. The Imperial Parliament's passage of the Statute of Westminster, 1931 (U.K.), 22 & 23 Geo. 5, c. 4, confirmed in law what had earlier been confirmed in fact by the Balfour Declaration of 1926, namely, that Canada was an independent country. Thereafter, Canadian law alone governed in Canada, except where Canada expressly consented to the continued application of Imperial legislation. Canada's independence from Britain was achieved through legal and political evolution with an adherence to the rule of law and stability. The proclamation of the *Constitution Act, 1982* removed the last vestige of British authority over the Canadian Constitution and re-affirmed Canada's commitment to the protection of its minority, aboriginal, equality, legal and language rights, and fundamental freedoms as set out in the *Canadian Charter of Rights and Freedoms.*

¶ 47 Legal continuity, which requires an orderly transfer of authority, necessitated that the 1982 amendments be made by the Westminster Parliament, but the legitimacy as distinguished from the formal legality of the amendments derived from political decisions taken in Canada within a legal framework which this

Court, in the *Patriation Reference*, had ruled were in accordance with our Constitution. It should be noted, parenthetically, that the 1982 amendments did not alter the basic division of powers in ss. 91 and 92 of the *Constitution Act, 1867*, which is the primary textual expression of the principle of federalism in our Constitution, agreed upon at Confederation. It did, however, have the important effect that, despite the refusal of the government of Quebec to join in its adoption, Quebec has become bound to the terms of a Constitution that is different from that which prevailed previously, particularly as regards provisions governing its amendment, and the *Canadian Charter of Rights and Freedoms*. As to the latter, to the extent that the scope of legislative powers was thereafter to be constrained by the *Charter*, the constraint operated as much against federal legislative powers as against provincial legislative powers. Moreover, it is to be remembered that s. 33, the "notwithstanding clause", gives Parliament and the provincial legislatures authority to legislate on matters within their jurisdiction in derogation of the fundamental freedoms (s. 2), legal rights (ss. 7 to 14) and equality rights (s. 15) provisions of the *Charter*.

¶ 48 We think it apparent from even this brief historical review that the evolution of our constitutional arrangements has been characterized by adherence to the rule of law, respect for democratic institutions, the accommodation of minorities, insistence that governments adhere to constitutional conduct and a desire for continuity and stability. We now turn to a discussion of the general constitutional principles that bear on the present Reference.

(3) Analysis of the Constitutional Principles

(a) Nature of the Principles

¶ 49 What are those underlying principles? Our Constitution is primarily a written one, the product of 131 years of evolution. Behind the written word is an historical lineage stretching back through the ages, which aids in the consideration of the underlying constitutional principles. These principles inform and sustain the constitutional text: they are the vital unstated assumptions upon which the text is based. The following discussion addresses the four foundational constitutional principles that are most germane for resolution of this Reference: federalism, democracy, constitutionalism and the rule of law, and respect for minority rights. These defining principles function in symbiosis. No single principle can be defined in isolation from the others, nor does any one principle trump or exclude the operation of any other.

¶ 50 Our Constitution has an internal architecture, or what the majority of this Court in *OPSEU v. Ontario (Attorney General)*, [1987] 2 S.C.R. 2, at p. 57, called a "basic constitutional structure". The individual elements of the Constitution are linked to the others, and must be interpreted by reference to the structure of the Constitution as a whole. As we recently emphasized in the *Provincial Judges Reference*, certain underlying principles infuse our Constitution and breathe life into it. Speaking of the rule of law principle in the *Manitoba Language Rights Reference*, supra, at p. 750, we held that "the principle is clearly implicit in the very nature of a Constitution". The same may be said of the other three constitutional principles we underscore today.

¶ 51 Although these underlying principles are not explicitly made part of the Constitution by any written provision, other than in some respects by the oblique reference in the preamble to the *Constitution Act, 1867*, it would be impossible to conceive of our constitutional structure without them. The principles dictate major elements of the architecture of the Constitution itself and are as such its lifeblood.

¶ 52 The principles assist in the interpretation of the text and the delineation of spheres of jurisdiction, the scope of rights and obligations, and the role of our political institutions. Equally important, observance of and respect for these principles is essential to the ongoing process of constitutional development and evolution of our Constitution as a "living tree", to invoke the famous description in *Edwards v. Attorney-General for Canada*, [1930] A.C. 123 (P.C.), at p. 136. As this Court indicated in *New Brunswick Broadcasting Co. v. Nova Scotia (Speaker of the House of Assembly)*, [1993] 1 S.C.R. 319, Canadians have long recognized the existence and importance of unwritten constitutional principles in our system of government.

¶ 53 Given the existence of these underlying constitutional principles, what use may the Court make of them? In the *Provincial Judges Reference*, supra, at paras. 93 and 104, we cautioned that the recognition of these constitutional principles (the majority opinion referred to them as "organizing principles" and described one of them, judicial independence, as an "unwritten norm") could not be taken as an invitation to dispense with the written text of the Constitution. On the contrary, we confirmed that there are compelling reasons to insist upon the primacy of our written constitution. A written Constitution promotes legal certainty and predictability, and it provides a foundation and a touchstone for the exercise of constitutional judicial review. However, we also observed in the *Provincial Judges Reference* that the effect of the preamble to the *Constitution Act, 1867* was to incorporate certain constitutional principles by reference, a point made earlier in *Fraser v. Public Service Staff Relations Board*, [1985] 2 S.C.R. 455, at pp. 462-63. In the *Provincial Judges Reference*, at para. 104, we determined that the preamble "invites the courts to turn those principles into the premises of a constitutional argument that culminates in the filling of gaps in the express terms of the constitutional text".

¶ 54 Underlying constitutional principles may in certain circumstances give rise to substantive legal obligations (have "full legal force", as we described it in the *Patriation Reference*, supra, at p. 845), which constitute substantive limitations upon government action. These principles may give rise to very abstract and general obligations, or they may be more specific and precise in nature. The principles are not merely descriptive, but are also invested with a powerful normative force, and are binding upon both courts and governments. "In other words", as this Court confirmed in the *Manitoba Language Rights Reference*, supra, at p. 752, "in the process of Constitutional adjudication, the Court may have regard to unwritten postulates which form the very foundation of the Constitution of Canada". It is to a discussion of those underlying constitutional principles that we now turn.

(b) Federalism

¶ 55 It is undisputed that Canada is a federal state. Yet many commentators have observed that, according to the precise terms of the *Constitution Act, 1867*, the federal system was only partial. See, e.g., K. C. Wheare, *Federal Government* (4th ed. 1963), at pp. 18-20. This was so because, on paper, the federal government retained sweeping powers which threatened to undermine the autonomy of the provinces. Here again, however, a review of the written provisions of the Constitution does not provide the entire picture. Our political and constitutional practice has adhered to an underlying principle of federalism, and has interpreted the written provisions of the Constitution in this light. For example, although the federal power of disallowance was included in the *Constitution Act, 1867*, the underlying principle of federalism triumphed early. Many constitutional scholars contend that the federal power of disallowance has been abandoned (e.g., P. W. Hogg, *Constitutional Law of Canada* (4th ed. 1997), at p. 120).

¶ 56 In a federal system of government such as ours, political power is shared by two orders of government: the federal government on the one hand, and the provinces on the other. Each is assigned respective spheres of jurisdiction by the *Constitution Act, 1867*. See, e.g., *Liquidators of the Maritime Bank of Canada v. Receiver-General of New Brunswick*, [1892] A.C. 437 (P.C.), at pp. 441-42. It is up to the courts "to control the limits of the respective sovereignties": *Northern Telecom Canada Ltd. v. Communication Workers of Canada*, [1983] 1 S.C.R. 733, at p. 741. In interpreting our Constitution, the courts have always been concerned with the federalism principle, inherent in the structure of our constitutional arrangements, which has from the beginning been the lodestar by which the courts have been guided.

¶ 57 This underlying principle of federalism, then, has exercised a role of considerable importance in the interpretation of the written provisions of our Constitution. In the *Patriation Reference*, supra, at pp. 905-9, we confirmed that the principle of federalism runs through the political and legal systems of Canada. Indeed, Martland and Ritchie JJ., dissenting in the *Patriation Reference*, at p. 821, considered federalism to be "the dominant principle of Canadian constitutional law". With the enactment of the *Charter*, that proposition may have less force than it once did, but there can be little doubt that the principle of federalism remains a central organizational theme of our Constitution. Less obviously, perhaps, but certainly of equal importance, federalism is a political and legal response to underlying social and political realities.

¶ 58 The principle of federalism recognizes the diversity of the component parts of Confederation, and the autonomy of provincial governments to develop their societies within their respective spheres of jurisdiction. The federal structure of our country also facilitates democratic participation by distributing power to the government thought to be most suited to achieving the particular societal objective having regard to this diversity. The scheme of the *Constitution Act, 1867*, it was said in *Re the Initiative and Referendum Act*, [1919] A.C. 935 (P.C.), at p. 942, was:

not to weld the Provinces into one, nor to subordinate Provincial Governments to a central authority, but to establish a central government in which these Provinces should be represented, entrusted with exclusive authority only in affairs in which they had a common interest. Subject to this each Province was to retain its independence and autonomy and to be directly under the Crown as its head.

More recently, in *Haig v. Canada*, [1993] 2 S.C.R. 995, at p. 1047, the majority of this Court held that differences between provinces "are a rational part of the political reality in the federal process". It was referring to the differential application of federal law in individual provinces, but the point applies more generally. A unanimous Court expressed similar views in *R. v. S. (S.)*, [1990] 2 S.C.R. 254, at pp. 287-88.

¶ 59 The principle of federalism facilitates the pursuit of collective goals by cultural and linguistic minorities which form the majority within a particular province. This is the case in Quebec, where the majority of the population is French-speaking, and which possesses a distinct culture. This is not merely the result of chance. The social and demographic reality of Quebec explains the existence of the province of Quebec as a political unit and indeed, was one of the essential reasons for establishing a federal structure for the Canadian union in 1867. The experience of both Canada East and Canada West under the *Union Act, 1840* (U.K.), 3-4 Vict., c. 35, had not been satisfactory. The federal structure adopted at Confederation enabled French-speaking Canadians to form a numerical majority in the province of Quebec, and so exercise the considerable provincial powers conferred by the *Constitution Act, 1867* in such a way as to promote their language and culture. It also made provision for certain guaranteed representation within the federal Parliament itself.

¶ 60 Federalism was also welcomed by Nova Scotia and New Brunswick, both of which also affirmed their will to protect their individual cultures and their autonomy over local matters. All new provinces joining the federation sought to achieve similar objectives, which are no less vigorously pursued by the provinces and territories as we approach the new millennium.

(c) Democracy

¶ 61 Democracy is a fundamental value in our constitutional law and political culture. While it has both an institutional and an individual aspect, the democratic principle was also argued before us in the sense of the supremacy of the sovereign will of a people, in this case potentially to be expressed by Quebeckers in support of unilateral secession. It is useful to explore in a summary way these different aspects of the democratic principle.

¶ 62 The principle of democracy has always informed the design of our constitutional structure, and continues to act as an essential interpretive consideration to this day. A majority of this Court in *OPSEU v. Ontario*, supra, at p. 57, confirmed that "the basic structure of our Constitution, as established by the *Constitution Act, 1867*, contemplates the existence of certain political institutions, including freely elected legislative bodies at the federal and provincial levels". As is apparent from an earlier line of decisions emanating from this Court, including *Switzman v. Elbling*, [1957] S.C.R. 285, *Saumur v. City of Quebec*, [1953] 2 S.C.R. 299, *Boucher v. The King*, [1951] S.C.R. 265, and *Reference Re Alberta Statutes*, [1938] S.C.R. 100, the democratic principle can best be understood as a sort of baseline against which the framers of our Constitution, and subsequently, our elected representatives under it, have always operated. It is perhaps for this reason that the principle was not explicitly identified in the text of the *Constitution Act, 1867* itself. To have done so might have appeared redundant, even silly, to the framers. As explained in the *Provincial Judges Reference*, supra, at para. 100, it is evident that our Constitution contemplates that Canada shall be a constitutional democracy. Yet this merely demonstrates the importance of underlying constitutional principles that are nowhere explicitly described in our constitutional texts. The representative and democratic nature of our political institutions was simply assumed.

¶ 63 Democracy is commonly understood as being a political system of majority rule. It is essential to be clear what this means. The evolution of our democratic tradition can be traced back to the *Magna Carta* (1215) and before, through the long struggle for Parliamentary supremacy which culminated in the *English Bill of Rights* in 1688-89, the emergence of representative political institutions in the colonial era, the development of responsible government in the 19th century, and eventually, the achievement of Confederation itself in 1867. "[T]he Canadian tradition", the majority of this Court held in *Reference Re Provincial Electoral Boundaries (Sask.)*, [1991] 2 S.C.R. 158, at p. 186, is "one of evolutionary democracy moving in uneven steps toward the goal of universal suffrage and more effective representation". Since Confederation, efforts to extend the franchise to those unjustly excluded from participation in our political system such as women, minorities, and aboriginal peoples have continued, with some success, to the present day.

¶ 64 Democracy is not simply concerned with the process of government. On the contrary, as suggested in *Switzman v. Elbling*, supra, at p. 306, democracy is fundamentally connected to substantive goals, most importantly, the promotion of self-government. Democracy accommodates cultural and group identities: *Reference Re Provincial Electoral Boundaries*, at p. 188. Put another way, a sovereign people exercises its right to self-government through the democratic process. In considering the scope and purpose of the *Charter*, the Court in *R. v. Oakes*, [1986] 1 S.C.R. 103, articulated some of the values inherent in the notion of democracy (at p. 136):

> The Court must be guided by the values and principles essential to a free and democratic society which I believe to embody, to name but a few, respect for the inherent dignity of the human person, commitment to social justice and equality, accommodation of a wide variety of beliefs, respect for cultural and group identity, and faith in social and political institutions which enhance the participation of individuals and groups in society.

¶ 65 In institutional terms, democracy means that each of the provincial legislatures and the federal Parliament is elected by popular franchise. These legislatures, we have said, are "at the core of the system of representative government": *New Brunswick Broadcasting*, supra, at p. 387. In individual terms, the right to vote in elections to the House of Commons and the provincial legislatures, and to be candidates in those elections, is guaranteed to "Every citizen of Canada" by virtue of s. 3 of the *Charter*. Historically, this Court has interpreted democracy to mean the process of representative and responsible government and the right of citizens to participate in the political process as voters (*Reference Re Provincial Electoral Boundaries*, supra) and as candidates (*Harvey v. New Brunswick (Attorney General)*, [1996] 2 S.C.R. 876). In addition, the effect of s. 4 of the *Charter* is to oblige the House of Commons and the provincial legislatures to hold regular elections and to permit citizens to elect representatives to their political institutions. The democratic principle is affirmed with particular clarity in that section 4 is not subject to the notwithstanding power contained in s. 33.

¶ 66 It is, of course, true that democracy expresses the sovereign will of the people. Yet this expression, too, must be taken in the context of the other institutional values we have identified as pertinent to this Reference. The relationship between democracy and federalism means, for example, that in Canada there may be different and equally legitimate majorities in different provinces and territories and at the federal level. No one majority is more or less "legitimate" than the others as an expression of democratic opinion, although, of course, the consequences will vary with the subject matter. A federal system of government enables different provinces to pursue policies responsive to the particular concerns and interests of people in that province. At the same time, Canada as a whole is also a democratic community in which citizens construct and achieve goals on a national scale through a federal government acting within the limits of its jurisdiction. The function of federalism is to enable citizens to participate concurrently in different collectivities and to pursue goals at both a provincial and a federal level.

¶ 67 The consent of the governed is a value that is basic to our understanding of a free and democratic society. Yet democracy in any real sense of the word cannot exist without the rule of law. It is the law that creates the framework within which the "sovereign will" is to be ascertained and implemented. To be accorded legitimacy, democratic institutions must rest, ultimately, on a legal foundation. That is, they must allow for the participation of, and accountability to, the people, through public institutions created under the Constitution. Equally, however, a system of government cannot survive through adherence to the law alone. A political system must also possess legitimacy, and in our political culture, that requires an interaction between the rule of law and the democratic principle. The system must be capable of reflecting the aspirations of the people. But there is more. Our law's claim to legitimacy also rests on an appeal to moral values, many of which are imbedded in our constitutional structure. It would be a grave mistake to equate legitimacy with the "sovereign will" or majority rule alone, to the exclusion of other constitutional values.

¶ 68 Finally, we highlight that a functioning democracy requires a continuous process of discussion. The Constitution mandates government by democratic legislatures, and an executive accountable to them, "resting ultimately on public opinion reached by discussion and the interplay of ideas" (*Saumur v. City of Quebec*, supra, at p. 330). At both the federal and provincial level, by its very nature, the need to build majorities necessitates compromise, negotiation, and deliberation. No one has a monopoly on truth, and our system is predicated on the faith that in the marketplace of ideas, the best solutions to public problems will rise to the top. Inevitably, there will be dissenting voices. A democratic system of government is committed to considering those dissenting voices, and seeking to acknowledge and address those voices in the laws by which all in the community must live.

¶ 69 The *Constitution Act, 1982* gives expression to this principle, by conferring a right to initiate constitutional change on each participant in Confederation. In our view, the existence of this right imposes a corresponding duty on the participants in Confederation to engage in constitutional discussions in order to acknowledge and address democratic expressions of a desire for change in other provinces. This duty is inherent in the democratic principle which is a fundamental predicate of our system of governance.

(d) Constitutionalism and the Rule of Law

¶ 70 The principles of constitutionalism and the rule of law lie at the root of our system of government. The rule of law, as observed in *Roncarelli v. Duplessis*, [1959] S.C.R. 121, at p. 142, is "a fundamental postulate of our constitutional structure." As we noted in the *Patriation Reference*, supra, at pp. 805-6, "[t]he 'rule of law' is a highly textured expression, importing many things which are beyond the need of these reasons to explore but conveying, for example, a sense of orderliness, of subjection to known legal rules and of executive accountability to legal authority". At its most basic level, the rule of law vouchsafes to the citizens and residents of the country a stable, predictable and ordered society in which to conduct their affairs. It provides a shield for individuals from arbitrary state action.

¶ 71 In the *Manitoba Language Rights Reference*, supra, at pp. 747-52, this Court outlined the elements of the rule of law. We emphasized, first, that the rule of law provides that the law is supreme over the acts of both government and private persons. There is, in short, one law for all. Second, we explained, at p. 749, that "the rule of law requires the creation and maintenance of an actual order of positive laws which preserves and embodies the more general principle of normative order". It was this second aspect of the rule of law that was primarily at issue in the *Manitoba Language Rights Reference* itself. A third aspect of the rule of law is, as recently confirmed in the *Provincial Judges Reference*, supra, at para. 10, that "the exercise of all public power must find its ultimate source in a legal rule". Put another way, the relationship between the state and the individual must be regulated by law. Taken together, these three considerations make up a principle of profound constitutional and political significance.

¶ 72 The constitutionalism principle bears considerable similarity to the rule of law, although they are not identical. The essence of constitutionalism in Canada is embodied in s. 52(1) of the Constitution Act, 1982, which provides that "[t]he Constitution of Canada is the supreme law of Canada, and any law that is inconsistent with the provisions of the Constitution is, to the extent of the inconsistency, of no force or effect." Simply put, the constitutionalism principle requires that all government action comply with the Constitution. The rule of law principle requires that all government action must comply with the law, including the Constitution. This Court has noted on several occasions that with the adoption of the *Charter*, the Canadian system of government was transformed to a significant extent from a system of Parliamentary supremacy to one of constitutional supremacy. The Constitution binds all governments, both federal and provincial, including the executive branch (*Operation Dismantle Inc. v. The Queen*, [1985] 1 S.C.R. 441, at p. 455). They may not transgress its provisions: indeed, their sole claim to exercise lawful authority rests in the powers allocated to them under the Constitution, and can come from no other source.

¶ 73 An understanding of the scope and importance of the principles of the rule of law and constitutionalism is aided by acknowledging explicitly why a Constitution is entrenched beyond the reach of simple majority rule. There are three overlapping reasons.

¶ 74 First, a Constitution may provide an added safeguard for fundamental human rights and individual freedoms which might otherwise be susceptible to government interference. Although democratic government is generally solicitous of those rights, there are occasions when the majority will be tempted to ignore fundamental rights in order to accomplish collective goals more easily or effectively. Constitutional entrenchment ensures that those rights will be given due regard and protection. Second, a Constitution may seek to ensure that vulnerable minority groups are endowed with the institutions and rights necessary to maintain and promote their identities against the assimilative pressures of the majority. And third, a Constitution may provide for a division of political power that allocates political power amongst different levels of government. That purpose would be defeated if one of those democratically elected levels of government could usurp the powers of the other simply by exercising its legislative power to allocate additional political power to itself unilaterally.

¶ 75 The argument that the Constitution may be legitimately circumvented by resort to a majority vote in a province-wide referendum is superficially persuasive, in large measure because it seems to appeal to some of the same principles that underlie the legitimacy of the Constitution itself, namely, democracy and self-government. In short, it is suggested that as the notion of popular sovereignty underlies the legitimacy of our existing constitutional arrangements, so the same popular sovereignty that originally led to the present Constitution must (it is argued) also permit "the people" in their exercise of popular sovereignty to secede by majority vote alone. However, closer analysis reveals that this argument is unsound, because it misunderstands the meaning of popular sovereignty and the essence of a constitutional democracy.

¶ 76 Canadians have never accepted that ours is a system of simple majority rule. Our principle of democracy, taken in conjunction with the other constitutional principles discussed here, is richer. Constitutional government is necessarily predicated on the idea that the political representatives of the people of a province have the capacity and the power to commit the province to be bound into the future by the constitutional rules being adopted. These rules are "binding" not in the sense of frustrating the will of a majority of a province, but as defining the majority which must be consulted in order to alter the fundamental balances of political power (including the spheres of autonomy guaranteed by the principle of federalism), individual rights, and minority rights in our society. Of course, those constitutional rules are themselves amenable to amendment, but only through a process of negotiation which ensures that there is an opportunity for the constitutionally defined rights of all the parties to be respected and reconciled.

¶ 77 In this way, our belief in democracy may be harmonized with our belief in constitutionalism. Constitutional amendment often requires some form of substantial consensus precisely because the content of the underlying principles of our Constitution demand it. By requiring broad support in the form of an "enhanced majority" to achieve constitutional change, the Constitution ensures that minority interests must be addressed before proposed changes which would affect them may be enacted.

¶ 78 It might be objected, then, that constitutionalism is therefore incompatible with democratic government. This would be an erroneous view. Constitutionalism facilitates indeed, makes possible a democratic political system by creating an orderly framework within which people may make political decisions. Viewed correctly, constitutionalism and the rule of law are not in conflict with democracy; rather, they are essential to it. Without that relationship, the political will upon which democratic decisions are taken would itself be undermined.

(e) Protection of Minorities

¶ 79 The fourth underlying constitutional principle we address here concerns the protection of minorities. There are a number of specific constitutional provisions protecting minority language, religion and education rights. Some of those provisions are, as we have recognized on a number of occasions, the product of historical compromises. As this Court observed in *Reference Re Bill 30, An Act to Amend the Education Act (Ont.)*, [1987] 1 S.C.R. 1148, at p. 1173, and in *Reference Re Education Act (Que.)*, [1993] 2 S.C.R. 511, at pp. 529-30, the protection of minority religious education rights was a central consideration in the negotiations leading to Confederation. In the absence of such protection, it was felt that the minorities in what was then Canada East and Canada West would be submerged and assimilated. See also *Greater Montreal Protestant School Board v. Quebec (Attorney General)*, [1989] 1 S.C.R. 377, at pp. 401-2, and *Adler v. Ontario*, [1996] 3 S.C.R. 609. Similar concerns animated the provisions protecting minority language rights, as noted in *Société des Acadiens du Nouveau-Brunswick Inc. v. Association of Parents for Fairness in Education*, [1986] 1 S.C.R. 549, at p. 564.

¶ 80 However, we highlight that even though those provisions were the product of negotiation and political compromise, that does not render them unprincipled. Rather, such a concern reflects a broader principle related to the protection of minority rights. Undoubtedly, the three other constitutional principles inform the scope and operation of the specific provisions that protect the rights of minorities. We emphasize that the protection of minority rights is itself an independent principle underlying our constitutional order. The principle is clearly reflected in the *Charter*'s provisions for the protection of minority rights. See, e.g., *Reference Re Public Schools Act (Man.)*, s. 79(3), (4) and (7), [1993] 1 S.C.R. 839, and *Mahe v. Alberta*, [1990] 1 S.C.R. 342.

¶ 81 The concern of our courts and governments to protect minorities has been prominent in recent years, particularly following the enactment of the *Charter*. Undoubtedly, one of the key considerations motivating the enactment of the *Charter*, and the process of constitutional judicial review that it entails, is the protection of minorities. However, it should not be forgotten that the protection of minority rights had a long history before the enactment of the *Charter*. Indeed, the protection of minority rights was clearly an essential consideration in the design of our constitutional structure even at the time of Confederation: *Senate Reference*, (cites omitted), at p. 71. Although Canada's record of upholding the rights of minorities is not a spotless one, that goal is one towards which Canadians have been striving since Confederation, and the process has not been without successes. The principle of protecting minority rights continues to exercise influence in the operation and interpretation of our Constitution.

¶ 82 Consistent with this long tradition of respect for minorities, which is at least as old as Canada itself, the framers of the *Constitution Act, 1982* included in s. 35 explicit protection for existing aboriginal and treaty rights, and in s. 25, a non-derogation clause in favour of the rights of aboriginal peoples. The "promise" of s. 35, as it was termed in *R. v. Sparrow*, [1990] 1 S.C.R. 1075, at p. 1083, recognized not only the ancient occupation of land by aboriginal peoples, but their contribution to the building of Canada, and the special commitments made to them by successive governments. The protection of these rights, so recently and arduously achieved, whether looked at in their own right or as part of the larger concern with minorities, reflects an important underlying constitutional value.

(4) The Operation of the Constitutional Principles in the Secession Context

¶ 83 Secession is the effort of a group or section of a state to withdraw itself from the political and constitutional authority of that state, with a view to achieving statehood for a new territorial unit on the international plane. In a federal state, secession typically takes the form of a territorial unit seeking to withdraw from the federation. Secession is a legal act as much as a political one. By the terms of Question 1 of this Reference, we are asked to rule on the legality of unilateral secession "under the Constitution of Canada". This is an appropriate question, as the legality of unilateral secession must be evaluated, at least in the first instance, from the perspective of the domestic legal order of the state from which the unit seeks to withdraw. As we shall see below, it is also argued that international law is a relevant standard by which the legality of a purported act of secession may be measured.

¶ 84 The secession of a province from Canada must be considered, in legal terms, to require an amendment to the Constitution, which perforce requires negotiation. The amendments necessary to achieve a secession could be radical and extensive. Some commentators have suggested that secession could be a change of such a magnitude that it could not be considered to be merely an amendment to the Constitution. We are not persuaded by this contention. It is of course true that the Constitution is silent as to the ability of a province to secede from Confederation but, although the Constitution neither expressly authorizes nor prohibits secession, an act of secession would purport to alter the governance of Canadian territory in a manner which undoubtedly is inconsistent with our current constitutional arrangements. The fact that those changes would be profound, or that they would purport to have a significance with respect to international law, does not negate their nature as amendments to the Constitution of Canada.

¶ 85 The Constitution is the expression of the sovereignty of the people of Canada. It lies within the power of the people of Canada, acting through their various governments duly elected and recognized under the Constitution, to effect whatever constitutional arrangements are desired within Canadian territory, including, should it be so desired, the secession of Quebec from Canada. As this Court held in the *Manitoba Language Rights Reference*, supra, at p. 745, "The Constitution of a country is a statement of the will of the people to be governed in accordance with certain principles held as fundamental and certain prescriptions restrictive of the powers of the legislature and government". The manner in which such a political will could be formed and mobilized is a somewhat speculative exercise, though we are asked to assume the existence of such a political will for the purpose of answering the question before us. By the terms of this Reference, we have been asked to consider whether it would be constitutional in such a circumstance for the National Assembly, legislature or government of Quebec to effect the secession of Quebec from Canada unilaterally.

¶ 86 The "unilateral" nature of the act is of cardinal importance and we must be clear as to what is understood by this term. In one sense, any step towards a constitutional amendment initiated by a single actor on the constitutional stage is "unilateral". We do not believe that this is the meaning contemplated by Question 1, nor is this the sense in which the term has been used in argument before us. Rather, what is claimed by a right to secede "unilaterally" is the right to effectuate secession without prior negotiations with the other provinces and the federal government. At issue is not the legality of the first step but the legality of the final act of purported unilateral secession. The supposed juridical basis for such an act is said to be a clear expression of democratic will in a referendum in the province of Quebec. This claim requires us to examine the possible juridical impact, if any, of such a referendum on the functioning of our Constitution, and on the claimed legality of a unilateral act of secession.

¶ 87 Although the Constitution does not itself address the use of a referendum procedure, and the results of a referendum have no direct role or legal effect in our constitutional scheme, a referendum undoubtedly may provide a democratic method of ascertaining the views of the electorate on important political questions on a particular occasion. The democratic principle identified above would demand that considerable weight be given to a clear expression by the people of

Quebec of their will to secede from Canada, even though a referendum, in itself and without more, has no direct legal effect, and could not in itself bring about unilateral secession. Our political institutions are premised on the democratic principle, and so an expression of the democratic will of the people of a province carries weight, in that it would confer legitimacy on the efforts of the government of Quebec to initiate the Constitution's amendment process in order to secede by constitutional means. In this context, we refer to a "clear" majority as a qualitative evaluation. The referendum result, if it is to be taken as an expression of the democratic will, must be free of ambiguity both in terms of the question asked and in terms of the support it achieves.

¶ 88 The federalism principle, in conjunction with the democratic principle, dictates that the clear repudiation of the existing constitutional order and the clear expression of the desire to pursue secession by the population of a province would give rise to a reciprocal obligation on all parties to Confederation to negotiate constitutional changes to respond to that desire. The amendment of the Constitution begins with a political process undertaken pursuant to the Constitution itself. In Canada, the initiative for constitutional amendment is the responsibility of democratically elected representatives of the participants in Confederation. Those representatives may, of course, take their cue from a referendum, but in legal terms, constitution-making in Canada, as in many countries, is undertaken by the democratically elected representatives of the people. The corollary of a legitimate attempt by one participant in Confederation to seek an amendment to the Constitution is an obligation on all parties to come to the negotiating table. The clear repudiation by the people of Quebec of the existing constitutional order would confer legitimacy on demands for secession, and place an obligation on the other provinces and the federal government to acknowledge and respect that expression of democratic will by entering into negotiations and conducting them in accordance with the underlying constitutional principles already discussed.

¶ 89 What is the content of this obligation to negotiate? At this juncture, we confront the difficult inter-relationship between substantive obligations flowing from the Constitution and questions of judicial competence and restraint in supervising or enforcing those obligations. This is mirrored by the distinction between the legality and the legitimacy of actions taken under the Constitution. We propose to focus first on the substantive obligations flowing from this obligation to negotiate; once the nature of those obligations has been described, it is easier to assess the appropriate means of enforcement of those obligations, and to comment on the distinction between legality and legitimacy.

¶ 90 The conduct of the parties in such negotiations would be governed by the same constitutional principles which give rise to the duty to negotiate: federalism, democracy, constitutionalism and the rule of law, and the protection of minorities. Those principles lead us to reject two absolutist propositions. One of those propositions is that there would be a legal obligation on the other provinces and federal government to accede to the secession of a province, subject only to negotiation of the logistical details of secession. This proposition is attributed either to the supposed implications of the democratic principle of the Constitution, or to the international law principle of self-determination of peoples.

¶ 91 For both theoretical and practical reasons, we cannot accept this view. We hold that Quebec could not purport to invoke a right of self-determination such as to dictate the terms of a proposed secession to the other parties: that would not be a negotiation at all. As well, it would be naive to expect that the substantive goal of secession could readily be distinguished from the practical details of secession. The devil would be in the details. The democracy principle, as we have emphasized, cannot be invoked to trump the principles of federalism and rule of law, the rights of individuals and minorities, or the operation of democracy in the other provinces or in Canada as a whole. No negotiations could be effective if their ultimate outcome, secession, is cast as an absolute legal entitlement based upon an obligation to give effect to that act of secession in the Constitution. Such a foregone conclusion would actually undermine the obligation to negotiate and render it hollow.

¶ 92 However, we are equally unable to accept the reverse proposition, that a clear expression of self-determination by the people of Quebec would impose no obligations upon the other provinces or the federal government. The continued existence and operation of the Canadian constitutional order cannot remain indifferent to the clear expression of a clear majority of Quebeckers that they no longer wish to remain in Canada. This would amount to the assertion that other constitutionally recognized principles necessarily trump the clearly expressed democratic will of the people of Quebec. Such a proposition fails to give sufficient weight to the underlying constitutional principles that must inform the amendment process, including the principles of democracy and federalism. The rights of other provinces and the federal government cannot deny the right of the government of Quebec to pursue secession, should a clear majority of the people of Quebec choose that goal, so long as in doing so, Quebec respects the rights of others. Negotiations would be necessary to address the interests of the federal government, of Quebec and the other provinces, and other participants, as well as the rights of all Canadians both within and outside Quebec.

¶ 93 Is the rejection of both of these propositions reconcilable? Yes, once it is realized that none of the rights or principles under discussion is absolute to the exclusion of the others. This observation suggests that other parties cannot exercise their rights in such a way as to amount to an absolute denial of Quebec's rights, and similarly, that so long as Quebec exercises its rights while respecting the rights of others, it may propose secession and seek to achieve it through negotiation. The negotiation process precipitated by a decision of a clear majority of the population of Quebec on a clear question to pursue secession would require the reconciliation of various rights and obligations by the representatives of two legitimate majorities, namely, the clear majority of the population of Quebec, and the clear majority of Canada as a whole, whatever that may be. There can be no suggestion that either of these majorities "trumps" the other. A political majority that does not act in accordance with the underlying constitutional principles we have identified puts at risk the legitimacy of the exercise of its rights.

¶ 94 In such circumstances, the conduct of the parties assumes primary constitutional significance. The negotiation process must be conducted with an eye to the constitutional principles we have outlined, which must inform the actions of all the participants in the negotiation process.

¶ 95 Refusal of a party to conduct negotiations in a manner consistent with constitutional principles and values would seriously put at risk the legitimacy of that party's assertion of its rights, and perhaps the negotiation process as a whole. Those who quite legitimately insist upon the importance of upholding the rule of law cannot at the same time be oblivious to the need to act in conformity with constitutional principles and values, and so do their part to contribute to the maintenance and promotion of an environment in which the rule of law may flourish.

¶ 96 No one can predict the course that such negotiations might take. The possibility that they might not lead to an agreement amongst the parties must be recognized. Negotiations following a referendum vote in favour of seeking secession would inevitably address a wide range of issues, many of great import. After 131 years of Confederation, there exists, inevitably, a high level of integration in economic, political and social institutions across Canada. The vision of those who brought about Confederation was to create a unified country, not a loose alliance of autonomous provinces. Accordingly, while there are regional economic interests, which sometimes coincide with provincial boundaries, there are also national interests and enterprises (both public and private) that would face potential dismemberment. There is a national economy and a national debt. Arguments were raised before us regarding boundary issues. There are linguistic and cultural minorities, including aboriginal peoples, unevenly distributed across the country who look to the Constitution of Canada for the protection of their rights. Of course, secession would give rise to many issues of great complexity and difficulty. These would have to be resolved within the overall framework of the rule of law, thereby assuring Canadians resident in Quebec and elsewhere a measure of stability in what would likely be a period of considerable upheaval and uncertainty. Nobody seriously suggests that our national existence, seamless in so many aspects, could be effortlessly separated along what are now the provincial boundaries of Quebec. As the Attorney General of Saskatchewan put it in his oral submission:

> A nation is built when the communities that comprise it make commitments to it, when they forego choices and opportunities on behalf of a nation, [...] when the communities that comprise it make compromises, when they offer each other guarantees, when they make transfers and perhaps most pointedly, when they receive from others the benefits of national solidarity. The threads of a thousand acts of accommodation are the fabric of a nation.

¶ 97 In the circumstances, negotiations following such a referendum would undoubtedly be difficult. While the negotiators would have to contemplate the possibility of secession, there would be no absolute legal entitlement to it and no assumption that an agreement reconciling all relevant rights and obligations would actually be reached. It is foreseeable that even negotiations carried out in conformity with the underlying constitutional principles could reach an impasse. We need not speculate here as to what would then transpire. Under the Constitution, secession requires that an amendment be negotiated.

¶ 98 The respective roles of the courts and political actors in discharging the constitutional obligations we have identified follows ineluctably from the foregoing observations. In the *Patriation Reference*, a distinction was drawn between the law of the Constitution, which, generally speaking, will be enforced by the courts, and other constitutional rules, such as the conventions of the Constitution, which carry only political sanctions. It is also the case, however, that judicial intervention, even in relation to the law of the Constitution, is subject to the Court's appreciation of its proper role in the constitutional scheme.

¶ 99 The notion of justiciability is, as we earlier pointed out in dealing with the preliminary objection, linked to the notion of appropriate judicial restraint. We earlier made reference to the discussion of justiciability in *Reference Re Canada Assistance Plan*, infra, at p. 545:

> In exercising its discretion whether to determine a matter that is alleged to be non-justiciable, the Court's primary concern is to retain its proper role within the constitutional framework of our democratic form of government.

In *Operation Dismantle*, supra, at p. 459, it was pointed out that justiciability is a "doctrine [...] founded upon a concern with the appropriate role of the courts as the forum for the resolution of different types of disputes". An analogous doctrine of judicial restraint operates here. Also, as observed in *Canada (Auditor General) v. Canada (Minister of Energy, Mines and Resources)*, [1989] 2 S.C.R. 49 (the *Auditor General's case*), at p. 91:

> There is an array of issues which calls for the exercise of judicial judgment on whether the questions are properly cognizable by the courts. Ultimately, such judgment depends on the appreciation by the judiciary of its own position in the constitutional scheme.

¶ 100 The role of the Court in this Reference is limited to the identification of the relevant aspects of the Constitution in their broadest sense. We have interpreted the questions as relating to the constitutional framework within which political decisions may ultimately be made. Within that framework, the workings of the political process are complex and can only be resolved by means of political judgments and evaluations. The Court has no supervisory role over the political aspects of constitutional negotiations. Equally, the initial impetus for negotiation, namely a clear majority on a clear question in favour of secession, is subject only to political evaluation, and properly so. A right and a corresponding duty to negotiate secession cannot be built on an alleged expression of democratic will if the expression of democratic will is itself fraught with ambiguities. Only the political actors would have the information and expertise to make the appropriate judgment as to the point at which, and the circumstances in which, those ambiguities are resolved one way or the other.

¶ 101 If the circumstances giving rise to the duty to negotiate were to arise, the distinction between the strong defence of legitimate interests and the taking of positions which, in fact, ignore the legitimate interests of others is one that also defies legal analysis. The Court would not have access to all of the information available to the political actors, and the methods appropriate for the search for truth in a court of law are ill-suited to getting to the bottom of constitutional negotiations. To the extent that the questions are political in nature, it is not the role of the judiciary to interpose its own views on the different negotiating positions of the parties, even were it invited to do so. Rather, it is the obligation of the elected representatives to give concrete form to the discharge of their constitutional obligations which only they and their electors can ultimately assess. The reconciliation of the various legitimate constitutional interests outlined above is necessarily committed to the political rather than the judicial realm, precisely because that reconciliation can only be achieved through the give and take of the negotiation process. Having established the legal framework, it would be for the democratically elected leadership of the various participants to resolve their differences.

¶ 102 The non-justiciability of political issues that lack a legal component does not deprive the surrounding constitutional framework of its binding status, nor does this mean that constitutional obligations could be breached without incurring serious legal repercussions. Where there are legal rights there are remedies, but as we explained in the *Auditor General's case*, supra, at p. 90, and *New Brunswick Broadcasting*, supra, the appropriate recourse in some circumstances lies through the workings of the political process rather than the courts.

¶ 103 To the extent that a breach of the constitutional duty to negotiate in accordance with the principles described above undermines the legitimacy of a party's actions, it may have important ramifications at the international level. Thus, a failure of the duty to undertake negotiations and pursue them according to constitutional principles may undermine that government's claim to legitimacy which is generally a precondition for recognition by the international community. Conversely, violations of those principles by the federal or other provincial governments responding to the request for secession may undermine their legitimacy. Thus, a Quebec that had negotiated in conformity with constitutional principles and values in the face of unreasonable intransigence on the part of other participants at the federal or provincial level would be more likely to be recognized than a Quebec which did not itself act according to constitutional principles in the negotiation process. Both the legality of the acts of the parties to the negotiation process under Canadian law, and the perceived legitimacy of such action, would be important considerations in the recognition process. In this way, the adherence of the parties to the obligation to negotiate would be evaluated in an indirect manner on the international plane.

¶ 104 Accordingly, the secession of Quebec from Canada cannot be accomplished by the National Assembly, the legislature or government of Quebec unilaterally, that is to say, without principled negotiations, and be considered a lawful act. Any attempt to effect the secession of a province from Canada must be undertaken pursuant to the Constitution of Canada, or else violate the Canadian legal order. However, the continued existence and operation of the Canadian constitutional order cannot remain unaffected by the unambiguous expression of a clear majority of Quebeckers that they no longer wish to remain in Canada. The primary means by which that expression is given effect is the constitutional duty to negotiate in accordance with the constitutional principles that we have described herein. In the event secession negotiations are initiated, our Constitution, no less than our history, would call on the participants to work to reconcile the rights, obligations and legitimate aspirations of all Canadians within a framework that emphasizes constitutional responsibilities as much as it does constitutional rights.

¶ 105 It will be noted that Question 1 does not ask how secession could be achieved in a constitutional manner, but addresses one form of secession only, namely unilateral secession. Although the applicability of various procedures to achieve lawful secession was raised in argument, each option would require us to assume the existence of facts that at this stage are unknown. In accordance with the usual rule of prudence in constitutional cases, we refrain from pronouncing on the applicability of any particular constitutional procedure to effect secession unless and until sufficiently clear facts exist to squarely raise an issue for judicial determination. [...]

IV. Summary of Conclusions

¶ 148 As stated at the outset, this Reference has required us to consider momentous questions that go to the heart of our system of constitutional government. We have emphasized that the Constitution is more than a written text. It embraces the entire global system of rules and principles which govern the exercise of constitutional authority. A superficial reading of selected provisions of the written constitutional enactment, without more, may be misleading. It is necessary to make a more profound investigation of the underlying principles that animate the whole of our Constitution, including the principles of federalism, democracy, constitutionalism and the rule of law, and respect for minorities. Those principles must inform our overall appreciation of the constitutional rights and obligations that would come into play in the event a clear majority of Quebeckers votes on a clear question in favour of secession.

¶ 149 The Reference requires us to consider whether Quebec has a right to unilateral secession. Those who support the existence of such a right found their case primarily on the principle of democracy. Democracy, however, means more than simple majority rule. As reflected in our constitutional jurisprudence, democracy exists in the larger context of other constitutional values such as those already mentioned. In the 131 years since Confederation, the people of the provinces and territories have created close ties of interdependence (economically, socially, politically and culturally) based on shared values that include federalism, democracy, constitutionalism and the rule of law, and respect for minorities. A democratic decision of Quebeckers in favour of secession would put those relationships at risk. The Constitution vouchsafes order and stability, and accordingly secession of a province "under the Constitution" could not be achieved unilaterally, that is, without principled negotiation with other participants in Confederation within the existing constitutional framework.

¶ 150 The Constitution is not a straitjacket. Even a brief review of our constitutional history demonstrates periods of momentous and dramatic change. Our democratic institutions necessarily accommodate a continuous process of discussion and evolution, which is reflected in the constitutional right of each participant in the federation to initiate constitutional change. This right implies a reciprocal duty on the other participants to engage in discussions to address any legitimate initiative to change the constitutional order. While it is true that some attempts at constitutional amendment in recent years have faltered, a clear majority vote in Quebec on a clear question in favour of secession would confer democratic legitimacy on the secession initiative which all of the other participants in Confederation would have to recognize.

¶ 151 Quebec could not, despite a clear referendum result, purport to invoke a right of self-determination to dictate the terms of a proposed secession to the other parties to the federation. The democratic vote, by however strong a majority, would have no legal effect on its own and could not push aside the principles of federalism and the rule of law, the rights of individuals and minorities, or the operation of democracy in the other provinces or in Canada as a whole. Democratic rights under the Constitution cannot be divorced from constitutional obligations. Nor, however, can the reverse proposition be accepted. The continued existence and operation of the Canadian constitutional order could not be indifferent to a clear expression of a clear majority of Quebeckers that they no longer wish to remain in Canada. The other provinces and the federal government would have no basis to deny the right of the government of Quebec to pursue secession, should a clear majority of the people of Quebec choose that goal, so long as in doing so, Quebec respects the rights of others. The negotiations that followed such a vote would address the potential act of secession as well as its possible terms should in fact secession proceed. There would be no conclusions predetermined by law on any issue. Negotiations would need to address the interests of the other provinces, the federal government, Quebec and indeed the rights of all Canadians both within and outside Quebec, and specifically the rights of minorities. No one suggests that it would be an easy set of negotiations.

¶ 152 The negotiation process would require the reconciliation of various rights and obligations by negotiation between two legitimate majorities, namely, the majority of the population of Quebec, and that of Canada as a whole. A political majority at either level that does not act in accordance with the underlying constitutional principles we have mentioned puts at risk the legitimacy of its exercise of its rights, and the ultimate acceptance of the result by the international community.

¶ 153 The task of the Court has been to clarify the legal framework within which political decisions are to be taken "under the Constitution", not to usurp the prerogatives of the political forces that operate within that framework. The obligations we have identified are binding obligations under the Constitution of Canada. However, it will be for the political actors to determine what constitutes "a clear majority on a clear question" in the circumstances under which a future referendum vote may be taken. Equally, in the event of demonstrated majority support for Quebec secession, the content and process of the negotiations will be for the political actors to settle. The reconciliation of the various legitimate constitutional interests is necessarily committed to the political rather than the judicial realm precisely because that reconciliation can only be achieved through the give and take of political negotiations. To the extent issues addressed in the course of negotiation are political, the courts, appreciating their proper role in the constitutional scheme, would have no supervisory role.

¶ 154 We have also considered whether a positive legal entitlement to secession exists under international law in the factual circumstances contemplated by Question 1, i.e., a clear democratic expression of support on a clear question for Quebec secession. Some of those who supported an affirmative answer to this question did so on the basis of the recognized right to self-determination that belongs to all "peoples". Although much of the Quebec population certainly shares many of the characteristics of a people, it is not necessary to decide the "people" issue because, whatever may be the correct determination of this issue in the context of Quebec, a right to secession only arises under the principle of self-determination of peoples at international law where "a people" is governed as part of a colonial empire; where "a people" is subject to alien subjugation, domination or exploitation; and possibly where "a people" is denied any meaningful exercise of its right to self-determination within the state of which it forms a part. In other circumstances, peoples are expected to achieve self-determination within the framework of their existing state. A state whose government represents the whole of the people or peoples resident within its territory, on a basis of equality and without discrimination, and respects the principles of self-determination in its internal arrangements, is entitled to maintain its territorial integrity under international law and to have that territorial integrity recognized by other states. Quebec does not meet the threshold of a colonial people or an oppressed people, nor can it be suggested that Quebeckers have been denied meaningful access to government to pursue their political, economic, cultural and social development. In the circumstances, the National Assembly, the legislature or the government of Quebec do not enjoy a right at international law to effect the secession of Quebec from Canada unilaterally.

¶ 155 Although there is no right, under the Constitution or at international law, to unilateral secession, that is secession without negotiation on the basis just discussed, this does not rule out the possibility of an unconstitutional declaration of secession leading to a de facto secession. The ultimate success of such a secession would be dependent on recognition by the international community, which is likely to consider the legality and legitimacy of secession having regard to, amongst other facts, the conduct of Quebec and Canada, in determining whether to grant or withhold recognition. Such recognition, even if granted, would not, however, provide any retroactive justification for the act of secession, either under the Constitution of Canada or at international law.

¶ 156 The reference questions are answered accordingly.

BEVERLEY McLACHLIN,[1] UNWRITTEN CONSTITUTIONAL PRINCIPLES: WHAT IS GOING ON?
Lord Cooke Lecture, Wellington, New Zealand, December 1st, 2005

[...]The contemporary concept of unwritten constitutional principles can be seen as a modern reincarnation of the ancient doctrines of natural law. Like those conceptions of justice, the identification of these principles seems to presuppose the existence of some kind of natural order. Unlike them, however, it

---

1   Chief Justice, Supreme Court of Canada.

does not fasten on theology as the source of the unwritten principles that transcend the exercise of state power. It is derived from the history, values and culture of the nation, viewed in its constitutional context.

[...]This "rich intellectual tradition" of natural law seeks to give the law minimum moral content. It rests on the proposition that there is a distinction between rules and the law. Rules and rule systems can be good, but they can also be evil. Something more than the very existence of rules, it is argued, is required for them to demand respect: in short, to transform rules into law. The distinction between rule by law, which is the state of affairs in certain developing countries, and rule of law, which developed democracies espouse, succinctly captures the distinction between a mere rules system and a proper legal system that is founded on certain minimum values. The debate about unwritten constitutional principles can thus be seen as a debate about the nature of the law itself and what about it demands our allegiance.

[...]Today's fundamental norms are cast more clearly and exclusively in terms of reason that take at their heart the notion, in some form, of basic human dignity. There is no doubt that the norms I mentioned earlier - government by consent, the protection of life and personal security, and freedom from discrimination - can all be advanced by moral argument. It is worth noting, however, that they can also be supported by a democratic argument grounded in conceptions of the state and fundamental human dignity that we have developed since John Stuart Mill.

[...]This brings us to the second problem: identifying those unwritten constitutional principles that can prevail over laws and executive action. At least three sources of unwritten constitutional principles can be identified: customary usage; inferences from written constitutional principles; and the norms set out or implied in international legal instruments to which the state has adhered.

Traditionally at common law, unwritten fundamental principles of constitutional or quasi-constitutional significance have been identified by past usage, chiefly the cases that have been decided by judges in the past. Judgments identifying or clarifying constitutional norms are typically supported by a culture in which Parliament and the executive accept the appropriateness of the norm and permit it to stand. Occasional exceptions, such as states of emergency, do not negate the general acceptance of these norms. As Dean Palmer of this Faculty of Law notes in a forthcoming paper, bureaucratic and political actors not only respond to constitutional interpretation, but they also engage in it themselves when they acknowledge and respect the legitimate constraints on their spheres of decision-making. Usage is thus not only about how judges view the constitution, but how decision-makers more generally understand their function in a broader system of governance.

[...]This brings me to the second source of unwritten constitutional principles – inference from the constitutional principles and values that have been set down in writing. While they may interpret their written constitutions, courts are never free to ignore them. Confronted with a new situation requiring a new norm, judges must look to the written constitution for the values that capture the ethos of the nation. In Canada, the 1998 *Secession Reference* provides an instructive example of how courts may draw unwritten constitutional principles from the written provisions of the constitution. The background was a provincial referendum ten years ago in which citizens in Quebec defeated the proposition that Quebec secede from Canada, but did so by a margin of just over 1%. Shocked, the Canadian government referred the question of the legality of unilateral secession to the Supreme Court.

The texts of Canada's constitution are silent on whether a province can secede from the federation. No written principles set the legal framework that would govern an attempt to secede. In order to answer the question before it, the Supreme Court turned to Canada's history and conventions, as well as the values that Canadians, through their governments, had entrenched in their written constitution. It examined these in the light of a long-recognized treatment of Canada's evolving constitution as a "living tree."

The Court identified four "fundamental and organizing principles of the Constitution" which were relevant to the question: federalism; democracy; constitutionalism and the rule of law; and respect for minorities. Although unwritten, the Court found that "it would be impossible to conceive of our written structure without them" and found that they were "not merely descriptive, but...also invested with a powerful normative force, and are binding upon both courts and governments." By exploring both the foundations and implications of each of these principles, the Court provided the answer to the question posed by the government: under Canadian law, unilateral succession by a province was not possible. However, the Court went on to state that these same organizing principles imposed an obligation on the federal and provincial governments to enter into negotiations if the citizens of Quebec were to provide "a clear expression of a clear majority" on the question of secession. By examining constitutional texts in light of the principles that underlay them and gave their content meaning, the Court ensured that an important legal gap was filled. This permitted the Court to suggest concrete steps that would have to be followed in a process that would provide the certainty, stability and predictability that are cornerstones of the rule of law.

The third source that may suggest and inform unwritten constitutional principles is international law. Customary international law has been accepted as a legitimate part of the common law without controversy, largely because it is based on both usage and on an acceptance of a sense of obligation: what we call *opinio juris*. As for treaties signed by the Crown, however, the traditional "dualism" of the common law has generally required the explicit incorporation of international norms into domestic law. Yet as British barrister Rabinder Singh has recently noted, judgments in the United Kingdom seem to reveal an increasing acceptance that even unincorporated treaties can be used not only to resolve ambiguity, but may establish a "presumption of compatibility" in the absence of express statutory language to the contrary. As courts continue to struggle to understand the precise legal effect of a country's international commitments, it surely must be the case that these can inform our understanding of the basic values that the state publicly and formally embraces. Where a country adheres to international covenants, such as the UN Convention Against Torture or the International Covenant on Civil and Political Rights, it thereby signals its intentions to be bound by their principles. This may amplify indications from usage and convention and the written text of the constitution and to help to establish the boundaries of certain unwritten principles.

I return to the question: how can unwritten constitution principles be identified? The answer is that they can be identified from a nation's past custom and usage; from the written text, if any, of the nation's fundamental principles; and from the nation's international commitments. Unwritten principles are not the arbitrary or subjective view of this judge or that. Rather, they are ascertained by a rigorous process of legal reasoning. Where, having regard to convention, written provisions and internationally affirmed values, it is clear that a nation and its people adhere to a particular fundamental principle or norm, then it is the court's duty to recognize it. This is not law-making in the legislative sense, but legitimate judicial work. [...]

- Note -
R. v. POWLEY

One example of how to use unwritten constitutional principle in constitutional argument may be seen in the Factum of the Congress of Aboriginal People in *R. v. Powley* argued in the Supreme Court of Canada. See http://www.constitutional-law.net/powley.pdf.

(b)   Constitutional Convention

- Research Note -
CONSTITUTIONAL CONVENTIONS

As explained in *Research Note – Sources of Constitutional Law*, supra, the Constitution comprises written texts, explanatory jurisprudence and a network of principles. Together, these provide an "exhaustive legal framework for our system of government".

The written texts establish executive, legislative and judicial offices; invest those offices with power; establish limits on state power; and specify how persons become qualified for the offices established by the Constitution.

Some of the written texts are very obscure in light of the way our government actually works.

To consider some examples: sec. 96 of the *Constitution Act, 1867* says that "The Governor General shall appoint the Judges", secs. 9 and 15 say that the executive government and command of "all Naval and Military Forces" are vested in the Queen and sec. 91 gives the Queen, as well as the Senate, an absolute veto over all legislation proposed in Parliament.

Also strange is what is missing from the written texts of the Constitution. Nowhere does the written constitution mention the most important constitutional actors in our system: Prime Minister, Leader of the Opposition, Cabinet. So too, our most important traditions of responsible government are entirely unknown to the written texts.

In brief, the written constitution does not reflect the way Canada's Constitution actually functions.

If the officer holders mentioned by the written Constitution attempted to exercise the power the Constitution vests in them, they would precipitate a constitutional crisis. The crisis would be immediate, deep and provocative. Such would be the case if the Queen exercised her veto over proposals agreed to by the House of Commons and Senate, or if she tried to tell the Generals and Admirals what to do. The Constitution would be immediately strained if the Governor General ignored the nominations of the Minister of Justice for appointment to the Judiciary, and appointed her cronies instead.

Canadians would regard these acts as fundamental breaches of our constitutional traditions.

Constitutional scholars and courts say that acting contrary to fundamental constitutional traditions is 'unconstitutional in the conventional sense'. In other words, the customary practices which reflect our fundamental constitutional traditions are called the *conventions* of the constitution.

Conventions of the Constitution operate by informing office holders how to exercise the wide powers and discretions the written Constitution vests in them. For example, the conventions of the Constitution instruct the Queen to assent to proposals agreed to by the Senate and House of Commons. The conventions tell the Governor General to appoint to the Judiciary only those persons recommended by the Minister of Justice, and none other.

In the *Patriation Reference*, [1981] 1 S.C.R. 753, the Court described all of this as follows:

> [Constitutional] rules create wide powers, discretions and
> rights which conventions prescribe should be exercised only
> in a certain limited manner, if at all.

A constitutional convention is generally regarded as obligatory by the official to whom the convention applies. This is why conventions seem like constitutional rules, and why breach of convention is called "unconstitutional in the conventional sense". However, unlike the rules of the written constitution, where courts give a sanction for breach, courts do not enforce constitutional conventions. Breach of a constitutional convention is "unconstitutional in the conventional sense", but no court will provide any remedy to anyone who claims to be injured by breach of a constitutional convention.

In the *Patriation Reference*, the Supreme Court of Canada described this interesting conundrum by saying:

> The main reason why conventional rules cannot be enforced
> by the Courts is that they are generally in conflict with the
> legal rules which they postulate and the Courts are bound to
> enforce the legal rules....if the remedy for breach of a
> convention does not lie with the Courts, still the breach is not

necessarily without a remedy. The remedy lies with some other institutions of Government; furthermore, it is not a formal remedy and it may be administered with less certainty or regularity that it would be by a Court.

All constitutional systems develop conventions which reflect how constitutional power is really expected to be used. Constitutional conventions are very important to the operation of the Constitution in that they govern the behavior of the political actors who operate the constitutional system.

While important to understanding how the constitution works in practice, constitutional conventions are not important in constitutional litigation. They are rarely mentioned in the constitutional cases. The reason why is simple: as courts do not enforce conventions, litigants do not rely on them. There is no reason to apply to a court for breach of constitutional convention because no remedy will be forthcoming.

Nevertheless, in certain spectacular constitutional crises, the courts were motivated to declare that certain constitutional conventions existed or did not exist. The most notable cases are the *Patriation Reference, supra,* and the *Quebec Veto Reference,* [1982] 2 S.C.R. 793. In these very dramatic cases, the Court essentially acted in a Statesman-like way, managing fractious political and constitutional crises by referring to the conventions, in effect reminding everybody of what our traditions are, and how the political actors were expected to behave. Even as it did so, the Court refrained from giving any remedy for breach of convention.

Interestingly in the *Patriation Reference,* the Court went so far to declare the conditions for establishing conventions. These are:

> We have to ask ourselves three questions: first, what are the precedents; secondly, did the actors in the precedents believe that they were bound by a rule; and thirdly, is there a reason for the rule?

This is important teaching for constitutional theory. It has little application in constitutional litigation.

The convention issue arose again in *Ontario Public Service Employees Union v. A.G. Ont.,* [1987] 2 S.C.R. 2. The issue was created out of confusion by counsel. Counsel claimed (erroneously) that a conventional rule of the Constitution stood on the same juridical plain as the written rules of the Constitution. On that footing counsel submitted that legislation restricting the political activities of public servants entrenched a constitutional convention.

The Court pointed out that counsel's submission was inaccurate.

Constitutional conventions do not stand on the same juridical plain as the rules of the written constitutional text. Conventions are merely norms of political behavior. They can be changed by the legislatures or by the political actors themselves. Unlike the written text of the Constitution conventions are not "entrenched". The written Constitution can only be changed in accordance with the constitutional amendment formula at Part V of the *Constitution Act, 1982.* By contrast, the conventions can be changed by ordinary legislative act.

REFERENCE RE AMENDMENT OF THE CONSTITUTION OF CAN.
(NOS. I, 2 AND 3)
"THE PATRIATION REFERENCE"
[1981] I S.C.R. 753.

[Prior to the *Patriation Reference*, the major constitutional document of Canada was *The British North America Act, 1867,* a statute of the United Kingdom Parliament. This statute organized the territories of what was then British North America into a federal union of four provinces and a central government. The Act endowed these newly created jurisdictions with executive, legislative and judicial power. As Canada gained increasing independence from Britain throughout the nineteenth and early twentieth centuries, a curious feature of the *British North America Act* came into increasing prominence. As a statute of the United Kingdom, the *British North America Act,* which effectively was Canada's Constitution, could only be amended by the United Kingdom Parliament. Canada did not have full responsibility for amendment of its own internal Constitution.

Thus, pressure began to be felt in Canada to "patriate" the Canadian Constitution — to end British responsibility for Canadian constitutional affairs, and the responsibility of the United Kingdom Parliament to amend the *British North America Act.* The difficulty with patriation was that jealousies between Ottawa and the provinces meant that Canadian political authorities could not agree among themselves as to the desired constitutional amending formula that would replace British responsibility.

The *Patriation Reference* concerned the unilateral attempt by the Government of Canada to patriate the Constitution on its own terms and to entrench its own ideas of the proper constitutional amending procedure, as well as a contentious *Charter of Rights and Freedoms.* Former constitutional amendments had been achieved by Canada requesting the Government of the United Kingdom to amend the *British North America Act, 1867,* which Britain unfailingly did. While most of these requests had involved the consent of the Provinces, the federal government took the view that provincial consent was unnecessary. The Government of Canada embarked on a project to achieve these reforms by using, for one last time, the old machinery: a request to the British Parliament by Resolution of the Canadian Senate and House of Commons, to amend the *British North America Act, 1867,* to end British authority for Canadian constitutional affairs (patriation) and to entrench a *Charter of Rights* and a domestic amending formula.

Canada's proposed Resolution was supported by only two provinces, Ontario and New Brunswick. The opposition of the other provinces was based on their assertion that constitutional law and constitutional convention required the consent of the provinces for the address to be forwarded to Her Majesty. The provinces of Manitoba, Newfoundland and Quebec directed references to their Courts of Appeal asking whether the proposed amendments, if enacted, would affect federal-provincial relationships within the Canadian federation; whether there was a legal requirement that provincial consent be obtained before such amendment could be requested of the U.K. Parliament; and whether there was a constitutional convention that such consent be obtained. The Court's treatment of federalism is dealt with at p. 91 in "Federalism - General Characteristics", infra.]

Prime Minister Pierre Elliot Trudeau at the 1981 Constitutional Conference where the Federal government negotiated the Constitution Act, 1982.

MARTLAND, RITCHIE, DICKSON, BEETZ, CHOUINARD AND LAMER JJ.: — The second question in the Manitoba Reference [...] is [...]

2.   Is it a constitutional convention that the House of Commons and Senate of Canada will not request Her Majesty the Queen to lay before the Parliament of the United Kingdom of Great Britain and Northern Ireland a measure to amend the Constitution of Canada affecting federal-provincial relationships or the powers, rights or privileges granted or secured by the Constitution of Canada to the provinces, their legislatures or governments without first obtaining the agreement of the provinces?

[...] The issue raised by the question is essentially whether there is a constitutional convention that the House of Commons and Senate of Canada will not proceed alone. The thrust of the question is accordingly on whether or not there is a conventional requirement for provincial agreement, not on whether the agreement should be unanimous assuming that it is required. [...]

THE NATURE OF CONSTITUTIONAL CONVENTIONS

A substantial part of the rules of the Canadian Constitution are written. They are contained not in a single document called a Constitution but in a great variety of statutes some of which have been enacted by the Parliament of Westminster, such as the *British North America Act, 1867*, 30 & 31 Vict., c. 3 (U.K.) (the *B.N.A. Act*), or by the Parliament of Canada, such as the *Alberta Act*, 1905, 4-5 Edw. VII, c. 3 (Can.); the *Saskatchewan Act*, 1905, 4-5 Edw. VII, c. 42 (Can.); the *Senate and House of Commons Act*, R.S.C. 1970, c. S-8, or by the provincial Legislatures, such as the provincial electoral Acts. They are also to be found in Orders in Council like the Imperial Order in Council of May 16, 1871, admitting British Columbia into the Union, and the Imperial Order in Council of June 26, 1873, admitting Prince Edward Island into the Union.

Another part of the Constitution of Canada consists of the rules of the common law. These are rules which the Courts have developed over the centuries in the discharge of their judicial duties. An important portion of these rules concerns the prerogative of the Crown. Sections 9 and 15 of the *B.N.A. Act* provide:

> 9. The Executive Government and authority of and over Canada is hereby declared to continue and be vested in the Queen. [...]

> 15. The Commander-in-Chief of the Land and Naval Militia, and of all Naval and Military Forces, of and in Canada, is hereby declared to continue and be vested in the Queen.

But the Act does not otherwise say very much with respect to the elements of "Executive Government and authority" and one must look at the common law to find out what they are, apart from authority delegated to the Executive by statute.

The common law provides that the authority of the Crown includes for instance the prerogative of mercy or clemency (*Re Royal Prerogative of Mercy upon Deportation Proceedings*, [1933] S.C.R. 269) and the power to incorporate by charter so as to confer a general capacity analogous to that of a natural person (*Bonanza Creek Gold Mining Co.* v. *The King*, [1916] 1 A.C. 566). The royal prerogative puts the Crown in a preferred position as a creditor (*Liquidators of Maritime Bank of Canada* v. *Receiver-General of New Brunswick*, [1892] A.C. 437) or with respect to the inheritance of lands for defect of heirs (*A.-G. Ont.* v. *Mercer* (1883), 8 App. Cas. 767) or in relation to the ownership of precious metals (*A.-G. B.C.* v. *A.-G. Can.* (1889), 14 App. Cas. 295) and *bona vacantia* (*R.* v. *A.-G. B.C.*, [1924] A.C. 213). It is also under the prerogative and the common law that the Crown appoints and receives ambassadors, declares war, concludes treaties and it is in the name of the Queen that passports are issued.

Those parts of the Constitution of Canada which are composed of statutory rules and common law rules are generically referred to as the law of the Constitution. In cases of doubt or dispute, it is the function of the Courts to declare what the law is and since the law is sometimes breached, it is generally the function of the Courts to ascertain whether it has in fact been breached in specific instances and, if so, to apply such sanctions as are contemplated by the law, whether they be punitive sanctions or civil sanctions such as a declaration of nullity. Thus, when a federal or a provincial statute is found by the Courts to be in excess of the legislative competence of the Legislature which has enacted it, it is declared null and void and the Courts refuse to give effect to it. In this sense it can be said that the law of the Constitution is administered or enforced by the Courts.

But many Canadians would perhaps be surprised to learn that important parts of the Constitution of Canada, with which they are the most familiar because they are directly involved when they exercise their right to vote at federal and provincial elections, are nowhere to be found in the law of the Constitution. For instance it is a fundamental requirement of the Constitution that if the Opposition obtains the majority at the polls, the Government must tender its resignation forthwith. But fundamental as it is, this requirement of the Constitution does not form part of the law of the Constitution.

It is also a constitutional requirement that the person who is appointed Prime Minister or Premier by the Crown and who is the effective head of the Government should have the support of the elected branch of the Legislature; in practice this means in most cases the leader of the political party which has won a majority of seats at a general election. Other ministers are appointed by the Crown on the advice of the Prime Minister or Premier when he forms or reshuffles his cabinet. Ministers must continuously have the confidence of the elected branch of the Legislature, individually and collectively. Should they lose it, they must either resign or ask the Crown for a dissolution of the Legislature and the holding of a general election. Most of the powers of the Crown under the prerogative are exercised only upon the advice of the Prime Minister or the Cabinet which means that they are effectively exercised by the latter, together with the innumerable statutory powers delegated to the Crown in council.

Yet none of these essential rules of the Constitution can be said to be a law of the Constitution. It was apparently Dicey who, in the first edition of his *Law of the Constitution, in 1885, called them "the conventions of the constitution"* (W.S. Holdsworth, "The Conventions of the Eighteenth Century Constitution", 17 Iowa Law Rev. 161 (1932)), an expression which quickly became current. What Dicey described under these terms are the principles and rules of responsible government, several of which are stated above and which regulate the relations between the Crown, the Prime Minister, the Cabinet and the two Houses of Parliament. These rules developed in Great Britain by way of custom and precedent during the nineteenth century and were exported to such British colonies as were granted self-government.

Dicey first gave the impression that constitutional conventions are a peculiarly British and modern phenomenon. But he recognized in later editions that different conventions are found in other constitutions. As Sir William Holdsworth wrote (W.S. Holdsworth, *op. cit.*, p. 162):

> In fact conventions must grow up at all times and in all places where the powers of government are vested in different persons or bodies – where in other words there is a mixed constitution. "The constituent parts of a state," said Burke, [French Revolution, 28] "are obliged to hold their public faith with each other and with all those who derive any serious interest under their engagements, as much as the whole state is bound to keep its faith with separate communities." Necessarily conventional rules spring up to regulate the working of the various parts of the constitution, their relations to one another, and to the subject.

Within the British Empire, powers of government were vested in different bodies which provided a fertile ground for the growth of new constitutional conventions unknown to Dicey whereby self-governing colonies acquired equal and independent status within the Commonwealth. Many of these culminated in the *Statute of Westminster*, 1931, 22 Geo. V, c. 4 (U.K.).

A federal Constitution provides for the distribution of powers between various Legislatures and Governments and may also constitute a fertile ground for the growth of constitutional conventions between those Legislatures and Governments. It is conceivable for instance that usage and practice might give birth to conventions in Canada relating to the holding of federal-provincial conferences, the appointment of Lieutenant-Governors, the reservation and disallowance of provincial legislation. It was to this possibility that Duff C.J.C. alluded when he referred to "constitutional usage or constitutional practice" in *Reference Re Power of Disallowance and Power of Reservation*, [1938] S.C.R. 71 at p. 78. He had previously called them "recognized constitutional conventions" in *Wilson v. E. & N. R. Co.*, [1922] 1 A.C. 202 at p. 210.

The main purpose of constitutional conventions is to ensure that the legal framework of the Constitution will be operated in accordance with the prevailing constitutional values or principles of the period. For example, the constitutional value which is the pivot of the conventions stated above and relating to responsible government is the democratic principle: the powers of the State must be exercised in accordance with the wishes of the electorate; and the constitutional value or principle which anchors the conventions regulating the relationship between the members of the Commonwealth is the independence of the former British colonies.

Being based on custom and precedent, constitutional conventions are usually unwritten rules. Some of them, however, may be reduced to writing and expressed in the proceedings and documents of Imperial conferences, or in the preamble of statutes such as the *Statute of Westminster, 1931*, or in the proceedings and documents of federal-provincial conferences. They are often referred to and recognized in statements made by members of governments.

The conventional rules of the Constitution present one striking peculiarity. In contradistinction to the laws of the Constitution, they are not enforced by the Courts. One reason for this situation is that, unlike common law rules, conventions are not judge-made rules. They are not based on judicial precedents but on precedents established by the institutions of government themselves. Nor are they in the nature of statutory commands which it is the function and duty of the Courts to obey and enforce. Furthermore, to enforce them would mean to administer some formal sanction when they are breached. But the legal system from which they are distinct does not contemplate formal sanctions for their breach.

Perhaps the main reason why conventional rules cannot be enforced by the Courts is that they are generally in conflict with the legal rules which they postulate and the Courts are bound to enforce the legal rules. The conflict is not of a type which would entail the commission of any illegality. It results from the fact that legal rules create wide powers, discretions and rights which conventions prescribe should be exercised only in a certain limited manner, if at all.

Some examples will illustrate this point.

As a matter of law, the Queen, or the Governor General or the Lieutenant-Governor could refuse assent to every bill passed by both Houses of Parliament or by a Legislative Assembly as the case may be. But by convention they cannot of their own motion refuse to assent to any such bill on any ground, for instance because they disapprove of the policy of the bill. We have here a conflict between a legal rule which creates a complete discretion and a conventional rule which completely neutralizes it. But conventions, like laws, are sometimes violated. And if this particular convention were violated and assent were improperly withheld, the Courts would be bound to enforce the law, not the convention. They would refuse to recognize the validity of a vetoed bill. This is what happened in *Gallant* v. *The King* (1949), 23 M.P.R. 48 (see also for a comment on the situation by K.M. Martin in 24 Can. Bar Rev. 434 (1946)), a case in keeping with the classic case of *Stockdale* v. *Hansard* (1839), 9 Ad. & E. 1, 112 E.R. 1112, where the English Court of Queen's Bench held that only the Queen and both Houses of Parliament could make or unmake laws. The Lieutenant-Governor who had withheld assent in *Gallant* apparently did so towards the end of his term of office. Had it been otherwise, it is not inconceivable that his withholding of assent might have produced a political crisis leading to his removal from office which shows that if the remedy for a breach of a convention does not lie with the Courts, still the breach is not necessarily without a remedy. The remedy lies with some other institutions of Government; furthermore, it is not a formal remedy and it may be administered with less certainty or regularity than it would be by a Court.

Another example of the conflict between law and convention is provided by a fundamental convention already stated above: if after a general election where the Opposition obtained the majority at the polls the Government refused to resign and clung to office, it would thereby commit a fundamental breach of conventions, one so serious indeed that it could be regarded as tantamount to a *coup d'État*. The remedy in this case would lie with the Governor General or the Lieutenant-Governor as the case might be who would be justified in dismissing the Ministry and in calling on the Opposition to form the Government. But should the Crown be slow in taking this course, there is nothing the Courts could do about it except at the risk of creating a state of legal discontinuity, that is a form of revolution. An order or a regulation passed by a Minister under statutory authority and otherwise valid could not be invalidated on the ground that, by convention, the Minister ought no longer to be a Minister. A writ of *quo warranto* aimed at Ministers, assuming that *quo warranto* lies against a Minister of the Crown, which is very doubtful, would be of no avail to remove them from office. Required to say by what warrant they occupy their ministerial office, they would answer that they occupy it by the pleasure of the Crown under a commission issued by the Crown and this answer would be a complete one at law for at law, the Government is in office by the pleasure of the Crown although by convention it is there by the will of the people.

This conflict between convention and law which prevents the Courts from enforcing conventions also prevents conventions from crystallizing into laws, unless it be by statutory adoption. It is because the sanctions of convention rest with institutions of government other than Courts, such as the Governor General or the Lieutenant-Governor, or the Houses of Parliament, or with public opinion and ultimately, with the electorate that it is generally said that they are political.

We respectfully adopt the definition of a convention given by the learned Chief Justice of Manitoba, Freedman C.J.M., in the Manitoba Reference at pp. 13-4:

> What is a constitutional convention? There is a fairly lengthy literature on the subject. Although there may be shades of difference among the constitutional lawyers, political scientists and Judges who have contributed to that literature, the essential features of a convention may be set forth with some degree of confidence. Thus there is general agreement that a convention occupies a position somewhere in between a usage or custom on the one hand and a constitutional law on the other. There is general agreement that if one sought to fix that position with greater precision he would place convention nearer to law than to usage or custom. There is also general agreement that "a convention is a rule which is regarded as obligatory by the officials to whom it applies". Hogg, *Constitutional Law of Canada* (1977), p. 9. There is, if not general agreement, at least weighty authority, that the sanction for breach of a convention will be political rather than legal.

It should be borne in mind, however, that, while they are not laws, some conventions may be more important than some laws. Their importance depends on that of the value or principle which they are meant to safeguard. Also they form an integral part of the Constitution and of the constitutional system. They come within the meaning of the word "Constitution" in the preamble of the *British North America Act, 1867*:

> Whereas the Provinces of Canada, Nova Scotia, and New Brunswick have expressed their Desire to be federally united [...] with a Constitution similar in principle to that of the United Kingdom:

That is why it is perfectly appropriate to say that to violate a convention is to do something which is unconstitutional although it entails no direct legal consequence. But the words "constitutional" and "unconstitutional" may also be used in a strict legal sense, for instance with respect to a statute which is found *ultra vires* or unconstitutional. The foregoing may perhaps be summarized in an equation: constitutional conventions plus constitutional law equal the total Constitution of the country. [...]

REQUIREMENTS FOR ESTABLISHING A CONVENTION

The requirements for establishing a convention bear some resemblance with those which apply to customary law. Precedents and usage are necessary but do not suffice. They must be normative. We adopt the following passage of Sir. W. Ivor Jennings in *The Law and the Constitution*, 5th ed. (1959), p. 136:

> We have to ask ourselves three questions: first, what are the precedents; secondly, did the actors in the precedents believe that they were bound by a rule; and thirdly, is there a reason for the rule? A single precedent with a good reason may be enough to establish the rule. A whole string of precedents without such a reason will be of no avail, unless it is perfectly certain that the persons concerned regarded them as bound by it.

[The Justices considered the precedents whereby federal-provincial relationships had been directly affected by constitutional amendment.]

Every one of these five amendments was agreed upon by each Province whose legislative authority was affected.

In negative terms, no amendment changing provincial legislative powers has been made since Confederation when agreement of a Province whose legislative powers would have been changed was withheld.

There are no exceptions.

Furthermore, in even more telling negative terms, in 1951, an amendment was proposed to give the Provinces a limited power of indirect taxation. Ontario and Quebec did not agree and the amendment was not proceeded with. [...]

The accumulation of these precedents, positive and negative, concurrent and without exception, does not of itself suffice in establishing the existence of the convention; but it unmistakedly points in its direction. Indeed, if the precedents stood alone, it might be argued that unanimity is required. [...]

THE ACTORS TREATING THE RULE AS BINDING

In the White Paper, one finds this passage at pp. 10-11:

PROCEDURES FOLLOWED IN THE PAST IN SECURING AMENDMENTS TO THE BRITISH NORTH AMERICA ACT. [...]

There follows a list of fourteen constitutional amendments thought to "have contributed to the development of accepted constitutional rules and principles." The White Paper then goes on to state these principles, at p. 15: [...]

> In our view, the fourth general principle equally and unmistakedly states and recognizes as a rule of the Canadian Constitution the convention referred to in the second question of the Manitoba and Newfoundland References as well as in Question B of the Quebec Reference, namely, that there is a requirement for provincial agreement to amendments which change provincial legislative powers.

This statement is not a casual utterance. It is contained in a carefully drafted document which had been circulated to all the Provinces prior to its publication and been found satisfactory by all of them. [...]

This statement is a recognition by all the actors in the precedents that the requirement of provincial agreement is a constitutional rule. In 1965, the White Paper had stated that: "The nature and the degree of provincial participation in the amending process... have not lent themselves to easy definition." Nothing has occurred since then which would permit us to conclude in a more precise manner. [...]

It would not be appropriate for the Court to devise in the abstract a specific formula which would indicate in positive terms what measure of provincial agreement is required for the convention to be complied with. Conventions by their nature develop in the political field and it will be for the political actors, not this Court, to determine the degree of provincial consent required.

It is sufficient for the Court to decide that at least a substantial measure of provincial consent is required and to decide further whether the situation before the Court meets with this requirement. The situation is one where Ontario and New Brunswick agree with the proposed amendments whereas the eight other Provinces oppose it. By no conceivable standard could this situation be thought to pass muster. It clearly does not disclose a sufficient measure of provincial agreement. Nothing more should be said about this.

A REASON FOR THE RULE

The reason for the rule is the federal principle. [The court's treatment of the federal principle is detailed at pp. 91 of this casebook below.] [...] The purpose of this conventional rule is to protect the federal character of the Canadian Constitution and prevent the anomaly that the House of Commons and Senate could obtain by simple resolutions what they could not validly accomplish by statute.

CONCLUSION

We have reached the conclusion that the agreement of the Provinces of Canada, no views being expressed as to its quantification, is constitutionally required for the passing of the "Proposed Resolution for a joint Address to Her Majesty respecting the Constitution of Canada" and that the passing of this Resolution without such agreement would be unconstitutional in the conventional sense. [...] NO.

[The Justices answered question 2 above as "No"]

LASKIN C.J.C., ESTEY AND McINTYRE JJ. [dissenting on question 2]:
[...]

From the wording of the questions [referred to the Court] and from the Course of argument it is clear that the questions meant the consent of *all* the Provinces. This then is the question which must be answered on this part of the References. An affirmative answer would involve a declaration that such a convention, requiring the consent of all the Provinces, exists, while a negative answer would, of course, deny its existence. No other answers can be open to the Court for, on a reference of this nature, the Court may answer only the questions put and may not conjure up questions of its own which, in turn, would lead to uninvited answers. [...]

[W]e are in agreement with much of what has been said as to the general nature of constitutional conventions in the reasons for judgment by the majority, which we have had the advantage of reading. We are in agreement, as well, with the words of Freedman C.J.M. in his reasons for judgment in the Manitoba Reference, referred to with approval and quoted by the majority. We cannot, however, agree with any suggestion that the non-observance of a convention can properly be termed unconstitutional in any strict or legal sense, or that its observance could be, in any sense, a constitutional requirement within the meaning of Question 3 of the Manitoba and Newfoundland References. In a federal State where the essential feature of the Constitution must be the distribution of powers between the two levels of government, each supreme in its own legislative sphere, constitutionality and legality must be synonymous, and conventional rules will be accorded less significance than they may have in a unitary State such as the United Kingdom. [...]

Conventions, while frequently unwritten, may none the less be reduced to writing. They may be reached by specific agreement between the parties to be bound, or they may more commonly arise from practice and usage. It is true, as well, that conventions can become law but this, in our view, would require some formal legal step such as enactment in statutory form. The *Statute of Westminster*, 1931 (U.K.), c. 4, affords an example of the enactment of conventions concerning constitutional relations between the United Kingdom and the various Dominions. However a convention may arise or be created, the essential condition for its recognition must be that the parties concerned regard it as binding upon them. While a convention, by its very nature, will often lack the precision and clearness of expression of a law, it must be recognized, known and understood with sufficient clarity that conformance is possible and a breach of conformance immediately discernible. It must play as well a necessary constitutional role. [...]

[R]ecognized conventions [...] are definite, understandable and understood. They have the unquestioned acceptance not only of the actors in political affairs but of the public at large. Can it be said that any convention having such clear definition and acceptance concerning provincial participation in the amendment of the Canadian Constitution has developed? It is in the light of this comparison that the existence of any supposed constitutional convention must be considered. It is abundantly clear, in our view, that the answer must be No. The degree of provincial participation in constitutional amendments has been a subject of lasting controversy in Canadian political life for generations. It cannot be asserted, in our opinion, that any view on this subject has become so clear and so broadly accepted as to constitute a constitutional convention. It should be observed that there is a fundamental difference between the convention in the Dicey concept and the convention for which some of the Provinces here contend. The Dicey convention relates to the functioning of individuals and institutions within a parliamentary democracy in unitary form. It does not qualify or limit the authority or sovereignty of Parliament or the Crown. The convention sought to be advanced here would truncate the functioning of the executive and legislative branches at the federal level. This would impose a limitation on the sovereign body itself within the Constitution. Surely such a convention would require for its recognition, even in the non-legal, political sphere, the clearest signal from the plenary unit intended to be bound, and not simply a plea from the majority of the beneficiaries of such a convention, the provincial plenary units.

An examination of the Canadian experience since Confederation will, bearing in mind the considerations above described serve to support our conclusion on this question.

[...]

The true test of the importance of the various amendments for our purpose is a consideration of the degree of provincial opposition they aroused, for whatever reason, the consideration that such opposition received, and the influence it had on the course of the amendment proceedings. [The Justices examined the precedents.]

[...] In summary, we observe that in the one hundred and fourteen years since confederation Canada has grown from a group of four somewhat hesitant colonies into a modern, independent State, vastly increased in size, power and wealth, and having a social and governmental structure unimagined in 1867. It cannot be denied that vast change has occurred in Dominion-Provincial relations over that period. Many factors have influenced this process and the amendments to the *B.N.A. Act* – all the amendments – have played a significant part and all must receive consideration in resolving this question. Only in four cases out of twenty-two amendments has full provincial consent been obtained and in many cases the federal Government has proceeded with amendments in the face of active provincial opposition. In our view, it is unrealistic in the extreme to say that the convention has emerged.

As a further support for the convention argument, the White Paper referred to above was cited and relied upon. It was asserted that the statement of principles set out, at p. 15, being an authoritative Government pronouncement, was decisive on the point. The summary of principles is set out hereunder: [...]

> The fourth general principle is that the Canadian Parliament will not request an amendment directly affecting federal-provincial relationships without prior consultation and agreement with the provinces. [...]

It is the fourth principle which is stressed by the objecting Provinces. In our view, they have attributed too much significance to this statement of the four principles. The author of the White Paper was at pains to say, at p. 11:

> Certain rules and principles relating to amending procedures have nevertheless developed over the years. They have emerged from the practices and procedures employed in securing various amendments to the *British North America Act* since 1867. *Though not constitutionally binding in any strict sense,* they have come to be recognized and accepted in practice as part of the amendment process in Canada. (emphasis added.)

It would not appear that he was satisfied that the principles had become so well-established that they had acquired strict constitutional force. [...]

A convention requires universal recognition by the actors in a scheme and this is certainly so where, as here, acceptance of a convention involves the surrender of a power by a sovereign body said to be a party to the convention. Furthermore, in recognizing uncertainty in specifying the degree of provincial participation, it denies the existence of any convention including that suggested by the Province of Saskatchewan. If there is difficulty in defining the degree of provincial participation, which there surely is, it cannot be said that any convention on the subject has been settled and recognized as a constitutional condition for the making of an amendment. It is the very difficulty of fixing the degree of provincial participation which, while it remains unresolved, prevents the formation or recognition of any convention. It robs any supposed convention of that degree of definition which is necessary to allow for its operation, for its binding effect upon the persons deemed to be bound, and it renders difficult if not impossible any clear discernment of a breach of the convention. In our view, then the fourth principle enunciated in the White Paper does not advance the provincial argument.

It was also argued that Canada was formed as a federal union and that the existence of a legal power of the central Government to unilaterally change the Constitution was inimical to the concept of federalism. The convention then, it was argued, arose out of the necessity to restrain such unilateral conduct and preserve the federal nature of Canada. In this connection, it must be acknowledged at once that, in a federal union, the powers and rights of each of the two levels of government must be protected from the assault of the other. The whole history of constitutional law and constitutional litigation in Canada since Confederation has been concerned with this vital question. We are asked to say whether the need for the preservation of the principles of Canadian federalism dictates the necessity for a convention, requiring consent from the Provinces as a condition of the exercise by the federal Government of its legal powers, to procure amendment to the Canadian Constitution. If the convention requires only partial consent, as is contended by Saskatchewan, it is difficult to see how the federal concept is thereby protected for, while those Provinces favouring amendment would be pleased, those refusing consent would claim coercion. If unanimous consent is required (as contended by the other objecting Provinces), while it may be said that in general terms the concept of federalism would be protected it would only be by overlooking the special nature of Canadian federalism that this protection would be achieved. The *B.N.A. Act* has not created a perfect or ideal federal State. [...]

It was argued that the federal authorities were assuming a power to act without restraint in disregard of provincial wishes which could go so far as to convert Canada into a unitary State by means of a majority vote in the Houses of Parliament. A few words will suffice to lay that argument at rest. What is before the Court is the task of answering the questions posed in three references. [...] [I]n our view [...] the federal constitutional proposals, which preserve a federal State without disturbing the distribution or balance of power, would create an amending formula which would enshrine provincial rights on the question of amendments on a secure, legal and constitutional footing, and would extinguish, as well, any presently existing power on the part of the federal Parliament to act unilaterally in constitutional matters. In so doing, it may be said that the parliamentary Resolution here under examination does not, save for the enactment of the *Charter of Rights*, which circumscribes the legislative powers of both the federal and provincial Legislatures, truly amend the Canadian Constitution. Its effect is to complete the formation of an incomplete Constitution by supplying its present deficiency, *i.e.*, an amending formula, which will enable the Constitution to be amended in Canada as befits a sovereign State. We are not here faced with an action which in any way has the effect of transforming this federal union into a unitary State. The *in terrorem* argument raising the spectre of a unitary State has no validity. [...]

OSBORNE v. CANADA (TREASURY BOARD)
[1991] 2 S.C.R. 69.

[These appeals concerned the constitutionality of s.33(1) of the *Public Service Employment Act*. Section 33(1)(a) prohibits public servants from working for or against a candidate. Section s.33(1)(b) prohibits public servants from working for a political party. Section 33(2) clarifies that public servants do not contravene s.33(1) by attending political meetings, or contributing money to a candidate or political party.

The respondents were federal public servants who wished to participate in various political activities. They brought an action in the Federal Court, Trial Division seeking a declaration that s.33 was of no force of effect because it violated secs.2(b) and 2(d) of the *Charter of Rights*. The Trial Division concluded that even if s.33 infringed the expression and association rights of public servants, it was justified under s.1. The Federal Court of Appeal reversed. The Court of Appeal ruled that the challenged provisions violated *Charter* rights. The Court declared s. 33(1)(a) of no force or effect, except as it applied to a deputy head. Section 33(1)(b) was ruled justifiable under s.1.]

SOPINKA J. [Cory, McLachlin JJ. concurring] — [...] The issues raised by these appeals are the following:

1.   Can a statutory provision, such as s. 33 of the *Act*, that implements a constitutional convention be considered to be inconsistent with the Constitution?

2.   If the response to the first question is in the affirmative, are the provisions of s. 33 of the *Act* inconsistent with ss. 2(*b*) or 2(*d*) of the *Charter*?

3.   If the response to the second question is in the affirmative, does s. 33 of the *Act* establish such reasonable limits as can be demonstrably justified in a free and democratic society?

1.   THE EFFECT OF THE CONSTITUTIONAL CONVENTION OF POLITICAL NEUTRALITY

The existence of a convention of political neutrality, central to the principle of responsible government, and the upholding of that convention in s. 33 of the *Act*, is not seriously disputed. Rather, the debate centres around the effect of the convention in assessing the validity of the impugned provision. The appellant contends that because s. 33 of the *Act* gives expression to the constitutional values embodied in the convention of public service neutrality, it forms "a part" of the Constitution and cannot therefore be "inconsistent" with the Constitution. Relying then on the words of Wilson J. in *Reference Re Bill 30, An Act to amend the Education Act (Ont.)*, [1987] 1 S.C.R. 1148, that "[i]t was never intended [...] that the *Charter* could be used to invalidate other provisions of the Constitution" (p. 1197), the appellant argues that there cannot be a breach of the *Charter* where there is a competing constitutional provision. The appellant's argument, which I may state at the outset to be untenable, is based on the decision of this Court in *Reference Re Resolution to amend the Constitution*, [1981] 1 S.C.R. 753 (the "*Patriation Reference*"), and on the decision of Beetz J. in *OPSEU v. Ontario (Attorney General)*, [1987] 2 S.C.R. 2.

In the *Patriation Reference*, this Court explored the nature of constitutional conventions and recognized that in contradistinction to the variety of statutes and common law rules which make up the "law of the constitution", conventions are not enforceable by the courts unless they are crystallized into laws by way of statutory adoption. Underlying this distinction between constitutional law and constitutional conventions is the contrast between legal and political constitutionalism. [...]

[W]hile conventions form part of the Constitution of this country in the broader political sense, i.e., the democratic principles underlying our political system and the elements which constitute the relationships between the various levels and organs of government, they are not enforceable in a court of law unless they are incorporated into legislation. Furthermore, statutes embodying constitutional conventions do not automatically become entrenched to become part of the constitutional law, but retain their status as ordinary statutes. If that were not the case, any legislation which may be said to embrace a constitutional convention would have the effect of an amendment to the Constitution which would have escaped the rigorous requirements of the constitutional amendment process.

In support of its argument, the appellant also draws attention to the decision of Beetz J. in *OPSEU*, supra. That case, which was argued and decided on the basis of the division of powers, dealt with the validity of provisions in the Ontario *Public Service Act*, R.S.O. 1970, c. 386, similar to those in the present case. Beetz J. found the provisions to be constitutional in nature, but I believe he made it clear (at p. 41) that the term "constitutional" in that context was not to be equated with constitutional law:

> It is clear to me that those provisions are constitutional in nature *in the sense that they bear on the operation of an organ of government in Ontario and that they impose duties on the members of a branch of government in order to implement a principle of government.* (emphasis added.)

Beetz J. thus recognized that the Constitution of Ontario is composed of ordinary statutes which are susceptible to being amended or repealed by ordinary statutes (at p. 46):

> In my opinion, the impugned provisions constitute an ordinary legislative amendment of the Constitution of Ontario, within the meaning of s. 92(1) of the *Constitution Act*, 1867.

In my view, there is nothing in his analysis which reveals an intention to confer on such ordinary statutes the status of constitutional entrenchment in the legal sense. Based on the foregoing, I am unable to agree with the appellant that s. 33 of the *Act* is immune from *Charter* scrutiny merely because it may be said to uphold a constitutional convention. Being a provision in an ordinary statute, it is subject to review under the *Charter* as any ordinary legislation. While the existence of a constitutional convention does not pre-empt scrutiny of the provision under the *Charter*, it is an important consideration in determining whether, in enacting s. 33, Parliament was seeking to achieve an important political objective.

2. IS S. 33 OF THE ACT INCONSISTENT WITH SS. 2(b) OR 2(d) OF THE CHARTER?

In my view, there is little doubt that s. 33 of the *Act*, which prohibits partisan political expression and activity by public servants under threat of disciplinary action including dismissal from employment, violates the right to freedom of expression in s. 2(b) of the *Charter*. [...]

I am of the view that s. 33 fails the minimum impairment test and it is therefore unnecessary to consider the third aspect of the proportionality test. I now proceed to consider the appropriate remedy. [...]

In these circumstances it is preferable to strike out the section to the extent of its inconsistency with s. 2(b). To maintain a section that is so riddled with infirmity would not uphold the values of the *Charter* and would constitute a greater intrusion on the role of Parliament. In my opinion it is Parliament that should determine how the section should be redrafted and not the Court. Apart from the impracticality of a determination of the constitutionality of the section on a case-by-case basis, Parliament will have available to it information and expertise that is not available to the Court. [...]

Accordingly, for the reasons I have expressed above, the appeals are dismissed with costs.

[The concurring judgments of Wilson and LaForest JJ. are omitted. The dissenting judgment of Stevenson J. is omitted.]

2. Federalism

The Constitution Act, 1867 united three British colonies — Canada, Nova Scotia and New Brunswick — into a *federation* which it styled Canada. The *Act* provided for executive, legislative and judicial organs of governance for Canada. The *Act* also created four Provinces in the same territory — Ontario, Quebec, Nova Scotia and New Brunswick — and established executive, legislative and judicial organs of governance for these provinces. The *Act* endowed Canada and the provinces with legislative powers, which it divided between them. By the terms of the *Constitution Act, 1867* the legislative powers conferred on the Federal Parliament are "exclusive"; so, too, does the *Act* "exclusively" confer legislative powers on the provinces. Because its powers are "exclusive, Canada's legislative power acts as a limit on provincial legislative power, and vice versa.

Canada's Constitution limits governmental power in other ways, most notably by Part I of the *Constitution Act, 1982* (the *Canadian Charter of Rights and Freedoms*) which guarantees certain rights to individuals and groups; by Part II of the *Constitution Act, 1982* and certain other constitutional statutes and rules of the common law which reserve rights and powers to Aboriginal persons and groups; and by other constitutional statutes which reserve further rights and powers to various individuals and groups. In this section we are concerned only with the limits to governmental power that derive from the creation of the Canadian state as a federation.

As will become clear from the readings that follow, there is a large debate about the nature of Canadian federalism. While there is considerable agreement about how Canadian federalism operates, there is considerable disagreement as to whether federalism promotes responsive and efficient government in this country. Does federalism encourage innovation and change, or does it promote stasis and conservatism? Does federalism promote prosperity in the Canadian economy, or does it squander our human and capital resources on multiple compliance costs and endless intergovernmental bickering? Does federalism promote toleration and happiness, or does it magnify ethnic and sectional rivalries? Does federalism have a future, or is it obsolete? The first section, "Characteristics and Trends" outlines these debates.

Proposals for modifications to the Canadian federation has been a natural outgrowth of these debates. Certain leaders in Quebec have outlined Quebec's problems with the Canadian federation. Their challenges, and the responses to those challenges are found in part one of the second section, "Federalism, Confederalism and Supranational Political Organizations". Other proposals have been more modest in scope. In the second part of this section, Peter Leslie squares off with Lucien Bouchard on the viability of a European Union-style arrangement for Canada.

Finally, this third section contains materials on "the Future of Federalism". The two most powerful changes to the Canadian union move in the same direction but vary in degree. The first is decentralization - a force which has taken hold of Canada for at least ten years. The second is the "ultimate decentralization" — secession. Secession is perhaps the most severe alternative to the Canadian union. The final part of this section looks at our neighbours in the U.S. and Latin America to see if Canada's future can be foreshadowed in federalisms operating elsewhere on this continent.

It is important for the Constitutional lawyer to understand the scope of these arguments and how Canadian federalism functions in practice. The bureaucratic, political and judicial officers who operate the Constitution require a network of principles and doctrines to guide their behaviours as they strive to promote efficient functioning of the federal system. This is particularly true for courts which superintend the federal system. The judiciary is responsible for developing rules for decision of disputes between actors in the federal system. To this purpose, the judiciary is receptive to constitutional arguments about what principles and policies will best promote efficient operation of Canadian federalism. The courts want to know what rules of constitutional decision- making will maximize the advantages of federalism, and minimize its unwanted costs. To that end, the following two chapters, "Devices for Intergovernmental Cooperation in a Federal State" and "Key Concepts in Constitutional Law" will prove instructive.

C-073717

Rioters burn the Parliament Buildings after the Rebellion Losses Bill was passed (Montreal, 1849).

(a)   General Characteristics and Trends

KEITH S. ROSENN, "FEDERALISM IN THE AMERICAS IN COMPARATIVE PERSPECTIVE"
((1994) 26 U. MIAMI INTER-AM. L. REV. 1)

THE ESSENTIAL FEATURES OF FEDERALISM

Despite the vast literature on the subject, federalism's essential nature remains elusive. Since the framers of the U.S. Constitution of 1787 invented modern federalism, theorists have tended to regard the basic federalist features of the U.S. Constitution as the essence of federalism. There are, however, several types of federalist systems, many of which differ from the U.S. model in important ways. Nevertheless, the essential characteristics of federalism can be reduced to two: (1) constitutional division of powers between the central and regional levels of government, and (2) entrenched regional representation in the central government. Federalism is a form of government in which sovereign powers are constitutionally divided between a central government and geographically defined, semi-autonomous levels of government. Generally, federalist constitutions allocate powers to large geographically defined units, such as states, provinces, cantons or *länder*, but a few also allocate governmental powers to smaller subdivisions such as federal districts, counties or municipalities. Typically, some powers are exercised exclusively by the central government, some are exercised exclusively by the states or counties, and some are exercised concurrently. Nothing in the concept of federalism, however, other than a vague notion that national government should be empowered to deal with national affairs and the state governments with local affairs, indicates how these powers should be divided. Hence, federal systems divide governmental powers differently. Even within the same country and under the same constitution, divisions of powers shift and evolve.

The second basic characteristic of federalism is that the states or provinces have entrenched representation within the national government. Federal states are almost invariably bicameral. Representation in the lower house is usually apportioned on the basis of population, but many guarantee each state or province equal representation in the upper house. Argentina and Brazil go one step further; the city of Buenos Aires and Brazil's Federal District are each entitled to elect three senators, the same representation as a province or state. Others, such as Canada or Germany, grant some provinces or Länder more delegates in the upper house than others.   Generally, federal constitutions may not be amended without the consent of a majority or extraordinary majority of the states or provinces. The U.S. Constitution goes further, categorically prohibiting any constitutional amendment from depriving any state without its consent of equal suffrage in the Senate.

THE ADVANTAGES OF FEDERALISM

Federalism has a number of advantages as a form of political organization. The most obvious reason for sovereign entities to form a federal nation is mutual protection against outside forces. Federalism facilitates the common defense. Second, it promotes economic growth through free internal trade, a single currency, freedom of travel, and reciprocal promises to enforce the laws and judicial decisions of the component units. Third, it helps safeguard against tyranny by preventing concentration of governmental power and providing countervailing centers of power. Fourth, it encourages participation in government at local levels, promoting greater citizen involvement with the tasks of governance. Fifth, it leads to development of new and imaginative solutions to societal problems because local units are more free to act as laboratories for experimentation. Sixth, it simplifies the process of dealing with linguistic, ethnic, religious, or cultural diversity, facilitating governance of large regions and pluralistic societies. Seventh, it promotes administrative efficiency by utilizing national uniform regulations, taxation and expenditures for national concerns, while allowing local legislatures to tailor regulations, taxation and expenditures to regional and local concerns.

THE DISADVANTAGES OF FEDERALISM

Federalism also has several disadvantages. First, it is an anachronistic form of government that makes it increasingly difficult for modern governments to cope with issues that were deemed local in another age but today transcend state or even national boundaries. Second, it impedes economic efficiency by subjecting businesses to a bewilderingly complex structure of overlapping and inconsistent legal regulation, thereby increasing the costs of doing business in more than one state. Third, states often vie with each other to attract businesses, capital and population, by enacting legislation that will be the least restrictive or burdensome, resulting in less than optimal levels of regulation. Fourth, states often seek to impose external costs, like pollution or taxes, on residents of other states. Fifth, federalism creates redundancy, making the costs of governance more expensive by adding numerous layers of bureaucracy. For example, the U.S. has more than 83,000 governments. Sixth, state or provincial governments are more likely to threaten the individual rights and guarantees of minorities than national governments because local constituencies are more homogeneous and cohesive than national ones. Seventh, federalism tends to be unstable, sometimes fragmenting into several nations or requiring military force to preserve the union.

Federalist systems have constant debates about the proper boundaries between national and regional powers. Few are satisfied with the existing scheme, and political forces are continually being marshaled to promote greater centralization or greater decentralization. The most difficult challenge confronting any federal system is to achieve and to maintain the appropriate balance between the resources and responsibilities of the central government and the resources and responsibilities of the constituent state and local governments.

In the past decade, political decentralization has become an important component of efforts to consolidate democracy in many Latin American countries. During this period, Brazil, Chile, Colombia, El Salvador, Mexico, Nicaragua, Peru, and Venezuela have instituted important political reforms aimed at transferring power and resources from the national government to local governmental units. These reforms were motivated by a desire to strengthen democratic institutions by dispersing political power more widely and increasing popular access to democratic decision-making. They were also motivated by a belief that local application and disbursement of governmental resources would lead to greater economic efficiency than centralized control.

Significant decentralization has also been taking place in the U.S. in the past fifteen years. High on the priorities of Ronald Reagan's presidency was revitalization of federalism by turning over responsibility for administering a number of federal programs and revenue sources to the states and eliminating much of the bureaucratic red tape surrounding federal programs. President Reagan, and his successor, George Bush, also sought to revitalize federalism by appointing to the federal judiciary a group of judges believed to be more sensitive to states' rights. In 1995, the Republican-led Congress enacted legislation restricting the power of the federal government to mandate activities by the state and local governments without transferring federal funds to pay for these mandates. The results of these actions are both complex and multidirectional, but the net result has been an important shift towards decentralization.

DANIEL J. ELAZAR, "FEDERALISM AND THE WAY TO PEACE"
(KINGSTON: INSTITUTE FOR INTERGOVERNMENTAL RELATIONS, 1996)

[...] [P]olitical science has identified three basic ways in which polities have come into existence: conquest ("force," in the words of *The Federalist*), organic development (for *The Federalist*, "accident"), and covenant or "reflection and choice." These questions of origins are not abstract; the mode of founding of a polity does much to determine the framework of its subsequent political life.

Conquest can be understood to include not only its most direct manifestation, a conqueror gaining control of a land or a people, but also such subsidiary ways as the revolutionary conquest of an existing state, a coup d'état, or even an entrepreneur conquering a market and organizing control through corporate means. Conquest tends to produce hierarchically organized regimes ruled in an authoritarian manner; power pyramids with the conqueror on top, his agents in the middle, and the people underneath the entire structure. [...]

Organic evolution involves the development of political life from its beginnings in families, tribes, and villages to large polities in such a way that institutions, constitutional relationships, and power alignments emerge in response to the interaction between past precedent and changing circumstances, with a minimum of deliberate constitutional choice. The end result tends to be a polity with a single centre of power organized in one of several ways. Classic Greek political thought emphasized the organic evolution of the polity and rejected any other means of polity-building as deficient or improper. The organic model is closely related to the concept of natural law in the political order.

The organic model has proved most attractive to political philosophers precisely because, at its best, it seems to reflect the natural order of things. Thus it has received the most intellectual and academic attention. However just as conquest tends to produce hierarchically organized regimes ruled in an authoritarian manner, organic evolution tends to produce oligarchic regimes which, at their best, have an aristocratic flavour, and, at their worst, are simply the rule of the many by the few. In the first, the goal is to control the top of the pyramid; in the second, the goal is to control the centre of power. [...]

Covenantal foundings emphasize the deliberate coming together of humans as equals to establish bodies politic in such a way that all reaffirm their fundamental equality and retain their basic rights. Even the Hobbesian covenant - and Hobbes specifically uses that term - which establishes a polity in which power is vested in a single sovereign, maintains this fundamental equality although, in practice, it would not be able to coexist with the system of rule that Hobbes proposes. Polities whose origins are covenantal reflect the exercise of constitutional choice and broad-based participation in constitutional design. Polities founded by covenant are essentially federal in character, in the original meaning of the term - whether they are federal in structure or not. That is to say, each polity is a matrix compounded of equal confederates who come together freely and retain their respective integrities even as they are bound in a common whole. Such polities are republican by definition, and power within them must be diffused among many centres or the various cells within the matrix. [...]

As many philosophers, theologians, and political theorists in the Western world have noted, the federal idea has its roots in the Bible. Indeed, the first usage of the term was for theological purposes, to define the partnership between man and God described in the Bible, which, in turn, gave form to the idea of a covenantal (or federal) relationship between individuals and families leading to the formation of a body politic, and between bodies politic leading to the establishment of compound polities. The political applications of the theological usage gave rise to the transformation of the term federal into an explicitly political concept.

The term "federal" is derived from the Latin *foedus*, which, like the Hebrew term *brit*, means covenant. In essence, a federal arrangement is one of partnership, established and regulated by covenant, whose internal relationships reflect the special kind of sharing which must prevail among the partners, namely one that both recognizes the integrity of each partner and seeks to foster a special kind of unity among them. Significantly, *shalom*, the Hebrew term for peace, is a cognate of brit, having to do with the creation of the covenantal wholeness that is true peace.

Federal principles are concerned with the combination of self-rule and shared rule. In the broadest sense, federalism involves the linkage of individuals, groups, and polities in lasting but limited union in such a way as to provide for the energetic pursuit of common ends while maintaining the respective integrities of all parties. As a political principle, federalism has to do with the constitutional diffusion of power so that the constituting elements in a federal arrangement share in the processes of common policy-making, and administration by right, while the activities of the common government are conducted in such a way as to maintain their respective integrities. Federal systems do this by constitutionally distributing power among general and constituent governing bodies in a manner designed to protect the existence and authority of all. In a federal system, basic policies are made and implemented through negotiation in some form so that all can share in the decision-making and executing process.

THE FEDERALIST REVOLUTION

The federalist revolution is among the most widespread - if one of the most unnoticed - of the various revolutions that are changing the face of the globe in our time. In the modern and postmodern epochs, federalism has emerged as a major means of accommodating the spreading desire of people to preserve or revive the advantages of small societies with the growing necessity for larger combinations to better mobilize the utilization of common resources, or to maintain or strengthen their cultural distinctiveness within more extensive polities. Consequently, federal arrangements have been widely applied, on one hand, to integrate new polities while preserving legitimate internal diversities and, on the other, to link established polities for economic advantage and greater security. Nearly 80 percent of the world's population now lives within polities that are formally federal, and that utilize federal arrangements in some way.

The phrase "federal arrangements" properly suggests that there is more than one way to utilize federal principles. Indeed, to use a biological analogy, federalism can be considered a genus of political organization of which there are several species. Premodern Europe knew of only one federal arrangement, confederation, whereby several pre-existing, polities joined together to form a common government for strictly limited purposes, usually foreign affairs and defence, that remained dependent upon its constituent polities. Two centuries ago, the United States invented modern federalism and added federation as a second form, one that was widely emulated in the nineteenth century. A federation is a polity compounded of strong constituent entities and a strong general government, each possessing powers to delegated to it by the people and empowered to deal directly with the citizenry in the exercise of those powers. Federations became the only successful way to apply federal principles during the modern epoch which emphasized the centralized nation-state as the norm.

In the twentieth century, especially since World War II, new federal arrangements have been developed, or federal elements have been recognized in older ones previously not well understood. Federacies, associated state arrangements, and common markets represent postmodern applications of the federal principal. In a federacy arrangement, a larger power and a smaller polity are linked asymmetrically in a federal relationship whereby the latter has greater autonomy than other segments of the former and, in return, has less of a role in the governance of the larger power. The relationship between them is more like that of a federation than a confederation and can only be dissolved by mutual agreement. Associated state arrangements are equally asymmetrical but are like confederations in that they can be dissolved unilaterally by either of the parties under certain conditions. Consequently the associated state has even less of a role in the governance of the associated power. Common markets are forms of confederation emphasizing shared economic rather than political functions. They have led the way toward the revival of confederation as a feasible form of federalism in the globally more interconnected world that encompasses new linkages but allows for loose arrangements.

Political scientists have rediscovered the federal characteristics present in *consociational polities, unions,* and *leagues.* Consociational polities are non-territorial federations in which polities divided into transgenerational religious, cultural, ethnic, or ideological groupings are constituted as federations of "camps," "sectors," or "pillars" and jointly governed by coalitions of the leaders of each. Unions are polities compounded in such a way that their constituent entities preserve their respective integrities primarily or exclusively through the common organs of the general government rather than through dual government structures. Leagues, on the other hand, are linkages of politically independent polities for specific purposes that function through a common secretariat rather than a government and from which members may unilaterally withdraw. While neither are species of federalism, properly speaking, both utilize federal principles in their constitution and governance.

New regional arrangements, which are essentially leagues that emphasize regional development, represent more limited applications of federal mechanisms. There is every reason to expect that the postmodern world will develop new applications of the federal principle in addition to the arrangements we already know, including *functional authorities* for the joint implementation of particular tasks and *condominiums* involving joint rule by two powers over a shared territory in such a way that the inhabitants of the latter have substantial self-rule. Thus, reality itself is coming to reflect the various faces of federalism.

A major reason for this lies in the reassertion of ethnic and regional identities, now worldwide in scope, which promises to be one of the major political issues of this generation and the next century. There are some 3000 ethnic or tribal groups in the world conscious of their respective identities. Of the over 180 politically "sovereign" states now in existence, over 160 are multiethnic in composition. Approximately 40 percent of those states are involved in formal arrangements utilizing federal principles in some way to accommodate demands for self-rule or shared rule within their boundaries or in partnership with other polities. In sum, while the ideology of the nation-state - a single state embracing a single nation - remains strong, the nation-state itself is rare enough.

The federalist revolution in Western Europe is taking on two forms. On one hand, Western Europe has established a new-style confederation of old states through the European Union and, on the other, there is a revival of even older ethnic and regional identities in the political arena within those states. As a result, Belgium, Italy, and Spain have constitutionally federalized or regionalized themselves and even France is being forced to move in that direction, at least in the case of Corsica and its overseas possessions. Portugal has devolved internal self-governing power to its island provinces - as the Netherlands and Denmark have long since done. Switzerland, Germany, and Austria, already federal systems, are undergoing an intensification of their federalist dimensions in one way or another. The issue also remains alive, if unresolved, in Britain. The idea of a Europe of ethnic regions is a potent force on that continent and the European Union has not only taken note of but fostered this movement.

Most of the new states of Asia and Africa must come to grips with the multiethnic issue. It is an issue that can be accommodated peacefully only through the application of federal principles that will combine kinship (the basis of ethnicity) and consent (the basis of democratic government) into politically viable, constitutionally protected, arrangements involving territorial and nonterritorial polities. Although only a few of those states have formally federal systems, as in India, Malaysia, Nigeria, and Pakistan, a number of others have adopted other federal arrangements internally and are combining in multinational arrangements on a regional basis.

Western Asia and the eastern Mediterranean region, known collectively as the Middle East, are no exceptions to this problem of ethnic diversity. Indeed many current problems can be traced to the breakdown of the Ottoman Empire, which had succeeded in accommodating communal diversity within a universal state for several centuries. The intercommunal wars in Cyprus, Iraq, Israel, Lebanon, and Sudan, not to speak of the minority problems in Egypt, Iran, and Syria, offer headline testimony to this reality. Federal solutions are no less relevant in the Middle East than elsewhere, but especially in the Middle East the need is greatest for a postmodern federalism, a federalism that is not simply based upon territorial boundaries but recognizes the existence of long enduring peoples as well.

On the other hand, in the older, more established federal systems of North America, the re-emphasis of ethnic and cultural differences has challenged accepted federal arrangements. In Canada, this challenge has taken the form of a provincial secessionist movement in Quebec, and in the United States, an emphasis on non-territorial as against territorial-based subnational loyalties on one hand and a revival of Native American (Indian) tribal aspirations on the other. Latin America, the first cultural area outside of the United States to adopt federal solutions to encourage political liberty, continues to struggle with the problems of reconciling the republican dimensions of federalism with a penchant for autocratic leadership. Venezuela has strengthened its federal structure by reintroducing popular election of state governors. Brazil's new constitution was avowedly designed to strengthen its states. Even Mexico has been moving toward more political autonomy for its states as part of a shift to democratic party politics. In sum, federal forms have been applied to a widening variety of relationships ranging from federation in support of group pluralism and individual liberties in the United States, to federalism in support of local liberties in Switzerland and federalism on a linguistic basis in India, to federalism as a means of gaining mild decentralization in Venezuela. Federal arrangements to accommodate ethnic differences are becoming more widespread than ever in Canada, Belgium, Spain, the United Kingdom (under other names), Malaysia, and Nigeria. In every case, these developments have emerged as practical responses to real situations.

In most, if not all of these cases, whether they know it or not, the various parties have arrived at the point which the late Martin Diamond described as the classic position of federalism - - the position expressed by the song that Jimmy Durante, the American comedian, belted out in the film, "The Man Who Came to Dinner": "Did you ever have the feeling that you want to go, and the feeling that you want to stay?" That is the classic problem for which federalism, as a technology, was invented.

RONALD L. WATTS, "COMPARING FEDERAL SYSTEMS"
(KINGSTON: INSTITUTE OF INTERGOVERNMENTAL RELATIONS, 1999), pp.4-6

[ ] Federalism is far from being an obsolete nineteenth century form of government inappropriate in the contemporary world. In fact, in the last decade it is the concept of the nation-state, developed in the seventeenth century, that more and more people have been coming to regard as obsolete. Observers have noted that we appear to be in the midst of a paradigm shift which is taking us from a world of sovereign nation-states to a world of diminished state sovereignty and increased interstate linkages of a constitutionally federal character. There are, at present among the approximately 180 politically sovereign states in the world, 24 federations containing about two billion people or 40 percent of the world population; they encompass about 480 constituent or federated states. In addition to these federations, there have emerged new variants in the application of the federal idea. Just one of the many examples is the European Union where individual federations, unions and unitary states have pooled their sovereignty (as they express it) in a hybrid structure which has come to involve elements of confederation and federation.[...]

There are a number of reasons for this international trend to increased pooling of sovereignty among states in various federal forms. First, modern developments in transportation, social communications, technology and industrial organization have produced pressures at one and the same time for larger political organizations and for smaller ones. The pressure for larger political units has been generated by the goals shared by most Western and non-Western societies today: a desire for progress, a rising standard of living, social justice, and influence in the world arena, and by a growing awareness of world-wide interdependence in an era whose advanced technology makes both mass destruction and mass construction possible. The desire for smaller, self-governing political units has risen from the desire to make governments more responsive to the individual citizen and to give expression to primary group attachments linguistic and cultural ties, religious connection, historical traditions and social practices which provide the distinctive basis for a community's sense of identity and yearning for self-determination. Given these dual pressures throughout the world, more and more peoples have come to see some form of federalism, combining a shared government for specified common purposes with autonomous action by constituent units of government for purposes related to maintaining their regional distinctiveness, as allowing the closest institutional approximation to the multinational reality of the contemporary world.

Second, and closely related, is the recognition that an increasingly global economy has itself unleashed economic and political forces strengthening both international *and* local pressures at the expense of the traditional nation-state. Global communications and consumership have awakened desires in the smallest and most remote villages around the world for access to the global marketplace of goods and services. As a result, governments have been faced increasingly with the desires of their people to be both *global* consumers and *local* citizens at the same time. Tom Courchene has labeled this trend *glocalization*. Thus, the nation-state itself is simultaneously proving both too small and too large to serve all the desires of its citizens. Because of the development of the world market economy, the old-fashioned nation-state can no longer deliver many of the benefits its citizens value, such as rising living standards and job security. Self-sufficiency of the nation-state is widely recognized as unattainable and nominal sovereignty is less appealing if it means that, in reality, people have less control over decisions that crucially affect them. At the same time, nation-states have come to be too remote from individual citizens to provide a sense of direct democratic control and to respond clearly to the specific concerns and preferences of their citizens. In such a context federalism with its different interacting levels of government has provided a way of mediating the variety of global and local citizen preferences.

Third, the spread of market-based economies is creating socioeconomic conditions conducive to support for the federal idea. Among these are the emphasis on contractual relationships; the recognition of the non-centralized character of a market-based economy; entrepreneurial self-governance and consumer rights consciousness; markets that thrive on diversity rather than homogeneity, on interjurisdictional mobility and on competition as well as cooperation; and the recognition that people do not have to like each other in order to benefit each other.

Fourth, changes in technology have been generating new and more federal models of industrial organization with decentralized and flattened hierarchies involving non-centralized interactive networks. This in turn has produced more favourable attitudes towards non-centralized political organization.

Fifth, increasing public attention, especially in Europe, has been given to the principle of subsidiarity, the notion that a higher political body should take up only those tasks that cannot be accomplished by the lower political bodies themselves. There are some problems in the concept: it is difficult to translate it into legal terms, it has a clearly hierarchical character, and it implies that ultimately it is for the higher body to decide at which level tasks should be performed. Nevertheless, the decentralist thrust of the subsidiarity principles has been instrumental in encouraging wider interest in a citizen-oriented federalism.

Yet another factor has been the resilience of the classical federations in the face of changing conditions. The constitutions of the United States (1789), Switzerland (1848), Canada (1867) and Australia (1901) are among the longest-surviving of any in the world today. In spite of problems experienced over the past three decades, these four federations along with Germany, another federation, have displayed a degree of flexibility and adaptability; they place high in international rankings of the most desirable countries in which to live.

For all these reasons, the federal idea is now more popular internationally than at any time in history. This suggests that Canadians should be wary of rejecting the advantages that so many elsewhere see in federal solutions.

A distinctive feature about the current popularity of federalism in the world is that the application of the federal idea has taken a great variety of forms. The degrees of centralization or decentralization differ across federation as do their financial arrangements, the character of their federal legislative and executive institutions, institutional arrangements for facilitating intergovern-mental relations, judicial arrangements for umpiring internal conflicts, and procedures for constitutional amendment. Among interesting recent developments and innovations has been the acceptance in an increasing number of instances of some degree of symmetry in the relationship of member units to federations or to supranational organization. Examples in practice include Belgium, Malaysia, Russia, Spain and, following the Maastricht Treaty, the European Union. Another has been the trend for federations themselves to become constituent members of even wider federations or supranational organizations. Examples are Germany, Belgium and Austria within the European Union. It is also worth noting that the three members of the North American Free Trade Agreement (NAFTA), Canada, the USA and Mexico are each themselves federations. Thus there has been an emerging trend towards three or even four (not just two) levels of federal organization to reconcile supranational, national, regional and local impulses in order to maximize the realization of citizen preferences.

All this suggests that to assume that a sovereign Quebec is the only alternative to the current structure of the Canadian federation is to deny the potential for a multitude of variations, not to mention innovations, that could be developed in the process of the political evolution of the Canadian federation. The choice is not necessarily limited to federation or sovereignty but encompasses a variety of possible relationships towards which the Canadian federation might evolve as a result of either non-constitutional political adaptation or constitutional adjustment or both. [...]

(b) Characteristics of Canadian Federalism

D.V. SMILEY, "THE FEDERAL CONDITION IN CANADA"
(MCGRAW-HILL RYERSON, 1987)

[...] I will consider Dicey's proposition that "federal government means weak government." Is the general impulse of federalism towards the non-interventionist state, towards sustaining the values which we now designate as neo-conservative?

Dicey gave plausible reasons for associating federalism with weak government:

> The distribution of all the powers of the state among co-ordinate authorities necessarily leads to the result that no one authority can wield the same amount of power as under a unitarian constitution is possessed by the sovereign. A scheme [...] of checks and balances in which the strength of the common government is [...] pitted against that of the state governments leads [...] to a certain waste of energy. A federation therefore will always be at a disadvantage in a contest with unitarian states of equal resources. [...] Federalism, as it defines, and therefore limits, the powers of each department of the administration, is unfavourable to the interference or to the activity of governments. Hence a federal government can hardly render services to the nation by undertaking for the national benefit

> functions which may be performed by individuals. [...] A system meant to maintain the status quo in politics is incompatible with schemes for wide social innovation.

He went on to state that "federalism tends to produce conservatism" because constitutional arrangements are hard to change, and this rigidity in itself was a barrier to the interventionist state.

In an influential article, "The Obsolescence of Federalism," published in 1939, Harold Laski supported the correctness of Dicey's association of federalism with weak government. He argued that the "contracting capitalism" of the period in which he wrote "cannot afford the luxury of federalism":

> It [federalism] is insufficiently positive in character; it does not provide for sufficient rapidity of action; it inhibits the emergence of necessary standards of uniformity: it relies upon compacts and compromises which take insufficient account of the urgent category of time; it leaves the backward areas a restraint, at once parasitic and poisonous, on those which seek to move forward; not least, its psychological results, especially in an age of crisis, are depressing to a democracy that needs the drama of positive achievement to retain its faith.

In general terms, Laski argued than in an age of "giant capitalism" federalism denied governments the necessary powers to deal with the problems confronting them. [...]

Nonetheless, federalism may, under certain circumstances, manifest impulses counterbalancing state interventionism. As we have seen, Pierre Trudeau argued that in federal states reform was more possible than otherwise because change was initiated by the more progressive sub-national jurisdictions. On this basis, it might plausibly be argued that because Saskatchewan had already put such programs in place, Canada established national schemes of medical and hospital insurance sooner than would have been the case if it had been a unitary state. It also seems reasonable to suggest that in the period of relatively buoyant public revenues between 1960 and 1980, both federal and provincial governments competed for the allegiance of Canadians through implementing measures of state intervention. In the present period of fiscal restraint, each order of government imposes obstacles to cut-backs the other wishes to make; for example, Ottawa has a stake in the provinces' maintaining existing levels of expenditures on health and post-secondary education; the provinces lobby for generous federal expenditures on unemployment insurance to forestall persons who have exhausted such benefits making claims for general welfare assistance.

Although much more investigation is needed to make any definitive judgements about the relation between federalism and the scope of government intervention, it is plausible to suggest that federalism results in unco-ordinated public policies. By co-ordination I mean the circumstance in which (1) the goals of public policy are explicitly formulated, (2) the goals of policy are ranked, and the less preferred are subsumed to more preferred objectives, and (3) scarce public resources are allocated to alternative uses in a context where the results of actual and proposed policies are measured as accurately as the existing state of such measurements permits. During the late 1960s and early 1970s there was a vast amount of effort expended in Ottawa and the provinces in pursuit of the rationalization and coordination of governmental operations on a jurisdiction-wide basis. It can be plausibly argued that such efforts resulted in intergovernmental conflicts becoming more widespread and less amenable to authoritative resolution than under the previous circumstances where many relations involved narrowly-defined measures outside the context of more comprehensive objectives.

To the extent that effective government requires the rationalization of public policy, federalism stands squarely in the way of this goal. Some partial reconciliation of federalism and policy effectiveness might be made in a regime where the overlapping of jurisdictions was minimized and where, so far as at all practical, the interdependence of central and state/provincial authorities was eliminated. However, in a remarkable article, "Can Federalism Make a Difference?" published in 1973, Vincent Ostrom argued that the fragmentation and overlapping responsibilities in the American federal system led to more effective public policies in respect to such matters as the quality of the natural environment and the control of crime and urban affairs than would exist under a regime in which public power was hierarchically organized. Ostrom's basic case rests on the limits of rationality in large bureaucratic organizations, the advantages of having organizations of differing sizes involved in meeting different kinds of public needs and the possibilities of integration through "quasi-market" relations among public authorities. Further, "conflicts among public jurisdictions in a highly federalized political system will elucidate larger amounts of information about alternative solutions to public problems." [...]

ALBERT BRETON, "SUPPLEMENTARY STATEMENT"
IN ROYAL COMMISSION ON THE ECONOMIC UNION AND DEVELOPMENT PROSPECTS FOR CANADA REPORT, v. 3, OTTAWA: MINISTER OF SUPPLY AND SERVICES CANADA, 1985, pp. 487-512 (footnotes omitted) .

[...] I wish to argue that parliamentarism and federalism are congruent; that the issue of having to give priority to either in opting for democracy is a false one; and that it is possible to reform our national and federal institutions in ways that increase their effectiveness, while remaining true to their fundamental genius. [...]

Parliamentary (that is, responsible or party) government was not designed. It evolved in response to pressures and influences applied first to monarchs by powerful interests and then, throughout history, to those in office by new emerging centres of power. The dynamics of parliamentarism are appropriately, if somewhat summarily, encapsulated by the expression "elite accommodation".

There is not much competition (or not many "checks and balances": the kinds of behaviours associated with political competition within governments, as distinguished from competition between governments) in such a system. There are, of course, the checks and balances that come from powerful interests, whether economic (like business and labour, though these are not usually of equal strength), religious (churches), intellectual (academics and research organizations), and so on. There are also the checks and balances that come from the Question Period in the House of Commons, from the log-rolling that takes place in caucus and from public opinion. Finally, and very importantly, there is the competition that originates in the requirement of popular support elicited in contested elections at more or less regular intervals.

All in all, however, competition is quite weak, especially when cabinet is supported by a good parliamentary majority. The weakness of the checks and balances that come from the lack of separation between the executive and legislative branches is aggravated by the "independence" of the judiciary, an independence which is reflected in the doctrine of "parliamentary supremacy", as contrasted to the doctrine of "judicial review". [...]

A necessary implication of the foregoing is that the preferences, aspirations and opinions of the public, unless they are adopted by the power elites, are not likely to be represented as vividly as they would be in a system in which competition was more vibrant. This overly schematic description of parliamentarism would be even more incomplete if I did not immediately add that the system is susceptible to improvements. The system is capable, as history documents, of absorbing further checks and balances, while at the same time remaining faithful to its own virtues and genius. [...]

The development of mainline economic thought in the Anglo-American tradition – by any measure the overwhelming tradition – has systematically restricted the notion of competition to price competition. This tradition has come to focus on the conditions under which this kind of competition leads to (Pareto) efficiency, that is, to that state in which no one individual can be made better off without someone else being made worse off. Significantly, this neo-classical tradition has not associated any particular behaviours or activities with its definition of competition. [...]

Price competition must be contrasted to other kinds of competition, which have from time to time retained the attention of economists and others. There are a number of strands in the literature associated with such labels as "working competition" and "countervailing power". One of the more important of these is the notion of entrepreneurial competition, sometimes also called Austrian or Schumpeterian competition. [...]

In the words of Schumpeter, one of the ablest analysts of this kind of competition:

> In capitalist reality as distinguished from its textbook picture, it is not that kind of competition (price competition) which counts but the competition from the new commodity, the new technology, the new source of supply, the new type of organization... competition which commands a decisive cost or quality advantage and which strikes not at the margins of the profits and the outputs of the existing firms but at their foundations and their very lives. This kind of competition is as much more effective than the other as a bombardment is in

> comparison with forcing a door, so much more important that it becomes a matter of comparative indifference whether competition in the ordinary sense functions more or less promptly; the powerful lever that in the long run expands output and brings down prices is in any case made of other stuff. [...]

It is not an accident that the extension of the analytical tools of economics to politics was initiated by Schumpeter (although Niccolo Machiavelli and John Stuart Mill, among others, had anticipated the possibility): it was a natural outgrowth of his work on entrepreneurial competition. Politicians, in that view, are entrepreneurs who compete for resources by introducing new politics, by developing new forms of organization, by heralding new unifying symbols, by structuring a new social consensus, etcetera. Recent writers have characterized entrepreneurial competition as "alertness to opportunities". If that is a good definition of entrepreneurship, it cannot be limited to the realm of economics, but extends naturally to politics and to other areas of life. [...]

[A] federal state can be formally defined as a type of political organization in which there are at least two levels of jurisdiction – in Canada, national and provincial – between which the entire set of constitutional powers is divided. The assignment of these powers between the governmental levels is not made by one level alone. That distinguishes federalism from confederalism, a system in which the assignment of powers is made by the provinces alone, and from unitary states, structures in which powers are assigned by senior governments acting in isolation. According to that definition, Canada is and has been a federation and never a confederation. The Canadian provinces, on the other hand, in their relationship with their municipalities, are unitary states.

The division of powers and the mode through which it is effected define federalism well, albeit in a way that is too formal to be very useful in understanding how such a system actually works. From that point of view, what is much more important are the implications of any division of powers for the operations of, and relationships between, the governments of the federation, all of which are responsible governments. The central and most important implication is that in the search for popular support – something that is as needed for the effectiveness of governing parties as revenue is essential for the effectiveness of business firms – the governments of a federation will find themselves competing with each other. Federalism thus adds more competition to that already present in responsible or party government.

One point needs emphasis. Political competition is not something that politicians choose or want, whatever their commitment to federalism and, more broadly, to liberty and to democracy. In that respect, they are exactly like business entrepreneurs who do not want competition either. Competition arises from the necessity to respond to the actions of others; it is "forced" on people by the environment. One does not even have to be aware that one is competing to be competitive. A business firm that adopts a new technology to reduce its costs is acting competitively; one that advertises and places some of its output on sale is acting in a competitive fashion; someone who supports a particular social movement or a particular lobby is competing; as is the politician who seeks harmony with provincial governments by removing the contentious questions from the agenda of federal-provincial encounters.

There is so much mystification about this that I must dwell on two corollary points, at the risk of seeming to insist on the obvious for those who have seen their way clear on the subject. First, there is the whole bag of issues that are best summarized by the words "co-operative federalism". What is co-operative federalism and how is it to be distinguished from other types of federalisms? To my knowledge, the expression has never been formally defined. That may not be a lacuna because we all have, from practical experience and observation, a good intuitive idea of what is meant by these two words. Two or more persons working together to lift a heavy object; two or more persons engaged in a search for something lost; two or more persons removing snow from a road; these are examples of the kind of behaviour we have in mind when we think of co-operation. In other words, someone helping someone else achieve a certain goal or objective.

Co-operative federalism by analogy would exist if all the politicians of a federation worked together to achieve some collective end. Instead of working on their own for their citizens, governments would work together for the betterment of all "the people". Before examining what is meant by co-operative federalism in more detail, I would like the reader to ask him or herself why it is that we do not, as societies, organize the search for justice on a co-operative basis, but instead set defence against prosecuting attorneys in courts of law? Why do we not organize the working of party politics on a co-operative basis, but instead set political parties against each other in grand electoral contests? Why do we not organize the search for truth on a co-operative basis, but instead require scholars and scientists to compete for research funds and for limited space in research publications? And, finally – though the list could go on – why do we not organize the production of goods and services on a co-operative basis, but instead implement laws that make co-operation an offence?

These examples underline the fact that in some areas, co-operation is not an efficient principle of social organization and that it is less efficient than competition, essentially because co-operation can easily degenerate into collusion, conspiracy and connivance and that this is not necessarily good! In the case of federalism, would co-operation be a better principle of social organization than competition? [...] To answer the question, it must be recognized that co-operative federalism is aimed at removing the competition which is a natural by-product of federal organization. Consequently, to be able to answer the question, it is necessary to know whether competition is a "good" feature of political organizations. [...]

I have posed the question here, however, because I wish to stress that the notion of co-operative federalism is part and parcel of the politics of "elite accommodation" which plays such an important role in the dynamics of party governments. Indeed, in practice, co-operative federalism is nothing but executive federalism. This has been defined by Smiley "as the relations between elected and appointed officials of the two orders of government in federal-provincial interactions and among the executives of the provinces in interprovincial interactions". I will argue later that there is a place for a limited executive federalism. The executive federalism contemplated by co-operative federalists, however, effectively extends to all the areas of federal-provincial contact. It transfers to executive and bureaucratic bargaining and negotiation what properly belongs to the realm of the political.

Co-operative federalism does not necessarily eliminate federalist competition, but by moving it into executive and bureaucratic offices and corridors, it mutes its public manifestations and its effectiveness. The heart of co-operative federalism is secret deals, not the stuff on which a lively democracy thrives! There are other implications of the doctrine of co-operative federalism; I mention two.

A first is a by-product of drumming into the psyche of Canadians the belief that federalism is or should be co-operative. Once that is achieved, it provides a fruitful background for the arguments of those, sometimes in one province, sometimes in another, who wish to promote and foster separatism. Indeed, a process that is inherently competitive, even if it is called co-operative, is bound to throw up incidents which separatists – themselves competitive individuals – will use to argue that "the system does not work", because on a particular matter the politicians of a province have been rebuffed or have simply lost in the competitive game. It would be relatively easy to document that the rhetoric of Canadian separatists is often based on the notion that federalism is not as co-operative as one had been led to believe it should be. I cannot undertake that documentation task here. I simply note that if Canadians had been helped to understand that federalist politics, like all politics, is inherently competitive, the propaganda of separatism would have fallen on more barren ground.

A second implication of the doctrine of co-operative federalism relates to the condemnation, by those who adhere to it, of unilateralism, that is, of independent action by any one government of the federation. Unilateral action by one government is, of course, a derogation from co-operation, since when one is acting alone one is not co-operating. Consequently, those who espouse co-operative federalism decry unilateral action on the part of any government in the federation. Although in principle, the condemnation applies to all, in practice it strikes much harder at the federal government, simply because the provinces, if they want to act in unison, have to come to an agreement – something that is not easy to do for essentially competitive entities. To put it differently, in the normal course of affairs, the central government is likely to act unilaterally more often than the provinces, to the extent that these wish to act as one, because the costs of co-ordination are positive. A condemnation of unilateralism, if enforced, would therefore affect the central government more than the provinces.

Co-operative federalism, because it proscribes unilateral action, is therefore a disguised ploy to shackle the federal government, to prevent it from addressing the problems it alone can resolve and is constitutionally responsible for resolving. Indeed, condemning federal unilateralism is condemning the federal government for acting constitutionally! This is so true that if one takes the trouble to go behind the language of co-operative federalism, to the reality of the arguments which it seeks to convey, one discovers either confederalism or a conservative view which seeks to reduce the role of the federal government and, indeed, of all governments in society.

In concluding this argument, I note that the condemnation of unilateralism is also a denial that the division of powers between orders of government is essential to federalism. That indeed is the crux of the matter. Co-operative federalism, if it came to pass, would deny federalism itself. Those who seek co-operative federalism and labour for its realization, seek and labour for a unitary state, disguised in the trappings of federalism, but from which competition would have been reduced to a minimum or even eliminated. [...]

There can be little doubt that from a *legal-constitutional* point of view, an optimal assignment of powers is one in which the degree of concurrency, of overlap or of joint occupation of any one power has been reduced to a minimum. Constitutions that embody such an assignment are sometimes said to be the hallmark of "classical federalism". The need for the smallest possible degree of *de jure* concurrency does not originate in a desire for neatness, nor is it a relic inherited from the long-dying nineteenth century conception of political sovereignty enshrined in early definitions of federal countries as states constituted of two "sovereign and independent orders of government".

Instead, a minimal degree of *de jure* concurrency is required by the necessity of "judicial accountability". Ultimately, when things come to a crunch, a court must be able to decide whether a government has the authority to implement a particular policy or not; whether it is acting *intra vires* or *ultra vires*. If there is no "compartmentalization" within which legal authority can be exercised, there will be no basis on which a court can make decisions and, in fact, no meaning to a juridical division of powers. I will insist below that courts, and in particular the Supreme Court, are often called upon to act as "monitors" of federalist competition and to insure that competition is efficient. They cannot play that role unless the degree of *de jure* concurrency is small, for if it is significant, the courts would find it harder to impute responsibility to one or the other governments involved. The fundamental democratic principle that parliament must be accountable becomes meaningless.

That much seems incontrovertible. But at the political or *de facto* level things are different: there, concurrency is the rule. We have to be clear about what that means if we do not want to become victims of the confusion between *de jure* and *de facto* concurrency which pervades the literature and which is used to argue against competitive federalism.

Before examining why an air-tight *de facto* division of powers is not possible in principle, let me illustrate the nature of the problem with a few examples. Consider the (welfare) economist's standard classification of powers into allocation, redistribution and stabilization, to which may or may not be added a revenue power, depending on how the first three have been defined. Now assume that for whatever reason, the redistribution and stabilization powers *de jure* are assigned to the federal jurisdictional level while allocation is somehow, again *de jure*, divided between the federal and provincial levels. If the division of the allocation powers is air-tight, we have "classical" assignment of powers.

Now suppose that some provincial governments decide to use some of their allocation powers – those in areas such as education, transportation, or urban land use – in ways that fully respect the Constitution, but which change the distribution of income in a direction that the federal government does not like, so that that government feels obliged to implement policies of its own to "re-establish" the distribution of income it desires. Would not the air-tight separation of powers have *de facto* been broken? I believe so, since the federal government's actions are now governed by decisions taken at the provincial level. [...]

We can now turn to general principles. As I hope the examples have made clear, the various day-to-day policies which can be implemented by the governments of a federation under the powers which have juridically been assigned to them, stand in all sorts of relationships to each other. In the way citizens look at these policies (formally, in the utility functions of citizens), some will be independent, while many others will be either substitutes or complements to each other. On the other side of decision making, in the way politicians and bureaucrats look at policies (formally at the technical level of "production" and implementation), policies will be independent, substitutes or complements, but not necessarily in the same way as they are for citizens.

That is the reason why *de facto* all powers tend to be concurrent. It is important to be clear about what that means and what it does not mean. It does not mean that both orders of government will, at the same time, legislate in the same policy area. It simply means that governments at the two jurisdictional levels will, in general, be legislating in policy areas that are closely related to each other. As noted, that "closeness" has two possible sources: the preferences of citizens and the technical properties of production and implementation technologies. In other words, policies can be related to each other in one fashion or another because of the way citizens value them: or they can be related, because their production and implementation connects them to each other. These connections create the *de facto* concurrency.

Once this is acknowledged, it is impossible not to recognize at the same time that governments at different jurisdictional levels will be in competition with each other. The competition originates in the desire of governments to obtain the support of citizens by providing them with the policies they want. Since these policies will not have the same relationships in the preferences of citizens and in the technical structure of the implementation technologies that they have in constitutional documents, governments at one level will be implementing policies which are substitutes or complements to policies that are the responsibility of governments at another level, hence the competition.

Does this *de facto* concurrency – the outcome of characteristics of policies and of the political process – imply that constitutions do not matter? That the juridical division of powers is meaningless? That any *de jure* division of powers would be equivalent to any other? The answer to these questions must be an emphatic no. There are better and there are worse *de jure* divisions of powers. There is a view – the outcome of the confusion between *de jure* and *de facto* concurrency – which holds that the best constitutional assignment of powers is the one which leads to the smallest degree of competition possible. The bookshelves of Canada's libraries are littered with constitutional blueprints aimed at working out a division of powers that would eliminate *de facto* concurrency, so as to eliminate federalist competition.

Such constitutional blueprints are impossible to design for the only reason that people and the environment change. A blueprint that succeeded in assigning powers so as to suppress competition today would be obsolete, in that respect, tomorrow. [...]

[...] I have already indicated some of the conditions that are necessary for efficient competition. Those that follow are additional.

The first of these conditions pertains to a notion of "competitive equality". To be sure, efficient horizontal competition does not require that all competing units be of equal size any more than efficient competition in markets requires that firms be of equal size. But it must be that the large units are not in a position to continually dominate, coerce, and in other ways prevent the smaller units from making independent, autonomous decisions; nor are they in a position to inflict "disproportionate" damage on them. The smaller units must be able to compete with the strong on an equal footing. This problem is more acute in some federations than in others, and is certainly an important one in the Canadian federation in which the disparity in the size of provinces is large and possibly growing.

The responsibility for insuring that the smaller units are able to compete against the larger ones cannot lie elsewhere than with the federal government. That is a first reason why the central government is different from provincial governments. How does the central government play this role or fulfill this responsibility? Before answering this question, let me note that it cannot be an easy role to play, because, as I have already indicated, the federal government, also competes with the provinces. We are faced with the situation in which a government, competing with those at another level, must act to insure that the competition between the latter is "fair" and "productive". That is necessarily a difficult task, one that cannot be left exclusively to the day-to-day push and pull of politics, but must be institutionally entrenched. [...]

Conventional wisdom about public policy in Canada is overlaid with the words "nation-building" and "province-building". When the view is not made explicitly, it is implicit that nation-building is the business of the central government, while province-building is that of the provinces. I would like to suggest that a look at the record would indicate that that attribution is largely wrong: the central government in Canada (and I would submit in other federal countries also) has been and continues to be engaged in province-building as much, if not more in certain instances, than the provinces themselves. That is one of the ways it acts as a "monitor" of horizontal competition. [...]

Besides competitive equality, another condition, this one pertaining to the appropriability of costs and benefits of public policies, must be satisfied. (A not dissimilar condition must also rule in markets if competition there is to be efficient.) The condition requires that the benefits and costs of decisions made by the government of a province be borne by the people living in the province, and, therefore, by the government of the province. This condition is particularly relevant for costs, so let me re-state it with respect to that variable. In competing to attract businesses to its jurisdiction, either by supplying particularly attractive local public goods, such as theatre, concerts, or dance, by offering tax advantages, or by buying part of the output of the sought-after enterprises, the government of a province should not be able to shift the burden of the offered amenities to the citizens of other jurisdictions. It is clear that otherwise the competition would be inefficient. There is already considerable machinery in place in Canada to ensure that benefits and costs are appropriated by decision makers themselves. This is particularly the case in the field of taxation. [...]

[S]enates play an absolutely central role in "monitoring" the vertical competition that exists in federations – the competition between the federal and provincial (state) governments. Because of that central role, it is desirable that senates be designed so as to guarantee that competition is as fair and as unbiased as possible.

The Senate acts as a "monitor" of vertical competition by injecting a provincial dimension in the central government. In a well-functioning federation, although it would always be an integral part of the central government, a senate would in some important sense be related to both orders of government. The Supreme Court was therefore right, and revealed a profound understanding of federalism, when it recently argued that the federal government could not alone, that is, without the provinces, change the basic structure of the Canadian Senate. [...]

A senate can only play a "monitoring" role if it has legitimacy, and, in our time, *that can be achieved only if it is popularly elected.* [...] However, legitimacy is not enough. If a senate is to inject a provincial dimension in the federal government and thus become capable of "monitoring" vertical competition efficiently, *the basis of representation must be provincial,* not regional, as is current practice. [...]

The primary role of the Senate should *not*, therefore, be that of a "chamber of sober second thought", although it would continue to play that role. *Its primary role should be to give saliency to the provincial dimensions of public policies.* I stress that this is not essentially a representation role; it is a "monitoring" function. In other words, in the competition over resources and policies that takes place in the national government, it is imperative, if the competition is to be efficient, that provincial interests be competing with each other on an equal footing. It is not sufficient, to put it still differently, that provincial interests be represented appropriately in national debates. They must be able to vie with each other on a basis of "competitive equality"; otherwise the checks and balances that characterize national politics will be biased against the weaker provinces, even if their points of view are represented. A capacity to compete is more than a capacity to talk; it is also, and radically, a capacity to exert a real influence on decisions. That is the real meaning underlying the notion of "monitored" competition. [...]

The Senate is not the only national body that serves to "monitor" vertical competition. That is also done by the Supreme Court. It is that body which interprets the division of powers and determines the competitive behaviours which, from a legal point of view, are constitutional and those which are not. In the absence of an efficient Senate, the burden which must be carried by the Supreme Court, in its role of "monitor" of vertical competition, tends to be too heavy. However, the remedy for the problem is not to reform the Supreme Court, as some have proposed, but to reform the Senate. [...]

JOHN A. MACDONALD ON THE FEDERAL SYSTEM
PARLIAMENTARY DEBATES ON THE SUBJECT OF CONFEDERATION OF THE BRITISH NORTH AMERICAN PROVINCES, 1865

[...] Now, as regards the comparative advantages of a Legislative and a Federal Union, I have never hesitated to state my own opinions. I have again and again stated in the House that, if practicable, I thought a Legislative Union would be preferable. (Hear, hear.) I have always contended that if we could agree to have one government and one parliament, legislating for the whole of these peoples, it would be the best, the cheapest, the most vigorous, and the strongest system of government we could adopt. (Hear, hear.) But, on looking at the subject in the Conference, and discussing the matter as we did, most unreservedly, and with a desire to arrive at a satisfactory conclusion, we found that such a system was impracticable. In the first place, it would not meet the assent of the people of Lower Canada, because they felt that in their peculiar position — being a minority, with a different language, nationality and religion from the majority, — in case of a junction with the other provinces, their institutions and their laws might be assailed, and their ancestral associations, on which they prided themselves, attacked and prejudiced; it was found that any proposition which involved the absorption of the individuality of Lower Canada — if I may use the expression — would not be received with favour by her people. We found too, that though their people speak the same language and enjoy the same system of law as the people of Upper Canada, a system founded on the common law of England, there was as great a disinclination on the part of the various Maritime Provinces to lose their individuality, as separate political organizations, as we observed in the case of Lower Canada herself. (Hear, hear). Therefore, we were forced to the conclusion that we must either abandon the idea of Union altogether, or devise a system of union in which the separate provincial organizations would be in some degree preserved. [...]

The Conference having come to the conclusion that a legislative union, pure and simple, was impracticable, our next attempt was to form a government upon federal principles, which would give to the General Government the strength of a legislative and administrative union, while at the same time it preserved that liberty of action for the different sections which is allowed by a Federal Union. And I am strong in the belief — that we have hit upon the happy medium in those resolutions, and that we have formed a scheme of government which unites the advantages of both, giving us the strength of a legislative union and the sectional freedom of a federal union, with protection to local interests. In so doing, we had the advantage of the experience of the United States. [...]

Sir John A. MacDonald,
Canada's First Prime Minister

Ever since the [United States] was formed the difficulty of what is called "State Rights" has existed, and this had much to do in bringing on the present unhappy war in the United States. They commence, in fact, at the wrong end. They declared by their Constitution that each state was a sovereignty in itself, and that all the powers incident to a sovereignty belonged to each state, except those powers which, by the Constitution, were conferred upon the General Government and Congress. Here we have adopted a different system. We have strengthened the General Government. We have given the General Legislature all the great subjects of legislation. We have conferred on them, not only specifically and in detail, all the powers which are incident to sovereignty, but we have expressly declared that all subjects of general interest not distinctly and exclusively conferred upon the local governments and local legislatures, shall be conferred upon the General Government and Legislature. [...]

[A]ny honourable member on examining the list of different subjects which are to be assigned to the General and Local Legislatures respectively, will see that all the great questions which affect the general interests of the Confederacy as a whole, are confided to the Federal parliament, while the local interests and local laws of each section are preserved intact, and entrusted to the care of the local bodies. As a matter of course, the General Parliament must have the power of dealing with the public debt and property of the Confederation. Of course, too, it must have the regulation of trade and commerce, of customs and exercise. The Federal Parliament must have the sovereign power of raising money and from such sources and by such means as the representatives of the people will allow. It will be seen that the local legislatures have the control of all local works; and it is a matter of great importance, and one of the chief advantages of the Federal Union and of local legislatures, that each province will have the power and means of developing its own resources and aiding its own progress after its own fashion and in its own way. Therefore all the local improvements, all local enterprises or undertakings of any kind, have been left to the are and management of the local legislatures of each province. (Cheers.) [...]

In conclusion, I would again implore the House not to let this opportunity pass. It is an opportunity that may never recur. At the risk of repeating myself, I would say, it was only by happy concurrence of circumstances, that we were enabled to bring this great question to its present position. If we do not take advantage of the time, if we show ourselves unequal to the occasion, it may never return, and we shall hereafter bitterly and unavailingly regret having failed to embrace the happy opportunity now offered of founding a great nation under the fostering care of Great Britain, and our Sovereign Lady, Queen Victoria. (Loud cheers, amidst which the honourable gentleman resumed his seat).

- Research Note -
FEDERALISM CASES

The most exhaustive consideration of the principles inspiring Canadian federalism occurred in two opinions of the Supreme Court of Canada — the *Patriation Reference Re Resolution to Amend the Constitution of Canada*, [1981] 1 S.C.R. 753 and the *Secession Reference*, [1998] 2 S.C.R. 217, particularly at paras. 55-60, 88-96. The *Patriation Reference* follows; the *Secession Reference* is reproduced supra. at p. 24.

$\Big[$ **REFERENCE RE AMENDMENT OF THE CONSTITUTION OF CANADA (NOS. I, 2, AND 3)** $\Big]$
["THE PATRIATION REFERENCE"]
[1981] 1 S.C.R. 753.

[A summary of the facts and issues in this case is contained at p. 53, supra. In ruling that there was a constitutional convention but that this convention was unenforceable by the courts, both the majority and the dissenting judges of the Court discussed the principles of federalism. Their response was divided in two parts: Part I considers the *legal* question; Part II considers the *convention* question.]

PART I

LASKIN C.J.C., DICKSON, BEETZ, ESTEY, McINTYRE, CHOUINARD AND LAMER JJ.: —

Support for a legal requirement of provincial consent to the Resolution that is before this Court, consent which is also alleged to condition United Kingdom response to the Resolution, is, finally, asserted to lie in the preamble of the *British North America Act* itself, and in the reflection, in the substantive terms of the Act, of what are said to be fundamental presuppositions in the preamble as to the nature of Canadian federalism. The preamble recites (and the whole of it is reproduced) the following:

> Whereas the Provinces of Canada, Nova Scotia, and New Brunswick have expressed their Desire to be federally united into One Dominion under the Crown of the United Kingdom of Great Britain and Ireland, with a Constitution similar in Principle to that of the United Kingdom:
>
> And whereas such a Union would conduce to the Welfare of the Provinces and promote the Interests of the British Empire:
>
> And whereas on the Establishment of the Union by Authority of Parliament it is expedient, not only that the Constitution of the Legislative Authority in the Dominion be provided for, but also that the Nature of the Executive Government therein be declared:
>
> And whereas it is expedient that Provision be made for the eventual Admission into the Union of other Parts of British North America:

What is stressed is the desire of the named provinces "to be federally united [...] with a Constitution similar in Principle to that of the United Kingdom". The preamble speaks also of union into "One Dominion" and of the establishment of the Union "by Authority of Parliament", that is the United Kingdom Parliament. What, then, is to be drawn from the preamble as a matter of law? A preamble, needless to say, has no enacting force but, certainly, it can be called in aid to illuminate provisions of the statute in which it appears.

Federal union "with a Constitution similar in Principle to that of the United Kingdom" may well embrace responsible government and some common law aspects of the United Kingdom's unitary constitutionalism, such as the rule of law and Crown prerogatives and immunities. The "rule of law" is a highly textured expression, importing many things which are beyond the need of these reasons to explore but conveying, for example, a sense of orderliness, of subjection to known legal rules and of executive accountability to legal authority.

Legislative changes may alter common law prescriptions, as has happened with respect to Crown prerogatives and immunities. There is also an internal contradiction in speaking of federalism in the light of the invariable principle of British parliamentary supremacy. Of course, the resolution of this contradiction lies in the scheme of distribution of legislative power, but this owes nothing to the preamble, resting rather on its own exposition in the substantive terms of the British North America Act.

There is not and cannot be any standardized federal system from which particular conclusions must necessarily be drawn. Reference was made earlier to what were called unitary features of Canadian federalism and they operate to distinguish Canadian federalism from that of Australia and that of the United States. Allocations of legislative power differ as do the institutional arrangements through which power is exercised. This Court is being asked by the provinces which object to the so-called federal "package" to say that the internal distribution of legislative power must be projected externally, as a matter of law, although there is no legal warrant for this assertion and, indeed, what legal authority exists (as in s. 3 of the *Statute of Westminster, 1931*) denies this provincial position.

At bottom, it is this distribution, it is the allocation of legislative power as between the central Parliament and the provincial legislatures, that the provinces rely on as precluding unilateral federal action to seek amendments to the *British North America Act* that affect, whether by limitation or extension, provincial legislative authority. The Attorney General of Canada was pushed to the extreme by being forced to answer affirmatively the theoretical question whether in law the federal government could procure an amendment to the *British North America Act* that would turn Canada into a unitary state. That is not what the present Resolution envisages because the essential federal character of the country is preserved under the enactments proposed by the Resolution.

That, it is argued, is no reason for conceding unilateral federal authority to accomplish, through invocation of legislation by the United Kingdom Parliament, the purposes of the Resolution. There is here, however, an unprecedented situation in which the one constant since the enactment of the *British North America Act* in 1867 has been the legal authority of the United Kingdom Parliament to amend it. The law knows nothing of any requirement of provincial consent, either to a resolution of the federal Houses or as a condition of the exercise of United Kingdom legislative power. [...]

MARTLAND AND RITCHIE JJ. [dissenting on this Part]:—

The contention of the Attorney General of Canada in the present proceedings is that only the federal Parliament can speak for Canada as a sovereign state. It is the Houses of Parliament which, alone, under the practice developed in the obtaining of amendments to the B.N.A. Act, can submit a request to the Imperial Parliament to amend the B.N.A. Act, and the Imperial Parliament by a firm and unbending convention must comply with such a request. There is therefore, it is contended, nothing which lawfully precludes the submission to the

Imperial Parliament by resolution of both Houses of a request for an amendment to the *B.N.A. Act* which affects the basic division of legislative powers enshrined in the *B.N.A. Act.*

In our opinion the accession of Canada to sovereign international status did not enable the federal Parliament, whose legislative authority is limited to the matters defined in s. 91 of the *B.N.A. Act,* unilaterally by means of a resolution of its two Houses, to effect an amendment to the *B.N.A. Act* which would offend against the basic principle of the division of powers created by that *Act.* The assertion of such a right, which has never before been attempted, is not only contrary to the federal system created by the *B.N.A. Act,* but also runs counter to the objective sought to be achieved by s. 7 of the *Statute of Westminster, 1931.*

The federal position in these appeals can be summarized in these terms. While the federal Parliament lacks legal authority to achieve the objectives set out in the Resolution by the enactment of its own legislation, that limitation upon its authority can be evaded by having the legislation enacted by the Imperial Parliament at the behest of a resolution of the two Houses of the federal Parliament. This is an attempt by the federal Parliament to accomplish indirectly that which it is legally precluded from doing directly by perverting the recognized resolution method of obtaining constitutional amendments by the Imperial Parliament for an improper purpose. In our opinion, since it is beyond the power of the federal Parliament to enact such an amendment, it is equally beyond the power of its two Houses to effect such an amendment through the agency of the Imperial Parliament.

John Robarts and Daniel Johnson shaking hands at a Federal-Provincial Constitutional Conference (Ottawa, 1970).

We would adopt the views expressed by the Right Honourable Louis St. Laurent, then Prime Minister of Canada, on January 31, 1949, when in the debate on the Address he said:

> With respect to all matters given by the Constitution to the provincial governments, nothing this house could do could take anything away from them. We have no jurisdiction over what has been assigned exclusively to the provinces. We cannot ask that what is not within our jurisdiction be changed. We have jurisdiction over the matters assigned to us and we can ask that the manner of dealing with those matters be changed. [...] (House of Commons Debates, 1949, vol. 1, at p. 85.)

This passage clearly defines the scope of the power of the federal Parliament to request, on its own motion, amendments to the *B.N.A. Act.* It is limited to matters which are assigned to the federal Parliament by the *B.N.A. Act.*

CONCLUSIONS:

The B.N.A. Act created a federal union. It was of the very essence of the federal nature of the Constitution that the Parliament of Canada and the provincial legislatures should have distinct and separate legislative powers. The nature of the legislative powers of the provinces under s. 92 and the status of the provincial legislatures was declared by the Privy Council in the *Hodge* case (supra) and in the *Maritime Bank* case (supra). We repeat the statement of Lord Watson in the latter case at pp. 441-42:

> The object of the *Act* was neither to weld the provinces into one, nor to subordinate provincial governments to a central authority, but to create a federal government in which they should all be represented, entrusted with the exclusive administration of affairs in which they had a common interest, each province retaining its independence and autonomy.

The continuation of that basic division of legislative powers was recognized in s. 7(3) of the *Statute of Westminster, 1931*. The Parliament of Canada has no power to trespass on the area of legislative powers given to the provincial legislatures. Section 7 of the *Statute* was intended to safeguard provincial legislative powers from possible encroachment by the federal Parliament as a result of the powers being conferred upon the Parliament of Canada by the *Statute*.

The fact that the status of Canada became recognized as a sovereign state did not alter its federal nature. It is a sovereign state, but its government is federal in character with a clear division of legislative powers. The Resolution at issue in these appeals could only be an effective expression of Canadian sovereignty if it had the support of both levels of government.

The two Houses of the Canadian Parliament claim the power unilaterally to effect an amendment to the *B.N.A. Act* which they desire, including the curtailment of provincial legislative powers. This strikes at the basis of the whole federal system. It asserts a right by one part of the Canadian governmental system to curtail, without agreement, the powers of the other part.

There is no statutory basis for the exercise of such a power. On the contrary, the powers of the Senate and the House of Commons, given to them by s. 4(a) of the Senate and House of Commons Act, excluded the power to do anything inconsistent with the *B.N.A. Act*. The exercise of such a power has no support in constitutional convention. The constitutional convention is entirely to the contrary. We see no other basis for the recognition of the existence of such a power. This being so, it is the proper function of this Court, in its role of protecting and preserving the Canadian constitution, to declare that no such power exists. We are, therefore, of the opinion that the Canadian Constitution does not empower the Senate and the House of Commons to cause the Canadian Constitution to be amended in respect of provincial legislative powers without the consent of the provinces.

PART II

LASKIN C.J.C., ESTEY AND McINTYRE JJ. [dissenting in this Part]: —

It was also argued that Canada was formed as a federal union and that the existence of a legal power of the central government to unilaterally change the Constitution was inimical to the concept of federalism. The convention then, it was argued, arose out of the necessity to restrain such unilateral conduct and preserve the federal nature of Canada. In this connection, it must be acknowledged at once that, in a federal union, the powers and rights of each of the two levels of government must be protected from the assault of the other. The whole history of constitutional law and constitutional litigation in Canada since Confederation has been concerned with this vital question. We are asked to say whether the need for the preservation of the principles of Canadian federalism dictates the necessity for a convention, requiring consent from the provinces as a condition of the exercise by the federal government of its legal powers, to procure amendment to the Canadian Constitution. If the convention requires only partial consent, as is contended by Saskatchewan, it is difficult to see how the federal concept is thereby protected for, while those provinces favouring amendment would be pleased, those refusing consent could claim coercion.

If unanimous consent is required (as contended by the other objecting provinces), while it may be said that in general terms the concept of federalism would be protected it would only be by overlooking the special nature of Canadian federalism that this protection would be achieved. The *B.N.A. Act* has not created a perfect or ideal federal state. Its provisions have accorded a measure of paramountcy to the federal Parliament. Certainly this has been done in a more marked degree in Canada than in many other federal states. For example, one need only look to the power of reservation and disallowance of provincial enactments; the power to declare works in a province to be for the benefit of all Canada and to place them under federal regulatory control; the wide powers to legislate generally for the peace, order and good government of Canada as a whole; the power to enact the criminal law of the entire country; the power to create and admit provinces out of existing territories and, as well, the paramountcy accorded federal legislation. It is this special nature of Canadian federalism which deprives the federalism argument described above of its force. This is particularly true when it involves the final settlement of Canadian constitutional affairs with an external government, the federal authority being the sole conduit for communication between Canada and the Sovereign and Canada alone having the power to deal in external matters. We therefore reject the argument that the preservation of the principles of Canadian federalism requires the recognition of the convention asserted before us.

While it may not be necessary to do so in dealing with Question 2, we feel obliged to make a further comment related to the federalism argument. It was argued that the federal authorities were assuming a power to act without restraint in disregard of provincial wishes which could go so far as to convert Canada into a unitary state by means of a majority vote in the Houses of Parliament. A few words will suffice to lay that argument at rest. What is before the Court is the task of answering the questions posed in three References. As has been pointed out, the

Court can do no more than that. The questions all deal with the constitutional validity of precise proposals for constitutional amendment and they form the complete subject-matter of the Court's inquiry and our comments must be made with reference to them. It is not for the Court to express views on the wisdom or lack of wisdom of these proposals. We are concerned solely with their constitutionality. In view of the fact that the unitary argument has been raised, however, it should be noted, in our view, that the federal constitutional proposals, which preserve a federal state without disturbing the distribution or balance of power, would create an amending formula which would enshrine provincial rights on the question of amendments on a secure, legal and constitutional footing, and would extinguish, as well, any presently existing power on the part of the federal Parliament to act unilaterally in constitutional matters. In so doing, it may be said that the parliamentary resolution here under examination does not, save for the enactment of the *Charter of Rights,* which circumscribes the legislative powers of both the federal and provincial legislatures, truly amend the Canadian Constitution. Its effect is to complete the formation of an incomplete constitution by supplying its present deficiency, i.e. an amending formula, which will enable the Constitution to be amended in Canada as befits a sovereign state. We are not here faced with an action which in any way has the effect of transforming this federal union into a unitary state. The in terrorem argument raising the spectre of a unitary state has no validity.

MARTLAND, RITCHIE, DICKSON, BEETZ, CHOUINARD AND LAMER JJ.:—

Canada is a federal union. The preamble of the *B.N.A. Act* states that

> [...] the Provinces of Canada, Nova Scotia, and New Brunswick have expressed their Desire to be federally united [...]

The federal character of the Canadian Constitution was recognized in innumerable judicial pronouncements. We will quote only one, that of Lord Watson in *Liquidators of the Maritime Bank of Canada v. Receiver-General of New Brunswick,* supra, at pp. 441-42:

> The object of the *Act* was neither to weld the provinces into one, nor to subordinate provincial governments to a central authority, but to create a federal government in which they should all be represented, entrusted with the exclusive administration of affairs in which they had a common interest, each province retaining its independence and autonomy.

The federal principle cannot be reconciled with a state of affairs where the modification of provincial legislative powers could be obtained by the unilateral action of the federal authorities. It would indeed offend the federal principle that "a radical change to [...] [the] Constitution [be] taken at the request of a bare majority of the members of the Canadian House of Commons and Senate" (Report of Dominion Provincial Conference, 1931, at p. 3).

This is an essential requirement of the federal principle which was clearly recognized by the Dominion-Provincial Conference of 1931. This conference had been convened to consider the proposed *Statute of Westminster* as well as a draft of s. 7 which dealt exclusively with the Canadian position.

At the opening of the conference, Prime Minister Bennett said:

> It should be noted that nothing in the *Statute* confers on the Parliament of Canada the power to alter the constitution.

> The position remained that nothing in the future could be done to amend the *British North America Act* except as the result of appropriate action taken in Canada and in London. In the past such appropriate action had been an address by both Houses of the Canadian Parliament to the Parliament at Westminster. It was recognized, however, that this might result in a radical change to our Constitution taken at the request of a bare majority of the members of the Canadian House of Commons and Senate. The original draft of the *Statute* appeared, in the opinion of some provincial authorities, to sanction such a procedure, but in the draft before the conference this was clearly not the case. (Report of Dominion-Provincial Conference, 1931, at pp. 3-4.)

[...] Furthermore, as was stated in the fourth general principle of the White Paper, the requirement of provincial consent did not emerge as early as other principles, but it has gained increasing recognition and acceptance since 1907 and particularly since 1930. This is clearly demonstrated by the proceedings of the Dominion-Provincial Conference of 1931.

Then followed the positive precedents of 1940, 1951 and 1964 as well as the abortive ones of 1951, 1960 and 1964, all discussed above. By 1965, the rule had become recognized as a binding constitutional one formulated in the fourth general principle of the White Paper already quoted reading in part as follows:

> The fourth general principle is that the Canadian Parliament will not request an amendment directly affecting federal-provincial relationships without prior consultation and agreement with the provinces.

The purpose of this conventional rule is to protect the federal character of the Canadian Constitution and prevent the anomaly that the House of Commons and Senate could obtain by simple resolutions what they could not validly accomplish by statute.

It was contended by counsel for Canada, Ontario and New Brunswick that the proposed amendments would not offend the federal principle and that, if they became law, Canada would remain a federation. The federal principle would even be reinforced, it was said, since the provinces would as a matter of law be given an important role in the amending formula.

It is true that Canada would remain a federation if the proposed amendments became law. But it would be a different federation made different at the instance of a majority in the Houses of the federal Parliament acting alone. It is this process itself which offends the federal principle.

It was suggested by counsel for Saskatchewan that the proposed amendments were perhaps severable; that the proposed *Charter of Rights* offended the federal principle in that it would unilaterally alter legislative powers whereas the proposed amending formula did not offend the federal principle.

To this suggestion we cannot accede. Counsel for Canada (as well as counsel for other parties and all interveners) took the firm position that the proposed amendment formed an unseverable package. Furthermore, and to repeat, whatever the result, the process offends the federal principle. It was to guard against this process that the constitutional convention came about.

CONCLUSION

We have reached the conclusion that the agreement of the provinces of Canada, no views being expressed as to its quantification, is constitutionally required for the passing of the "Proposed Resolution for a Joint Address to Her Majesty the Queen respecting the Constitution of Canada" and that the passing of this Resolution without such agreement would be unconstitutional in the conventional sense. [...]

(c) Federalism, Confederalism, and Supra-National Political Association

(i) Quebec's Grievances and Proposals

- Research Note -

QUEBEC'S GRIEVANCES AND PROPOSALS

Why do a substantial number of Quebecers favour sovereignty-association, sovereignty-partnership or independence for Quebec? There are perhaps many reasons. Professor Watts (supra at p. 110) thinks that there are two motives: the desire for large political units that facilitate economic and social progress, and the desire for smaller self-governing political units that "give expression [...] to historical traditions and social practices."

General de Gaulle, "Vive Le Québec Libre!" Montreal, 1967

FEDERALISM, CONFEDERALISM, AND SUPRA-NATIONAL POLITICAL ASSOCIATION

It is undeniable that the attachment to community is strong in Quebec. The sense of community is strengthened by the shared history of a small and tightly knit population, a common and distinctive language, the experience of an extraordinarily active church in domestic and institutional life and its dramatic, recent decline through a process of deconfessionalisation, a lively oral, written and visual culture and many unique, common traditions. The attachment to community beats on the pulses of many people resident in Quebec as a strong attachment to Quebec — as nationalism. But for many of these same Quebec residents, the attachment to community is felt equally strong as an attachment to Canada, an identification as "French-Canadians" or "Quebecois" within Canada. Many Quebecers share a profound "rêve d'une nation", as well as the dream of being one of the two founding people of a great Canadian state.

Quebec's political leaders have consistently voiced the idea of Canada as an association of equals, as a bi-national state. For example, Premier Daniel Johnson addressed the Federal Provincial Conference in Ottawa, in 1968 in this way:

> The object of the Constitution must not solely be to federate territories, but also to associate as equals two linguistic and cultural communities, two founding peoples, two societies, two nations in the sociological sense of the term. A Canadian Constitution must be the product of an agreement between the two nations that make up the people of Canada, and must recognize the principle of the legal equality of the two cultural communities

This idea has worked its way deep into the French Canadian mind. It is associated with a bundle of grievances which French Canadians have been encouraged by their political and intellectual leaders to bear against the federal government in Ottawa. The core idea of these grievances is that the federal infrastructure is chipping away at the autonomy of Quebec, and eroding the community of equals which confederation is supposed to represent. Therefore, proponents of the sovereignty idea have been able to generate a sizable political following behind the following grievances articulated over the years:

Canadian Identity has not Developed under Federalism: Quebec separatists allege that federalism has been incapable of resolving Canada's "identity problem". It united the East and West although both the East and West have more North-South interactions. It unites the French and English yet the institutions are British, the British monarch is the head of state. The country is officially bilingual and multicultural and gives no respect to the founding people or aboriginals. In short, Canadian federalism has failed to "give birth to one united people".[1]

The Federal Government Retains the Key Instruments of Government Policy[2]: Objectives, priorities, and norms for Quebec's economy are determined by that

---

1   Jean Louis Bourque, *Demain, la république: Le projet du Québec profond* (Sainte-Foy, PQ: Les Editions La Liberté, 1992), pp. 17-18.

2   Pierre Renaud, "Il nous fait tous les pouvoirs," in A. Ferretti and G. Miron (eds.), *Les grands textes indépendantistes* (Montreal: Editions de l'Hexagone, 1992), p. 359.

level of government that controls the great economic levers: money, credit, customs, and most taxes. This is the federal government, and the federal government will never let go of those powers. In effect, Premier Lucien Bouchard argues, "English speaking Canada has a veto on the future development of Quebec within the federation."[1]

Quebecers Do Not Believe in the Equality Inherent in Canadian Federalism: Quebecers do not accept guarantees of equality in the same way that the rest of Canada does. Former Premier Jacques Parizeau suggests that "it is not that rights and obligations are any less important than in Canada, but there must be a place for differences."[2] Therefore the equality guarantees in the *Charter*, calls for a Triple-E senate, and other things held dearly by the Rest of Canada are antithetical to Quebec's aspirations.

Federalism Creates Overlap and Duplication: Beyond the waste involved in intergovernmental conflict, federalism creates too much government. Overlapping jurisdictions are "naturally very costly."[3] It is a "waste of money and energy that is difficult to measure accurately."[4] In order to eliminate this overlap and duplication, the federal government would have to transfer virtually all of its powers to Quebec.

Quebec Cannot Develop Economically, Culturally, Socially and Politically under Canadian Federalism: These areas are still controlled, in a large part, by the financial resources of the federal government that seeks to create a concept of Canada against the desire of Quebecers in a parliament where Quebec has a minority voice.[5]

Multiple Levels of Government Authority in Canadian Federalism is Bad for Quebec Business: Businesses do not understand which level of government has jurisdiction and usually has to negotiate with both, and this hinders the development of Quebec business.[6]

Quebec is Getting More Cuts than the Rest of Canada: Deficit-cutting in Canada is felt harder in Quebec than in the rest of Canada. Reduction of transfer payments means that Quebec will receive 32 percent less in 1997-1998 than it did in 1994-1995. Between 1982 and 1993, Quebecers paid 143% more in tax. Meanwhile, regional development has increased by only 50 percent in Quebec while they increased by 250% in Maritimes and 300% in Western Canada.[7]

1   *Debates of the House of Commons* (June 7, 1994), p. 4917.

2   Jacques Parizeau, "Who's Afraid of Sovereignty Association?" *Canadian Speeches*, January 1991.

3   Gouvernement de Québec, Conseil Exécutif, *Québec-Canada: A New Deal* (Québec, Editeur officiel du Quebec, 1979), pp. 24-25.

4   *Ibid.* See also Parti Québécois, *La souveraineté: des réponses à vos questions* (Québec: Service des communications du Parti Québécois, 1995), p. 10.

5   Parti Québecois, *La sourveraineté: des réponses à vos questions* (Quebec: Service des communications du Parti Québécois, 1995).

6   Jean Campeau, "L'indépendance du Québec pour bâtir deux pays à leur image," *Action Nationale* 82(7) (Spring 1992), pp. 846-851.

7   Gaston Leroux (BQ), *Debates of the House of Commons* (May 2, 1995).

FEDERALISM, CONFEDERALISM, AND SUPRA-NATIONAL POLITICAL ASSOCIATION

The grievances which French Canadians are encouraged to bear against Ottawa have a certain traditional or mythical cast about them, and nationalism is a traditional or mythical response to the perceptions of French Canadians that they are not getting a fair deal out of Confederation. But there is a separate sense in which the grievances of French Canadians against Ottawa are not misconceived ideology — a sense in which the grievances of French Canada are real and quantifiable. Prior to the quiet revolution the two nations inhabiting the Canadian state did so on the basis of inequality. The English Canadian nation dominated the civil service and the private economy, and did so with the quiet concurrence of the Catholic church, the dominant voice in French Canada. After the quiet revolution, French Canada rapidly de-confessionalised. As it did so, the new French Canadian intellectuals rejected the domination of English Ottawa and the English corporations. While the inequality of incomes and the unequal participation of French Canadians in the Federal civil service has been largely eradicated in the past thirty years, the legacy of domination lives on in certain minds and hearts.

To a certain extent, the problems of Canada resemble those of all large polities. All large political systems engender economic and political competition between regional subdivisions. However, in Canada, regional competition is exacerbated by five additional factors: (1) Canada's regions have distinctive linguistic identities. In Canada, therefore, regional economic competition is superimposed over a division of linguistic identities. This makes it possible to perceive commonplace regional competitions as contests of English against French. This makes regional economic competition in Canada at times supercharged; the competition of English against French tends to be perceived as intensely political and all-pervasive. The feelings generated by this competition become fierce. Canadians are capable of carrying on this imagined rivalry between English and French everywhere in their political life, even where it has little rational application, as, for example, in majority-minority relations in the overwhelmingly English-speaking provinces. The competition is perceived as a zero-sum game — one community wins; the other community loses.

(2) Canadian demography places the English and French *languages* in contact. The sociology of language well understands that when diverse languages come into contact, unique effects are produced. The most important of these effects is "language shift," which may be defined as the switching from the language habitually used by a speaker to the language better understood by that speaker's audience. Language shift occurs as a result of the need to communicate in a commonly understood language. Over time, language shift leads to assimilation of weaker languages by stronger languages. Canadian history offers a potent illustration of how this works. Outside of Quebec, the weaker French language has been assimilated by the stronger English language for over one-hundred-twenty-five years, to the point where most provincial French-speaking communities are diminished and some provincial French-speaking communities have ceased to exist. More recently, a similar process has been eclipsing the weaker English language inside of Quebec.

Canada's political system does not have the institutional strength to manage this competition well. (3) The Upper Chamber's design does not allow it to broker regional economic interests (as in other federations). (4) Canada's extensive use of executive federalism as brokerage machinery has democratic deficits which obscure the brokerage process. This tempts regional actors to attack the regime, as well as the process, for brokerage failures; (5) From the perspective of all major actors, the regime — Canada's Constitution — is incompletely manufactured. Proposals for its completion generate strenuous political competition between the regions.

The presence in Canada of all these factors simultaneously exaggerates regional and linguistic competition to unusually severe levels. Regional economic competition (which is superimposed over competition between the language communities) plays out repeatedly to enlarge local incidents involving minority linguistic communities. Local linguistic clashes all progress basically the same. The conflicts emerge seemingly out of nowhere: at a school board meeting, in an exchange between a speeding motorist and a police officer, in a hospital restructuring exercise. The arena of contest is overwhelmingly controlled by the linguistic majority. The majority uses its power in a seemingly injurious spirit. The local minority has inadequate constitutional weight in the balance of power. Local actors have incentives to fan the flames. National actors appear to give the incident weighty national significance, but no forum for national resolution. Nor does the constitutional and institutional machinery meant to control linguistic conflict work well. Counter-intuitively, in many instances the machinery amplifies local conflicts: by drawing them out over time, by failing to provide clear, unambiguous outcomes, by failing to insulate linguistic minorities from aggressive provincial majorities, by under-weighting minorities in the balance of constitutional power and by expanding the stage to national debate without resolution machinery that operates in the national interest. The repeated flare-up of these local firestorms throughout Canadian history have made for difficult relations between the linguistic communities, and in Quebec, it has deepened suspicion of 'English Canada' and Canada's federal system.

In light of these grievances, perceived or real, it is worth asking why a substantial number of Quebecers favour sovereignty-association, sovereignty-partnership, or independence as an antidote to these grievances. Sovereigntists find fertile ground in merchandising nationalism to the Quebec polity. They find ready consumers of the idea in various quarters: older Quebecers, particularly in rural areas, still smarting from the domination by an exclusively English managerial and entrepreneurial class, French business people competing with rivals in English Canada, old time clerics longing for the *ancien regime* of church supremacy, provincial bureaucrats and workers in the para-public sector (schools, municipalities, hospitals, universities) who associate their upward mobility with the almost exclusively French provincial government and resist any encroachment on their jurisdictions by Ottawa.

There is a large body of literature concerning Quebec's grievances with federalism. It is interesting to visit the web-sites of the Bloc Québécois and Parti Québécois. One finds there the themes that motivate the desire for sovereignty in Quebec. Distilled down to the core ideas, this literature amounts to assertions that federalism:

- pays insufficient respect to the Quebec people as a distinctive national community;

- makes vulnerable Quebec's institutions, language, culture, and national identity;
- devolves insufficient power to Quebec, and
- gives Ottawa too much control over Quebec's economy.

The desirability of sovereignty as a solution to Quebec's grievances about Canada's federal system is also advanced by certain political thinkers in Quebec. The Parti Québécois stated in a 1994 pamphlet what a sovereign Quebec would look like. This was developed by the Comité National pour OUI for the 1995 Referendum. Finally, the PQ published another document in 1995 that purported to explain the reasons why Quebecers should vote for sovereignty. This was the PQ's answer to the charge, "Why would sovereignty be better than federalism?"

POSITION OF THE PARTIS QUÉBÉCOIS ON THE SEPARATIST MOVEMENT TODAY
Source: Partis Québécois online: http://www.pq.org/nv/index.php?pq=57

1. What does The Parti Québécois want?

The Parti Québécois wants Québec to become a sovereign country and for it to have all the political, judicial and fiscal instruments to become master of its own destiny. It wants the government to be able to legitimately promote and defend the interests of the Québec people, and participate in international forums, like other nations, a necessity more and more pronounced in the context of globalization. Québec is the only North American State where Francophones constitute the majority of the population, and where a specific model of culture, development, institutions, legal system and civil law exists. The sovereignty project is legitimate, as recognized by the Canadian Supreme Court in August 1998 and Canada has, according this Court, an obligation to negotiate in good faith Quebec's accession to sovereignty.

2. Where does the Québec sovereignty project come from?

Since the birth of Canada in 1867, there have always been supporters of independence who thought Québec was not just another province within the Canadian borders, but rather constituted a nation and should become a country. Negotiations in the 1960's to amend Canada's Constitution in order to recognize Québec as one of the founding nations and to give it the necessary powers to develop itself within Canada failed. These failures occurred even when negotiations were conducted by Québec federalist governments in favour of Québec staying within Canada. Elected in 1976, the Parti Québécois government held a referendum on sovereignty in 1980, obtaining 40.6% support. In 1982, Canada modified its Constitution without National Assembly's and the

René Lévesque, the founder of the Parti Québécois, speaking to supporters on election night (October, 1973).

Québec government's assent. To this day, no Québec political party has accepted to adhere to this Constitution. In 1994 the Parti Québécois regained power and in 1995 held another referendum, where the support for sovereignty climbed to 49.4%. On November 30th, 1998, the Parti Québécois was re-elected and once again formed the government.

3. Why does the Parti Québécois still want Québec to achieve sovereignty?

Since the October 1995 referendum, the governments of Canada have ignored the will of the people of Québec to reform Canadian federalism. The federal government in Ottawa decided to maintain the status quo, accentuating problems which have existed for the last forty years. Furthermore, this government has multiplied attacks against Québec and continues to intervene in its areas of its exclusive jurisdiction, which causes severe problems in the planning of public services. It has also attempted to intimidate the Québec population by threatening not to recognize any future referendum result, notwithstanding the fact that Québec's democratic traditions are flawless and that its legislation on the financing of political parties and referendums are exemplary.

4. Who in Québec is considered a Quebecker?

Québec nationalism is not ethnic but civic. All citizens residing on Québec territory are Quebeckers. Québec has a Charter of Rights and Freedoms which guarantees equality to all citizens. Québec's official language is French and new immigrants are obligated by law to send their children to French-speaking schools. The English-speaking community has its own complete educational system, from preschool to university, and has access to all services in its own language. It manages on their own its learning, health and social services institutions, along with numerous radio and television stations, newspapers and magazines. As for Aboriginal nations, Québec's National Assembly recognized in 1985 the existence of eleven aboriginal nations, along their right of self-government. Conventions and agreements were concluded with a number of aboriginal nations in matters related to education and health and provide also for joint economical development projects.

COMITÉ NATIONAL DU OUI, "TO BUILD A QUEBEC SOCIETY: OUR HEARTS INTO WORK"
(Internet Publication: Sept. 7, 1995)

CHANGE, FOR A TRUE PARTNERSHIP WITH CANADA

Comedian Yvon Deschamps once said that "Quebecers want an independent Québec inside a strong Canada!" It's no accident that his quip has become famous: it contains a strong grain of truth.

And it's a fact: a very large majority of us want to control our own taxes, vote our own laws, sign our own treaties. Which is the definition of sovereignty. At the same time we worked hard to build Canada, to create its institutions, contribute to its reputation around the world. In particular, it was Montrealers who invented the Canadian dollar. Before the federal government got involved, paper money was printed by the Bank of Montreal!

FEDERALISM, CONFEDERALISM, AND SUPRA-NATIONAL POLITICAL ASSOCIATION

In the past, many Quebecers thought it was possible to combine our two objectives — by remaining a province in Canada but on condition that we make in Quebec a larger proportion of our own decisions. For a while, it seemed possible.

During the 1960s, Liberal Premier Jean Lesage said Quebecers had to be Masters in Our Own House. Then his successor as Premier, Daniel Johnson Senior, of the Union Nationale, said what was needed was Equality or Independence. After that, Robert Bourassa asked first for cultural sovereignty, then for recognition of Québec as a distinct society. All these attempts had just one goal: to allow Quebecers to make their own choices on a certain number of important matters.

But they all failed. Every time, English Canada's No was expressed a little louder. Canadians elsewhere believe that if Quebecers stay in Canada, they have to behave exactly like the others, and submit to the decisions of the majority, without having any unique rights or status. In fact the vast majority of Canadians are convinced that Quebecers do not form a distinct people.

Even worse, when the other provinces got together to change the Constitution in 1982, they did so without our agreement and they took powers away from us, particularly in the areas of language and education. All political parties in Québec were opposed to that measure. Recently Daniel Johnson, leader of the Quebec Liberal Party, wrote that the 1982 Constitution created among Quebecers "a sense of betrayal and isolation."

Another Québec federalist, former Liberal cabinet minister Claude Forget, calculates that since we are increasingly a minority, we're increasingly vulnerable to the Canadian majority. Recently he wrote in La Presse that it is "an illusion" to think we'll obtain more autonomy if we remain in Canada, because, in fact, that "any change will worsen the situation, not improve it." At the present time, Québec has one seat in four in the federal Parliament. Over the next 50 years, because of the evolution of the population, we'll be down to one in five or six.

And it's true that at any time, seven Anglophone provinces together with the federal government can modify the Canadian Constitution without our approval, thereby weakening Québec. This is more or less what the Supreme Court of Canada did last year when it declared that Québec had no power in one of the areas most important for our future, our culture, and our language: telecommunications.

SOVEREIGNTY AND PARTNERSHIP: THE WINNING COMBINATION

So we can see that the longer we remain a province in Canada like the others, the less we'll be able to make decisions that reflect us. And we would pass on to our children the never-ending debate on the future of Québec, because we'll have decided not to settle it ourselves.

Even if we've been unable to reach an agreement on some fundamental political subjects over the past 30 years, we and the Canadians have forged significant economic ties. The jobs of hundreds of thousands of Canadians depend on us, and the reverse is true as well. Every fifteen minutes we buy a million dollars worth of goods manufactured in the rest of Canada, which is why it's as important for them as for us to maintain economic exchanges. The Québec government was in fact in the forefront in the negotiations in recent months that led to freer trade between the provinces of Canada.

Even if the Canadians refuse to recognize our existence and our identity, there are things on which we can agree, areas in which it's preferable to act in common. We hold no animosity towards Canadians. We'd even like to maintain a new, permanent political link with our neighbours, to properly manage our common interests.

Which is where the proposal of a political and economic Partnership with Canada comes in. Inside of joint, light, effective institutions, this partnership will consolidate free trade between Québec and Canada. It will confirm the absence of customs at the borders with the provinces. It will allow mobility of manpower. It will oversee the monetary union and provide arrangements on Québec and Canadian citizenship. A joint tribunal will also be charged with resolving possible disputes, particularly in commercial matters.

Inside a Partnership Council, made up equally of ministers from Québec and Canada, and with the views of a Parliamentary Assembly consisting of Members delegated by the two countries, we will be able to choose to act jointly in other areas too.

First come all the areas involved in being good neighbours. We'll have to cooperate so we can facilitate transportation between the two States, join forces for example against cross-border pollution or to stop the trafficking in weapons and drugs.

On the international scene, Québec will have its own seat in the United Nations, in the Francophonie and elsewhere, so that its own unique, distinct voice can be heard. But thanks to the Partnership, Québec and Canada will be able to speak in a single voice at certain international forums, when they decide it will give them more weight. We can also decide to associate with Canadians during peacekeeping operations, for example.

The big difference with the current situation is that every time it will be our choice whether we act independently or jointly with Canada inside the partnership. They won't be able to impose their decisions on us and we won't be able to impose ours on them. Which is what a true partnership is.

To get there we need the agreement of the rest of Canada, naturally. But we know that the Canadian people aren't opposed to this idea. As far as the basic components of an economic association are concerned, the vast majority of English Canadians think an arrangement with Québec is inevitable. After a Yes perhaps they'll have their own proposal to make on how to organize the partnership, what scope it will have, and how it will operate. And Quebecers will welcome these proposals with the open and constructive spirit that characterizes them.

It's in all our interests to build a partnership with the minimum of frictions and the maximum of mutually advantageous cooperation. A Yes vote means wanting a sovereign Québec in a strong Partnership with Canada. And it means proving that Yvon Deschamps was essentially right!

(ii)   Federalism and its Alternatives

PETER LESLIE, THE MAASTRICHT MODEL: A CANADIAN PERSPECTIVE ON THE EUROPEAN UNION
(KINGSTON: INSTITUTE OF INTERGOVERNMENTAL RELATIONS, 1996)

Both the historical context of European integration and the inner logic of the institutional system that has been built up are pertinent to making comparisons with other complex systems (federal states, supranational organizations, forms of economic association — to establish a free trade area, for example). North American comparisons may be made at several levels: with the Canadian (or American) federal system, with the North American Free Trade Agreement (NAFTA), and with a hypothetical association between an independent Quebec and "Canada" or its various successor states.

The last of these comparisons - an "associated states" concept linking an independent Quebec with a surviving but diminished Canadian state - has recently received a good deal of attention from Quebec secessionists. Clearly, what one might call "the Maastricht model" is attractive to those Quebecers who find the federal system too constraining, but who want to preserve some links with Canada. If the Parti Quebecois (PQ) wins the next election in Quebec, one may anticipate another referendum on the principle of independence, probably (as in 1995) with the commitment that if the "Yes" side wins, the Government of Quebec would propose a form of economic and political association with "Canada". Such an association would presumably be nested within the NAFTA (of which both Quebec and the truncated Canadian state would be members in their own right). In 1995, at least in official documents, comparisons with the European Union remained implicit, but the institutional arrangements were then sketched out bear a striking resemblance to those in the EU. There was not enough detail in the relevant documents to be precise about this. However, there are no official sources suggesting that the PQ envisions the creation of legislative, executive, and judicial institutions with anything like the range of powers that have been found necessary in the EU. Although the party program envisions a ministerial council, along with a secretariat to assist in, seemingly no attention has been paid to creating a genuine analogue to the European Commission; that is, there has apparently been no recognition of the need for a bureaucracy with the size, powers, and capacity to play a supervisory and negotiating role vis-à-vis the governments of Quebec and Canada if the proposed economic union were to function effectively. In brief, the political aspect of the association that has been envisioned for Canada-Quebec is less well developed than the supranationalism that exists today in western Europe, while the economic aspect is in some respects more fully developed than in the EU of 1996 (in particular, the persistence of the monetary union is proposed and assumed).

As might be inferred from the preceding parts of this report, experience in the EC/EU indicates a number of potential difficulties that would have to be resolved if an attempt were made to link Quebec and the new Canada through a Maastricht-inspired form of economic and political association.

Some of the greatest potential difficulties of "Maastricht in Canada" are not appropriate to this report. However, it may be useful to note (briefly, at least) that the PQ and its allies have assumed that, as soon as the province signals its intention to secede, Canada will be ready to sit down and negotiate a two-member economic and political association. This assumption, however, is unwarranted. There is no one with the constitutional authority or the necessary political base to enter such negotiations on behalf of Canada. It is a near certainty that provinces would insist on being involved in any bargaining with Quebec in order to protect or advance their own interests. They would refuse to stand aside while a federal government bargained on their behalf. [...] As numerous commentators have remarked, if Quebec ever appears to be irrevocably committed to independence, the rest of Canada would probably be far more preoccupied with its own political arrangements than with any agreement it might strike with the future independent state of Quebec. [...]

The problem of the fragility of a regional grouping of states would arise whether Quebec was seeking economic and political association with several other successor-states of Canada, with a barely federal or confederal system (a system with a central political authority mainly controlled by the states), or with a truncated but still clearly federal Canada. One may reasonably conclude that those who are showing interest in a Maastricht-inspired form of economic and political association linking Quebec and Canada are neglecting some of the most important economic and political facts of life in North America. It is not suggested that secessionists have failed to factor in the NAFTA when they think about Quebec's economic future - on the contrary, they emphasize the opportunities it offers. But they seem not to have reflected on how the NAFTA (or simply the presence of the United States) might affect the working of any Quebec-Canada economic/political association. Fragmentation would be a strong possibility, since all the provinces or former provinces of Canada would be more concerned about their ties with the United States than about their ties with each other. Every province except Prince Edward Island now exports more to foreign trading partners, mainly the United States, than to other provinces of Canada. [...]

FEDERALISM, CONFEDERALISM, AND SUPRA-NATIONAL POLITICAL ASSOCIATION

The preceding paragraphs have shown that a Canada-Quebec economic association or economic union strong enough to preserve the existing Canadian economic space intact would comprise several elements:

- There would be a customs union with a common commercial policy and therefore with a single agency to conduct international trade negotiations and to ratify agreements. Both under the NAFTA and under the World Trade Organization, negotiations and agreements can be expected to cover such a wide range of issues that it will be impossible to make a clear distinction between trade policy and management or control of the domestic economy.

- There would be a common market, providing for free movement of services, persons and capital, as well as goods. As demonstrated by the European Union, to achieve this degree of economic integration a wide range of policies must be decided in common, or mechanisms must exist to ensure harmonization of policies in areas as diverse as consumption taxes, product standards, subsidies to economic enterprises of all kinds, working conditions, and environmental protection. However, even if the many loopholes in Canada's 1994 Agreement on Internal Trade were plugged and it were rigorously enforced, the agreement would not be adequate to prevent the emergence of barriers inconsistent with a common market.

- The common or agreed regulatory framework for economic activity, required to make a common market work, would be sufficiently well developed to allow for open borders (absence of controls).

- If the Maastricht provisions on monetary union are any guide, there would have to be controls on member states' budgetary policies to ensure the stability and strength of the common currency.

In each of these areas, both Canada and Quebec would necessarily be restricted in their economic policies, essentially as the EU states are today. The constraints within which both would have to operate, at least if they followed the Maastricht model, would leave them with less control over their economies than the provinces of Canada - including, of course, Quebec - have today. [...]

The difficulties of making Maastricht-type institutions work in the Canada-Quebec context would be especially great, given that what is envisioned is an association of only two states. In the EU, the essence of the political decision-making process is the give and take that is involved in continuing, multi-issue negotiations among multiple partners. Introduction of the qualified majority voting rule led to the success of the Single Market program, and it was the key reform in the relaunching of the Community in the mid-1980s. Today, qualified majority voting lies at the heart of the institutional system in the EU; without it, the institutions and processes would lack the flexibility to work effectively.

A two-member association cannot have such flexibility. A proportional weighting of votes (by population) could not be acceptable to the smaller state, as it would be outvoted every time. To the smaller state, then, the only conceivably acceptable voting rule would be unanimity, as Quebec separatists have proposed. This would give each state an almost comprehensive veto over the other's economic policies. In the Canada-Quebec case, Quebec would gain a voice equal to that of the nine provinces and two territories combined. This would be so obviously unacceptable to Canada as to be not worth discussing. "Maastricht for two" is an impossible concept.

RONALD L. WATTS, COMPARING FEDERAL SYSTEMS
(McGill-Queen's University Press: 1999) at pp.113-114.

[...] In the current Canadian context, the experience of bipolar federations and confederations is relevant because proposals have been advanced [...] for converting Canada into a confederation composed of two units: Quebec and a nine-province federation of the "Rest of Canada." [...]

The experience of bipolar or dyadic federal systems elsewhere is, however, not encouraging. Pakistan prior to the secession of East Pakistan in 1971 and Czechoslovakia prior to is segregation in 1991 have provided examples of the difficulties which arise in bipolar federations. Another relevant case was the bipolar racial and ideological Malaysia-Singapore relationship within the Malaysian federation which culminated in Singapore's expulsion after only two years. All three of these cases resulted in the end in the splitting of these federations. Indeed the particular difficulties of dyadic federations and unions have generally been recognized.

The problem within two-unit federations generally has been that insistence upon parity in all matters between the two units has usually tended to produce impasses and deadlocks. This is because there is no opportunity for shifting alliances and coalitions among the constituent units which is one of the ways in which multi-unit federations are able to resolve issues. Furthermore, since invariably one of the two units is less populous than the other (e.g. West Pakistan and Slovakia) that unit has usually been particularly conscious of the continuous need to insist upon equality of influence in federal policy making, while the larger unit (and in the case of Czechoslovakia, the wealthier unit) has developed a sense of grievance over the constraints imposed upon it to accommodate the smaller unit. The resulting cumulatively intensifying bipolarity in these examples led ultimately to their terminal instability. Such tendencies would appear likely to be accentuated in a two-unit confederation , since it is a normal characteristic of confederations that each member unit possesses a veto on all major policy decisions in the confederation. The existence of mutual vetoes where there are only two units is likely to be a recipe for repeated impasses and deadlocks contributing to cumulatively sharpening frustrations. Thus, the application of the European Union Maastricht model, which despite its difficulties works for a confederation of 15 member states, is likely to be much less workable when applied to a confederation of two units. [...]

FEDERALISM, CONFEDERALISM, AND SUPRA-NATIONAL POLITICAL ASSOCIATION

LUCIEN BOUCHARD, WHY WE ARE SOVEREIGNTISTS
((1994), 17 CDN. PARLIAMENTARY REV.)

[...] The close economic integration between Quebec and Canada forces us to take a careful look at what is happening in Europe. What lessons can we draw from the European model?

Some pundits like to believe the European Community will gradually transform itself into something resembling Canadian federalism, and use this as an argument against Quebec sovereignty. Thus they reveal their lack of familiarity with European developments. In fact the other way around appears much more likely. To solve the Canadian political crisis our present institutions should evolve along the lines of the European Community.

A few facts seem in order. The European Commission in Brussels has a budget that amounts to 1.2 per cent of the global GNP of the community. It has no fiscal powers and cannot run a deficit. The federal government in Ottawa spends 22 per cent of GNP and has the whole gamut of fiscal powers. As for deficits we all know what has happened. The commission in Brussels has no army, no police, and a small bureaucracy when compared to national governments. Community decisions are in fact executed by national bureaucracies. If we exclude trade matters, national sovereignty remains the basic ingredient of the community.

For instance the 12 members could modify the structure and the workings of the EC without the commission having any say in the decision. For these countries co-operation is the master word, not subordination. This is a far cry from the Canadian brand of federalism. Who will pretend, for example, that only the provincial governments determine the future of Canada? Who will pretend that the federal government is but a benevolent arbitrator of inter-regional conflicts? For Quebec, the central government is the problem. For English Canada, it is part of the solution.

The Maastricht treaty extended the process of economic integration to the field of monetary policy by setting the objective of a common currency before the end of the century, and the process of political co-operation by specifying the objective of a common thread in the fields of defence and foreign policy. These sensitive fields will remain the prerogative of the heads of state assembled in the European Council.

Hence the following question: If the European union is indeed the wave of the future as is frequently alleged in the Canadian media, why not propose this model as a solution to Canada's national problem? If Maastricht represents the embodiment of the next century, why does English Canada not propose the same kind of arrangement to Quebec? The Maastricht arrangements would be much easier to implement between Quebec and Canada than among 12 very diverse countries.

Let there be no mistake. Bloc members will not forget that their commitment to sovereignty constitutes the real reason for their presence in this House. One could say that as far as we are concerned, the pre-referendum campaign has begun. Meanwhile, we will not let the recession be dissociated from its causes.

- Research Note -

NATION RESOLUTION

On November, 2007, the House of Commons resolved that "Québécois form a nation within a united Canada."

For sixty years, Canadians have been trying to answer the question: "What does Quebec want?" Since patriation of the Constitution in 1982, many have thought that the answer to this question was recognition - especially recognition in the Constitution of Canada.

This thinking lay behind the *Meech Lake Accord*. That constitutional settlement attempted reconciliation of Quebec to Canada by, among other things, recognizing Quebec as a "distinct society".

A significant number of Canadians disapproved of the *Meech Lake Accord*, and it failed. Some argued that that the *Accord* gave Quebec too much power; others argued that it was the first step down a perilous road to disintegration of Canada.

In 1995, the separatist Parti Québécois, which formed the Quebec government at the time, held a provincial referendum on separation. Separatists lost the vote by a very narrow margin.

The matter rested there - an uneasy cease fire, with Quebec, politically, never having formally agreed to the Constitutional reforms effected by Patriation in 1982, and Canadians having the sense that the question "What does Quebec want?" remained unanswered.

Will the "Nation Declaration" make a difference?

The Quebec government, now led by federalists, maintains that the territory of Quebec (not Quebecers) constitutes a nation. The "nation resolution" maintains that Quebeckers form a nation. It is probable that at some point these views will clash in a renewed attempt to insert some form of recognition into the Constitution.

The Prime Minister introduced the Nation Resolution with the following speech. The incoming leader of the Liberal Party of Canada also spoke.

HANSARD, VOL. 14, NO 086, IST SESS, 39TH PARL, NOV. 24, 2006.
RIGHT HON. STEPHEN HARPER (PRIME MINISTER, CPC)

[...] Mr. Speaker, the real intent behind the motion by the leader of the Bloc and the sovereignist camp is perfectly clear. It is to recognize not what the Québécois are, but what the sovereignists would like them to be.

To the Bloc, the issue is not that Quebec is a nation-the National Assembly has already spoken on that subject; the issue is separation. To them, "nation" means "separation". We saw its true intent on October 27, when it said that the NDP had recognized for decades that Quebec was a nation, but that every time there was a referendum its actions contradicted the positions it had taken....

The former PQ premier, Bernard Landry, asked this question:

> — once that recognition is achieved, you must know, in all honesty, that you will then be faced with the question: why should the nation of Quebec be satisfied with the status of province of another nation and forego equality with yours and every other nation?

Mr. Speaker, the answer is clear. Quebeckers have always played an historic role in Canada's progress, through their public spirit, courage and vision, by building a confident, autonomous and proud Quebec showing its solidarity within a strong, united, independent and free Canada. [...]

Quebeckers know who they are. They know that they have participated in the founding of Canada and in its development and its greatness. They know that they have preserved their language and their unique culture, and that they have advanced their values and their interests within Canada. The real question is simple: do the Québécois form a nation within a united Canada? The answer is yes. Do the Québécois form a nation independent of Canada? The answer is no, and it will always be no...

I say to my federalist colleagues and to the separatist side that we here will do what we must and what our forefathers have always done to preserve this country, Canada, strong, united, independent and free.

HANSARD, 39TH PARLIAMENT, IST SESSION, NOV 27, 2006. P. 2005

Hon. Stéphane Dion [T]he motion that the Prime Minister has put before us reads as follows:

> That this House recognize that the Québécois form a nation within a united Canada.

Before voting on a text that some of our fellow citizens believe will be of great significance, we have a duty to tell them clearly what that text means.

In French, according to *Le Petit Robert*, "nation" has at least three meanings.

First, there is the ethnic sense of the word:

> Group of men presumed to have a common origin.

Second, there is the state sense of the word:

> Group of people constituting a political unit, established in a defined territory..., and personified by a sovereign authority.

113

Third, there is the sociological sense of the word

Group of people, generally large, characterized by awareness of its unity and a desire to live together.

...In the first sense, the ethnic sense, Quebec and Canada are not nations, but French-Canadians are a nation, one that is concentrated primarily in Quebec but is present everywhere in Canada.

There are several other groups of people in our country that can also be considered to be nations in ethnic terms. I would therefore vote in favour of a motion that said: In Canada, including in the province of Quebec, there are several nations in the ethnic sense of the word.

In the second sense of the word "nation", the state sense, the only sense that confers legal existence in international law, Canada and Canada alone is a nation. I would therefore vote for a motion that said: Canada forms a single nation which holds a seat at the United Nations.

In the third sense of the word "nation", the sociological sense, we, the Québécois, are a nation, because we form a large group within Canada—nearly a quarter of the population—and we have an awareness of our unity and a desire to live together. In that sense, it is correct to say that the Québécois form a nation within a united Canada. I will therefore vote for the motion that is before us.

However, I add that the entire Canadian population is also a nation in the sociological sense of the term. As Canadians, we have the sense of our unity and the will to live together, and there is nothing that prevents the same individual to be part of different nations in the sociological sense of the term.

... I am a proud member of the Quebec nation and a proud member of the Canadian nation. I say that these identities are cumulative and indivisible, and that I will fight with every resource that democracy gives me against anyone who wants to make me choose between these two wonderful identities: Québécois and Canadian.

I know all too well the game that the independentist leaders want to play. They want to persuade us that we cannot be part of the Canadian nation because we, the Québécois, form a nation. In other words, they want to shift from the sociological to the state sense of the word "nation": from the "community" sense to the "country" sense. As usual, they want to conflate the meaning of words in order to sow confusion in people's minds.

...[I]n proclaiming my identity as a proud Quebecker today, I am proclaiming my identity as a proud Canadian. Let us work together to ensure that this noble and generous interpretation of the motion that we will vote on today will prevail.

FEDERALISM, CONFEDERALISM, AND SUPRA-NATIONAL POLITICAL ASSOCIATION

THOMAS M. FRANCK, WHY FEDERATIONS FAIL
(NEW YORK: NYU PRESS, 1968)

[...] [I]n this study, failure is specifically a non-achievement of the necessary conditions for survival of a federation as initially conceived. But again, as with human beings, failures are seldom absolute. An old British army saying has it that "No man is ever a complete failure — he can always serve as a horrible example." Besides the lessons failed federations teach, they also frequently accomplish some very important objectives during their brief lifetimes — objectives which could arguably be said to be more important than the continuation of federation itself. [...]

The principal cause for failure, or partial failure, of each of the federations studied cannot, it thus seems, be found in an analysis of economic statistics or in an inventory of social, cultural, or institutional diversity. It can only be found in the absence of a sufficient political-ideological commitment to the *primary* concept or value of federation itself. How one can account for the absence of this primary commitment is left to be discussed in a later part of this chapter in which the four failed federations are for this purpose compared to the classical federations of Canada, Australia and the United States. Suffice it here to repeat that such a commitment might spring from the people — charismatically caused by events or gradually by a growth and confluence of secondary values and factors—or be generated by charismatic national leaders, and that the former appears to occur rarely except in a situation of overwhelming common threat from external forces or other passionate historic challenge to the collective imagination. It is, however, important to stress that, in each of our studies, this commitment to primary goals appears to have been shown not to exist at the moment of federation and not to have been generated subsequently.

[...] If there is, indeed, a common factor in the failures of the four federations here studied it is this: federations are apt to fail when they are justified to the participants only in terms of immediately realizable practical advantages. If the practical advantages accrue, the need for federation may be at an end. If, as more often proved the case, they do not, the federation stands exposed as a fraud. And the supposed short-run advantages expected by each unit and each leader of a federation are likely, on investigation or implementation, to prove different and contradictory one to another, thus giving rise to destructive conflicts. It has been said by J.P. Morgan of a certain expensive yacht that if you have to ask its price, you can't afford it. Something comparable may be said of federalism. If one has to justify it in terms of specific secondary and tertiary short-term benefits: tariffs, subventions, votes, jobs, racial balance, it probably cannot succeed. A nation can neither be fully explained nor constituted in accountants' terms. Where what is wanted is not a new *nation* but a pragmatic solution to certain problems of trade and marketing, population movement, defense or foreign policy, some other solution different from classic federalism may be more realistic and so, more successful.

3. Devices for Intergovernmental Cooperation in a Federal State

(a) General

-Research Note-

FEDERALISM AND FLEXIBILITY

In 1937 the Privy Council portrayed Canada's federal system in a severe metaphor. The Canadian federation, Lord Atkin said, "still retains the watertight compartments which are an essential part of her original structure".[1] The metaphor is powerfully evocative, suggesting impermeable jurisdictions vigorously policed by the Courts. Suggestive as it is, the metaphor could only have been conceived in constitutional litigation, a process which offers perspective from where intergovernmental processes become dysfunctional and break down. The metaphor is unimaginable from within Canada's operating constitution. A more accurate image would be the meshing of interlocking and interpenetrating jurisdictions as constitutional power is geared into political action. As in all federations, Canadian governments treat each other as partners (or competitors); it is only in rare cases that federal and provincial authorities experience the circle of their constitutional jurisdiction as closed.[2] Throughout the framework of Canadian governance the norm is that federal and provincial authorities consult, coordinate and co-operate to bring the totality of governmental power to bear on practical subject matters, notwithstanding that in theory Canadian political power may be riven with jurisdictional divides.

It is useful to ask: what are the instruments by which governments coordinate in Canada?

Canadian federalism has created numerous constitutional, legislative and administrative tools to overcome the watertight division of responsibilities supposedly essential to federal union. These are:

- formal constitutional amendment
- *de facto* constitutional amendment, utilizing:

  ☐ court interpretation and adaptation of constitutional limitations
  ☐ creation and modification of constitutional usages, customs and conventions
  ☐ creation of quasi-constitutional requirements

---

1   *A.G. Canada v. A.G. Ontario*, [1937] A.C. 326, 354.
2   J. Peter Meekison, formerly Deputy Minister of Alberta's Department of Federal and Intergovernmental Affairs gives an interesting and insightful explanation for this. "While jurisdiction may be important," he writes, "it may not be in anybody's interest to seek a clarification of where the boundaries lie. Thus, it may be better to cooperate than to risk losing jurisdiction:" "Distribution of Functions and Jurisdiction: A Political Scientist's Analysis," in Watts and Brown (eds.), *Options for a New Canada* (Toronto: U of T Press, 1991), p. 259 at 264.

- concurrent exercise of power
- fiscal arrangements, including

  ☐ federal spending in areas of provincial jurisdiction;
  ☐ provincial spending in areas of federal jurisdiction
  ☐ intergovernmental transfers and equalization schemes

- creation of conjoint regulatory schemes harmonized by

  ☐ formal delegation of power
  ☐ informal administrative cooperation
  ☐ intergovernmental agreements

- bureaucratic, ministerial and First Ministers conferences
- limited opting out of and into fiscal and regulatory schemes, with compensation

HERPERGER, "DISTRIBUTION OF POWERS AND FUNCTIONS IN FEDERAL SYSTEMS"
IN SHAPING CANADA'S FUTURE TOGETHER: PROPOSALS (1991)
(OTTAWA: SUPPLY AND SERVICES CANADA) at pp. 21-24.

DEVICES FOR FLEXIBILITY AND ADJUSTMENT

In most federal systems, the constitutional enumeration of the distribution of government powers and functions established at the time of federation has proven to be remarkably enduring. The United States constitution, for example, has over two centuries continued to provide the basic blueprint for the workings of a very successful federal system. Change, however, is as much a function of the life of governments as it is of societies, and so the distribution of powers must respond to this dynamic. Formal constitutional amendment is the most obvious means to effect such change when deemed necessary, and it has been employed occasionally in most federations. However, it is not the only means by which federal systems adapt their distribution of powers and functions to changing circumstances. What follows is a cursory examination of several devices for flexibility and adjustment evident in federal systems. [...]

1. Extensive Concurrency

[Editor's note: Concurrency refers to the fact that both Parliament and the provincial legislatures may regulate particular subjects. Concurrency may arise by specific constitutional provision, such as s. 95 of the Constitution Act relating to agriculture and immigration, or by judicial interpretation of a particular subject. Because both orders of government may regulate the same subject, there is potential for conflict in the rules provided by each order of government. Generally speaking, such conflicts are resolved by a constitutional rule which stipulates that the federal law prevails in the case of conflict.]

In the context of the current constitutional debate in Canada, recent proposals have suggested that increased recourse to concurrent powers could provide an effective means of accommodating the competing demands for constitutional reform evident in Quebec and the rest of Canada. According to advocates of these proposals, a significantly expanded list of concurrent powers with provincial paramountcy ... would allow a province such as Quebec to achieve additional jurisdictional powers to protect and enhance its distinctiveness within the country, while at the same time allowing other jurisdiction to retain the benefits of common or than through federal jurisdiction. While such a device could result in a *de facto* degree of jurisdictional asymmetry, provinces would retain equality of constitutional status, as the opportunity for enhanced provincial autonomy would remain equally available to all provinces within the federation.

2. Intergovernmental Delegation

As noted above, several federal systems have constitutionally assigned the federal government legislative authority in certain fields of jurisdiction, while leaving the executive and administrative responsibility for the delivery of programs, services or regulations in these areas with the constituent units of the federation. Another means by which federal systems may be made more adaptable to changing circumstances is the device of a temporary delegation of powers. Delegation can be either from the federal government to the regional governments or vice versa; to or from one or more of the constituent units (i.e., not requiring unanimous consent of all units); for both legislative and executive powers; for varying periods of time (with an opportunity for formal review); and for one or more subject matters. The advantage of such arrangements is that they enable the temporary transfer of authority to meet the needs of special circumstances. The use of delegation does not violate the federal principle as long as there are provisions for the consent of affected governments and for proper fiscal compensation.

Most federal systems provide for the delegation of executive authority. If not explicitly stated in the constitution, the practice has usually been sanctioned by the courts. In terms of legislative authority, provisions for delegation are not as widespread, and usually occur only from the federal to state governments. Of the established federations, only the Australian constitution provides for the delegation of legislative authority, and then only from a state to the federal legislature. However, in all newer Commonwealth federations, with the exception of Nigeria, the constitutions have generally permitted the delegation of legislative authority from the federal to state legislatures. In Canada, proposals to revise the Constitution to allow for legislative delegation have been advanced by the Rowell-Sirois Commission, the 1964 First Ministers' Conference (which produced the Fulton-Favreau amending formula) and, most recently, the 1991 Beaudoin-Edwards Special Joint Committee on the Process for Amending the Constitution.

3. Federal-Provincial Agreements or Accords

It has been proposed that the Canadian Constitution recognize the ability of the federal and provincial governments to enter into agreements or accords relating to specified subject matters and to provide the protection of the Constitution to such agreements under certain circumstances. The device of federal-provincial agreements is intended to satisfy competing jurisdictional claims without resorting to a formal amendment of the Constitution. Canada has had a long history of intergovernmental agreements, covering matters such as tax collection and economic and regional development. An example of the potential of this approach is the recently concluded agreement between the federal government and the province of Quebec on immigration. Considered a major step in resolving federal-provincial differences in this area, the agreement nonetheless remains subject to legislative override and is not entrenched in the Constitution. [See *Canada Assistance Plan Reference,* infra]

In its final report released in 1985, the Macdonald Commission advocated the inclusion of a provision allowing for the constitutional entrenchment of federal-provincial agreements. It cited the example of the 1985 Atlantic Accord reached by the federal and Newfoundland governments, which provides for the joint management of offshore resources and the sharing of revenues. It is interesting to note that the wording of the Atlantic Accord actually anticipates the possibility that its provisions may eventually become constitutionally entrenched.

4. Optional Occupation of Jurisdiction: "Opting Out" and "Opting In"

The device of optional occupation of jurisdiction is foreseen in specific provisions in *Canada's Constitution Acts, 1867 to 1982* and in some recent proposals for constitutional reform. Two approaches to this device are possible. First, there is the concept of "opting out", which can apply to matters of concurrent jurisdiction (such as pensions and survivors' benefits, as enumerated in section 94A), to the application of constitutional amendments (sections 38(2) and 40 of the *Constitution Act, 1982*), or to fields in which the federal government exercises its spending power in areas of exclusive provincial jurisdiction (for example, the proposed section 106A of the Meech Lake Accord). In principle, such "opting out" could allow provinces to establish programs parallel to federal initiatives and could provide for reasonable fiscal compensation.

The second approach, "opting in", finds its conceptual origins in two provisions of the Canadian Constitution: section 94 of the *Constitution Act, 1867*, which provides for the authority of the federal Parliament to pass uniform laws in relation to property and civil rights in three of the four original provinces of the federation (never invoked); and section 23(1)(a) of the *Charter of Rights and Freedoms* in the *Constitution Act, 1982*, which enumerates certain minority language educational rights which do not come into effect in Quebec until that province gives its consent.

5. Interstate Agreements

An interstate agreement (or compact) is another example of a device allowing for flexibility in the distribution of powers, and it finds its origins in the United States constitution. The device permits two or more states to enter into an agreement for joint action, and becomes effective upon achieving Congressional consent. Applied to the Canadian context, these arrangements could establish federation-wide standards for such matters as interprovincial trade barriers and professional certification. The advantage of this approach is that it allows for the achievement of an interprovincial consensus in relation to certain subjects without the direct intervention of the federal government, whose initiative might be perceived by the constituent units of the federation as merely an attempt to expand its own jurisdiction.

(b)   Delegation

(I)   General

G. V. LA FOREST, "DELEGATION OF LEGISLATIVE POWER IN CANADA"
(1975), 21 MCGILL L.J. 131.

The *British North America Act, 1867,* makes no general provision for the delegation of legislative power from one level of government to the other. [...]

JUDICIAL DECISIONS RESPECTING DELEGATION

It has long been firmly settled that both the federal Parliament and the provincial legislatures are sovereign within their spheres, and concomitantly that they can freely delegate to their respective Governors in Council, municipalities and bodies of their own creation. However, from a very early period, there have been several judicial and academic assertions (the weightiest being a statement of Lord Watson during the argument in *C.P.R.* v. *Bonsecours* in 1899) that the federal Parliament could not give legislative jurisdiction to a provincial legislature, and that the provinces laboured under the converse disability. But most of these statements could be explained away by saying that either Parliament or a legislature was prevented from divesting itself of jurisdiction in favour of the other. Such divesting can be distinguished from delegation, which may be defined "as entrusting by a person or body of persons, of the power residing in that person or body of persons, *with complete power of revocation or amendment remaining in the grantor (or delegator)*". In a word, since the delegator may at any time revoke, the power remains in him, the delegatee being simply an agent.

Serious interest in delegation began developing in the 1920's and 1930's when the existence of a divided legislative jurisdiction made comprehensive regulation of vital areas of the economy extremely difficult... Satisfactory results, said the Privy Council, "can only be obtained by co-operation". But even where co-operation could be achieved, the careful manner in which legislation had to be drawn made implementation difficult. [...] Not unnaturally, numerous commentators looked to delegation as a way of avoiding these difficulties. [...]

The issue was squarely raised before the Supreme Court of Canada in 1951 in *Attorney-General of Nova Scotia* v. *Attorney-General of Canada*. This was an appeal from the Supreme Court of Nova Scotia on a reference regarding the validity of the *Delegation of Legislative Jurisdiction Act*, a proposed *Act* of that province which, *inter alia*, empowered the province

(a)   to delegate to the federal Parliament authority to make laws relating to employment in industries falling within provincial jurisdiction;

(b)   to apply provincial laws relating to unemployment to industries within federal jurisdiction if the federal Parliament delegated authority to the province to do so; and

(c)   to impose an indirect retail sales tax if the federal Parliament should delegate authority to the province to do so.

The Supreme Court of Nova Scotia, by a majority, held the statute *ultra vires*, and the decision was affirmed by the Supreme Court of Canada.

The decision rests largely on an appeal to authority and arguments of a textual nature. Rinfret C.J. and Kerwin and Kellock JJ. thought that if a power of delegation had been intended, it would have been expressly given. Rinfret C.J. and Taschereau and Fauteux JJ. stressed that legislative powers under sections 91 and 92 are given "exclusively" to the appropriate legislature. Kerwin and Fauteux JJ. also noted that it had been thought necessary to insert section 94 to provide for Parliament's jurisdiction to make uniform laws in certain circumstances. Finally, Rand, Estey and Fauteux JJ. questioned the ability of the federal Parliament or the provinces to accept delegation in view of their status; each was sovereign within its sphere, but delegation involves subordination to the delegator.

[...] Some of the judges advanced more fundamental arguments for their position. Rand J. thought that, responsibility for a particular area of jurisdiction having been vested in a particular body, it was intended that it should deliberate upon it and ultimately be responsible for the discharge of that function to the electorate. Taschereau J. made a similar point, and Estey and Fauteux JJ. also noted that delegation would divest one level of government of responsibility and give it to the other. Rand J. also referred to the fundamental distinction between delegation to a subordinate body when a detailed scheme is considered and a broad delegation to another legislative body. He said:

> In the generality of actual delegation to its own agencies, Parliament, recognizing the need of the legislation, lays down the broad scheme and indicates the principles, purposes and scope of the subsidiary details to be supplied by the delegate: under the mode of enactment now being considered, the real and substantial analysis and weighing of the political considerations which would decide the actual provisions adopted, would be given by persons chosen to represent local interests.

He also underlined the danger that once a power was delegated, there would be a tendency for the power to remain with the delegatee. Taschereau J. seemed to think there was a danger that general delegation could lead to a unitary state and, on the other hand, that different laws might be enacted in the various provinces on matters in which the framers of the Constitution thought uniformity imperative. An appraisal of these various arguments will be made later.

OTHER DEVICES

Interdelegation between the federal Parliament and provincial legislatures, therefore, appears impossible. However, other legislative devices have been used to achieve flexibility. These are:

(1)   conditional legislation;
(2)   incorporation by reference (or adoption); and
(3)   conjoint schemes with administrative cooperation.

Conditional Legislation

A conditional statute is one whose operation is determined by a condition, for example, the existence of a state of fact or the action of an individual or body. Thus, the common provision that an *Act* shall come into force on proclamation is conditional legislation. The issue is the extent to which the federal Parliament or the provinces may employ one another to decide upon an action on which a statute is conditional. Here the courts have found no constitutional limitation... As the Supreme Court of Canada underlined in the... case of *Lord's Day Alliance of Canada* v. *Attorney-General for British Columbia*, Parliament can limit the operation of its own *Act* to an event or condition, but it cannot extend the jurisdiction of the provincial legislatures by delegation.

Considerable use has been made in recent years of this device, under which provinces were permitted to "opt out" of social service schemes devised by the federal authorities and to instead accept tax credits permitting them to devise their own schemes.

Incorporation or Adoption

A legislature may choose to employ the device of incorporating by reference (or adopting) another statute rather than repeat the whole of its provisions. Since the incorporated or adopted provisions derive their authority from the incorporating or adopting legislature, and that legislature has considered them, there seems no logical ground (other than ease in finding the material) for invalidating such legislation even though the incorporated material appears in a statute of another legislature. The courts have long upheld statutes incorporating existing legislation of another legislature, but a different problem is raised where a legislature purports to adopt the law of another legislature as it exists or is amended from time to time: then the legislature whose legislation is adopted is the one exercising discretion in respect of change, not the adopting legislature. The situation is clearly quite similar to delegation. [...]

[T]he Supreme Court of Canada in *Attorney-General of Ontario* v. *Scott* [...] upheld the validity of the Ontario *Reciprocal Enforcement of Maintenance Orders Act*, which incorporated defences available to maintenance orders made in reciprocating countries. [...] The matter is, therefore, settled. One point, however, should be emphasized. This device does not extend the legislative sphere of the adopting legislature; it can only adopt legislation that it would have been able to enact itself.

The device has raised some minor problems relating to such matters as the manner of charging an individual with an offence, the reconciliation of provisions where a matter is dealt with under both the adopting and adopted legislation (for example, where penalties are provided under both), and the exercise of powers in relation to interprovincial undertakings in a manner different from their exercise in relation to intraprovincial undertakings. But these are the types of problems that will vanish as more familiarity with the technique develops.

Conjoint Schemes

Finally, much can be done to avoid the restraints on interdelegation by administrative cooperation and conjoint schemes. The simplest form of this device is where an official is given power to enforce or administer both federal and provincial laws in relation to one subject matter. For example, the federal government may assign to a provincial fishery officer the task of enforcing fishery laws; such delegation of administrative responsibility may also take place in the reverse.

Cooperation may similarly be effected by parallel legislation intended to secure a common end, through employing independent or combined administrative structures. Problems respecting parallel legislation arise at three levels:

(a)   in securing initial federal-provincial cooperation;
(b)   in drafting legislation that truly meshes without overstepping the legislative bounds of either legislature; and
(c)   in securing efficient and continuing cooperation of administrative officers.

So far as the latter is concerned, it is obvious that if parallel administrative structures are employed, duplication is likely to result. Moreover, administrative officers responsible to different bodies will almost inevitably have differences of view. These problems can be avoided by a single administration, but even here the maintenance of continuing cooperation cannot be effected if the government that hires the administrative officers concerned seeks to follow policies adverse to those of the other government. But most of the other problems have in fairly recent years been overcome by one level of government delegating executive and administrative authority (including the power to make regulations) to administrative agencies created by the other. The validity of this device [...] was approved by the Supreme Court of Canada in 1952 in *P.E.I. Potato Marketing Board v. H.B. Willis Inc.* [...]

In a comment on this case, Professor Laskin (now Laskin C.J.) suggested that it could be interpreted as permitting interdelegation between the federal Parliament and provincial legislatures in relation to matters on which the delegated body is independently competent [...] What Laskin was proposing was the principle (discussed in the preceding section but not then established) that a province acting within its legislative competence (*e.g.*, respecting property and civil rights) could adopt by reference federal legislation (*e.g.*, criminal law) not only when it was already in existence, but also future amendments.

In truth this amounts, for practical purposes, to a limited form of legislative delegation, for it permits a legislature other than that giving the law ultimate power to exercise effective discretion. But this is an oblique and highly convenient transgression against the principle prohibiting interdelegation. It permits uninterrupted uniformity of laws as regards a scheme the general structure of which has been considered by the adopting legislature. In a word, the technique does not substantially offend against the underlying reasons for the rule against delegation and the gains in flexibility are extensive. [...]

It may be well to add that the Supreme Court of Canada has at its disposal a weapon against a delegation of administrative power or an adoption of future legislation so broad as to amount in substance to a grant of legislative power: it could declare such a device void as being a colourable attempt to escape the restraints imposed by the *Nova Scotia* delegation case.

ADVANTAGES AND DISADVANTAGES OF DELEGATION

The major advantage of delegation of legislative power is that it gives flexibility to a federal system by making it possible to overcome the difficulties of a water tight division of legislative power. This is particularly so where constitutional amendment is difficult. It can permit one level of government, rather than the other, to deal with a particular matter where experience or circumstances dictate that this is wiser. There may be situations where one level of government is not equipped or prepared to deal with a problem. This was one of the reasons given for empowering provincial boards to deal with extraprovincial motor transport. Again, the different situations of the various provinces may make it desirable to have delegation to or from some but not all provinces with respect to certain matters. In this way delegation may achieve another type of flexibility.

Delegation may also make legislative action easier where a single activity, looked at from a functional point of view, could be regulated in its entirety by different levels of government because the entire activity falls under several constitutional rubrics. Delegation can avoid duplication of effort, both at the legislative and administrative levels, and prevent the confusion that inevitably results even when there is cooperation. As already mentioned, without some kind of delegation, difficulties in cooperation arise at three different levels:

(a)   at the political level, where agreement may be difficult;
(b)   at the legislative level, where the legislation must be made workable while avoiding passage into a forbidden legislative sphere; and
(c)   at the administrative level, where cooperation has to be maintained over a long period, with the dangers of different approaches being developed by political and administrative authorities of both levels of government.

There are, however, important disadvantages to interdelegation. On the one hand, it may be argued that delegation may destroy the federation because the abandonment of powers by the provinces may create a virtually all-powerful federal Parliament. On the other hand, the federation could be reduced to a loose confederacy were the federal Parliament to delegate too many of its powers to the provinces. It is true that delegation in its proper sense involves the power to take back jurisdiction, but this is always difficult, particularly where administrative machinery has been developed.

The mere existence of a power of interdelegation may give rise to difficulties. It may lead to pressures by one level of government on the other to transfer powers, and give rise to friction when there is refusal, and possible unproductive work in deciding whether delegation is wise or unwise whenever such pressures exist.

124

Also weighing against delegation is the consideration (so well expressed by Rand J. in the passage quoted earlier) that the Constitution obviously intended that discretion and financial responsibility respecting certain matters be given to one level of government, rather than the other. This applies more strongly where general powers are delegated as in the *Nova Scotia* delegation case than where delegation is restricted to a particular scheme. Not only is responsibility dispersed in a manner that may be difficult to define, but so are the financial implications. The argument is fortified by the fact that what is delegated may be related to other powers which should be considered in a generalized scheme. For example, in devising general policies respecting interprovincial transport, interprovincial motor transport must be considered; yet the fact that this is currently administered by provincial boards may well inhibit the formulation of policy.

A further dimension to this argument is that the giving of power to one level of government may have been done to prevent the other from having that power. Thus, one of the reasons for not granting indirect taxation to the provinces is that this may have the effect of creating tariff walls and imposing the primary burden of taxation on non-residents of a province. In other words, the grant of power may not only be looked upon as a positive vesting of power in the federal Parliament but as an implied prohibition against the provinces.

Flowing from the argument that a particular legislature is intended by the Constitution to exercise discretion in a particular area is the more fundamental one that that legislature is looked upon by the electorate as having responsibility in the area. Though one must not exaggerate the degree of sophistication of the electorate (particularly where a Constitution has many overlapping areas), there is a good measure of truth in the argument.

Another argument against delegation relates to situations where there is delegation to or from one or several, but not all, provinces. This, it may be argued, would create a constitutional "hodge podge", a result the Fulton-Favreau formula tried to minimize by requiring at least four provinces to participate in a scheme. In truth, however, the many administrative federal-provincial arrangements may already have resulted in a hodge podge. Thus, the federal Department of Insurance acts as a delegate for some provinces in certain matters but not for others. This diversity may indeed be the best way to cope with many situations where wide differences exist among the provinces. In one respect, however, the argument has special cogency. Delegation could be used as a means of giving special status to a province, which could undermine the influence and responsibilities of the Parliamentary representatives from the province given such status. A hodge podge could also occur where all the provinces delegated power to the federal Parliament, but later one withdrew. This could result in the dismantling of complicated and expensive programmes.

SUMMARY AND APPRAISAL

As can be seen, there are weighty arguments for and against delegation. Not surprisingly, the first reaction of the courts both here and in other federations (for example, the United States) is to attempt to protect the general structure of the Constitution by finding a constitutional bar to delegation. Even where there is a general clause under which a general transfer of power could be made, as is the case under the Australian Constitution and to a more limited extent under section 94 of the B.N.A. Act, such clause tends to become a dead letter because of the felt need to maintain the integrity of the federation.

Yet a division of legislative responsibility effected in one era cannot be expected to foresee all future problems, and overlap of authority in relation to emerging social problems is bound to occur. Changing conditions may make it desirable that different levels of government should deal with a problem at different periods. Moreover, the needs of one province may not coincide with those of another at all times, and some accommodation must be made. Accordingly, devices are invented to permit some transfer of functions. This has been true not only in Canada but also in other federations, such as the United States and Australia.

The practical result achieved by the courts may well be as good as we are likely to get. Transfer of functions between federal and provincial authorities is necessary, but the equilibrium of the federation must be preserved. The legislature given a power by the Constitution should exercise a measure of discretion in the various schemes it transfers. This is, in effect, what the courts have achieved, and consequently constitutional tinkering in this area is not recommended.

However, if in future constitutional discussions it is thought advisable to provide expressly for delegation, the best balance between the advantages and disadvantages would be to permit one level of government to make laws within the legislative competence of the other if that other consents to the particular statute. [...] This requirement for consent would make for a certain uniformity and help to avoid the creation of a special status for any province, but it would tend to limit seriously the use of the express delegation power and make it more restrictive than the techniques to transfer authority now available under the constitution. A scheme for delegation should also provide that a province cannot revoke delegated power for a certain period. Otherwise it could, in some cases, effectively dismantle a national scheme constructed at considerable expense.

(ii)   Administrative Delegation

HODGE v. R.
(1883), 9 A.C. 117 (P.C.).

[The appellant, a Toronto tavern owner, was convicted of an offence pursuant to the *Liquor Licence Act of Ontario* (R.S.O. 1877, c. 181). The act provided for the appointment of a Licence Commissioner empowered to pass resolutions for the regulation of taverns and shops. A Licence Commissioners Board was authorized to impose penalties for breach of the resolutions. Hodge appealed against conviction on the ground that the provincial legislature had no authority to delegate its legislative power to regulate taverns to a Licence Commissioner. Thus, the offence was beyond the power of the Licence Commissioner to create. The Court of Appeal for Ontario reversed the Queen's Bench Division and sustained the conviction. Hodge appealed to the Privy Council.]

SIR BARNES PEACOCK [for the Court]: – [...] Assuming that the local legislature had power to legislate to the full extent of the resolutions passed by the License Commissioners, and to have enforced the observance of their enactments by penalties and imprisonment with or without hard labour, it was further contended that the Imperial Parliament had conferred no authority on the local legislature to delegate those powers to the License Commissioners, or any other persons. In other words, that the power conferred by the Imperial Parliament on the local legislature should be exercised in full by that body, and by that body alone. The maxim *delegatus non potest delegare* was relied on.

It appears to their Lordships, however, that the objection thus raised by the appellants is founded on an entire misconception of the true character and position of the provincial legislatures. They are in no sense delegates of or acting under any mandate from the Imperial Parliament. When the *British North America Act* enacted that there should be a legislature for Ontario, and that its legislative assembly should have exclusive authority to make laws for the Province and for provincial purposes in relation to the matters enumerated in sect. 92, it conferred powers not in any sense to be exercised by delegation from or as agents of the Imperial Parliament, but authority as plenary and as ample within the limits prescribed by sect. 92 as the Imperial Parliament in the plenitude of its power possessed and could bestow. Within these limits of subjects and area the local legislature is supreme, and has the same authority as the Imperial Parliament, or the Parliament of the Dominion, would have had under like circumstances to confide to a municipal institution or body of its own creation authority to make by-laws or resolutions as to subjects specified in the enactment, and with the object of carrying the enactment into operation and effect.

PA-069901

Toronto Police arresting a man for possession of alcohol while the Canada Temperance Act was in force.

It is obvious that such an authority is ancillary to legislation, and without it an attempt to provide for varying details and machinery to carry them out might become oppressive, or absolutely fail. The very full and very elaborate judgment of the Court of Appeal contains abundance of precedents for this legislation, entrusting a limited discretionary authority to others, and has many illustrations of its necessity and convenience. It was argued at the bar that a legislature committing important regulations to agents or delegates effaces itself. That is not so. It retains its powers intact, and can, whenever it pleases, destroy the agency it has created and set up another, or take the matter directly into his own hands. How far it shall seek the aid of subordinate agencies, and how long it shall continue them, are matters for each legislature, and not for Courts of Law, to decide.

Their Lordships do not think it necessary to pursue this subject further, save to add that, if by ~~two or~~ resolutions are warranted, power to enforce them seems necessary and equally lawful. Their Lordships have now disposed of the real questions in the cause. [...]

The provincial legislature having thus the authority to impose imprisonment, with or without hard labour, had also power to delegate similar authority to the municipal body which it created, called the License Commissioners. [...]

Their Lordships do not think it necessary or useful to advert to some minor points of discussion, and are, on the whole, of opinion that the decision of the Court of Appeal of Ontario should be affirmed, and this appeal dismissed, with costs, and will so humbly advise Her Majesty.

- Research Note -
ADMINISTRATIVE DELEGATION

In 1690, John Locke wrote this important passage in his *Second Treatise of the Civil Government*:

> "[...] The legislative cannot transfer the power of making laws to any other hands; for it being but a delegated power from the people, they who have it cannot pass it over to others. The people alone can appoint the form of the commonwealth, which is by constituting the legislative and appointing in whose hands that shall be. And when the people have said, we will submit to rules and be governed by laws made by such men, and in such forms, nobody else can say other men shall make laws for them; nor can the people be bound by any laws but such as are enacted by those whom they have chosen and authorized to make laws for them.

> The power of the legislative, being derived from the people by a positive voluntary grant and institution, can be no other than what the positive grant conveyed, which being only to make laws, and not to make legislators, the legislative can have no power to transfer their authority of making laws and place it in other hands. [...]"

In the 1930s, United States constitutional law moulded this dictum into an operative constitutional doctrine. *Panama Refining Co. v. Ryan*, 293 U.S. 388 (1935) considered s. 9 of the *National Industrial Recovery Act* of 1933, an aggressive statute meant to deal with the crippling economic crisis of the depression. Section 9 of the *Act* dealt with overproduction and consequent collapsing prices in the petroleum industry by allowing federal enforcement of state conservation orders. President Roosevelt exercised the power by an implementing Executive Order. This order was challenged in the *Panama Refining* case. The United States Supreme Court invalidated s. 9 of the *Act* on the ground that it unlawfully delegated legislative power. Chief Justice Hughes found that s. 9 provided no standard for the

President to follow; "disobedience to his order is made a crime punishable by fine and imprisonment;" "among the numerous and diverse objectives broadly stated [in the *Act*] the President was not required to choose;" "the Congress left the matter to the President without standard or rule, to be dealt with as he pleased."

> "There are limits of delegation which there is no constitutional authority to transcend. We think that s. 9(c) goes beyond those limits. [...] The Congress has declared no policy, has established no standard, has laid down no rule. There is no requirement, no definition of circumstance and conditions in which the transportation is to be allowed or prohibited. If s. 9(c) were held valid, it would be idle to pretend that anything would be left of limitations upon the power of the Congress to delegate its law-making function. [...] Instead of performing its law-making function, the Congress could at will and as to such subjects as it chose transfer that function to the President or other officer or to an administrative body. The question is not of the intrinsic importance of the particular statute before us but of the constitutional processes of legislation which are an essential part of our system of government."

Five months later, the United States Supreme Court considered s. 3 of the same *Act* in *A.L.A. Schechter Poultry Corp. v. United States*, 295 U.S. 495 (1935). Section 3 authorized the President to approve various trade association codes of fair competition. The codes vigorously regulated various trades, but the approval process for the Codes was secretive and without supervision. In a concurring opinion, Justice Cardozo (who dissented in *Panama Refining*) stated:

> "The delegated power of legislation which has found expression in this code is not canalized within banks that keep it from overflowing. It is unconfined and vagrant. [...] Here, in the case before us, is an attempted delegation not confined to any single act nor to any class or group of acts identified or described by reference to a standard. Here in effect is a roving commission to inquire into evils and upon discovery correct them."

Panama Refining and *Schechter* remain on the books, and subsequent cases acknowledge their authority. However, later cases appear to restrict the non-delegation doctrine to a hortatory principle. The principle seems to be a caution to the legislative architects who create administrative power, rather than a constitutional knife used by courts to cut away offensive statutes. The leading modern cases are *Mistretta v. United States*, 488 U.S. 361 and *Industrial Union Department, AFL-CIO v. American Petroleum Institute*, 448 U.S. 607. In *Mistretta*, the court noted that in the aftermath of *Panama Refining* and *Schechter*, the court "upheld, again without deviation, Congress's ability to delegate power under broad standards." In *Industrial Union Department*, the Court overturned the statute at issue for reasons unrelated to the non-delegation doctrine. Interestingly, Justice Rehnquist, in a concurring decision, would have applied the non-delegation doctrine as an additional lever to upset the *Occupational Safety and Health Act* at issue. Justice Rehnquist stated:

"The non-delegation doctrine serves three important functions. First, and most abstractly, it insures to the extent consistent with orderly governmental administration that important choices of social policy are made by Congress, the branch of our Government most responsive to the popular will. [...] Second, the doctrine guarantees that, to the extent Congress finds it necessary to delegate authority, it provides the recipient of that authority with an 'intelligible principle' to guide the exercise of the delegated discretion. [...] Third, and derivative of the second, the doctrine insures that courts charged with reviewing the exercise of delegated legislative discretion will be able to test that exercise against ascertainable standards."

The hortatory principle appears to be well formulated in the words of Chief Justice Taft who observed that the limits of delegation "must be fixed according to common sense and the inherent necessities of the governmental co-ordination:" *J.W. Hampton, Jr. and Co. v. United States*, 276 U.S. 394, 406 (1928).

In the 1982 Supplement to his *Administrative Law Treatise*, Professor Davis put forward five possible views with respect to delegation of legislative power to an administrative agency. These five positions are summarized as follows:

1. A doctrine that legislative power may not be delegated is unthinkable. Almost the whole of the Code of Federal Regulations [analogous to the Consolidated Regulations of Canada] would be invalidated. Adoption of the idea would be irresponsible.

2. Delegation to an administrative body must be accompanied by meaningful standards.

3. The Constitution [of the United States] requires that Congress make all major policy decisions.

4. Major policymaking cannot be delegated to the courts.

5. Legislative power may be delegated to agencies as Congress chooses, including the power to make major policy.

Sir Barnes Peacock dealt with one critical argument against delegation of important regulation making power to administrative or executive agencies in *Hodge v. The Queen* (1883-4), 9 A.C. 117. Considering the argument that by such delegation the legislature "effaces itself," Sir Barnes Peacock replied:

"That is not so. It [the legislature] retains its powers intact, and can, whenever it pleases, destroy the agency it has created and set up another, or take the matter directly into its own hands."

His Lordship's conclusion that only legislatures, and not courts of law, must decide how far delegation may go is perhaps too strong. It is possible to conceive of a legislature committing virtually unlimited power to make regulations to administrative entities in particular fields. It may prove useful for the court to assist legislative partners to develop a hortatory principle against creation of autocratic power. Clearly, any use of a non-delegation doctrine in Canada would have to be extremely rare. Still, in a spirit of earnest partnership with the legislative branch, courts may develop norms of delegation that prohibit the creation of despotic or tyrannous power in executive entities, and, if the rare case calls for it, overturn legislation offensive to it.

(iii)   Interlegislative Delegation

A.G.N.S. v. A.G. CAN.
[1951] S.C.R. 31.

[Reference on a Bill which empowered the Lieutenant Governor of Nova Scotia to delegate to Parliament the province's legislative power over local employment. The Bill also permitted the Nova Scotia Legislature to receive and exercise delegated powers from Parliament in relation to federal employment and indirect taxation.]

RINFRET C.J.: In each of the supposed cases either the Parliament of Canada, or the Legislature of Nova Scotia, would be adopting legislation concerning matters which have not been attributed to it but to the other by the Constitution of the country. [...]

The Parliament of Canada and the Legislatures of the several Provinces are sovereign within their sphere defined by *The British North America Act*, but none of them has the unlimited capacity of an individual. They can exercise only the legislative powers respectively given to them by sections 91 and 92 of the Act, and these powers must be found in either of these sections.

The Constitution of Canada does not belong either to Parliament, or to the Legislatures; it belongs to the country and it is there that the citizens of the country will find the protection of the rights to which they are entitled. It is part of that protection that Parliament can legislate only on the subject matters referred to it by section 91 and that each Province can legislate exclusively on the subject matters referred to it by section 92. The country is entitled to insist that legislation adopted under section 91 should be passed exclusively by the Parliament of Canada in the same way as the people of each Province are entitled to insist that legislation concerning the matters enumerated in section 92 should come exclusively from their respective Legislatures. In each case the Members elected to Parliament or to the Legislatures are the only ones entrusted with the power and the duty to legislate concerning the subjects exclusively distributed by the constitutional Act to each of them.

No power of delegation is expressed either in section 91 or in section 92, nor, indeed, is there to be found the power of accepting delegation from one body to the other; and I have no doubt that if it had been the intention to give such powers it would have been expressed in clear and unequivocal language. Under the scheme of the *British North America Act* there were to be, in the words of Lord Atkin in *The Labour Conventions Reference*, "watertight compartments which are an essential part of the original structure."

Neither legislative bodies, federal or provincial, possess any portion of the powers respectively vested in the other and they cannot receive it by delegation. In that connection the word "exclusively" used both in section 91 and in section 92 indicates a settled line of demarcation and it does not belong to either Parliament, or the Legislatures, to confer powers upon the other [...]

The appeal should be dismissed with costs.

KERWIN J.: [...] The *British North America Act* divides legislative jurisdiction between the Parliament of Canada and the Legislatures of the Provinces and there is no way in which these bodies may agree to a different division. The fact that section 94 was considered necessary to provide in certain contingencies for the uniformity in some of the provinces of laws relating to property and civil rights and court procedure, indicates that an agreement for such a delegation as is here contended for was never intended. To permit of such an agreement would be inserting into the Act a power that is certainly not stated and one that should not be inferred. The appeal should be dismissed with costs.

TASCHEREAU J.: [...] The *British North America Act, 1867*, and amendments has defined the powers that are to be exercised by the Dominion Parliament and by the Legislatures of the various provinces. There are fields where the Dominion has exclusive jurisdiction, while others are reserved to the provinces. This division of powers has received the sanction of the Imperial Parliament, which was then and is still the sole competent authority to make any alterations to its own laws. If Bill 136 were *intra vires*, the Dominion Parliament could delegate its powers to any or all the provinces, to legislate on commerce, banking, bankruptcy, militia and defence, issue of paper money, patents, copyrights, indirect taxation, and all other matters enumerated in Section 91; and on the other hand, the Legislatures could authorize the Dominion to pass laws in relation to property and civil rights, municipal institutions, education, etc. etc., all matters outside the jurisdiction reserved to the Dominion Parliament. The powers of Parliament and of the Legislatures strictly limited by the *B.N.A. Act*, would thus be considerably enlarged, and I have no doubt that this cannot be done, even with the joint consent of Parliament and of the Legislatures.

It is a well settled proposition of law that jurisdiction cannot be conferred by consent. None of these bodies can be vested directly or indirectly with powers which have been denied them by the *B.N.A. Act*, and which therefore are not within their constitutional jurisdiction. [...]

It has been further argued that as a result of the delegation made by the Federal Government to the Provinces, the laws enacted by the Provinces as delegatees would be federal laws and that they would, therefore, be constitutionally valid. With this proposition I cannot agree. These laws would not then be enacted "with the advice and consent of the Senate and House of

Commons", and would not be assented to by the Governor General, but by the Lieutenant Governor, who has no power to do so. Moreover, as already stated, such a right has been denied the Provinces by the *B.N.A. Act.*

If the proposed legislation were held to be valid, the whole scheme of the Canadian Constitution would be entirely defeated. The framers of the *B.N.A. Act* thought wisely that Canada should not be a unitary state, but it would be converted into one, as Mr. Justice Hall says, if all the Provinces empowered Parliament to make laws with respect to *all matters* exclusively assigned to them. Moreover, it is clear that the delegation of legislative powers by Parliament to the ten Provinces on matters enumerated in Section 91 of the *B.N.A. Act* could bring about different criminal laws, different banking and bankruptcy laws, different military laws, different postal laws, different currency laws, all subjects in relation to which it has been thought imperative that uniformity should prevail throughout Canada.

For the above reasons, I have come to the conclusion that this appeal should be dismissed.

RAND J.: [...]That Canadian legislatures may delegate has long been settled: *Hodge* v. *The Queen* [(1883), 9 App. Cas. 117]. Notwithstanding the plenary nature of the jurisdiction enjoyed by them, it was conceded that neither Parliament nor Legislature can either transfer its constitutional authority to the other or create a new legislative organ in a relation to it similar to that between either of these bodies and the Imperial Parliament. [...]

These bodies were created solely for the purposes of the Constitution by which each, in the traditions and conventions of the English Parliamentary system, was to legislate, in accordance with its debate and judgment, on the matters assigned to it and on no other. To imply a power to shift this debate and this judgment of either to the other is to permit the substance of transfer to take place, a dealing with and in jurisdiction utterly foreign to the conception of a federal organization.

So exercising delegated powers would not only be incompatible with the constitutional function with which Nova Scotia is endowed and an affront to constitutional principle and practice, it would violate, also, the interest in the substance of Dominion legislation which both the people and the legislative bodies of the other provinces possess. In a unitary state, that question does not arise; but it seems to be quite evident that such legislative absolutism, except in respects in which, by the terms express or implied of the constituting Act, only one jurisdiction is concerned, is incompatible with federal reality. If a matter affects only one, it would not be a subject for delegation to the other; matters of possible delegation, by that fact, imply a common interest. Dominion legislation in relation to employment in Nova Scotia enacted by the legislature may affect interests outside of Nova Scotia; by delegation Nova Scotia might impose an indirect tax upon citizens of Alberta in respect of matters arising in Nova Scotia; or it might place restrictions on foreign or interprovincial trade affecting Nova Scotia which impinge on interests in Ontario. The incidence of laws of that nature is intended by the Constitution to be determined by the deliberations of Parliament and not of any Legislature. In the generality of actual delegation to its own agencies,

Parliament, recognizing the need of the legislation, lays down the broad scheme and indicates the principles, purposes and scope of the subsidiary details to be supplied by the delegate: under the mode of enactment now being considered, the real and substantial analysis and weighing of the political considerations which would decide the actual provisions adopted, would be given by persons chosen to represent local interests.

Since neither is a creature nor a subordinate body of the other, the question is not only or chiefly whether one can delegate, but whether the other can accept. Delegation implies subordination and in *Hodge* v. *The Queen,* (supra), the following observations (at p. 132) appear:–

> Within these limits of subjects and area the local legislature is supreme, and has the same authority as the Imperial Parliament, or the parliament of the Dominion, would have had under like circumstances to confide to a municipal institution or body of its own creation authority to make by-laws or resolutions as to subjects specified in the enactment, and with the object of carrying the enactment into operation and effect. [...]

> It was argued at the bar that a legislature committing important regulations to agents or delegates effaces itself. That is not so. It retains its powers intact, and can, whenever it pleases, destroy the agency it has created and set up another, or take the matter directly into his own hands. How far it shall seek the aid of subordinate agencies, and how long it shall continue them, are matters for each legislature, and not for Courts of Law, to decide.

Subordination, as so considered, is constitutional subordination and not that implied in the relation of delegate. Sovereign states can and do confer and accept temporary transfers of jurisdiction under which they enact their own laws within the territory of others; but the exercise of delegation by one for another would be an incongruity; for the enactments of a state are of its own laws, not those of another state.

Subordination implies duty: delegation is not made to be accepted or acted upon at the will of the delegate; it is ancillary to legislation which the appropriate legislature thinks desirable; and a duty to act either by enacting or by exercising a conferred discretion not, at the particular time, to act, rests upon the delegate. No such duty could be imposed upon or accepted by a co-ordinate legislature and the proposed bill does no more than to proffer authority to be exercised by the delegate solely of its own volition and, for its own purposes, as a discretionary privilege. Even in the case of virtually unlimited delegation as under the *Poor Act of England,* assuming that degree to be open to Canadian legislatures, the delegate is directly amenable to his principal for his execution of the authority. [...]

The practical consequences of the proposed measure, a matter which the Courts may take into account, entail the danger, through continued exercise of delegated power, of prescriptive claims based on conditions and relations established in reliance on the delegation. Possession here as elsewhere would be nine points of law and disruptive controversy might easily result. The power of revocation might in fact become no more feasible, practically, than amendment of the Act of 1867 of its own volition by the British Parliament.

I would, therefore, dismiss the appeal with costs.

[The judgments of Kellock, Estey and Fauteux JJ. are omitted.]

R. v. FURTNEY
[1991] 3 S.C.R. 89.

STEVENSON, J. [for the Court]: — [...] The appellants were charged in an information that, on five occasions, they counseled licensees of bingo lottery schemes to violate the terms and conditions of their licences relating to bingo lotteries, contrary to s. 190(3) of the *Criminal Code*.

The appellants challenged the provisions of ss. 190(1)(b) and (2) (now ss. 207(1)(b) and (2)). They submitted that Parliament exceeded its powers of delegation in permitting exemptions from criminality for charitable or religious organizations operating a lottery pursuant to a licence issued by the Lieutenant Governor-in-Council of a province. [...]

Criminal Code, R.S.C. 1985, c. C-46:

"207(1) Notwithstanding any of the provisions of this Part relating to gaming and betting, it is lawful. [...]

(b) for a charitable or religious organization, pursuant to a licence issued by the Lieutenant Governor-in-Council of a province or by such other person or authority in the province as may be specified by the Lieutenant Governor-in-Council thereof, to conduct and manage a lottery scheme in that province if the proceeds from the lottery scheme are used for a charitable or religious object or purpose; [...]

"(2) Subject to this Act, a licence issued by or under the authority of the Lieutenant Governor-in-Council of a province as described in paragraph (1)(b), (c), (d) or (f) may contain such terms and conditions relating to the conduct, management and operation of or participation in the lottery scheme to which the licence relates as the Lieutenant Governor-in-Council of that province, the person or authority in the province designated by the Lieutenant Governor-in-Council thereof or any law enacted by the legislature of that province may prescribe.

"(3) Every one who, for the purpose of a lottery scheme, does anything that is not authorized by or pursuant to a provision of this section

(a) in the case of the conduct, management or operation of that lottery scheme,

(i) is guilty of an indictable offence and liable to imprisonment for a term not exceeding two years, or

(ii) is guilty of an offence punishable on summary conviction; or

(b) in the case of participating in that lottery scheme, is guilty of an offence punishable on summary conviction." [...]

The appellants were acquitted at trial as a result of their seeking and obtaining, on an agreed statement of facts, a determination that there was an *ultra vires* delegation of criminal law. [...]

The leading authority on what is best described as prohibited interdelegation is *Attorney General of Nova Scotia* v. *Attorney General of Canada*, [1951] S.C.R. 31. It establishes that Parliament cannot delegate its legislative authority to a provincial legislature. We must, then, ask whether the impugned provisions of the Code delegate legislative authority over some aspect of the criminal law to the provincial legislature.

On the other hand, if what Parliament does is not characterized as a delegation of a legislative power to a provincial legislature, this authority does not govern. [...]

In *Coughlin* v. *Ontario Highway Transport Board*, [1968] S.C.R. 569, this court recognized that Parliament may incorporate by reference provincial legislation as it may from time to time exist. That is not a delegation. There, federal legislation gave the provincial transport board authority to license extra-provincial undertakings upon like terms and conditions as if the undertaking were a local one within the province. Cartwright, J., for the majority, upholding the legislation said, at p. 575:

> [...] there is here no delegation of lawmaking power, but rather the adoption by Parliament, in the exercise of its exclusive power, of the legislation of another body as it may from time to time exist. [...]

> Thus, in the exercise of its powers generally, and the criminal law specifically, Parliament is free to define the area in which it chooses to act and, in so doing, may leave other areas open to valid provincial legislation.

If a province legislates in respect of an open area, it is not doing so as a delegate, but in the exercise of its powers under s. 92 of the *Constitution Act, 1867*. That proposition is discussed in the context of the exercise of the criminal law power in *Lord's Day Alliance of Canada* v. *Attorney General of British Columbia*, [1959] S.C.R. 497. There the federal *Lord's Day Act* made it unlawful to engage in public games or contests "except as provided in any provincial Act or law now or hereafter in force." This court held that provincial laws permitting the otherwise prohibited conduct were not *ultra vires*, but rather provided a condition of fact that Parliament had provided as a limitation on its own statute. The permissive legislation fell within s. 92 and there was no delegation to the province. In *Lord's Day Alliance of Canada* v. *Attorney General for Manitoba*, [1925] A.C. 384, the Privy Council had recognized that Parliament was free to prohibit and to forbear from prohibiting in the exercise of its legislative authority over criminal law.

In my view, the regulation of gaming activities has a clear provincial aspect under s. 92 of the *Constitution Act, 1867* subject to Parliamentary paramountcy in the case of a clash between federal and provincial legislation. [...]

I agree with Dreidger in *The Interaction of Federal and Provincial Laws* (1976), 54 Can. Bar Rev. 695, when he concludes that inter-delegation is constitutionally impermissible because there is a constitutional prohibition founded upon the granting of exclusive powers to the Parliament on one hand, and the provincial legislatures on the other.

The prohibition is against delegation to a legislature. There is no prohibition against delegating to any other body. The power of Parliament to delegate its legislative powers had been unquestioned, at least since the *Reference as to the Validity of the Regulations in Relation to Chemicals*, [1943] S.C.R. 1. The delegate is, of course, always subordinate in that the delegation can be circumscribed and withdrawn. The Lieutenant Governor-in-Council has capacity or status to receive a delegated power: *R.* v. *Wilson* (1980), 119 D.L.R. (3d) 558 (B.C.C.A.), at p. 568. He is not subject to any constitutional prohibition against the acceptance of delegated authority. It may be that in some instances a delegation to the Lieutenant Governor would be tantamount to a delegation to a legislature. That question need not be resolved in this case, because the essential elements of the substantial federal scheme are spelled out in the Code and what was done by Lieutenant Governor was to make administrative decisions relating to matters of essentially provincial concern. These decisions fall within the ambit of the decision in *Re Peralta*, (cites omitted).

Thus Parliament may delegate legislative authority to bodies other than provincial legislatures; it may incorporate provincial legislation by reference and it may limit the reach of its legislation by a condition, namely the existence of provincial legislation.

I now analyze and characterize the sections in question here.

Section 207(1)(b) does not impose any right or duty on a provincial legislature. It gives authority to the Lieutenant Governor-in-Council or a person or authority specified by him. Regardless of the nature of the delegation, it is not a prohibited inter-delegation.

Section 207(2) similarly does not impose any right or duty on a provincial legislature, with the exception of the last phrase which provides that a licence issued by or under the authority of the Lieutenant Governor-in-Council may contain such relevant terms and conditions as "any law enacted by the legislature of that province may prescribe".

I do not read that provision as a delegation of legislative authority by Parliament. In my view, the provision may be read as incorporating by reference provincial legislation authorizing the Lieutenant Governor-in-Council to issue licences containing relevant terms and conditions or as excluding from the reach of the criminal law prohibition, lotteries licensed under provincial law so long as that licensing is by or under the authority of the Lieutenant Governor-in-Council. Dreidger, in the article to which I have referred, notes that the *Criminal Code* exemption for lotteries conducted in accordance with a provincial statute is not a delegation. I agree. [...]

I would answer the constitutional questions as follows: [...]

2. Are paragraphs 207(1)(b), (2) or (3) of the *Criminal Code* of Canada, R.S.C. 1985, c. C-46, or any combination thereof, *ultra vires* Parliament as improper delegation to a provincial body of a matter within the exclusive competence of the Federal Government?

A. No.

BRITISH COLUMBIA (MILK BOARD) v. GRISNICH
[1995] 2 S.C.R. 895.

[The B.C. Milk Board (the Appellant) challenged a decision of the B.C. Court of Appeal, which held that in every order made by an administrative tribunal, the tribunal had to state on the face of the order the legislative source of its authority. Both the federal and the provincial government had delegated authority to the B.C. Milk Board. Gilbert and Ronald Grisnich were dairy farmers who challenged one of the Milk Board's orders, which had collected over $100,000 in levies from the Grisnich family, due to the Grisnich's over-quota production of milk.

The majority, led by Iacobucci J., held that there was no requirement on administrative tribunals to state their source of authority. LaForest, L'Heureux-Dubé, and Gonthier JJ. concurred, but in so doing, also discussed a point not commented on by the majority — the validity of a tribunal being endowed with powers from both the federal and provincial governments in light of the doctrine emanating from the *Nova Scotia Inter-delegation* case and its progeny.]

LaFOREST J.: [...] The very point of an administrative inter-delegation scheme such as the one in the case at bar is to ensure that a provincial marketing board is possessed of the totality of regulatory power over one agricultural product. The very reason such joint federal-provincial schemes are necessary is because no one level of government is constitutionally empowered to regulate all aspects of intraprovincial and extraprovincial trade. As the respondents noted, the administrative inter-delegation scheme is a means of allowing Parliament to delegate administrative powers to a body created by the provincial legislature in a manner that avoids the rule against legislative inter-delegation established by this Court in *Attorney General of Nova Scotia v. Attorney General of Canada*, [1951] S.C.R. 31 ("*Nova Scotia Inter-delegation*"). The constitutionality of such arrangements has been repeatedly endorsed by this Court; see for example *P.E.I. Potato Marketing Board v. H. B. Willis Inc.*, [1952] 2 S.C.R. 392, and *Reference Re Agricultural Products*

Marketing Act, [1978] 2 S.C.R. 1198. To require an administrative agency overseeing and implementing a national marketing scheme to "choose" between its federal and provincial authority would defeat the very *raison d'être* of the scheme.

The respondents, however, suggest that a system of dual, or "mirror", legislation, with both federal and provincial regulations clearly identified, could accomplish the objectives served by the current joint delegation scheme, while at the same time allowing the citizen to know more clearly what level of government was responsible in any given situation. Not only does this proposal strike me as being duplicative and expensive, but it is also hard to understand how such a scheme would assist the individual citizen. There is a certain simplicity, and indeed a form of accountability, that results from Parliament and the provincial legislatures having empowered *one* expert body, with authority derived from both sources, to regulate a particular and complicated technical area of the law. Citizens affected by milk regulations benefit from a scheme that requires them to comply with the regulations of only one administrative body, rather than two. A system of dual legislation would likely only increase the number of subordinate regulations, rules and orders in this area, thus potentially contributing to greater frustration and malcontent on the part of the citizenry.

In his oral presentation, counsel for the respondents relied in support of his position on certain principles emphasized by this Court in the *Nova Scotia Inter-delegation* case. He argued that the basic principles of Parliamentary democracy and accountability that motivated the Court in reaching its decision in that case should be extended to the current situation. Just as Parliament and the provincial legislatures are obliged to frame their own legislation carefully, so that it falls squarely within a permissible head of authority under the Constitution, so too, he urged, should subordinate bodies exercise care and discipline in drafting their subordinate orders and regulations. He suggested that our constitutional order requires the imposition of this discipline on subordinate bodies, in order that the twin principles of Parliamentary democracy and accountability are met.

In my view, the *Nova Scotia Inter-delegation* case is not determinative in the present case for two reasons. First, unlike the *Nova Scotia Inter-delegation* case, the present case is not a *legislative* delegation case. We are not talking here of one level of government delegating powers over one of its areas of jurisdiction to another government. Instead, the case at bar involves an administrative inter-delegation scheme, where Parliament and provincial legislatures have both chosen to empower one subordinate body to implement the details of a national marketing strategy, the broad outlines of which they have co-operatively established. There was no question in the *Nova Scotia Inter-delegation* case that each level of government was free, acting within its own constitutional sphere, to delegate authority to a subordinate body. That the same subordinate body can accept and exercise powers from both levels of government is evident from the decisions of this Court in *P.E.I. Potato Marketing Board* and the *Agricultural Products Reference* referred to above.

Second, I do not believe the principles of Parliamentary democracy and accountability emphasized by the Court in the *Nova Scotia Inter-delegation* case warrant imposing on administrative bodies the kind of requirement advocated by the respondents. All that is constitutionally required of subordinate bodies — as of federal and provincial governments — is that they act within their jurisdiction, not that they state the source of this jurisdiction. As for the question of accountability, in the *Nova Scotia Inter-delegation* case, the Court was concerned with this principle at its most fundamental level. At issue was the accountability of federal and provincial governments for law-making in broad and substantive policy areas exclusively reserved to them under the Constitution. In the present case, the appellant is responsible for filling in the details of a national scheme, already agreed to in principle by both levels of government. By nature, the appellant's orders are technical and specific. They are not designed to establish broad policy directions or strategies, for this more general course has already been set by the federal and provincial governments acting co-operatively. In so far as it may be somewhat confusing for the citizen to sort out the question of jurisdiction because two levels of government are ultimately accountable for the appellant's actions, that is the very nature of a national marketing scheme. If we are going to tolerate joint delegation arrangements — permissible as a matter of constitutional law and desirable, in my view, as a matter of practice — then we must accept that the details of these arrangements will be implemented by marketing boards empowered from multiple sources. Citizens must look first to these boards to be accountable for their actions, and then to the two levels of government that have constituted them. In my view any potential loss in accountability that results in this situation is more than made up for by the benefits and practicalities of the joint delegation arrangement.

Appeal allowed with costs.

(c) Executive Federalism

-Research Note-
DEMOCRATIC DEFICIT

The division of powers in Canada's federal system means that most issues of major public importance straddle the responsibilities of the federal and provincial orders of government. To deal with issues comprehensively and to produce rational policy responses, both governments must act. To coordinate action into a focused policy response requires negotiations between both provincial and federal governments.

Federal provincial negotiations are actually conducted by bureaucratic officials of the governments. Bureaucrats from each level of government meet, discuss, negotiate and more often than not — agree. All of this occurs behind closed doors.

Michael Jenkin wrote: "More than any other federation, Canada relies on intergovernmental negotiation to help resolve political differences." Professor Smiley referred to this phenomenon as "executive federalism." He observed that this characteristic of Canada's governance produced a parliamentary system that was "executive dominated."

Professor Smiley went further. Executive federalism, he wrote, "contributes to undue secrecy in the conduct of the public's business" and to "an unduly low level of citizen-participation in public affairs." More, "it weakens and dilutes the accountability of governments to their respective legislatures and to the wider public" and "leads to continuous and often unresolved conflicts among governments."

It is true that Canada relies on executive federalism to power the federal system. It is also true that executive federalism is quite secretive and that this produces a substantial democratic deficit. It is also true that Canadians become annoyed about this secrecy when made aware of it.

What follows from these observations? First, given the existing democratic deficit executive federalism produces in Canada, it is hard to see why there is any need to entrench executive federalism deeper into constitutional forms. The *Meech Lake Accord* of 1987 would have done this by introducing requirements for a First Ministers Conference each year on the "Canadian Economy and such other matters as may be appropriate," and a second First Ministers Conference on various subjects, in addition to an open agenda.[1] If these conferences are to evolve, they should evolve by custom, and hopefully will do so in a way and by means that respond to the perceived democratic deficits they produce. Entrenchment in the Constitution would increase the democratic deficit, and make responding with curative procedures more difficult.

Second, it is hard to see that the democratic deficit can be removed by any legal or constitutional prohibition on intergovernmental interchanges. These practices are the outgrowth of Canadian governmental culture. A better way to shake the democratic deficit out of intergovernmental culture would be to experiment with oversight by representative institutions. Representative institutions are where the democratic spirit runs strongest in Canada's governmental system. It might be profitable to try strengthening legislative committee oversight of executive federalism patterns. Other useful experiments would be to allow representative institutions to review key intergovernment appointments; and to require intergovernmental ministries to report annually to a legislative committee.

Perhaps reforms with legislative oversight would reduce the democratic deficit of Canadian style executive federalism and imbue its culture with more accountability and a stronger democratic spirit. If these experiments were tried, undoubtedly, they would themselves have to be reviewed continually to judge what worked and what did not.

---

1   *Constitution Amendment, 1987* [Meech Lake Accord]. Secs. 8 and 12 (proposed but not proclaimed). The *Charlottetown Accord, Draft Legal Text*, Oct. 9, 1992, s.31, would have added s.37.1 to the *Constitution Act, 1982* which simply would have required an annual first ministers conference with nothing said about the agenda.

(d)   Intergovernmental Agreements

REFERENCE RE CANADA ASSISTANCE PLAN
[1991] 2 S.C.R. 525.

[The *Canada Assistance Plan* authorized the federal government to enter into agreements with provincial governments to pay them contributions toward their social assistance and welfare expenditures. Canada entered into agreements with each province in 1967. The *Canada Assistance Plan* provided for a procedure for alteration or termination of the contribution. Canada unilaterally terminated its contribution. Canada's termination was by an act of Parliament, the *Government Expenditures Restraint Act*, S.C. 1991, c. 9, which did not follow the stipulated procedure. British Columbia, Alberta, and Ontario challenged the unilateral cancellation on various grounds.

The challenge raised two issues: whether Canada had authority to cancel its contribution, and whether Canada had followed the correct procedure when it canceled its contribution. The Supreme Court of Canada held that Canada did have the necessary authority to cancel its contribution, but did not follow the correct procedure. However, the court went on to hold that the *Restraint Act* was nevertheless effective to terminate Canada's contribution.]

SOPINKA J. [for the Court]: – [...] In general, the language of the Plan is duplicated in the Agreement. But the contribution formula, which actually authorizes payments to the provinces, does not appear in the Agreement. It is only in s. 5 of the Plan. Clause 3(1)(a) of the Agreement provides that "Canada agrees [...] to pay to the province of British Columbia the contributions or advances [...] that Canada is authorized to pay to that province under the Act and the Regulations". That means, of course, the contributions or advances authorized by s. 5 of the Plan, an instrument that is to be construed as subject to amendment. This is the effect of s. 42(1) of the *Interpretation Act* which states:

> 42(1) Every Act shall be so construed as to reserve to Parliament the power of repealing or amending it, and of revoking, restricting or modifying any power, privilege or advantage thereby vested in or granted to any person.

In my view this provision reflects the principle of parliamentary sovereignty. The same results would flow from that principle even in the absence or non-applicability of this enactment. But since the *Interpretation Act* governs the interpretation of the Plan and all federal statutes where no contrary intention appears, the matter will be resolved by reference to it.

It is conceded that the government could not bind Parliament from exercising its powers to legislate amendments to the Plan. To assert the contrary would be to negate the sovereignty of Parliament. This basic fact of our constitutional life was, therefore, present to the minds of the parties when the Plan and Agreement were enacted and concluded. The parties were also aware that an amendment to the Plan would have to be initiated by the government by reason of the provisions of s. 54 of the *Constitution Act, 1867*. If it had been the intention of the parties to arrest this process, one would have expected clear language in the Agreement that the payment formula was frozen. Instead, the payment formula was left out of the Agreement and placed in the statute where it was, by virtue of s. 42, subject to amendment. In these circumstances the natural meaning to be given to the words "authorized to pay [...] under the Act" in cl. 3(1)(a) is that the obligation is to pay what is authorized from time to time. The government was, therefore, not precluded from exercising its powers to introduce legislation in Parliament amending the Plan. [...]

If this appears to deprive the Agreement of binding effect or mutuality, which are both features of ordinary contracts, it must be remembered that this is not an ordinary contract but an agreement between governments. Moreover, s. 8 itself contains an amending formula that enables either party to terminate at will. In lieu of relying on mutually binding reciprocal undertakings which promote the observance of ordinary contractual obligations, these parties were content to rely on the perceived political price to be paid for non-performance.

The result of this is that the Government of Canada, in presenting Bill C-69 to Parliament, acted in accordance with the Agreement and otherwise with the law which empowers the Government of Canada to introduce a money bill in Parliament. [...]

- Research Note -
INTERGOVERNMENTAL AGREEMENTS
(REVISED BY MEGAN BRADY)

Intergovernmental agreements are one of the more important instruments by which intergovernmental relations are conducted in the Canadian political system. Interestingly, intergovernmental agreements are not specifically protected by the Constitution. They have received weak protection from the Courts (*Reference Re Canada Assistance Plan*, [1991] 2 S.C.R. 525).

Intergovernmental agreements are quite diverse as concerns the parties involved. Some agreements are federal-provincial. Others are between provinces. Still others are tri-partite, i.e. between federal, provincial and aboriginal governments. The agreements concern many diverse subject matters.

There is no standard form for Canadian intergovernmental agreements. No central secretariat monitors them. While the Internet makes them more available than formerly, they are not always easy to find. Some are, or seem, secret.

Notwithstanding the bewildering complexity of form, content and ongoing compliance management, the agreements are a major instrument by which Canadian governments coordinate policy objectives.

Conservative estimates of federal-provincial agreements in Canada place the number at about one thousand.[1] Add to this the thousands of municipal-

---

1   Nigel Banks, "Co-operative Federalism: Third Parties and Inter-governmental Agreements and Arrangements in Canada and Australia" (1991), 29 Alta. L. Rev. 792.

municipal, regional-municipal, and provincial municipal agreements, and a number of at least 5,000 intergovernmental agreements seems more in order. This leaves out the diverse array of agreements with First Nations.

Some of the intergovernmental agreements are enacted into implementing statutes. For example, the James Bay and Northern Quebec Agreement, to which the federal government, Quebec, the Grand Council of the Crees and the Northern Quebec Inuit Association are all parties, was ratified by federal and provincial legislation. The legal status of the agreement was considered in *Cree Regional Authority v. Quebec* (1991), 47 F.T.R. 251, where Rouleau J. stated that the Agreement itself imposed obligations and duties amendable only by way of statute (at 267).

In addition to legislation which implements the agreements, there are also statutes which grant authority to designated Ministers to enter into intergovernmental agreements. The provinces generally provide for complementary enabling legislation within existing statutes. Some provinces, Saskatchewan for example, have enacted specific legislation which allows the provincial minister to enter into all intergovernmental agreements.[1]

Signing of the Federal-Provincial Agreement that returned the control of natural resources to Alberta (December, 1929)

The legal capacity of governments to enter into intergovernmental agreements and to delegate this power to officials has been unambiguously upheld by the Courts. In *Re Anastan and the Queen* (1977), 15 O.R. (2d) 1977, the Ontario Court of Appeal upheld the delegated authority of the Acting Director of Corrections authorized by a federal-provincial agreement between the province of Saskatchewan and the federal government. "There is no question of delegation of legislative jurisdiction" the Court held, as "each [level of government] was operating properly within its own sphere dealing with [these] situations" (at 520).

While the capacity to enter into the agreements is clear, the legal status of the intergovernmental agreements themselves is much less so. It remains to be seen whether, or how far third parties can sue the governments concerned for non-performance of the agreements. Agreements implementing constitutional obligations – for example, the obligation to provide minority language education – must conform closely to the constitutional obligation, and may be challenged as failing to do so.

---

1   *Federal-Provincial Agreements Act*, R.S.S. 1978, c. F-13.

INTERGOVERNMENTAL COOPERATION: INTERGOVERNMENTAL AGREEMENTS

The agreements have been challenged rarely. In addition to the *Reference Re CAP* (reproduced within), the agreements have given rise to challenges by third parties who might receive the benefits accorded by the agreements. In *Finlay v. Minister of Finance*, [1986] 2 S.C.R. 607, the Court granted standing to an individual who would receive welfare benefits under Manitoba's *Social Allowance Act*, as funded by the Canada Assistance Plan. For the Court, Le Dain J. had no question of the suitability of Finlay's challenge of government action under the CAP:

> There will no doubt be cases in which the question of provincial compliance with the conditions of federal cost-sharing will raise issues that are not appropriate for judicial determination, but the particular issues of provincial non-compliance raised by the respondent's statement of claim are questions of law and as such are clearly justiciable. [at 632]

The justiciability of federal compliance with the conditions of federal-provincial cost-sharing agreements was confirmed by the Supreme Court of Canada in *Reference Re Canada Assistance Plan, supra*, a decision which appears to leave intergovernmental agreements vulnerable to unilateral amendment or abrogation by fickle or subsequent governments. In refusing to uphold British Columbia's challenge to unilateral federal modification of the contribution formula associated with the CAP agreement, Mr. Justice Sopinka stated:

> If this appears to deprive the Agreement of binding effect or mutuality, which are both features of ordinary contracts, it must be remembered that this is not an ordinary contract but an agreement between governments [...] In lieu of relying on mutually binding reciprocal undertakings which promote the observance of ordinary contractual obligations, these parties were content to rely on the perceived political price to be paid for non-performance.

The Supreme Court of Canada's decision in *Reference Re Canada Assistance Plan* does not conclusively affirm the right of one party to an intergovernmental agreement to unilaterally derogate from the terms of the agreement itself. The fact that the agreement failed to specify a precise contribution formula enabled the Court to conclude that unilateral changes to the contribution formula by the federal government was not, in fact, a derogation from the agreement at all.

The Court determined that the principles of parliamentary sovereignty, codified in s. 42(1) of the *Interpretation Act*, R.S.C. 1985, c. I-21, confirmed Parliament's right to repeal or amend any ordinary federal legislation and revoke, restrict or modify any rights conferred thereunder. This was not, however, a particularly vexing point. Sopinka J. noted that "[i]t is conceded that the government could not bind Parliament from exercising its powers to legislate amendments to the [*Canada Assistance*] *Plan*".

What remained contentious was the fact that by exercising its power to amend federal legislation, the federal government had effectively, though not technically, unilaterally altered what had been a core component of British

Columbia's agreement with Canada. The Supreme Court's decision provides no
conclusive guidance as to whether the federal government's unilateral legislative
amendment would have been permitted to stand had it violated express terms in
the CAP agreement. The Supreme Court avoided this question by reading the
terms of the intergovernmental agreement in question as compatible with
unilateral federal government alteration of the formula by which its contributions
to British Columbia's social welfare spending were determined. The fact that the
intergovernmental agreement only obliged the federal government to contribute
the amount authorized under federal legislation, combined with the principle of
parliamentary sovereignty, lead the Court to conclude that the agreement merely
obliged the federal government to pay those contributions that were authorized
from time to time under federal legislation and not those contributions that were
authorized at the time the agreement was struck. As federal legislation could be
amended, so too could the amount of the federal government's contributions to
British Columbia's social welfare spending, without upsetting the terms of the
agreement.

Where unilateral action by a party to an intergovernmental agreement
would violate express terms in that agreement, the judiciary has upheld the terms
of the agreement as binding where those agreements were ratified by statute. In
Cree Regional Authority (supra, at p. 267), Rouleau J. said that "the [James Bay &
Northern Quebec] agreement cannot be amended or supplanted without
participation of all of the original signatories." This conclusion is consistent with
the fact that an express provision in that agreement (22.6.7) governing the matter
in issue (environmental assessments) permitted an amendment to the terms of the
agreement by the federal and provincial government and the Cree Regional
Authority "by mutual agreement".

The *Beaudoin-Dobbie* report[1] explored the constitutional position of
unilateral amendment of intergovernmental agreements. The report
recommended recognition of the constitutional principle of parliamentary
sovereignty but suggested certain constitutional modifications that would make
the agreements more stable. The Report advocated for an approval process for the
intergovernmental agreements, giving them heightened public scrutiny and to
allow for an informed debate on the agreements. This process would also apply to
changes or modifications to the agreement. Agreements that went through this
process would have constitutional force for a certain period.

It is doubtful whether the criticism that intergovernmental agreements
can be annulled unilaterally reflects real problems in current Canadian
federalism. Almost every international treaty (including the U.N. Declaration of
Human Rights, the GATT, and the NAFTA) that the Canadian government enters
into can also be unilaterally annulled. It is rare that governments withdraw from
these treaties, absent extraordinary circumstances. Moreover, in a *flexible* system,
opting-out should be within the powers of the party. Rigid adherence to
agreements made decades ago without regard to the current environment is not

---

1   Canada, *Report of the Special Joint Committee on a Renewed Canada
[Beaudoin-Dobbie Report]* (Ottawa: Queen's Printer, 1992), p. 67

necessarily positive, especially when the agreements made are as detailed as the *Agreement on Internal Trade*, which consists of over 1800 articles. Perhaps the death of this recommendation in the *Beaudoin-Dobbie Report* does not require any extensive grief.

In Australia, Germany and the United States, the power to enter into intergovernmental agreements is found in the constitution. Canada has reached the same position without a specific constitutional text. A Charlottetown-type of provision advocated in the *Beaudoin-Dobbie Report* goes further than merely making intergovernmental agreements resistant to unilateral governmental abrogation; in essence the specified procedure would give governments easier access to a limited form of constitutional amendment.

Were there a serious problem here (which there is not) such a text might attract few objections. Given the remarkable rigidity Canada's Constitution already imposes on constitutional amendments, more rigidity for aligning jurisdictional responsibilities is probably not advisable. A constitutional procedure to entrench the agreements makes the agreements too rigid. The rigidity of other policy instruments is what has led these governments to use the flexible intergovernmental agreements as a policy instrument of choice in the first place. Proposals for a new constitutional procedure to stiffen intergovernmental agreements seem to be more of a theoretical solution to a non-existent problem, and are more likely to damage Canadian federalism by draining away some of its flexibility, than to improve it.

Some changes are desirable for intergovernmental agreements to find their proper fit in the political fabric of Canada. One problem concerns accessibility to intergovernmental agreements. It would be helpful to have a central registry for intergovernmental agreements to make them accessible. A legal databank of litigation on the agreements also seems in order to improve accessibility. Research on the form and content of the agreements might help us understand if the agreements have any lowest common denominators which could assist governments in the future.

Changes to the status of intergovernmental agreements could also be made to improve their democratic-deficit problems. Currently, the agreements are made with little public scrutiny or debate. They do not require ratification by legislatures; no notice or hearing need be given to any parties. The answer to these problems likely does not lie in the machinery of constitutional law. The better solution would be for provincial legislatures or Parliament to enact their own legislation mandating an approval or consultative process. When individuals were concerned with the tight control over information held by governments up to the 1980s, the solution was not found in the Constitution — it was found in statutory *Freedom of Information Acts*. There is no reason to think that this situation is any different.

4. Key Concepts in Constitutional Law

(a) Supremacy of the Constitution

> **CONSTITUTION ACT, 1982**
> s. 52(1)
>
> 52.(1) The Constitution of Canada is the supreme law of Canada, and any law that is inconsistent with the provisions of the Constitution is, to the extent of the inconsistency, of no force or effect.

- Research Note -
LAWS INCONSISTENT WITH THE CONSTITUTION

Section 52(1) of the *Constitution Act, 1982* states that any law that is inconsistent with the provisions of the Constitution is of no force or effect. Statutes which conflict with the Constitution are invalid in the most radical sense; they do not become law. In Strayer, *The Canadian Constitution and the Courts* (3d ed., 1988) the author states at p. 32:

> Now we need look no further than s. 52 of the *Constitution Act, 1982* for the principle of supremacy of the Constitution [...] and for the intended consequence of supremacy; that is, the invalidity of inconsistent laws.

In *R. v. Therens*, [1985] 1 S.C.R. 613 at 638, the Supreme Court of Canada, speaking through Le Dain J. stated:

> [...] the *Charter* must be regarded, because of its constitutional character, as a new affirmation of rights and freedoms and of judicial power and responsibility in relation to their protection. This results from s. 52 of the *Constitution Act, 1982*, which removes any possible doubt or uncertainty as to the general effect which the *Charter* is to have by providing that it is part of the supreme law of Canada and that any law that is inconsistent with its provisions is to the extent of such inconsistency of no force and effect.

In *Hunter v. Southam Inc.*, [1984] 2 S.C.R. 145 at 148, Dickson J. emphasized the importance of s. 52(1):

> [...] The Constitution of Canada, which includes the *Canadian Charter of Rights and Freedoms*, is the supreme law of Canada. Any law inconsistent with the provisions of the Constitution is, to the extent of the inconsistency, of no force or effect. Section 52(1) of the *Constitution Act, 1982* so mandates.

Again in *R. v. Big M Drug Mart*, [1985] 1 S.C.R. 295 at 312, Dickson C.J.C. said:

> Section 24(1) sets out a remedy for individuals (whether real persons or artificial ones such as corporations) whose rights under the *Charter* have been infringed. It is not, however, the only recourse in the face of unconstitutional legislation. Where, as here, the challenge is based on the unconstitutionality of the legislation, recourse to s. 24 is unnecessary and the particular effect on the challenging party is irrelevant.

> Section 52 sets out the fundamental principle of constitutional law that the Constitution is supreme. The undoubted corollary to be drawn from this principle is that no one can be convicted of an offence under an unconstitutional law.

These cases seem to indicate that section 52 operates in two ways. First, s. 52 states that the constitutional law is supreme — when legislation comes into conflict with the constitution, there are certain effects. These "effects" are the second branch of section 52: constitutional remedies. When legislation comes into conflict with the constitution, what should the petitioner receive? The second part of section 52 is dealt with in the "Constitutional Remedies" section at Part V of this volume.

The first arm of section 52 - constitutional supremacy - is not a phenomenon unique to Canada. In the United States, Chief Justice Marshall stated this principle in *Marbury v. Madison* (1803), 5 U.S. (1 Cranch 137):

> [T]he people have an original right to establish, for their future government, such principles, as, in their opinion, shall most conduce to their own happiness [and this] is the basis on which the whole American fabric has been erected. The exercise of this original right is a very great exertion; nor can it, nor ought it, to be frequently repeated. And as the authority from which they proceed is supreme, and can seldom act, they are designed to be permanent. [...]

> The Constitution is either a superior paramount law, unchangeable by ordinary means, or it is on a level with ordinary legislative acts, and, like other acts, is alterable when the legislature shall please to alter it.

> If the former part of the alternative be true, then a legislative act contrary to the Constitution is not law: if the latter part be true, then written constitutions are absurd attempts, on the part of the people, to limit a power in its own nature illimitable.

> Certainly all those who have framed written constitutions contemplate them as forming the fundamental and paramount law of the nation, and consequently, the theory of every such government must be that an act of the legislature, repugnant to the constitution, is void.

LAW SOCIETY OF UPPER CANADA v. SKAPINKER
[1984] 1 S.C.R. 357.

[Skapinker was a South African citizen who had met all of the requirements to become a member of the Ontario Bar except the Canadian citizenship requirement. Skapinker challenged the constitutional validity of this requirement of the *Law Society Act* under section 6(2)(b) of the *Charter*. As *Charter* litigation was still new for the courts, Justice Estey took the opportunity to discuss the principle of supremacy of the Constitution in his opinion.

ESTEY J. [Ritchie, Dickson, Beetz, McIntyre, Lamer, Wilson JJ. concurring]: We are here engaged in a new task, the interpretation and application of the *Canadian Charter of Rights and Freedoms* as adopted first as an appendage to the Resolution of Parliament on December 8, 1981 and then as an appendix to the *Canada Act 1982,* 1982 (U.K.), c. 11. This is not a statute or even a statute of the extraordinary nature of the *Canadian Bill of Rights*, R.S.C. 1970, Appendix III. It is a part of the Constitution of a nation adopted by constitutional process which, in the case of Canada in 1982, took the form of a statute of the Parliament of the United Kingdom.

The adoptive mechanisms may vary from nation to nation. They lose their relevancy or shrink to mere historical curiosity value on the ultimate adoption of the instrument as the Constitution. The *British North America Act of 1867* was such a law, albeit but a statute of the Parliament of the United Kingdom and albeit incomplete in the absence of an intra-national amending mechanism. In the interpretation and application of this document the Judicial Committee of the Privy Council of the United Kingdom, which until 1949 was the highest level of the judicial branch engaged in resolving constitutional issues, said: "The *British North America Act* planted in Canada a living tree capable of growth and expansion within its natural limits": *Edwards v. Attorney-General for Canada*, [1930] A.C. 124, per Lord Sankey at p. 136, who reiterated this judicial attitude towards a "constituent or organic statute such as the [B.N.A.] Act" in *British Coal Corporation v. The King*, [1935] A.C. 500, at p. 518. This Court recognized the distinction between simple "statutory interpretation" and "a constitutional role" when the Court was called upon to determine the effect of the Canadian Bill of Rights: *Curr v. The Queen*, [1972] S.C.R. 889, at p. 899, per Laskin J. as he then was. The Canadian Bill of Rights is, of course, in form, the same as any other statute of Parliament. It was designed and adopted to perform a more fundamental role than ordinary statutes in this country. It is, however, not a part of the Constitution of the country. It stands, perhaps, somewhere between a statute and a constitutional instrument. Nevertheless, it attracted the principles of interpretation developed by the courts in the constitutional process of interpreting and applying the Constitution itself.

There are some simple but important considerations which guide a Court in construing the *Charter*, and which are more sharply focused and discernible than in the case of the federal Bill of Rights. The *Charter* comes from neither level of the legislative branches of government but from the Constitution itself. It is part of the fabric of Canadian law. Indeed, it "is the supreme law of Canada": *Constitution Act, 1982*, s. 52. It cannot be readily amended. The fine and constant adjustment process of these constitutional provisions is left by a tradition of necessity to the judicial branch.

Flexibility must be balanced with certainty. The future must, to the extent foreseeably possible, be accommodated in the present. The *Charter* is designed and adopted to guide and serve the Canadian community for a long time. Narrow and technical interpretation, if not modulated by a sense of the unknowns of the future, can stunt the growth of the law and hence the community it serves. All this has long been with us in the process of developing the institutions of government under the *B.N.A. Act, 1867* (now the *Constitution Act, 1867*). With the *Constitution Act, 1982* comes a new dimension, a new yardstick of reconciliation between the individual and the community and their respective rights, a dimension which, like the balance of the Constitution, remains to be interpreted and applied by the Court.

The courts in the United States have had almost two hundred years experience at this task and it is of more than passing interest to those concerned with these new developments in Canada to study the experience of the United States courts. Where the United States Supreme Court was first concerned with the supervision of constitutional development through the application of the recently adopted Constitution of the United States, the Supreme Court of the United States speaking through Chief Justice Marshall stated:

> The question, whether an act, repugnant to the constitution, can become the law of the land, is a question deeply interesting to the United States; but, happily, not of an intricacy proportioned to its interest. It seems only necessary to recognize certain principles, supposed to have been long and well established, to decide it. [*Marbury v. Madison*, 5 U.S. (1 Cranch) 137 (1803), at p. 175.]

There followed a lengthy discussion not dissimilar to that engaged in by the Privy Council and by this Court in considering the allocation of powers and institutional provisions in the Constitution as it existed, at least to 1981. As to the nature of a written Constitution in relation to the component governments, the Chief Justice continued at pp. 176-77:

> Certainly all those who have framed written constitutions contemplate them as forming the fundamental and paramount law of the nation, and, consequently, the theory of every such government must be, that an act of the legislature, repugnant to the constitution, is void.

> This theory is essentially attached to a written constitution, and, is consequently, to be considered, by this court, as one of the fundamental principles of our society. It is not therefore to be lost sight of in the further consideration of this subject.

The Court then turned, at p. 177, to the role of the court:

> It is emphatically the province and duty of the judicial department to say what the law is. Those who apply the rule to particular cases, must of necessity expound and interpret that rule. If two laws conflict with each other, the courts must decide on the operation of each.

So if a law be in opposition to the constitution; if both the law and the Constitution apply to a particular case, so that the court must either decide that case conformably to the law, disregarding the constitution; or conformably to the constitution, disregarding the law; the court must determine which of these conflicting rules governs the case. This is of the very essence of judicial duty.

The Court having staked out its constitutional ground then moved on in *M'Culloch v. State of Maryland*, 17 U.S. (4 Wheaton's) 316 (1819), to consider the techniques of interpretation to be applied in construing a constitution. Again speaking through Chief Justice Marshall at p. 407:

A constitution, to contain an accurate detail of all the subdivisions of which its great powers will admit, and of all the means by which they may be carried into execution, would partake of the prolixity of a legal code, and could scarcely be embraced by the human mind. It would probably never be understood by the public. Its nature, therefore, requires, that only its great outlines should be marked, its important objects designated, and the minor ingredients which compose those objects be deduced from the nature of the objects themselves. [...] In considering this question, then, we must never forget, that it is a Constitution we are expounding.

In recognizing that both legislative and judicial power under the Constitution is limited, the Chief Justice observed, at p. 421, that the Court must allow the legislative branch to exercise that discretion authorized by the Constitution which will:

[...] enable that body to perform the high duties assigned to it, in the manner most beneficial to the people. Let the end be legitimate, let it be within the scope of the constitution, and all means which are appropriate, which are plainly adapted to that end, which are not prohibited, but consist with the letter and spirit of the constitution, are constitutional.

REFERENCE RE MANITOBA LANGUAGE RIGHTS
[1985] 1 S.C.R. 721.

[For a full report of the facts and issues, see infra, p. 167]

THE COURT: — [...] Section 23 of the *Manitoba Act*, 1870, 33 Vict., c. 3 entrenches a mandatory requirement to enact, print, and publish all Acts of the Legislature in both official languages (see *Blaikie v. A.G. Que.; Laurier v. A.G. Que.*, [1979] 2 S.C.R. 1016, 101 D.L.R. (3d) 394 (*Blaikie No. 1*)). It establishes a constitutional duty on the Manitoba Legislature with respect to the manner and form of enactment of its legislation. This duty protects the substantive rights of all Manitobans to equal access to the law in either the French or the English language.

The constitutional entrenchment of a duty on the Manitoba Legislature to enact, print and publish in both French and English in s. 23 of the *Manitoba Act, 1870* confers upon the judiciary the responsibility of protecting the correlative language rights of all Manitobans, including the Franco-Manitoban minority. The judiciary is the institution charged with the duty of ensuring that the government complies with the Constitution. We must protect those whose constitutional rights have been violated, whomever they may be, and whatever the reasons for the violation.

The Constitution of a country is a statement of the will of the people to be governed in accordance with certain principles held as fundamental and certain prescriptions restrictive of the powers of the legislature and government. It is, as s. 52 of the *Constitution Act, 1982* declares, the "supreme law" of the nation, unalterable by the normal legislative process, and unsuffering of laws inconsistent with it. The duty of the judiciary is to interpret and apply the laws of Canada and each of the provinces, and it is thus our duty to ensure that the constitutional law prevails.

As this Court said in *Amax Potash Ltd. v. Saskatchewan*, [1977] 2 S.C.R. 576 at p. 596, 71 D.L.R. (3d) 1:

> A state, it is said, is sovereign and it is not for the courts to pass upon the policy or wisdom of legislative will. As a broad statement of principle that is undoubtedly correct, but the general principle must yield to the requisites of the Constitution in a federal state. By it the bounds of sovereignty are defined and supremacy circumscribed. The court will not question the wisdom of enactments which, by the terms of the Canadian Constitution, are within the competence of the legislatures, *but it is the high duty of the court to insure that the legislatures do not transgress the limits of their constitutional mandate and engage in the illegal exercise of power.*

See also *Re Resolution to Amend the Constitution*, [1981] 1 S.C.R. 753 (the *Patriation Reference*), at pp. 841, 848, 877.

Since April 17, 1982, the mandate of the judiciary to protect the Constitution has been embodied in s. 52 of the *Constitution Act, 1982*. This section reads:

> 52(1) The Constitution of Canada is the supreme law of Canada, and any law that is inconsistent with the provisions of the Constitution is, to the extent of the inconsistency, of no force or effect.

Prior to enactment of the *Constitution Act, 1982*, the government provision was, pursuant to the *Statute of Westminster, 1931*, s. 2 of the *Colonial Laws Validity Act, 1865* (U.K.), 28 & 29 Vict., c. 63, which provides:

2. Any Colonial Law which is or shall be in any respect repugnant to the Provisions of any Act of Parliament extending to the Colony to which such Law may relate, or repugnant to any Order or Regulation made under Authority of such Act of Parliament, or having in the Colony the Force and Effect of such Act, shall be read subject to such Act, Order, or Regulation, and shall, to the Extent of such Repugnancy, but not otherwise, be and remain *absolutely void and inoperative.*

Invalidity doctrine

The constitutional jurisprudence, developed under the *Colonial Laws Validity Act, 1865,* was based on the invalidity doctrine. If Parliament or a provincial legislature was *ultra vires* its constitutionally allocated powers in enacting a certain Act, then the repugnancy of that Act with the provisions of the *British North America Act, 1867* would mean that the Act was "absolutely void and inoperative".

Section 52 of the *Constitution Act, 1982* does not alter the principles which have provided the foundation for judicial review over the years. In a case where constitutional manner and form requirements have not been complied with, the consequence of such non-compliance continues to be invalidity. The words "of no force or effect" mean that a law thus inconsistent with the Constitution has no force or effect because it is invalid.

Canadian courts have been unanimous in finding that failure to respect mandatory requirements to enact, print and publish statutes and regulations in both official languages leads to inconsistency and thus invalidity. See *Société Asbestos Ltée v. Société Nationale de L'Amiante,* [1980] C.S. 331; affirmed [1981] C.A. 43, 128 D.L.R. (3d) 405; *P.G. du Qué. v. Collier,* [1983] C.S. 366; *P.G. du Qué. v. Brunet,* J.E. 83-510 reversed on other grounds, J.E. 84-62 (Que. S.C.). These cases accord with the general principle that failure to comply with constitutional provisions dealing with the manner and form of the enactment of legislation will result in inconsistency and thus invalidity. See *Bribery Commr. v. Ranasinghe,* [1965] A.C. 172, [1964] 2 All E.R. 758 (P.C.).

In the present case the unilingual enactments of the Manitoba Legislature are inconsistent with s. 23 of the *Manitoba Act, 1870* since the constitutionally required manner and form for their enactment has not been followed. Thus, they are invalid and of no force or effect. [...]

The conclusion that the Acts of the Legislature of Manitoba are invalid and of no force or effect means that the positive legal order which has purportedly regulated the affairs of the citizens of Manitoba since 1890 will be destroyed and the rights, obligations and other effects arising under these laws will be invalid and unenforceable. As for the future, since it is reasonable to assume that it will be impossible for the Legislature of Manitoba to rectify *instantaneously* the constitutional defect, the Acts of the Manitoba Legislature will be invalid and of no force or effect until they are translated, re-enacted, printed and published in both languages. [...]

The only appropriate solution for preserving the rights, obligations and other effects which have arisen under invalid Acts of the Legislature of Manitoba and which are not saved by the *de facto* or other doctrines is to declare that, in order to uphold the rule of law, these rights, obligations and other effects have, and will continue to have, the same force and effect they would have had if they had arisen under valid enactments, for that period of time during which it would be impossible for Manitoba to comply with its constitutional duty under s. 23 of the *Manitoba Act, 1870*. The Province of Manitoba would be faced with chaos and anarchy if the legal rights, obligations and other effects which have been relied upon by the people of Manitoba since 1890 were suddenly open to challenge. The constitutional guarantee of rule of law will not tolerate such chaos and anarchy. [...]

(b)   The Rule of Law

- Research Note -
OVERVIEW OF THE RULE OF LAW

The "rule of law" is a principle of longstanding constitutional value. It is recognized in the preamble of the *Constitution Act, 1982*, and has been utilized by the courts as important constitutional rhetoric, and also as a doctrine that produced juridical effects in various contexts

At a minimum, the inspiration behind the "rule of law" is a sense of order and hierarchy. The modern concept was developed in the nineteenth century writings of A.V. Dicey, and has since undergone several metamorphoses. In *Roncarelli v. Duplessis*, [1959] S.C.R. 121, the Supreme Court of Canada relied upon the doctrine to assert that all official acts must be authorized by law. In *Reference Re Proposed Resolution Respecting the Constitution of Canada*, [1981] 1 S.C.R. 753, 805, the Court explained that

> The "rule of law" is a highly textured expression [...] conveying, for example, a sense of orderliness, of subjection to known legal rules and of executive accountability to legal authority.

Mature development of the rule of law as the underpinning of the Canadian public law system means that the constitutional review jurisdiction vested in the courts must extend to ensuring that constitutional obligations are performed, in addition to checking illegal exercises of power. Failure of governments to discharge the few affirmative duties imposed on them by the Constitution, as, for example, failure to print and publish legislative records, journals and acts in both English and French (*Manitoba Act, 1870*, s. 23), gives rise to difficult and novel questions as to public law remedies. These issues were explored by the Supreme Court of Canada in *Reference Re Manitoba Language Rights*, at p. 167, infra. In that case at S.C.R. p. 749, the Supreme Court established as a second branch of the rule of law doctrine that "the rule of law requires the creation and maintenance of an actual order of positive laws which preserves and embodies the more general principle of normative order". A third aspect of the rule of law doctrine was established in the *Provincial Judges Reference*, para. 10 and the *Secession Reference*, para. 71. In these cases the Supreme Court attributed to the rule of law doctrine the requirement that " 'the exercise of all public power must find its ultimate source in a legal rule . Put another way, the relationship between the state and the individual must be regulated by law." The Court went on to note that, taken together, the three branches of the rule of law doctrine "make up a principle of profound constitutional and political significance;" (*Secession Reference*, para. 71).

The theory of the rule of law is interesting. Some argue that the rule of law is a procedural concept. The rule of law implies a sense of order and hierarchy in the sense that each act of the authorities must be authorized by legal rules which are legitimate. The only way legal rules can be recognized as legitimate is if they are procedurally correct – i.e. the rule has been stipulated by the required legal procedure. Thus, for example, the police may only arrest if they are authorized to do so by some rule of statute or common law. The authorizing rule itself must ultimately have its source in a grant of power in the Constitution. The rule of law is said to require procedural regularity in the sense that one can trace the source of all official acts ultimately to an authorizing grant of power in the Constitution. In this sense, the rule of law requires that each legal step, beginning with the exercise of constitutional power by the legislature, through to orders given to officials, to have been followed in legally and procedurally correct form. If there is any break in the chain of legality, the action is not in accordance with law, and may be controlled by the Courts.

Others would say that the rule of law concept goes beyond procedural regularity. In addition to commanding procedural correctness, the rule of law concept is said to require that the law obligate. Persons can only be obligated by laws that are fundamentally just. Even if all procedural steps required by the Constitution, statutes and regulations authorize the state to do something fundamentally unjust, such as torture, this would still be inconsistent with the rule of law because people would not feel obligated to comply. In this second sense it is said that the rule of law implies that the law must be consistent with at least certain minimal substantive norms, those norms which we recognize as fundamental tenets of justice.

The jurisprudence of the Supreme Court of Canada contains comments which indicate both a procedural and substantive approach to the rule of law. In the *Manitoba Language Rights Reference*, for example, the court referred to two senses of the rule of law:

1. the rule of law which precludes the influence of arbitrary power;
2. the rule of law which "preserves and embodies the more general principle of normative order [...] which [...] is linked with basic democratic notions".

In the *Secession Reference*, para. 95 the Court added a duty to negotiate the profound political proposal of separation if demanded by political action in Quebec. "Those who quite legitimately insist upon the importance of upholding the rule of law," the Court noted, cannot at the same time be oblivious to the need to act in conformity with constitutional principles and values, and so do their part to contribute to the maintenance and promotion of an environment in which the rule of law may flourish.

Although undeveloped, these comments suggest that the Supreme Court may well utilize the rule of law as a doctrine that supplies normative principles, as a doctrine that requires compliance with at least certain minimal principles deemed fundamental to the legal system. This is what makes *Vanguard Coatings and Chemicals v. M.N.R.*, [1986] 2 C.T.C. 431 (Fed. T.D.) so interesting. In that case, the Federal Court Trial Division was moved to find violation of the rule of law by a statute which offended both procedural and substantive norms in the sense that the statute created arbitrary unlimited power (a procedural violation), and also unfairly deprived a citizen of his property. Justice Muldoon stated:

> Thus it may be seen that section 34 of the *Excise Tax Act* is no paradigm of the rule of law. It is, indeed, so contrary to the rule of law that it can surely be declared to be unconstitutional. It accords arbitrary administrative discretion, without any guidelines or directives, to the Minister whose determination is not subject to any objective second opinion as is inherent in an appeal provision. Even if, in fact and theory, section 34 does not transgress the specific rights and freedoms proclaimed in the *Charter*, that constitutional document itself, in section 26, claims no monopoly in the promulgation of Canadians' other existing rights and freedoms. The rule of law is a central principle of our Constitution and it is transgressed by section 34....By levying his determination of "fair price" against Vanguard, the Minister at a stroke of the pen imposes a heavy burden of tax debt. Since the Minister did not agree with Vanguard's submissions, it and its shareholders and directors are left with the burdensome decree of the one-and-only, far-from-disinterested and uncontradictable authority whom section 34 recognizes in conjuring the "fair price on which the tax should be imposed". The "tax should be imposed" in the sole judgment of the Minister whose duty is to collect tax? Section 34 certainly makes a despot of the Minister. If this formulation be so decent and reasonable as the Minister's counsel say it is, why Parliament could provide that all Canadians should subject their lives and livelihoods to some chosen official who finds himself in as paramount a conflict of official interest as does the Minister of National Revenue when determining that taxpayers should really contribute more revenue to the Crown, pursuant to section 34 of the *Excise Tax Act*.

This novel and potent use of the doctrine was reversed on appeal on the narrow point that "the rule of law has never been taken to include a right of appeal." The decisions are helpful in reminding us of how prone are some Courts to reach for available doctrines to deal with perceptions of unfairness, and how circumspect are other Courts when confronted with openings for seemingly unlimited judicial discretion.

While there is much rhetoric about the rule of law in Canadian jurisprudence, the doctrine has been pressed into service as an operative principle only rarely. There are but few examples where the rule of law concept creates a Constitutional standard to which other legal rules must conform.

UNIMPEDED ACCESS TO THE COURTS

The Supreme Court of Canada found within the rule of law a requirement that the public have unimpeded access to the courts. In *N.A.P.E. v. A.G. Nfld.*, [1988] 2 S.C.R. 204, the Court held that picketing a courthouse constituted criminal contempt to the extent it interfered with such access. Dickson C.J. said:

> [C]ourts of record have from time immemorial had the power to punish for contempt those whose conduct is such as to interfere with or obstruct the due course of justice; the courts have this power in order that they may effectively defend and protect the rights and freedoms of all citizens in the only forums in which those rights and freedoms can be adjudicated, the courts of civil and criminal law. Any action taken to prevent, impede or obstruct access to the courts runs counter to the rule of law and constitutes criminal contempt. The rule of law, enshrined in our Constitution, can only be maintained if persons have unimpeded, uninhibited access to the courts of this country.

Dickson C.J. repeated this view in *B.C.G.E.U. v. B.C. (A.G.)*, [1988] 2 S.C.R. 214 at 230.

This led Professor Monahan to suggest that:

> [R]ight of access to the courts is in no way limited to the vindication of rights set out in the *Charter*. Rather, the rule of law encompasses the right of citizens to a "separate and independent branch of government" -- the judiciary -- for determination of rights and obligations. Therefore, to deprive citizens of access to the courts for the determination of their rights, even if this is accomplished through legislation, must be inconsistent with the rule of law. ("Is the Pearson Airport Legislation Unconstitutional?", (1995), 33 *Osgoode Hall L. J.* 411, 427).

This same point was pressed by Professor Monahan as counsel before the Ontario Court (General Division) in *Reclamation Systems Inc. v. Rae* (1996), 27 O.R. (3d) 419, 432-433. The submission was neither adopted nor rejected by the Court, as that case was decided on other grounds.

The submissions made in *Reclamation Systems*, supra, are probably untenable. Dickson C.J.'s statements in *B.C.G.E.U.* and *N.A.P.E.* were made in the context of unions picketing in front of courthouses, essentially prohibiting entry to the courthouses. The Court was upholding an inherent power of the court to order injunctions for individuals seeking to bar entry to the courthouse. McLachlin J. developed this concept by stating in *United Nurses of Alberta v. Alberta (Attorney General)*, [1992] 1 S.C.R. 901: "[t]he rule of law is directly dependent on the ability of the courts to enforce their process and maintain their dignity and respect."

It is difficult to see how this aspect of the rule of law can be stretched to embody the dubious principle that statutes which create a form of Crown immunity offend the rule of law. While the Court will use the rule of law to prohibit general closures of the Courts, they will not use it, for example, to strike down privative or limitation clauses which remove the right of access to certain classes of claimants, in certain situations or at certain times, just as they will not use it to strike down short limitation periods or limits on damages less than full compensation. In *Reclamation Systems*, the plaintiff alleged that the statute "denies access to the court for citizens who may have suffered wrongs [...]". The same could be said of many statutes of the type noted above, all of which are beyond controversy. The only possible justification for the contrary view would be based on the distinguishing characteristic in *Reclamation Systems* that the right of access denied in that case had been pre-existing.

This would involve analogizing the case to a civil attainder — a legislative act directed against a designated person which extinguishes civil rights. While in theory a civil attainder of this nature — an act which extinguishes specific civil rights of a specific person with respect to a specific controversy with the government could be found contrary to the rule of law, this has never happened. As for the general case — legislation which modifies, or extinguishes contractual rights, or creates Crown immunities — the Courts hold that the rule of law does not impose a limit on the power of Canadian legislatures.

In *Bacon et al. v. Saskatchewan Crop Insurance Corp.*, [1999] 65 C.R.R. (2d) 170 (Sask. C.A.), Wakeling, J.A., for the Saskatchewan Court of Appeal, reviewed earlier Supreme Court cases referring to the rule of law before rejecting the contention that the doctrine can be used to upset legislation which extinguishes contractual rights. Wakeling J.A. stated that a contrary ruling "would reduce the supremacy of Parliament by subjecting it to the scrutiny of superior court judges to be sure it did not offend the rule of law" (p. 181). Wakeling J.A. went on to say that to advance the submission "is to misunderstand the democratic process by downgrading the importance of holding a government responsible to the will of the electors."

In *JTI-MacDonald Corp. v. B.C. (A.G.)* (2000), 184 D.L.R. (4th) 335 (B.C.S.C.) Justice Holmes considered a rule of law attack on the *Tobacco Damages Recovery Act*, S.B.C. 1997, c. 41 as amended. S. 13(1) of the challenged Act gave the government a direct cause of action against tobacco manufacturers for the cost of health care benefits provided to smokers. The Act significantly altered the law of procedure and evidence in a s. 13(1) action. In particular, the Act exposed tobacco companies to an "aggregate action;" in such an action government could recover benefits paid to individuals based on the portion of the population that suffered disease from smoking without having to identify particular individuals or prove the cause of their illnesses.

The tobacco companies specifically complained that retroactive legislation violates the rule of law because it changes the law applied to past events, making the citizenry unable to know the conduct required until after the event. Interestingly, Justice Holmes replied to this submission as follows:

[¶124] The manufacturers' position is that retroactive legislation obviously violates the rule of law, on which the Constitution rests, as it changes the law in respect of past events making discovery of law unascertainable until after the event.

[¶125] The rule against Bills of Attainder is suggested by the manufacturers to represent one of the component parts of an implied bill of rights. The manufacturers equate any non-compensatory view of s. 13 of the Act as targeting tobacco manufacturers for punishment for acts that attracted no penalty at the suit of government at the time they occurred.

[¶126] Bills of Attainder are expressly prohibited under the American Constitution Article 1, s. 9, CL. 3. Although there is no equivalent written *Charter* or constitutional prohibition in Canada:

> [...] it would surely be unthinkable today that Parliament could enact a Bill of Attainder or a Bill of Pains and Penalties [...] even apart from the *Charter*, such a method of finding guilt and imposing punishment would be generally regarded as beyond the power of Parliament in a country like Canada which has "a Constitution similar in Principle to that of the United Kingdom" (*R. v. Bowen*, [1989] 2 W.W.R. 213 (Alta.Q.B.) at 259-60, aff'd at [1991] 1 W.W.R. 466 (Alta.C.A.))

[¶127] The experience in American law has been that governments should not be permitted to manipulate the form of proceeding and Courts have recognized that criminal prohibition in the guise of a civil statute will not succeed. [...]

[¶128] I do not consider that any party has raised a serious issue as to the Act being interpreted as other than compensatory legislation intended to recoup health care costs incurred by the government. In my view, no reasonable interpretation of the Act would make it penal legislation.

Justice Holmes then reviewed the jurisprudence at length, and concluded, as did Wakeling J.A. in *Bacon*, that "the rule of law of itself is not a basis for setting aside legislation as unconstitutional."

These views were considered at length by the Supreme Court in *British Columbia v. Imperial Tobacco Ltd.*, [2005] 2 S.C.R. 473. Justice Major there replied to the rule of law attack on *B.C.'s Tobacco Damages and Health Care Costs Recovery Act* as follows:

> [¶58] This Court has described the rule of law as embracing three principles. The first recognizes that "the law is supreme over officials of the government as well as private individuals,

and thereby preclusive of the influence of arbitrary power": *Reference re Manitoba Language Rights*, at p. 748. The second "requires the creation and maintenance of an actual order of positive laws which preserves and embodies the more general principle of normative order": *Reference re Manitoba Language Rights*, at p. 749. The third requires that "the relationship between the state and the individual ... be regulated by law": *Reference re Secession of Quebec*, at para. 71.

[¶59] So understood, it is difficult to conceive of how the rule of law could be used as a basis for invalidating legislation such as the Act based on its content. That is because none of the principles that the rule of law embraces speak directly to the terms of legislation. The first principle requires that legislation be applied to all those, including government officials, to whom it, by its terms, applies. The second principle means that legislation must exist. And the third principle, which overlaps somewhat with the first and second, requires that state officials' actions be legally founded....

[¶60] This does not mean that the rule of law as described by this Court has no normative force. As McLachlin C.J. stated in *Babcock*, at para. 54, "unwritten constitutional principles", including the rule of law, "are capable of limiting government actions".... But the government action constrained by the rule of law as understood in *Reference re Manitoba Language Rights* and *Reference re Secession of Quebec* is, by definition, usually that of the executive and judicial branches. Actions of the legislative branch are constrained too, but only in the sense that they must comply with legislated requirements as to manner and form (i.e. the procedures by which legislation is to be enacted, amended and repealed).

[¶61] Nonetheless, considerable debate surrounds the question of what additional principles, if any, the rule of law might embrace, and the extent to which they might mandate the invalidation of legislation based on its content.

In *British Columbia (Attorney General) v. Christie*, 2007 SCC 21 the Supreme Court of Canada considered B.C.'s *Social Service Tax Amendment Act*, which imposed a seven per cent tax on the fees billed by members of the legal profession to their clients for legal service. The tax applied only to the legal profession. This tax was questioned on the basis that it offended the rule of law. The Supreme Court of Canada replied:

"... general access to legal services is not a currently recognized aspect of the rule of law. However, in *Imperial Tobacco*, this Court left open the possibility that the rule of law may include additional principles.... The issue [here] is whether general access to legal services in relation to court and tribunal proceedings dealing with rights and obligations is a fundamental aspect of the rule of law.... [A] review of the constitutional text, the jurisprudence and the history of the concept does not support the respondent's contention that there is a broad general right to legal counsel as an aspect of, or precondition to, the rule of law...[T]he *Charter* ... provides for a right to legal services in one specific situation. Section 10(b) of the *Charter* provides that everyone has the right to retain and instruct counsel, and to be informed of that right "on arrest or detention". If the reference to the rule of law implied the right to counsel in relation to all proceedings where rights and obligations are at stake, s. 10(b) would be redundant.... Nor has the rule of law historically been understood to encompass a general right to have a lawyer in court or tribunal proceedings affecting rights and obligations. The right to counsel was historically understood to be a limited right that extended only, if at all, to representation in the criminal context...We conclude that the text of the constitution, the jurisprudence and the historical understanding of the rule of law do not foreclose the possibility that a right to counsel may be recognized in specific and varied situations. But at the same time, they do not support the conclusion that there is a general constitutional right to counsel in proceedings before courts and tribunals dealing with rights and obligations; (paras 21-27).

Justice Major's statement in *Imperial Tobacco* that the rule of law can never be used to check parliamentary action is perhaps useful as a reminder of how unusual it would be for the rule of law doctrine to overturn legislative action. *Christie* shows that it is inaccurate to read *Imperial Tobacco* as a *per se* ruling that the rule of law doctrine can never void legislative acts. *Christie* reinforces that it would be an unusual case which would warrant the use of this power.

The *Manitoba Language Rights Reference*, which was very unusual, called forth the rule of law doctrine to uphold Manitoba legislation enacted in violation of constitutional requirements. An obverse case -- using the rule of law doctrine to void legislation, such as a civil attainder -- is not inconceivable. Allowing for the possibility that the rule of law doctrine might serve as an emergency switch to overturn legislation in such unusual circumstances may provide useful flexibility in Canada's constitutional system.

CONSISTENCY IN APPLICATION OF THE LAW

Justice McLachlin saw various values inspired by the rule of law in her analysis that follows at p. 164. She stated:

> We expect our administrative tribunals to be bound by the law, to render decisions in an equal and predictive manner and to act in accordance with law and social values.

There are qualifications to this aspect of the rule of law. As Harry Arthurs pointed out in his seminal book, *"Without the Law": Administrative Justice and Legal Pluralism in 19th Century England*, a large degree of pluralism is characteristic of the modern legal system. Various administrative regimes have relative autonomy from the Courts. They are epicentres of power, creating rules and speciality regulatory regimes which are designed by the legislature to act without close supervision by the Courts As with any large rule-administering or rule creating bureaucracy, they generate a degree of inconsistency. The rule of law tolerates this inconsistency. In *Domtar Inc. v. Quebec*, [1993] 2 S.C.R. 756, Madam Justice L'Heureux-Dubé explained:

> The requirement of consistency in the application of the law is unquestionably a valid objective and so a persuasive argument. For litigants to receive diametrically opposite answers to the same question, depending on the identity of the members of administrative tribunals, may seem unacceptable to some and even difficult to reconcile with several objectives, including the rule of law. Yet, as the courts have held, consistency in decision-making and the rule of law cannot be absolute in nature regardless of context. So far as judicial review is concerned, the problem of inconsistency in decision-making by administrative tribunals cannot be separated from the decision-making autonomy, expertise and effectiveness of those tribunals.

In a later article, "The Roles of Administrative Tribunals and Courts in Maintaining the Rule of Law" (1999), 12 *C.J.A.L.P.* 171 Chief Justice McLachlin added a further core element to her concept of the rule of law — a culture of justification. She put this interesting point as follows:

> societies governed by the Rule of Law are marked by a certain ethos of justification. [...] Where a society is marked by a culture of justification, an exercise of public power is only appropriate where it can be justified to citizens in terms of rationality and fairness [...] the ability to call for such a justification as a precondition to the legitimate exercise of public power is regarded by citizens as their right, a right which only illegitimate institutions and laws venture to infringe. The prevalence of such a cultural expectation is, in my view, the definitive marker of a mature Rule of Law. [...] once a culture of justification is recognized, it affects the relationships among institutions of the state almost as much as it affects the relationship between those institutions and the citizens living under their rules. [...] I believe that one of the most intriguing aspects of the new Rule of Law is that it makes it possible for institutions other than courts to play key roles in maintaining it. [...] The new Rule of Law has an element of positivity. It requires proactive efforts to maintain it. Fair procedures, equitable treatment, and responsiveness to the public are the cornerstones of a system of administrative tribunals built according to the Rule of Law. I suggests that, in many important ways, it falls to the members and support staff of those administrative boards to ensure that every person dealing with the state is treated fairly and with respect. Only if decisions can be defended rationally with reasons or some other imprint of rationality can the Rule of Law survive.

DEVELOPING THE RULE OF LAW DOCTRINE

Undoubtedly the judiciary's infrequent resort to the rule of law concept is caused by the familiar legitimacy debate. While it is always tempting for the judiciary to pour substantive content into elastic constitutional concepts like the rule of law, the temptation is dangerous. Frequent use of unbridled judicial power contains the seeds of its own destruction because it ultimately will erode the perceived legitimacy of the judiciary. Robert Bork, a controversial conservative judge, tells a story of Justice Holmes and Judge Learned Hand, who one day lunched together.

> Afterwards, as Holmes began to drive off in his carriage, Hand, in a sudden onset of enthusiasm, ran after him, crying, "Do justice, sir, do justice." Holmes stopped the carriage and reproved Hand: "That is not my job. It is my job to apply the law." I meant something like that when I dissented from a decision that seemed to proceed from sympathy rather than law: We administer justice according to law. Justice in a larger sense, justice according to morality, is for Congress and the President to administer, if they see fit, through the creation of new law; (R. Bork, The Tempting of America (1990), 6).

The legitimacy debate is probably not resolvable in any ultimate sense, and as such, it will always serve as a caution to the judiciary in utilizing open-ended concepts like the rule of law to overturn statutes enacted by the legislature. Nevertheless, advocates for use of the doctrine in a substantive sense are also persuasive. Rodger Beehler's article at p. 165 provides a good example of that school.

MADAM JUSTICE BEVERLEY MCLACHLIN, "RULES AND DISCRETION IN THE GOVERNANCE OF CANADA"
(1992), 56 SASK. L. REV. 167

The term "Rule of Law" means many things to many people. Dicey's definition of over a hundred years ago is a valuable starting point in understanding the modern concept of the rule of law. Dicey used the term to denote a procedure-based assurance of "government under law." For him, the rule of law consisted of the supremacy of "ordinary law" over arbitrary power, the equality before the law of all persons, and the recognition of constitutional law as the fundamental law of the land.

Since then, scholars have enlarged the concept of the rule of law, with many defining it less in terms of a dichotomy between ordinary law and administrative fiat, than as a concept embodying the fundamental expectations for decision-making in a democratic society. Professor J. Raz has proposed that the substantive content of the rule of law is premised on two basic propositions: 1) the people, including the state, should be ruled by the law and should conform to it; and 2) the people should be able (and, in essence, willing) to be guided by the law.

Upon reviewing and analyzing the various definitions proposed since Dicey, Professor G. Walker identifies twelve basic "requirements" of the rule of law which provide an adequate context within which to address the exercise of administrative discretion. The rule of law may be said to include the following principles:

1. Freedom from private lawlessness (coercion).
2. Government under law: the state must be bound by the ordinary law.
3. Ordinary (substantive) law should possess certainty, generality and equality.
4. Mechanisms must ensure the congruence of law with social values.
5. The effective and impartial enforcement of law and order (against private coercion).
6. The enforcement, through procedures and institutions, of government under law.
7. The assurance of the independence of the judiciary.
8. A system of legal representation: an independent legal profession.
9. The application (and enforcement) of the principles of natural justice.
10. The accessibility of the courts.
11. The assurance of "impartial and honest" law enforcement.
12. An "attitude of legality": the application of law in spirit as well as in letter.

Chief Justice Beverly McLachlin
(Joe Plaskett, 2002).

These principles of general application should apply to all public decision-making in a democratic society. We expect our administrative tribunals to be bound by the law, to render decisions in an equal and predictive manner and to act in accordance with law and social values.

The conclusion we then arrive at is that the modern concept of the rule of law provides a structure of legal and political values applicable not only to the courts, but also to the administrative decisions of governments. Dicey's view, that courts embody the rule of law and administrative decision-making embodies the rule of arbitrariness, is too categoric to conform with our modern conception of the rule of law.

RODGER BEEHLER, "WAITING FOR THE RULE OF LAW"
(1988), 38 U.T.L.J. 298.

Two conceptions of the rule of law continue to compete. One may be termed the procedural conception, according to which the rule of law is rule by due process. The other may be termed the substantive conception, according to which the rule of law is rule by right reason.

Adherents of both conceptions may claim to trace their positions back to Aristotle. [...]

[Aristotle wrote in the *Politics*:]

> There are some who hold that it is not even in accordance with nature that one man should be sovereign over all the citizens, when the state is made up of persons who are alike. For, they say, those who are by nature alike must get the same natural justice and deserts; and so, if it is bad for the health of unequal persons to have equal food or clothing, this is also applicable to honours; and the converse also is true. Justice therefore demands that no one should do more ruling than being ruled, but that all should have their turn. So we are back again with law, for organization *is* law.

Note the argument. Since justice demands that each person rule in turn, we are back at law – that is, organization. Law is organization, but it is not necessarily *any* organization. It is, in the instance, the organization whose purpose is to achieve what justice demands. [...]

[Aristotle also wrote:]

> He who asks law to rule is asking God and intelligence and no others to rule; while he who asks [as we cannot escape asking] for the rule of a human being is importing a wild beast too; for desire is like a wild beast, and anger perverts rulers and the very best of men. Hence law is intelligence without appetition.

For Aristotle, then, law is that intelligent organization which orders justly, and which is not perverted by individual appetite or preference. It is precisely to circumvent such perversion that the organization takes a quite specific form. [...]

In any case, there is no need to invoke ancient theory to show the procedural conception of the rule of law to be inadequate. [...]

The basic tenet of the procedural conception (as of the substantive conception) is that the rule of law is the opposite of arbitrary rule. The procedural conception construes "arbitrary" here quite narrowly as "unregulated". It accordingly puts all the stress on such preventive regulatory features as public promulgation of laws, indictment only for duly promulgated offences, opportunity for defence if accused, an independent judiciary, and so on. But this emphasis is itself quite sufficient to introduce a substantive moral content to the (allegedly) neutral procedural conception, since it entails denying the description "rule of law" to processes that do not preclude arbitrary rule – a denial that proceeds from the moral recognition that arbitrary rule is unjust. [...]

The substantive conception of the rule of law from the beginning construes arbitrary rule more widely than does the procedural conception. Arbitrary rule is not merely unregulated rule, but non-legitimated rule. On the substantive conception, what distinguishes the rule of law from any other social circumstance is that the rule is legitimate. What makes the rule legitimate is, partly the substance of the rule: what it exacts and confers. This alone can relevantly command the free assent of the intelligent beings who are thus ruled, can alone move them freely to subject themselves to that rule by their acceptance of it as what they ought to submit to and observe. Whoever rules in a regular manner in the procedural sense, but without legitimate right, still rules arbitrarily in this stronger sense. [...]

In short, the rule of law is rule of a certain kind. It is that rule which is just. Therefore, it is legitimate and not arbitrary to require human beings to submit to it. This is both the oldest and the only defensible definition of the rule of law, which even the procedural conception falls within. For even the procedural conception accepts that only some kinds of putative legal process are sufficient to meet the procedural requirements of the rule of law, which procedural requirements are in fact moral requirements. [...]

It is a basic tenet of legal thought, at least in the West, that a ruling regime whose subjects are not obligated but only coerced to obey is not a regime of law. This fact is one additional reason that the rule of law cannot be reduced solely to regulated procedure, but must encompass the content and social relations of the ruling regime. Confronted with a regime that (let us suppose) aims at justice but does not achieve justice, the answer to the question "Is it still law?" is bound up with the question "Does it obligate?"

Yet the fact that a regime aims at justice does not establish that anyone is obligated to comply with it. On the contrary, it is entirely possible that a rule (or act) that aims at justice is nevertheless not just, and that one is in fact obligated to oppose it, despite the sincerity of the aim. In short, a conception of the rule of law as any regime that aims at justice appears manifestly inadequate, for the reason that what aims at justice does not *eo ipso* obligate, while law (as virtually everyone affirms) does obligate. It seems, therefore, that only the conception of the rule of law as rule that achieves justice is compatible with the dictum that law is not mere coercion but a structure of obligation.

REFERENCE RE MANITOBA LANGUAGE RIGHTS
[1985] I S.C.R. 721.

THE COURT: — [...] Section 23 of the Manitoba Act, 1870 provides:

> Either the English or the French language may be used by any person in the debates of the Houses of the Legislature, and both those languages shall be used in the respective Records and Journals of those Houses; and either of those languages may be used by any person, or in any Pleading or Process, in or issuing from any Court of Canada established under the *Constitutional Act, 1867*, or in or from all or any of the Courts of the Province. The Acts of the Legislature shall be printed and published in both those languages.

[Section 23 of the *Manitoba Act, 1870* was the result of years of struggle and co-existence between the English, the French and the Metis in Red River Colony, what is now known as the province of Manitoba. An attempt was made to unite the various segments of the Colony and a "Bill of Rights" was drawn up to be used in negotiations with Canada. A Convention of delegates made up of equal members of French and English was elected to prepare the terms on which the Colony would join the Confederation.

The final version of the Bill of Rights contained a clause stating that both the English and French languages be used in the Legislature and the courts, and that all public documents and Acts of the Legislature be published in both languages. This became s. 23 of the *Manitoba Act, 1870*. The *Manitoba Act, 1870* is now entrenched in the Constitution of Canada by virtue of s. 52(2)(b) of the *Constitution Act, 1982*.

In 1890 the Manitoba Legislature enacted the *Official Languages Act*, S.M. 1890, c. 14 which stated that the English language only need be used in the records and journals of the House of Assembly and that the Acts of the Legislature of the province of Manitoba need only be printed and published in English.

The *Official Languages Act* was challenged and ruled ultra vires but the ruling was not followed. The Act was attacked again in 1909 and 1976, and in both instances was ruled unconstitutional. Nevertheless, the 1890 Act remained on the books and in force. In 1979 the constitutionality of the *1890 Act* was challenged before the Supreme Court of Canada and was held unanimously to be unconstitutional.

After this decision, the Legislature of Manitoba continued to enact its statutes and regulations in English only, which raised questions, the subject of this Reference, as to the validity of all Manitoba Legislation.]

THE RULE OF LAW

1. The Principle

The difficulty with the fact that the unilingual Acts of the Legislature of Manitoba must be declared invalid and of no force or effect is that, without going further, a legal vacuum will be created with consequent legal chaos in the province of Manitoba. The Manitoba Legislature has, since 1890, enacted nearly all of its laws in English only. Thus, to find that the unilingual laws of Manitoba are invalid and of no force or effect would mean that only laws enacted in both French and English *before 1890*, would continue to be valid, and would still be in force even if the law had purportedly been repealed or amended by a post-1890 unilingual statute; matters that were not regulated by laws enacted before 1890 would now be unregulated by law, unless a pre-confederation law or the common law provided a rule.

The situation of the various institutions of provincial government would be as follows: the courts, administrative tribunals, public officials, municipal corporations, school boards, professional governing bodies, and all other bodies created by law, to the extent that they derive their existence from or purport to exercise powers conferred by Manitoba laws enacted since 1890 in English only, would be acting without legal authority.

Questions as to the validity of the present composition of the Manitoba Legislature might also be raised. [...]

Finally, all legal rights, obligations and other effects which have purportedly arisen under all Acts of the Manitoba Legislature since 1890 would be open to challenge to the extent that their validity and enforceability depends upon a regime of unconstitutional unilingual laws.

In the present case, declaring the Acts of the Legislature of Manitoba invalid and of no force or effect would, without more, undermine the principle of the Rule of Law. The Rule of Law, a fundamental principle of our Constitution, must mean at least two things. First, that the law is supreme over officials of the government as well as private individuals, and thereby preclusive of the influence of arbitrary power. Indeed, it is because of the supremacy of law over the government, as established in s. 23 of the *Manitoba Act, 1870* and s. 52 of the *Constitution Act, 1982*, that this Court must find the unconstitutional laws of Manitoba to be invalid and of no force and effect.

Second, the Rule of Law requires the creation and maintenance of an actual order of positive laws which preserves and embodies the more general principle of normative order. Law and order are indispensable elements of civilized life. "The Rule of Law in this sense implies[...] simply the existence of public order". (I. Jennings, *The Law and the Constitution*, 5th ed., 1959, at p. 43). As John Locke once said, "A government without laws is, I suppose, a mystery in politics, inconceivable to human capacity and inconsistent with human society". (quoted by Lord Wilberforce in *H.L. Carl Zeiss-Stiftung v. Rayner and Keeler Ltd. (No. 2)*, [1966] 2 All E.R. 536 at 577 (H.L.)). According to Wade and Phillips, *Constitutional and Administrative Law* (9th ed., 1977), at p. 89: "The Rule of Law expresses a preference for law and order within a community rather than anarchy, warfare and constant strife. In this sense, the Rule of Law is a philosophical view of society which in the Western tradition is linked with basic democratic notions".

It is this second aspect of the Rule of Law that is of concern in the present situation. The conclusion that the Acts of the Legislature of Manitoba are invalid and of no force or effect means that the positive legal order which has purportedly regulated the affairs of the citizens of Manitoba since 1890 will be destroyed and the rights, obligations and other effects arising under these laws will be invalid and unenforceable. As for the future, since it is reasonable to assume that it will be impossible for the Legislature of Manitoba to rectify *instantaneously* the constitutional defect, the Acts of the Manitoba Legislature will be invalid and of no force or effect until they are translated, re-enacted, printed and published in both languages.

Such results would certainly offend the Rule of Law. As we stated in the *Patriation Reference*, supra, at pp. 805-806 S.C.R.:

> The "rule of Law" is a highly textured expression [...] conveying, for example, *a sense of orderliness, of subjection to known legal rules* and of executive accountability to legal authority.

Dr. Raz has said: "'The rule of law' means literally what it says: the rule of the law [...] It has two aspects: (1) that people should be ruled by the law and obey it, and (2) that the law should be such that people will be able to be guided by it."

(*The Authority of Law*, (1979), at pp. 212-13). The Rule of Law simply cannot be fulfilled in a province that has no positive law.

The constitutional status of the Rule of Law is beyond question. The preamble to the *Constitution Act, 1982* states:

> Whereas Canada is founded upon principles that recognize the supremacy of God and the *rule of law*.

This is explicit recognition that "the rule of law [is] a fundamental postulate of our constitutional structure". (Per Rand J. *Roncarelli v. Duplessis*, [1959] S.C.R. 121 at 142, 16 D.L.R. (2d) 689). "The Rule of Law has always been understood as the very basis of the English Constitution, characterising the political institutions of England from the time of the Norman Conquest". (A.V. Dicey, *The Law of the Constitution*, 10th ed., 1959, at p. 183). It becomes a postulate of our own constitutional order by way of the preamble to the *Constitution Act, 1982*, and its implicit inclusion in the preamble to the *Constitution Act, 1867* by virtue of the words "with a Constitution similar in principle to that of the United Kingdom".

Steven Scott, Counsel for Alliance Quebec, Joseph Magnet, Counsel for Société Franco Manitobaine during argument of the Reference

Additional to the inclusion of the Rule of Law in the preambles of the Constitution Acts of 1867 and 1982, the principle is clearly implicit in the very nature of a Constitution. The Constitution, as the Supreme Law, must be understood as a purposive ordering of social relations providing a basis upon which an actual order of positive laws can be brought into existence. The founders of this nation must have intended, as one of the basic principles of nation building, that Canada be a society of legal order and normative structure: one governed by Rule of Law. While this is not set out in a specific provision, the principle of the Rule of Law is clearly a principle of our Constitution.

This Court cannot take a narrow and literal approach to constitutional interpretation. The jurisprudence of the Court evidences a willingness to supplement textual analysis with historical, contextual and purposive interpretation in order to ascertain the intent of the makers of our Constitution.

The Court has in the past inferred constitutional principles from the preambles to the Constitution Acts and the general object and purpose of the Constitution. [...] [I]n the process of constitutional adjudication, the Court may have regard to unwritten postulates which form the very foundation of the Constitution of Canada. In the case of the *Patriation Reference*, supra, this unwritten postulate was the principle of federalism. In the present case, it is the principle of Rule of Law.

2. Application of the Principle of the Rule of Law

It is clear from the above that: (i) the law as stated in s. 23 of the *Manitoba Act, 1870* and s. 52 of the *Constitution Act, 1982* requires that the unilingual Acts of the Manitoba Legislature be declared to be invalid and of no force or effect, and (ii) without more, such a result would violate the Rule of Law. The task the Court faces is to recognize the unconstitutionality of Manitoba's unilingual laws and the Legislature's duty to comply with the "supreme law" of this country, while avoiding a legal vacuum in Manitoba and ensuring the continuity of the Rule of Law. [...]

The only appropriate resolution to this Reference is for the Court to fulfill its duty under s. 52 of the *Constitution Act, 1982* and declare all the unilingual Acts of the Legislature of Manitoba to be invalid and of no force and effect and then to take such steps as will ensure the Rule of Law in the province of Manitoba.

There is no question that it would be impossible for all the Acts of the Manitoba Legislature to be translated, re-enacted, printed and published overnight. There will necessarily be a period of time during which it would not be possible for the Manitoba Legislature to comply with its constitutional duty under s. 23 of the *Manitoba Act, 1870*.

The vexing question, however, is what will be the legal situation in the province of Manitoba for the duration of this period. The difficulties faced by the province of Manitoba are two-fold: first, all of the rights, obligations and other effects which have arisen under the repealed, spent and current Acts of the Manitoba Legislature will be open to challenge, since the laws under which they purportedly arise are invalid and of no force or effect; and, second, the province of Manitoba has an invalid and therefore ineffectual legal system until the Legislature is able to translate, re-enact, print and publish its current Acts. [...]

The only appropriate solution for preserving the rights, obligations and other effects which have arisen under invalid Acts of the Legislature of Manitoba and which are not saved by the *de facto* or other doctrines is to declare that, in order to uphold the Rule of Law, these rights, obligations and other effects have, and will continue to have, the same force and effect they would have had if they had arisen under valid enactments, for that period of time during which it would be impossible for Manitoba to comply with its constitutional duty under s. 23 of the *Manitoba Act, 1870*. The province of Manitoba would be faced with chaos and anarchy if the legal rights, obligations and other effects which have been relied upon by the people of Manitoba since 1890 were suddenly open to challenge. The constitutional guarantee of Rule of Law will not tolerate such chaos and anarchy.

Nor will the constitutional guarantee of Rule of Law tolerate the province of Manitoba being without a valid and effective legal system for the present and future. Thus, it will be necessary to deem temporarily valid and effect the unilingual Acts of the Legislature of Manitoba which would be currently in force, were it not for their constitutional defect, for the period of time during which it would be impossible for the Manitoba Legislature to fulfill its constitutional duty. Since this temporary validation will include the legislation under which the

Manitoba Legislature is presently constituted, it will be legally able to re-enact, print and publish its laws in conformity with the dictates of the Constitution once they have been translated. [...]

The cases on the necessity doctrine in all three circumstances discussed above point to the same conclusion: the Courts will recognize unconstitutional enactments as valid where a failure to do so would lead to legal chaos and thus violate the constitutional requirement of the Rule of Law. [...]

The doctrine of necessity is not used in these cases to support some law which is above the Constitution; it is, instead used to ensure the unwritten but inherent principle of Rule of Law which must provide the foundation of any constitution.

In every case in which the doctrine of state necessity has been applied it has been either the executive or the legislative branch of government which has responded to the necessitous circumstances, later to have its actions tested in the courts. This fact does not, however, detract from the general relevance of these cases in demonstrating that the courts will not allow the Constitution to be used to create chaos and disorder.

Turning back to the present case, because of the Manitoba Legislature's persistent violation of the constitutional dictates of the *Manitoba Act, 1870*, the province of Manitoba is in a state of emergency: all of the Acts of the Legislature of Manitoba, purportedly repealed, spent and current (with the exception of those recent laws which have been enacted, printed and published in both languages), are and always have been invalid and of no force or effect, and the legislature is unable to immediately re-enact these unilingual laws in both languages. The Constitution will not suffer a province without laws. Thus, the Constitution requires that temporary validity and force and effect be given to the current Acts of the Manitoba Legislature from the date of this judgment, and that rights, obligations and other effects which have arisen under these laws and the repealed and spent laws of the province prior to the date of this judgment, which are *not* saved by the *de facto* or some other doctrine, are deemed temporarily to have been and continue to be effective and beyond challenge. It is only in this way that legal chaos can be avoided and the Rule of Law preserved.

To summarize, the legal situation in the province of Manitoba is as follows. All unilingually enacted Acts of the Manitoba Legislature are, and always have been, invalid and of no force or effect. All Acts of the Manitoba Legislature which would currently be valid and of force and effect, were it not for their constitutional defect, are deemed temporarily valid and effective from the date of this judgment to the expiry of the minimum period necessary for translation, re-enactment, printing and publishing. Rights, obligations and any other effects which have arisen under these current laws by virtue of reliance on acts of public officials, or on the assumed legal validity of public or private bodies corporate, are enforceable and forever beyond challenge under the *de facto* doctrine. The same is true of those rights, obligations and other effects which have arisen under current laws and are saved by doctrines such as *res judicata* and mistake of law.

Rights, obligations and any other effects which have arisen under purportedly repealed or spent laws by virtue of reliance on acts of public officials, or on the assumed legal validity of public or private bodies corporate are enforceable and forever beyond challenge under the *de facto* doctrine. The same is true of those rights, obligations and other effects which have arisen under purportedly repealed or spent laws and are saved by doctrines such as *res judicata* and mistake of law.

All rights, obligations and any other effects which have arisen under Acts of the Manitoba Legislature which are purportedly repealed, spent, or would currently be in force were it not for their constitutional defect, and which are not saved by the *de facto* doctrine, or doctrines such as *res judicata* and mistake of law, are deemed temporarily to have been, and to continue to be, enforceable and beyond challenge from the date of their creation to the expiry of the minimum period of time necessary for translation, re-enactment, printing and publishing of these laws. At the termination of the minimum period these rights, obligations and other effects will cease to have force and effect unless the Acts under which they arose and have been translated, re-enacted, printed and published in both languages. As a consequence, to ensure the continuing validity and enforceability of rights, obligations and any other effects not saved by the *de facto* or other doctrines, the repealed or spent Acts of the Legislature, under which these rights, obligations and other effects have purportedly arisen, may need to be enacted, printed and published, and then repealed, in both official languages.

As concerns the future, the Constitution requires that, from the date of this judgment, all new Acts of the Manitoba Legislature be enacted, printed and published in both French and English. Any Acts of the Legislature that do not meet this requirement will be invalid and of no force or effect.

THE DURATION OF THE TEMPORARY PERIOD

The difficult question, then, is what is the duration of the minimum period necessary for translation, re-enactment, printing and publishing of the unilingual Acts of the Manitoba Legislature? It was argued by the Attorney General of Canada and by the Fédération Des Francophones Hors Québec that this Court fix some arbitrary period such as a year or two years during which the Manitoba Legislature could re-enact its unilingual legislation in both languages.

This solution would not be satisfactory. We do not know how many of the Acts of the Legislature have already been translated. We know nothing as to the availability of translators or their daily output. We thus have no factual basis for determining a period during which compliance with s. 23 of the *Manitoba Act, 1870* would not be possible.

As presently equipped, the Court is incapable of determining the period of time during which it would not be possible for the Manitoba Legislature to comply with its constitutional duty. The Court will, however, at the request of either the Attorney General of Canada, or the Attorney General of Manitoba, made within one hundred and twenty days of the date of this judgment, make such a determination. The Attorney General of Canada was granted carriage of this *Reference* and the Attorney General of Manitoba represents the province whose laws are in issue in this case. Following such a request, a special hearing will be set and submissions will be accepted from the Attorney General of Canada and the Attorney General of Manitoba and the other intervenors.

The period of temporary validity will not apply to any unilingual Acts of the Legislature enacted after the date of judgment. From the date of judgment, laws which are not enacted, printed, and published in both languages will be invalid and of no force and effect *ab initio*.

Note: See supra. at p. 24, Reference Re Secession of Quebec, [1998] 2 S.C.R. 217, at paras. 67, 70-78, 95-6. There, the Supreme Court of Canada added further detail to the Rule of Law doctrine expounded in the *Patriation* and *Manitoba Language Rights References*.

BRITISH COLUMBIA V. IMPERIAL TOBACCO CANADA LTD. ET. AL.
[2005] 2 S.C.C. 49.

[The *Tobacco Damages and Health Care Costs Recovery Act* (the "Act") authorizes an action by the government of British Columbia against a manufacturer of tobacco products for the recovery of health care expenditures incurred by the government in treating individuals exposed to those products. The appellants were sued by the government pursuant to the Act, and challenged its constitutional validity, inter alia, on the grounds that it violated the rule of law.]

The judgment of the Court was delivered by

¶ 1 **MAJOR J.** — The *Tobacco Damages and Health Care Costs Recovery Act*, S.B.C. 2000, c. 30 (the "Act"), authorizes an action by the government of British Columbia against a manufacturer of tobacco products for the recovery of health care expenditures incurred by the government in treating individuals exposed to those products. Liability hinges on those individuals having been exposed to tobacco products because of the manufacturer's breach of a duty owed to persons in British Columbia, and on the government of British Columbia having incurred health care expenditures in treating disease in those individuals caused by such exposure.

¶ 2 These appeals question the constitutional validity of the Act. The appellants, each of which was sued by the government of British Columbia pursuant to the Act, challenge its constitutional validity on the basis that it violates (1) territorial limits on provincial legislative jurisdiction; (2) the principle of judicial independence; and (3) the principle of the rule of law....

¶ 5 Section 2(1) is the keystone of the Act. It reads:

> The government has a direct and distinct action against a manufacturer to recover the cost of health care benefits caused or contributed to by a tobacco related wrong...

¶ 14 Pursuant to s. 10, all provisions of the Act operate retroactively...

¶ 57 The rule of law is "a fundamental postulate of our constitutional structure" (*Roncarelli v. Duplessis*, [1959] S.C.R. 121, at p. 142) that lies "at the root of our system of government" (*Reference re Secession of Quebec*, [1998] 2 S.C.R. 217, at para. 70). It is expressly acknowledged by the preamble to the *Constitution Act, 1982*, and implicitly recognized in the preamble to the *Constitution Act, 1867*: see *Reference re Manitoba Language Rights*, [1985] 1 S.C.R. 721, at p. 750.

¶ 58 This Court has described the rule of law as embracing three principles. The first recognizes that "the law is supreme over officials of the government as well as private individuals, and thereby preclusive of the influence of arbitrary power": *Reference re Manitoba Language Rights*, at p. 748. The second "requires the creation and maintenance of an actual order of positive laws which preserves and embodies the more general principle of normative order": *Reference re Manitoba Language Rights*, at p. 749. The third requires that "the relationship between the state and the individual ... be regulated by law": *Reference re Secession of Quebec*, at para. 71.

¶ 59 So understood, it is difficult to conceive of how the rule of law could be used as a basis for invalidating legislation such as the Act based on its content. That is because none of the principles that the rule of law embraces speak directly to the terms of legislation. The first principle requires that legislation be applied to all those, including government officials, to whom it, by its terms, applies. The second principle means that legislation must exist. And the third principle, which overlaps somewhat with the first and second, requires that state officials' actions be legally founded....

¶ 60 This does not mean that the rule of law as described by this Court has no normative force. As McLachlin C.J. stated in *Babcock*, at para. 54, "unwritten constitutional principles", including the rule of law, "are capable of limiting government actions".... But the government action constrained by the rule of law as understood in *Reference re Manitoba Language Rights* and *Reference re Secession of Quebec* is, by definition, usually that of the executive and judicial branches. Actions of the legislative branch are constrained too, but only in the sense that they must comply with legislated requirements as to manner and form (i.e. the procedures by which legislation is to be enacted, amended and repealed).

¶ 61 Nonetheless, considerable debate surrounds the question of what additional principles, if any, the rule of law might embrace, and the extent to which they might mandate the invalidation of legislation based on its content. P. W. Hogg and C. F. Zwibel write in "The Rule of Law in the Supreme Court of Canada" (2005), 55 *U.T.L.J.* 715, at pp. 717-18:

> Many authors have tried to define the rule of law and explain its significance, or lack thereof. Their views spread across a wide spectrum.... T.R.S. Allan, for example, claims that laws that fail to respect the equality and human dignity of individuals are contrary to the rule of law. Luc Tremblay asserts that the rule of law includes the liberal principle, the democratic principle, the constitutional principle, and the federal principle. For Allan and Tremblay, the rule of law demands not merely that positive law be obeyed but that it embody a particular vision of social

justice. Another strong version comes from David Beatty, who argues that the "ultimate rule of law" is a principle of "proportionality" to which all laws must conform on pain of invalidity (enforced by judicial review). In the middle of the spectrum are those who, like Joseph Raz, accept that the rule of law is an ideal of constitutional legality, involving open, stable, clear, and general rules, even-handed enforcement of those laws, the independence of the judiciary, and judicial review of administrative action. Raz acknowledges that conformity to the rule of law is often a matter of degree, and that breaches of the rule of law do not lead to invalidity....

¶ 62   This debate underlies Strayer J.A.'s apt observation in *Singh v. Canada (Attorney General)*, [2000] 3 F.C. 185 (C.A.), at para. 33, that "[a]dvocates tend to read into the principle of the rule of law anything which supports their particular view of what the law should be".

¶ 63   The appellants' conceptions of the rule of law can fairly be said to fall at one extreme of the spectrum of possible conceptions and to support Strayer J.A.'s thesis. They submit that the rule of law requires that legislation (1) be prospective; (2) be general in character; (3) not confer special privileges on the government, except where necessary for effective governance; and (4) ensure a fair civil trial. And they argue that the Act breaches each of these requirements, rendering it invalid.

¶ 64   A brief review of this Court's jurisprudence will reveal that none of these requirements enjoy constitutional protection in Canada. But before embarking on that review, it should be said that acknowledging the constitutional force of anything resembling the appellants' conceptions of the rule of law would seriously undermine the legitimacy of judicial review of legislation for constitutionality. That is so for two separate but interrelated reasons.

¶ 65   First, many of the requirements of the rule of law proposed by the appellants are simply broader versions of rights contained in the *Charter*. For example, the appellants' proposed fair trial requirement is essentially a broader version of s. 11(d) of the *Charter*, which provides that "[a]ny person charged with an offence has the right ... to ... a fair and public hearing". But the framers of the *Charter* enshrined that fair trial right only for those "charged with an offence". If the rule of law constitutionally required that all legislation provide for a fair trial, s. 11(d) and its relatively limited scope (not to mention its qualification by s. 1) would be largely irrelevant because everyone would have the unwritten, but constitutional, right to a "fair ... hearing". (Though, as explained in para. 76, infra, the Act provides for a fair trial in any event.) Thus, the appellants' conception of the unwritten constitutional principle of the rule of law would render many of our written constitutional rights redundant and, in doing so, undermine the delimitation of those rights chosen by our constitutional framers. That is specifically what this Court cautioned against in *Reference re Secession of Quebec*, at para. 53:

Given the existence of these underlying constitutional principles, what use may the Court make of them? In [Reference re Remuneration of Judges of the Provincial Court of Prince Edward Island], at paras. 93 and 104, we cautioned that the recognition of these constitutional principles ... could not be taken as an invitation to dispense with the written text of the Constitution. On the contrary, we confirmed that there are compelling reasons to insist upon the primacy of our written constitution. A written constitution promotes legal certainty and predictability, and it provides a foundation and a touchstone for the exercise of constitutional judicial review. [Emphasis added.]

¶ 66   Second, the appellants' arguments overlook the fact that several constitutional principles other than the rule of law that have been recognized by this Court — most notably democracy and constitutionalism — very strongly favour upholding the validity of legislation that conforms to the express terms of the Constitution (and to the requirements, such as judicial independence, that flow by necessary implication from those terms). Put differently, the appellants' arguments fail to recognize that in a constitutional democracy such as ours, protection from legislation that some might view as unjust or unfair properly lies not in the amorphous underlying principles of our Constitution, but in its text and the ballot box....

¶ 67 The rule of law is not an invitation to trivialize or supplant the Constitution's written terms. Nor is it a tool by which to avoid legislative initiatives of which one is not in favour. On the contrary, it requires that courts give effect to the Constitution's text, and apply, by whatever its terms, legislation that conforms to that text.

¶ 68 A review of the cases showing that each of the appellants' proposed requirements of the rule of law has, as a matter of precedent and policy, no constitutional protection is conclusive of the appellants' rule of law arguments.

(1) Prospectivity in the Law

¶ 69 Except for criminal law, the retrospectivity and retroactivity of which is limited by s. 11(g) of the Charter, there is no requirement of legislative prospectivity embodied in the rule of law or in any provision of our Constitution. Professor P. W. Hogg sets out the state of the law accurately (in *Constitutional Law of Canada* (loose-leaf ed.), vol. 1, at p. 48-29):

> Apart from s. 11(g), Canadian constitutional law contains no prohibition of retroactive (or ex post facto laws). There is a presumption of statutory interpretation that a statute should not be given retroactive effect, but, if the retroactive effect is clearly expressed, then there is no room for interpretation and the statute is effective according to its terms. Retroactive statutes are in fact common...

¶ 71   The absence of a general requirement of legislative prospectivity exists despite the fact that retrospective and retroactive legislation can overturn settled expectations and is sometimes perceived as unjust: see E. Edinger, "Retrospectivity in Law" (1995), 29 U.B.C. L. Rev. 5, at p. 13. Those who perceive it as such can perhaps take comfort in the rules of statutory interpretation that require the legislature to indicate clearly any desired retroactive or retrospective effects. Such rules ensure that the legislature has turned its mind to such effects and "determined that the benefits of retroactivity [or retrospectivity] outweigh the potential for disruption or unfairness"...

¶ 72 It might also be observed that developments in the common law have always had retroactive and retrospective effect. Lord Nicholls of Birkenhead recently explained this point in *In re Spectrum Plus Ltd.*, [2005] 3 W.L.R. 58, [2005] UKHL 41, at para. 7:

> A court ruling which changes the law from what it was previously thought to be operates retrospectively as well as prospectively. The ruling will have a retrospective effect so far as the parties to the particular dispute are concerned, as occurred with the manufacturer of the ginger beer in Donoghue v Stevenson [1932] AC 562. When Mr Stevenson manufactured and bottled and sold his ginger beer the law on manufacturers' liability as generally understood may have been as stated by the majority of the Second Division of the Court of Session and the minority of their Lordships in that case. But in the claim Mrs Donoghue brought against Mr Stevenson his legal obligations fell to be decided in accordance with Lord Atkin's famous statements. Further, because of the doctrine of precedent the same would be true of everyone else whose case thereafter came before a court. Their rights and obligations would be decided according to the law as enunciated by the majority of the House of Lords in that case even though the relevant events occurred before that decision was given.

This observation adds further weight, if needed, to the view that retrospectivity and retroactivity do not generally engage constitutional concerns.

(2) Generality in the Law, Ordinary Law for the Government and Fair Civil Trials

¶ 73 Two decisions of this Court defeat the appellants' submission that the Constitution, through the rule of law, requires that legislation be general in character and devoid of special advantages for the government (except where necessary for effective governance), as well as that it ensure a fair civil trial.

¶ 74   The first is *Air Canada*. In it, a majority of this Court affirmed the constitutionality of 1981 amendments to the *Gasoline Tax Act*, 1948, R.S.B.C. 1960, c. 162, that retroactively taxed certain companies in the airline industry. The amendments were meant strictly to defeat three companies' claims, brought in 1980, for reimbursement of gasoline taxes paid between 1974 and 1976, the collection of which was ultra vires the legislature of British Columbia. The legislative amendments, in addition to being retroactive, were for the benefit of the Crown, aimed at a particular industry with readily identifiable members and totally destructive of that industry's ability to pursue successfully their claims filed a year earlier. Nonetheless, the constitutionality of those amendments was affirmed by a majority of this Court.

¶ 75 The second is *Authorson v. Canada (Attorney General)*, [2003] 2 S.C.R. 40, 2003 SCC 39, in which this Court unanimously upheld a provision of the *Department of Veterans Affairs Act*, R.S.C. 1985, c. V-1, aimed specifically at defeating certain disabled veterans' claims, the merits of which were undisputed, against the federal government. The claims concerned interest owed by the government on the veterans' benefit accounts administered by it, which interest it had not properly credited for decades. Though the appeal was pursued on the basis of the *Canadian Bill of Rights*, S.C. 1960, c. 44, the decision confirmed that it was well within Parliament's power to enact the provision at issue — despite the fact that it was directed at a known class of vulnerable veterans, conferred benefits on the Crown for "undisclosed reasons" (para. 62) and routed those veterans' ability to have any trial — fair or unfair — of their claims. See para. 15:

> The *Department of Veterans Affairs Act*, s. 5.1(4) takes a property claim from a vulnerable group, in disregard of the Crown's fiduciary duty to disabled veterans. However, that taking is within the power of Parliament. The appeal has to be allowed.

¶ 76 Additionally, the appellants' conception of a "fair" civil trial seems in part to be of one governed by customary rules of civil procedure and evidence. As should be evident from the analysis concerning judicial independence, there is no constitutional right to have one's civil trial governed by such rules. Moreover, new rules are not necessarily unfair. Indeed, tobacco manufacturers sued pursuant to the Act will receive a fair civil trial, in the sense that the concept is traditionally understood: they are entitled to a public hearing, before an independent and impartial court, in which they may contest the claims of the plaintiff and adduce evidence in their defence. The court will determine their liability only following that hearing, based solely on its understanding of the law as applied to its findings of fact. The fact that defendants might regard that law (i.e. the Act) as unjust, or the procedural rules it prescribes as unprecedented, does not render their trial unfair.

¶ 77 The Act does not implicate the rule of law in the sense that the Constitution comprehends that term. It follows that the Act is not unconstitutional by reason of interference with it.

V. Conclusion

¶ 78 The Act is constitutionally valid. The appeals are dismissed, with costs to the respondents throughout. Each constitutional question is answered "no"...

(c)   Limited Authority of Government Officials

RONCARELLI v. DUPLESSIS
[1959] S.C.R. 121.

RAND J. [Judson J. concurring]: — [...] The appellant was the proprietor of a restaurant in a busy section of Montreal which in 1946 through its transmission to him from his father had been continuously licensed for the sale of liquor for approximately 34 years; he is of good education and repute and the restaurant was of a superior class. On December 4 of that year, while his application for annual renewal was before the Liquor Commission, the existing license was canceled and his application for renewal rejected, to which was added a declaration by the respondent that no future license would ever issue to him. These primary facts took place in the following circumstances.

For some years the appellant had been an adherent of a rather militant Christian religious sect known as the Witnesses of Jehovah. Their ideology condemns the established church institutions and stresses the absolute and exclusive personal relation of the individual to the Deity without human intermediation or intervention.

The first impact of their proselytizing zeal upon the Roman Catholic church and community in Quebec, as might be expected, produced a violent reaction. Meetings were forcibly broken up, property damaged, individuals ordered out of communities, in one case out of the province, and generally, within the cities and towns, bitter controversy aroused. The work of the Witnesses was carried on both by word of mouth and by the distribution of printed matter, the latter including two periodicals known as "The Watch Tower" and "Awake", sold at a small price.

In 1945 the provincial authorities began to take steps to bring an end to what was considered insulting and offensive to the religious beliefs and feelings of the Roman Catholic population. Large scale arrests were made of young men and women, by whom the publications mentioned were being held out for sale, under local by-laws requiring a licence for peddling any kind of wares. Altogether almost one thousand of such charges were laid. The penalty involved in Montreal, where most of the arrests took place, was a fine of $40, and as the Witnesses disputed liability, bail was in all cases resorted to. [...]

Beyond the giving of bail and being an adherent, the appellant is free from any relation that could be tortured into a badge of character pertinent to his fitness or unfitness to hold a liquor licence. The mounting resistance that stopped the surety bail sought other means of crushing the propagandist invasion and among the circumstances looked into was the situation of the appellant. Admittedly an adherent, he was enabling these protagonists to be at large to carry on their campaign of publishing what they believed to be the Christian truth as revealed by the Bible; he was also the holder of a liquor licence, a "privilege" granted by the Province, the profits from which, as it was seen by the authorities, he was using to promote the disturbance of settled beliefs and arouse community disaffection generally. Following discussions between the then Mr. Archambault, as the personality of the Liquor Commission, and the chief prosecuting officer in Montreal, the former, on or about November 21, telephoned to the respondent, advised him of those facts, and queried what should be done. Mr. Duplessis answered that the matter was serious and that the identity of the person furnishing bail and the liquor licensee should be put beyond doubt. A few days later, that identity being established through a private investigator, Mr. Archambault again communicated with the respondent and, as a result of what passed between them, the licence, as of December 4, 1946, was revoked.

In the meantime, about November 25, 1946, a blasting answer had come from the Witnesses. In an issue of one of the periodicals, under the heading "Quebec's Burning Hate", was a searing denunciation of what was alleged to be the savage persecution of Christian believers. Immediately instructions were sent out from the department of the Attorney-General ordering the confiscation of the issue and proceedings were taken against one Boucher charging him with publication of a seditious libel.

It is then wholly as a private citizen, an adherent of a religious group, holding a liquor licence and furnishing bail to arrested persons for no other purpose than to enable them to be released from detention pending the determination of the charges against them, and with no other relevant considerations to be taken into account, that he is involved in the issues of this controversy.

The complementary state of things is equally free from doubt. From the evidence of Mr. Duplessis and Mr. Archambault alone, it appears that the action taken by the latter as the general manager and sole member of the Commission was dictated by Mr. Duplessis as Attorney-General and Prime Minister of the province; that that step was taken as a means of bringing to a halt the activities of the Witnesses, to punish the appellant for the part he had played not only by revoking the existing licence but in declaring him barred from one "forever", and to warn others that they similarly would be stripped of provincial "privileges" if they persisted in any activity directly or indirectly related to the Witnesses and to the objectionable campaign. The respondent felt that action to be his duty, something which his conscience demanded of him; and as representing the provincial government his decision became automatically that of Mr. Archambault and the Commission. [...]

In these circumstances, when the *de facto* power of the Executive over its appointees at will to such a statutory public function is exercised deliberately and intentionally to destroy the vital business interests of a citizen, is there legal redress by him against the person so acting? [...]

Section 35 [of *An Act Respecting Alcoholic Liquor*, R.S.Q. 1941, c. 255] [...] provides that the "Commission may cancel any permit at its discretion". [...]

The field of licensed occupations and businesses of this nature is steadily becoming of greater concern to citizens generally. It is a matter of vital importance that a public administration that can refuse to allow a person to enter or continue a calling which, in the absence of regulation, would be free and legitimate, should be conducted with complete impartiality and integrity; and that the grounds for refusing or canceling a permit should unquestionably be such and such only as are incompatible with the purposes envisaged by the statute: the duty of a Commission is to serve those purposes and those only. A decision to deny or cancel such a privilege lies within the "discretion" of the Commission, but that means that decision is to be based upon a weighing of considerations pertinent to the object of the administration.

In public regulation of this sort there is no such thing as absolute and untrammeled "discretion", that is that action can be taken on any ground or for any reason that can be suggested to the mind of the administrator; no legislative Act can, without express language, be taken to contemplate an unlimited arbitrary power exercisable for any purpose, however capricious or irrelevant, regardless of the nature or purpose of the statute. Fraud and corruption in the Commission may not be mentioned in such statutes but they are always implied as exceptions. "Discretion" necessarily implies good faith in discharging public duty; there is always a perspective within which a statute is intended to operate; and any clear departure from its lines or objects is just as objectionable as fraud or corruption. Could an applicant be refused a permit because he had been born in another province, or because of the colour of his hair? The ordinary language of the legislature cannot be so distorted.

The Hon. Maurice Duplessis speaking during the Quebec Legislative Assembly election campaign, July 1952.

To deny or revoke a permit because a citizen exercises an unchallengeable right totally irrelevant to the sale of liquor in a restaurant is equally beyond the scope of the discretion conferred. There was here not only revocation of the existing permit but a declaration of a future, definitive disqualification of the appellant to obtain one: it was to be "forever". This purports to divest his citizenship status of its incident of membership in the class of those of the public to whom such a privilege could be extended. [...] [W]hat could be more malicious than to punish this licensee for having done what he had an absolute right to do in a matter utterly irrelevant to the *Liquor Act*? Malice in the proper sense is simply acting for a reason and purpose knowingly foreign to the administration, to which was added here the element of intentional punishment by what was virtually vocation outlawry. [...]

The act of the respondent through the instrumentality of the Commission brought about a breach of an implied public statutory duty toward the appellant; it was a gross abuse of legal power expressly intended to punish him for an act wholly irrelevant to the statute, a punishment which inflicted on him, as it was intended to do, the destruction of his economic life as a restaurant keeper within the province. Whatever may be the immunity of the Commission or its member from an action for damages, there is none in the respondent. He was under no duty in relation to the appellant and his act was an intrusion upon the functions of a statutory body. The injury done by him was a fault engaging liability within the principles of the underlying public law of Quebec: *Mostyn v. Fabrigas,* and under art. 1053 of the Civil Code. That, in the presence of expanding administrative regulation of economic activities, such a step and its consequences are to be suffered by the victim without recourse or remedy, that an administration according to law is to be superseded by action dictated by and according to the arbitrary likes, dislikes and irrelevant purposes of public officers acting beyond their duty, would signalize the beginning of disintegration of the rule of law as a fundamental postulate of our constitutional structure. An administration of licences on the highest level of fair and impartial treatment to all may be forced to follow the practice of "first come, first served", which makes the strictest observance of equal responsibility to all of even greater importance; at this stage of developing government it would be a danger of high consequence to tolerate such a departure from good faith in executing the legislative purpose. It should be added, however, that that principle is not, by this language, intended to be extended to ordinary governmental employment: with that we are not here concerned.

It was urged by Mr. Beaulieu that the respondent, as the incumbent of an office of state, so long as he was proceeding in "good faith", was free to act in a matter of this kind virtually as he pleased. The office of Attorney-General traditionally and by statute carries duties that relate to advising the Executive, including here, administrative bodies, enforcing the public law and directing the administration of justice. In any decision of the statutory body in this case, he had no part to play beyond giving advice on legal questions arising. In that role his action should have been limited to advice on the validity of a revocation for such a reason or purpose and what that advice should have been does not seem to me to admit of any doubt. To pass from this limited scope of action to that of bringing about a step by the Commission beyond the bounds prescribed by the legislature for its exclusive action converted what was done into his personal act.

"Good faith" in this context, applicable both to the respondent and the general manager, means carrying out the statute according to its intent and for its purpose; it means good faith in acting with a rational appreciation of that intent and purpose and not with an improper intent and for an alien purpose; it does not mean for the purposes of punishing a person for exercising an unchallengeable right; it does not mean arbitrarily and illegally attempting to divest a citizen of an incident of his civil status.

[The concurring opinion of Martland J., with whom Kerwin C.J. concurred, has been omitted. The concurring opinion of Abbott J. has been omitted. The dissenting opinions of Taschereau, Cartwright and Fauteux JJ. have been omitted.]

R. v. CATAGAS
[1978] 1 W.W.R. 282, 81 D.L.R. (3D) 396 (MAN. C.A.).

FREEDMAN, C.J.M. [for the Court]: — In Maitland's classic work on *Constitutional History of England* (1909), Cambridge University Press, he discusses the subject of the Royal dispensing power as well as the allied subject of the Royal suspending power. These subjects take us back to the 17th century and earlier. They represent a dark chapter in English legal and constitutional history. They were a part of the struggle for sovereignty between the Crown and Parliament, a struggle in which, fortunately, Parliament emerged the victor, as exemplified by the enactment of the *Bill of Rights*, 1688, 1 Will. & Mar., c. 2.

The legal status of these powers today is well described in 7 Hals., 3rd ed., p. 230, para. 486, thus:

> 486. The Crown may not suspend laws or the execution of laws without the consent of Parliament; nor may it dispense with laws, or the execution of laws; and dispensations by *non obstante* of or to any statute or part thereof are void and of no effect, except in such cases as are allowed by statute.

That is clearly the law today. But Maitland's discussion centres upon a much earlier period when the Crown, as part of the Royal prerogative, suspended some laws and dispensed with obedience to others. The distinction between these two ancient powers may be briefly noted. By virtue of the suspending power the Crown suspended the operation of a duly enacted law of Parliament, and such suspension could be for an indefinite period. Very often the power was called into play in religious matters, James II frequently resorting to it for the purpose of annulling statutes which excluded Roman Catholics and others from office. But he was not always successful in his attempts, as will be recalled from the celebrated *Seven Bishops' Case* (1688), 12 State Tr. 183, on which it is not necessary to linger here.

Under the dispensing power the Crown purported to declare that a law enacted by Parliament would be inapplicable to certain named individuals or groups. By virtue of dispensation in their favour the law would not apply to them, but it would continue to apply to all others. It has been said that the dispensing power "was derived from the Papal practice of issuing bulls *non obstante statuto*, 'any law to the contrary notwithstanding": *Chalmers and Hood Phillips' Constitutional Laws of Great Britain*, 6th ed. (1946), p. 16.

To return to Maitland this is what he said about the suspending and dispensing powers (pp. 304-5):

> The Bill of Rights condemned absolutely the suspending power; its condemnation of the dispensing power was qualified. "The pretended power of dispensing with laws or the execution of laws by regal authority as it hath been assumed and exercised of late, is illegal." It would have been going too far to declare that every exercise of the dispensing power had been illegal – many private rights and titles must have been acquired on the faith of

dispensations. No attempt, however, was made to settle what dispensations had been legal; the words used were those which I have just read. As to the future, it was declared that no dispensation by *non obstante* of any statute shall be allowed, "except a dispensation be allowed of in such statute, and except in such cases as shall be specially provided for by one or more bill or bills, to be passed during this present session of parliament." There was some intention, at least among the lords, of passing an act defining in what cases dispensations should be valid: but the project fell to the ground – and so the words about a bill to be passed in the then session of parliament, never took effect. This is the last of the dispensing power.

"This is the last of the dispensing power." Maitland could never have thought that in the year 1968, nearly three centuries after the *Bill of Rights*, a certain departmental official of Manitoba, acting in fact or in law under the authority of his Minister, would purport to grant a dispensation in favour of a certain group, exempting them from obedience to a particular law to which all others continued to remain subject. That sorry episode must now be recounted.

Perhaps its proper starting point should be a reference to the case of *Daniels v. The Queen*, [1968] S.C.R. 517. That case concerned the right of an Indian to hunt game for food at all seasons of the year on all unoccupied Crown lands and on any other lands to which Indians might have a right of access. [...] If [...] the *Migratory Birds Convention Act* prevailed, the Indian would lose; and his loss would mean the loss also of all other Indians in the Prairie Provinces in similar situations to his.

The Supreme Court of Canada reached the conclusion that the *Migratory Birds Convention Act* prevailed. [...] So Daniels, the Indian in question, lost. He had hunted for and captured game birds out of season and he had these birds in his possession, contrary to the provisions of the *Act* and the Regulations thereunder. [...] Four of the nine Judges held that [...] Daniels [...] committed no offence. [...] But of course it is the judgment of the majority of the Court that is decisive, not that of the minority. [...]

The decision of the Supreme Court of Canada was delivered on April 29, 1968. Not many weeks later – on June 14, 1968 – a senior official of the Department of Mines and Natural Resources for the Province of Manitoba, under ministerial responsibility, announced to field staff the adoption of a policy whose avowed object was to overcome and negate the *Daniels* decision and to exempt Indians from compliance with the *Migratory Birds Convention Act*. In other words, it was a policy of dispensation in favour of Indians. [...]

The record makes it clear that this dispensation policy had the active concurrence of officialdom at the federal level. [...]

So what we have here is a clear case of the exercise of a purported dispensing power by executive action in favour of a particular group. Such a power does not exist. The dispensation which it sought to create was, in the words of Halsbury, "void and of no effect".

Two points must here be noted. The first is that the attempted dispensation was no doubt benevolent in purpose. It flowed from a recognition of the Indian's historic right to hunt game for food at all seasons of the year. But that was precisely the position taken by the minority Judges in the *Daniels* case. The purported dispensation would have given legal validity to the judgment of the minority and negated the judgment of the majority. And that of course cannot legally be done, no matter how sympathetic one may be towards the Indian and his hunting rights.

The other point is that nothing here stated is intended to curtail or affect the matter of prosecutorial discretion. [...] It is the particular facts of a given case that call that discretion into play. But that is a far different thing from the granting of a blanket dispensation in favour of a particular group or race. Today the dispensing power may be exercised in favour of Indians. Tomorrow it may be exercised in favour of Protestants, and the next day in favour of Jews. Our laws cannot be so treated. The Crown may not by Executive action dispense with laws. The matter is as simple as that, and nearly three centuries of legal and constitutional history stand as the foundation for that principle.

(d)   Separation of Powers

- Research Note -
THE SEPARATION OF POWERS

DEVELOPMENT OF THE DOCTRINE

The *separation of powers* doctrine was well developed in antiquity. Aristotle considered that the well-ordered constitution results from proper mixing of three factors: the deliberative body, the magistracies, and the judiciary (*Politics*, 1297b). The 'mixed' constitution was thought to conduce towards greater stability, an important value in a society characterized by constant warfare and frequent constitutional revision. Cicero added another important thought – that the mixed constitution keeps each of the three powers in check:

> For the primary forms already mentioned degenerate easily into
> the corresponding perverted forms, the king being replaced by
> a despot, the aristocracy by an oligarchical faction, and the
> people by a mob and anarchy; but whereas these forms are
> frequently changed into new ones, this does not usually happen
> in the case of the mixed and evenly balanced constitution; (Rep.,
> 1.69).

It was not until Montesquieu's great work, *L'Esprit des Lois,* that a vital connection was made between the separation of powers and political liberty. Montesquieu's study of ancient constitutions hardened his opinion "that every man invested with power is apt to abuse it." To prevent abuse of authority, he reasoned, it is necessary "that power should be a check to power." In order to achieve liberty under law, and to prevent concentration of power incompatible with liberty, the three departments of government must be separated.

> In order to have [political] liberty, it is requisite the government be so constituted as one man need not be afraid of another.
>
> When the legislative and executive powers are united in the same person, or in the same body of magistrates, there can be no liberty; because apprehensions may arise, lest the same monarch or senate should enact tyrannical laws, to execute them in a tyrannical manner.
>
> Again, there is no liberty, if the judiciary power be not separated from the legislative and executive. Were it joined with the legislative, the life and liberty of the subject would be exposed to arbitrary control; for the judge would be then the legislator. Were it joined to the executive power, the judge might behave with violence and oppression.
>
> There would be an end of everything, were the same man or the same body, whether of the nobles or of the people, to exercise those three powers, that of enacting laws, that of executing the public resolutions, and of trying the causes of individuals; (*The Spirit of the Laws* (1751), Bk. XI).

Montesquieu advocated a strict, formal separation of the three branches of government. Strict and formal, but not complete – the separation Montesquieu called for was a prohibition on the *same persons* exercising the whole powers of different branches. This would be the case, according to the American writers;

> if the king, who is the sole executive magistrate, had possessed also the complete legislative power, or the supreme administration of justice; or if the entire legislative body had possessed the supreme judiciary, or the supreme executive authority (*The Federalist*, no. 47).

The same persons should not exercise the whole powers of different branches. The authors of *The Federalist*, nos. 47-51 observed that Montesquieu's injunction would be respected by a constitution where the different departments "have not been kept absolutely separate and distinct," but where "some deviations from the principle" of separation were allowed. They had constructed and were defending a constitution where the different departments were separated formally, but connected functionally "as to give to each a constitutional control over the others." The object was to thwart the tendency of power to expand beyond "the limits assigned to it." *The Federalist*, no. 51 explained that the "partition of power among the several departments" was necessary both as "the means of keeping each other in their proper places" and also as "essential to the preservation of liberty" – the purposes established by the classical writers of antiquity. *The Federalist* evolved Montesquieu's formal separation, which prohibited the same persons from exercising different powers, into a functional separation where the different branches were both separated and connected in order to protect liberty. The means employed was to create for each department "a will of its own," so that power would be motivated to check power.

AMERICAN IMPLEMENTATION

This model of separated and divided powers was enthusiastically embraced in the design of the American Constitution. The American constitution created the "presidential model" of government. The presidential model establishes the most rigorous separation of powers in the history of government, with entrenched constitutional status and powers for each of the three branches of government. This model also contains 'deviations' from a pure separation model, 'deviations' which are intended to balance the power of each branch with 'constitutional control' by other branches.

In keeping with the separated but connected theory of *The Federalist*, the separate powers vested in each branch are made subject to a checking power in other branches. The President is invested with constitutional power to nominate departmental secretaries and judges, to command the armed forces and to make treaties. He is checked by constitutional power in the legislative branch to refuse to confirm presidential nominations, to declare war, to reject treaties and to impeach the President. The legislative branch is invested with constitutional power to enact all federal laws and to establish federal courts. The legislative branch is checked by constitutional power in the President to call the Congress into session, to veto any bill (subject to override by 2/3rds vote of both houses of Congress), and also by power in the judiciary to declare laws enacted unconstitutional. The Judicial branch has constitutional power to try federal cases, to interpret the laws in those cases and to declare any law or executive act unconstitutional. The judiciary is checked by power in the President to nominate its members; and also by power in the legislative branch to approve Presidential nominations, to impeach judges and to enact legislation, or propose constitutional amendments that overturn judicial decisions.

Any undue mixing of any two branches can be set aside as unconstitutional, as the United States Supreme Court explained in *Buckley v. Valeo*, 424 U.S. 1, 96 S. Ct. 612, 682 (1976).

> The Framers regarded the checks and balances that they had built into the tripartite Federal Government as a self-executing safeguard against the encroachment or aggrandizement of one branch at the expense of the other. As Madison put it in Federalist No. 51:

>> "This policy of supplying, by opposite and rival interests, the defect of better motives, might be traces through the whole system of human affairs, private as well as public. We see it particularly displayed in all the subordinate distributions of power, where the constant aim is to divide and arrange the several offices in such a manner as that each may be a check on the other – that the private interest of every individual may be sentinel over the public rights. These inventions of prudence cannot be less requisite in the distribution of the supreme powers of the State."

This Court has not hesitated to enforce the principle of separation of powers embodied in the Constitution when its application has proved necessary for the decisions of cases or controversies properly before it. The Court has held that executive or administrative duties of a nonjudicial nature may not be imposed on judges holding office under Art. III of the Constitution. The Court has held that the President may not execute and exercise legislative authority belonging only to Congress. *Youngstown Sheet & Tube Co. v. Sawyer, supra*. In the course of its opinion in that case, the Court said:

> "In the framework of our Constitution, the President's power to see that the laws are faithfully executed refutes the idea that he is to be lawmaker. The Constitution limits his functions in the lawmaking process to the recommending of laws he thinks wise and the vetoing of laws he thinks bad. And the Constitution is neither silent nor equivocal about who shall make laws which the President is to execute. The first section of the first article says that "All legislative Powers herein granted shall be vested in a Congress of the United States[...]" 343 U.S., at 587-588, 72 S.Ct., at 867.

This is a doctrine that has had to do much heavy lifting in the construction of American institutions in the last quarter century. The separation of powers significantly impacted the design of programs responding to many pressing American political concerns, and influenced the evolution of institutional relationships in American government. A sample of the institutions attacked by the separation of powers doctrine in the United States Supreme Court in the last twenty five years is startling: the power to appoint members of the Federal Election Commission, authority of the Comptroller General in a deficit reduction scheme, power to remove officials, congress-people participating in the administration of airports, the design of bankruptcy courts, the details of civil fraud actions for securities violations, the legislative veto and Presidential line item veto (all invalidated); establishment of an independent counsel in the executive branch, sentencing guidelines by a sentencing commission and the adjudication of common-law counter-claims by an administrative tribunal (all sustained).[1] Many more institutions collided with the separation of powers

---

1   *Buckley v. Valeo*, 424 U.S. 1 (1976) - elections; *Bowsher v. Synar*, 478 U.S. 714 (1986) - deficit; *Metropolitan Washington Airports Auth. v. Citizens for the Abatement of Aircraft Noise*, 501 U.S. 252 (1991) - airports; *Northern Pipeline Constr. Co. v. Marathon Pipe Line Co.*, 458 U.S. 50 (1982) - bankruptcy; *Plaut v. Spendthrift Farm*, 514 U.S. 211 (1995)- fraud; *INS v. Chadha*, 462 U.S. 919 (1983) - legislative veto; *Clinton v. City of New York*, 524 U.S. 417 (1998) - line item veto; *Morrison v. Olson*, 487 U.S. 654 (1988) - independent prosecutor; *Mistretta v. United States*, 488 U.S. 361 (1989) - sentencing; *Commodity Futures Trading Comm'n v. Schor*, 478 U.S. 833 (1986) - counter-claims.

doctrine in the lower courts. The separation model also continues to be significant for expounding those doctrines which are meant to shield the president from the judiciary – the 'executive privilege' doctrine, and the Presidential immunity theory. The Supreme Court cases on this branch of the doctrine led directly to the resignation of President Nixon and the impeachment of President Clinton.[1] In the *Line Item Veto case*, which entitled the President, on specified grounds, to cancel portions of statutes enacted by Congress, the Supreme Court described the separation of powers issue as "profoundly important." The cancellation authority that the *Act* vested in the President offended procedures governing the enactment of statutes. The relationships established by these procedures, said the Court, were a "single, finely wrought" system.

The United States Supreme Court's work on the separation of powers is carried out in the context of a presidential system of government. Presidential systems characterize a small minority – about 15% – of countries in the family of the democracies: see A. Lijphart, *Patterns of Democracy: Government Forms and Performance in Thirty-Six Countries* (1999). The constitutions of the presidential democracies establish an executive power that is very unique, in that it is (1) elected for a constitutionally prescribed period not dependent on the confidence of the legislative branch; (2) popularly elected as opposed to being selected by the legislative branch; (3) one-person, non collegial executives. These three elements stand in marked contrast to the constitution of executive power in parliamentary democracies. In the parliamentary systems of government the executive power (1) has no fixed term, but depends on the confidence of the legislative branch; (2) is not popularly elected but blooms from the legislative branch; (3) has a high (if varying) degree of collegiality.

Because presidential systems are so particular, it is difficult to transport the separation of powers doctrine elaborated in presidential systems to parliamentary systems without careful adaptation.

Nevertheless, the purposes served by the separation of powers doctrine – checking power and protecting liberty – will always have their champions. It is thus relevant to consider to what extent these purposes pursued in presidential systems can or should be pursued by constructing a closely similar doctrine for Parliamentary systems of government.

Before we delve into this complicated problem, some objections to the separation model should be considered.

---

1   *United States v. Nixon*, 418 U.S. 683 (1974); *Nixon v. Fitzgerald*, 457 U.S. 731 (1982); and *Clinton v. Jones*, 520 U.S. 681 (1997).

MODERN CRITICS

The separation of powers doctrine is controversial. Michel Troper, *The Development of the Notion of Separation of Powers* (1992), 26 Israel L. Rev. 1 observed that critics of the doctrine:

> emphasize first of all the conflict between the principle of separation of powers and the unity and indivisibility of sovereignty. How is it conceivable that sovereignty be thus divided into three distinct powers? Either the division is impossible and the unity of sovereignty is maintained, or the division is possible and sovereignty is destroyed. Any attempt to reconcile between the two principles can but founder into bad metaphysics.

> Secondly, critics of separation of powers point out the principle's inefficacy and its inability to protect liberty. Any imperfection in the equilibrium between the powers, and the domination of one of them, is fatal, it is claimed, to the cause of liberty; and even if the powers are able to check one another, the inevitable result is a paralysis of the state, which in turn leads to anarchy or coups d'état. Invoked as an example to support this proposition is the directorate regime of the year III, which knew a series of coups d'état and in the end succumbed.

> Finally, the separation of powers is set opposite the principle of democracy: if the legislative power is in the hands of the people's elected representatives, any mechanism which allows another power, executive or judicial, to effectively oppose the legislative power is by hypothesis antidemocratic. The liberty of the people is realized through the exercise of power, not through its limitation.

Bruce Ackerman, *The New Separation of Powers* (2000), 113 Harv. L. Rev. 633, at p. 640 ff. added insights from comparative constitutional law. The model of separated power, he pointed out, is implemented in order to pursue three values: democracy (or self-government), promoting professional competence and bureaucratic impartiality, and enhancing fundamental rights. Support for the doctrine must stand or fall on the success its implementation has had in promoting these values.

Ackerman believed that presidential separationism works well in United States, largely because of atypical American traditions and the system's "deep roots in American culture". He observed that attempts to export it to other countries have "proved nothing less than disastrous." Interestingly, Ackerman also rejected the typical foil to American style separationism – the British model of concentrating power in the House of Commons, which gives "the Prime Minister and her Cabinet effective control over the legislative agenda." Ackerman proffered "constrained parliamentarism," as a model of a "new" separation of powers. Investigation of the new model "has only just begun," nevertheless, It is possible to see that the powers of parliament may be constrained by other institutions of democratic self-government, including popular referenda and the representation of provincial governments in federal systems;" (pp. 640-2). Canada is one of the examples Ackerman examined (briefly) in order to add these institutions to the inventory of separationism's techniques.

Ackerman concluded that "the separation of powers is a good idea, but there is no reason to suppose that the classical writers have exhausted its goodness." He summarized his theory of constrained parliamentarism in this way:

> At the centerpiece of my model of constrained parlia-mentarianism is a democratically elected house in charge of selecting a government and enacting ordinary legislation. The power of this center is checked and balanced by a host of special-purpose branches, each motivated by one or more of the three basic concerns of separationist theory.
>
> From the side of democratic legitimacy, the center is constrained by the previous decisions of the people rendered through serial referenda and enforced by a constitutional court. It may also be checked by a subordinate federal senate or a more powerful second chamber organized on national lines.
>
> From the side of functional specialization, the center is constrained not only by an independent court system, but also by an integrity branch scrutinizing the government for corruption and similar abuses, as well as a regulatory branch forcing the bureaucracy to explain how its supplemental rulemaking will actually improve upon the results generated by the invisible hand.
>
> From the side of liberal rights, the center is constrained by a democracy branch seeking to safeguard each citizen's participatory rights, a distributive justice branch focusing on minimum economic provision for those citizens least able to defend their rights politically, and a constitutional court dedicated to the protection of fundamental human rights for all.
>
> At first glance, this may seem like an overly complicated structure. But is this first impression merely a product of the scheme's novelty? ... my model hives off a number of special functions from direct parliamentary control without generating the pervasive bureaucratic disruptions characteristic of the American system.... is there any good reason to suppose that a sensible modern government should divide power among only three or four branches? (pp. 727-8)

THE SEPARATION OF POWERS IN CANADA

Separatism and Parliamentarism

Canada's system of government is based on a parliamentary model quite distinct from the presidential system operating in the United States. One of our leading constitutional writers said that Canada's retention of the British system of responsible government is "utterly inconsistent with any separation of the executive and legislative functions;" (Hogg, *Constitutional Law of Canada*, 1999 student ed., p. 321). While this is one important view, it has never been approved by the Supreme Court of Canada. Indeed, the Supreme Court of Canada has made passing reference to the doctrine of the separation of powers in several cases, including *Fraser v. P.S.S.R.B.*, [1985] 2 S.C.R. 455, 479 and *Provincial Judges Reference*, [1997] 3 S.C.R. 3 at para. 108. On occasion, the Court has used muscular language, as in *Operation Dismantle v. The Queen*, [1985] 1 S.C.R. 441, 491 when the Court referred to the doctrine as one of the "essential features of our constitution". In *R. v. Power*, below, the separation of powers was actually harnessed by the court for use as an operative doctrine to reinforce the independence of Crown Attorney decisions as against judicial interference with prosecutorial decisions.

Because Canadian parliamentary democracy increasingly trends towards power concentration in the executive branch – a tendency that has disturbed many observers – it may be time to reconsider the corrective role that could be played by the separation of powers theory in Canadian constitutional doctrine.

Constitutional Convention, Branch Fusion and the Democratic Deficit

First, we need to understand how it is that parliamentary government fuses the legislative and the executive branches. In a parliamentary system the executive springs from the legislature, is part of it and is responsible to it as a confidence chamber.

> The Lieutenant-Governor is part and parcel of the Legislature (*B.N.A. Act*, s. 71; the *Legislature Act*, R.S.Q. 1977, c. L-1, s. 1). He appoints members of the Executive Council and Ministers (*B.N.A. Act*, s. 63; Executive Power Act, R.S.Q. 1977, c. E-18, ss. 3 to 5) and these, according to constitutional principles of a customary nature referred to in the preamble of the *B.N.A. Act* as well as in some statutory provisions (*Executive Power Act*, R.S.Q. 1977, c. E-18, ss. 3 to 5, 7 and 11(1); *Legislature Act*, R.S.Q. 1977, c. L-1, s. 56(1)), must be or become members of the Legislature and are expected, individually and collectively, to enjoy the confidence of its elected branch. There is thus a considerable degree of integration between the Legislature and the Government; (*Blaikie v. A.G. Quebec (No. 2)* (1981), 123 D.L.R. (3d) 15 at 122 (S.C.C.)).

Although *Blaikie* dealt specifically with the provincial executive power, the Court's description applies equally to the federal executive. The Court's observations in *Blaikie* are interesting because the Court focuses on the institutions of parliamentary government established by constitutional convention, particularly the institutions of responsible government. It is at the conventional level that integration between the executive and legislative branches occurs.

Constitutional convention enhances integration between the legislature and executive in two respects. First, the formal executive, the Governor General, is controlled by responsible ministers of the Crown, creatures unknown to the formal constitution. Second, the legislature's powers and priorities are in practice controlled by other executive instrumentalities unknown to the formal constitution – the PMO (office of the Prime Minister), PCO (Privy Council Office) and Cabinet. These institutions, particularly PMO and PCO, act as a clutch that meshes the gears of formal constitutional institutions into the full force of operating political power. Donald Savoie, *Governing From the Centre: The Concentration of Power in Canadian Politics* (1999) describes the real situation.

> Central agencies stand at the apex of the machinery of government.... they have a licence to roam wherever they wish and to raise whatever issue they may choose; (p. 5) ... The prime minister alone thus has access to virtually every lever of power in the federal government, and when he put his mind to it he can get his way on almost any issue; (p. 87).

In other words, the central agencies, particularly PMO, PCO and, to a lesser extent, Cabinet, are the conventional executive. It is the conventional executive which in practice controls the legislature, and which allows the writers to speak about the integration between the executive and legislature.

> The Queen of Canada is our head of state, and under our Constitution she is represented in most capacities within the federal sphere by the Governor General. The Governor General's executive powers are of course exercised in accordance with constitutional conventions. For example, after an election he asks the appropriate party leader to form a government. Once a government is in place, democratic principles dictate that the bulk of the Governor General's powers be exercised in accordance with the wishes of the leadership of that government, namely the Cabinet. So the true executive power lies in the Cabinet. And since the Cabinet controls the government, there is in practice a degree of overlap among the terms "government", "Cabinet" and "executive". In these reasons, I have used all of these terms, as one or another may be more appropriate in a given context. The government has the power to introduce legislation in Parliament.

In practice, the bulk of the new legislation is initiated by the government. By virtue of s. 54 of the *Constitution Act, 1867*, a money bill, including an amendment to a money bill, can only be introduced by means of the initiative of the government; (*Reference Re Canada Assistance Plan*, [1991] 2 S.C.R. 525, *per* Sopinka, J.).

It is at the conventional level, not the formal level or the text of the constitution, that the operation of Canada's constitution exhibits a high degree of integration between the executive and legislative branches of government. At the conventional level, where the constitution actually functions, it is accurate to say that Canadian government is characterized by a high degree of control by the executive over the legislative branch, particularly as contrasted with presidential systems. It is perhaps this situation that was in the mind of the Supreme Court of Canada when it commented that "the Canadian Constitution does not insist on a strict separation of powers;" (*Reference Re Secession of Quebec*, S.C.C. Aug. 20, 1998, para 15).

It is also at the level of the operating conventional constitution that the writers observe worrisome signals of a deterioration in accountability and transparency of governmental processes – what is commonly referred to as the democratic deficit. The democratic deficit is enhanced by the extensive use of executive federalism to coordinate the actions of the thirteen governments in the federation. Executive federalism, the negotiation of issues of the day between senior officials and ministers, takes place behind closed doors; it is not visible. For this reason Canadian governance tends to be unduly secretive, and lacking in reliable structures of accountability. Also, despite the pre-eminent role central agencies play in government

> we know very little about central agencies, about what they do, why they do it, and how they do it.... there is evidence to suggest that elected politicians themselves do not fully understand how the machinery of government or bureaucracy actually works even after several years in office; (Savoie, supra., p. 5).

Given the simultaneous growth of Canada's democratic deficit and the concentration of political power in somewhat mysterious central agencies, it is not surprising that there should be a renewed interest in the separation of powers. It is at root a concept designed to guard against tyrannical concentrations of power and to protect political liberty.

The Formal Constitution and Separationism

The conventional machinery that integrates the executive and legislative branches in Canada obscures the very real structural separation of powers that the text of the constitution ordains. The *Constitution Act, 1867* sets out separate and divided powers that, at least textually and formally, have close parallels to presidentialism. *Blaikie* drew attention to this. After describing the conventional machinery which integrates the legislative and executive branches, the Supreme Court went on to observe:

> The Government of the province is not a body of the Legislature's own creation. It has a constitutional status and is not subordinate to the Legislature in the same sense as other provincial legislative agencies established by the Legislature (*Blaikie v. A.G. Quebec (No. 2)* (1981), 123 D.L.R. (3d) 15 at 122 (S.C.C.)).

It is useful to elaborate further on the Court's observations about formal separation and conventional integration. The *Constitution Act, 1867* establishes executive power by ss. 9-16. These provisions vest the executive power in the Queen, and call for its exercise by the Governor General and Privy Council. The *Constitution Act, 1867* establishes significant power in the executive branch, including, by s. 15, the command of the armed forces. *The Constitution Act, 1867* identifies and organizes separate constitutional status as well for the legislature (sections 17-52) and judiciary (sections 96-101) and specifies their respective powers and limits.

This is why it is accurate to say that, at least textually and formally, the *Constitution Act, 1867* has close parallels to presidentialism. Although the realities of conventional integration have made Canada's formal separation of powers little noticed, it is worth remembering that within the text of the *Constitution Act, 1867*, powers *are* formally and structurally separated, as we find in presidential systems. This provides a textual basis for any court that in future decides to improvise a separation of powers doctrine specific to Canada's parliamentary system.

It is also worth remembering that within the text of the *Constitution Act, 1867* the three branches of government are connected functionally "as to give to each a constitutional control over the others." Parliament is invested with constitutional power to enact all federal laws and to establish federal courts. Parliament is checked by the power of the executive to call the House of Commons into session (s. 38) and by the power of the judiciary to declare laws enacted unconstitutional. Parliament is also checked by power in the executive to reserve Bills passed by the Houses of Parliament and to disallow laws enacted (secs. 55-7). These veto-like powers, designed for British control of Canadian law-making, have long since fallen into disuse, but they still exist in the text and structure of the Constitution. The Judicial branch has constitutional power to try all cases, to interpret the laws in those cases and to declare any law or executive act unconstitutional. The judiciary is checked by power in the executive to appoint its members; by power in the legislature to enact amendments that overturn judicial decisions, including many constitutional decisions (*Charter of Rights*, s. 33); and also by the combined power of the executive and legislative branches to remove judges.

The Constitution of Ceylon is drawn from the same British colonial sources as the Constitution of Canada. It is interesting to observe in that Constitution's structure a closely similar formal constitutional separation of powers. It was this structural separation, which, setting out executive, legislative and judicial powers in separate chapters that motivated the Privy Council to find "an intention to secure in the judiciary a freedom from political, legislative and executive control." Because of that intention their Lordships overturned special legislation that would have intruded the legislative power too deeply into the judicial sphere (*Liyanage v. The Queen*, [1967 1 A.C. 259). Perhaps this ruling is further evidence that the separation of powers doctrine is capable of more operational development in parliamentary systems, including Canada. Indeed, there is some dicta in this case which shapes Canada's important doctrine of judicial independence out of separationist language.

Constitutional Dialogue and the Separation of Powers

Still, beyond protecting the independence of the judiciary, it is unusual to conceive of the separation of powers doctrine as an operative doctrine that controls any undue mixing of the three branches in parliamentary systems of government. However, it has become common in constitutional doctrine to conceive that the institutions of government have proper roles to play in Canadian democracy. In carrying out their functions, each branch should have proper regard and "mutual respect" for the role of the other branches:

> respect by the courts for the legislature and executive role is as important as ensuring that the other branches respect each others' role and the role of the courts; (*Vriend v. Alberta*, [1998] 1 S.C.R. 493, para. 136).

In modern constitutional doctrine, the rise of this mutual respect "gives rise to a more dynamic interaction among the branches of government," what is also called "a dialogue" between the institutions of government.

> In reviewing legislative enactments and executive decisions to ensure consti- tutional validity, the courts speak to the legislative and executive branches. ... most of the legislation held not to pass constitutional muster has been followed by new legislation designed to accomplish similar objectives ... By doing this, the legislature responds to the courts; hence the dialogue among the branches; (para. 138).

An important value of this mutual respect, dynamic interaction and dialogue is that "each of the branches is made somewhat accountable to the other."

> This dialogue between and accountability of each of the
> branches have the effect of enhancing the democratic
> process (para. 139)

In *Mills*, this perspective of dynamic interaction was applied to alter the normal suspicious posture reviewing courts sometimes adopt with respect to legislative acts alleged to be unconstitutional.

> Courts do not hold a monopoly on the protection and
> promotion of rights and freedoms; Parliament also
> plays a role in this regard and is often able to act as a
> significant ally for vulnerable groups.... If
> constitutional democracy is meant to ensure that due
> regard is given to the voices of those vulnerable to
> being overlooked by the majority, then this court has an
> obligation to consider respectfully Parliament's
> attempt to respond to such voices; (*R. v. Mills*, [1993] 3
> S.C.R. 668).

Dialogue and dynamic interaction may be newly minted constitutional doctrine to explain to the citizenry why courts are sometimes obliged to overturn policies enacted into law by the representative branch. This is legitimacy theory, consciously meant to blunt attack on the constitutional review function repeatedly heard from the right and left. It is interesting to note that this theory is wrapped in separationism concepts. Is this really part of the sculpting of a separation of powers theory appropriate to parliamentary systems? To ask the question in other terms, is there anything in this separation of powers talk from the courts that can respond to the real problem that Canadian governance confronts today – democratic deficits being rung up by the fusing of political power in executive agencies?

Trend Lines

In the *Provincial Judges Reference*, [1997] 3 S.C.R. 3 the Supreme Court observed:

> ¶138 These different components of the institutional financial
> security of the courts inhere, in my view, in a fundamental
> principle of the Canadian Constitution, the separation of
> powers. As I discussed above, the institutional independence of
> the courts is inextricably bound up with the separation of
> powers, because in order to guarantee that the courts can
> protect the Constitution, they must be protected by a set of
> objective guarantees against intrusions by the executive and
> legislative branches of government.

¶139 The separation of powers requires, at the very least, that some functions must be exclusively reserved to particular bodies: see *Cooper, supra,* at para. 13. However, there is also another aspect of the separation of powers -- the notion that the principle requires that the different branches of government only interact, as much as possible, in particular ways. In other words, the relationships between the different branches of government should have a particular <u>character</u>. For example, there is a hierarchical relationship between the executive and the legislature, whereby the executive must execute and implement the policies which have been enacted by the legislature in statutory form: see *Cooper, supra,* at paras. 23 and 24. In a system of responsible government, once legislatures have made political decisions and embodied those decisions in law, it is the constitutional duty of the executive to implement those choices.

¶140 What is at issue here is the character of the relationships between the legislature and the executive on the one hand, and the judiciary on the other. These relationships should be depoliticized. When I say that those relationships are <u>depoliticized</u>, I do not mean to deny that they are political in the sense that court decisions (both constitutional and non-constitutional) often have political implications, and that the statutes which courts adjudicate upon emerge from the political process. What I mean instead is the legislature and executive cannot, and cannot appear to, exert political pressure on the judiciary, and conversely, that members of the judiciary should exercise reserve in speaking out publicly on issues of general public policy that are or have the potential to come before the courts, that are the subject of political debate, and which do not relate to the proper administration of justice.

¶141 To be sure, the depoliticization of the relationships between the legislature and the executive on the one hand, and the judiciary on the other, is largely governed by convention. And as I said in *Cooper, supra,* at para. 22, the conventions of the British Constitution do not have the force of law in Canada: *Reference re Resolution to Amend the Constitution, supra.* However, to my mind, the depoliticization of these relationships is so fundamental to the separation of powers, and hence to the Canadian Constitution, that the provisions of the Constitution, such as s. 11(d) of the *Charter,* must be interpreted in such a manner as to protect this principle.

This is a more developed idea of the role of the courts as resolver of disputes, interpreter of the law and defender of the Constitution that the Supreme Court explained earlier. In *R. v. Beauregard,* [1986] 2 S.C.R. 56, 73 the Court required that as a result of these functions, the courts be completely separate in authority and function from *all* other participants in the justice system.

Doucet-Boudreau v. Nova Scotia, [2003] 3 S.C.R. 3, reproduced below, swims in the current animated by many of the ideas canvassed in this note. The majority and minority debate what version of the separation of powers is appropriate for Canada's Parliamentary system. In so doing the Court helps to illuminate the ideas discussed here better.

R. V. POWER
[1994] I S.C.R. 601.

[The accused was charged with impaired driving causing death, and two counts of impaired driving causing bodily harm. The trial judge held that the accused's right to counsel under s. 10(b) of the *Charter* was violated because the accused was not advised of the specific charges against him. The trial judge excluded the breathalyzer certificate evidence under s. 24(2). The Crown elected not to call other evidence of impairment. The trial judge directed the jury to return a verdict of acquittal. The Crown appealed. The Newfoundland Court of Appeal, Goodridge, C.J.N., dissenting, dismissed the appeal. The Court of Appeal held that although the trial judge erred in finding that the accused's right to counsel was violated, the Crown was nevertheless precluded from appealing because of it's election to not proceed with the trial by calling other evidence. The Court of Appeal held that this failure to call further evidence constituted an abuse of process. The Crown appealed to the Supreme Court of Canada, claiming the Court of Appeal erred in not ordering a new trial.]

L'HEUREUX-DUBÉ J. [La Forest, Gonthier and McLachlin JJ. Concurring] —: [...] I cannot agree with my colleague [Sopinka J.] that s. 686(4) of the *Code* confers any discretion on a court of appeal other than the discretion to dismiss or allow an appeal. In particular, I cannot agree, as a matter of law, principle and policy, that a court of appeal is empowered to inquire into prosecutorial discretion.

Section 686(4) of the *Criminal Code* reads as follows:

> 686.(4) Where an appeal is from an acquittal, the court of appeal may
>> (a) dismiss the appeal; or
>> (b) allow the appeal, set aside the verdict and
>>> (i) order a new trial, or
>>> (ii) except where the verdict is that of a court composed of a judge and jury, enter a verdict of guilty with respect to the offence of which, in its opinion, the accused should have been found guilty but for the error in law, and pass a sentence that is warranted in law, or remit the matter to the trial court and direct the trial court to impose a sentence that is warranted in law. ...

[I]n criminal cases, courts have a residual discretion to remedy an abuse of the court's process but only in the "clearest of cases", which, in my view, amounts to conduct which shocks the conscience of the community and is so detrimental to the proper administration of justice that it warrants judicial intervention.

To conclude that the situation "is tainted to such a degree" and that it amounts to one of the "clearest of cases", as the abuse of process has been characterized by the jurisprudence, requires overwhelming evidence that the proceedings under scrutiny are unfair to the point that they are contrary to the interest of justice. As will be developed in more detail further in these reasons, the Attorney General is a member of the executive and as such reflects, through his or her prosecutorial function, the interest of the community to see that justice is properly done. The Attorney General's role in this regard is not only to protect the public, but also to honour and express the community's sense of justice. Accordingly, courts should be careful before they attempt to "second-guess" the prosecutor's motives when he or she makes a decision. Where there is conspicuous evidence of improper motives or of bad faith or of an act so wrong that it violates the conscience of the community, such that it would genuinely be unfair and indecent to proceed, then, and only then, should courts intervene to prevent an abuse of process which could bring the administration of justice into disrepute. Cases of this nature will be extremely rare.

Applying this test to the facts of this case, it is evident that in no way did the conduct of the prosecution meet the high threshold required to constitute an abuse of process. There is not one iota of evidence that the Crown prosecutor's conduct was prompted by bad faith or an improper motive, a fact recognized by Cameron J.A., nor did the prosecution intend to frustrate the administration of justice or even to circumvent the rules of criminal law regarding interlocutory appeals. [...]

That the Crown prosecutor may have acted precipitously or may have exercised poor judgment in deciding not to adduce further evidence, even if true, fails to establish misconduct of such a nature as to shock the community's sense of fairness or to warrant the application of the doctrine of abuse of process. [...]

[M]y colleague [states] [...] at p. 646, "there is support in our jurisprudence for a limited discretion on the part of the Court of Appeal to decline to allow an appeal in some circumstances in which the Crown unreasonably shuts down its case with the result that a verdict of acquittal is directed". I respectfully disagree. [...]

In holding that under s. 686(4) of the *Code* an appellate court is entitled to consider whether the Crown has acted unreasonably, my colleague invites the courts of appeal to invade the exclusive domain of the Crown and to interfere with prosecutorial discretion, as well as to foster rulings based on pure speculation as to what might have happened had the prosecution chosen a different path. This, in my view, is not only impermissible and contrary to the rule of law but also contrary to the interest in a good and efficient administration of justice. [...]

My colleague himself, at p. 649, alluding to the type of discretion he sees in s. 686(4) of the *Criminal Code*, warns that courts "should be mindful of the fact that exercising this power must be done sparingly in that it constitutes a review of prosecutorial discretion". This, at a minimum, indicates the danger with which such interference by courts is fraught. There are other dangers, not the least of which involves the possibility of interfering with the separation of powers under our constitution.

In contrast to the U.S. Constitution, no general "separation of powers" doctrine is spelled out in the *Constitution Act, 1867*. However, as Professor Peter W. Hogg notes in *Constitutional Law of Canada* (3rd ed. 1992), at pp. 184-85, such a separation of powers does in fact exist. As Dickson C.J. wrote, for the Court, in *Fraser v. Public Service Staff Relations Board*, [1985] 2 S.C.R. 455, at pp. 469-70:

> There is in Canada a separation of powers among the three branches of government — the legislature, the executive and the judiciary. In broad terms, the role of the judiciary is, of course, to interpret and apply the law; the role of the legislature is to decide upon and enunciate policy; the role of the executive is to administer and implement that policy. (emphasis added.) [...]

It is manifest that, as a matter of principle and policy, courts should not interfere with prosecutorial discretion. This appears clearly to stem from the respect of separation of powers and the rule of law. Under the doctrine of separation of powers, criminal law is in the domain of the executive, as Jean-Claude Hébert explains in "Le contrôle judiciaire de certains pouvoirs de la couronne", in *Droit pénal - Orientations nouvelles* (1987), 129, at pp. 136-37:

> [translation] *In Canada, it is the executive which assumes primary responsibility for administering the criminal law*, as was held by a majority of the Supreme Court in *Skogman v. The Queen*. This stems from the fact that there must be an authority which decides whether the judicial process should be set in motion and what form the prosecution will take. *Decisions concerning the operation of criminal justice involve important considerations relating to the public interest.* From this perspective, the actions of the Attorney General are hybrid in that there is a perpetual moving to and fro between his legal and political functions. That is why the Attorney General must answer politically to Parliament for the manner in which the Crown exercises its powers. (emphasis added.) [...]

In *Re Balderstone and The Queen* (1983), 8 C.C.C. (3d) 532 (Man. C.A.), (leave to appeal refused by the Supreme Court of Canada on December 15, 1983, [1983] 2 S.C.R. v), Monnin C.J. wrote, at p. 539:

> The judicial and the executive must not mix. These are two separate and distinct functions. The accusatorial officers lay informations or in some cases prefer indictments. Courts or the curia listen to cases brought to their attention and decide them on their merits or on meritorious preliminary matters. *If a judge should attempt to review the actions or conduct of the Attorney-General — barring flagrant impropriety — he could be falling into a field which is not his and interfering with the administrative and accusatorial function of the Attorney-General or his officers. That a judge must not do.* (emphasis added.)

La Forest J. stated in *R. v. Beare*, [1988] 2 S.C.R. 387, at pp. 410-11:

> Discretion is an essential feature of the criminal justice system. A system that attempted to eliminate discretion would be unworkably complex and rigid. Police necessarily exercise discretion in deciding when to lay charges, to arrest and to conduct incidental searches, as prosecutors do in deciding whether or not to withdraw a charge, enter a stay, consent to an adjournment, proceed by way of indictment or summary conviction, *launch an appeal* and so on.
>
> The *Criminal Code* provides no guidelines for the exercise of discretion in any of these areas. *The day to day operation of law enforcement and the criminal justice system nonetheless depends upon the exercise of that discretion.*
>
> *This Court has already recognized that the existence of prosecutorial discretion does not offend the principles of fundamental justice*; see *R. v. Lyons*, infra, at p. 348; see also *R. v. Jones*, [1986] 2 S.C.R. 284, at pp. 303-4. The Court did add that if, in a particular case, it was established that a discretion was exercised for improper or arbitrary motives, a remedy under s. 24 of the *Charter* would lie (emphasis added.) [...]

Our Court in *R. v. T. (V.)*, [1992] 1 S.C.R. 749, at p. 761, commented on the rationale for not interfering with prosecutorial discretion:

> It is important to understand the rationale for this judicial deference to the prosecutor's discretion. In this regard, the reasons of Viscount Dilhorne in *Director of Public Prosecutions v. Humphrys*, [1976] 2 All E.R. 497 (H.L.), at p. 511, are instructive:
>
>> A judge must keep out of the arena. He should not have or appear to have any responsibility for the institution of a prosecution. The functions of prosecutors and of judges must not be blurred. *If a judge has power to decline to hear a case because he does not think it should be brought, then it soon may be thought that the cases he allows to proceed are cases brought with his consent or approval.* (emphasis added.) [...]

Since a myriad of factors can affect a prosecutor's decision either to bring charges, to prosecute, to plea bargain, to appeal, etc., courts are ill-equipped to evaluate those decisions properly. (See: Steven Alan Reiss, "Prosecutorial Intent in Constitutional Criminal Procedure" (1987), 135 *U. Pa. L. Rev.* 1365, at p. 1373.)

The judicial review of prosecutorial discretion may also involve disclosure by the Crown of precise details about the process by which it decides to charge, to prosecute and to take other actions. Such a procedure could generate masses of documents to review and could eventually reveal the Crown's confidential strategies and preoccupations. [...] Indeed, confidentiality permits prosecutors to employ flexible and multifaceted enforcement policies, while disclosure promotes inflexible and static policies which are not necessarily desirable.

Moreover, should judicial review of prosecutorial discretion be allowed, courts would also be asked to consider the validity of various rationales advanced for each and every decision, involving the analysis of policies, practices and procedure of the Attorney General. The court would then have to "second-guess" the prosecutor's judgment in a variety of cases to determine whether the reasons advanced for the exercise of his or her judgment are a subterfuge. This method of judicial review is not only improper and technically impracticable, but, as Kozinski J. observed in *United States v. Redondo-Lemos*, 955 F.2d 1296 (9th Cir. 1992), at p. 1299:

> Such decisions [to charge, to prosecute and to plea-bargain] are normally made as a result of *a careful professional judgment as to the strength of the evidence*, the availability of resources, the visibility of the crime and the likely deterrent effect on the particular defendant and others similarly situated. Even were it able to collect, understand and balance all of these factors, a court would find it nearly impossible to lay down guidelines to be followed by prosecutors in future cases. We would be left with *prosecutors not knowing when to prosecute and judges not having time to judge.* (emphasis added.)

Such a situation would be conducive to a very inefficient administration of justice. Furthermore, the Crown cannot function as a prosecutor before the court while also serving under its general supervision. The court, in turn, cannot both supervise the exercise of prosecutorial discretion and act as an impartial arbitrator of the case presented to it. Judicial review of prosecutorial discretion, which would enable courts to evaluate whether or not a prosecutor's discretion was correctly exercised, would destroy the very system of justice it was intended to protect (*United States v. Redondo-Lemos*, supra, at p. 1300).

In *Director of Public Prosecutions v. Humphrys*, supra, at p. 511, Viscount Dilhorne provides a further reason why judicial screening of prosecutorial discretion is not mandated:

> *A judge must keep out of the arena.* He should not have or appear to have any responsibility for the institution of a prosecution. The functions of prosecutors and of judges must not be blurred. *If a judge has power to decline to hear a case because he does not think it should be brought, then it soon may be thought that the cases he allows to proceed are cases brought with his consent or approval.* (emphasis added.)

In our system, a judge does not have the authority to tell prosecutors which crimes to prosecute or when to prosecute them. [...]

I agree with Sidney I. Lezak and Maureen Leonard ("The Prosecutor's Discretion: Out of the Closet — Not Out of Control" (1984), 63 *Or. L. Rev.* 247, at p. 251) that:

> Fifth, *law enforcement considerations* support continued prosecutorial discretion. The need to obtain information about other crimes or other criminals, and the difficulty of proving the crime at trial often play a part in decisions to grant immunity or reduce charges.
>
> Sixth, although the *pressure of public* opinion is a "wild card" factor which is difficult to evaluate, aggressive news coverage or oversight of specific criminal proceedings by special interest groups affects the exercise of discretion. *Hence, public opinion assumes an increasingly important position in the prosecutor's decisional matrix.* An interesting example is the change in prosecution policies that appeared when it became increasingly unpopular to convict draft evaders and protesters of the Vietnam War. (emphasis added.)

(See, also: Ian Temby, Q.C., *"Prosecution Discretions and the Director of Public Prosecutions Act 1983"* (1985), 59 *Austl. L.J.* 197, at pp. 197, 199-200 and 202.)

My colleague's invitation to the court of appeal to interfere with prosecutorial discretion, absent abuse of process, goes against the grain of doctrine and jurisprudence. It also carries with it the dangers that have been outlined above. In my view, there is neither a need nor a justification for an interpretation of s. 686(4) of the *Criminal Code* which extends the discretion of the courts in this manner. As Goodridge C.J. underlined, the wording of s. 686(4) of the *Criminal Code* does not warrant such an interpretation, particularly in view of our Court's decision in *Welch v. The King*, [1950] S.C.R. 412. Principle and policy dictate against it, and the case law does not favour it.

For these reasons, I conclude that courts of appeal possess no residual discretion under s. 686(4). [...]

I conclude, therefore, that even had I shared my colleague's view that s. 686(4) of the *Criminal Code* confers a residual discretion to a court of appeal, which I do not, I would hold that the facts of this case do not point to an unreasonable decision on the part of the Crown such as to warrant the exercise of that discretion.

I base my reasons, however, on the fact that a court of appeal does not have the discretion, under s. 686(4) of the *Criminal Code*, absent abuse of process, to decline to allow an appeal when a reversible error of law is found in the trial judge's decision.

In the result, I would allow the appeal, reverse the judgment of the Court of Appeal and order a new trial.

[The dissenting reasons of Sopinka J. (Cory and Major JJ. concurring) are omitted]

DOUCET-BOUDREAU v. NOVA SCOTIA (MINISTER OF EDUCATION)
[2003] 3 S.C.R. 3.

[The appellants are Francophone parents living in five school districts in Nova Scotia. They applied for an order directing the Province and the Conseil scolaire acadien provincial to provide, out of public funds, homogeneous French-language facilities and programs at the secondary school level. The trial judge noted that the government did not deny the existence or content of the parents' rights under s. 23 of the *Canadian Charter of Rights and Freedoms* but rather failed to prioritize those rights and delayed fulfilling its obligations, despite clear reports showing that assimilation was "reaching critical levels". He found a s. 23 violation and ordered the Province and the Conseil to use their "best efforts" to provide school facilities and programs by particular dates. He retained jurisdiction to hear reports on the status of the efforts. The Province appealed the part of the order in which the trial judge retained his jurisdiction to hear reports to the Nova Scotia Court of Appeal which allowed the appeal. This is an appeal from the Nova Scotia Court of Appeal.]

The judgment of McLachlin C.J. and Gonthier, Iacobucci, Bastarache and Arbour JJ. was delivered by

IACOBUCCI AND ARBOUR JJ. –

¶ 30 ... To put the matter of judicial remedies in greater context, it is useful to reflect briefly on the role of courts in the enforcement of our laws.

¶ 31 Canada has evolved into a country that is noted and admired for its adherence to the rule of law as a major feature of its democracy. But the rule of law can be shallow without proper mechanisms for its enforcement. In this respect, courts play an essential role since they are the central institutions to deal with legal disputes through the rendering of judgments and decisions. But courts have no physical or economic means to enforce their judgments. Ultimately, courts depend on both the executive and the citizenry to recognize and abide by their judgments.

¶ 32 Fortunately, Canada has had a remarkable history of compliance with court decisions by private parties and by all institutions of government. That history of compliance has become a fundamentally cherished value of our constitutional democracy; we must never take it for granted but always be careful to respect and protect its importance, otherwise the seeds of tyranny can take root.

¶ 33 This tradition of compliance takes on a particular significance in the constitutional law context, where courts must ensure that government behaviour conforms with constitutional norms but in doing so must also be sensitive to the separation of function among the legislative, judicial and executive branches. While our Constitution does not expressly provide for the separation of powers [cites omitted], the functional separation among the executive, legislative and judicial branches of governance has frequently been noted. [cites omitted] In *New Brunswick Broadcasting Co. v. Nova Scotia (Speaker of the House of Assembly)*, [1993] 1 S.C.R. 319 , McLachlin J. (as she then was) stated, at p. 389:

> Our democratic government consists of several branches: the Crown, as represented by the Governor General and the provincial counterparts of that office; the legislative body; the

executive; and the courts. It is fundamental to the working of government as a whole that all these parts play their proper role. It is equally fundamental that no one of them overstep its bounds, that each show proper deference for the legitimate sphere of activity of the other.

¶ 34 In other words, in the context of constitutional remedies, courts must be sensitive to their role as judicial arbiters and not fashion remedies which usurp the role of the other branches of governance by taking on tasks to which other persons or bodies are better suited. Concern for the limits of the judicial role is interwoven throughout the law. The development of the doctrines of justiciability, and to a great extent mootness, standing, and ripeness resulted from concerns about the courts overstepping the bounds of the judicial function and their role vis-à-vis other branches of government.

¶ 35 In addition, it is unsurprising, given how the Charter changed the nature of our constitutional structure by requiring that all laws and government action conform to the Charter, that concerns about the limits of the judicial role have animated much of the Charter jurisprudence and commentary surrounding it [cites omitted]. Thus, in Vriend [1998] 1 S.C.R. 493, this Court stated, at para. 136:

> In carrying out their duties, courts are not to second-guess legislatures and the executives; they are not to make value judgments on what they regard as the proper policy choice; this is for the other branches. Rather, the courts are to uphold the Constitution and have been expressly invited to perform that role by the Constitution itself. But respect by the courts for the legislature and executive role is as important as ensuring that the other branches respect each others' role and the role of the courts.

¶ 36 Deference ends, however, where the constitutional rights that the courts are charged with protecting begin. As McLachlin J. stated in *RJR-MacDonald Inc. v. Canada (Attorney General)*, [1995] 3 S.C.R. 199 , at para. 136:

> Parliament has its role: to choose the appropriate response to social problems within the limiting framework of the Constitution. But the courts also have a role: to determine, objectively and impartially, whether Parliament's choice falls within the limiting framework of the Constitution. The courts are no more permitted to abdicate their responsibility than is Parliament.

Determining the boundaries of the courts' proper role, however, cannot be reduced to a simple test or formula; it will vary according to the right at issue and the context of each case.

¶ 37 Returning to this appeal, we believe that LeBlanc J. was duly guided by historical and contextual factors in crafting a remedy that would meaningfully protect, indeed implement, the applicants' rights to minority official language education for their children while maintaining appropriate respect for the proper roles of the executive and legislative branches....

¶ 54 While it would be unwise at this point to attempt to define, in detail, the words "appropriate and just" or to draw a rigid distinction between the two terms, there are some broad considerations that judges should bear in mind when evaluating the appropriateness and justice of a potential remedy. These general principles may be informed by jurisprudence relating to remedies outside the Charter context, such as cases discussing the doctrine of functus and overly vague remedies, although, as we have said, that jurisprudence does not apply strictly to orders made under s. 24(1).

¶ 55 First, an appropriate and just remedy in the circumstances of a Charter claim is one that meaningfully vindicates the rights and freedoms of the claimants....

¶ 56 Second, an appropriate and just remedy must employ means that are legitimate within the framework of our constitutional democracy. As discussed above, a court ordering a Charter remedy must strive to respect the relationships with and separation of functions among the legislature, the executive and the judiciary. This is not to say that there is a bright line separating these functions in all cases. A remedy may be appropriate and just notwithstanding that it might touch on functions that are principally assigned to the executive. The essential point is that the courts must not, in making orders under s. 24(1), depart unduly or unnecessarily from their role of adjudicating disputes and granting remedies that address the matter of those disputes.

¶ 57 Third, an appropriate and just remedy is a judicial one which vindicates the right while invoking the function and powers of a court. It will not be appropriate for a court to leap into the kinds of decisions and functions for which its design and expertise are manifestly unsuited. The capacities and competence of courts can be inferred, in part, from the tasks with which they are normally charged and for which they have developed procedures and precedent....

(b) The Reporting Order Respected the Framework of our Constitutional Democracy

¶ 68 The remedy granted by LeBlanc J. took into account, and did not depart unduly or unnecessarily from, the role of the courts in our constitutional democracy. LeBlanc J. considered the government's progress toward providing the required schools and services (see, e.g., paras. 233-34). Some flexibility was built into the "best efforts" order to allow for unforeseen difficulties. It was appropriate for LeBlanc J. to preserve and reinforce the Department of Education's role in providing school facilities as mandated by s. 88 of the Education Act, as this could be done without compromising the entitled parents' rights to the prompt provision of school facilities.

¶ 69 To some extent, the legitimate role of the court vis-à-vis various institutions of government will depend on the circumstances. In these circumstances, it was appropriate for LeBlanc J. to craft the remedy so that it vindicated the rights of the parents while leaving the detailed choices of means largely to the executive.

¶ 70 Our colleagues LeBel and Deschamps JJ. appear to consider that the issuance of an injunction against the government under s. 24(1) is constitutionally suspect and represents a departure from a consensus about Charter remedies (see para. 134 of the dissent). With respect, it is clear that a court may issue an injunction under s. 24(1) of the Charter. The power of courts to issue injunctions against the executive is central to s. 24(1) of the Charter which envisions more than declarations of rights. Courts do take actions to ensure that rights are enforced, and not merely declared. Contempt proceedings in the face of defiance of court orders, as well as coercive measures such as garnishments, writs of seizure and sale and the like are all known to courts. In this case, it was open to the trial judge in all the circumstances to choose the injunctive remedy on the terms and conditions that he prescribed.

(c) The Reporting Order Called on the Function and Powers of a Court

¶ 71 Although it may not be common in the context of Charter remedies, the reporting order issued by LeBlanc J. was judicial in the sense that it called on the functions and powers known to courts....

¶ 73 As academic commentators have pointed out, the range of remedial orders available to courts in civil proceedings demonstrates that constitutional remedies involving some degree of ongoing supervision do not represent a radical break with the past practices of courts ...

¶ 74 The order in this case was in no way inconsistent with the judicial function. There was never any suggestion in this case that the court would, for example, improperly take over the detailed management and co-ordination of the construction projects. Hearing evidence and supervising cross-examinations on progress reports about the construction of schools are not beyond the normal capacities of courts....

¶ 88 The remedy crafted by LeBlanc J. meaningfully vindicated the rights of the appellant parents by encouraging the Province's prompt construction of school facilities, without drawing the court outside its proper role. The Court of Appeal erred in wrongfully interfering with and striking down the portion of LeBlanc J.'s order in which he retained jurisdiction to hear progress reports on the status of the Province's efforts in providing school facilities by the required dates.

V. Disposition

¶ 89 In the result, we would allow the appeal, set aside the judgment of the Court of Appeal, and restore the order of the trial judge.

The reasons of Major, Binnie, LeBel and Deschamps JJ. were delivered by

LeBEL AND DESCHAMPS JJ. (dissenting) —

I. Introduction

¶ 91 The devil is in the details.... Courts should not unduly encroach on areas which should remain the responsibility of public administration and should avoid turning themselves into managers of the public service. Judicial interventions should end when and where the case of which a judge is seized is brought to a close....

1. The Separation of Powers

¶ 106 Courts are called upon to play a fundamental role in the Canadian constitutional regime. When needed, they must be assertive in enforcing constitutional rights. At times, they have to grant such relief as will be required to safeguard basic constitutional rights and the rule of law, despite the sensitivity of certain issues or circumstances and the reverberations of their decisions in their societal environment. Despite — or, perhaps, because of — the critical importance of their functions, courts should be wary of going beyond the proper scope of the role assigned to them in the public law of Canada. In essence, this role is to declare what the law is, contribute to its development and to give claimants such relief in the form of declarations, interpretation and orders as will be needed to remedy infringements of constitutional and legal rights by public authorities. Beyond these functions, an attitude of restraint remains all the more justified, given that, as the majority reasons acknowledge, Canada has maintained a tradition of compliance by governments and public servants with judicial interpretations of the law and court orders.

¶ 107 Given the nature of the Canadian parliamentary system, the existence of a true doctrine of separation of powers in Canada was sometimes put in doubt [cites omitted]. It is true that Canadians have never adopted a watertight system of separation of judicial, legislative and executive functions. In the discharge of their functions, courts have had to strike down laws, regulations or administrative decisions. They have imposed liability on the Crown or public bodies and have awarded damages against them. Forms of administrative justice or adjudication have grown out of the development of executive functions [cites omitted]. Such developments may be said to have blurred theoretical distinctions between government functions. Nevertheless, in a broad sense, a separation of powers is now entrenched as a cornerstone of our constitutional regime.

¶ 108 More particularly, the distinction clearly stands out in respect of the relationship of courts on one side and of the legislatures and executive or public administration on the other [cites omitted]. Our Court has acknowledged the fundamental nature of the separation of powers, although some of its pronouncements emphasize its functional nature [cites omitted]. Indeed, our Court has recently characterized this principle as a defining feature of the Canadian Constitution [cites omitted].

¶ 109 Our Court has strongly emphasized and vigorously applied the principle of separation of powers in order to uphold the independence of the judiciary [cites omitted]. In that context, the principle was viewed as a shield designed to protect the judiciary in order to allow it to discharge its duties under the Constitution with complete independence and impartiality. Nothing less was required to maintain the normative ordering of the Canadian legal system.

¶ 110 However, the principle of separation of powers has an obverse side as well, which equally reflects the appropriate position of the judiciary within the Canadian legal system. Aside from their duties to supervise administrative tribunals created by the executive and to act as vigilant guardians of constitutional rights and the rule of law, courts should, as a general rule, avoid interfering in the management of public administration.

¶ 111 More specifically, once they have rendered judgment, courts should resist the temptation to directly oversee or supervise the administration of their orders. They should generally operate under a presumption that judgments of courts will be executed with reasonable diligence and good faith. Once they have declared what the law is, issued their orders and granted such relief as they think is warranted by circumstances and relevant legal rules, courts should take care not to unnecessarily invade the province of public administration. To do otherwise could upset the balance that has been struck between our three branches of government.

¶ 112 This is what occurred in the present case....

V. Application of the Relevant Principles to the Present Case

¶ 119 [T]he separation of powers was ... breached....

¶ 120 By purporting to be able to make subsequent orders, the trial judge would have assumed a supervisory role which included administrative functions that properly lie in the sphere of the executive. These functions are beyond the capacities of courts. The judiciary is ill equipped to make polycentric choices or to evaluate the wide-ranging consequences that flow from policy implementation. This Court has recognized that courts possess neither the expertise nor the resources to undertake public administration....

¶ 121 In addition, if he purported to adopt a managerial role, the trial judge undermined the norm of co-operation and mutual respect that not only describes the relationship between the various actors in the constitutional order, but defines its particularly Canadian nature, and invests each branch with legitimacy....

¶ 123 This Court has recognized that in the Canadian parliamentary system, the executive is inextricably tied to the legislative branch. The Court in *Attorney General of Quebec v. Blaikie*, [1981] 1 S.C.R. 312 , at p. 320, observed that "[t]here is thus a considerable degree of integration between the Legislature and the Government". In *Wells v. Newfoundland*, [1999] 3 S.C.R. 199, at para. 53, the Court held: "On a practical level, it is recognized that the same individuals control both the executive and legislative branches of government."

¶ 124 Therefore, just as the legislature should, after a judicial finding of a Charter breach retain independence in writing its legislative response, the executive should after a judicial finding of a breach, retain autonomy in administering government policy that conforms with the Charter. In our constitutional order, the legislature and the executive are intimately interrelated and are the principal loci of democratic will. Judicial respect for that will should extend to both branches.

¶ 125 Thus, if the trial judge's initial suggestion that he could continue to make orders, and thereby effectively engage in administrative supervision and decision making accurately characterizes the nature of the reporting sessions, the order for reporting sessions breached the constitutional principle of separation of powers. Since no part of the Constitution can be interpreted to conflict with another, that order cannot be considered appropriate and just in the circumstances, under s. 24(1). The trial judge's order for reporting sessions should also be considered inappropriate because it put into question the Canadian tradition of mutual respect between the judiciary and the institutions that are the repository of democratic will.

¶ 126 If, however, the trial judge's statement in the last session that he could not make further orders correctly characterized his remedial order, then he breached the separation of powers in another way.

¶ 127 The appellants argued that the trial judge retained jurisdiction <u>only</u> to hear reports, and that these hearings had purely "suasive" value. They also argued that the hearings were designed to hold "the Province's feet to the fire" (SCC hearing transcripts). They further suggested that the threat of having to report to the trial judge functioned as an incentive for the government to comply with the best efforts order....

¶ 128 If this characterization of the trial judge's activity is accurate, then ... it resulted in activity that can be characterized as political. According to the appellants' characterization, a primary purpose of the hearings was to put public pressure on the government to act. This kind of pressure is paradigmatically associated with political actors. Indeed, the practice of publicly questioning a government on its performance, without having any legal power to compel it to alter its behaviour, is precisely that undertaken by an opposition party in the legislature during question period....

¶ 130 In Provincial Court Judges Reference, supra, Lamer C.J. described the separation of powers as providing that "the relationships between the different branches of government should ... be depoliticized....

¶ 131 In that case, Lamer C.J. remarked that the legislature and the executive cannot exert, and cannot appear to exert political pressure on the judiciary (para. 140). The reciprocal proposition applies to the immediate case. With the reporting hearings, the trial judge may have sought to exert political or public pressure on the executive, and at least appeared to do so. In our view, such action would tend to politicize the relationship between the executive and the judiciary.

¶ 132 If the reporting hearings were intended to hold "the Province's feet to the fire", the character of the relationship between the judiciary and the executive was improperly altered and, as per the Provincial Court Judges Reference, the constitutional principle of separation of powers was breached. Once again, since no part of the Constitution can conflict with another, the trial judge's order for reporting hearings cannot be interpreted as appropriate and just under s. 24(1)....

VI. Neither a Breach of Procedural Fairness nor of the Separation of Powers Was Appropriate

¶ 134 ...We do not deny that in the appropriate factual circumstances, injunctive relief may become necessary....

¶ 135 One might argue that such a breach is appropriate where it is the only way that a claimant's rights can be vindicated. Alternatively, one might suggest that if a government has ignored previous, less intrusive judicial measures, and thereby put into question their efficacy, a court might be justified in abandoning the presumption of governmental good will that we referred to above. In our view, the present case gave rise to neither of these arguments.

¶ 136 ...If the claimants felt that the government was not complying with any part of the order, then they could have brought an application for contempt. ...[E]xpedited applications are possible in Nova Scotia and other jurisdictions to deal with cases quickly and efficiently. In addition, the reporting order at issue in this case precluded applying to any other judge for relief.... Most importantly, contempt proceedings are more consistent with our adversarial system, which is based on the common law norm of giving the parties primary control over the proceedings [cites omitted]. In contrast, the present order for reporting sessions placed the trial judge in an inappropriate, ongoing supervisory and investigative role...

¶ 145 In the result, the trial judge breached both a principle of procedural fairness and the constitutional principle of separation of powers, and it is not clear that alternative, less-intrusive remedial measures, would not have achieved the ends sought....The Court of Appeal was correct in declaring that the order to retain jurisdiction for the purposes of reporting sessions was of no force and effect.

- Research Note -
CROWN PRIVILEGE AND THE SEPARATION OF POWERS

A recurring constitutional issue which arises from the separation of powers doctrine is whether a court can compel the executive or one of its members to release private documents within the context of judicial proceedings: for example, for purposes of discovery prior to litigation.

In *Smallwood v. Sparling*, [1982] 2 S.C.R. 686 the Supreme Court of Canada held that any privilege enjoyed by the executive was relative only, and must wait upon examination of the contents of the documents. Where such documents are *prima facie* relevant to the issues before the court, the court must review the documents in order to balance the competing interests of preventing harm to the state by disclosure, and preventing frustration of the administration of justice by withholding disclosure.

This principle was further explained by the Supreme Court of Canada in *Carey v. R.*, [1986] 2 S.C.R. 637. The case involved a conflict between the public interest claimed by a person who asserts a legal claim to access to all information relevant to prove that claim, and the public interest against disclosure of confidential communications of the executive branch of government.

The immediate issue was whether the appellant Carey was entitled to compel production of documents in an action against the Crown in right of Ontario and the other respondents of Cabinet documents in the possession of the executive government of the province which, he contends, would support his claim. Mr. Justice La Forest referred to the *Smallwood* case and stated:

> That case determines that Cabinet documents like other evidence must be disclosed unless such disclosure would interfere with the public interest. The fact that such documents concern the decision-making process at the highest level of government cannot, however be ignored. Courts must proceed with caution in having them produced. But the level of the decision-making process concerned is only one of many variables to be taken into account. The nature of the policy concerned and the particular contents of the document are, I would have thought, even more important. [...]
>
> In the present case [...] we are dealing with a claim based solely on the fact that the documents concerned are of a class whose revelation might interfere with the proper functioning of the public service. [...] The development of a tourist policy is undoubtedly of some importance, but it is hardly worldshaking. [...]
>
> Divulgence is all the more important in our day when more open government is sought by the public. It serves to reinforce the faith of the citizen in his governmental institutions. [...] [I]t has a bearing on the perception of the litigant and the public on whether justice has been done.

5. Judicial Power

(a) Protected Status of Constitutional Review

AMAX POTASH LTD. v. SASK.
[1977] 2 S.C.R. 576.

[The government of Saskatchewan collected tax from appellant, Amax Potash, under the *Potash Reserve Tax Regulations, 1974*. Amax Potash sought a declaration that the *Regulations* were *ultra vires*, and that the tax money paid be repaid. The government argued that s. 5(7) of *The Proceedings against the Crown Act* prevented any taxes being repaid, even if the taxing regulations were *ultra vires*. Section 5(7) provided that no proceedings could be taken against the Crown, even if a statute authorizing the doing of an act was beyond the powers of the province.]

DICKSON J. [for the Court]: — [...] The respondent government of Saskatchewan submits that s. 5(7) is valid under head (1) of s. 92 of the *B.N.A. Act*, i.e., amendment from time to time of the Constitution of the province and that it draws authority from heads (13), (14) and (16) of s. 92. The question of validity of s. 5(7) is characterized as one turning on a legislature's authority to legislate with respect to Crown immunity. It is argued that a provincial legislature can expand or contract the scope of litigation against the Crown and that s. 5(7) is only a limitation on actions against the Crown. [...]

A state, it is said, is sovereign and it is not for the courts to pass upon the policy or wisdom of legislative will. As a broad statement of principle that is undoubtedly correct, but the general principle must yield to the requisites of the Constitution in a federal state. By it the bounds of sovereignty are defined and supremacy circumscribed. The courts will not question the wisdom of enactments which, by the terms of the Canadian Constitution, are within the competence of the legislatures, but it is the high duty of this court to insure that the legislatures do not transgress the limits of their constitutional mandate and engage in the illegal exercise of power. Both Saskatchewan and Alberta inform the court that justice and equity are irrelevant in this case. If injustice results, it is the electorate which must administer a rebuke, and not the courts. The two provinces apparently find nothing inconsistent or repellent in the contention that a subject can be barred from recovery of sums paid to the Crown under protest, in response to the compulsion of the legislation later found to be ultra vires.

Section 5(7) of *The Proceedings against the Crown Act*, in my opinion, has much broader implications than mere Crown immunity. In the present context, it directly concerns the right to tax. It affects, therefore, the division of powers under the *B.N.A. Act*. It also brings into question the right of a province, or the federal Parliament for that matter, to act in violation of the Canadian Constitution. Since it is manifest that if either the federal Parliament or a provincial legislature can tax beyond the limit of its powers, and by prior or ex post facto legislation give itself immunity from such illegal act, it could readily place itself in the same position as if the act had been done within proper constitutional limits. To allow moneys collected under compulsion, pursuant to an ultra vires statute, to be retained would be tantamount to allowing the provincial legislature to do indirectly what it could not do directly, and by covert means to impose illegal burdens.

There are no Canadian constitutional law precedents addressed directly to the present issue but an analogy can be drawn to the inability of the provinces to limit judicial review of constitutionality [...] and some authority can be drawn from the case of *B.C. Power Corpn. Ltd. v. B.C. Electric Co. Ltd.*, [1962] S.C.R. 642:

> In a federal system, where legislative authority is divided, as are also the prerogatives of the Crown, as between the Dominion and the Provinces, it is my view that it is not open to the Crown, either in right of Canada or of a province, to claim a Crown immunity based upon an interest in certain property, where its very interest in that property depends completely and solely on the validity of the legislation which it had itself passed, if there is a reasonable doubt as to whether such legislation is constitutionally valid. To permit it to do so would be to enable it, by the assertion of rights claimed under legislation which is beyond its powers, to achieve the same results as if the legislation were valid. In a federal system it appears to me that, in such circumstances, the court has the same jurisdiction to preserve assets whose title is dependent on the validity of the legislation as it has to determine the validity of the legislation itself.

[...] The principle governing this appeal can be shortly and simply expressed in these terms: if a statute is found to be ultra vires the legislature which enacted it, legislation which would have the effect of attaching legal consequences to acts done pursuant to that invalid law must equally be ultra vires because it relates to the same subject matter as that which was involved in the prior legislation. If a state cannot take by unconstitutional means, it cannot retain by unconstitutional means. [...]

For the foregoing reasons, I have concluded that s. 5(7) of *The Proceedings against the Crown Act* is *ultra vires* the Province of Saskatchewan insofar as it purports to bar the recovery of taxes paid under a statute or statutory provision which is beyond the legislative jurisdiction of the legislature of Saskatchewan.

KINGSTREET INVESTMENTS LTD. v. NEW BRUNSWICK (DEPARTMENT OF FINANCE)
[2007] S.C.J. No. 1

[K Ltd. operated night clubs in New Brunswick that sell alcoholic beverages. K Ltd. purchased alcohol from the provincial liquor corporation's retail stores. In addition to the retail price, K Ltd. paid a user charge, as prescribed by regulation. K Ltd. challenged the constitutional validity of the user charge. It sought reimbursement of all amounts paid with compound interest.]

The judgment of the Court was delivered by

BASTARACHE J.: —

... This case is about the consequences of the injustice created where a government attempts to retain unconstitutionally collected taxes. ... Taxes were illegally collected. Taxes must be returned subject to limitation periods and remedial legislation, when such a measure is deemed appropriate....

The Court's central concern must be to guarantee respect for constitutional principles. One such principle is that the Crown may not levy a tax except with authority of the Parliament or the legislature: *Constitution Act, 1867,* ss. 53 and 90. This principle of "no taxation without representation" is central to our conception of democracy and the rule of law....

When the government collects and retains taxes pursuant to *ultra vires* legislation, it undermines the rule of law. To permit the Crown to retain an *ultra vires* tax would condone a breach of this most fundamental constitutional principle. As a result, a citizen who has made a payment pursuant to *ultra vires* legislation has a right to restitution...

This Court has previously recognized this right [in In *Amax Potash Ltd. v. Government of Saskatchewan*] ... However, the general availability of restitution for ultra vires taxes has to date not been clearly established. In *Air Canada v. B.C.* [1989] 1 S.C.R. 1161, La Forest J. was of the opinion that policy considerations operated to take claims for taxes paid pursuant to unlawful legislation outside of the restitutionary context [...] But La Forest J. did not command a majority in that case and so the status of his proposed immunity rule was never clear.

As Professor Hogg explained:

> Where a tax has been paid to government under a statute subsequently held to be unconstitutional, can the tax be recovered by the taxpayer? In principle, the answer should be yes. The government's right to the tax was destroyed by the holding of unconstitutionality, and the tax should be refunded to the taxpayer...

[T]he immunity rule proposed by La Forest J. amounts to saying that "the principle should be reversed *for policy reasons* in the case of payments made to governmental bodies"... Those policy reasons, according to La Forest J., included the fact that the unconstitutional tax at issue in *Air Canada* came close to raising a merely technical issue. ... In my view, privileging policy considerations in the case of *ultra vires* taxes threatens to undermine the rule of law.

Professor Hogg has explained that

> the constitutional principle that ought to dominate all others in this context is the principle that the Crown may not levy a tax except by the authority of the Parliament or Legislature. This principle, enshrined in the Bill of Rights of 1688, ensures not

merely that the executive branch is subject to the rule of law, but also that the executive branch must call the legislative branch into session to raise taxes (and vote supply). To permit the Crown to retain a tax that has been levied without legislative authority is to condone a breach of one of the most fundamental constitutional principles.

Another policy reason given by La Forest J. for the immunity rule was a concern for fiscal inefficiency and fiscal chaos (p. 1207). My view is that concerns regarding potential fiscal chaos are best left to Parliament and the legislatures to address, should they choose to do so. Where the state leads evidence before the court establishing a real concern about fiscal chaos, it is open to the court to suspend the declaration of invalidity to enable government to address the issue.... Moreover, this Court's decision in *Air Canada* demonstrates that it will be open to Parliament and to the legislatures to enact valid taxes and apply them retroactively, so as to limit or deny recovery of *ultra vires* taxes. Obviously, such legislation must also be constitutionally sound....

Turning to La Forest J.'s concern about potential fiscal inefficiency, I agree with Wilson J. in *Air Canada*, where she queries:

> Why should the individual taxpayer, as opposed to taxpayers as a whole, bear the burden of government's mistake?... The loss should not fall on the totally innocent taxpayer whose only fault is that it paid what the legislature improperly said was due....

Concerns about fiscal chaos and inefficiency should not be incorporated into the applicable rule.... For these reasons, I would not adopt the general immunity rule proposed by La Forest J....

Having rejected the immunity rule, this raises the question of whether claims for the recovery of unconstitutional taxes should be analysed on the basis of the private law rules of unjust enrichment or constitutional principles. As explained above, the recovery of unconstitutional taxes is warranted on the basis of limitations to the state's constitutional authority to tax, and in particular on the fundamental constitutional principle that there shall be no taxation without representation... This would place the restitutionary right clearly within a public law context. However, there is no question that the law of unjust enrichment, although developed in the private law context, can apply to public bodies.... In my view, an unjust enrichment analysis is inappropriate in this case...

Restitution is a tool of corrective justice. When a transfer of value between two parties is normatively defective, restitution functions to correct that transfer by restoring parties to their pre-transfer positions....

However, a technical interpretation of "benefit" and "loss" is hard to apply in tax recovery cases. Furthermore, in the context of this case, the unjust enrichment framework adds an unnecessary layer of complexity to the real legal issues. Some of the components of the modern doctrine are of little use to a principled disposition of the matter, but are rather liable to confuse the proper application of the key principles of constitutional law at issue....

For the above reasons, I would conclude that the ordinary principles of unjust enrichment should not be applied to claims for the recovery of monies paid pursuant to a statute held to be unconstitutional....

My view is that claims such as the present may be subject to an applicable limitation period. The New Brunswick *Limitation of Actions Act* provides that:

> **9.**   No other action shall be commenced but within six years after
> the cause of action arose.

Section 9 was clearly intended to cover all other actions not specifically provided for in the legislation. There is no reason why modern restitutionary claims ought not to be subject to s. 9. I agree with Robertson J.A. that such a result does not run afoul of the principles developed by this Court in *Amax Potash*:

> In my view, the reasoning adopted in *Amax Potash* has no application to cases in which the provinces are relying on a pre-existing statutory prescription period. There is a substantive difference between existing legislation that bars potential claims, unless brought within a fixed period, and legislation enacted for the specific purpose of barring restitutionary claims based on an invalid or unconstitutional tax. A prescription statute is adopted for purposes of providing a defendant with "peace of mind"; to be secure in the knowledge that he or she is no longer at risk from a stale claim accompanied by stale testimony. It is not adopted for the purpose of barring claims outright. A *Limitation of Actions Act* is valid legislation adopted for a valid purpose. It does not seek to achieve indirectly what cannot be achieved directly. [para. 42]

The appellants are entitled to recover all user charges paid on or after May 25, 1995, with interest.

(b)   Reference Cases

- Research Note -
REFERENCE PROCEDURE

By s. 53 of the *Supreme Court Act* the Governor-in-Council may refer constitutional questions directly to the Supreme Court of Canada for "hearing and consideration." The *Act* provides that when a question is referred:

> it is the duty of the Court to hear and consider it and to answer each question so referred, and the Court shall certify to the Governor in Council, for his information, its opinion on each question, with the reasons for each answer, and the opinion shall be pronounced in like manner as in the case of a judgment on an appeal

Each province has a look-alike statute authorizing the provincial executive to refer questions to the Provincial Courts of Appeal

This process is known as 'the reference procedure.' The reference procedure has proven very convenient for helping to resolve thorny questions of public policy, particularly where constitutional issues form part of the policy considerations. For example, the Federal Government referred questions to the Supreme Court concerning whether Quebec can unilaterally secede from Canada; whether and to what extent Parliament has legislative authority in relation to same sex marriage; and whether Manitoba statutes are constitutionally required to be in both English and French.

All these questions vexed governments of the day, and to a certain extent were not being satisfactorily dealt with in the political process. The reference procedure provided a convenient means of de-politicizing the issues somewhat, and providing a foundation of reasoned constitutional opinion as a guide for the formation of public policy.

The reference procedure is a process open only to governments. Private persons cannot direct a reference to any court. Only the Federal government can by pass the lower courts and refer questions directly to the Supreme Court of Canada. Only Provincial governments may by pass provincial trial courts and refer questions directly to the Provincial Court of Appeal.

Courts have the discretion to refuse to answer a question referred to the court under certain conditions (see *Reference Same Sex Marriage*, infra.).

To put the reference procedure in perspective, it is helpful to consider how constitutional question "normally" arise in the courts. Constitutional questions arise in "actions" and "applications". These are typical lawsuit between private parties or between a private party and government. References differ from actions and applications in significant ways.

- *Initiation*. Governments (and only governments) initiate references by Order-in-Council. Private parties or governments initiate actions and application that raise constitutional issues by issuing Statements of Claim or Notices of Application.

- *Outcome*. The outcome of a reference is that the Court gives an "advisory opinion" to government, i.e. the Court answers the question asked in the Order in Council. The Court answers the question asked; it does not make a traditional order. As the Court does not make an order in a reference, there is nothing to enforce. By contrast, the outcome of an action or application is a Court order to pay money, do something or refrain from doing something. The court order is enforceable. It may be placed in the hands of enforcement officials which have an execution process to enforce the Court's orders.

- *Procedure*. Actions and applications are subject to procedural statutes relating to procedure, evidence, time limitation, remedies, execution and appeals. References are not subject to these statutes.

- *Evidence*. Governments may provide the evidentiary basis of references by including statements of fact in the initiating Order in Council. This may be supplemented by the Court, which has discretion to allow parties to file additional evidence. Usually the evidentiary base is quite constricted.

- *Evidentiary limits*. Proof of facts in the reference procedure is difficult. Carriage of the reference is with the government, which alone has rights to present facts in the Order of Reference. All other parties are interveners without rights to present facts. As the proceeding originates in an appellate court, interested parties do not have full opportunity to prove their version of the necessary facts or to contest the factual basis by cross examination.

- *Stare decisis*. When the Court answers a reference question the doctrine of *stare decisis* applies and the question is considered settled. This gives references high utility even though the formal result is an "advisory opinion". Knowing that other courts will follow the Court's advisory opinion means that, in practice, the question is decided with as much authority as a case originated by statement of claim or notice of application.

- *Provincial references*. Reference questions originating in a provincial Order in Council and answered by a provincial Court of Appeal may be appealed as of right to the Supreme Court of Canada.

REFERENCE RE SECESSION OF QUEBEC
[1998] 2 S.C.R. 217

THE COURT: – [...]

The questions posed by the Governor in Council by way of Order in Council P.C. 1996-1497, dated September 30, 1996, read as follows:

1. Under the Constitution of Canada, can the National Assembly, legislature or government of Quebec effect the secession of Quebec from Canada unilaterally?

2. Does international law give the National Assembly, legislature or government of Quebec the right to effect the secession of Quebec from Canada unilaterally? In this regard, is there a right to self-determination under international law that would give the National Assembly, legislature or government of Quebec the right to effect the secession of Quebec from Canada unilaterally?

3.	In the event of a conflict between domestic and international law on the right of the National Assembly, legislature or government of Quebec to effect the secession of Quebec from Canada unilaterally, which would take precedence in Canada? [...]

In *Re References by Governor-General in Council* (1910), 43 S.C.R. 536, affirmed on appeal to the Privy Council, [1912] A.C. 571 (*sub nom. Attorney-General for Ontario v. Attorney-General for Canada*), the constitutionality of this Court's special jurisdiction was twice upheld. The Court is asked to revisit these decisions. In light of the significant changes in the role of this Court since 1912, and the very important issues raised in this Reference, it is appropriate to reconsider briefly the constitutional validity of the Court's reference jurisdiction.

Section 3 of the *Supreme Court Act* establishes this Court both as a "general court of appeal" for Canada and as an "additional court for the better administration of the laws of Canada". These two roles reflect the two heads of power enumerated in s. 101 of the *Constitution Act, 1867*. However, the "laws of Canada" referred to in s. 101 consist only of <u>federal</u> law and statute: see *Quebec North Shore Paper Co. v. Canadian Pacific Ltd.*, [1977] 2 S.C.R. 1054, at pp. 1065-66. As a result, the phrase "additional courts" contained in s. 101 is an insufficient basis upon which to ground the special jurisdiction established in s. 53 of the *Supreme Court Act*, which clearly exceeds a consideration of federal law alone (see, e.g., s. 53(2)). Section 53 must therefore be taken as enacted pursuant to Parliament's power to create a "general court of appeal" for Canada.

Section 53 of the *Supreme Court Act* is *intra vires* Parliament's power under s. 101 if, in "pith and substance", it is legislation in relation to the constitution or organization of a "general court of appeal". Section 53 is defined by two leading characteristics -- it establishes an original jurisdiction in this Court and imposes a duty on the Court to render advisory opinions. Section 53 is therefore constitutionally valid only if (1) a "general court of appeal" may properly exercise an original jurisdiction; and (2) a "general court of appeal" may properly undertake other legal functions, such as the rendering of advisory opinions.

(1)	May a Court of Appeal Exercise an Original Jurisdiction?

The words "general court of appeal" in s. 101 denote the status of the Court within the national court structure and should not be taken as a restrictive definition of the Court's functions. In most instances, this Court acts as the exclusive ultimate appellate court in the country, and, as such, is properly constituted as the "general court of appeal" for Canada. Moreover, it is clear that an appellate court can receive, on an exceptional basis, original jurisdiction not incompatible with its appellate jurisdiction.

The English Court of Appeal, the U.S. Supreme Court and certain courts of appeal in Canada exercise an original jurisdiction in addition to their appellate functions. See *De Demko v. Home Secretary*, [1959] A.C. 654 (H.L.), at p. 660; *Re Forest and Registrar of Court of Appeal of Manitoba* (1977), 77 D.L.R. (3d) 445 (Man. C.A.), at p. 453; United States Constitution, art. III, § 2. Although these courts are not constituted under a head of power similar to s. 101, they certainly provide examples which suggest that there is nothing inherently self-contradictory about an appellate court exercising original jurisdiction on an exceptional basis.

It is also argued that this Court's original jurisdiction is unconstitutional because it conflicts with the original jurisdiction of the provincial superior courts and usurps the normal appellate process. However, Parliament's power to establish a general court of appeal pursuant to s. 101 is plenary, and takes priority over the province's power to control the administration of justice in s. 92(14). See *Attorney-General for Ontario v. Attorney-General for Canada*, [1947] A.C. 127 (P.C.). Thus, even if it could be said that there is any conflict between this Court's reference jurisdiction and the original jurisdiction of the provincial superior courts, any such conflict must be resolved in favour of Parliament's exercise of its plenary power to establish a "general court of appeal" provided, as discussed below, advisory functions are not to be considered inconsistent with the functions of a general court of appeal.

(2)   May a Court of Appeal Undertake Advisory Functions?

The *amicus curiae* submits that

> [TRANSLATION] [e]ither this constitutional power [to give the highest court in the federation jurisdiction to give advisory opinions] is expressly provided for by the Constitution, as is the case in India (*Constitution of India*, art. 143), or it is not provided for therein and so it simply does not exist. This is what the Supreme Court of the United States has held. [Emphasis added.]

However, the U.S. Supreme Court did not conclude that it was unable to render advisory opinions because no such express power was included in the United States Constitution. Quite the contrary, it based this conclusion on the express limitation in art. III, § 2 restricting federal court jurisdiction to actual "cases" or "controversies". See, e.g., *Muskrat v. United States*, 219 U.S. 346 (1911), at p. 362. This section reflects the strict separation of powers in the American federal constitutional arrangement. Where the "case or controversy" limitation is missing from their respective state constitutions, some American state courts do undertake advisory functions (e.g., in at least two states -- Alabama and Delaware -- advisory opinions are authorized, in certain circumstances, by statute: see Ala. Code 1975 § 12-2-10; Del. Code Ann. tit. 10, § 141 (1996 Supp.)).

In addition, the judicial systems in several European countries (such as Germany, France, Italy, Spain, Portugal and Belgium) include courts dedicated to the review of constitutional claims; these tribunals do not require a concrete dispute involving individual rights to examine the constitutionality of a new law -- an "abstract or objective question" is sufficient. See L. Favoreu, "American and European Models of Constitutional Justice", in D. S. Clark, ed., *Comparative and Private International Law* (1990), 105, at p. 113. The European Court of Justice, the European Court of Human Rights, and the Inter-American Court of Human Rights also all enjoy explicit grants of jurisdiction to render advisory opinions. See *Treaty establishing the European Community*, Art. 228(6); Protocol No. 2 of the

Convention for the Protection of Human Rights and Fundamental Freedoms, Europ. T.S. No. 5, p. 36; *Statute of the Inter-American Court of Human Rights*, Art. 2. There is no plausible basis on which to conclude that a court is, by its nature, inherently precluded from undertaking another legal function in tandem with its judicial duties.

Moreover, the Canadian Constitution does not insist on a strict separation of powers. Parliament and the provincial legislatures may properly confer other legal functions on the courts, and may confer certain judicial functions on bodies that are not courts. The exception to this rule relates only to s. 96 courts. Thus, even though the rendering of advisory opinions is quite clearly done outside the framework of adversarial litigation, and such opinions are traditionally obtained by the executive from the law officers of the Crown, there is no constitutional bar to this Court's receipt of jurisdiction to undertake such an advisory role. The legislative grant of reference jurisdiction found in s. 53 of the *Supreme Court Act* is therefore constitutionally valid. [...]

REFERENCE RE SAME SEX MARRIAGE
[2004] 3 S.C.R. 698

[Pursuant to s. 53 of the *Supreme Court Act*, the Governor in Council referred four questions to the Supreme Court, including, "4. Is the opposite-sex requirement for marriage for civil purposes, as established by the common law and set out for Quebec in section 5 of the Federal Law-Civil Law Harmonization Act, No. 1, consistent with the Canadian Charter of Rights and Freedoms? If not, in what particular or particulars and to what extent?" Certain interveners urged the Court to decline to answer the questions on the ground that they are essentially political and are for Parliament.]

THE COURT:–

¶ 61 The first issue is whether this Court should answer the fourth question, in the unique circumstances of this reference. This issue must be approached on the basis that the answer to Question 4 may be positive or negative; the preliminary analysis of the discretion not to answer a reference question cannot be predicated on a presumed outcome. The reference jurisdiction vested in this Court by s. 53 of the Supreme Court Act is broad and has been interpreted liberally: see, e.g., Secession Reference, supra. The Court has rarely exercised its discretion not to answer a reference question reflecting its perception of the seriousness of its advisory role.

¶ 62 Despite this, the Court may decline to answer reference questions where to do so would be inappropriate, either because the question lacks sufficient legal content (which is not the case here) or because attempting to answer it would for other reasons be problematic.

¶ 63 In the Secession Reference, supra, at para. 30, we noted that instances where the Court has refused to answer reference questions on grounds other than lack of legal content tend to fall into two broad categories: (1) where the question is too ambiguous or imprecise to allow an accurate answer...; and (2) where the parties have not provided the Court with sufficient information to provide a complete answer...These categories highlight two important considerations, but are not exhaustive.

¶ 64 A unique set of circumstances is raised by Question 4, the combined effect of which persuades the Court that it would be unwise and inappropriate to answer the question.

¶ 65 The first consideration on the issue of whether this Court should answer the fourth question is the government's stated position that it will proceed by way of legislative enactment, regardless of what answer we give to this question. In oral argument, counsel reiterated the government's unequivocal intention to introduce legislation in relation to same-sex marriage, regardless of the answer to Question 4. The government has clearly accepted the rulings of lower courts on this question and has adopted their position as its own. The common law definition of marriage in five provinces and one territory no longer imports an opposite-sex requirement. In addition, s. 5 of the Federal Law-Civil Law Harmonization Act, No. 1, S.C. 2001, c. 4, no longer imports an opposite-sex requirement. Given the government's stated commitment to this course of action, an opinion on the constitutionality of an opposite-sex requirement for marriage serves no legal purpose. On the other hand, answering this question may have serious deleterious effects, which brings us to our next point.

¶ 66 The second consideration is that the parties to previous litigation have now relied upon the finality of the judgments they obtained through the court process. In the circumstances, their vested rights outweigh any benefit accruing from an answer to Question 4. Moreover, other same-sex couples acted on the finality of EGALE, Halpern and Hendricks to marry, relying on the Attorney General of Canada's adoption of the result in those cases. While the effects of the EGALE and Hendricks decisions were initially suspended, the suspensions were lifted with the consent of the Attorney General. As a result of these developments, same-sex marriages have generally come to be viewed as legal and have been regularly taking place in British Columbia, Ontario and Quebec. Since this reference was initiated, the opposite-sex requirement for marriage has also been struck down in the Yukon, Manitoba, Nova Scotia and Saskatchewan... In each of those instances, the Attorney General of Canada conceded that the common law definition of marriage was inconsistent with s. 15(1) of the Charter and was not justifiable under s. 1, and publicly adopted the position that the opposite-sex requirement for marriage was unconstitutional.

¶ 67 As noted by this Court in Nova Scotia (Attorney General) v. Walsh, [2002] 4 S.C.R. 325, 2002 SCC 83, at para. 43:

> The decision to marry or not is intensely personal and engages a complex interplay of social, political, religious, and financial considerations by the individual.
>
> The parties in EGALE, Halpern and Hendricks have made this intensely personal decision. They have done so relying upon the finality of the judgments concerning them. We are told that thousands of couples have now followed suit. There is no compelling basis for jeopardizing acquired rights, which would be a potential outcome of answering Question 4.

¶ 68 There is no precedent for answering a reference question which mirrors issues already disposed of in lower courts where an appeal was available but not pursued. Reference questions may, on occasion, pertain to already adjudicated disputes...In those cases, however, no appeal to the Supreme Court was possible....

¶ 69 The final consideration is that answering this question has the potential to undermine the government's stated goal of achieving uniformity in respect of civil marriage across Canada. There is no question that uniformity of the law is essential. This is the very reason that Parliament was accorded legislative competence in respect of marriage under s. 91(26) of the Constitution Act, 1867. However, as discussed, the government has already chosen to address the question of uniformity by means of the Proposed Act, which we have found to be within Parliament's legislative competence and consistent with the Charter. Answering the fourth question will not assist further. Given that uniformity is to be addressed legislatively, this rationale for answering Question 4 fails to compel.

¶ 70 On the other hand, consideration of the fourth question has the potential to undermine the uniformity that would be achieved by the adoption of the proposed legislation. The uniformity argument succeeds only if the answer to Question 4 is "no". By contrast, a "yes" answer would throw the law into confusion. The decisions of the lower courts in the matters giving rise to this reference are binding in their respective provinces. They would be cast into doubt by an advisory opinion which expressed a contrary view, even though it could not overturn them. The result would be confusion, not uniformity.

¶ 71 In sum, a unique combination of factors is at play in Question 4. The government has stated its intention to address the issue of same-sex marriage by introducing legislation regardless of our opinion on this question. The parties to previous litigation have relied upon the finality of their judgments and have acquired rights which in our view are entitled to protection. Finally, an answer to Question 4 would not only fail to ensure uniformity of the law, but might undermine it. These circumstances, weighed against the hypothetical benefit Parliament might derive from an answer, convince the Court that it should exercise its discretion not to answer Question 4...

¶ 72 For the reasons set out above, the Court exercises its discretion not to answer this question.

(c)   Interpretation of Section 96

> **CONSTITUTION ACT, 1867**
>
> **96. The Governor General shall appoint the Judges of the Superior, District, and County Courts in each Province, except those of the Courts of Probate in Nova Scotia and New Brunswick.**

REFERENCE RE RESIDENTIAL TENANCIES ACT
[1981] 1 S.C.R. 714.

DICKSON J. [for the Court]: — The resolution of disputes between landlords and tenants has long been a central preoccupation of the common law Courts. [...]

Within the past few years the Province of Ontario, in common with a number of other Provinces, had enacted legislation to redress what was perceived to be an imbalance, in favour of landlords, in the landlord and tenant relationship. On June 21, 1979, the Legislative Assembly of Ontario enacted the *Residential Tenancies Act, 1979* (Ont.), c. 78 [now R.S.O. 1980, c. 452], to come into effect on proclamation. The Act contains a detailed legislative code to govern landlords and tenants and establishes a tribunal, bearing the name the Residential Tenancy Commission, to oversee and enforce the newly enunciated rights and obligations. [...] [T]he Executive Council of the Province, pursuant to s. 1 of the *Constitutional Questions Act*, R.S.O. 1980, c. 86, referred the following questions to the Court of Appeal of Ontario: [...]

1.   Is it within the legislative authority of the Legislative Assembly of Ontario to empower the Residential Tenancy Commission to make an order evicting a tenant as provided in the *Residential Tenancies Act*.

2.   Is it within the legislative authority of the Legislative Assembly of Ontario as provided in the *Residential Tenancies Act, 1979* to empower the Residential Tenancy Commission to make orders requiring landlords and tenants to comply with obligations imposed under that Act? [...]

As Professor Hogg has noted in his work on *Constitutional Law in Canada* (1977), at p. 129, there is no general "separation of power" in the *British North America Act, 1867*. Our Constitution does not separate the legislative, executive, and judicial function and insist that each branch of Government exercise only its own function. Thus it is clear that the Legislature of Ontario may confer non-judicial functions on the Courts of Ontario and, subject to s. 96 of the *British North America Act, 1867*, which lies at the heart of the present appeal, confer judicial functions on a body which is not a Court.

Under s. 92(14) of the *British North America Act, 1867*, the provincial Legislatures have the legislative power in relation to the administration of justice in the Province. This is a wide power but subject to subtraction of ss. 96 to 100 in favour of the federal authority. Under s. 96 the Governor-General has the sole power to appoint the Judges of the Superior, District and County Courts in each Province. Under s. 97 the Judges who are to be appointed to the Superior, District and County Courts are to be selected from the respective bars of each Province. Under s. 100 the Parliament of Canada is obliged to fix and provide for their salaries. Section 92(14) and ss. 96 to 100 represent one of the important compromises of the Fathers of Confederation. It is plain that what was sought to be achieved through this compromise, and the intended effect of s. 96, would be destroyed if a Province could pass legislation creating a tribunal, appoint members thereto, and then confer on the tribunal the jurisdiction of the Superior Courts. What was conceived as a strong constitutional base for national unity, through a unitary judicial system, would be gravely undermined. Section 96 has thus come to be regarded as limiting provincial competence to make appointments to a tribunal exercising s. 96 judicial powers and therefore as implicitly limiting provincial competence to endow a provincial tribunal with such powers. [...]

In *Tomko v. Labour Relations Board (Nova Scotia) et al.*, [1977] 1 S.C.R. 112, the issue was the validity of the Nova Scotia Labour Relations Board's authority to issue a "cease and desist order". It was argued that this jurisdiction was analogous to the jurisdiction of 96 Courts to issue mandatory injunctions to halt illegal activity. The Chief Justice, speaking for eight members of the Court, held that this consideration was not conclusive, since "it is not the detached jurisdiction or power alone that is to be considered but rather its setting in the institutional arrangements in which it appears and is exercisable under the provincial legislation". A consideration of the "institutional setting" indicated that the power to make cease and desist orders was merely one aspect of a broad legislative scheme for the peaceful regulation of collective bargaining, an area which the Courts had not entered. Thus, the Labour Relations Board had been validly clothed with the power impugned.

The recent decision of this Court, *City of Mississauga v. Regional Municipality of Peel et al.*, [1979] 2 S.C.R. 244, is, in the words of the Chief Justice in that case, "a prime illustration of the proposition laid down in *Tomko*". In *Mississauga*, the Ontario Municipal Board had been given certain powers to resolve disputes over assets between amalgamating municipalities. [...] [I]t was stated that the power to adjudicate was merely one "incident in the overall picture of the general restructuring of the municipalities in which the Municipal Board is given an important part to play". Viewed in their "institutional setting, the 'judicial powers' to determine rights and liabilities under provincial legislation had been validly granted to the Municipal Board".

I do not think it can be doubted that the Courts have applied an increasingly broad test of constitutional validity in upholding the establishment of administrative tribunals within provincial jurisdiction. In general terms it may be said that it is now open to the Provinces to invest administrative bodies with "judicial functions" as part of a broader policy scheme. There will still be situations, however, as in *A.-G. Qué. v. Farrah*, [1978] 2 S.C.R. 638, where a s. 96 "judicial function" is isolated from the rest of the administrative structure of the relevant legislation. In *Farrah*, a transport tribunal was given appellate jurisdiction over the Quebec Transport Commission. The tribunal performed no function other than deciding questions of law. Since this function was normally performed by s. 96 Courts and divorced from the broader institutional framework of the Act, the impugned sections were held to be unconstitutional. Subject to this type of situation, s. 96 can no longer be construed as a bar to a Province seeking to vest an administrative tribunal with ancillary "judicial" powers formerly exercised by s. 96 Courts. [...]

The Privy Council in [*Labour Relations Bd. of Sask. v. John East Iron Works Ltd.*, [1948] 2 W.W.R. 1055], suggested that the application of s. 96 required a determination as to whether or not the powers being exercised were judicial or administrative and if judicial, whether or not the administrative body was "broadly analogous" to a Superior, District or County Court. *Tomko* added a further dimension. An administrative tribunal may be clothed with power formerly exercised by s. 96 Courts, so long as that power is merely an adjunct of, or ancillary to, a broader administrative or regulatory structure. If, however, the impugned power forms a dominant aspect of the function of the tribunal, such that the tribunal itself must be considered to be acting "like a Court", then the conferral of the power is *ultra vires*.

The jurisprudence since *John East* leads one to conclude that the test must now be formulated in three steps. The first involves consideration, in the light of the historical conditions existing in 1867, of the particular power or jurisdiction conferred upon the tribunal. The question here is whether the power of jurisdiction conforms to the power or jurisdiction exercised by Superior, District or County Courts at the time of Confederation. This temporary segregation, or isolation, of the impugned power is not for the purpose of turning back the clock and restoring *Toronto v. York* as the governing authority, an approach deplored in *Mississauga*. It is rather the first step in a three step process.

If the historical inquiry leads to the conclusion that the power or jurisdiction is not broadly conformable to jurisdiction formerly exercised by s. 96 Courts, that is the end of the matter. As Rand J. noted in *A.E. Dupont et al. v. Inglis et al.*, [1958] S.C.R. 535 at p. 512: "Judicial power, not of that type [i.e., that exercised by s. 96 Courts at Confederation], such as that exercised by inferior Courts, can be conferred on a Provincial tribunal whatever its primary character." If, however, the historical evidence indicates that the impugned power is identical or analogous to a power exercised by s. 96 Courts at Confederation, then one must proceed to the second step of the inquiry.

Step two involves consideration of the function within its institutional setting to determine whether the function itself is different when viewed in that setting. In particular, can the function still be considered to be a "judicial" function? In addressing the issue, it is important to keep in mind the further statement by Rand J. in *Dupont v. Inglis* [at p. 543 S.C.R.] that "it is the subject-matter rather than the apparatus of adjudication that is determinative". Thus the question of whether any particular function is "judicial" is not to be determined simply on the basis of procedural trappings. The primary issue is the nature of the question which the tribunal is called upon to decide. Where the tribunal is faced with a private dispute between parties, and is called upon to adjudicate through the application of a recognized body of rules in a manner consistent with fairness and impartiality, then, normally, it is acting in a "judicial capacity". To borrow the terminology of Professor Ronald Dworkin, the judicial task involves questions of "principle", that is, consideration of the competing rights of individuals or groups. This can be contrasted with questions of "policy" involving competing views of the collective good of the community as a whole: see Dworkin, *Taking Rights Seriously* (1977), at pp. 82-90 (Duckworth).

If, after examining the institutional context, it becomes apparent that the power is not being exercised as a "judicial power" then the inquiry need go no further for the power, within its institutional context, no longer conforms to a power or jurisdiction exercisable by a s. 96 Court and the provincial scheme is valid. On the other hand, if the power or jurisdiction is exercised in a judicial manner, then it becomes necessary to proceed to the third and final step in the analysis and review the tribunal's function as a whole in order to appraise the impugned function in its entire institutional context. The phrase – "it is not the detached jurisdiction or power alone that is to be considered but rather its setting in the institutional arrangements in which it appears" – is the central core of the judgment in *Tomko*. It is no longer sufficient simply to examine the particular power or function of a tribunal and ask whether this power or function was once exercised by s. 96 Courts. This would be examining the power or function in a "detached" manner, contrary to the reasoning in *Tomko*. What must be considered is the "context" in which this power is exercised. *Tomko* leads to the following result: it is possible for administrative tribunals to exercise powers and jurisdiction which once were exercised by the s. 96 Courts. It will all depend on the context of the exercise of the power. It may be that the impugned "judicial powers" are merely subsidiary or ancillary to general administrative functions assigned to the tribunal (*John East, Tomko*) or the powers may be necessarily incidental to the achievement of a broader policy goal of the Legislature (*Mississauga*). In such a situation, the grant of judicial power to provincial appointees is valid. The scheme is only invalid when the adjudicative function is a sole or central function of the tribunal (*Farrah*) so that the tribunal can be said to be operating "like a s. 96 Court".

The matter was well expressed in the Ontario Court of Appeal:

> 7. Where judicial powers are conferred by a provincial legislature on a provincially constituted and appointed tribunal, the fact that the tribunal may not be curial in its essential functions but rather an administrative tribunal entrusted with the making of decisions that are primarily of an administrative nature will not, of itself, insulate the judicial powers from a finding that the legislation conferring them is, to that extent, invalid. Whether such a finding may be escaped will tend to depend on whether the judicial powers are seen to be merely incidents of, or adjuncts to, a scheme for the administration of a matter that is otherwise within provincial legislative competence, albeit that as incidents of or adjuncts to the scheme they may be necessary for its effective functioning.

V

Step one, the historical inquiry. The Residential Tenancy Commission is given a broad range of powers under the Act: in this reference, as I have noted, we are concerned with only two, power to make an eviction order and power to make a "compliance" order. [...]

The Attorney-General for Ontario conceded that the powers given to the Residential Tenancy Commission "are not merely analogous to those (pre-1867) powers but are the same powers".

We start therefore with the proposition that the power to order eviction in the 1979 Act is broadly conformable to pre-1867 jurisdiction in ejectment, and the power to order compliance is broadly conformable to the pre-1867 jurisdiction to award damages or specific performance. It is true that the Tenancy Commission ordering an eviction in 1981 would look to different considerations than a Court ordering an ejectment in 1867, the rules surrounding the granting of these remedies having altered somewhat since 1867, but mere alteration in rules cannot change the substance of things or prevent the drawing of analogies. [...]

The question whether the powers or jurisdiction conferred by the statute are analogous to, in broad conformity with, the kind of powers or jurisdiction historically exercised by the Superior, County or District Courts admits of only one answer – "yes". [...]

VI

We pass now to the second step of the inquiry, to consideration of the impugned powers within their institutional setting. Is the power to order eviction or compliance when so viewed still a "judicial power"? I have already indicated that the hallmark of a judicial power is a *lis* between parties in which a tribunal is called upon to apply a recognized body of rules in a manner consistent with fairness and impartiality. The adjudication deals primarily with the rights of the parties to the dispute, rather than considerations of the collective good of the community as a whole.

With very few exceptions, the Residential Tenancy Commission is not free to intervene of its own motion in disputes between landlords and tenants. Virtually all of the provisions of the Act require that either a landlord or a tenant apply to the Commission before any action be taken. Moreover, the power to order eviction or compliance will, in all cases, be exercised in the context of a *lis* between parties. [...]

When confronted with a *lis*, the task of the Commission will be to determine the respective rights and obligations of the parties according to the terms of the legislation. The Commission does not have an untrammeled discretion to "set matters right". The powers which it may invoke and the remedies which it may award are circumscribed by the terms of the Act. At no point is the individual's right at law surrendered for the benefit of a common group or policy. The Commission deals exclusively with matters of contract and land law as they arise between landlords and tenants. [...]

The Commission has authority to hear and determine disputes in accordance with rules of law, and by the authority of the law. It authorizes actions for which application is made. It has the power to impose penalties and sanctions and to award remedies for the infringement of rights. Disobedience of an order of the Commission is a penal offence. The Commission decides contractual and property rights between individual landlords and tenants and in so doing determines not only the right to land and property, but also other rights. In each case, there is an analysis of the law, an application of the applicable law to the particular facts, and then a judicial decision and a consequent order. It is difficult to conceive that when so acting the Commission acts otherwise than as a curial tribunal. In substance the tribunal is exercising judicial powers roughly in the same way as they are exercised by the Courts. [...]

I conclude that the impugned powers, when viewed in their institutional setting, remain essentially "judicial powers".

VII

We now face the most difficult aspect of this appeal – an examination of the interrelationship between the Commission's impugned "judicial powers" and the other powers and jurisdiction conferred under the Act.

Prior to 1979, [...] [t]he function of adjudicating disputes between landlords and tenants was handled by s. 96 Courts. The 1979 Act effected relatively minor changes in the substantive law of landlord and tenant. [...]

The Attorney-General for Ontario argues that the Commission is essentially an administrative body charged with "supervising and regulating" the relationship of landlord and tenant in the Province of Ontario. The function of adjudicating disputes, it is contended, is merely a subsidiary or ancillary aspect of the Commission's role. [...]

It appears upon reading the Act as a whole that the central function of the Commission is that of resolving disputes, in the final resort by a judicial form of hearing between landlords and tenants. The bulk of the Act is taken up with defining the rights and obligations of landlords and tenants and with prescribing a method for resolving disputes over those obligations. Dispute resolution is achieved through application to the Commission. [...]

There is no broad legislative scheme as there was in *Mississauga, supra*, to subsume the judicial functions of the Commission. It was argued that the powers vested in the Residential Tenancy Commission were merely incidental or ancillary to the policy of "security of tenure" for tenants. This submission is unconvincing. The primary purpose and effect of the 1979 Act was to transfer jurisdiction over a large and important body of law, affecting landlords and tenants of 1,000,000 rental units, from the s. 96 Courts where it has been administered since Confederation to a provincially appointed tribunal.

Here the chief role of the Commission is not to administer a policy or to carry out an administrative function. Its primary role is to adjudicate. The administrative features of the legislation can be characterized as ancillary to the main adjudicative function. The power of the Commission to mediate disputes is aimed at the speedy resolution of differences between the parties. So too is the informal nature of the proceedings. The goal of these provisions is to enable the Commission to "process" controversies in an expeditious manner. As such, they are merely incidental to the main purpose of the legislation.

In the case at bar, as the Court of Appeal observed, powers until now exercised by the Courts have simply been transferred to the Commission as the "chosen vehicle for their exercise". In the instant case the impugned powers are the nuclear core around which other powers and functions are collected. In *Tomko*, supra, the tribunal was composed of persons familiar with labour relations matters and presumably better able than the Courts to weigh the interests involved and to assess the implications of cease and desist orders upon the parties. In the present case the Act imposes no particular qualifications or experience as essential to appointment to the Commission. There is no requirement of legal training or occupational experience for any member of the Commission and the process of selection is not based on any bipartite or tripartite principle. The Commission is in no way a specialized agency. In the instant case the whole of a s. 96 Court's jurisdiction in a certain area, however limited, has been transferred to provincially appointed officials. The provincial Legislature has sought to withdraw historically entrenched and important judicial functions from the Superior Court and vest them in one of its own tribunals. Although the Legislature may undoubtedly contract, as well as enlarge, Court jurisdiction it cannot lift wholesale from the Superior Courts and bestow on a tribunal of its own making the resolution of disputes theretofore handled by Superior Courts in respect of rights and obligations in the nature of eviction orders and orders for compliance with contractual mandates.

The Residential Tenancy Commission is charged with the function of interpreting contracts and enforcing contractual rights through the exercise of the impugned powers. The Commission is to be empowered to do what a Superior Court has always done. It is clearly a Superior Court *quoad* those powers. The statutory provisions conferring those powers are therefore invalid. In *Farrah*, supra, the jurisdiction which the statute sought to transfer was, in the words of Pigeon J. at pp. 656-7 S.C.R., "precisely the same as that which was previously exercised by the Quebec Court of Appeal". In the present case the jurisdiction sought to be transferred is precisely the same as that which was previously, and is presently, exercised by the Courts. [...]

Implicit throughout the argument advanced on behalf of the Attorney-General of Ontario is the assumption that the Court system is too formal, too cumbersome, too expensive and therefore unable to respond properly to the social needs which the *Residential Tenancies Act, 1979* is intended to meet. All statutes respond to social needs. The Courts are not unfamiliar with equity and the concepts of fairness, justice, convenience, reasonableness. Since the enactment in 1976 of the legislation assuring "security of tenure" the County Court Judges of Ontario have been dealing with matters arising out of that legislation, apparently with reasonable dispatch, as both landlords and tenants in the present proceedings have spoken clearly against transfer of jurisdiction in respect of eviction and compliance orders from the Courts to a special commission. It is perhaps also of interest that there is no suggestion in the material filed with us that the Law Reform Commission favoured removal from the Courts of the historic functions performed for over 100 years by the Courts.

I am neither unaware of, nor unsympathetic to the arguments advanced in support of a view that s. 96 should not be interpreted so as to thwart or unduly restrict the future growth of provincial administrative tribunals. Yet, however worthy the policy objectives, it must be recognized that we, as a Court, are not given the freedom to choose whether the problem is such that provincial, rather than federal, authority should deal with it. We must seek to give effect to the Constitution as we understand it and with due regard for the manner in which it has been judicially interpreted in the past. If the impugned power is violative of s. 96 it must be struck down. [...]

In the result, I would dismiss the appeal, and answer in the negative the constitutional questions which have been posed by the Executive Council of the Province of Ontario.

NOVA SCOTIA (A.G.) V. SOBEYS' STORES LTD.
[1989] 1 S.C.R. 238.

[An employee of the respondent company complained to the Director of Labour Standards for Nova Scotia that he had been dismissed from Sobeys' "without just cause" within the meaning of s. 67A of the *Labour Standards Code*. The Director ordered that the employee be reinstated and paid lost wages stemming from unjust dismissal.

The Director's decision was upheld by the Labour Standards Tribunal. However, the Appeal Division of the N.S. Supreme Court held that ss. 67(2) and (3) of the *Code* were *ultra vires* the province, as they conferred a s. 96 power on a provincially-appointed tribunal. The Supreme Court of Canada held that these provisions did not contravene s. 96: although the tribunal carried out a judicial function in regard to s. 67A of the *Code*, that function was found to be necessarily incidental to the implementation of broader policy goals.]

WILSON J. [Dickson C.J.C., McIntyre and Lamer JJ. concurring]: — [...]

THE HISTORICAL INQUIRY

The Appeal Division correctly held that the test to be applied in s. 96 cases is that laid down by this Court in the *Residential Tenancies* case. This three-step test represents a consolidation of the principles enunciated in a number of previous decisions, in particular *The Adoption Reference*, [1938] S.C.R. 398; *John East Ironworks*; and *Tomko v. Labour Relations Board (Nova Scotia)*, [1977] 1 S.C.R. 112. The first stage requires us to consider whether "the challenged power or jurisdiction broadly conform[s] to the power or jurisdiction exercised by Superior, District or County Courts at the time of Confederation": per Laskin C.J. in *Massey-Ferguson Industries Ltd. v. Saskatchewan*, [1981] 2 S.C.R. 413, at p. 429. But before addressing this question it is necessary to examine three preliminary issues which were raised during the hearing of the appeal:

(1)   how broadly should the power or jurisdiction be characterized for purposes of the historical analysis?

(2)   do the words "broadly conform" to Superior Court jurisdiction mean that such jurisdiction must have been exclusive to those courts at Confederation?

(3)   should the court look only at the jurisdiction of the courts of the province in which the case arose or should the inquiry embrace all or most of the provinces?

(i) Characterization of the Power or Jurisdiction at Issue

[...] It seems to me that this raises two problems pertaining to the characterization of the jurisdiction. How broadly should it be characterized, and can a broader or narrower characterization be used for the different steps of the *Residential Tenancies* test? These questions do not appear to have been canvassed in any previous decision of the Court, yet they could clearly be important. The way in which the power or jurisdiction is characterized can have significant consequences for the historical inquiry in which the courts must search for analogous jurisdiction in inferior courts. Although in the present case both the Attorney General and Sobeys saw an advantage for themselves in a narrow characterization, that is probably only so because of the unusual remedy at issue. In general, those challenging legislation will probably favour the narrower view as more likely to bring success through the historical test. Those supporting the legislation will no doubt advocate a more expansive view on the assumption that the broader the characterization the more likely it will be that at least some aspects of the jurisdiction will have been within the purview of inferior courts at Confederation.

To resolve these questions on characterization one must look to the different purposes served by the three stages of the *Residential Tenancies* test. The test represents a reconciliation of jurisprudence from two different types of cases, those that dealt with attempted expansions of inferior court jurisdiction and those that involved the assignment of subject areas of superior court jurisdiction to administrative tribunals. This distinction between the two principal types of s. 96 cases was noted in a different context by then Chief Justice Laskin in *Re B.C. Family Relations Act*, [1982] 1 S.C.R. 62, at p. 68. The first line of cases establish the proposition that, while the jurisdiction of the inferior courts will not be frozen as of the date of Confederation, neither will it be substantially expanded so as to undermine the independence of the judiciary which s. 96 protects: see *Adoption Reference; Re B.C. Family Relations Act; Séminaire de Chicoutimi v. Attorney General of Quebec*, [1973] S.C.R. 681; *Re Cour de Magistrat de Québec*, [1965] S.C.R. 772; *Canadian Broadcasting Corporation v. Quebec Police Commission*, [1979] 2 S.C.R. 618. The second line of cases, those dealing with administrative tribunals, provide what might be called permissible exceptions to the constitutional stricture against the reduction of superior court jurisdiction. The courts have recognized that s. 96 should not stand in the way of new institutional approaches to social or political problems. Departures from the strict rule against devolving superior court jurisdiction on inferior tribunals are permitted only if the scheme meets the criteria of the second or third stage of the test. Otherwise bald grants of superior court jurisdiction to inferior courts are precluded.

Viewed against this background the first step of the *Residential Tenancies* test, which is drawn from the "inferior court" cases, represents a kind of threshold test, a method of deciding whether, in a formal sense, s. 96 has been violated at all. The second and third steps serve to validate some legislative schemes *despite* the fact that they trench on the traditional jurisdiction of s. 96 courts. The purposes of s. 96 require a strict, that is to say a narrow, approach to characterization at the first stage. Given what I have to say below on concurrent superior/inferior court jurisdiction at Confederation, any other approach would potentially open the door to large accretions of jurisdiction and thereby defeat the purposes of the constitutional provision. I would therefore reject as too broad characterizations of the s. 67A jurisdiction as being in relation to employer/employee relations or labour standards. [...]

At the first stage the search is for "broad conformity" with the powers of s. 96 courts at Confederation. It is a search for analogous, not precisely the same, jurisdiction. Even if I were to accept the appellant's contention that the remedy of reinstatement was outside the purview of s. 96 courts, as was done in *Asselin,* I do not think that should be determinative in s. 96 cases. To do so would be to freeze the jurisdiction of those courts at 1867 by a technical analysis of remedies. It is, in my view, the type of dispute that must guide us and not the particular remedy sought. The question of new remedies for traditional causes of action is better suited to the second and third steps of the *Residential Tenancies* test which are specifically designed to allow the courts to consider new approaches to old problems, approaches which are more responsive to changing social conditions. Thus, the jurisdiction in this case should, in my view, be characterized as jurisdiction in relation to unjust dismissal.

(ii) **Must the Superior Court Jurisdiction at Confederation be exclusive?**

[...] It is obvious that at the first stage s. 96 will be violated if provincial tribunals are accorded a power or jurisdiction that belonged *exclusively* to s. 96 courts at Confederation. It is equally trite law that there will be no violation if the power or jurisdiction was the exclusive preserve of inferior courts. These propositions, however, leave unclear what the consequences are of discovering a shared, or concurrent, jurisdiction between the two levels of court. Moreover, if concurrent jurisdiction will enable the provincial tribunal to pass the historical test, it is necessary to ask how much shared jurisdiction will suffice for this purpose. [...]

The foregoing [review of the cases] leads me to conclude that a certain gloss must be added to the *Residential Tenancies* test. At the first step, the threshold question is whether at Confederation superior courts exercised an exclusive jurisdiction. This test accords with the general principle that inferior court jurisdiction need not be frozen at its pre-Confederation level: see *Re Cour de Magistrat de Québec*. If the jurisdiction was exclusive to superior courts, then the inquiry must pass on to the second and third stages of the test. If the jurisdiction was shared, the legislation under challenge may, in some circumstances, be held valid by the historical test.

How much concurrent jurisdiction is necessary for the purposes of the test? It would obviously largely defeat the purpose of s. 96 if a finding of one small aspect of jurisdiction, limited, for example, by subject matter, geography or monetary amount, in an inferior court were sufficient to permit legislatures to oust the jurisdiction of today's superior courts. However, the dangers of this are not as great as they might at first sight appear, given what I have said earlier about the need to characterize the power or jurisdiction relatively narrowly for the purposes of the historical test. Yet they must be borne in mind in fashioning a test of general application. [...]

It seems to me that in *Grondin* this Court laid down a test which requires the practical involvement of inferior courts to have been broadly coextensive with the work of superior courts. This is not to suggest that jurisdiction must have been entirely or even generally concurrent, for the nature of the inferior-superior court distinction will invariably mean that the former's jurisdiction was limited in some way. But some limits will be more significant than others. A significant geographical limitation would tell against the legislative scheme much more than a purely pecuniary limit. The former might well have prevented recourse to the inferior courts for the majority of colonial residents, while the latter, given inflation, would be a much less dramatic bar. The courts must search for what I would term a general shared involvement in a jurisdiction, not concurrent jurisdiction in all respects. It is impossible to define with precision just how much jurisdiction is enough for a finding of shared involvement in all cases. But the following questions, in my view, are relevant:

(a) was the inferior court jurisdiction geographically restricted? Was it confined to certain municipal or district courts or was it being exercised province-wide?

(b) was the inferior court jurisdiction limited to a few specific situations? For example, in the area of unjust dismissal, did only certain types of employees have recourse to the inferior courts?

(c) was the inferior court jurisdiction restricted by pecuniary limits so as to reduce its scope even after allowing for inflation?

These are by no means the only questions the courts should address and I proffer them by way of illustration only. Others will appear germane in different contexts. In all cases, however, the inquiry should be directed to the question whether or not the work of the inferior courts at the time of Confederation was broadly co-extensive with that of the superior courts. Only if this standard is met will the history of shared jurisdiction validate the contemporary scheme under the historical test.

(iii) Extent of the Historical Inquiry

In argument before us counsel for the parties and some of the intervenors also raised the issue of which jurisdiction(s) should be examined in the historical test. It was suggested that the correct approach was a "global" one in which more than one province's pre-confederation jurisdiction should be considered. [...]

It seems to me that this issue should be resolved by answering a somewhat broader question – does pre-confederation jurisdiction refer to pre-1867 jurisdiction or to jurisdiction in a particular province immediately prior to that province joining confederation? If the former approach is adopted, the courts must consider only the four original confederating provinces (Quebec, Ontario, Nova Scotia and New Brunswick) irrespective of which present-day province is involved in the litigation. If the latter approach is adopted, the test will involve perhaps only one colony, perhaps as many as eight, and a potential chronological span of as many as 72 years, from 1867 to 1949. I note that on all of these points past decisions of this Court have been somewhat inconsistent. [...]

[T]he Residential Tenancies test of 1867 jurisdiction should be expanded somewhat to include examination of the general historical conditions in all four original confederating provinces. I say this for two reasons. The first is a practical one. While it might make sense to examine only Ontario in an Ontario case (as was done in Residential Tenancies) or Quebec in a Quebec case (as was done in Grondin) there would be no reason to choose one or the other in deciding a case emanating from Alberta, Prince Edward Island or elsewhere.

The second and more important reason is that implicit in what I have said above is the principle that s. 96 should apply in the same way across the country. The "strong constitutional basis for national unity, through a unitary judicial system" (Residential Tenancies, p. 728) would indeed be undermined by inconsistent results derived from a jurisprudence developed province by province. I do not wish to suggest that there must be uniformity of result for all s. 96 challenges to provincial initiatives in a given area. It is entirely possible that different results may emerge from analyzing contemporary schemes in light of the second and third stages of the Residential Tenancies test. I am suggesting only that consistency at the level of the historical analysis would seem to be desirable and that it is best achieved by measuring each s. 96 challenge against the same historical yardstick. The test at this stage should be national, not provincial.

There remains only to consider one practical problem – the difficulties created if, as in this case, the four original provinces produce a "tie", two upholding jurisdiction and two denying it. While there is probably no ideal solution to such a problem, I am persuaded that the best approach would be to examine jurisdiction in the United Kingdom at the time of Confederation. The inquiry is one generally into jurisdiction in 1867 and our court structure is derived from the British model. Moreover, this Court certainly considered U.K. jurisdiction relevant in its judgments in the Adoption Reference and Re B.C. Family Relations Act.

[The judgment of La Forest J., Beetz and L'Heureux-Dubé JJ. concurring, has been omitted.]

MCEVOY v. A.G. N.B. AND A.G. CAN.
[1983] I S.C.R. 704.

BY THE COURT. — This is an appeal from a unanimous judgment of the New Brunswick Court of Appeal [...] answering in the affirmative three questions put before that court on a reference by the provincial Lieutenant-Governor in Council. [...]

The three questions posed to the court in New Brunswick, and the very same questions are now before this court on appeal, read as follows:

1. Is it *intra vires* the Parliament of Canada to amend the *Criminal Code* to confer upon a court constituted by the legislature of a province, the judges of which are appointed by the Lieutenant Governor in Council, exclusive jurisdiction to try all indictable offences under that Act?

2. Is it *intra vires* the Parliament of Canada to amend the *Criminal Code* to confer upon a court constituted by the legislature of a province, the judges of which are appointed by the Lieutenant-Governor in Council, jurisdiction to try all indictable offences under that Act, if that jurisdiction is concurrent with that of courts whose judges are appointed pursuant to section 96 of the *British North America Act*?

3. Is it *intra vires* the legislature of a province to constitute a court, the judges of which are appointed by the Lieutenant-Governor in Council, to exercise such jurisdiction in criminal law matters as is conferred upon it by the Parliament of Canada, if the jurisdiction conferred by Parliament is to try all indictable offences under the *Criminal Code*, and is either

   (a) exclusive; or
   (b) concurrent with that of courts whose judges are appointed pursuant to section 96 of the *British North America Act*? [...]

In general terms the issue is whether s. 96 of the *Constitution Act, 1867* is a bar to a plan whereby the federal government and a provincial government would by conjoint action transfer the criminal jurisdiction of provincial superior courts to a new court to be called the "unified criminal court" the judges of which would be provincially appointed. [...]

There is no doubt that jurisdiction to try indictable offences was part of the superior court's jurisdiction in 1867; none of the parties suggests otherwise. Nor does anyone argue that inferior courts had concurrent jurisdiction to try indictable offences in 1867. Although this fact is not conclusive (see *Reference Re Residential Tenancies Act*, [1981] 1 S.C.R. 714) none of the other considerations which might save the scheme from the force of s. 96 applies here. The proposed court is obviously a judicial body; its judicial aspect does not change colour when considered in the factual setting in which the court will operate; nor will the court exercise administrative powers to which its adjudicative functions are incidental. The proposed body is clearly and only a criminal court. [...]

What is proposed in the New Brunswick proposals is the establishment of a statutory court. As distinguished from what? Certainly not from existing provincial courts which must be fed criminal jurisdiction by federal legislation. No doubt, however, to separate the new court from provincial superior courts. Will that help or advance the matter if functional considerations have to be considered? It has long been the rule that s. 96, although in terms an appointing power, must be addressed in functional terms lest its application be eroded. What then, is the relation between the proposed new statutory court and s. 96? This is the key constitutional issue in the present case and, as we view the matter, the result is to defeat the new statutory court because it will effectively be a s. 96 court.

Sections 96, 97, 98, 99 and 100 are couched in mandatory terms. They do not rest merely on federal statutory powers as does s. 91(27). [See Appendix for the text of these sections]

What is being contemplated here is not one or a few transfers of criminal law power, such as has already been accomplished under the *Criminal Code*, but a complete obliteration of superior court criminal law jurisdiction. Sections 96 to 100 do not distinguish between courts of civil jurisdiction and courts of criminal jurisdiction. They should not be read as permitting the Parliament of Canada through use of its criminal law power to destroy superior courts and to deprive the Governor-General of appointing power and to exclude members of the bar from preferment for superior court appointments.

Parliament can no more give away federal constitutional powers, than a province can usurp them. Section 96 provides that "The Governor General *shall* appoint the Judges of the Superior, District and County Courts in *each* Province" (emphasis added). The proposal here is that Parliament transfers the present superior courts' jurisdiction to try indictable offences to a provincial court. The effect of this proposal would be to deprive the Governor-General of his power under s. 96 to appoint the judges who try indictable offences in New Brunswick. That is contrary to s. 96. Section 96 bars Parliament from altering the constitutional scheme envisaged by the judicature sections of the *Constitution Act, 1867* just as it does the provinces from doing so.

The traditional independence of English superior court judges has been raised to the level of a fundamental principle of our federal system by the *Constitution Act, 1982* and cannot have less importance and force in the administration of criminal law than in the case of civil matters. Under the Canadian Constitution the superior courts are independent of both levels of government. The provinces constitute, maintain and organize the superior courts; the federal authority appoints the judges. The judicature sections of the *Constitution Act, 1867* guarantee the independence of the superior courts; they apply to Parliament as well as to the provincial Legislatures.

Both sides of the proposal under review are flawed. Parliament cannot in effect give away the Governor-General's s. 96 appointing power under colour of legislation vesting jurisdiction to try all indictable offences in a provincial court. New Brunswick cannot exercise an appointing power in respect of courts with s. 96 jurisdiction under colour of legislation in relation to the constitution, maintenance and organization of courts with criminal jurisdiction.

Nor is much gained for the proposed new provincial statutory court by providing for concurrent superior court jurisdiction. The theory behind the concurrency proposal is presumably that a provincial court with concurrent rather than exclusive powers would not oust the superior court's jurisdiction, at least not to the same extent; since the superior courts' jurisdiction was not frozen as of 1867, it would be permissible to alter that jurisdiction so long as the essential core of the superior courts' jurisdiction remained; s. 96 would be no obstacle because the superior court would retain jurisdiction to try indictable offences. With respect, we think this overlooks the fact that what is being attempted here is the transformation by conjoint action of an inferior court into a superior court. Section 96 is, in our view, an insuperable obstacle to any such endeavour. [...]

There is, in our view, a cardinal difference between mere alteration or diminution of criminal jurisdiction and complete exclusion of such jurisdiction. In so far as this latter point was taken by Taschereau J., [in *Valin v. Langlois* (1879), 3 S.C.R. 1] we find it unacceptable.

It is hardly necessary to say that the proposed provincial scheme is not saved by preserving civil jurisdiction for the provincial superior courts.

We have taken perhaps a limited view of the important issues that are thrown up by the three referred questions but, having decided to address them, we felt it best to consider only those provisions of the Constitution which we think are beyond conjoint provincial and federal action. We would, therefore, allow the appeal and answer all three questions in the negative.

MACMILLAN BLOEDEL LTD. v. SIMPSON
[1995] 4 S.C.R. 725.

[Simpson contravened an injunction of the British Columbia Supreme Court prohibiting protest activities interfering with MacMillan Bloedel's logging operations in the Clayoquot Sound area of Vancouver Island. He was charged with contempt of court and, at trial, made an application to be tried in youth court pursuant to s. 47(2) of the *Young Offenders Act*. This section states that exclusive jurisdiction over *ex facie* contempt of court committed by a young person is transferred to the youth court. The application was dismissed and the appellant was later convicted and sentenced to 45 days imprisonment and a fine. He appealed his conviction on the ground that the British Columbia Supreme Court had no jurisdiction to try him. The Court of Appeal upheld the conviction.]

LAMER C.J. [La Forest, Sopinka, Gonthier and Cory JJ. Concurring]: — This case requires us to decide whether Parliament, pursuant to its criminal law power, can confer upon youth courts the exclusive power to try youths for contempt *ex facie* of superior courts. To put the question another way, must superior courts retain the power to try charges of contempt, both *in facie* and *ex facie*. The problematic aspect of the impugned legislative provision is precisely the exclusivity of the grant of jurisdiction. The historical evolution of the provincial superior courts and their importance to our constitutional structure require that these superior courts retain the full range of their inherent contempt powers. While it need not have exclusive jurisdiction, curbing the power of a superior court to control its own process alters its essence, making it something less than a superior court. Such an alteration is impermissible in Canada in the absence of a constitutional amendment.

To resolve this issue we must consider both whether the grant of jurisdiction to the youth court is permissible and whether removing the corresponding jurisdiction from the superior court is equally so. The jurisprudence concerning s. 96 of the *Constitution Act, 1867* gives guidance in considering the grant of jurisdiction. The removal of jurisdiction is better analyzed in a broader constitutional context, considering this jurisprudence along with the preamble to the *Constitution Act, 1867*, the principle of the rule of law, and the central place of the superior courts in our system of governance. [...]

A Clayoquot fisherman catching flounders and other flat fish, which lie half-covered by the sand.

I agree in part with McEachern C.J.B.C.'s analysis [at the B.C. Court of Appeal], particularly with his consideration of the inherent jurisdiction of superior courts and the nature of the contempt power. Nonetheless, in keeping with my conclusion that the essence of the problem before us is the *exclusivity* of the grant of jurisdiction to the youth court, I find that our jurisprudence on this question mandates a two-part analysis. [...]

THE SECTION 96 JURISPRUDENCE

This Court's decision in *McEvoy, supra*, establishes that s. 96 of the *Constitution Act, 1867*, limits both Parliament and the provincial legislatures. Accordingly, the first analytic step is to consider the s. 96 jurisprudence to date to determine how that limitation takes effect.

Writing for the Court in *Re Residential Tenancies Act, 1979*, [1981] 1 S.C.R. 714, Dickson J. (as he then was) reviewed the s. 96 jurisprudence up to that time and fashioned its principles into a three-part test for determining which powers, under which circumstances, can be transferred to inferior courts or to administrative tribunals without infringing the guarantee of judicial independence which s. 96 has come to stand for. Dickson J. asserted that the judicature sections of the *Constitution Act, 1867* limit the power of the provincial legislatures under s. 92(14) over the administration of justice in a province and provide a unifying force to the Canadian judicial system (at p. 728):

> Section 92(14) and ss. 96 to 100 represent one of the important compromises of the Fathers of Confederation. It is plain that what was sought to be achieved through this compromise, and the intended effect of s. 96, would be destroyed if a province could pass legislation creating a tribunal, appoint members thereto, and then confer on the tribunal the jurisdiction of the superior courts. What was conceived as a strong constitutional base for national unity, through a unitary judicial system, would be gravely undermined.

After reviewing the jurisprudence, Dickson J. concluded that there was a general trend towards an increasingly broad test of constitutional validity, except in cases where the judicial function in question is isolated from the rest of the administrative structure of the legislation in question. Having thus stated his view of the purpose of the constitutional provisions and the directions in the jurisprudence, he elaborated the test which is now our standard for analysing grants of jurisdiction to tribunals not presided over by s. 96 judges. [Lamer C.J. then reviewed the three-part test, and then considered Sobeys Stores.] [...]

The decision in *Reference Re Young Offenders Act* is important to my analysis in this case both because it continues the development of the s. 96 jurisprudence and because it addresses in a broad manner the same Act which is before the Court now. I opened my analysis in *Reference Re Young Offenders Act* by stating (at p. 264):

> Section 96 of the *Constitution Act, 1867* is regarded as a means of protecting the "core" jurisdiction of the superior courts so as to provide for some uniformity throughout the country in the judicial system. The case law has developed principles to ensure that s. 96 would not be rendered meaningless through the use of the provincial competence to constitute, maintain and organize provincial courts staffed with provincially appointed judges having the same jurisdiction and powers as superior courts. [...]

> [I]f the jurisdiction conferred on Youth Courts by Parliament is within the core of jurisdiction of superior courts, Parliament cannot confer such jurisdiction on courts presided over by judges not appointed in accordance with s. 96.

While there were three judgments in the case, none of my colleagues took issue with my statement of the law regarding the core jurisdiction of the superior courts. The superior courts have a core or inherent jurisdiction which is integral to their operations. The jurisdiction which forms this core cannot be removed from the superior courts by either level of government, without amending the Constitution. Without this core jurisdiction, s. 96 could not be said either to ensure uniformity in the judicial system throughout the country or to protect the independence of the judiciary. Furthermore, the power of superior courts to fully control their own process is, in our system where the superior court of general jurisdiction is central, essential to the maintenance of the rule of law itself. I discuss the contents and contours of the core jurisdiction below.

The second aspect of the *Reference Re Young Offenders Act* decision which figures in my analysis here is the precise issue which was determined at that time. [...] The *Reference Re Young Offenders Act* decision states explicitly that there is a core jurisdiction of superior court powers which cannot be removed by either level of government in the absence of a constitutional amendment. It also leaves open the specific question of whether individual provisions of the Act may offend s. 96 even though the overall scheme of the Act does not. While it was not required in that case, *Reference Re Young Offenders Act* mandates a two-stage analysis in cases like the present. The first stage, following the jurisprudence of *Residential*

Tenancies and *Sobeys Stores*, is to consider whether the <u>grant</u> of jurisdiction is permissible. The second stage, considering the emphasis on core jurisdiction in *Reference Re Young Offenders Act*, is to decide whether the superior court's jurisdiction can be <u>ousted</u>. In other words, the second stage weighs whether an exclusive grant of jurisdiction is permissible.

IS THE GRANT OF JURISDICTION PERMISSIBLE?

1. Characterization

The first step in analysing whether a grant of jurisdiction infringes s. 96 is to properly characterize the provision in question. [Lamer C.J. then reviewed the law and academic commentary] [...]

On the basis of the history of contempt of court, academic commentary, and the overall scheme of the *Criminal Code* and the *Young Offenders Act*, I am persuaded that criminal contempt of court has distinct characteristics from other crimes. By history and procedure, as well as its links with the inherent jurisdiction of superior courts which I discuss below, criminal contempt of court can be distinguished from other criminal offences. While other crimes occur in society and the law merely defines or criminalizes them, contempt of court does not occur in the absence of a court. Having considered the nature of criminal contempt of court, I will now proceed to characterize the power transferred by s. 47(2) of the *Young Offenders Act* and apply the test outlined in *Residential Tenancies*.

A proper characterization for s. 96 purposes must be narrow and consider the nature of the dispute. While I noted in *Reference Re Young Offenders Act* that the nature of the dispute provides little assistance in criminal law, this is not the case here as contempt of court is distinctive. The dispute is one between the individual and the court itself. *Ex facie* criminal contempt of superior courts committed by youths has some aspects of a crime and some aspects of a *sui generis* court power. A proper characterization must be narrow enough to reflect both these aspects. I would therefore characterize the jurisdiction transferred by s. 47(2) as the power to punish youths for *ex facie* contempt of a superior court.

2. The *Residential Tenancies* Test

Having settled on a characterization of the power being transferred, the three branches of the *Residential Tenancies* test are quickly dealt with in this case. Power to punish youths for *ex facie* contempt of superior courts was within the jurisdiction of superior courts at Confederation. Under the second branch of the test, this power obviously remains judicial in nature even in its new institutional setting. Nonetheless, when considering the institutional function of the youth courts, a transfer of this power is permissible. As we elaborated in *Reference Re Young Offenders Act*, the policy objectives of the youth court system are clear and laudable. Our society wishes to establish different treatment for youths accused of criminal offences than for adults. Youth courts have an expertise in providing procedural protections appropriate for youths and in deciding punishments for convicted young offenders. The power to punish youths for *ex facie* contempt of superior courts is indeed a mere ancillary to these primary functions.

Accordingly, granting jurisdiction to punish youth for *ex facie* contempt of superior courts does not infringe s. 96. What remains to be considered, however, is whether this jurisdiction can be granted to the exclusion of superior courts.

CAN THE SUPERIOR COURTS' JURISDICTION BE REMOVED?

In the case of transfers of jurisdiction *which are within the inherent powers* of a superior court, the *Residential Tenancies* test does not provide a framework for analysing the most important aspect of constitutional infringement. The true problem in this case is the exclusivity of the grant. The impugned section of the *Young Offenders Act* clearly states that *exclusive* jurisdiction over *ex facie* contempt of court is transferred to the youth court. [...] The requirement to consider whether the corresponding removal of jurisdiction is valid only arises when the core jurisdiction of superior courts is affected. In many instances, therefore, the *Residential Tenancies* test provides a complete answer to the constitutional query.

To determine whether either Parliament or a provincial legislature may remove part of the superior court's jurisdiction, we must consider the contours and contents of the "core" or "inherent" jurisdiction of superior courts. On the facts of this appeal, the British Columbia Supreme Court being the superior court involved, we need only consider whether this jurisdiction can be removed from superior courts of general jurisdiction, that is, the provincial superior courts. Whether jurisdiction to punish youth for *ex facie* contempt of statutorily constituted superior courts can be removed from those courts is a question for another day since neither the parties nor the courts below addressed the issue of whether a distinction might exist between these two kinds of superior courts.

The seminal article on the core or inherent jurisdiction of superior courts is I. H. Jacob's "The Inherent Jurisdiction of the Court" (1970), 23 *Current Legal Problems* 23. Jacob's work is a starting point for many discussions of the subject, figures prominently in analyses of contempt of court, and was cited with approval by Dickson C.J. in *B.C.G.E.U. v. British Columbia (Attorney General)*, [1988] 2 S.C.R. 214. [...] Regarding the basis of inherent jurisdiction, Jacob states (at p. 27):

> [...] the jurisdiction to exercise these powers was derived, not from any statute or rule of law, but from the very nature of the court as a superior court of law, and for this reason such jurisdiction has been called "inherent." This description has been criticised as being "metaphysical" [cite omitted], but I think nevertheless that it is apt to describe the quality of this jurisdiction. For the essential character of a superior court of law necessarily involves that it should be invested with a power to maintain its authority and to prevent its process being obstructed and abused. *Such a power is intrinsic in a superior court; it is its very life-blood, its very essence, its immanent attribute. Without such a power, the court would have form but would lack substance. The jurisdiction which is inherent in a superior court of law is that which enables it to fulfil itself as a court of law.* (emphasis added.)

While inherent Jurisdiction may be difficult to define, it is of paramount importance to the existence of a superior court. The full range of powers which comprise the inherent jurisdiction of a superior court are, together, its "essential character" or "immanent attribute". To remove any part of this core emasculates the court, making it something other than a superior court. [...]

This Court's jurisprudence has also contributed to outlining the contours of the inherent jurisdiction of superior courts. In *Crevier v. Attorney General of Québec*, [1981] 2 S.C.R. 220, the Court considered whether the provincial legislature could grant the power to make final decisions on questions of jurisdiction to an appeal tribunal under Quebec's *Professional Code*. Writing for the Court, Laskin C.J. stated (at pp. 236-37):

> It is true that this is the first time that this Court has declared unequivocally that a provincially constituted statutory tribunal cannot constitutionally be immunized from review of decisions on questions of jurisdiction. In my opinion, this limitation, arising by virtue of s. 96, stands on the same footing as the well-accepted limitation on the power of provincial statutory tribunals to make unreviewable determinations of constitutionality. There may be differences of opinion as to what are questions of jurisdiction but, in my lexicon, they rise above and are different from errors of law, whether involving statutory construction or evidentiary matters or other matters. [...] [G]iven that s. 96 is in the *British North America Act* and that it would make a mockery of it to treat it in non-functional formal terms as a mere appointing power, *I can think of nothing that is more the hallmark of a superior court than the vesting of power in a provincial statutory tribunal to determine the limits of its jurisdiction without appeal or other review.* (emphasis added.)

This decision establishes, therefore, that powers which are `hallmarks of superior courts' cannot be removed from those courts. [...]

In the constitutional arrangements passed on to us by the British and recognized by the preamble to the *Constitution Act, 1867*, the provincial superior courts are the foundation of the rule of law itself. Governance by rule of law requires a judicial system that can ensure its orders are enforced and its process respected. In Canada, the provincial superior court is the only court of general jurisdiction and as such is the centre of the judicial system. None of our statutory courts has the same core jurisdiction as the superior court and therefore none is as crucial to the rule of law. To remove the power to punish contempt *ex facie* by youths would maim the institution which is at the heart of our judicial system. Destroying part of the core jurisdiction would be tantamount to abolishing the superior courts of general jurisdiction, which is impermissible without constitutional amendment.

The core jurisdiction of the provincial superior courts comprises those powers which are essential to the administration of justice and the maintenance of the rule of law. It is unnecessary in this case to enumerate the precise powers which compose inherent jurisdiction, as the power to punish for contempt *ex facie* is obviously within that jurisdiction. The power to punish for all forms of contempt is one of the defining features of superior courts. [...]

In light of its importance to the very existence of a superior court, no aspect of the contempt power may be removed from a superior court without infringing all those sections of our Constitution which refer to our existing judicial system as inherited from the British, including ss. 96 to 101, s. 129, and the principle of the rule of law recognized both in the preamble and in all our conventions of governance. [...]

DISPOSITION

I would dismiss the appeal on the grounds that s. 47(2) is unconstitutional to the extent that it purports to confer exclusive jurisdiction on the youth court and to deprive a superior court of general jurisdiction of its *ex facie* contempt power. Section 47(2) is valid to the extent that it confers jurisdiction on the youth court. The section should be read down accordingly. As read down, the section is inoperative to deprive the superior court of its jurisdiction to convict the appellant of contempt in this case. [...]

McLACHLIN J. [L'Heureux-Dubé, Iacobucci and Major JJ. concurring] — [...] [T]he heart of the problem posed on this appeal [is]: when may Parliament or the provincial legislatures confer powers exercised by s. 96 courts on inferior tribunals created for special purposes? Clearly, Parliament and the legislatures cannot be allowed to set up shadow courts exercising all or some of the powers of s. 96 courts. [...] What is required is a test for transfer of s. 96 powers which balances the need to maintain a strong constitutional position of s. 96 courts with the need to provide sufficient scope for the creation of effective administrative tribunals. [...]

The *Residential Tenancies* test is based on the premise that any judicial power can be transferred from a s. 96 court to an inferior tribunal, provided that the power is ancillary to the tribunal's larger mandate. Shadow courts, devoted exclusively or primarily to rendering judgments which s. 96 courts have traditionally rendered, are forbidden. Only if the tribunal's major focus is a larger one and the powers can be said to lose their judicial character in the administrative context, is the tribunal permitted to incidentally exercise judicial powers traditionally exercised by s. 96 courts.

THE PROPOSED "CORE" TEST

The Court of Appeal below and the Chief Justice in this Court propose a modification of this test. Acknowledging that the *Residential Tenancies* test is satisfied in this case, the Chief Justice argues that an additional question must be asked: is the power transferred a "core" power of s. 96 courts? The boundaries and constituent elements of this core are unspecified but seem to extend at least to the inherent powers of s. 96 courts. This is a new test which in my respectful opinion needlessly derogates from the functional approach of the *Residential Tenancies* test. As I understand the proposed test, it would no longer be sufficient that the transfer of judicial power historically exercised by s. 96 courts be ancillary to the larger function of inferior tribunal; it would also be necessary to show that the particular power transferred is not one of the "core" powers of s. 96 courts. This "core" is not defined by reference to the functions of the tribunal, but by the nature of the s. 96 power transferred. What is proposed is a class of "core" powers which, by their very nature, are essential to s. 96 courts and cannot be transferred to other courts regardless of whether or not the three inquiries of the *Residential Tenancies* test are satisfied. This marks a shift from the functional approach of the *Residential Tenancies* test for transfer of s. 96 powers toward a more categorical approach. [...]

The significance of this change should not be underestimated. If accepted, it would amount to an important new fetter on the ability of Parliament and the provincial legislatures to create effective tribunals to ensure compliance with regulatory schemes. The significance of the additional fetter is enhanced by the fact that it is constitutional, and hence incapable of being legislatively overridden, as well as by the fact that what falls within the core remains largely undefined. [...]

The crux of the Chief Justice's argument is that the superior courts can never be deprived of their "core" powers, which include the power to regulate their own process, including contempt not in the face of the court.

The difficulty which this argument faces is that it has long been settled that under the rule of law Parliament and the legislatures may limit and structure the ways in which the superior courts exercise their powers. These inherent powers of superior courts are simply innate powers of internal regulation which courts acquire by virtue of their status as courts of law. The inherent power of superior courts to regulate their process does not preclude elected bodies from enacting legislation affecting that process. The court's inherent powers exist to complement the statutory assignment of specific powers, not override or replace them: [...]

All of this is simply to restate the general principle that courts must conform to the rule of law. They can exercise more power in the control of their process, in different ways, than is expressly provided by statute, but must generally abide by the dictates of the legislature. It follows that Parliament and the legislatures can legislate to limit the superior courts' powers, including their powers over contempt, provided that the legislation is not otherwise unconstitutional. If this is so, then it is wrong to posit a core of inherent superior court powers to regulate the process of the courts which the legislators cannot touch. [...]

Before leaving the policy argument, it may be useful to ask whether, when all is considered, it can be said that the *Residential Tenancies* test might fail to maintain the protection of s. 96 courts which the Constitution requires. I would not suggest that the *Residential Tenancies* test is forever cast in stone, nor that situations may not arise affecting the stature and integrity of the superior court, which could require the court to invoke its inherent power to safeguard its own process in a manner which was not contemplated by the *Residential Tenancies* test. This said, the current test for transfer, developed in response to Canadian needs over a period of several decades, strikes a reasonable balance between the need to permit Parliament and the legislatures to annex effective administrative tribunals to their legislative schemes, and the need to maintain the constitutional position of the s. 96 courts. The test permits only incidental derogations of powers from s. 96 courts, and then only to the extent that their judicial nature is transformed by the administrative context in which they are exercised. The greater the powers sought to transferred, the greater the curtailment of the inherent powers of the s. 96 courts, the more likely the powers are to be seen as judicial rather than administrative, barring their transfer from s. 96 courts to inferior tribunals.

On the other hand, the revised "core" test proposed would impose significant new restrictions on the power of Parliament and the legislatures to endow specialized tribunals with sufficient powers to meet particular problems and deprive many tribunals of powers which they have long exercised. The alternative of dual powers exercised by the tribunals and the courts would encourage forum shopping and contribute to expense and delay in the resolution of problems within these specialized areas. At the same time, the addition of a concept of a category of core of inherent powers which can never be transferred would add a new element of uncertainty to the law. As the Chief Justice admits, inherent jurisdiction "may be difficult to define" (para. 30). He declines, quite understandably, "to enumerate the precise powers which compose inherent jurisdiction" (para. 38). What is clear is that this concept of inherent jurisdiction includes some of what administrative tribunals now do. What is not clear is how far beyond this the penumbra of inherent powers may extend.

For these reasons, I remain unpersuaded that the *Residential Tenancies* test for transfer s. 96 judicial powers to inferior tribunals should be supplemented by the concept of immutable core powers which can never constitutionally be transferred from s. 96 courts, no matter how incidental their role in the overall administrative scheme. I would maintain the *Residential Tenancies* test.

APPLICATION OF THE RESIDENTIAL TENANCIES TEST IN THIS CASE

As the Chief Justice concedes, application of the *Residential Tenancies* test in this case leads to the result that the transfer of contempt not in the face of the court committed by juveniles from s. 96 courts to the youth courts is valid and constitutional. The power was historically possessed by s. 96 courts, it is judicial, and it is merely ancillary to the larger role of the youth courts in relation to the special problems and needs of young offenders.

A number of assaults were made on the proposition that conferral of this power is ancillary only. None, in my view, succeed. [...]

[Appeal dismissed, McLachlin, L'Heureux-Dubé, Iacobucci and Major JJ. dissenting]

(d)   Judicial Independence

SHETREET, "JUDICIAL INDEPENDENCE.
NEW CONCEPTUAL DIMENSIONS AND CONTEMPORARY CHALLENGES"
IN SHETREET AND DESCHÊNES, EDS., JUDICIAL INDEPENDENCE (MARTINUS NIJHOFF, 1985) 590 AT 593.

THE CONTEMPORARY SIGNIFICANCE OF JUDICIAL INDEPENDENCE

The importance of the principle of judicial independence has grown, and the attention which it has received has continuously increased as a result, among other things, of the ever increasing role of the judiciary in our society. This general trend of increasing judicialization is shared by many countries, including Holland, Belgium, Israel, Australia, and the United States, to mention only a few.

The increasing role of the judiciary is partially a result of social developments. Professor Cappelletti mentions several such developments. Firstly, the expansion of the welfare state with wide ranging legislation and administrative regulations and a corresponding expansion in litigation against government services. Secondly, the development of "social rights," a typical legal by-product of the welfare state. Thirdly, the development of collective procedures, the American class action, or the German Verbandsklagen, or the French action collective, which brought about a process of massification of the law, transforming what has been once a simple two-party litigation to a major multi-party complex litigation. Fourthly, the industrialization and "massification of society."

While these developments which increased judicialization of society, such as the process of urbanization and industrialization, which has called for greater recourse to the courts, could be viewed as natural and objective developments, one might also mention causes for greater judicialization which may be referred to as "convenience-based processes of judicialization." This refers to judicialization of issues for reasons of largely political convenience of the other branches of government. As Sir Ninian Stephen writes, "both the legislature and the executive may find it very convenient to shift to the judiciary the task of initiative-taking in [sensitive] areas. Elected bodies may have much to fear if they have to decide such issues for themselves; wise politicians may well prefer to avoid the issue for fear of electoral backlash." [...]

Some writers view this trend with disfavour and suggest that the legislature and the executive should not shift to the courts the burden of resolving social issues for which they, not the judiciary, bear the primary responsibility. I personally believe that we should not frown at this development. If the community has more confidence in the judiciary than in the political branches, and if the other branches shift the burden of resolving embarrassing issues to the judiciary, it falls on the judiciary to serve a useful social function. It is seized with the duty of filling a vacuum left by the other branches, either because they lost public confidence, or because they refrain from assuming the responsibility of determining the issue.

250

Whatever the approach one may wish to adopt towards this trend of increasing judicialization, it has confronted the courts with challenges which they have not faced before, and it has increased the social interest in promoting judicial independence.

DEFINING THE "INDEPENDENCE" OF THE "JUDICIARY"

Much reference is made in legal literature, as well as in public debate and discussion, to "an independent judiciary" and to the vital importance of the independence of the judiciary to a free society. But what do we mean when we say "an independent judiciary?" [...]

Sir Ninian Stephen defines an independent judiciary as "a judiciary which dispenses justice according to law without regard to the policies and inclinations of the government of the day." Erkki Juhani Taipale, a European jurist, found the focus of judicial independence in "that the organs administering justice can only be subordinate to the law, and that only the law can influence the contents of the decisions made by these organs. No other state authority, not even the highest, is allowed to influence the decisions made by the judicial organs. This judicial independence is a guarantee for the fulfillment of the legal security of the individual."

With all due respect, the definitions offered above for judicial independence by the various writers mentioned are not complete. They generally focus on the independence of the judges in the decision-making process. But this aspect of judicial independence, though of vital importance, is only one aspect of the concept of judicial independence. This is the substantive independence of the judge. [...] In addition to this aspect, there are other, essential aspects of judicial independence, including personal independence, collective independence and internal independence, which must be complied with so that a judiciary may be conceptually viewed as "independent." [...]

In the enumeration of the essential elements of judicial independence a distinction must be made between two aspects of the concept of the independence of the judiciary: the independence of the individual judges and the collective independence of the judiciary as a body. The independence of the individual judge is comprised of two essential elements: substantive independence and personal independence. Substantive independence means that in the making of judicial decisions and exercising other official duties, individual judges are subject to no other authority but the law.

Personal independence means that the judicial terms of office and tenure are adequately secured. Personal independence is secured by judicial appointment during good behaviour terminated at retirement age, and by safeguarding judicial remuneration. Thus, executive control over terms of service of the judges, such as remuneration, pensions, or travel allowance is inconsistent with the concept of judicial independence. Still much less acceptable is any executive control over case assignment, court scheduling, or moving judges from one court to another, or from one locality to another.

Independence of the judiciary implies not only that a judge should be free from executive or legislative encroachment and from political pressures and entanglements but also that he should be removed from financial or business entanglement likely to affect or rather to seem to affect him in the exercise of his judicial functions. To this end, statutory rules as well as judicial traditions and conventions have been established to remove judges from political and business entanglements. A modern conception of judicial independence cannot be confined to the individual judge and to his substantive and personal independence, but must include collective independence of the judiciary as a whole. The concept of collective judicial independence may require a greater measure of judicial participation in the central administration of the courts, including the preparation of budgets for the courts, and depending on one's view of the nature of judicial independence, the extent of judicial participation may range from consultation, sharing responsibility with the executive (or the legislature) and exclusive judicial responsibility. [...]

IV. THE CONSTITUTIONAL POSITION OF THE JUDICIARY

THE NORMATIVE LEVEL: CONSTITUTIONAL V. LEGISLATIVE

The constitutional position of the judiciary depends on the normative level of the legal norms which provide for the courts and their jurisdiction, and for the terms of office and tenure of the judges. When these are provided for in constitutional provisions then one could speak of constitutional courts, or constitutional judges. Normally any change in such provisions would require a constitutional amendment. Sometimes the existence of certain courts is provided for in the constitution, but the jurisdiction of such a court is defined by ordinary legislature. In such a case one can speak of a constitutional court and legislative jurisdiction. The same may occur with regard to judges. Some of them may be constitutional judges, others may be the creation of ordinary statutes ("legislative judges"). Constitutionally speaking, legislative freedom to abolish courts to change their jurisdiction or affect terms of judicial independence by ordinary legislation depends on the normative position of the provision in question, as explained. [...]

Judicial independence is viewed in Canada as a most significant principle which lies at the foundation of the legal order. As Chief Justice Howland, of the Ontario Court of Appeal said in the recent case of *R. v. Valente* "judicial independence, like the rule of law, is one of the corner stones of our legal system. The courts stand between the state and the individual to maintain the supremacy of the law. They safeguard the rights of the individual and ensure that there is no interference with his or with her liberty which is not justified by the laws."

The Canadian constitution vests significant powers in the courts. Thus under the *Canadian Charter of Rights and Freedoms* (section 1) the courts are established as the final constitutional arbitrators on whether the reasonable limits on the individual rights and freedoms prescribed by law are "demonstrably justified in a free and democratic society." At the same time, the courts in Canada are entrusted with the function of constitutional arbitration between the provinces and the federal government.

In spite of the central role that Canadian courts play in the constitutional order and in the system of government, the role of the judiciary as a constitutional branch of the government is not expressly provided for and secured in the Canadian Constitution. Certain constitutional provisions refer to "an independent and impartial tribunal" which alone can pronounce a person guilty of a criminal offence as provided by Section 11(d) of the *Charter*, and Section 2(f) of the *Canadian Bill of Rights*. However, there is no general express constitutional provision in Canada which states that the judiciary shall be independent and defines its powers. Instead, legal arrangements of different normative value lay down judicial tenure and terms of judicial office including judicial appointment, removal, discipline, retirement age and judicial remuneration, or the control over judicial administration. Some of these matters are embodied in constitutional provisions such as the good behaviour tenure of the judges of the superior courts of the provinces and their retirement age at 75 (under section 99 of the *Constitution Act, 1867*): the appointing authority is the Governor General (under section 96) and the judges should be appointed from the Bars of the respective provinces (under sections 97, 98). The *Constitution Act, 1867* (section 100) also requires that the salaries and pensions of the judges of the superior and county courts be fixed and provided by the Parliament of Canada. [...]

An implied reference to judicial independence can also be found in Section 7 of the *Charter* which provides that every one has the right to life, liberty and security of the person and the right not to be deprived thereof, except in accordance with the "principles of fundamental justice," which must also include judicial independence. It can be argued, however, that Section 11(d) by specific reference to judicial independence excludes it from Section 7, which is more general.

This constitutional development which should be generally acclaimed, does not, however, rectify the constitutional deficiency in Canada, to which I have referred earlier, namely the absence of substantive express protection of judicial independence against possible encroachment by the legislature or the executive when they exercise ordinary constitutional and statutory powers over the judges. *Beauregard v. The Queen* serves as a good illustration of this deficiency. The constitutional ambiguity whether Parliament may properly reduce judicial salaries or, put in broader terms, introduce detrimental changes in judicial terms of service is indicative of an objectionable situation and deserves criticism under the better view as to the proper conception of judicial independence. The decision of the Federal Court of Appeal sustained the judgment of Justice Addy in *Beauregard* but reversed his holding that Parliament cannot constitutionally reduce salaries of sitting judges. If the Federal Court of Appeal is upheld on appeal, it means that judicial terms of office are at the mercy of Parliament, subject to the limitations which emanate from the language of the *Constitution Act of 1867*, as suggested by the majority opinion in the Federal Court of Appeal in the *Beauregard* case.

By way of contrast, I wish to refer again to the United States where the existence of an adequate constitutional protection removes the ambiguities regarding the legislative interference with judicial remuneration. *U.S. v. Will* held that congressional legislation which purported to freeze judicial pay increases was unconstitutional when the increase had already been in force, but was perfectly proper with regard to increase which had not yet come into force. The name will apply to any detrimental change in the conditions of judicial service applicable to sitting judges. [...]

THE ENVELOPE OF RULES: ACTUAL AND APPEARANCE OF IMPARTIALITY

In the process of decision-making the judge should be free from any irrelevant controls, overt and covert. Two dimensions should be recognized. First, there is a significant social interest of attaining actual impartiality and neutrality of the judge. Second, but no less important, is the appearance of impartiality. The necessity of maintaining not only the actual but also the appearance of, impartiality is mandated by the value of public confidence in the courts, the judges and the judicial process. From this emanates a theoretical approach, which requires the creation of an envelope of rules, which covers the judge and protects his substantive independence. This envelope of rules covers the judge's official and non-official sphere of activity and shields his substantive independence from dependencies, associations or even less intensive involvements which might cast doubts on his neutrality.

Because of the need to maintain the appearance of impartiality, when shaping the contents of the rules of the "envelope" covering the judicial office, the tendency has been to err on the side of caution. This is why we find a series of protective rules, some which restrict the judges in their conduct, and others which restrict the conduct of others when it relates to judges. Thus, we find restrictive rules of conduct excluding judges from association with the other branches of the government, limiting their business association, and excluding them from, matters of public controversy or matters which might put into question the dignity and the integrity of the judiciary. As illustrations of such protective or restrictive rules one can mention the doctrine of judicial immunity, the sub judice rule, and the limitations on parliamentary comments on judge except upon a specific motion.

Other illustrations are also the disqualification of judges from serving as members of legislative bodies or in executive offices.

THE PRINCIPLE OF FAIR REFLECTION OF SOCIETY

There are many illustrations of a requirement of inclusion of judges with certain characteristics on the bench of a given court, or on the bench in general. This model is often found in federal, or multi-cultural countries where the constituent political units, cultures or geographical regions are expected to be reflected on the bench. The inclusion of the required judges is secured at times by an express statutory provision, and at times by conventions which are strictly followed. The Canadian scene offers again an instructive example. By statute, three judges of the nine Supreme Court justices must come from Quebec, and by convention three judges come from Ontario, two from the western provinces of Canada, and one from the Atlantic provinces. [...]

The support for a principle of fair reflection comes also from the criticism which has been directed in many countries at the social composition of the judiciary, coming predominantly from the upper middle class. The response to the challenge of a judiciary which fails to reflect society might come from a doctrinal approach based on an inclusionary principle of fair reflection which is mandated by the doctrine of substantive independence and the value of public confidence in the court.

Criticism of the narrow social, ideological or geographical background of judges has been recorded in numerous countries such as in England, Canada, Greece, France and West Germany, to mention a few. [...]

An important duty lies upon the appointing authorities to ensure a balanced composition of the judiciary, ideologically, socially, culturally and the like. This is based on a doctrinal ground, which has been suggested: the principle of fair reflection. This doctrinal approach may be supported by additional arguments. The judiciary is a branch of the government, not merely a dispute resolution institution. As such, it cannot be composed in total disregard of the society. Hence, due regard must be given to the consideration of fair reflection. There are other grounds for ensuring well balanced composition of the judiciary. First, the need to preserve public confidence in the courts. Secondly, the need to insure balanced panels in appellate courts, particularly in cases with public or political overtones.

I believe that a reflective judiciary is an imperative factor for maintaining the important value of public confidence in the courts. I do not share the school of thought which unduly emphasizes the impact of personal values on judicial decision-making and disregards the balancing effect of social controls, system factors and institutional controls. But even the balanced proposition to which I adhere, that adjudication involves a certain degree of imposition of the judges' own values, must lead to a well supported claim for a reflective judiciary. The process and standards of judicial selection must ensure fair reflection of social classes, ethnic and religious groups, ideological inclinations and, where appropriate, geographical areas. The reflection should be fair and not numerical or accurately proportional. Likewise, the compliance with this principle of a reflective judiciary is subject to the requirements of maintaining the professional quality and the moral integrity of the judiciary.

- Research Note -
INDEPENDENCE OF THE JUDICIARY

The core concepts of judicial independence are "impartiality" and "independence". These are distinct values. Each imposes separate constitutional requirements.

"Impartiality" refers to the state of mind or attitude of the tribunal in relation to the issues and the parties in a particular case. Impartiality requires absence of bias, actual or perceived. The test is what would reasonable and right minded persons think if, having become fully informed, they viewed the matter realistically and practically, and thought the matter through. If, under those conditions, the reasonable, right minded person would think the judge is biased, the constitutional requirement for impartiality is violated.

"Independence" refers to a status or relationship to others – particularly the relationship of the judiciary to the executive branch of government. The independent status of the judiciary must be protected by objective guarantees, including security of tenure, financial security and institutional independence with respect to matters of administration bearing directly on the exercise of its judicial function. Perception still governs, but independence requires that a reasonable and right minded person perceive that the tribunal enjoys the essential objective conditions or guarantees of judicial independence. It is insufficient to perceive that the tribunal will act rightly regardless of whether it enjoys such conditions or guarantees.

The leading case to set this out is *Valente v. The Queen*, [1985] 2 S.C.R. 673. *Valente* raised the issue of whether a judge of the Ontario Provincial Court hearing criminal cases, whose independence and impartiality are expressly guaranteed by s. 11(*d*) of the *Canadian Charter*, was an independent tribunal within the meaning of that provision. Justice Le Dain observed that while desirable, it is not constitutionally required to implement the most elaborate and rigorous conditions of judicial independence. His reason was that the constitutional guarantees will be applied to a variety of tribunals, and should allow for flexible construction to respect that diversity.

The diversity which *Valente* allowed, and which existed in fact, spawned a large jurisprudence, as municipal court judges, provincial court judges, superior court judges, masters and prothonotaries contested salaries, pensions, working conditions, removals and related matters. A significant number of these cases reached the Supreme Court of Canada. The Supreme Court's now lengthy jurisprudence have refashioned some of the constitutional requirements first elaborated by *Valente*, and added detail and complexity to certain other matters *Valente* first explored. The constitutional challenges continue to engage the courts.

The essence of security of tenure, Justice Le Dain said in *Valente*, is that the appointment be made until an age of retirement, for a fixed term, or for a specific adjudicative task, and that the tenure be secure against interference by the Executive or other appointing authority in a discretionary manner (p. 698).

The most important cases concerning financial security are the two *Provincial Court Judges References* of 1997 and 2005. The 1997 *Reference* is reproduced in chapter I(1) above. The 2005 *Reference* follows below.

PROVINCIAL JUDGES REFERENCE II
[2005] 2 S.C.R. 286.

[Provincial Court judges in New Brunswick, Ontario and Quebec, justices of the peace in Alberta and municipal court judges in Quebec sought judicial review of their provincial governments' decisions to reject certain compensation commission recommendations relating to their salaries and benefits.]

The following is the judgment delivered by

The Court: —

I. Introduction

¶ 1 These appeals again raise the important question of judicial independence and the need to maintain independence both in fact and in public perception. Litigants who engage our judicial system should be in no doubt that they are before a judge who is demonstrably independent and is motivated only by a search for a just and principled result.

¶ 2 The concept of judicial independence has evolved over time. Indeed, "[c]onceptions have changed over the years as to what ideally may be required in the way of substance and procedure for securing judicial independence.... Opinions differ on what is necessary or desirable, or feasible": *Valente v. The Queen*, [1985] 2 S.C.R. 673, at p. 692, per Le Dain J.

¶ 3 This evolution is evident in the context of judicial remuneration. In *Valente*, at p. 706, Le Dain J. held that what was essential was not that judges' remuneration be established by an independent committee, but that a provincial court judge's right to a salary be established by law. By 1997 this statement had proved to be incomplete and inadequate. In *Reference re Remuneration of Judges of the Provincial Court of Prince Edward Island*, [1997] 3 S.C.R. 3 ("*Reference*"), this Court held that independent commissions were required to improve the process designed to ensure judicial independence but that the commissions' recommendations need not be binding. These commissions were intended to remove the amount of judges' remuneration from the political sphere and to avoid confrontation between governments and the judiciary. The *Reference* has not provided the anticipated solution, and more is needed....

A. *The Principle of Judicial Independence*

¶ 4 The basis for the principle of judicial independence can be found in both our common law and the Canadian Constitution; see *Beauregard v. Canada*, [1986] 2 S.C.R. 56, at pp. 70-73; *Ell v. Alberta*, [2003] 1 S.C.R. 857, at paras. 18-23. Judicial independence has been called "the lifeblood of constitutionalism in democratic societies" (*Beauregard*, at p. 70), and has been said to exist "for the benefit of the judged, not the judges" (*Ell*, at para. 29). Independence is necessary because of the judiciary's role as protector of the Constitution and the fundamental values embodied in it, including the rule of law, fundamental justice, equality and preservation of the democratic process; *Beauregard*, at p. 70.

¶ 5 There are two dimensions to judicial independence, one individual and the other institutional. The individual dimension relates to the independence of a particular judge. The institutional dimension relates to the independence of the court the judge sits on. Both dimensions depend upon objective standards that protect the judiciary's role: *Valente*, at p. 687; *Beauregard*, at p. 70; *Ell*, at para. 28.

¶ 6 The judiciary must both be and be seen to be independent. Public confidence depends on both these requirements being met: *Valente*, at p. 689. Judicial Independence serves not as an end in itself, but as a means to safeguard our constitutional order and to maintain public confidence in the administration of justice": *Ell*, at para. 29.

¶ 7 The components of judicial independence are: security of tenure, administrative independence and financial security; see *Valente*, at pp. 694, 704 and 708; the *Reference*, at para. 115; *Ell*, at para. 28.

¶ 8 The *Reference*, at paras. 131-35, states that financial security embodies three requirements. First, judicial salaries can be maintained or changed only by recourse to an independent commission. Second, no negotiations are permitted between the judiciary and the government. Third, salaries may not fall below a minimum level....

¶ 10 The often spirited wage negotiations and the resulting public rhetoric had the potential to deleteriously affect the public perception of judicial independence. However independent judges were in fact, the danger existed that the public might think they could be influenced either for or against the government because of issues arising from salary negotiations. The *Reference* reflected the goal of avoiding such confrontations. Lamer C.J.'s hope was to "depoliticize" the relationship by changing the methodology for determining judicial remuneration (para. 146).

¶ 11 Compensation commissions were expected to become the forum for discussion, review and recommendations on issues of judicial compensation. Although not binding, their recommendations, it was hoped, would lead to an effective resolution of salary and related issues. Courts would avoid setting the amount of judicial compensation, and provincial governments would avoid being accused of manipulating the courts for their own purposes.

¶ 12 Those were the hopes, but they remain unfulfilled. In some provinces and at the federal level, judicial commissions appear, so far, to be working satisfactorily. In other provinces, however, a pattern of routine dismissal of commission reports has resulted in litigation. Instead of diminishing friction between judges and governments, the result has been to exacerbate it. Direct negotiations no longer take place but have been replaced by litigation. These regrettable developments cast a dim light on all involved. In order to avoid future conflicts such as those at issue in the present case, the principles of the compensation commission process elaborated in the *Reference* must be clarified.

B. *The Fundamental Principles of the Commission Process*

¶ 13 The principles stated in the *Reference* remain valid. The *Reference* focused on three themes: the nature of compensation commissions and their recommendations; the obligation of the government to respond; and the scope of judicial review of the government's response and the related remedies.

(1) The Nature of the Compensation Commission and Its Recommendations

¶ 14 The *Reference* laid the groundwork to ensure that provincial court judges are independent from governments by precluding salary negotiations between them and avoiding any arbitrary interference with judges' remuneration. The commission process is an "institutional sieve" (*Reference*, at paras. 170, 185 and 189) - a structural separation between the government and the judiciary. The process is neither adjudicative interest arbitration nor judicial decision making. Its focus is on identifying the appropriate level of remuneration for the judicial office in question. All relevant issues may be addressed. The process is flexible and its purpose is not simply to "update" the previous commission's report. However, in the absence of reasons to the contrary, the starting point should be the date of the previous commission's report.

¶ 15 Each commission must make its assessment in its own context.... The reports of previous commissions and their outcomes form part of the background and context that a new compensation committee should consider....

¶ 16 It is a constitutional requirement that commissions be independent, objective and effective. One requirement for independence is that commission members serve for a fixed term which may vary in length. Appointments to a commission are not entrusted exclusively to any one of the branches of government. The appointment process itself should be flexible. The commission's composition is legislated but it must be representative of the parties.

¶ 17 The commission must objectively consider the submissions of all parties and any relevant factors identified in the enabling statute and regulations. Its recommendations must result from a fair and objective hearing. Its report must explain and justify its position.

¶ 18 A number of criteria that must be met to ensure effectiveness are identified in the *Reference*. Once the process has started, the commission must meet promptly and regularly. As well there must be no change in remuneration until the commission has made its report public and sent it to the government. The commission's work must have a "meaningful effect" on the process of determining judicial remuneration (*Reference*, at para. 175).

¶ 19 What is a "meaningful effect"? Some of the appellants submit that "meaningful effect" means a binding effect on the government. A number of Attorneys General, by contrast, submit that "meaningful effect" requires a public and open process of recommendation and response. They urge that governments be permitted to depart from the report for a rational reason, but not to manipulate the judiciary. The essence of this appeal depends on whether "meaningful effect" means a binding effect or refers to an open process. For the reasons that follow, we conclude that it is the latter.

¶ 20 "Meaningful effect" does not mean binding effect. In the *Reference*, the Court addressed this question and stated that a recommendation could be effective without being binding. It held that the Constitution does not require that commission reports be binding, as decisions about the allocation of public resources belong to legislatures and to the executive (para. 176).

¶ 21 A commission's report is consultative. The government may turn it into something more. Unless the legislature provides that the report is binding, the government retains the power to depart from the commission's recommendations as long as it justifies its decision with rational reasons. These rational reasons must be included in the government's response to the commission's recommendations.

(2) The Government's Response to the Recommendations

¶ 22 If the government departs from the commission's recommendations, the Reference requires that it respond to the recommendations. Uncertainties about the nature and scope of the governments' responses are the cause of this litigation. Absent statutory provisions to the contrary, the power to determine judicial compensation belongs to governments. That power, however, is not absolute.

¶ 23 The commission's recommendations must be given weight. They have to be considered by the judiciary and the government. The government's response must be complete, must respond to the recommendations themselves and must not simply reiterate earlier submissions that were made to and substantively addressed by the commission. The emphasis at this stage is on what the commission has recommended.

¶ 24 The response must be tailored to the commission's recommendations and must be "legitimate" (*Reference*, at paras. 180-83), which is what the law, fair dealing and respect for the process require. The government must respond to the commission's recommendations and give legitimate reasons for departing from or varying them.

¶ 25 The government can reject or vary the commission's recommendations, provided that legitimate reasons are given. Reasons that are complete and that deal with the commission's recommendations in a meaningful way will meet the standard of rationality. Legitimate reasons must be compatible with the common law and the Constitution. The government must deal with the issues at stake in good faith. Bald expressions of rejection or disapproval are inadequate. Instead, the reasons must show that the commission's recommendations have been taken into account and must be based on facts and sound reasoning. They must state in what respect and to what extent they depart from the recommendations, articulating the grounds for rejection or variation. The reasons should reveal a consideration of the judicial office and an intention to deal with it appropriately. They must preclude any suggestion of attempting to manipulate the judiciary. The reasons must reflect the underlying public interest in having a commission process, being the depoliticization of the remuneration process and the need to preserve judicial independence.

¶ 26 The reasons must also rely upon a reasonable factual foundation. If different weights are given to relevant factors, this difference must be justified. Comparisons with public servants or with the private sector may be legitimate, but the use of a particular comparator must be explained. If a new fact or circumstance arises after the release of the commission's report, the government may rely on that fact or circumstance in its reasons for varying the commission's recommendations. It is also permissible for the government to analyse the impact of the recommendations and to verify the accuracy of information in the commission's report.

¶ 27 The government's reasons for departing from the commission's recommendations, and the factual foundations that underlie those reasons, must be clearly and fully stated in the government's response to the recommendations. If it is called upon to justify its decision in a court of law, the government may not advance reasons other than those mentioned in its response, though it may provide more detailed information with regard to the factual foundation it has relied upon, as will be explained below.

(3) The Scope and Nature of Judicial Review

¶ 28 Once the commission has made its recommendations and the government has responded, it is hoped that, with the guidance of these reasons for judgment, the courts will rarely be involved. Judicial review must nonetheless be envisaged.

¶ 29 The *Reference* states that the government's response is subject to a limited form of judicial review by the superior courts. The government's decision to depart from the commission's recommendations must be justified according to a standard of rationality. The standard of judicial review is described in the *Reference* as one of "simple rationality" (paras. 183-84). The adjective "simple" merely confirms that the standard is rationality alone.

¶ 30 The reviewing court is not asked to determine the adequacy of judicial remuneration. Instead, it must focus on the government's response and on whether the purpose of the commission process has been achieved. This is a deferential review which acknowledges both the government's unique position and accumulated expertise and its constitutional responsibility for management of the province's financial affairs.

¶ 31 In the Reference, at para. 183, a two-stage analysis for determining the rationality of the government's response is set out. We are now adding a third stage which requires the reviewing judge to view the matter globally and consider whether the overall purpose of the commission process has been met. The analysis should be as follows:

(1) as the government articulated a legitimate reason for departing from the commission's recommendations?

(2) Do the government's reasons rely upon a reasonable factual foundation? and

(3) Viewed globally, has the commission process been respected and have the purposes of the commission - preserving judicial independence and depoliticizing the setting of judicial remuneration - been achieved?

261

¶ 32 The first stage of the process described in the *Reference* is a screening mechanism. It requires the government to provide a "legitimate" reason for any departure from the commission's recommendation. What constitutes a "legitimate" reason is discussed above (paras. 23-27).

¶ 33 The second stage of the review consists of an inquiry into the reasonableness and sufficiency of the factual foundation relied upon by the government in rejecting or varying the commission's recommendations....

¶ 36 In analysing these two factors as part of the second stage of the judicial review process, the reviewing court must determine whether the government has explained the factual foundation of its reasons in its response....

¶ 37 The reviewing court should also... determine whether it is rational for the government to rely on the stated facts or circumstances to justify its response. This is done by looking at the soundness of the facts in relation to the position the government has adopted in its response.

¶ 38 At the third stage, the court must consider the response from a global perspective. Beyond the specific issues, it must weigh the whole of the process and the response in order to determine whether they demonstrate that the government has engaged in a meaningful way with the process of the commission and has given a rational answer to its recommendations. Although it may find fault with certain aspects of the process followed by the government or with some particular responses or lack of answer, the court must weigh and assess the government's participation in the process and its response in order to determine whether the response, viewed in its entirety, is impermissibly flawed even after the proper degree of deference is shown to the government's opinion on the issues. The focus shifts to the totality of the process and of the response.

¶ 39 It is obvious that, on the basis of the test elaborated above, a bald expression of disagreement with a recommendation of the commission, or a mere assertion that judges' current salaries are "adequate", would be insufficient.... The response can reweigh factors the commission has already considered as long as legitimate reasons are given for doing so. The focus is on whether the government has responded to the commission's recommendations with legitimate reasons that have a reasonable factual foundation.

¶ 40 In a judicial review context, the court must bear in mind that the commission process is flexible and that, while the commission's recommendations can be rejected only for legitimate reasons, deference must be shown to the government's response since the recommendations are not binding. If, in the end, the reviewing court concludes that the response does not meet the standard, a violation of the principles of judicial independence will have been made out.

¶ 41 In the *Reference*, Lamer C.J. briefly commented in passing on the justification under s. 1 of the *Canadian Charter of Rights and Freedoms* (paras. 277-85). Since the parties have not raised this issue in the case at bar, consideration of it, if it is indeed applicable, should await the proper case....

(4) Remedies

¶ 42 The limited nature of judicial review dictates the choice of remedies. The remedies must be consistent with the role of the reviewing court and the purpose of the commission process. The court must not encroach upon the commission's role of reviewing the facts and making recommendations. Nor may it encroach upon the provincial legislature's exclusive jurisdiction to allocate funds from the public purse and set judicial salaries unless that jurisdiction is delegated to the commission.

¶ 43 A court should not intervene every time a particular reason is questionable, especially when others are rational and correct. To do so would invite litigation, conflict and delay. This is antithetical to the object of the commission process. If, viewed globally, it appears that the commission process has been effective and that the setting of judicial remuneration has been "depoliticized", then the government's choice should stand.

¶ 44 In light of these principles, if the commission process has not been effective, and the setting of judicial remuneration has not been "depoliticized", then the appropriate remedy will generally be to return the matter to the government for reconsideration. If problems can be traced to the commission, the matter can be referred back to it. Should the commission no longer be active, the government would be obliged to appoint a new one to resolve the problems. Courts should avoid issuing specific orders to make the recommendations binding unless the governing statutory scheme gives them that option. This reflects the conclusion in *Mackin v. New Brunswick (Minister of Finance)*, [2002] 1 S.C.R. 405, 2002 SCC 13, that it is "not appropriate for this Court to dictate the approach that should be taken in order to rectify the situation. Since there is more than one way to do so, it is the government's task to determine which approach it prefers" (para. 77).

III. Application of the Principles to the Cases

[The Court ruled that New Brunswick, Ontario and Alberta's reasons for rejecting the Commissions' recommendations met the standard of rationality. Quebec's reasons for rejecting the Commissions' recommendations did not meet the standard of rationality as the government's response failed to address the Committee's most important recommendations and the justifications given for them. The Quebec matter was remitted to the Government and the National Assembly of Quebec for reconsideration in accordance with the Court's reasons.]

RE APPLICATION UNDER S. 83.28 OF THE *CRIMINAL CODE*
[2004] 2 S.C.R. 248.

[Two acts of alleged terrorism occurred in 1985. An explosion killed two baggage handlers, and injured four others, at the Narita Airport in Japan, as baggage was being transferred onto Air India Flight 301. A second explosion one hour later caused Air India Flight 182 to crash off the west coast of Ireland. All 329 passengers and crew perished.

Reyat, was arrested in England, extradited to Canada, tried and convicted of manslaughter and the use of explosive substances. Malik and Bagri were jointly charged with offences in relation to both explosions and the intended explosion of Air India Flight 301. Reyat pleaded guilty to aiding or abetting the construction of the explosive that was placed on Air India Flight 182 and the manslaughter of the 329 passengers and crew. He was sentenced to five years imprisonment in addition to time already spent in custody.

The trial of Malik and Bagri (the "Air India Trial") continues to date. Shortly after that trial began, the Crown brought an *ex parte* application seeking an order that a Named Person, a potential Crown witness at the Air India trial, attend a judicial investigative hearing for examination pursuant to s. 83.28 of the *Criminal Code* (sec. 83.28 was added to the *Code* by the *Anti-terrorism Act* in 2001). The application judge granted the order and set terms and conditions to govern the judicial investigative hearing. The hearing was to be conducted *in camera* and notice of the hearing was not to be given to the accused in the Air India trial, to the press or to the public. Fortuitously, counsel for the accused became aware of the order. They and counsel for the Named Person challenged the constitutional validity of s. 83.28 at an *in camera* hearing.

The judge concluded that the order was validly issued and s. 83.28 was constitutionally sound. One question at issue in this appeal was whether s. 83.28 of the *Criminal Code* infringed the principles of independence and impartiality of the judiciary.]

The judgment of McLachlin C.J. and Iacobucci, Major and Arbour JJ. was delivered by

IACOBUCCI AND ARBOUR JJ.: − [...]

¶ 33 [...] This appeal marks the first known instance where the s. 83.28 judicial investigative hearing power has been invoked.... [T]he provision in its entirety represents a new addition to the Canadian legal landscape....

¶ 41 Section 83.28 provides for a two stage process, whereby an order for the gathering of information from a named individual is first issued, and an examination of the individual so named is subsequently held. ... At its core, s. 83.28 permits the investigation of terrorism offences, at both a pre and post charge stage through testimonial compulsion on the part of the named witness. Consequently, the purpose of the provision is to confer greater investigative powers upon the state in its investigation of terrorism offences.

¶ 42 The procedure is initiated at the behest of a peace officer who, with the Attorney General's consent, applies to a judge for an order for the gathering of information: s. 83.28(2) and (3). The judge may so order, and thereby initiate the hearing, if he or she is satisfied (a) that there are reasonable grounds to believe either that a terrorism offence has been committed and that information concerning the offence or concerning the whereabouts of a suspect is likely to be obtained; or (b) that there are reasonable grounds to believe that a terrorism offence will be committed, that there are reasonable grounds to believe that the witness has direct and material information relating to the terrorism offence or in relation to the whereabouts of a suspect, and reasonable prior attempts have been made to obtain that information from the witness: s. 83.28(4). The scope of the order will ultimately dictate the parameters of the subsequent hearing.

¶ 43 Pursuant to s. 83.28(5), the judge may (a) order the examination, under oath or not, of the person named in the order (the "named person"); (b) order the named person to attend for the examination and to remain in attendance until excused by the presiding judge; (c) order the named person to bring to the examination anything in their possession or control and produce it to the presiding judge; (d) designate another judge as the judge to preside over the examination; and

(e) include any other terms or conditions considered desirable, including those for the protection of the named person, third parties, and an ongoing investigation. Under s. 83.28(7), the terms of the order may be varied.

¶ 44 The powers of the presiding judge and the Attorney General at the judicial investigative hearing itself also fall within the ambit of s. 83.28. Under s. 83.28(8), the named person must answer questions put to him or her by the Attorney General and produce tangibles he or she was ordered to bring to the examination. The named person may refuse to answer a question or produce any such thing that would violate any law relating to the non disclosure of information or to privilege: s. 83.28(8). Section 83.28(9) empowers the presiding judge to rule on any objection or other issue relating to a refusal to answer a question or produce an item. Section 83.28(10) provides the named person with use and derivative use immunity with respect to self incrimination which will be discussed below in the context of s. 7 of the *Charter*. The named person has a right to retain and instruct counsel at any stage of the proceedings: s. 83.28(11). The presiding judge may also order tangibles to be given into police custody if satisfied that any such item is relevant to the investigation of any terrorism offence: s. 83.28(12)....

¶ 53 [T]he judge is present at the judicial investigative hearing to ensure that the procedure is carried out in accord with constitutional protections.

(3)   The Independence of the Judiciary

¶ 80 Judicial independence is the "lifeblood of constitutionalism in democratic societies": *Beauregard v. Canada*, [1986] 2 S.C.R. 56, at p. 70. The importance of judicial independence to the promotion and preservation of the rule of law cannot be overstated.   In this respect, as the late Professor Lederman noted, judicial independence is one of the original principles of the English Constitution.... An independent judiciary is absolutely necessary to "ensure that the power of the state is exercised in accordance with the rule of law and the provisions of our Constitution. In this capacity, courts act as a shield against unwarranted deprivations by the state of the rights and freedoms of individuals" ...

¶ 81   This principle exists in Canadian law in a number of forms.   In the Constitution, it is explicitly referenced in ss. 96 to 100 of the *Constitution Act, 1867* and in s. 11(*d*) of the *Charter*. The application of these provisions, however, is limited. The former applies to judges of superior courts, and the latter to courts and tribunals charged with trying the guilt of persons charged with criminal offences...   Judicial independence has also been implicitly recognized as a residual right protected under s. 7, as it, along with the remaining protections in ss. 8 to 14, are specific examples of broader principles of fundamental justice... Moreover, the commitment to the "foundational principle" of judicial independence has also been referenced by way of the Preamble to the *Constitution Act, 1867*.... Judicial independence further represents the cornerstone of the common law duty of procedural fairness, which attaches to all judicial, quasi judicial and administrative proceedings, and is an unwritten principle of the Constitution.

¶ 82 The twin aspects of judicial independence and impartiality are relevant to this appeal. The first is the requirement that the judiciary function independently from the executive and legislative branches of government. *Ellahaleguru, supra*, at pp. 72-73. The second is the recognition that judicial independence is necessary to uphold public confidence in the administration of justice.... The relationship between judicial independence and impartiality was considered by the Court in *R. v. Lippé*, [1991] 2 S.C.R. 114, at p. 139:

> The overall objective of guaranteeing judicial independence is to ensure a reasonable perception of impartiality; judicial independence is but a "means" to this "end". If judges could be perceived as "impartial" without judicial "independence", the requirement of "independence" would be unnecessary. However, judicial independence is critical to the public's perception of impartiality. Independence is the cornerstone, a necessary prerequisite, for judicial impartiality.

¶ 83 In this respect, we must ultimately consider whether a reasonable and informed person would conclude that the court under s. 83.28 is independent ...

¶ 84 One of the criticisms levied against s. 83.28 is that it co opts the judiciary into performing executive, investigatory functions in place of its usual adjudicative role: see, e.g., Paciocco, *supra*, at p. 232. Essentially, the assertion is that judges acting under s. 83.28 lack institutional independence or impartiality. The institutional dimension of judicial independence was recognized in *Ell, supra*, at para. 22, where Major J. described it as "the need to maintain the independence of a court or tribunal as a whole from the executive and legislative branches of government"....

¶ 86 We find that the substance of such a criticism is not made out in the context of the s. 83.28 judicial investigative hearing. Judges routinely play a role in criminal investigation by way of measures such as the authorization of wire taps (s. 184.2 of the *Code*), search warrants (s. 487 of the *Code*), and in applications for DNA warrants (s. 487.05 of the *Code*). The thrust of these proceedings is their investigatory purpose, and the common underlying thread is the role of the judge in ensuring that such information is gathered in a proper manner. The place of the judiciary in such investigative contexts is to act as a check against state excess.

¶ 87 However, once legislation invokes the aid of the judiciary, we must remain vigilant to ensure that the integrity of its role is not compromised or diluted. ... The function of the judge in a judicial investigative hearing is not to act as "an agent of the state", but rather, to protect the integrity of the investigation and, in particular, the interests of the named person *vis à vis* the state.

¶ 88 The parameters of the judicial role under s. 83.28 must be clearly delineated and understood. As discussed above, the judge is empowered to ensure that questioning is fair and relevant, as required by the *CEA* and the common law. The scope of the order under s. 83.28(5), any exercise of judicial discretion under s. 83.28(5)(e) and the terms and conditions set under s. 83.28(7) must take as a starting point the rights and interests of the named person. Where a judge, acting pursuant to s. 83.28, imposes terms and conditions or exercises his or her discretion in a manner which goes beyond the role of the judiciary as guardian of the Constitution, that judge will have acted unconstitutionally. This accords with Parliamentary intention. During the third reading of Bill C 36 in the House of Commons, the Parliamentary Secretary to the Minister of Justice characterized the direct judicial supervision of s. 83.28 as one of the "very significant limits and controls" that brought the legislation into compliance with the *Charter: House of Commons Debates*, vol. 137, 1st Sess., 37th Parl., November 28, 2001, at p. 7620.

¶ 89 We conclude that judicial independence is not compromised in this case. Under a broad and purposive interpretation, s. 83.28 requires the judge to act "judicially", in accordance with constitutional norms, and the historic role of the judiciary in criminal proceedings. Moreover, the provision confers upon the judge considerable flexibility and discretion to set and vary the terms and conditions of the initiating order and the subsequent hearing. In light of the mandatory exercise of such discretion with respect to rules of evidence, and use and derivative use immunity being extended to extradition and deportation hearings, judges bring the full weight of their authority as impartial adjudicators to the hearing to provide the witness with all the constitutional guarantees of the *Charter*. A failure on the part of a hearing judge to exercise his or her discretion in this manner will constitute reviewable error.

¶ 90 The ultimate question, however, is "whether a reasonable and informed person, viewing the relevant statutory provisions in their full historical context, would conclude that the court or tribunal is independent... Professor Paciocco states that, "[e]ven though the legislation does not purport to command judges to perform this function, but leaves them with the discretion as to whether to conduct such a hearing, the appearance of independence is compromised...

¶ 91 The concern about the judicial investigative hearing stems largely from its being held *in camera*. However, in the media appeal, we discuss the fundamental principle of openness of the courts, a hallmark of the Canadian judicial system. In that appeal, we conclude that judicial investigative hearings are to be held presumptively in open court and that the onus is on the Crown to rebut that presumption .... In our view, the presumptive openness of the judicial investigative hearing is another factor that militates in favour of our conclusion that judicial investigative hearings do not compromise the independence or impartiality of the judiciary.

¶ 92 ... a reasonable and informed person would conclude, on the facts of this case, and in light of the institutional function of the judiciary, that judicial impartiality and independence have not been compromised or diluted. Where a hearing is held within the parameters discussed above, justice will not only be done, but will also manifestly be seen to be done....

¶ 106 The constitutional questions are answered as follows...

> 5. Does s. 83.28 of the *Criminal Code* infringe the principles of independence and impartiality established by the Preamble to the *Constitution Act, 1867*?
>
> No.

The reasons of Bastarache and Deschamps JJ. were delivered by

¶ 107 BASTARACHE J — I agree with the majority reasons subject to my comments on the openness of investigative hearings.

I.   The Independence of the Judiciary

¶ 108   In my view, where a judicial investigative hearing is closed, the independence or impartiality of the judiciary will not be compromised as several other factors promote independence and impartiality. Further, the subsequent release of the information disclosed during these proceedings promote the accountability of the judiciary....

The following are the reasons delivered by

¶ 111 **BINNIE J.** (dissenting): — ... In my view, the s. 83.28 order in this case was sought by the Crown for an inappropriate purpose, it was granted on inappropriate terms, and its impropriety was not cured (although the terms were much improved) by the amendments made by the hearing judge. Accordingly, while I agree that s. 83.28 of the *Code*, as interpreted by my colleagues, is constitutionally valid, in my opinion the Crown's resort to it in the circumstances of this case was an abuse of process. I would therefore allow the appeal.

¶ 112 The Air India trial commenced on April 28, 2003. It has therefore been open to the Crown for more than a year to call the appellant as a witness for the prosecution. As of the date of the hearing of this appeal, the Crown had not done so. ... [I]t is clear that the *timing* of the Crown's attempt to obtain the appellant's s. 83.28 evidence was driven by trial tactics. By that I mean the Crown's desire to obtain a mid-trial examination for discovery of the appellant before a different judge to determine in advance precisely what the appellant will say or not say in the witness box. This is an abuse of the extraordinary powers granted under the *Anti-terrorism Act*, S.C. 2001, c. 41. In my view the s. 83.28 hearing should have been stayed until after the appellant testified at the Air India trial or the Crown declared that the appellant would not be called as a prosecution witness.

I.   The Fundamental Issue

¶ 115   ...The challenge posed to our legal institutions by the current "war on terrorism" promises to be more enduring and difficult to manage than the more traditional wartime challenges to civil liberties previously experienced. The terrorist threat had no announced point of commencement and may have no end. The enemy is not conveniently dressed in uniforms or arranged in battlefield order. They operate among us in guerilla-style networks, where decisions can be made, adjusted, improvised and implemented in lower level cells. They are, it seems, everywhere and yet they are nowhere to be seen. There may be no dramatic final battle in which victors and losers are made manifest. We are told that there will be a long, slow process of attrition. Efforts to counteract terrorism are likely to become part of our everyday existence for perhaps generations to come. In these circumstances we can take limited comfort from the declared intention of the government that the *Anti-terrorist Act* is a temporary measure.

While its continued existence will depend on Parliament's appreciation of developments in the "war on terrorism", such temporary measures may well slide into a state of *de facto* permanence. The role of s. 83.28 in our criminal law should be approached with that unhappy prospect firmly in mind.

¶ 116 The danger in the "war on terrorism" lies not only in the actual damage the terrorists can do to us but what we can do to our own legal and political institutions by way of shock, anger, anticipation, opportunism or overreaction....

D. *Use of Section 83.28 to Obtain Mid-Trial Discovery of an Uncooperative Witness Was an Abuse of Process*

¶ 138 It is apparent that in this case an investigative procedure designed for the purpose of gathering information at the pre-charge stage was invoked behind the backs of the accused in part at least to obtain advance discovery of an uncooperative prosecution witness not only after charges were laid but during the Air India trial itself.

¶ 139 ... [T]here is nothing in s. 83.28 to suggest that Parliament intended to confer on the Crown a right of mid-trial discovery of uncooperative witnesses before a different judge where the Crown proceeds by direct indictment in the trial of criminal offences, even if those offences involve terrorist acts....

¶ 140 ...[T]he s. 83.28 order was itself "state excess". So far as Malik and Bagri are concerned, the presence of the judge presiding over the examination adds weight to its coercive potential and strengthens the hand of the prosecution. The Crown's trial tactic to use s. 83.28 to deal with an uncooperative witness in the ongoing Air India trial, on the facts of this particular case, was abusive of the proper role of the judiciary....

¶ 168 I would therefore allow the appeal, affirm the constitutional validity of s. 83.28 of the *Criminal Code* when correctly interpreted and properly applied, but I would have entered a stay against the s. 83.28 hearing in this proceeding until after the appellant had testified at the trial of Malik and Bagri, or the Crown otherwise had indicated that the appellant would not be called as a prosecution witness.

¶ 169 **LeBEL J.** (Fish J. concurring), dissenting: - I agree with Binnie J. that the appeal should be allowed because of the abuse of process by the Crown and would reach the same conclusion as him on that issue.... In my opinion, s. 83.28 of the *Criminal Code*, R.S.C. 1985, c. C 46 ("*Cr. C.*"), compromises judicial independence and should, for this reason, be declared unconstitutional. Due to the manner in which this provision structures relations between the judiciary, the investigative arm of the police and the Crown, it will inevitably lead to the abuses and irregularities....

¶ 170 As noted by Iacobucci and Arbour JJ., the principle of judicial independence has a variety of sources. Judicial independence is guaranteed by s. 11(*d*) of the *Canadian Charter of Rights and Freedoms* and the Preamble to and ss. 96 to 100 of the *Constitution Act, 1867*, and it plays an essential role in the proper functioning of Canada's constitutional democracy ... This principle, which serves to maintain public confidence in the court system and the rule of law, was established to prevent interference by the executive and legislative branches in the exercise of judicial powers. The judiciary must remain completely independent of the other branches of government in the performance of its functions....

¶ 171 The courts have identified three fundamental characteristics of judicial independence: security of tenure, financial security, and administrative independence. Security of tenure means that a judge can be removed from office only for serious and very specific reasons following an independent review process that affords the judge the opportunity to be heard and to defend him- or herself. Financial security safeguards judges' salaries or other remuneration and pensions. Administrative independence, which is not to be confused with institutional independence, a point I will discuss below, gives courts necessary power over matters of administration bearing directly on the exercise of their functions (*Valente, supra,* at pp. 694 712).

¶ 172 Judicial independence also has two dimensions, individual independence and institutional independence, which are distinct from its core characteristics (*Reference re Judges of the Provincial Court, supra,* at para. 119). On the one hand, individual independence attaches to the individual judge. Judges must be able to discharge their judicial functions without outside interference. Thus, this dimension of independence is concerned with the personal attributes of a judge, such as security of tenure. On the other hand, institutional independence attaches to courts as institutions. Courts must be independent, and appear to be independent, of the legislative and executive branches of government. The institutional dimension of judicial independence thus ensures the separation of powers ...

¶ 173 This Court has often stressed the need to safeguard the institutional dimension of judicial independence so that the courts can continue to fulfill their role as guardians of the Constitution (*Reference re Judges of the Provincial Court, supra,* at para. 123; *Mackin, supra,* at para. 39). If the courts are to retain the ability to provide individuals with effective protection against unwarranted deprivations of their rights and freedoms by the executive and legislative branches, they must necessarily be independent of those branches (*Ell, supra,* at para. 22).

¶ 174 In the case before us, it is important, indeed essential, that these two dimensions of judicial independence not be confused. Thus, although a judge may be independent in fact and act with the utmost impartiality, judicial independence will not exist if the court of which he or she is a member is not independent of the other branches of government on an institutional level. To determine whether judicial independence has been maintained in a specific case, both dimensions of judicial independence therefore have to be reviewed.

¶ 175 As noted by Iacobucci and Arbour JJ., the principle of judicial independence is essential to the preservation of the fundamental normative order of a society founded on the principles of constitutionalism and the rule of law. Judicial independence effectively ensures the maintenance of public confidence in the administration of justice, which is itself an essential precondition for respect for and acceptance of the justice system and the rule of law. Thus, public confidence guarantees the effectiveness of our justice system, while at the same time putting the principle of the rule of law into practice ... The maintenance of public confidence in the administration of justice is therefore central to concerns relating to judicial independence.

¶ 176 To determine whether a measure compromises judicial independence, it must be asked whether the judicial institution, meaning, on the one hand, the individual judges and, on the other hand, collectively, the institution *per se*, is perceived by the public to be independent:

> Confidence in our system of justice requires a healthy perception of judicial independence to be maintained amongst the citizenry. Without the perception of independence, the judiciary is unable to "claim any legitimacy or command the respect and acceptance that are essential to it" [cites omitted]

The appropriate test for this purpose is whether a reasonable person who is informed of the relevant statutory provisions would conclude, after viewing the matter realistically and practically, that the judiciary is independent. ... It is important to note, however, that "reasonable person" does not for this purpose mean an experienced legal professional who understands the intricacies of legal issues based on subtle distinctions of which lay persons would generally be unaware. In short, the objective test of the reasonable person should serve to determine whether the public has a positive perception of judicial independence.

¶ 177 When analysed from this perspective, s. 83.28 *Cr. C.* compromises the institutional dimension of judicial independence. To conclude otherwise, it would be necessary to ignore the fundamental distinction between the two dimensions of judicial independence when applying the law to the facts of this case. Although they do discuss the institutional dimension of judicial independence, Iacobucci and Arbour JJ. seem to have inferred the existence of judicial independence from the individual independence of the judge acting pursuant to s. 83.28 without considering whether the institutional dimension was in fact protected. In my colleagues' view, if a judge conducting an investigation pursuant to this provision fails, in exercising his or her discretion, to uphold the rights and freedoms of the person being examined, then, and only then, could it be concluded, after the fact, that judicial independence had been compromised (para. 88).

¶ 178 Holmes J. concluded that s. 83.28 *Cr. C.* does not compromise judicial independence, because the judge conducting the investigation will not be the same as the one who presides at the trial, and because the two proceedings will very rarely take place in the same jurisdiction. This reasoning overlooks the institutional dimension of judicial independence and fails to consider the impact of the statutory provisions in question on that dimension and of the perception a reasonable, well informed person would have with respect thereto. This analysis considers only the actions of individual judges and their personal impartiality in the conduct of the investigation process.

¶ 179 Without institutional independence or, in other words, without the appearance of a clear separation of powers between the judicial, executive and legislative branches, judicial independence cannot be said to exist. In my view, preserving the appearance of a separation of powers is a necessary condition for concluding that judicial independence exists.

¶ 180 Section 83.28 *Cr. C.* requires judges to preside over police investigations; as such investigations are the responsibility of the executive branch, this cannot but leave a reasonable person with the impression that judges have become allies of the executive branch. This perception that the judicial and executive branches are allied when conducting an investigation pursuant to this provision results, in my view, from the difficulty that a judge presiding over such a process will have protecting the rights and freedoms of the person being examined, the overly broad discretionary powers wielded by the judge, the legislative objectives behind the provision and the very nature of these proceedings, which may be held *in camera*.

¶ 181 Iacobucci and Arbour JJ. found that a judge exercises a judicial function when carrying out such an examination, since ss. 83.28(7) and 83.28(9) *Cr. C.* provide that he or she has the power to vary the terms and conditions of the order and to rule on objections relating to a refusal to answer a question. My colleagues thus conclude that the judge's role here is to protect the interests of the person being examined and thereby act as a shield against unwarranted deprivations thereof by the executive branch. I do not agree. Even if the impugned statutory provisions are interpreted as my colleagues propose, the judge will not have the necessary means to ensure that the rights and freedoms of the person being examined are protected.

¶ 182 First, I question how effective the judge's power to rule on objections to evidence in the course of these investigations will actually be. I am sceptical[sic] about the view that the rules of evidence set out in the *Canada Evidence Act*, R.S.C. 1985, c. C 5, such as ss. 8 to 12, 19 to 36 and 42, and the common law rules can govern the conduct of such an examination. These rules were created, first and foremost, to govern the building of a case to prove an accused's guilt. They are ill suited to the gathering of information relating to the commission of an offence or to fears that one may have been committed.

¶ 183 Next, even if I agreed with Iacobucci and Arbour JJ. as to the application of these rules of evidence, the rules would not create a framework allowing judges to effectively protect the rights and freedoms of the person being examined. Indeed, as my colleagues noted, the application of these rules of evidence is not mandatory. Moreover, some of the rules will not apply, as they are incompatible with the type of investigation provided for in s. 83.28. This is true of the rule against hearsay evidence. Finally, although the rules relating to the relevance of questions asked and to their probative value could be useful in theory, the judge will not be in a position to apply them. The judge presiding over the examination will undoubtedly not have access to the full record of the police investigation. It would therefore be easy for a Crown prosecutor to contend that a question is relevant or that its probative value outweighs its prejudicial effects. Without knowledge of the investigation's sources, framework and objectives, it will be virtually impossible for the judge to rule on such objections. Thus, the power to limit the scope of questions put to the person being examined could prove illusory. Even based on my colleagues' interpretation, the impugned provisions do not give the judge the means to effectively protect the rights and freedoms of the person being examined.

¶ 184 Moreover, if it were possible to conclude that the judge could effectively rule on certain objections, the fluidity and vagueness of the investigation procedure would still give too much discretion to the judge. Without a specific rule that can be applied uniformly to all cases, judges will have to rely on their own discretion, if not their own subjective preferences, when deciding which solution to apply to a given objection. To my mind, a judge's individual perception of his or her role will necessarily affect the nature and conduct of the examination. Thus, some judges will be more inclined to protect the fundamental rights of the person being examined, while others, who are more conservative, will adopt a contrary approach.

¶ 185 As the judiciary is unable to defend the fundamental rights and freedoms of a person being examined under s. 83.28 *Cr. C.* against interference from the executive branch, the judiciary's role is then, on its face, no different from that of the executive branch. In my view, a reasonable, well informed person could conclude that the purpose of having a judge at such an investigation is to help the executive branch compel the witness to answer questions. The judiciary's symbolic and legal weight will assist the police in their investigations. The judiciary will then no longer be playing the role of an independent arbiter.

¶ 186 This perception is also justified by the legislative objectives of the *Anti terrorism Act*, S.C. 2001, c. 41, and s. 83.28 *Cr. C.* As Iacobucci and Arbour JJ. have stated, Parliament's intent in enacting this legislation was to prevent and punish acts of terrorism. In enacting s. 83.28, Parliament gave increased powers to the executive branch to enable it to investigate such acts effectively. In light of these legislative objectives, a reasonable person might conclude that Parliament intended to use the judiciary to make the prevention and suppression of acts of terrorism more effective by sacrificing some of the judiciary's institutional independence. Professor Paciocco has given a clear description of how the judiciary's role in investigations conducted pursuant to s. 83.28 might be perceived by the public:

> The government is clearly counting on the oath of the witness and the threat of contempt of court to enforce this system, and it is using the power of the judicial office, not to obtain a legal ruling or to resolve a question of fact, but as a form of coercion to compel information in the advancement of the executive, investigative function....

¶ 187 In light of the procedural framework established by s. 83.28 *Cr. C.*, it would be reasonable for the public to perceive the judicial and executive branches as allies. This public perception is heightened by the fact that the judge's duties under s. 83.28 are unlike any of the duties traditionally discharged by the judiciary....

¶ 189 ...A judge who presides over an examination under s. 83.28 *Cr. C*...take[s] part in the exercise of a power of the executive branch and has no way to counterbalance the exercise thereof. In the pursuit of the unarguably important objective of suppressing and preventing terrorism, the distinction between the judicial and executive branches has been blurred.

¶ 190 The public's perception that the judicial and the executive branches do not act separately in an investigation under s. 83.28 *Cr. C.* will be heightened when the investigation is held *in camera*. In such a case, a reasonable, well informed person would be justified in questioning the role the judge is really playing in the investigation. The judge is therefore at risk of being perceived as a true ally of the executive branch in a secret investigation that is not subject to scrutiny.

¶ 191 In short, I do not believe it is possible to uphold the constitutional validity of the legislation in question by isolating individual cases in which judges will act unconstitutionally. When faced with the problems raised by s. 83.28 *Cr. C.*, it will not suffice to state that judicial independence will be compromised only in those specific cases, as such a conclusion would be based on an analysis restricted to the individual dimension of judicial independence. For the reasons I have stated above, I believe that s. 83.28 compromises the institutional dimension of judicial independence. In my view, the public will perceive the judicial and executive branches as allies rather than as separate branches of government. The implementation of s. 83.28, which is the source of this perception that there is no separation of powers, could therefore lead to a loss of public confidence in Canada's justice system. The tension and fears resulting from the rise in terrorist activity do not justify such an alliance. It is important that the criminal law be enforced firmly and that the necessary investigative and punitive measures be taken, but this must be done in accordance with the fundamental values of our political system. The preservation of our courts' institutional independence belongs to those fundamental values.

¶ 192 Therefore, it is my view that s. 83.28 *Cr. C.* compromises the judicial independence guaranteed by the Preamble to the *Constitution Act, 1867* and must be declared unconstitutional. For this reason, I would have allowed the appeal and found, as did Binnie J., that there was an abuse of process.

PART II

TECHNIQUES OF FEDERALISM REVIEW

1. Matters Coming Within Classes of Subjects

(a) General

W.R. LEDERMAN, "THE BALANCED INTERPRETATION OF THE FEDERAL DISTRIBUTION OF LEGISLATIVE POWERS IN CANADA"
IN LEDERMAN, CONTINUING CANADIAN CONSTITUTIONAL DILEMMAS
(TORONTO: BUTTERWORTHS, 1981).

The federal distribution of legislative powers and responsibilities in Canada is one of the facts of life when we concern ourselves with the many important social, political, economic or cultural problems of our country. Over the whole range of actual and potential law-making, our constitution distributes powers and responsibilities by two lists of categories or classes – one list for the federal parliament (primarily section 91 of the *BNA Act*), the other for each of the provincial legislatures (primarily section 92 of the *BNA Act*). [...]

These federal and provincial categories of power are expressed, and indeed have to be expressed, in quite general terms. This permits considerable flexibility in constitutional interpretation, but also it brings much overlapping and potential conflict between the various definitions of powers and responsibilities. [...]

Accordingly the courts must continually assess the competing federal and provincial lists of powers against one another in the judicial task of interpreting the constitution. [...]

Nearly all laws or legislative schemes have a multiplicity of features, characteristics, or aspects by which they may be classified in a number of different ways, and hence potentialities of cross-classification are ever present. The more complex the statute, the greater the number of logical possibilities in this regard. So, in the case of a particular law challenged for validity, one aspect of it points to a federal category of power with logical plausibility, but, with equal logical plausibility, another aspect points to a provincial category of power. [...]

[T]his partial but multiple coincidence of categories is the usual and not the exceptional situation for a classification system such as that embodied in the *BNA Act*. Those who make a federal constitution must generalize in some degree the concepts to be used to distribute law-making powers. But, once such lists have been made, those who must interpret the constitution encounter the broad extensions of meaning and the overlapping of concepts that generalized thought makes inevitable. At this point it is clear that such generalized concepts must be used with care if we would preserve the balance of our federal constitution – preserve, that is, a proper equilibrium between significant provincial autonomy and adequate central power.

The danger is this, that some of the categories of federal power and some of those of provincial power are capable of very broadly extended ranges of meaning. If one of these concepts of federal power should be given such a broadly extended meaning, *and also priority over any competing provincial concept*, then federal power would come close to eliminating provincial power. The converse could happen just as easily, with the federal power suffering virtual eclipse. Take for example the federal category of criminal law. If all that is necessary for valid legislation under this head is that the federal Parliament should prohibit something with penal consequences for breach, then Parliament can enact any legislative scheme it pleases provided it sprinkles the statute concerned with a few prohibitions and penalties. There would be very little left of independent provincial power if the federal Parliament could really get away with this. And the attempt has been made. [...]

[I]f we would maintain a balanced federal system here, there are two dilemmas of classification for the distribution of legislative powers that one must solve. They have been revealed in the foregoing analysis and may be briefly recapitulated as follows.

1. *The categories of legislative power*. No one of the general concepts by which power is given should be allowed to prevail to the extreme limits of its potential meaning, regardless of the competing scope of other concepts. There must be some mutual limitations of definition, and even then much overlapping will remain.

2. *The laws to be classified*. The laws challenged for validity, the particular items to be classified, are almost invariably ambivalent in the logical sense, in that they exhibit both federal and provincial aspects or characteristics. Different aspects of the same particular law point to categories in both the federal and provincial lists respectively, even though no one category in those lists is allowed an extremely extended meaning. So, on this account alone, there must be some further step in the classification process whereby the federal aspect is made to prevail over the provincial one, or *vice versa*, for purposes of decisive classification.

Let us now consider the solutions of these problems. [...]

[T]he courts have indeed tended to avoid extremely extended meanings for categories of federal power at the expense of those of provincial power, and *vice versa*. Definitions have tended to be mutually restrained. [...]

Nevertheless, in spite of mutual modification of definitions because of the whole context of the *BNA Act*, much overlapping of concepts inevitably remains. In other words, the ambivalent character of particular laws or statutes persists. This constitutes the second dilemma of classification. The first step towards solution is to construe the challenged statute itself carefully to be sure of having determined its full meaning, that is, the full range of features by any one of which or by any combination of which it may be classified. [...]

Pith & Substance

[H]aving thus determined the full range of features of the challenged statute, we find the usual situation, that federal aspects and provincial aspects are both present and compete to control characterization of the statute for purposes of determining the power to enact it. To resolve this competition, the courts must now assess the relative importance of the respective federal and provincial features of the statute in contrast with the other. Accordingly, criteria of relative value enter the picture. If the judges find a clear contrast, if for instance they deem the federal aspects clearly more important than the provincial ones, then the conclusion is that power to pass the statute is exclusively federal. For the purpose of distributing legislative power then, the challenged statute is decisively classified by its leading feature, by its more important characteristic, by its primary aspects, by its pith and substance. These are synonymous phrases. And if, on the other hand, the provincial features are deemed clearly more important than the federal ones, the power to pass the law in question is exclusively provincial. In this way exclusive power can be assigned to federal parliament or provincial legislature in spite of the purely logical ambivalence of the challenged statute because of its different aspects. [...]

Concurrent Power

But, what if the contrast between the federal and provincial features respectively of the challenged law is not so sharp that one can be selected as the leading feature? What if both seem to be leading features? [...] In these circumstances, federal and provincial laws are permitted to operate concurrently, provided they do not conflict in what they prescribe for the persons subject to them. [...]

Federal Paramountcy

Nevertheless, if there is conflict between federal and provincial statutes in a concurrent field, the doctrine of dominion paramountcy is to the effect that the federal statute prevails and the provincial one is thereby displaced and suspended. So, in the end, federal power is over-riding in a concurrent field. [...]

[F]ederal constitutional interpretation in Canada might be said to call for mutual exclusion of powers if practical, but concurrency if necessary. Moreover, whether one finds mutual exclusion or concurrency, the process requires decisions about the relative values represented by the competing federal and provincial aspects of the challenged statute. Often these are difficult decisions indeed, but they are inescapable. So the question becomes: Is the statutory scheme at issue something that is better done province by province on the basis of provincial autonomy, or is it something better done uniformly over the whole country on a nation-wide basis? What criteria of value move the judges in this respect? In an earlier essay, the writer attempted the following answer to this.

> In this inquiry the judges are beyond the aid of logic, because logic merely displays the many possible classifications; it does not assist in a choice between them. If we assume that the purpose of the constitution is to promote the well-being of the people then some of the necessary criteria will start to emerge. When a particular rule has features of meaning relevant to both federal and provincial classes of laws, then the question must be asked. Is it better for the people that this thing be done on a national level, or on a provincial level? In other words, is the feature of the challenged law which falls within the federal class more important to the well-being of the country than that which falls within the provincial class of laws? Such considerations as the relative value of uniformity and regional diversity, the relative merit of local *versus* central administration, and the justice of minority claims, would have to be weighed. Inevitably, widely prevailing beliefs in the country about these issues will be influential and presumably the judges should strive to implement such beliefs. [...]

Once again, the importance is apparent of exploring all aspects of the challenged law as a matter of meaning and evidence. A legal system must in general be related to the social, economic, and cultural realities, and to the accepted values and beliefs, of the country concerned. Indeed a legal system exists to take account of these realities in a way that advances those values and beliefs as far as laws can do so. In a federal country like Canada this applies to the special issues concerning which legislative body – the central or the provincial – should be responsible for this or that statutory scheme. Professor Bora Laskin seems to have all this in mind when he speaks of "constitutional values" in a special sense. He says:

> What the process of constitutional adjudication involves is a distillation of the "constitutional value" represented by challenged legislation (the "matter" in relation to which it is enacted) and its attribution to a head of power (or class of subject). This is not to say that the process is mechanical or that there are logically-discoverable essences which go to make up a class of subject. The distribution of legislative power must surely be envisaged as an instrumental or operating scheme, ample enough to embrace any subject or object of legislation. The classes of subjects must hence be conceived as vehicles through which social or economic or political policy is expressed, and these considerations (however they may be inarticulate or concealed in precedent or logic) cannot be ignored when the courts give content to the classes of subjects and measure the validity of legislation accordingly.

At this point one may well ask: Why all the emphasis on the analytical logic of classification that characterizes the present essay, if in the end logic alone is indecisive? The answer is that such analytical reasoning is necessary to prepare the way for and to reveal the need of the value judgments that are in the end decisive. Good analytical jurisprudence isolates issues of form and reveals issues of substance in their true colours. If you can frame the right questions and put them in the right order, you are half way to the answers. In other words, by proper questions and analysis, the issues requiring value decisions are rendered specific and brought into focus one by one in particular terms, so that ordinary mortals of limited wisdom and moral insight can cope with them. This is the reason for insisting that if you would distribute law-making powers you must classify laws, and that if you would classify laws you must at least draft the terms of the statute you are talking about and then ascertain all its aspects of meaning as a rule for social action of some kind.

In any event, it ought to be clear that a judge interpreting a federal constitution is no mere automaton – that, on the contrary, he has critical choices to make at different stages of the process. Nevertheless, authoritative precedent does enter the picture in a very important way, and by this factor the guide lines of the distribution of legislative powers are given considerable stability and even rigidity. Writing of this factor elsewhere, I said:

> Lest a false impression of complete uncertainty and fluidity be conveyed by the foregoing, the importance of the rules of precedent that obtain in our courts should be remembered. However open logically the classification of a given type of law may have been when first it was considered by the highest court, that decision will in all probability foreclose the question of the correct classification should the same type of law come up again. [...]

STRAYER, THE CANADIAN CONSTITUTION AND THE COURTS
(TORONTO: BUTTERWORTHS) 3D ED. (1988) AT pp. 335-341.

THE FUTURE OF JUDICIAL REVIEW

It can be assumed that the distribution of powers between federal and provincial authorities will continue to generate regular disputes. In spite of suggestions such as that "continual negotiations and political compromise" are generally a better device than judicial review for solving such disputes, experience has shown that political resolution is not always possible. [...]

Longer term constitutional solutions through agreed constitutional amendment have also been modest in scope.

While it is unlikely that federalism issues will fail to be discussed in federal-provincial fora before litigation occurs, it is difficult to envisage negotiations as a substitute for all judicial review. Indeed, judicial review provides both an ultimate alternative to, and a framework for, political negotiation. The agenda of negotiations and the relative negotiating strength of the parties are strongly influenced by what the courts have done or may be expected to do. [...]

So without minimizing the importance of political compromise, judicial review can be seen as an important adjunct to the negotiation process in the solution of federal-provincial conflicts. It cannot preclude political solutions, nor need it detract from their use. [...]

RICHARD E. SIMEON, "CRITERIA FOR CHOICE IN FEDERAL SYSTEMS"
(1982) 8 QUEEN'S L.J. AT pp. 131-157.

INTRODUCTION

One of the recurring themes in William Lederman's work is the question of what criteria are we to use in assessing, weighing, judging whether "it is better for the people that this thing be done on a national level or on a provincial level." He emphasizes that no single set of criteria will suffice; there is no neat theory from which decisions about centralization or decentralization, the division of powers, or the best structure of federal institutions can be deduced. We can "slice up" the political and policy world according to a multitude of categories and schemes of classification. Judges, like other decision-makers, must compare apples and oranges, compare the incomparable. Lederman relies, ultimately, on the wisdom and good sense of judges, aided by the law and by precedent, to maintain a "balanced" federalism. That, in the real world of politics, is as it should be.

This paper takes a somewhat different tack. It seeks to make explicit some of the normative criteria and assumptions which underlie debates about federalism. It asks: By what standards or yardsticks can we assess, evaluate, justify, defend, or attack the structure and operation of a federal system? [...]

Federalism (and its many variations in the view taken here) is valued or criticized because it is felt to promote (or constrain) other important values, and is believed to have certain kinds of effects. Federalism, as a doctrine, is thus often associated with a number of other political values, such as liberty or pluralism; federalism as a set of institutions is felt to enhance the likelihood of approximating these values in practice. Moreover, if this is true, then it should also be true that proposals for change in a federal system like Canada's can be judged by whether they serve or block these wider values, and perhaps even that if we had clear normative criteria in mind we should be able to deduce proposals for reform from them. [...]

Federalism can be evaluated first from the perspective of *community*. Here the question is: what implications do different forms of federalism have for different images of the ideal or preferred community with which people identify and to which they feel loyalty? Linguistic dualism and regional diversity have made this perspective the overwhelming focus of both practitioners and students of Canadian federalism, especially since the 1960s. Second, federalism can be evaluated from the perspective of democratic theory: does federalism promote democracy; do different conceptions of democracy generate different images of the good federal system? The prominence of the *Charter of Rights* and opposition from groups "frozen out" of the constitutional settlement together with more general critiques of the elitism of "executive federalism" have recently given a new prominence to such democratically-based perspectives on federalism. Third, federalism can be assessed from the vantage point of functional effectiveness: does it enhance or frustrate the capacity of government institutions to generate effective policy and respond to citizen needs? [...]

The relative emphasis among the three perspectives tends to vary considerably from country to country and time to time. Thus, if Canadians have been preoccupied with accommodating rival conceptions of community, Americans have – with the major exception of the Civil War period – debated federalism overwhelmingly in terms of its implications for democracy. Australians and Germans have emphasized the functional dimension – though the establishment of the Bonn republic sought the restoration of federalism as one means to diffuse power and thus inhibit the reemergence of totalitarianism. In Canada, while community has been central, English-Canadian academics of the thirties concentrated largely on federalism and effective government, rather than federalism and community. [...]

CONCEPTIONS OF COMMUNITY

The first set of criteria asks what conception of the political *community* is to be embodied in political arrangements. Federalism is thus assessed largely in terms of its ability to defend and maintain a balance between regional and national political communities. Conflict arises out of competing models of community: between a vision of a single pan-Canadian community, a vision of a union of ten provincial communities and a vision of two distinct national communities, each with full sovereignty. Within the perspective of community, moreover, is the controversy about whether the communities in Canada are to be defined largely in political terms, or in terms of the relationship of linguistic and ethnic communities. In the present context, the competing images of community can be summarized in terms of a conflict between three drives: country-building, province-building, and two-nation or Quebec nation-building. Federalism itself represents, from this point of view, a dynamic balance between regional and national communities, reflected in the relationship between federal and provincial governments. The tension threatens the federal system itself when residents of different parts of the country hold fundamentally clashing conceptions of the balance; or when residents of one or more regions develop a conception of community in which their identification or links with other regions and the central government become weak. [...]

THE FUNCTIONAL PERSPECTIVE

The second set of criteria may be labeled *functional*. [...] [F]ederal and provincial governments are seen to be different elements within a single system. Together – either through independent action, or through various forms of cooperation – they are responsible for governing the country and for satisfying the needs of citizens. Powers are allocated, at least in principle, not according to what different communities need to express and protect themselves but rather according to a division of labour criterion: which level can most efficiently and effectively carry out any given responsibility of contemporary government? The system as a whole is evaluated in terms of its ability to respond to the needs of citizens – to provide them with the mix of public policies which they prefer. And citizen interests in terms of economic and social goals – as consumers, workers, businessmen, homeowners, etc. – are held to be more important to them than their interests as members of territorially-defined communities. Does the federal system facilitate or frustrate governmental responsiveness, does it promote or block desires for more effective economic planning, control over foreign ownership, environmental protection, a fair welfare system, or any other set of objectives? Does it impose unacceptably high delays or uncertainties in decision-making, or impose heavy organizational and decision costs? [...]

The constitutional problem, then, is to allocate powers and erect machinery that maximizes the capacity of governments collectively to satisfy citizen needs. [...]

THE DEMOCRATIC PERSPECTIVE

The third perspective is that of democratic theory. It asks: what are the consequences of alternative federal arrangements for different conceptions of democracy – for participation, responsiveness, liberty and equality? There are several strands to such arguments. The first approach is primarily concerned with protecting citizens *from* governments; it stresses preservation of liberty and of minority rights against oppression by the majority. The classic defence of federalism as it emerged in the United States suggests that its fundamental purpose is to minimize the possibility of tyranny, especially majority tyranny, by ensuring that power would be fragmented among competing governmental authorities. It is thus part of the complex ideas of Madisonian liberalism, along with the division of powers, checks and balances, a constitutional Bill of Rights, and so on. In this view federalism is a device to place limits on government, in part by ensuring that "ambition" will be checked by ambition, and in part by ensuring that diverse jurisdictions will offer different packages of services from which mobile individuals can choose. This approach tends to argue for considerable decentralization and makes a virtue out of divided jurisdiction and competing governments. [...]

A second strand of democratic theorizing stresses the advantages of smaller units in terms of governmental responsiveness and citizen participation. In Montesquieu's view:

> In a large republic, the common good is subject to a thousand considerations; it is subordinated to various exceptions; it depends on accidents. In a small republic, the public good is more strongly felt, better known and closer to each citizen; abuses are less extensive, and consequently less protected.

Smaller units are likely to be more homogeneous, so a clear majority interest is more likely to emerge. The political weight of an individual citizen is greater if he is one of a small rather than a large number. Political leaders are more sensitive to public opinion with small constituencies. The advantage of a decentralized federal system, then, is that it maximizes opportunities for effective citizen participation. [...]

[D]emocratic theory also produces important critiques of federalism. Most prominent recently in Canada is the argument that the Canadian pattern of "executive federalism" in which relations between governments are conducted primarily through the negotiations of political executives limits citizen participation and effectiveness in many ways. Confusion about which level of government is responsible for what makes rational intervention difficult. The mixing of responsibilities reduces accountability and allows governments to pass the buck. The secrecy of the process has similar effects and freezes out interest groups. The dominance of executives strengthens the role of bureaucrats as against politicians, and cabinets as against legislatures and opposition parties. Citizens' interests, it is argued, get lost in governmental competition for status and power. Such considerations underlie some of the proposals of "disentanglement" and for change in the mechanisms of intergovernmental relations to make them more open. They also underline the view that the process of constitutional change should not be entirely dominated by the process of executive federalism itself. [...]

The second critique of federalism is that it frustrates majority rule; indeed, it does so almost by definition. It does so by denying a level of government the jurisdiction or resources to achieve certain ends, or by providing inadequate mechanisms for joint decision-making. [...]

A related argument, advanced by Porter and others, is that the federal structure, by fragmenting groups and institutionalizing the territorial dimension of politics, has inhibited the emergence of national majorities or of majorities and minorities based on non-regional cleavages, such as class. Both these views argue for more centralization. [...]

CONCLUSION

It is clear that we have a wealth – indeed perhaps a surfeit – of alternative criteria for choice. This variety is frustrating mainly because of the diversity of criteria which are available and because of the inability of most theorists fully to make them operational. Thus we have three clearly different normative standpoints: conceptions of community, of functional efficacy and of democracy. Within each of these we have differing assumptions and goals yielding very different prescriptions. Differences exist not only at the normative level, but also at the empirical level: given a set of goals it is not clear what institutional changes would have the desired effect, or whether, indeed, any conceivable set of changes *could* succeed.

We have also seen how difficult it is to move from statements of principles to specific proposals. While the economic criteria, for example, are reasonably precise, they are far from providing constitution-makers a clear guide to the allocation of powers, and they are especially weak in suggesting how problems of multi-level government will be dealt with.

Does this suggest that analysis from fundamental principles is useless? I think not. First, they may be more useful as rough guides, or rules of thumb, and as tools to apply. They direct the observer to ask himself: what in my conception of community? Does a given proposal look as if it will enhance or frustrate it? Given my economic and social interests and my view about the role of government, is a given change likely to increase or decrease the chances of my preferences being met? Similarly, is any particular proposal likely to enhance or threaten my view of democracy – is it likely to induce more or less clarity, more or less accountability, more or less legislative control over executives? While definitive answers cannot be given to all such questions, some of the general directions are clear. The criteria are valuable primarily as questions to ask of various alternatives, and perhaps commonsense answers to them are as good as more sophisticated ones. [...]

In a sense, all four sets of basic normative criteria are equal – we want simultaneously to maximize democracy, effectiveness, our image of community, and our ability to manage conflict. At given times one or other may be dominant – as in the growing concern with the functional dimensions of federalism after a long period of preoccupation with community. Yet in another sense, community is most fundamental. It is competing conceptions here which have generated the most dissatisfaction and conflict and which have threatened the fabric of Confederation. Moreover, [we] have seen that a great many elements in both the economic and democratic models depend on a prior – if often implicit – view of community and so cannot be discussed in isolation from it. This is especially evident with respect to equity, stabilization, and redistribution in functionalist models, and with views about which kinds of majority should prevail in democratic theory.

By their very nature, final answers about the normative issues raised here cannot be given. They are, after all, the great questions of politics. But one of the virtues of the constitutional debate of the past few years was to raise and force us to think about the broad principles underlying federalism. We were forced to ask: what is federalism for? One hopes that debate about such principles will remain a prominent feature of constitutional discussion, and that further work will clarify the relationship between federalism and other political values.

(b) Judicial Tools For Resolving Federalism Disputes

(i) "In Relation to" and "Ancillary" Doctrines

CONSTITUTION ACT, 1867 (U.K.)

c. 3, ss. 91-2

VI. – DISTRIBUTION OF LEGISLATIVE POWERS

Powers of Parliament

---

91. It shall be lawful for the Queen, by and with the Advice and Consent of the Senate and House of Commons, to make Laws for the Peace, Order, and good Government of Canada, in relation to all Matters not coming within the Classes of Subjects by this Act assigned exclusively to the Legislatures of the Provinces; and for greater Certainty, but not so as to restrict the Generality of the foregoing Terms of this Section, it is hereby declared that (notwithstanding anything in this Act) the exclusive Legislative Authority of the Parliament of Canada extends to all Matters coming within the Classes of Subjects next hereinafter enumerated: that is to say, –

[31 ENUMERATIONS FOLLOW]

92. In each Province the Legislature may exclusively make Laws in relation to Matters coming within the Classes of Subject next hereinafter enumerated; that is to say, -

[16 ENUMERATIONS FOLLOW]

- Research Note -
PITH AND SUBSTANCE

Canada's constitution divides law making power between the Parliament of Canada and provincial legislatures. This is the essence of Canadian federalism.

The division of legislative powers is done mainly by secs. 91-5 of the *Constitution Act, 1867*. The language of these sections is quite broad, using phrases like "Trade and Commerce," "Property and Civil Rights" and "Generally all Matters of a merely local or private Nature". In some cases the language granting law making power is antique – "Asylums" and "Eleemosynary Institutions," for example. Still, in responding to a challenge that a particular law is beyond the constitutional power of either Parliament or a provincial legislature, a court must consult secs. 91-5 – even if they are antique and not precise, for they are the main sources by which law making power is given to Canadian legislatures.

A court that consults these provisions will scrutinize the opening words of secs. 91 and 92 particularly. These opening phrases use several concepts to create law making power, the main ones of which are:

- law making power is in relation to matters
- matters come within classes of subjects
- classes of subjects are assigned by the *Constitution Act, 1867*
- law making powers are exclusive.

These four concepts – *in relation to, matters, coming within classes of subjects assigned by the Constitution Act, exclusivity* – are not of universal intellectual interest, but they are crucial here because they are found in the text of the constitutional provisions that assign law making power to Canadian legislatures. For example, the opening words of s. 92 assigns power to the provincial legislatures in this way:

> In each Province the Legislature may <u>exclusively</u> make Laws <u>in relation to Matters coming within the Classes of Subjects</u> next hereinafter enumerated; that is to say...
>
> [emphasis added]

Sixteen classes of subjects then follow. Section 91 grants law making power to Parliament in similar, if more convoluted language, and by using the same the same four concepts – *in relation to, matters, coming within classes of subjects, exclusivity.*

The courts have built a method for dividing constitutional power out of this language and these four concept. The method is now well settled. It is specific to Canadian federalism for two reasons: the language and the concepts used are specific to Canada's constitution; and the balance of power struck between the federal and provincial governments is a uniquely Canadian balance responsive to uniquely Canadian imperatives. Other federations confront similar problems of dividing and balancing power, but each solves this problem with its own technique to arrive at its own specific balance.

"Matter"

The concepts of 'matter' and 'in relation to' require some explanation."Matters" are constructed by the courts. They are intellectual fabrications. Courts build them by taking a cue from the constitutional text, which requires that matters *come within* the 16 provincial and 31 federal "classes of subjects." To meet the requirement that a matter come within a class of subject, a court must insure that the matter it constructs is not too big. For example, 'the environment' is too big to be a matter. It does not come within any of the 16 provincial or 31 federal classes of subjects. But 'pollution of inland rivers by the dumping of substances in them' is a matter. So is 'control of the emissions of smokestacks of heavy industry'. These easily fit with in the enumerated classes of subjects.

Another way to think about this is that if 'the environment' were allowed to be a matter, it would be exclusively federal or exclusively provincial. This would disturb the necessary balance between federal and provincial governments that Canadian courts have found necessary for the Canadian federal system. *Balance* is really the whole point. All the rest is technique.

In relation to

"In relation to" must be understood in light of an opposing concept – *ancillary*. The constitutional jurisprudence makes this clear. *In relation to* – meaning that the law is really all about this matter. The law is really all about this matter as opposed to "ancillary" to it. *Ancillary* – meaning that while the law may affect the matter, that is not its central focus, or what it is really all about. A law is in relation to a matter when its dominant or most important characteristics, its leading features, its pith and substance are really all about that matter. Perhaps the law affects the matter in an ancillary or incidental way; perhaps the law impacts on the matter in passing, or in ways that are beside the real thrust of the law, but that does not make the law "in relation to" the matter. Laws affect many things in a variety of ways, large and small. These side winds do not determine what matter a law is in relation to. That is determined by analysing the central focus of the law, what it is really all about.

Pith and Substance

In order to analyse what matter a challenged law is "in relation to" – to separate it from matters incidentally affected by the law – requires a "pith and substance analysis".

Pith and substance??? A pith and substance analysis scrutinizes the law to discover:

- the purpose of the law

- the legal effect of the law, that is, impacts that are expected to happen if the statute works as planned

- the practical effect of the law, that is, impacts the statute actually causes as it operates, anticipated or unanticipated. The effects may arise from imperfect administration, discriminatory enforcement, or unanticipated side effects caused by the law on the universe of behaviours.

For example, in *Saumur v. City of Quebec*, [1953] 2 S.C.R. 299, the Court struck down a municipal by-law that prohibited leafleting because it had been applied so as to suppress the religious views of Jehovah's Witnesses. Similarly, in *Attorney-General for Alberta v. Attorney-General for Canada*, [1939] A.C. 117, the Privy Council struck down a law imposing a tax on banks because the effects of the tax were so severe that the true purpose of the law could only be to destroy banks, not taxation. However, merely incidental effects will not disturb the constitutionality of a law otherwise in relation to a matter that comes within the classes of subjects assigned to the enacting legislature.

WALTER v. A.G. ALTA.; FLETCHER v. A.G. ALTA.
[1969] S.C.R. 383.

MARTLAND J. [for the Court]: — The question in issue in both these appeals is as to the constitutional validity of *The Communal Property Act*, R.S.A. 1955, c. 52, as amended, hereinafter referred to as "the Act". In each of the two actions the real purpose was to obtain a declaration that this statute was *ultra vires* of the Legislature of the Province of Alberta and they were consolidated for trial.

The facts are not in issue. The appellants, other than the Fletchers, are Hutterians. The Fletchers are owners of land in Alberta which their fellow plaintiffs sought to purchase. The plaintiffs in the other action also sought to purchase Alberta lands. It is conceded that the lands in each case sought to be acquired would be held in common as defined in s. 2(b)(i) of the Act and that the

C-036153

Hutterite Settlers
(Winnipeg, 1920-1930)

operation of the Act prevents the acquisition of the lands. The appellants, other than the Fletchers, in each case formed part of a religious community which based its community life and its holding of property on religious principles.

As of December 31, 1963, Hutterite colonies held approximately 480,000 acres of land in Alberta and over 10,000 acres had been added in 1964. The approximate population of Hutterites in Alberta as of December 31, 1963, was 6,000.

The Act is described as "An Act respecting Lands in the Province Held as Communal Property". "Communal Property" is defined in s. 2 of the Act, which states:

2. In this Act,
(a) "colony"

(i) means a number of persons who hold land or any interest therein as communal property, whether as owners, lessees or otherwise, and whether in the name of trustees or as a corporation or otherwise.

(ii) includes a number of persons who propose to acquire land to be held in such manner, and

(iii) includes Hutterites or Hutterian Brethren and Doukhobors;

(b) "communal property" means

(i) land held by a colony in such a manner that no member of the colony has any individual or personal ownership or right of ownership in the land, and each member shares in the distribution of profits or benefits according to his needs or in equal measure with his fellow members, and

(ii) land held by a member of the colony by personal ownership or right of ownership or under a lease, if the land is used in conjunction with and as part of other land held in the manner described in subclause (i);

(c) "Board" means the Communal Property Control Board established pursuant to this Act.

The general scheme of the Act for controlling the holding of land as communal property is as follows: Unless otherwise authorized by the Lieutenant Governor in Council in the public interest (s. 5(2)) no colony existing on the 1st day of May, 1947, may increase the holdings of its land beyond its holdings on the 1st day of March, 1944 (s. 4(1)), or, if on that date the holdings were less than 6,400 acres, they may be extended thereto (s. 4(5)). The significance of the dates May 1, 1947, and March 1, 1944, referred to in the statute is as follows: The first Alberta legislation in relation to acquisition of land by Hutterites to come into force was *The Land Sales Prohibition Act*, 1944 (Alta.), c. 15, which came into force on March 1, 1944. In general that statute prohibited the selling of land to and the purchase of land by Hutterites. That Act, as amended, remained the law until it expired on May 1, 1947, and on that date *The Communal Property Act*, 1947 (Alta.), c. 16, came into force. So that between March 1, 1944, and May 1, 1947, no Hutterite could acquire any land in Alberta, but by virtue of the provisions of *The Communal Property Act* which came into force on the latter date the restrictions on the acquisition of land were lessened somewhat in relation to Hutterites and the new provisions were made applicable to all "colonies", whether Hutterite or otherwise.

The general scheme of the Act goes on to provide as follows:

> No "colony" which exists or existed outside the province may acquire land without the consent of the Lieutenant Governor in Council (s. 6).
> No land may be acquired for the purpose of establishing a new "colony" without the consent of the Lieutenant Governor in Council (s. 7). [...]

The submission of the appellants is that the Act is legislation in respect of religion and, in consequence, is beyond the legislative powers of a provincial legislature. The respondent contends that the Act is legislation in respect of property in Alberta, controlling the way in which land is to be held, by regulating the acquisition and disposition of land to be acquired by colonies to be held as communal land.

The learned trial judge, Milvain J. (as he then was), held that, in pith and substance, the Act relates to land tenure in the province and is, therefore, intra vires of the Legislature of the Province of Alberta under s. 92(13) of the *British North America Act*. This judgment was sustained on appeal.

[...] In my opinion, the Act was enacted in relation to the ownership of land in Alberta and the Legislature had jurisdiction, under s. 92(13) of the *British North America Act*, because it deals with property in the province. The scheme of the legislation indicates that the Legislature considered the use of large areas of land in Alberta for the purposes of communal living was something which, in the public interest, required to be regulated and controlled. The Act restricts, but does not prohibit, the use of land for such purposes.

It would seem to me to be clear that a provincial legislature can enact laws governing the ownership of land within the province and that legislation enacted in relation to that subject must fall within s. 92(13), and must be valid unless it can be said to be in relation to a class of subject specifically enumerated in s. 91 of the *British North America Act* or otherwise within exclusive Federal jurisdiction.

There is no suggestion in the present case that the Act relates to any class of subject specifically enumerated in s. 91. [...]

It was submitted by the appellants that the Act is aimed at preventing the spread of Hutterite colonies in Alberta, that, because the maintenance of such colonies is a cardinal tenet of the Hutterite religion, the Act seeks to deal with religion, and that the subject of religion is within the exclusive jurisdiction of the Parliament of Canada. Their position is stated in the reasons of Johnson J.A., in the Court below, as follows:

> This Act then in its pith and substance is legislation restricting the acquisition by Hutterites of more land in the province. If a by-law which prevents the distribution of religious tracts (the *Saumur* case) was an interference with religion, I find it difficult to say that legislation which is aimed at the restriction of new and existing colonies and the holding of land in common as practised by these colonies when living in such colonies and holding lands in that manner are the principal tenets of Hutterian faith, does not also deal with religion.

With respect, I do not share this view. [...]

The purpose of the legislation in question here is to control the use of Alberta lands as communal property. While it is apparent that the legislation was prompted by the fact that Hutterites had acquired and were acquiring large areas of land in Alberta, held as communal property, it does not forbid the existence of Hutterite colonies. What it does is to limit the territorial area of communal land to be held by existing colonies and to control the acquisition of land to be acquired by new colonies which would be held as communal property. The Act is not directed at Hutterite religious belief or worship, or at the profession of such belief. It is directed at the practice of holding large areas of Alberta land as communal property, whether such practice stems from religious belief or not. The fact that Hutterites engage in that practice was the circumstance which gave rise to the necessity for the Legislature's dealing generally with the holding of land as communal property, but that does not mean that legislation controlling the holding of land in that way is not in relation to property in the Province of Alberta.

It is a function of a provincial legislature to enact those laws which govern the holding of land within the boundaries of that province. It determines the manner in which land is held. It regulates the acquisition and disposition of such land, and, if it is considered desirable in the interests of

Doukhobor women breaking the prairie sod by pulling a plow themselves (Thunder Hill, Manitoba, 1899).

the residents in that province, it controls the extent of the land holdings of a person or group of persons. The fact that a religious group upholds tenets which lead to economic views in relation to land holding does not mean that a provincial legislature, enacting land legislation which may run counter to such views, can be said, in consequence, to be legislating in respect of religion and not in respect to property

Religion, as the subject-matter of legislation, wherever the jurisdiction may lie, must mean religion in the sense that it is generally understood in Canada. It involves matters of faith and worship, and freedom of religion involves freedom in connection with the profession and dissemination of religious faith and the exercise of religious worship. But it does not mean freedom from compliance with provincial laws relative to the matter of property holding. There has been no suggestion that mortmain legislation by a provincial legislature is incompetent as interfering with freedom of religion. In *Carnation Company Limited v. The Quebec Agricultural Marketing Board*, reference was made at p. 252, to the distinction between legislation "affecting" the appellant's interprovincial trade and legislation "in relation to" the regulation of trade and commerce. In my opinion, the legislation in question here undoubtedly affects the future expansion and creation of Hutterite colonies in Alberta, but that does not mean it was enacted in relation to the matter of religion. The Act is in relation to the right to acquire land in Alberta, if it is to be used as communal property, and, in consequence, it is within provincial jurisdiction under s. 92(13). [...]

I would dismiss the appeals with costs.

MUNRO v. NAT. CAPITAL COMM.
[1966] S.C.R. 663.

CARTWRIGHT J. [for the Court]: — This is an appeal from a judgment of Gibson J. in the Exchequer Court pronounced on April 28, 1965, answering in the negative the following question which, by order of the President of the Court, had been directed to be tried before the trial of the other questions raised in the action:

> Whether, on the special case stated by the parties, the expropriation of the lands of the defendant by the National Capital Commission therein referred to is a nullity because the legislative authority of the Parliament of Canada under the *British North America Act*, 1867 to 1960, does not extend to authorizing the expropriation.

On June 25, 1959, the respondent, with the approval of the Governor in Council, expropriated a farm of 195 acres in the Township of Gloucester in the Province of Ontario owned by the appellant. In so doing the respondent was acting under subs. (1) of s. 13 of the *National Capital Act*, Statutes of Canada 1958, 7 Elizabeth II, Chap. 37, hereinafter sometimes referred to as "the Act", which came into force on February 6, 1959.

By information filed in the Exchequer Court on January 31, 1963, the respondent recited the taking of the lands for the purposes of the Act and stated its willingness to pay $200,000 by way of compensation.

In his statement of defence filed on October 13, 1964, the appellant asked, firstly, a declaration that the expropriation "was illegal, null and void because it was beyond the jurisdiction of the Parliament of Canada to grant to the Plaintiff (the respondent) powers of expropriation for establishing a Green Belt outside the limits of the said City of Ottawa", secondly, in the alternative, that compensation be awarded to him in the sum of $420,000. [...]

The main ground relied on by counsel who support the appeal is that the power of expropriation which the Act gives to the respondent has been exercised, in the case of the appellant's land, for the imposition upon the use of land within the National Capital Region of controls or restrictions of the nature of zoning regulations contemplated by the Planning Acts passed by the Provinces. It is said, more particularly, that the power has been used for the purpose of the establishment of a "Green Belt" in the Region. It is argued that such a use of the power of expropriation is in its nature, character and purpose a use in relation to a matter falling within the classes of subjects assigned exclusively to the Legislatures of the Provinces by the *British North America Act* and that, consequently, if the *National Capital Act* purports to confer such a power upon the Commission it is, *pro tanto, ultra vires* of Parliament.

[I] accept the following conclusions that counsel for the appellant and for the intervenant seek to draw, in part, from that history: (i) that the making of zoning regulations and the imposition of controls of the use of land situate in any province of the sort provided, for example, in the *Planning Act* (Ontario) are matters which, generally speaking, come within the classes of subjects assigned to the Legislature by s. 92 of the *British North America Act*; (ii) that the legislative history of the predecessors of the *National Capital Act* indicates that Parliament, up to the time of the passing of that Act, contemplated that the "zoning" of the lands comprised in the National Capital Region should be effected by co-operation between the Commission established by Parliament and the municipalities which derive their powers from the Provincial Legislatures; and (iii) that it was only after prolonged and unsuccessful efforts to achieve the desired result by such co-operation that Parliament decided to confer upon the National Capital Commission the powers necessary to enable it to carry out the zoning contemplated in the Master Plan. [...]

Section 10 defines the objects and purposes of the Commission and confers the powers to be used for the purposes of the Act. It reads as follows:

> 10.(1) The objects and purposes of the Commission are to prepare plans for and assist in the development, conservation and improvement of the National Capital Region in order that the nature and character of the seat of the Government of Canada may be in accordance with its national significance.

Section 13(1) reads as follows:

> Section 13.(1) The Commission may, with the approval of the Governor in Council, take or acquire lands for the purpose of this Act without the consent of the owner, and, except as otherwise provided in this section, all the provisions of the

> *Expropriation Act*, with such modifications as circumstances require, are applicable to and in respect of the exercise of the powers conferred by this section and the lands so taken or acquired. [...]

In my view, it is clear, from a reading of the Act as a whole, that the matter in relation to which it is enacted is the establishment of a region consisting of the seat of the Government of Canada and the defined surrounding area which are formed into a unit to be known as the National Capital Region which is to be developed, conserved and improved "in order that the nature and character of the seat of the Government of Canada may be in accordance with its national significance". [...]

I find it difficult to suggest a subject matter of legislation which more clearly goes beyond local or provincial interests and is the concern of Canada as a whole than the development, conservation and improvement of the National Capital Region in accordance with a coherent plan in order that the nature and character of the seat of the Government of Canada may be in accordance with its national significance. Adopting the words of the learned trial judge, it is my view that the Act "deals with a single matter of national concern".

There is no doubt that the exercise of the powers conferred upon the Commission by the *National Capital Act* will affect the civil rights of residents in those parts of the two provinces which make up the National Capital Region. In the case at bar the rights of the appellant are affected. But once it has been determined that the matter in relation to which the Act is passed is one which falls within the power of Parliament it is no objection to its validity that its operation will affect civil rights in the provinces. As Viscount Simon, adopting what had been pointed out by Rand J., said in *Attorney-General for Saskatchewan v. Attorney General for Canada*:

> Consequential effects are not the same thing as legislative subject matter. It is "the true nature and character of the legislation" – not its ultimate economic results – that matters.

The passage from the judgment of Duff J., as he then was, in *Gold Seal Limited v. Dominion Express Company and Attorney-General for Alberta*, quoted by the learned trial judge, correctly states the law. It is as follows:

> The fallacy lies in failing to distinguish between legislation affecting civil rights and legislation "in relation to" civil rights. Most legislation of a repressive character does incidentally or consequentially affect civil rights. But if in its true character it is not legislation "in relation to" the subject matter of "property and civil rights" within the provinces, within the meaning of section 92 of the *British North America Act*, then that is no objection although it be passed in exercise of the residuary authority conferred by the introductory clause. [...]

For these reasons I would dismiss the appeal with costs.

R. V. MORGENTALER
[1993] 3 S.C.R. 463.

[In 1989, Dr. Morgentaler was charged with fourteen counts of violating the Nova Scotia *Medical Services Act*, R.S.N.S. 1989, c. 281 and certain regulations passed under that and other *Acts*. The *Act* and the regulations prohibited, *inter alia*, the performance of an abortion anywhere other than in a place approved as a hospital under the *Hospitals Act*.]

SOPINKA J. [for the Court]: — [...] The relevant portions of the [*Medical Services*] *Act* are as follows:

> 2 The purpose of this Act is to prohibit the privatization of the provision of certain medical services in order to maintain a single high-quality health-care delivery system for all Nova Scotians.
>
> 3 In this Act,
> (a) "designated medical service" means a medical service designated pursuant to the regulations; [...]
>
> 4 No person shall perform or assist in the performance of a designated medical service other than in a hospital approved as a hospital pursuant to the *Hospitals Act*.
>
> 5 Notwithstanding the *Health Services and Insurance Act*, a person who performs or for whom is performed a medical service contrary to this Act is not entitled to reimbursement pursuant to that Act.
>
> 6 (1) Every person who contravenes this Act is guilty of an offence and liable upon summary conviction to a fine of not less than ten thousand dollars nor more than fifty thousand dollars. [...]

The Medical Society was consulted after the passage of the Act, and a list of medical services was finalized. On July 20, 1989, the *Medical Services Designation Regulation*, N.S. Reg. 152/89, was made, designating the following medical services for the purposes of the Act:

> (a) Arthroscopy
> (b) Colonoscopy (which, for greater certainty, does not include flexible sigmoidoscopy)
> (c) Upper Gastro-Intestinal Endoscopy
> (d) Abortion, including a therapeutic abortion, but not including emergency services related to a spontaneous abortion or related to complications arising from a previously performed abortion
> (e) Lithotripsy
> (f) Liposuction
> (g) Nuclear Medicine
> (h) Installation or Removal of Intraocular Lenses
> (i) Eletromyography, including Nerve Conduction Studies

The appellant argued that the *Medical Services Act* and the regulation are valid provincial legislation enacted pursuant to the province's legislative authority over hospitals, health, the medical profession and the practice of medicine. It relies particularly on heads (7), (13), and (16) of s. 92 of the *Constitution Act, 1867*. [...] The ground on which the legislation is challenged is head (27) of s. 91, which reserves "The Criminal Law [...]" to Parliament. [...]

Classifications of Laws

Classification of a law for purposes of federalism involves first identifying the "matter" of the law and then assigning it to one of the "classes of subjects" in respect to which the federal and provincial governments have legislative authority under ss. 91 and 92 of the *Constitution Act, 1867*. This process of classification is "an interlocking one, in which the *British North America Act* and the challenged legislation react on one another and fix each other's meaning": (cites omitted). Courts apply considerations of policy along with legal principle; the task requires "a nice balance of legal skill, respect for established rules, and plain common sense. It is not and never can be an exact science": (cites omitted)

A law's "matter" is its leading feature or true character, often described as its pith and substance (cites omitted). There is no single test for a law's pith and substance. The approach must be flexible and a technical, formalistic approach is to be avoided. See Hogg, *Constitutional Law of Canada* (3rd ed. 1992), vol. 1, at p. 15-13. While both the purpose and effect of the law are relevant considerations in the process of characterization (cites omitted) it is often the case that the legislation's dominant purpose or aim is the key to constitutional validity. Rand J. put it this way in *Switzman v. Elbling*, [1957] S.C.R. 285, at pp. 302-3:

> The detailed distribution made by ss. 91 and 92 places limits to direct and immediate purposes of provincial action. [...] The settled principle that calls for a determination of the "real character", the "pith and substance", of what purports to be enacted and whether it is "colourable" or is intended to effect its ostensible object, means that the true nature of the legislative act, its substance in purpose, must lie within s. 92 or some other endowment of provincial power. [...]

"LEGAL EFFECT" OR STRICT LEGAL OPERATION

Evidence of the "effect" of legislation can be relevant in two ways: to establish "legal effect" and to establish "practical effect". The analysis of pith and substance necessarily starts with looking at the legislation itself, in order to determine its legal effect. "Legal effect" or "strict legal operation" refers to how the legislation as a whole affects the rights and liabilities of those subject to its terms, and is determined from the terms of the legislation itself. See Hogg, supra, at pp. 15-13 and 15-15. Legal effect is often a good indicator of the purpose of the legislation (cites omitted) but is relevant in constitutional characterization even when it is not fully intended or appreciated by the enacting body. Thus in *Starr v. Houlden*, supra, the terms of reference of the Patricia Starr inquiry were held to duplicate the purposes and functions of a police investigation and preliminary inquiry into criminal allegations against specific individuals, which are criminal law matters, even though the province may not have intended that result.

The analysis of pith and substance is not, however, restricted to the four corners of the legislation (cites omitted). Thus the court "will look beyond the direct legal effects to inquire into the social or economic purposes which the statute was enacted to achieve", its background and the circumstances surrounding its enactment (Hogg, supra, at p. 15-13) and, in appropriate cases, will consider evidence of the second form of "effect", the actual or predicted practical effect of the legislation in operation (cites omitted). The ultimate long-term, practical effect of the legislation will in some cases be irrelevant. (cites omitted)

THE USE OF EXTRINSIC MATERIALS   *Practical Effect*

In determining the background, context and purpose of challenged legislation, the court is entitled to refer to extrinsic evidence of various kinds provided it is relevant and not inherently unreliable: (cites omitted) This clearly includes related legislation (such as, in this case, the March regulations and the former s. 251 of the *Criminal Code*), and evidence of the "mischief" at which the legislation is directed: (cites omitted). It also includes legislative history, in the sense of the events that occurred during drafting and enactment; as Ritchie J., concurring in *Reference Re Anti-Inflation Act, supra,* wrote at p. 437, it is "not only permissible but essential" to consider the material the legislature had before it when the statute was enacted.

The former exclusionary rule regarding evidence of legislative history has gradually been relaxed (*Reference Re Upper Churchill Water Rights Reversion Act,* [1984] 1 S.C.R. 297, at pp. 317-19), but until recently the courts have balked at admitting evidence of legislative debates and speeches. [...] The main criticism of such evidence has been that it cannot represent the "intent" of the legislature, an incorporeal body, but that is equally true of other forms of legislative history. Provided that the court remains mindful of the limited reliability and weight of Hansard evidence, it should be admitted as relevant to both the background and the purpose of legislation. Indeed, its admissibility in constitutional cases to aid in determining the background and purpose of legislation now appears well established. [...]

I would therefore hold, as did Freeman J.A. in the Court of Appeal, that the excerpts from Hansard were properly admitted by the trial judge in this case. In a nutshell, this evidence demonstrates that members of all parties in the House understood the central feature of the proposed law to be prohibition of Dr. Morgentaler's proposed clinic on the basis of a common and almost unanimous opposition to abortion clinics *per se*. [...]

In the present case the Attorney General of Nova Scotia submits that the evidence shows that the future administration of the Act will not result in a restriction on abortion services; the respondent submits the opposite. This raises the question of the relevance of evidence of practical effect. I have noted that the legal effect of the terms of legislation is always relevant. Barring material amendments, it does not change over time. The practical effect of legislation, on the other hand, has a less secure status in constitutional analysis. Practical effect consists of the actual or predicted results of the legislation's operation and administration (see, e.g., *Saumur*, supra). Courts are often asked to adjudicate the constitutionality of legislation which is not yet in force or which, as here, has only been in force a short time. In such cases any prediction of future practical effect is necessarily short-term, since the court is not equipped to predict accurately the future consequential impact of legislation.

[...] The difficulty with practical effect is that whereas in one context practical effect may reveal the true purpose of the legislation (see *Saumur*, supra), in another context it may be incidental and entirely irrelevant even though it is drastic (cites omitted); and in yet another context provincial and federal enactments with the same practical impact may both stand if the matter to which they relate has two "aspects" of roughly equivalent importance, one within federal and the other within provincial competence (cites omitted).

In the majority of cases the only relevance of practical effect is to demonstrate an *ultra vires* purpose by revealing a serious impact upon a matter outside the enacting body's legislative authority and thus either contradicting an appearance of *intra vires* or confirming an impression of ultra vires.

[...] If, however, pith and substance can be determined without reference to evidence of practical effect, the absence of evidence that the legislation has a practical effect in line with this characterization will not displace the conclusion as to the legislation's invalidity. In such a case, "evidence as to the likely effect of legislation would not add anything useful to the task of characterization, but would merely bear on the wisdom or efficacy of the statute. In those cases the evidence is not relevant" (cites omitted). Such evidence will not change the legislation's "matter", and only goes to the effectiveness of the statute to fulfil its

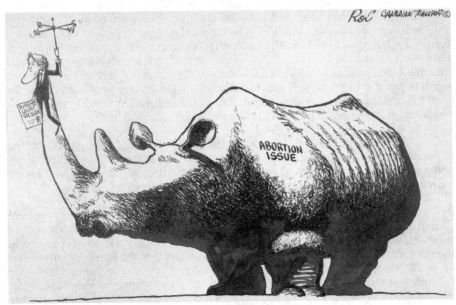

On the Horn of Dilemma

object. The court is not concerned with the wisdom of a statute, and the government surely cannot justify legislation already determined to be *ultra vires* by arguing that it will not realize its aim or objective. Moreover, as I have said, legislation is often considered before experience has shown its actual impact, and prediction of future impact is necessarily short-term. I would adapt what La Forest J. said in another context (*R. v. Edwards Books and Art Ltd.*, supra, at p. 803) to this situation: "[i]t is undesirable that an Act be found constitutional today and unconstitutional tomorrow" simply because of the absence of conclusive evidence as to future impact or the possibility of a change in practical effect. [...]

Scope of the Applicable Heads of Power

The issue we face in the present case is whether Nova Scotia has, by the present legislation, regulated the place for delivery of a medical service with a view to controlling the quality and nature of its health care delivery system, or has attempted to prohibit the performance of abortions outside hospitals with a view to suppressing or punishing what it perceives to be the socially undesirable conduct of abortion. The former would place the legislation within provincial competence; the latter would make it criminal law. [...] The presence or absence of a criminal public purpose or object is thus pivotal. [...]

The provinces have general legislative jurisdiction over hospitals by virtue of s. 92(7) of the *Constitution Act, 1867,* and over the medical profession and the practice of medicine by virtue of ss. 92(13) and (16). Section 92(16) also gives them general jurisdiction over health matters within the province: *Schneider v. The Queen,* [1982] 2 S.C.R. 112, at p. 137. The *Schneider* case gives an indication of the watershed between valid health legislation and criminal law. In that case, British Columbia's *Heroin Treatment Act* was held to be *intra vires* because its object was not to punish narcotics addicts, but to treat their addiction and ensure their safety and security. Narcotic addiction was targeted not as a public evil but as a "physiological condition necessitating both medical and social intervention" (at p. 138). Accordingly, if the central concern of the present legislation were medical treatment of unwanted pregnancies and the safety and security of the pregnant woman, not the restriction of abortion services with a view to safeguarding the public interest or interdicting a public harm, the legislation would arguably be valid health law enacted pursuant to the province's general health jurisdiction.

In addition, there is no dispute that the heads of s. 92 invoked by the appellant confer on the provinces jurisdiction over health care in the province generally, including matters of cost and efficiency, the nature of the health care delivery system, and privatization of the provision of medical services. [...]

The two *Morgentaler* decisions focus attention on the purpose or concern of abortion legislation to determine if it is truly criminal law: Is the performance or procurement of abortion prohibited as socially undesirable conduct? Is protecting the state interest in the foetus or balancing the interests of the foetus against those of women seeking abortions a primary objective of the legislation? Is the protection of the woman's health only an ancillary concern? And are other provincial concerns such as the establishment of hospitals or the regulation of the medical profession or the practice thereof merely incidental? [...]

The appellant argues that even if the object of the legislation was to suppress free-standing abortion clinics on grounds of public morals, this is not fatal to provincial jurisdiction. Although there has been some recognition of a provincial "morality" power, it is clear that the exercise of such a power must be firmly anchored in an independent provincial head of power: *Rio Hotel Ltd. v. New Brunswick*, supra, at pp. 71-80; *Attorney General for Canada and Dupond v. City of Montreal*, [1978] 2 S.C.R. 770; R. Pepin, "Le pouvoir des provinces canadiennes de légiférer sur la moralité publique" (1988), 19 R.G.D. 865; *Attorney General of Canada v. Law Society of British Columbia*, [1982] 2 S.C.R. 307, at p. 364.

While legislation which authorizes the establishment and enforcement of a local standard of morality does not *ipso facto* "invade the field of criminal law" (see *Nova Scotia Board of Censors v. McNeil*, supra, at pp. 691-92), it cannot be denied that interdiction of conduct in the interest of public morals was and remains one of the classic ends of the criminal law, as established in the *Margarine Reference*, supra, at p. 50: see *Westendorp v. The Queen*, supra, and *Johnson v. Attorney General of Alberta*, [1954] S.C.R. 127, at pp. 148-49.

As Wilson J. recognized in *Morgentaler (1988)*, supra, at p. 171, a woman's decision to have an abortion is "profound[ly] social and ethical;" indeed it is "essentially a moral decision" (cf. M.L. McConnell, "'Even by Commonsense Morality': *Morgentaler, Borowski* and the Constitution of Canada" (1989), 68 *Can. Bar Rev.* 765, at p. 766) and it seems clear to me that the present legislation, whose primary purpose is to prohibit abortions except in certain circumstances, treats of a moral issue.

In view of the foregoing, there is a strong inference that the purpose of the legislation and its true nature relate to a matter within the federal head of power in respect of criminal law. In order to determine whether this is its dominant purpose or characteristic, it is necessary to compare the above indicia of federal subject matter with indications of provincial objectives.

This legislation deals, by its terms, with a subject historically considered to be part of the criminal law — the prohibition of the performance of abortions with penal consequences. It is thus suspect on its face. Its legal effect partially reproduces that of the now defunct s. 251 of the *Criminal Code*, in so far as both precluded the establishment and operation of free-standing abortion clinics. Its legislative history, the course of events leading up to the Act's passage and the making of N.S. Reg. 152/89, the Hansard excerpts and the absence of evidence that privatization and the cost and quality of health care services were anything more than incidental concerns, lead to the conclusion that the *Medical Services Act* and the *Medical Services Designation Regulation* were aimed primarily at suppressing the perceived public harm or evil of abortion clinics. The legislation meets the tests set out in the *Margarine Reference*, supra, and of *Morgentaler (1975)* and *Morgentaler (1988)*, supra. The primary objective of the legislation was to prohibit abortions outside hospitals as socially undesirable conduct, and any concern with the safety and security of pregnant women or with health care policy, hospitals or the regulation of the medical profession was merely ancillary. This legislation involves the regulation of the place where an abortion may be obtained, not from the viewpoint of health care policy, but from the viewpoint of public wrongs or crimes, to echo Cannon J.'s words in *Reference Re Alberta Statutes,* [1938] S.C.R. 100, at p. 144 (appeal dismissed as moot in *Alberta Bank Taxation Reference,* at pp. 127-20) (cases omitted):

> I agree with the submission of the Attorney-General for Canada that this bill deals with the regulation of the press of Alberta, *not from the viewpoint of private wrongs or civil injuries* resulting from any alleged infringement or privation of civil rights which belong to individuals, considered as individuals *but from the viewpoint of public wrongs or crimes,* i.e., involving a violation of the public rights and duties to the whole community, considered as a community, in its social aggregate capacity. (emphasis added.)

Paraphrasing what Lamer J. said in *Starr v. Houlden,* supra, at p. 1405: I find unpersuasive the argument that this legislation is solidly anchored in s. 92(7), (13) or (16) of the *Constitution Act, 1867.* There is nothing on the surface of the legislation or in the background facts leading up to its enactment to convince me that it is designed to protect the integrity of Nova Scotia's health care system by preventing the emergence of a two-tiered system of delivery, to ensure the delivery of high-quality health care, or to rationalize the delivery of medical services so as to avoid duplication and reduce public health care costs. Any such objectives are clearly incidental to the central feature of the legislation, which is the prohibition of abortions outside hospitals as socially undesirable conduct subject to punishment.

PRACTICAL EFFECT

This legislation will certainly restrict abortion in the sense that it makes abortions unavailable in any place other than hospitals. But will it lead to a practical restriction of access to abortion in Nova Scotia? Will the present hospital system be able and willing to accommodate all the women who desire to terminate a pregnancy, given among other things that the hospital in which 83 percent of all abortions are performed has lost half of its medical staff willing to perform the procedure? These are questions that the trial judge did not answer, and on which the parties are resolutely divided. Women may not wish to have an abortion in a hospital for any number of legitimate reasons. Clearly restrictions as to place can have the effect of restricting abortions in practice, and indeed it was the operation of s. 251 of the *Criminal Code* in restricting abortions to certain hospitals that contributed largely to its demise. One of the reasons that the former s. 251 of the *Criminal Code* was struck down in *Morgentaler (1988),* supra, was that the in-hospital requirement in that section led to unacceptable delays, undue stress and trauma, and a severe practical restriction of access to abortion services. Several years of experience under s. 251 showed that the combined decisions and actions of individual anti-abortion hospital boards could render access to legal abortion non-existent in large areas of the country. Something similar may occur in Nova Scotia but that is something we have no way of predicting. One of the effects of the legislation is consolidation of abortions in the hands of the provincial government, largely in one provincially controlled institution. This renders free access to abortion vulnerable to administrative erosion.

Having applied the ordinary tests as to the matter of the present legislation, I am able to conclude that the legislation was an *ultra vires* invasion of the field of criminal law. I am able to reach this conclusion without predicting the ultimate practical effect of this legislation, and it is consequently unnecessary to adjudicate the intractable dispute between the parties as to whether this legislation will, in fact, restrict access to abortion in Nova Scotia. The appellant's evidence that the legislation will not have the practical effect of restricting abortions is simply evidence that the legislation will not actually accomplish what it set out to do. In view of my conclusion as to the pith and substance of the legislation, I am not concerned with whether the legislation is effective and such evidence can no more be used to validate ultra vires legislation than to invalidate *intra vires* legislation, as was held in *Reference Re Anti-Inflation Act*, supra.

WARD v. CANADA (ATTORNEY GENERAL) ET AL.
[2002] 1 S.C.R. 569.

McLACHLIN, C.J.C. [for the Court]: —

¶ 3 Ford Ward is a licensed fisherman and sealer who resides in La Scie, a town on the north coast of Newfoundland. During the period in question, he held a commercial sealing license issued under the authority of the *Fisheries Act*, R.S.C. 1985, c. F-14, which permitted him to harvest hooded and harp seals. During March and April of 1996, Ward engaged in the seal hunt off the northeast coast of Newfoundland in an area known as "the Front". On the voyage in question, Ward harvested approximately 50 seals, a number of which included hooded "blueback" seals.

¶ 4 On November 20, 1996, Ward was charged with selling blueback seal pelts contrary to s. 27 of the *Marine Mammal Regulations*, SOR/93-56 (the "*Regulations*"), which prohibits the sale, trade or barter of whitecoat and blueback seals. Ward applied to the Supreme Court of Newfoundland, Trial Division, for a declaration that s. 27 was *ultra vires* the Parliament of Canada.[...]

¶ 8 The past 30 years have seen vigorous anti-sealing campaigns directed largely at the killing of seal pups at the Front and in the Gulf of St. Lawrence. In 1983, the Council of the European Communities issued a directive banning the import of whitecoat and blueback skins. A second directive in 1985 extended the ban to October 1989. The campaigns all but destroyed the traditional markets for Canadian seal products and threatened to spread to other fish products, particularly canned fish. In June of 1984, the federal government established the Royal Commission on Seals and the Sealing Industry in Canada, also known as the Malouf Commission. In light of the circumstances surrounding the campaigns and the market threat to other fish products, the Malouf Commission recommended in its Report that the large-scale commercial hunting of whitecoats and bluebacks "should not be permitted", and non-commercial hunting, "to the extent it occurs at all, should be carefully regulated and strictly limited" [...]

¶ 9 The government responded by passing new regulations, including the ban on the sale, trade or barter of whitecoats and bluebacks here at issue. [...]

V. Issue

¶ 15 The issue on this appeal is whether the federal regulation prohibiting the sale, trade or barter of blueback seals is a valid exercise of the federal fisheries power or the federal criminal law power.

VI. Analysis

¶ 16 In order to resolve the issue posed by this appeal, we must determine whether s. 27, in pith and substance, falls under the federal power over fisheries or the criminal law. The pith and substance analysis asks two questions: first, what is the essential character of the law? Second, does that character relates to an enumerated head of power granted to the legislature in question by the *Constitution Act, 1867*? [...] We must address these questions first with respect to the federal fisheries power, second with respect to the federal criminal law power.

> A. *The Pith and Substance of Section 27 of the Regulations in Relation to the Fisheries Power*

> (1) The Essential Character of the Law

¶ 17 The first task in the pith and substance analysis is to determine the pith and substance, or essential character of the law. What is the true meaning or dominant feature of the impugned legislation? This is resolved by looking at the purpose and the legal effect of the regulation or law: see *Reference re Firearms Act, supra*, at para. 16. The purpose refers to what the legislature wanted to accomplish. Purpose is relevant to determine whether, in this case, Parliament was regulating the fishery, or venturing into the provincial area of property and civil rights. The legal effect refers to how the law will affect rights and liabilities, and is also helpful in illuminating the core meaning of the law.... The effects can also reveal whether a law is "colourable", i.e. does the law in form appear to address something within the legislature's jurisdiction, but in substance deal with a matter outside that jurisdiction... In oral argument, Ward expressly made clear that he is not challenging the law on the basis of colourability.

¶ 18 The pith and substance analysis is not technical or formalistic [...]. It is essentially a matter of interpretation. The court looks at the words used in the impugned legislation as well as the background and circumstances surrounding its enactment [...]. In conducting this analysis, the court should not be concerned with the efficacy of the law or whether it achieves the legislature's goals [...].

¶ 19 Section 27 of the *Regulations*, read alone, is simply a prohibition of sale, trade or barter, suggesting it might fall within the provincial rather than federal domain. However, we cannot stop at this point. We must go further. What is the purpose of s. 27, and what is its effect? How does it fit into the regulatory scheme as a whole? The question is not <u>whether</u> the *Regulations* prohibit the sale so much as <u>why</u> it is prohibited.

¶ 20 To answer this question, we need go no further than the findings of the trial judge. Wells J. found that the purpose of s. 27 of the *Regulations* was to control the killing of bluebacks and whitecoats by prohibiting their sale, thus making it largely pointless to harvest them. In other words, the prohibition on sale, trade or barter is directed not to controlling commerce, but to preventing the harvesting of these seals.

¶ 21 This purpose is clear from both the *Regulations* as a whole and the legislative history. As discussed, s. 27 of the *Regulations* was adopted in response to the Malouf Commission, which recommended that the commercial harvest of bluebacks and whitecoats be curtailed. The reaction to this harvest destroyed the traditional seal markets and was threatening the markets for Canadian fish products abroad.

¶ 22 The method the government chose to curtail the commercial harvest of bluebacks and whitecoats was a prohibition on their sale, trade or barter. This, as Wells J. found, was because prohibiting the killing of bluebacks simply would not have worked. The seals are harvested while in the sea by hunters on boats. It is impossible to distinguish bluebacks from other seals in the water. Not until a blueback is brought aboard the boat does the seal-hunter know that he has taken one. When this happens, the seal-hunter knows that the seals in the area are bluebacks. Since he cannot sell, trade or barter bluebacks, he will stop killing them. This will tend to stop the commercial harvest of bluebacks, as recommended by the Malouf Commission. As Wells J. conceded, the method chosen may be imperfect. However, it is the only practical method for curtailing the commercial taking of bluebacks. In any event, as noted, the efficacy of the law is not a valid consideration in the pith and substance analysis.

¶ 23 Situating s. 27 in its context supports the view that it is neither directed at property nor at trade, but at curtailing the commercial hunting of bluebacks and whitecoats. The *Regulations* are enacted under the authority of s. 43 of the *Fisheries Act*, which permits the government to make regulations "for the proper management and control of the sea-coast and inland fisheries" and "respecting the conservation and protection of fish" (emphasis added). This notion of "management and control" of the fisheries is again reflected in s. 3 of the *Regulations*. The *Regulations* as a whole are concerned not with property, but with generally regulating the fishery, including details as to who may kill (with exemptions for Indians, Inuk and "beneficiaries" under certain aboriginal claim settlements), methods of killing, quotas and seasons for killing, allowable fishing areas, reporting duties, and provisions for observation of the seal fishery. Included are restrictions on the disposition of the edible parts of cetaceans or walruses, narwhal tusks and the prohibition on the sale, trade or barter of whitecoats and bluebacks at issue here. In short, the prohibition we are concerned with exists in the context of a scheme that is concerned with the overall "management and control" of the marine fisheries resource.

¶ 24 I conclude that Parliament's object was to regulate the seal fishery by eliminating the commercial hunting of whitecoats and bluebacks through a prohibition on sale, while at the same time allowing for limited harvesting of these animals for non-commercial purposes. Stated another way, the "mischief" that Parliament sought to remedy was the large-scale commercial hunting of whitecoats and bluebacks. This was done to preserve the economic viability of not only the seal fishery, but the Canadian fisheries in general.

¶ 25 Turning to the effects of the legislation, s. 27 affects the legal rights of its subjects by prohibiting the sale of whitecoats and bluebacks that have otherwise been legally harvested. Ward submits that the legal effect of s. 27 is to regulate the property and processing of a harvested seal product. The argument amounts to saying that because the legislative measure is a prohibition on sale, it must be in pith and substance concerned with the regulation of sale. This confuses the purpose of the legislation with the means used to carry out that purpose. Viewed in the context of the legislation as a whole and the legislative history, there is nothing to suggest that Parliament was trying to regulate the local market for trade of seals and seal products. Ward's argument that s. 27 is directed at regulating an already processed product because the seals are skinned and the meat preserved on the vessel similarly confuses the purpose of s. 27 with the means chosen to achieve it.

¶ 26 Ward also argues that the "close time" variation method would better avoid newborn seals being killed on the ice and the negative reaction the government was seeking to avoid than a prohibition on sale. This argument also fails. As previously mentioned, an inquiry into efficacy does not advance the pith and substance inquiry. The purpose of legislation cannot be challenged by proposing an alternate, allegedly better, method for achieving that purpose.

¶ 27 Finally, Ward submits that the purpose of s. 27 -- saving Canada's markets for seal products -- had already eroded by the time it was introduced in 1993, citing the Malouf Commission in support. This is a variant on the efficacy argument. It was for the government to determine if a problem existed and if the means chosen would address it. Moreover, the evidence shows that the danger of damage to other sea products, like canned fish, continued to exist at the time the Regulations were adopted.

¶ 28 I conclude that the s. 27 prohibition on sale is essentially concerned with curtailing the commercial hunting of whitecoats and bluebacks for the economic protection of the fisheries resource. As such, it is in pith and substance concerned with the management of the Canadian fishery.

(2) Does the Pith and Substance of Section 27 of the *Regulations* Fall within the Federal Fisheries Power?

¶ 29 Having determined the pith and substance of s. 27, we must ask whether it fits within the federal fisheries power. This requires us to consider the scope of the fisheries power and its relationship to the provincial power over property and civil rights. More precisely, does the fisheries power extend beyond measures relating to conservation to the management of the resource to preserve its economic viability?

¶ 30 Before examining the scope of the federal fisheries power in relation to property and civil rights, it may be useful to consider the principles that guide the exercise. They are well known and I content myself with briefly summarizing them.

1. The Constitution must be interpreted flexibly over time to meet new social, political and historic realities [...].

2. The principle of federalism must be respected: see *Reference re Secession of Quebec, supra,* at para. 55. Power is shared by two orders of government, each autonomous in developing policies and laws within their own jurisdiction subject to the courts which "control the limits of the respective sovereignties" [...]. In cases where federal and provincial classes of subjects contemplate overlapping concepts, meaning may be given to both through the process of "mutual modification" [...]. Classes of subjects should not be construed so broadly as to expand jurisdiction indefinitely [...]

¶ 31 With these principles in mind – flexibility and respect for the proper powers of both the federal government and the provinces – I approach the question at hand, the scope of the federal fisheries power.

¶ 32 Three different views on the scope of the federal fisheries power are presented:

1. The federal fisheries power extends only to conservation measures directed to preserving numbers (the conservation theory, espoused by the majority of the Newfoundland Court of Appeal).

2. The fisheries power extends only to the management of the fisheries resource in its natural state to the point of harvest and sale. This would include setting the permissible times and methods of extracting the resource, but it would not extend to the regulation of sale, processing and "markets" (the "point of sale" theory, espoused by Ward).

3. The fisheries power extends beyond conservation to measures intended to carry out economic goals and policies associated with the fisheries as a resource (the economic policy theory, advanced by the federal Crown).

¶ 33 Only the last theory is capable of supporting a regulation directed in pith and substance at curtailing the commercial hunting of young seals to protect the economic viability of the resource from retaliatory boycotts. The issue is therefore whether this theory of the fisheries power is valid. The jurisprudence suggests that it is. [...]

[Chief Justice McLachlin reviewed the cases.]

¶ 41 These cases put beyond doubt that the fisheries power includes not only conservation and protection, but also the general "regulation" of the fisheries, including their management and control. They recognize that "fisheries" under s. 91(12) of the *Constitution Act, 1867* refers to the fisheries as a resource; "a source of national or provincial wealth" [...]; "a common property resource" to be managed for the good of all Canadians [...]. The fisheries resource includes the animals that inhabit the seas. But it also embraces commercial and economic interests, aboriginal rights and interests, and the public interest in sport and recreation

¶ 42 Although broad, the fisheries power is not unlimited. The same cases that establish its broad parameters also hold that the fisheries power must be construed to respect the provinces' power over property and civil rights under s. 92(13) of the *Constitution Act, 1867*. This too is a broad, multi-faceted power, difficult to summarize concisely. For our purposes, it suffices to note that the regulation of trade and industry within the province generally (with certain exceptions) falls within the province's jurisdiction over property and civil rights [...].

¶ 43 Thus we have before us two broad powers, one federal, one provincial. In such cases, bright jurisdictional lines are elusive. Whether a matter best conforms to a subject within federal jurisdiction on the one hand, or provincial jurisdiction on the other, can only be determined by examining the activity at stake. Measures that in pith and substance go to the maintenance and preservation of fisheries fall under federal power. By contrast, measures that in pith and substance relate to trade and industry within the province have been held to be outside the federal fisheries power and within the provincial power over property and civil rights.

¶ 44 The cases bear this out. Measures whose essence went to the regulation of fish processing and labour relations in the fishery have been held to fall outside the federal power. On the other hand, measures primarily related to the regulation of the fisheries resource but incidentally touching the sale of fish have been upheld as valid federal legislation. [...]

[Chief Justice McLachlin reviewed the cases.]

¶ 47 These cases suggest that measures essentially directed to regulating fish processing and labour relations fall under the provincial power over property and civil rights, and outside the federal fisheries power. If the activity is in pith and substance a matter of trade and industry within the province, it will not fall under the federal fisheries power merely because some aspects of the activity touch upon the fishery. Conversely, measures that are in pith and substance directed to the fishery fall within the federal fisheries power even though they possess aspects relating to property and civil rights.

¶ 48 It follows that the federal fisheries power is not confined to measures directed at conserving the resource, nor limited by the distinction between control of the resource in its natural state and at "point of sale". While Parliament must respect the provincial power over property and civil rights, the approach to be adopted is not simply drawing a line between federal and provincial powers on the basis of conservation or sale. The issue is rather whether the matter regulated is essentially connected -- related in pith and substance -- to the federal fisheries power, or to the provincial power over property and civil rights.

¶ 49 We earlier established that the regulation here at issue, while on its face a simple ban on sale, trade or barter, is in pith and substance concerned with curtailing commercial hunting of young seals to preserve the fisheries as an economic resource, vitally connected to protecting the economic viability of the Canadian fishery as a whole. It follows that s. 27 is a valid federal measure. This result fully respects the constitutional right of the provinces to control property and civil rights. If the essential character of the measure was directed toward regulating business or property within the province, it would be in pith and substance a matter of property and civil rights and outside federal jurisdiction. However, that is not the case. Section 27 of the *Regulations* is thus a valid exercise of the federal fisheries power. [...]

VII. Conclusion and Disposition

57 I conclude that s. 27 of the *Regulations*, prohibiting the sale, trade or barter of whitecoat and blueback seals, is a valid measure under the federal fisheries power. I would therefore allow the appeal, restore the decision of the trial judge, and find that s. 27 of the *Regulations* is a valid exercise of Parliament's jurisdiction under sea coast and inland fisheries contained in s. 91(12) of the *Constitution Act, 1867*. [...]

[**Note**: See *Reference Re Firearms Act*, infra under Criminal Law, for a further example of the technique by which courts classify statutes for the purpose of the federal distribution of powers.]

(ii) "Necessarily Incidental" Doctrine,
"Rational Functional Connection" Test

GENERAL MOTORS v. CITY NATIONAL LEASING
[1989] 1 S.C.R. 641.

[Respondent (CNL), a company leasing fleets of automobiles and trucks nation-wide in competition with other national fleet leasing companies, sued General Motors under s. 31.1 of the *Combines Investigation Act*. CNL alleged that GM had been paying "preferential" interest rate support to CNL's competitors in respect of their purchases of GM vehicles. CNL alleged this to be price discrimination contrary to s. 34(1)(a) of the *Combines Investigation Act*. Section 31.1 creates a civil cause of action for infractions of the Act notwithstanding the fact that the creation of civil causes of action lies within the domain of the provinces. CNL claimed damages equivalent to monies saved by its competitors.

The motions court judge found s. 31.1 of the *Act* to be *ultra vires* Parliament as the right to sue was not truly necessary for the *Combines Investigation Act*. The Court of Appeal found s. 31.1 to be *intra vires* Parliament.

The Court considered the following constitutional questions: (1) whether the *Combines Investigation Act* or any part of it is *intra vires* Parliament under s. 91(2) of the *Constitution Act, 1867*, and (2) whether s. 31.1 is within the competence of Parliament.]

DICKSON C.J.C. [for the Court]: — [Justice scrutinized the *Combines Investigation Act* and found it to be *intra vires* Parliament under s. 91(2). (see p. 541, infra). He then continued:]

The final question is whether the provision [s. 31.1] can be constitutionally justified by reason of its connection with valid legislation. As Laskin C.J. remarked in *Vapour Canada, supra*, inclusion of an invalid provision in a valid statute does not necessarily stamp the provision with validity. Here the court must focus on the relationship between the valid legislation and the impugned provision. Answering the question first requires deciding what test of "fit" is appropriate for such a determination. By "fit" I refer to how well the provision is integrated into the scheme of the legislation and how important it is for the efficacy of the legislation. The same test will not be appropriate in all circumstances. In arriving at the correct standard the court must consider the degree to which the provision intrudes on provincial powers. The case law, to which I turn below, shows that in certain circumstances a stricter requirement is in order, while in others, a looser test is acceptable. For example, if the impugned provision only encroaches marginally on provincial powers, then a "functional" relationship may be sufficient to justify the provision. Alternatively, if the impugned provision is highly intrusive *vis à vis* provincial powers then a stricter test is appropriate. A careful case by case assessment of the proper test is the best approach.

In determining the proper test it should be remembered that in a federal system it is inevitable that, in pursuing valid objectives, the legislation of each level of government will impact occasionally on the sphere of power of the other level of government; overlap of legislation is to be expected and accommodated in a federal state. Thus a certain degree of judicial restraint in proposing strict tests which will result in striking down such legislation is appropriate. I reiterate what I said on this general theme (although in a slightly different context) in *OPSEU v. Ontario (Attorney General)*, [1987] 2 S.C.R. 2, at p. 18:

> The history of Canadian constitutional law has been to allow for a fair amount of interplay and indeed overlap between federal and provincial powers. It is true that doctrines like interjurisdictional and Crown immunity and concepts like "watertight compartments" qualify the extent of that interplay. But it must be recognized that these doctrines and concepts have not been the dominant tide of constitutional doctrines: rather they have been an undertow against the strong pull of pith and substance, the aspect doctrine and, in recent years, a very restrained approach to concurrency and paramountcy issues.

The above comments also emphasize that the question in this appeal of how far federal legislation may validly impinge on provincial powers is one part of the general notion of the "pith and substance" of legislation; i.e., the doctrine that a law which is federal in its true nature will be upheld even if it affects matters which appear to be a proper subject for provincial legislation (and vice versa). On p. 334 of his book *Constitutional Law of Canada* (2nd ed. 1985), Professor Hogg explains this in the following way:

The pith and substance doctrine enables a law that is classified as "in relation to" a matter within the competence of the enacting body to have incidental or ancillary effects on matters outside the competence of the enacting body.

I emphasize that these comments should not be seen as altering the balance of constitutional powers. Both provincial and federal governments have equal ability to legislate in ways that may incidentally affect the other government's sphere of power. I quote from Professor Hogg again, where at p. 336 he states: "I think it is plain both on principle and on authority that the provincial enumerated powers have exactly the same capacity as the federal enumerated powers to `affect' matters allocated to the other level of government."

In the present appeal, the appellant focuses its attack on a particular section of the Act. The issue is not whether the Act as a whole is rendered *ultra vires* because it reaches too far, but whether a particular provision is sufficiently integrated into the Act to sustain its constitutionality. In numerous cases courts have considered the nature of the relationship which is required, between a provision which encroaches on provincial jurisdiction and a valid statute, for the provision to be upheld. In different contexts courts have set down slightly different requirements, *viz*: "rational and functional connection" in *Papp v. Papp*, [1970] 1 O.R. 331, *R. v. Zelensky*, [1978] 2 S.C.R. 940, and *Multiple Access Ltd. v. McCutcheon*, [1982] 2 S.C.R. 161; "ancillary", "necessarily incidental" and "truly necessary" in the *Regional Municipality of Peel v. MacKenzie*, supra; "intimate connection", "an integral part" and "necessarily incidental" in *Northern Telecom Ltd. v. Communications Workers of Canada*, [1980] 1 S.C.R. 115; "integral part" in *Clark v. Canadian National Railway Co.*, [1988] 2 S.C.R. 680; "a valid constitutional cast by the context and association in which it is fixed as a complementary provision" in *Vapour Canada*, supra; and "truly necessary" in *R. v. Thomas Fuller Construction Co.* (1958) Ltd., [1980] 1 S.C.R. 695. I believe the approach I have outlined is consistent with the results of this jurisprudence. These cases are best understood as setting out the proper test for the particular context in issue, rather than attempting to articulate a test of general application with reference to all contexts. Thus the tests they set out are not identical. As the seriousness of the encroachment on provincial powers varies, so does the test required to ensure that an appropriate constitutional balance is maintained. In surveying past jurisprudence it is to be expected that some example of patterns between the appropriate test of fit, and the head of power under which the federal legislation is valid, will be found. Such patterns exist not only because of a possible degree of similarity between the federal legislation which falls under any one head of power, but also for the reason that certain federal heads of power, for example, s. 92(10), are narrow and distinct powers which relate to particular works and undertakings and are thus quite susceptible to having provisions "tacked-on" to legislation which is validated under them, while other federal heads of power, for example, trade and commerce, are broad and therefore less likely to give rise to highly intrusive provisions.

The steps in the analysis may be summarized as follows. First, the court must determine whether the impugned provision can be viewed as intruding on provincial powers, and if so to what extent (if it does not intrude, then the only possible issue is the validity of the act). Second, the court must establish whether the act (or a severable part of it) is valid, in cases under the second branch of s. 91(2) this will normally involve finding the presence of a regulatory scheme and then ascertaining whether that scheme meets the requirements articulated in *Vapour Canada*, supra, and in *Canadian National Transportation*, supra. If the scheme is not valid, that is the end of the inquiry. If the scheme of regulation is declared valid, the court must then determine whether the impugned provision is sufficiently integrated with the scheme that it can be upheld by virtue of that relationship. This requires considering the seriousness of the encroachment on provincial powers, in

Assembling army vehicles in the General Motors Oshawa Plant (1943).

order to decide on the proper standard for such a relationship. If the provision passes this integration test, it is *intra vires* Parliament as an exercise of the general trade and commerce power. If the provision is not sufficiently integrated into the scheme of regulation, it cannot be sustained under the second branch of s. 91(2). I note that in certain cases it may be possible to dispense with some of the afore-mentioned steps if a clear answer to one of them will be dispositive of the issue. For example, if the provision in question has no relation to the regulatory scheme then the question of its validity may be quickly answered on that ground alone. The approach taken in a number of past cases is more easily understood if this possibility is recognized.

KITKATLA BAND v. BRITISH COLUMBIA (MINISTER OF SMALL BUSINESS, TOURISM AND CULTURE)
[2002] 2 S.C.R. 146.

The opinion of the Court was delivered by

LeBEL J. —

I. <u>Introduction</u>

¶ 1 This case concerns a constitutional challenge to the application of provincial legislation on the protection of cultural heritage property. The dispute relates to culturally modified trees or CMTs. These trees have often been altered by aboriginal people as part of their traditional use and have cultural, historical and scientific importance for a number of First Nations in British Columbia. In the opinion of the appellants, legislation authorizing the removal or modification of these cultural objects would fall beyond the scope of provincial legislative powers. Hence, the *Heritage Conservation Act*, R.S.B.C. 1996, c. 187 ("the Act"), should be struck down in part to the extent that it allows for the alteration and destruction of native cultural objects. [...]

II. The Origins of the Case

¶ 2 [...] The respondent, International Forest Products Limited ("Interfor"), had long held a forest licence over land in the central coast of British Columbia which included an area known as the Kumealon. Provincial forestry legislation required Interfor, as the holder of a forest licence, to propose sequential forest development plans. The legislation also granted the public some participatory rights in the creation of these plans. Interfor provided direct notification of its development plans to the appellant Kitkatla Band ("the Band") since early 1994, but these plans never specifically identified the Kumealon area. The appellants claimed aboriginal rights in this area and had been engaged in treaty negotiations with the province. In early 1998, aware of its obligations under the Act, Interfor hired a firm of archaeologists in order to report on the impact of future logging operations in an area that included the Kumealon. Coincidentally, it appears, the appellants expressed an interest in the Kumealon at roughly the same time. Interfor was alerted to this claim, and, shortly thereafter, the firm it hired contacted the Band in order to ascertain their views. The Band designated two persons for this purpose. Interfor was concerned with the possible presence of native heritage sites and objects including CMTs in the area to be harvested. The archaeologist eventually reported the presence of a significant number of these trees in seven cutblocks Interfor intended to harvest.

¶ 3 Meanwhile, Interfor applied to the respondent, the Minister of Small Business, Tourism and Culture ("the Minister"), for a site alteration permit under s. 12 of the Act, to authorize the cutting and processing of CMTs during logging operations. The Minister forwarded Interfor's application to the Band, along with a cover letter requesting its written submissions on the application. No submissions were received by the deadline. One week later, on March 31, 1998, and without having considered a single archaeological report, the Minister issued a site alteration permit.

¶ 4 At this stage, the Band commenced proceedings to challenge the legality of the permit. They began judicial review proceedings. These proceedings raised administrative law arguments asserting that the Minister had failed to address all relevant issues -- and had violated his fiduciary obligations towards the appellants by failing to provide them with proper notification and the opportunity to consult -- before issuing the permit. The Band also challenged the Act as being *ultra vires* the province.

¶ 5 The administrative law challenge succeeded. A judgment of the British Columbia Supreme Court ordered the Minister to reconsider the part of its decision which affected the CMTs, after giving the Band an adequate opportunity to be consulted and to make representations. At the same time, the trial court dismissed the constitutional challenge.

¶ 6 The Minister went through the reconsideration process. During this process, the Band asserted a claim of aboriginal rights in the continued existence of the CMTs. It petitioned for an order in the nature of prohibition, to restrain the Minister from granting the site alteration permit. The Minister took the position that this issue fell outside the scope of the permit granting procedure and should be left to the courts. Wilson J. agreed with the Minister and dismissed the petition.

In the end, the Minister issued a site alteration permit in accordance with the CMTs management plan proposed by Interfor which provided that all fallen CMTs should be preserved together with 76 of 116 trees still standing in the cutblocks. This led to the present appeal. Meanwhile, the Band launched another judicial review application on the basis that the Minister should have considered native rights in the permit granting procedure. This new challenge also failed.[...]

Heritage Conservation Act, R.S.B.C. 1996, c. 187

> ...12(2) The minister may
>
> (a) issue a permit authorizing an action referred to in section 13, or
>
> (b) refuse to issue a permit for an action that, in the opinion of the minister, would be inconsistent with the purpose of the heritage protection of the property.
>
> 13(1) Except as authorized by a permit issued under section 12 or 14, a person must not remove, or attempt to remove, from British Columbia a heritage object that is protected under subsection (2) or which has been removed from a site protected under subsection (2).
>
> (2) Except as authorized by a permit issued under section 12 or 14, or an order issued under section 14, a person must not do any of the following:[...]
>
> (c) damage, alter, cover or move an aboriginal rock painting or aboriginal rock carving that has historical or archaeological value;
>
> (d) damage, excavate, dig in or alter, or remove any heritage object from, a site that contains artifacts, features, materials or other physical evidence of human habitation or use before 1846...

V. Constitutional Questions

¶ 30 On January 22, 2001, the Chief Justice stated the following constitutional questions:

> (1) Is s. 12(2)(a) in respect of the subject matter of s. 13(2)(c) and (d) of the *Heritage Conservation Act* in pith and substance law in relation to Indians or Lands reserved for the Indians, or alternatively, is the law in relation to property, and, therefore, within the exclusive legislative competence of the Province under s. 92(13) of the *Constitution Act, 1867*? [...]

¶ 42 The *Heritage Conservation Act* is designed to grant a broad protection to the cultural heritage of British Columbia in a very comprehensive manner [...]

¶ 45 The Act considers First Nations' culture as part of the heritage of all residents of British Columbia. It must be protected, not only as an essential part of the collective material memory which belongs to the history and identity of First Nations, but also as part of the shared heritage of all British Columbians. [ ] At the same time, heritage conservation schemes such as the Act here must strike a balance between conservation and other societal interests, which may require the destruction of heritage objects or sites after a careful review by the Minister. [...] This is what is at issue here. Is the power to order the alteration or even destruction of a cultural object beyond provincial powers when it affects native cultural objects?

D. *Evidentiary Problems*

¶ 46 Constitutional questions should not be discussed in a factual vacuum. Even in a division of powers case, rights must be asserted and their factual underpinnings demonstrated. [...]

¶ 48 The appellants' claim in this case is concerned with what archaeologists refer to as culturally modified trees (CMTs). From the evidence, large numbers of CMTs are found in British Columbia. Thousands are reported and registered every year in British Columbia in the archaeology branch of the ministry. For ministry purposes, CMTs are trees which bear the marks of past aboriginal intervention occurring as part of traditional aboriginal use. Bark may have been stripped from them. Pieces or chunks of wood may have been removed from the trees to make tools or build canoes. Sap or pitch may have been collected from the trees.... In this appeal, the CMTs that the archaeologists were able to identify were generally categorized as either "bark-stripped trees" or "aboriginally-logged trees". [...]

¶ 49 Even if there is evidence of native intervention, it is next to impossible to tell which aboriginal group modified them [...] In this case, in particular, the trees are found in an area covered by the conflicting claims of the Band and another group, the Lax Kw'alaams, which, like the appellants, also belong to the Tsimshian Tribal Council. This second group has agreed with the forestry management plan proposed by Interfor, and approved by the Minister.

¶ 50 The appellants, in support of their claim, assert that the preservation of the CMTs as living trees is required in order to safeguard evidence of their cultural heritage including the work, activities and endeavours of their forebears... Unfortunately, the evidence supporting these claims is sparse. Aside from an affidavit sworn by the appellant Chief Hill, there is very little evidence as to the extent to which these trees in the Kumealon had been related to or incorporated into the culture of the Band. [...]

E. *The Division of Powers Issue*

¶ 51 The constitution of Canada does not include an express grant of power with respect to "culture" as such. Most constitutional litigation on cultural issues has arisen in the context of language and education rights. However, provinces are also concerned with broader and more diverse cultural problems and interests. In addition, the federal government affects cultural activity in this country through the exercise of its broad powers over communications and through the establishment of federally funded cultural institutions. Consequently, particular cultural issues must be analyzed in their context, in relation to the relevant sources of legislative power. In this case, the issues raised by the parties concern the use and protection of property in the province. The Act imposes limitations on property rights in the province by reason of their cultural importance. At first blush, this would seem to be a provincial matter falling within the scope of s. 92(13) of the *Constitution Act, 1867*. This view will have to be tested through a proper pith and substance analysis, in order to establish the relationship between the impugned provisions and the federal power on Indian affairs.

F. *The Pith and Substance of the Provisions of the Heritage Conservation Act*

¶ 52 The beginning of any division of powers analysis is a characterization of the impugned law to determine the head of power within which it falls. This process is commonly known as "pith and substance analysis".... By thus categorizing the impugned provision, one is able to determine whether the enacting legislature possesses the authority under the constitution to do what it did.

¶ 53 A pith and substance analysis looks at both (1) the purpose of the legislation as well as (2) its effect. First, to determine the purpose of the legislation, the Court may look at both intrinsic evidence, such as purpose clauses, or extrinsic evidence, such as Hansard or the minutes of parliamentary committees.

¶ 54 Second, in looking at the effect of the legislation, the Court may consider both its legal effect and its practical effect. In other words, the Court looks to see, first, what effect flows directly from the provisions of the statute itself; then, second, what "side" effects flow from the application of the statute which are not direct effects of the provisions of the statute itself: see *R. v. Morgentaler*, [1993] 3 S.C.R. 463, at pp. 482-83. Iacobucci J. provided some examples of how this would work in *Global Securities Corp. v. British Columbia (Securities Commission)*, [2000] 1 S.C.R. 494, at para. 23:

> The effects of the legislation may also be relevant to the validity of the legislation in so far as they reveal its pith and substance. For example, in *Saumur v. City of Quebec*, [1953] 2 S.C.R. 299, the Court struck down a municipal by-law that prohibited leafleting because it had been applied so as to suppress the religious views of Jehovah's Witnesses. Similarly, in *Attorney-General for Alberta v. Attorney-General for Canada*, [1939] A.C. 117, the Privy Council struck down a law imposing a tax on banks because the effects of the tax were so severe that the true purpose of the law could only be in relation to banking, not taxation. However, merely incidental effects will not disturb the constitutionality of an otherwise *intra vires* law.

¶ 55 There is some controversy among the parties to this case as to the appropriate approach to the pith and substance analysis where what is challenged is not the Act as a whole but simply one part of it. The appellants tend to emphasize the characterization of the impugned provisions outside the context of the Act as a whole. The respondents and interveners take the opposite view, placing greater emphasis on the pith and substance of the Act as a whole. The parties also disagree as to the order in which the analysis should take place: the appellants favour looking at the impugned provisions first, while the respondents and interveners tend to prefer to look at the Act first.

¶ 56 In my opinion, the proper approach to follow in a case such as this is to look first to the challenged provisions. Such a rule is stated in the dictum of Dickson J. (as he then was) in *Attorney General of Canada v. Canadian National Transportation Ltd.*, [1983] 2 S.C.R. 206, at p. 270 (quoted by Dickson C.J. in *General Motors of Canada Ltd. v. City National Leasing*, [1989] 1 S.C.R. 641, at p. 665):

> It is obvious at the outset that a constitutionally invalid provision will not be saved by being put into an otherwise valid statute, even if the statute comprises a regulatory scheme under the general trade and commerce branch of s. 91(2). The correct approach, where there is some doubt that the impugned provision has the same constitutional characterization as the Act in which it is found, is to start with the challenged section rather than with a demonstration of the validity of the statute as a whole. I do not think, however, this means that the section in question must be read in isolation. If the claim to constitutional validity is based on the contention that the impugned provision is part of a regulatory scheme it would seem necessary to read it in its context. If it can in fact be seen as part of such a scheme, attention will then shift to the constitutionality of the scheme as a whole.

¶ 57 Laskin C.J. took the same view but put it in somewhat different words in referring to the appropriate analysis of a section of the Trade Marks Act in an earlier case, *MacDonald v. Vapor Canada Ltd.*, [1977] 2 S.C.R. 134 at p. 159 (quoted by Dickson C.J. in *General Motors of Canada Ltd., supra*, at p. 665):

> If [the impugned provision] can stand alone, it needs no other support; if not, it may take on a valid constitutional cast by the context and association in which it is fixed as complementary provision [sic] serving to reinforce other admittedly valid provisions.

¶ 58 Dickson C.J. set out in *General Motors of Canada Ltd., supra*, at pp. 666-69, a three-part test for determining the pith and substance of an impugned provision. Iacobucci J. discussed and adopted this test in *Global Securities, supra*, at para. 19:

> While *GM Canada* itself was concerned with federal legislation, Dickson C.J. made it very clear, at p. 670, that the same analysis applied to determining the constitutionality of provincial legislation. With respect to the first step, Dickson C.J. said the following (at pp. 666-67):
>
> > The first step should be to consider whether and to what extent the impugned provision can be charac-

terized as intruding into provincial powers. If it cannot be characterized as intruding at all, i.e., if in its pith and substance the provision is federal law, and if the act to which it is attached is constitutionally valid (or if the provision is severable or if it is attached to a severable and constitutionally valid part of the act) then the investigation need go no further.

If, on the other hand, the legislation is not in pith and substance within the constitutional powers of the enacting legislature, then the court must ask if the impugned provision is nonetheless a part of a valid legislative scheme. If it is, at the third stage the impugned provision should be upheld if it is sufficiently integrated into the valid legislative scheme.

In my view, Dickson C.J.'s test could be re-stated in the following form:

1 Do the impugned provisions intrude into a federal head of power, and to what extent?

2 If the impugned provisions intrude into a federal head of power, are they nevertheless part of a valid provincial legislative scheme?

3 If the impugned provisions are part of a valid provincial legislative scheme, are they sufficiently integrated with the scheme?

In the rest of this section, I will consider these questions and apply the test in the context of this appeal.

G. *Purpose of the Provisions Test*

¶ 59 The first stage of the analysis requires a characterization of the impugned provisions in isolation, looking at both their purpose and effect. [...]

¶ 60 Paragraphs (c) and (d) of s. 13(2) have as their purpose the protection of certain aboriginal heritage objects from damage, alteration, or removal. In other words, the purpose of these paragraphs is heritage conservation, specifically the heritage of the aboriginal peoples of British Columbia. The protection extends to all aboriginal rock paintings or aboriginal rock carvings that have historical or archaeological value, as well as to heritage objects, including artifacts, features, materials or other physical evidence of human habitation or use before 1846, which in effect consists almost entirely of aboriginal cultural artifacts.

¶ 61 Paragraph (a) of s. 12(2), on the other hand, provides the minister responsible for the operation of the Act as a whole with the discretion to grant a permit authorizing one of the actions prohibited under s. 13(2)(c) and (d). In other words, this paragraph provides a tempering of the absolute protection otherwise provided by s. 13(2)(c) and (d).

¶ 62 The purpose of such a provision seems obvious when one considers the nature of heritage conservation legislation generally and its specific application in the context of British Columbia. No heritage conservation scheme can provide absolute protection to all objects or sites that possess some historical, archaeological, or cultural value to a society. To grant such an absolute protection would be to freeze a society at a particular moment in time. It would make impossible the need to remove, for example, buildings or artifacts of heritage value which, nevertheless, create a public health hazard or otherwise endanger lives. In other cases, the value of preserving an object may be greatly outweighed by the benefit that could accrue from allowing it to be removed or destroyed in order to accomplish a goal deemed by society to be of greater value. It cannot be denied that ss. 12(2)(a) and 13(2)(c) could sometimes affect aboriginal interests. As will be seen below, these provisions form part of a carefully balanced scheme. As recommended by the Court in *Delgamuukw, supra,* it is highly sensitive to native cultural interests. At the same time, it appears to strike an appropriate balance between native and non-native interests. Native interests must be carefully taken into account at every stage of a procedure under the Act. The Act clearly considers them as an essential part of the interests to be preserved and of the cultural heritage of British Columbia as well as of all First Nations.

¶ 63 Consequently, any heritage conservation scheme inevitably includes provisions to make exceptions to the general protection the legislation is intended to provide. Such a permissive provision strikes a balance among competing social goals.

H. *Effect of the Provisions*

¶ 64 Having looked at the purpose of these provisions, I turn now to consider their effects. Sections 12(2)(a) and 13(2)(c) and (d) grant the Minister a discretion to allow the alteration or removal of aboriginal heritage objects. We have no evidence before us with respect to the total number of aboriginal heritage objects which may be covered by this legislation. Nor do we have any evidence as to how often the Minister has exercised the discretion to permit the removal or destruction of aboriginal heritage objects of whatever type. We know only that, in the present case, the permit granted to the respondent Interfor allowed it to cut 40 out of about 120 standing CMTs within seven identified cutblocks. Thus, the practical effect, in this case anyway, is to permit the destruction of what are alleged to be Kitkatla heritage objects (although there is no specific proof here that the 40 CMTs in question were indeed the products of Kitkatla ancestors) while protecting 80 CMTs from alteration and removal. In addition, all CMTs allowed to be logged must be catalogued and an archival record of them must be retained. In other words, the effect here is the striking of a balance between the need and desire to preserve aboriginal heritage with the need and desire to promote the exploitation of British Columbia's natural resources.

I. *Effect on Federal Powers*

¶ 65 Given this analysis of the purpose and effect of the legislation in order to characterize the impugned provisions, the Court must then determine whether the pith and substance of ss. 12(2)(*a*) and 13(2)(*c*) and (*d*) fall within a provincial head of power or if, rather, they fall within a federal head of power. If the Court characterizes these provisions as a heritage conservation measure that is designed to strike a balance between the need to preserve the past while also allowing the exploitation of natural resources today, then they would fall squarely within the provincial head of power in s. 92(13) of the *Constitution Act, 1867* with respect to property and civil rights in the province.

¶ 66 On the other hand, one cannot escape the fact that the impugned provisions directly affect the existence of aboriginal heritage objects, raising the issue of whether the provisions are in fact with respect to Indians and lands reserved to Indians, a federal head of power under s. 91(24) of the *Constitution Act, 1867*. In considering this question, the Court must assess a number of factors. First, the Court must remember the basic assumption that provincial laws can apply to aboriginal peoples; First Nations are not enclaves of federal power in a sea of provincial jurisdiction: see *Cardinal v. Attorney General of Alberta*, [1974] S.C.R. 695. The mere mention of the word "aboriginal" in a statutory provision does not render it *ultra vires* the province.

¶ 67 Second, it is clear that legislation which singles out aboriginal people for special treatment is *ultra vires* the province. [...] For example, a law which purported to affect the Indian status of adopted children was held to be *ultra vires* the province. [...] Similarly, laws which purported to define the extent of Indian access to land for the purpose of hunting were *ultra vires* the provinces because they singled out Indians: ... Further, provincial laws must not impair the status or capacity of Indians. [...]

¶ 68 Nevertheless, "singling out" should not be confused with disproportionate effect. Dickson J. (as he then was) said in *Kruger, supra*, at p. 110, that "the fact that a law may have graver consequence to one person than to another does not, on that account alone, make the law other than one of general application".

¶ 69 In the present case, the impugned provisions cannot be said to single out aboriginal peoples, at least from one point of view. The provisions prohibit everyone, not just aboriginal peoples, from the named acts, and require everyone, not just aboriginal peoples, to seek permission of the Minister to commit the prohibited acts. In that respect, the impugned provisions treat everyone the same. The impugned provisions' disproportionate effects can be attributed to the fact that aboriginal peoples have produced by far the largest number of heritage objects in British Columbia. These peoples have been resident in British Columbia for thousands of years; other British Columbians arrived in the last two hundred years. [...]

¶ 75 I thus find that there is no intrusion on a federal head of power. It has not been established that these provisions affect the essential and distinctive core values of Indianness which would engage the federal power over native affairs and First Nations in Canada. They are part of a valid provincial legislative scheme. The legislature has made them a closely integrated part of this scheme. The provisions now protect native interests in situations where, before, land owners and business undertakings might have disregarded them, absent evidence of a constitutional right.[...]

VII. Conclusion and Disposition

¶ 78 Heritage properties and sites may certainly, in some cases, turn out to be a key part of the collective identity of people. In some future case, it might very well happen that some component of the cultural heritage of a First Nation would go to the core of its identity in such a way that it would affect the federal power over native affairs and the applicability of provincial legislation. This appeal does not raise such issues, based on the weak evidentiary record and the relevant principles governing the division of powers in Canada. In the circumstances of this case, the overall effect of the provision is to improve the protection of native cultural heritage and, indeed, to safeguard the presence and the memory of the cultural objects involved in this litigation, without jeopardizing the core values defining the identity of the appellants as Indians. For these reasons, I would dismiss the appeal, without costs.[...]

CANADIAN WESTERN BANK v. ALBERTA
2007 S.C.C. 22.

[In 2000, Alberta amended its *Insurance Act* to make federally chartered banks subject to the provincial licensing scheme governing the promotion of insurance products. The appellant banks brought an application for a declaration that their promotion of certain insurance products authorized by the *Bank Act* was banking within the meaning of s. 91(15) of the *Constitution Act, 1867* and that the *Insurance Act* and its associated regulations were constitutionally inapplicable to the banks' promotion of insurance by the doctrine of interjurisdictional immunity or, alternatively, inoperative by the doctrine of federal paramountcy.]

The judgment of McLachlin C.J. and Binnie, LeBel, Fish, Abella and Charron JJ. was delivered by

BINNIE and LeBEL JJ. — [...]

¶ 25 It is now well established that the resolution of a case involving the constitutionality of legislation in relation to the division of powers must always begin with an analysis of the "pith and substance" of the impugned legislation. [...] The analysis may concern the legislation as a whole or only certain of its provisions. [...]

¶ 27 To determine the pith and substance, two aspects of the law must be examined: the purpose of the enacting body and the legal effect of the law. [...] Equally, the courts may take into account the effects of the legislation. [...]

¶ 28 ... [L]egislation whose pith and substance falls within the jurisdiction of the legislature that enacted it may, at least to a certain extent, affect matters beyond the legislature's jurisdiction without necessarily being unconstitutional. At this stage of the analysis of constitutionality, the "dominant purpose" of the legislation is still decisive. Its secondary objectives and effects have no impact on its constitutionality: "merely incidental effects will not disturb the constitutionality of an otherwise *intra vires* law". [...] By "incidental" is meant effects that may be of significant practical importance but are collateral and secondary to the mandate of the enacting legislature... Such incidental intrusions into matters subject to the other level of government's authority are proper and to be expected. [...]

¶ 29 The "pith and substance" doctrine is founded on the recognition that it is in practice impossible for a legislature to exercise its jurisdiction over a matter effectively without incidentally affecting matters within the jurisdiction of another level of government. For example ... it would be impossible for Parliament to make effective laws in relation to copyright without affecting property and civil rights, or for provincial legislatures to make effective laws in relation to civil law matters without incidentally affecting the status of foreign nationals. [...]

¶ 30 Also, some matters are by their very nature impossible to categorize under a single head of power: they may have both provincial and federal aspects. Thus the fact that a matter may for one purpose and in one aspect fall within federal jurisdiction does not mean that it cannot, for another purpose and in another aspect, fall within provincial competence: *Hodge v. The Queen* (1883), 9 App. Cas. 117 (P.C.), at p. 130; *Bell Canada v. Quebec (Commission de la santé et de la securité du travail)*, [1988] 1 S.C.R. 749 ("*Bell Canada (1988)*"), at p. 765. The double aspect doctrine, as it is known, which applies in the course of a pith and substance analysis, ensures that the policies of the elected legislators of both levels of government are respected. A classic example is that of dangerous driving: Parliament may make laws in relation to the "public order" aspect, and provincial legislatures in relation to its "Property and Civil Rights in the Province" aspect. [...] The double aspect doctrine recognizes that both Parliament and the provincial legislatures can adopt valid legislation on a single subject depending on the perspective from which the legislation is considered, that is, depending on the various "aspects" of the "matter" in question.

¶ 31 When problems resulting from incidental effects arise, it may often be possible to resolve them by a firm application of the pith and substance analysis. The scale of the alleged incidental effects may indeed put a law in a different light so as to place it in another constitutional head of power. The usual interpretation techniques of constitutional interpretation, such as reading down, may then play a useful role in determining on a case-by-case basis what falls exclusively to a given level of government. In this manner, the courts incrementally define the scope of the relevant heads of power. The flexible nature of the pith and substance analysis makes it perfectly suited to the modern views of federalism in our constitutional jurisprudence.

¶ 32 That being said, it must also be acknowledged that, in certain circumstances, the powers of one level of government must be protected against intrusions, even incidental ones, by the other level. For this purpose, the courts have developed two doctrines. The first, the doctrine of interjurisdictional immunity, recognizes that our Constitution is based on an allocation of exclusive powers to both levels of government, not concurrent powers, although these powers are bound to interact in the realities of the life of our Constitution. The second, the doctrine of federal paramountcy, recognizes that where laws of the federal and provincial levels come into conflict, there must be a rule to resolve the impasse. [...]

¶ 76 The above review of constitutional doctrines inevitably raises questions about the logical order in which they should be applied. It would be difficult to avoid beginning with the "pith and substance" analysis, which serves to determine whether the legislation in question is in fact *valid*. The other two doctrines serve merely to determine whether a valid law is *applicable* or *operative* in specific circumstances.

¶ 77 Although our colleague Bastarache J. takes a different view on this point, we do not think it appropriate to *always* begin by considering the doctrine of interjurisdictional immunity. To do so could mire the Court in a rather abstract discussion of "cores" and "vital and essential" parts to little practical effect. As we have already noted, interjurisdictional immunity is of limited application and should in general be reserved for situations already covered by precedent. This means, in practice, that it will be largely reserved for those heads of power that deal with federal things, persons or undertakings, or where in the past its application has been considered absolutely indispensable or necessary to enable Parliament or a provincial legislature to achieve the purpose for which exclusive legislative jurisdiction was conferred, as discerned from the constitutional division of powers as a whole, or what is absolutely indispensable or necessary to enable an undertaking to carry out its mandate in what makes it specifically of federal (or provincial) jurisdiction. If a case can be resolved by the application of a pith and substance analysis, and federal paramountcy where necessary, it would be preferable to take that approach, as this Court did in *Mangat*.

¶ 78 In the result, while in theory a consideration of interjurisdictional immunity is apt for consideration after the pith and substance analysis, in practice the absence of prior case law favouring its application to the subject matter at hand will generally justify a court proceeding directly to the consideration of federal paramountcy. [...]

¶ 80 The Alberta *Insurance Act* is a valid law. As the banks acknowledge, the business of insurance in general falls within the authority of the provinces as a matter of property and civil rights. See, e.g., *Parsons* and *Canadian Pioneer Management*. As noted earlier, a federally incorporated company remains subject to provincial regulation in respect of its insurance business: *Canadian Indemnity*. The banks say however that the promotion of their eight lines of "authorized" insurance products is integral to their lending practices, and thus to banking, which is a federally regulated activity.

¶ 81 Nevertheless, banks, as such, are not exempt from provincial law. [...] Accordingly, the mere fact that the banks now participate in the promotion of insurance does not change the essential nature of the insurance activity, which remains a matter generally falling within provincial jurisdiction.

[Justices Binnie and LeBel then considered the interjurisdictional immunity argument]

¶ 82 In this respect, the banks' argument is also that while insurance is generally a provincial matter, when used as collateral for bank loans, credit-related insurance is "integrated" into banking ... This integration contention fails on the facts...

¶ 85 Banks are institutions of great importance. [...] Courts have recognized that in its regulation of banks, Parliament may well trench on matters that would otherwise lie within provincial jurisdiction such as property and civil rights in the province, including insurance. [...] Such considerations, however, should not lead to confusion between the scope of the federal power and its basic, minimum and unassailable content. [...]

¶ 88 T]he appellants centred their argument on the provincial licensing requirement. However if, as we conclude, the promotion of insurance is not vital or essential to the banking activity, there is no reason why the banks *should* be shielded from the consequences of non-compliance with the provincial *Insurance Act*. If a bank were to misrepresent the amount of a policy premium, or wrongfully disclose confidential information to third parties, or engage in other market practices considered by the Alberta Legislature to be unfair, there is no reason why it should escape the regulatory discipline to which all other promoters of insurance in the province are subject. [...]

¶ 89 [J]ust because Parliament *can* create innovative forms for financing does not mean that s. 91(15) grants Parliament *exclusive* authority to regulate their promotion. [...] The rigid demarcation sought by the banks between federal and provincial regulations would not only risk a legal vacuum, but deny to lawmakers at both levels of government the flexibility to carry out their respective responsibilities. [...]

[Justices Binnie and LeBel then considered the paramountcy argument]

¶ 98 The banks' alternative argument is that if the provincial law is applicable to the promotion of insurance by banks, it is nevertheless rendered inoperative by virtue of the doctrine of paramountcy. They argue that the federal *Bank Act* authorizes the banks to promote insurance, subject to enumerated restrictions, and that these enactments are comprehensive and paramount over those of the province. In our view, neither operational incompatibility nor the frustration of a federal purpose [which activate the paramountcy doctrine] have been made out. [...]

¶ 110 For these reasons, we would dismiss the appeal...

BASTARACHE J. —

¶ 111 I have read the reasons of Justices Binnie and LeBel and concur in the result. I disagree, however, with their approach to the doctrine of interjurisdictional immunity and with their appreciation of the doctrine within the general methodological approach to division of powers questions.

¶ 112 [M]y analysis in *Lafarge* was to set out the proper methodological approach to division of powers questions. As I noted at para. 10, all constitutional legal challenges to legislation should follow the same pattern. First, the pith and substance of the provincial statutory provisions and the federal statutory provisions should be examined to ensure that they are both validly enacted laws and to determine the nature of the overlap, if any, between them. Second, the applicability of the provincial law to the federal undertaking or matter in question must be resolved with reference to the doctrine of interjurisdictional immunity. Third, only if both the provincial law and the federal law have been found to be valid pieces of legislation, and only if the provincial law is found to be applicable to the federal matter in question, then both statutes must be compared to determine whether the overlap between them constitutes a "conflict" sufficient to trigger the application of the doctrine of federal paramountcy.

¶ 113 These steps should take place in the sequence listed, such that if the impugned law is found to be invalid on the pith and substance test, there is no need to move on to consider applicability. Similarly, as demonstrated in my reasons in *Lafarge*, where an impugned law is found inapplicable to a federal matter or undertaking on account of interjurisdictional immunity, there is no need to go on to consider operability. I cannot agree with Justices Binnie and LeBel's suggestion at paras. 76-78 that considerations of operability should generally precede considerations of applicability in the division of powers analytical framework absent "situations already covered by precedent" and that the interjurisdictional immunity analysis should be exceptional to the general methodological approach. In my view, it is impossible to find a federal law paramount over a provincial law, or to conclude that the provincial law is inoperable, if the provincial law is not even applicable to the federal matter at issue. This is a matter of practicality as much as it is one of logic.

¶ 114 Regarding the option of considering paramountcy first, J. E. Magnet, in "Research Note: The Difference Between Paramountcy and Interjurisdictional Immunity" in *Constitutional Law of Canada: Cases, Notes and Materials* (8th ed. 2001), at p. 338, convincingly notes the differences between the doctrines of immunity and paramountcy. He writes that immunity "is different from the paramountcy doctrine in that even where there is no contradiction or meeting of legislation, the provincial legislation offers significant obstruction to the federal thing, person or undertaking, affects its status, or drains off essential federal attributes which make them within federal jurisdiction" (p. 339). I agree that there is clearly a need for different types of constitutional legal inquiries.

¶ 116 The *Insurance Act* is clearly a law "in pith and substance" about the regulation of the insurance industry within the province, and the particular provisions at issue are concerned with the licensing and regulation of insurance providers, promoters and agents. The provincial law applies to all persons providing or promoting insurance services, including banks. It is therefore valid legislation of general application enacted under the provincial legislative authority over "property and civil rights" in the province under s. 92(13). Nevertheless, the effects of the provincial law do create some overlap with federal areas of jurisdiction, given that it is potentially applicable to banks as one class of persons or institutions involved in the business of insurance. Thus, the provincial law has some "incidental effects" on banks and, by implication, on the federal banking power; such overlap is generally permissible and should not disturb the constitutionality of an otherwise *intra vires* statute: see *Kitkala Band v. British Columbia ... at para. 64.* The extent of these incidental effects, however, and whether they affect the "core" of the banking power and whether they frustrate Parliament's purpose in amending the *Bank Act* to permit banks to promote certain types of authorized insurance, will be discussed under the application of the doctrine of interjurisdictional immunity and the doctrine of federal paramountcy.

[Justice Bastarache then considered the interjurisdictional immunity issue.]

¶ 120 In my view, the courts below were correct to conclude that the promotion of authorized insurance does not come within the "core" of banking. [...]

¶ 123 If the promotion of insurance did go to the core of banking, a more in-depth analysis would have to be undertaken, as was done in *Lafarge* (see paras. 48-50), to determine the severity of the impact. Therefore, no immunity arises in the circumstances. [...]

[Justice Bastarache then considered the paramountcy issue.]

¶ 125 In this case, it is clear that there is no express conflict between the provincial and federal schemes concerning the promotion of insurance by banks and that on the face of the relevant statutory provisions involved, dual compliance with both schemes is possible and in fact is to be encouraged. This is in large part due to the fact that the federal scheme is in fact permissive and empowering, rather than a complete regulatory code concerning the banks' ability to promote authorized forms of insurance.

¶ 127 Finally, there is no evidence here that the application of the provincial law to the banks' promotion of authorized insurance products would frustrate Parliament's legislative intent in allowing banks to engage in this activity. [...]The evidence discloses specific instances of Parliamentary committees and reports explicitly recommending that the banks' promotion of authorized insurance products continues to be subject to valid provincial regulatory regimes (see paras. 80-82 of trial reasons). [...]

¶ 129 I would dismiss the appeal. [...]

2. Paramountcy

(a) Double Aspect Theory

LEDERMAN, "THE CONCURRENT OPERATION OF FEDERAL AND PROVINCIAL LAWS IN CANADA"
(1963), 9 MCGILL L.J. 185.

DEFINITION OF CONCURRENT FIELDS

The federal distribution of legislative powers and responsibilities in Canada is one of the facts of life when we concern ourselves with the many important social, political, economic or cultural problems of our country. Over the whole range of actual and potential law-making, our Constitution distributes powers and responsibilities by two lists of categories or classes – one list for the federal parliament (primarily section 91 of the *B.N.A. Act*), the other for each of the provincial legislatures (primarily section 92 of the *B.N.A. Act*). For instance, the federal list includes regulation of trade and commerce, criminal law, and a general power to make laws in all matters not assigned to the provinces. Examples from the provincial list are property and civil rights in the province, local works and undertakings, and all matters of a merely local or private nature in the province.

These federal and provincial categories of power are expressed, and indeed have to be expressed, in quite general terms. This permits considerable flexibility in constitutional interpretation, but also it brings much overlapping and potential conflict between the various definitions of powers and responsibilities. [...]

Accordingly the courts must continually assess the competing federal and provincial lists of powers against one another in the judicial task of interpreting the constitution. In the course of judicial decisions on the *B.N.A. Act*, the judges have basically done one of two things. First, they have attempted to define mutually exclusive spheres for federal and provincial powers, with partial success. But, where mutual exclusion did not seem feasible or proper, the courts have implied the existence of concurrent federal and provincial powers in the overlapping area, with the result that either or both authorities have been permitted to legislate provided their statutes did not in some way conflict one with the other in the common area. It is the problems arising from such concurrency that are the primary concern of this article.

But, before proceeding specifically to the problems that arise after concurrency has been found, it is necessary to examine carefully the interpretative process whereby the courts strive first to establish mutually exclusive spheres of federal and provincial law-making powers. The words "exclusive" or "exclusively" occur in section 91 of the *B.N.A. Act* respecting federal powers and in section 92 respecting provincial powers, hence the priority for the attempt at mutual exclusion. Only if this attempt fails do the judges then proceed to define by necessary implication certain spheres of common powers to regulate the same matter.

Here we encounter important considerations that go under the name of 'the aspect theory'. As Lord Fitzgerald said long ago in *Hodge v. The Queen*, "subjects which in one aspect and for one purpose fall within Sect. 92, may in another aspect and for another purpose fall within Sect. 91." For instance, a law providing for suspension or revocation of the right to drive a car upon a highway because the driver was drunk has the provincial aspects of control of highways as local works and of the right to drive as a civil right in the province, these things reflecting the provincial responsibility for safe and efficient circulation of traffic. The law mentioned has also the federal aspect of criminal law, reflecting the federal responsibility to forbid and punish such dangerous anti-social conduct. Where does the power to suspend and revoke drivers' licences reside, or do both parties have it? Such laws with double aspects in the logical sense are the usual and not the exceptional case.

In other words, simply as a rational or logical matter, the challenged law displays several features of meaning some one of which at least falls within a federal class of laws, and another one of which falls within a provincial class of laws. Rationally the challenged law is classified both ways – how then do we determine whether power to pass such a law is exclusively federal or exclusively provincial or is something both legislative authorities have? The basic solution here comes by decisions on the relative importance of the federal features and the provincial features respectively of the challenged law in contrast to one another. Respecting the detailed aspects raised by the challenged law, one must ask – when does the need for a national standard by federal law outweigh the need for provincial autonomy and possible variety as developed by the laws of the several provinces, or vice versa? The criteria of relative importance here arise from the social, economic, political, and cultural conditions of the country and its various regions and parts, and of course involve the systems of value that obtain in our society. The answers must be guided by and related to the categories and concepts of the *British North America Act*, and so at this point we find that the two interpretative situations mentioned earlier emerge.

MUTUAL MODIFICATION AND EXCLUSIVE POWERS

If the federal features of the challenged law are deemed clearly to be more important than the provincial features of it, then the power to pass that law is exclusively federal. In other words, for this purpose the challenged law is classified by its leading feature, by its more important characteristic, by its pith and substance. And if, on the other hand, the provincial features are deemed clearly more important than the federal ones, then power to pass the law in question is exclusively provincial.

In some instances, the solution to this dilemma of competing classifications may be grammatically obvious if one simply reads sections 91 and 92 together. For example, the provincial power 'Solemnization of Marriage' (92(12)) is obviously to be read as an exception to the federal power 'Marriage and Divorce' (91(26)). As a matter of construction the former is a particular subclass completely comprehended by and carved out of the latter as a more general class or category.

Only the provincial legislatures then can make law for marriage ceremonies, but only the federal parliament can make divorce law. Another example is afforded by 'Patents' and 'Copyrights' (91(22) and (23)) as small subdivisions of the general category of 'Property' (92(13)). In these cases the *B.N.A. Act* seems explicit enough on the priorities between competing classifications, and to the extent that the words of the *Act* are clear on such issues they are conclusive.

Nevertheless, most of the problems of competing classifications that arise are not so easily soluble. Take for instance the competition between 'Trade and Commerce' (91(2)) and 'Property and Civil Rights' (92(13)) considered in the *Parsons* case. Neither of these classes of laws is grammatically or logically an all-inclusive general category of which the other is obviously a subdivision. As a matter of construction it can properly be said that each is to be read subject to the other, that neither should be permitted to push the other out of the picture completely, but the question remains: where is the line to be drawn? There is no answer to this to be found by a simple reading of the statutory words. The answer is not grammatically internal to the *Act*. These are simply two wide or general categories that overlap a large common area – all property or civil rights laws that are also trading or commercial laws fall both ways as a matter of simple logic. From the legal point of view, most trade and commerce is the transfer of property rights by contract, or the provision of services by contract. In the *Parsons* case, the judgment of relative importance called for at this point was a compromise. The general line of distinction between section 91(2) and section 92(13) was drawn as follows: given that the challenged law is both property or contract law and trading or commercial law, if the trade or commerce is internal to a single province, then the property and civil rights aspect is the more important and provincial power is exclusive. But, if the challenged law is property or contract law about interprovincial or international trade or commerce, then its trading or commercial aspect is the more important and the federal power is exclusive. In this way an issue of relative importance originally open so far as the words of the Act are concerned becomes settled as a matter of judicial precedent.

Accordingly, if there is sufficient contrast in relative importance between the competing federal and provincial features of the challenged law, then in spite of extensive overlap the interpretative tribunal can still allot exclusive legislative power one way or the other. Once exclusive power has been determined to exist for either legislature, then the so-called doctrine of abstinence simply expresses the implication of this negatively. If the federal parliament does not choose to use its power of regulation in a particular exclusive federal field, nevertheless a province cannot enter the field with provincial legislation. The activity concerned simply remains unregulated.

But what if the federal and provincial aspects of the challenged law seem to be of equivalent importance? What if there is no real contrast in this respect? This leads to the second main interpretative situation.

THE DOUBLE-ASPECT DOCTRINE AND CONCURRENT POWERS

If [the above] has been attempted, but it develops that the federal and provincial aspects of the challenged law are of equivalent importance – that they are on the same level of significance – then the allocation of *exclusive* power one way or the other is not possible. For example, in the *Voluntary Assignments* case, the Court pointed out that the federal parliament must be able to deal with priority among the execution creditors of an insolvent debtor from the point of view of effective bankruptcy legislation, but that, equally, provincial legislatures had to deal with priorities among such execution creditors from the point of view of the provincial responsibility for civil procedure and civil rights. Hence the provincial legislation was valid, there being no federal bankruptcy statute at the time.

Accordingly the idea of mutual exclusion if practical, but concurrency if necessary, explains much of Canadian constitutional law. [...]

There seems a definite increase in the number and importance of concurrent fields being presently established by the courts. Of course, agriculture and immigration are expressly concurrent fields by section 95 of the B N A Act, while temperance and insolvency have been with us by judicial implication since the nineteenth century. Recent cases have added concurrency concerning conduct on highways, sale of securities, validity of trading stamps in retail stores, and aspects of Sunday observance. This list is by no means exhaustive. So, precisely what concurrency means requires and deserves careful analysis. In 1907 in the Judicial Committee of the Privy Council, Lord Dunedin said that two propositions were established:

> First, that there can be a domain in which provincial and Dominion legislation may overlap, in which case neither legislation will be ultra vires, if the field is clear; and secondly, that if the field is not clear, and in such a domain the two legislations meet, then the Dominion legislation must prevail.

The word 'meet' is used here in the sense of collision, but there may be joint occupation of a concurrent field without collision necessarily occurring. The different conditions of joint legislative tenancy will be discussed in Part II under the headings *conflict, supplement* and *duplication*.

CONFLICT, SUPPLEMENT AND DUPLICATION RESPECTING FEDERAL AND PROVINCIAL LAWS IN CONCURRENT FIELDS

Given that a concurrent sphere or field has been established, what if both the federal parliament and a provincial legislature have entered the field with statutes? What if 'the two legislations meet'?

If the meeting is a collision, *i.e.* if conflict or inconsistency or repugnancy is the result, the federal statute prevails and the provincial one is displaced and inoperative. But it is far from obvious what amounts to sufficient conflict or inconsistency or repugnance to effect this result.

We start with two statutes that are somehow concerned with the same matter, that matter being the respect in which a concurrent field has been found to exist. The two statutes may differ in what they prescribe about the concurrent matter, or they may be the same in what they prescribe about it. This can soon be discovered by construing and comparing their respective terms, remembering that the search is for substantial differences or substantial identities. As in other constitutional matters, one must not be put off by merely verbal differences or identities. Does the provincial statute differ from the federal one or does it duplicate the federal one? That is the first question, because the reasoning appropriate to difference is not the same as that appropriate to duplication.

And even difference has its variations. The provincial statute may differ from the federal one in either one of two ways – it may be inconsistent with the federal one or it may be merely supplemental to the federal one, adding something to what the federal statute does but not contradicting it. So, in considering the relation of a provincial statute to a federal one in a concurrent field, there are three basic states: (A) conflict, (B) supplement, and (C) duplication. For the sake of developing the analysis clearly, it is assumed to start with that we have provincial statutes that are pure examples of each of these states, *i.c.* first a provincial statute that is purely conflicting, second a provincial statute that is purely supplemental and finally a provincial statute that is purely duplicative. The problems presented by a mixed provincial statute – one that combines any two or all three of these types of provisions – can be disposed of if we know what is appropriate for the pure cases.

CONFLICT

The situation envisaged here is actual conflict between the comparable terms of the provincial statute and the federal one. One finds that the same citizens are being told to do inconsistent things. One statute blows hot and the other cold. For example, a provincial statute says that a certain creditor is a secured creditor, but the federal *Bankruptcy Act* says he is an unsecured creditor. There can only be one scheme for priority among creditors in the event of bankruptcy of the debtor, hence the federal statute prevails and the provincial one is inoperative for repugnancy. [...]

Thus the pure case of express conflict is clear on the authorities – the federal statute prevails. At least the doctrine of Dominion paramountcy must go this far, but there has been some suggestion recently that it goes no further – that this is *all* it means. In the recent case of *Smith v. The Queen* (1960), which concerned federal and provincial offences of knowingly issuing a false prospectus to induce the sale of company shares, Mr. Justice Martland of the Supreme Court of Canada said that, unless the federal and provincial provisions in question conflict "in the sense that compliance with one law involves breach of the other," they can operate concurrently. If only such patent and positive conflict of comparable terms can invoke the doctrine of Dominion paramountcy, then that doctrine is indeed confined to the narrowest significance it could possibly be given. On this view, any supplemental or duplicative provincial legislation could operate concurrently with the federal legislation it supplemented or duplicated, and our enquiry into the scope of the doctrine of Dominion paramountcy could end right here. But, as we shall see, this does not seem to be the state of the authorities.

In addition to the patent and positive conflict of terms just considered, there is another type of conflict or inconsistency to be examined. The federal legislation in a concurrent field may carry the express or tacit implication that there shall not be any other legislation on the concurrent subject by a province. If this negative implication is present, any supplemental provincial statute would be in conflict with it, though there is no conflict between comparable terms of the two statutes. It would be normal to find this implication in a federal statute that could properly be construed as a complete code for the concurrent subject. To revert to the matter of priority among various kinds of creditors in a bankruptcy, the federal code of priorities would clearly have this negative implication, even if there were gaps in it here or there where something might be added or even if there were room for further refinements. It should be noted at this point that Mr. Justice Cartwright of the Supreme Court of Canada has carried this idea of conflict by negative implication to its ultimate limit. In *O'Grady v. Sparling* (1960), the

Supreme Court was considering the relation of two different dangerous driving offences. The *Criminal Code of Canada* at this time made it an offence to drive a car with "wanton or reckless disregard for the lives or safety of other persons." The *Highway Traffic Act* of Manitoba made it an offence to drive a car on a highway "without due care and attention or without reasonable consideration for other persons using the highway." The provincial offence is much wider than the federal one, but overlaps and includes it. Mr. Justice Cartwright (dissenting) said:

> In my opinion when Parliament has expressed in an Act its decision that a certain kind or degree of negligence in the operation of a motor vehicle shall be punishable as a crime against the state it follows that it has decided that no less culpable kind or degree of negligence in such operation shall be so punishable. By necessary implication the Act says not only what kinds or degrees of negligence shall be punishable but also what kinds or degrees shall not.

In other words, he is saying that if there is a federal statute of any kind in a concurrent field, this alone necessarily and invariably implies that there shall be no other legal regulation by a province of the concurrent subject. To carry negative implication this far would ban all supplemental or duplicative provincial legislation. To use the metaphor of the 'field', the effect of this view is that any federal statute touching a concurrent field constitutes total excluding occupation of that field by the federal Parliament. This is the opposite extreme from the view of Mr. Justice Martland and thus represents the broadest sweep that could possibly be given the doctrine of Dominion paramountcy. Mr. Justice Cartwright's view is not the law, but, as stated, it does mark out one of the two extreme positions possible and so aids this attempt at analysis.

As suggested earlier, the negative implication discussed here is legitimate and realistic in some circumstances, and when it is present, the rule of Dominion paramountcy operates to cause the exclusion or suspension of any provincial legislation on the subject in hand. But this is by no means automatically the case for every federal statute in a concurrent field.

Finally, if one has a provincial statute that mixes repugnant provisions with supplemental or duplicative ones, it may be that the repugnant provisions can be severed. This depends on the normal tests for severance in a constitutional case – does the provincial statute still constitute a viable and sensible legislative scheme without the obnoxious section or sections? If severance is not proper, then the whole provincial statute becomes inoperative. If severance is possible, then one goes on to the question whether the supplemental or duplicative provisions are respectively valid in their own right. The case of pure supplement is then next.

SUPPLEMENT

The situation envisaged here is that of a provincial statute which simply adds something to regulation of the concurrent matter without contradicting the federal statute in the field in either the positive or the negative sense explained in [the above]. A.H.F. Lefroy gives a good example of this.

Thus, where the *Dominion Companies Act* provided a method for serving summonses, notices, and other documents on a company incorporated under that Act, this was held not to prevent provincial, or rather North-West Territorial, legislation, providing that such companies must file a power of attorney to some person in the Territories upon whom process might be served, before they could be registered and enabled to carry on their business in the Territories, thus providing another and more convenient method for the service of process upon such company.

Accordingly, provincial supplemental legislation in these circumstances is valid and operates concurrently with the relevant federal legislation. A refinement of this position was approved by the Supreme Court of Canada in the case of *Lord's Day Alliance of Canada v. Attorney General of British Columbia*. The federal statute in question was the *Lord's Day Act*, section 6(1) of which is as follows:

6(1) It is not lawful for any person on the Lord's Day [except as provided in any provincial Act or law now or hereafter in force] to engage in any public game or contest for gain, or for any prize or reward, or to be present thereat, or to provide, engage in, or be present at any performance or public meeting elsewhere than in a church, at which any fee is charged, directly or indirectly, either for admission to such performance or meeting, or to any place within which the same is provided, or for any service or privilege thereat.

If it were not for the words *except as provided in any provincial law now or hereafter in force*, the field of regulation of Sunday commercial sports and movies would be completely occupied by the federal prohibition by virtue of the federal criminal law power. The Supreme Court considered that permissive Sunday observance legislation would also be proper for a province as a matter of civil rights in the province or as a matter of merely a local nature in the province, and that the federal parliament had deliberately and effectively made room for such permissive provincial legislation by the statutory words just quoted. Here then we have the federal parliament explicitly drawing back from full occupation of the concurrent field to allow a different provincial provision on the subject to operate without conflict. It is the strongest possible case for the validity of non-repugnant and supplemental provincial legislation because, on the facts, a prohibition was withdrawn to make room for a permission to operate. The extreme view of the scope of negative implication explained earlier under [the above], is inconsistent with the *Lord's Day Alliance* case of 1959. [...]

The position of provincial legislation in a concurrent field then may be summarized as follows. Provincial legislation may operate if there is no federal legislation in the field or if the provincial legislation is merely supplemental to federal legislation that is in the field. [...]

In conclusion, it should be noted that the existence of a concurrent field means that there is room for political agreement between provincial and federal governments about whether the federal parliament or a provincial legislature undertakes the regulation of this or that phase of a concurrent matter. The precise equilibrium point in practice then would become a matter for political and administrative decision. As governmental activities continue to expand in our modern urban and industrial society, we can expect much more concurrent operation of federal and provincial laws in the old areas of joint occupation and in new areas as well. The adjustments involved will continue to call for both judicial and political decisions of a high order.

LAW SOCIETY OF BRITISH COLUMBIA V. MANGAT
[2001] 3 S.C.R. 113.

[The respondent M was an immigration consultant carrying on his work through an immigration consulting company ("Westcoast"). He had not studied law in Canada and was not a member of the B.C. Law Society. M and other Westcoast employees engaged in a number of activities involving immigration proceedings, including appearing as counsel or advocating on behalf of aliens, for or in the expectation of a fee from the persons for whom the acts were performed, before the Immigration and Refugee Board ("IRB"). The Law Society brought an application seeking a permanent injunction against M and Westcoast to prevent them from engaging in the ongoing practice of law, in contravention of the B.C. *Legal Profession Act.* M and Westcoast admitted that they were engaged in the practice of law within the meaning of s. 1 of the *Legal Profession Act*, but contended that their conduct was sanctioned by ss. 30 and 69(1) of the *Immigration Act*, which permit non-lawyers to appear on behalf of clients before the IRB.]

The judgment of the court was delivered by

GONTHIER J.: — [...]

III. Relevant Statutory Provisions

¶ 10 *Legal Profession Act*, S.B.C. 1987, c. 25 (subsequently R.S.B.C. 1996, c. 255, ss. 1, 26, 109; now S.B.C. 1998, c. 9, ss. 1, 15, 85(5)-(8))

1. In this Act

. . . . .

"practice of law" includes

(*a*) appearing as counsel or advocate [...]

[...] no person, other than a member of the society in good standing, shall engage in the practice of law [...]

Immigration Act, R.S.C. 1985, c. I-2

30. Every person with respect to whom an inquiry [by an adjudicator] is to be held shall be informed of the person's right to obtain the services of a barrister or solicitor or other counsel and to be represented by any such counsel at the inquiry and shall be given a reasonable opportunity, if the person so desires, to obtain such counsel at the person's own expense.

. . . . .

69(1) In any proceedings before the Refugee Division, the Minister may be represented at the proceedings by counsel or an agent and the person who is the subject of the proceedings may, at that person's own expense, be represented by a barrister or solicitor or other counsel.

. . . . .

114(1) The Governor in Council may make regulations

. . . . .

(*v*) requiring any person, other than a person who is a member of the bar of any province, to make an application for and obtain a licence from such authority as is prescribed before the person may appear before an adjudicator, the Refugee Division or the Appeal Division as counsel for any fee, reward or other form of remuneration whatever [...]

A. Are Sections 30 and 69(1) of the Immigration Act Intra Vires Parliament? [...]

[Justice Gonthier considered the authorities and concluded:]

¶ 37 Both ss. 30 and 69(1) relate to the delineation of the procedural rights of aliens, as refugee claimants, permanent residents, or visitors. Since the pith and substance of these provisions is the rights that aliens possess in front of certain divisions of the IRB and the procedure before those divisions, they therefore fall under [*Constitution Act, 1867*] s. 91(25), given that section's granting of jurisdiction over aliens and naturalization. [...]

¶ 38 Representation before a tribunal has as its object the determination of legal rights. It falls within the scope of legal representation and the practice of law. Parliament itself has acknowledged that legal aspect by imposing certain quotas of lawyers' membership in the Refugee Division and Appeal Division, as well as providing a right of representation by barristers or solicitors. Sections 30 and 69(1) relate to the legal profession and therefore to professions in general. The parties agree that the provinces have legislative authority to regulate the practice of law in the province under s. 92(13) as part of the provinces' jurisdiction over professional regulation. [...]

¶ 41 Provincial law societies or bars are entrusted with the mandate of governing the legal profession with a view towards protecting the public when professional services are rendered. [...] This is the purpose behind s. 26 of the *Legal Profession Act* (s. 15 in the current incarnation). Insofar as appearing before the IRB in the capacity of counsel involves the practice of law, the subject matter is as much covered by s. 26 of the *Legal Profession Act* as it is by ss. 30 and 69(1) of the *Immigration Act*.

¶ 42 While provinces may regulate professions as part of their jurisdiction over property and civil rights, the legal profession is also part of the administration of justice in the province, which s. 92(14) attributes to the provinces. [...]

¶ 47 The subject matter of the representation of aliens by counsel before the IRB has federal and provincial aspects. Parliament and the provincial legislatures can both legislate pursuant to their respective jurisdiction and respective purpose. The federal and provincial statutes and rules or regulations in this regard will coexist insofar as there is no conflict.

B. Double Aspect Doctrine

¶ 48 The Privy Council first enunciated the doctrine of double aspect in the case of *Hodge v. The Queen* (1883), 9 App. Cas. 117, at p. 130, where it was said that "subjects which in one aspect and for one purpose fall within sect. 92, may in another aspect and for another purpose fall within sect. 91". Dickson J., as he then was, canvassed the same doctrine in *Multiple Access Ltd. v. McCutcheon*, [1982] 2 S.C.R. 161, at pp. 180-82, 138 D.L.R. (3d) 1, where he said:

> Because "[t]he language of [ss. 91 and 92] and of the various heads which they contain obviously cannot be construed as having been intended to embody the exact disjunctions of a perfect logical scheme" (*John Deere Plow Co. v. Wharton, supra*, at p. 338, per Viscount Haldane), a statute may fall under several heads of either s. 91 or s. 92. For example, a provincial statute will often fall under both s. 92(13), property and civil rights and s. 92(16), a purely local matter, given the broad generality of the language. There is, of course, no constitutional difficulty in this. *The constitutional difficulty arises, however, when a statute may be characterized, as often happens, as coming within a federal as well as a provincial head of power.*
>
> . . . . .
>
> I incline to the view that the impugned insider trading provisions have both a securities law and a companies law aspect and would adopt as the test for applying the double aspect doctrine to validate both sets of legislative provisions, that formulated by Professor Lederman:
>
> > "But if the contrast between the relative importance of the two features is not so sharp, what then? Here we come upon the double-aspect theory of inter- pretation, which constitutes the second way in which the courts have dealt with inevitably overlapping categories. When the court considers that the federal and provincial features of the challenged rule are of roughly equivalent importance so that neither should be ignored respecting the division of legislative powers, the decision is made that the challenged rule could be enacted by either the federal Parliament or provincial legislature. In the language of the Privy Council, *'subjects which in one aspect and for one purpose fall within sect. 92, may in another aspect and for another purpose fall within sect. 91'.*" [Emphasis added.] [...]

¶ 50 Both the federal and provincial features of the challenged provisions are of equivalent importance, and so neither should be ignored in the analysis of the division of powers. Parliament must be allowed to determine who may appear before tribunals it has created, and the provinces must be allowed to regulate the practice of law as they have always done. Having determined that there are both federal and provincial constitutional aspects to the subject matter in ss. 30 and 69(1) of the *Immigration Act*, the sections are validly enacted by Parliament under the double aspect doctrine. Accordingly, the three-step test set out by Dickson C.J. in *General Motors, supra*, at pp. 666-72, is not applicable since no issue of intrusion into the provincial power arises.

C. Application of the Paramountcy Doctrine

¶ 51 There was much argument submitted by the parties regarding the respective preferability of the doctrines of paramountcy and interjurisdictional immunity in determining the manner in which the federal provisions would prevail over the provincial legislation. The latter doctrine has received its classical application in *Bell Canada, supra*. The authority for the former is *Multiple Access, supra*.

¶ 52 [...] Paramountcy is the more appropriate doctrine in this case. The existence of a double aspect to the subject matter of ss. 30 and 69(1) favours the application of the paramountcy doctrine rather than the doctrine of interjurisdictional immunity. While the role for provincially regulated lawyers is non-exclusive, it is nonetheless inconsistent with interjurisdictional immunity, which would exclude provincial legislation, even if Parliament did not legislate in the area. The application of the interjurisdictional immunity doctrine in such a context might lead to a bifurcation of the regulation and control of the legal profession in Canada. The application of the paramountcy doctrine safeguards the control by Parliament over the administrative tribunals it creates. At the same time, it preserves the principle of a unified control of the legal profession by the various law societies throughout Canada. By the very statutory scheme for immigration tribunals in the *Immigration Act*, Parliament contemplated a role for provincially regulated lawyers. While I have determined the pith and substance of the provisions in question to be in relation to aliens and naturalization under s. 91(25), immigration in general is subject to a joint federal and provincial jurisdiction. Section 95 establishes this and itself contains a paramountcy provision. Thus, there is no clear boundary between the federal and provincial jurisdiction in this matter generally. Finally, the immigration aspects of the legal affairs of aliens are not easily distinguishable from the non-immigration aspects of their legal affairs.

¶ 53 The respondent Sparling brought to the attention of this Court the decision of the Ontario Court of Appeal in *R. v. Lewis* (1997), 155 D.L.R. (4th) 442, where Rosenberg J.A. applied the interjurisdictional immunity doctrine in holding that provincial legislation could not limit the range of persons qualified to be auditors for the purpose of the *Canada Elections Act*, R.S.C. 1985, c. E-2. While the latter Act permitted a wide range of accounting practitioners, as defined by provincial legislation, to carry out an audit for federal election candidates, such a task was reserved for chartered accountants by the provincial legislation.

¶ 54 The result achieved in that case is certainly agreed with by this Court. However, the same result could have been achieved by the more supple paramountcy doctrine rather than the interjurisdictional immunity doctrine, especially since the federal legislation was itself resorting to provincial definitions of accounting professionals in determining the range of persons qualified to act, thus creating a role for provincial regulatory legislation.

> 1. *Is Section 26 of the Legal Profession Act Constitutionally Inoperative to Persons Acting Under Sections 30 and 69(1) of the Immigration Act and its Associated Rules and Regulations?*

[...]

¶ 67 [T]here is no obligation for Parliament to regulate the "other counsel", even though it may be wise and advisable to do so. The enactment of ss. 30 and 69(1) and of s. 114(1)(*v*) illustrates Parliament's intention to address the subject of who may appear before the IRB. Aside from the situations where Parliament refers to provincial legislation (as it does for barristers and solicitors), the federal government has defined "other counsel" as being "a person", and the provinces cannot intervene in that sphere. Moreover, by the enactment of s. 114, Parliament has demonstrated its intent to regulate such counsel if and when needed. It has not yet done so, but that does not mean that the provinces can enact conflicting legislation in the meantime. However, to the extent that Parliament refers to the provincial statutes and regulations or leaves the matter unaddressed, the provinces can regulate that matter in accordance with their own powers.

(b) Is There an Operational Conflict?

¶ 68 As I mentioned above, the controlling authority with respect to federal paramountcy is *Multiple Access, supra*. At pp. 189-91, Dickson J. (as he then was) explained that a central assessment to be made in the application of this doctrine is to ascertain whether there is a conflict between the federal and provincial legislation. If there is none, then paramountcy is of course not relevant.

¶ 69 There will be a conflict in operation where the application of the provincial law will displace the legislative purpose of Parliament. The test is stated at p. 191: "one enactment says 'yes' and the other says 'no'; 'the same citizens are being told to do inconsistent things'; compliance with one is defiance of the other".

¶ 70 In *Bank of Montreal v. Hall*, [1990] 1 S.C.R. 121, 65 D.L.R. (4th) 361, this Court reiterated the test of the "actual conflict in operation" and the rationale for the application of the doctrine of paramountcy. At p. 152, La Forest J. held that the question before the Court was reducible to asking whether there is an actual conflict in operation "in the sense that the legislative purpose of Parliament stands to be displaced in the event that the appellant bank is required to defer to the provincial legislation in order to realize on its security". The Court put a gloss at pp. 154-55 on the argument that compliance with both laws was possible by obeying the stricter one:

For, as we have seen, dual compliance will be impossible when application of the provincial statute can fairly be said to frustrate Parliament's legislative purpose.

. . . . .

A showing that conflict can be avoided if a provincial Act is followed to the exclusion of a federal Act can hardly be determinative of the question whether the provincial and federal [A]cts are in conflict, and, hence, repugnant. That conclusion, in my view, would simply beg the question. The focus of the inquiry, rather, must be on the broader question whether operation of the provincial Act is compatible with the federal legislative purpose. Absent this compatibility, dual compliance is impossible

¶ 71 In *M & D Farm Ltd. v. Manitoba Agricultural Credit Corp.*, [1999] 2 S.C.R. 961, 176 D.L.R. (4th) 585, Binnie J. at para. 41 applied the reasoning of the Privy Council in *Crown Grain Co. v. Day*, [1908] A.C. 504, as "rationalized" by Hogg, *supra*, at pp. 16-6.1 to 16-7:

"... on a superficial analysis, the dual compliance test is not satisfied: the two laws imposed no duties on the parties to litigation, and both laws could be complied with by the losing litigant in a mechanics lien case not taking an appeal to the Supreme Court. But if the laws are recast as *directives to a court* that has to determine whether or not an appeal to the Supreme Court is available, the contradiction emerges. A court cannot decide that there is a right of appeal (as directed by federal law) and that there is not a right of appeal (as directed by provincial law). For the court, there is an impossibility of dual compliance and therefore an express contradiction." [My emphasis.]

Applying this reasoning to the facts before him, Binnie J. concluded, "In summary, we have here an 'express contradiction' within the extended meaning of the relevant jurisprudence" where a federal farm act gives the farmer a short standstill period but the relevant provincial act allows for immediate foreclosure.

¶ 72 In this case, there is an operational conflict as the provincial legislation prohibits non-lawyers to appear for a fee before a tribunal but the federal legislation authorizes non-lawyers to appear as counsel for a fee. At a superficial level, a person who seeks to comply with both enactments can succeed either by becoming a member in good standing of the Law Society of British Columbia or by not charging a fee. Complying with the stricter statute necessarily involves complying with the other statute. However, following the expanded interpretation given in cases like *M & D Farm* and *Bank of Montreal, supra*, dual compliance is impossible. To require "other counsel" to be a member in good standing of the bar of the province or to refuse the payment of a fee would go contrary to Parliament's purpose in enacting ss. 30 and 69(1) of the *Immigration Act*. In those provisions, Parliament provided that aliens could be represented by non-lawyers acting for a fee, and in this respect it was pursuing the legitimate objective of establishing an informal, accessible (in financial, cultural, and linguistic terms), and expeditious process, peculiar to administrative tribunals. Where there is an enabling federal law, the provincial law cannot be contrary to Parliament's purpose. Finally, it would be impossible for a judge or an official of the IRB [who need not be a lawyer] to comply with both Acts. [...]

¶ 74 As this case dealt with hearings before the Adjudication and Refugee Divisions only, I would hold that the Legal Profession Act's prohibition on non-lawyers from collecting a fee to act as representatives and to provide services in that regard is inoperative to that extent. The provision of services means document preparation and advice on matters relevant to the individual's case. [...]

¶ 76 The Court finds that there is a basis to grant a declaratory order that ss. 30 and 69(1) of the *Immigration Act* and its associated Rules and Regulations are *intra vires* Parliament and that s. 26 (now s. 15) of the *Legal Profession Act* is inoperative to non-lawyers who collect a fee acting under ss. 30 and 69(1) for the purposes of representation before the Adjudication Division or Refugee Division and the provision of services to that end. [...]

¶ 79 I would answer the constitutional question as follows:

> 1. Is s. 26 of the *Legal Profession Act*, S.B.C. 1987, c. 25 constitutionally inoperative or inapplicable to persons acting under ss. 30 and 69 of the *Immigration Act*, R.S.C. 1985, c. I-2 and its associated Rules and Regulations and, if so, are the latter provisions *ultra vires* Parliament?

> Section 26 of the *Legal Profession Act* is constitutionally inoperative to persons acting under ss. 30 and 69(1) of the *Immigration Act* and its associated Rules and Regulations. It is not necessary to determine whether this disposition is constitutionally inapplicable. The provisions are *intra vires* Parliament.

Appeal dismissed.

(b) Duplication

MULTIPLE ACCESS LTD. v. McCUTCHEON
[1982] 2 S.C.R. 161.

DICKSON J. [Laskin C.J.C. and McIntyre, Lamer, Martland and Ritchie JJ. concurring]: Multiple Access Limited (the Company) is a public company incorporated under the laws of Canada having its head office in Metropolitan Toronto and capital stock listed for trading by the public on the Toronto Stock Exchange. The defendant McCutcheon was president and director, Lowrie a director and the other defendants senior managing officers of the Company. By an order of Addy J., on a motion made by two shareholders of the Company pursuant to s. 114(1) of the *Securities Act*, it was ordered that the Ontario Securities Commission commence action, in the name of and on behalf of the Company, to enforce the liability created by the alleged "insider trading" of the defendants.

It is alleged that (i) it was known to the defendants but not the public that the Company made a formal written offer to purchase certain radio and television assets of Canadian Marconi Limited for a purchase price of $18 million dollars, (ii) the offer was accepted, (iii) the defendants made use of such confidential knowledge to their own advantage by purchasing securities in the capital stock of the Company at $1.76, and the stock rose to $7 and later to $10. The cause of action is based on the allegation that the defendants were "insiders" of the Company as that term is defined in the *Securities Act* of Ontario, s. 109(1)(*c*) [now s. 101], and, as such, were liable to the Company for losses suffered as a result of the use of confidential information in connection with transactions relating to the capital securities of the Company in accordance with ss. 113 and 114 of the *Securities Act*.

The defendants, in their statement of defence, maintained that ss. 113 and 114 of the *Securities Act* of Ontario were duplications of ss. 100.4 and 100.5 of the *Canada Corporations Act* and therefore, with respect to the plaintiff, ss. 113 and 114 are suspended and inoperative due to the doctrine of paramountcy, and also *ultra vires* the Legislature of Ontario with respect to the plaintiff, a federally-incorporated company.

[The Justice then considered whether ss. 113 and 114 of the *Securities Act* of Ontario and ss. 100.4 and 100.5 of the *Canada Corporations Act* were within the powers of Ontario and Canada respectively, and concluded that they were constitutionally valid in that sense.]

[...] [T]here remains but to respond to the third and final question. Are ss. 113 and 114 of the *Ontario Act* suspended and rendered inoperative in respect of corporations incorporated under the laws of Canada? [...]

Although the appellant argues, weakly, that there are minor differences in the legislation, Henry J. found an identity of purpose, conduct and remedy. Does mere duplication constitute "the conflict" required by the paramountcy doctrine in order to render a provincial statutory provision inoperative? This is the issue upon which Mr. Justice Henry at trial and Mr. Justice Morden in the Divisional Court parted ways. The same difference of opinion is reflected by the commentators.

Mr. Justice Henry chose a more narrow and if I may say so, more modern, test of conflict with the concomitant result of leaving to the provinces ample legislative room. He adopted the test propounded by Mr. Justice Martland in *Smith v. The Queen*, supra (at p. 246 D.L.R., p. 800 S.C.R.):

> It may happen that some acts might be punishable under both provisions and in this sense that these provisions overlap. However, even in such cases, there is no conflict in the sense that compliance with one law involves breach of the other. It would appear, therefore, that they can operate concurrently.

Parenthetically, and interestingly, the test adopted by Martland J. in *Smith v. The Queen* was the very test propounded by the Attorney-General of Canada in *Smith*. If one refers to the factum of the federal Attorney-General in *Smith*, prepared by W. R. Jackett and S. Samuels, one will find the following passage (at p. 8):

It might happen that the same facts might be punishable under both provisions. In this sense they overlap. However there is no conflict in the sense that compliance with one law involves breach of the other. That being so, it is submitted that they can live together and are not only both valid but are operative concurrently.

The express contradiction test was reaffirmed in *Montcalm Construction v. Minimum Wage Com'n,* supra, by Mr. Justice Beetz (at p. 661 D.L.R., p. 800 S.C.R.):

> Montcalm's third submission cannot succeed unless the impugned provisions are in conflict with the *Fair Wages and Hours of Labour Act: Ross v. Registrar of Motor Vehicles et al.* (1973), 42 D.L.R. (3d) 68, 14 C.C.C. (2d) 322, [1975] 1 S.C.R. 5. Here again, it was incumbent upon Montcalm to establish that it could not comply with provincial law without committing a breach of the federal Act. Montcalm did not even attempt any such demonstration. It argues in its factum that the federal Act provides not only for wages but also for overtime, unfair labour practices, etc., and that, in several instances, such provisions "may" differ from those of provincial law. This is not good enough. Montcalm had to prove that federal and provincial law were in actual conflict for the purposes of this case. It did not so prove.

See also *Robinson v. Countrywide Factors Ltd.* (1977), 72 D.L.R. (3d) 500, [1978] 1 S.C.R. 753, [1977] 2 W.W.R. 111.

On the basis of the "overwhelming weight of recent authority" Mr. Justice Henry found that the two sets of statutory provisions could "live together and operate concurrently". Any "diseconomies" resulting from the proliferation of laws and administration were inherent in the federal system. Double liability would be avoided by "cooperation between administrators and the ordinary supervision of the courts over duplication of proceedings before them".

Mr. Justice Henry and Professor Hogg are of one mind. Professor Hogg writes:

> There is no reason why duplication should be a case of inconsistency once the negative implication or covering the field test is rejected. On the contrary, duplication is "the ultimate in harmony". The argument that it is untidy, wasteful and confusing to have two laws when only one is needed reflects a value which in a federal system often has to be subordinated to that of provincial autonomy. Nor does the latter value disappear when provincial law merely duplicates federal law, because the suspension of a provincial law may create a gap in a provincial scheme of regulation which would have to be filled by federal law " a situation as productive of untidiness, waste and confusion as duplication. (Hogg, *Constitutional Law of Canada,* supra, at p. 110).

He continued (at p. 111):

> In any event, arguments against duplication of federal and provincial laws can have little weight once overlapping is admitted. After all, overlapping legislation is duplicative to the extent of the overlap; and yet it is clear that provincial law is not inoperative to the extent of its overlap with federal law. It must be remembered too that the differences between the federal and provincial laws in *O'Grady*, and *Stephens* were small, and in Smith and *Mann* they were virtually non-existent. If paramountcy does not apply when 999 cases out of 1,000 are covered by both laws, why should the paramountcy apply when all 1,000 are covered by both laws? It is submitted that duplication is not a test of inconsistency. The one case which decides that it is should be treated as overruled by the recent decisions, especially *Smith* and *Mann*.

Morden J. adopts the older and more prevalent view of the commentators that "The authorities establish one of the implications of Dominion paramountcy to be that provincial duplicative legislation is suspended and inoperative. Simple duplication by a province is not permitted": Lederman, "The Concurrent Operation of Federal and Provincial Laws in Canada, supra", at p. 195; see also "Abel, *Laskin's Canadian Constitutional Law*" (1975), at p. 117: "If member and federal measures are substantial duplicates, every situation covered by one is likewise covered by the other and there is no provincial room left, given full operation of the federal law." Morden J. finds [78 D.L.R. (3d) at p. 709] that "Resort to one statute, from a practical point of view, precludes the other from having any application."

The conflict between the reasons of Mr. Justice Henry and the reasons of Mr. Justice Morden lies in large measure upon the opinion of the latter that the paramountcy doctrine became applicable because a plaintiff could resort to one set of provisions only and, having done so, there would be no scope for the other to have operational effect. That is unquestionably an important consideration but it is not, in my view, conclusive. The provincial legislation merely duplicates the federal; it does not contradict it. The fact that a plaintiff may have a choice of remedies does not mean that the provisions of both levels of government cannot "live together" and operate concurrently. In the *Smith* case the provincial and federal provisions were virtually identical in substance, and the law authorities could prosecute the proscribed conduct as a provincial offence or as a federal offence under the *Criminal Code*.

I agree with the submissions of counsel for Saskatchewan that it would be ironic if a province, by adding elements of differentiation in its legislation (which do not conflict with federal provisions governing the same conduct but which, in effect, go further than the federal) could create valid operative provisions whereas in regard to the same legislative field, it could not merely duplicate the federal provisions; the cases where overlapping provincial legislation has not been rendered inoperative cannot be validly distinguished on the basis that in each of them there were elements of difference between the provincial and the federal legislation; there is no true repugnancy in the case of merely duplicative provisions since it does not matter which statute is applied; the legislative purpose of Parliament will be fulfilled regardless of which statute is invoked by a remedy-seeker; application of the provincial law does not displace the legislative purpose of Parliament.

The respondents strenuously support Mr. Justice Morden's reasons on this court. Counsel for the respondent McCutcheon argues: "Where two actions are brought under the federal and provincial legislation against the insider, either concurrently or *seriatum*, the Court will not permit both to proceed to judgment. Both pieces of legislation cannot operate concurrently in that resort to one precludes resort to the other. The legislation under which one action is commenced operates to prevent the application of the other. In such case, the two statutes meet and are in conflict." I am not of that opinion.

With Mr. Justice Henry I would say that duplication is, to borrow Professor Lederman's phrase, "the ultimate in harmony". The resulting "untidiness" or "diseconomy" of duplication is the price we pay for a federal system in which economy "often has to be subordinated to [...] provincial autonomy" (Hogg, at p. 110). Mere duplication without actual conflict or contradiction is not sufficient to invoke the doctrine of paramountcy and render otherwise valid provincial legislation inoperative.

The following passage from Professor Lederman's article "The Concurrent Operation of Federal and Provincial Laws in Canada," supra, at p. 199 (fn. 39), is apposite:

> As Dr. J.A. Corry has pointed out, our country is increasingly moving away from the older classical federalism of "watertight compartments" with provincial legislatures and federal parliament carefully keeping clear of one another. We seem to be moving towards a co-operative federalism. "The co-ordinate governments no longer work in splendid isolation from one another but are increasingly engaged in co-operative ventures in which each relies heavily on the other". See J.A. Corry, "Constitutional Trends and Federalism, in the volume of essays *Evolving Canadian Federalism* (Durham, N.C., U.S.A., 1958), p. 96. The multiplication of concurrent fields is one of the facets of this trend.

In principle, there would seem to be no good reason to speak of paramountcy and preclusion except where there is actual conflict in operation as where one enactment says "yes" and the other says "no"; "the same citizens are being told to do inconsistent things"; compliance with one is defiance of the other. The courts are well able to prevent double recovery in the theoretical and unlikely event of plaintiffs trying to obtain relief under both sets of provisions. The fact that a court must authorize proceedings under the *Ontario Act* provides a safeguard against double recovery if the company has already proceeded under the federal Act. In addition the court at the final stage of finding and quantifying liability could prevent double recovery if in fact compensation and an accounting had already been made by a defendant. No court would permit double recovery.

I find that ss. 113 and 114 of the *Securities Act* of Ontario are not suspended or rendered inoperative in respect of corporations incorporated under the laws of Canada by ss. 100.4 and 100.5 of the *Canada Corporations Act*.

For the reasons stated above, I would answer the questions in this manner:

> Question 1: No
> Question 2: No
> Question 3: No

The appeal should be allowed. The judgments of the Divisional Court and of the Ontario Court of Appeal should be set aside. The declaration made by the Honourable Mr. Justice Henry that the Honourable Mr. Justice Addy had jurisdiction to commence the action herein should be reinstated.

[The judgment of Estey J. (Beetz and Chouinard JJ. concurring) dissenting in part, is omitted.]

R. V. CHIASSON
(1982), 135 D.L.R. (3D) 499 (N.B.C.A.); AFFIRMED [1984] I S.C.R. 266.

La FOREST J.A. [for the Court]: — This case raises the question whether s. 50(1) of the *Fish and Wildlife Act*, 1980 (N.B.), c. F-14.1, is *intra vires* the provincial Legislature, and if so whether it is inoperative owing to the fact that s. 84(2) of the *Criminal Code*, as enacted by 1976-77, c. 53, s. 3, substantially covers the whole field of its operation. Section 50(1) of the provincial Act makes it an offence of careless hunting to handle or cause the discharge of a firearm without due care and attention. It reads as follows:

> 50(1) Every person who, being in possession of a firearm for the purpose of hunting, discharges, causes to be discharged or handles a firearm without due care and attention commits the offence of careless hunting. [...]

Section 84(2) of the *Criminal Code* reads as follows:

> 84(2) Every one who, without lawful excuse, uses, carries, handles, ships or stores any firearm or ammunition in a careless manner or without reasonable precautions for the safety of other persons
>
> (a) is guilty of an indictable offence and is liable to imprisonment
>> (i) in the case of a first offence, for two years,
>> and
>> (ii) in the case of a second or subsequent offence, for five years;
>> or
>>> (b) is guilty of an offence punishable on summary conviction. [...]

The case arose under the following circumstances. On December 3, 1980, an information was laid against the respondent André Chiasson charging that on November 1st he "being in possession of a firearm for the purpose of hunting, did discharge a firearm without due care and attention and did commit the offence of careless hunting contrary to and in violation of s. 50(1) of the *Fish and Wildlife Act*". [...]

DUPLICATION

The major attack against the legislation, however, was that it was completely duplicative of s. 84(2) of the *Code* and inoperative.

Like Mr. Justice Stevenson, I see no significant difference between the acts prohibited by the two sections other than that, of course, the *Code* provision has a general field of application, as contrasted with the provincial Act which is confined to persons possessed with firearms for the purpose of hunting, as well as minor differences in the definition of "firearm". Nor do I see any great difference between the mental element in the two offences. In any event, for the reasons I will be giving, I see no reason to indulge in this kind of casuistry in assessing the constitutional validity of the legislation.

It follows from the doctrine of paramountcy of federal legislation, of course, that where federal and provincial legislation conflict, the federal legislation must prevail. That, we saw, is really the basis on which *R. v. Leonard* was decided. The principle that provincial legislation that conflicts with, or is repugnant to federal legislation must give way to the latter goes at least as far back as the *Local Prohibition* case: *A.-G. Ont. v. A.-G. Can.*, [1896] A.C. 348. But here, of course, there is no conflict. There is simply a provincial prohibition that covers conduct also prohibited under federal law.

The genesis of the notion that provincial legislation that does not conflict with, but is merely duplicative of federal legislation, is by reason of that duplication inoperative can be traced back to a series of vague statements of principle by the Privy Council. The history of this development has been traced in detail by Professor, now Chief Justice, Laskin, in his article "Occupying the Field: Paramountcy in Penal Legislation", 41 *Can. Bar Rev.* 234 (1963). Suffice it to say that it began with the statements of Lord Dunedin in *Grand Trunk R. Co. of Canada v. A.-G. Can.*, [1907] A.C. 65 at p. 68, 7 C.R.C. 472, when he speaks of "a domain in which provincial and Dominion legislation may overlap", and adds that "if the field is not clear, and in such a domain the two legislations meet, then the Dominion legislation must prevail". Similar mixed imagery was later used by Lord Tomlin in his famous but, as Professor Laskin put it, "now somewhat badly battered" four principles of constitutional interpretation in the *Fish Canneries* case: *Re Fisheries Act, 1914*; *A.-G. Can. v. A.-G. B.C.*, [1930] 1 D.L.R. 194, [1930] A.C. 111, [1929] 3 W.W.R. 449.

This led a number of Courts to declare provincial legislation inoperative when, in their view, Parliament had already covered the same ground. An example in this context is the New Brunswick case of *R. v. Beach* (1948), 92 C.C.C. 40, 5 C.R. 294. There White Co. Ct. J. held *ultra vires* s. 83(a) of the *Game Act* which made it an offence to obstruct a game warden in the discharge of his duties, because this duplicated a *Criminal Code* offence: see also *R. v. Smith,* supra. The doctrine in fact found some echo in statements in the Supreme Court of Canada although these do not appear to have been necessary to the decision: see *Home Ins. Co. of New York et al. v. Lindal & Beattie,* [1934] 1 D.L.R. 497, at p. 503, [1934] S.C.R. 33 at p. 40, *per* Lamont J.; *Johnson v. A.-G. Alta.* (1954), 108 C.C.C. 1, [1954] 2 D.L.R. 625, [1954] S.C.R. 127. The doctrine, if valid, has the effect of constraining provincial power over local matters, and expanding the influence of federal enactments. [...]

Beginning in the early 1940s the Supreme Court of Canada began to extricate itself from the statements asserting that provincial measures duplicating federal legislation were by that very fact inoperative. The first steps were taken in relation to highway traffic legislation. In *Provincial Secretary of P.E.I. v. Egan* (1941), 76 C.C.C. 227, [1941] 3 D.L.R. 305, [1941] S.C.R. 396, the Court upheld a provincial statute providing for the suspension of the driver's licence of a person on his conviction for driving while under the influence of liquor or drugs, even though the *Criminal Code* provided that the Judge presiding at the trial could, in addition to other penalties, prohibit a person from driving. This was followed in *O'Grady v. Sparling,* supra, where the Court upheld a provincial offence of careless driving despite the existence in the *Criminal Code* of the offence of criminal negligence in the operation of a motor vehicle, and by *Stephens v. The Queen* (1960), 128 C.C.C. 21, 25 D.L.R. (2d) 296, [1960] S.C.R. 823, where it also held valid and operative a provincial highway traffic offence of failing to remain at the scene of an accident even though the *Criminal Code* made it an offence not to stop at the scene of an accident with intent to escape civil or criminal liability.

In *Mann v. The Queen,* [1966] 2 C.C.C. 273, 56 D.L.R. (2d) 1, [1966] S.C.R. 238, an attempt was made by counsel to distinguish *O'Grady v. Sparling* on the ground that the *Code* now contained a provision prohibiting driving in a manner dangerous to the public. The effect of this change, it was argued, was that Parliament had now gone beyond dealing solely with "advertent negligence" but also dealt with "inadvertent negligence". Parliament had thus covered the field so there was no room for the operation of provincial legislation. The Court, however, rejected the argument.

In *Smith v. The Queen* (1960), 25 D.L.R. (2d) 225, 128 C.C.C. 145, [1960] S.C.R. 776, 33 C.R. 318, the Court followed the same approach in another field of legislation. There it upheld a penal prohibition of furnishing false information in a prospectus, which formed part of a provincial scheme regulating the securities business, in the face of a *Criminal Code* provision punishing the making or publishing of false statements in a prospectus with intent to induce persons to become shareholders of, or advance money to, or enter into any security for the benefit of the company.

In all these cases, the provincial legislation was held *intra vires* as regulating an activity, for provincial legislative purposes, while the federal legislation was held *intra vires* as criminal law. It also appears to have been conceded that federal legislation could validly have been enacted to cover the ground dealt with in the provincial legislation. In short, they exemplify the principle that there are areas where provincial legislation may be valid if enacted to effect a provincial legislative purpose permitted under the *B.N.A. Act, 1867,* even though similar federal legislation to effect a federal legislative purpose could also validly be enacted. But in all these cases, a distinction could be made between the two pieces of legislation in question although in the *Smith* case it was rather hard to find and three Judges dissented. Until that case, at least, all the Judges emphasized the differences between the two enactments. That, however, was the fact situation before them. Besides when one is finding one's way out of a morass, one does not always tread a straight path.

In any event, in the *Smith* case, Martland J., in a separate concurring judgment, took what has been widely considered as a different approach. He found no repugnancy between the two provisions because compliance with one law did not involve breach of the other. They could exist side by side. He thus put it, at p. 168 C.C.C., p. 246 D.L.R., p. 342 C.R.:

> The fact that both provisions prohibit certain acts with penal consequences does not constitute a conflict. It may happen that some acts might be punishable under both provisions and in this sense that these provisions overlap. However, even in such cases, there is no conflict in the sense that compliance with one law involves breach of the other. It would appear, therefore, that they can operate concurrently.

The subsequent *Mann* case can be looked at both as supporting this new approach, or as adopting it as a different formulation of the preceding position. However, the disposition to hold provincial legislation valid despite the existence of federal legislation covering the same area of activity is clearly underlined. Fauteux J., speaking for himself, Abbott and Judson JJ., categorically asserted that federal and provincial powers [at p. 284 C.C.C., p. 11 D.L.R.] "must be rationalized in principle and reconciled in practice whenever possible", and Spence J., after citing Martland J.'s comment in the *Smith* case, added that [at p. 286 C.C.C., pp. 12-3 D.L.R.]:

> [...] a practical test is to consider whether there may be cases in which the accused's conduct would justify a conviction under the provisions of the [provincial Act] but where no conviction would be possible under the provisions of [...] the *Cr. Code*.

The facts of the present case clearly fall within the test propounded by Spence J. but that simply means that the former distinction had now become so threadbare that one is left with the feeling that the Court had irrevocably moved toward a test of operational conflict, as opposed to one of mere overlap. [...]

The same theory of conflict again found expression in Beetz J.'s judgment in *Robinson v. Countrywide Factors Ltd.* (1977), 72 D.L.R. (3d) 500, [1978] 1 S.C.R. 753, [1977] 2 W.W.R. 111. There the Court had to deal with the operation of certain provisions of the Saskatchewan *Fraudulent Preferences Act* in the light of other provisions in the federal *Bankruptcy Act*. In a separate concurring judgment, Beetz J. set forth his views on the operation of provincial laws in a field where there is federal legislation, at pp. 538-9 D.L.R., p. 808 S.C.R., as follows:

[...] [L]aws provincial in their purpose, object and nature as those under attack cannot be rendered *ultra vires* because of virtual federal paramountcy: they can only become inoperative in case of actual repugnancy with valid federal laws.

On this latter point, I believe the test of repugnancy to be applied in this case should not differ from the one which was... admitted in *Provincial Secretary of Prince Edward Island v. Egan; O'Grady v. Sparling* [...] provincial law gives way to federal law in case of operational conflict. [...]

The language in these recent cases seems far removed from that used in earlier cases. Operational conflict with federal laws, it is clearly stated, must now be shown for the operation of otherwise valid provincial legislation to be affected. The subsequent case of *Re Nova Scotia Board of Censors et al. and McNeil* (1978), 44 C.C.C. (2d) 316, 84 D.L.R. (3d) 1, 19 N.R. 570, may, however, arguably be looked upon as bringing an end to this recent development. There certain provincial provisions covered substantially the whole area already dealt with in the *Criminal Code*. They prohibited theatre owners from permitting indecent or improper performances, and performers from taking part in such performances, and authorized the provincial Board of Censors to define what constituted such a performance. The *Criminal Code* provision, which was found substantially identical, made it an offence to knowingly, without lawful justification, publicly exhibit an indecent show. Though Ritchie J., speaking for the majority, does assert that he now recognizes as authority the above-quoted statement of Martland J. in the *Smith* case, he later goes on to say that *Johnson v. A.-G. Can.* (cites omitted), constitutes authority against the validity of provincial legislation that is virtually identical to federal legislation.

The *McNeil* case does not, however, appear to me to be authority for the statement that otherwise valid provincial legislation duplicating federal legislation is *ipso facto* inoperative. As already mentioned there may be situations where the existence of provincial legislation can inhibit enforcement of federal legislation, and the former must then give way. This may, in some cases, occur where the provisions are substantially identical. It should be noted that the sections considered by Ritchie J. were considered by the four minority Judges to constitute criminal law and so invalid quite apart from duplication, and that in the *Johnson* case on which he relied a majority had found the provisions there to be essentially criminal law. In areas such as this where the object of the legislation is almost exclusively addressed to underlining and protecting fundamental social values – the primary purpose of criminal law – the Courts may at times decide in Rand J.'s words in the *Johnson* case (p. 12 C.C.C., p. 636 D.L.R., p. 138 S.C.R.) that the existence of duplicate provincial legislation would tend to weaken or confuse enforcement of legislation of Parliament. It could in such a case confuse the citizen about the purpose of Parliament in insisting on certain behaviour to underline certain social values rather than for simple administrative or other purposes.

This was clearly in Rand J.'s mind in the *Johnson* case when in the course of his discussion he stated (p. 12 C.C.C., p. 635 D.L.R., p. 138 S.C.R.) that "Criminality is primarily personal and sanctions are intended not only to serve as deterrents but to mark a personal delinquency". In the *McNeil* case, Ritchie J. drew particular attention to indecency as being the common factor in both statutes. The task of setting public standards for personal delinquency falls to Parliament under its criminal law power, though the Provinces may for their own purposes regulate the same conduct. In doing so, however, they cannot enact legislation interfering with, or impeding the operation of federal laws covering the same ground by creating confusion about the purpose, and thereby weakening the operation of the federal laws. As already mentioned, however, the Courts should not, in my view, be overly astute in attempting to find such interference or impediment. However, there can be no confusion about the purposes of the legislation in the present case and so no interference with federal law. The two pieces of legislation can operate side by side.

However that may be, the Supreme Court of Canada has since the *McNeil* case reiterated its view that operational conflict must be established to warrant declaring a provincial law inoperative. In *Montcalm Construction Inc. v. Minimum Wage Com'n et al.* (1978), D.L.R. (3d) 641, [1979] 1 S.C.R. 754 *sub nom. Construction Montcalm Inc. v. Minimum Wage Com'n et al.*, 25 N.R. 1, a case dealing with the application of the Quebec *Minimum Wage Act* to a contractor working on a federal project, Beetz J., speaking for the majority, had this to say at p. 661 D.L.R., p. 15 N.R.:

> Montcalm's third submission cannot succeed unless the impugned provisions are in conflict with the *Fair Wages and Hours of Labour Act: Ross v. Registrar of Motor Vehicles et al.* (1973), 42 D.L.R. (3d) 68, 14 C.C.C. (2d) 322, [1975] 1 S.C.R. 5. Here again, it was incumbent upon Montcalm to establish that it could not comply with provincial law without committing a breach of the federal Act. Montcalm did not even attempt any such demonstration. It argues in its factum that the federal Act provides not only for wages but also for overtime, unfair labour practices, etc., and that, in several instances, such provisions "may" differ from those of provincial law. This is not good enough. Montcalm had to prove that federal and provincial law were in actual conflict for the purposes of this case. It did not so prove.

The dissenting judgments in the case turned on other points. [...]

For the foregoing reasons, I have concluded that s. 50 of the *Fish and Wildlife Act, 1980* is *intra vires* and continues in operation notwithstanding the existence of s. 84(2) of the *Criminal Code*. I would allow the appeal. The question asked in the stated case should, in my view, be answered yes.

I would direct that the case together with this opinion be remitted to the trial Judge with instructions to render a decision consistent with this opinion.

I would make no order as to costs on the proceedings by way of stated case.

[In affirming the decision of the Court of Appeal, the Supreme Court of Canada adopted the judgment of La Forest J.A. (as he was then), 8 D.L.R. (4th) 767.]

(c)   Contradiction

[See *Multiple Access Ltd. v. McCutcheon, supra.*]

ROSS V. REG. OF MOTOR VEHICLES
[1975] I S.C.R. 5.

PIGEON J. [Abbott, Martland, Ritchie and Dickson JJ. concurring] — On August 22, 1972, Gordon Russell Ross was convicted under s. 234 of the *Criminal Code* of driving while his ability was impaired. As varied on appeal, his sentence provides:

> The accused shall be prohibited from driving for a period of six months except Monday to Friday, 8:00 a.m. to 5:45 p.m., in the course of employment and going to and from work.

The order thus made on January 3, 1973 further provided that Ross' operator's licence was not to be suspended and that the Registrar of Motor Vehicles be advised of the order. However, s. 21 of the *Highway Traffic Act*, R.S.O. 1970, c. 202, provides that, subject to s. 25, the licence of a person who is convicted of an offence under any of several sections of the *Criminal Code* including s. 222 (now 234) is thereupon suspended for a period of, upon the first offence, three months, but where personal injury, death or damage to property occurred in connection with the offence, six months. A six or twelve-month suspension is provided for a second offence. Section 25 contemplates the issue in some cases of a restricted licence for the last three months of a six-month suspension or the last six months of a twelve-month suspension, upon the recommendation of the provincial judge, leaving mandatory the complete suspension for the first three or six months.

On January 29, 1973, Ross instituted an action in the Supreme Court of Ontario claiming against the Registrar of Motor Vehicles and the Attorney General for Ontario a declaration that s. 21 of the *Highway Traffic Act* is inoperative and that the suspension of his operator's licence is of no effect. [...]

In 1941, a substantially similar question concerning the validity and effect of provincial motor vehicle legislation was raised in the case of *Provincial Secretary of Prince Edward Island v. Egan*. Although a conclusion on the appeal could have been reached on a question of jurisdiction of the court below, this Court went on unanimously to determine that the operation and validity of provincial legislation suspending driving licences upon conviction of certain offences under the *Criminal Code* remained unaffected by the enactment, by the Parliament of Canada, of a provision for the making of orders prohibiting a convicted person from driving a motor vehicle during a period not exceeding three years. [...]

The provisions of the *Criminal Code* presently in force concerning the making of orders prohibiting a person from driving are in s. 238. As amended by 1972, c. 13, s. 18, the first four subsections read as follows:

238.(1) Where an accused is convicted of an offence under section 203, 204 or 219 committed by means of a motor vehicle or of an offence under section 233, 234, 235, 236 or subsection (3) of this section, the court, judge, justice or magistrate, as the case may be, may, in addition to any other punishment that may be imposed for that offence, make an order prohibiting him from driving a motor vehicle in Canada *at all times or at such times and places as may be specified in the order*
(*a*) during any period that the court, judge, or magistrate considers proper, if he is liable to imprisonment for life in respect of that offence, or
(*b*) during any period not exceeding three years, if he is not liable to imprisonment for life in respect of that offence. [...]

(3) Every one who drives a motor vehicle in Canada while he is disqualified or prohibited from driving a motor vehicle by reason of
(*a*) the legal suspension or cancellation, in any province, of his permit or licence or of his right to secure a permit or licence to drive a motor vehicle in that province, or
(*b*) an order made pursuant to subsection (1),
is guilty of
(*c*) an indictable offence and is liable to imprisonment for two years, or
(*d*) an offence punishable on summary conviction.

(3.1) Subsection (3) does not apply to a person who drives a motor vehicle in Canada while he is disqualified or prohibited from driving a motor vehicle by reason of the legal suspension or cancellation, in any province, of his permit or licence or of his right to secure a permit or licence to drive a motor vehicle in that province, where that suspension or cancellation is inconsistent with an order made with respect to him under subsection (1).

The material changes made by the 1972 amendments in the above-quoted provisions consisted in the insertion of the words I have underlined in subs. (1) immediately before paragraph (*a*) and in the addition of subs. (3.1). Prior to these amendments, it had been decided by the Court of Appeal in three provinces that s. 238 authorized only an order for a single continuous period (*R. v. Adamowiez* (Alta.), *R. v. Lloyd,* (N.B.), *R. v. Herbert,* (Ont.)). A contrary judgment had been rendered only by the British Columbia Court of Appeal in *R. v. Kazakoff.*

The question in the present case is as to the effect of the 1972 amendments. The direction that Ross' operator's licence was not to be suspended shows that the judge who made the prohibitory order considered not only that the prohibition may be limited as to time and place, but also that the person to whom the order is directed should enjoy the right to drive at specified time and place, irrespective of provincial legislation concerning the suspension of driving privileges. In terms, the *Criminal Code* merely provides for the making of prohibitory orders limited as to time and place. If such an order is made in respect of a period of time during which a provincial licence suspension is in effect, there is, strictly speaking, no repugnancy. Both legislations can fully operate simultaneously. It is true that this means that as long as the provincial licence suspension is in effect, the person concerned gets no benefit from the indulgence granted under the federal legislation. But, is the situation any different in law from that which was considered in the *Egan* case namely, that due to the provincial legislation, the right to drive was lost by reason of the conviction, although the convicting magistrate had made no prohibitory order whatsoever? [...]

Subs. (3.1) indicates that in enacting the 1972 amendments, Parliament was conscious of the differences that could arise between prohibitory orders and licence suspensions. The subsection goes no further than to provide that in such case, the penalty provided under the *Criminal Code* for driving while under suspension shall not apply. [...]

In my view, it should be said in the present case that Parliament did not by the amendments to s. 238 of the *Criminal Code* purport to deal generally with the right to drive a motor vehicle after a conviction for certain offences. The only change effected was that a larger area of discretion was given to the convicting magistrate. Instead of being authorized only to make an order prohibiting driving for a definite length of time not exceeding the period stated, the magistrate was empowered to issue an order limited as to time and place. No authorization was given to make an order such as made in the present case, directing that the licence of the person convicted be not suspended. It seems clear to me that this order was made by an inferior court completely without jurisdiction and is to be ignored.

On my view of the enactment, I can see no reason for which it could be considered as going beyond parliament's competence. Apparently, the contention that Parliament thereby invaded provincial jurisdiction was advanced solely on the basis that s. 238 might operate to prevent the application of provincial legislation either of itself or by virtue of orders made hereunder.

It may be of some interest to observe that under the Australian constitution, a principle was developed to determine whether a field of legislation is to be considered as occupied by federal legislation so as to exclude or make inoperative State legislation. The rule was stated by Dixon J. in *Ex Parte McLean* (at p. 483), in the following statement that was subsequently approved by the Privy Council (*O'Sullivan v. Noarlunga Ltd.*, at p. 28):

> [...] The inconsistency does not lie in the mere co-existence of two laws which are susceptible of simultaneous obedience. It depends upon the intention of the paramount Legislature to express by its enactment, completely, exhaustively, or exclusively, what shall be the law governing the particular conduct or matter to which its attention is directed. When a Federal statute discloses such an intention, it is inconsistent with it for the law of a State to govern the same conduct or matter.

Of course, if we were to apply that rule, it would have to be said that Parliament did not purport to state exhaustively the law respecting motor driving licences, or the suspension or cancellation for driving offences. Therefore, the question whether this could validly be done by Parliament does not arise.

For those reasons, I would answer the questions of law stated in the order of the Supreme Court of Ontario by stating that s. 21 of the *Highway Traffic Act*, R.S.O. 1970, c. 202 is valid and operative legislation, and that s. 238 of the *Criminal Code*, R.S.C. 1970, c. C-34 as amended is also valid. I would make no order as to costs as none were demanded.

JUDSON J. (dissenting): — Three questions are before this Court for decision. They are: [...]

> (3) Whether section 21 of the *Highway Traffic Act*, R.S.O. 1970, c. 202 is rendered inoperative by subsection (1) of Section 238 of the *Criminal Code*, R.S.C., 1970, c. C-34. [...]

The 1972 amendment to s. 238(1) of the *Criminal Code*, referred to above, introduced a new element into this problem. Before the amendment there had been conflicting decisions. [...]

The 1972 amendment enabled the convicting court to make an order allowing a person to drive intermittently. The section as amended provided for this in these terms:

> [...] the court, judge, justice or magistrate, as the case may be, may, in addition to any other punishment that may be imposed for that offence, make an order prohibiting him from driving a motor vehicle in Canada at all times or at such times and places as may be specified in the order.

This was the type of order made in the present case, the *Ross* case. In my opinion, the section as amended gives the court the power to make such an order. [...] The difficulty arises with respect to the third question, whether s. 21 of the *Highway Traffic Act* is rendered inoperative by s. 238(1) of the *Criminal Code*. The order made by the convicting court permits intermittent driving. In s. 21 of the *Highway Traffic Act* there is an automatic and complete suspension of the licence for a stated period.

In the *Ross* case, the *Criminal Code*, as applied, and the provincial statute, s. 21 of the *Highway Traffic Act*, are in direct conflict and the federal legislation must prevail. This situation did not arise in the *Egan* case, where there was no order for the suspension of the licence made by the convicting magistrate. The power of the province to impose an automatic suspension must give way to an order for punishment validly made under the *Criminal Code* and to that extent the provincial suspension is inoperative.

The *Bell* case from Prince Edward Island is in a different category. No order of any kind was made by the convicting magistrate. There is no conflict, therefore, between the punishment imposed under the *Criminal Code* and the automatic suspension imposed by the provincial legislation. The provincial legislation is not inoperative in such a case. This was the *Egan* case and it is the *Bell* case, and everything said in the *Egan* case applies with equal force to the *Bell* case.

[The judgment of Spence J. is omitted.]

BANK OF MONTREAL v. HALL
[1990] 1 S.C.R. 121.

[Hall obtained a loan for farm machinery from the Bank of Montreal. He gave the Bank a security interest in the machinery under s. 88 of the *Bank Act*, R.S.C. 1985, c. B-1. Hall defaulted on the loan and the bank repossessed the farm machinery. However, the bank did not follow the procedures for repossession set out in the provincial *Limitation of Civil Rights Act*, R.S.S. 1978, c. L-16. Section 27 of the *Limitation of Civil Rights Act* provided that failure to follow the provincial *Act's* procedures terminates a security interest and the debtor is released from any further obligation. Hall claimed that the security the Bank held in his farm machinery was terminated because of the failure to follow the procedures of the provincial *Act*.

The Supreme Court of Canada determined that both the Federal and Provincial Acts were constitutionally valid. A further issue arose as to whether the provincial legislation should be declared inoperative because it conflicted with the federal legislation.]

La FOREST J. [Wilson, L'Heureux-Dubé, Sopinka and Cory JJ. concurring]: — Do ss. 178 and 179 of the *Bank Act* conflict with ss. 19 to 36 of the *Limitation of Civil Rights Act* so as to render inoperative ss. 19 to 36 in respect of security taken pursuant to s. 178 by a chartered bank?

The decision of this Court in *Multiple Access Ltd. v. McCutcheon,* supra, has delimited the circumstances that will justify application of the doctrine of paramountcy, whereby otherwise validly enacted provincial legislation will be held to be inoperative to the extent that it conflicts with federal legislation. In a widely quoted passage, Dickson J., as he then was, espoused the view that the doctrine of paramountcy would only need to be invoked in instances where it is impossible to comply with both legislative enactments. He stated, at p. 191:

> In principle, there would seem to be no good reasons to speak of paramountcy and preclusion except where there is actual conflict in operation as where one enactment says "yes" and the other says "no"; "the same citizens are being told to do inconsistent things"; compliance with one is defiance of the other.

Multiple Access Ltd. v. McCutcheon was a case involving duplicative federal and provincial legislation. This Court rejected the view that such enactments could not operate concurrently simply because resort to the one would preclude resort to the other. On the contrary, Dickson J., borrowing the phrase coined by Professor Lederman in his seminal article "The Concurrent Operation of Federal and Provincial Laws in Canada" (1963) 9 McGill L.J. 185, expressed the view that in a federal system such legislation was expressive of the "ultimate in harmony". In the following excerpt Dickson J. provides a cogent and succinct rationale for this view, at pp. 189-90:

> [...] the cases where overlapping provincial legislation has not been rendered inoperative cannot be validly distinguished on the basis that in each of them there were elements of difference between the provincial and the federal legislation; *there is no true repugnancy in the case of merely duplicative provisions since it does not matter which statute is applied; the legislative purpose of*

Parliament will be fulfilled regardless of which statute is invoked by a remedy-seeker; application of the provincial law does not displace the legislative purpose of Parliament. (emphasis added.)

On the basis of these principles, the question before me is thus reducible to asking whether there is an "actual conflict in operation" between the *Bank Act* and the *Limitation of Civil Rights Act* in the sense that the legislative purpose of Parliament stands to be displaced in the event that the appellant bank is required to defer to the provincial legislation in order to realize on its security. This calls for an examination of the provincial legislation.

As is apparent from s. 20, the purpose of ss. 21 to 35 of the *Limitation of Civil Rights Act* is to prescribe, in a comprehensive manner, the procedure which a secured creditor must follow in Saskatchewan in order to take possession of his security. Failure to follow the prescribed procedure results in the imposition of a sweeping penalty provision; s. 27 provides, in these circumstances, for the determination of the security agreement and the release of the debtor from all liability. I shall assume for the purposes of this appeal that the Court of Appeal correctly interpreted the provision as applying to federally created securities.

The most salient feature of the procedure set out in ss. 21 to 35 of the Act, as I understand it, is that it is designed to ensure that a judge determine the terms and conditions under which a creditor may repossess and seize articles. Section 33 makes this clear. It is a judge who is to decide if, when, and under what circumstances the pledged article is to be returned to the secured party.

The contrast with the comprehensive regime provided for in ss. 178 and 179 of the *Bank Act* could not be more striking. The essence of that regime, it hardly needs repeating, is to assign to the bank, on the taking out of the security, right and title to the goods in question, and to confer, on default of the debtor, an *immediate* right to seize and sell those goods, subject only to the conditions and requirements set out in the *Bank Act*.

On a comparison of the two enactments, can it be said that there is an "actual conflict in operation" between them, giving that phrase the meaning above described, I am led inescapably to the conclusion that there is. The *Bank Act* provides that a lender may, on the default of his borrower, seize his security, whereas *The Limitation of Civil Rights Act* forbids a creditor from immediately repossessing the secured article on pain of determination of the security interest. There could be no clearer instance of a case where compliance with the federal statute necessarily entails defiance of its provincial counterpart. The necessary corollary to this conclusion is that to require the bank to defer to the provincial legislation is to displace the legislative intent of Parliament. As the dissenting judge, Wakeling J., put it in the Court of Appeal, at pp. 34-35:

> The provincial legislation obviously intends that the unqualified right of seizure granted to the bank is to be restricted. It does so by saying a bank may exercise the right of seizure given by s. 178(3) but only by leave of a judge, who will apply criteria formulated by the Province as to when and under what circumstances seizure can take place.

I do not think it is open to a provincial legislature to qualify in this way a right given and defined in a federal statute; see *Attorney-General for Alberta and Winstanley v. Atlas Lumber Co.*, [1941] S.C.R. 87, *per* Duff C.J., at p. 95.

I am not, with respect, dissuaded from this conclusion by the reasoning of the majority in the Court of Appeal to the effect that requiring a bank to defer to the provisions of the *Limitation of Civil Rights Act* would, in any given instance, have, in all likelihood, the sole effect of delaying the bank's ability to take possession of its security. As Sherstobitoff J.A. put it, at p. 40:

> The *Limitations of Civil Rights Act* simply requires that a creditor give notice to a debtor before seizure of property so as to enable the debtor to make application to the court. The application and resulting order may have the effect of delaying the taking of possession by the creditor. It does not affect the amount of the indebtedness or liability for payment of same except in cases of noncompliance with the terms of the Act so as to bring s. 27 into play. Put simply, it requires the Bank to follow certain procedures before realizing upon its security, and nothing more.

The reasoning of the majority on this point cannot be determinative of the question of paramountcy. Such a view, with respect, rests on a misinterpretation of what was said in *Multiple Access Ltd. v. McCutcheon*. For, as we have seen, dual compliance will be impossible when application of the provincial statute can fairly be said to frustrate Parliament's legislative purpose. In this instance, as I have already noted, Parliament's legislative purpose in defining the unique security interest created by ss. 178 and 179 of the *Bank Act* was manifestly that of creating a security interest susceptible of uniform enforcement by the banks nationwide, that is to say a lending regime sui generis in which, to borrow the phrase of Muldoon J. in *Canadian Imperial Bank of Commerce v. R.*, supra, at p. 159, the "bank obtains and may assert its right to the goods and their proceeds against the world, *except as only Parliament itself may reduce or modify those rights*" (emphasis added.). This, of course, is merely another way of saying that Parliament, in its wisdom, wished to guard against creating a lending regime whereby the rights of the banks would be made to depend solely on provincial legislation governing the realization and enforcement of security interests.

I can only conclude that it was Parliament's manifest legislative purpose that the sole realization scheme applicable to the s. 178 security interest be that contained in the *Bank Act* itself. Again, as I pointed out earlier, I am firmly of the view that the security interest and realization procedure must, in essence, be viewed as a single whole in that both components of the legislation are fully integral to Parliament's legislative purpose in creating this form of financing. In other words, a s. 178 security interest would no longer be cognizable as such the moment provincial legislation might operate to superadd conditions governing realization over and above those found within the confines of the *Bank Act*. To allow this would be to set at naught the very purpose behind the creation of the s. 178 security interest.

Accordingly, the determination that there is no repugnancy cannot be made to rest on the sole consideration that, at the end of the day, the bank might very well be able to realize on its security if it defers to the provisions of the provincial legislation. A showing that conflict can be avoided if a provincial Act is followed to the exclusion of a federal Act can hardly be determinative of the question whether the provincial and federal acts are in conflict and, hence, repugnant. That conclusion, in my view, would simply beg the question. The focus of the inquiry, rather, must be on the broader question whether operation of the provincial Act is compatible with the federal legislative purpose. Absent this compatibility, dual compliance is impossible. Such is the case here. The two statutes differ to such a degree in the approach taken to the problem of realization that the provincial cannot substitute for the federal.

I have dealt with this case on the basis of paramountcy to meet the arguments put forward by counsel. But the issue can, I think, be answered more directly. At the end of the day, I agree with counsel for the Attorney General of Canada that this is simply a case where Parliament, under its power to regulate banking, has enacted a complete code that at once defines and provides for the realization of a security interest. There is no room left for the operation of the provincial legislation and that legislation should, accordingly, be construed as inapplicable to the extent that it trenches on valid federal banking legislation.

In response to the third question, then, I would hold that ss. 19 to 36 of the *Limitation of Civil Rights Act*, if interpreted to include a s. 178 security, conflict with ss. 178 and 179 of the *Bank Act* so as to render ss. 19 to 36 inoperative in respect of the security taken pursuant to s. 178 by a chartered bank. To put it another way, ss. 19 to 36 of the *Limitation of Civil Rights Act* are inapplicable to security taken pursuant to ss. 178 and 179 of the *Bank Act*.

ROTHMAN'S BENSON & HEDGES INC. v. SASKATCHEWAN
[2005] 1 S.C.R. 188.

The judgment of the Court was delivered by

¶ 1 **MAJOR J.**: — The question on this appeal is whether Saskatchewan legislation, and in particular s. 6 of *The Tobacco Control Act*, S.S. 2001, c. T-14.1, is sufficiently inconsistent with s. 30 of the federal *Tobacco Act*, S.C. 1997, c. 13, so as to be rendered inoperative pursuant to the doctrine of federal legislative paramountcy. [...]

¶ 2 In 1997, Parliament enacted the *Tobacco Act*. Section 4 of the statute speaks to its purpose as follows:

> **4.** The purpose of this Act is to provide a legislative response to a national public health problem of substantial and pressing concern and, in particular,
>
> (*a*) to protect the health of Canadians in light of conclusive evidence implicating tobacco use in the incidence of numerous debilitating and fatal diseases;

(*b*) to protect young persons and others from inducements to use tobacco products and the consequent dependence on them;

(*c*) to protect the health of young persons by restricting access to tobacco products; and

(*d*) to enhance public awareness of the health hazards of using tobacco products.

¶ 3 Section 19 of the *Tobacco Act* prohibits the promotion of tobacco products and tobacco product-related brand elements, except as authorized elsewhere in the *Tobacco Act* or its regulations. Section 18 of the *Tobacco Act* defines "promotion" as:

> ... a representation about a product or service by any means, whether directly or indirectly, including any communication of information about a product or service and its price and distribution, that is likely to influence and shape attitudes, beliefs and behaviours about the product or service.

¶ 4 The provisions that follow s. 19 both prohibit specific types of tobacco product promotion, and permit other types of promotion that s. 19 would otherwise prohibit. Among those provisions, s. 30(1) provides that, "[s]ubject to the regulations, any person may display, at retail, a tobacco product or an accessory that displays a tobacco product-related brand element." Section 30(2) further provides that retailers may post signs indicating the availability and price of tobacco products.

¶ 5 On March 11, 2002, *The Tobacco Control Act* came into force in Saskatchewan. Section 6 of that Act bans all advertising, display and promotion of tobacco or tobacco-related products in any premises in which persons under 18 years of age are permitted.

¶ 6 The respondent sued the appellant in the Saskatchewan Court of Queen's Bench, seeking two forms of relief: a declaration that s. 6 of *The Tobacco Control Act* is inoperative in light of s. 30 of the *Tobacco Act*, and a declaration that ss. 6 and 7 of *The Tobacco Control Act* are of no force and effect in light of s. 2(b) of the *Canadian Charter of Rights and Freedoms*. The respondent applied pursuant to Rule 188 of *The Queen's Bench Rules* of Saskatchewan for a summary determination by the court as to whether s. 6 of *The Tobacco Control Act* is inoperative in light of s. 30 of the *Tobacco Act* by virtue of the doctrine of federal legislative paramountcy. [...]

¶ 11 The doctrine of federal legislative paramountcy dictates that where there is an inconsistency between validly enacted but overlapping provincial and federal legislation, the provincial legislation is inoperative to the extent of the inconsistency. *Multiple Access Ltd. v. McCutcheon*, [1982] 2 S.C.R. 161, is often cited for the proposition that there is an inconsistency for the purposes of the doctrine if it is impossible to comply simultaneously with both provincial and federal enactments. Dickson J. (as he then was) wrote, at p. 191:

> In principle, there would seem to be no good reasons to speak of paramountcy and preclusion except where there is actual conflict in operation as when one enactment says "yes" and the other says "no"; "the same citizens are being told to do inconsistent things"; compliance with one is defiance of the other.[...]

¶ 12 However, subsequent cases indicate that impossibility of dual compliance is not the sole mark of inconsistency. Provincial legislation that displaces or frustrates Parliament's legislative purpose is also inconsistent for the purposes of the doctrine. In *Bank of Montreal v. Hall*, [1990] 1 S.C.R. 121, at p. 155, La Forest J. wrote:

> A showing that conflict can be avoided if a provincial Act is followed to the exclusion of a federal Act can hardly be determinative of the question whether the provincial and federal acts are in conflict, and, hence, repugnant. That conclusion, in my view, would simply beg the question. The focus of the inquiry, rather, must be on the broader question whether operation of the provincial Act is compatible with the federal legislative purpose.[...]

¶ 13 This concern about frustration of Parliament's legislative purpose may find its roots in *McCutcheon*, in which Dickson J. stated, at p. 190:

> ... [T]here is no true repugnancy in the case of merely duplicative provisions since it does not matter which statute is applied; the legislative purpose of Parliament will be fulfilled regardless of which statute is invoked by a remedy-seeker; application of the provincial law does not displace the legislative purpose of Parliament. [Emphasis added.]

¶ 14 In my view, the overarching principle to be derived from *McCutcheon* and later cases is that a provincial enactment must not frustrate the purpose of a federal enactment, whether by making it impossible to comply with the latter or by some other means. In this way, impossibility of dual compliance is sufficient but not the only test for inconsistency.

¶ 15 It follows that in determining whether s. 6 of *The Tobacco Control Act* is sufficiently inconsistent with s. 30 of the *Tobacco Act* so as to be rendered inoperative through the paramountcy doctrine, two questions arise. First, can a person simultaneously comply with s. 6 of *The Tobacco Control Act* and s. 30 of the *Tobacco Act*? Second, does s. 6 of *The Tobacco Control Act* frustrate Parliament's purpose in enacting s. 30 of the *Tobacco Act*?

¶ 16 Before answering those questions, it is necessary to examine the character of s. 30 of the *Tobacco Act*.

¶ 17 Read in the context of the *Tobacco Act* as a whole, it is clear that the purpose and effect of s. 30 is to define with greater precision the prohibition on the promotion of tobacco products contained in s. 19. Specifically, it serves to exclude from the wide net of s. 19 promotion by way of retail display. In this way, it is like ss. 22(2), 26(1) and 28(1) of the *Tobacco Act*, which also exclude from the s. 19 prohibition certain types of tobacco product promotion that it might otherwise capture. This demarcation of the s. 19 prohibition represents a measured approach to protecting "young persons and others from inducements to use tobacco products", one of the purposes of the *Tobacco Act* set out in s. 4.

¶ 18 However, in demarcating the scope of the s. 19 prohibition through s. 30, Parliament did not grant, and could not have granted, retailers a positive entitlement to display tobacco products. That is so for two reasons.

¶ 19 First, like the *Tobacco Products Control Act*, S.C. 1988, c. 20, before it, the *Tobacco Act* is directed at a public health evil and contains prohibitions accompanied by penal sanctions. Accordingly, and as the Saskatchewan courts correctly concluded in light of this Court's decision in *RJR-MacDonald Inc. v. Canada (Attorney General)*, [1995] 3 S.C.R. 199, it falls within the scope of Parliament's criminal law power contained in s. 91(27) of the *Constitution Act, 1867*. [...] As the criminal law power is essentially prohibitory in character, provisions enacted pursuant to it, such as s. 30 of the *Tobacco Act*, do not ordinarily create freestanding rights that limit the ability of the provinces to legislate in the area more strictly than Parliament. [...]

¶ 20 Second, it is difficult to imagine how granting retailers a freestanding right to display tobacco products would assist Parliament in providing "a legislative response to a national public health problem of substantial and pressing concern" (*Tobacco Act*, s. 4). To put it slightly differently, an interpretation of s. 30 as granting retailers an entitlement to display tobacco products is unsupported by, and perhaps even contrary to, the stated purposes of the *Tobacco Act*.

¶ 21 I do not accept the respondent's argument that Parliament, in enacting s. 30, intended to make the retail display of tobacco products subject only to its own regulations. In my view, to impute to Parliament such an intention to "occup[y] the field" in the absence of very clear statutory language to that effect would be to stray from the path of judicial restraint in questions of paramountcy that this Court has taken since at least *O'Grady* (p. 820).

A. Impossibility of Dual Compliance

¶ 22 It is plain that dual compliance is possible in this case. A retailer can easily comply with both s. 30 of the *Tobacco Act* and s. 6 of *The Tobacco Control Act* in one of two ways: by admitting no one under 18 years of age on to the premises or by not displaying tobacco or tobacco-related products.

¶ 23 Similarly, a judge called upon to apply one of the statutes does not face any difficulty in doing so occasioned by the existence of the other. The judge, like this Court, can proceed on the understanding that *The Tobacco Control Act* simply prohibits what Parliament has opted not to prohibit in its own legislation and regulations.

¶ 24 For an impossibility of dual compliance to exist, s. 30 of the *Tobacco Act* would have to require retailers to do what s. 6 of *The Tobacco Control Act* prohibits — i.e., to display tobacco or tobacco-related products to young persons.

B. Frustration of Legislative Purpose

¶ 25 Section 6 of *The Tobacco Control Act* does not frustrate the legislative purpose underlying s. 30 of the *Tobacco Act*. Both the general purpose of the *Tobacco Act* (to address a national public health problem) and the specific purpose of s. 30 (to circumscribe the *Tobacco Act*'s general prohibition on promotion of tobacco products set out in s. 19) remain fulfilled. Indeed, s. 6 of *The Tobacco Control Act* appears to further at least two of the stated purposes of the *Tobacco Act*, namely, "to protect young persons and others from inducements to use tobacco products" (s. 4(*b*)) and "to protect the health of young persons by restricting access to tobacco products" (s. 4(*c*)).

¶ 26 The conclusion that s. 6 of *The Tobacco Control Act* does not frustrate the purpose of s. 30 of the *Tobacco Act* is consistent with the position of the Attorney General of Canada, who intervened in this appeal to submit that the *Tobacco Act* and *The Tobacco Control Act* were enacted for the same health-related purposes and that there is no inconsistency between the two provisions at issue. While the submissions of the federal government are obviously not determinative of the legal question of inconsistency, there is precedent from this Court for bearing in mind the other level of government's position in resolving federalism issues: see *Kitkatla Band v. British Columbia (Minister of Small Business, Tourism and Culture)*, [2002] 2 S.C.R. 146, 2002 SCC 31, at paras. 72-73.

IV. Conclusion

¶ 27 There is no inconsistency between s. 6 of *The Tobacco Control Act* and s. 30 of the *Tobacco Act* that would render the former inoperative pursuant to the doctrine of federal legislative paramountcy. The appeal is allowed with costs to the appellant throughout.

¶ 28 The constitutional question is answered as follows:

> Is s. 6 of *The Tobacco Control Act*, S.S. 2001, c. T-14.1, constitutionally inoperative under the doctrine of federal legislative paramountcy, having regard to s. 30 of the *Tobacco Act*, S.C. 1997, c. 13?

No.

Appeal allowed with costs.

CANADIAN WESTERN BANK v. ALBERTA
2007 S.C.C. 22

[In 2000, Alberta amended its *Insurance Act* to make federally chartered banks subject to the provincial licensing scheme governing the promotion of insurance products. The appellant banks brought an application for a declaration that their promotion of certain insurance products authorized by the *Bank Act* was banking within the meaning of s. 91(15) of the *Constitution Act, 1867* and that the *Insurance Act* and its associated regulations were constitutionally inapplicable to the banks' promotion of insurance by the doctrine of interjurisdictional immunity or, alternatively, inoperative by the doctrine of federal paramountcy.]

The judgment of McLachlin C.J. and Binnie, LeBel, Fish, Abella and Charron JJ. was delivered by

BINNIE and LeBEL JJ. — [...]

F. *Doctrine of Federal Paramountcy*

¶ 69 According to the doctrine of federal paramountcy, when the operational effects of provincial legislation are incompatible with federal legislation, the federal legislation must prevail and the provincial legislation is rendered inoperative to the extent of the incompatibility. The doctrine applies not only to cases in which the provincial legislature has legislated pursuant to its ancillary power to trench on an area of federal jurisdiction, but also to situations in which the provincial legislature acts within its primary powers, and Parliament pursuant to its ancillary powers. This doctrine is much better suited to contemporary Canadian federalism than is the doctrine of interjurisdictional immunity, as this Court has expressly acknowledged in the "double aspect" cases (*Mangat*, at para. 52).

¶ 70 Of course, the main difficulty consists in determining the degree of incompatibility needed to trigger the application of the doctrine of federal paramountcy. The answer the courts give to this question has become one of capital importance for the development of Canadian federalism. To interpret incompatibility broadly has the effect of expanding the powers of the central government, whereas a narrower interpretation tends to give provincial governments more latitude.

¶ 71 In developing its approach, this Court, despite the problems occasionally caused by certain relevant aspects of its case law, has shown a prudent measure of restraint in proposing strict tests: *General Motors*, at p. 669. In *Multiple Access Ltd. v. McCutcheon*, [1982] 2 S.C.R. 161, the Court defined the fundamental test for determining whether there is sufficient incompatibility to trigger the application of the doctrine of federal paramountcy. Dickson J. stated:

> In principle, there would seem to be no good reasons to speak of paramountcy and preclusion except where there is actual conflict in operation as where one enactment says "yes" and the other says "no"; "the same citizens are being told to do inconsistent things"; compliance with one is defiance of the other. [p. 191]

¶ 72 Thus, according to this test, the mere existence of a duplication of norms at the federal and provincial levels does not in itself constitute a degree of incompatibility capable of triggering the application of the doctrine. Moreover, a provincial law may in principle add requirements that supplement the requirements of federal legislation (*114957 Canada Ltée (Spraytech, Société d'arrosage)*). In both cases, the laws can apply concurrently, and citizens can comply with either of them without violating the other.

¶ 73 Nevertheless, there will be cases in which imposing an obligation to comply with provincial legislation would in effect frustrate the purpose of a federal law even though it did not entail a direct violation of the federal law's provisions. The Court recognized this in *Bank of Montreal v. Hall*, [1990] 1 S.C.R. 121, in noting that Parliament's "intent" must also be taken into account in the analysis of incompatibility. The Court thus acknowledged that the impossibility of complying with two enactments is not the sole sign of incompatibility. The fact that a provincial law is incompatible with the purpose of a federal law will also be sufficient to trigger the application of the doctrine of federal paramountcy. This point was recently reaffirmed in *Mangat* and in *Rothmans, Benson & Hedges Inc. v. Saskatchewan*, [2005] 1 S.C.R. 188, 2005 SCC 13.

¶ 74 That being said, care must be taken not to give too broad a scope to *Hall*, *Mangat* and *Rothmans*. The Court has never given any indication that it intended, in those cases, to reverse its previous decisions and adopt the "occupied field" test it had clearly rejected in *O'Grady* in 1960. The fact that Parliament has legislated in respect of a matter does not lead to the presumption that in so doing it intended to rule out any possible provincial action in respect of that subject. As this Court recently stated, "to impute to Parliament such an intention to 'occup[y] the field' in the absence of very clear statutory language to that effect would be to stray from the path of judicial restraint in questions of paramountcy that this Court has taken since at least *O'Grady*" (*Rothmans*, at para. 21).

¶ 75 An incompatible federal legislative intent must be established by the party relying on it, and the courts must never lose sight of the fundamental rule of constitutional interpretation that, "[w]hen a federal statute can be properly interpreted so as not to interfere with a provincial statute, such an interpretation is to be applied in preference to another applicable construction which would bring about a conflict between the two statutes" (*Attorney General of Canada v. Law Society of British Columbia*, at p. 356). To sum up, the onus is on the party relying on the doctrine of federal paramountcy to demonstrate that the federal and provincial laws are in fact incompatible by establishing either that it is impossible to comply with both laws or that to apply the provincial law would frustrate the purpose of the federal law. [...]

Application to the Facts of this Case

(4) Federal Paramountcy Does Not Apply on the Facts of this Case

¶ 98 The banks' alternative argument is that if the provincial law is applicable to the promotion of insurance by banks, it is nevertheless rendered inoperative by virtue of the doctrine of paramountcy. They argue that the federal *Bank Act* authorizes the banks to promote insurance, subject to enumerated restrictions, and that these enactments are comprehensive and paramount over those of the province. In our view, neither operational incompatibility nor the frustration of a federal purpose have been made out.

(a) *No Operational Incompatibility*

¶ 99 Since 2000, the banks have been promoting insurance in Alberta while complying with both the federal *Bank Act* and the provincial *Insurance Act*. All of the appellants presently hold the provincial restricted certificates of authority and are actively promoting insurance in Alberta. It cannot be said, in the words of Dickson J., that one enactment says "yes" and the other says "no"; or that compliance with one is defiance of the other: *Multiple Access*, at p. 191.

¶ 100 The appellants say there is conflict between s. 416(2) of the *Bank Act*, which *prohibits* banks from acting as "agents", and the provincial *Insurance Act* which *requires* the banks to hold a "restricted insurance agent's certificate" (s. 454(1)). However, it is apparent that the term "agent" is not used in the same sense in the two enactments. The term "agent" in the *Bank Act* is undefined and bears the common law meaning of a person who can legally bind his or her principal. This the banks cannot do. They cannot bind an insurance underwriter. They merely "promote" insurance. By contrast, the term "insurance agent" is a defined term in the provincial *Insurance Act* and includes a person "who, for compensation, [...] solicits insurance on behalf of an insurer, insured or potential insured" (s. 1). Accordingly, the banks may properly act as an insurance agent within the meaning of the provincial *Insurance Act* by promoting (soliciting) insurance and transmitting applications without binding the insurer or potential insured within the prohibition of the *Bank Act*. This is not a case where the provincial law prohibits what the federal law permits.

(b) *No Frustration of Federal Purpose*

¶ 101 A classic example of a provincial law that frustrates a federal purpose is *Mangat*. In that case, the provincial prohibition against non-lawyers appearing before a tribunal for a fee would, if applied, frustrate Parliament's intention to enable non-lawyers to appear before immigration proceedings so as to promote hearings that are informal, accessible and expeditious.

¶ 102 The banks argue that the *Bank Act* and its *IBRs* are similar to the legislation in *Mangat* and should be taken to express Parliament's intent that its regulations are exhaustive. However, this is not borne out by the record.

¶ 103 Here, as in *Rothmans*, the federal legislation is permissive. Section 416(1) provides that "[a] bank shall not undertake the business of insurance <u>except to the extent permitted</u> by this Act or the regulations". ...[T]he federal legislation at issue in this case, while permitting the banks to promote authorized insurance, contains references that assume the relevant provincial law to be applicable. [...]

¶ 104 The relevant legislative history may be used to shed light on Parliament's object and purpose in passing the 1991 amendment. [...]

¶ 108 The intention of the 1991 amendments is clear on their face. The appellants argue that Parliament intended to create a unified national "banking" scheme for the promotion of insurance, but there is nothing in the record to support such a conclusion. Parliamentarians were concerned as early as 1985 to maintain a level playing field among all financial service providers participating in the same business. To hold the banks immune from provincial market conduct regulation would give them a privileged position in the marketplace. Every indication is that Parliament wished to avoid this result.

¶ 110 For these reasons, we would dismiss the appeal...

BASTARACHE J: —

¶ 124 ... the doctrine of paramountcy is triggered when there is "conflict" between a provincial law and a federal law, and this only *after* they have both been found valid and the provincial law found to be applicable. The meaning of "conflict" was disputed between the parties, but it is fairly clear in the jurisprudence. Conflict should be considered equivalent to "inconsistency" between the statutes, and inconsistency is generally present when Parliament's legislative purpose has been frustrated or displaced, either by making it impossible to comply with both statutes or through some other means notwithstanding the theoretical possibility of complying with both statutes... If there is conflict or inconsistency, the provincial law will be inoperable to the extent of the conflict or inconsistency, and the federal law will be paramount.

¶ 125 In this case, it is clear that there is no express conflict between the provincial and federal schemes concerning the promotion of insurance by banks and that on the face of the relevant statutory provisions involved, dual compliance with both schemes is possible and in fact is to be encouraged. This is in large part due to the fact that the federal scheme is in fact permissive and empowering, rather than a complete regulatory code concerning the banks' ability to promote authorized forms of insurance. There is in fact virtually nothing in the *Bank Act* or in the regulations about the conduct of such promotion of insurance and how it is to be regulated and governed. [...]

¶ 126 Nor is there any express or "operational" conflict ...

¶ 127 Finally, there is no evidence here that the application of the provincial law to the banks' promotion of authorized insurance products would frustrate Parliament's legislative intent in allowing banks to engage in this activity. There is nothing to indicate that Parliament enacted the legislative amendments to the *Bank Act* with the intent that the promotion of authorized insurance products should be immune from provincial regulation. [...] The evidence discloses specific instances of Parliamentary committees and reports explicitly recommending that the banks' promotion of authorized insurance products continues to be subject to valid provincial regulatory regimes ...

¶ 128 Overall, the application of the provincial law in this case would not frustrate Parliament's legislative intent in enacting the amendments to the *Bank Act* and the associated regulations, because the aim of those amendments was to permit the banks to engage in the promotion of authorized insurance products and to spell out the types of products which could be validly promoted, not to set out the precise manner in which the promotion of insurance would be governed and regulated. Conversely, the aim of the provincial legislation is to provide a regulatory scheme for the promotion of insurance, but not to exercise any control over the kinds of insurance that banks may promote, or the extent to which they may do so, thereby maintaining the integrity of Parliament's legislative purpose. The interaction between the two statutory schemes is therefore one of harmony and complementarity, rather than frustration or displacement of legislative purpose. [...]

¶ 129 For all of the foregoing reasons, I would dismiss the appeal. [...]

3. Interjurisdictional Immunity

- Research Note -
PARAMOUNTCY AND INTERJURISDICTIONAL IMMUNITY

THE PARAMOUNTCY DOCTRINE

The paramountcy doctrine may be stated in this way. From constitutionally valid power bases in their own respective catalogues of powers, both Parliament and a provincial legislature enact valid legislation. The legislations meet in the sense that they regulate similar activities. The legislations contradict: in a strong sense the two statutes command a citizen to do inconsistent things and the citizen cannot comply with both statutes. One statute says "go right", the other says "go left", and the citizen cannot go in both directions. In a weaker version — *R. v. Chiasson*, supra at p. 343 — the legislations contradict in that the provincial legislation weakens the enforcement of, or violates or confuses the citizen about the purpose of the federal legislation.

The central point of the paramountcy doctrine is that two pieces of legislation meet, regulate the same activities, and conflict. When they do, the federal legislation is paramount, prevails and renders the provincial legislation inoperative.

INTERJURISDICTIONAL IMMUNITY

Interjurisdictional immunity is different. The interjurisdictional immunity doctrine does not premise a meeting of legislation competently enacted by Parliament and a province. Rather, the interjurisdictional immunity doctrine becomes relevant where valid legislation of general application embraces a thing, person or undertaking specifically within the jurisdiction of the other order of government. This could occur where provincial legislation of general application applies to an interprovincial undertaking, an Indian, or a federally established park. The provincial legislation regulates the federal thing, person or undertaking along with everything else to which it applies in the province. As a more specific example, a provincial wildlife statute regulates hunting throughout the province. It applies to Indians as well as to everyone else. The statute is obviously valid, but questions are raised concerning its application to Indians because s. 91(24) confers exclusive legislative jurisdiction over Indians on Parliament.

The questions become acute when laws of general application significantly impact the thing, person or undertaking within the jurisdiction of the other order of government. This may happen without provincial legislation meeting any federal legislation regulating the thing or person, and without the provincial legislation contradicting federal legislation. For example, members of a First Nation follow a traditional lifestyle; hunting and trapping form a significant part of their economy and lifestyle. No federal legislation deals with Indian hunting. But the provincial *Wildlife Act* requires a licence, and limits the kill. The impact is significant.

In this situation the paramountcy doctrine is not relevant since there is no conflict between federal and provincial legislation. Nevertheless, this situation invites application of the interjurisdictional immunity doctrine. Interjurisdictional immunity prevents the provincial law of general application from applying to the federal thing, person or undertaking. It renders the provincial *Wildlife Act* inapplicable.

The interjurisdictional immunity doctrine differs from the paramountcy doctrine in that even where there is no meeting of legislation or contradiction between federal and provincial statutes, and where the provincial legislation impacts significantly on federal things, persons or undertakings, the doctrine is activated. It renders inapplicable legislation of general application which affect affects the rights and obligations, impacts the status, or regulates the essential parts of things, persons or undertakings exclusively within the core of the jurisdiction of the other order of government.

AVOIDING CONFUSION

It is easy to confuse the interjurisdictional immunity doctrine with paramountcy. Federal jurisdiction is sometimes implemented by statutes that intend there should be no interference by supplementary or conflicting provincial standards. In such cases the federal statute intends to express "completely, exhaustively or exclusively what shall be the law governing the particular conduct or matter to which [the federal legislature's] attention is directed;" *Ross v. Reg. of Motor Vehicles*. Provincial statutes that seek to provide supplementary rules would contradict the purpose of the federal legislation.

Any provincial statute which attempted to enter a field exhaustively regulated by such a federal statute would be superceded by the paramountcy doctrine. One might be tempted to say that the provincial statute is rendered *inapplicable*. That, however, is inaccurate because this is a paramountcy situation. As a paramountcy situation, the provincial law is rendered *inoperative*, not *inapplicable* as would be the case in an interjurisdictional immunity situation. The rule for paramountcy is that paramount federal statutes render conflicting provincial statutes inoperative. The interjurisdictional immunity doctrine is not engaged.

HOW MUCH IMPACT IS REQUIRED?

There is some question as to how much impact provincial statutes must have on federal undertakings, things, or persons before the provincial law is rendered inapplicable. The original approach was that the provincial law had to "sterilize" the federal undertaking. The legislation had to inflict the regulatory equivalent to a death blow to the federal undertaking to be rendered inapplicable. This was modified in later cases: the legislation needed only to "impair" the federal undertaking.

Various descriptions of this were developed in the cases: the legislation would be rendered inapplicable if it "affected a vital part of the federal undertaking." These various verbal concoctions can be seen in the materials that follow. There is a significant split on this issue in the Supreme Court opinions in the *Canadian Western Bank* and *Lafarge* cases that follow. The split appears to be motivated by controversy as to views about federalism, how extensive the interjurisdictional immunity doctrine should be, and how far the doctrine should be permitted to grow.

TWO VIEWS

On one view interjurisdictional immunity applies in two circumstances. It applies when the adverse impact of a law adopted by one level of government *impairs* the "core" of the legislative power of the other lever of government – the basic, minimum and unassailable content of the power in question. It also applies when the adverse impact of a law adopted by one level of government *impairs* the vital or essential part of an undertaking duly constituted by the other level of government.

In this view *impairs* is contrasted with *affects*; impairment is a more stringent condition. The requirement of impairment is satisfied even if the impairment does not go so far as to *sterilize* or *paralyse* the other government's core competence or undertaking.

This is the view of Justices Binnie and Lebel in *Canadian Western Bank*, which follows.

On a second view interjurisdictional immunity applies to render inapplicable an impugned provincial law which *affects* a vital aspect of the core of a federal power or undertaking. On this view *affects* means that the provincial law "intrudes heavily" upon core areas of federal jurisdiction or federal subject matters.

This is the view of Justice Bastarache in *Lafarge, infra.*, para 108. Justice Bastarache left open the question of whether indirect effects could engage the interjurisdictional immunity doctrine. This question was discussed in *Irwin Toy*.

INCIDENTAL OR IMPLEMENTING REGULATION

Whatever view eventually prevails, it is free from doubt that in order to render statutes inapplicable, the impacts that engage the interjurisdictional immunity doctrine must be *significant*. The requirement is that legislation *significantly* embrace things, undertakings or persons exclusively in the jurisdiction of the other order of government. On any view, the interjurisdictional immunity doctrine will not render inapplicable insignificant impacts caused by legislation of general application.

Nor will the interjurisdictional immunity doctrine render inapplicable provincial laws that assist to implement rights belonging to persons specifically within federal jurisdiction. This may become quite important concerning the interface that persons possessing aboriginal rights may have with the network of provincial statutes and regulations that apply to hunting, land and related matters. This issue was discussed in *R. v. Morris*, infra.

CANADIAN WESTERN BANK v. ALBERTA
2007 S.C.C. 22

[Parliament amended the *Bank Act* in 1991 to permit banks to promote insurance products, an activity historically closed to them. In 2000, Alberta amended its *Insurance Act* to make banks subject to provincial legislation governing the promotion of insurance products.

The banks brought an application for a declaration that their promotion of certain insurance products authorized by the *Bank Act* was banking within the meaning of s. 91(15) of the *Constitution Act, 1867* and that the *Insurance Act* and regulations were constitutionally inapplicable to the banks' promotion of insurance by the doctrine of interjurisdictional immunity or, alternatively, inoperative by the doctrine of federal paramountcy.]

The judgment of McLachlin C.J., Binnie, LeBel, Fish, Abella and Charron JJ. was delivered by

BINNIE and LeBEL JJ. — [...]

¶ 32 [I]n certain circumstances, the powers of one level of government must be protected against intrusions, even incidental ones, by the other level. For this purpose, the courts have developed ... the doctrine of interjurisdictional immunity [and] the doctrine of federal paramountcy. [...]

¶ 33 Interjurisdictional immunity is a doctrine of limited application, but its existence is supported both textually and by the principles of federalism. The leading modern formulation of the doctrine of interjurisdictional immunity is found in the judgment of this Court in *Bell Canada (1988)* where Beetz J. wrote that "classes of subject" in ss. 91 and 92 must be assured a "basic, minimum and unassailable content" (p. 839) immune from the application of legislation enacted by the other level of government. Immunity from such intrusion, Beetz J. observed in the context of a federal undertaking, is an integral and vital part of [Parliament's] primary legislative authority over federal undertakings. If this power is exclusive, it is because the Constitution, which could have been different but is not, expressly specifies this to be the case; and it is because this power is exclusive that it pre-empts that of the legislatures both as to their legislation of general and specific application, in so far as such laws affect a vital part of a federal undertaking. [p. 840]

¶ 34 The doctrine is rooted in references to "exclusivity" throughout ss. 91 and 92 of the *Constitution Act, 1867*. The opening paragraph of s. 91 refers to the "exclusive [l]egislative [a]uthority of the Parliament of Canada" in relation to matters coming within the listed "classes of subjects" including "Banking, Incorporation of Banks, and the Issue of Paper Money" (s. 91(15)). If that authority is truly exclusive, the reasoning goes, it cannot be invaded by provincial legislation even if the federal power remains unexercised...

¶ 35 In theory, the doctrine is reciprocal: it applies both to protect provincial heads of power and provincially regulated undertakings from federal encroachment, and to protect federal heads of power and federally regulated undertakings from provincial encroachment. However, it would appear that the jurisprudential application of the doctrine ... has been invoked in favour of federal immunity at the expense of provincial legislation...

¶ 36 A view of federalism that puts greater emphasis on the legitimate interplay between federal and provincial powers was championed by the late Chief Justice Dickson, who described the doctrine of interjurisdictional immunity as "not [...] particularly compelling" (*OPSEU v. Ontario (Attorney General)*, [1987] 2 S.C.R. 2, at p. 17):

> The history of Canadian constitutional law has been to allow for a fair amount of interplay and indeed overlap between federal and provincial powers. It is true that doctrines like interjurisdictional and Crown immunity and concepts like "watertight compartments" qualify the extent of that interplay. But it must be recognized that these doctrines and concepts have not been the dominant tide of constitutional doctrines; rather they have been an undertow against the strong pull of pith and substance, the aspect doctrine and, in recent years, a very restrained approach to concurrency and paramountcy issues. [p. 18]...

¶ 37 The "dominant tide" finds its principled underpinning in the concern that a court should favour, where possible, the ordinary operation of statutes enacted by *both* levels of government. In the absence of conflicting enactments of the other level of government, the Court should avoid blocking the application of measures which are taken to be enacted in furtherance of the public interest. Professor Paul Weiler wrote over 30 years ago that

> the court should refuse to try to protect alleged, but as yet unoccupied, enclaves of governmental power against the intrusions of another representative legislature which has ventured into the area. Instead, the court should try to restrict

itself to the lesser but still important role of interpreting statutes of different jurisdictions in the same area, in order to avoid conflict, and applying a doctrine of paramountcy in the few situations which are left. [...]

¶ 38 In our view, the sweeping immunity argued for by the banks in this appeal is not acceptable in the Canadian federal structure. The argument exposes the dangers of allowing the doctrine of interjurisdictional immunity to exceed its proper (and very restricted) limit and to frustrate the application of the pith and substance analysis and of the double aspect doctrine. The latter have the ability to resolve most problems relating to the validity of the exercise of legislative powers under the heads of power applicable to the activities in question. [...]

¶ 41 [Historically] the doctrine of interjurisdictional immunity was used to protect that which makes certain works or undertakings things (e.g., Aboriginal lands) or persons (e.g., Aboriginal peoples and corporations created by the federal Crown) specifically of federal jurisdiction. As Gonthier J. observed in *Commission de transport de la Communauté urbaine de Québec v. Canada (National Battlefields Commission)*, [1990] 2 S.C.R. 838:

> The immunity pertaining to federal status applies to <u>things or persons falling within federal jurisdiction</u>, some specifically federal aspects of which would be affected by provincial legislation. This is so because these specifically federal aspects are an integral part of federal jurisdiction <u>over such things or persons</u> and this jurisdiction is meant to be exclusive. [Emphasis added; p. 853.]

Of course, what is of specific federal interest may well be the federally regulated activity itself rather than the identity of the participants. In *Natural Parents*, at p. 760, Laskin C.J. observed:

> It cannot be said therefore that because a provincial statute is general in its operation, in the sense that its terms are not expressly restricted to <u>matters</u> within provincial competence, it may embrace matters within exclusive federal competence. [...] This is because to construe the provincial legislation to embrace such activities would have it encroaching on an exclusive federal legislative area. [...]

In *Ordon Estate v. Grail*, [1998] 3 S.C.R. 437, in the course of considering federal jurisdiction over maritime law, the Court acknowledged that the doctrine could potentially apply to all "activities" within Parliament's jurisdiction...

¶ 42 While the text and logic of our federal structure justifies the application of interjurisdictional immunity to certain federal "activities"; nevertheless, a broad application of the doctrine to "activities" creates practical problems of application much greater than in the case of works or undertakings, things or persons, whose limits are more readily defined. A broad application also appears inconsistent, as stated, with the flexible federalism that the constitutional doctrines of pith and substance, double aspect and federal paramountcy are designed to promote.... It is these doctrines that have proved to be most consistent with contemporary views of Canadian federalism, which recognize that overlapping powers are unavoidable. Canadian federalism is not simply a matter of legalisms. The Constitution, though a legal document, serves as a framework for life and for political action within a federal state, in which the courts have rightly observed the importance of co-operation among government actors to ensure that federalism operates flexibly.

¶ 43 Excessive reliance on the doctrine of interjurisdictional immunity would create serious uncertainty. It is based on the attribution to every legislative head of power of a "core" of indeterminate scope — difficult to define, except over time by means of judicial interpretations triggered serendipitously on a case-by-case basis. The requirement to develop an abstract definition of a "core" is not compatible, generally speaking, with the tradition of Canadian constitutional interpretation, which favours an incremental approach. While it is true that the enumerations of ss. 91 and 92 contain a number of powers that are precise and not really open to discussion, other powers are far less precise, such as those relating to the criminal law, trade and commerce and matters of a local or private nature in a province. Since the time of Confederation, courts have refrained from trying to define the possible scope of such powers in advance and for all time... For example, while the courts have not eviscerated the federal trade and commerce power, they have, in interpreting it, sought to avoid draining of their content the provincial powers over civil law and matters of a local or private nature. A generalized application of interjurisdictional immunity related to "trade and commerce" would have led to an altogether different and more rigid and centralized form of federalism. It was by proceeding with caution on a case-by-case basis that the courts were gradually able to define the content of the heads of power of Parliament and the legislatures, without denying the unavoidable interplay between them, always having regard to the evolution of the problems for which the division of legislative powers must now provide solutions.

¶ 44 Moreover, as stated, interjurisdictional immunity means that despite the absence of law enacted at one level of government, the laws enacted by the other level cannot have even incidental effects on the so-called "core" of jurisdiction. This increases the risk of creating "legal vacuums"... Generally speaking, such "vacuums" are not desirable.

¶ 45 Further, a broad use of the doctrine of interjurisdictional immunity runs the risk of creating an unintentional centralizing tendency in constitutional interpretation. As stated, this doctrine has in the past most often protected federal heads of power from incidental intrusion by provincial legislatures. The "asymmetrical" application of interjurisdictional immunity is incompatible with the flexibility and co-ordination required by contemporary Canadian federalism. Commentators have noted that an extensive application of this doctrine to protect federal heads of power and undertakings is both unnecessary and "undesirable in a federation where so many laws for the protection of workers, consumers and the environment (for example) are enacted and enforced at the provincial level". [...] The asymmetrical effect of interjurisdictional immunity can also be seen as undermining the principles of subsidiarity, i.e. that decisions "are often best [made] at a level of government that is not only effective, but also closest to the citizens affected". [...]

¶ 46 Finally, the doctrine would seem as a general rule to be superfluous in that Parliament can always, if it sees fit to do so, make its legislation sufficiently precise to leave those subject to it with no doubt as to the residual or incidental application of provincial legislation. As we shall see, sufficient confirmation of this can be found in the history and operation of the doctrine of federal paramountcy.

¶ 47 For all these reasons, although the doctrine of interjurisdictional immunity has a proper part to play in appropriate circumstances, we intend now to make it clear that the Court does not favour an intensive reliance on the doctrine, nor should we accept the invitation of the appellants to turn it into a doctrine of first recourse in a division of powers dispute.

D. *A More Restricted Approach to Interjurisdictional Immunity*

(1) Impairment Versus Affects

¶ 48 Even in situations where the doctrine of interjurisdictional immunity is properly available, we must consider the level of the intrusion on the "core" of the power of the other level of government which would trigger its application. In *Bell Canada (1988)*, Beetz J. wrote, at pp. 859-60:

> In order for the inapplicability of provincial legislation rule to be given effect, it is sufficient that the provincial statute which purports to apply to the federal undertaking affects a vital or essential part of that undertaking without necessarily going as far as impairing or paralyzing it. [Emphasis added.]

Our colleague Bastarache J. agrees with the substitution in *Bell Canada (1988)* of "affects" for "impairs". He writes:

> ... the meaning of the word "affects" should be interpreted as a kind of middle ground between the perhaps overly vague or broad standard of "touches on" and the older and overly restrictive standard of "sterilizes" or "impairs". Without requiring complete paralysis of the core of the federal power or the operations of the undertaking, the impact of the application of the by-law must be sufficiently severe and serious to trigger immunity.
>
> (*British Columbia (Attorney General) v. Lafarge Canada Inc.*, 2007 SCC 23, at para. 48)

With great respect, we cannot agree. We believe that the law as it stood prior to *Bell Canada (1988)* better reflected our federal scheme. In our opinion, it is not enough for the provincial legislation simply to "affect" that which makes a federal subject or object of rights specifically of federal jurisdiction. The difference between "affects" and "impairs" is that the former does not imply any adverse consequence whereas the latter does. The shift in *Bell Canada (1988)* from "impairs" to "affects" is not consistent with the view subsequently adopted in Mangat that "[t]he existence of a double aspect to the subject matter ... favours the application of the paramountcy doctrine rather than the doctrine of interjurisdictional immunity" (para. 52)... It is when the adverse impact of a law adopted by one level of government increases in severity from "affecting" to "impairing" (without necessarily "sterilizing" or "paralyzing") that the "core" competence of the other level of government (or the vital or essential part of an undertaking it duly constitutes) is placed in jeopardy, and not before.

¶ 49 In *Irwin Toy Ltd. v. Quebec (Attorney General)*, [1989] 1 S.C.R. 927, Dickson C.J. and Lamer and Wilson JJ. observed in passing that a distinction could be drawn between the direct application of provincial law (where the operative verb is "affects") and the indirect application (where the operative verb may still be "impairs") (p. 957). This further exercise in line drawing signalled a measure of dissatisfaction with the "affects" test without doing anything about it. At this point, we should complete the reassessment begun in *Irwin Toy* and hold that, in the absence of impairment, interjurisdictional immunity does not apply.

(2) Identification of the "Basic, Minimum and Unassailable" Content of a Legislative Power

¶ 50 One of the important contributions of *Bell Canada (1988)* was to limit the scope of the doctrine to the "basic, minimum and unassailable content" (p. 839) sometimes referred to as the "core" of the legislative power in question. (By "minimum", we understand that Beetz J. meant the minimum content necessary to make the power effective for the purpose for which it was conferred.) This is necessary, according to Beetz J., to give effect to what he called "the principle of federalism underlying the Canadian Constitution" (p. 766). Thus, the success of the appellants' argument in this appeal depended in part on locating the promotion of "peace of mind" insurance at the core of banking. For the reasons already discussed, and particularized below, we do not believe that this aspect of the appellants' argument can be sustained.

(3) The Vital or Essential Part of an Undertaking

¶ 51 In the exercise of their legislative powers, federal and provincial legislators bring into existence "undertakings". The appellant banks are "federal undertakings" constituted pursuant to the s. 91(15) banking power. In *Bell Canada (1988)*, Beetz J. spoke of interjurisdictional immunity in relation to "essential and vital elements" of such undertakings (pp. 839, 859-60). In our view, some text writers and certainly the appellants have been inclined to give too wide a scope to what should be considered "vital or essential" to a federal undertaking. We believe that Beetz J. chose his words carefully and intended to use "vital" in its ordinary grammatical sense of "[e]ssential to the existence of something; absolutely indispensable or necessary; extremely important, crucial"... The word "essential" has a similar meaning, e.g. "[a]bsolutely indispensable or necessary"... The words "vital" and "essential" were not randomly chosen. [...] What is "vital" or "essential" is, by definition, not co-extensive with every element of an undertaking incorporated federally or subject to federal regulation. In the case of federal undertakings, Beetz J. referred to a "general rule" that there is *no* interjurisdictional immunity, provided that "the application of [the] provincial laws does not bear up on those [federal] subjects in what makes them specifically of federal jurisdiction" (*Bell Canada (1988)*, at p. 762 (emphasis added)). In the present appeal, for example, the appellants' argument inflates out of all proportion what could reasonably be considered "vital or essential" to their banking undertaking. The promotion of "peace of mind" insurance can hardly be considered "absolutely indispensable or necessary" to banking activities unless such words are to be emptied of their ordinary meaning.

¶ 52 In this respect, following the sage common law adage that it is wise to look at what the courts do as distinguished from what they say, a useful approach to understanding the limited scope of the doctrine of interjurisdictional immunity in respect of undertakings is to see how it has been applied to the facts. A comparison between *Bell Canada (1988)* and the present case is instructive. In *Bell Canada (1988)*, the Court concluded that the application of a provincial *Act respecting occupational health and safety* could not apply to a federal telephone undertaking because such application would "enter directly and massively into the field of working conditions and labour relations ... and ... management and operation" of the federal utility (p. 798). Amongst other things, the provincial Act would impose "a system of partial co-management of the undertaking by the workers and the employer" (p. 810), thereby regulating the federal undertaking in a manner not sanctioned by Parliament. [...]

¶ 53 Nor do the other authorities relied on by the appellants, in our view, justify their expansive view of the elements that are vital and essential to their banking operations. It is simply not credible, in our view, to suggest that the promotion of "peace of mind" insurance is "absolutely indispensable or necessary" to enable the banks to carry out their undertakings in what makes them specifically of federal jurisdiction. [...]

¶ 67 In our view, the above review of the case law cited by the appellants and other parties and interveners shows that not only *should* the doctrine of interjurisdictional immunity be applied with restraint, but with rare exceptions it *has* been so applied. Although the doctrine is in principle applicable to all federal and provincial heads of legislative authority, the case law demonstrates that its natural area of operation is in relation to those heads of legislative authority that confer on Parliament power over enumerated federal things, people, works or undertakings. In most cases, a pith and substance analysis and the application of the doctrine of paramountcy have resolved difficulties in a satisfactory manner.

H. *Application to the Facts of this Case*

(1) The Pith and Substance of the Alberta *Insurance Act* Relates to Property and Civil Rights in the Province

¶ 80 The Alberta *Insurance Act* is a valid law. As the banks acknowledge, the business of insurance in general falls within the authority of the provinces as a matter of property and civil rights. ... [A] federally incorporated company remains subject to provincial regulation in respect of its insurance business. [...] The banks say however that the promotion of their eight lines of "authorized" insurance products is integral to their lending practices, and thus to banking, which is a federally regulated activity.

¶ 81 Nevertheless, banks, as such, are not exempt from provincial law. ...[T]he mere fact that the banks now participate in the promotion of insurance does not change the essential nature of the insurance activity, which remains a matter generally falling within provincial jurisdiction...

(2) The onus lies on the proponent of interjurisdictional immunity on the facts of a particular case to demonstrate that credit-related insurance is part of the basic, minimum and unassailable content of the banking power.

¶ 83 The purpose of allocating "Banking, Incorporation of Banks and the Issue of Paper Money" to Parliament under s. 91(15) of the *Constitution Act, 1867* was to create an orderly and uniform financial system, subject to exclusive federal jurisdiction and control in contrast to a regionalized banking system which in "[t]he years preceding the Canadian Confederation were characterized in the United States by 'a chaotic era of wild-cat state banking'"...

¶ 84 At least in part, the importance of national control was because of "the peculiar status of bankers [as financial intermediaries], their importance at the centre of the financial community [and] the expectation of the public that it can grant them implicit and utmost confidence"... In 1914, the High Court of Australia said:

> The essential characteristics of the business of banking ... may be described as the collection of money by receiving deposits upon on loan, repayable when and as expressly or impliedly agreed upon, and the utilization of the money so collected by lending it again in such sums as are required...

¶ 85 It is unnecessary, for present purposes, to delve deeply into the notoriously difficult task of defining banking. It includes the incorporation of banks. It certainly includes, as the banks argue, the securing of loans by appropriate collateral. At issue is the difference between *requiring* collateral (a banking activity) and promoting the acquisition of a certain type of product (e.g. insurance) that could then be *used* as collateral. The respondent, for its part, complains that the appellants' argument would render the "basic, minimum and unassailable" content of the banking power more or less co-extensive with what bankers are authorized to do. There is no doubt that banking is crucial to the economy and that even the basic, minimum and unassailable content of the exclusive power conferred on Parliament in this regard must not be given a cramped interpretation. [...] Such considerations, however, should not lead to confusion between the scope of the federal power and its basic, minimum and unassailable content.

(3) Credit-related insurance is not a vital or essential element of the banking undertaking

¶ 88 ... [T]he appellants centred their argument on the provincial licensing requirement. However if, as we conclude, the promotion of insurance is not vital or essential to the banking activity, there is no reason why the banks *should* be shielded from the consequences of non-compliance with the provincial *Insurance Act*. [...] [T]here is no reason why [banks] should escape the regulatory discipline to which all other promoters of insurance in the province are subject. [...]

¶ 110 For these reasons, we would dismiss the appeal with costs and answer the constitutional questions as follows:

1. Are Alberta's *Insurance Act*, R.S.A. 2000, c. I-3, and the regulations made thereunder, in whole or in part, constitutionally inapplicable to the promotion by banks of an "authorized type of insurance" or "personal accident insurance" as defined in the *Insurance Business (Banks and Bank Holding Companies) Regulations*, SOR/92-330, by reason of the doctrine of interjurisdictional immunity?

Answer: No.

BASTARACHE J. (concurring):– [...]

¶ 118 The proper analytical approach to the applicability analysis was set out at para. 27 of my reasons in *Lafarge*:

> The first step is to identify the "core" of the federal head of power; that is, to determine what the federal power encompasses within its primary scope, and then to determine whether the impugned federal undertaking or matter at issue falls within that core. The second step is to determine whether the impugned provincial law ... impermissibly affects a vital aspect of the federal core of [the] head of power, so as to render it inapplicable to the federal undertaking or matter. [...]

Thus, the first step is to identify the "core" of the federal head of power in issue, which here is "banking" under s. 91(15). I do not support a concept of the "core" that is overly restrictive; nor do I support a concept of the "core" that is defined too widely (para. 36 of my reasons in *Lafarge*). Ultimately, my view is that the extent of the "core" is very context specific; it depends on the federal head of power in question. For example, in *Lafarge*, I concluded that the federal power over navigation and shipping (s. 91(10)) is broad and comprehensive and as a result its core must be defined in a more global and comprehensive fashion (para. 40). While the federal power over "banking" in s. 91(15) has similarly been found to be quite extensive ... I do not think its core is so imprecise. Certainly, just because something is permitted by the *Bank Act* does not make it essential to the core of banking. What will be protected under the core from impermissible intrusions by the provinces are only those elements of federal jurisdiction which are "essential and vital" to the proper functioning of the federal undertaking or matter... After a thorough examination of the jurisprudence, the trial judge found that the lending of money, the taking of deposits, the extension of credit in the form of granting loans, as well as the taking of security for those loans were core elements of banking (paras. 129-30). I agree. When one considers these "essential" elements of the federal banking power, one is naturally drawn towards a consideration of the activities and operations performed by banks which are central to the reasons why they fall under federal jurisdiction. Thus, deposit taking and credit granting easily fall at the heart of this core set of operations and activities, since these activities constitute in many ways the *raison d'être* of banks. It is also possible to see these activities as part of the core of banking because this is so clearly and palpably the "domain" of banks as federal undertakings. The question thus becomes whether the particular matter in issue falls within this core.

¶ 119 Here I endorse the characterization of the particular matter in issue as the promotion of authorized insurance. It may appear that I am focussing on a specific activity as opposed to a subject matter or jurisdiction — a position I criticized in *Lafarge* (para. 18). However, the problem with Justices Binnie and LeBel's analysis in *Lafarge* was that they focused on the Vancouver Port Authority's regulatory power over land-use planning *as exercised in a particular case by deciding to approve the Lafarge proposal*. The corresponding "prohibited" line of inquiry here would thus be a focus on the power of banks to promote the sale of authorized insurance products *as exercised in a particular factual context* (such as a specific manner in which the insurance is promoted, or a specific insurance product or type of insurance). Just as the particular activity of the Vancouver Port Authority approving the development was technically not relevant to the immunity analysis in *Lafarge*, the particular way in which the banks promote the authorized insurance products or the particular type of authorized insurance would not be relevant to the immunity analysis here. Thus, the particular subject matter or power at the heart of this interjurisdictional immunity analysis is the ability of the banks to promote the purchase of authorized insurance products, regardless of whether or how they actually exercise that power.

¶ 120 In my view, the courts below were correct to conclude that the promotion of authorized insurance does not come within the "core" of banking. ... First, the nature of the promotion of authorized insurance products renders it "one step removed" from generally-accepted "core" areas of banking identified above, to use the language of the trial judge (para. 164). While the granting of credit in exchange for collateral and the taking of "security" can be seen as being clearly at the core of the banking power ..., the promotion, sale or creation of insurance as collateral for the exercise of such security is not part of the core of the banking power. As recognized by the trial judge, at para. 118, insurance can never be "security". The insurance is rather the collateral created in relation to the granting of a bank loan. Thus, the provincial law in question cannot be interpreted as affecting the promotion of security, but rather the promotion of collateral (see the trial judge's reasons, at para. 121). [...]

¶ 121 Second, although not a determinative factor (because Parliament cannot, for constitutional purposes, determine the content of the core of a federal head of power), the structure and language of the federal statutory provisions which permit banks to engage in the promotion of insurance suggests that Parliament clearly intended to allow only a limited participation in the insurance industry, recognizing that such participation would in fact constitute an encroachment of banks into an area not traditionally associated with the core of "banking". [...] Parliament appears to have drawn a clear distinction between the business of banking and the business of insurance.

¶ 122 Third, the aim of promoting insurance yields another clue as to its exclusion from the core of the banking power. Matters that fall within the core of a federal head of power would normally be expected to have a purpose or goal which is consistent with the exercise of that head of power and consistent with its maintenance and use. Here, the promotion of insurance by the banks does not seek to permit the continued use and maintenance of the federal banking power; rather, the sole purpose of engaging in the promotion of insurance appears to be to generate additional revenue as a separate product line and profit centre, thereby maintaining and enhancing a bank's competitive edge in an economic world of "universal banking". I would also raise the fact that the insurance promoted is optional and can be cancelled at any time, as well as the fact that the overall impact of the promotion of insurance on the banks' portfolio risk is quite minimal, as further evidence that the matter does not come within the core of banking. Clearly, the promotion of authorized insurance is not part of the core of banking because it is not essential to the function of banking.

¶ 123 The analysis should not stop here, however, because the second step set out in Lafarge is to determine whether the impugned provincial law impermissibly affects a vital aspect of the federal core of the head of power, so as to render it inapplicable to the federal undertaking or matter. The benefit of such a two-step inquiry, rather than focussing almost exclusively on the question of whether a federal matter comes within the "core" to determine immunity, is that it promotes greater flexibility in assessing whether immunity should arise. Even if a matter is found to be essential to a federal undertaking, immunity from a provincial law will not arise unless its "affect" on the federal power is "sufficiently severe": the federal legislative authority needs to be "attacked", "hindered" or "restrained" (paras. 17 and 48 of my reasons in *Lafarge*). Because the promotion of insurance does not go to the core of banking, it is obvious that in the present case, Alberta's *Insurance Act* is not affecting in any important way the core of banking. If the promotion of insurance did go to the core of banking, a more in-depth analysis would have to be undertaken, as was done in *Lafarge* (see paras. 48-50), to determine the severity of the impact. Therefore, no immunity arises in the circumstances. [...]

BRITISH COLUMBIA (ATTORNEY GENERAL) V. LAFARGE CANADA INC.
2007 S.C.C. 23

[Lafarge Canada Inc. wished to build an integrated ship offloading/concrete batching facility on waterfront lands owned by the Vancouver Port Authority ("VPA"), a federal undertaking constituted by federal legislation. A group of ratepayers opposed the project. The ratepayers filed argued in the British Columbia Supreme Court that the City of Vancouver wrongly declined to require Lafarge to obtain a City development permit. The VPA replied that no City permit was necessary because VPA lands enjoy interjurisdictional immunity as "public property" within the meaning of s. 91(1A) of the *Constitution Act, 1867*, or because the management of those lands is vital to the VPA's "federal undertaking" pursuant to the federal s. 91(10) jurisdiction over "navigation and shipping". In the alternative, the VPA contended that there was an operational conflict and that, according to the doctrine of federal paramountcy, the conflict must be resolved in favour of federal jurisdiction.]

The judgment of Binnie, LeBel, Deschamps, Fish, Abella and Charron JJ. was delivered by

BINNIE and LeBEL JJ. — [...]

¶ 36 There is no separate head of legislative power over "ports". The federal government enjoys exclusive jurisdiction in relation to its public property and over shipping and navigation activities. The province exercises jurisdiction over "property and civil rights" and "municipal institutions" within the province but it has, of course, been long recognized that the power to control navigation and shipping conferred by s. 91(10) is "capable of allowing the Dominion Parliament to restrict very seriously the exercise of proprietary rights"...

¶ 37 The development of waterfront land could potentially fall under either provincial or federal jurisdiction, depending on the ownership and the use to which the land is proposed to be put. [...]

¶ 38 The potential for conflict in mixed land-use development along urban waterfronts is considerable. [...] Federal-provincial-municipal cooperation in such matters is not unconstitutional. It is essential. [...]

¶ 41 As discussed in *Canadian Western Bank*, there are circumstances in which the powers of one level of government must be protected against intrusions, even incidental ones, by the other level (para. 32). This is called interjurisdictional immunity and is an exception to the ordinary rule under which legislation whose pith and substance falls within the jurisdiction of the legislature that enacted it may, at least to a certain extent, affect matters beyond the legislature's jurisdiction without necessarily being unconstitutional (para. 26). [...]

¶ 42 In this case, we are dealing with a federal undertaking, the Vancouver Port Authority, constituted pursuant to two heads of federal legislative power, the authority in relation to public property (*Constitution Act, 1867*, s. 91(1A)) and the federal authority in relation to navigation and shipping (s. 91(10)). In *Bell Canada v. Quebec (Commission de la santé et de la securité du travail)*, [1988] 1 S.C.R. 749 ("*Bell Canada (1988)*"), the Court restricted interjurisdictional immunity to "essential and vital elements" of such undertakings (pp. 839, 859-60). In our view, as explained in *Canadian Western Bank*, Beetz J. chose his words carefully, and intended to use "vital" in its ordinary grammatical sense of "[e]ssential to the existence of something; absolutely indispensable or necessary; extremely important, crucial". [...] The word "essential" has a similar meaning, e.g. "[a]bsolutely indispensable or necessary" (p. 860). [...] What is "vital" or "essential" is, by definition, not co-extensive with every element of an undertaking incorporated federally or subject to federal regulation. In the case of federal undertakings, that would include the VPA. Beetz J. referred to a "general rule" that there is no interjurisdictional immunity, provided "the application of [the] provincial laws does not bear upon those [federal] subjects <u>in what makes them specifically of federal jurisdiction</u>". [...]

¶ 43 The question before us, therefore, is whether it can be said that federal jurisdiction over all development on VPA lands within the port area of Vancouver, even non-Crown lands not used for shipping and navigation purposes, is "absolutely indispensable or necessary" to the discharge by the VPA of its responsibilities in relation to federal "public property" or "shipping and navigation". We concluded in *Canadian Western Bank* that interjurisdictional immunity is not essential to make these federal powers effective for the purposes for which they were conferred and therefore this appeal should be decided on the basis of federal paramountcy, not interjurisdictional immunity. [...]

¶ 62 The methodology for reconciling the exercise of federal power and provincial power is ... [first] to identify the "pith and substance" of the respective enactments... [T]he CMA [Canada Marine Act] in relation to non-Crown lands is supported by the federal legislative power relating to navigation and shipping under s. 91(10)... The federal power ... enables the federal government to build or regulate the necessary facilities like ports. [...] [T]he CMA may have "incidental effects" in matters that would otherwise fall within provincial authority, such as the planning and development of land uses within the municipality of Vancouver.

¶ 63 On the provincial side, the power involved is the authority over municipal institutions and matters of local interest. The province of British Columbia has delegated broad powers to the City on zoning and construction within its boundaries. [...] [T]he Parliament of Canada and the legislature of British Columbia have validly exercised their legislative powers. The regulatory and decision-making power of the VPA and the City flow from them. The question before our Court is their applicability. [...]

¶ 66 Our jurisprudence holds that a matter otherwise subject to provincial jurisdiction may be brought within federal jurisdiction if it is "closely integrated" with shipping and navigation. [...] This test of "close integration" [allows] ... jurisdiction over "marine-related port uses", properly circumscribed and interpreted by reference to the shipping component [to] come within the reach of the federal power over navigation and shipping. [...]

¶ 67 The issue is not necessity but integration. As Rand J. pointed out in the *Stevedoring* case:

> Actual necessity need not appear as the contracting out case shows; it is the appropriateness, on a balance of interests and convenience, to the main subject matter or the legislation. [Emphasis added; p. 548-49.]

¶ 68 In our view, the CMA [*Canada Marine Act*] land-use controls can constitutionally extend to the Lafarge project, which has from the outset been conceived of by both the City and the VPA as an integrated transportation/mixing facility in which the marine transportation aspect dominates. [...]

¶ 72 The CMA is a federal law in pith and substance related to the management of public property and shipping and navigation. Its land-use controls reach beyond Crown property to embrace uses that are "closely integrated" with shipping and navigation. This covers the Lafarge project. However, land-use jurisdiction asserted by the VPA in this case, while valid, does not attract interjurisdictional immunity. The port is not a federal enclave. VPA lands are held and leased for a variety of activities. Authorizing the construction of a cement plant on these port lands does not fall within the core or vital functions of VPA. On the facts of this case, it rather belongs to an incidental port development business, which because of its integration in marine transportation is reached by federal jurisdiction, but which certainly lies beyond the core of s. 91(10).

¶ 73 In the absence of valid and applicable federal regulatory land-use controls, there would be no regulatory vacuum on the former Sterling shipbuilding site. The provincial land-use controls would apply. [...]

The Application of Federal Paramountcy to CMA Section 48 and *Port 2010*

¶ 75 The provincial Attorneys General argue that there is no operational conflict because Lafarge could apply for and obtain building permits from both the VPA and the City. But that argument overlooks the fact that the Lafarge project in its present form does not comply with the City's By-law. The By-law imposes a 30-foot height restriction. It would be within the City's discretion to waive the height limit up to 100 feet, but that would impose the condition precedent of an exercise of a discretion by the City to approve a project that has already been approved by the VPA This would create an operational conflict that would flout the federal purpose, by depriving the VPA of its final decisional authority on the development of the port, in respect of matters which fall within the legislative authority of Parliament. [...]

¶ 77 We restated the requirements for federal paramountcy in our reasons in *Canadian Western Bank*. The party raising the issue must establish the existence of valid federal and provincial laws and the impossibility of their simultaneous application by reasons of an operational conflict or because such application would frustrate the purpose of the enactment...

(i) The Existence of an Operational Conflict

¶ 81 Operational conflict is present here. Reference has already been made to the City's 30-foot height restriction. The record confirms other areas of conflict in respect of noise and pollution from the offloading activity and the subsequent loading of the aggregates.

¶ 82 If the Ratepayers had succeeded in persuading the City to seek an injunction to stop the Lafarge project from going ahead without a city permit, the judge could not have given effect both to the federal law (which would have led to a dismissal of the application) and the municipal law (which would have led to the granting of an injunction). That is an operational conflict, as held in *M & D Farm Ltd. v. Manitoba Agricultural Credit Corp.*, [1999] 2 S.C.R. 961.

(ii) Frustration of Federal Legislative Purpose

¶ 83 Such an application of the relevant municipal standards would frustrate the federal purpose. Although the VPA should seek to cooperate with the municipalities of the Greater Vancouver area, it retains the final say in respect of all matters falling within valid federal jurisdiction, in case of conflict.

¶ 84 Assistance can be drawn from *Mangat* where provincial legislation prohibited non-lawyers from appearing for a fee before a tribunal, but the federal legislation authorized non-lawyers to appear as counsel for a fee. *Mangat* confirms that the second prong of the test should not be interpreted as a return to the doctrine of the "occupied field". Rather it intends to capture those instances where it might be possible to comply with the letter of both laws, but where such compliance would frustrate the purpose intended by Parliament. In *Mangat*, it was argued that both enactments could be complied with, if would – be advocates either became a member in good standing of the Law Society of British Columbia or refrained from charging a fee. However, Gonthier J. held at para. 22 that "[t]o require "other counsel" to be a member in good standing of the bar of the province or to refuse the payment of a fee would go contrary to Parliament's purpose in enacting ss. 30 and 69(1) of the *Immigration Act*. [...] Where there is an enabling federal law, the provincial law cannot be contrary to Parliament's purpose." Here, the CMA has authorized the VPA to make its decision about the project and has enabled Lafarge to proceed on the basis of that authorization. [...]

¶ 85 Given the operational conflict and its impact on the achievement of the federal purpose, the preconditions of federal paramountcy are met and the Ratepayers' petition should be rejected on that ground.

¶ 91 For these reasons, we would dismiss the appeal with costs...

The following are the reasons delivered by

BASTARACHE J. — [...]

¶ 101 [A]ll constitutional legal challenges to legislation should follow the same pattern: considerations of validity, considerations of applicability and, where two laws are potentially in conflict, considerations of operability in terms of federal paramountcy. [...]

¶ 104 [S]ome critics of interjurisdictional immunity have argued that it is unnecessary and irrelevant in light of the doctrine of federal paramountcy. Magnet convincingly notes the differences between the two doctrines discussed in the preceding paragraphs. Magnet writes that immunity "is different from the paramountcy doctrine in that even where there is no contradiction or meeting of legislation, the provincial legislation offers significant obstruction to the federal thing, person or undertaking, affects its status, or drains off essential federal attributes which make them within federal jurisdiction" (p. 339). Preserving the application of the immunity doctrine in certain contexts demonstrates the full extent and breadth of different types of constitutional legal inquiries. [...]

¶ 106 [T]here are those who would argue that the concerns addressed by the doctrine of immunity are already resolved by the "double aspect" doctrine. Once again, those criticisms appear to be misguided in that the double aspect doctrine merely recognizes that some laws may have a purpose corresponding to a valid head of provincial jurisdiction, but may also have a purpose corresponding to a valid head of federal jurisdiction. With respect, I believe Binnie and LeBel JJ. mischaracterize this doctrine, at para. 4 of their reasons. The recognition of an apparent double aspect to a provincial law does not render it inapplicable or inoperative (nor invalid). Those matters must still be determined using the concepts of federal immunity and paramountcy. Likewise, a finding that a provincial law has only "incidental effects" on a federal head of power is merely a statement about the law's validity; it says nothing about the *impact* of the provincial law — its effects on federal matters when it is *applied* to those matters. It may in fact be possible for a provincial law to be valid to the extent that its true or essential nature can be seen as having merely "incidental" effects on a federal head of power (pursuant to the pith and substance analysis), but then to be rendered inapplicable because of "impermissible" effects on the *core of a federal head of power when it is applied* to certain federal undertakings. Immunity would therefore play a role in preventing constitutionally impermissible applications of provincial laws to federal matters, without the need to strike down such laws and without the need for competing and conflicting federal legislation. [...]

¶ 108 Notwithstanding this defence of the doctrine, I would agree with some critics of interjurisdictional immunity who allege that its application is often difficult and who in particular allege that the criterion for determining when a provincial law "affects" the core of a federal power or vital part of a federal undertaking is often vague or overly broad. It is no doubt time to recognize that defining the word "affects" as simply or merely "touches on" leads to an overly wide scope of immunity in many contexts. While the former standard of "impairment" or "sterilization" appears to be too narrow and restrictive (with the possible exception of special cases like *Irwin Toy Ltd. v. Quebec (Attorney General)*, [1989] 1 S.C.R. 927, where the provincial law has only "indirect" effects on the federal matter, which is not the case here), an overly broad or vague notion of whether a provincial law "affects" the core of a federal power might confer federal immunity in wholly inappropriate scenarios. Some middle ground should therefore be sought out. In my view, the effect of the application of a provincial law on the core of a federal head of legislative power must be sufficiently severe to justify a finding of immunity. Without going so far as to require the federal core or matter or undertaking to be "sterilized", I would suggest that we should interpret *Bell Canada (1988)*'s determination of a vital part of the federal core being "affected" to mean that the full or plenary exercise (or potential exercise) of the federal legislative authority in question would need to be "attacked", "hindered" or "restrained" before immunity could attach. The key, to return to the language used by Beetz J. in *Bell Canada (1988)*, at p. 856, is whether the provincial law "bears upon" a federal matter or subject in what makes it "specifically of federal jurisdiction" (p. 762). As Professor Hogg suggests, the provincial law in its application to the federal matter must "intrude heavily" upon core federal areas of jurisdiction and/or upon core aspects of federal subject matters in order for immunity to be triggered ... In my view, these qualifying descriptions of the word "affects" will give more teeth to the notion of immunity and respond to critics of the doctrine who have expressed concern over its overly broad and limitless application. I will not discuss the matter of indirect effects described in *Irwin Toy*; it raises a number of difficulties in its own right that are better left to another day.

¶ 109 Regarding the application of the immunity doctrine in cases like the present one, I would disagree with Justices Binnie and LeBel's treatment of the operation of interjurisdictional immunity, at para. 46 of their reasons, where they focuses on an "activities" based notion of jurisdiction. This indicates a focus on the specific nature of the Lafarge proposal and the activities it would carry out. This concern is repeated at para. 71, where the core of the federal power here is found not to include "uses that ... cannot be said to be absolutely indispensable and necessary to its shipping and navigation undertaking". With respect, this analysis is problematic because the test for immunity should not focus on any specific *activity* or operation at issue (i.e. the Lafarge proposal for a concrete batch facility or any other particular use of port lands) and whether this activity or use is immune from the municipal by-law, but rather on whether the federal *power* over navigation and shipping (expressed in this case as the federal power over land-use planning and development decisions by a port authority, a federally regulated undertaking) is immune from the application of the municipal by-law. The immunity doctrine is about jurisdiction; what matters is whether or not a provincial law affects the core of a *federal head of legislative power*, regardless of whether or how that federal power is exercised or will be exercised, if at all, with respect to a particular project or activity. The only relevance of the activity is that discussed further on in these reasons, i.e. whether approval of the project by the VPA as a federal undertaking is consistent with the regulation of land-use planning and development of port lands in support of port operations (which I believe falls within the core of s. 91(10)). But even that determination says nothing of the applicability of the municipal by-law.

¶ 110 Because of this focus on jurisdiction rather than action, there need not be any federal legislation or executive action "occupying the field" for federal immunity to be triggered with respect to an area of federal legislative authority. This is one of the key facets of the immunity doctrine; the mere fact that a provincial law or municipal by-law affects a vital part of an area of exclusive federal jurisdiction is enough to render it inapplicable with respect to a federal undertaking, regardless of whether or not Parliament has itself enacted any laws or taken any specific action with respect to the jurisdictional area or the undertaking. [...]

¶ 111 This conclusion (that a provincial law, if it is found inapplicable to a federal undertaking or matter by reason of interjurisdictional immunity, cannot "fill the gap" left by the absence of any federal legislation or action) is consistent with the principle of "exclusivity" whereby subject matters enumerated in ss. 91 and 92 of the *Constitution Act, 1867* are assigned to one level of government only. According to Monahan, this principle means that "constitutional jurisdiction over a particular work or undertaking is to be undivided: for the purposes of section 92(10), jurisdiction is allocated to a single level of government. The courts have consistently rejected the idea of dividing jurisdiction between the federal and the provincial governments over a single undertaking" (p. 357). The same could be said of undertakings or subject matters covered by a particular head of power under s. 91, such as navigation and shipping in this case. [...]

¶ 118 The first step is to identify the "core" of the federal head of power; that is, to determine what the federal power encompasses within its primary scope, and then to determine whether the impugned federal undertaking or matter at issue falls within that core. The second step is to determine whether the impugned provincial law (or in this case, the impugned municipal by-law) impermissibly affects a vital aspect of the federal core of either head of power, so as to render it inapplicable to the federal undertaking or matter. [...]

¶ 126 The alternative ground for federal immunity from the application of the municipal by-law is that the by-law cannot apply by virtue of Parliament's exclusive legislative jurisdiction over navigation and shipping under s. 91(10), and in particular over the VPA's regulation of land-use planning and development of port lands in respect of port operations, as a federally regulated undertaking rooted in s. 91(10). [...]

¶ 128 [T]he jurisprudence clearly establishes that ports and harbours with interprovincial dimensions fall within the core of s. 91(10) as facilities or undertakings in which various aspects of the federal power over navigation and shipping would logically be exercised. [...]

¶ 130 If ports and harbours are part of the core of s. 91(10), then, in my view, it is clear that the regulation of land use within ports also falls within the core when such regulation concerns port lands and port operations and, thus, navigation and shipping. Clearly, if ports themselves are a vital aspect of navigation and shipping, then the use and development of surrounding port lands for port operations must be as well. More specifically, the land-use planning activities and operations of port authorities as federally created and regulated undertakings charged with managing and operating ports, and ensuring their commercial viability, must also fall within the core of s. 91(10). The federal power over navigation and shipping must therefore also include and extend to federally regulated port authorities such as the VPA, whose creation, role and mandate are undeniably at the core of Parliament's legislative authority over navigation and shipping. [...]

¶ 131 Even further, in my view, the federal regulation of port lands *in support* of port operations also falls within the core of s. 91(10) — not just federal regulation of port lands used directly or strictly for port "activities" *per se*. As discussed above, the federal power over navigation and shipping is broad and comprehensive; as a result, its core must be defined in a more global and coherent fashion... [L]and-use planning and development of all port lands, regardless of the specific status of individual parcels of land, lies at the core of s. 91(10). As for concerns over certain "uses" of land which might not seem closely connected to navigation and shipping, as discussed earlier, those concerns fail to recognize the nature of the doctrine of interjurisdictional immunity as being concerned with areas of potential legislative jurisdiction, not specific executive action or activities. If immunity extends to the regulation of land-use planning on all port lands, then ... it should not matter what is the specific status of a particular parcel of port lands, and what its specific intended use would be. [...]

¶ 136 In my view, the VPA's decision to approve the Lafarge project is consistent with a valid exercise of the power to regulate land-use planning for port lands in support of port operations. [...]

¶ 137 In my view, Justices Binnie and LeBel's conclusion (at para. 71) that the regulation of land-use on port lands for activities "in support" of port operations and for a "port service industry reliant on waterfront access" does not fall within the core of s. 91(10) because it is not "absolutely indispensable and necessary" to the VPA's federal undertaking is really a reflection of their concern that certain possible uses of land (plazas, parks, restaurants, condominiums, etc.) should not receive federal immunity because they would be unconnected to navigation and shipping. With respect, as previously discussed, I do not understand how the regulation of land-use planning for <u>port</u> lands "in <u>support of port operations</u>" does not fall within the core of the navigation and shipping power; nor can I understand how certain land uses which support "<u>port</u> service industries <u>reliant on waterfront access</u>" could also be excluded from the core, even if those uses in and of themselves do not appear to be "navigation and shipping" activities. By definition, such uses of land, even if they do not appear at first blush to be part of the core of navigation and shipping, are destined to support the operations of a port. Which falls within the core of s. 91(10), and would occur on port lands, the development and planning of which also falls within the core of s. 91(10). The concern over apparently non-marine related uses of port lands (such as plazas, condominiums, parks, industrial facilities, etc.) seems rooted in the fear that uses of port lands which merely act as additional sources of income are not sufficiently "marine related" to count as "shipping and navigation". [...] In the present case, however, even if some "purely" economic or commercial uses of Schedule C lands could result from the VPA's regulation of land-use planning and development on port lands, such uses are still designed to support port operations and are still occurring on port lands; these factors establish a strong connection to core matters within the federal navigation and shipping power. [...] Immunity still protects activities which appear to be at the outer limits of the core of a federal power, even those apparently aimed at generating revenue or increasing the competitive edge of a federal undertaking, but only if such activities can be tied to a core function of the federal power (in this case, the regulation of land-use planning and development on port lands, including lands for activities in support of port operations).

¶ 138 In addition, and more importantly, I do not think this is the correct lens through which to frame the inquiry. Specific uses of land are relevant to the immunity analysis only to the extent that they might not reflect a proper exercise of the core federal power over the regulation of land use for port lands, including for activities in support of port operations. If certain uses should not receive federal immunity, that is because they lack a sufficient connection to navigation and shipping and are likely inconsistent with the federal power to regulate land use *in support of port operations*, and would therefore constitute an excess of federal jurisdiction. That would not change the fact that the provincial law in question here (the municipal by-law) affects a vital part of the federal navigation and shipping power because it hinders (by its application to the Port of Vancouver) the regulation of land-use planning on port lands in support of operations, a protected "core" matter within s. 91(10) which is intended to be performed exclusively by a federal authority — i.e. the VPA.

3.2.2.2 *The By-law's Effect on the Core of Section 91(10)*

¶ 139 The second step in the interjurisdictional immunity test with respect to navigation and shipping is to determine whether the application of the municipal by-law in this case would "affect" a vital part of the federal legislative authority over navigation and shipping under s. 91(10) — that is, whether it would affect the core of that head of power as defined above. More specifically, the question is whether the application of the by-law would impermissibly affect the power (as exercised by the VPA as a federal undertaking) to regulate land-use planning of port lands, including for activities in support of port operations, as a "vital part" of the federal navigation and shipping power under s. 91(10). As noted earlier, the meaning of the word "affects" should be interpreted as a kind of middle ground between the perhaps overly vague or broad standard of "touches on" and the older and overly restrictive standard of "sterilizes" or "impairs". Without requiring complete paralysis of the core of the federal power or the operations of the undertaking, the impact of the application of the by-law must be sufficiently severe and serious to trigger immunity.

¶ 140 In my view, this question must be answered in the affirmative here. The by law clearly and significantly affects the VPA's regulation of land-use planning and development for port lands in support of port operations by imposing a zoning regime and an approvals process for development proposals and projects on such lands. This regulation of land-use planning and development within the port for purposes related to navigation and shipping is at the core of the federal power over navigation and shipping under s. 91(10). If the by-law were applied to the Port of Vancouver, the VPA's ability to regulate the land-use planning and development of the port would be severely affected (see para. 108 of Finch C.J.B.C.'s reasons on this point). From a practical perspective, it would create a jurisdictional nightmare, given that the port itself lies at the intersection of eight separate municipalities, all of whom could conceivably enforce a land-use planning by-law regime which would apply to port lands. It is therefore clear that the application of any of these by-laws would seriously affect or hinder a vital part of the federal navigation and shipping power under s. 91(10) by affecting the ability of the VPA as a federal undertaking to regulate land-use planning of port lands in support of port operations. The ideal of federal-provincial co-operation discussed by Justices Binnie and LeBel at para. 38 must be concerned with actual facts.

¶ 141 It should also be noted that even if this were an "impairment" situation where the provincial law in question applied only "indirectly" to the federal matter (see *Irwin Toy*), immunity would still attach. If the by-law were only indirectly applicable to the VPA's regulation of land-use planning and development within the port, it would still be impossible to exercise the s. 91(10) federal power over navigation and shipping (and more specifically over the regulation of land-use planning and development on port lands by a federally regulated port authority) in any rational way. The federal power would consistently be subject to interference, and thus impairment, by municipal legislation and action in the form of delays, lengthy approvals processes, inconsistent municipal zoning norms and the possibility of a "patchwork" of separate rules over the same relatively small land mass. Thus, even under the *Irwin Toy* version of the doctrine, interjurisdictional immunity should attach to the VPA's regulation of land use in the port for port lands in support of port operations.

3.3 *The Operation of the Municipal By-law*

¶ 142 Having concluded that the by-law in question is constitutionally inapplicable in this case, by reason of interjurisdictional immunity, it is neither necessary nor possible to consider whether the by-law is also constitutionally inoperable by reason of the doctrine of federal paramountcy... [C]onsideration of the doctrine of federal paramountcy is only triggered when there are two valid and applicable laws which overlap and appear to conflict. That is not the case here, given that the municipal by-law is inapplicable.

4. Conclusion

¶ 143 Accordingly, I would dismiss the Attorney General of British Columbia's appeal. [...]

PART III

DIVISION OF LEGISLATIVE POWERS

1.　Property and Civil Rights in the Province

(a)　Sections 92(13) and 92(16)

MCCONNELL, COMMENTARY ON THE BRITISH NORTH AMERICA ACT
(MACMILLAN, 1977) AT 270, 286.

13. Property and Civil Rights in the Province.

　　　A consideration of the expansible category of "Property and Civil Rights in the Province" illustrates the substantial influence which judicial interpretation may have on the development of a federal constitution. Writing sixty years after the enactment of the *B.N.A. Act*, Professor H. A. Smith reflected on the intervening current of Judicial Committee interpretation:

> The result of the decisions is that the real residuary power is now to be found in the words "property and civil rights", over which s. 92 gives exclusive jurisdiction to the provinces. Considered grammatically and apart from their historical context, these words are amply sufficient to cover the whole field of possible legislation outside pure criminal law, and it then becomes necessary to treat the matters specifically enumerated in s. 91 as so many exceptions to the general legislative power of the provinces. In other words, the principle of American federalism has been substituted for that agreed upon at Quebec in 1865 ("Interpretation in English and Continental Law", [1927] 9 *J. Comp. Leg. & Int. Law*, 153 at 163).

In the half century since Professor Smith wrote the above lines, much has happened that would confirm his analysis, but there are also indications of a new centralizing tendency. After the abolition of Privy Council appeals in 1949, some of the recent decisions by the Supreme Court of Canada have uncharacteristically favoured the peace, order, and good government clause (the *actual* residuary power) and the trade and commerce power when they came into competition with property and civil rights (see the commentaries on the preamble to ss. 91 and 91(2)).

The first expansive phase in the judicial construction of s. 92(13) began with Sir Montague Smith's judgment in an early insurance case *Citizens' Ins. Co. v. Parsons* (1881), 9 App. Cas. 96. One of the important issues in that case was whether statutory conditions prescribed by the Ontario legislature for inclusion in insurance contracts validly fell within the provincial head of property and civil rights or were, in effect, a usurpation by the province of the federal trade and commerce power. The enormously important subject of "contracts" was nowhere expressly allocated in the *B.N.A. Act* to either the federal government or the provinces, and it was necessary to consider under which of the rival heads of ss. 91 and 92 contracts of fire insurance could appropriately be classified. The appellants contended that s. 92(13) conferred on the provinces the right to regulate the ownership of property and to legislate on such civil rights as flowed from the operation of law, such as matters of status, leaving the control of contracts to the Dominion under s. 91(2). The Privy Council, however, rejected this contention, holding that s. 92(13) embraced "rights" arising from contracts. Two important supporting reasons given by the Justices involved the consideration of (a) s. 94 of the *B.N.A. Act*, and (b) s. 8 of the *Quebec Act*, 1774, 14 Geo. III, c. 83. It was pointed out, concerning (a), that s. 94 empowered parliament to provide for the uniformity of laws relative to "property and civil rights" in Ontario, Nova Scotia, and New Brunswick, and that Quebec was intentionally omitted because of her distinct civil law system. As the nomenclature in ss. 92(13) and 94 was identical, if one assumed that contracts were not included within the former subsection it would follow that parliament could, under s. 91(2), legislate respecting contracts in Quebec which are now governed by the provincial Civil Code, founded on French law. With respect to (b), it was emphasized that by s. 8 of the *Quebec Act* Her Majesty's subjects in Quebec were to enjoy their property, usages, and other civil rights, and that in all matters of controversy resort would be had to the local law (*ibid.*, 110-11). Sir Montague concluded that the words "property" and "civil rights" were plainly used in their largest sense; in his opinion the latter term was certainly elastic enough to include local contracts. The reasoning of the Privy Council on this latter point would seem to be that while the *Quebec Act* maintained English public and criminal law in the province, it extended virtually the whole range of private law to Quebec, including commercial and contractual law, and hence, unless other provisions in the *B.N.A. Act* later expressly divested the provinces of such rights, the phrase should be understood as possessing the full amplitude of meaning it had in the *Quebec Act*. In acknowledging the jurisdiction of the provinces over matters of local contract, the *Parsons* decision was later to have a highly decentralizing effect.

Both "property" and "civil rights", especially when the latter is defined as in *Parsons*, are broad, generic terms of potentially vast signification. The former would include, really, everything subject to ownership. It would include real property such as land and things affixed to land or growing on land, as well as corporeal and incorporeal personal property, the former being movable and tangible, such as animals, liquor, vehicles, and merchandise, while the latter would include ownership of intangible property such as stocks, bonds, trade marks, and various related abstract interests. "Civil rights" would embrace local contracts including such related things as the sale of goods and the regulation of activities governed by local contracts, such as many business relationships, labour-management disputes, marketing, employment, sports, hoarding, prices, debtor-credit relationships, torts, and matters of status such as adoption. Extensive jurisdiction over the labour relations and social welfare fields has also gravitated to the provinces by judicial decision. Most collective bargaining, certification of locals, strikes, social assistance, child welfare matters, pensions, health care, and unemployment relief, for example, has gone to the provinces under ss. 92(13) and (16).

The great breadth of the above categories has led, at times, to a sober judicial re-examination of their appropriate extension. In upholding the validity of the *Canada Temperance Act*, 1878, although the appellant had argued that the federal prohibition of the sale of intoxicating liquors was an interference with "property and civil rights", Sir Montague Smith observed, "Few, if any, laws could be made by Parliament for the peace, order and good government of Canada which did not in some incidental way affect property and civil rights; and it could not have been intended, when assuring to the provinces exclusive legislative authority on the subjects of property and civil rights, to exclude the Parliament from the exercise of this general power whenever any such incidental interference would result from it. The true nature and character of the legislation in the particular instance under discussion must always be determined, in order to ascertain the class of subject to which it really belongs" (*Russell v. R.* [1882], 7 A.C. 829 at 839-40). One would have to characterize the main features of a law, in other words, in order to determine whether "property" or "civil rights" or some other element was predominant. Similarly, referring to the term "civil rights" in *John Deere Plow Company v. Wharton* (1915), A.C. 330 at 340, Viscount Haldane said: "An abstract logical definition of their scope is, not only, having regard to the context of ss. 91 and 92 of the Act, impracticable, but is certain, if attempted, to cause embarrassment and possible injustice in future cases." When legislating on property and civil rights, in other words, the provinces must take care not to intrude on spheres confided to the federal power which, like copyright (see s. 91(23)), or various agreements concluded by the Government of Canada with its employees, may have proprietary or civil rights aspects, but which more appropriately fall under other heads of the *B.N.A. Act*. Haldane, in fact, coupled his above caveat on the futility of "abstract logical definition" with his characteristic "aspect" approach to ss. 91 and 92: "It must be borne in mind in construing the two sections that matters which in a special aspect and for a particular purpose may fall within one of them may in a different aspect and for different purpose fall within the other" (*ibid.*, 339). The sale of firearms for hunting purposes, for example, would be purely a matter of local contract under property and civil rights, but if the same firearms were knowingly sold for seditious purposes the transaction would fall under the peace, order, and good government clause and the criminal law power. Because of federal paramountcy, in a possible ⟨⟨⟨⟩⟩⟩ of conflict a valid federal law would prevail over a valid provincial one, and provisions ordinarily in the provincial domain but properly ancillary to a valid federal law would, when enacted as part of a valid federal statute, result in the suspension of the provincial law, insofar as there was a repugnancy, as long as the federal law remained in force.[...]

16. Generally matters of a merely local or private nature in the Province.

The term "local" in this subsection may mean either that a law is (a) confined in its incidence and direct effects within the boundaries of the whole province, or (b) of significance only to some locality in a particular part of the province. In *L'Union St-Jacques de Montréal v. Belisle* (1874), L.R. 6 P.C. 31, the granting of financial relief by a provincial statute to a distressed local benefit society incorporated in Quebec was said to be sustainable under s. 92(16), Lord Selborne observing, "Clearly this matter is private; clearly it is local, so far as the locality is to be considered, because it is in the province and the City of Montreal". In a curious 1909 Prince Edward Island case a local statute banning the use of motor vehicles on highways and purporting to be enacted "in the public interest" and for "the safety of the traveling public" was upheld under s. 92(16), the construction, repair, management, and control of highways being described as of "a merely local or private nature in the province". It has been held also that provincial game laws enacted for the conservation of fur-bearing species did not encroach on ss. 91(2) or (27), falling under provincial jurisdiction over woods and forests (ss. 92(5) or 92(16)).

In the *Local Prohibition* case (1896), A.C. 348, Lord Watson upheld Ontario local option legislation for the suppression of the liquor traffic in part under s. 92(16), saying "[i]t is not impossible that the vice of intemperance may prevail in particular localities within a province to such an extent as to constitute its cure by restricting or prohibiting the sale of liquor a matter of a merely local or private nature, and therefore falling prima facie within No. 16". In the same case Watson suggested the logically somewhat implausible "four-compartment" view that clause 16 was performing "the same office" in relation to s. 92 as the peace, order, and good government, or federal "residuary" clause did in s. 91, being supplementary to the enumerated provincial subjects and assigning to the local legislatures all "remaining" matters local or private in the provinces (see the commentary on the preamble to s. 91).

And although, as G.P. Browne has pointed out, it is difficult in a "structural" sense to argue that s. 92(16) has a provincial "residuary" character, since it is on the same textual footing as the other 15 heads of s. 92, all of which precede it, it may come to the same thing. The very generality of the words "[g]enerally all matters of a merely local or private nature in the province" lends the subsection an elasticity or expansibility enabling it to embrace many, though perhaps not all, subjects which are not allocated to the other heads of s. 92. Where, for instance, there are specific limitations on provincial jurisdiction arising from the words used to define a specific head, neither ss. 92(13) or (16) could be used in supplement of that head to fill in the gaps created by such limiting words. Rand's observation in *Reference Re Farm Products Marketing Act* (1957), S.C.R. 198 at 208, that "local trade" could be assigned more aptly to s. 92(16) rather than to s. 92(13), the former having something akin to a provincial residuary character, is instructive. [some cites omitted]

- Research Note -
SECTION 92(16) - THE PROVINCIAL RESIDUARY CLAUSE?

Other writers have made even broader claims with respect to s. 92(16). Professor Lysyk, as he then was, expressed the view that s. 92(16) was intended to function as a provincial counterpart to the "peace, order and good government" clause of section 91, which constitutes a residual category of federal law-making power.

According to this view, the Constitution contains two parallel legislative residua which compete for jurisdiction over matters which are not specifically enumerated in sections 91 and 92. The parallel function of these provisions, however, is not reflected in the format of the Constitutional text: whereas the federal residuum is located in the introductory clause of section 91, the provincial residuum takes the form of an enumerated class of subject assigned to the provinces by section 92.

In the following excerpt from "Constitutional Reform and the Introductory Clause of Section 91" (1979) 57 *Can. Bar Rev.* 531 at 535-537, Professor Lysyk argues that the dissimilar form of the two clauses should not detract from the intention of the Constitutional draughtsmen to create complementary federal and provincial residua.

KENNETH LYSYK, "CONSTITUTIONAL REFORM AND THE INTRODUCTORY CLAUSE OF SECTION 91: RESIDUAL AND EMERGENCY LAW-MAKING AUTHORITY"
(1979) 57 CAN. BAR REV. 531.

The relevant constitutional provisions of the *B.N.A. Act* that I have described as being parallel in function are not parallel in form. As already noted, the federal residuum is located in the introductory clause of section 91, while the provincial residual category takes the form of an enumerated class of subject – the sixteenth and last – assigned to the provincial sphere by section 92 of the *B.N.A. Act*.

The lack of symmetry in these provisions appears to be attributable to "improvements" in form effected by the draughtsman of the *B.N.A. Act*. Both the Resolutions adopted at the London Conference of 1866 and the Resolutions of the Quebec Conference of 1864 by adopting a parallel structure clearly demonstrated an intention to provide for complementary federal and provincial residuums. The antecedents of sections 91 and 92 of the *B.N.A. Act* in the London Resolutions, numbered respectively 28 and 41, read as follows:

28. The federal Parliament shall have power to make laws for the peace, welfare, and good government of the Confederation (saving the sovereignty of England), and especially laws respecting the following subjects: [...]

(36) And generally respecting all matters of a general character not specially and exclusively reserved for the Local Legislatures.

41. The Local Legislatures shall have power to make the following laws respecting the following subjects: [...]

(18) And generally all matters of a private or local nature not assigned to the General Parliament.

The above quoted provisions from the London Resolutions were unchanged from the version adopted earlier at the Quebec Conference. In each case, the final item in the list of subjects assigned to Parliament is a residuum of matters with only two identifying characteristics: first, the matters must be "of a general character" and, second, they must not be matters "specially and exclusively reserved for the Local Legislatures". Similarly, the final item in the list of subjects assigned to the Legislatures is a residuum of matters with just two distinguishing features: first, they comprise matters "of a private or local nature" and, second, they must not be matters "assigned to the General Parliament". The parallel structure of these resolutions makes the intent unmistakable. The first complementary feature is that the federal residuum comprises matters "of a general character" as compared with the provincial residuum which catches matters of "a private or local nature". Assuming that the two clauses were to cover all legislative matters not expressly dealt with in the enumerations or elsewhere in the constitution, it would follow that the reference to matters "of a general character" was intended to be synonymous with, and a shorthand way of describing, all such residual matters other than those "of a private or local nature". The second component of the two residuums is the matching qualifier, making it clear that for purposes of allocating legislative authority specific assignments effected by the enumerations were to be determinative regardless of whether the particular matter was one of a "general character" or one of a "private or local nature".

In casting sections 91 and 92 of the *B.N.A. Act*, the draughtsman departed from the strictly parallel structure of the London and Quebec Resolutions. With respect to the list of provincial powers in section 92, the residuum of local-private matters retained its position as the final item in the enumerations:

92. In each Province the Legislature may exclusively make laws in relation to Matters coming within the Classes of Subject next hereinafter enumerated; that is to say, [...]

(16) Generally all Matters of a merely local or private Nature in the Province.

However, in the section 91 description of Parliament's legislative authority, the residuum appears not as the last of the enumerated classes of subjects but, instead, is contained within the introductory clause.

Relocation of the federal residual power no doubt made the complementary nature of the two residuums somewhat less obvious, but not so obscure as to escape the attention of Lord Watson in the *Local Prohibition* case, where he stated:

> In s. 92, No. 16 appears to [the Justices] to have the same office which the general enactment with respect to matters concerning the peace, order, and good government of Canada, so far as supplementary of the enumerated subjects, fulfils in s. 91. It assigns to the provincial legislature all matters in a provincial sense local or private which have been omitted from the preceding enumeration, and, although its terms are wide enough to cover, they were obviously not meant to include, provincial legislation in relation to the classes of subjects already enumerated.

Lord Watson, evidently (and, it is submitted, quite properly) read sections 91 and 92 as effecting essentially the same kind of distribution which the London and Quebec Resolutions patently called for, that is to say, specific allocations of subjects or classes of subjects to Parliament and to the Legislatures, together with complementary residuums for all matters not caught by the enumerations, such matters outside the enumerations being divided between those local or private in nature (and therefore within provincial competence) and all other matters (assigned to Parliament).

(b)   Matters 'Coming Within' Section 92(13)

CITIZENS INS. CO. v. PARSONS; QUEEN INS. CO. v. PARSONS
(1881), 7 A.C. AT 109-113.

SIR MONTAGUE SMITH [for the Court]: — The main contention on the part of the respondent was that the *Ontario Act* in question had relation to matters coming within the class of subjects described in No. 13 of sect. 92, viz., "Property and civil rights in the province." The Act deals with policies of insurance entered into or in force in the province of Ontario for insuring property situate therein against fire, and prescribes certain conditions which are to form part of such contracts. These contracts, and the rights arising from them, it was argued, came legitimately within the class of subject, "Property and civil rights." The appellants, on the other hand, contended that civil rights meant only such rights as flowed from the law, and gave as an instance the status of persons. Their Lordships cannot think that the latter construction is the correct one. They find no sufficient reason in the language itself, nor in the other parts of the Act, for giving so narrow an interpretation to the words "civil rights." The words are sufficiently large to embrace, in their fair and ordinary meaning, rights arising from contract, and such rights are not included in express terms in any of the enumerated classes of subjects in s. 91.

It becomes obvious, as soon as an attempt is made to construe the general terms in which the classes of subjects in sects. 91 and 92 are described, that both sections and the other parts of the Act must be looked at to ascertain whether language of a general nature must not by necessary implication or reasonable intendment be modified and limited. In looking at the Act, it will be found not only that there is no class including, generally, contracts and the rights arising from them, but that one class of contracts is mentioned and enumerated, viz., "18, bills of exchange and promissory notes," which it would have been unnecessary to specify if authority over all contracts and the rights arising from them had belonged to the dominion parliament.

The provision found in sect. 94 of the *British North America Act*, which is one of the sections relating to the distribution of legislative powers, was referred to by the learned counsel on both sides as throwing light upon the sense in which the words "property and civil rights" are used. By that section the parliament of Canada is empowered to make provision for the uniformity of any laws relative to "property and civil rights" in Ontario, Nova Scotia, and New Brunswick, and to the procedure of the Courts in those three provinces, if the provincial legislatures choose to adopt the provision so made. The province of Quebec is omitted from this section for the obvious reason that the law which governs property and civil rights in Quebec is in the main the French law as it existed at the time of the cession of Canada, and not the English law which prevails in the other provinces. The words "property and civil rights" are, obviously, used in the same sense in this section as in No. 13 of sect. 92, and there seems no reason for presuming that contracts and the rights arising from them were not intended to be included in this provision for uniformity. If, however, the narrow construction of the words "civil rights," contended for by the appellants were to prevail, the dominion parliament could, under its general power, legislate in regard to contracts in all and each of the provinces and as a consequence of this the province of Quebec, though now governed by its own Civil Code, founded on the French law, as regards contracts and their incidents, would be subject to have its law on that subject altered by the dominion legislature, and brought into uniformity with the English law prevailing in the other three provinces, notwithstanding that Quebec has been carefully left out of the uniformity section of the Act.

It is to be observed that the same words, "civil rights," are employed in the Act of 14 Geo. 3, c. 83, which made provision for the Government of the province of Quebec. Sect. 8 of that Act enacted that His Majesty's Canadian subjects within the province of Quebec should enjoy their property, usages, and other civil rights, as they had before done, and that in all matters of controversy relative to property and civil rights resort should be had to the laws of Canada, and be determined agreeably to the said laws. In this statute the words "property" and "civil rights" are plainly used in their largest sense; and there is no reason for holding that in the statute under discussion they are used in a different and narrower one.

The next question for consideration is whether, assuming the *Ontario Act* to relate to the subject of property and civil rights, its enactments and provisions come within any of the classes of subjects enumerated in sect. 91. The only one which the Appellants suggested as expressly including the subject of the *Ontario Act* is No. 2, "the regulation of trade and commerce."

A question was raised which led to much discussion in the Courts below and this bar, viz., whether the business of insuring buildings against fire was a trade. This business, when carried on for the sake of profit, may, no doubt, in some sense of the word, be called a trade. But contracts of indemnity made by insurers can scarcely be considered trading contracts, nor were insurers who made them held to be "traders" under the English bankruptcy laws; they have been made subject to those laws by special description. Whether the business of fire insurance properly falls within the description of a "trade" must, in their Lordships' view, depend upon the sense in which that word is used in the particular statute to be construed; but in the present case their Lordships do not find it necessary to rest their decision on the narrow ground that the business of insurance is not a trade.

The words "regulation of trade and commerce," in their unlimited sense are sufficiently wide, if uncontrolled by the context and other parts of the Act, to include every regulation of trade ranging from political arrangements in regard to trade with foreign governments, requiring the sanction of parliament, down to minute rules for regulating particular trades. But a consideration of the Act shews that the words were not used in this unlimited sense. [...]

Construing therefore the words "regulation of trade and commerce" by the various aids to their interpretation above suggested, they would include political arrangements in regard to trade requiring the sanction of parliament, regulation of trade in matters of interprovincial concern, and it may be that they would include general regulation of trade affecting the whole dominion. Their Lordships abstain on the present occasion from any attempt to define the limits of the authority of the dominion parliament in this direction. It is enough for the decision of the present case to say that, in their view, its authority to legislate for the regulation of trade and commerce does not comprehend the power to regulate by legislation the contracts of a particular business or trade, such as the business of fire insurance in a single province, and therefore that its legislative authority does not in the present case conflict or compete with the power over property and civil rights assigned to the legislature of Ontario by No. 13 of sect. 92.

[In result, their Lordships held that the *Act* was *intra vires* the Province of Ontario.]

BÉDARD v. DAWSON
[1923] S.C.R. 681.

IDINGTON J.: — This action was taken by the respondent Dawson under and by virtue of 10 Geo. V, c. 81 of the Quebec Legislature, entitled "An Act respecting the owners of houses used as disorderly houses," which provides, by sections 2, 3, 4, and 7, as follows: –

> 2. It shall be illegal for any person who owns or occupies any house or building of any nature whatsoever, to use or to allow any person to use the same as a disorderly house. A certified copy of any judgment convicting any person of an offence under section 228, 228*a*, 229 or 229*a* of the *Criminal Code* shall be *prima facie* proof of such use of the house in respect of which such conviction was had.

3. Any person knowing or having reason to believe that any building or part of a building is being made use of as a disorderly house, may send to the registered owner, or to the lessor, or to the agent of the registered owner, or to the lessee of such building, a notice, accompanied by a certified copy of any conviction as aforesaid, if any there be, by registered mail to the last known address of the said owner, agent or lessee, as the case may be.

4. Ten days after the mailing of such notice, if such building or any part thereof still continues to be used as a disorderly house, any person may apply for and obtain an injunction directed to the owner, lessor, lessee or occupant of such building, or to all such persons, restraining them, their heirs, assigns or successors from using or permitting the use of such building or any other building for the purposes above-mentioned.

7. If the judge finds that the use of such building as a disorderly house continues, he shall by his final judgment, in addition to all other orders he is by law empowered to make, order the closing of the said building against its use for any purpose whatsoever for a period of not more than one year from the date of judgment. [...]

I have long entertained the opinion that the provincial legislatures have such absolute power over property and civil rights, as given them by section 92 of the *B.N.A. Act*, item 13 thereof, that so long as they did not in fact encroach upon the powers assigned by the said Act to the Dominion Parliament it would be almost impossible to question any such exercise of power so given unless by the exercise of the veto power given the Dominion Government. That veto power was originally designed to prevent an improper exercise of legislative power by the provincial legislatures.

I, therefore, do not see that if properly interpreted and construed the said Act now in question herein can be said to be *ultra vires*.

There is, however, one aspect of it which rather disturbs me, and that is this: The Act takes certain sections of the *Criminal Code* as the basis of its subject matter and then proceeds to apply convictions thereunder as the basis of its application.

And if, as might well happen, the keeper of the disorderly house so penalized should also be the owner thereof, and this Act applied in such a case, it would look very much like adding as a matter of course to the penalties imposed by Parliament for the offence in question, when Parliament alone is endowed with the power and has imposed on it in so doing the sole responsibility of determining what is the proper measure of punishment.

That, however, is not the case presented on the facts in question herein. I point it out as being the possible cause of future embarrassment and would have preferred to see its enactment somewhat differently framed.

As to the argument addressed to us that the local legislatures cannot legislate to prevent crime, I cannot assent thereto for in a very wide sense it is the duty of the legislature to do the utmost it can within its power to anticipate and remove, so far as practicable, whatever is likely to tend to produce crime; and yet not produce worse forms of it, or tending thereto.

Sometimes we may doubt the wisdom of what is done in that direction and find it in fact productive of crime or a lowering of the usual standard observed by mankind. That possibility may exist in regard to many phases of social life. What we are concerned with herein, however, is merely the question of the power of the legislature so far as the relevant facts raise same. It certainly has, I think, the power called in question herein so far as the relevant facts require. Indeed the duty to protect neighbouring property owners in such cases as are involved in this question before us renders the question hardly arguable.

There are many instances of other nuisances which can be better rectified by local legislation within the power of the legislatures over property and civil rights than by designating them crimes and leaving them to be dealt with by Parliament as such.

Mr. Justice Maclennan and others in the court below have so well presented the exposition of the law as it has been expounded in many well known cases relative to the overlapping of the powers of Parliament and local legislatures, that I need not repeat the citation of cases here.

I think the appeal should be dismissed with costs to the intervenant. [...]

ANGLIN J. — [...] I am of the opinion that this statute in no wise impinges on the domain of criminal law but is concerned exclusively with the control and enjoyment of property and the safeguarding of the community from the consequences of an illegal and injurious use being made of it – a pure matter of civil right. In my opinion in enacting the statute now under consideration the legislature exercised the power which it undoubtedly possesses to provide for the suppression of a nuisance and the prevention of its recurrence by civil process.

The appeal fails and should be dismissed with costs.

[The concurring opinions of Duff, Brodeur and Mignault JJ. are omitted.]

MCNEIL v. N.S. BD. OF CENSORS
[1978] 2 S.C.R. 662.

RITCHIE J. [Martland, Pigeon, Beetz and de Grandpré JJ. concurring]: — This is an appeal brought with leave of this Court from a judgment of the Appeal Division of the Supreme Court of Nova Scotia rendered pursuant to an application made at the instance of the respondent McNeil whose standing to initiate the proceedings in a representative capacity on behalf of other Nova Scotians was confirmed by order of this Court (see [1976] 2 S.C.R. 265).

The respondent's application was for a declaration that certain sections of the *Theatres and Amusements Act*, R.S.N.S. 1967, c. 304 as amended, and certain Regulations made thereunder were ultra virus and beyond the legislative competence of the Province of Nova Scotia.

The exciting cause of the application appears to have been the exercise by the Nova Scotia Amusements Regulation Board (hereinafter referred to as "the Board") of the authority which the Act purports to confer on it, to prevent a film entitled "Last Tango in Paris" from being exhibited in the theatres of Nova Scotia.

Maria Schneider and Marlon Brando in
Last Tango in Paris

It is the statutory provisions purporting to authorize the Board to regulate and control the film industry within the Province of Nova Scotia according to standards fixed by it, which are challenged by the respondent on the ground that the citizens of Nova Scotia are thereby denied, on moral grounds, their right to exercise their freedom of choice in the viewing of films and theatre performances which might otherwise be available to them, and it is further alleged that the legislation constitutes an invasion of fundamental freedoms. [...]

When the Act and the Regulations are read as a whole, I find them to be primarily directed to the regulation, supervision and control of the film business within the Province of Nova Scotia, including the use and exhibition of films in that Province. To this end the impugned provisions are in my view enacted for the purpose of reinforcing the authority vested in a provincially appointed Board to perform the task of regulation which includes the authority to prevent the exhibition of films which the Board, applying its own local standards, has rejected as unsuitable for viewing by provincial audiences. This legislation is concerned with dealings in and the use of property (i.e. films) which take place wholly within the Province and in my opinion it is subject to the same considerations as those which were held to be applicable in such cases as *Shannon v. Lower Mainland Dairy Products Board, Home Oil Distributors Limited v. A.G. of British Columbia* and *Caloil Inc. v. Attorney General of Canada*.

In the *Shannon* case, the Natural Products Marketing legislation was put in issue as constituting an encroachment on "the regulation of trade and commerce" a subject assigned exclusively to the Parliament of Canada by s. 91(2), and in the course of delivering the opinion of the Judicial Committee, Lord Atkin had occasion to say of this ground:

> It is sufficient to say upon first ground that it is apparent that the legislation in question is confined to regulating transactions that take place wholly within the Province, and are therefore within the sovereign powers granted to the Legislature in that respect by s. 92 of the *British North America Act*.

More recently, in commenting on that case and the *Home Oil* case (supra) Mr. Justice Pigeon had occasion to say in *Caloil Inc. v. Attorney General of Canada*, at p. 519:

> It is to be noted that the *Shannon* and *Home Oil* cases both dealt with the validity of provincial regulation of local trades. They hold that provincial authority over transactions taking place wholly within the province is, as a rule, applicable to products imported from another country, or brought in from another province, as well as to local products. However, it must be borne in mind that the division of constitutional authority under the Canadian Constitution often results in overlapping legislation.

It will be seen that, in my opinion, the impugned legislation constitutes nothing more than the exercise of provincial authority over transactions taking place wholly within the province and it applies to the "regulating, exhibition, sale and exchange of films" whether those films have been imported from another country or not.

We are concerned however in this appeal with a decision of the Appeal Division of the Supreme Court of Nova Scotia in which the majority quite clearly struck down the legislation as *ultra vires* on the sole ground that it was concerned with morality and as such constituted an invasion of the criminal law field reserved to the exclusive legislative authority of Parliament under s. 91(27) of the *B.N.A. Act*. [...]

Issue

Simply put, the issue raised by the majority opinion in the Appeal Division is whether the Province is clothed with authority under s. 92 of the *British North America Act* to regulate the exhibition and distribution of films within its own boundaries which are considered unsuitable for local viewing by a local Board on grounds of morality or whether this is a matter of criminal law reserved to Parliament under s. 91(27). [...]

[M]orality and criminality are far from coextensive and it follows in my view that legislation which authorizes the establishment and enforcement of a local standard of morality in the exhibition of films is not necessarily "an invasion of the federal criminal field" as Chief Justice MacKeigan thought it to be in this case.

Even if I accepted the view that the impugned legislation is concerned with criminal morality, it would still have to be noted that it is preventive rather than penal and the authority of the Province to pass legislation directed towards prevention of crime is illustrated by the case of *Bédard v. Dawson*, which was concerned with the validity of a statute of the Province of Quebec entitled "An Act respecting the owners of houses used as disorderly houses", by which the judge was authorized to order the closing of a disorderly house. The legislation was held to be *intra vires* on the ground that it was concerned with property within the Province and Mr. Justice Anglin said, at p. 685:

[...] I am of the opinion that this statute in no wise impinges on the domain of criminal law but is concerned exclusively with the control and enjoyment of property and the safeguarding of the community from the consequences of an illegal and injurious use being made of it – a pure matter of civil right. In my opinion in enacting the statute now under consideration the legislature exercised the power which it undoubtedly possesses to provide for the suppression of a nuisance and the prevention of its recurrence by civil process. [...]

As I have already said, I take the view that the impugned legislation is not concerned with criminality. The rejection of films by the Board is based on a failure to conform to the standards of propriety which it has itself adopted and this failure cannot be said to be "an act prohibited with penal consequences" by the Parliament of Canada either in enacting the *Criminal Code* or otherwise. This is not to say that Parliament is in any way restricted in its authority to pass laws penalizing immoral acts or conduct, but simply that the provincial government in regulating a local trade may set its own standards which in no sense exclude the operation of the federal law.

There is, in my view, no constitutional barrier preventing the Board from rejecting a film for exhibition in Nova Scotia on the sole ground that it fails to conform to standards of morality which the Board itself has fixed notwithstanding the fact that the film is not offensive to any provision of the *Criminal Code*; and, equally, there is no constitutional reason why a prosecution cannot be brought under s. 163 of the *Criminal Code* in respect of the exhibition of a film which the Board of Censors has approved as conforming to its standards of propriety. [...]

Holding

It will be seen that in my view the impugned legislation "has for its true object, purpose, nature and character" the regulation and control of a local trade and that it is therefore valid provincial legislation. [...]

As I have said, I take the view that the legislation here in question is in pith and substance directed to property and civil rights and therefore valid under s. 92(13) of the *British North America Act*. [...]

LASKIN C.J.C. [Judson, Spence and Dickson JJ. concurring]: — What is involved, as I have already noted, is an unqualified power in the Nova Scotia Board to determine the fitness of films for public viewing on considerations that may extend beyond the moral and may include the political, the social and the religious. Giving its assertion of power the narrowest compass, related to the film in the present case, the Board is asserting authority to protect public morals, to safeguard the public from exposure to films, to ideas and images in films, that it regards as morally offensive, as indecent, probably as obscene.

The determination of what is decent or indecent or obscene in conduct or in a publication, what is morally fit for public viewing, whether in films, in art or in a live performance is, as such, within the exclusive power of the Parliament of Canada under its enumerated authority to legislate in relation to the criminal law. This has been recognized in a line of cases in which, beginning with the seminal case of *Attorney-General of Ontario v. Hamilton Street Rwy.*, (where it was said that it is the criminal law in the widest sense that falls within exclusive federal authority), the criminal law power has been held to be as much a brake on provincial legislation as a source of federal legislation. [...]

It is beside the point to urge that morality is not co-extensive with the criminal law. Such a contention cannot of itself bring legislation respecting public morals within provincial competence. Moreover, the federal power in relation to the criminal law extends beyond control of morality, and is wide enough to embrace anti-social conduct or behaviour and has, indeed, been exercised in those respects.

Films have been held to fall within s. 159 of the *Criminal Code*, dealing with obscene publications: see *R. v. Fraser; R. v. Goldberg and Reitman; Daylight Theatre Co. Ltd. v. The Queen*. Indeed, the very film, Last Tango in Paris, out of which this case arose, was the subject of a prosecution under s. 159 which was unsuccessful: see *R. v. Odeon Morton Theatres Ltd.* I draw attention as well to s. 163 of the *Criminal Code* dealing with the presentation or giving of immoral, indecent or obscene performances, entertainments or representations, and it seems to me that if films are within s. 159 they are *a fortiori* within s. 163. This is indicated in *St. Leonard v. Fournier*, where the New Brunswick Appeal Division held that a municipal theatre licensing by-law, which authorized cancellation of a licence for a moving picture theatre where an immoral, profane or indecent show or performance takes place, was invalid in the face of what is now s. 163 of the *Criminal Code*. The by-law provisions considered in *St. Leonard v. Fournier* are similar to the provisions of Regulation 32 herein coupled with the sanction of s. 20 of the *Nova Scotia Act* by way of cancellation of licence. This is not a case where civil consequences are attached to conduct defined and punished as criminal under federal legislation, as in *McDonald v. Down*, but rather a case where a provincially authorized tribunal itself defines and determines legality, what is permissible and what is not. This, in my view, is a direct intrusion into the field of criminal law. At best, what the challenged Nova Scotia legislation is doing is seeking to supplement the criminal law enacted by Parliament, and this is forbidden: see *Johnson v. Attorney-General of Alberta*, per Rand J. at p. 138 (see also *St. Leonard v. Fournier*, supra, at p. 320). [...]

It does not follow from all of the foregoing that provincial legislative authority may not extend to objects where moral considerations are involved, but those objects must in themselves be anchored in the provincial catalogue of powers and must, moreover, not be in conflict with valid federal legislation. It is impossible in the present case to find any such anchorage in the provisions of the Nova Scotia Statute that are challenged, and this apart from the issue of conflict which, I think, arises in relation to ss. 159 and 163 of the *Criminal Code*. What is asserted, by way of tying the challenged provisions to valid provincial regulatory control, is that the Province is competent to licence the use of premises, and entry into occupations, and may in that connection determine what shall be exhibited in those premises. This hardly touches the important issue raised by the present case and would, if correct, equally justify control by the Province of any conduct and activity in licensed premises even if not related to the property aspect of licensing, and this is patently indefensible. Moreover, what is missing from this assertion by the appellant is a failure to recognize that the censorship of films takes place without relation to any premises and is a direct prior control of public taste. *Bédard v. Dawson,* which was heavily relied on by the appellant, does not assist the provincial contention because there, in the view of this Court at the time, the challenged provincial legislation related to the occupation and enjoyment of premises, and it was distinguished on that account from the wider legislation that was invalidated by this Court in *Switzman v. Elbling,* supra. [...]

Much more relevant here than the principle sought to be applied on the basis of *Bédard v. Dawson,* supra, is that which is reflected in *Henry Birks and Sons (Montreal) Ltd. v. Montreal.* In invalidating provincial prohibitory legislation directed to compulsory observance of certain religious or feast days this Court made it clear that a tenuous connection with property (the operation of shops and businesses) will not save provincial legislation which is paramountly directed to religious or moral observance. Even the tenuous connection with property in the Birks case is absent here. [...] It is not enough to save the challenged prohibitory provisions of the Nova Scotia Statute, if they are otherwise invalid, that they are part of a legislative scheme which embraces licensing of theatres and of motion picture projectionists. As I have already noted, the provisions now challenged go beyond the licensing provisions and engage the public directly. [...]

[**Note**: See *Westendorp v. R.,* infra at p. 753. See also *R. v. Morgentaler* (1993), p. 704 for further consideration of provincial power to regulate morality as a "local and private matter in the province".]

- Research Note -
RIO HOTEL LTD. v. N.B. (LIQUOR LICENSING BD.) AND LOCAL MORALITY

In *Rio Hotel Ltd. v. N.B. (Liquor Licensing Bd.),* [1987] 2 S.C.R. 59, the Supreme Court of Canada upheld as a valid exercise of provincial jurisdiction over property and civil rights a provincial liquor licensing board's prohibition of nude dancing as a condition on entertainment licences. See, infra, at p. 671 under "Criminal Law".

In the principal judgment of the Court, Dickson C.J.C. (McIntyre, Wilson and Le Dain JJ. concurring) stated at p. 65:

> The legislation is [...] *prima facie* related to property and civil rights within the Province and to matters of a purely local nature. The Legislature seeks only to regulate the forms of entertainment that may be used as marketing tools by the owners of licensed premises to boost sales of alcohol. Although there is some overlap between the licence condition precluding nude entertainment and various provisions of the [*Criminal*] *Code,* there is no direct conflict.

As the provincial regulations could easily operate concurrently with the federal *Criminal Code* provisions, Dickson C.J.C. held that the federal paramountcy doctrine did not operate to render the provincial regulations invalid.

In a separate judgment, Estey J. (Lamer J. concurring) did not find it necessary to rely on the doctrine of paramountcy to uphold the provincial regulations. He held that the licensing system did not purport to establish an offence criminal in character, but was instead related entirely to the local operations of premises engaged in the business of selling alcohol.

At p. 75, Estey J. considered the case of *McNeil v. N.S. Bd. of Censors*, [1978] 2 S.C.R. 662, and raised some doubt as to the ability of the provinces to regulate with respect to local morality under the authority of s. 92(16):

> The five member majority of the Court [in *McNeil*] held the legislation (except for one regulation) to be *intra vires* the province on the basis that the impugned legislation addressed the regulation of a trade or business within the province, properly falling within the scope of s. 92(13) of the *Constitution Act, 1867*. The Court also found the legislation valid on the grounds that it was regulatory and preventative rather than penal; the legislation was not concerned with creating a criminal offence or providing for its punishment. [...] Finally, the Court upheld the legislation as addressing the determination of "what is and what is not acceptable for public exhibition on moral grounds", this being a matter of a "local and private nature in the Province" within the meaning of s. 92(16) of the *Constitution Act, 1867*. The most persuasive ground upon which to uphold this legislation is that the regulation relates to the valid regulation of a trade or business within the province. It is possible that the reference to the provincial jurisdiction over the morality of the public exhibition in question, as being a matter of a "local and private nature", could be distinguished. It may well be (although it is not necessary, in my view, to decide so now) that this point in *McNeil* will be confined by the courts to the precise facts of that case.

A.G. QUE. V. KELLOGG'S CO.
[1978] 2 S.C.R. 211.

[The Quebec government adopted a regulation under the *Consumer Protection Act* aimed at regulating, *inter alia*, advertising intended for children. Paragraph (n) of s. 11.53 of this regulation provided that no one shall "use [...] advertising intended for children which [...] employs cartoons". The Attorney General of Quebec filed four complaints against Kellogg's Co., alleging breaches of this regulation in connection with televised advertisements of their products. The Attorney General of Quebec also sought an injunction against Kellogg's to restrain the commission of further infractions.]

MARTLAND J. [Ritchie, Pigeon, Dickson, Beetz and de Grandpré JJ. concurring]: — [...] [It] is not necessary to consider the general power of a province to exercise control over advertising in Quebec intended for children. The provincial power to enact such legislation under s. 92(13) and (16), if not under s. 93, of the *British North America Act* would appear to be clear. The basic issue is as to whether a provincial law restricting the type of advertising intended for children which may be used by a manufacturer or vendor of goods within the province can preclude him from advertising, by means of television, in breach of the restriction.

The majority of the Court of Appeal took the view that the regulation in question was an attempt to legislate on the content of broadcasting, that this was a matter exclusively within federal legislative power and that the appellant was not entitled to its injunction. [...]

[The Justice next reviewed the decision of the Supreme Court of Canada in *Capital Cities Communications Inc. v. C.R.T.C.*, [1978] 2 S.C.R. 141; *Public Service Bd. v. Dionne*, [1978] 2 S.C.R. 191].

The cases to which I have referred specifically above all dealt with the legislative power to regulate and control broadcast undertakings engaged in the transmission and reception of radio or television signals. That power is not in issue in the present case. What is in issue here is the power of a provincial legislature to regulate and control the conduct of a commercial enterprise in respect of its business activities within the province. The majority of the Court of Appeal appears to hold the view that the federal power in respect of the broadcast undertaking is decisive. I do not think that it is. [...]

As its name indicates, the purpose of the *Consumer Protection Act* is the protection of consumers in Quebec by regulating the commercial conduct of persons engaged in the sale of goods in that province. Part of this regulation involves the control of the advertising which is used in effecting such sales. Paragraph (*n*), under attack in this case, is one of several restrictions imposed in connection with advertising intended for children. It forbids the use of a particular kind of advertising considered to have a special appeal to children.

In my opinion this regulation does not seek to regulate or to interfere with the operation of a broadcast undertaking. In relation to the facts of this case it seeks to prevent Kellogg from using a certain kind of advertising by any means. It aims at controlling the commercial activity of Kellogg. The fact that Kellogg is precluded from using televised advertising may, incidentally, affect the revenue of one or more television stations but it does not change the true nature of the regulation. In this connection the case of *Carnation Company Ltd. v. The Quebec Agricultural Marketing Board* is analogous.

Kellogg is not exempted from the application of restriction upon its advertising practices because it elects to advertise through a medium which is subject to federal control. A person who caused defamatory material to be published by means of a televised program would not be exempted from liability under provincial law because the means of publication were subject to federal control. Further, he could be enjoined from repeating the publication. In my opinion the position of Kellogg in relation to this regulation is analogous. It cannot justify conduct which has been rendered illegal because it is using the medium of television.

In my opinion par. (*n*) is within the power of the province to enact and applies to all persons who employ advertising as a means of selling their goods in the Province of Quebec.

(c)   The Territorial Limit: "Within the Province"

ROYAL BANK v. R.
[1913] A.C. 283 (P.C.).

[In 1909, an Act of the Legislature of Alberta incorporated the Alberta and Great Railway Company. A second Act of the same year authorized the Government of Alberta to guarantee the principal and interest on bonds to be issued by the railway, the proceeds of which were to be used to construct a rail line wholly within the province. A subsequent Order in Council designated certain banks, including the appellant, to receive the proceeds arising from the issue of the bonds in London. To this end, a special railway account was opened in the Alberta branch of the appellant bank in the name of the Provincial Treasurer. The proceeds of the bond issue in London were received at the New York branch of the appellant bank and were credited to the railway account. No money *in specie* was sent to the branch office in Alberta.

Following a change of government in Alberta in 1910, new legislation was enacted. After setting out in its preamble that the railway company had defaulted in payment of interest on the bonds and in the construction of the line, the Act (1 Geo. 5, c. 9) provided that the whole of the proceeds of the sale of the bonds and all interest thereon standing in the bank in the name of the Provincial Treasurer should form part of the general revenue fund of the province free from all claims of the railway company, and should be paid over to the Treasurer without deduction. Shortly thereafter, notice was served on the bank claiming payment of the money. The bank refused. In the ensuing action by the Crown and Provincial Treasurer, the appellant bank pleaded that the Act of 1910 was *ultra vires* in that, *inter alia*, it was not confined to property and civil rights within the province.

The trial judge rejected this defence and found for the plaintiffs. The appellants appealed to the Court of Appeal, which unanimously dismissed the appeal. A further appeal was then taken to the Privy Council.]

VISCOUNT HALDANE L.C. [for the Court]: — [...] Their Lordships are not concerned with the merits of the political controversy which gave rise to the statute the validity of which is impeached. What they have to decide is the question whether it was within the power of the Legislature of the province to pass the Act of 1910. They agree with the contention of the respondents that in a case such as this it was in the power of that Legislature subsequently to repeal any Act which it had passed. If this were the only question which arose the appeal could be disposed of without difficulty. But the Act under consideration does more than modify existing legislation. It purports to appropriate to the province the balance standing at the special accounts in the banks, and so to change its position under the scheme to carry out which the bondholders had subscribed their money. Elaborately as the case was argued in the judgments of the learned judges in the Courts below, their Lordships are not satisfied that what appears to them to be the fundamental question at issue has been adequately considered.

Richard Burdon Haldane,
Viscount Haldane (1856-1928),
Author of many Privy Council
opinions on Canada's
Constitution.

It is a well-established principle of the English common law that when money has been received by one person which in justice and equity belongs to another, under circumstances which render the receipt of it a receipt by the defendant to the use of the plaintiff, the latter may recover as for money had and received to his use. The principle extends to cases where the money has been paid for a consideration that has failed. It applies, as was pointed out by Brett L.J. in *Wilson v. Church*, when money has been paid to borrowers in consideration of the undertaking of a scheme to be carried into effect subsequently to the payment and which has become abortive. The lender has in this case a right to claim the return of the money in the hands of the borrowers as being held to his use. *Wilson v. Church*, which was affirmed in the House of Lords under the name of *National Bolivian Navigation Co. v. Wilson*, is an excellent illustration of the principle. A loan had been raised to make a foreign railway, on a prospectus which set out a concession by the foreign Government in virtue of which the bondholders were to have the benefit of certain Customs duties. The foreign Government, finding that the railway had not been made, revoked the concession. The trustees, to whom the money had been paid to be expended on the gradual construction of the railway, contended that it was not apparent that they could not with certain variations substantially carry out the scheme. It was held that while the Government had a right to revoke the concession, which could not be questioned, the effect of its so doing was materially to vary the prospects and terms of security of the bondholders, and that the question whether the scheme had become so abortive that the consideration for the advances had failed must be determined, not merely by a survey of physical or financial consideration, but by reference to the conditions originally stipulated for. The bondholders were declared to be entitled to recover their money.

The present case appears to their Lordships to fall within the broad principle on which the judgments in that case proceeded. The lenders in London remitted their money to New York to be applied in carrying out the particular scheme which was established by the statutes of 1909 and the Orders in Council, and by the contracts and mortgage of that year. The money claimed in the action was paid to the appellant bank as one of those designated to act in carrying out the scheme. The bank received the money at its branch in New York, and its general manager then gave instructions from the head office in Montreal to the manager of one of its local branches, that at Edmonton in the Province of Alberta, for the opening of the credit for the special account. The local manager was told that he was to act on instructions from the head office, which retained control. It appears to their Lordships that the special account was opened solely for the purposes of the scheme, and that when the action of the Government in 1910 altered its conditions, the lenders in London were entitled to claim from the bank at its head office in Montreal the money which they had advanced solely for a purpose which had ceased to exist. Their right was a civil right outside the province, and the Legislature of the province could not legislate validly in derogation of that right. These circumstances distinguish the case from that of *Rex v. Lovitt*, where the point decided was in reality quite a different one.

In the opinion of their Lordships the effect of the statute of 1910, if validly enacted, would have been to preclude the bank from fulfilling its legal obligation to return their money to the bondholders, whose right to this return was a civil right which had arisen, and remained enforceable outside the province. The statute was on this ground beyond the powers of the Legislature of Alberta, inasmuch as what was sought to be enacted was neither confined to property and civil rights within the province nor directed solely to matters of merely local or private nature within it. [...]

Their Lordships will humbly advise His Majesty that the appeal should be allowed and the action dismissed. [...]

LADORE v. BENNETT
[1939] A.C. 468 (P.C.).

[*The City of Windsor (Amalgamation) Act, 1935*, S.O. 1935, c. 74 amalgamated four municipalities into the City of Windsor. Those municipalities were in financial difficulties and were unable to meet their debenture interest and maturing principle, part of which was payable outside the province. A second Act, *The City of Windsor (Amalgamation) Amendment Act, 1936, S.O. 1936*, c. 66 gave power to the Ontario Municipal Board to order the exchange of new debentures for outstanding debentures and to vary the terms of payment and interest rate in the outstanding indebtedness of any municipality which had failed to meet its debentures or interest due to financial difficulties. The Ontario Municipal Board approved a scheme for restructuring the debts of the old independent municipalities, under which former creditors of the old municipalities would receive debentures of the new City of an equal amount to those formerly held, but with the interest reduced. The *Amalgamation Acts* were challenged by the debenture holders on the grounds, *inter alia*, that the legislation deals with rights outside the province.]

LORD ATKIN: — [...] The Province has exclusive legislative power in relation to municipal institutions in the Province: s. 92(8) of the *British North America Act, 1867*. Sovereign within its constitutional powers, the province is charged with the local government of its inhabitants by means of municipal institutions. If local government in any particular area becomes ineffective or non-existent because of the financial difficulties of one or more municipal institutions, or for any other reason, it is not only the right, but it would appear to be the duty, of the Provincial Legislature to provide the necessary remedy, so that the health of the inhabitants and the necessities of organized life in communities should be preserved. If corporation A or B or C is unable to function satisfactorily it would appear to be elementary that the Legislature must have power to provide that the functions of one or all should be transferred to some other body or corporation. For this purpose, as the corporation could be created by the Province, so it could be dissolved, and a new corporation created as a municipal institution to perform the duties performed by the old. The result of dissolution is that the debts of the dissolved corporation disappear. Amalgamation of municipalities for the purpose of more effective administration, whether for financial or other reasons, is a common incident of local government. It is necessarily accompanied by an adjustment of financial relations. Where the former bodies are dissolved it is inevitable that the old debts disappear, to be replaced by new obligations of the new body. And in creating the new corporation with the powers of assuming new obligations it is implicit in the powers of the Legislature (sovereign in this respect) that it should place restrictions and qualifications on the obligations to be assumed. Efficient local government could not be provided in similar circumstances unless the Province were armed with these very powers, and if for strictly Provincial purposes debts may be destroyed and new debts created, it is inevitable that debtors should be affected whether the original creditors reside within or without the Province. They look for their debtor a corporation which at the will of the Province could lawfully be dissolved, and of its destruction they took the risk. That for the purpose of keeping control over municipal institutions the Legislature provided that a department of the Provincial government should have the means of ascertaining whether a particular municipal body was solvent or insolvent does not make its legislative provision in that regard an encroachment on the general powers of the Dominion over bankruptcy and insolvency. It is of the essence of its control over local government administered by municipalities that it should have these powers of inquiry and decision. In other words, the pith and substance of both the Amalgamation Acts and the *Municipal Board Act, 1932,* and the *Department of Municipal Affairs Act, 1935,* are that the Acts are passed in relation to municipal institutions in the Province. They would also, so far as the public utility commissions are concerned, be justified as having been passed in relation to local works and undertakings under s. 92(10) of the *British North America Act.*

It was suggested in argument that the impugned provisions should be declared invalid because they sought to do indirectly what could not be done directly – namely, to facilitate repudiation by Provincial municipalities of obligations incurred outside the Province. It is unnecessary to repeat what has been said many times by the Courts in Canada and by the Board, that the Courts will be careful to detect and invalidate any actual violation of constitutional restrictions under pretence of keeping within the statutory field. A colourable device will not avail. But in the present case nothing has emerged even to suggest that the Legislature of Ontario at the respective dates had any purpose in view other than to legislate in times of difficulty in relation to the class of subject which was its special care – namely, municipal institutions. For the reasons given the attack upon the Acts and scheme on the ground either that they infringe the Dominion's exclusive power relating to bankruptcy and insolvency, or that they deal with civil rights outside the Province, breaks down. The statutes are not directed to insolvency legislation; they pick out insolvency as one reason for dealing in a particular way with unsuccessful institutions; and though they affect rights outside the Province they only so affect them collaterally, as a necessary incident to their lawful powers of good government within the Province.

The question of interest does not present difficulties. The above reasoning sufficiently disposes of the objection. If the Provincial Legislature can dissolve a municipal corporation and create a new one to take its place, it can invest the new corporation which such powers of incurring obligations as it pleases, and incidentally may define the amount of interest which such obligations may bear. Such legislation, if directed bona fide to the effective creation and control of municipal institutions, is in no way an encroachment upon the general exclusive power of the Dominion Legislature over interest.

For these reasons their Lordships will humbly advise His Majesty that the appeal should be dismissed. The appellants must pay the costs of the appeal.

INTERPROVINCIAL CO-OP. LTD. v. R.
[1976] 1 S.C.R. 477.

PIGEON J. [Martland and Beetz, JJ, concurring]: — The action herein is founded on the allegation that the defendants, the appellants in this Court, caused damage to Manitoba's fisheries by allowing mercury to be discharged from their respective chlor-alkali plants in Saskatchewan and Ontario which mercury was carried into Manitoba by the natural flow of the rivers in which the discharge took place.

In addition to the common law, Manitoba relies on what I will call the *Assistance Act*, a statute passed by its Legislature in 1970, entitled the *Fishermen's Assistance and Polluters' Liability Act*, 1970 (Man.), c. 32 [Continuing Consolidation F100]. It is there provided that Manitoba may recover as damages caused by pollution the amount of assistance payments made to fishermen or the actual loss, whichever is greater.

[Section 4(1) of this Act reads:

In any suit in which the government is a plaintiff wherein the pollution of water is in issue, if it is established by the degree of proof required in a civil suit that the defendant has without lawful excuse, the proof whereof lies on him, discharged or permitted the discharge of any contaminant is carried into waters in the province, and that thereafter fishing those waters have suffered death, disease or injury, or contamination rendering them unfit or unsafe for human consumption, or any adverse effect whereby they are rendered less marketable, the defendant is liable for all financial loss occasioned thereby to any person whose loss is a subject matter of the suit, notwithstanding any one or more of the following circumstances: (a) At no time did that person have any proprietary interest in the fishery containing the affected fish; (b) A regulatory authority has forbidden or refused to permit the taking of fish from that fishery by reason of the pollution of the waters thereof; (c) Those waters have been, or are being polluted from any other cause or by any other person; (d) It cannot be established that the contaminant affecting the fish derived from the actual volume of contaminant which the defendant discharged or permitted to be discharged from premises occupied by him, provided the deleterious effect on the fish is of a nature consistent with a contaminant of that kind being the total or partial, immediate or mediate cause.

Section 4(2) of the Act reads:

For the purposes of subsection (1) it is not a lawful excuse for the defendant to show that the discharge of the contaminant was permitted by the appropriate regulatory authority having jurisdiction at the place where the discharge occurred, if that regulatory authority did not also have jurisdiction at the place where the contaminant caused damage to the fishery.]

A statutory liability is created against any person having discharged a contaminant either "into waters in the province or into any waters whereby it is carried into waters in the province". It is also provided that it is not a lawful excuse "to show that the discharge of the contaminant was permitted by the appropriate regulatory authority having jurisdiction at the place where the discharge occurred, if that regulatory authority did not also have jurisdiction at the place where the contaminant caused damage to the fishery."

On a motion to strike out the allegations related to the *Assistance Act*, Matas, J. (as he then was), held that the Act was beyond the powers of the Manitoba Legislature as purporting to deny to the defendants the benefit of civil rights outside of Manitoba, that is the authorization presumably issued by the appropriate authority under the laws of the Province in which each plant was operated [[1972] 5 W.W.R. 541].

On appeal, the majority upheld the validity of the *Assistance Act*, Guy, J.A., dissenting [[1973] 3 W.W.R. 673]. Freedman, C.J.M., with whom Dickson, J.A. (as he then was), expressed agreement, said [at p. 383], after referring to *Cowen et al. v. A.-G. B.C. et al.*, [1941] S.C.R. 321: "The *Assistance Act* is similarly directed against acts done within the Province." Hall, J.A., with whom Monnin, J.A., concurred, said [at p. 400]:

> In my opinion, the impugned statute in the context of the assumed facts is valid provincial legislation and does not offend any doctrine of territorial limitation. To the extent that such limitation may exist it does not debar the Manitoba Legislature from enacting legislation imposing obligations in respect of acts done outside the Province on persons or corporations who are domiciled or resident in the Province. The Courts of Manitoba can and do entertain actions and award damages for torts committed abroad, from which it follows that the Manitoba Legislature is competent to define the conditions on which damages in such actions should be awarded, in so far as the matter relates to property and civil rights in the Province and to subjects of a local and private nature therein.

With respect, I fail to see how the *Assistance Act* can be said in the present case to be directed against acts done within Manitoba. The essential provision on which Manitoba relies to claim against the appellants is the discharge of a contaminant from premises outside Manitoba into waters whereby it is carried into waters in the Province. While it can be said that the legislation is aimed at damage caused in Manitoba, it is not directed against acts done in that Province: the basic provision on which the claim is founded is an act done outside the Province, namely, the discharge of the contaminant. In my view, the situation is totally unlike that which obtained in the *Cowen* case. He was a dentist practicing in Spokane, State of Washington, but the acts complained of were advertisements published in a newspaper at Nelson, B.C. Duff C.J.C., speaking for the Court, carefully delineated the ambit of the decision saying (at pp. 689-90 D.L.R., pp. 323-4 S.C.R.):

> The decisive [sic] consideration, in my opinion, is that the prohibitions are directed against acts done within the Province, *prima facie* the legislation is within the provincial legislative sphere. Nor do I think (subject to an observation to be made upon one feature of the amending statute) there is any

circumstance present here which has the effect of rebutting this *prima facie* conclusion. The statute does not profess to prohibit people going beyond the limits of British Columbia for the purpose of getting the benefit of the services of a dentist, or to regulate their conduct in doing so; nor does it prohibit the sending into British Columbia from abroad of newspapers and journals containing the advertising cards of practising dentists; nor does it prohibit any communication with British Columbia from abroad. *Such prohibitions would present an entirely different question.*

There is one feature of the statute to which it is desirable to advert. By s. 63 of the principal Act, which is now s. 63(1), there is a definition of "practising the profession of dentistry within the meaning of this Act." By s. 2 of the amending Act of 1939, s. 63 is amended by bringing within the category of persons who are deemed to be practising dentistry within the meaning of the Act. "Any person. [...] who supplies or offers to supply to the public artificial teeth, dentures or repairs therefor."

It would seem to be at least arguable that the statute as amended in 1939 prohibits the publication in British Columbia by persons carrying on business outside the Province of advertisements stating that they are manufacturers of or dealers in dental supplies of the description or descriptions mentioned. It is unnecessary to consider this aspect of the amendments of 1939. It might be argued, not without plausibility, that any prohibition of the publication in British Columbia of such advertisements in respect of articles of commerce is legislation in relation to a matter that is not a local British Columbia matter, within the contemplation of ss. 91 and 92 of the *B.N.A. Act*. Assuming the amending legislation is to be *pro tanto* invalid by reason of this particular feature of it, the offending parts seem to be plainly severable; and no such question is raised by the advertisements before us. (Italics added).

As to the extent of the constitutional authority that can be derived from the presence of the appellants within Manitoba, it is necessary, in my view, to bear in mind that the fact that a party is amenable to the jurisdiction of the Courts of a Province does not mean that the Legislature of that Province has unlimited authority over the matter to be adjudicated upon. The authority conferred by s. 92(14), *British North America Act, 1867*, is limited to "The Administration of Justice in the Province, including the Constitution, Maintenance, and Organization of Provincial Courts, both of Civil and of Criminal Jurisdiction, and including Procedure in Civil Matters in those Courts." This certainly does not include the substantive law to be applied. The authority over substantive law must be derived from the other enumerated heads. This is implicit in the judgment of the Privy Council in *Royal Bank of Canada et al. v. The King* (1913), [1913] A.C. 283. The bank had a place of business in Alberta and was undoubtedly amenable to the jurisdiction of the Supreme Court of that Province in which the action was brought. Nevertheless, it was held that the Legislature could not preclude the bank from fulfilling its legal obligation to return the money to the bond owners whose right to this return was a civil right which had arisen and remained enforceable outside the Province. [...]

In my view, a statement of great importance with respect to the territorial limitation of provincial legislative authority is to be found in the judgment delivered for the Court by Duff, C.J.C., in *The King v. National Trust Co.*, [1933] S.C.R. 670. In that case, the question was as to the extent of the power of "Direct Taxation within the Province" as applicable to property. At p. 673 S.C.R., one reads:

> Some propositions pertinent to that issue may, we think, be collected from the judgments of the Judicial Committee of the Privy Council, if not laid down explicitly, at least, as implicit in them. First, property, whether movable or immovable, can, for the purposes of determining *situs* as among the different Provinces of Canada in relation to the incidence of a tax imposed by a provincial law upon property transmitted owing to death, have only one local situation. In applying this proposition, of course, it is necessary to distinguish between a tax upon property and a tax upon persons domiciled or resident in the Province (*Toronto Gen'l Trusts Corp. v. The King*, 46 D.L.R. 318, [1919] A.C. 679; *Brassard v. Smith*, [1925] 1 D.L.R. 528, [1925] A.C. 371; *Provincial Treasurer of Alberta v. Kerr*, [1933] 4 D.L.R. 81).

> Then, it seems to be a corollary of this proposition that *situs*, in respect of intangible property (which has no physical existence) must be determined by reference to some principle or coherent system of principles: and again, the Courts appear to have acted upon the assumption that the British Legislature, in defining, in part, at all events, by reference to the local situation of such property, the authority of the Province in relation to taxation, must be supposed to have had in view the principles of, or deductible from, those of the common law (*The King v. Lovitt*, [1912] A.C. 212; *Toronto Gen'l Trusts Corp. v. The King*, 46 D.L.R. 318, [1919] A.C. 679; *Brassard v. Smith*, [1925] 1 D.L.R. 528, [1925] A.C. 371; *Royal Trust Co. v. A.-G. Alta.*, [1930] 1 D.L.R. 868, [1930] A.C. 144).

> We think it follows that a provincial Legislature is not competent to prescribe the conditions fixing the *situs* of intangible property for the purpose of defining the subjects in respect of which its powers of taxation under the *B.N.A. Act, 1867*, s. 92(2), may be put into effect.

It seems to me that the same reasoning should be applied in the construction of "Property and Civil Rights in the Province". It is not within the authority of a provincial Legislature to define or to extend the scope of its constitutional jurisdiction. Hence the fact that a person is amenable to the jurisdiction of its Courts cannot serve as a basis for imposing obligations in respect of torts any more than with respect to taxation. On its face s. 4(2) of the *Assistance Act* purports to destroy the effect of legislation passed in adjacent Provinces. It was agreed on all sides in argument that the question raised in this case is to be answered on the assumption that the appellants' activities complained of were properly licensed under the laws of the Province in which they were performed, but this essential provision of the *Assistance Act* declares that this will afford no defence to Manitoba's claim. Thus, the situation is that, although presumably the appellants' operations are authorized by the law of the Province where they are effected, they are sought to be enjoined under the laws of another Province by virtue of an enactment of that other Province.

In the circumstances of this case, I find it necessary to say that it does not appear to me that a Province can validly license on its territory operations having an injurious effect outside its borders so as to afford a defence against whatever remedies are available at common law in favour of persons suffering injury thereby in another Province. In *K.V.P. Co. v. McKie*, [1949] S.C.R. 698, this Court upheld the common law right of riparian owners to claim an injunction and damages against the owner of a polluting plant. [...] In my view, that judgment is authority for the proposition that, at common law, pollution of waters to an injurious degree is a tort that gives rise to a cause of action for those whose property rights are affected thereby. I fail to see how a provincial authority could, by licensing the polluting operations, destroy this cause of action as against persons whose rights are affected outside its borders. It seems to me that there is decisive authority, especially *Composers, Authors & Publishers Ass'n of Canada Ltd. v. Int'l Good Music, Inc. et al.* (1963), 37 D.L.R. (2d) 1, [1963] S.C.R. 136, 40 C.P.R. 1, in favour of the proposition that a cause of action arises where damage is caused by acts performed in another State or Province. Such a cause of action is, I think, a right enforceable outside that State or Province which its Legislature cannot take away under the principle stated in *Royal Bank of Canada v. The King*. The legal situation would not be different if, instead of polluting plants, we were faced with dams flooding lands in an adjoining Province. It could certainly not be contended that the Province in which the dam was erected could validly license the flooding in the other.

As between sovereign countries, such problems can be settled only by international agreement such as was done in the case of damages caused in the U.S. by the smelter at Trail, B.C. The Courts of the respective States would be bound to consider their own laws as conclusive. However, as between different Canadian Provinces, the situation is not in all respects the same as if they were independent States. There is a constitutional limitation on their legislative authority and there is a common forum to enforce it. What was said in *British Coal Corp. et al. v. The King*, [1935] A.C. 500 at p. 520, about the doctrine forbidding extraterritorial legislation being "a doctrine of somewhat obscure extent" was in relation to the powers of the federal Parliament, not of the provincial Legislatures. In this respect, it must be noted that s. 7(2) of the *Statute of Westminster, 1931* has made applicable to the provincial Legislatures only the provisions of s. 2 dealing with conflict with Imperial statutes, not those of s. 3 which declare that the federal Parliament "has full power to make laws having extra-territorial operation".

The basic principle of the division of legislative powers in Canada is that all legislative power is federal except in matters over which provincial Legislatures are given exclusive authority. Such authority is under every head expressly or impliedly restricted to the provincial territory. In deciding what is "within a Province", the Courts must obviously look for guidance at decisions rendered in matters of private international law. However, there is a very important difference between those cases and those that arise under our Constitution. When a Court is called upon to choose as between the laws of two countries the proper laws to be applied for the solution of some private dispute, it must in the end be guided by the laws of the State that created it. But the superior Courts of the Canadian Provinces are not State Courts. "They are", as Ritchie, C.J., said in *Valin v. Langlois* (1879), 3 S.C.R. 1 at p. 20; affirmed 5 App. Cas. 115, "the Queen's Courts, bound to take cognizance of and execute all laws, whether enacted by the Dominion Parliament or the Local Legislatures". Hence, when the question before them is where does the legislative authority reside over a given subject in Canada, there is always the possibility for them to find that it is not in any provincial Legislature but in the Parliament of Canada.

It has been determined in *Citizens Ins. Co. of Canada v. Parsons* (1881), 7 App. Cas. 96, that the power to regulate by legislation the contracts of a particular business or trade is within the scope of provincial legislative authority over property and civil rights. However, where business contracts affect interprovincial trade, it is no longer a question within provincial jurisdiction. The matter becomes one of federal jurisdiction. Such is the substance of our recent judgment in *Burns Foods Ltd. et al. v. A.-G. Man. et al.*, [1974] 2 W.W.R. 537, 1 N.R. 147. In my opinion, the same view ought to be taken in respect of pollution of interprovincial waters as with respect to interprovincial trade. Even if the enumerated power, s. 91(12), "Sea Coast and Inland Fisheries", is not quite as explicit as s. 91(2), "The Regulation of Trade and Commerce", the paramount consideration is that the specific powers are only "for greater certainty", the basic rule is that general legislative authority in respect of all that is not within the provincial field is federal. The importance of this basic rule is such that, although s. 91(2) is in terms unlimited, it has in fact been construed as limited to interprovincial or international trade and commerce. Here, we are faced with a pollution problem that is not really local in scope but truly interprovincial. The legal situation is not without analogy with that of interprovincial pipelines which were held to be excluded from the operation of provincial *Mechanics' Lien Acts* by reason of their interprovincial character: *Campbell-Bennett Ltd. v. Comstock Midwestern Ltd. et al.*, [1954] S.C.R. 207.

It seems to me that in the present case, the question from the point of view of constitutional legislative authority, is not at all the same as in a lawsuit between private parties where the question arises whether the proper law to be applied is the law of the place where the tortious act was committed or that of the place where the damage was suffered. In such a situation, a choice has to be made and regard must sometimes be had for both to a certain extent. If the two elements have occurred in different countries and there are bases on which the Courts of both countries can take jurisdiction, there is no guarantee against conflicting decisions: see The *"Atlantic Star"*, [1974] A.C. 436. Fortunately in Canada, no such situation exists. There is a common forum having unifying authority over all superior Courts. Concurrent jurisdiction will not therefore authorize the Courts of one Province to disregard the authority of those of another. [...]

Coming back to the facts of the present case, it appears to me equally impossible to hold that Saskatchewan and Ontario can license the contaminant discharge operations so as to preclude a legal remedy by those who suffered injury in Manitoba, or to hold that Manitoba can, by prohibiting the discharge of *any contaminant* into waters flowing into its territory, require the shutting down of plants erected and operated in another Province in compliance with the laws of that province. I have italicized the words "any contaminant" because as previously noted, I accept the view that Manitoba is entitled at common law to complain of injury to its fisheries done by pollution of waters flowing into its territory. The judgment of Matas, J., it should be remembered, does not strike out the claim for injury at common law. However, under the *Assistance Act*, there is no quantity of contaminant that may be lawfully discharged and the consequence might be that the injunction prayed for could be obtained even if the discharge was cut down to a degree that would cause no substantial injury and would comply with the Regulations enacted under federal authority.

[...] [In] respect of injury caused by acts performed outside its territory, I cannot accede to the view that this can be treated as a matter within [a province's] legislative authority when those acts are done in another Province any more than when they are accomplished in another country. In my view, although the injurious acts cannot be justified by or under legislation adopted in the Province or State where the plants are operated, by the same token, Manitoba is restricted to such remedies as are available at common law or under federal legislation.

For those reasons, I would allow the appeals and restore the judgment of Matas, J., with costs in this Court and in the Court of Appeal; there should be no costs to or against any of the intervenants. [...]

RITCHIE J. — [...] Legislation in respect of water quality and of pollution, including the permitting thereof in interprovincial rivers is clearly within the exclusive legislative authority of the Parliament of Canada under s. 91(12), whereas provincial legislation dealing exclusively with the effect of pollution, including the proof thereof and the measure of damage resulting therefrom, has controlling effect within the territorial limits of the Province by which it is enacted. It follows, in my view, that provincial legislation relating to the recovery of damages for pollution, and indeed creating and controlling an action therefor, against a polluter whose acts done within the Province have occasioned the pollution, is clearly within the provincial domain, whereas the overall authority seized with the regulation and control of pollution in interprovincial waters just as clearly rests with Parliament.

Subsection 4(2) of the *Assistance Act* clearly contemplates the discharge of a contaminant into waters outside of the Province of Manitoba at a place where such discharge is permitted "by the appropriate regulatory authority having jurisdiction" at that place and having no jurisdiction in the Province of Manitoba where the contaminant allegedly caused the damage to the fishery. I think it of first importance to observe that this motion has been argued in all Courts on the supposition that in enacting the subsection the Legislature did contemplate the existence of the permission of such an appropriate regulatory authority and that it is unnecessary to decide in this case whether such authority be federal or provincial or indeed to make any final decision as to its validity. What is accepted here is that the provincial Legislature purported to nullify the effect of permission duly granted by the regulatory authority of another jurisdiction and I agree with Mr. Justice Matas that in so doing it purported to legislate with respect to conduct and rights of the defendants outside the territorial limits of the Province of Manitoba with the result that the statute of which it forms part has no application to the appellants in the present case.

It is perhaps trite to observe that under the *British North America Act, 1867* each Province of Canada enjoys sovereign authority within the spheres enumerated in s. 92 of that Act and that this authority is limited by the territorial boundaries of the Provinces respectively. It follows in my view that in considering the law applicable in any particular case, the common law principles established in the general field of conflict of laws must govern.

I agree with Chief Justice Freedman that "the case of *Phillips v. Eyre* (1870), L.R. 6 Q.B. 1, must be our starting point" in determining the applicable law. In that case Willes, J., stated the following rule [at pp. 28-9]:

> As a general rule, in order to found a suit in England for a wrong alleged to have been committed abroad, two conditions must be fulfilled. First, the wrong must be of such a character that it would have been actionable if committed in England. [...] Secondly, the act must not have been justifiable by the law of the place where it was done.

This general rule has been adopted as applicable between two Provinces of Canada in a considered series of cases of undoubted authority. [...]

In my view, the question in the present case is not only whether a tort was committed in Manitoba, but whether the acts of the appellants done in Saskatchewan and Ontario amounted to actionable torts at all. If the acts were authorized by licence and therefore justifiable in the places where they were done, they were not civil wrongs and can form no basis for a damage action.

There is, as I have said, an unbroken line of authority in this Court accepting the rule in *Phillips v. Eyre* (1870), L.R. 6 Q.B. 1, without question and I am not prepared to depart from it. If that rule is to be adhered to it follows that if there were licences making the appellants' "mercury discharging activities" in Saskatchewan and Ontario justified, this not only gave rise to the civil right under the law of those Provinces, but to a concomitant civil right to have those licences recognized in the Courts of Manitoba in determining whether or not the action is properly founded in that Province. As to the authority of the Legislature of that Province to nullify these civil rights and convert an act lawfully done in another Province under the laws of that Province into an unlawful one while at the same time disregarding rights established under private international law, I share the view of Mr. Justice Matas that the case of *Royal Bank of Canada et al. v. The King,* [1913] A.C. 283, has direct application to the circumstances.

The facts of the *Royal Bank* case have been extensively explored in the judgments in the Court of Appeal and by the Chief Justice of this Court and it would be superfluous for me to repeat them so that it is perhaps enough for me to say that in my opinion I agree with the basic proposition asserted by Viscount Haldane, L.C., at p. 298 A.C., where he said of the appellants:

> Their right was a civil right outside the province; and the legislature of the province could not legislate validly in derogation of that right.

In distinguishing that case, Chief Justice Freedman had this to say [38 D.L.R. (3d) at p. 376]:

> In the *Royal Bank* case the right of the bondholders in England to claim the return of their money from the bank at its head office in Montreal was held to be a civil right arising and enforceable extra-provincially – that is, outside the Province of Alberta. Here, on the other hand, the effect of any licence or permit which the defendants may possess would necessarily have to be tested and determined intra-provincially – that is, within the Province of Manitoba. The place where the rights are enforceable – in the *Royal Bank* case, outside the Province, in the present case, within the Province – constitutes a clear distinction between the two cases, a distinction that goes to the very root of the constitutional issue now before us.

The first portion of these observations appears to me to be based on the assumption that the present case is concerned with a civil right arising in Manitoba, but as I view the appellants' civil right as stemming from the licences which are assumed to have been granted to them in Ontario and Saskatchewan respectively, I cannot subscribe to this distinction.

The extra-provincial character of the right of action asserted by the respondent against the appellants is most dramatically illustrated by the fact that the first claim for relief under the statement of claim is for

> An injunction restraining each from continuing to discharge mercury or mercury compounds from their respective chlor-alkali plants into the two aforementioned rivers respectively, or into any other watercourse directly or indirectly draining into or connecting with the Manitoba waters. [...]

This to me is a clear assertion of a right of one Province to enter into another and there invoke its own law so as to restrain companies who have a presence in all three Provinces from exercising rights which they are assumed to have under licences from the Province where the discharge took place.

For all these reasons I would allow this appeal, set aside the judgment rendered by the Court of Appeal for Manitoba on March 21, 1973, and restore the judgment of the Honourable Mr. Justice Matas of the Court of Queen's Bench of Manitoba pronounced on June 16, 1972.

Mr. Justice Pigeon, as I understand his reasons, has reached the same conclusion on the ground that as the acts of the appellants necessarily have an interprovincial effect they are a subject-matter within the exclusive authority of Parliament in accordance with its residual power over matters of inter-provincial concern not specifically allocated to either federal or provincial authority under the *British North America Act, 1867*. He concludes therefore that the Province of Ontario and Saskatchewan were without authority to license the appellants' acts of contamination, and as a corollary to this reasoning, he concludes that the legislation in question is *ultra vires* the Province as involving the exclusively federal field of the pollution of interprovincial rivers. This argument was not advanced by either of the parties at any stage and it formed no part of the submissions made by any of the intervenants as all concerned proceeded throughout on the assumption that the acts of pollution were duly permitted by the appropriate regulatory authority having jurisdiction where they took place. I am unable to share the view of my brother Pigeon because I take the view that while the control of pollution of such rivers is a federal matter, the legislation here impugned has to do with its effect in damaging property within the Province of Manitoba and it only becomes inapplicable by reason of the extra-territorial aspect to which I have made reference. The action here was instituted by the Crown as assignee of the rights of private individuals and in my view the applicable law is that of the place where the acts complained of were done.

Altogether, apart from the provisions of the *Assistance Act*, the statement of claim alleges an action at common law, and if this action should be pursued and it should develop that the appellants were not licensed by the appropriate regulatory authorities in Ontario and Manitoba, then I have no doubt that the Courts in Manitoba would have jurisdiction to entertain the suit in accordance with the reasoning expounded by Mr. Justice Dickson in *Moran et al. v. Pyle National (Canada) Ltd.*, decided in this Court on December 21, 1973, [1974] 2 W.W.R. 586. [...]   *Dissent*

LASKIN C.J.C. [Judson and Spence, JJ, concurring (dissenting)]: — [...] Jurisdiction *in personam* being uncontested, the issue in this case turns therefore on applicable law, on the choice of law to govern the liability of the appellants for the damage and loss suffered in Manitoba. I do not see how it can be said that the *Manitoba Act* denies to the appellants any legal rights they acquired in Saskatchewan or in Ontario in respect of the operation there of their respective chlor-alkali plants. If, as is assumed for the purposes of this case, they are respectively licensed to discharge contaminants to the extent that they did, that licence, local to each of the Provinces, does not have an extra-territorial reach to entitle each of them with impunity to send their pollutants into the waters of another Province. That would be to assert against Manitoba an extra-territorial privilege and to use it as a basis for denying to Manitoba any local internal power to charge Ipco and Dryden with civil liability for damage produced in Manitoba to Manitoba property interests.

There is, of course, no title in flowing water, and if any regulatory authority to have interprovincial effect is to exist in respect of pollution of interprovincial waters it would have to be established under federal legislation. It may be (and this does not appear in the record) that the licence to discharge pollutants into the South Saskatchewan and the Wabigoon rivers came from a federal source but, as in the case of federal fishery Regulations, it did not purport to have more than a local intra-provincial force; and hence no nourishment for their constitutional position can be found by Ipco and Dryden in the fact that they were licenced to pollute in Saskatchewan and Ontario. One might argue, with equal want of logic, that an American State could authorize pollution of an international river flowing into Manitoba and thus immunize the polluter against liability in Manitoba for damage caused in Manitoba. To put the matter in tort terms, Ipco and Dryden in discharging a pollutant into waters that flow into an adjoining Province created a risk of harm there that could not be justified by reliance on permission that was necessarily limited to the waters and the fisheries in the licensing Provinces.

What must be the resort of Ipco and Dryden is that Manitoba law does not, or does not alone, govern the liability of the appellants for the damage and loss that occurred in Manitoba. What, then, is the law that governs this liability, or is it, in any event, open to Manitoba to determine for itself, having jurisdiction over the appellants, how their liability should be determined for damage and loss in Manitoba? In respect of this latter point, the constitutional issue, if any, has a similarity to that which this Court and the Privy Council considered in cases touching the power of a Province to fix for itself the *situs* of intangibles for the purpose of provincial taxation: see, for example, *The King v. National Trust Co.*, [1933] S.C.R. 670. However, for the reasons that follow, I do not think such an issue has to be met in this case. In my opinion, choice of law principles relative to the place of commission of the tort in the present case make it appropriate for Manitoba to apply its own law, whether common law or statute law, to the liability of Ipco and Dryden; and, moreover, I find no excess of constitutional power in the way in which the impugned legislation operates. In short, I do not regard this as a case where Manitoba has purported to bring within its borders a tort which could not justifiably be litigated there under Manitoba law by common law choice of law principles. Certainly, in proceedings originating in a motion to strike out the major part of the statement of claim it would be rash (as Chief Justice Freedman noted in his reasons) to view the facts in the present case as giving rise to a tort actionable under Saskatchewan and under Ontario law but not under Manitoba law.

Manitoba's predominant interest in applying its own law, being the law of the forum in this case, to the question of liability for injury in Manitoba to property interests therein is undeniable. Neither Saskatchewan nor Ontario can put forward as strong a claim to have their provincial law apply in the Manitoba action; in other words, the wrong in this case was committed, or the cause of action arose in Manitoba and not in Saskatchewan or in Ontario. There is hence no need to consider either *Phillips v. Eyre* (1870), L.R. 6 Q.B. 1, or other cases in which it has been considered or reconsidered such as *Chaplin v. Boys*, [1971] A.C. 356, since these cases involve the situation where the tort or wrong or the cause of action had arisen outside the forum or the jurisdiction in which suit was brought. The question whether the rules in *Phillips v. Eyre* are jurisdictional (and this is unlikely), or are indeed choice of law rules, does not arise in the present case upon the conclusion being reached that there is here no tort that has arisen outside of Manitoba and is being sued upon in Manitoba. To the extent that the recent judgment of this Court in *Moran et al. v. Pyle National (Canada) Ltd.*, judgment pronounced December 21, 1973, but not yet reported [now reported [1974] 2 W.W.R. 696], may be said to relate to choice of law principles as well as to jurisdiction, it supports the view I take here as to the place where the cause of action arose.

If, as I would hold, Manitoba law is applicable to redress the injury suffered in that Province, how can there be constitutional infirmity in its imposition of liability merely because the cause of the damage arose outside Manitoba, or because as a result of the damage fishing in Manitoba has been halted by the governing regulatory authority or because Manitoba refuses to recognize within Manitoba the lawfulness of the discharge of the pollutant outside Manitoba? I do not regard any of these circumstances, not even that last-mentioned (reflected in s. 4(2) of the *Manitoba Act*) as involving legislation in relation to any civil rights or interests of the appellants outside of Manitoba. Of course, the *Manitoba Act* has an effect upon them, but its purpose is to strike at the damage and loss produced in Manitoba to Manitoba property.

None of the cases cited by the appellants as a basis for their constitutional position support it. [...]

This brings me to *Royal Bank of Canada et al. v. The King*, [1913] A.C. 283, such later cases as *Ottawa Valley Power Co. v. A.-G. Ont. et al.*, [1937] O.R. 265 *sub nom. Ottawa Valley Power Co. v. Hydro-Electric Power Com'n et al.; Beauharnois Light Heat & Power Co. et al. v. Hydro-Electric Power Com'n et al.*, [1937] O.R. 796, and *Crédit Foncier Franco-Canadien v. Ross et al.*, [1937] 2 W.W.R. 353. The first observation I would make is that all these cases involved contractual undertakings which later provincial legislation sought to abrogate, and the invalidation of the legislation proceeded on the footing that the contracts created civil rights outside the territory of the Provinces which those Provinces were powerless to destroy. Whatever be the merit of the criticism of the *Royal Bank of Canada* case in particular, its principle does not touch the present case which involved no promissory undertakings. Second, as Freedman, C.J.M., pointed out in his reasons, if there be analogy by reference to where the rights in issue in each case were enforceable, it is obvious that in the present case they were enforceable only in Manitoba and not outside, as was the situation in the *Royal Bank of Canada* case. [...]

In my view, the appellants' contention of constitutional invalidity based on alleged deprivation or divestment of a "right" outside Manitoba proceeds upon a misconception. What the appellants are claiming is an immunity in Manitoba based on a licence to pollute granted outside. That licence was not granted as against the respondent herein or against any of the assignor fishermen, nor could it be. Manitoba, in enacting s. 4(2), simply took care to exclude any possible contention that a licence granted in another Province could provide a defence against liability for injury to Manitoba property. Whether the result would have been the same without s. 4(2) need not be decided, but there is bound to be doubt whether a foreign jurisdiction can licence the pollution of waters in a neighbouring State so as to provide a defence to an action brought in the latter for injury to property therein.

For all the foregoing reasons, I would dismiss the appeals herein with costs.

Appeal allowed.

- Research Note -
THE TREATMENT OF POLLUTION AND CROWN ZELLERBACH

The limitation which Pigeon J. would have placed upon the ability of the provinces to legislate in relation to subject matters having interprovincial effects, and the corresponding legislative power granted to Parliament under the p.o.g.g. clause, has failed to become a source of a broad federal jurisdiction over pollution.

The Supreme Court of Canada has made it clear that *Interprovincial Co-operatives* has little precedential value. In *R. v. Crown Zellerbach Can. Ltd.*, [1988] 1 S.C.R. 401 (which is reproduced, infra, at p. 444) LeDain J., for the majority of the Court, refers to *Interprovincial Co-operatives*, and then states at p. 435:

> Because of the nature of the Manitoba legislation and the facts of the case, I think it must be assumed, as submitted by the respondent, that in referring to the pollution of interprovincial rivers Pigeon J. had in mind pollution that crossed provincial boundaries Moreover, the opinion that there was federal jurisdiction based on the peace, order and good government power to control the pollution of interprovincial rivers was not that of a majority of the Court. Ritchie J., the other member of the majority in favour of allowing the appeal, was of the view that the Manitoba statute was inapplicable to the defendants, in so far as it sought to deny a right arising outside of the province, but he declined to hold, with Pigeon J., that it was *ultra vires* as being in relation to a matter within federal legislative jurisdiction, a point which he said had not been argued. In the course of his reasons he did express the opinion that Parliament had jurisdiction to control pollution in interprovincial rivers but he referred only to s. 91(12) of the *Constitution Act, 1867* as the basis of such jurisdiction.

CHURCHILL FALLS (LAB.) CORP. v. A.G. NFLD.
[1984] 1 S.C.R. 297.

[During the 1960s Newfoundland granted certain leases to Churchill Falls (Labrador) Corp. (CFLCo) to enable it to develop the hydro-electric resources at Churchill Falls. CFLCo was to construct facilities for the generation and transmission of electricity, most of which would be exported from the province. The money to finance this construction was raised chiefly through the sale of bonds to lenders outside the province. In 1969 CFLCo negotiated an agreement with Hydro-Quebec (the Power Contract) under which the latter agreed to participate in the Churchill Falls development and to purchase nearly all the power it would produce at a price based on the capital cost of the project. The contract was for a term of 40 years and could be extended to 65 years at the option of Hydro-Quebec.

By 1974 Newfoundland was unhappy with the Power Contract and particularly with the small amount of power CFLCo was entitled to retain for use within Newfoundland. It tried to obtain improved terms from Hydro-Quebec and from the government of Quebec. These efforts failed however, and in 1980 the Legislature of Newfoundland enacted *The Upper Churchill Water Rights Reversion Act*, S.N. 1980, c. 40. In essence this Act provides for the revesting in the provincial Crown of all rights granted to CFLCo in connection with the Churchill Falls development and the expropriation of the company's hydro-electric works. It also provides for the payment of CFLCo's creditors and the compensation of its shareholders for any loss in the value of their shares resulting from the coming into force of the Act.

Various questions concerning the validity of the *Reversion Act* were referred to the Newfoundland Court of Appeal which held that the Act was in all respects valid. On appeal to the Supreme Court of Canada the appellants alleged that the Act was *ultra vires* because it interferes with civil rights outside the province of Newfoundland.]

McINTYRE J. [Ritchie, Dickson, Beetz, Estey, Chouinard, Lamer and Wilson JJ., concurring]: — The appellants argued, firstly, that any provincial legislation that has extra-territorial effect is *ultra vires*. Alternatively, it was argued that the true purpose and intent of the legislation, its pith and substance, governs in the issue of territorial limitation just as it does in other constitutional cases involving division of powers. The appellants contended that the *Reversion Act* is aimed at the destruction of the rights of Hydro-Quebec under the Power Contract, rights situate outside Newfoundland. Consequently, the Act is beyond the legislative competence of the province. [...]

The appellants relied heavily on the case of *Royal Bank v. R.*, [1913] A.C. 283, 3 W.W.R. 994, 23 W.L.R. 315, 9 D.L.R. 337 (P.C.), and the cases which followed it, including *Ottawa Valley Power Co. v. H.E.P.C.*, [1937] O.R. 265, [1936] 4 D.L.R. 594 (C.A.); *Beauharnois Light, Heat & Power Co. v. H.E.P.C. of Ont.*, [1937] O.R. 796, [1937] 3 D.L.R. 458 (C.A.) and *Credit-Foncier Franco-Can. v. Ross; Netherlands Invt. Co. of Can. v. Fife*, [1937] 2 W.W.R. 353, 18 C.B.R. 368, [1937] 3 D.L.R. 365 (Alta. C.A.). These cases have been considered to be strong authority for the proposition that a provincial legislature may not validly legislate in derogation of extra-provincial rights. In the *Royal Bank* case the proceeds of a bond issue made by a railway company were held by the appellant bank. The railway company had made default in the payment or interest and in the construction of the railway line, and the Alberta government, which had guaranteed the bonds, enacted a statute ratifying the guarantee and requiring payment of the money from the bank into the General Revenue Fund of the province. It was not entirely clear from the report whether the funds were held by the bank in an account in Montreal or in an account in Alberta, but the judgment seems to proceed on the basis that the monies were, in fact, held in Montreal. The bank refused to pay on the ground that the right to the money upon default of the railway company revested in the bondholders and this right was a right outside Alberta. The statute was held by the Judicial Committee of the Privy Council to be *ultra vires* upon that ground.

In the *Ottawa Valley Power* case, on facts somewhat similar to those at Bar, contracts were made between the Hydro-Electric Power Commission of Ontario and Ottawa Valley Power Company, a Quebec company distributing power in Quebec. An *Ontario Act* which declared the contracts "to be and always to have been illegal, void, and unenforceable as against The Hydro-Electric Power Commission of Ontario" was held to be *ultra vires* in the Court of Appeal of

Ontario as being legislation in derogation of extra-provincial rights. In the *Beauharnois* case a similar result was reached on similar facts, and in the *Credit-Foncier* case the Appellate Division of the Supreme Court of Alberta held that an Act affecting interest payable on certain debts, owing by residents of Alberta to creditors outside of Alberta, was *ultra vires* as derogating from extraprovincial civil rights.

It has been said that the courts in these cases did not differentiate, at least expressly, between statutes which are directed at extra-provincial rights and statutes which only incidentally affect those rights. See, for example, the words of Viscount Haldane, at p. 298 [A.C.] of the *Royal Bank* case:

> In the opinion of the Justices the effect of the statute of 1910, if validly enacted, would have been to preclude the bank from fulfilling its legal obligation to return their money to the bondholders, whose right to this return was a civil right which had arisen, and remained enforceable outside the province. The statute was on this ground beyond the powers of the Legislature of Alberta, inasmuch as what was sought to be enacted was neither *confined* to property and civil rights within the province nor directed *solely* to matters of merely local or private nature within it. (emphasis added.)

There is other authority which is frequently referred to on this question and it was heavily relied on in argument by Newfoundland. The leading case is *Ladore v. Bennett*, [1939] A.C. 468, [1939], 3 All E.R. 98, [1939] 2 W.W.R. 566, 21 C.B.R. 1, [1939] 3 D.L.R. 1. This case concerned provincial legislation which amalgamated certain municipalities in Ontario into the city of Windsor. In the process of this amalgamation the securities for the debts of the various component municipalities were replaced by new bonds issued by the new city of Windsor with modifications in interest rates and other terms of the indebtedness. There was no question that the rights of many municipal creditors situate outside of Ontario were affected and, in some degree at least, derogated from. Lord Atkin held that the pith and substance of the Acts was in relation to municipal institutions within the province and that, in addition, as far as they affected public utility commissions, they were justified as having been passed in relation to local works and undertakings under s. 92(10) of the *British North America Act*. He rejected the argument of colourability with these words, at p. 482 [A.C.]:

> It was suggested in argument that the impugned provisions should be declared invalid because they sought to do indirectly what could not be done directly – namely, to facilitate repudiation by Provincial municipalities of obligations incurred outside the Province. It is unnecessary to repeat what has been said many times by the Courts in Canada and by the Board, that the Courts will be careful to detect and invalidate any actual violation of constitutional restrictions under pretence of keeping within the statutory field. A colourable device will not avail. But in the present case nothing has emerged even to

* "do indirectly what could not be done directly"

suggest that the Legislature of Ontario at the respective dates had any purpose in view other than to legislate in times of care – namely, municipal institutions.

He went on to reject the argument that the legislation was *ultra vires* as being in derogation of extraprovincial rights by saying, at pp. 482-3:

> [A]nd though they affect rights outside the Province they only so affect them collaterally, as a necessary incident to their lawful powers of good government within the Province. [...]

It will be seen that there is an apparent conflict between the *Royal Bank* line of cases and *Ladore v. Bennett*. In *Royal Bank* the view expressed by Viscount Haldane (see quotation from p. 298, supra) would appear to be that any provincial enactment not wholly confined in its effect to the province would on that account be *ultra vires*. The same reasoning appears to have been applied in *Ottawa Valley* and *Beauharnois* as well as *Credit-Foncier*. [...]

It should be noted that the other cases referred to above which followed *Royal Bank* were all decided before *Ladore v. Bennett*, which case in my view states the law correctly.

"A colourable device will not prevail"

Where the pith and substance of the provincial enactment is in relation to matters which fall within the field of provincial legislative competence, incidental or consequential effects on extra-provincial rights will not render the enactment *ultra vires*. Where, however, the pith and substance of the provincial enactment is the derogation from or elimination of extra-provincial rights then, even if it is cloaked in the proper constitutional form, it will be *ultra vires*. A colourable attempt to preserve the appearance of constitutionality in order to conceal an unconstitutional objective will not save the legislation. I refer to the words of Lord Atkin quoted above that "a colourable device will not avail."

The appellants argued that the *Reversion Act* is colourable legislation aimed at the Power Contract. In support of this argument reference was made to the extrinsic evidence which has already been mentioned. That part of the evidence which I have held to be reliable and therefore admissible indicates the true purpose and intent of the Act. Newfoundland attempted to recall more power than was provided for in the Power Contract, first by a request to Hydro-Quebec and then to the Quebec Premier. These attempts failed. A demand to CFLCo by Order in Council was also refused. A whole section in the government pamphlet, "The Energy Priority of Newfoundland and Labrador," deals with the price paid by Hydro-Quebec for Churchill Falls power under the Power Contract and the benefits realized by Hydro-Quebec from its investment. The section concludes:

> The foregoing financial estimates have been included here to illustrate the harsh inequity created by the Power Contract since 1972. This inequity will clearly magnify to unconscionable proportions and amounts over the remaining 61 years of the Power Contract. It is this very Power Contract which

Hydro-Quebec is using to deny Newfoundland's right to access 800 MW of Churchill Falls power at this time. The increasing inequity of the Power Contract adds impetus to the Government's determination to reach a resolution to its right of access. Such access would only begin to reduce the inequity and to move towards a fair and equitable utilization of the Churchill Falls resource.

Another section is entitled, "Newfoundland's Case for Fairness and Equity," and outlines Newfoundland's attempt to renegotiate the Power Contract in terms of both price and Newfoundland's access to Churchill Falls power. Even the *Reversion Act* itself provides for compensation to shareholders and creditors directly, rather than to CFLCo, thus depriving the company of any assets upon which recovery by Hydro-Quebec for breach of the Power Contract could be effected. As soon as the *Reversion Act* came into force, Hydro-Quebec's right to receive power according to the terms of the Power Contract would be effectively destroyed. Even if the flow of electricity to Quebec continued at the same rate and for the same price after the coming into force of the Act, it would then be in the form of a privilege rather than an enforceable right. All of this, in my opinion, points to one conclusion: the *Reversion Act* is a colourable attempt to interfere with the Power Contract and thus to derogate from the rights of Hydro-Quebec to receive an agreed amount of power at an agreed price. It was also argued by the appellants that the *Reversion Act* is *ultra vires* in that it affects the rights of secured creditors outside the province. In my opinion, there is nothing in the Act itself nor in the extrinsic evidence to indicate that the Act is aimed at the rights of secured creditors. Any effect on these rights would be of an incidental nature and, in accordance with the principle of *Ladore v. Bennett* discussed above, would not of itself be grounds for declaring the Act *ultra vires*.

A finding that the *Reversion Act* is aimed at the rights of Hydro-Quebec under the Power Contract would render the contract *ultra vires* only if the rights so attacked are situate in Quebec, beyond the jurisdiction of the legislature of Newfoundland. Little argument was advanced on this issue and the case seemed to proceed on the general assumption that the rights of Hydro-Quebec were situated in Quebec. The fact, of course, is that Hydro-Quebec has the right under the Power Contract to receive delivery in Quebec of hydro-electric power and thereafter to dispose of it for use in Quebec or elsewhere as it may choose. If these facts are not sufficient for the purpose of the constitutional characterization of the *Reversion Act*, it may be noted in any event that ordinarily the rule is that rights under contracts are situate in the province or country where the action may be brought: see Castel, *Canadian Conflict of Laws*, vol. 2, p. 347, and Dicey & Morris, *The Conflict of Laws*, vol. 2, 10th ed., p. 533, and cases cited therewith. It will be recalled that the Power Contract provided that the courts of Quebec would have jurisdiction to adjudicate disputes arising under it and it is, therefore, the province of Quebec where enforcement of the contract may be ordered and where the intangible rights arising under the contract are situate.

It was argued by the Attorney General of Newfoundland that control over the power generated at Churchill Falls is essential for the effective management by Newfoundland of its water resources and to meet the energy needs of the province. However, it is not for this Court to consider the desirability of legislation from a social or economic perspective where a constitutional issue is raised. [...] It follows that the *Reversion Act* is *ultra vires*.

HUNT v. T&N PLC
[1993] 4 S.C.R. 289.

[The appellant suffered from cancer which he alleged was caused by the inhalation of asbestos fibres to which he was exposed while working as an electrician in British Columbia. These fibres were allegedly contained in products manufactured and sold by the respondents. The appellant sued the respondents for damages in British Columbia. He requested production of documents relating to the action. The respondents did not respond, because the Quebec *Business Concerns Records Act* prohibited the removal of any documents from Quebec relating to any business concern in Quebec pursuant to any requirement of a judicial authority outside the province. The appellant then served demands for discovery of documents on the Respondents pursuant to Rule 26(1) of the British Columbia *Rules of Court*. The Quebec Provincial Court granted orders preventing the respondent companies from sending documents out of the province. The appellant then applied to the British Columbia Supreme Court for an order compelling production of the documents. The application was dismissed, and the Court of Appeal upheld that judgment. Both courts acted on the basis that the *Quebec Act* was valid, ruling that the British Columbia courts did not have jurisdiction over the constitutional validity of a Quebec statute. The fundamental issue in the appeal was whether the statute is *ultra vires* the province as being in relation to a matter outside the province, or constitutionally inapplicable to judicial proceedings in other provinces.]

La FOREST J. [for the Court]: — [...] The respondents and the intervener the Attorney General of Quebec submit that the Act falls within provincial legislative competence by virtue of ss. 92(13), (14) and (16), which empower a province to legislate in relation to the following matters in the province: property and civil rights, the administration of justice, including the creation and organization of provincial courts and the procedure in civil matters, and matters of a merely local or private nature. These provisions, they say, empower a province to legislate respecting the enforcement of judicial and other orders emanating from another province.

A necessary inference, they say, is that the province has legislative jurisdiction to prevent the enforcement in its jurisdiction of any order in relation to property located in the province, even if that affects rights recognized outside the province.

This position, of course, raises issues about the extent to which a province may give extraterritorial effect to legislation, issues that have traditionally been considered in the context of the limitation in every head of provincial power to legislation "in the province". As well, so far as the extraterritorial application of judicial pronouncements in another province is concerned, it raises issues concerning whether the doctrine propounded in *Morguard* is of a constitutional character and whether that doctrine applies in the circumstances. Before turning to these extraterritorial concerns, however, I should observe that I have considerable reservations about some of the suggested constitutional justifications for the Act. First, it is difficult to view the Act as concerned with the administration of justice in Quebec pursuant to s. 92(14). That section relates to the creation of courts in the province and their procedures. The impugned Act does not, however, relate to the administration of justice or procedure in the courts in Quebec; rather it purports to control property in the province that might be affected by proceedings outside the province. It has nothing to do with the court procedure in Quebec. It is instead concerned with impeding legal processes of courts outside the province by preventing their enforcement in the province.

Similarly, s. 92(16) seems an implausible head of power under which the Act could be authorized because the refusal to allow discovery of documents related to court orders or legislative acts emanating from outside the province is hardly a matter of a "merely local or private Nature in the Province". Rather the Act is specifically concerned with orders and acts from outside the province, and the response of parties in Quebec to them.

The most promising constitutional basis for the Act is s. 92(13), as it relates to the substantive property and civil rights in the province. The documents and information in question may certainly form the subject of legislation as property in the province of Quebec. This indeed was the basis principally relied on by those seeking to uphold the Act. The purpose of the Act, it was said, was to prohibit execution of decisions made outside the province that affected the communication of records of business concerns located in the province.

This argument is understandable in terms of traditional approaches to private international law as it operates between foreign states. It is well established that judgments and orders of a state must be recognized and enforced in order to have effect in a foreign jurisdiction. But the traditional conflicts rules, which were designed for an anarchic world that emphasized forum independence, must be assessed in light of the principles of our constitutional law mentioned above. First, the statute must conform to the requirement that it be "in the Province" as required by s. 92, a requirement that involves a balancing under the "pith and substance" approach to determine if it exceeds provincial jurisdiction to enact legislation with extraprovincial effect. Secondly, the courts must consider appropriate policy in relation to recognition and enforcement of judgments issued in other provinces in light of the legal interdependence under the scheme of confederation established in 1867. It is the latter issue I now wish to explore.

THE MORGUARD DECISION

It was the situation of total autonomy over recognition and enforcement, and the consequent disruption it could cause for any litigation involving interprovincial or international elements, that was the concern of this Court's decision in *Morguard,* supra. Morguard was concerned with tempering this source of unfairness and inconvenience to litigants in conformity with the changing nature of the world community and, in particular, in light of the Canadian constitutional structure.

A central idea in that judgment was comity. But as I stated, at p. 1098, "I do not think it much matters whether one calls these rules of comity or simply relies directly on the reasons of justice, necessity and convenience" that underlie them. In my view, the old common law rules relating to recognition and enforcement were rooted in an outmoded conception of the world that emphasized sovereignty and independence, often at the cost of unfairness. Greater comity is required in our modern era when international transactions involve a constant flow of products, wealth and people across the globe.

In any event, I indicated, at p. 1099, that the traditional rules emphasizing sovereignty seem to "fly in the face of the obvious intention of the Constitution to create a single country". Among the factors I identified that would also support a more cooperative spirit in recognition and enforcement were (1) common citizenship, (2) interprovincial mobility of citizens, (3) the common market created by the union as reflected in ss. 91(2), 91(10), 121 and the peace, order and good government clause, and (4) the essentially unitary structure of our judicial system with the Supreme Court of Canada at its apex to which I have earlier referred. The following passage, at p. 1099 of *Morguard*, sets out these factors:

> In any event, the English rules seem to me to fly in the face of the obvious intention of the Constitution to create a single country. This presupposes a basic goal of stability and unity where many aspects of life are not confined to one jurisdiction. A common citizenship ensured the mobility of Canadians across provincial lines, a position reinforced today by s. 6 of the *Charter*; see *Black v. Law Society of Alberta*, [1989] 1 S.C.R. 591. In particular, significant steps were taken to foster economic integration. One of the central features of the constitutional arrangements incorporated in the *Constitution Act, 1867* was the creation of a common market. Barriers to interprovincial trade were removed by s. 121. Generally trade and commerce between the provinces was seen to be a matter of concern to the country as a whole; see *Constitution Act, 1867*, s. 91(2). The Peace, Order and Good Government clause gives the federal Parliament powers to deal with interprovincial activities (see *Interprovincial Co-Operatives Ltd. v. The Queen*, [1976] 1 S.C.R. 477; as well as my reasons in *R. v. Crown Zellerbach Canada Ltd.*, [1988] 1 S.C.R. 401 (dissenting but not on this point); see also *Multiple Access Ltd. v. McCutcheon*, [1982] 2 S.C.R. 161). And the combined effect of s. 91(29) and s. 92(10) does the same for interprovincial works and undertakings.
>
> These arrangements themselves speak to the strong need for the enforcement throughout the country of judgments given in one province. But that is not all. [The judgment then goes on, at pp. 1099-1100, with the passage cited supra regarding the essentially unitary structure of the Canadian court system, which allays any concerns about differential quality of justice among the provinces.]

The importance of adapting the traditional procedural limits of common law rules in light of the demands of the structural requirements of the Canadian Constitution was not something invented in *Morguard*. For example, I noted then, and repeat now, what was said by Estey J. in *Aetna Financial Services Ltd. v. Feigelman*, [1985] 1 S.C.R. 2, at pp. 34-35, in relation to *Mareva* injunctions designed to prevent the removal of assets from one jurisdiction to another:

> All the foregoing considerations, while important to an understanding of the operation of this type of injunction, leave untouched the underlying and basic question: do the principles, as developed in the United Kingdom courts, survive intact a transplantation from that unitary state to the federal state of Canada?

He concluded that the rules intended to deal with the removal of assets and "fend off the depredations of shady mariners operating out of far-away havens, usually on the fringe of legally organized commerce" were not applicable to situations where a corporate defendant was seeking to move assets for legitimate business purposes to another jurisdiction in Canada. Similarly, I do not think litigation engendered against a corporate citizen located in one province by its trading and commercial activities in another province should necessarily be subject to the same rules as those applicable to international commerce. In particular, when a corporate citizen situate in one province chooses to engage in trading and commercial activities in other provinces, the rules governing consequential litigation, specifically rules for the recognition and enforcement of judgments, should be adapted to the specific nature of the Canadian federation. And it is difficult to believe that ordinary individuals moving across Canada in the exercise of their common right of citizenship should be treated differently; see *Black v. Law Society of Alberta*, [1989] 1 S.C.R. 591.

Morguard was not argued in constitutional terms, so it was sufficient there to infuse the constitutional considerations into the rules that might otherwise have governed issues of enforcement and recognition of judgment. But the issue was very clearly raised in this case and in fact a constitutional question was framed. Now, as perusal of the last cited passage from *Morguard* reveals, the constitutional considerations raised are just that. They are constitutional imperatives, and as such apply to the provincial legislatures as well as to the courts. [...]

In short, to use the expressions employed in *Morguard*, at p. 1100, the "integrating character of our constitutional arrangements as they apply to interprovincial mobility" calls for the courts in each province to give "full faith and credit" to the judgments of the courts of sister provinces. This, as also noted in *Morguard*, is inherent in the structure of the Canadian federation, and, as such, is beyond the power of provincial legislatures to override. This does not mean, however, that a province is debarred from enacting any legislation that may have some effect on litigation in other provinces or indeed from enacting legislation respecting modalities for recognition of judgments of other provinces. But it does mean that it must respect the minimum standards of order and fairness addressed in *Morguard*. I turn briefly then to the relevant principles after which I shall consider whether the statute impugned in this case offends these standards.

The basic thrust of *Morguard* was that in our federation a greater degree of recognition and enforcement of judgments given in other provinces was called for. *Morguard* was careful to indicate, however, that a court must have reasonable grounds for assuming jurisdiction. One must emphasize that the ideas of "comity" are not an end in themselves, but are grounded in notions of order and fairness to participants in litigation with connections to multiple jurisdictions.

In *Morguard*, a more accommodating approach to recognition and enforcement was premised on there being a "real and substantial connection" to the forum that assumed jurisdiction and gave judgment. Contrary to the comments of some commentators and lower court judges, this was not meant to be a rigid test, but was simply intended to capture the idea that there must be some limits on the claims to jurisdiction. Indeed I observed (at p. 1104) that the "real and substantial connection" test was developed in *Indyka v. Indyka*, [1969] 1 A.C. 33, in a case involving matrimonial status (where sound policy demands generosity in recognition), and that in a personal action a nexus may need to be sought between the subject-matter and the territory where the action is brought. I then considered the test developed in *Moran v. Pyle National (Canada) Ltd.*, supra, for products liability cases as an example of where jurisdiction would be properly assumed. The exact limits of what constitutes a reasonable assumption of jurisdiction were not defined, and I add that no test can perhaps ever be rigidly applied; no court has ever been able to anticipate all of these. However, though some of these may well require reconsideration in light of *Morguard*, the connections relied on under the traditional rules are a good place to start. More than this was left to depend on the gradual accumulation of connections defined in accordance with the broad principles of order and fairness; V. Black, "The Other Side of *Morguard*: New Limits on Judicial Jurisdiction" (1993), 22 *Can. Bus. L.J.* 4. But I think that the general approach was solidly based. [...]

Finally, I noted in *Morguard* (at p. 1100) that a number of commentators had suggested that the federal Parliament had power to legislate respecting the recognition and enforcement of judgments, and in my view that suggestion is well founded. This issue is ultimately related to the rights of the citizen, trade and commerce and other federal legislative powers, including that encompassed in the peace, order and good government clause. But subject to these overriding powers, I see no reason why the provinces should not be able to legislate in the area, subject, however, to the principles in *Morguard* and to the demands of territoriality as expounded in the cases, most recently in *Reference Re Upper Churchill Water Rights Reversion Act*, supra.

APPLICATION OF MORGUARD PRINCIPLES TO THE IMPUGNED STATUTE

I now turn to the issue whether the impugned statute is consistent with the principles I have just set forth. I say at the outset that I do not think it is. A province undoubtedly has an interest in protecting the property of its residents within the province, but it cannot do so by unconstitutional means. Here the means chosen are intended to unconditionally refuse recognition to orders and thereby impede litigation, not only in foreign countries but in other provinces. At least when a court order is sought, if not before, a judicial order in another province will be denied effect. There are no qualifications. No discretion is given so it can scarcely be said that the Act respects the principles of order and fairness which must, under the *Morguard* principle, inform the procedures required for litigation having extraprovincial effects. Apart from the legislative aspect, the situation in *Morguard* differed in that the appellant there sought refusal of recognition after the judgment was rendered. But the constitutional mandate cannot be avoided by a preemptive strike. The whole purpose of a blocking statute is to impede successful litigation or prosecution in other jurisdictions by refusing recognition and compliance with orders issued there. Everybody realizes that the whole point of blocking statutes is not to keep documents in the province, but rather to prevent compliance, and so the success of litigation outside the province that that province finds objectionable. This is no doubt part of sovereign right, but it certainly runs counter to comity. In the political realm it leads to strict retaliatory laws and power struggles. And it discourages international commerce and efficient allocation and conduct of litigation. It has similar effects on the interprovincial level, effects that offend against the basic structure of the Canadian federation. [...]

If blocking statutes of the type now in effect in both Ontario and Quebec were possible under the Constitution, they would have the potential of affecting the rights of litigants in all the other provinces, whenever the defendant was a Quebec or Ontario business. Discovery is a very important tool of civil litigation. It is especially important in cases of this type, where there are allegations of some sort of product liability. The ultimate plaintiff must have a tool to access the otherwise internal documents, especially of large corporate monoliths. And given that there are allegations of civil conspiracy in this case, it is all the more necessary. [...]

If constitutionally permissible, this approach would effectively immunize the business concerns located in Quebec and Ontario from *ever* having to produce documents sought for the purposes of litigation in other provinces. All they, or their shareholders, would need to do to escape discovery would be to simply seek an order as provided in the Act. When one considers that Ontario and Quebec are the headquarters for many of the largest corporations in this country, many of which will properly be subject to tort and other actions in other provinces, the impact would be serious. The essential effect then, and indeed the barely shielded intent, is to impede the substantive rights of litigants elsewhere. It would force parties to conduct litigation in multiple fora and compel more plaintiffs to choose to litigate in the courts of Ontario and Quebec. Other provinces could, of course, follow suit. It is inconceivable that in devising a scheme of union comprising a common market stretching from sea to sea, the Fathers of Confederation would have contemplated a situation where citizens would be effectively deprived of access to the ordinary courts in their jurisdiction in respect of transactions flowing from the existence of that common market. The resultant higher transactional costs for interprovincial transactions constitute an infringement on the unity and efficiency of the Canadian marketplace (see Finkle and Labrecque, supra), as well as unfairness to the citizen.

The lack of order and fairness in the present situation is evident in a further incongruity. It is that full rights of discovery are available to parties in the civil procedure of Ontario and Quebec. It is not as if these jurisdictions have a totally different tradition of civil procedure. If the litigation was proceeding in either of those provinces there would be full discovery. And if both parties to the action had been from British Columbia there would be discovery. But somehow, because of the fortuitous combination of litigation in British Columbia involving a defendant from Quebec or Ontario, the discovery process is barred.

In light of the foregoing, I conclude that the Quebec *Business Concerns Records Act* is constitutionally inapplicable to other provinces, and consequently in the present case.

[...]

For these reasons, I would allow the appeal with costs throughout and order the respondents to produce for inspection within 30 days, in British Columbia, copies of all documents in their possession and control relating to the matters in question in this action, regardless of whether those documents are located inside or outside the province of Quebec. I would answer the constitutional question by saying that the Act should be read as not applying to the provinces since such application would be *ultra vires* under the constitutional principle set forth in the *Morguard* case.

MUSCUTT ET. AL. v. COURCELLES ET. AL.
[2002] 60 O.R. (3d) 20 (C.A.).

The judgement of the court was delivered by

¶ 1 **SHARPE J.A.:** — This appeal argued together with four other appeals, involves the important issue whether the Ontario courts should assume jurisdiction over out-of-province defendants in claims for damage sustained in Ontario as a result of a tort committed elsewhere.

¶ 2 The fact situation common to these appeals is as follows. An Ontario resident suffers serious personal injury in another province or in another country. The injured party returns home to Ontario, endures pain and suffering, receives medical treatment, and suffers loss of income and amenities of life, all as a result of the injury sustained outside the province. The question is whether the courts of Ontario should entertain the injured party's suit against the out-of-province defendants who are alleged to be liable in tort for damages.

¶ 3 The following are the relevant Rules of Civil Procedure, R.R.O. 1990, Reg.194:

> 17.02 A party to a proceeding may, without a court order, be served outside Ontario with an originating process or notice of a reference where the proceeding against the party consists of a claim or claims,

• • • • •

(h) Damage sustained in Ontario-in respect of damage sustained in Ontario arising from a tort, breach of contract, breach of fiduciary duty or breach of confidence, wherever committed.

• • • • •

17.06 (1) A party who has been served with an originating process outside Ontario may move, before delivering a defense, notice of intent to defend or notice of appearance,

(a) for an order setting aside the service and any order that authorized the service; or

(b) for an order staying the proceeding.

(2) The court may make an order under subrule (1) or such other order as is just where it is satisfied that,

(a) service outside Ontario is not authorized by there rules;

(b) an order granting leave to serve outside Ontario should be set aside; or

(c) Ontario is not a convenient forum for the hearing of the proceeding.

(3) Where on a motion under subrule (1) the court concludes that service outside Ontario is not authorized by these rules, but the case is one in which it would have been appropriate to grant leave to serve outside Ontario under rule 17.03, the court may make an order validating the service.

(4) The making of a motion under subrule (1) is not in itself a submission to the jurisdiction of the court over the moving party.

¶ 4 On November 27, 1999, the plaintiff Chris Muscott, was a passenger in a motor vehicle that was involved in an accident in Cochrane, Alberta. The vehicle was owned by the defendant Simpson and was being driven by the defendant Ducharme-Gullins. The vehicle was struck by an ambulance driven by the defendant Guardian Ambulance. Muscott suffered a serious spinal process fracture as a result of the accident.

¶ 5 Three weeks prior to the accident, Muscott had moved to Alberta from London, Ontario. He had gone to Alberta to work on a contract for his Ontario-based employer. While in Alberta, he accepted his employer's offer to work at a new Alberta office and would have moved to Alberta to take that job if not for the accident. However, when he was released from a Calgary hospital soon after the accident, he returned to London, Ontario to live with his mother. He has required extensive ongoing medical care in Ontario. At the time of the accident, all of the defendants were resident in Alberta. Following the accident, the defendant Ducharme-Gullins moved to Ontario.

¶ 6 Muscott brought this action in Ontario, claiming damages for pain and suffering, loss of income and loss of business opportunity. His statement of claim was served on the defendants in Alberta without leave under rule 17.02(h), which provides that an originating process may be served outside Ontario where there is a claim in respect of damage sustained in Ontario arising from a tort.

¶ 7 The defendants Simpson and Ducharme-Gullins moved pursuant to rule 17.06 and s. 106 of the Courts of Justice Act, R.S.O. 1990, c.43 to set aside service out of the jurisdiction and to stay the action. They argued that the action should be stayed for want of jurisdiction, since the plaintiff's expenses, loss of income and pain and suffering in Ontario did not amount to a "real and substantial connection" with Ontario. They also argued that the Ontario Superior Court should decline jurisdiction on the ground that Ontario is not the convenient forum for the action. [...]

¶ 12 The jurisdictional issues that arise on this appeal emerge from a rapidly emerging area of law. Until the early 1990s, this area was governed by a set of rigid common law rules developed in England in the 19th century. These rules, discussed below, were shaped by the sovereignty concerns of a dominant 19th-century world power anxious to safeguard its territorial sovereignty and jealous of any attempt by foreign states to intrude.

¶ 13 Towards the end of the 20th century, it became increasingly apparent that these rules were out of keeping with the reality of modern interprovincial and international commerce and the frequent and rapid movement of people, goods and services across borders. The rules were especially ill-suited for resolving issues of jurisdiction, enforcement and choice of law between the interdependent sister provinces of Canada.

¶ 14 In four seminal decisions between 1990 and 1994, the Supreme Court of Canada radically changed the entire area of law. The decisions recognized that a new approach was necessary for a modern federal state with integrated national markets and justice system that featured closely-shared values, a common appointment process for judges and a single final court of appeal for all courts.

¶ 15 *Morguard* and *Hunt* rewrote the law of jurisdiction and enforcement. For the first time, jurisdiction and enforcement were recognized as being governed by common values. The Supreme Court held that the principles of "order and fairness" require limits on the reach of provincial jurisdiction can only be asserted against an out-of-province defendant on the basis of a "real and substantial connection". However, the court also held that the courts of a province must give "full faith and credit" to the judgements of the courts of a sister province where the real and substantial connection test is satisfied.

¶ 16 In *Tolofson v. Jenson*, [1994] 3 S.C.R. 1022, 120 D.L.R. (4th) 289, the Supreme Court of Canada dramatically altered choice of law in tort cases. The court overruled the common law rule that gave the law of the forum prominence and introduced the rule that tort cases should be governed by the law of the place where the tort was committed.

¶ 17 In *Amchem Products Inc. v. British Columbia (Workers' Compensation Board)*, the [1993] 1 S.C.R. 897, 102 D.L.R. (4th) 96, the Supreme Court of Canada elaborated the doctrine of *forum non conveniens*, the discretionary power of the courts to decline to exercise jurisdiction where the case is more appropriately dealt with in another jurisdiction. [...]

¶ 20 This appeal raises the issue of assumed jurisdiction. Assumed jurisdiction is initiated by service of the court's process out of the jurisdiction pursuant to rule 17.02. Unlike presence- based jurisdiction and consent-based jurisdiction, prior to *Morguard* and *Hunt*, assumed jurisdiction did not provide a basis for recognition and enforcement. [...]

¶ 27 Rule 17.02(h) was enacted in 1975. As mentioned above, this rule allows for service out of jurisdiction in respect of a claim for damage sustained in Ontario arising from a tort committed elsewhere. This "damage sustained" rule represented a legislative response to the of problem confronted by the Supreme Court of Canada in *Moran v. Pyle*.

¶ 28 Courts have given the "damage sustained" rule a generous and liberal interpretation. [...]

¶ 29 As will be explained below, the "damage sustained" rule is now subject to the principles articulated in *Morguard* regarding the need for a real and substantial connection and the need for order, fairness and jurisdictional restraint. [...]

¶ 31 In *Morguard*, La Forest J. ... La Forest J. held that the traditional preoccupation with the notion of sovereignty and the desire to protect nationals from unfair treatment by foreign courts were out of keeping with modern social and economic reality. At pp.1095, 1097 and 1098 S.C.R., he stated that " [m]odern states [...] cannot live in splendid isolation", that the law had to be "adjusted in the light of a changing world order", and that "[a]ccomodating the flow of wealth, skills and people across state lines has now become imperative".

¶ 32 Further, [at p. 1099 S.C.R] La Forest J. held that the application of the traditional approach to the judgements of the courts of sister provinces failed to reflect the values of Canadian confederation, seemed "to fly in the face of the obvious intention of the Constitution to create a single country", and was inconsistent with the common citizenship of the residents of all provinces and with mobility rights, economic integration and a common market for goods, services and capital. In La Forest J.'s view, Canada's integrated system of justice, under which superior court judges are appointed by the federal government and their judgements are subject to review by a single Supreme Court, minimized the risk of unfairness.

¶ 33 La Forest J. concluded [at p. 1100 S.C.R.] that although Canada's constitution does not include a "full faith and credit" clause such as those of the United States or Australia, where a court in one province has properly exercised jurisdiction in an action, the courts of another province should accord the judgement full faith and credit.

¶ 34 *Morguard* establishes that the proper exercise of jurisdiction depends upon two principles. First, there is a need for "order and fairness" and jurisdictional restraint. Second, there must be a "real and substantial connection". [...]

¶ 35 *Morguard* did not deal explicitly with constitutional limits on the reach of provincial laws. In Hunt, the court considered a constitutional challenge to the operation of a Quebec statute that purported to forbid removing certain corporate records from Quebec to British Columbia for production in litigation. The Supreme Court of Canada found that by frustrating the normal discovery process in British Columbia, the Quebec statute failed to respect the "full faith and credit" principles established in *Morguard*. The court gave the principles from *Morguard* constitutional force, holding that these principles are "constitutional imperatives" that apply to the legislatures as well as the courts. At pp.324 and 328 S.C.R., the court held that provinces are required to "respect the minimum standards of order and fairness addressed in *Morguard*" and that "courts are required, by constitutional restraints, to assume jurisdiction only where there are real and substantial connections to that place".

¶ 36 The language that the Supreme Court has used to describe that real and substantial connection test is deliberately general to allow for flexibility in the application of the test. In *Morguard*, at pp. 1104-09 S.C.R., the court variously described a real and substantial connection as a connection "between the *subject-matter of the action* and the territory where the action is brought", "between the jurisdiction and the *wrongdoing*", "between the *damages suffered* and the jurisdiction", between the *defendant* and the forum province", "with the *transaction or the parties*", and "with the *action*" (emphasis added) [...]

¶ 37 In *Hunt*, at p. 325 S.C.R., the court held:

> The exact limits of what constitutes a reasonable assumption of jurisdiction were not defined [in Morguard], and I add that no test can perhaps ever be rigidly applied; no court has ever been able to anticipate all of these.

The court also held that the real and substantial connection test "was not meant to be a rigid test, but was simply intended to capture the idea that there must be some limits on the claims to jurisdiction" and that "the assumption of and the discretion not to exercise jurisdiction must ultimately be guided by the requirements of order and fairness, not a mechanical counting of contacts or connections". This plea for flexibility echoes Dickson J.'s comments in *Moran v. Pyle* that it would be "unnecessary, and unwise, to have resort to any arbitrary set of rules" for jurisdiction and that an "arbitrary and inflexible" approach is to be avoided.

(c) *The Relationship Between Assumed Jurisdiction and Recognition and Enforcement*

¶ 38 Although *Morguard* dealt with the proper exercise of jurisdiction from the perspective of recognition and enforcement, La Forest J. made it clear that precisely the same real and substantial connection test applies to the assumption of jurisdiction against an out-of-province defendant. As La Forest J. held at p. 1103 S.C.R., "the taking of jurisdiction by a court in one province and its recognition in another must be viewed as correlatives". Likewise, La Forest J. made it clear that the need for order, fairness and jurisdictional restraint also applies to assumed jurisdiction. At pp. 1103-04 S.C.R., La Forest J. wrote:

> [I]t hardly accords with principles of order and fairness to permit a person to sue another in any jurisdiction, without regard to the contacts that jurisdiction may have to the defendant of the subject-matter of the suit... Thus, fairness to the defendant requires that the judgement be issued by a court acting through fair process and with properly restrained jurisdiction.

• • • • •

> [I]f the courts of one province are to be expected to give effect to judgements given in another province, there must be some limits to the exercise of jurisdiction against persons outside the province

¶ 39 In *Tolofson*, the Supreme Court reaffirmed that the same test and the same need for restraint apply to both assumed jurisdiction and jurisdiction for recognition and enforcement purposes. Further, at p. 1049 S.C.R., La Forest J. held that it is the real and substantial connection test that prevents jurisdictional overreaching: "This test has the effect of preventing a court from unduly entering into matters in which the jurisdiction it is located has little interest."

(d) *The Distinction Between Assumed Jurisdiction and Forum Non Conveniens*

¶ 40 Very often there is more than one forum capable of assuming jurisdiction and it is necessary to determine where the action should be litigated.... Where more that one forum is capable of assuming jurisdiction, the most appropriate forum is determined through the *forum non conveniens* doctrine, which allows a court to decline to exercise its jurisdiction on the ground that there is another forum more appropriate to entertain the action.

¶ 41 Courts have developed a list of several factors that may be considered in determining the most appropriate forum for the action [Justice Sharpe set out a list of factors that guide courts in exercising their discretion to choose the most convenient forum under the *forum non conveniens* doctrine] [...]

¶ 42 It is important to distinguish the real and substantial connection test from the discretionary *forum non conveniens* doctrine. In *Tolofson*, at p. 1049 S.C.R., La Forest J. explained the distinction as follows:

> [The real and substantial connection] test has the effect of preventing a court from unduly entering into matters in which the jurisdiction in which it is located has little interest. *In addition,* through the doctrine of *forum non conveniens,* a court may refuse to exercise jurisdiction where, under the rule elaborated in *Amchem*...there is a more convenient or appropriate forum elsewhere. (Emphasis Added)

¶ 43 In "*Morguard v. De Savoye*: Subsequent Developments" (1993) 22 C.B.L.J. 29 at p. 33, Professor Elizabeth Edinger explains that "[j]urisdictional decisions are comprised of two elements: rules and discretion". While the real and substantial connection test is a legal rule, the *forum non conveniens* test is discretionary. The real and substantial connection test involves a fact-specific inquiry, but the test ultimately rests upon legal principles of general application. The question is whether the forum can assume jurisdiction over the claims of plaintiffs in general against defendants in general given the sort of relationship between the case, the parties and the forum. By contrast, the *forum non conveniens* test is a discretionary test that focuses upon the particular facts of the parties and the case. The question is whether the forum should assert jurisdiction at the suit of this particular plaintiff against this particular defendant. [...]

¶ 44 In G.D. Watson and F. Au, "Constitutional Limits on Service *Ex Juris*: Unanswered Questions from Morguard" (2000) 23 Adv. Q.167 at pp. 211-14, the authors explain the implications of a two-stage approach that first considers assumed jurisdiction and then considers *forum non conveniens.* I agree with their analysis of this issue. The residual discretion to decline jurisdiction where the real and substantial connection test is met assumes that the forum in question is not the only one that has jurisdiction over the case. The real and substantial connection test requires only a real and substantial connection, not the most real and substantial connection. See also J.-G. Castel & J. Walker, *Canadian Conflict of Laws,* 5th ed. (Markham: Butterworths, 2002) at p.1.40. Further, the residual discretion to decline jurisdiction also suggests that the consideration of fairness and efficiency is not exhausted at the stage of assumed jurisdiction and that there is scope for considering these factors at the forum non conveniens stage. The residual discretion therefore provides both a significant control on assumed jurisdiction and a rationale for lowering the threshold required for the real and substantial connection test. [...]

Issue 1: Is Rule 17.02(h) Ultra Vires the Province?

¶ 46 The appellants submit that rule 17.02 (h) should be struck down as *ultra vires* the province of Ontario. They submit that rule 17.02(h) asserts jurisdiction against extra-provincial defendants on a basis that exceeds the limits of the principles of order and fairness and the real and substantial connection test articulated in *Morguard* and *Hunt.*

¶ 47 The motions court judge dismissed the constitutional challenge on the basis that rule 17.02 (h) is purely procedural and does not confer jurisdiction on the court. By contrast, in *Duncan (Litigation Guardian of) v. Neptunia Corp.* (2001), 53 O.R. (3d) 754, 199 D.L.R. (4th) 354 (S.C.J.), the court held that rule 17.02 (h) does confer jurisdiction on the court.

¶ 48 For the reasons that follow, I agree with the motions court judge that rule 17.02 (h) is procedural in nature and does not by itself confer jurisdiction. I would therefore dismiss this ground of appeal and hold the rule 17.02 (h) is not *ultra vires* the province.

¶ 49 It is clear that *Morguard* and *Hunt* together impose constitutional limits on the assumption of jurisdiction against extra-provincial defendants. As P.W. Hogg states in *Constitutional Law in Canada*, looseleaf (Toronto: Carswell, 2000) at p. 13-15, " the constitutional rule of extraterritoriality requires that the only causes of action in respect of which service *ex juris* is available are those in which there is a substantial connection between the defendant and the forum province." It follows that provincial rules of court allowing for service out of the jurisdiction, including rule 17.02 (h), must now be read in the light of the constitutional principles of "order and fairness" and "real and substantial connection".

¶ 50 In fact, it has long been accepted that service in according with the rules of court does not determine the issue of jurisdiction: see *Singh v. Howden Petroleum, supra*. Service merely ensures that the parties to an action receive timely notice of the proceeding so that they have an opportunity to participate. Moreover, the constitutional validity of rule 17.02 (h) cannot be determined by reading the rule in isolation. Rule 17.02(h) is part of a procedural scheme that operates within the limits of the real and substantial connection test.

¶ 51 In G.D. Watson & L. Jeffrey, *Holmested and Watson: Ontario Civil Procedure* (Toronto: Carswell, 2001) at p. 17-9, the authors explain that the grounds outlined in rule 17.02 "provide a rough guide to the kinds of cases in which persons outside Ontario will be regarded as subject to the jurisdiction of the Ontario courts". However, these grounds do not determine the issue of jurisdiction.

¶ 52 Several subsections of rule 17.02 indicate that the rule was not intended as a complete description of the requirements for assumed jurisdiction. For example, rules 17.02 (j), (k) and (l) provide for service outside Ontario for support claims, claims for custody of or access to a minor, and claims to declare the invalidity of a marriage. Each of these claims has well-established legal standards governing jurisdiction must be satisfied notwithstanding the fact that the defendant has been served in accordance with the rule. In my view, the same conclusion follows for rule 17.02 (h), which must now be read as being subject to the real and substantial connection requirement.

¶ 53 A party who is served in accordance with rule 17.02 (h) has several means of challenging the jurisdiction of the court on the basis that the real and substantial connection test has not been met. First, rule 17.06 (l) allows a party who has been served outside Ontario to move for an order setting aside the service of staying the proceeding. Second, s.106 of the Courts of Justice Act provides for a stay of proceedings, and it is well established that a defendant may move for a stay on the ground that the court lacks jurisdiction. Third, rule 21.01 (3)(a) allows a defendant to move to have the action stayed or dismissed on the ground that "the court has no jurisdiction over the subject matter of the action." Together, this procedural scheme adequately allows for jurisdictional challenges to ensure that he interpretation and application of rule 17.02 (h) will comply with the constitutional standards prescribed by *Morguard* and *Hunt*.

Issue 2: Did the Motions Court Judge Err in Finding that the Ontario Superior Court Could Assume Jurisdiction Against the Out-of-Province Defendants?

¶ 54 The appellants urge us to adopt an interpretation of the real and substantial connection test that focuses on the nature and extent of the defendant's contacts with the jurisdiction. The appellants submit that a court can only assume jurisdiction against an extra-provincial defendant where it is reasonable to infer that the defendant has voluntarily submitted to Ontario's jurisdiction or where it was reasonably within the defendant's contemplation that his or her conduct could cause an injury in Ontario and give rise to a claim in Ontario courts.

¶ 55 The respondents contend that an approach that focuses solely upon the nature and extent of the defendant's contacts with the jurisdiction would be unduly restrictive and would fail to pay adequate heed to the interests of the injured plaintiff. They submit that the connection between the forum and the damages suffered by the plaintiff are equally relevant in determining whether there is a real and substantial connection. [...]

¶ 63 The weight of post-*Morguard* appellate authority holds that a real and substantial connection may be found on a broader basis that personal subjection. [...]

¶ 72 In "Constitutional Limits on Service *Ex Juris*: Unanswered Questions from *Morguard*", *supra*, Watson and Au argue that Canadian court should not adopt a personal subjection approach that required "minimum contacts" between the defendant and the forum. At pp. 198-211, they outline several objections to the adoption of this American approach:

1. In the United Stated, the Constitution's due process guarantee explicitly protects property rights, and due process jurisprudence focuses on the defendant's liberty interest. By contrast, s.7 of the *Canadian Charter of Rights and Freedoms* does not protect property rights, and the Canadian approach to jurisprudence does not rest on constitutionally-entrenched individual rights but on the territorial concerns of a federal state.

2. Insisting on a substantial connection between the defendant and the forum may result in multiple actions and inconsistent judgements in complex litigation involving several defendants in different jurisdictions.

3. In the United Stated, the personal subjection approach to jurisdiction has led to practical uncertainty and frequent preliminary challenges to jurisdiction, which are often used strategically to prolong litigation. Watson and Au argue that "courts should exercise care in interpreting rules and developing legal principles so as not to encourage unnecessary motions". To this end, they suggest that Canadian courts should show greater deference to the policy underlying provincial service *ex juris* rules that American courts do.

4. A narrow focus on the defendant's connection with the forum could lead to decisions that are contrary to "common sense and practicability". Watson and Au argue that "cases should be allowed to be heard in a forum which, having regard to *all relevant circumstances*, is one appropriate to hear the dispute. The defendant's interest should be *among* the factors to be weighed, and should not itself be determinative of the choice of forum" (emphasis in original).

5. Deciding jurisdictional questions primarily on the defendant's connection with the forum may pay insufficient attention to the fairness component of the *forum non conveniens* analysis. The threshold of the jurisdiction test should be sufficiently low as to allow for the more detailed weighing of factors that occurs under the *forum non conveniens* test.

¶ 73 On the basis of these objections, Watson and Au conclude that the real and substantial connection test should be interpreted as requiring a connection either between the forum and the defendant or between the forum and the subject matter of the action. In their view, the defendant's connection with the forum should not determine the choice of forum. Rather, the defendant's connection should simply be a relevant factor to be weighed together with other factors.

¶ 74 I find these arguments to be persuasive. While the defendant's contact with the jurisdiction is an *important* factor, it is not a necessary factor. In my view, to hold otherwise would be contrary to the Supreme Court of Canada's direction that the real and substantial connection test is flexible. It would also be contrary to the weight of Canadian appellate authority outlined above.

(e) *The relevant factors under the broader approach*

¶ 75 It is apparent from *Morguard*, *Hunt* and subsequent case law that it is not possible to reduce the real and substantial connection test to a fixed formula. A considerable measure of judgement is required in assessing whether the real and substantial connection test has been met on the facts of a given case. Flexibility is therefore important.

¶ 76 But clarity and certainty are also important. As such, it is useful to identify the factors emerging from the case law that are relevant in assessing whether a court should assume jurisdiction against an out-of-province defendant on the basis of damage sustained in Ontario as a result of a tort committed elsewhere. No factor is determinative. Rather, all relevant factors should be considered and weighed together. In my view, a weighing of the factors in the present case favours the assumption of jurisdiction against the out-of-province defendants in this case.

[Justice Sharpe considered seven factors relevant to the question whether the Court should assume jurisdiction in this case, before concluding.]

¶ 111 In my view, a fair weighing of the factors I have outlined clearly favours assumed jurisdiction in the present case. Accordingly, I would affirm the finding of the motions court judge that the real and substantial connection test has been met.

¶ 116 I would dismiss the appeal and affirm the motions court judge's dismissal of the motion to stay the action on the ground that the Ontario Superior Court lacks jurisdiction or that jurisdiction should be declined on the basis of *forum non conveniens*.

INSURANCE CORPORATION OF BRITISH COLUMBIA v. UNIFUND ASSURANCE COMPANY
[2003] 2 S.C.R. 63.

The opinion of McLachlin C.J. and Iacobucci, Binnie and LeBel JJ. was delivered by

BINNIE J.: — [...]

¶ 4 Marcia and Ronald Brennan, who made their home in Cambridge, Ontario, flew to Vancouver in August 1995 for the wedding of one of their sons. While in British Columbia, they rented a car. Driving along the Upper Levels Highway in North Vancouver, the Brennans' rental car was struck from behind by a tractor trailer driven by Baljinder Singh, the impact of which catapulted their car across the centre line concrete barrier into the path of oncoming traffic. In a collision the trial judge described as "horrendous", the Brennans, particularly Mrs. Brennan, suffered terrible injuries....

¶ 5 [T]he Brennans brought an action for damages in the Supreme Court of British Columbia and, on March 4, 1999, were awarded approximately $2.5 million.

¶ 6 The respondent, Unifund Assurance Company ("Unifund"), had issued a motor vehicle insurance policy to the Brennans in Ontario. The policy included the mandatory, no-fault coverage (or SAB) payments [here, about $750,000], for which the Brennans paid a premium. The *Ontario Insurance Act*, R.S.O. 1990, c. I.8 (..."the Ontario Act"), provides that SABs are payable under an Ontario policy when insured persons are injured in motor vehicle accidents occurring anywhere in North America. Unifund, a Newfoundland company, was licensed to carry on business in Ontario, but not, at the time of the accident, in British Columbia.

¶ 7 The appellant Insurance Corporation of British Columbia ("ICBC") insured the negligent truck owner, truck driver, and truck repair shop in British Columbia. It is on the hook for the $2.5 million award of damages, but, under the law of that province, it is entitled to deduct any no-fault payments paid to the Brennans, even though it actually paid no part of that amount.

¶ 8 Unifund understandably feels aggrieved that the appellant, having contributed nothing to the payment of the no-fault benefits, is nevertheless taking a $750,000 deduction created at Unifund's expense. Unifund contends that the appellant should pay it the $750,000. [...]

¶ 9 Unifund's problem is to find a cause of action.... S. 275 of the Ontario Act ... provides a statutory mechanism for transferring losses between Ontario insurance companies arising out of the payment of "SABs" under the Ontario Act. [...]

¶ 10 Unifund either has a statutory cause of action against the British Columbia insurer under the Ontario Act or it has no cause of action at all.

¶ 11 The deduction of about $750,000 claimed by the appellant, ICBC, is [provided for by] ... the *British Columbia Insurance (Motor Vehicle) Act* [...]

¶ 14 The constitutional question of whether the *Ontario Insurance Act* applies to provide Unifund with a statutory cause of action is therefore dispositive of the respondent's claim. [...]

IX. <u>Analysis</u>

¶ 23 It is well established that motor vehicle insurance within a province is a matter within provincial legislative competence: *Citizens Insurance Co. of Canada v. Parsons* [...]

¶ 26 In this case, the accident and all the lawsuits arising directly from the accident took place in British Columbia. It is only the quite separate statutory procedure initiated by Unifund against the appellant that is brought in Ontario.

¶ 27 The constitutional question stated by the Chief Justice identifies the dispositive issue:

> Is section 275 of the *Insurance Act*, R.S.O. 1990, c. I.8, as amended, constitutionally inapplicable to the appellant because its application in the circumstances of this case would not accord with territorial limits on provincial jurisdiction?

While at one level, the argument is about which court has jurisdiction over the dispute (and if more than one court qualifies, then whether Ontario is the convenient forum for its resolution), the underlying issue is whether, in light of the territorial limitation on provincial legislation, the respondent, Unifund, has a viable cause of action at all against the out-of-province appellant. If it is concluded, as the constitutional question asks, that s. 275 of the Ontario Act is "constitutionally inapplicable to the appellant ... [because of] territorial limits on provincial jurisdiction", then Unifund's action under the Ontario Act should be stopped irrespective of where it is brought. [...]

¶ 50 It is well established that a province has no legislative competence to legislate extraterritorially. If the Ontario Act purported to regulate civil rights in British Columbia arising out of an accident in that province, this would be an impermissible extraterritorial application of provincial legislation [...]

¶ 51 This territorial restriction is fundamental to our system of federalism in which each province is obliged to respect the sovereignty of the other provinces within their respective legislative spheres, and expects the same respect in return.

It flows from the opening words of s. 92 of the Constitution Act, 1867, which limit the territorial reach of provincial legislation: "In each Province the Legislature may exclusively make Laws in relation to" the enumerated heads of power (emphasis added). The authority to legislate in respect of insurance is founded in s. 92(13), which confers on each legislature the power to make laws in relation to "Property and Civil Rights in the Province" (emphasis added).

¶ 52 Unifund does not take issue with these basic propositions. Its contention is that it seeks only to enforce its Ontario civil rights in Ontario, namely the right to indemnification created by s. 275 of the Ontario Act. It says it is entitled to do so under ordinary constitutional law principles because there is "a real and substantial connection" between the appellant and Ontario, or, alternatively, under the PAU.

¶ 53 I therefore turn to the first of the two grounds on which the respondent alleges the Ontario statutory scheme applies. *R's position*

   (a) The respondent says that there is a "real and substantial connection" between the appellant and Ontario that makes it appropriate for Ontario law to regulate the outcome of their dispute.

¶ 54 The "real and substantial connection" test has been adopted and developed by this Court in *Morguard* ... and *Hunt* [...]

¶ 55 In this case, however, we are asked to apply the "real and substantial connection test" in the different context of the applicability of a provincial regulatory scheme to an out-of-province defendant. The issue is not just the competence of the Ontario court to entertain the appointment of an arbitrator (as in the choice of forum cases) but, as the constitutional question asks, whether the "connection" between Ontario and the respondent is sufficient to support the application to the appellant of Ontario's regulatory regime.

¶ 56 Consideration of constitutional applicability can conveniently be organized around the following propositions:

   1. The territorial limits on the scope of provincial legislative authority prevent the application of the law of a province to matters not sufficiently connected to it;

   2. What constitutes a "sufficient" connection depends on the relationship among the enacting jurisdiction, the subject matter of the legislation and the individual or entity sought to be regulated by it;

   3. The applicability of an otherwise competent provincial legislation to out-of-province defendants is conditioned by the requirements of order and fairness that underlie our federal arrangements;

   4. The principles of order and fairness, being purposive, are applied flexibly according to the subject matter of the legislation.

¶ 57 I propose to address each of these elements to the extent necessary to resolve this aspect of the appeal.

1. The Sufficient Connection

¶ 58 The territorial limits on the scope of provincial legislative authority prevent the application of the law of a province to matters not sufficiently connected to it [...]

¶ 62 [E]arly formulations conceive of the territorial limitation in very physical terms, as was still the case in 1913 in *Royal Bank of Canada, supra*, where the court struck down an Alberta statute which purported to direct monies raised for a failed railway project to be paid over to provincial government coffers instead of having the monies returned to the lenders, most of whom resided in the United Kingdom. Lord Haldane considered it notable that "[n]o money in specie was sent to the branch office" in Alberta (p. 294). He concluded that the debts were recoverable by the bondholders at the Bank's head office in Montreal. Accordingly, the right of the foreign bondholders to receive back their money

> ... was a civil right which had arisen, and remained enforceable outside the province. The statute was on this ground beyond the powers of the Legislature of Alberta, inasmuch as what was sought to be enacted was neither confined to property and civil rights within the province nor directed solely to matters of merely local or private nature within it. [At p. 298] ...

2. What Constitutes a "Sufficient Connection" Depends on the Relationship Among the Enacting Jurisdiction, the Subject Matter of the Law, and the Persons Sought To Be Regulated By It.

¶ 63 Later formulations of the extraterritoriality rule put the focus less on the idea of actual physical presence and more on the relationships among the enacting territory, the subject matter of the law, and the person sought to be subjected to its regulation. The potential application of provincial law to relationships with out-of-province defendants became more nuanced. The evolution of the rule was perhaps inevitable given the reality, as La Forest J. commented in *Morguard*, that modern states "cannot live in splendid isolation" (p. 1095). The focus on the relationship, as something that did not necessarily require actual physical presence within the jurisdiction, was identified by Dixon J., speaking for the High Court of Australia in *Broken Hill South Ltd. v. Commissioner of Taxation* (N.S.W.) (1936-1937), 56 C.L.R. 337 (Aust. H.C.), at p. 375, who said it was

> ... also within the competence of the [state] legislature to base the imposition of liability on no more than the relation of the person to the territory. The relation may consist in presence within the territory, residence, domicil, carrying on business there, or even remoter connections.

¶ 64 Viewed in this way, the problem in *Royal Bank of Canada*, supra, was not physical presence as such but that there was insufficient connection between the province of Alberta, on the one hand, and the out of province bondholders and their money on deposit with the bank's head office in Quebec, on the other hand, to justify the regulation of the debt by Alberta.

¶ 65 It appears from the case law that different degrees of connection to the enacting province may be required according to the subject matter of the dispute. [...]

¶ 66 In *Ladore v. Bennett* ... Ontario legislation that reduced the rate of interest on out-of-province bondholders was upheld. Purchasers, wherever situated, of Ontario municipal bonds had created a relationship between themselves and Ontario which was sufficient to ground jurisdiction in respect of the particular subject matter of the legislation. On the facts, *Ladore* is difficult to distinguish from *Royal Bank of Canada v. King*. The different result can only be explained, from the perspective of the out-of-province parties, by an evolving sophistication in respect of the true scope of the territorial limitation. *Ladore*, supra, was expressly approved by this Court in *Reference Re Upper Churchill Water Rights Reversion Act*. [...]

¶ 67 A further complication arises when the issue is not the validity of provincial legislation, but its applicability to out-of-province entities. In this case, the appellant does not at all challenge the validity of the *Ontario Insurance Act* which on its face regulates an aspect of "Property and Civil Rights in the Province" (emphasis added) (*Constitution Act, 1867*, s. 92(13)). The appellant says only that the Ontario Act must be confined to its proper constitutional sphere, and its reach cannot validly be extended to an out-of-province insurer to govern the outcome of the present dispute.

3. *The Applicability of Otherwise Competent Provincial Legislation to Out-of-Province Defendants is Conditioned by the Requirements of Order and Fairness that Underlie Our Federal Arrangements.*

¶ 68 The more flexible view of extraterritorial application evident in the later cases will, at least to some extent, increase the potential among the provinces for conflict. In *Hunt*, supra, an organizing principle of the federation was found in the requirements of order and fairness, described by the Court as "constitutional imperatives" (p. 324). Within the Canadian federation, comity requires adherence to "principles of order and fairness, principles that ensure security of transactions with justice" (*Morguard*, supra, at p. 1097). As La Forest J. explained in Tolofson, supra, at p. 1051:

> Many activities within one state necessarily have impact in another, but a multiplicity of competing exercises of state power in respect of such activities must be avoided.

¶ 69 To similar effect is the concern expressed by La Forest J. in *Tolofson*, supra, at p. 1066:

... it is arguable that it is not constitutionally permissible for both the province where certain activities took place and the province of the residence of the parties to deal with civil liability arising out of the same activities. Assuming both provinces have legislative power in such circumstances, this would open the possibility of conflicting rules in respect of the same incident.

¶ 70 The issue in *Hunt* was whether a Quebec statute, which purported to prohibit the removal from Quebec of business records required by judicial process outside the province, excused compliance in a British Columbia court with documentary production. Noting (at p. 330) that this approach would effectively immunize the business concerns located in Quebec from ever having to produce documents sought for the purposes of litigation in other provinces, La Forest J. held that the Quebec "blocking statute" was "constitutionally inapplicable [in British Columbia] because it offends against the principles enunciated in *Morguard*" (p. 331).

¶ 71 Similarly, in my view, order in the federation would be undermined if every provincial jurisdiction took it upon itself to regulate aspects of the financial impact of the British Columbia car crash in relation to its own residents at the expense of the British Columbia insurer.... All it would take is a collision involving Mr. Singh's truck and one 58-passenger tourist bus filled with out-of-province skiers heading along the Upper Levels Highway towards Whistler. Such "competing exercises" of regulatory regimes "must be avoided". The cost of such regulatory uncertainties undermines economic efficiency.

¶ 72 Fairness to the out-of-province defendant is also an important factor in the federation. Here, if the respondent is correct, the appellant would be obliged to respond to insurance regimes in each province or state claiming some sort of insured interest in the financial fall-out from the British Columbia accident arising out of whatever financial obligations those other provincial or state legislatures have seen fit for whatever reason to impose on their own insurance companies.

¶ 73 Adoption of the principles of order and fairness as a mechanism to regulate extraterritoriality concerns differentiates Canada somewhat from Australia ...and the United States. [...]

¶ 74 In *Broken Hill*, for example, Dixon J. went on to say, "If a connection exists, it is for the legislature to decide how far it should go in the exercise of its powers" (p. 375). We would say ... that, within our federal structure, it is not only the view of the enacting legislature that must be considered, but the collective interest of the federation as a whole in order and fairness.

¶ 75 Cases dealing with extraterritorial application from the courts of Australia and the United States should therefore be read with an eye to the differences in our constitutional arrangements. [...]

4. *The Principles of "Order and Fairness", Being Purposive, Are Applied Flexibly.*

¶ 80 The required strength of the relationship varies with the type of jurisdiction being asserted. A relationship that is inadequate to support the application of regulatory legislation may nevertheless provide a sufficient "real and substantial connection" to permit the courts of the forum to take jurisdiction over a dispute. This happens regularly. The courts, having taken jurisdiction, then apply the law of the other province applying rules of conflict resolution governing choice of law issues. Thus, in *Tolofson* itself, there was a sufficient relationship between British Columbia and the parties for the British Columbia courts to hear the case, but it was determined that Saskatchewan law should apply to determine the outcome of the dispute.

¶ 81 It would be unwise in this case to embark on a general discussion of "order and fairness". The question before us is quite specific: Does the respondent have a statutory cause of action against the appellant given the constitutional limitations on the reach of the *Ontario Insurance Act*?

5. Application of These Principles to the Facts of this Case

¶ 82 The respondent, Unifund, points to the fact that the payments for which reimbursement is claimed were paid in Ontario by an Ontario insurer to an Ontario resident. This is true, but it leaves out of consideration the relationship between Ontario and the party sought to be made to pay, the out-of-province appellant. Not only is the appellant not authorized to sell insurance in Ontario, it does not in fact do so. Its insured vehicles in this case did not venture into Ontario. The accident did not take place in Ontario, and the appellant did not benefit from the $750,000 deduction by virtue of Ontario law but by the law of British Columbia.

¶ 83 The most that can be said for the respondent in this case is that the fact of a motor vehicle accident in British Columbia triggered certain payments in Ontario under Ontario law. However, the fact the Ontario legislature has chosen to attach legal consequences in Ontario to an event (the motor vehicle accident) taking place elsewhere does not extend its legislative reach to a resident of "elsewhere". It can also be said that these payments in Ontario, in turn, triggered a deduction of an equivalent amount under the laws of British Columbia. Again, however, the decision of the British Columbia legislature to attach legal consequences (the deduction) in that province to an event that occurred in Ontario (the SAB payments) does not bring the appellant (beneficiary under the British Columbia legislation) into the orbit of the Ontario legislature for the purpose of taking away the British Columbia benefit in favour of an Ontario insurance company.

¶ 84 Here ...the appellant had not hired anyone in Ontario to promote its products. It was not in the Ontario marketplace and, in my view, it was not required to "comply with the rules of the [Ontario] game". The decision of the Ontario legislature to impose no-fault benefits on Unifund could not be bootstrapped into legislative jurisdiction to impose a corresponding debt on the appellant, which (leaving aside the PAU argument) was beyond the territorial jurisdiction of the province. [...]

¶ 91 I therefore conclude that under ordinary constitutional principles the *Ontario Act* is inapplicable to the out-of-province appellant in this case. [...]

[Justice Binnie held that the Power of Attorney and Undertaking ("PAU") signed by the appellant had no application to the facts of this case.]

¶ 108 The constitutional question should be answered as follows:

> Q. Is section 275 of the *Insurance Act*, R.S.O. 1990, c. I.8, as amended, constitutionally inapplicable to the appellant because its application in the circumstances of this case would not accord with territorial limits on provincial jurisdiction?

> Answer: Yes.

The opinion of Major, Bastarache and Deschamps JJ. was delivered by

BASTARACHE J. (dissenting):— [...]

¶ 110 For the reasons that follow, I am of the view that [...] on the facts of this case, ICBC has accepted the jurisdiction of Ontario in this matter by signing a "Power of Attorney and Undertaking" ("PAU"). That instrument, interpreted in light of the principles of private international law set out in *Morguard* [...] constitutes a sound foundation for the application of the *Ontario Insurance Act* to the parties in this case. By virtue of the fact of attornment through the PAU, amongst other factors, I conclude that the subject matter which the *Insurance Act* covers is sufficiently connected to Ontario so as to render the Act applicable to ICBC. [...]

¶ 114 The "Power of Attorney and Undertaking" ("PAU"), titled "Canada Non-Resident Inter-Province Motor Vehicle Liability Insurance Card", provides that when an insured is sued in another province or territory, the Superintendent of Insurance of that province will accept service on behalf of the insurer or its insured, and that the insurer undertakes to appear in the action. As a signatory to the PAU, the insurer further undertakes not to set up any defence in respect of any action under a motor vehicle liability contract which might not be set up in the province in which the action is instituted, and to satisfy judgment up to the greater of the amounts and limits of coverage provided for in the contract, or the minimum for that kind or class of coverage provided for by the laws of the province or territory in which the action is filed. This reciprocal scheme provides a uniform basis for the enforcement of motor vehicle insurance claims in Canada and, to a lesser extent, in North America. [...]

¶ 115 *Insurance Act*, R.S.O. 1990, c. I.8

> 275(1) The insurer responsible under subsection 268 (2) for the payment of statutory accident benefits ... is entitled ... to indemnification in relation to such benefits paid by it from the insurers of [...] automobiles as may be named in the regulations involved in the incident from which the responsibility to pay the statutory accident benefits arose. [...]

V. Analysis

¶ 119 The law of interprovincial jurisdiction and enforcement was changed drastically in *Morguard*, supra, where the Court held that the principles of order and fairness require limits on the reach of provincial legislation facilitating the enforcement of an extraprovincial judgment, but that extraprovincial jurisdiction can nevertheless be asserted on the basis of a real and substantial connection. The territoriality issue arose again in *Hunt* ... However, the principles developed in *Hunt* ... are of little help in the case at bar as it concerns consent based jurisdiction in the context of a conflict between insurers. The difficulty with this appeal is that there is a disagreement between the parties about the effect of the PAU and whether signing it constituted attornment by the parties to Ontario's jurisdiction. [...]

¶ 129 In the present case ... what is relevant is the fact that the insurers, by signing the PAU, have recognized the interrelationship of insurance regimes across Canada and accepted that insurers in one province will sometimes be sued in other provinces. In my opinion it is therefore reasonably foreseeable that the appellant will sometimes have to appear in Ontario to defend an action brought in that jurisdiction as a result of an accident having occurred in British Columbia. The appellant is, at least notionally, an insurer in Ontario, or one carrying out business in that province. In fact, the appellant has facilitated service and agreed, in limited circumstances, not to raise certain defences in Ontario courts. I do not find it unfair that insurers involved in the interprovincial scheme underlying this appeal, and having accepted the risk of harm to extraprovincial parties to the agreement, be considered to have attorned to the jurisdiction of Ontario's courts. I think that all of the reasons justifying a widened jurisdiction in *Morguard* apply in this case. Most importantly, the demands of Canadian federalism strongly favour this result. I wish to clarify at this juncture that my conclusion does not interfere with the right of the appellant in this case to argue that Ontario is forum non conveniens, or that the law of Ontario should not apply. [...]

D) *The Constitutional Issue*

¶ 140 I do not propose to deal at any length with the question of the permissible reach of Ontario's *Insurance Act*. In *Reference re Upper Churchill Water Rights Reversion Act*, [1984] 1 S.C.R. 297 , the Court opined that valid provincial legislation can affect extra-provincial rights in an "incidental" manner. I am of the view that valid provincial laws can affect "matters" which are "sufficiently connected" to the province. ... In my view, the respondent has shown that the subject matter which the *Insurance Act* covers, interinsurer indemnification, falls within provincial jurisdiction and is sufficiently connected to Ontario so as to render the statute applicable to the ICBC. [...]

¶ 141 [...] The constitutional question should be answered in the negative.

BRITISH COLUMBIA v. IMPERIAL TOBACCO CANADA LTD. ET. AL.
[2005] 2 S.C.C. 49.

The judgment of the Court was delivered by

¶ 1 **MAJOR J.** — The *Tobacco Damages and Health Care Costs Recovery Act*, S.B.C. 2000, c. 30 (the "Act"), authorizes an action by the government of British Columbia against a manufacturer of tobacco products for the recovery of health care expenditures incurred by the government in treating individuals exposed to those products. Liability hinges on those individuals having been exposed to tobacco products because of the manufacturer's breach of a duty owed to persons in British Columbia, and on the government of British Columbia having incurred health care expenditures in treating disease in those individuals caused by such exposure.

¶ 2 These appeals question the constitutional validity of the Act. The appellants, each of which was sued by the government of British Columbia pursuant to the Act, challenge its constitutional validity on the basis that it violates (1) territorial limits on provincial legislative jurisdiction; (2) the principle of judicial independence; and (3) the principle of the rule of law. [...]

¶ 5 Section 2(1) is the keystone of the Act. It reads:

> The government has a direct and distinct action against a manufacturer to recover the cost of health care benefits caused or contributed to by a tobacco related wrong.

¶ 6 The terms "manufacturer", "cost of health care benefits" and "tobacco related wrong" are defined in s. 1(1) of the Act. Their definitions in turn refer to other defined terms. Incorporating the definitions into s. 2, then paraphrasing to some degree, the section provides as follows:

> The government has a direct and distinct action against a manufacturer for the present value of existing and reasonably expected future expenditures by the government for
>
> (a) benefits as defined under the Hospital Insurance Act or the Medicare Protection Act;
>
> (b) payments under the Continuing Care Act; and
>
> (c) programs, services or benefits associated with disease,
>
> where
>
> (a) such expenditures result from disease or the risk of disease caused or contributed to by exposure to a tobacco product; and
>
> (b) such exposure was caused or contributed to by
>
>> (i) a tort committed in British Columbia by the manufacturer; or
>>
>> (ii) a breach of a common law, equitable or statutory duty or obligation owed by the manufacturer to persons in British Columbia who have been or might have become exposed to a tobacco product.

¶ 7 Viewed in this light, s. 2(1) creates a cause of action by which the government of British Columbia may recover from a tobacco manufacturer money spent treating disease in British Columbians, where such disease was caused by exposure to a tobacco product (whether entirely in British Columbia or not), and such exposure was caused by that manufacturer's tort in British Columbia, or breach of a duty owed to persons in British Columbia.

¶ 8 The cause of action created by s. 2(1), besides being "direct and distinct", is not a subrogated claim: s. 2(2). Nor is it barred by the *Limitation Act*, R.S.B.C. 1996, c. 266 s. 6(1). Crucially, it can be pursued on an aggregate basis — i.e. in respect of a population of persons for whom the government has made or can reasonably be expected to make expenditures: s. 2(4)(b).

¶ 9 Where the government's claim is made on an aggregate basis, it may use statistical, epidemiological and sociological evidence to prove its case: s. 5(b). It need not identify, prove the cause of disease or prove the expenditures made in respect of any individual member of the population on which it bases its claim: s. 2(5)(a). Furthermore, health care records and related information in respect of individual members of that population are not compellable, except if relied upon by an expert witness: ss. 2(5)(b) and (c). However, the court is free to order the discovery of a "statistically meaningful sample" of the health care records of individual members of that population, stripped of personal identifiers: ss. 2(5)(d) and (e).

¶ 10 Pursuant to ss. 3(1) and (2), the government enjoys a reversed burden of proof in respect of certain elements of an aggregate claim. Where the aggregate claim is, like the one brought against each of the appellants, to recover expenditures in respect of disease caused by exposure to cigarettes, the reversed burden of proof operates as follows. Once the government proves that

> (a) the defendant manufacturer breached a common law, equitable or statutory duty or obligation it owed to persons in British Columbia who have been or might become exposed to cigarettes;
>
> (b) exposure to cigarettes can cause or contribute to disease; and
>
> (c) during the manufacturer's breach, cigarettes manufactured or promoted by the manufacturer were offered for sale in British Columbia,

the court will presume that

> (a) the population that is the basis for the government's aggregate claim would not have been exposed to cigarettes but for the manufacturer's breach; and
>
> (b) such exposure caused or contributed to disease in a portion of the population that is the basis for the government's aggregate claim.

¶ 11 In this way, it falls on a defendant manufacturer to show that its breach of duty did not give rise to exposure, or that exposure resulting from its breach of duty did not give rise to the disease in respect of which the government claims for its expenditures. The reversed burden of proof on the manufacturer is a balance of probabilities: s. 3(4).

¶ 12 Where the aforementioned presumptions apply, the court must determine the portion of the government's expenditures after the date of the manufacturer's breach that resulted from exposure to cigarettes: s. 3(3)(a). The manufacturer is liable for such expenditures in proportion to its share of the market for cigarettes in British Columbia, calculated over the period of time between its first breach of duty and trial: ss. 3(3)(b) and 1(6).

¶ 13 In an action by the government, a manufacturer will be jointly and severally liable for expenditures arising from a joint breach of duty (i.e. for expenditures caused by disease, which disease was caused by exposure, which exposure was caused by a joint breach of duty to which the manufacturer was a party): s. 4(1).

¶ 14 Pursuant to s. 10, all provisions of the Act operate retroactively. [...]

IV. Analysis

A. *Extra-territoriality*

¶ 26 Section 92 of the *Constitution Act, 1867* is the primary source of provincial legislatures' authority to legislate. Provincial legislation must therefore respect the limitations, territorial and otherwise, on provincial legislative competence found in s. 92. The opening words of s. 92 — "In each Province" — represent a blanket territorial limitation on provincial powers. That limitation is echoed in a similar phrase that qualifies a number of the heads of power in s. 92: "in the Province".

¶ 27 The territorial limitations on provincial legislative competence reflect the requirements of order and fairness underlying Canadian federal arrangements and discussed by this Court in *Morguard* ... *Hunt* ... and *Unifund*.... They serve to ensure that provincial legislation both has a meaningful connection to the province enacting it, and pays respect to "the sovereignty of the other provinces within their respective legislative spheres". [...]

¶ 28 Where the validity of provincial legislation is challenged on the basis that it violates territorial limitations on provincial legislative competence, the analysis centres on the pith and substance of the legislation. If its pith and substance is in relation to matters falling within the field of provincial legislative competence, the legislation is valid. Incidental or ancillary extra-provincial aspects of such legislation are irrelevant to its validity. [...]

¶ 29 In determining the pith and substance of legislation, the court identifies its essential character or dominant feature... This may be done through reference to both the purpose and effect of the legislation [...]

¶ 30 Where the pith and substance of legislation relates to a tangible matter — i.e., something with an intrinsic and observable physical presence — the question of whether it respects the territorial limitations in s. 92 is easy to answer. One need only look to the location of the matter. If it is in the province, the limitations have been respected, and the legislation is valid. If it is outside the province, the limitations have been violated, and the legislation is invalid.

¶ 31 Where legislation's pith and substance relates to an intangible matter, the characterization is more complicated. That is the case here.

¶ 32 The pith and substance of the Act is plainly the creation of a civil cause of action. More specifically, it is the creation of a civil cause of action by which the government of British Columbia may seek compensation for certain health care costs incurred by it. Civil causes of action are a matter within provincial legislative jurisdiction under s. 92(13) of the *Constitution Act, 1867*: "Property and Civil Rights in the Province". See *General Motors of Canada Ltd. v. City National Leasing* [...]

¶ 33 But s. 92(13) does not speak to "Property and Civil Rights" located anywhere. It speaks only to "Property and Civil Rights in the Province". And, to reiterate, it is, like all provincial heads of power, qualified by the opening words of s. 92: "In each Province". The issue thus becomes how to determine whether an intangible, such as the cause of action constituting the pith and substance of the Act, is "in the Province".

¶ 34 *Churchill Falls* dealt with a similar issue. In that case, McIntyre J. was confronted with a Newfoundland statute, the pith and substance of which was the modification of rights existing under a contract between Churchill Falls (Labrador) Corporation Limited and Quebec Hydro-Electric Commission. Since the entity possessing those rights (namely, the Commission) was constituted in Quebec, and the parties had agreed that the Quebec courts had exclusive jurisdiction to adjudicate disputes concerning their contract, McIntyre J. regarded the rights created by that contract as situated in Quebec. The Newfoundland law that purported to modify them was thus invalid. It related to civil rights, but not to civil rights "in the Province".

¶ 35 McIntyre J.'s approach to locating the civil rights constituting the pith and substance of the Newfoundland legislation illustrates the role, pointed out by Binnie J. in *Unifund*, at para. 63, that "the relationships among the enacting territory, the subject matter of the law, and the person[s] sought to be subjected to its regulation" play in determining the validity of legislation alleged to be impermissibly extra-territorial in scope. In *Churchill Falls*, an examination of those relationships indicated that the intangible civil rights constituting the pith and substance of the Newfoundland legislation at issue were not meaningfully connected to the legislating province, and could properly be the subject matter only of Quebec legislation. Put slightly differently, if the impugned Newfoundland legislation had been permitted to regulate those civil rights, neither of the purposes underlying s. 92's territorial limitations would be respected. It followed that those civil rights should be regarded as located beyond the territorial scope of Newfoundland's legislative competence under s. 92.

Roadmap — Real & Substantial Connection Test

¶ 36 From the foregoing it can be seen that several analytical steps may be required to determine whether provincial legislation in pith and substance respects territorial limits on provincial legislative competence. The first step is to determine the pith and substance, or dominant feature, of the impugned legislation, and to identify a provincial head of power under which it might fall. Assuming a suitable head of power can be found, the second step is to determine whether the pith and substance respects the territorial limitations on that head of power — i.e. whether it is in the province. If the pith and substance is tangible, whether it is in the province is simply a question of its physical location. If the pith and substance is intangible, the court must look to the relationships among the enacting territory, the subject matter of the legislation and the persons made subject to it, in order to determine whether the legislation, if allowed to stand, would respect the dual purposes of the territorial limitations in s. 92 (namely, to ensure that provincial legislation has a meaningful connection to the enacting province and pays respect to the legislative sovereignty of other territories). If it would, the pith and substance of the legislation should be regarded as situated in the province.

Analysis / Application

¶ 37 Here, the cause of action that is the pith and substance of the Act serves exclusively to make the persons ultimately responsible for tobacco-related disease suffered by British Columbians — namely, the tobacco manufacturers who, through their wrongful acts, caused those British Columbians to be exposed to tobacco — liable for the costs incurred by the government of British Columbia in treating that disease. There are thus strong relationships among the enacting territory (British Columbia), the subject matter of the law (compensation for the government of British Columbia's tobacco-related health care costs) and the persons made subject to it (the tobacco manufacturers ultimately responsible for those costs), such that the Act can easily be said to be meaningfully connected to the province.

¶ 38 The Act respects the legislative sovereignty of other jurisdictions. Though the cause of action that is its pith and substance may capture, to some extent, activities occurring outside of British Columbia, no territory could possibly assert a stronger relationship to that cause of action than British Columbia. That is because there is at all times one critical connection to British Columbia exclusively: the recovery permitted by the action is in relation to expenditures by the government of British Columbia for the health care of British Columbians.

¶ 39 In assessing the Act's respect for the territorial limitations on British Columbia's legislative competence, the appellants and the Court of Appeal placed considerable emphasis on the question of whether, as a matter of statutory interpretation, the breach of duty by a manufacturer that is a necessary condition of its liability under the cause of action created by the Act must occur in British Columbia. That emphasis was undue, for two reasons.

¶ 40 First, the driving force of the Act's cause of action is compensation for the government of British Columbia's health care costs, not remediation of tobacco manufacturers' breaches of duty. While the Act makes the existence of a breach of duty one of several necessary conditions to a manufacturer's liability to the government, it is not the mischief at which the cause of action created by the Act is aimed. The Act leaves breaches of duty to be remedied by the law that gives rise to the duty. Thus, the breaches of duty to which the Act refers are of subsidiary significance to the cause of action created by it, and the locations where those breaches might occur have little or no bearing on the strength of the relationship between the cause of action and the enacting jurisdiction.

¶ 41 Second, and in any event, the only relevant breaches under the Act are breaches of duties (or obligations) owed "to persons in British Columbia" (s. 1(1) "tobacco related wrong", s. 3(1)(a)) that give rise to health care expenditures by the government of British Columbia. Thus, even if the existence of a breach of duty were the central element of the Act's cause of action (it is not), the cause of action would remain strongly related to British Columbia.

¶ 42 The question of whether other matters, such as exposure and disease, to which the Act refers, must occur or arise in British Columbia is equally or more irrelevant to the Act's validity. Those matters too are conditions precedent to success in an action brought pursuant to the Act and of subsidiary significance to it.

¶ 43 It follows that the cause of action that constitutes the pith and substance of the Act is properly described as located "in the Province". The Act is not invalid by reason of extra-territoriality, being in pith and substance legislation in relation "Property and Civil Rights in the Province" under s. 92(13) of the *Constitution Act, 1867.* ...

V. Conclusion

¶ 78 The Act is constitutionally valid. The appeals are dismissed, with costs to the respondents throughout. Each constitutional question is answered "no". [...]

2. Residuary and Emergency Powers

(a) General

LYSYK, "CONSTITUTIONAL REFORM AND THE INTRODUCTORY CLAUSE OF SECTION 91: RESIDUAL AND EMERGENCY LAW-MAKING AUTHORITY"
(1979), 57 CAN. BAR REV. 531.

INTRODUCTION

No provision of the *British North America Act* has attracted more attention or sparked more controversy among legal commentators than has the introductory clause of section 91, together with its overlay of judicial interpretation. The introductory clause is the enacting portion of section 91 and it provides, with disarming simplicity, that Parliament shall have authority "to make laws for the Peace, Order and good Government of Canada, in relation to all Matters not coming within the Classes of Subjects by this Act assigned exclusively to the Legislatures of the Provinces". By its terms the clause constitutes a residual category of federal law-making authority.

Further, it carries the judicially assigned responsibility of providing a constitutional base for the so-called emergency doctrine, the thrust of which is that Parliament may, to meet an emergency, enact laws which in ordinary circumstances would be beyond its constitutional reach.

Both varieties of law-making power – residual and emergency – have been the subject of proposals for change in a new or revised Canadian constitution. With respect to residual powers the government of Quebec has on a number of occasions taken the position that all powers not expressly conferred on the central government ought to be assigned to the provincial legislatures, pointing out that in the case of most other federal constitutions residual legislative authority is assigned to the constituent units of the federation. That position found support in the recent Pepin-Robarts Task Force recommendations for a single legislative residuum assigned to the provincial legislatures. The Task Force rejected the possibility of residual authority shared by Parliament and the provincial legislatures, but this latter option has found other sponsorship. Insofar as the emergency power is concerned, recent recommendations have included proposals to the effect that this exceptional legislative authority ought to be expressly dealt with, and more sharply defined, in a new constitutional clause, and some provinces are on record as advocating new constraints, either of form or substance, or of both, upon exercise of this power. [...]

PEACE, ORDER AND GOOD GOVERNMENT

A closer examination of section 91 of the *B.N.A. Act* is called for at this point. It consists of three distinct segments: (i) the introductory (or enacting) clause; (ii) the declaratory clause, together with the 31 (originally 29) enumerations incorporated within it; and (iii) the deeming clause. Compartmentalized in that way for convenience, section 91 reads as follows:

Introductory Clause:
It shall be lawful for the Queen, by and with the Advice and Consent of the Senate and House of Commons, to make laws for the Peace, Order and good Government of Canada, in relation to all matters not coming within the Classes of Subjects by this Act assigned exclusively to the Legislatures of the Provinces;

Declaratory Clause:
and for greater Certainty, but not so as to restrict the Generality of the foregoing terms of this Section, it is hereby declared that (notwithstanding anything in this Act) the exclusive Legislative Authority of the Parliament of Canada extends to all Matters coming within the Classes of Subjects next hereinafter enumerated, that is to say, [enumerations 1 to 29].

Deeming Clause:
And any Matter coming within any of the Classes of Subjects enumerated in this section shall not be deemed to come within the Class of Matters of a local or private Nature comprised in the Enumeration of the Classes of Subjects by this Act assigned exclusively to the Legislatures of the Provinces.

As noted above, the introductory clause is the enacting, or power-conferring, portion of section 91. The thrust of the introductory clause is that Parliament can make laws relating to matters "not coming within the classes of subjects which the Act assigns exclusively to the Provinces. In form, at least, the only function of the balance of section 91 is to aid in determining the scope of the classes of subjects assigned exclusively to the provincial legislatures, the central question being whether the "matter" to which an enactment is found to relate is one "coming within" the classes of subjects allocated to the provinces. The second (declaratory) and third (deeming) clauses of section 91 perform that function in the following ways.

The declaratory clause stipulates that Parliament can (notwithstanding anything in the Act) exclusively legislate on matters coming within specified classes of subjects: the thirty-one enumerations. These enumerations, according to the opening words of the declaratory clause, are made "for greater certainty". This might be imagined to indicate that since the items have been listed in section 91 only to provide greater certainty, they are all ones which, by their very nature, might have been deduced to fall outside the classes of subjects assigned to the provinces even if the draughtsman of the *B.N.A. Act* had not thoughtfully provided us with a checklist by way of reminder. Of course, this is not the case, for without the enumerations in the declaratory clause, what governing constitutional principle would have disclosed that penitentiaries lay beyond provincial legislative competence? Or Sable Island? Or marriage and divorce? Or intellectual property? In fact, many of the enumerations of section 91 do not merely add "greater certainty"; they supply new information in that they carve out exceptions or exclusions from the provincial classes of subjects which the latter, read in isolation, would not disclose or even permit, much less require. [...]

Returning now to the question of what assistance can be derived from the language of the introductory clause itself, it will be recalled that it provides that it shall be lawful for Parliament to make laws, "for the Peace, Order and good Government of Canada, in relation to all Matters not coming within the Classes of Subjects by this Act assigned exclusively to the Legislatures of the Provinces. [...]" The clause is sometimes referred to as the "peace, order and good government clause", but this does not capture its essence. It may be noted, to begin, that the clause does not authorize Parliament to enact laws *in relation to* peace, order and good government. It confers authority to legislate for the peace, order and good government of Canada, but only in relation to matters not coming within provincial classes of subjects. The point is not merely technical, but one of substance. An examination of Part VI of the *B.N.A. Act* ("Distribution of Legislative Powers", sections 91 to 95, inclusive) discloses that the power-conferring provisions invariably employ the phrase *"in relation to"* for the purpose of identifying the matters or subjects or classes of subjects which are being allocated. What the introductory clause assigns to Parliament, to repeat, is not authority to make laws in relation to peace, order and good government but authority to make laws in relation to matters "not coming within" the provincial heads of power. In other words, Parliament is not authorized to legislate in relation to a matter caught by the provincial categories simply because it might in some sense be thought to qualify as contributing toward the "peace, order and good government of Canada".

Further, it would have been quite inappropriate to assign to Parliament authority to make laws in relation to "peace, order and good government" because that phrase had been used throughout British colonial history to confer the full range of legislative authority characteristic of a unitary, not a federal, state. Prior to Confederation the "peace, order and good government" phraseology had been used repeatedly in British North America to confer law-making authority. The words were not intended to be descriptive of the power granted in the sense that it invited the question of whether a particular local enactment was conducive to peace or to order or to good government. The salient point, however, is simply that the phrase could hardly be thought to have any relevance to the federal principle, for prior to 1867 it had never been employed with respect to a federation. What it denotes in the introductory clause, as in the case of the earlier enactments, is simply plenitude of legislative authority, subject to expressed limitations and to overriding Imperial legislation. And what Parliament is authorized to make laws in relation to is not the totality – not peace, order and good government generally – but only that portion of the whole which consists of matters "not coming within" the classes of subjects assigned to the provinces. While use of the "peace, order and good government" expression carries the thought that the entirety of legislative authority is bestowed on Parliament and Legislatures together, it provides no assistance at all on the question of where the line between their respective areas of competence is to be drawn. Insofar as the distribution of legislative authority is concerned, in other words, the reference to "peace, order and good government" contributes nothing.

In sum, for purposes of allocating legislative authority, the introductory clause stripped to essentials simply provides that Parliament can "make laws [...] in relation to all matters not coming within the classes of subjects [...] assigned exclusively to the Legislatures of the Provinces." If one wished to epitomize Parliament's law-making authority thereunder one might wish to describe it (were the phrase not so awkward) as the "not coming within" clause. Labeling it the "peace, order and good government" clause, on the other hand, focuses upon a phrase that performs no useful function in drawing the constitutional boundary between federal and provincial legislative authority. Moreover, it diverts attention from the central thrust of the introductory clause, which calls for determining the scope of the provincial enumerations in order to ascertain what remains for Parliament after the provincial heads of power, properly construed in light of the Act as a whole, have been exhausted. [...]

THE EMERGENCY DOCTRINE

Simply stated, the "emergency doctrine" amounts to this: to meet an emergency (by definition a temporary and abnormal situation), Parliament may legislate in relation to matters which would ordinarily come within the classes of subjects assigned to the provinces. [...] From the outset [...] the emergency doctrine was advanced not in substitution for, but in supplement of, the capacity of the introductory clause of section 91 to support federal legislation relating to residual matters.

The emergency doctrine was developed primarily in nine decisions of the Judicial Committee of the Privy Council reviewing federal enactments, and in each of those cases the legislation was characterized as being in relation to matters ordinarily coming within the property and civil rights clause. The result of that characterization was that in none of those cases could the purely residuary capacity of the introductory clause be relied upon. In six of the cases the enactments did not purport to deal with, or to be limited to the duration of, an emergency, and a finding of ultra vires resulted. In the other three cases, due to abnormal circumstances (war and the aftermath of war), the legislation was sustained as directed toward meeting an emergency.

How is the special legislative power available to Parliament to deal with emergencies to be reconciled with the limitation in the introductory clause restricting federal authority to matters "not coming within" the provincial enumerations? The inventor of the emergency doctrine, Viscount Haldane, employed expressions which suggest a temporary transcending of the confines of the provincial heads of power. [...] Haldane was clearly of the view that a federal Constitution must accommodate centralized power in an emergency situation even if (as in the case of the United States) residuary powers are at the local level.

The course of decision on the emergency doctrine makes it abundantly clear, therefore, that there are two separate and wholly distinct strands to the legislative authority that the introductory clause of section 91 confers on Parliament. They are entirely compatible and cumulative. If a federal enactment is characterized as being in relation to a matter ordinarily coming within a provincial head of power, and would therefore be ultra vires, it may still be possible to sustain the enactment by demonstrating that it is responsive to an emergency situation.

RECENT DEVELOPMENTS

[...] The reasons for judgment in the *Anti-Inflation Reference* [...] clearly drew a distinction between the special and temporary legislative authority accruing to Parliament in emergency situations on the one hand and, on the other, the authority it enjoys at all times to enact legislation over matters which are residual in the sense of falling outside the classes of subjects assigned to the provinces. [...] [T]he fundamental difference between the two functions of the clause, supported by two distinct lines of judicial decisions, was accepted, and any attempt to fashion a single test for applicability of the introductory clause, à la Viscount Simon in the *Canadian Temperance Federation* case, may now be taken to have been abandoned. [...]

It seems abundantly clear in the wake of the *Anti-Inflation* judgment that in peacetime, as well as in circumstances associated with war, the courts will be strongly inclined to defer to Parliament's appraisal of whether or not a particular situation qualifies as an emergency, and the appropriateness of the legislative response aimed at meeting it.

One [...] aspect of the *Anti-Inflation Reference* [...] has to do with the task of characterizing a challenged enactment for purposes of constitutional categorization. This stage in the process of constitutional analysis can effectively be dispensed with whenever a federal enactment is sustainable on the basis of the emergency doctrine since, by hypothesis, the ordinary distribution of legislative authority stands in abeyance during the course of the emergency. As the dissenting reasons for judgment authored by Beetz J. rejected the emergency doctrine option, it became necessary for him to address the question of the "matters" to which the *Anti-Inflation Act* related and in the course of doing so he offered some observations concerning considerations to be taken into account when the federal residuary power is invoked.

A more intriguing element in the Beetz analysis is the attention paid to the question of whether the legislation addresses a "new" matter, and the relevance of that question in determining whether or not constitutional support will be forthcoming from the federal residual power. Having reviewed instances in which the introductory clause of section 91 has been invoked successfully with respect to matters of "national concern" (federally incorporated companies, aeronautics, radio, National Capital Region) he stated:

> [These authorities] had the effect of adding by judicial process new matters or new classes of matters to the federal list of powers. However, this was done only in cases where a new matter was not an aggregate but had a degree of unity that made it indivisible, an identity which made it distinct from provincial matters and a sufficient consistence to retain the bounds of form. [...] The "containment and reduction of inflation" does not pass muster as a new subject matter. It is an aggregate of several subjects some of which form a substantial part of provincial jurisdiction. It is totally lacking in specificity. It is so pervasive that it knows no bounds. Its recognition as a federal head of power would render most provincial powers nugatory.

> I should add that inflation is a very ancient phenomenon, several thousands years old, as old probably as the history of currency. The Fathers of Confederation were quite aware of it.

This passage reflects the theme, already noted, that a candidate for characterization as a new matter or class of matters assignable to the residuary power ought to have a relative coherence or "degree of unity". But beyond that the above quoted passage, and in particular the last paragraph of it, carries the suggestion that the "newness" of the matter is relevant not only to whether the characterization of a particular enactment arises as a matter of first impression for the courts, but whether the problem which the legislation addresses is new or old and, more particularly, whether the phenomenon is or is not one which has emerged since Confederation. This latter element – the novelty or lack of novelty in the problem with which the enactment is concerned – reappears in the *Hauser* decision. [...]

[Note: "Newness" is also discussed in detail in the majority and minority opinions in *Crown Zellerbach*, infra p. 485, which adds modifications and clarifications.]

(b) The Residuary Power

(i)   Early Development

RUSSELL v. R.
(1882) 7 APP. CAS. 829 (P.C.).

[Charles Russell was convicted under the *Canada Temperance Act, 1878* of unlawfully selling liquor in Fredericton, New Brunswick. Russell challenged the constitutional validity of the *Canada Temperance Act, 1878* as beyond Parliament's jurisdiction under the division of powers. The preamble of the *Act* states that "it is very desirable to promote temperance in the dominion and that there should be uniform legislation in all the provinces respecting the traffic in intoxicating liquors." The *Act* prohibits traffic in intoxicating liquors and provides for the prosecution and penalties for offences. The *Act* provides that the prohibition comes into force by petition of one-fourth of the qualified federal electors in any county or city in the Dominion asking that the *Act* be in force, followed by voting by all electors. If the petition is adopted, the Governor General is authorized to proclaim the *Act* in force in that county or city.]

SIR MONTAGUE E. SMITH [for the Court]: — [...] The effect of the Act when brought into force in any county or town within the Dominion is, describing it generally, to prohibit the sale of intoxicating liquors, except in wholesale quantities, or for certain specified purposes, to regulate the traffic in the excepted cases, and to make sale of liquors in violation of the prohibition and regulations contained in the Act criminal offences, punishable by fine, and for the third or subsequent offence by imprisonment. [...]

The general question of the competency of the Dominion Parliament to pass the act depends on the construction of the 91st and 92nd sections of the *British North America Act, 1867*, which are found in Part VI of the statute under the heading, "Distribution of Legislative Powers." [...]

The general scheme of the *British North America Act* with regard to the distribution of legislative powers, and the general scope and effect of sects. 91 and 92, and their relation to each other, were fully considered and commented on by this Board in the case of the *Citizens Insurance Company v. Parsons*. According to the principle of construction there pointed out, the first question to be determined is, whether the Act now in question falls within any of the classes of subjects enumerated in sect. 92 and assigned exclusively to the Legislatures of the Provinces. If it does, then the further question would arise, viz., whether the subject of the Act does not also fall within one of the enumerated classes of subjects in sect. 91, and so does not still belong to the Dominion Parliament. But if the Act does not fall within any of the classes of subjects in sect. 92, no further question will remain, for it cannot be contended, and indeed was not contended at the Justices' bar that, if the Act does not come within one of the classes of subjects assigned to the Provincial Legislatures, the Parliament of Canada had not, by its general power "to make laws for the peace, order and good government of Canada", full legislative authority to pass it.

Three classes of subjects enumerated in sect. 92 were referred to, under each of which, it was contended by the appellant's counsel, the present legislation fell. These were:

9. Shop, saloon, tavern, auctioneer, and other licenses in order to the raising of a revenue for provincial, local or municipal purposes.

13. Property and civil rights in the province.

16. Generally all matters of a merely local or private nature in the province.

With regard to the first of these classes, No. 9, it is to be observed that the power of granting licenses is not assigned to the Provincial Legislatures for the purpose of regulating trade, but "in order to the raising of a revenue for provincial, local or municipal purposes."

The Act in question is not a fiscal law; it is not a law for raising revenue; on the contrary, the effect of it may be to destroy or diminish revenue; indeed it was a main objection to the Act that in the city of Fredericton it did in point of fact diminish the sources of municipal revenue. It is evident, therefore, that the matter of the Act is not within the class of subject No. 9, and consequently that it could not have been passed by the Provincial Legislature by virtue of any authority conferred upon it by that sub-section. [...]

Next, their Lordships cannot think that the *Temperance Act* in question properly belongs to the class of subjects, "Property and Civil Rights." It has in its legal aspect an obvious and close similarity to laws which place restrictions on the sale or custody of poisonous drugs, or of dangerously explosive substances. These things, as well as intoxicating liquors, can, of course, be held as property, but a law placing restrictions on their sale, custody or removal, on the ground that the free sale or use of them is dangerous to public safety, and making it a criminal offense punishable by find or imprisonment to violate these restrictions, cannot properly be deemed a law in relation to property in the sense in which those words are used in the 92nd section. What Parliament is dealing with in legislation of this kind is not a matter in relation to property and its rights, but one relating to public order and safety. That is the primary matter dealt with, and though incidentally the free use of things in which men may have property is interfered with, that incidental interference does not alter the character of the law. Upon the same considerations, the Act in question cannot be regarded as legislation in relation to civil rights. In however large a sense these words are used, it could not have been intended to prevent the Parliament of Canada from declaring and enacting certain uses of property, and certain acts in relation to property, to be criminal and wrongful. Laws which make it a criminal offence for a man wilfully to set fire to his own house on the ground that such an act endangers the public safety, or to overwork his horse on the ground of cruelty to the animal, though affecting in some sense property and the right of a man to do as he pleases with his own, cannot properly be regarded as legislation in relation to property or to civil rights. Nor could a law which prohibited or restricted the sale or exposure of cattle having a contagious disease be so regarded. Laws of this nature designed for the promotion of public order, safety or morals, and which subject those who contravene them to criminal procedure and punishment, belong to the subject of public wrongs rather than to that of civil rights. They are of a nature which fall within the general authority of Parliament to make laws for the order and good government of Canada, and have direct relation to criminal law, which is one of the enumerated classes of subjects assigned exclusively to the Parliament of Canada. It was said in the course of the judgment of this Board in the case of the *Citizens Insurance Company of Canada v. Parsons*, that the two sections (1 and 92) must be read together, and the language of one interpreted, and, where necessary, modified by that of the other. Few, if any, laws could be made by Parliament for the peace, order and good government of Canada which did not in some incidental way affect property and civil rights; and it could not have been intended, when assuring to the provinces exclusive legislative authority on the subject of property and civil rights, to exclude the Parliament from the exercise of this general power whenever any such incidental interference would result form it. The true nature and character of the legislation in the particular instance under discussion must always be determined, in order to ascertain the class of subject to which it really belongs. In the present case it appears to their Lordships, for the reasons already given, that the matter of the Act in question doe not properly belong to the class of subjects "Property and Civil Rights" within the meaning of sub-sect. 13.

It was lastly contended that this Act fell within sub-sect. 16 of sect. 92, - "Generally all matters of a merely local or personal nature in the province." [...] Their Lordships cannot concur in this view. [...]

The manner of bringing the prohibitions and penalties of the Act into force, which Parliament has thought fit to adopt, does not alter its general and uniform character. Parliament deals with the subject as one of general concern to the Dominion, upon which uniformity of legislation is desirable, and the Parliament alone can so deal with it. There is no ground or pretence for saying that the evil or vice struck at by the Act in question is local or exists only in one province, and that Parliament, under colour of general legislation, is dealing with a provincial matter only. It is therefore unnecessary to discuss the considerations which a state of circumstances of this kind might present. The present legislation is clearly meant to apply a remedy to an evil which is assumed to exist throughout the Dominion, and the local option, as it is called, no more localizes the subject and scope of the Act than a provision in an Act for the prevention of contagious diseases in cattle that a public officer should proclaim in what districts it should come in effect, would make the statute itself a mere local law for each of these districts. In statutes of this kind the legislation is general, and the provision for the special application of it to particular places does not alter its character.

Their Lordships having come to the conclusion that the Act in question does not fall within any of the classes of subjects assigned exclusively to the Provincial Legislatures, it becomes unnecessary to discuss the further question whether its provisions also fall within any of the classes of subjects enumerated in sect. 91. In abstaining from this discussion, they must not be understood as intimating any dissent from the opinion of the Chief Justice of the Supreme Court of Canada and the other Judges, who held that the Act, as a general regulation of the traffic in intoxicating liquors throughout the Dominion, fell within the class of subject, "the regulation of trade and commerce," enumerated in that section, and was, on that ground, a valid exercise of the legislative power of the Parliament of Canada.

In the result, their Lordships will humbly recommend Her Majesty to affirm the judgment of the Supreme Court of Canada, and with costs.

A.G. ONT. V. A.G. CAN.
[1896] A.C. 348 (P.C.).

[The Governor-General in Council referred seven questions to the Supreme Court of Canada. Generally, these questions asked whether a provincial legislature had jurisdiction to prohibit the sale, manufacture and importation of intoxicating liquors into the province. The seventh question asked whether Ontario had jurisdiction to enact s. 18 of the *Liquor Licence Act*. Section 18 empowered township councils, following approval by municipal electors, to prohibit the sale of liquor in taverns and shops.]

LORD WATSON [for the Court]: — [...] The *Canada Temperance Act of 1886* (Revised Statutes of Canada, 49 Vict. c. 106) is applicable to all the provinces of the Dominion. Its general scheme is to give to the electors of every county or city the option of adopting, or declining to adopt, the provisions of the second part of the Act, which make it unlawful for any person "by himself, his clerk, servant or agent, to expose or keep for sale, or directly or indirectly, on any pretence or upon any device, to sell or barter, or in consideration of the purchase of any other property, give to any other person any intoxicating liquor." It expressly declares that no violation of these enactments shall be made lawful by reason of any licence of any description whatsoever. Certain relaxations are made in the case of sales of liquor for sacramental or medicinal purposes, or for exclusive use in some art, trade, or manufacture. The prohibition does not extend to manufacturers, importers, or wholesale traders who sell liquors in quantities above a specified limit, when they have good reason to believe that the purchasers will forthwith carry their purchase beyond the limits of the county or city, or of any adjoining county or city in which the provisions of the Act are in force.

For the purpose of bringing the second part of the Act into operation an order of the Governor-General of Canada in Council is required. The order must be made on the petition of a county or city, which cannot be granted until it has been put to the vote of the electors of such county or city. When a majority of the votes pulled are adverse to the petition, it must be dismissed, and no similar application can be made within the period of three years from the day on which the poll was taken. When the vote is in favour of the petition, and is followed by an Order in Council, one-fourth of the qualified electors of the county or city may apply to the Governor-General in Council for a recall of the order, which is to be granted in the event of a majority of the electors voting in favour of the application. Power is given to the Governor-General in Council to issue in the like manner, and after similar procedure, an order repealing any by-law passed by any municipal council for the application of the *Temperance Act of 1864*.

The *Dominion Act* also contains an express repeal of the prohibitory clauses of the provincial *Act* of 1864, and of the machinery thereby provided for bringing them into operation, (1.) as to every municipality within the limits of Ontario in which, at the passing of the *Act* of 1886, there was no municipal by-law in force, (2.) as to every municipality within these limits in which a prohibitive by-law then in force shall be subsequently repealed under the provisions of either Act, and (3.) as to every municipality having a municipal by-law which is included in the limits of, or has the same limits with, any county or city in which the second part of the *Canada Temperance Act* is brought into force before the repeal of the by-law, which by-law, in that event, is declared to be null and void.

With the view of restoring to municipalities within the province whose powers were affected by that repeal the right to make by-laws which they had possessed under the law of the old province, the Legislature of Ontario passed s. 18 of 53 Vict. c. 56, to which the seventh question in this case relates. The enacting words of the clause are introduced by a preamble which recites the previous course of legislation, and the repeal by the *Canada Temperance Act* of the *Upper Canada Act* of 1864 in municipalities where not in force, and concludes thus: "it is expedient that municipalities should have the powers by them formerly possessed." Issue

The seventh question raises the issue, whether, in the circumstances which have just been detailed, the provincial legislature had authority to enact s. 18. In order to determine that issue, it becomes necessary to consider, in the first place, whether the Parliament of Canada had jurisdiction to enact the *Canada Temperance Act*; and, if so, to consider in the second place, whether, after that Act became the law of each province of the Dominion, there yet remained power with the Legislature of Ontario to enact the provisions of s. 18.

The authority of the Dominion Parliament to make laws for the suppression of liquor traffic in the provinces is maintained, in the first place, upon the ground that such legislation deals with matters affecting "the peace, order, and good government of Canada," within the meaning of the introductory and general enactments of s. 91 of the *British North America Act*. [...]

It was apparently contemplated by the framers of the *Imperial Act* of 1867, that the due exercise of the enumerated powers conferred upon the Parliament of Canada by s. 91 might, occasionally and incidentally, involve legislation upon matters which are *prima facie* committed exclusively to the provincial legislatures by s. 92. In order to provide against that contingency, the concluding part of s. 91 enacts that "any matter coming within any of the classes of subjects enumerated in this section shall not be deemed to come within the class of matters of a local or private nature comprised in the enumeration of the classes of subjects by this Act assigned exclusively to the legislatures of the provinces." It was observed by this *Board in Citizens' Insurance Co. of Canada v. Parsons* that the paragraph just quoted "applies in its grammatical construction only to No. 16 of s. 92." The observation was not material to the question arising in that case, and it does not appear to their Lordships to be strictly accurate. It appears to them that the language of the exception in s. 91 was meant to include and correctly describes all the matters enumerated in the sixteen heads of s. 92, as being, from a provincial point of view, of a local or private nature. It also appears to their Lordships that the exception was not meant to derogate from the legislative authority given to provincial legislatures by these sixteen subsections, save to the extent of enabling the Parliament of Canada to deal with matters local or private in those cases where such legislation is necessarily incidental to the exercise of the powers conferred upon it by the enumerative heads of clause 91.

The general authority given to the Canadian Parliament by the introductory enactments of s. 91 is "to make laws for the peace, order, and good government of Canada, in relation to all matters not coming within the classes of subjects by this Act assigned exclusively to the legislatures of the provinces"; and it is declared, but not so as to restrict the generality of these words, that the exclusive authority of the Canadian Parliament extends to all matters coming within the classes of subjects which are enumerated in the clause. There may, therefore, be matters not included in the enumeration, upon which the Parliament of Canada has power to legislate, because they concern the peace, order, and good government of the Dominion. But to those matters which are not specified among the enumerated subjects of legislation, the exception from s. 92, which is enacted by the concluding words of s. 91, has no application; and, in legislating with regard to such matters, the Dominion Parliament has no authority to encroach upon any class of subjects which is exclusively assigned to provincial legislatures by s. 92. These enactments appear to their Lordships to indicate that the exercise of legislative power by the Parliament of Canada, in regard to all matters not enumerated in s. 91, ought to be strictly confined to such matters as are unquestionably of Canadian interest and importance, and ought not to trench upon provincial legislation with respect to any of the classes of subjects enumerated in s. 92. To attach any other construction to the general power which, in supplement of its enumerated powers, is conferred upon the Parliament of Canada by s. 91, would, in their Lordships' opinion, not only be contrary to the intendment of the Act, but would practically destroy the autonomy of the provinces. If it were once conceded that the Parliament of Canada has authority to make laws applicable to the whole Dominion, in relation to matters which in each province are substantially of local or private interest, upon the assumption that these matters also concern the peace, order, and good government of the Dominion, there is hardly a subject enumerated in s. 92 upon which it might not legislate, to the exclusion of the provincial legislatures.

In construing the introductory enactments of s. 91, with respect to matters other than those enumerated, which concern the peace, order, and good government of Canada, it must be kept in view that s. 94, which empowers the Parliament of Canada to make provision for the uniformity of the laws relative to property and civil rights in Ontario, Nova Scotia, and New Brunswick does not extend to the province of Quebec; and also that the Dominion legislation thereby authorized is expressly declared to be of no effect unless and until it has been adopted and enacted by the provincial legislature. These enactments would be idle and abortive, if it were held that the Parliament of Canada derives jurisdiction from the introductory provisions of s. 91, to deal with any matter which is in substance local or provincial, and does not truly affect the interest of the Dominion as a whole. Their Lordships do not doubt that some matters, in their origin local and provincial, might attain such dimensions as to affect the body politic of the Dominion, and to justify the Canadian Parliament in passing laws for their regulation or abolition in the interest of the Dominion. But great caution must be observed in distinguishing between that which is local and provincial, and therefore within the jurisdiction of the provincial legislatures, and that which has ceased to be merely local or provincial, and has become matter of national concern, in such sense as to bring it within the jurisdiction of the Parliament of Canada. An Act restricting the right to carry weapons of offence, or their sale to young persons, within the province would be within the authority of the province legislature. But traffic in arms, or the possession of them under such circumstances as to raise a suspicion that they were to be used for seditious purposes, or against a foreign State, are matters which, their Lordships conceive, might be competently dealt with by the Parliament of the Dominion.

Analysis

The judgment of this Board in *Russell v. Reg.* has relieved their Lordships from the difficult duty of considering whether the *Canada Temperance Act* of 1886 relates to the peace, order, and good government of Canada, in such sense as to bring its provisions within the competency of the Canadian Parliament. In that case the controversy related to the validity of the *Canada Temperance Act* of 1878; and neither the Dominion nor the Provinces were represented in the argument. It arose between a private prosecutor and a person who had been convicted, at his instance, of violating the provisions of the *Canadian Act* within a district of New Brunswick, in which the prohibitory clauses of the Act had been adopted. But the provisions of the *Act* of 1878 were in all material respects the same with those which are now embodied in the *Canada Temperance Act* of 1886; and the reasons which were assigned for sustaining the validity of the earlier, are, in their Lordships' opinion, equally applicable to the later Act. It therefore appears to them that the decision in *Russell v. Reg.* must be accepted as an authority to the extent to which it goes, namely, that the restrictive provisions of the Act of 1886, when they have been duly brought into operation in any provincial area within the Dominion, must receive effect as valid enactments relating to the peace, order, and good government of Canada. [...]

Their Lordships [...] are of opinion that the Ontario Legislature had jurisdiction to enact s. 18, subject to this necessary qualification, that its provisions are or will become inoperative in any district of the province which has already adopted, or may subsequently adopt, the second part of the *Canada Temperance Act* of 1886.

(ii)   Matters "Not Coming Within" Section 92

A.G. ONT. v. CANADA TEMPERANCE
[1946] A.C. 193 at 202 et seq. (P.C.).

VISCOUNT SIMON [for the Court]: — On June 1, 1939, the Lieutenant-Governor of Ontario in Council referred to the Supreme Court of Ontario under the provisions of the *Constitutional Questions Act*, R.S.O., c. 130, the following question: "Are Parts I., II. and III. of the *Canada Temperance Act*, R.S.C. 1927, c. 196, constitutionally valid in whole or in part, and if in part, in what respect?". [...]

The object of the appeal is to challenge the decisions of this Board in the case of *Russell v. The Queen* or at any rate to deny its applicability to the Act now in question. The majority of the Supreme Court held that that decision governed the present case and obliged it to answer the question referred to it in the affirmative. The statute which was declared to be within the legislative competence of the Dominion Parliament in *Russell's* case was the *Canada Temperance Act, 1878*.

The object of the *Act* of 1878 was to authorize the adoption of a system of local option in regard to the sale of intoxicating liquor in counties and cities throughout the Dominion. By Part I elaborate provisions are made for bringing the Act into force within the area of any county or city. Following on a petition to the Governor-General in Council supported by a certain proportion of the electors in the area, a poll is to be taken, and if a majority supports the petition an Order in Council is passed bringing the Act into effect in that area for a minimum of three years. Amendments have from time to time been passed dealing with portions of the Dominion which were not divided into counties and substituting electoral districts as the area in such cases, but it is unnecessary to set these out in detail. Part II. prohibits the sale of liquors in the areas in which the Act is brought into force, and Part III. provides for prosecution and penalties, which in some cases are severe, for breaches of the Act.

The Act having been passed in 1878, its constitutional validity was challenged in 1882 in *Russell's* case, which arose out of a conviction of the appellant Russell for unlawfully selling intoxicating liquor contrary to the provisions of Part II. of the Act. It was argued in that case that the Act was *ultra vires* of the Dominion Parliament on the ground that the matter was one which fell within s. 92 of the *British North America Act* and was therefore within the exclusive jurisdiction of the provincial legislatures. The Board, however, held that the Act did not deal with any of the matters exclusively reserved to the provinces and upheld the validity of the statute on the ground that it related to the peace, order, and good government of Canada. This decision has stood unreversed for sixty-three years. More than that, it has received the express approval of the Board in subsequent cases.

[...] But in 1925 *Russell's* case was commented on in a judgment of the Judicial Committee delivered by Lord Haldane in *Toronto Electric Commissioners v. Snider*, and it is on this comment that the present appellants largely rely in support of their contention that it was wrongly decided. After contrasting that case with other decisions of the Board already mentioned above, Lord Haldane said:

> It appears to their Lordships that it is not now open to them to treat *Russell v. The Queen* as having established the general principle that the mere fact that Dominion legislation is for the general advantage of Canada, or is such that it will meet a mere want which is felt throughout the Dominion, renders it competent if it cannot be brought within the head enumerated specifically in s. 91. [...] No doubt there may be cases arising out of some extraordinary peril to the national life of Canada, as a whole, such as the cases arising out of a war, where legislation is required of an order that passes beyond the head of exclusive Provincial competency.

And later he said:

> Their Lordships think that the decision in *Russell v. The Queen* can only be supported to-day, not on the footing of having laid down an interpretation, such as has sometimes been invoked, of the general words at the beginning of s. 91, but on the

assumption of the Board, apparently made at the time of deciding the case of *Russell v. The Queen*, that the evil of intemperance at that time amounted in Canada to one so great and so general that at least for the period it was a menace to the national life of Canada so serious and pressing that the National Parliament was called on to intervene to protect the nation from disaster. An epidemic of pestilence might conceivably have been regarded as analogous.

The first observation which their Lordships would make on this explanation of *Russell's* case is that the *British North America Act* nowhere gives power to the Dominion Parliament to legislate in matters which are properly to be regarded as exclusively within the competence of the provincial legislatures merely because of the existence of an emergency. Secondly, they can find nothing in the judgment of the Board in 1882 which suggests that it proceeded on the ground of emergency; there was certainly no evidence before that Board that one existed. The *Act* of 1878 was a permanent, not a temporary, Act, and no objection was raised to it on that account. In their Lordships' opinion the true test must be found in the real subject matter of the legislation: if it is such that it goes beyond local or provincial concern or interests and must from its inherent nature be the concern of the Dominion as a whole (as, for example, in the *Aeronautics* case and the *Radio* case), then it will fall within the competence of the Dominion Parliament as a matter affecting the peace, order, and good government of Canada, though it may in another aspect touch on matters specially reserved to the provincial legislatures. War and pestilence, no doubt, are instances; so, too, may be the drink or drug traffic, or the carrying of arms. In *Russell v. The Queen*, Sir Montague Smith gave as an instance of valid Dominion legislation a law which prohibited or restricted the sale or exposure of cattle having a contagious disease. Nor is the validity of the legislation, when due to its inherent nature, affected because there may still be room for enactments by a provincial legislature dealing with an aspect of the same subject in so far as it specially affects that province.

It is to be noticed that the Board in *Snider's* case nowhere said that *Russell v. The Queen* was wrongly decided. What it did was to put forward an explanation of what it considered was the ground of the decision, but in their Lordships' opinion the explanation is too narrowly expressed. True it is that an emergency may be the occasion which calls for the legislation, but it is the nature of the legislation itself, and not the existence of emergency, that must determine whether it is valid or not. The appellants' first contention is that *Russell's* case was wrongly decided and ought to be overruled. [...] In the present case the decision now sought to be overruled has stood for over sixty years; the Act has been put into operation for varying periods in many places in the Dominion; under its provisions businesses must have been closed, fines and imprisonments for breaches of the Act have been imposed and suffered. Time and again the occasion has arisen when the Board could have overruled the decision had it thought it wrong. Accordingly, in the opinion of their Lordships, the decision must be regarded as firmly embedded in the constitutional law of Canada, and it is impossible now to depart from it. [...]

Accordingly, their Lordships are not prepared to hold either that *Russell v. The Queen* was wrongly decided or that it has ceased to be a binding authority by reason that the *Act* of 1878 has been re-enacted in 1927. It is by repeal by the Dominion Legislature, and not by appeal to the Judicial Committee, that the enactment might cease to be effective. Their Lordships will humbly advise His Majesty that this appeal should be dismissed.

- Research Note -
MATTERS OF NATIONAL CONCERN

The "national concern" doctrine, as developed in the *Local Prohibitions* and *Canada Temperance* cases, has been applied by the Supreme Court of Canada to provide a basis for legislation under the introductory clause of section 91 of the Constitution. Generally speaking, the cases do seem to follow Lord Watson's warning in *Local Prohibitions*, above, that use of the power "ought to be strictly confined to such matters as are unquestionably of Canadian interest and importance" and that "great caution must be observed in distinguishing between matters that are 'local and provincial' and matters that are of 'national concern'."

In *Johannesson v. West St. Paul*, [1952] 1 S.C.R. 292, [1951] 4 D.L.R. 609 the Court held that aeronautics satisfied the national concern test. Locke J. discussed the characteristics which made the field of aeronautics one which concerned the country as a whole. He cited the increasing volume of passenger and freight traffic, the use of aircraft in the carriage of mail, and the importance of air traffic, particularly to remote northern areas, to the opening up of the country and the development of national resources. Locke J. then stated, at p. 327:

> It is an activity, which to adopt the language of Lord Simon in the *Attorney General for Ontario v. Canada Temperance Federation*, must from its inherent nature be a concern of the Dominion as a whole. The field of legislation is not, in my opinion, capable of division in any practical way.

In *Munro v. National Capital Commission*, [1966] S.C.R. 663, 57 D.L.R. (3d) 753 the Court held that the development of a legislatively designated area surrounding Ottawa was of sufficient national concern to be encompassed by the federal residuary power. Cartwright J. stated, at p. 671:

> I find it difficult to suggest a subject-matter of legislation which more clearly [...] is the concern of Canada as a whole than the development, conservation and improvement of the National Capital Region in accordance with a coherent plan in order that the nature and character of the seat of the Government of Canada may be in accordance with its national significance. Adopting the words of the learned trial judge, it is my view that the Act "deals with a single matter of national concern".

The similarity between these two cases is noted by Beetz J. in *Re Anti-Inflation Act*, [1976] 2 S.C.R. 373, below. In that case, Mr. Justice Beetz added detail and refinement to Lord Watson's cautions.

REFERENCE RE ANTI-INFLATION ACT
[1976] 2 S.C.R. 373.

[Following a 20-month period of double-digit inflation, the federal government announced a comprehensive "wage and price control" program. *The Anti-Inflation Act,* and regulations made thereunder, controlled increases in wages, fees, prices, profits and dividends in certain areas of the private sector. The Act applied directly to the federal public sector, and authorized the government to enter into agreements with the provinces to apply the program to provincial public sectors. Most of the private sector relations regulated by the Act were under provincial jurisdiction, as a long series of judicial decisions had given the provinces regulatory power over most business and commercial transactions in the province.

A majority of the Court upheld the constitutional validity of the Act as an exercise of the federal emergency power, see infra, p. 497.

While Laskin C.J.C. (Spence, Dickson and Judson JJ. concurring) left open the possibility that the legislation could be supported by the residuary branch of the peace, order and good government clause, a majority of the court rejected that assertion.]

LASKIN C.J.C. [Spence, Dickson and Judson JJ. concurring]: — By Order in Council P.C. 1976-581 dated March 11, 1976, the Governor-General in Council invoked the authority conferred by s. 55 of the *Supreme Court Act,* R.S.C. 1970, c. S-19, and referred the following two questions to this Court for its opinion:

1. Is the *Anti-Inflation Act,* Statutes of Canada 1974-75-76, Chapter 75 (a copy of which act and the *Anti-Inflation Guidelines* made thereunder are attached hereto as Annex "A") *ultra vires* the Parliament of Canada either in whole or in part, and, if so, in what particular or particulars and to what extent?

2. If the *Anti-Inflation Act* is *intra vires* the Parliament of Canada, is the Agreement entitled "Between the Government of Canada and the Government of the Province of Ontario", entered into on January 13, 1976, (a copy of which is annexed hereto together with copies of the Orders of the Governor in Council and the Lieutenant Governor in Council as Annex "B") effective under the *Anti-Inflation Act* to render that Act binding on, and the *Anti-Inflation Guidelines* made thereunder applicable to, the provincial public sector in Ontario as defined in the Agreement.

Attached to the Order of Reference as annex A were a copy of the *Anti-Inflation Act,* 1974-75 (Can.), c. 75, and a copy of the *Anti-Inflation Guidelines,* SOR/76-1, made thereunder; and attached as annex B were a copy of the agreement involved in the second question and copies of orders of the Governor-General in Council and of the Lieutenant-Governor in Council approving the entry into the agreement by the Governments of Canada and of Ontario which are the respective parties thereto. Nothing else appears in or is attached to the Order of Reference.

The Bill which became the *Anti-Inflation Act* was introduced into the House of Commons on October 16, 1975 (notice having been given on October 14th), and was passed on December 15, 1975, but with effect to a degree from October 14, 1975. Its long title and preamble are as follows:

An Act to provide for the restraint of profit margins, prices, dividends and compensation in Canada.

WHEREAS the Parliament of Canada recognizes that inflation in Canada at current levels is contrary to the interests of all Canadians and that the containment and reduction of inflation has become a matter of serious national concern;

AND WHEREAS to accomplish such containment and reduction of inflation it is necessary to restrain profit margins, prices, dividends and compensation;

Its scope is indicated in ss. 3 [since am. 1974-75-76, c. 98, s. 2] and 4. Sufficient indication of that scope for the purposes of this Reference is provided by quoting s. 3(1), (2) and s. 4(1), (2), (3), (4). They are as follows:

3(1) The Governor in Council may from time to time cause to be published and made known guidelines for the guidance of all Canadians in restraining profit margins, prices, dividends and compensation.

(2) The Governor in Council may, by regulation, establish guidelines for the restraint of
(a) prices and profit margins of
(i) public sector suppliers of commodities or services,
(ii) private sector suppliers of commodities or services who employ five hundred or more persons in Canada.
[...]
(b) compensation of
(i) (employees of suppliers and persons whose prices or profit margins are subject to restraint in accordance with guidelines established pursuant to any of subparagraphs (*a*)(i), (ii), (iv) or (v),
(ii) employees, who are members of a profession, of persons whose prices or profit margins are subject to restraint in accordance with guidelines established pursuant to subparagraph (*a*)(iii), and [...]

The Act as supplemented by the Guidelines, which were promulgated on December 22, 1975, and amended on February 3, 1976, establishes supervision, control and regulation of prices, profits, wages, salaries, fees and dividends by way of monitoring and limiting increases in order to combat inflation. Flexibility in administration is built into the Guidelines by making allowance for such matters as cost increases and productivity factors. The Guidelines are complex in their detail as well as in their language, and it is consoling that an elaboration of their terms is not a prerequisite to the determination of the answers to the two questions referred to this Court. [...]

I turn, therefore, for the purposes of the present case and in order to answer the first question referred to this Court, to an examination of the constitutional basis for the *Anti-Inflation Act* and its implementing Guidelines put forward by the Attorney-General of Canada, who was fully supported in his submissions by the Attorney-General of Ontario. Simply put, the *Anti-Inflation Act* is supported by the Attorney-General of Canada under the opening words of s. 91 of the *British North America Act, 1867*, as being a law for the peace, order and good government of Canada in relation to matters not coming within the classes of subjects assigned exclusively to the Legislatures of the Provinces. There are two prongs to this assertion, and they relate to two lines of judicial decision which have both given substance and placed limitation on the so-called general power of Parliament. Fully spelled out, this general power, which is operative outside of the powers assigned to the provincial Legislatures, is also fed by a catalogue of exclusive enumerated federal powers which are declared to be paramount to and thus diminish the scope of provincial legislative authority. Among the federal enumerated powers that are material here are the powers in relation to the regulation of trade and commerce, in relation to currency and coinage, in relation to banking and the issue of paper money, in relation to interest, in relation to the raising of money by any mode or system of taxation and in relation to the borrowing of money on the public credit, *i.e.*, of Canada.

Although it is conceded that the Parliament of Canada could validly legislate as it has done if it had limited the legislation to the federal public service and to enterprises or undertakings which are within exclusive federal legislative authority, such as interprovincial transportation and communication services, radio operations, aerial navigation, atomic energy enterprises, banks and works declared to be for the general advantage of Canada, the *Anti-Inflation Act* embraces sectors of industry and of services, including employers and employees therein, which are admittedly subject in respect of their intra-provincial operation to provincial regulatory authority. I take it as undeniable that it would have been open to each Province to impose the price and wage restraints in these sectors, to the extent to which there was no invasion of federal powers such as that in relation to the regulation of trade and commerce. It is equally undeniable that each Province could have validly dealt with restraint of salaries and wages of persons in its public service. It is part of the submission of the Attorney-General of Canada that Parliament could have brought the members of the provincial public service under the *Anti-Inflation Act* and Guidelines without permitting Provinces to "contract in" under s. 4(3) and (4), and that the validity of the Act is not affected by their express exclusion from its coverage subject to inclusion under an agreement as prescribed by s. 4(3) or (4). [...]

The Attorney-General of Canada, supported by the Attorney-General of Ontario, put his position in support of the *Anti-Inflation Act* on alternative bases. He relied, primarily, on the *Canada Temperance Federation* case, contending that the

Act, directed to containment and reduction of inflation, concerned a matter which went beyond local or private or provincial concern and was of a nature which engaged vital national interests, among them the integrity of the Canadian monetary system which was unchallengeably within exclusive federal protection and control. He urged, in the alternative, that there was an economic crisis amounting to an emergency or exceptional peril to economic stability sufficient to warrant federal intervention, and, if not an existing peril, there was a reasonable apprehension of an impending one that justified federal intervention through the legislation in question which was designed to support measures and policies of a fiscal and monetary character which were undoubtedly within Parliament's legislative authority.

The Attorney-General of Quebec and the Attorney-General of Saskatchewan contended that the Act could be supported only on an "emergency" basis but took no position on whether such a basis of support was shown. The Attorney-General of British Columbia and the Attorney-General of Alberta both took the position that the legislation *ex facie* was an unconstitutional interference with the provincial private sector, being an interference with provincial regulatory authority, with contractual arrangements in the Provinces and with the operation of businesses within provincial legislative authority. They conceded that the Parliament of Canada could enact such legislation in an emergency, but the mere existence or persistence of inflation did not, in their submission, evidence an emergency which required federal action only and, in any event, there was no sufficient evidence, either from the terms of the *Anti-Inflation Act* or otherwise, to show that an emergency existed. [...]

Since there was, in general, a concession by those opposing the legislation that it would be valid if it were what I may call crisis legislation, and since the proponents of the legislation urged this as an alternative ground on which its validity should be sustained, it appears to me to be the wise course to consider first whether the *Anti-Inflation Act* can be supported on that footing. If it is sustainable as crisis legislation, it becomes unnecessary to consider the broader ground advanced in its support, and this because, especially in constitutional cases, Courts should not, as a rule, go any farther than is necessary to determine the main issue before them. [The Justice proceeded to hold that the Act was valid as a measure to meet a temporary emergency. See infra under emergencies.]

[De Grandpré J. concurs with Beetz J. on Question No. 1 and concurs with Laskin C.J.C. on Question No. 2. Ritchie J. upheld the legislation as an emergency measure.]

RITCHIE J. [Pigeon and Martland, JJ, concurring]: — I do not consider that the validity of the Act rests upon the constitutional doctrine exemplified in earlier decisions of the Privy Council, to all of which the Chief Justice has made reference, and generally known as the "national dimension" or "national concern" doctrine. It is not difficult to envisage many different circumstances which could give rise to national concern, but at least since the *Japanese Canadians* case, I take it to be established that unless such concern is made manifest by circumstances amounting to a national emergency, Parliament is not endowed under the cloak of the "peace, order and good government" clause with the authority to legislate in relation to matters reserved to the Provinces under s. 92 of the *British North America Act, 1867*. In this regard I am in full agreement with the reasons for judgment prepared for delivery by my brother Beetz which I have had the advantage of reading, and I have little to add to what he has said.

BEETZ, J. (dissenting on Question No. 1): – The first of the two questions referred to this Court for its opinion, relates to the constitutional validity of the *Anti-Inflation Act*, 1974-75 (Can.), c. 75. Two main submissions were advanced in support of the Act. The Chief Justice whose reasons I have had the advantage of reading takes the view that the Act is valid on the basis of the second submission and he does not express an opinion with respect to the first. As my conclusions differ from those of the Chief Justice on the second submission, I find it necessary to deal with both. My task on the other hand is lightened since the Chief Justice quotes the two questions referred to us, the relevant parts of the Act and so many of the authorities. [...]

The first submission made by counsel for Canada and for Ontario is that the subject-matter of the *Anti-Inflation Act* is the containment and the reduction of inflation. This subject-matter, it is argued, goes beyond local provincial concern or interest and is from its inherent nature the concern of Canada as a whole and falls within the competence of Parliament as a matter affecting the peace, order and good government of Canada. It was further submitted that the competence of Parliament over the subject of inflation may be supported by reference to the following heads of s. 91 of the Constitution:

2. The regulation of trade and commerce.
3. The raising of money by any mode or system of taxation.
4. The borrowing of money on the public credit. [...]
14. Currency and coinage.
15. Banking, incorporation of banks and the issue of paper money.
16. Savings banks. [...]
19. Interest.
20. Legal tender.

These heads of powers were invoked as indicative of the breadth of Parliament's competence in economic matters and as giving additional assistance to the *Anti-Inflation Act*. [...]

Some of the extremely far-reaching consequences of this submission must be underlined with respect to the so-called subject-matter of inflation or its containment as well as in relation to the principles underlying the distribution of powers between Parliament and the provincial Legislatures. If the first submission is to be accepted, then it must be conceded that the *Anti-Inflation Act* could be compellingly extended to the provincial public sector. Parliament has not done so in this case as a matter of legislative policy but it could decide to control and regulate at least the maximum salaries paid to all provincial public servants notwithstanding any provincial appropriations, budgets and laws. Parliament could also regulate wages paid by municipalities, educational institutions, hospitals and other provincial services as well as tuition or other fees charged by some of these institutions for their services. Parliament could occupy the whole field of rent controls. Since in time of inflation there can be a great deal of speculation to certain precious possessions such as land or works of arts, Parliament could move to prevent or control that speculation not only in regulating the trade or the price of those possessions but by any other efficient method reasonably connected with the control of inflation. For example Parliament could presumably enact legislation analogous to mortmain legislation and even extend it to individuals. Parliament could control all inventories in the largest as in the smallest undertakings, industries and trades. Parliament could ration not only food but practically everything else in order to prevent hoarding and unfair profits. One could even go further and argue that since inflation and productivity are greatly interdependent, Parliament could regulate productivity, establish quotas and impose the output of goods or services which corporations, industries, factories, groups, areas, villages, farmers, workers, should produce in any given period. Indeed, since practically any activity or lack of activity affects the gross national product, the value of the Canadian dollar and, therefore, inflation, it is difficult to see what would be beyond the reach of Parliament. Furthermore, all those powers would belong to Parliament permanently; only a constitutional amendment could reduce them. Finally, the power to regulate and control inflation as such would belong to Parliament to the exclusion of the Legislatures if, as is contended, that power were to vest in Parliament in the same manner as the power to control and regulate aeronautics or radio communication or the power to develop and conserve the national capital (*Aeronautics*, *Radio*, *Johannesson* and *Munro* cases); the Provinces could probably continue to regulate profit margins, prices, dividends and compensation if Parliament saw fit to leave them any room; but they could not regulate them in relation to inflation which would have become an area of exclusive federal jurisdiction.

Such are the constitutional imports of the first submission in terms of the so-called subject-matter of inflation.

Its effects on the principles which underlie the distribution of other powers between Parliament and the Legislatures are even more far-reaching assuming there would be much left of the distribution of powers if Parliament has exclusive authority in relation to the "containment and reduction of inflation."

If the first submission is correct, then it could also be said that the promotion of economic growth or the limits to growth or the protection of the environment have become global problems and now constitute subject-matters of national concern going beyond local provincial concern or interest and coming within the exclusive legislative authority of Parliament. It could equally be argued that older subjects such as the business of insurance or labour relations, which are not specifically listed in the enumeration of federal and provincial powers and have been held substantially to come within provincial jurisdiction have outgrown provincial authority whenever the business of insurance or labour has become national in scope. It is not difficult to speculate as to where this line of reasoning would lead: a fundamental feature of the Constitution, its federal nature, the distribution of powers between Parliament and the provincial Legislatures, would disappear not gradually but rapidly.

479

I cannot be persuaded that the first submission expresses the state of the law. It goes against the persistent trend of the authorities. It is founded upon an erroneous characterization of the *Anti-Inflation Act*. As for the cases relied upon by counsel to support the submission, they are quite distinguishable and they do not, in my view, stand for what they are said to stand.

I have mentioned above several of the authorities relating to the control and regulation of local trade, to marketing, to the contract of employment and to property and civil rights, which are in contradiction with the first submission. There is no need to repeat them. But I should like to add a few quotations drawn from those authorities and others. [...]

[The Justice referred to the *Board of Commerce, Natural Products Marketing Act* and the *Insurance Reference* cases.]

Those authorities, particularly the *Board of Commerce* case, upon which Parliament, the Provinces and the Courts have relied for so many years as expressing the state of the law are totally incompatible with the first submission.

This submission is predicated upon the proposition that the subject-matter of the *Anti-Inflation Act*, its pith and substance, is inflation or the containment and reduction of inflation.

To characterize a law is but to give a name to its content or subject-matter in order to classify it into one or the other of the classes of matters mentioned in s. 91 or s. 92 of the Constitution. These classes of matters are themselves so many labels bearing a more or less specific name, except the general power of Parliament to make laws in relation to matters not coming within the classes of matters exclusively assigned to the Provinces – a label specific only in a negative way – and except the power of the Provinces in relation to all matters of a merely local or private nature – a label unspecific except mainly with regard to dimensions. This leaves some forty-six specific labels, thirty-one of which are in the federal list and fifteen of which are in the provincial list.

But there are in language a great many expressions other than those used for the labels in the federal and the provincial lists. Those innumerable other expressions, often broader and more extensive than those of s. 91 and s. 92, may, apart from any issue of colourability, be employed in the title of a statute or to describe a statute. The expressions "inflation" or "the containment and reduction of inflation" are of that nature. Needless to say, their use in the title of a statute or as an attempt to characterize a statute does not suffice by far in disposing of the characterization or in taking the matter with which in fact they deal outside the ambit of provincial jurisdiction. It is necessary to look at the reality of the matter or of the matters with which in effect they deal.

It is possible to invent such matters by applying new names to old legislative purposes. There is an increasing tendency to sum up a wide variety of legislative purposes in single, comprehensive designations. Control of inflation, environmental protection, and preservation of the national identity or independence are examples.

Many matters within provincial jurisdiction can be transformed by being treated as part of a larger subject or concept for which no place can be found within that jurisdiction. This perspective has a close affinity to the notion that there must be a single, plenary power to deal effectively and completely with any problem. The future of the general power, in the absence of emergency, will depend very much on the approach that the courts adopt to this issue of characterization.

"Sir Lyman Duff and the Constitution", by Professor Gerald LeDain, Q.C., as he then was, 12 *Osgoode Hall Law Journal* 261 (1974) at p. 293. (See also "Unity and Diversity in Canadian Federalism: Ideals and Methods of Moderation", by Professor W.R. Lederman, Q.C., 53 *Can. Bar Rev.* 596 (1975). I am much indebted to these two articles.)

The "containment and reduction of inflation" can be achieved by various means including monetary policies, a federal field; the reduction of public expenditures, federal, provincial and municipal; and the restraint of profits, prices and wages, a federal or a provincial field depending on the sector.

I have no reason to doubt that the *Anti-Inflation Act* is part of a more general programme aimed at inflation and which may include fiscal and monetary measures and Government expenditure policies. I am prepared to accept that inflation was the occasion or the reason for its enactment. But I do not agree that inflation is the subject-matter of the Act. In order to characterize an enactment, one must look at its operation, at its effects and at the scale of its effects rather than at its ultimate purpose where the purpose is practically all-embracing. If for instance Parliament is to enact a tax law or a monetary law as a part of an anti-inflation programme no one will think that such laws have ceased to be a tax law or a monetary law and that they have become subsumed into their ultimate purpose so that they should rather be characterized as "anti-inflation laws", an expression which, in terms of actual content, is not meaningful. They plainly remain and continue to be called a tax law or a monetary law, although they have been enacted by reason of an inflationary situation. When the Bank of Canada changes its rate of interest, it must obviously take inflation into account; even if inflation is the main reason for such a measure, the measure will still be characterized by everyone as a central banking measure relating to interest. The same would also be said of a measure relating to the issue of currency; although it may have been dictated by inflationary trends, it remains a measure relating to currency, coinage or the issue of paper money. Similarly, the *Anti-Inflation Act* is, as its preamble states, clearly a law relating to the control of profit margins, prices, dividends and compensation, that is, with respect to the provincial private sector, a law relating to the regulation of local trade, to contract and to property and civil rights in the Provinces, enacted as part of a programme to combat inflation. Property and civil rights in the Provinces are, for the greater part, the pith and substance or the subject-matter of the *Anti-Inflation Act*. According to the Constitution, Parliament may fight inflation with the powers put at its disposal by the specific heads enumerated in s. 91 or by such powers as are outside of s. 92. But it cannot, apart from a declaration of national emergency or from a constitutional amendment, fight inflation with powers exclusively reserved to the Provinces, such as the power to make laws in relation to property and civil rights. This is what Parliament has in fact attempted to do in enacting the *Anti-Inflation Act*.

The authorities relied upon by Counsel for Canada and Ontario in support of the first submission are connected with the constitutional doctrine that became known as the national concern doctrine or national dimension doctrine. Sir Montague Smith was the first, I believe, to use the expression "a subject of general concern to the Dominion" in *Russell v. The Queen* (1882), 7 App. Cas. 829 at p. 841, and Lord Watson, in the *Local Prohibition* case, *A.-G. Ont. v. A.-G. Can.*, [1896] A.C. 348, coined the two names later given to the doctrine (at p. 361):

> The Justices do not doubt that some matters, in their origin local and provincial, might attain such dimensions as to affect the body politic of the Dominion, and to justify the Canadian Parliament in passing laws for their regulation or abolition in the interest of the Dominion. But great caution must be observed in distinguishing between that which is local and provincial, and therefore within the jurisdiction of the provincial legislatures, and that which has ceased to be merely local or provincial, and has become a matter of national concern, in such sense as to bring it within the jurisdiction of the Parliament of Canada.

The *Russell* case is a special case. It is not easy to reconcile with the *Local Prohibition* case unless it be thought that the promotion of temperance is a matter of concurrent jurisdiction such as agriculture and immigration. Lord Watson implied some reservations about the *radio* in *Russell* when he wrote as follows in the *Local Prohibition* case (at p. 362):

> The judgment of the Board in *Russell v. Reg.* has relieved the Justices from the difficult duty of considering whether the *Canada Temperance Act* of 1886 relates to the peace, order and good government of Canada, in such sense as to bring its provisions within the competency of the Canadian Parliament. [...] neither the Dominion nor the Provinces were represented in the argument. [...] It [...] appears [...] that the decision in *Russell v. Reg.* must be accepted as an authority to the extent to which it goes, namely, that the restrictive provisions of the Act of 1886, when they have been duly brought into operation in any provincial area within the Dominion, must receive effect as valid enactments relating to the peace, order and good government of Canada. [...]

Even before the *Russell* case, it had been assumed by the Judicial Committee in *Citizens Ins. Co. of Canada v. Parsons* (1881), 7 App. Cas. 96 at pp. 116-7, that the incorporation of companies for objects other than provincial falls within the general power of Parliament as it does not come within the enumerated powers of the Provinces. This was affirmed later in *John Deere Plow Co. v. Wharton*,

Precedents

[1915] A.C. 330 at p. 340, with the additional comment that this subject "may be properly regarded as a matter affecting the Dominion generally and covered by the expression 'the peace, order, and good government of Canada.'" [...]

In the *Canada Temperance Federation* case, the Judicial Committee was asked to overrule *Russell*. This the Judicial Committee was not prepared to do, *Russell* having stood for over sixty years and the *Canada Temperance Act* having been put in operation for varying periods in many places. It fell upon Viscount Simon again to explain *Russell*. He quoted Viscount Haldane's explanation according to which *Russell* could only be supported on the assumption that, in 1878, the evil of intemperance was so great and general as to amount to a situation of national emergency, and he wrote (at p. 205 A.C.):

> The first observation which the Justices would make on this explanation of *Russell's* case is that the *B.N.A. Act* nowhere gives power to the Dominion Parliament to legislate in matters which are properly to be regarded as exclusively within the competence of the Provincial Legislatures, merely because of the existence of an emergency. Secondly, they can find nothing in the judgment of the Board in 1882 which suggests that it proceeded on the ground of emergency; there was certainly no evidence before that Board that one existed. The *Act* of 1878 was a permanent, not a temporary Act and no objection was raised to it on that account. In the Justice's opinion, the true test must be found in the real subject-matter of the legislation: if it is such that it goes beyond local or provincial concern or interests and must from its inherent nature be the concern of the Dominion as a whole (as, for example, in the *Aeronautics* case and the *Radio* case, then it will fall within the competence of the Dominion Parliament as a matter affecting the peace, order and good government of Canada, though it may in another aspect touch on matters specially reserved to the Provincial Legislatures. War and pestilence, no doubt, are instances, so too may be the drink or drug traffic, or the carrying of arms.

It is to be doubted that Viscount Simon intended to formulate an important constitutional doctrine on the basis of a case as exceptional as *Russell*. But he had to find a form of words that would account for *Russell*. It is significant that, less than a year later, the Judicial Committee was to revert to the national emergency doctrine in *Co-operative Committee on Japanese Canadians et al. v. A.G. Can. et al.*, [1947] A.C. 87.

In *Johannesson*, this Court upheld exclusive federal jurisdiction over the subject of aeronautics even though this jurisdiction could no longer be supported by an imperial treaty and by s. 132 of the Constitution. The approaches taken by various members of this Court vary. The *Canada Temperance Federation* case was referred to and quoted together with the *Radio* case and the *Aeronautics* case. It was pointed out that in *obiter* the *Aeronautics* case supported federal jurisdiction apart from s. 132 and this view seems to have met with the approval of the majority.

In the Munro case, this Court referred to the Canada Temperance case and to *Johannesson.* It held that the subject-matter of the *National Capital Act* was the establishment of a region consisting of the seat of the Government of Canada and a surrounding area which was to be developed, conserved and improved "in order that the nature and character of the seat of the Government of Canada may be in accordance with its national significance". That subject was a "single" matter of national concern and was not mentioned in s. 91 and s. 92 of the Constitution; it therefore came within the sole jurisdiction of Parliament.

DISTINCT SUBJECT MATTERS

In my view, the incorporation of companies for objects other than provincial, the regulation and control of aeronautics and of radio, the development, conservation and improvement of the National Capital Region are clear instances of distinct subject-matters which do not fall within any of the enumerated heads of s. 92 and which, by nature, are of national concern.

I fail to see how the authorities which so decide lend support to the first submission. They had the effect of adding by judicial process new matters or new classes of matters to the federal list of powers. However, this was done only in cases where a new matter was not an aggregate but had a degree of unity that made it indivisible, an identity which made it distinct from provincial matters and a sufficient consistence to retain the bounds of form. The scale upon which these new matters enabled Parliament to touch on provincial matters had also to be taken into consideration before they were recognized as federal matters: if an enumerated federal power designated in broad terms such as the trade and commerce power had to be construed so as not to embrace and smother provincial powers (*Parson's* case) and destroy the equilibrium of the Constitution, the Courts must be all the more careful not to add hitherto unnamed powers of a diffuse nature to the list of federal powers.

The "containment and reduction of inflation" does not pass muster as a new subject matter. It is an aggregate of several subjects some of which form a substantial part of provincial jurisdiction. It is totally lacking in specificity. It is so pervasive that it knows no bounds. Its recognition as a federal head of power would render most provincial powers nugatory.

I should add that inflation is a very ancient phenomenon, several thousand years old, as old probably as the history of currency. The Fathers of Confederation were quite aware of it.

It was argued that other heads of power enumerated in s. 91 of the Constitution and which relate for example to the regulation of trade and commerce, to currency and coinage, to banking, incorporation of banks and the issue of paper money may be indicative of the breadth of Parliament's jurisdiction in economic matters. They do not enable Parliament to legislate otherwise than in relation to their objects and it was not argued that the *Anti-Inflation Act* was in relation to their objects. The Act does not derive any assistance from those powers any more than the legislation found invalid in the *Board of Commerce* case.

For those reasons, the first submission fails.

R. v. CROWN ZELLERBACH CAN. LTD.
[1988] 1 S.C.R. 401.

[While carrying out its logging operations, the respondent dumped woodwaste into the waters of Beaver Cove, an area within the province of British Columbia, and was charged with contravening s. 4(1) of the federal *Ocean Dumping Control Act*. The provision prohibited the dumping of any substance in the sea except in accordance with the terms and conditions of a permit. The sea was defined in the Act as including the internal waters of Canada other than fresh waters.

The respondent challenged the authority of Parliament to enact legislation that controlled the dumping in provincial waters of substances that were not shown to have a pollutant effect in extra-provincial waters. The federal government contended that the control of dumping in provincial marine waters was an integral part of a single matter of national concern – the prevention of marine pollution.]

Le DAIN J. [Dickson C.J.C. McIntyre and Wilson JJ. concurring]: – Before considering the relationship of the subject-matter of the Act to the possible bases of federal legislative jurisdiction something more should be said about the characterization of that subject-matter, according to the respective contentions of the parties. As I have indicated, the appellant contends that the Act is directed to the control or regulation of marine pollution, the subject-matter of the *Convention on the Prevention of Marine Pollution by Dumping of Wastes and other Matter*. The respondent, on the other hand, contends that by its terms the Act is directed at dumping which need not necessarily have a pollutant effect. It prohibits the dumping of *any* substance, including a substance not specified in Schedule I or Schedule II, except in accordance with the terms and conditions of a permit. In my opinion, despite this apparent scope, the Act, viewed as a whole, may be properly characterized as directed to the control or regulation of marine pollution, in so far as that may be relevant to the question of legislative jurisdiction. The chosen, and perhaps only effective, regulatory model makes it necessary, in order to prevent marine pollution, to prohibit the dumping of any substance without a permit. Its purpose is to require a permit so that the regulatory authority may determine before the proposed dumping has occurred whether it may be permitted upon certain terms and conditions, having regard to the factors or concerns specified in ss. 9 and 10 of the Act and Schedule III. The Act is concerned with the dumping of substances which may be shown or presumed to have an adverse effect on the marine environment. The Minister and not the person proposing to do the dumping must be the judge of this, acting in accordance with the criteria or factors indicated in ss. 9 and 10 and Schedule III of the Act. There is no suggestion that the Act purports to authorize the prohibition of dumping without regard to perceived adverse effect or the likelihood of such effect on the marine environment. The nature of the marine environment and its protection from adverse effect from dumping is a complex matter which must be left to expert judgment. [...]

[The Justices found that s. 91(12) of the Constitution, with respect to seacoast and inland fisheries, could not support the constitutional validity of s. 4(1) of the Act.]

It is necessary then to consider the national dimensions or national concern doctrine (as it is now generally referred to) of the federal peace, order and good government power as a possible basis for the constitutional validity of s. 4(1) of the Act, as applied to the control of dumping in provincial marine waters. [...]

The national concern doctrine was the subject of important commentary in this Court in the *Anti-Inflation Act* reference. A majority of the Court (Laskin C.J. and Martland, Judson, Ritchie, Spence, Pigeon and Dickson JJ.) upheld the Act on the basis of the emergency doctrine of the federal peace, order and good government power as legislation required to meet a "crisis" (the word used by Laskin C.J.) or "national emergency" (the words used by Ritchie J.). In the course of a comprehensive review of the judicial decisions with respect to the federal peace, order and good government power, Laskin C.J., with whom Judson, Spence and Dickson JJ. concurred, referred, with implicit approval, to the dictum of Viscount Simon in *Canada Temperance Federation*, but indicated that if he found, as he did, that the Act was valid on the basis of the emergency doctrine, as "crisis" legislation, he did not intend to express an opinion as to its possible validity on the basis of the national concern doctrine, on which the Attorney General of Canada had principally relied. He said at p. 419: "If it is sustainable as crisis legislation, it becomes unnecessary to consider the broader ground advanced in its support, and this because, especially in constitutional cases, Courts should not, as a rule, go any farther than is necessary to determine the main issue before them." He indicated, however, that he did not think it wise to attempt to define the scope of the federal peace, order and good government power in such precise or fixed terms as to make it incapable of application to changing or unforeseen circumstances. There is, moreover, a hint that he was disposed to seek a unified theory of the peace, order and good government power and that he regarded the emergency doctrine as a particular application of the national concern doctrine. Referring to the use of the word "emergency" in *Fort Francis Pulp & Power Co. v. Manitoba Free Press Co.*, [1923] A.C. 695, he said at p. 407: "Here then was a particular application of what Lord Watson said in the *Local Prohibition* case." [...]

Ritchie J., with whom Martland and Pigeon JJ. concurred, held that the validity of the Act could rest only on the emergency doctrine of the peace, order and good government power and that the national concern doctrine, in the absence of national emergency, could not give Parliament jurisdiction with respect to matters which would otherwise fall within provincial legislative jurisdiction. He said that he was in agreement with what was said by Beetz J. with reference to the national concern doctrine. Beetz J., with whom de Grandpré J. concurred, was obliged to consider the contention based on the national concern doctrine because he was of the view that the validity of the *Anti-Inflation Act* could not be supported on the basis of national emergency. He held that the national concern doctrine applied, in the absence of national emergency, to single, indivisible matters which did not fall within any of the specified heads of provincial or federal legislative jurisdiction. He held that the containment and reduction of inflation did not meet the test of singleness or indivisibility. [...]

[The Justice proceeded to consider the Court's references to the federal residuary power in *Labatt Breweries of Can. Ltd. v. A.G. Can.*, [1980] 1 S.C.R. 914, *Schneider v. R.*, [1982] 2 S.C.R. 112, *R. v. Wetmore*, [1983] 2 S.C.R. 284.]

In *Labatt Breweries*, in which a majority of the full Court held that certain provisions of the *Food and Drugs Act* and regulations thereunder were *ultra vires*, Estey J., with whom Martland, Dickson and Beetz JJ. concurred, had occasion to consider the peace, order and good government power as a possible basis of validity. He summed up the doctrine with respect to that basis of federal legislative jurisdiction as falling into three categories: (a) the cases "basing the federal competence on the existence of a national emergency"; (b) the cases in which "federal competence arose because the subject matter did not exist at the time of Confederation and clearly cannot be put into the class of matters of a merely local or private nature", of which aeronautics and radio were cited as examples; and (c) the cases in which "the subject matter `goes beyond local or provincial concern or interest and must, from its inherent nature, be the concern of the Dominion as a whole'", citing *Canada Temperance Federation*. Thus Estey J. saw the national concern doctrine enunciated in *Canada Temperance Federation* as covering the case, not of a new subject matter which did not exist at Confederation, but of one that may have begun as a matter of a local or provincial concern but had become one of national concern. He referred to that category as "a matter of national concern transcending the local authorities' power to meet and solve it by legislation", and quoted in support of this statement of the test a passage from Professor Hogg's *Constitutional Law of Canada* (1977), at p. 261, in which it was said that "the most important element of national dimension or national concern is a need for one national law which cannot realistically be satisfied by cooperative provincial action because the failure of one province to cooperate would carry with it grave consequences for the residents of other provinces."

In *Schneider*, in which the Court unanimously held that the *Heroin Treatment Act* of British Columbia was *intra vires*, Dickson J. (as he then was), with whom Martland, Ritchie, Beetz, McIntyre, Chouinard and Lamer JJ. concurred, indicated, with particular reference to the national concern doctrine and what has come to be known as the "provincial inability" test, why he was of the view that the treatment of heroin dependency, as distinct from the traffic in narcotic drugs, was not a matter falling within the federal peace, order and good government power. He referred to the problem of heroin dependency as follows at pp. 131-32:

> It is largely a local or provincial problem and not one which has become a matter of national concern, so as to bring it within the jurisdiction of the Parliament of Canada under the residuary power contained in the opening words of the *B.N.A. Act* (now, *Constitution Act, 1867*).

> There is no material before the Court leading one to conclude that the problem of heroin dependency as distinguished from illegal trade in drugs is a matter of national interest and dimension transcending the power of each province to meet and solve its own way. It is not a problem which "is beyond the power of the provinces to deal with" (Professor Gibson (1976-77), 7 Man. L.J. 15, at p. 33). Failure by one province to provide treatment facilities will not endanger the interest of another province. The subject is not one which "has attained

such dimensions as to affect the body politic of the Dominion" (*In re Regulation and Control of Aeronautics in Canada*, [1932] A.C. 54, at p. 77). It is not something that "goes beyond local or provincial concern or interests and must from its inherent nature be the concern of the Dominion as a whole (as, for example, in the *Aeronautics* case and the *Radio* case)" *per* Viscount Simon in *Attorney-General for Ontario v. Canada Temperance Federation*, [1946] A.C. 193, at p. 205. [...]

In *Wetmore*, where the issue was whether the federal Attorney General was entitled to conduct the prosecution of charges for violation of the *Food and Drugs Act*, Dickson J., dissenting, considered whether the applicable provisions of the *Food and Drugs Act* had their constitutional foundation in the federal criminal law power, or as was held in *Hauser* with respect to the *Narcotic Control Act*, in the peace, order and good government power. [...]

Dickson J. noted that there was no question of emergency or of a new matter that did not exist at Confederation and rejected the national concern doctrine of the peace, order and good government as a basis for the constitutional validity of the provisions in question for the following reasons at p. 296:

> Finally, it cannot be maintained that ss. 8(*a*), 9(1) and 26 address a subject that goes beyond local or provincial interest and must from its intrinsic nature be the concern of the Dominion as a whole, as that concept has been interpreted in the cases. Their subject matter would clearly not satisfy the requirements cited by Beetz J. in the *Reference Re Anti-Inflation Act,* supra, nor would it come within the criteria proposed by Hogg, *Constitutional Law of Canada* (1977), at p. 261, in a passage cited by Estey J. in *Labatt*, supra, at p. 945:
>
>> These cases suggest that the most important element of national dimension or national concern is a need for one national law which cannot realistically be satisfied by cooperative provincial action because the failure of one province to co-operate would carry with it grave consequences for the residents of other provinces. A subject matter of legislation which has this characteristic has the necessary national dimension or concern to justify invocation of the p.o.g.g. power.

From this survey of the opinion expressed in this Court concerning the national concern doctrine of the federal peace, order and good government power I draw the following conclusions as to what now appears to be firmly established:

1. The national concern doctrine is separate and distinct from the national emergency doctrine of the peace, order and good government power, which is chiefly distinguishable by the fact that it provides a constitutional basis for what is necessarily legislation of a temporary nature;

2.   The national concern doctrine applies to both new matters which did not exist at Confederation and to matters which, although originally matters of a local or private nature in a province, have since, in the absence of national emergency, become matters of national concern;

3.   For a matter to qualify as a matter of national concern in either sense it must have a singleness, distinctiveness and indivisibility that clearly distinguishes it from matters of provincial concern and a scale of impact on provincial jurisdiction that is reconcilable with the fundamental distribution of legislative power under the Constitution;

4.   In determining whether a matter has attained the required degree of singleness, distinctiveness and indivisibility that clearly distinguishes it from matters of provincial concern it is relevant to consider what would be the effect on extra-provincial interests of a provincial failure to deal effectively with the control or regulation of the intra-provincial aspects of the matter.

This last factor, generally referred to as the "provincial inability" test and noted with apparent approval in this Court in *Labatt, Schneider* and *Wetmore*, was suggested, as Professor Hogg acknowledges, by Professor Gibson in his article, "Measuring 'National Dimensions'" (1976), 7 *Man. L.J.* 15, as the most satisfactory rationale of the cases in which the national concern doctrine of the peace, order and good government power has been applied as a basis of federal jurisdiction. As expounded by Professor Gibson, the test would appear to involve a limited or qualified application of federal jurisdiction. As put by Professor Gibson at pp. 34-35, "By this approach, a national dimension would exist whenever a significant aspect of a problem is beyond provincial reach because it falls within the jurisdiction of another province or of the federal Parliament. It is important to emphasize however that the *entire* problem would not fall within federal competence in such circumstances. Only that aspect of the problem that is beyond provincial control would do so. Since the "P.O. & G.G." clause bestows only residual powers, the existence of a national dimension justifies no more federal legislation than is necessary to fill the gap in provincial powers. For example, federal jurisdiction to legislate for pollution of interprovincial waterways or to control "pollution price-wars" would (in the absence of other independent sources of federal competence) extend only to measures to reduce the risk that citizens of one province would be harmed by the non-co-operation of another province or provinces." To similar effect, he said in his conclusion at p. 36: "Having regard to the residual nature of the power, it is the writer's thesis that 'national dimensions' are possessed by only those aspects of legislative problems which are beyond the ability of the provincial legislatures to deal because they involve either federal competence or that of another province. Where it would be possible to deal fully with the problem by co-operative action of two or more legislatures, the "national dimension" concerns only the risk of non-co-operation, and justifies only federal legislation addressed to that risk." This would appear to contemplate a concurrent or overlapping federal jurisdiction which, I must observe, is in conflict with what was emphasized by Beetz J. in the *Anti-Inflation Act* reference – that where a matter falls within the national concern doctrine of the peace, order and good government power, as distinct from the emergency doctrine, Parliament has an exclusive jurisdiction of a plenary nature to legislate in relation to that matter, including its intra-provincial aspects.

As expressed by Professor Hogg in the first and second editions of his *Constitutional Law of Canada*, the "provincial inability" test would appear to be adopted simply as a reason for finding that a particular matter is one of national concern falling within the peace, order and good government power: that provincial failure to deal effectively with the intra-provincial aspects of the matter could have an adverse effect on extra-provincial interests. In this sense, the "provincial inability" test is one of the indicia for determining whether a matter has that character of singleness or indivisibility required to bring it within the national concern doctrine. It is because of the interrelatedness of the intra-provincial and extra-provincial aspects of the matter that it requires a single or uniform legislative treatment. The "provincial inability" test must not, however, go so far as to provide a rationale for the general notion, hitherto rejected in the cases, that there must be a plenary jurisdiction in one order of government or the other to deal with any legislative problem. In the context of the national concern doctrine of the peace, order and good government power, its utility lies, in my opinion, in assisting in the determination whether a matter has the requisite singleness or indivisibility from a functional as well as a conceptual point of view. [...]

Marine pollution, because of its predominantly extra-provincial as well as international character and implications, is clearly a matter of concern to Canada as a whole. The question is whether the control of pollution by the dumping of substances in marine waters, including provincial marine waters, is a single, indivisible matter, distinct from the control of pollution by the dumping of substances in other provincial waters. The *Ocean Dumping Control Act* reflects a distinction between the pollution of salt water and the pollution of fresh water. The question, as I conceive it, is whether that distinction is sufficient to make the control of marine pollution by the dumping of substances a single, indivisible matter falling within the national concern doctrine of the peace, order and good government power.

Marine pollution by the dumping of substances is clearly treated by the *Convention on the Prevention of Marine Pollution by Dumping of Wastes and other Matter* as a distinct and separate form of water pollution having its own characteristics and scientific considerations. This impression is reinforced by the United Nations Report of the Joint Group of Experts on the Scientific Aspects of Marine Pollution, Reports and Studies No. 15, *The Review of the Health of the Oceans* (UNESCO 1982) (hereinafter referred to as the "U. N. Report"), which forms part of the materials placed before the Court in the argument. It is to be noted, however, that, unlike the *Ocean Dumping Control Act*, the Convention does not require regulation of pollution by the dumping of waste in the internal marine waters of a state. Article III, para. 3, of the Convention defines the "sea" as "all marine waters other than the internal waters of the States." The internal marine waters of a state are those which lie landward of the baseline of the territorial sea, which is determined in accordance with the rules laid down in the United Nations *Convention on the Law of the Sea* (1982). The limitation of the undertaking in the

Convention, presumably for reasons of state policy, to the control of dumping in the territorial sea and the open sea cannot, in my opinion, obscure the obviously close relationship, which is emphasized in the U.N. Report, between pollution in coastal waters, including the internal marine waters of a state, and pollution in the territorial sea. Moreover, there is much force, in my opinion, in the appellant's contention that the difficulty of ascertaining by visual observation the boundary between the territorial sea and the internal marine waters of a state creates an unacceptable degree of uncertainty for the application of regulatory and penal provisions. This, and not simply the possibility or likelihood of the movement of pollutants across that line, is what constitutes the essential indivisibility of the matter of marine pollution by the dumping of substances.

There remains the question whether the pollution of marine waters by the dumping of substances is sufficiently distinguishable from the pollution of fresh waters by such dumping to meet the requirement of singleness or indivisibility. In many cases the pollution of fresh waters will have a pollutant effect in the marine waters into which they flow, and this is noted by the U.N. Report, but that report, as I have suggested, emphasizes that marine pollution, because of the differences in the composition and action of marine waters and fresh waters, has its own characteristics and scientific considerations that distinguish it from fresh water pollution. Moreover, the distinction between salt water and fresh water as limiting the application of the *Ocean Dumping Control Act* meets the consideration emphasized by a majority of this Court in the *Anti-Inflation Act* reference – that in order for a matter to qualify as one of national concern falling within the federal peace, order and good government power it must have ascertainable and reasonable limits, in so far as its impact on provincial jurisdiction is concerned.

For these reasons I am of the opinion that s. 4(1) of the *Ocean Dumping Control Act* is constitutionally valid as enacted in relation to a matter falling within the national concern doctrine of the peace, order and good government power of the Parliament of Canada, and, in particular, that it is constitutional in its application to the dumping of waste in the waters of Beaver Cove. I would accordingly allow the appeal, set aside the judgments of the Court of Appeal and Schmidt Prov. Ct. J. and refer the matter back to the Provincial Court judge. The constitutional question should be answered as follows:

> Is section 4(1) of the *Ocean Dumping Control Act*, S.C. 1974-75-76, c. 55, *ultra vires* of the Parliament of Canada, and, in particular, is it *ultra vires* of the Parliament of Canada in its application to the dumping of waste in the waters of Beaver Cove, an area within the province of British Columbia?

Answer: No.

La FOREST J. (dissenting) [Beetz. and Lamer JJ. concurring]: – The issue raised in this appeal involves the extent to which the federal Parliament may constitutionally prohibit the disposal of substances not shown to have a pollutant effect in marine waters beyond the coast but within the limits of a province. [...]

For his part, the respondent does not deny Parliament's power to regulate ocean pollution, but submits that s. 4(1) of the Act extends beyond the control of ocean pollution to encompass the dumping of all substances, whether pollutants or not. Much of the subject-matter of the section, the respondent continues, particularly as it relates to the facts of the present case, falls within the classes of subjects assigned exclusively to the provincial legislatures. The reality, it adds, is that while s. 4(1) deals with some matters falling within federal jurisdiction, such as extra-provincial dumping and extra-provincial pollution, which is clearly federal, it does not do so directly, but encompasses as well matters such as intra-provincial depositing of substances and intra-provincial pollution. It thus invades the following heads of provincial legislative power: provincial public lands (s. 92(5)), local works and undertakings (s. 92(10)), property and civil rights (s. 92(13)), and matters of a local or private nature (s. 92(16)).

I start with the proposition that what is sought to be regulated in the present case is an activity wholly within the province, taking place on provincially owned land. Only local works and undertakings are involved, and there is no evidence that the substance made subject to the prohibition in s. 4(1) is either deleterious in any way or has any impact beyond the limits of the province. It is not difficult, on this basis, to conclude that the matter is one that falls within provincial legislative power unless it can somehow be established that it falls within Parliament's general power to legislate for the peace, order and good government of Canada.

PEACE, ORDER AND GOOD GOVERNMENT

There are several applications of the peace, order and good government power that may have relevance to the control of ocean pollution. One is its application in times of emergency. The federal Parliament clearly has power to deal with a grave emergency without regard to the ordinary division of legislative power under the Constitution. The most obvious manifestation of this power is in times of war or civil insurrection, but it has in recent years also been applied in peacetime to justify the control of rampant inflation; see *Re: Anti-Inflation Act*, supra. But while there can be no doubt that the control of ocean pollution poses a serious problem, no one has argued that it has reached such grave proportions as to require the displacement of the ordinary division of legislative power under the Constitution.

A second manner in which the power to legislate respecting peace, order and good government may be invoked in the present context is to control that area of the sea lying beyond the limits of the provinces. The federal government may not only regulate the territorial sea and other areas over which Canada exercises sovereignty, either under its power to legislate respecting its public property, or under the general power respecting peace, order and good government under s. 91 (*Reference Re Offshore Mineral Rights of British Columbia*, [1967] S.C.R. 792) or under s. 4 of the *Constitutional Act, 1871* (U.K.), 34 & 35 Vict., c. 28. I have no doubt that it may also, as an aspect of its international sovereignty, exercise legislative jurisdiction for the control of pollution beyond its borders; see *Reference Re Newfoundland Continental Shelf*, [1984] 1 S.C.R. 86.

In legislating under its general power for the control of pollution in areas of the ocean falling outside provincial jurisdiction, the federal Parliament is not confined to regulating activities taking place within those areas. It may take steps to prevent activities in a province, such as dumping substances in provincial waters that pollute or have the potential to pollute the sea outside the province. Indeed, the exercise of such jurisdiction, it would seem to me, is not limited to coastal and internal waters but extends to the control of deposits in fresh water that have the effect of polluting outside a province. Reference may be made here to *Interprovincial Co-operatives Ltd. v. The Queen*, [1976] 1 S.C.R. 477, where a majority of this Court upheld the view that the federal Parliament had exclusive legislative jurisdiction to deal with a problem that resulted from the depositing of a pollutant in a river in one province that had injurious effects in another province. This is but an application of the doctrine of national dimensions triggering the operation of the peace, order and good government clause. [...]

The power above described can be complemented by provisions made pursuant to the criminal law power. Thus specific provisions prohibiting the deposit of particular substances could be devised in a manner similar to the prohibitions in the *Food and Drugs Act*, R.S.C. 1970, c. F-27. The combination of the criminal law power with its power to control pollution that has extra-provincial dimensions gives the federal Parliament very wide scope to control ocean pollution. While it would not be proper for me to enter into the validity of the provisions of the *Clean Air Act*, S.C. 1970-71-72, c. 47, which were upheld in *Re Canada Metal Co. and The Queen* (1982), 144 D.L.R. (3d) 124 (Man. Q.B.), those provisions do indicate that a combination of the general federal legislative power and the criminal power could go a long way towards prohibiting the pollution of internal waters as well as those in territorial waters and the high seas.

In fact, as I see it, the potential breadth of federal power to control pollution by use of its general power is so great that, even without resort to the specific argument made by the appellant, the constitutional challenge in the end may be the development of judicial strategies to confine its ambit. It must be remembered that the peace, order and good government clause may comprise not only prohibitions, like criminal law, but regulation. Regulation to control pollution, which is incidentally only part of the even larger global problem of managing the environment, could arguably include not only emission standards but the control of the substances used in manufacture, as well as the techniques of production generally, in so far as these may have an impact on pollution. This has profound implications for the federal-provincial balance mandated by the Constitution. The challenge for the courts, as in the past, will be to allow the federal Parliament sufficient scope to acquit itself of its duties to deal with national and international problems while respecting the scheme of federalism provided by the Constitution. [...]

However widely one interprets the federal power to control ocean pollution along the preceding line of analysis, it will not serve to support the provision impugned here, one that, as in the *Fowler* case, supra, is a blanket prohibition against depositing *any* substance in waters without regard to its nature or amount, and one moreover where there is, in Martland J.'s words, at p. 226 of that case, "no attempt to link the proscribed conduct to actual or potential harm" to what is sought to be protected; in *Fowler*, the fisheries, here, the ocean. As in *Fowler*, too, there is no evidence to indicate that the full range of activities caught by the provision serve the harm sought to be prevented. Whether one views this in terms of protecting federal marine property or as an attempted application of the national dimensions doctrine in the matter somewhat akin to that in the *Interprovincial Co-operatives* case, supra, the second proposition of Lord Tomlin in *Attorney-General for Canada v. Attorney-General for British Columbia* (the *Fish Canneries* case), [1930] A.C. 111, at p. 118, has relevance here. It reads:

> (2) The general power of legislation conferred upon the Parliament of the Dominion by s. 91 of the Act in supplement of the power to legislate upon the subjects expressly enumerated must be strictly confined to such matters as are unquestionably of national interest and importance, and must not trench on any of the subjects enumerated in s. 92 as within the scope of provincial legislation, unless these matters have attained such dimensions as to affect the body politic of the Dominion: see *Attorney-General for Ontario v. Attorney-General for the Dominion* ([1896] A.C. 348).

(Cited by Martland J. in *Fowler*, supra, at p. 220.) Here, Parliament may undoubtedly prohibit the dumping of anything into federal waters, but unless a more comprehensive theory for applying the national dimensions doctrine can be found, prohibitions against dumping substances into provincial waters must be linked to some federal power.

Why Parliament should have chosen to enact a prohibition in such broad terms is a matter upon which one is left to speculate. It may be that, in view of the lack of knowledge about the effects of various substances deposited in water, it may be necessary to monitor all such deposits. We have no evidence on the extent to which it is necessary to monitor all deposits into the sea to develop an effective regime for the prevention of ocean pollution. A system of monitoring that was necessarily incidental to an effective legislative scheme for the control of ocean pollution could constitutionally be justified. But here not only was no material advanced to establish the need for such a system, the Act goes much further and prohibits the deposit of any substance in the sea, including provincial internal waters. If such a provision were held valid, why would a federal provision prohibiting the emission of any substance in any quantity into the air, except as permitted by federal authorities, not be constitutionally justifiable as a measure for the control of ocean pollution, it now being known that deposits from the air are a serious source of ocean pollution? [...]

Counsel for the appellant did not, of course, frame the issue in the manner in which I have thus far discussed it. I have examined it in this way, however, to show that on a more traditional approach to the underlying issues than he suggests Parliament has very wide powers to deal with ocean pollution, whether within or outside the limits of the province, but that even if one stretches this traditional approach to its limits, the impugned provision cannot constitutionally be justified. It requires a quantum leap to find constitutional justification for the provision, one, it seems to me, that would create considerable stress on Canadian federalism as it has developed over the years. What he argues for, we saw, is that the dumping of any substance in the sea beginning, apparently, from the coasts of the provinces and the mouths of provincial rivers falls exclusively within the legislative jurisdiction of Parliament as being a matter of national concern or dimension even though the sea-bed is within the province and whether or not the substance is noxious or potentially so.

Le Dain J. has in the course of his judgment discussed the cases relating to the development of the "national concern or dimension" aspect of the peace, order and good government clause, and I find it unnecessary to review that development in any detail. It is sufficient for my purpose to say that this development has since the 1930s particularly been resorted to from time to time to bring into the ambit of federal power a number of matters, such as radio (In *re Regulation and Control of Radio Communication in Canada*, [1932] A.C. 304), aeronautics (*Johannesson v. Municipality of West St. Paul*, [1952] 1 S.C.R. 292), and the national capital region (*Munro v. National Capital Commission*, [1966] S.C.R. 663), that are clearly of national importance. They do not fit comfortably within provincial power. Both in their workings and in their practical implications they have predominantly national dimensions. Many of these subjects are new and are obviously of extra-provincial concern. They are thus appropriate for assignment to the general federal legislative power. They are often related to matters intimately tied to federal jurisdiction. Radio (which is relevant to the power to regulate interprovincial undertakings) is an example. The closely contested issue of narcotics control (cf. *R. v. Hauser*, [1979] 1 S.C.R. 984, and *Schneider v. The Queen*, [1982] 2 S.C.R. 112, *per* Laskin C.J.) is intimately related to criminal law and international trade.

The need to make such characterizations from time to time is readily apparent. From this necessary function, however, it is easy but, I say it with respect, fallacious to go further, and, taking a number of quite separate areas of activity, some under accepted constitutional values within federal, and some within provincial legislative capacity, consider them to be a single indivisible matter of national interest and concern lying outside the specific heads of power assigned under the Constitution. By conceptualizing broad social, economic and political issues in that way, one can effectively invent new heads of federal power under the national dimensions doctrine, thereby incidentally removing them from provincial jurisdiction or at least abridging the provinces' freedom of operation. This, as I see it, is the implication of the statement made by my colleague, then Professor Le Dain, in his article, "Sir Lyman Duff and the Constitution" (1974), 12 *Osgoode Hall L.J.* 261. He states, at p. 293:

> As reflected in the *Munro* case, the issue with respect to the general power, where reliance cannot be placed on the notion of emergency, is to determine what are to be considered to be single, indivisible matters of national interest and concern lying outside the specific heads of jurisdiction in sections 91 and 92. It is possible to invent such matters by applying new names to old legislative purposes. There is an increasing tendency to sum up a wide variety of legislative purposes in single, comprehensive designations. Control of inflation, environmental protection, and preservation of the national identity or independence are examples.

Professor Le Dain was there merely posing the problem; he did not attempt to answer it. It seems to me, however, that some of the examples he gives, notably the control of inflation and environmental protection, are all-pervasive, and if accepted as items falling within the general power of Parliament, would radically alter the division of legislative power in Canada. The attempt to include them in the federal general power seems to me to involve fighting on another plane the war that was lost on the economic plane in the Canadian new deal cases. My colleague Beetz J. has, in *Re. Anti-Inflation Act,* supra, fully supported this way of viewing things in rejecting the control of inflation as a proper subject for incorporation into the peace, order and good government clause under the national dimension doctrine. (His was, we saw, a dissenting judgment, but on this issue too, his views were shared by a majority of the Court.) He there revealed the fallacy of looking at inflation as a single source of federal power in the following passage, at pp. 457-58:

> In my view, the incorporation of companies for objects other than provincial, the regulation and control of aeronautics and of radio, the development, conservation and improvement of the National Capital Region are clear instances of distinct subject matters which do not fall within any of the enumerated heads of s. 92 and which, by nature, are of national concern.

> I fail to see how the authorities which so decide lend support to the first submission. They had the effect of adding by judicial process new matters or new classes of matters to the federal list of powers. However, this was done only in cases where a new matter was not an aggregate but had a degree of unity that made it indivisible, an identity which made it distinct from provincial matters and a sufficient consistence to retain the bounds of form. The scale upon which these new matters enabled Parliament to touch on provincial matters had also to be taken into consideration before they were recognized as federal matters: if an enumerated federal power designated in broad terms such as the trade and commerce power had to be construed so as not to embrace and smother provincial powers (*Parsons'* case) and destroy the equilibrium of the Constitution, the Courts must be all the more careful not to add hitherto unnamed powers of a diffuse nature to the list of federal powers.

> The "containment and reduction of inflation" does not pass muster as a new subject matter. It is an aggregate of several subjects some of which form a substantial part of provincial jurisdiction. It is totally lacking in specificity. It is so pervasive that it knows no bounds. Its recognition as a federal head of power would render most provincial powers nugatory.

> I should add that inflation is a very ancient phenomenon, several thousand years old, as old probably as the history of currency. The Fathers of Confederation were quite aware of it.

What was there said by Beetz J. seems to me to apply, *a fortiori*, to the control of the environment, a subject more germane to the present issue. All physical activities have some environmental impact. Possible legislative responses to such activities cover a large number of the enumerated legislative powers, federal and provincial. [...]

To allocate environmental pollution exclusively to the federal Parliament would, it seems to me, involve sacrificing the principles of federalism enshrined in the Constitution. As Professor William R. Lederman has indicated in his article, "Unity and Diversity in Canadian Federalism: Ideals and Methods of Moderation" (1975), 53 *Can. Bar Rev.* 597, at p. 610, environmental pollution "is no limited subject or theme, [it] is a sweeping subject or theme virtually all-pervasive in its legislative implications". If, he adds, it "were to be enfranchised as a new subject of federal power by virtue of the federal general power, then provincial power and autonomy would be on the way out over the whole range of local business, industry and commerce as established to date under the existing heads of provincial powers". And I would add to the legislative subjects that would be substantially eviscerated the control of the public domain and municipal government. Indeed as Beetz J. in *Re. Anti-Inflation Act,* supra, at p. 478, stated of the proposed power over inflation, there would not be much left of the distribution of power if Parliament had exclusive jurisdiction over this subject. For similar views that the protection of environmental pollution cannot be attributed to a single head of legislative power, see P.W. Hogg, *Constitutional Law of Canada* (2nd ed. 1985), at pp. 392 and 598; Gérald A. Beaudoin, "La protection de l'environnement et ses implications en droit constitutionnel" (1977), 23 *McGill L.J.* 207.

It is true, of course, that we are not invited to create a general environmental pollution power but one restricted to ocean pollution. But it seems to me that the same considerations apply. I shall, however, attempt to look at it in terms of the qualities or attributes that are said to mark the subjects that have been held to fall within the peace, order and good government clause as being matters of national concern. Such a subject, it has been said, must be marked by a singleness, distinctiveness and indivisibility that clearly distinguishes it from matters of provincial concern. In my view, ocean pollution fails to meet this test for a variety of reasons. In addition to those applicable to environmental pollution generally, the following specific difficulties may be noted. First of all, marine waters are not wholly bounded by the coast; in many areas, they extend upstream into rivers for many miles. The application of the Act appears to be restricted to waters beyond the mouths of rivers (and so intrude less on provincial powers), but this is not entirely clear, and if it is so restricted, it is not clear whether this distinction is based on convenience or constitutional imperative. Apart from this, the line between salt and fresh water cannot be demarcated clearly; it is different at different depths of water, changes with the season and shifts constantly; see U.N. Report, op. cit., at p. 12. [...]

This leads me to another factor considered in identifying a subject as falling within the general federal power as a matter of national domain: its impact on provincial legislative power. Here, it must be remembered that in its supposed application within the province the provision virtually prevents a province from dealing with certain of its own public property without federal consent. A wide variety of activities along the coast or in the adjoining sea involves the deposit of some substances in the sea. In fact, where large cities like Vancouver are situated by the sea, this has substantial relevance to recreational, industrial and municipal concerns of all kinds. As a matter of fact, the most polluted areas of the sea adjoin the coast; see U.N. Report, *op. cit.*, at pp. 3-4. Among the major causes of this are various types of construction, such as hotels and harbours, the development of mineral resources and recreational activities (*id.*, at p. 3). These are matters of immediate concern to the province. They necessarily affect activities over which the provinces have exercised some kind of jurisdiction over the years. Whether or not the "newness" of the subject is a necessary criterion for inventing new areas of jurisdiction under the peace, order and good government clause, it is certainly a relevant consideration if it means removing from the provinces areas of jurisdiction which they previously exercised. As I mentioned, pollution, including coastal pollution, is no new phenomenon, and neither are many of the kinds of activities that result in pollution.

A further relevant matter, it is said, is the effect on extra-provincial interests of a provincial failure to deal effectively with the control of intra-provincial aspects of the matter. I have some difficulty following all the implications of this, but taking it at face value, we are dealing here with a situation where, as we saw earlier, Parliament has extensive powers to deal with conditions that lead to ocean pollution wherever they occur. The difficulty with the impugned provision is that it seeks to deal with activities that cannot be demonstrated either to pollute or to have a reasonable potential of polluting the ocean. The prohibition applies to an inert substance regarding which there is no proof that it either moves or pollutes. The prohibition in fact would apply to the moving of rock from one area of provincial property to another. I cannot accept that the federal Parliament has such wide legislative power over local matters having local import taking place on provincially owned property. The prohibition in essence constitutes an impermissible attempt to control activities on property held to be provincial in *Reference Re Ownership of the Bed of the Strait of Georgia and Related Areas* (cites omitted). It may well be that the motive for enacting the provision is to prevent ocean pollution, but as Beetz J. underlines in *Re. Anti-Inflation Act*, supra, Parliament cannot do this by attempting to regulate a local industry, although it can, of course, regulate the activities of such an industry that fall within federal power, whether such activities are expressly encompassed within a specific head of power, e.g., navigation, or affect areas of federal concern, e.g., health under the criminal law power, or cause pollution to those parts of the sea under federal jurisdiction. But here the provision simply overreaches. In its terms, it encompasses activities – depositing innocuous substances into provincial waters by local undertakings on provincial lands – that fall within the exclusive legislative jurisdiction of the province.

Finally, it was argued that the provision might be read down to apply to federal waters only, but I do not think this is possible. One need only look at the broad definition of "the sea" in s. 2(2) and (3) to appreciate the comprehensive reach of the Act. Besides it is well known that many bays and other internal bodies of waters in Canada fall within the limits of the provinces. Many of the federal internal waters are located in the Arctic and have been expressly dealt with by the federal government.

I would dismiss the appeal with costs and reply to the constitutional question in the affirmative. (Yes - ultra vires)

- Research Note -

THE FUTURE OF THE NATIONAL CONCERN DOCTRINE

The *Anti-Inflation Act* Reference gave new definition to the national concern branch of the p.o.g.g. clause. Crown Zellerbach appeared to solidify that definition, although the Court divided deeply about how to apply the reworked doctrine to the analysis of challenged legislation.

Some commentators contended that the Supreme Court's development of the national concern doctrine in Crown Zellerbach would threaten provincial jurisdiction. The Supreme Court has been sensitive to this particular criticism and has been careful in later cases to avoid any complaint that the Court will use the national concern branch of the p.o.g.g. clause to threaten provincial jurisdiction. Perhaps for that reason, application of the doctrine continues to split the Court.

In *Ontario Hydro v. Ontario (Labour Relations Board)*, [1993] 3 S.C.R. 327, the Court held that labour relations in Ontario Hydro's nuclear generating stations was sustainable, *inter alia*, on the federal government's P.O.G.G. power. Speaking for the majority, La Forest J. stated:

> There can surely be no doubt that the production, use and application of atomic energy constitute a matter of national concern. It is predominantly extra-provincial and international in character and implications, and possesses sufficiently distinct and separate characteristics to make it subject to Parliament's residual power.

Mr. Justice Iacobucci [Sopinka and Cory JJ. concurring] disagreed, focusing on Le Dain J.'s third conclusion on the p.o.g.g. power from Crown Zellerbach: "it must have a singleness, distinctiveness and indivisibility." While Iacobucci J. agreed that the federal government generally had jurisdiction over atomic energy under the p.o.g.g. power,

> [...] that jurisdiction does not extend to the labour relations between Ontario Hydro and those of its employees employed in the nuclear electrical generating stations. The federal government does not require control over labour relations at Ontario Hydro's nuclear facilities for the exercise of jurisdiction over atomic energy. In other words, the labour relations at issue in this case are not part of the single, distinctive and indivisible matter identified as atomic energy.

In *A.G. Canada v. Hydro Quebec et. al.*, [1997] 3 S.C.R. 213 Hydro Quebec, which had been charged under s. 6(a) of the Chlorobiphenyls Interim Order, challenged s. 6(a) and ss. 34 and 35 of the *Canadian Environmental Protection Act* pursuant to which s. 6(a) was made. One basis of the attack was that the provision did not fall within the national concern branch of the peace, order and good government clause of s. 91 of the *Constitution Act, 1867*; another was that the provisions did not fall within Parliaments criminal law power at. s. 91.27. A majority of the Court found the provisions were justified by s. 91:27 and thus found it unnecessary to consider the national concern branch of the p.o.g.g. power. However, Justice La Forest, for the majority did say in passing:

> In considering how the question of the constitutional validity of a legislative enactment relating to the environment should be approached, this Court in *Oldman River* (cites omitted), made it clear that the environment is not, as such, a subject matter of legislation under the *Constitution Act, 1867*. As it was put there, "the *Constitution Act, 1867* has not assigned the matter of 'environment' sui generis to either the provinces or Parliament" (p. 63). Rather, it is a diffuse subject that cuts across many different areas of constitutional responsibility, some federal, some provincial (pp. 63-64).
>
> [...]
>
> Some heads of legislation may support a wholly different type of environmental provision than others. Notably under the general power to legislate for the peace, order and good government, Parliament may enact a wide variety of environmental legislation in dealing with an emergency of sufficient magnitude to warrant resort to the power. But the emergency would, of course, have to be established. So too with the "national concern" doctrine, which formed the major focus of the present case. A discrete area of environmental legislative power can fall within that doctrine, provided it meets the criteria first developed in *Reference Re Anti-Inflation Act*, [1976] 2 S.C.R. 373, and thus set forth in *Crown Zellerbach*, supra, at p. 485:
>
> > For a matter to qualify as a matter of national concern in either sense it must have a singleness, distinctiveness and indivisibility that clearly distinguishes it from matters of provincial concern and a scale of impact on provincial jurisdiction that is reconcilable with the fundamental distribution of legislative power under the Constitution.
>
> Thus in the latter case, this Court held that marine pollution met those criteria and so fell within the exclusive legislative power of Parliament under the peace, order and good government clause. While the constitutional necessity of characterizing certain activities as beyond the scope of provincial legislation and falling within the national domain was accepted by all the members of the Court, the danger of too readily adopting this course was not lost on the minority. Determining that a particular subject matter is a matter of national concern involves the consequence that the matter falls within the exclusive and

paramount power of Parliament and has obvious impact on the balance of Canadian federalism. In *Crown Zellerbach*, the minority (at p. 485) expressed the view that the subject of environmental protection was all-pervasive, and if accepted as falling within the general legislative domain of Parliament under the national concern doctrine, could radically alter the division of legislative power in Canada.

The minority position on this point (which was not addressed by the majority) was subsequently accepted by the whole Court in *Oldman River* at p. 64 (cites omitted). The general thrust of that case is that the Constitution should be so interpreted as to afford both levels of government ample means to protect the environment while maintaining the general structure of the Constitution. This is hardly consistent with an enthusiastic adoption of the "national dimensions" doctrine. That doctrine can, it is true, be adopted where the criteria set forth in *Crown Zellerbach* are met so that the subject can appropriately be separated from areas of provincial competence.

I have gone on at this length to demonstrate the simple proposition that the validity of a legislative provision (including one relating to environmental protection) must be tested against the specific characteristics of the head of power under which it is proposed to justify it. For each constitutional head of power has its own particular characteristics and raises concerns peculiar to itself in assessing it in the balance of Canadian federalism. This may seem obvious, perhaps even trite, but it is all too easy (see *Fowler v. The Queen*, [1980] 2 S.C.R. 213) to overlook the characteristics of a particular power and overshoot the mark or, again, in assessing the applicability of one head of power to give effect to concerns appropriate to another head of power when this is neither appropriate nor consistent with the law laid down by this Court respecting the ambit and contours of that other power. In the present case, it seems to me, this was the case of certain propositions placed before us regarding the breadth and application of the criminal law power. There was a marked attempt to raise concerns appropriate to the national concern doctrine under the peace, order and good government clause to the criminal law power in a manner that, in my view, is wholly inconsistent with the nature and ambit of that power as set down by this Court from a very early period and continually reiterated since, notably in specific pronouncements in the most recent cases on the subject.

[...]

In saying that Parliament may use its criminal law power in the interest of protecting the environment or preventing pollution, there again appears to have been confusion during the argument between the approach to the national concern doctrine and the criminal law power. The national concern doctrine operates by assigning full power to regulate an area to Parliament. Criminal law does not work that way. Rather it seeks by discrete prohibitions to prevent evils falling within a broad purpose, such as, for example, the protection of health. In the criminal law area, reference to such broad policy objectives is simply a means of ensuring that the prohibition is legitimately aimed at some public evil Parliament wishes to suppress and so is not a colourable attempt to deal with a matter falling exclusively within an area of provincial legislative jurisdiction.

Lamer, C.J.C. and Iacobucci, J. for the minority wrote joint reasons which concluded that the challenged provisions could not be justified by s. 91:27. Accordingly they went on to consider whether the national concern branch of the p.o.g.g. clause could support the challenged provisions. After reciting the four enumerated points by which Justice LeDain summarized the national concern doctrine in *Crown Zellerbach*, [1988] 1 S.C.R. 401 at 431-2, Lamer C.J.C. and Iacobucci, J. continued:

Assuming that the protection of the environment and of human life and health against any and all potentially harmful substances could be a "new matter" which would fall under the P.O.G.G. power, we must then determine whether that matter has the required "singleness, distinctiveness and indivisibility that clearly distinguishes it from matters of provincial concern" and whether its "impact on provincial jurisdiction [...] is reconcilable with the fundamental distribution of legislative power under the Constitution". Only if these criteria are satisfied will the matter be one of national concern.

(i) Singleness, Distinctiveness and Indivisibility

The test for singleness, distinctiveness and indivisibility is a demanding one. Because of the high potential risk to the Constitution's division of powers presented by the broad notion of "national concern", it is crucial that one be able to specify precisely what it is over which the law purports to claim jurisdiction. Otherwise, "national concern" could rapidly expand to absorb all areas of provincial authority. As Le Dain J. noted in *Crown Zellerbach*, supra, at p. 485, once a subject matter is qualified of national concern, "Parliament has an exclusive jurisdiction of a plenary nature to legislate in relation to that matter, including its intra-provincial aspects."

The appellant submits that the object of Part II of the Act is limited in scope in that there is a clear distinction between chemical substances whose pollutant effects are diffuse and persist in the environment and other types of pollution whose effects are temporary and more local in nature. Therefore, being a single, distinct and indivisible form of pollution which can cross provincial boundaries, chemical pollution requires particular national measures for its proper control. However, as we have shown above, Part II of the Act applies to a wide array of substances, not only to chemical pollutants. Moreover, the impugned legislation is not limited to substances having interprovincial effects.

The definition of "toxic substances" in s. 11, combined with the definition of "substance" found in s. 3, is an all-encompassing definition with no clear limits. [...]

Furthermore, by virtue of s. 11(a), a "toxic substance" may be any form of distinguishable matter which has or even simply may have "an immediate or long-term harmful effect on the environment." [...]

In sum, the investigatory guidelines contemplated by s. 15 do not effectively narrow the broad definitions given to "toxic substances" in ss. 11 and 3; that is, they do not guarantee that only the most serious, diffuse and persistent toxic substances will be caught by the regulatory power conferred by ss. 34 and 35. [...]

With respect to geographical limits, although the preamble of the Act suggests that its ambit is restricted to those substances that "cannot always be contained within geographic boundaries", nowhere in Part II or the enabling provisions at issue is there any actual limitation based on territorial considerations. The notion of "environment" as defined in s. 3 includes all conceivable environments without regard to provincial boundaries. Thus, Part II applies with equal force to "toxic substances" that are wholly situated within a province or whose effects are localized or entirely intraprovincial and to those which move across interprovincial or international borders.

The majority of this Court in *Crown Zellerbach*, supra, at pp. 436-37, found marine pollution to constitute a single, distinct, and indivisible subject-matter, on the basis that the *Ocean Dumping Control Act*, S.C. 1974-75-76, c. 55, distinguished between the pollution of salt water and the pollution of fresh water, both types of waters having different compositions and characteristics. In Part II of the *Canadian Environmental Protection Act*, there is no analogous clear distinction between types of toxic substances, either on the basis of degree of persistence and diffusion into the environment and the severity of their harmful effect or on the basis of their extraprovincial aspects. The lack of any distinctions similar to those in the legislation upheld in *Crown Zellerbach* means that the Act has a regulatory scope which can encroach widely upon several provincial heads of power, notably, s. 92(13) "property and civil rights", s. 92(16) "matters of a merely local or private nature", and s. 92(10) "local works and undertakings." In our view, this failure to circumscribe the ambit of the Act demonstrates that the enabling provisions lack the necessary singleness, distinctiveness and indivisibility.

Another criterion that can be used to determine whether the subject matter sought to be regulated can be sufficiently distinguished from matters of provincial interest is to consider whether the failure of one province to enact effective regulation would have adverse effects on interests exterior to the province. This indicator has also been named the "provincial inability" test (see *Crown Zellerbach*, at pp. 432-34). If the impugned provisions of the Act were indeed restricted to chemical substances, like PCBs, whose effects are diffuse, persistent and serious, then a *prima facie* case could be made out as to the grave consequences of any one province failing to regulate effectively their emissions into the environment. However, the s. 11(a) threshold of "immediate or long-term harmful effect on the environment" also encompasses substances whose effects may only be temporary or local. Therefore, the notion of "toxic substances" as defined in the Act is inherently divisible. Those substances whose harmful effects are only temporary and localized would appear to be well within provincial ability to regulate. To the extent that Part II of the Act includes the regulation of "toxic substances" that may only affect the particular province within which they originate, the appellant bears a heavy burden to demonstrate that provinces themselves would be incapable of regulating such toxic emissions. It has not discharged this burden before this Court.

The s. 34(6) equivalency provision also implicitly undermines the appellant's submission that the provinces are incapable of regulating toxic substances. If the provinces were unable to regulate, there would be even more reason for the federal government not to agree to withdraw from the field. Section 34(6) demonstrates that the broad subject matter of regulating toxic substances, as defined by the Act, is inherently or potentially divisible.

These reasons confirm that the subject matter does not fulfill the characteristics of singleness, distinctiveness and indivisibility required to qualify as a national concern matter.

(ii) Impact on Provincial Jurisdiction

Having concluded that the requirement of singleness, distinctiveness and indivisibility was not satisfied, it is unnecessary to examine the second criterion of the national concern test. The subject matter at issue does not qualify as a national concern matter and, since it was not suggested that it could be upheld as a matter of national emergency, it is therefore not justified by the peace, order and good government power.

[Note: See Malmo-Levine v. The Queen, infra under Criminal law, at paras 67 ff. for further elaboration of the POGG power.]

(c)   Emergency

RE BOARD OF COMMERCE ACT, 1919, AND COMBINES AND FAIR PRICES ACT, 1919
[1922] I A.C. 191 at 193 et seq., 60 D.L.R. 513 (P.C.).

[In 1919, the Parliament of Canada passed legislation creating a "Board of Commerce." The Board was empowered to prohibit the operation of combines and to make orders to that effect. Also, the Board had power to control the distribution and sale of the necessities of life. It could make determinations as to the amount of such commodities that could be withheld from sale. Further, the Board could deem profits to be unfairly high and could order return of the unfair profit. Upon the Board prohibiting profits on sales from an Ottawa clothier of more than a certain percentage of costs, the constitutional validity of the Board was attacked.]

VISCOUNT HALDANE [for the Court]: — [...] The first question to be answered is whether the Dominion Parliament could validly enact such a law. Their Lordships observe that the law is not one enacted to meet special conditions in wartime. It was passed in 1919, after peace had been declared, and it is not confined to any temporary purpose, but is to continue without limit in time, and to apply throughout Canada. No doubt the initial words of s. 91 of the *British North America Act* confer on the Parliament of Canada power to deal with subjects which concern the Dominion generally, provided that they are not withheld from the powers of that Parliament to legislate, by any of the express heads in s. 92, untrammeled by the enumeration of special heads in s. 91. It may well be that the subjects of undue combination and hoarding are matters in which the Dominion has a great practical interest. In special circumstances, such as those of a great war, such an interest might conceivably become of such paramount and overriding importance as to amount to what lies outside the heads in s. 92, and is not covered by them. The decision in *Russell v. The Queen* appears to recognize this as constitutionally possible, even in time of peace; but it is quite another matter to say that under normal circumstances general Canadian policy can justify interference, on such a scale as the statutes in controversy involve, with the property and civil rights of the inhabitants of the Provinces. It is to the Legislatures of the Provinces that the regulation and restriction of their civil rights have in general been exclusively confided, and as to these the Provincial Legislatures possess quasi-sovereign authority. It can, therefore, be only under necessity in highly exceptional circumstances, such as cannot be assumed to exist in the present case, that the liberty of the inhabitants of the Provinces may be restricted by the Parliament of Canada, and that the Dominion can intervene in the interests of Canada as a whole in questions such as the present one. For, normally, the subject-matter to be dealt with in the case would be one falling within s. 92. [...]

As their Lordships have already indicated, the jurisdiction attempted to be conferred on the new Board of Commerce appears to them to be *ultra vires* for the reasons now discussed. It implies a claim of title, in the cases of non-traders as well as of traders, to make orders prohibiting the accumulation of certain articles required for every-day life, and the withholding of such articles from sale at prices to be defined by the Board, whenever they exceed the amount of the material which appears to the Board to be required for domestic purposes or for the ordinary purposes of business. The Board is also given jurisdiction to regulate profits and dealings which may give rise to profit. The power sought to be given to the Board applies to articles produced for his own use by the householder himself, as well as to articles accumulated, not for the market but for the purposes of their own processes of manufacture by manufacturers. The Board is empowered to inquire into individual cases and to deal with them individually, and not merely as the result of applying principles to be laid down as of general application. This would cover such instances as those of coal mines and of local Provincial undertakings for meeting Provincial requirements of social life.

Legislation setting up a Board of Commerce with such powers appears to their Lordships to be beyond the powers conferred by s. 91. They find confirmation of this view in s. 41 of the *Board of Commerce Act*, which enables the Dominion Executive to review and alter the decisions of the Board. It has already been observed that circumstances are conceivable, such as those of war or famine, when the peace, order and good Government of the Dominion might be imperilled under conditions so exceptional that they require legislation of a character in reality beyond anything provided for by the enumerated heads in either s. 92 or s. 91 itself. Such a case, if it were to arise would have to be considered closely before the conclusion could properly be reached that it was one which could not be treated as falling under any of the heads enumerated. Still, it is a conceivable case, and although great caution is required in referring to it, even in general terms, it ought not, in the view their Lordships take of the *British North America Act*, read as a whole, to be excluded from what is possible. For throughout the provisions of that Act there is apparent the recognition that subjects which would normally belong exclusively to a specifically assigned class of subject may, under different circumstances and in another aspect, assume a further significance. Such an aspect may conceivably become of paramount importance, and of dimensions that give rise to other aspects. This is a principle which, although recognized in earlier decisions, such as that of *Russell v. The Queen*, both here and in the Courts in Canada, has always been applied with reluctance, and its recognition as relevant can be justified only after scrutiny sufficient to render it clear that the circumstances are abnormal. In the case before them, however important it may seem to the Parliament of Canada that some such policy as that adopted in the two Acts in question should be made general throughout Canada, their Lordships do not find any evidence that the standard of necessity referred to has been reached, or that the attainment of the end sought is practicable, in view of the distribution of legislative powers enacted by the *Constitution Act*, without the co-operation of the Provincial Legislatures.

FORT FRANCIS PULP & POWER CO. v. MAN. FREE PRESS CO.
[1923] A.C. 695 (P.C.).

VISCOUNT HALDANE [for the Court]: — This appeal raises questions of some novelty and delicacy. The appellants are manufacturers of newsprint paper in Ontario, and the respondents are publishers of newspapers, carrying on business at various places in Canada. The action out of which the appeal arises was brought by the respondents against the appellants to recover sums the former had paid for paper delivered to them at controlled prices. These sums, which the respondents alleged to represent margins in excess of the prices regulated by law, they claimed to be repayable to them as the result of orders of the Paper Control Tribunal of Canada, the final order having been made on July 8, 1920. The sums represented the amounts due after an adjustment of accounts in accordance with the above-mentioned final order and previous orders which it modified. For the balance so arrived at the action was brought in the Supreme Court of Ontario. It was tried before Riddell J., who gave judgment for the plaintiffs, the respondents. [...]

It is therefore necessary to consider in the first place the validity of the legislation and Orders in Council by which the controlling tribunals were set up and invested with the powers exercised. Purporting to act under the provisions of the *War Measures Act* passed by the Parliament of the Dominion in August, 1914, the Governor-General made an Order in Council, dated April 16, 1917, authorizing the Minister of Customs to fix the quantity and price of newsprint paper in sheets or rolls furnished or to be furnished to those who required it for publishing. The Order was to be operative from March 1, 1917, to June 1 in the same year. By further Orders this power was extended to December 1 in that year. Acting in accordance with these Orders the Minister ordered deliveries and fixed prices, and this procedure continued until Mr. R.A. Pringle K.C. was, by Order in Council dated November 3, 1917, appointed Controller as well as Commissioner, with power to fix the quantities to be delivered and the prices, such prices, however, to be approved by the Governor-General in Council.

By various Orders Mr. Pringle fixed prices for a period extending from July 1, 1918, to December 1 in that year. By Order in Council dated September 16, 1918, prices were directed no longer to be supervised by the Governor in Council, inasmuch as a new tribunal called the Paper Control Tribunal was set up, and a right of appeal to it from any Order of the Controller was given. The Paper Control Tribunal made various Orders on appeals from the Controller, and on July 8, 1920, made an Order fixing a price for a period ending on December 31, 1919, and directing the appellants to refund all sums received in excess of the prices fixed. It was the amount of the excess that was the subject of the present action.

On the construction and validity of these Orders points have been made in argument, but the most general question to be decided is definitely raised by the appellants, and is whether the Orders in Council, the statutory basis on which they rest, and the proceedings founded on them by the Controller and the Paper Control Tribunal, were *intra vires* of the Dominion executive and Legislature.

So far as the relevant legislation of the Parliament of the Dominion is concerned, this consists of two statutes. The first of these is the *War Measures Act, 1914*. It enacts that the provisions of s. 6 (to be presently referred to) are only to be in force during war, invasion or insurrection, real or apprehended. The issue of a Government proclamation is to be conclusive evidence that these exist and are continuing, until the issue of a subsequent proclamation declaring them to exist no longer. War is to be deemed to have existed since August 4, 1914. By s. 6 the Governor in Council is to have power to do and authorize such acts and things and to make such orders and regulations as he may, by reason of the existence of real or apprehended war, invasion or insurrection, deem necessary or advisable for the security, defence, peace, order and welfare of Canada. These powers are to extend, among other matters, to trading, exportation, importation, production, manufacture, and also to appropriation, control, forfeiture, and disposition of property and of its use.

By a later Act of the Dominion Parliament, passed on July 7, 1919, relating to paper control, after referring to certain of the Orders in Council already mentioned and to the *War Measures Act* of 1914, on the recital that there had been investigations and work begun by the Paper Commissioner and Controller which were not completed, and with respect to which appeals would lie to the Paper Control Tribunal, and that there were then matters pending before and undetermined by that tribunal, it was enacted that the powers, jurisdiction and authority of the Commissioner and Controller of Paper were confirmed and extended so as to enable him to complete all work and investigations begun by him prior to the declaration of peace, and to determine all questions and to make all necessary Orders with respect to matters coming before him prior to the publication in the Canada Gazette of a proclamation by the Governor in Council declaring the war to no longer exist.

It was further enacted that the powers, jurisdiction and authority of the Paper Control Tribunal were so confirmed and extended as to enable it to determine finally after the declaration of peace all matters pending before and not finally determined by it at the date of such declaration, and to dispose of all appeals brought before it subsequent to such declaration from any act done by or order or decision of the Commissioner and Controller under the Act. It was also provided that, except for the purpose of finally completing all matters undertaken, and determining all matters arising prior to the declaration of peace, the powers, the authority and jurisdiction of the Commissioner and Controller of Paper and of the Paper Control Tribunal should cease upon the publication of the said proclamation. [...]

The question, therefore, becomes one of constitutional law, as to whether the procedure thus established had a valid basis. This depends, in the first place, on whether the two statutes already quoted were *intra vires* of the Dominion Parliament.

It is clear that in normal circumstances the Dominion Parliament could not have so legislated as to set up the machinery of control over the paper manufacturers which is now in question. The recent decision of the Judicial Committee in the *Board of Commerce* case, as well as earlier decisions, show that as the Dominion Parliament cannot ordinarily legislate so as to interfere with property and civil rights in the Provinces, it could not have done what the two statutes under consideration purport to do had the situation been normal. But it does not follow that in a very different case, such as that of sudden danger to social order arising from the outbreak of a great war, the Parliament of the Dominion cannot act under other powers which may well be implied in the Constitution. The reasons given in the *Board of Commerce* case recognize exceptional cases where such a power may be implied.

In the event of war, when the national life may require for its preservation the employment of very exceptional means, the provision of peace, order and good government for the country as a whole may involve effort on behalf of the whole nation, in which the interests of individuals may have to be subordinated to that of the community in a fashion which requires s. 91 to be interpreted as providing for such an emergency. The general control of property and civil rights for normal purposes remains with the Provincial Legislatures. But questions may arise by reason of the special circumstances of the national emergency which concern nothing short of the peace, order and good government of Canada as a whole.

The overriding powers enumerated in s. 91, as well as the general words at the commencement of the section, may then become applicable to new and special aspects which they cover of subjects assigned otherwise exclusively to the Provinces. It may be, for example, impossible to deal adequately with the new questions which arise without the imposition of special regulations on trade and commerce of a kind that only the situation created by the emergency places within the competency of the Dominion Parliament. It is proprietary and civil rights in new relations, which they do not present in normal times, that have to be dealt with; and these relations, which affect Canada as an entirety, fall within s. 91, because in their fullness they extend beyond what s. 92 can really cover. The kind of power adequate for dealing with them is only to be found in that part of the Constitution which establishes power in the State as a whole. For it is not one that can be reliably provided for by depending on collective action of the Legislatures of the individual Provinces agreeing for the purpose. That the basic instrument on which the character of the entire Constitution depends should be construed as providing for such centralized power in an emergency situation follows from the manifestation in the language of the Act of the principle that the instrument has among its purposes to provide for the State regarded as a whole, and for the expression and influence of its public opinion as such. This principle of a power so implied has received effect also in countries with a written and apparently rigid Constitution such as the United States, where the strictly federal character of the national basic agreement has retained the residuary powers not expressly conferred on the Federal Government for the component States. The operation of the scheme of interpretation is all the more to be looked for in a Constitution such as that established by the *British North America Act*, where the residuary powers are given to the Dominion Central Government, and the preamble of the statute declares the intention to be that the Dominion should have a Constitution similar in principle to that of the United Kingdom.

Their Lordships, therefore, entertain no doubt that however the wording of ss. 91 and 92 may have laid down a framework under which, as a general principle, the Dominion Parliament is to be excluded from trenching on property and civil rights in the Provinces of Canada, yet in a sufficiently great emergency such as that arising out of war, there is implied the power to deal adequately with that emergency for the safety of the Dominion as a whole. The enumeration in s. 92 is not in any way repealed in the event of such an occurrence, but a new aspect of the business of Government is recognized as emerging, an aspect which is not covered or precluded by the general words in which powers are assigned to the Legislatures of the Provinces as individual units. Where an exact line of demarcation will lie in such cases it may not be easy to lay down a priori, nor is it necessary. For in the solution of the problem regard must be had to the broadened field covered, in case of exceptional necessity, by the language of s. 91, in which the interests of the Dominion generally are protected. As to these interests the Dominion Government, which in its Parliament represents the people as a whole, must be deemed to be left with considerable freedom to judge.

The other point which arises is whether such exceptional necessity as must be taken to have existed when the war broke out, and almost of necessity for some period subsequent to its outbreak, continued through the whole of the time within which the questions in the present case arose.

When war has broken out it may be requisite to make special provision to ensure the maintenance of law and order in a country, even when it is in no immediate danger of invasion. Public opinion may become excitable, and one of the causes of this may conceivably be want of uninterpreted information in newspapers. Steps may have to be taken to ensure supplies of these and to avoid shortage, and the effect of the economic and other disturbance occasioned originally by the war may thus continue for some time after it is terminated. The question of the extent to which provision for circumstances such as these may have to be maintained is one of which a Court of law is loath to enter. No authority other than the central Government is in a position to deal with a problem which is essentially one of statesmanship. It may be that it has become clear that the crisis which arose is wholly at an end and that there is no justification for the continued exercise of an exceptional interference which becomes *ultra vires* when it is no longer called for. In such a case the law as laid down for distribution of powers in the ruling instrument would have to be invoked. But very clear evidence that the crisis had wholly passed away would be required to justify the judiciary, even when the question raised was one of *ultra vires* which it had to decide, in overruling the decision of the Government that exceptional measures were still requisite. In saying what is almost obvious, their Lordships observe themselves to be in accord with the view taken under analogous circumstances by the Supreme Court of the United States, and expressed in such decisions as that in October, 1919, in *Hamilton v. Kentucky Distilleries Co.*

When then, in the present instance, can it be said that the necessity altogether ceased for maintaining the exceptional measure of control over the newspaper print industry introduced while the war was at its height? At what date did the disturbed state of Canada which the war had produced so entirely pass away that the legislative measures relied on in the present case became *ultra vires?* It is enough to say that there is no clear and unmistakable evidence that the Government was in error in thinking that the necessity was still in existence at the dates on which the action in question was taken by the Paper Control Tribunal. No doubt late in 1919 statements were made to the effect that the war itself was at an end. For example, in the Order in Council made at Ottawa on December 20, 1919, it is stated that it must "be realized that although no proclamation has been issued declaring that the war no longer exists, actual war conditions have in fact long ago ceased to exist, and consequently existence of war can no longer be urged as a reason in fact for maintaining these extraordinary regulations as necessary or advisable for the security of Canada."

The Order in Council then goes on to say that in consequence of the armistice of November, 1918, the Expeditionary Force had since been withdrawn and demobilized, and the country generally is devoting its energies to re-establishment in the ordinary avocations of peace. In these circumstances, it states, the Minister of Justice considers that the time has arrived when the emergency Government legislation should cease to operate. This was in December, 1919. The Order then goes on to declare repealed all Orders and Regulations of the Governor in Council which depend for their sanction upon s. 6 of the *War Measures Act, 1914*, and repeals them as from January 1, 1920. But from this repeal it expressly excepts, among other Orders and Regulations specified, those relating to paper control, which are to remain in force until the end of another session of Parliament.

It will be observed that this Order in Council deals only with the results following from the cessation of actual war conditions. It excepts from repeal certain measures concerned with consequential conditions arising out of war, which may obviously continue to produce effects remaining in operation after war itself is over. *(Intravires)*

Their Lordships find themselves unable to say that the Dominion Government had no good reason for thus temporarily continuing the paper control after actual war had ceased, but while the effects of war conditions might still be operative. They are, therefore, unable to accept the propositions submitted to them in the powerful argument for the appellants.

REFERENCE RE ANTI-INFLATION ACT
[1976] 2 S.C.R. 373.

[For a report of the facts, see supra, p. 474.]

LASKIN C.J.C.: [Spence, Dickson and Judson JJ., concurring] — [...] The Attorney-General of Canada relied upon the preamble to the *Anti-Inflation Act* both in respect of his primary argument and in respect of his alternative argument. He emphasized the words therein "that the containment and reduction of inflation has become a matter of *serious* national concern" and as well the following words that "to accomplish such containment and reduction of inflation it is *necessary* to restrain profit margins, prices, dividends and compensation" (the italicized words were especially emphasized). I do not regard it as telling against the Attorney-General's alternative position that the very word "emergency" was not used. Forceful language would not carry the day for the Attorney-General of Canada if the circumstances attending its use did not support the constitutional significance sought to be drawn from it. Of course, the absence of any preamble would weaken the assertion of crisis conditions, and I have already drawn attention to the fact that no preamble suggesting a critical economic situation, indeed no preamble at all was included in the legislation challenged in the *Board of Commerce* case.

The preamble in the present case is sufficiently indicative that Parliament was introducing a far-reaching programme prompted by what in its view was a serious national condition. The validity of the *Anti-Inflation Act* does not, however, stand or fall on that preamble, but the preamble does provide a base for assessing the gravity of the circumstances which called forth the legislation.

This brings me to the third of the four issues above-mentioned, namely, the relevancy and weight of the extrinsic evidence and the assistance to be derived from judicial notice. When, as in this case, an issue is raised that exceptional circumstances underlie resort to a legislative power which may properly be invoked in such circumstances, the Court may be asked to consider extrinsic material bearing on the circumstances alleged, both in support of and in denial of the lawful exercise of legislative authority. In considering such material and assessing its weight, the Court does not look at it in terms of whether it provides proof of the exceptional circumstances as a matter of fact. The matter concerns social and economic policy and hence governmental and legislative judgment. It may be that the existence of exceptional circumstances is so notorious as to enable the Court, of its own motion, to take judicial notice of them without reliance on extrinsic material to inform it. Where this is not so evident, the extrinsic material need go only so far as to persuade the Court that there is a rational basis for the legislation which it is attributing to the head of power invoked in this case in support of its validity. [...]

In my opinion, this Court would be unjustified in concluding, on the submissions in this case and on all the material put before it, that the Parliament of Canada did not have a rational basis for regarding the *Anti-Inflation Act* as a measure which, in its judgment, was temporarily necessary to meet a situation of economic crisis imperiling the well-being of the people of Canada as a whole and requiring Parliament's stern intervention in the interests of the country as a whole. That there may have been other periods of crisis in which no similar action was taken is beside the point.

The rationality of the judgment so exercised is, in my view, supported by a consideration of the fourth of the issues which I enumerated above. The fact that there had been rising inflation at the time federal action was taken, that inflation is regarded as a monetary phenomenon and that monetary policy is admittedly within exclusive federal jurisdiction persuades me that the Parliament of Canada was entitled, in the circumstances then prevailing and to which I have already referred, to act as it did from the springboard of its jurisdiction over monetary policy and, I venture to add, with additional support from its power in relation to the regulation of trade and commerce. The Government White Paper refers to a prices and incomes policy as one element in a four-pronged programme of which the first engages its fiscal and monetary authority; and although the White Paper states that the Government rejects the use of severe monetary and fiscal restraints to stop inflation because of the alleged heavy immediate cost in unemployment and foregone output, it could seek to blend policies in those areas with a prices and incomes policy under the circumstances revealed by the extrinsic material.

Since no argument was addressed to the trade and commerce power I content myself with observing only that it provides the Parliament of Canada with a foothold in respect of "the general regulation of trade affecting the whole dominion", to use the words of the Privy Council in *Citizens Ins. Co. of Canada v. Parsons* (1881), 7 App. Cas. 96 at p. 113. The *Anti-Inflation Act* is not directed to any particular trade. It is directed to suppliers of commodities and services in general and to the public services of governments, and to the relationship of those suppliers and of the public services to those employed by and in them, and to their overall relationship to the public. With respect to some of such suppliers and with respect to the federal public service, federal legislative power needs no support from the existence of exceptional circumstances to justify the introduction of a policy of restraint to combat inflation.

The economic interconnection with other suppliers and with provincial public services, underlined by collective bargaining conducted by, or under the policy umbrella of trade unions with Canada-wide operations and affiliations, is a matter of public general knowledge of which the Court can take judicial notice. The extrinsic material does not reveal any distinction in the operation and effect of inflation in respect of those economic areas which are ordinarily within and those ordinarily outside of effective federal regulatory control. In enacting the *Anti-Inflation Act* as a measure for the peace, order and good government of Canada, Parliament is not opening an area of legislative authority which would otherwise have no anchorage at all in the federal catalogue of legislative powers but, rather, it is proceeding from legislative power bases which entitle it to wage war on inflation through monetary and fiscal policies and entitle it to embrace within the *Anti-Inflation Act* some of the sectors covered thereby but not all. The circumstances recounted above justify it in invoking its general power to extend its embrace as it has done.

For all the foregoing reasons, I would hold that the *Anti-Inflation Act* is valid legislation for the peace, order and good government of Canada and does not, in the circumstances under which it was enacted and having regard to its temporary character, invade provincial legislative jurisdiction. It is open to this Court to say, at some future time, as it in effect said in the *Margarine* case, [1949] S.C.R. 1; affirmed [1951] A.C. 179, that a statutory provision valid in its application under circumstances envisaged at the time of its enactment can no longer have a constitutional application to different circumstances under which it would, equally, not have been sustained had they existed at the time of its enactment.

[De Grandpré J. concurs with Laskin C.J.C. on Question No. 2 (the 'emergency' doctrine); De Grandpré J. concurs with Beetz J. on Question No. 1. (the 'national concern' doctrine)]

RITCHIE J. [Pigeon and Martland JJ., concurring]: — I have had the privilege of reading the reasons for judgment of the Chief Justice and his comprehensive review of the authorities satisfies me that the answer to the question of whether or not the *Anti-Inflation Act*, 1974-75 (Can.), c. 75, hereinafter referred to as the "Act", is *ultra vires* the Parliament of Canada, must depend upon whether or not the legislation was enacted to combat a national economic emergency. I use the phrase "national emergency" in the sense in which I take it to have been used by Lord Wright in *Co-Operative Committee on Japanese Canadians et al. v. A.-G. Can. et al.*, [1947] A.C. 87, (hereinafter referred to as the *Japanese Canadians* case), and accepted by this Court in *Reference Re Wartime Leasehold Regulations*, [1950] S.C.R. 124. In those cases the "emergency" was occasioned by war and the aftermath of war, but I see nothing to exclude the application of the principles there enunciated from a situation created by highly exceptional economic conditions prevailing in times of peace.

In my opinion such conditions exist where there can be said to be an urgent and critical situation adversely affecting all Canadians and being of such proportions as to transcend the authority vested in the Legislatures of the Provinces and thus presenting an emergency which can only be effectively dealt with by Parliament in the exercise of the powers conferred upon it by s. 91 of the *British North America Act, 1867*, "to make laws for the peace, order and good government of Canada". The authority of Parliament in this regard is, in my opinion, limited to dealing with critical conditions and the necessity to which they give rise and must perforce be confined to legislation of a temporary character. [...]

I should also say, however, that I cannot find that the authority of Parliament to pass legislation such as the present Act stems from any of the enumerated classes of subjects referred to in s. 91. The source of the federal power in relation to the *Anti-Inflation Act* must, in my opinion, be found in the "peace, order and good government" clause, and the aura of federal authority to which that clause relates can in my view only be extended so as to invade the provincial area when the legislation is directed to coping with a genuine emergency in the sense to which I have made reference.

In order to determine whether the legislation here in question was enacted to combat such an emergency, it is necessary to examine the legislation itself, but in so doing I think it not only permissible but essential to give consideration to the material which Parliament had before it at the time when the statute was enacted for the purpose of disclosing the circumstances which prompted its enactment.

[The Justice then considered the materials which were before Parliament.]

[...]

I am accordingly satisfied that the record discloses that in enacting the *Anti-Inflation Act* the Parliament of Canada was motivated by a sense of urgent necessity created by highly exceptional circumstances and that a judgment declaring the Act to be *ultra vires* could only be justified by reliance on very clear evidence that an emergency had not arisen when the statute was enacted. In this regard I reiterate what was said by Lord Wright in the *Japanese Canadians* case, supra, at pp. 101-2 A.C., in the following passage:

Again, if it be clear that an emergency has not arisen, or no longer exists, there can be no justification for the exercise or continued exercise of the exceptional powers. The rule of law as to the distribution of powers between the Parliaments of the Dominion and the Parliaments of the Provinces comes into play. But very clear evidence that an emergency has not arisen or that the emergency no longer exists, is required to justify the judiciary, even though the question is one of *ultra vires*, in overruling the decision of the Parliament of the Dominion that exceptional measures were required or were still required.

[...]

In my opinion, the evidence presented to the Court by those opposed to the validity of the legislation did not meet the requirements set by Lord Wright and I am unable to say that the exceptional measures contained in the Act were not required.

It is for these reasons I am in agreement with the Chief Justice that the first question posed by this Reference should be answered in the negative.

As to the second question posed by the Reference, I am in complete agreement with the reasons for judgment of the Chief Justice. [...]

BEETZ J. (dissenting on Question No. 1): — [...] The second submission made in support of the validity of the *Anti-Inflation Act* is that the inflationary situation was in October of 1975, and still is such as to constitute a national emergency of the same significance as war, pestilence or insurrection and that there is in Parliament an implied power to deal with the emergency for the safety of Canada as a whole; that such situation of exceptional necessity justified the enactment of the impugned legislation. [...]

Before I deal with this second submission I should state at the outset that I am prepared to assume the validity of the following propositions:

- the power of Parliament under the national emergency doctrine is not confined to war situations or to situations of transition from war to peace; an emergency of the nature contemplated by the doctrine may arise in peace time;

- inflation may constitute such an emergency;

- Parliament may validly exercise its national emergency powers before an emergency actually occurs; a state of apprehended emergency or crisis suffices to justify Parliament in taking preventive measures including measures to contain and reduce inflation where inflation amounts to state of apprehended crisis.

In order to decide whether the *Anti-Inflation Act* is valid as a national emergency measure, one must first consider the way in which the emergency doctrine operates in the Canadian Constitution; one must find in the second place whether the *Anti-Inflation Act* was in fact enacted on the basis that it was a measure to deal with a national emergency in the constitutional sense.

I disagree with the proposition that the national concern or national dimension doctrine and the emergency doctrine amount to the same. Even if it could be said that "where an emergency exists it is the emergency which gives the matter its dimension of national concern or interest" (LeDain, *op. cit.*, p. 291) the emergency does not give the matter the same dimensions as the national concern doctrine applied for instance in the *Aeronautics* case, in the *Johannesson* case or in the *Munro* case. The national concern doctrine illustrated by these cases applies in practice as if certain heads such as aeronautics or the development and conservation of the national capital were added to the categories of subject-matters enumerated in s. 91 of the Constitution when it is found by the Courts that, in substance, a class of subjects not enumerated in either s. 91 or s. 92 lies outside the first fifteen heads enumerated in s. 92 and is not of a merely local or private nature. Whenever the national concern theory is applied, the effect is permanent although it is limited by the identity of the subject newly recognized to be of national dimensions. By contrast, the power of Parliament to make laws in a great crisis knows no limits other than those which are dictated by the nature of the crisis. But one of those limits is the temporary nature of the crisis.

In my view, the verbal precautions taken by the Judicial Committee in the *Fort Frances* case, pp. 704-6 A.C., and in other cases reflect its concern over the fact that a power of such magnitude as the national emergency power had to be inferred. But further passages, some of which are even to be found in the very judgments which in other parts appear to say the contrary, make clear that, in practice, the emergency doctrine operates as a partial and temporary alteration of the distribution of powers between Parliament and the provincial Legislatures. [...]

Perhaps it does not matter very much whether one chooses to characterize legislation enacted under the emergency power as legislation relating to the emergency or whether one prefers to consider it as legislation relating to the particular subject-matter which it happens to regulate. But if one looks at the practical effects of the exercise of the emergency power, one must conclude that it operates so as to give to Parliament for all purposes necessary to deal with the emergency, concurrent and paramount jurisdiction over matters which would normally fall within exclusive provincial jurisdiction. To that extent, the exercise of that power amounts to a temporary *pro tanto* amendment of a federal Constitution by the unilateral action of Parliament. The legitimacy of that power is derived from the Constitution: when the security and the continuation of the Constitution and of the nation are at stake, the kind of power commensurate with the situation "is only to be found in that part of the Constitution which establishes power in the state as a whole" (Viscount Haldane in the *Fort Frances* case, p. 704 A.C.).

The extraordinary nature and the constitutional features of the emergency power of Parliament dictate the manner and form in which it should be invoked and exercised. It should not be an ordinary manner and form. At the very least, it cannot be a manner and form which admits of the slightest degree of ambiguity to be resolved by interpretation. In cases where the existence of an emergency may be a matter of controversy, it is imperative that Parliament should not have recourse to its emergency power except in the most explicit terms indicating that it is acting in the basis of that power. Parliament cannot enter the normally forbidden area of provincial jurisdiction unless it gives an unmistakable signal that it is acting pursuant to its extraordinary power. Such a signal is not conclusive to support the legitimacy of the action of Parliament but its absence is fatal. It is the duty of the Courts to uphold the Constitution, not to seal its suspension, and they cannot decide that a suspension is legitimate unless the highly exceptional power to suspend it has been expressly invoked by Parliament. Also, they cannot entertain a submission implicitly asking them to make findings of fact justifying even a temporary interference with the normal constitutional process unless Parliament has first assumed responsibility for affirming in plain words that the facts are such as to justify the interference. The responsibility of the Courts begins after the affirmation has been made. If there is no such affirmation, the Constitution receives its normal application. Otherwise, it is the Courts which are indirectly called upon to proclaim the state of emergency whereas it is essential that this be done by a politically responsible body.

We have not been referred to a single judicial decision, and I know of none, ratifying the exercise by Parliament of its national emergency power where the constitutional foundation for the exercise of that power had not been given clear utterance to. And, apart from judicial decisions, I know of no precedent where it could be said that Parliament had attempted to exercise such an extraordinary power by way of suggestion or innuendo.

The use of the national emergency power enables Parliament to override provincial laws in potentially every field: it must be explicit.

This is not to say that Parliament is bound to use ritual words. Words such as "emergency" are not necessarily required. [...]

In such cases, urgent or emergency legislation is enacted by Parliament under its ordinary powers. What is required from Parliament when it purports to exercise its extraordinary emergency power in any situation where a dispute could arise as to the existence of the emergency and as to the constitutional foundation of its action, is an indication, I would even say a proclamation, in the title, the preamble or the text of the instrument, which cannot possibly leave any doubt that, given the nature of the crisis, Parliament in fact purports to act on the basis of that power. The Statutes of Canada and the Canada Gazette contain several examples of laws, proclamations and Orders in Council which leave room for no doubt that they have been enacted pursuant to the exceptional emergency power of Parliament, or issued or passed under the authority of an Act of Parliament enacted by virtue of that power. Those dealing with wartime or post-wartime conditions usually present no difficulty given the global aspect of modern warfare, the total conscription of activities which it is susceptible to impose upon nations, and the general recognition of the factual situation. [...]

The *Anti-Inflation Act* fails in my opinion to pass the test of explicitness required to signal that it has been enacted pursuant to the national emergency power of Parliament.

The preamble has been much relied upon:

WHEREAS the Parliament of Canada recognizes that inflation in Canada at current levels is contrary to the interests of all Canadians and that the containment and reduction of inflation has become a matter of serious national concern;

AND WHEREAS to accomplish such containment and reduction of inflation it is necessary to restrain profit margins, prices, dividends and compensation;

The words "a matter of serious national concern" have been emphasized. I remain unimpressed.

The death penalty is a matter of national concern. So is abortion. So is the killing or maiming of innumerable people by impaired drivers. So is the traffic in narcotics and drugs. One can conceive of several drastic measures, all coming within the ordinary jurisdiction of the Parliament of Canada, and which could be preceded by a preamble reciting that a given situation had become a matter of serious national concern. I fail to see how the adding of the word "serious" can convey the meaning that Parliament has decided to embark upon an exercise of its extraordinary emergency power. [...] It does not seem to present itself as such. How is a matter of serious national concern to be distinguished from a matter of urgent national concern? I cannot read the preamble of the *Anti-Inflation Act* as indicating that the act was passed to deal with a national emergency in the constitutional sense.

Counsel for Canada has also insisted upon the temporary nature of the *Anti-Inflation Act*. I note that the duration of the Act could, under s. 46 [since am. 1974-75-76, c. 98, s. 11], be extended by Order in Council with the approval of both Houses of Parliament, although I am not inclined to attach undue importance to this point. None the less, while it would be essential to the validity of a measure enacted under the national emergency power of Parliament that it be not permanent, still the temporary character of an Act is hardly indicative and in no way conclusive that it constitutes a measure passed to deal with a national emergency: Parliament can and often does enact temporary measures relating to matters coming within its normal jurisdiction.

3.   Trade and Commerce

(a)   General

BRIAN MORGAN, "THE TRADE AND COMMERCE POWER", 2006
(ORIGINAL CONTRIBUTION)

I. INTRODUCTION

By section 91(2) of the *Constitution Act*, 1867 the federal Parliament was given the power to make laws in relation to the "regulation of trade and commerce" without qualification.

In *Citizens Insurance Company of Canada v. Parsons* (1881), 7 A.C. 96, the Privy Council considered provincial legislation which required certain conditions to be included in all fire insurance policies. The Privy Council held that the Ontario Act was valid law in relation to property and civil rights in the province under section 92(13), and in so doing rejected the unlimited potential implicit in the wording of the federal trade and commerce power.

The Court established that federal power consisted of two branches:

(1) international and inter-provincial trade; and
(2) general regulation of trade affecting the whole country.

The regulation of any particular business or trade, however, and intra-provincial trade and commerce were determined to be within provincial power under section 92(13).

II. INTERNATIONAL AND INTERPROVINCIAL TRADE

While *Parsons* established the framework for the trade and commerce power, it failed to define the point at which trade and commerce became sufficiently inter-provincial so as to come within federal power. This task was left to the Privy Council during the Haldane period.

Constitutional interpretation is rooted in history and varying views of the nature of Canadian Federalism. The prevailing theory of political economy in the early years of confederation was laissez-faire. Initial cases tended to strike down both federal and provincial laws alike. Inasmuch as the majority of legislation considered (and struck down) was federal, the result was an increase in provincial power and a fostering of regionalization.

The first case of note is the *Insurance Reference (A.-G. Can. v. A.-G. Alta.)*, [1916] 1 A.C. 588. This case considered the federal *Insurance Act* of 1910, which established a licensing system for insurance companies, other than provincial companies carrying on business wholly within the province of incorporation. Viscount Haldane laid down the following principle (at p. 596):

> ... it must now be taken that the authority to legislate for the regulation of trade and commerce does not extend to the regulation by a licensing system of a particular trade in which Canadians would otherwise be free to engage in the provinces.

Consequently, the fact that the insurance industry spanned the country was not sufficient to uphold federal regulation under the trade and commerce power.

In *Re Board of Commerce*, [1922] 1 A.C. 191 is the next example of the narrow interpretation of the federal trade and commerce power in the Haldane era. At issue was federal legislation which included anti-combines provisions and restrictions on hoarding and excessive prices for various necessaries of life. Viscount Haldane said that section 91(2) "did not, by itself, enable interference with particular trades in which Canadians would, apart from any right of interference conferred by these words above, be free to engage in the Provinces". Viscount Haldane also made the striking suggestion that the trade and commerce power had no independent content; it could only be invoked as ancillary to other federal powers.

In *Toronto Electric Commissioners v. Snider*, [1925] A.C. 396 Viscount Haldane again rejected the trade and commerce power as support for federal legislation, this time in respect of a federal act relating to compulsory arbitration of labour disputes. In holding that the Act was within property and civil rights in the provinces under section 92(13), Viscount Haldane stated, more clearly this time, that the trade and commerce power could not be relied on as enabling Parliament to regulate civil rights in the provinces, unless it could be invoked in aid of another federal power.

Professor Hogg suggested that the statutes considered in the *Board of Commerce* and *Snider* cases were inter-provincial inasmuch as they attempted to control combinations, prices and labour, not particular trades. The statutes dealt in general aspects of the economy which ignored provincial boundaries. However, the Court did not consider the pervasiveness and interdependence of the subject matters of the legislation sufficient to carry them out of property and civil rights and into federal jurisdiction.

The *King v. Eastern Terminal Elevator Company*, [1925] S.C.R. 434 is the first of a succession of cases considering the commerce power in light of schemes for the marketing of natural products. In this case, as part of more comprehensive regulation, federal legislation required the licensing of grain elevators. In holding the Act *ultra vires*, Duff J. stated that Parliament's jurisdiction over a trade is not warranted by the fact that a certain percentage of the trade is exported.

In the *Proprietary Articles Trade Association v. A.G. Canada (P.A.T.A.)*, [1931] A.C. 310 the *Combines Investigation Act* was sought to be upheld under the trade and commerce power. This was a narrower form of anti-combines law than that considered in the *Board of Commerce* case. Having held legislation intra vires in relation to criminal law, the Court found it unnecessary to discuss section 91(2). In so stating, however, the judges made the following significant observation (at p. 326):

> Their Lordships merely propose to disassociate themselves from the construction suggested in argument of a passage in the judgment in the *Board of Commerce* case under which it was contended that the power to regulate trade and commerce could be invoked only in furtherance of a general power which Parliament possessed independently of it. No such restriction is properly to be inferred from that judgment. The words of the statute must receive their proper construction where they stand as giving an independent authority to Parliament over the particular subject-matter.

Thus, the effect of Viscount Haldane's statement in the *Board of Commerce* and *Snider* cases, which had threatened to rob the trade and commerce power of its independence, was checked.

Chief Justice Duff then laid the ground for the "necessary incidental" doctrine, which was to prove fruitful later as a support for federal legislation, in his analysis of the Parsons decision in *Reference Re: Natural Products Marketing Act (Canada)* [1936], S.C.R. 398 (at pp. 406 407):

> ... nor is there anything to suggest, whatever the precise scope of the power may be, that, when Parliament is legislating with reference to matters strictly within the regulation of trade and commerce, it is disabled from legislating in regard to matters otherwise exclusively within the provincial authority if such legislation is necessarily incidental to the exercise of the exclusive powers in relation to that subject.

The Privy Council upheld the Supreme Court of Canada.

By this time, both federal and provincial attempts to regulate the grain trade had been invalidated. Weiler (1973), 23 *U.T.L.J.* 307 commented that "by the end of 1949, a constitutional straitjacket had been placed on the ability of governmental authority from either source - dominion or provincial - to exercise meaningful control over private enterprise", and as a result the country was faced with a "regulatory 'no man's land'".

The *Margarine Reference (Can. Fed. of Agriculture v. A.G. Que.)*, [1951] A.C. 179 was the last case in which the Privy Council considered the trade and commerce power. The Justices exhibited concern for the autonomy of the provinces as they once again narrowed the power. Provincial power was considered more important than centralization of economic regulation covering more than one province. There was little perception that legislative schemes such as those struck down might be important to the building of a national economy in Canada.

The role of the Privy Council in interpreting the Constitution has been defended by Lysyk. He commented:

> While a high degree of centralism might be suitable for a unilingual country which has seen itself as a "melting pot", is it equally appropriate for a country with two official languages, two distinct legal systems, and a small multicultural population thinly distributed over a huge land mass? Or is it just possible that the jurisprudence passed on to us by the Privy Council, so roundly condemned as ignorant or perverse, may in fact have reflected an appreciation that an attempt to impose complete domination from the centre would have imposed strains on the Canadian federation which, quite simply, would have proved unacceptable? ...

After the abolition of appeals to the Privy Council in 1949, there was a resurgence in the federal trade and commerce power. The first case in which this new attitude of the courts is discernible is *Reference Re Farm Products Marketing Act*, [1957] S.C.R. 198. This case questioned the validity of a provincial marketing statute, on the assumption that the statute applied only to intra-provincial transactions. While the majority of the Court held the legislation to be *intra vires*, four judges indicated by implication that the federal power would extend to some transactions which were completed within a province. Rand J. stated that there is a field of trade within provincial power, such power being a subtraction from that comprehended within section 91(2). Kerwin C.J. laid down the "flow of commerce" concept (at p. 205):

> The concept of trade and commerce, the regulation of which is confided to Parliament, is entirely separate and distinct from the regulation of mere sale and purchase agreements. Once an article enters into the flow of interprovincial or external trade, the subject-matter and all its attendant circumstances cease to be a mere matter of local concern.

In *Murphy v. C.P.R. Co.*, [1958] S.C.R. 626 the Court considered a second attempt by Parliament to regulate the grain trade. Federal jurisdiction was invoked successfully pursuant to a statutory declaration that all elevators and mills involved in the grain trade were works for the general advantage of Canada. Under section 92(10)(c) of the *Constitution Act, 1867,* such declarations terminate provincial jurisdiction. *Murphy* did not hold that substantial extra-provincial interest in the intra-provincial aspects of trade might on that ground alone come under federal jurisdiction.

In *R. v. Klassen* (1959), 20 D.L.R. (2d) 406 (Man. C.A.) the Court considered section 16 of the *Canadian Wheat Board Act,* which provided for a quota scheme respecting delivery of grain by producers to elevators and feed mills and required the recording of such deliveries in permit books issued to the producers by the Board. This quota scheme was designed to ensure equal access to inter-provincial and export markets. The Court had to decide whether the Act could apply to a purely local work, that is, to a mill not engaged in export or inter-provincial trade and which received a delivery of grain produced locally, processed as feed and sold in intra-provincial trade. Using the necessarily incidental doctrine developed in the *Natural Products Marketing* case, the Court held that the Act could validly apply to such intra-provincial transactions. The Court found that the quota scheme was necessarily incidental to the principal purpose of the Act (i.e., the orderly marketing system envisaged by the Act) and to the equitable rationing of delivering opportunity which is a feature of the control system.

Weiler (1973), 23 U.T.L.J. 307, 331 commented that *R. v. Klassen* is the first time a Canadian court, having declared the main thrust or "aspect" of legislation to be valid federal regulation of marketing beyond provincial borders, went on to uphold the related intra-provincial activity or controls, as functionally desirable in the overall scheme. Rather than holding that federal regulation of trade or marketing could begin only at the point of interprovincial or export movement, the Court instead adopted a functional approach. It is this new approach which makes Klassen so significant. The Court seems to have realized that trade in wheat is essentially a matter of export and interprovincial trade and consequently any marketing of wheat, intra-provincial or interprovincial, could and should reasonably be subjected to federal regulation. The Klassen case represents an important departure from previous Privy Council decisions which had consistently struck down federal attempts to regulate wholly intra-provincial transactions. Leave to appeal to the Supreme Court of Canada was denied.

Caloil v. A.G. Can., [1971] S.C.R. 543 gave the Supreme Court of Canada the opportunity to confirm *Klassen*. In *Caloil*, regulations under the *National Energy Board Act* controlled the importation of oil west of the Ottawa Valley with the purpose of protecting the domestic industry in the West from then cheaper imported products. The Court upheld the legislation as "an incident in the administration of an extraprovincial marketing scheme" and as "an integral part of the control of imports in furtherance of an extraprovincial trade policy".

In *A.G. Man. v. Manitoba Egg and Poultry Association*, [1971] S.C.R. 689 the Court dealt with certain provincial regulations proposed to be made by the Produce Board aimed at establishing a marketing plan to regulate the sale in Manitoba of all eggs, wherever produced. Inasmuch as the plan was designed to regulate interprovincial trade in eggs and would restrict the free flow of interprovincial trade, the Supreme Court held it to constitute an invasion of exclusive federal authority over trade and commerce.

Burns Foods Ltd. v. A.G. Man. (1973), 40 D.L.R. (3d) 731 (S.C.C.) concerned a provincial attempt to regulate interprovincial trade in hogs. The legislation prohibited processors from purchasing hogs from producers in another province except through the agency of the Provincial Marketing Board. The Court held the legislation to be *ultra vires* the province. The scheme, said the Court, was not a case of subjecting all goods of a certain kind to uniform regulation. Rather, it directly regulated extra-provincial trade operations in their essential aspects, that is, the price and all other conditions of sale. In effect, the Court held that direct regulation of interprovincial trade cannot be treated as an accessory of local trade.

The *Manitoba Egg and Poultry Association* and *Burns Foods* cases, by their rejection of provincial power, were also a part of the courts' recognition of a larger role for the federal trade and commerce power. These and the preceding cases which had upheld federal marketing and economic regulatory schemes, exhibited a different attitude of the courts. Particularly through the 1960s and early 1970s the courts appeared to accept that such federal legislation was a necessary and desirable part of economic nation-building. Perhaps the then current perception that Canada had come of age as a country encouraged the courts to accept a federal economic role beyond that tolerable to the Privy Council.

In *MacDonald v. Vapour Canada Ltd.*, [1977] 2 S.C.R. 134 the Court considered, and struck down, section 7(e) of the federal *Trade Marks Act* which provided that: "No person shall [...] do any other act or adopt any other business practice contrary to honest industrial or commercial usage in Canada". Laskin C.J.C. pointed out that the inclusion of section 7(e) in an Act whose main provisions were unchallenged did not thereby render it valid. He stated (at pp. 164-165):

> I do not read s. 91(2) as in itself authorizing federal legislation that merely creates a statutory tort, enforceable by private action, and applicable, as here, to the entire range of business relationships in any activity, whether the activity be itself within or beyond federal legislative authority. [...]

The provision is not directed to trade but to the ethical conduct of persons engaged in trade or in business, and, in my view, such a detached provision cannot survive along unconnected to a general regulatory scheme to govern trading relations going beyond merely local concern.

Laskin C.J.C. implied that a connection to a regulatory scheme administered by a federally-appointed agency is necessary to support a provision under the trade and commerce power. This was a notable departure from the results of previous Privy Council decisions in which such connections existed, but where the federal legislation was invalidated nevertheless.

Section 7(e) of the Act was not directed to interprovincial trade. This precluded resort to the first branch of the trade and commerce power. The Court, therefore, turned to the second branch. In the Federal Court of Appeal, Jackett C.J. commented that "a law laying down a set of general rules as to the conduct of businessmen in their competitive activities in Canada" was within the second branch of the power.

Canadian Industrial Gas & Oil Ltd. (CIGOL) v. Government of Saskatchewan, [1978] 2 S.C.R. 545 dealt with provincial legislation which imposed a mineral income tax and royalty surcharge on the production of oil and gas in the province. The effect of the legislation was to set a floor price for Saskatchewan oil in the international market. The legislation was held to be ultra vires the province as imposing indirect taxes and as coming within exclusive federal authority under section 91(2). The latter conclusion turned on the fact that virtually all oil produced in the province was destined for export; the legislation, therefore, aimed at the export market and controlled the export price.

CIGOL further broadened the federal commerce power. The Supreme Court of Canada appeared to be centralizing Canadian federalism, eschewing provincial control of economic matters affecting other parts of the country. CIGOL produced bitter protest from the Saskatchewan government, and was eventually reversed by constitutional amendment in 1982 (*Constitution Act, 1982*, s. 50).

Central Canada Potash Co. Ltd. v. Government of Saskatchewan, [1979] 1 S.C.R. 42 dealt with Saskatchewan regulations controlling the production and price of potash, and included a prorationing scheme. The scheme limited the production of the respondent company and, therefore, prevented the company from fulfilling a contract with a U.S. co-operative. The Court invalidated the provincial scheme because, as it held, provincial control cannot extend to fixing the price to be charged in the export market, a point earlier made in *CIGOL*. However, the Court noted that production controls and conservation measures with respect to natural resources in a province are, usually, matters within provincial legislative authority.

Turnbull (1980), 6 *Queens L.J.* 295 suggested that *Central Canada Potash* follows a principle earlier advanced in *Re The Grain Marketing Act, 1931*, [1931] 2 W.W.R. 146 (Sask. C.A.) that transactions completed wholly within the province are valid subjects of provincial regulation. *Central Canada Potash*, he reasons, is the other side of this principle. Transactions which are not completed within one province fall within federal jurisdiction. Mr. Turnbull thinks the principle is erroneous: it reverts to the `water-tight compartments' approach which choked the creativity of the Privy Council. Mr. Turnbull's major criticism is that this approach precludes the Court from developing a serious functional approach, based on the economic and social needs of provincial and national economies, to allocating commerce jurisdiction.

Reference Re Agricultural Products Marketing Act, [1978] 2 S.C.R. 1198 (the "Egg Reference" case) placed in issue the validity of certain provisions of the federal Agricultural Products Marketing Act and Farm Products Marketing Agencies Act, the provincial Farm Products Marketing Act, and orders and regulations passed under these Acts. This legislation had been enacted as a result of an agreement between the federal and provincial Ministers of Agriculture as well as the federal and provincial marketing boards; it established a comprehensive programme for the marketing of eggs. The agreement contained provision for provincial and federal marketing plans to establish agreed-upon quotas for intra-provincial, interprovincial and export trade. The Court invalidated section 2(2)(a) of the federal Agricultural Products Marketing Act, which provided for levies in respect of intra-provincial trade, but upheld the balance of the legislation. This case continued the general trend, dating from the Murphy case in 1958, of broadening the first branch of the commerce power, thus breaking away from the paralysis of federal power resulting from the Privy Council legacy.

GENERAL TRADE AND COMMERCE

The development of the second branch of the commerce power has lagged far behind the first branch. In fact, the resistance on the part of courts to "breath life into the second branch of the Parsons trade and commerce description" (terminology used by Estey, J. to describe John Deere Plow case in Labatts Breweries of Canada v. A.-G. of Canada (1979), 110 D.L.R. (3d) 594, [1980] 1 S.C.R. 914) has lead at least one commentator to conclude that the general trade an commerce power was "a badly endangered species" (See J.C. MacPherson, "Economic Regulation and the British North America Act", (1980-81) 5 Can. Bar L.J. 172 at 191-2). However, in recent years the second branch has assumed greater significance.

The first occasion that the second branch was used as support for legislation was in John Deere Plow Co. v. Wharton, [1915] A.C. 330. In that case the Privy Council invalidated the British Columbia Companies Act, which required federally incorporated companies to obtain a provincial license to carry on business in the province. The legislation dealt with "a question of general interest throughout the Dominion" and thus fell under federal commerce jurisdiction. This statement became the test for application of the second branch of the power in subsequent case law.

In A.G. Ont. v. A.G. Canada, [1937] A.C. 405 the Privy Council upheld the creation of a national trade mark as within the second branch of federal commerce jurisdiction. Clearly it was appropriate for such a matter to be regulated at the federal level, rather than being subject to possibly varying treatment in each province.

While acknowledgment of the existence of a "general power to regulate trade" can be found in *Bank of Toronto v. Lambe*; *Hodge v. The Queen*; *Toronto Electric Commissioners v. Snider*, and *Reference Re Natural Products Marketing Act*, the Courts never defined the scope of the power until *Reference Re Anti-Inflation Act Reference*, [1976] 2 S.C.R. 373. There, Laskin C.J. referred in *obiter* to "the general regulation of trade affecting the whole dominion" as a head of power which would justify a policy of restraint to combat inflation.

In *MacDonald v. Vapour Canada Ltd.*, Chief Justice Laskin suggested that, to be upheld under the second branch of the power, a federal act must fulfill the following conditions:

(1) the challenged provision must be part of a regulatory scheme administered by a federally appointed agency, and

(2) the enforcement of the scheme must not be left to the chance of private redress without public monitoring by the continuous oversight of a regulatory agency.

Several cases introduced uncertainty by the absence of a clear and consistent analysis of this branch of the trade and commerce power. *R. v. Dominion Stores Ltd.*, [1980] 1 S.C.R. 844 dealt with section 3 of the *Canadian Agricultural Products Standards Act*, which established a grading system for agricultural products. The scheme was compulsory in interprovincial and international trade, but required provincial consent to apply locally. In separate opinions the Supreme Court held section 3 invalid in relation to purely intra-provincial transactions. Kushner (1981), 19 *O.H.L.J.* 118 criticizes both opinions for failing to address the proper scope of the second branch of the commerce power. While both opinions accept the authority of the Trademarks case, Mr. Justice Estey distinguished the case on its facts. Chief Justice Laskin simply applied the case without discussion of the test to apply. *Labatt Breweries of Canada Ltd. v. A.G. Can.* (1980), 30 N.R. 496 (S.C.C.) contains an important discussion of the second branch of the commerce power. The case concerned plaintiff's use of the label "Labatts Special Lite" for a beer which was not a "light beer" within the grade standards defined in the regulations under the federal *Food and Drugs Act*. Plaintiff argued that the regulations were *ultra vires* Parliament. The majority confirmed that the test of whether the second branch of the trade and commerce power applies is to be found in the *John Deere Plow* case. The majority added that the "trade and commerce head cannot be applied to the regulation of a single trade, even though it be on a national basis". Nor do minute rules for regulating particular trades come within the second branch. Unrestricted geographic play of an Act is not sufficient to find legislative authority under section 91(2). Neither national ownership nor national advertising of a product alone will suffice to invoke use of federal commerce power. Since the provisions in issue in Labatt purported to establish such a detailed single industry regulatory pattern, they could not be justified under the trade and commerce power.

Kushner, *supra*, commented that Chief Justice Laskin's dissent in *Labatt's* reflects a constitutional view concerned with preserving a federal commerce power that is not limited to the marketing of goods. This is a perception of Canada which differs from that adopted by the Privy Council, and, apparently, also from that of Mr. Justice Estey. In his dissenting judgment in *Labatt's*, the Chief Justice did not follow the route suggested in *MacDonald v. Vapour Canada*, which he might have done by supporting the validity of compulsory commodity standards legislation on the basis of a scheme of public control in association with a regulatory authority. Instead he supported the federal legislation on the basis that it was a method of equalizing competitive advantages for businesses concerned with the manufacture of foods, drugs, cosmetics and therapeutic devices. As stated by Mr. Kushner (at p. 128):

> Although the different interpretation of the second category of 91(2) adopted by the Chief Justice and Mr. Justice Estey may derive from differing views on their role in interpreting the Constitution (provincial rights, co-operative federalism, functional necessities), both the Chief Justice and Mr. Justice Estey seem inclined to the view that marketing legislation should be treated as coming exclusively within the first category of 91(2).

Thus, in *Dominion Stores* and *Labatt's*, the Court broke the pattern of broadening the trade and commerce power. This may be seen in part as a reflection of a general social and political period during which the pendulum was swinging back after the heady days of nationalism, expanding economic activity and increased centralization of the 1960s and early 1970s. In part, also, it may reflect an ambivalence of the judges to the values at stake in the competing demands of federal uniformity and centralization as against provincial diversity and decentralization.

Kushner further notes that the judgments in *Dominion Stores* and *Labatt's* reveal the concern of the Court to protect provincial jurisdiction under section 92. It is consistent with this view to restrict the scope for federal legislation which affects local trade; hence to narrow the federal general trade power, to restrict the necessarily incidental doctrine, and to create provincial paramountcy.

In *R. v. Hoffman-La Roche Ltd. (Nos. 1 and 2)* (1981), 125 D.L.R. 607 the Ontario Court of Appeal cited with approval the conclusions of the trial judge that section 34(1)(c) of the *Combines Investigation Act* could be constitutionally supported on the federal commerce power. Section 34(1)(c) provides that everyone engaged in a business who sells items at unreasonably low prices which has, or is designed to have, the effect of lessening competition or eliminating a competitor is guilty of an offence. The trial Judge stated that section 34(1)(c) is part of a legislative scheme aimed at deterring a wide range of unfair competitive practices that affect trade and commerce generally across Canada, and is not limited to a single industry, commodity or area. The conduct which it prohibits is generally of national and international scope and the presence or absence of healthy competition may affect the welfare of the economy of the entire nation. Thus, the Court held it is within the sphere of the federal Parliament to seek to regulate such competition in the interests of all Canadians.

In *A.G. Can. v. Canadian National Transportation Limited* (1983), 3 D.L.R. (4th) 16 (S.C.C.), the accused were charged with conspiracy under section 32(1)(c) of the *Combines Investigation Act*. Laskin C.J.C., for the majority, dealt with the section as criminal law and consequently did not have to decide whether it could also be upheld under the trade and commerce power. Dickson J., in a concurring judgment, viewed section 32(1)(c) as regulation of trade and commerce, stating that the "long disuse of this second branch does not impugn its constitutional validity". Dickson J. stated (at p. 58) that it was necessary to have a restrictive reading of the *John Deere Plow* test inasmuch as:

> [T]here is hardly an economic issue, which, if only by virtue of its recurrence in locations around the country, could not be characterized as a matter of general interest throughout the Dominion.

Mr. Justice Dickson considered that the proper approach to characterization is, as suggested in *Parsons*, a careful case-by-case assessment, but indicated the following to be indicia for a valid exercise of the general trade and commerce power.

(a) presence of a national regulatory scheme;
(b) oversight of a regulatory agency;
(c) concern with trade in general rather than an aspect of particular business;
(d) the provinces jointly or severally would be constitutionally incapable of passing such an enactment;
(e) failure to include one or more provinces or localities would jeopardize successful operation in other parts of the country.

He stated that this list was not meant to be exhaustive, nor any of the indicia necessarily decisive.

Dickson J.'s judgment in *Canadian National Transportation* represented a change with respect to competition law, and possibly other matters of economic legislation as well. Until that point, federal competition law had been upheld as criminal law. The criminal law characterization of competition law, however, creates serious administration and enforcement problems. MacDonald (1969), 47 *Can. Bar Rev.* 161 pointed out the procedural advantages from justifying combines legislation under the commerce power. [...]

Since Mr. Justice Dickson's decision in *C.N. Transportation* there has been an expansion of the general trade and commerce power and to some extent the "necessarily incidental" doctrine at the Federal Court of Appeal level. *C.N. Transportation* has proved to be a turning point in the development of the second branch of section 91(2) and increased the federal government's ability to regulate the national economy at a time when national and international trade occupy important positions on the federal government's political agenda.

The Supreme Court of Canada returned to elaboration of the second branch of *Parsons* in *General Motors of Canada Limited v. City National Leasing*, [1989] 1 S.C.R. 641. The Court reinforced its liberal interpretation, and held section 31.1 of the *Combines Investigation Act intra vires* Parliament. The section was stated to be sufficiently related to a valid federal regulatory scheme aimed at controlling anti-competitive activity nationwide.

In *General Motors v. City National Leasing*, 1989 ([1989] 1 S.C.R. 641), and its companion case *Quebec Ready Mix v. Rocois Construction* ([1989] 1 S.C.R. 695), Dickson C.J. continued to develop the second branch of the trade and commerce power. Writing for a unanimous court in both cases, Dickson C.J. held that the *Combines Investigation Act* was a valid exercise of the federal government's "general" trade and commerce power.

In determining whether this legislation was *intra vires* the federal government Dickson C.J. applied five indicia he previously set out in *Canadian National Transportation*. The court held that the sections of the *Combines Investigation Act* creating a civil remedy satisfied each of the indicia, the purpose of the civil remedy being to provide for "a more complete and more effective system of enforcement in which public and private initiative can both operate to motivate and effectuate compliance". (*Quebec Ready Mix*, at p. 400 D.L.R.). This test for constitutional validity under s. 91(2) set out in *General Motors* was applied by the Quebec Court of Appeal in *Alex Courture Inc. v. Canada (Attorney-General)* ((1991), 83 D.L.R. (4th) 577 at 601-611), another case involving the *Competition Act*.

In *General Motors* Dickson C.J. quoted Professor Hogg in his book *Constitutional Law of Canada*, for the proposition that the pith and substance doctrine, which upholds federal legislation that incidentally affects a matter that appears to be the proper subject of provincial legislation, applies equally to uphold provincial legislation:

> I think it is plain both on principle and on authority that the provincial enumerated powers have exactly the same capacity as the federal enumerated powers to "affect" matters allocated to the other level of government.

This principle was followed in *Re It's Adult Video v. B.C. (Dir. of Film Classification)* ((1991), 81 D.L.R. (4th) 436), wherein the British Columbia Supreme Court upheld the provisions of the *Motion Picture Act* requiring the submission of adult films to a director of film Classification before distribution. The Court held that the pith and substance of the legislation was to regulate the content of a product and that any effects the legislation had on the regulation of interprovincial trade "was merely incidental to the proper exercise of jurisdiction in a provincial matter" (at D.L.R. p. 454). This "Dickson Period" aimed at creating national economic unity is in sharp contrast to the "Haldane Period" which aimed at protecting provincial autonomy.

In *Kirkbi AG v. Ritvik Holdings Inc.* [2005], 3 S.C.R. 302, the Supreme Court of Canada recently returned to the second branch of the commerce power to uphold the constitutionality of s. 7(b) of the *Trade-marks Act*. The impugned section enforced the substantive aspects of that statute as it relates to unregistered trade-marks. Applying the five indicia of Dickson C.J. in the *Canadian National Transportation* and *General Motors* cases to determine whether the statute fell within the federal commerce power or the provincial property and civil rights power, the court found that the pith and substance of the Act was well within the jurisdiction of the federal government. The court observed that trade-marks apply to trade as a whole, across and between industries in different provinces. It also cautioned that divided federal and provincial jurisdiction in this sphere could lead to an uneven protection of trade-marks. As the remedial provision of s. 7(b) represented only a minimal intrusion into the provincial realm of power, the court found that the functional relationship between the statute as a whole and this section in particular demonstrated that the regulation was sufficiently integrated into the statutory framework so as to be a valid exercise of federal power.

IV. NEW DIRECTIONS

Attempts were made in the Charlottetown Agreement (August 28, 1992 text) to include new provisions in the Constitution describing the commitment of the governments, Parliament and legislatures within the federation to the principle of the preservation and development of Canada's social and economic union. The new provision was to be entitled *The Social and Economic Union*. The policy objectives were to include inter alia the free movement of persons, goods, services and capital. The provision was not to be justiciable. Rather, a mechanism for monitoring the Social and Economic Union was to be determined by a First Ministers' Conference. With the rejection of the Charlottetown Agreement in a national referendum, the need to address the continuing tension between the federal and provincial governments over the division of powers remained. Although repeated attempts at constitutional reform had failed, some moderate success was achieved in the area of trade and commerce with the adoption of the Agreement on Internal Trade.

Signed in July of 1994 and coming into effect one year later, this agreement represented an attempt to ensure the primacy of the Canadian common market by promoting unrestricted movement of persons, goods, services and investments. Although the Agreement on Internal Trade did not require the removal of all existing trade barriers within the federation, it does restrict the adoption of any new trade obstacles, unless the purpose of these is to achieve legitimate objectives which are not determined to be unduly restrictive.

Another issue which has been raised on many occasions during the past several decades has been the establishment of a federal securities commission. Since first proposed in 1964, this issue has highlighted some of the many challenges which lie in attempting to delineate the overlapping areas of "trade and commerce" and "property and civil rights." One of the particular considerations among various supporters of the proposal is the need to ensure constitutional validity of the legislation. It is not unlikely that participants in the heavily regulated industry will challenge any federal intervention in the area of securities regulation and will carry with them the significant case history of jurisdictional exclusivity for the provinces. Despite renewed interest in the field, and various efforts to resolve their differences, negotiations between the federal and the provincial governments remain to this day, unsuccessful.

Although the area no longer receives the amount of judicial attention it did in previous times, questions concerning trade and commerce have recently been raised before the Canadian courts, including in the Supreme Court of Canada.

In *Federation des producteurs de volailles du Quebec v. Pelland* [2005], 1 S.C.R. 292, the court addressed the issue of whether a production and marketing quota that is set by a provincial body, and that applies to all production regardless of whether it is to be sold within the province or interprovincially, is constitutional. Drawing on the *Egg Reference* case as precedent, the court found that the core character of the impugned provision was to regulate the production and marketing of chicken in Quebec as part of a cooperative federal-provincial agreement. Having determined that the object of the provincial legislation was to regulate local undertakings and not interprovincial or international trade, the court proceeded to hold that any impact upon such trade was incidental to the legitimate purposes of the provision and that it was therefore constitutional. In particular, the court emphasized the fact that the provincial legislation left Quebec chicken producers free to market their produce within the province, extraprovincially, or in some combination thereof, provided that they adhered to their individual quotas.

The decision of the Supreme Court in *Pelland* affirmed the analysis of the Court of Appeal for *Alberta in Leth Farms Ltd. v. Alberta (Turkey Growers Marketing Board)*, [2000] A.J. No. 59 (QL). The plaintiffs in Leth Farms claimed that provincial legislation imposing levies upon them for producing and marketing turkeys was unconstitutional because most of their turkeys were sold outside of Alberta. The court rejected this argument and declared the provincial legislation to be a valid exercise of provincial power. Explaining that most of the operations of turkey producers that are covered by the legislation have to be undertaken regardless of the final destination of the product, the court found that the regulation sought to control production within the province and not interprovincial trade. Finally, the court reasoned that the validity of the legislation should not be called into question simply because one producer allocated most of his production for sale outside of Alberta and thereby caused the provision to have an incidental effect upon interprovincial trade.

Soon after the Supreme Court released its decision in *Pelland*, an analogous Ontario provision was found to be constitutional upon the strength of that precedent in *Allan v. Ontario (Attorney General)* (2005), 76 O.R. (3d) 616 (Div. Ct.). The impugned regulation in *Allan* required that all milk producers in Ontario abide by a quota system and sell their entire output to the provincial marketing board. The court found that the primary purpose of the legislation was to control the volume of milk produced and marketed in Ontario. While the court acknowledged that the legislation required producers to sell their entire output to the marketing board and therefore prevented producers from independently exporting milk from Ontario, this effect on interprovincial trade was deemed not to render the regulation *ultra vires*. As in *Pelland*, and *Leth Farms*, the court held that producers could not circumvent provincial regulation of production and marketing by simply exporting their product.

The Newfoundland and Labrador courts have followed suit in applying the *Pelland* rationale to uphold provincial regulations licensing crab processors and limiting the output of fish processors, even though over 95% of the fish processed in Newfoundland and Labrador was exported. See *Port Enterprises v. Newfoundland (Minister of Fisheries and Aquaculture)*, [2006] N.J. No. 171 (QL) (C.A.); *Dandy Dan's Fish Market Ltd. v. Newfoundland*, [2005] N.J. No. 249 (QL) (S.C. (T.D.)).

In *R. v. Pickering*, [1999] M.J. No. 377 (QL), the Manitoba Court of Queen's Bench upheld provincial legislation forbidding the possession of more than a prescribed amount of tobacco products that were marked by the authorities of another province for sale in that province or for export out of Canada. The court found that the purpose of the legislation was to enforce related provisions taxing tobacco products and not to regulate interprovincial trade. Furthermore, the court emphasized that the impugned regulation was an essential element of the taxing scheme and that the province was entitled to pass such legislation to give force to its constitutional powers of taxation.

Conversely, in the earlier case of *British Columbia (Milk Marketing Board) v. Bari Cheese Ltd.*, [1996] B.C.J. No. 1789 (QL) (C.A.), the B.C. Court of Appeal upheld a ruling of the B.C. Supreme Court which had determined that a British Columbia's Marketing Board Regulation and the Board's orders relating to the marketing of industrial milk were *ultra vires* the Province as legislation aimed at interprovincial trade.

It is also important to note that s. 121 of the *Constitution Act, 1867* presently provides for a common market:

> All Articles of the Growth, Produce, or Manufacture of any one of the Provinces shall, from and after the Union, be admitted free into each of the other Provinces.

In 1989, the Supreme Court of Canada expressed the relationship between the Trade and Commerce power and s. 121 in the following terms:

> A dominant intention of the drafters of the British North America Act (now the Constitution Act, 1867) was to establish "a new political nationality" and, as the counterpart to national unity, the creation of a national economy [...] (*Black v. Law Society of Alberta*, [1989] 1 S.C.R. 591 per La Forest, J. at p. 609). [...]

> The creation of a central government, the trade and commerce power, s. 121 and the building of a transcontinental railway were expected to help forge this economic union. The concept of Canada as a single country comprising what one would now call a common market was basic to the Confederation arrangements and the drafters of the *British North America Act* attempted to pull down the existing internal barriers that restricted movement within the country. (*Ibid.*, at p. 609; see also *Morguard Investments v. De Savoye*, [1990] 2 S.C.R. 1077, 46 C.P.C. (2d) 1 per La Forest at pages 19-20).

Notwithstanding these statements, the full impact of s. 121 on presently existing trade barriers, and its relation to the Trade and Commerce power, have yet to be developed by the courts.

(b)   Intraprovincial Trade and Commerce

(i)   Provincial Competence "in relation to"

CITIZENS INS. CO. v. PARSONS; QUEEN INS. CO. v. PARSONS
(1881) 7 APP. CAS. 96 (P.C.).

SIR MONTAGUE SMITH [for the Court]: — The questions in these appeals arise in two actions brought by the same plaintiff (the respondent) upon contracts of insurance against fire of buildings situate in the province of Ontario, in the dominion of Canada. [...]

The statute impeached by the appellants, as being an excess of legislative power, is an Act of the legislature of the province of Ontario (39 Vict. c. 24), entitled "An Act to secure uniform Conditions in Policies of Fire Insurance." [...]

The main contention on the part of the respondent was that the *Ontario Act* in question had relation to matters coming within the class of subjects described in No. 13 of sect. 92, viz., "Property and civil rights in the province." The Act deals with policies of insurance entered into or in force in the province of Ontario for insuring property situate therein against fire, and prescribes certain conditions which are to form part of such contracts. These contracts, and the rights arising from them, it was argued, came legitimately within the class of subject, "Property and civil rights." The appellants, on the other hand, contended that civil rights meant only such rights as flowed from the law, and gave as an instance the status of persons. Their Lordships cannot think that the latter construction is the correct one. They find no sufficient reason in the language itself, nor in the other parts of the Act, for giving so narrow an interpretation to the words "civil rights." The words are sufficiently large to embrace, in their fair and ordinary meaning, rights arising from contract, and such rights are not included in express terms in any of the enumerated classes of subjects in sect. 91. [...]

The next question for consideration is whether, assuming the *Ontario Act* to relate to the subject of property and civil rights, its enactments and provisions come within any of the classes of subjects enumerated in sect. 91. The only one which the Appellants suggested as expressly including the subject of the *Ontario Act* is No. 2, "the regulation of trade and commerce."

A question was raised which led to much discussion in the Courts below and this bar, viz., whether the business of insuring buildings against fire was a trade. This business, when carried on for the sake of profit, may, no doubt, in some sense of the word, be called a trade. But contracts of indemnity made by insurers can scarcely be considered trading contracts, nor were insurers who made them held to be "traders" under the English bankruptcy laws; they have been made subject to those laws by special description. Whether the business of fire insurance properly falls within the description of a "trade" must, in their Lordships' view, depend upon the sense in which that word is used in the particular statute to be construed; but in the present case their Lordships do not find it necessary to rest their decision on the narrow ground that the business of insurance is not a trade.

The words "regulation of trade and commerce," in their unlimited sense are sufficiently wide, if uncontrolled by the context and other parts of the Act, to include every regulation of trade ranging from political arrangements in regard to trade with foreign governments, requiring the sanction of parliament, down to minute rules for regulating particular trades. But a consideration of the Act shows that the words were not used in this unlimited sense. In the first place the collocation of No. 2 with classes of subjects of national and general concern affords an indication that regulations relating to general trade and commerce were in the mind of the legislature, when conferring this power on the dominion parliament. If the words had been intended to have the full scope of which in their literal meaning they are susceptible, the specific mention of several of the other classes of subjects enumerated in sect. 91 would have been unnecessary; as, 15, banking; 17, weights and measures; 18, bills of exchange and promissory notes; 19, interest; and even 21, bankruptcy and insolvency. [...]

Construing therefore the words "regulation of trade and commerce" by the various aids to their interpretation above suggested, they would include political arrangements in regard to trade requiring the sanction of parliament, regulation of trade in matters of interprovincial concern, and it may be that they would include general regulation of trade affecting the whole dominion. Their Lordships abstain on the present occasion from any attempt to define the limits of the authority of the dominion parliament in this direction. It is enough for the decision of the present case to say that, in their view, its authority to legislate for the regulation of trade and commerce does not comprehend the power to regulate by legislation the contracts of a particular business or trade, such as the business of fire insurance in a single province, and therefore that its legislative authority does not in the present case conflict or compete with the power over property and civil rights assigned to the legislature of Ontario by No. 13 of s. 92.

Having taken this view of the present case, it becomes unnecessary to consider the question how far the general power to make regulations of trade and commerce, when competently exercised by the dominion parliament, might legally modify or affect property and civil rights in the provinces, or the legislative power of the provincial legislatures in relation to those subjects.

HOME OIL DISTRIBUTORS LTD. v. A.G.B.C.
[1940] S.C.R. 444.

KERWIN J. [Rinfret J. concurring]: — The plaintiffs (appellants) brought action against the Attorney-General of British Columbia, Coal and Petroleum Control Board, and Dr. William Alexander Carrothers (the sole member of the Board), for a declaration that the *Coal and Petroleum Products Control Board Act of British Columbia* (chapter 8 of the statutes of 1937), or that certain sections of it, were *ultra vires* the legislature of the province. The plaintiffs also asked a declaration that an amending *Act* of 1938 was *ultra vires* the legislature, and that a certain regulation was *ultra vires* the Board. [...]

The *Principal Act* provides for the appointment of a Board with power to regulate and control within the province the "coal and petroleum industries." That expression is stated to include: —

the carrying-on within the Province of any of the following industries or businesses: The mining of coal; the preparation of coal for the market; the storage of coal; the wholesale and retail distribution and selling of coal, the distillation, refining, and blending of petroleum; the manufacture, refining, preparation, and blending of all products obtained from petroleum; the storage of petroleum and petroleum products; and the wholesale and retail distribution and selling of petroleum products.

Sections 14 and 15, which are the ones declared *ultra vires* the provincial legislature by the trial judge, are as follows: —

> 14.(1) The Board may from time to time, with the approval of the Lieutenant-Governor in Council, fix the price or prices, maximum price or prices, minimum price or prices at which coal or petroleum products may be sold in the Province either at wholesale or retail or otherwise for use in the Province.

Home Oil Company's No. 1 Gas Well (June, 1934)

> (2) Without limiting the generality of the powers conferred by subsection (1), the Board may: –
> (a) Fix different prices for different parts of the Province;
> (b) Fix different prices for licenses notwithstanding that they are in the same class of occupation;
> (c) Fix schedules of prices for different qualities, quantities, standards, grades, and kinds of coal and petroleum products.

> 15. Where the Board has fixed a price for coal or for petroleum or for any petroleum product, it may, with the approval of the Lieutenant-Governor in Council, declare that any covenant or agreement for the purchase or sale within the Province of coal or petroleum or a petroleum product for use in the Province contained in any agreement in existence at the time of fixing such price shall be varied so that the price shall conform to the price fixed by the Board, and the agreement, subject only to the variation declared by the Board, shall in all other respects remain in full force and effect.

By section 2 of the Act: —

> "Petroleum products" includes petroleum, gasoline, naphtha, benzene, kerosene, lubricating-oils, stove oil, fuel oil, furnace-oil, paraffin, and all derivatives of petroleum and all products obtained from petroleum, whether blended with or added to other things or not.

Reading these sections in the light of all the other provisions of the Act, I am of opinion that, to quote the judgment of the Judicial Committee in *Shannon v. Lower Mainland Dairy Products Board*: —

> the legislation in question is confined to regulating transactions that take place wholly within the Province, and are therefore within the sovereign powers granted to the Legislature in that respect by s. 92 of the *British North America Act*;

or to quote again from the same judgment, at page 720: —

> The pith and substance of this Act is that it is an Act to regulate particular businesses entirely within the Province and it is therefore *intra vires* of the Province. [...]

CROCKET J. — Notwithstanding Mr. Farris's ingenious and able argument regarding the integrated character of the oil production, refining and sales industry and the apprehended effect of the impugned legislation upon the profits of that industry as an integrated whole outside the limits of British Columbia, I am unable to discover any substantial or satisfactory reason for holding that the legislation is anything else than what it plainly purports to be, namely, an enactment constituting a board with power to fix maximum and minimum wholesale and retail prices of all coal and petroleum products sold in the Province of British Columbia or for use in that Province. This, in my judgment, the Provincial Legislature clearly had the right to do under the exclusive legislative powers assigned to it by s. 92 of the *B.N.A. Act*.

The fact that the motive of the Legislature may have been, as was suggested, to empower the Coal and Petroleum Products Board, by fixing an arbitrary maximum price for the sale of gasoline and a minimum price for the sale of crude fuel oil within the Province, to afford some needed protection for the important coal mining industry of the Province against the menacing competition of the sale of the latter product at the then current prices, cannot in my opinion alter the character of the legislation as legislation for purely provincial purposes. Neither can the fact that the legislation was calculated to compel all international or external corporations desiring and authorized to do business within the limits of the Province to alter their methods and policy regarding the allocation of profits as between the gasoline and fuel oil branches of their so-called integrated industry. If they desire to carry on their business in the Province of British Columbia, they must comply with provincial laws in common with all provincial and independent dealers in the same commodities. In my opinion the judgment of the Judicial Committee in *Shannon v. Lower Mainland Dairy Products Board* is in all essential points indistinguishable from and decisive of the present appeal.

I think the appeal should be dismissed with costs.

[The concurring judgments of Duff C.J., Davis and Hudson JJ. have been omitted.]

REFERENCE RE FARM PRODUCTS MARKETING ACT
[1957] S.C.R. 198.

THE CHIEF JUSTICE: — This is a reference by His Excellency the Governor General in Council as to the validity of one clause of one section of *The Farm Products Marketing Act* of the Province of Ontario, R.S.O. 1950, c. 131, of certain regulations made thereunder, of an order of The Ontario Hog Producers' Marketing Board, of a proposed amendment to the Act, and of a suggested authorization by the Farm Products Marketing Board if that amendment be held to be *intra vires*. [...]

Subsequent to the date of the order of reference, the Act was amended by c. 20 of the statutes of 1956, which came into force the day it received Royal Assent, s. 1 of which reads as follows:

> 1. *The Farm Products Marketing Act* is amended by adding thereto the following section:
> 1(*a*). The purpose and intent of this Act is to provide for the control and regulation in any or all respects of the marketing within the Province of farm products including the prohibition of such marketing in whole or in part.

Without entering into a discussion as to what is a declaratory law, since the term may have different connotations depending upon the matter under review, it is arguable that, for present purposes, this amendment should be read as part of *The Farm Products Marketing Act*, but, in any event, the first question submitted to us directs us to assume that that Act as amended down to the date of the reference applies only in the case of "intra-provincial transactions". This term means "existing or occurring within a province"; see Shorter Oxford English Dictionary, including "intra-parochial" as an example under the word "intra". As will appear later, the word "marketing" is defined in the Act, but, in accordance with what has already been stated, I take it as being confined to marketing within the Province.

Question 1 is as follows:

> 1. Assuming that the said Act applies only in the case of intra-provincial transactions, is clause (*l*) of subsection 1 of section 3 of *The Farm Products Marketing Act*, R.S.O. 1950 chapter 131 as amended by Ontario Statutes 1951, chapter 25, 1953, chapter 36, 1954, chapter 29, 1955, chapter 21, *ultra vires* the Ontario Legislature?

Clause (*l*) of subs. (1) of s. 3 referred to, as re-enacted by 1955, c. 21, s. 2, provides:

> 3.(1) The board may. [...]
> (*l*) authorize any marketing agency appointed under a scheme to conduct a pool or pools for the distribution of all moneys received from the sale of the regulated product and requiring any such marketing agency, after deducting all necessary and proper disbursements and expenses, to distribute the proceeds

of sale in such manner that each person receives a share of the total proceeds in relation to the amount, variety, size, grade and class of the regulated product delivered by him and to make an initial payment on delivery of the product and subsequent payments until the total net proceeds are distributed.

For a proper understanding of the terms used in this clause and of the provisions of the Act it is necessary to refer to what is proposed by the latter.

The Board is the Farm Products Marketing Board and " 'farm products' includes animals, meats, eggs, poultry, wool, dairy products, grains, seeds, fruit, fruit products, vegetables, vegetable products, maple products, honey, tobacco and such articles of food or drink manufactured or derived in whole or in part from any such product and such other natural products of agriculture as may be designated by the regulations" (s. 1(*b*)). " 'Regulated product' means a farm product in respect of which a scheme is in force" (s. 1(*g*)). Provision is made for the formulation of a scheme for the marketing or regulating of any farm product upon the petition of at least 10 per cent of all producers engaged in the production of the farm product in Ontario, or in that part thereof to which the proposed scheme is to apply. " 'Marketing' means buying, selling and offering for sale and includes advertising, assembling, financing, packing and shipping for sale or storage and transporting in any manner by any person, and 'market' and 'marketed' have corresponding meanings" (s. 1(*c*), as re-enacted by 1955, c. 21, s. 1). The scheme may provide for a "marketing agency" designated by the Board in its regulations. Once the scheme is approved by the Board the latter's regulations will apply according to the farm products dealt with thereby.

It seems plain that the Province may regulate a transaction of sale and purchase in Ontario between a resident of the Province and one who resides outside its limits; that is, if an individual in Quebec comes to Ontario and there buys a hog, or vegetables, or peaches, the mere fact that he has the intention to take them from Ontario to Quebec does not deprive the Legislature of its power to regulate the transaction, as is evidenced by such enactments as *The Sale of Goods Act*, R.S.O. 1950, c. 345. That is a matter of the regulation of contracts and not of trade as trade and in that respect the intention of the purchaser is immaterial. However, if the hog be sold to a packing plant or the vegetables or peaches to a cannery, the products of those establishments in the course of trade may be dealt with by the Legislature or by Parliament depending, on the one hand, upon whether all the products are sold or intended for sale within the Province or, on the other, whether some of them are sold or intended for sale beyond Provincial limits. It is, I think, impossible to fix any minimum proportion of such last-mentioned sales or intended sales as determining the jurisdiction of Parliament. This applies to the sale by the original owner. Once a statute aims at "regulation of trade in matters of inter-provincial concern" (*The Citizens Insurance Company of Canada v. Parsons; The Queen Insurance Company v. Parsons*), it is beyond the competence of a Provincial Legislature. The ambit of head 2 of s. 91 of the *British North America Act*, "The Regulation of Trade and Commerce" has been considerably enlarged by decisions of the Judicial Committee and expressions used in some of its earlier judgments must be read in the light of its later pronouncements, as is pointed out by Sir Lyman Duff in *Re Alberta Statutes*. In fact, his judgment in *Re The Natural Products Marketing Act, 1934*, which is justly considered as the *locus classicus*, must be read in conjunction with and subject to his remarks in the later case. The concept of trade and commerce, the regulation of which is confided to Parliament, is entirely separate and distinct from the regulation of mere sale and purchase agreements. Once an article enters into the flow of interprovincial or external trade, the subject-matter and all its attendant circumstances cease to be a mere matter of local concern. No change has taken place in the theory underlying the construction of the *British North America Act* that what is not within the legislative jurisdiction of Parliament must be within that of the Provincial Legislatures. This, of course, still leaves the question as to how far either may proceed, and, as Lord Atkin pointed out in the *Natural Products Marketing Act* case, supra, at p. 389, neither party may leave its own sphere and encroach upon that of another. [...]

In view of the wording of question 1, I take clause (*l*) of subs. (1) of s. 3 of *The Farm Products Marketing Act* as being a successful endeavour on the part of the Ontario Legislature to fulfil its part while still keeping within the ambit of its powers. On the assumption directed to be made and reading the clause so as not to apply to transactions which I have indicated would be of a class beyond the powers of the Legislature, my answer to the first question is "No". [...]

RAND J. (concurring in the result): — This reference raises questions going to the scope of Provincial authority over trade. They arise out of *The Farm Products Marketing Act*, R.S.O. 1950, c. 131, as amended, which deals comprehensively with the matter connoted by its name and out of certain schemes formed under it. Its object is to accord primary producers of farm products the advantages of various degrees of controlled marketing, for which it provides provincial and local machinery. [...]

Although not specifically mentioned in s. 92 of the *British North America Act*, there is admittedly a field of trade within provincial power, and the head or heads of s. 92 from which it is to be deduced will be considered later. The power is a subtraction from the scope of the language conferring on the Dominion by head 2 of s. 91 exclusive authority to make laws in relation to the regulation of trade and commerce, and was derived under an interpretation of the Act which was found necessary:

> in order to preserve from serious curtailment, if not from virtual extinction, the degree of autonomy which, as appears from the scheme of the Act as a whole, the provinces were intended to possess

(*per* Duff J. in *Lawson v. Interior Tree, Fruit and Vegetable Committee of Direction*). In examining the legislation for the purpose mentioned we should bear in mind Lord Atkin's admonition in *Attorney-General for British Columbia v. Attorney-General for Canada et al.* that:

the legislation will have to be carefully framed, and will not be achieved by either party leaving its own sphere and encroaching upon that of the other.

The definitive statement of the scope of Dominion and Provincial jurisdiction was made by Duff C.J. in *Re The Natural Products Marketing Act, 1934*. The regulation of particular trades confined to the Province lies exclusively with the Legislature subject, it may be, to Dominion general regulation affecting all trade, and to such incidental intrusion by the Dominion as may be necessary to prevent the defeat of Dominion regulation; interprovincial and foreign trade are correspondingly the exclusive concern of Parliament. That statement is to be read with the judgment of this Court in *The King v. Eastern Terminal Elevator Company*, approved by the Judicial Committee in *Attorney-General for British Columbia v. Attorney-General for Canada*, supra, at p. 387 to the effect that Dominion regulation cannot embrace local trade merely because in undifferentiated subject-matter the external interest is dominant. But neither the original statement nor its approval furnishes a clear guide to the demarcation of the two classes when we approach as here the origination, the first stage of trade, including certain aspects of manufacture and production.

That demarcation must observe this rule, that if in a trade activity, including manufacture or production, there is involved a matter of extraprovincial interest or concern its regulation thereafter in the aspect of trade is by that fact put beyond Provincial power. This is exemplified in *Lawson v. Interior Tree Fruit and Vegetable Committee of Direction*, supra, where the Province purported to regulate the time and quantity of shipment, the shippers, the price and the transportation of fruit and vegetables in both unsegregated and segregated local and interprovincial trade movements.

A producer is entitled to dispose of his products beyond the Province without reference to a provincial marketing agency or price, shipping or other trade regulation; and an outside purchaser is entitled with equal freedom to purchase and export. Processing is one of a number of trade services that may be given products in the course of reaching the consumer: milling (as of grain or lumber), sorting, packing, slaughtering, dressing, storing, transporting, etc. The producer or purchaser may desire to process the product either within or beyond the Province and if he engages for that with a local undertaking (using that expression in a non-technical sense), such as a packing plant – and it would apply to any sort of servicing – he takes that service as he finds it but free from such Provincial impositions as are strictly trade regulations such as prices or the specification of standards, which could no more be imposed than Provincial trade marks. Regulation of that nature could directly nullify external trade vital to the economy of the country. Trade arrangements reaching the dimensions of world agreements are now a commonplace; interprovincial trade, in which the Dominion is a single market, is of similar importance, and equally vital to the economic functioning of the country as a whole. The Dominion power implies responsibility for promoting and maintaining the vigour and growth of trade beyond Provincial confines, and the discharge of this duty must remain unembarrassed by local trade impediments. If the processing is restricted to external trade, it becomes an instrumentality of that trade and its single control as to prices, movements, standards, etc., by the Dominion follows: *Re The Industrial Relations and Disputes Investigation Act.* The licensing of processing plants by the Province as a trade regulation is thus limited to their operations in local trade. Likewise the licensing of shippers, whether producers or purchasers and the fixing of the terms and conditions of shipment, including prices, as trade regulation, where the goods are destined beyond the Province, would be beyond Provincial power.

Local trade has in some cases been classed as a matter of property and civil rights and related to head 13 of s. 92, and the propriety of that allocation was questioned. The production and exchange of goods as an economic activity does not take place by virtue of positive law or civil right; it is assumed as part of the residual free activity of men upon or around which law is imposed. It has an identity of its own recognized by head 2 of s. 91. I cannot agree that its regulation under that head was intended as a species of matter under head 13 from which by the language of s. 91 it has been withdrawn. It happened that in *The Citizens Insurance Company of Canada v. Parsons, The Queen Insurance Company v. Parsons,* assuming insurance to be a trade, the commodity being dealt in was the making of contracts, and their relation to head 13 seemed obvious. But the true conception of trade (in contradistinction to the static nature of rights, civil or property) is that of a dynamic, the creation and flow of goods from production to consumption or utilization, as an individualized activity. [...]

Head 16 contains what may be called the residuary power of the Province: *Attorney-General for Ontario v. Attorney-General for the Dominion et al.,* and it is within that residue that the autonomy of the Province in local matters, so far as it might be affected by trade regulation, is to be preserved. As was recognized in the *Parsons* case, supra, this points up the underlying division of the matters of legislation into those which are primarily of national and those of local import. But this is not intended to derogate from regulation as well as taxation of local trade through licence under head 9 of s. 92, nor from its support under head 13.

It is important to keep in mind, as already observed, that the broad language of head 2 of s. 91 has been curtailed not by any express language of the statute but as a necessary implication of the fundamental division of powers effected by it. The interpretation of this head has undergone a transformation. When it was first considered by this Court in *Severn v. The Queen* and *The City of Fredericton v. The Queen,* the majority views did not envisage the limitation now established; that was introduced by the judgment in the *Parsons* case, supra. The nadir of its scope was reached in what seemed its restriction to a function ancillary to other Dominion powers; but that view has been irretrievably scotched. [...]

The reaches of trade may extend to aspects of manufacture. In *Attorney-General for Ontario v. Attorney-General for the Dominion et al.,* [*Local Prohibitions*] supra, the Judicial Committee dealt with the question whether the Province could prohibit the manufacture within the Province of intoxicating liquor, to which the answer was given that, in the absence of conflicting legislation of Parliament, there would be jurisdiction to that effect if it were shown that the manufacture was carried on under such circumstances and conditions as to make its prohibition a merely local matter in the Province. This involves a limitation of a power of the Province to interdict, as a trade matter, the manufacture or production of articles destined for external trade. Admittedly, however, local regulation may affect that trade: wages, workmen's compensation, insurance, taxes and other items that furnish what may be called the local conditions underlying economic activity leading to trade.

The federal character of our Constitution places limits on legislative acts in relation to matters which as an entirety span, so to speak, the boundary between the two jurisdictions. In *The King v. Eastern Terminal Elevator Company*, supra, for example, there was a common storage of grain destined both to local and external trade. The situation in *City of Montreal v. Montreal Street Railway* was equally striking: there Parliament was held incapable of imposing through rates over a local railway on traffic passing between points on that line and points on a connecting Dominion railway; the only regulation open was declared to be parallel action by Legislature and Parliament, each operating only on its own instrumentality. Although by that means the substantial equivalent of a single administration may be attained, there is a constitutional difference between that co-operating action and action by an overriding jurisdiction.

It follows that trade regulation by a Province or the Dominion, acting alone, related to local or external trade respectively, before the segregation of products or manufactures of each class is reached, is impracticable, with the only effective means open, apart from conditional regulation, being that of co-operative action; this, as in some situations already in effect, may take the form of a single board to administer regulations of both on agreed measures. [...]

[Rand J. concluded that the Act, with respect to intraprovincial transactions at issue, was not ultra vires.]

LOCKE J. (concurring in the result): − [...] The first question is directed to clause (*l*) of subs. (1) of s. 3 of the Act. This authorizes the Board to:

> authorize any marketing agency appointed under a scheme to conduct a pool or pools for the distribution of all moneys received from the sale of the regulated product and requiring any such marketing agency, after deducting all necessary and proper disbursements and expenses, to distribute the proceeds of sale in such manner that each person receives a share of the total proceeds in relation to the amount, variety, size, grade and class of the regulated product delivered by him and to make an initial payment on delivery of the product and subsequent payments until the total net proceeds are distributed.

Construing the reference to intraprovincial transactions in the question and the words "control and regulation in any or all respects of the marketing within the Province of farm products including the prohibition of such marketing in whole or in part" in the 1956 amendment, as referring to purchases and sales of the controlled product, whether hogs, fruit or vegetables in their natural form, for consumption in the Province, and sales to processors, manufacturers or dealers proposing to sell such products, either in their natural form or after they have been processed by canning, preserving or otherwise treating them, for consumption within the Province, I consider the clause to be within the powers of the Province.

Such transactions are, in my opinion, matters of a merely local or private nature in the Province within head 16 of s. 92, and such regulation is in relation to property and civil rights in the Province within head 13. [...]

In answering this question I exclude sales of produce where the producer himself ships his product to other Provinces or countries for sale by any means of transport, or sells his product to a person who purchases the same for export. To illustrate, I exclude a shipment by a hog producer of his hogs, alive or dead, to the Province of Quebec and transactions between such producer and a buyer for a packing plant carrying on business in Hull who purchases the hog intending to ship it to Hull, either alive or dead, and transactions between a hog producer and a packing plant operating in Ontario purchasing the hog for the purpose of producing pork products from it and exporting them from the Province to the extent that the carcass is so used.

The passage from the judgment in *Lawson's* case which is above quoted makes it clear that to attempt to control the manner in which traders in other Provinces will carry out their transactions within the Province, or to prohibit them from purchasing natural products for export, is not a matter of merely Provincial concern but also directly and substantially the concern of the other Provinces. I cannot think that from a constitutional standpoint the fact that the buyer for the packing house elects to have the hog killed before it is exported or cut up and, after treatment, exported as hams, bacon or other pork products, can affect the matter.

[...]

[Locke J. held that the Act was *intra vires*.]

FAUTEUX J. (dissenting): — [...] Certain general principles, related to the validity of marketing legislation, may expediently be stated before entering into the individual consideration of each of the questions.

The regulation of the marketing of farm products within the Province exclusively is within the legislative competence of the Provincial Legislature and not of Parliament. In *Attorney-General of British Columbia v. Attorney-General of Canada et al.*, the *Natural Products Marketing Act, 1934*, enacted by Parliament, was held to be *ultra vires* substantially for the reason that it covered transactions completed within the Province and having no connection with interprovincial or export trade. Later, in *Shannon et al. v. Lower Mainland Dairy Products Board*, the *Natural Products Marketing (British Columbia) Act*, 1936, providing for the regulation of marketing within the Province, was held *intra vires*. Such valid regulatory scheme may be carried out and enforced through the means of a licence scheme provided for by a Provincial Legislature for, as stated by Lord Atkin in the *Shannon* case, supra, at p. 721:

> If regulation of trade within the Province has to be held valid,
> the ordinary method of regulating trade, *i.e.*, by a system of
> licences, must also be admissible. [...]

The main submission is that the scheme is applicable to the sale of hogs generally, for import and export as well, and as such regulates trade within the meaning of head 2 of s. 91 of the *British North America Act* and therefore to ultra vires. [...]

With respect to importation: It is clear from the [statutory] provisions that hogs produced elsewhere than in Ontario are not covered by the scheme. It is equally clear from [the statutory] scheme, which for the whole purpose thereof provides for the grouping of hog producers by districts within the Province, that producers beyond its boundaries are not affected either. In the result, anyone in Ontario is free to import therein and anyone beyond its boundaries to export thereto the regulated product.

With respect to exportation: Were the words "within the Province", expressed or held to be implied after each of the words "marketed" and "processing" appearing in the opening provision of [the *Act*], the submission that an Ontario producer is barred from marketing the regulated product elsewhere than in the Province would fail; and in my view it must be so held. [...]

Having reached the view that the transaction covered by the scheme is intraprovincial, I do not find it necessary or expedient to define in general terms what constitutes an intraprovincial transaction. The suggestion that to be intraprovincial a transaction must be completed within the Province, in the sense that the product, object of the transaction, must be ultimately and exclusively consumed or be sold for delivery therein for such consumption, is one which would, if carried to its logical conclusion, strip from a Province its recognized power to provide for the regulation of marketing within such Province in disregard of the decisions of the Judicial Committee in *Attorney-General for British Columbia v. Attorney-General for Canada et al.*, supra, and in *Shannon v. Lower Mainland Dairy Products Board*, supra. [...]

[Fauteux J. held that the Act was *ultra vires*.]

ABBOTT J.: — [...] [T]he principal attack made on the validity of these schemes was that they purport to regulate extraprovincial trade.

It is hard to conceive of any important article of commerce, produced in any Province, which would not, to some extent at least, enter into interprovincial or export trade. Certainly milk, which was the product regulated in *Shannon's* case, in its processed form at any rate, must be exported from British Columbia. Similarly it is common knowledge that potatoes in substantial quantities are shipped out of Prince Edward Island.

The power to regulate the sale within a Province of specific products, is not, in my opinion, affected by reason of the fact that some, or all, of such products may subsequently, in the same or in an altered form, be exported from that Province, unless it be shown, of course, that such regulation is merely a colourable device for assuming control of extraprovincial trade. Similarly, the power to regulate the wages of those engaged in processing such products within a Province, is not affected by the fact that the resulting product may be exported, although it is obvious that the scale of such wages would have a significant effect upon the export price. It is the immediate effect, object or purpose, not possible consequential effects, that are relevant, in determining whether *The Farm Products Marketing Act* of Ontario and the three schemes adopted under it, which are the subject of the present reference, are laws in relation to a matter falling within Provincial legislative competence. As Viscount Simon said in *Attorney-General for Saskatchewan v. Attorney-General for Canada et al.*:

> Consequential effects are not the same thing as legislative subject-matter. It is "the true nature and character of the legislation" – not its ultimate economic results – that matters.

What is regulated under these schemes is not the farm product itself but certain transactions involving that product, and the transaction which is regulated is completed before the product is consumed either in its original or in some processed form. Processing may take many forms and the original product may be changed out of all recognition. The place where the resulting product may be consumed, therefore, is not in my opinion conclusive, as a test to determine by what legislative authority a particular transaction involving such farm product may validly be regulated.

As I have stated, the fact that some, or all, of the resulting product, after processing, may subsequently enter into extraprovincial or export trade does not, in my view, alter the fact that the three schemes submitted in this reference, regulate particular businesses carried on entirely within Provincial legislative jurisdiction, and are therefore *intra vires*.

[Mr. Justice Taschereau agreed with Fauteux and Abbott JJ. The dissenting opinion of Cartwright J. is omitted, as is the opinion of Nolan J., who concurred with Locke J.]

REFERENCE RE AGRICULTURAL PRODUCTS MARKETING ACT
[1978] 2 S.C.R. 1198.

[At issue in this litigation was the validity of the *Agricultural Products Marketing Act*, R.S.C. 1970, c. A-7. The Act established a comprehensive supply-managed marketing scheme which placed quotas on production in intra-provincial, inter-provincial and international trade in eggs. Although the Court upheld the general scheme, s. 2 ran into particular difficulty. Section 2 empowered the Governor-in-Council by order to authorize provincial boards to impose expense and adjustment levies in both intraprovincial (s. 2(2)(*a*)) and interprovincial (s. 2(2)(*b*)) trade.]

PIGEON J. [Martland, Ritchie, Beetz and De Grandpré JJ. concurring]: — [...] Question 1 asks whether ss. 2 and 3 of the *Agricultural Products Marketing Act* (Canada) are *ultra vires*. [...] Section 2(2) provides for levies in respect of products in intraprovincial trade (sub-para. (*a*)) and in extraprovincial trade (sub-para. (*b*)). [...]

I agree with the Chief Justice that sub-para. (*a*) of s. 2(2) of the *Agricultural Products Marketing Act*, is invalid. This sub-paragraph purports to authorize the granting to a provincial board or agency of the authority to impose and to use levies or charges "in relation to the powers granted to such board or agency under the laws of any province with respect to the marketing of any agricultural product locally within the province." As previously stated, I agree that such levies are not taxes when they are not collected for purposes other than defraying expenses or effecting adjustment or redistribution among producers. [...]

I agree with the Chief Justice that the orders mentioned in question 2 come within the scope of the Act.

Question 3 concerns the validity of the *Farm Products Marketing Agencies Act*. I have to disagree with the Chief Justice's observations on s. 23(1)(*a*) in relation to the surplus disposal program of CEMA. It is not immaterial that surpluses are marketable in local trade and I do not agree that a federal agency may lawfully be authorized to purchase in any market and to dispose of its purchases as an ordinary trader. In the *Shannon* case, Lord Atkin said, at p. 719:

> [...] It is now well settled that the enumeration in s. 91 of "the regulation of trade and commerce" as a class of subject over which the Dominion has exclusive legislative powers does not give the power to regulate for legitimate Provincial purposes particular trades or businesses so far as the trade or business is confined to the province. [...]

In my view federal intrusion into local trade is just as unconstitutional when done by buying and selling, as when done through any other method. Viscount Simon's and Lord Halsbury's observations are just as applicable to federal as to provincial powers. Of course, this does not preclude operations by federal agencies acting for proper federal purposes. It does not appear to me that my disagreement on this point in any way affects the conclusion on the question namely that the Act is not invalid. [...]

Questions 8 and 9 concern the validity of the egg producers quota regulations. In my view, the control of production, whether agricultural or industrial, is *prima facie* a local matter, a matter of provincial jurisdiction. Egg farms, if I may use this expression to designate the kind of factories in which feed is converted into eggs and fowl, are local undertakings subject to provincial jurisdiction under section 92(10) *B.N.A. Act*, unless they are considered as within the scope of "agriculture" in which case, by virtue of s. 95, the jurisdiction is provincial subject to the overriding authority of Parliament. In my view the *Carnation* case is conclusive in favour of provincial jurisdiction over undertakings where primary agricultural products are transformed into other food products. In that case, the major portion of the production was shipped outside the province ([1968] S.C.R. 238, at p. 242). In view of the reasons given, the conclusion could not be different even if the whole production had been going into extraprovincial trade.

In *The King v. Eastern Terminal Elevator Co.*, it was decided that, for constitutional jurisdiction purposes, trade in grain was to be considered as distinct from production. Mignault J. said (at p. 457): "I have not overlooked the appellant's contention that the statute can be supported under s. 95 of the *British North America Act* as being legislation concerning agriculture. It suffices to answer that the subject matter of the Act is not agriculture but a product of agriculture considered as an article of trade". Duff J. as he then was, said with respect to legislative authority over a trade: "that is not a principle the application of which can be ruled by percentages". It was therefore decided that Parliament could not assume legislative authority over grain elevators by setting up a licensing system. It was, however, pointed out that Parliament could subject grain elevators to its authority by a declaration under s. 92(10)(*c*). Parliament acted on the suggestion and thereby acquired complete control of the grain trade as is related in *Jorgenson v. Attorney General of Canada*. In the absence of a similar declaration applicable to a quarry supplying rock for ballast on an interprovincial railway, this quarry was held not to form part of the railway (*C.N.R. v. Nor-Min Supplies*). The Chief Justice said (at p. 333):

> [...] The mere economic tie-up between the C.N.R.'s quarry and the use of the crushed rock for railway line ballast does not make the quarry a part of the transportation enterprise in the same sense as railway sheds or switching stations are part of that enterprise. The exclusive devotion of the output of the quarry to railway uses feeds the convenience of the C.N.R., as would any other economic relationship for supply of fuel or materials or rolling stock, but this does not make the fuel refineries or depots or the factories which produce the materials or the rolling stock parts of the transportation system.

"I suppose there will be those who will try to raise a stink about it."

In my view a similar reasoning must be made with respect to egg farms. No operator can claim exemption from provincial control by electing to devote his entire output to extraprovincial trade. I can find no basis for the view that there must be a division of authority at the stage of production between what will be going into intraprovincial and what will be going into extraprovincial trade. As I read it, the *Eastern Terminal Elevator* case stands squarely against such a contention. Eggs are a commodity like grain and they are treated in trade as fungible things. As a rule the person who is obliged to deliver grain of a given grade is not obliged to deliver any identified grain. (See *Canada Grain Act*, R.S.C. 1970, c. G-16, ss. 111, 115.) He satisfies his obligation by delivering the required quantity of proper grade. One of the purposes of the grading is precisely that goods of the same grade may be considered interchangeable. This holds true for eggs as for grain. The consequence is that any workable control scheme has to be effective with respect to all eggs irrespective of intended disposition. In *Reference Re The Farm Products Marketing Act of Ontario*, Rand J. said at p. 214:

> [...] trade regulation by a Province or the Dominion, acting alone, related to local or external trade respectively, before the segregation of products or manufactures of each class is reached, is impracticable, with the only effective means open, apart from conditional regulation, being that of co-operative action

> [...]

We are not called upon to decide in the present case whether the federal Parliament could assume control over egg farms devoted exclusively to the production of eggs for extraprovincial trade. Under the present circumstances such farms are, like any other farms, local undertakings subject to provincial authority, irrespective of the destination of their output. I can see no reason why such legislative authority would not extend to the control of production as to quantity just as it extend undoubtedly to the price to be paid for raw materials.

This does not mean that such power is unlimited, a province cannot control extraprovincial trade, as was held in the *Manitoba Egg Reference* and in the *Burns Foods* case. However, "Marketing" does not include production and, therefore, provincial control of production is *prima facie* valid. In the instant case, the provincial regulation is not aimed at controlling the extraprovincial trade. In so far as it affects this trade, it is only complementary to the regulations established under federal authority. In my view this is perfectly legitimate, otherwise it would mean that our Constitution makes it impossible by federal-provincial cooperative action to arrive at any practical scheme for the orderly and efficient production and marketing of a commodity which all governments concerned agree requires regulation in both intraprovincial and extraprovincial trade. As early as 1912, it was asserted by the Privy Council that "whatever belongs to self-government in Canada belongs either to the Dominion or to the provinces". (*References* case, at p. 583). I do not overlook the admonition in the *Natural Products Marketing Act* case, at p. 389, that the legislation has to be carefully framed but, when after 40 years a sincere cooperative effort has been accomplished, it would really be unfortunate if this was all brought to nought.

While I adhere to the view that provinces may not make use of their control over local undertakings to affect extraprovincial marketing, this does not, in my view, prevent the use of provincial control to complement federal regulation of extraprovincial trade.

In so far as the producer quotas are to be viewed as marketing quotas rather than as production quotas, it seems to me that their validity is established by the principle of the *Willis* case. Those quotas are fixed by the provincial board so the total will equal what the plan, established under the federal Act, provides for Ontario in respect of extraprovincial trade in addition to what comes under intraprovincial trade. The Board is properly empowered by provincial authority to regulate the intraprovincial trade and it has delegated authority from the federal in respect of the extraprovincial trade. I fail to see what objection there can be to overall quotas established by a board thus vested with dual authority, unless it is said that our Constitution precludes any businesslike marketing of products in both local and extraprovincial trade except under a federal assumption of power, something which I think, is directly contrary to the basic principle of the *B.N.A. Act*.

In the result I would answer questions 8 and 9 in the negative, as the Court of Appeal unanimously did. [...]

[The judgment of Laskin C.J.C. (Judson, Spence, and Dickson JJ. concurring) is omitted.]

FÉDÉRATION DES PRODUCTEURS DE VOLAILLES DU QUÉBEC v. PELLAND
[2005] 1 S.C.R. 292.

The judgment of the court was delivered by

¶ 1 **ABELLA J.**:— [...]

¶ 2 In a landmark 1978 case which has come to be known as the "*Egg Reference*" (*Reference re Agricultural Products Marketing Act*, [1978] 2 S.C.R. 1198), this Court unanimously affirmed the constitutional validity of a national agricultural marketing scheme collaboratively crafted by Parliament and the provinces in response to the Court's evolving jurisprudence. The *Egg Reference* has since become the blueprint for federal-provincial marketing schemes.

¶ 3 After the release of the *Egg Reference*, the federal and provincial governments entered into the 1978 *Federal-Provincial Agreement with respect to the establishment of a Comprehensive Chicken Marketing Program in Canada* ("Federal-Provincial Agreement").

¶ 4 To ensure effective marketing and a dependable supply of chicken to Canadian consumers, the Federal-Provincial Agreement was designed to weave together the legislative jurisdiction of both levels of government in order to ensure a seamless regulatory scheme. The integration of the federal and provincial components of the scheme is achieved through s. 22(3) of the *Farm Products Agencies Act*, R.S.C. 1985, c. F-4. ..Section 22(3) enables a federal marketing agency to authorize a provincial body to perform any function relating to interprovincial or export trade in the regulated product that the federal agency is authorized to perform. Pursuant to the *Canadian Chicken Marketing Agency Quota Grant of Administrative Authority* ("Grant of Authority"), P.C. 1991-1090, June 13, 1991, the federal marketing agency delegated its authority to Quebec's chicken marketing board, the Fédération des producteurs de volailles du Québec ("Fédération"). The Grant of Authority authorized the provincial body to allocate and administer federal quotas in accordance with both the federal *Canadian Chicken Marketing Quota Regulations*, 1990, SOR/90-556, and such relevant rules as were in force from time to time in the province.

¶ 5 Implementing its part of the terms of the Federal-Provincial Agreement, and pursuant to what is now s. 16(1) of the *Farm Products Agencies Act*, the federal government created a federal chicken marketing agency, then known as the Canadian Chicken Marketing Agency and now called the Chicken Farmers of Canada ("CFC"). It was expressly empowered by s. 22(1) of the *Farm Products Agencies Act* to implement a marketing plan and make such orders and regulations, subject to the approval of the Governor in Council, as were necessary for the execution of the plan.

¶ 6 The provincial component of the scheme in Quebec is the subject of the constitutional challenge before us ... The Plan is administered by the Fédération and governs all production and marketing of chicken within the province of Quebec.

¶ 7 The function of the federal body is to assess the national market and set a global production quota for each province. It assigns a marketing quota to each province representing that province's share of the national market.

¶ 8 Each provincial body then adopts as its intraprovincial production quota the exact share federally assigned to it. It agrees to authorize its local producers to globally produce and market no more chicken than the quantity fixed by the federal body as that province's share of the national marketing target. To produce and market chickens in Quebec, a farmer must receive a quota allocation from the Fédération and produce no more than his or her allocated quota for a given period. A producer in a province receives a single quota applicable to all of his or her production and marketing of chicken, regardless of intended destination.

¶ 9 In order to facilitate the integration of production and marketing quotas, the federal body delegates its authority to regulate the marketing of chickens in interprovincial and export trade to the provincial body, in this case the Fédération. Once producers obtain a production and marketing quota from the Fédération, they are free to decide where their product will be sold. Neither the federal nor the provincial body sets distinct intraprovincial or extraprovincial marketing quotas.

¶ 10 In this way, the federal-provincial scheme combines in one body, the Fédération, provincial jurisdiction over production and intraprovincial marketing, and federal jurisdiction over extraprovincial marketing. The federally and provincially assigned quotas dovetail so that the total quantity of chicken produced in Canada does not exceed the agreed-upon national marketing total.

¶ 11 Because Mr. Pelland produced 4,425,030 kg in excess of his allotted quota for the relevant periods, the Fédération, in accordance with the penalty provisions found in the provincial regulations, automatically reduced his quota to zero and imposed a monetary penalty in the amount of $2,433,766.50. In addition, it sought an interlocutory injunction...

¶ 15 In my view, the 1978 Federal-Provincial Agreement, like the scheme in the *Egg Reference*, both reflects and reifies Canadian federalism's constitutional creativity and cooperative flexibility. For the reasons that follow, and based largely on a generation of constitutional jurisprudence from this Court, I would dismiss the appeal. ...

The Constitutional Validity of the Provincial Production and Marketing Legislation

¶ 16 Mr. Pelland does not dispute that he grossly exceeded his allocated quota. Rather, he challenges the interlocutory injunction obtained by the Fédération on the grounds that the entirety of his produce is exported to Ontario and not marketed in the province of Quebec. He argues that the provincial marketing Act and regulations can only apply to the production of chickens destined for Quebec markets, not those intended exclusively for interprovincial markets.

¶ 17 Mr. Pelland does not base his argument on the pith and substance of the provincial marketing Act and the provincial chicken regulation; instead, he urges the Court to conclude that placing quota restrictions on products destined for export is not a provincial matter. He does not challenge the validity of the provincial scheme , but argues that it cannot apply to the production of chicken destined solely for interprovincial markets. The scheme he proposes as an alternative would be bifurcated: a federal quota for export production and a provincial one for intraprovincial trade.

¶ 18 Mr. Pelland relies on Laskin C.J.'s statement in the *Egg Reference* that the provincial law and regulations at issue there would not be valid if they occurred "with a view to limiting interprovincial or export trade" (p. 1287). However, this comment was made in the context of considering whether the law and regulations were in pith and substance a provincial matter. Ultimately, as explained later in these reasons, Laskin C.J. found that they were. This comment, therefore, does not support the proposition that provincial laws found valid under a pith and substance analysis are inapplicable to export trade.

¶ 19 Contrary to Mr. Pelland's submissions, in my view the pith and substance of the provincial marketing Act and the provincial chicken regulations are at the heart of this appeal. In order to determine whether the provincial component of the scheme is unconstitutional because it intrudes into a federal head of power, it is necessary first to determine its core character.

¶ 20 The requisite approach was recently discussed by LeBel J. in *Kitkatla Band* ...

> A pith and substance analysis looks at both (1) the purpose of the legislation as well as (2) its effect. First, to determine the purpose of the legislation, the Court may look at both intrinsic evidence, such as purpose clauses, or extrinsic evidence, such as Hansard or the minutes of parliamentary committees.

Second, in looking at the effect of the legislation, the Court may consider both its legal effect and its practical effect [ ]

¶ 21 The essential character of an analogous scheme was scrutinized in the *Egg Reference*. Under the scheme at issue in that case, the Canadian Egg Marketing Agency set overall quotas for each province. It was created as a result of an agreement between the federal Minister of Agriculture, the federal marketing agency, and their counterparts in all provinces. The goal was to establish a comprehensive national egg marketing scheme . The federal Agency was given authority to set overall provincial quotas and to impose levies or charges on the marketing of eggs by egg producers, to be collected on its behalf by the provincial egg marketing boards. In Ontario, the Ontario Farm Products Marketing Board was the provincial board setting individual egg production quotas for its producers based on the province's assigned quota. The Ontario legislation also prohibited egg production by anyone who did not have a quota.

¶ 22 In the *Egg Reference*, this Court confirmed that the regulation of agricultural production is essentially a local matter within provincial jurisdiction pursuant to s. 92(10) of the *Constitution Act, 1867*. The Court reached the following relevant conclusions: although constitutional jurisdiction over marketing is divided, agricultural production is *prima facie* a local matter under provincial jurisdiction; the provincial scheme was not aimed at controlling extraprovincial trade, but was deemed to be coordinated and integrated with the regulations established under federal authority; and, most pertinently, producers could not claim exemption from provincial control over production by electing to devote their entire output to extraprovincial trade.

¶ 23 Any effect of the provincial egg marketing and production scheme on extraprovincial trade was found to be incidental to the constitutionally permissible purpose of controlling agricultural production within the context of a cooperative federal-provincial agreement.

¶ 24 While disagreeing about the exact scope of the relevant provincial head of power, Pigeon J., for the five-person majority, and Laskin C.J., in a minority concurring opinion, agreed that the provincial component of this marketing scheme was constitutional because its purpose did not extend beyond production and trade within the province. They also both accepted that if the true purpose of the provincial legislation had been to regulate interprovincial and export trade, it would have been *ultra vires*.

¶ 25 Pigeon J. held that because agricultural production is *prima facie* within provincial jurisdiction, production quotas could be imposed by a province on all its producers, regardless of the ultimate destination of the goods produced. A producer could not evade a province's jurisdictional authority over production by producing goods destined for an export or extraprovincial market:

> No operator can claim exemption from provincial control by electing to devote his entire output to extraprovincial trade. I can find no basis for the view that there must be a division of authority at the stage of production between what will be going into intraprovincial and what will be going into extraprovincial trade. [Emphasis added; p. 1295.]

¶ 26 This is the conclusion Mr. Pelland seeks to set aside, primarily on the basis of Laskin C.J.'s minority opinion expressing the concern that if the focus of the provincial legislation had been the regulation of extraprovincial interests, it would have been beyond the province's jurisdiction. The possibility that specifically caused Laskin C.J. to articulate a caveat to Pigeon J.'s opinion was that of a province using its regulatory jurisdiction over production [page304] to "choke off" interprovincial trade at its very source:

> It is true that a Province cannot limit the export of goods from the Province, and any provincial marketing legislation must yield to this. How then, it may be asked, can it be allowed to accomplish this forbidden end by choking off interprovincial trade at its very source, at the point of production? [p. 1286]

¶ 27 Based on this analysis, Mr. Pelland submits that this Court ought to reconsider the constitutionality of a marketing scheme like the one he is regulated by, find the provincial component of the scheme to be unconstitutional, and confine the jurisdiction of provincial marketing boards to production for provincial marketing only.

¶ 28 It seems to me that the impugned legislation is constitutionally valid whether the majority or minority opinion in the *Egg Reference* is applied. Pigeon J. did not dispute that provincial legislation which is aimed at regulating extraprovincial trade is *ultra vires*. He held only that agricultural production is *prima facie* a provincial matter:

> In my view, the control of production, whether agricultural or industrial, is *prima facie* a local matter, a matter of provincial jurisdiction. [p. 1293]

He qualified this position, however, by stating:

> This does not mean that such power is unlimited, a province cannot control extraprovincial trade, as was held in the *Manitoba Egg Reference* [[1971] S.C.R. 689] and in the *Burns Foods* case [[1975] 1 S.C.R. 494] . However, "Marketing" does not include production and, therefore, provincial control of production is *prima facie* valid. In the instant case, the provincial regulation is not aimed at controlling the extraprovincial trade. In so far as it affects this trade, it is only complementary to the regulations established under federal authority. In my view this is perfectly legitimate, otherwise it would mean that our Constitution makes it impossible by federal-provincial cooperative action to arrive at any practical scheme for the orderly and efficient production and marketing of a commodity which all governments concerned agree requires [page305] regulation in both intraprovincial and extraprovincial trade. [Emphasis added; p. 1296.]

Laskin C.J. was in substantial agreement with this analysis:

> The primary object is to regulate marketing in intraprovincial trade. *Although it would not be a valid regulation of such marketing to impose quotas on production with a view to limiting interprovincial or export trade,* I am not persuaded that I should give s. 21a, seen in the context of the *Ontario Farm Products Marketing Act* of which it is part, that construction. [Emphasis added; pp. 1286-87.]

¶ 29 With respect, I have difficulty seeing how Laskin C.J.'s reasons in the *Egg Reference* assist Mr. Pelland or yield a fertile basis for reconsidering the constitutionality of the provincial component of the scheme in this case. In a passage of equal applicability to the present case, Laskin C.J. wrote that:

> It is clear that the intention was to mesh federal and provincial regulatory control so as to embrace both the producers who market their production in a particular Province and those who seek to export their production to another Province or beyond Canada. It was certainly open to the federal authorities to fix the respective provincial shares of Canadian egg production for the purpose of regulating the movement of eggs in interprovincial or export trade. The share so fixed for a particular Province would establish a limitation for that Province in respect of its own marketing policies. Hence, the fact that a Province has adopted the same share percentage does not *per se* rule out its connection with intraprovincial trade. The adoption provides no more than a reference point by which to measure the provincial approach to marketing quotas for producers in the Province. I do not think that the use of this reference point amounts to an invasion of federal authority in relation to interprovincial trade. Rather, and the terms of the challenged Regulation so indicate, it is enacted under a recognition of that authority and an appreciation of the control of that trade under federal legislation. In short, <u>it envisages that there will be interprovincial and export marketing by producers in Ontario</u>. [Emphasis added; pp. 1282-83.]

¶ 30 As a substantive matter, neither judgment in the *Egg Reference* deviated from this Court's defining prior analysis in *Carnation Co. v. Quebec Agricultural Marketing Board*, [1968] S.C.R. 238 . In Carnation, Martland J., writing for a unanimous Court, undertook a careful review of this Court's jurisprudence, including *Reference re The Farm Products Marketing Act*, [1957] S.C.R. 198 , and concluded that:

> The view of the four judges in the *Ontario Reference* was that the fact that a transaction took place wholly within a province did not necessarily mean that it was thereby subject solely to provincial control. The regulation of some such transactions relating to products destined for interprovincial trade could constitute a regulation of interprovincial trade and be beyond provincial control.

While I agree with the view of the four judges in the *Ontario Reference* that a trade transaction, completed in a province, is not necessarily, by that fact alone, subject only to provincial control, I also hold the view that the fact that such a transaction incidentally has some effect upon a company engaged in interprovincial trade does not necessarily prevent its being subject to such control.

I agree with the view of Abbott J., in the *Ontario Reference*, that each transaction and each regulation must be examined in relation to its own facts... . They did not purport directly to control or to restrict such trade. There was no evidence that, in fact, they did control or restrict it. The most that can be said of them is that they had some effect upon the cost of doing business in Quebec of a company engaged in interprovincial trade, and that, by itself, is not sufficient to make them invalid. [Emphasis added; pp. 253-54.]

¶ 31 This analysis underlies the concern expressed by Laskin C.J. in the *Egg Reference*, and it arises whenever there is overlapping jurisdiction. Laws enacted under the jurisdiction of one level of government often overflow into or have incidental impact on the jurisdiction of the other governmental level. That is why a reviewing court is required to focus on the core character of the impugned legislation [...]

¶ 32 Turning to an examination of the essence of the provincial component of the 1978 federal-provincial chicken marketing scheme, one observes at the outset that the scheme is functionally identical to Ontario's egg marketing and production legislation considered in the *Egg Reference*. Like that case, the parties agree that the provisions of the *Constitution Act, 1867* engaged by the federal-provincial chicken marketing scheme at issue here are s. 91(2), which confers jurisdiction over trade and commerce to the federal government, and s. 92(10), which gives provincial governments jurisdiction over local works and undertakings.

¶ 33 As previously indicated, once the national quota for chicken production is divided among the provinces, a producer must be allotted an individual production quota in order to produce chicken in the province. Chicken producers within each province receive only one individual marketing and production quota.

¶ 34 The provincial chicken regulation expresses quotas in square meters of barn space, clearly tying quotas to physical production within Quebec. The quota assigned to each producer in a province does not distinguish between what can be marketed within the province and what can be marketed extraprovincially; rather, the decision whether to market internally or externally is up to each producer once he or she obtains the proper licences (*Canadian Chicken Licensing Regulations*, SOR/81-517). Quebec's chicken producers are free to market their products intraprovincially, extraprovincially or in some combination of the two, so long as they do not exceed their individual quotas.

¶ 35 The only requirements imposed on provincial producers wishing to export their product are that they obtain a marketing and production quota from the Fédération and a licence from the federal body. A producer may not engage in the marketing of [page308] chicken in interprovincial or export trade without the appropriate licence. The licensing requirement, however, is not onerous. On receipt of a valid application, the federal body is required to issue a licence. For its part, the producer is required to abide by the applicable laws and to make regular reports detailing its extraprovincial sales. The amount of chicken that a producer may export is not specified on the licence and is, in theory, limited solely by the quota amount assigned by the Fédération.

¶ 36 It is important to stress that in examining the provincial laws at issue in the *Egg Reference*, both Laskin C.J. and Pigeon J. agreed that they were constitutional because they did not purport to, nor did they in fact, directly control or restrict export trade. The same is true of the provincial scheme in this case.

¶ 37 The core character of the provincial legislative component of the federal-provincial chicken marketing scheme is not to set quotas or fix prices for exported goods or to attempt to regulate interprovincial or export trade. As in the *Egg Reference*, its purpose is to establish rules that allow for the organization of the production and marketing of chicken within Quebec and to control chicken production to fulfill provincial commitments under a cooperative federal-provincial agreement. Any impact of this legislation on extraprovincial trade is incidental.

¶ 38 With respect, I see no principled basis for disentangling what has proven to be a successful federal-provincial merger. Because provincial governments lack jurisdiction over extraprovincial trade in agricultural products, Parliament authorized the creation of federal marketing boards and the delegation to provincial marketing boards of regulatory jurisdiction over interprovincial and export trade. Each level of government enacted laws and regulations, based on their respective legislative competencies, to create a unified and coherent regulatory scheme. [page309] The quota system is an attempt to maintain an equilibrium between supply and demand and attenuate the inherent instability of the markets. To achieve this balance, it cannot exempt producers who seek to avoid production control limits by devoting all or any of their production to extraprovincial trade. [...]

¶ 41 In Mr. Pelland's case, however, quotas are not being imposed on production with a view to limiting interprovincial trade, the hypothetical situation left open by Laskin C.J.'s minority judgment in the *Egg Reference*.... [T]he cooperative scheme at issue in this case is designed, like the scheme in the *Egg Reference*, to integrate federal and provincial marketing and production programmes. [...]

¶ 44 Accordingly ... the provincial legislation is constitutional and can operate to limit the production of chickens destined exclusively for the interprovincial market. [...]

[Justice Abella then considered, and rejected, arguments founded on improper administrative delegation and referential incorporation.]

¶ 63 I would dismiss the appeal with costs to Fédération des producteurs de volailles du Québec.

(ii)   Ancillary Federal Competence

R. V. EASTERN TERMINAL ELEVATOR CO.
[1925] S.C.R. 434.

DUFF J. — The *Grain Act* was passed in 1912. The authors of the legislation proceeded upon the view upon which the Dominion Parliament had acted in 1910 in enacting the *Insurance Act*, that, in exercise of the powers given by sec. 91(2), for the regulation of trade and commerce, the Dominion Parliament could, by a system of licences and otherwise, regulate individual trades, both locally and in respect of interprovincial and external trade. The Act provides for a Board, to be known as the Board of Grain Commissioners, to be appointed by the Governor in Council, and this Board is invested with very wide powers. By sec. 20, the Board is empowered, with the consent of the Governor in Council, to make rules and regulations for the government, control and licensing of terminal and other elevators. [...]

In addition to the power of regulation conferred upon the Board, the Act contains elaborate substantive provisions defining the duties of persons engaged in the business of operating elevators, in respect of the cleaning of grain, the grading of it, the storage of it; defines the effect of warehouse receipts, the rights of holders of them.

By secs. 210 *et seq.*, provision is made for licensing persons in the Western Division to carry on the business of selling grain on commission; and persons not so licensed are prohibited from engaging in that occupation. By secs. 218 *et seq.* there is provision for licensing track-buyers, and prohibition against engaging in the occupation of a track-buyer without such a licence. By secs. 219(a) *et seq.* there is a prohibition against carrying on the business of a primary grain dealer without first having obtained a licence to do so from the Board.

The Act is an attempt to regulate, directly and through the instrumentality of Grain Commissioners the occupations mentioned. It is also an attempt to regulate generally elevators as warehouses for grain, and the business of operating them; and it seems, ex facie, to come within the decision of the Judicial Commit- tee, Attorney General for *Canada v. Attorney General for Alberta,* condemning the *Insurance Act* of 1910 as *ultra vires.*

Grain elevators at Pilot Mound, Manitoba, 1900, on the Pembina branch of the C.P.R. South of Winnipeg.

Mr. Symington, in a very able argument, attempted to support the Act on the ground that the trade in grain is largely an external trade (between seventy and eighty per cent, apparently, of the grain produced in the country is exported); and that the provisions of the Act are, on the whole, an attempt to regulate a branch of external trade, the provisions dealing with local matters being, as a rule, subsidiary and reasonably ancillary to the main purpose of the Act.

It is undeniable that one principal object of this Act is to protect the external trade in grain, and especially in wheat, by ensuring the integrity of certificates issued by the Grain Commission in respect of the quality of grain, and especially of wheat; and the beneficent effect and the value of the system provided by the legislation as a whole is not at all disputed by anybody. I do not think it is fairly disputable, either, that the Dominion possesses legislative powers, in respect of transport (by its authority over Dominion railways, over lines of ships connecting this country with foreign countries, over navigation and shipping); in respect of weight and measures; in respect of trade and commerce, interpreted as that phrase has been interpreted; which would enable it effectively, by properly framed legislation, to regulate this branch of external trade for the purpose of protecting it, by ensuring correctness in grading and freedom from adulteration, as well as providing for effective and reliable public guarantees as to quality. It does not follow that it is within the power of Parliament to accomplish this object by assuming, as this legislation does, the regulation in the provinces of particular occupations, as such, by a licensing system and otherwise, and of local works and undertakings, as such, however important and beneficial the ultimate purpose of the legislation may be. There are, no doubt, many provisions of this statute which, as they stand, can be sustained; with them we are not concerned at this moment. The particular provision which is sought to be enforced is one of a series of provisions which are designed to regulate elevators and the occupations of those who make it their business to operate elevators. The particular provision, if it stood alone, might, perhaps, be sustained as a tax, but it cannot be separated from its context; it is only one part of a scheme for the regulation of elevators. There is one way in which the Dominion may acquire authority to regulate a local work such as an elevator; and that is, by a declaration properly framed under section 92(10) of the *B.N.A. Act*. See *Union Colliery Co. of B.C. v. Bryden*. This, of course, is not to say that there may not be elevators subject to Dominion control, as being, for example, adjuncts of the undertaking of a Dominion railway or of a company operating a line of steamships under Dominion jurisdiction; but the general regulation of all elevators is a different matter.

There are two lurking fallacies in the argument advanced on behalf of the Crown; first, that, because in large part the grain trade is an export trade, you can regulate it locally in order to give effect to your policy in relation to the regulation of that part of it which is export. Obviously that is not a principle the application of which can be ruled by percentages. If it is operative when the export trade is seventy per cent of the whole, it must be equally operative when that percentage is only thirty; and such a principle in truth must postulate authority in the Dominion to assume the regulation of almost any trade in the country, provided it does so by setting up a scheme embracing the local, as well as the external and interprovincial trade; and regulation of trade, according to the conception of it which governs this legislation, includes the regulation in the provinces of the occupations of those engaged in the trade, and of the local establishments in which it is carried on. Precisely the same thing was attempted in the *Insurance Act* of 1910, unsuccessfully. The other fallacy is (the two are, perhaps, different forms of the same error) that the Dominion has such power because no single province, nor, indeed, all the provinces acting together, could put into effect such a sweeping scheme. The authority arises, it is said, under the residuary clause because of the necessary limits of the provincial authority. This is precisely the view which was advanced in the *Board of Commerce Case* and, indeed, is the view which was unsuccessfully put forward in the *Montreal Street Railway Case*, where it was pointed out that in a system involving a division of powers such as that set up by the *British North America Act*, it may often be that subsidiary legislation by the provinces or by the Dominion is required to give full effect to some beneficial and necessary scheme of legislation not entirely within the powers of either.

In one respect there is a close analogy between this case and the *Montreal Street Railway Case*. The expedient which their Lordships there pointed out as the appropriate one in order to enable the Dominion to acquire the authority it was seeking to exercise, is precisely that by which the Dominion could invest itself with the authority over such elevators as it might be considered necessary to regulate; that is to say, by resorting, as already suggested, to the power conferred by section 92(10) to assume, through the procedure there laid down, jurisdiction in respect of "local works".

Fortunately, however, to repeat what has been said above, the control possessed by the Dominion over the subject matters mentioned, and especially over transport (both land transport and water transport) and over external trade, would really appear to be amply sufficient to enable the Dominion, by appropriately framed legislation, effectively to secure the essential objects of this statute.

[The appeal was dismissed. The concurring opinions of Rinfret, Idington and Mignault JJ. and the dissenting opinion of Anglin C.J. have been omitted.]

REFERENCE RE NATURAL PRODUCTS MARKETING ACT, 1934
[1936] S.C.R. 398 AFF'D (SUB NOM. A.-G. B.C. v. A.-G. CAN.;) [1937] A.C. 377 (P.C.).

DUFF C.J. [for the Court]: — [...] By section 3 [of the statute], the Governor General is empowered to:

> establish a Board to be known as the Dominion Marketing Board to regulate the marketing of natural products as hereinafter provided.

By section 4(1) the Board is invested with power:

> a) to regulate the time and place at which, and to designate the agency through which the regulated product shall be marketed, to determine the manner of distribution, the quantity and quality, grade or class of the regulated product that shall be marketed by any person at any time, and to prohibit the marketing of any of the regulated product of any grade, quality or class;

"Marketed" is used in an extended sense as embracing "buying and selling, shipping for sale or storage and offering for sale."

The Board is also empowered:

> (c) to conduct a pool for the equalization of returns received from the sale of the regulated product; [...]

For the purposes of the discussion, it will not be necessary further to particularize the enactments of the statute. These enactments, in our opinion, are not enactments within the contemplation of the second head of section 91. "The regulation of trade and commerce" in the sense which has been ascribed to those words by decisions which are binding upon us and which it is our duty to follow. [...]

The judgment of the Board in *Parsons* case contains the well known elucidation of the words "regulation of trade and commerce" which received the express approval of the Judicial Committee in *Wharton's* case. [...]

The actual decision, it will be observed was that the authority to legislate for the regulation of trade and commerce does not contemplate the power to regulate by legislation the contracts of a particular business or trade in a single province. But the judgment suggests, although it does not decide, that this power of regulation does not extend to the unlimited regulation of particular trades and occupations. On the other hand, there is nothing in the judgment to indicate that the regulation of external trade is excluded from the scope of the authority, nor is there anything to suggest, whatever the precise scope of the power may be, that, when Parliament is legislating with reference to matters strictly within the regulation of trade and commerce, it is disabled from legislating in regard to matters otherwise exclusively within the provincial authority if such legislation is necessarily incidental to the exercise of its exclusive powers in relation to that subject. [...]

[The Justice discussed the *Montreal Street Railway* case and *A.-G. B.C. v. A.-G. Can.*, [1924] A.C. 222.]

It would appear to result from these decisions that the regulation of trade and commerce does not comprise, in the sense in which it is used in section 91, the regulation of particular trades or occupations or of a particular kind of business such as the insurance business in the provinces, or the regulation of trade in particular commodities or classes of commodities in so far as it is local in the provincial sense; while, on the other hand, it does embrace the regulation of external trade and the regulation of inter-provincial trade and such ancillary legislation as may be necessarily incidental to the exercise of such powers. [...]

Obviously, these propositions do not furnish a complete definition of the authority given by the second subdivision of section 91. Logically, they leave scope for a possible jurisdiction in relation to "general trade and commerce" or in relation to "general regulations of trade applicable to the whole Dominion" – phrases employed in the judgment in *Parsons* case. Broadly speaking, they have their basis in the consideration mentioned in *Parsons* case arising from the specification of particular subjects in section 91 and from the necessity to limit the natural scope of the words,

> in order to preserve from serious curtailment, if not from virtual extinction, the degree of autonomy, which as appears from the scheme of the Act as a whole, the provinces were intended to enjoy. (*Lawson's* case).

Restrictions upon the natural meaning of the words, in so far as they are dictated by force of such considerations, may properly be accepted as the necessary result of the application of settled principles of construction pursuant to which, from the beginning, it has been recognized that, in considering sections 91 and 92, the language of each must be read in light of the other and in some cases even modified for the purpose of giving effect to the two sections.

The necessity for some such restriction seems to be demonstrable by reference to the concluding clause of s. 91 which is in these words:

> Any matter coming within any of the classes of subjects enumerated in this section shall not be deemed to come within the class of matters of a local or private nature comprised in the enumeration of the classes of subjects by this Act assigned exclusively to the legislatures of the provinces. [...]

The decision in *Hodge v. The Queen* that it is competent to a province to regulate by a local licensing system the trade in liquor seems incompatible with the contention that such local regulation of the trade in particular commodities is strictly within any of the classes of matters comprehended under the general words "The regulation of trade and commerce"; and this was the view taken by the Board in the case of *A.G. for Alberta v. A.G. for Canada*. Such was also, it would appear, the necessary effect of the judgment of the Board on the Reference in 1885 in relation to the *Dominion Licensing Acts* which has already been mentioned.

It does not seem to admit of serious dispute that, if, regards natural products, as defined by the Act, the provinces are destitute of the powers to regulate the dealing with natural products in respect of the matters designated in section 4(1)a the powers of the provinces are much more limited than they have generally been supposed to be. If this defect of power exists in relation to natural products it exists in relation to anything that may be the subject of trade. Furthermore, if the Dominion has power to enact section 4(1)f, as a provision falling strictly within "the regulation of trade and commerce," then the provinces are destitute of the power to regulate, by licensing persons engaged in the production, the buying and selling, the shipping for sale or storage and the offering for sale, in an exclusively local and provincial way of business of any commodity or commodities. The acceptance of this view of the powers of the provinces would seem to be inconsistent, not only with *Hodge v. The Queen*, but with the judgment in the *Montreal Street Railway* case as well as with the judgment in the *Board of Commerce* case. The judgment in this latter case seems very plainly to declare that in the absence of very special circumstances such as those indicated in the judgment of the Board, such matters as subjects of legislation fall within the jurisdiction of the provinces under section 92.

The enactments in question, therefore, in so far as they relate to matters which are in substance local and provincial are beyond the jurisdiction of Parliament. Parliament cannot acquire jurisdiction to deal in the sweeping way in which these enactments operate with such local and provincial matters by legislating at the same time respecting external and interprovincial trade and committing the regulation of external and interprovincial trade and the regulation of trade which is exclusively local and of traders and producers engaged in trade which is exclusively local to the same authority (*King v. Eastern Terminal Elevators*).

It should also be observed that these enactments operate by way of the regulation of dealings in particular commodities and classes of commodities. The regulations contemplated are not general regulations of trade as a whole or regulations of general trade and commerce within the sense of the judgment in *Parsons* case. [...]

There is one further observation which, perhaps, ought not to be omitted although it may be a mere corollary of what has already been said. Legislation necessarily incidental to the exercise of the undoubted powers of the Dominion in respect of the regulations of trade and commerce is competent although such legislation may trench upon subjects reserved to the province by section 92, but it cannot, we think, be seriously contended that sweeping regulation in respect of local trade, such as we find in this enactment, is, in the proper sense, necessarily incidental to the regulation of external trade or interprovincial trade or both combined.

The scheme of this statute in respect of its essential enactments would not appear to be practicable as a legislative scheme.

in view of the distribution of legislative powers enacted by the *Constitution Act*, without the cooperation of the provincial legislatures to quote from the judgment of the Judicial Committee in *Re the Board of Commerce Act*.

[The judgment of Duff C.J. was affirmed on appeal to the Privy Council: [1937] A.C. 377. Lord Atkin said, at p. 387: "The Justices agree with this and find it unnecessary to add anything."]

(c)   Interprovincial Trade and Commerce

(i)   Federal Competence "in relation to"

CALOIL INC. v. A.G. CAN. (NO. 2)
[1971] S.C.R. 543.

[Section 20 of the National Energy Board Part VI Regulations conferred upon the Board the power to regulate the importation of oil into certain parts of Canada. Under the amended Regulations, the Board refused applications for licences to import gasoline into certain areas of Ontario. It also refused to issue import licences for other areas unless the importer declared that the gasoline imported would be consumed in those areas. The appellant challenged the validity of the Legislation and the decisions of the Board requiring him to make the declaration on the ground that this was an unconstitutional interference with intraprovincial trade.]

PIGEON J. [Fauteux C.J. and Abbott, Ritchie, Hall and Spence JJ. concurring]: — [...] The appellant did not challenge federal authority over imports as such. The attack was exclusively directed against the regulation of trade in the imported commodity at the level of distribution for consumption. On this, I would first quote the following from what Duff J. (as he then was) said in the *Lawson* case:

> The scope which might be ascribed to head 2, s. 91 (if the natural meaning of the words, divorced from their context, were alone to be considered), has necessarily been limited, in order to preserve from serious curtailment, if not from virtual extinction, the degree of autonomy which, as appears from the scheme of the Act as a whole, the provinces were intended to possess. Therefore, it has been found necessary to say that this head does not comprise the regulation, by a system of licences, of a particular business within any one or within all of the provinces. But there is no lack of authority for the proposition that regulations governing external trade, that is, trade between Canada and foreign countries, as well as regulations in matters affected with an interprovincial interest, or regulations which are necessary as auxiliary to some Dominion measure relating to trade generally throughout the Dominion, and dealing with matters not falling within s. 92, such as, for example, the incorporation of Dominion companies, are within the purview of that head. [...]

In *Shannon v. Lower Mainland Dairy Products Board* (1938 A.C. 708), after holding that the provincial marketing scheme there under attack did not encroach on section 91(2) of the *British North America Act* because the legislation was "confined to regulating transactions that take place wholly within the province, and are therefore within the sovereign powers granted to the legislature", Lord Atkin said, at pp. 718-9:

> [...] The Justices do not accept the view that natural products as defined in the Act are confined to natural products produced in British Columbia. [...] But the Act is clearly confined to dealings with such products as are situate within the Province.

In *Home Oil Distributors Ltd. v. Attorney-General Of British Columbia* (1940 S C R 444), a provincial scheme for regulating and controlling the coal and petroleum industries within British Columbia and which expressly authorized a Board to fix the prices of coal or petroleum products at wholesale or retail, was held to be good, by its application of the *Shannon* (supra) case, although the attack had been made on it that it was a provincial attempt to interfere with international trade in petroleum products and there can be no doubt that at least part, if not all, of the regulated product under consideration was imported.

I reach the conclusion then that, on the authorities to which my attention has been drawn, once goods are imported into Canada, they ordinarily fall, from the point of view of trade regulation, into the same category as goods produced in Canada and, fall to be regulated, from the trade point of view, by Parliament or the legislatures depending on whether they find their way into paths leading to destinations in or outside the province where they are situate.

It is to be noted that the *Shannon* and *Home Oil* cases both dealt with the validity of provincial regulation of local trades. They hold that provincial authority over transactions taking place wholly within the province is, as a rule, applicable to products imported from another country, or brought in from another province, as well as to local products. However, it must be borne in mind that the division of constitutional authority under the Canadian Constitution often results in overlapping legislation. [...]

This principle was recently applied by this Court in such cases as *Smith v. The Queen; O'Grady v. Sparling* and *Stephens v. The Queen*. It is clear, therefore, that the existence and extent of provincial regulatory authority over specific trades within the province is not the sole criterion to be considered in deciding whether a federal regulation affecting such a trade is invalid. On the contrary, it is no objection when the impugned enactment is an integral part of a scheme for the regulation of international or interprovincial trade, a purpose that is clearly outside provincial jurisdiction and within the exclusive federal field of action. [...]

In the present case, subs. 2 of s. 20 of the Regulations clearly shows that the policy intended to be implemented by the impugned enactment is a control of the imports of a given commodity to foster the development and utilization of Canadian oil resources. The restriction on the distribution of the imported product to a defined area is intended to reserve the market in other areas for the benefit of products from other provinces of Canada. Therefore, the true character of the enactment appears to be an incident in the administration of an extraprovincial marketing scheme as in *Murphy v. C.P.R.* Under the circumstances, the interference with local trade restricted as it is to an imported commodity, is an integral part of the control of imports in the furtherance of an extraprovincial trade policy and cannot be termed "an unwarranted invasion of provincial jurisdiction". [...]

LASKIN J. [Martland and Judson JJ. concurring]: — I support the dismissal of the appeal, as announced by the Chief Justice at the conclusion of the hearing, and do so on the ground taken by my brother Pigeon that the admitted authority of Parliament to regulate importation of goods from foreign countries was validly exercised in this case in including as part of the regulatory scheme a provision restricting the area of distribution of the goods within Canada by their importer.

(ii)   Ancillary Provincial Competence

[See also *Carnation Co. v. Que. Agricultural Marketing Bd.*, [1968] S.C.R. 238.]

A.G. MAN. v. MAN. EGG & POULTRY ASSN.
[1971] S.C.R. 689.

[The *Manitoba Egg Reference* arose out of the notorious "chicken and egg" war which began when Quebec, a major importer of eggs, established a marketing plan restricting egg imports so as to protect Quebec producers. In retaliation, the Ontario government enacted restrictions on the importation of broiler chickens, of which Quebec was a major exporter.

Claiming to be injured by both these schemes, Manitoba enacted an egg marketing plan based on the Quebec model. The legislation required that all out-of-province eggs be channeled through the provincial marketing board regulations, which controlled all marketing conditions (grading, packaging, level of supply, etc.). The government of Manitoba referred the legislation to the courts for a determination of its constitutional validity, thereby determining the validity of the Quebec and Ontario regulations.]

MARTLAND, J. [Fauteux C.J.C. and Abbott, Judson, Ritchie and Spence JJ. concurring] : — This is an appeal from an opinion pronounced, unanimously, by the Court of Appeal for Manitoba on a matter referred to it by an Order of the Lieutenant-Governor in Council [relating to the Manitoba Egg Producers Marketing Plan]. [...]

Section 3(*a*) and (*c*) provides that the purpose of the Plan is: "To obtain for producers the most advantageous marketing conditions for the regulated product" and also that its purpose is to regulate production to "avoid overproduction thereof".

Section 4(1) and (2) provides:

4.(1) There is hereby established a producer board to be known as The Manitoba Egg Producers' Marketing Board. [...]

The relevant portions of s. 8 are as follows:

8. The Producer Board may with respect to the regulated product: –
(b) Issue production and marketing quotas to producers:
   (i)   Establish quotas for production and sale, fix the time and place of marketing, prohibit marketing outside the fixed time or place or in violation of the established quota or standard, and prohibit the offering for sale of a particular regulated product to ensure the orderly marketing of the regulated product; [...]

The Order of the Manitoba Egg Producers' Marketing Board, referred to in the Order in Council, contains the following provisions:

1. In this Order:
> (c) "distributor" means any person having a contract with the Producer Board and who is engaged in the selling of regulated product to retailers;
>
> (j) "retailer" means any person engaged in the sale of any regulated product to consumers, regardless of the form under which such regulated product is sold. The term includes all government organizations, hospital, religious or school institutions, as well as all restaurants, hotels or enterprises which use any regulated product in their business.

2. A producer shall send his whole production to the grading station specified by the Producer Board.

3. A producer shall market his production through the Producer Board acting as his selling agent.

4. No person shall sell or offer for sale any regulated product except through the Producer Board acting as his selling agent. [...]

The foregoing are the provisions of the Regulation and of the order which are relevant to the consideration of this appeal. The Regulation and the Order, together, constitute what I shall refer to as "the Plan".

[...] [A]s it is clear that the Manitoba Legislature does not have the constitutional power to regulate the activities outside Manitoba of persons outside Manitoba, and having in mind the nature of the regulation of "producers", which many of the provisions of the Plan seek to impose, it is my view that, generally, the word [producer] as used in the Regulation and in the Order, means a Manitoba producer.

The Plan, none the less, contemplates that it shall be applicable to all eggs marketed in Manitoba, whether or not they are produced in that Province. While the provincial Legislature could not control, or permit the Producer Board (hereinafter referred to as "the Board") to control the production of eggs in another Province, the terms of the Plan are applicable to the produce of another Province once it is within Manitoba and available for marketing.

That this is the position is illustrated by the fact that, whereas s. 8(b) of the Regulation authorizes the Board to issue production and marketing quotas to producers, para. (i) of the same section goes on to give a general authority to the Board to establish quotas for production and sale, to prohibit marketing in violation of an established quota and to prohibit the offering for sale of a particular regulated product to ensure the orderly marketing of the regulated product.

Sections 2 and 3 of the Order require a producer to send his whole production to a grading station specified by the Board and to market such production through the Board acting as his selling agent. Sections 4 and 5 provide that "no person" shall sell or offer for sale any regulated product except through the Board acting as his selling agent and that "no person" shall sell or offer for sale any regulated product not graded, packed and marked in a grading or packing station, the operator of which is under contract with the Board.

These provisions make it clear that the Plan is intended to apply not only to eggs produced by Manitoba producers, but to any eggs in Manitoba, wherever they may have been produced. This intent is placed beyond doubt by the provisions of ss. 12, 14 and 15 of the Order, which require the regulated product to be packed in containers, provided by the Board, which shall carry an inscription showing the place of origin of the regulated product and indicating whether such place of origin was in Manitoba, in another country, or in another Province.

Complete control of the marketing of all eggs in Manitoba is vested in the Board. It is only through the Board, as selling agent, that any eggs may be sold or offered for sale. It has the authority, as already noted, to impose marketing quotas and to prohibit the offering for sale of a particular regulated product to ensure the orderly marketing of the regulated product. No eggs can be sold or offered for sale unless graded, packed and marked by a grading or packing station under contract with the Board. All eggs must be offered for sale to distributors, under contract with the Board, at prices set, from time to time, by the Board.

The Board, to which the Plan proposes to grant these broad powers, is not one which is to be appointed by the Manitoba Government, but is to be elected by the Manitoba producers. Its members must be actively engaged in the production of eggs. The main purpose of the Plan, to be achieved through the Board, is "to obtain for producers the most advantageous marketing conditions for the regulated product".

We have, therefore, a Plan which is intended to govern the sale in Manitoba of all eggs, wherever produced, which is to be operated by and for the benefit of the egg producers of Manitoba, to be carried out by a Board armed with the power to control the sale of eggs in Manitoba, brought in from outside Manitoba, by means of quotas, or even outright prohibition.

The issue which has to be considered in this appeal is as to whether the Plan is *ultra vires* the Manitoba Legislature because it trespasses upon the exclusive legislative authority of the Parliament of Canada to legislate on the matter of the regulation of trade and commerce conferred by s. 91(2) of the *B.N.A. Act, 1867*. [...]

The earlier authorities on the matter of provincial marketing regulation were considered by various members of this Court in the *Reference Re Farm Products Marketing Act, R.S.O. 1950, c. 131, as amended*, 7 D.L.R. (2d) 257, [1957] S.C.R. 198 [*the Ontario Reference*], which case, as well as some of those authorities, was reviewed in the judgment of this Court in *Carnation Co. Ltd. v. Quebec Agricultural Marketing Board et al.*, 67 D.L.R. (2d) 1, [1968] S.C.R. 238. It was said, in that case, at p. 15:

While I agree with the view of the four Judges in the Ontario Reference that a trade transaction, completed in a Province, is not necessarily, by that fact alone, subject only to provincial control, I also hold the view that the fact that such a transaction incidentally has some effect upon a company engaged in interprovincial trade does not necessarily prevent its being subject to such control.

Our conclusion was that each transaction and regulation had to be examined in relation of its own facts, and that, in determining the validity of the regulatory legislation in issue in that appeal, the issue was not as to whether it might affect the interprovincial trade of the appellant company, but whether it was made in relation to the regulation of interprovincial trade and commerce. There was cited the following passage from the reasons of Kerwin, C.J.C., in the *Ontario Reference* (at p. 264):

> Once a statute aims at "regulation of trade in matters of interprovincial concern" (*Citizens Ins. Co. v. Parsons* (1881), 7 App. Cas. 96 at p. 113) it is beyond the competence of a Provincial Legislature.

It is my opinion that the Plan now in issue not only affects interprovincial trade in eggs, but that it aims at the regulation of such trade. It is an essential part of this scheme, the purpose of which is to obtain for Manitoba producers the most advantageous marketing conditions for eggs, specifically to control and regulate the sale in Manitoba of imported eggs. It is designed to restrict or limit the free flow of trade between Provinces as such. Because of that, it constitutes an invasion of the exclusive legislative authority of the Parliament of Canada over the matter of the regulation of trade and commerce.

That being so, I would hold that the Regulation and order are not ones which are within the legislative competence of the Manitoba Legislature to authorize, and the answer to Q. (1)(a) should be: No. [...]

[The opinion of Pigeon J., concurring with Martland J., is omitted.]

LASKIN J. [Hall J. concurring]: — [...] The absence of what I regard as relevant data leaves the position as one where, on the face of the legislative scheme and in the light of the arguments thereon addressed to the Court, the contemplated Regulations and Order purport to embrace out-of-Province eggs sent or brought into the Province. Moreover, the embrace would extend to out-of-Province eggs of whatever quantity, and to whatever extent they might engulf the Manitoba retailer and consumer market. On this view of the situation, there is the naked constitutional question to be faced, namely, there being no federal regulatory legislation in force with the same thrust, is the proposed scheme offensive to the legislative power of Parliament in relation to "the regulation of trade and commerce" under s. 91(2) of the *B.N.A. Act, 1867*, and, if not or if so, is it in any event offensive to the prescriptions of s. 121 of that Act? [...]

I adopt the position put by Rand, J., in *Reference Re Farm Products Marketing Act*, R.S.O. 1950, c. 131, as amended, 7 D.L.R. (2d) 257 at pp. 268-9, [1957] S.C.R. 198, that there is a field of trade within provincial power, such power being a subtraction from that comprehended within s. 91(2). The subtraction is, to me, quite rational under the scheme of the *B.N.A. Act, 1867*, although stronger terms, referable to a necessary degree of provincial autonomy, have been used in the cases to support it. That there is such subtraction if a provincial regulatory field is to be recognized was obvious to this Court in its earliest years.

[...]

The stage of dealing at which the Regulation is imposed and its purpose, on which economic data would be relevant, are important considerations in assessing provincial competence. This emerges clearly from *Carnation Milk Co. Ltd. v. Quebec Agricultural Marketing Board*, supra, where this Court rejected a contention that the regulatory scheme, as reflected in three challenged orders, constituted an unlawful invasion of federal power in relation to export. What was there involved was the fixing of prices, by arbitration if agreement could not otherwise be reached, at which milk and dairy products produced in the Province were to be sold by provincial producers, operating under a joint marketing plan, to a distributor and processor in the Province. The fact that the processed products were largely distributed and sold outside the Province did not react upon the validity of the scheme whose purpose was to improve the bargaining position in the Province of provincial producers in their dealings with manufacturers or processors in the Province. The regulatory scheme under attack did not involve a marketing control which extended through the various stages of production, distribution and consumption.

What was raised in the *Carnation Milk* case was the meaning, for constitutional purposes, of an intraprovincial transaction where the issue was seen in the context of goods leaving the Province. The present Reference raises this question in the context of goods entering the Province and their subjection, in consequence, to the same regulatory scheme that operates upon like goods produced in the Province. This was a matter which had been considered in the *Shannon* case, supra, and in *Home Oil Distributors Ltd., et al. v. A.-G. B.C.*, [1940] 2 D.L.R. 609, [1940] S.C.R. 444, in both of which the impugned schemes were held to be within provincial legislative competence. [...]

Neither in the *Shannon* case nor in the *Home Oil* case was there any attempt to examine the various elements or sets of relationships in a marketing or price fixing scheme with a view to elucidating the meaning, for constitutional purposes, of intra-provincial trade and commerce. This exercise fell to this Court in the *Ontario Farm Products Marketing Act Reference*, supra. What emerges from the various reasons of the members of the Court is that (1) individual contracts for the sale and purchase of goods in a Province do not engage federal power under s. 91(2) where any applicable provincial legislation relates merely to the terms of the contract; (2) regulation of the marketing, or the processing and marketing, of products in a Province for consumption therein is within provincial competence; (3) regulation of the marketing of provincial produce intended for export or sought to be purchased for export is beyond that competence; (4) regulation of production or manufacture must be distinguished from regulation of transactions in the product and it cannot be said that the former is so wholly within provincial regulatory competence as in all cases to cover production or manufacture for export, and (5) even in respect of the latter, it cannot be categorically stated that ultimate extra-provincial destination will foreclose provincial regulation of intermediate steps in the marketing process. The matter was put in the following words by Martland, J., speaking for the Court in the *Carnation Co.* case (at p. 15 of 67 D.L.R. (2d)):

> While I agree with the view of the four Judges in the Ontario Reference that a trade transaction, completed in a Province, is not necessarily, by that fact alone, subject only to provincial control, I also hold the view that the fact that such a transaction incidentally has some effect upon a company engaged in interprovincial trade does not necessarily prevent its being subject to such control.

The *Ontario Farm Products Marketing Act Reference*, although refining the meaning of an intraprovincial transaction, did not expressly address itself to the position of an extra-provincial producer, or a purchaser from him, seeking to bring his production into a Province free of a regulatory scheme applicable to local product. Fauteux, J., as he then was, noted in that Reference that the hog marketing scheme which was the subject of the Court's concern did not cover hogs produced outside the Province nor were producers outside the Province affected thereby. "In the result", he said, "any one in Ontario is free to import therein and one beyond its boundaries to export thereto the regulated product" (at p. 310 of 7 D. L. R. (2d)). This is, however, precisely the issue that must be faced in the present Reference. [...]

Although the emphasis is on control of the Manitoba producers and distributors in order (as stated in the proposed measures) "to obtain for producers the most advantageous marketing conditions" and "to avoid overproduction", the scheme brings into its grasp "persons" as well as producers, that is, those outside the Province who are either producers or distributors seeking to enter the Manitoba market, or those inside the Province who are not themselves producers but who bring in out-of-Province eggs for disposition in Manitoba. This view is reinforced by the provision for indicating the origin of eggs, including eggs other than those produced in Manitoba.

There may be a variety of reasons which impel a Province to enact regulatory legislation for the marketing of various products. For example, it may wish to secure the health of the inhabitants by establishing quality standards; it may wish to protect consumers against exorbitant prices; it may wish to equalize the bargaining or competitive position of producers or distributors or retailers, or all three classes; it may wish to ensure an adequate supply of certain products. These objects may not all nor always be realizable through legislation which fastens on the regulated product as being within the Province. That is no longer, if it ever was, the test of validity. Just as the Province may not, as a general rule, prohibit an owner of goods from sending them outside the Province, so it may not be able to subject goods to a regulatory scheme upon their entry into the Province. This is not to say that goods that have come into a Province may not, thereafter, be subject to the same controls in, for example, retail distribution to consumers as apply to similar goods produced in the Province.

Assuming such controls be open to a Province, the scheme before this Court is not so limited. It embraces products which are in the current of interprovincial trade and, as noted at the beginning of these reasons, it embraces them in whatever degree they seek to enter the provincial market. It begs the question to say that out-of-Province producers who come in voluntarily (certainly they cannot be compelled by Manitoba) must not expect to be treated differently from local producers. I do not reach the question of discriminatory standards applied to out-of-Province producers or distributors (that is, the question of a possibly illegal administration of the scheme as bearing on its validity) because I am of opinion that the scheme is on its face an invasion of federal power in relation to s. 91(2).

There are several grounds upon which I base this conclusion. The proposed scheme has as a direct object the regulation of the importation of eggs, and it is not saved by the fact that the local market is under the same regime. Anglin, J., said in *Gold Seal Ltd. v. Dominion Express Co. and A.-G. Alta.*, 62 S.C.R. 424, that "It is common ground that the prohibition of importation is beyond the legislative jurisdiction of the Province."

Conversely, the general limitation upon provincial authority to exercise of its powers within or in the province precludes it from intercepting either goods moving into the province or goods moving out, subject to possible exceptions, as in the case of danger to life or health. Again, the Manitoba scheme cannot be considered in isolation from similar schemes in other provinces; and to permit each province to seek its own advantage, so to speak, through a figurative sealing of its borders to entry of goods from others would be to deny one of the objects of Confederation, evidence by the catalogue of federal powers and by s. 121, namely, to form an economic unit of the whole of Canada: see the *Lawson* case [[1931] S.C.R. 357 at 373, 2 D.L.R. 193.]. The existence of egg marketing schemes in more than one province, with objectives similar to the proposed Manitoba scheme, makes it clear that interprovincial trade in eggs is being struck at by the provincial barriers to their movement into various provincial markets. If it be thought necessary or desirable to arrest such movement at any provincial border then the aid of the Parliament of Canada must be sought, as was done through Part V of the *Canada Temperance Act*, R.S.C. 1952, c. 30, in respect of provincial regulation of the sale of intoxicating liquor.

I do not find it necessary in this case to invoke s. 121, and hence say nothing about its applicability to the marketing scheme under review. I would also note at this point that nothing is added to provincial competence by the fact (under the assumptions stated in the Order of Reference) that the Producer Board was to have authority under the federal *Agricultural Products Marketing Act*, already mentioned, to regulate the marketing in interprovincial and export trade of eggs produced in Manitoba. The combined effect of *Murphy v. C.P.R.*, supra, and *P.E.I. Potato Marketing Board v. H.B. Willis Inc.* [[1952] 2 S.C.R. 392, [1952] 4 D.L.R. 146] gives federal authority for the delegation of power to act in respect of matters within federal jurisdiction] none is needed from the province, nor is there any accretion to its legislative authority. [...]

I turn now to the questions put before the Manitoba Court of Appeal and to the answers thereto by Dickson, J.A., who spoke for that Court. They are as follows:

(1) (a) Are the Regulation and the Order ones that it is within the legislative competence of the Manitoba Legislature to authorize the Lieutenant-Governor-in-Council and the Producer Board respectively, to make?

ANSWER: No.

As is evident from my reasons, I concur with Dickson, J.A., in the answer which he gave to Q. 1(a). [...]

BURNS FOODS LTD. v. A.G. MAN.
[1975] 1 S.C.R. 494.

PIGEON J. [Fauteux C.J.C. and Abbott, Martland, Judson and Spence JJ. concurring]: — This appeal [concerns an injunction which] [...] restrains the Packers from slaughtering hogs in Manitoba unless same have been purchased from the respondent Manitoba Hog Producers' Marketing Board (the Board). The Packers' counterclaim is for a declaration that the *Natural Products Marketing Act*, R.S.M. 1970, c. N20 [and certain regulations thereunder [...] are invalid by reason of being *ultra vires* the Province of Manitoba. [...]

Under date 17th July 1972 the Board made an order, known as Manitoba Reg. 4/72, adding to Reg. 4/72 after s. 2:

2A. No Manitoba processor shall prepare hogs for slaughter in Manitoba or slaughter hogs in Manitoba unless same have been purchased from the producer board and where hogs have been brought into the province they shall, for the purpose of the Act, be deemed to be hogs produced in Manitoba and shall be subject to the same provisions of the Act and regulation as hogs produced in Manitoba. [...]

The effect of the Regulation under attack must, therefore, be taken to be that the Packers are prohibited from slaughtering in Manitoba hogs raised in Saskatchewan or in any other province, unless those hogs are purchased *from the producer through the Board*. It is true that this prohibition does not apply unless the hogs are slaughtered in Manitoba, but that is the only purpose for which they are bought by the Packers. At the hearing in this Court, the position taken by those who sought to support the validity of the Regulation was that the order under attack was made by the Board with the conscious realization that it would affect hogs brought from another province. [...]

The question then becomes whether, as an incident of its authority over the local matter of hog slaughter by the Packers in Manitoba, this province can regulate the buying of hogs by the Packers from producers in another province. As we have seen, the injunction is aimed at preventing the Packers from buying hogs in Saskatchewan, direct from the producer, for slaughter in Manitoba. Such acquisition is a contract made outside Manitoba. Of course, the parties could choose to make it in that province, but they would certainly choose to make it in Saskatchewan when desirous, as the Packers are, of avoiding subjection to the Manitoba Plan. However, if the order is valid, the conditions of the sale will be regulated by the Manitoba Plan, even when the Packers deal with the Saskatchewan producers in that province. Such a contract is clearly not within the legislative authority of the Province of Manitoba: *Royal Bank of Canada v. The King,* [1913] A.C. 283. Can it be brought in because, as Tritschler C.J.Q.B. puts it [p. 54]: "If the Manitoba processor could bypass the system the Plan would be destroyed with great damage to the industry which has been built up?" In my view the answer to this question is to be found in the following sentence quoted in Lord Atkin's judgment in *Attorney General for British Columbia v. Attorney General for Canada (Reference Re Natural Products Marketing Act, 1934),* [1937] A.C. 377 at 387:

> Parliament cannot acquire jurisdiction to deal in the sweeping way in which these enactments operate with such local and provincial matters by legislating at the same time respecting external and interprovincial trade and committing the regulation of external and interprovincial trade and the regulation of trade which is exclusively local and of traders and producers engaged in trade which is exclusively local to the same authority. *Rex v. Eastern Terminal Elevator Co.,* [1925] S.C.R. 434.

If the federal Parliament cannot regulate local trade because it would be more efficient to regulate it together with the extra-provincial trade, *a fortiori* a provincial legislature cannot regulate interprovincial trade in a given product because this appears desirable for the effective control of intra-provincial trade. In other words, the direct regulation of interprovincial trade is of itself a matter outside the legislative authority of any province and it cannot be treated as an accessory of the local trade. This is not a case of subjecting all goods of a certain kind within a province to uniform regulations, such as the retail sale price (as in *Home Oil Distributors Ltd. v. Attorney General for British Columbia,* [1940] S.C.R. 444). It is a case of directly regulating extra-provincial trade operations in their essential aspects, namely, the price and all the other conditions of sale. In effect, the impugned Regulation does not really deal with goods already brought within the province. What it seeks to accomplish is to require that their acquisition from the producer in another province be made in accordance with the law of Manitoba, not with the law of the province of origin. It is true that it does not purport to prohibit the bringing in if that requirement is not complied with, but the same result is sought by providing that the goods cannot then be used for sole purpose for which they are brought in, namely, immediate slaughter.

Nothing that was said in any previous case supports the proposition that such direct interference with interprovincial trade may be effected by a provincial authority. This is not an insignificant interference. On the contrary, it is not denied that the interprovincial trade in hogs between Saskatchewan and Manitoba is substantial. It is no answer to say that there is no discrimination, not only because this is due to a policy decision subject to alteration at the will of the Board, but also because it is the substance of the interprovincial trade that is being regulated, not some accessory or unessential aspect. To make a comparison with the trucking industry, it is the equivalent of rate-fixing for interprovincial transport as opposed to the setting of the speed limits. [...]

I cannot, therefore, accede to the argument submitted by Mr. Hilton that the restriction is valid because it is imposed in aid of the object to ensure a fair price for the sale of the local product. [...]

[I]n *Carnation Co. Ltd. v. Quebec Agricultural Marketing Board*, [1968] S.C.R. 238, all the producers were within the province in which the processing plant was operating. The basis of the attack was not that extra-provincial producers were affected, but that a large part of the plant's production was sold outside the province. From that point of view, the situation is much the same in the present case. It is conceded that two-thirds of the Packers' production is sold outside Manitoba. However, in view of what was decided in the *Carnation* case, this was not the basis of the challenge on constitutional grounds.

The Regulation was sought to be supported because it applies only to hogs brought within the province. The difficulty is that what the order in question does is really to prescribe the conditions under which the hogs may be brought in from outside and that is, in itself, interprovincial trade. It is not an incident of the operation of slaughter taking place within the province.

It was also said that the pith and substance is not to erect any barrier against the free flow of trade but to stabilize the price of hogs in Manitoba. The difficulty is that such regulation by subjecting the price of "imports" to the same regulations as local sales is, of itself, a regulation of the interprovincial trade. The fact that this is presently being done without the features of discrimination present in the *Egg* case (*Attorney General for Manitoba v. Manitoba Egg & Poultry Assn.*, ([1971] S. C. R. 689]) cannot make a real difference, not only because discrimination could at any time be established at the discretion of the Board but also because what is sought to be regulated in all its essential aspects is the trade in hogs between the Packers in Manitoba and hog producers in any other province.

For those reasons, I would allow the appeal, set aside the judgments in the Courts below, dissolve the injunction, dismiss the action and allow the counterclaim to the extent of declaring Manitoba Reg. 97/72 null and void. [...]

RITCHIE J. (dissenting): — I am in agreement with the Court of Appeal of Manitoba [[1973] 5 W.W.R. 60, 35 D.L.R. (3d) 581] that the impugned legislation primarily directed to the slaughter of hogs within the province which is a local matter, and that it only affects interprovincial trade as an incident of a scheme for controlling local trade within the province and does not aim at the regulation of trade in matters of interprovincial concern.

For these reasons I would dismiss this appeal with costs.

CANADIAN INDUSTRIAL GAS AND OIL LTD. v. SASK.
[1978] 2 S.C.R. 545.

[For a fuller report of the facts see infra at p. 637.]

MARTLAND J. [Laskin C.J.C. and Judson, Ritchie, Spence, Pigeon and Beetz JJ. concurring]: — [...] In considering this issue the important fact is, of course, that practically all of the oil to which the mineral income tax or the royalty surcharge becomes applicable is destined for interprovincial or international trade. Some of this oil is sold by producers at the well-head and thereafter transported from the Province by pipeline. Some of the oil is not sold at the well-head, but is produced by companies for their own purposes, and is likewise transported out of the Province by pipeline. In either case the levy becomes applicable. The producer in the first case must, if he is to avoid pecuniary loss, sell at the well-head at the well-head value established. The company which has its own oil production transported from the Province must, if it is to avoid pecuniary loss, ultimately dispose of the refined product at a price which will recoup the amount of the levy. Thus, the effect of the legislation is to set a floor price for Saskatchewan oil purchased for export by the appropriation of its potential incremental value in interprovincial and international markets, or to ensure that the incremental value is not appropriated by persons outside the province.

Chief Justice Kerwin in the *Reference Re Farm Products Marketing Act*, [1957] S.C.R. 198 at p. 204, said:

> Once a statute aims at "regulation of trade in matters in inter-provincial concern" [...] it is beyond the competence of a Provincial Legislature.

At p. 204 S.C.R., he said:

> The concept of trade and commerce, the regulation of which is confided to Parliament, is entirely separate and distinct from the regulation of mere sale and purchase agreements. Once an article enters into the flow of interprovincial or external trade, the subject-matter and all its attendant circumstances cease to be a mere matter of local concern.

The purpose of the legislation under review was accurately defined by Chief Justice Culliton in the Court of Appeal [at p. 98]:

> There is no doubt in my mind that both the mineral income tax and the royalty surcharge were imposed for one purpose, and one purpose only – to drain off substantial benefits that would have accrued to the producers due to the sudden and unprecedented price of crude oil.

The means used to achieve this end are to compel a Saskatchewan oil producer to effect the sale of the oil at a price determined by the Minister. The mineral income tax is defined as the difference between the basic well-head price and the price at which the oil is sold, but with the important proviso that if the

575

Minister is of the opinion that the oil has been sold at less then its fair value, he can determine the price at which it should have been sold, and that price governs in determining the amount of the tax. The royalty surcharge, as provided under the Regulations requires the payment of the surcharge on oil produced on the basis of the difference between its well-head value, as established by the Minister, less the basic well-head price. In either case the Minister is empowered to determine the well-head value of the oil which is produced which will govern the price at which the producer is compelled to sell the oil which he produces. In an effort to obtain for the provincial treasury the increases in the value of oil exported from Saskatchewan which began in 1973, in the form of a tax upon the production of oil in Saskatchewan, the legislation gave power to the Minister to fix the price receivable by Saskatchewan oil producers on their export sales of a commodity that has almost no local market in Saskatchewan. Provincial legislative authority does not extend to fixing the price to be charged or received in respect of the sale of goods in the export market. It involves the regulation of interprovincial trade and trenches upon s-s. 91(2) of the *British North America Act, 1867*.

This is not a case similar to *Carnation Co. Ltd. v. Quebec Agricultural Marketing Board*, [1968] S.C.R. 238, where the effect of the Regulations was to increase the cost of the milk purchased by Carnation in Quebec and processed there, mostly for sale outside Quebec. The legislation there indirectly affected Carnation's export trade in the sense that its costs of production were increased, but was designed to establish a method for determining the price of milk sold by Quebec milk producers, to a purchaser in Quebec, who processed it there. Here the legislation is directly aimed at the production of oil destined for export and has the effect of regulating the export price, since the producer is effectively compelled to obtain that price on the sale of his product.

DICKSON J. [(de Grandpré J. concurring) dissenting]: — [...] Counsel for appellant urged the Court to strike down the legislation as an infringement of Parliament's exclusive authority respecting the regulation of trade and commerce. Appellant says:

> [...] the tax and surcharge are established in a way which enables the Province of Saskatchewan to control the minimum price at which Saskatchewan crude oil is sold. This control is imposed on a commodity almost exclusively consumed outside of Saskatchewan, either in the Canadian or international marketplace. This imposition of a minimum price by the Province to be passed on to consumers outside of the Province is an interference with the free flow of trade between provinces [...] so as to prevent producers in Saskatchewan from dealing unhampered with purchasers outside of Saskatchewan.

Section 91, head 2 of the *British North America Act, 1867*, has undergone a jurisprudential renaissance during the past fifty years. Appellant asks the Court to extend that revivification to an unprecedented degree. In *Home Oil Distributors Ltd. v. A.-G. B.C.*, [1940] S.C.R. 444, the Court held *intra vires* the *Coal and Petroleum Products Control Board Act* 1937 (B.C.), c. 8, which provided for the appointment of a Board to regulate and control provincial coal and petroleum industries. The Board was empowered to fix the prices at which coal or petroleum products might be sold in the Province either at well-head or retail or otherwise for use in the Province. Raw supplies for the British Columbia refineries originated extra-provincially. Extra-provincial producers were dumping surplus fuel oil into British Columbia at low prices to the detriment of the local coal industry. The contention advanced was that the legislation was aimed at extraterritorial sources of supply and that it was an attempt to control through price fixing the interprovincial movement of products. That submission was rejected upon the authority of *Shannon v. Lower Mainland Dairy Product Board*, [1938] A. C. 708. The point was made that a degree of price regulation in support of legitimate provincial interests was tolerable even though affecting the entry of foreign oil.

The notion that a Province may incidentally affect goods in interprovincial or international trade was developed in *Carnation Co. Ltd. v. Quebec Agricultural Marketing Board*, [1968] S.C.R. 238. In that case it was held that a Province could obliquely affect such goods by increasing their cost if the legislation in object and purpose was in relation to a valid head of provincial power. Mr. Justice Martland, speaking for a unanimous Court said, at pp. 252-3 S.C.R.:

> That the price determined by the orders may have a bearing upon the appellant's export trade is unquestionable. It affects the cost of doing business. But so, also, do labour costs affect the cost of doing business of any company which may be engaged in export trade and yet there would seem to be little doubt as to the power of a Province to regulate wage rates payable within a Province, save as to an undertaking falling within the exceptions listed in s. 92(10) of the *B.N.A. Act*. It is not the possibility that these orders might "affect" the appellant's interprovincial trade which should determine their validity, but, rather, whether they were made "in relation to" the regulation of trade and commerce. This was a test applied, in another connection, by Duff, J. (as he then was), in *Gold Seal Ltd. v. Dominion Express Co. and A.-G. Alta.*, 62 D.L.R. 62 at pp. 81-2, 62 S.C.R. 424, [1921] 3 W.W.R. 710.

The argument that the orders of the marketing board might have impact upon interprovincial trade was disposed of in these words, at p. 253 S.C.R.:

> I am not prepared to agree that, in determining that aim, the fact that these orders may have some impact upon the appellant's interprovincial trade necessarily means that they constitute a regulation of trade and commerce within s. 91(2) and thus renders them invalid. The fact of such impact is a matter which may be relevant in determining their true aim and purpose, but it is not conclusive.

It is now well established that incidental effect is not a quantum measurement. It is tested by the design or aim of the legislation. That was held in *Brant Dairy Co. Ltd. et al. v. Milk Commission of Ontario et al.*, [1973] S.C.R. 131 at p. 166, where Mr. Justice Judson said:

The test that determines whether a marketing plan or its administration is ultra vires the Province is the test applied in the *Manitoba Egg Reference* (Mr. Justice Martland at p. 703 S.C.R.). Is it "designed to restrict or limit the free flow of trade between provinces as such"?

and in *A.-G. Man. v. Manitoba Egg & Poultry Ass'n.*, [1971] S.C.R. 689 at p. 703, where the following observation appears, quoting Kerwin, C.J.C., in the *Reference Re Farm Products Marketing Act*, [1957] S.C.R. 198:

> Once a statute aims at "regulation of trade in matters of interprovincial concern" [...] it is beyond the competence of a Provincial Legislature.

The concept of a "current of commerce" as an aid to the interpretation of the commerce power in the United States is of long standing. The concept originated with Holmes, J., in *Swift & Co. v. United States* (1905), 196 U.S. 375. It was applied in *Stafford & Wallace* (1922), 258 U.S. 496, and in *Chicago Board of Trade v. Olsen* (1923), 262 U.S. 1. That idea as applied to s. 91, head 2 of the *British North America Act, 1867* was considered in the *Farm Products Marketing Reference*, supra, although no majority opinion is reflected in the judgments. Kerwin, C.J.C., recognized the right of a Province to regulate a transaction of purchase and sale within the Province even if the purchaser had the intention of taking the product out of the Province. He said, at p. 204 S.C.R.: "That is a matter of the regulation of contracts and not of trade as trade and in that respect the intention of the purchaser is immaterial." Later in his judgment, however, the following passage appears, at p. 205 S.C.R.: "Once an article enters into the flow of interprovincial or external trade, the subject-matter and all its attendant circumstances cease to be a mere matter of local concern." Mr. Justice Rand spoke to the same effect in these words, at p. 210 S.C.R.: " [...] if in a trade activity, including manufacture or production, there is involved a matter of extra-provincial interest or concern its regulation thereafter in the aspect of trade is by that fact put beyond provincial power". Mr. Justice Locke (with whom Mr. Justice Nolan agreed) would exclude from provincial regulatory power sales of produce where the producer sells his product to a person who purchased the same for export. Mr. Justice Fauteux (with whom Mr. Justice Taschereau agreed) held a different view, which he expressed in these words, at p. 256 S.C.R.:

> The suggestion that to be intra-provincial a transaction must be completed within the Province, in the sense that the product, object of the transaction, must be ultimately and exclusively consumed or be sold for delivery therein for such consumption, is one, which would, if carried to its logical conclusion, strip from a Province its recognized power to provide for the regulation of marketing within such Province in disregard of the decisions of the Judicial Committee in *A.-G. B.C. v. A.-G. Can.* (supra) and in *Shannon v. Lower Mainland Dairy Products Bd.* (supra).

Mr. Justice Abbott had this to say, at p. 264 S.C.R.:

> The power to regulate the sale within a Province, of specific products, is not, in my opinion, affected by reason of the fact that some, or all, of such products may subsequently, in the same or in an altered form, be exported from that Province, unless it be shown, of course, that such regulation is merely a colourable device for assuming control of extra-provincial trade.

The conceptual tool of a "flow," or "current," or "stream" of commerce has been referred to by the Court in a number of subsequent cases, the most recent being *MacDonald et al. v. Vapour Canada Ltd. et al.*, [1977] 2 S.C.R. 134. The real question, unsettled in the jurisprudence, is the determination of when the product enters the export stream marking the start of the process of exportation. American jurisprudence has held that the distinguishing mark of an export product is shipment or entry with a common carrier for transportation to another jurisdiction: *Coe v. Errol*, 116 U.S. 517 at 527; *Richfield Oil Corp. v. State Board of Equalization*, 329 U.S. 69; *Empresa Siderurgica v. Merced Co.*, 337 U.S. 154. Implicit in the argument of the appellant is the assumption that federal regulatory power pursuant to s. 91(2) follows the flow of oil backward across provincial boundaries, back through provincial gathering systems and finally to the well-head. A secondary assumption is that sale at the well-head marks the start of the process of exportation. In the view I take of the case it is unnecessary to reach any conclusion as to the validity of either of these assumptions. It is, however, worth noting that neither American nor Canadian jurisprudence has ever gone that far.

I can find nothing in the present case to lead me to conclude that the taxation measures imposed by the Province of Saskatchewan were merely a colourable device for assuming control of extra-provincial trade. The language of the impugned statutes does not disclose an intention on the part of the Province to regulate, or control, or impede the marketing or export of oil from Saskatchewan. "Oil produced and sold" means produced and sold within the Provinces. "Well-head price" by definition means the price at the well-head of a barrel of oil produced in Saskatchewan. The mineral income tax and the royalty surcharge relate only to oil produced within Saskatchewan. The transactions are well-head transactions. There are no impediments to the free movement of goods as were found objectionable in *A.-G. Man. v. Manitoba Egg & Poultry Ass'n*, supra, and in *Burns Foods Ltd. et al. v. A.-G. Man. et al.*, [1975] 1 S.C.R. 494.

Nor is there anything in the extraneous evidence to form the basis of an argument that the impugned legislation in its *effect* regulated interprovincial or international trade. The evidence is all to the contrary and that evidence comes entirely from witnesses called on behalf of the appellant. Production and export of oil increased after the legislative scheme was implemented. Sales of oil by the appellant were continued in 1974 as in 1973 and previously.

The trial Judge, Hughes, J., made the following finding of fact [[1975] 2 W.W.R. 481 at p. 578]:

[...] I do emphasize that nothing has happened to suggest any intrusion or invasion on the part of the defendant with respect to the export of crude oil from this province unless it is to be suggested that it is to be found in price regulation.

Chief Justice Culliton, speaking for a unanimous Court of Appeal, made a further finding [[1976] 2 W.W.R. 356]:

Neither of the charges [*i.e.*, mineral income tax and royalty surcharge] have any effect on price. As a matter of fact, the true situation is that the tax does not influence the price but rather, the price determines the tax.

On the basis of such concurrent findings it is hard to say that the flow of commerce was in any way impeded, unless it can be said to relate to price.

It was contended in argument that the effect was to place a floor price under Saskatchewan oil and thereby interfere with interprovincial trade. So far as mineral income tax is concerned the incidence of taxation is pegged to the price received for the oil at the well-head. Section 4A is an "after-the-event" provision which comes into play only if there was a sale at less than fair value. The emphasis on fair value ensures that the tax will not change the export oil price. The price of oil subject to the tax and the price of oil free of the tax, *i.e.*, from the exempted 1,280-acre tracts, will be the same as the product crosses the provincial border. The ultimate position of consumers is unaffected. The only way in which extra-provincial consumers could have benefitted would have been in the event of the Province freezing the price of oil, assuming constitutional competence to do so.

One is free to speculate that, to the extent producers would be prepared to undercut the fair market value of their oil, the legislation discourages them from doing so by virtue of the constant tax liability. The possibility of price-cutting is highly theoretical, unsupported by evidence and in view of the inelasticity of demand for petroleum products, highly unlikely.

In *Burns Foods Ltd. v. A.-G. Man.*, supra, in striking down a regulation under the *Natural Products Marketing Act of Manitoba* which required packers in Manitoba to buy hogs only from the Manitoba Hog Producers Marketing Board, Mr. Justice Pigeon said this, at pp. 504-5 S.C.R.:

It is a case of directly regulating extra-provincial trade operations in their essential aspects, namely, the price and all the other conditions of sale. [...] The situation here is totally unlike that which obtained in *Brant Dairy Co. Ltd. et al. v. Milk Commission of Ontario* (1972), 30 D.L.R. (3d) 559, [1973] S.C.R. 131. In that case, the challenge on constitutional grounds was dismissed because there was no evidence that the orders had any extra-provincial effect.

The key word is "directly" for it leaves open the possibility for a scheme to affect incidentally interprovincial trade, so long as the scheme is not in pith and substance in relation to interprovincial trade. This last proposition, while obvious in other areas of constitutional law, was remarkably absent in the cases respecting trade and commerce decided in the first half of this century.

The Province of Saskatchewan had a *bona fide* legitimate and reasonable interest of its own to advance in enacting the legislation in question, as related to taxation and natural resources, out of all proportion to the burden, if there can be said to be a burden, imposed on the Canadian free trade economic unit through the legislation. The effect, if any, on the extra-provincial trade in oil is merely indirectly and remotely incidental to the manifest revenue-producing object of the legislation under attack. [...]

I would dismiss the appeal.

- Research Note -
THE AFTERMATH OF CIGOL

In the 1970s federal policy initiatives in the natural resources field contributed to political irritation in Western Canada. The judgment of the Supreme Court in *CIGOL* and a similar ruling in *Central Canada Potash v. A.G. Saskatchewan*, [1979] 1 S.C.R. 42 added to this disaffection. The Western provinces agitated for constitutional reform. The result was the inclusion of s. 92A of the *Constitution Act, 1982* as part of the total package of constitutional reforms introduced with patriation. Among other things, section 92A reversed the *CIGOL* and *Potash* decisions by constitutional amendment. Section 92A increases provincial jurisdiction in relation to natural resources exploitation and taxation. It reads:

> 92A. (1) In each province, the legislature may exclusively make laws in relation to
>> (*a*) exploration for non-renewable natural resources in the province;
>> (*b*) development, conservation and management of non-renewable natural resources and forestry resources in the province, including laws in relation to the rate of primary production therefrom; and
>> (*c*) development, conservation and management of sites and facilities in the province for the generation and production of electrical energy.
>
> (2) In each province, the legislature may make laws in relation to the export from the province to another part of Canada of the primary production from non-renewable natural resources and forestry resources in the province and the production from facilities in the province for the generation of electrical energy, but such laws may not authorize or provide for discrimination in prices or in supplies exported to another part of Canada.

(3) Nothing in subsection (2) derogates from the authority of Parliament to enact laws in relation to the matters referred to in that subsection and, where such a law of Parliament and a law of a province conflict, the law of Parliament prevails to the extent of the conflict.

(4) In each province, the legislature may make laws in relation to the raising of money by any mode or system of taxation in respect of

> (a) non-renewable natural resources and forestry resources in the province and the primary production therefrom, and
> (b) sites and facilities in the province for the generation of electrical energy and the production therefrom

whether or not such production is exported in whole or in part from the province, but such laws may authorize or provide for taxation that differentiates between production exported to another part of Canada and production not exported from the province,

(5) The expression "primary production" has the meaning assigned by the Sixth Schedule.

(6) Nothing in subsections (1) to (5) derogates from any powers or rights that a legislature or government of a province had immediately before the coming into force of this section.

(d) General Trade and Commerce Affecting the Dominion

LABATT'S BREWERIES OF CAN. LTD. v. A.G. CAN.
[1980] 1 S.C.R. 91.

ESTEY J. [Martland, Dickson, Beetz and Pratte JJ. concurring]: — The appellant seeks a declaration that its product "Labatt's Special Lite" as labeled, packaged and sold "is not likely to be mistaken for a 'light beer' within the standards set out [...] " in the regulations under the *Food and Drugs Act*, R.S.C. 1970, c. F-27 ("the Act"). [...] [T]he appellant takes the position that this product [...] is not likely to be mistaken for a light beer within [...] s. B.02.134 of the *Food and Drug Regulations* C.R.C., c. 807, [...] enacted pursuant to s. 25(1) of the Act [...] Section 6 of the Act states as follows:

> Where a standard has been prescribed for a food, no person shall label, package, sell or advertise any article in such a manner that it is likely to be mistaken for such food, unless the article complies with the prescribed standard.

The second position taken by the appellant is that s. 6 of the Act and regulation B.02.134 are *ultra vires* the Parliament of Canada, and to the extent that it authorizes such regulation, s. 25 is likewise *ultra vires*. [...]

I turn now to the constitutional issue. The appellant challenges the constitutional validity of s. 6 and S. 25(1)(c) of the *Food and Drug Act* and the regulations promulgated thereunder with reference to the production and sale of beer. [...]

The statute and its implementing regulations [...] construct a detailed code governing the manufacture of malt liquors, the labels or display panels on the article so produced, and the name under which the end product shall be sold. [...]

What then is the constitutional basis for the enactment of the contested portions of this statute by Parliament? [...]

[The *Parsons* case makes] clear that "minute rules for regulating particular trades" are not within the trade and commerce competence. The statute and regulation with which we are here concerned purport to establish such a detailed single industry regulatory pattern. [...]

The principles developed in the natural products marketing judgments only obliquely deal with the second branch of the *Parsons* description of trade and commerce, supra, and hence are not of direct application here. The impugned regulations in and under the *Food and Drugs Act* are not concerned with the control and guidance of the flow of articles of commerce through the distribution channels, but rather with the production and local sale of the specified products of the brewing industry. There is no demonstration by the proponent of these isolated provisions in the *Food and Drugs Act* and its regulations of any interprovincial aspect of this industry. The labels in the record reveal that the appellant produces these beverages in all provinces but Quebec and Prince Edward Island. From the nature of the beverage, it is apparent, without demonstration, that transportation to distant markets would be expensive, and hence the local nature of the production operation. This distinction between the flow of commerce, and production and local sale, if I may say so with respect, is pointedly made by Pigeon, J. in *Reference Re Agricultural Products Marketing Act*, [1978] 2 S.C.R. 1198 at p. 1293:

> In my view, the control of production, whether agricultural or industrial, is prima facie a local matter, a matter of provincial jurisdiction. Egg farms, if I may use this expression to designate the kind of factories in which feed is converted into eggs and fowl, are local undertakings subject to provincial jurisdiction under section 92(10) *B.N.A. Act* [...] ;

and at p. 1296:

> "Marketing" does not include production and, therefore, provincial control of production is prima facie valid.

The first successful attempt to breathe life into the second branch of the *Parsons* trade and commerce description, *supra*, is found in *John Deere Plow Co. v. Wharton*, [1915] A.C. 330. The provincial legislature had attempted to establish regulation in a limited sense of federally incorporated companies within the provincial boundaries. The Court determined that such provincial action was *ultra vires* as being an invasion of the power of Parliament to regulate the exercise by federal companies of their powers throughout the Dominion. This subject should not be left without adding that the Court there found the constitutional basis for legislation authorizing the establishment of federal incorporations in the peace, order and good government clause while the regulation of their activities fell into the trade and commerce category. Viscount Haldane, speaking in the *Wharton* case, supra, stated at p. 340:

> [...] the power to regulate trade and commerce at all events enables the Parliament of Canada to prescribe to what extent the powers of companies the objects of which extend to the entire Dominion should be exercisable, and what limitations should be placed on such powers. For if it be established that the Dominion Parliament can create such companies, then it becomes *a question of general interest throughout the Dominion* in what fashion they should be permitted to trade (emphasis added).

To this date this is still the test in determining whether the second branch of the trade and commerce power applies; *vide* Laskin C.J. in *Reference Re the Anti-Inflation Act*, [1978] 2 S.C.R. 373, at p. 426.

What clearly is not of general national concern is the regulation of a single trade or industry. *Vide In Re Insurance Act 1910* (1913), 48 S.C.R. 260, at 308-9; *Eastern Terminal Elevator Co.*, supra. [...]

In more modern times, the Court in *MacDonald v. Vapour Canada Ltd.*, [1977] 2 S.C.R. 134, struck down that part of the *Trade Marks Act of Canada* purporting to create a cause of action in connection with "any business practice contrary to honest industrial or commercial usage in Canada". Unrestricted geographic play of the provision was not sufficient to find legislative authority under the trade and commerce heading. *Vide* Chief Justice Laskin at pp. 156 and 159.

The *Wharton* judgment, supra, came in for examination in *Re The Board of Commerce Act* (1920), 60 S.C.R. 456, where Duff J., as he then was, stated at p. 500:

> [...] the regulation in question in *Wharton's* case, was not a regulation relating to any particular kind of trade or business, but a regulation touching the trading powers of all dominion companies engaged in any kind of business and applying to all such companies alike and thus at least potentially affecting Dominion trade and commerce in general through one of its most important instrumentalities.

This is of major importance in the disposition of the appeal now before us. As we have seen, the trade and commerce head cannot be applied to the regulation of a single trade, even though it be on a national basis, and in the *Board of Commerce* disposition, supra, the invocation of the trade and commerce head of federal jurisdiction is forbidden in the regulation of elements of commerce such as contracts, in an individual trade or concern even though the control was imposed in a series of separate regulatory codes each purporting to regulate a separate trade or industry. [...]

In the result, the trade and commerce power has been rescued from near oblivion following the *Citizens Insurance* case, supra, by the extension or development of the *obiter* or afterthought of Sir Montague Smith in that case. The application of the power to this stage in our constitutional development finds illustration firstly in general regulation of an element of trade such as the regulation of federal incorporations. With respect to legislation relating to the support, control or regulation of the various levels or components in the marketing cycle of natural products, the provincial authority is *prima facie* qualified to legislate with reference to production (*vide* Pigeon J. in the *Reference Re Agricultural Products Marketing Act*, supra, at p. 1296), and the federal Parliament with reference to marketing in the International and Interprovincial levels of trade. In between, the success or failure of the legislator depends upon whether the pith and substance or primary objective of the statute or regulation is related to the heads of power of the legislative authority in question. Incidental effect on the other legislative sphere will no longer necessarily doom the statute to failure. Several indicia of the proper tests have evolved. For example, if contractual rights within the province are the object of the proposed regulation, the province has the authority. On the other hand, if regulation of the flow in extra-provincial channels of trade is the object, then the federal statute will be valid. Between these spectrum ends, the shadings cannot be foretold in anything approaching a constitutional formula. The majority of the illustrated tests thus far encountered are largely in the distribution, and not the production, of farm products. Here, however, we are concerned with the proper regulatory authority in connection with the production process of a single industry and, to some extent, with the sale of its products, the latter being concerned largely with the use of labels or identification. Nowhere are the impugned statutory regulations or provisions concerned with the control or regulation of the extra-provincial distribution of these products or their movement through any channels of trade. On the contrary, their main purpose is the regulation of the brewing process itself by means of a "legal recipe", as counsel for the appellant put it. Indeed, if the industry is substantially local in character, as seems to be the case from the sparse record before the court (as noted above), the regulations are, in fact, confined to the regulation of a trade within a province.

In the end, the effort of the respondent here is simply to build into these regulations a validity essentially founded upon the embryonic definition of the application of the trade and commerce heading in the *Citizens Insurance* case, supra. That observation and the subsequent references thereto are all predicated upon the requirement that the purported trade and commerce legislation affected industry and commerce at large or in a sweeping, general sense. In the context of the *Food and Drugs Act*, it follows that even if this statute were to cover a substantial portion of Canadian economic activity, one industry or trade at a time, by a varying array of regulations or trade codes applicable to each individual sector, there would not, in the result, be at law a regulation of trade and commerce in the sweeping general sense contemplated in the *Citizens Insurance* case, supra. That, in my view, is the heart and core of the problem confronting the respondent in this appeal. Thus the provisions regulating malt liquors relate either to a single industry or a sector thereof, while other regulations appear to concern themselves in a similar way with other individual industries; the former being condemned by the *Citizens Insurance* case, supra, and the latter does not rescue the malt liquor regulations by reason of the *Board of Commerce* case, supra.

I conclude, therefore, in this part, that the impugned sections as they relate to malt liquors cannot be founded in the trade and commerce head of jurisdiction. [...]

For these reasons, I would therefore answer the following question in the negative:

Is it within the competence of the Parliament of Canada to enact sections 6 and 25(1)(c) of the *Food and Drugs Act*, R.S.C. 1970, c. F-27, and are regulations B.02-130 to R.02-135 inclusive thereunder validly made?

LASKIN C.J.C. (dissenting): — [...] The matter therefore comes down to whether this Court views the federal trade and commerce power as a sufficient support for the legislation and Regulations which are attacked in the present case. I would hold that it does, and, in so doing I would adopt the statement in the *Parsons* case (1881), 7 App. Cas. 96, at 113 which envisages competent federal legislation by way of "general regulation of trade affecting the whole Dominion".

It may be that the present case can be disposed of on the ground taken by my brother Pigeon that the regulations that are attacked amount to no more than labeling provisions. We are not concerned with a marketing situation, and hence this case is distinguishable from cases like the *Natural Products Marketing Act* case, [1937] A.C. 377, and *Shannon v. Lower Mainland Dairy Products Board*, [1938] A.C. 708, or even the *Ontario Marketing* case decided by this Court in [1957] S.C.R. 198. There are, however, other matters that must be brought into account, matters which I think are relevant to the recognition of the federal trade and commerce power as a fully independent source of authority when viewed against the catalogue of provincial powers, especially the power in relation to "property and civil rights in the Province" under s. 92(13) of the *British North America Act*.

In the *Board of Commerce* case, [1922] 1 A.C. 191, at p. 201, the Privy Council indicated that it might be open to Parliament "to call [...] for statistical and other information which may be valuable for guidance in questions affecting Canada as a whole. Such information may be required before any power to regulate trade and commerce can be properly exercised [...]" I do not press any perfect analogy to the prescription of common standards for an article of food which is produced throughout the country and which is also imported from abroad, but it does appear to me that if Parliament can set up standards for required returns for statistical purposes, it should be able to fix standards that are common to all manufacturers of foods, including beer, drugs, cosmetics and therapeutic devices, at least to equalize competitive advantages in the carrying on of businesses concerned with such products. I find some reinforcement in this view of the scope of the federal trade and commerce power in s. 121 of the *British North America Act* which precludes interprovincial tariffs, marking Canada as a whole as an economic union.

The operations of Labatt Breweries and of other brewers of beer extend throughout Canada, and I would not attenuate the federal trade and commerce power any further than has already been manifested in judicial decisions by denying Parliament authority to address itself to uniform prescriptions for the manufacture of food, drugs, cosmetics, therapeutic devices in the way, in the case of beer, of standards for its production and distribution according to various alcoholic strengths under labels appropriate to the governing regulations.

Appeal allowed.

[The dissenting opinions of Pigeon J. (McIntyre J. concurring) and Ritchie J. have been omitted.]

A.G. CAN. V. C.N. TRANSPORT LTD.; A.G. CAN. V. C.P. TRANSPORT CO.
[1983] 2 S.C.R. 206.

[CN Transport and CP Transport were charged with unlawful "conspiracy to prevent or lessen unduly competition" in the interprovincial transportation of general merchandise, contrary to s. 32 of the *Combines Investigation Act*. Section 15(2) of this *Act* grants the authority to prosecute *Combines Investigation Act* violations to the Attorney General of Canada. CN and CP Transports challenged the validity of the legislation on the grounds that it was *ultra vires* the Parliament as legislation in relation to 92(14) of the *Constitution Act, 1867*. The criminal law issue of this case is dealt with in section III.6 "Criminal Law" in this casebook.]

DICKSON J. (concurring in the result): — If the constitutional validity of s. 32(1)(*c*) of the *Combines Investigation Act* depends on a federal head of power other than s. 91(27), then following the majority judgment in *Hauser*, [1979] 1 S.C.R. 984, with regard to this section there can be no doubt that s. 15(2) of the *Combines Investigation Act* and s. 2 of the *Criminal Code* are *intra vires* and the Attorney General of Canada is competent to prefer indictments and to conduct proceedings in respect of alleged violations of the Act. If, on the other hand, the validity of s. 32(1)(*c*) depends solely on the federal criminal law power, then this court will have to deal with the issue of the competing federal and provincial claims for constitutional authority to prosecute criminal cases which the majority decision in *Hauser* left moot. [...]

GENERAL REGULATION OF TRADE AFFECTING THE WHOLE DOMINION

In the present case, [...] even on the most generous definition, s. 32(1)(c) of the *Combines Investigation Act* cannot be seen as a regulation of interprovincial trade and commerce. The appellant Attorney General of Canada concedes that if it is to be justified under s. 91(2) this enactment must fall within what has been called the "second branch" of the *Parsons* classification, namely "the general regulation of trade affecting the whole dominion". Although in *Parsons* this second branch is presented as merely a possibility ("and it may be that they would include [...] "), the existence of a "general trade and commerce" power seems to have been widely assumed in subsequent cases. [...]

If every economic issue that could be characterized as a "question of general interest throughout the Dominion" were to fall under federal competence by virtue of s. 91(2), then the extent of the power would hardly be narrower than it would on a literal reading of the words "regulation of trade and commerce" alone. There is hardly an economic issue which, if only by virtue of its recurrence in locations around the country, could not be characterized as a matter of general interest throughout the Dominion.

In the *Labatt* case ([1980] 1 S.C.R. 914 at 940, 9 B.L.R. 181, 30 N.R. 496), Estey J. states that the criterion of constituting a question of general interest throughout the Dominion is still the correct test in determining whether the second branch of the trade and commerce power applies. I agree with this statement, just as I am of opinion that the long disuse of this second branch does not impugn its constitutional validity. But I am also of the view – as Estey J.'s treatment of the issue in *Labatt* confirms – that the same considerations which led Sir Montague Smith to limit the scope of the words "regulation of trade and commerce" in *Parsons'* case also necessitate a restrictive reading of the Wharton test of "general interest throughout the Dominion." [See *John Deere Plow Co. v. Wharton* (1914), 18 D.L.R. 353.] The question, of course, is how much is to be subtracted from these words, and on what basis?

REGULATING THE CONTRACTS OF A PARTICULAR BUSINESS OR TRADE

Although the Privy Council in *Parsons* was unwilling to consider in detail the boundary between ss. 91(2) and 92(13) it did go as far as holding that "regulation of trade and commerce" could not include "the power to regulate by legislation the contracts of a particular business or trade." [...] [T]he starting point of Duff J.'s reasoning in *Bd. of Commerce [Re Board of Commerce Act, 1919 and Combines and Fair Prices Act, 1919,* [1922] 1 A.C. 191], namely a subtraction from s. 91(2) of what *Parsons* found to be within provincial jurisdiction, has gained general acceptance and is to be found prominently in most cases dealing with s. 91(2) and the general trade and commerce power. [...]

Every general enactment will necessarily have some local impact, and if it is true that an overly literal conception of "general interest" will endanger the very idea of the local, there are equal dangers in swinging the telescope the other way around. The forest is no less a forest for being made up of individual trees. Whatever the constitutional flaws in the *Board of Commerce Act* and *Combines and Fair Prices Act*, they cannot be attributed, as Duff J. seems to contend, to the fact that any individual order made by the board would have its effect on a business or trade in the province. Were that the test then no economic legislation could ever qualify under the general trade and commerce power. Such a conception is merely the obverse of the equally unacceptable proposition that economic legislation qualifies under the general trade and commerce rubric merely because it applies equally and uniformly throughout the country.

The reason why the regulation of a single trade or business in the province cannot be a question of general interest throughout the Dominion, is that it lies at the very heart of the local autonomy envisaged in the *Constitution Act, 1867*. That a federal enactment purports to carry out such regulation in the same way in all the provinces or in association with other regulatory codes dealing with other trades or businesses does not change the fact that what is being created is an exact overlapping and hence a nullification of a jurisdiction conceded to the provinces by the Constitution. A different situation obtains, however, when what is at issue is general legislation aimed at the economy as a single integrated national unit rather than as a collection of separate local enterprises. Such legislation is qualitatively different from anything that could practically or constitutionally be enacted by the individual provinces either separately or in combination. The focus of such legislation is on the general, though its results will obviously be manifested in particular local effects any one of which may touch upon "property and civil rights in the province". Nevertheless, in pith and substance such legislation will be addressed to questions of general interest throughout the Dominion. The line of demarcation is clear between measures validly directed at a general regulation of the national economy and those merely aimed at centralized control over a large number of local economic entities. The regulations in the *Labatt's* case were probably close to the line. It may also well be that, given the state of the economy in 1920 and the actual mechanics of the legislation, the *Board of Commerce Act* and *Combines and Fair Prices Act* amounted simply to an attempt to authorize the issuance of an uncoordinated series of local orders and prohibitions.

In approaching this difficult problem of characterization it is useful to note the remarks of the Chief Justice in *MacDonald v. Vapour Can. Ltd.* (1976), 66 D.L.R. (3d) 1 at 25-26, in which he cites as possible indicia for a valid exercise of the general trade and commerce power the presence of a national regulatory scheme, the oversight of a regulatory agency and a concern with trade in general rather than with an aspect of a particular business. To this list I would add what to my mind would be even stronger indications of valid general regulation of trade and commerce, namely (i) that the provinces jointly or severally would be constitutionally incapable of passing such an enactment and (ii) that failure to include one or more provinces or localities would jeopardize successful operation in other parts of the country.

The above does not purport to be an exhaustive list, nor is the presence of any or all of these indicia necessarily decisive. The proper approach to the characterization is still the one suggested in *Parsons*: a careful case by case assessment. Nevertheless, the presence of such factors does at least make it far more probable that what is being addressed in a federal enactment is genuinely a national economic concern and not just a collection of local ones.

It is with these considerations in mind that I turn to the question of whether s. 32(1)(c) can be said validly to depend on the federal trade and commerce power. [...]

It is obvious at the outset that a constitutionally invalid provision will not be saved by being put into an otherwise valid statute, even if the statute comprises a regulatory scheme under the general trade and commerce branch of s. 91(2). The correct approach, where there is some doubt that the impugned provision has the same constitutional characterization as the Act in which it is found, is to start with the challenged section rather than with a demonstration of the validity of the statute as a whole. I do not think, however, this means that the section in question must be read in isolation. If the claim to constitutional validity is based on the contention that the impugned provision is part of a regulatory scheme it would seem necessary to read it in its context. If it can in fact be seen as part of such a scheme, attention will then shift to the constitutionality of the scheme as a whole. [...]

Having found that s. 32(1)(c) is not an isolated provision, but rather part of a regulatory scheme, it still remains to assess whether this scheme is valid under the second branch of s. 91(2). The fact of forming part of such a scheme is but one indicium of validity and not in itself determinative. A number of cases have found that the scheme embodied by the Act also displays such additional indicia as a national scope, a general application and a concern with the trade as a whole rather than with a single business. [...]

[I]t is still necessary even in the face of all these factors to consider the issue of constitutional balance, and whether a finding of validity under the trade and commerce power might not erode the local autonomy in economic regulation contemplated by the Constitution. [...]

For the reasons cited earlier I would in any event be inclined to reject this contention. To give it heed would amount to a denial of the possibility of a Parliament ever validly exercising its general trade and commerce power, a power which if properly understood and properly constrained does not erode local autonomy but rather complements it. I would also, however, mention an additional factor. A scheme aimed at the regulation of competition is in my view an example of the genre of legislation that could not practically or constitutionally be enacted by a provincial government. Given the free flow of trade across provincial borders guaranteed by s. 121 of the *Constitution Act, 1867*, Canada is, for economic purposes, a single huge marketplace. If competition is to be regulated at all it must be regulated federally. This fact leads to the syllogism cited by Hogg and Grover, "The Constitutionality of the Competition Bill" (1977), 1 Can. Bus. L.J. 197 at 200:

> [R]egulation of the competitive sector of the economy can be effectively accomplished only by federal action. If there is no federal power to enact a competition policy, then Canada cannot have a competition policy. The consequence of a denial of federal constitutional power is, therefore, in practical effect, a gap in the distribution of legislative powers.

All these considerations lead to the conclusion that s. 32(1)(c) is valid federal legislation under s. 91(2) of the *Constitution Act, 1867*, as well as s. 91(27). [...]

AUTHORITY TO PROSECUTE S. 32(1)(C)

The result of holding *s. 32(1)(c)* to be valid under both the criminal law and the trade and commerce power is in my view a finding of concurrent federal and provincial prosecutorial authority. The majority in *Hauser* held that the authority to prefer indictments and conduct prosecutions with reference to legislation other than that enacted under s. 91(27) was validly vested in the Attorney General of Canada. Therefore, insofar as s. 32(1)(c) depends on the trade and commerce power, the federal Attorney General is the proper prosecutor. As to prosecutorial authority by virtue of the characterization of s. 32(1)(c) as criminal law, I am still of the opinion that only the provincial Attorney General can validly prosecute criminal enactments: see my reasons in *R. v. Wetmore Co. Ct. J.*, judgment in which is being delivered concurrently herewith [appeal from *A.G. Can. v. Wetmore Co. Ct. J.*, [1982] 1 W.W.R. 487, 24 C.R. (3d) 244, 32 B.C.L.R. 283, 64 C.C.C. (2d) 25 (*sub nom. Re R. and Kripps Pharmacy Ltd.*), 129 D.L.R. (3d) 566 (B.C. C.A.)]. [...]

In *Hauser* I observed that there is a certain unity and cohesion between the three aspects of law enforcement, investigation, policing and prosecution, which would be imperilled if the investigatory function were discharged at one level of government and the prosecutorial function at the other level. In *Hauser* this reasoning would have worked to the benefit of the provincial position, as I was of opinion that the *Narcotic Control Act* was criminal law. My opinion was then and is now, that under s. 92(141 of the *Constitution Act* the police can investigate criminal activity, and that authority to conduct and oversee criminal prosecutions is an inherent and essential part of such jurisdiction.

[Laskin, C.J. (Ritchie, Estey and McIntyre JJ., concurring) held that the Federal Attorney General is entitled to prosecute even if the *Combines Investigation Act* rests only on the criminal law power, and thus did not address trade and commerce issues. Beetz and Lamer, JJ. held that the *Combines Investigations Act* was validly enacted under the federal trade and commerce power, and therefore its validity did not depend on the criminal law of power, whether or not the Act could also be supported under that power.]

- Research Note -
REGULATORY SCHEMES AND THE TRADE & COMMERCE POWER

It is well-established that there are several indicia for characterizing a matter as a valid exercise of the general trade and commerce power. As Dickson J. noted in *A.G. Canada v. CN Transport Ltd.*, the indicia are:

1. The presence of a national "regulatory scheme"
2. The oversight of a regulatory agency
3. The concern with trade in general, not a particular aspect of a business
4. Whether the provinces jointly or severally would be constitutionally incapable of passing the enactment
5. Whether failure to include one or more provinces would jeopardize successful operation in other parts of Canada.

The constitutional concept of a "valid regulatory scheme" is part of the arsenal of techniques constitutional law utilizes to overcome the difficulties of divided jurisdiction in a federal state. That being said, there has been surprisingly little pronouncement on what constitutes a "regulatory scheme". This is even more surprising when one considers that a "regulatory scheme" is also required in the context of indirect tax (see pp. 635 below). However, by examining the factual context of all of the trade and commerce and taxation cases, it may be seen that certain characteristics are present whenever a regulatory scheme exists.

First, the party being regulated has caused the need for the regulation and receives some benefit from the regulation. In the *Reference Re Agricultural Products Marketing Act* and *Shannon v. Lower Mainland Dairy Products Board* cases, it was the appellants' economic activities that caused chaotic markets. It was also the appellants who benefitted from the introduction of order into these markets. In the tax cases, the appellants do some activity which causes the need for regulation. For example, in *Allard Contractors v. Coquitlam*, (infra p. 660), gravel truck operators caused damage to the municipal roads which required levying a tax on those truck operators.

Second, the challenged statute delineates certain required or prohibited conduct, creates an investigatory procedure supervised by public regulators, and establishes remedial or punitive mechanisms. In *General Motors v. City National Leasing*, the orders at issue prohibited conduct - activities which tended to reduce competition in the marketplace. In the tax cases, businesses are prohibited from operating without a licence, and to obtain a licence one must pay a tax. Where there is a prohibited conduct in a regulatory scheme, there must also be a punitive sanction — either a fine or other sanction. In *Macdonald v. Vapour Canada*, Chief Justice Laskin stated that:

> One looks in vain for any regulatory scheme in s.7 let alone s. 7(e) [of the challenged legislation]. Its enforcement is left to the chance of private redress without public monitoring by the continuing oversight of a regulatory agency which would at least lend some colour to the alleged national or Canada-wide sweep of s.7(e). The provision is not directed to trade but to the ethical conduct of persons engaged in trade or business, and, in my view, such a detached provision cannot survive alone unconnected to a general regulatory scheme to govern trading relations going beyond merely local concern. Even on the footing of being concerned with practices in the context of trade, its private enforcement by civil action gives it a local cast because it is as applicable in its terms to local or intraprovincial competitors as it is to competitors in interprovincial trade.

Third, the major elements of the regulatory scheme should be statutory. A totally discretionary ability to regulate, coupled with an absence of any specific legislation on how to regulate, should not be upheld as a "regulatory scheme". There is no reason to believe that the regulatory scheme must be found within *one* statute: in the tax case *Ontario Home Builders*, the regulatory scheme was found in any provincial legislation from the *Planning Act* to the *Fire Marshall's Act*. Laskin

C.J.C.'s comment above, "such a detached provision cannot survive alone unconnected to a general regulatory scheme" is also indicative of the court's attention to this element.

Finally, as is obvious, the scheme must be a "national" regulatory scheme. In either its design or effect the regulatory scheme should not be limited to one local area. Moreover, the effect of the legislation should be regulating interprovincial trade more than it does intraprovincial trade (see Laskin C.J.C.'s comments above). Presumably ancillary effects on intraprovincial trade would be acceptable.

MACDONALD v. VAPOUR CAN. LTD.
[1977] 2 S.C.R. 134.

LASKIN C.J.C. [Spence, Pigeon, Dickson and Beetz JJ. concurring]: — [T]he main issue involves the question whether [...] relief, under ss. 7(e), 53 and 55 [...] of the *Trade Marks Act*, R.S.C. 1970, c. T-10, is [a remedy] [...] that the Parliament of Canada may prescribe. [...]

The constitutional issue raised in this case, one of high importance as to the scope of federal legislative power, especially as it arises under s. 91(2) of the *British North America Act, 1867*. [...] Proper perspective requires a reference to the whole of s. 7 and, indeed, to the scheme of the *Trade Marks Act* and to some legislative history. I reproduce here ss. 7, 53 and 55 before proceeding to examine their context and the constitutional issue arising upon the whole of the case. They are as follows:

> 7. No person shall
> (*a*) make a false or misleading statement tending to discredit the business, wares or services of a competitor;
> (*b*) direct public attention to his wares, services or business in such a way as to cause or be likely to cause confusion in Canada, at the time he commenced so to direct attention to them, between his wares, services or business and the wares, services or business of another;
> (*c*) pass off other wares or services as and for those ordered or requested;
> (*d*) make use, in association with wares or services, of any description that is false in a material respect and likely to mislead the public as to
> > (i) (the character, quality, quantity or composition,
> > (ii) the geographical origin, or
> > > the mode of the manufacture, production or performance of such wares or services; or
> (*e*) do any other act or adopt any other business practice contrary to honest industrial or commercial usage in Canada.

53. Where it is made to appear to a court of competent jurisdiction that any act has been done contrary to this Act, the court may make any such order as the circumstances require including provision for relief by way of injunction and the recovery of damages or profits, and may give directions with respect to the disposition of any offending wares, packages, labels and advertising material and of any dies used in connection therewith.

56. The Federal Court of Canada has jurisdiction to entertain any action or proceeding for the enforcement of any of the provisions of this Act or of any right or remedy conferred or defined thereby. [...]

The contention of the appellant and of the supporting intervenants, briefly put, was that s. 7(e), if not also the whole of s. 7, was legislation in relation to property and civil rights in the Province or, alternatively, legislation in relation to matters of a local or private nature in the Province, within s. 92(13) or (16) of the *British North America Act, 1867*. The respondent and the Attorney-General for Canada supported s. 7(e) as being (1) legislation in relation to the regulation of trade and commerce within s. 91(2) of that Act; (2) supportable as legislation in implementation of a Canadian international obligation arising out of a treaty or convention, and thus falling within federal power for the peace, order and good government of Canada in relation to a matter not coming within s. 92; and (3) legislation in relation to the criminal law within s. 91(27).

This last-mentioned basis of validity deserves no more than a brief statement of reasons for rejecting it. Assuming that s. 7(e) (as, indeed, the other paragraphs of s. 7) proscribe anti-social business practices, and are thus enforceable under the general criminal sanction of s. 115 of the *Criminal Code* respecting disobedience of a federal statute, the attempt to mount the civil remedy of s. 53 of the *Trade Marks Act* on the back of the *Criminal Code* proves too much, certainly in this case. The principle which would arise from such a result would provide an easy passage to valid federal legislation to provide and govern civil relief in respect of numerous sections of the *Criminal Code* and would, in the light of the wide scope of the federal criminal law power, debilitate provincial legislative authority and the jurisdiction of provincial Courts so as to transform our constitutional arrangements on legislative power beyond recognition. It is surely unnecessary to go into detail on such an extravagant posture. [...]

Over all, whether s. 7(e) be taken alone or, more properly, as part of a limited scheme reflected by s. 7 as a whole, the net result is that the Parliament of Canada has, by statute, either overlaid or extended known civil causes of action, cognizable in the provincial Courts and reflecting issues falling within provincial legislative competence. In the absence of any regulatory administration to oversee the prescriptions of s. 7 (and without coming to any conclusion on whether such an administration would in itself be either sufficient or necessary to effect a change in constitutional result), I cannot find any basis in federal power to sustain the unqualified validity of s. 7 as a whole or s. 7(e) taken alone. It is not a sufficient peg on which to support the legislation that it applies throughout Canada when there is nothing more to give it validity.

The cases to which I have referred indicate some association of s. 7(*a*), (*b*) and (*d*) with federal jurisdiction in relation to patents and copyrights arising under specific heads of legislative power, and with its jurisdiction in relation to trade marks and trade names, said to arise (as will appear later in these reasons) under s. 91(2) of the *British North America Act, 1867*. If, however, this be enough to give a limited valid application to those subparagraphs it would not sweep them into federal jurisdiction in respect of other issues that may arise thereunder not involving matters that are otherwise within exclusive federal authority. Certainly, it would not engage s. 7(*e*) which, as interpreted in the cases which have considered it, does not have any such connection with the enforcement of trade marks or trade names or patent rights or copyright as may be said to exist in s. 7(*a*), (*b*) and (*d*). Even if it be possible to give a limited application to s. 7, in respect of all its subparagraphs, to support existing regulation by the Parliament of Canada in the fields of patents, trade marks, trade names and copyright, the present case falls outside of those fields because it deals with breach of confidence by an employee and appropriation of confidential information.

It was emphasized again and again by counsel for the respondent that s. 7(*e*) deals with predatory practices in competition, in a competitive market, that it postulates two or more aspirants or competitors in business and that it involves misappropriation and a dishonest use, in competition, of information or documents so acquired. This may equally be said of the tort of conversion where it involves persons in business or in competition. The fact that Parliament has hived off a particular form of an existing tort or has enlarged the scope of the liability does not determine constitutionality. The relevant questions here are whether the liability is imposed in connection with an enterprise or an activity, for example, banking or bills of exchange, that is itself expressly within federal legislative power; or, if not, whether the liability is dealt with in such a manner as to bring it within the scope of some head of federal legislative power.

This depends not only on what the liability is, but as well on how the federal enactment deals with its enforcement. What is evident here is that the predatory practices are not under administrative regulation of a competent federally-appointed agency, nor are they even expressly brought under criminal sanction in the statute in which they are prohibited. It is, in my opinion, difficult to conceive them in the wide terms urged upon the Court by the respondent and by the Attorney-General of Canada when they are left to merely private enforcement as a private matter of business injury which may arise, as to all its elements including damage, in a small locality in a Province or within a Province. I do not see any general cast in s. 7(*e*) other than the fact that it is federal legislation and unlimited (as such legislation usually is) in its geographic scope. Indeed, the very basis upon which s. 7(*e*) is analyzed by the respondent, namely, that it postulates two or more competitors in business, drains it, in my opinion, of the generality that would have been present if the legislation had established the same prescriptions to be monitored by a public authority irrespective of any immediate private grievance as to existing or apprehended injury.

The source of authority for s. 7, alleged to be in s. 91(2) of the *British North America Act, 1867*, may now be examined. The reasons for judgment of the Federal Court of Appeal, delivered by Jackett, C.J., are adopted by the respondent and by the Attorney-General of Canada and I turn to them. The initial proposition stated in those reasons as a base for what follows is not one which I can accept. Jackett C.J., says this [9 C.P.R. (2d) 18 at p. 21]:

> The primary question is whether the *Trade Marks Act*, as a whole, is a valid exercise of Parliament's legislative powers. If the answer to that question were in the negative, the further question that would arise is whether s. 7, or s. 7(*e*), is severable from the rest of the statute and, taken by itself, is a valid exercise of Parliament's legislative powers.

No attack has been made on the *Trade Marks Act* as a whole, and the validity of its provisions in so far as they deal with trade marks is not in question. Since s. 7(*e*) is not a trade mark provision, its inclusion in the *Trade Marks Act* does not stamp it with validity merely because that Act in its main provisions is quantitatively unchallenged. I come back to the question whether s. 7, and particularly s. 7(*e*), can stand as part of the scheme of the *Trade Marks Act* and other related federal legislation. If it can stand alone, it needs no other support; if not, it may take on a valid constitutional cast by the context and association in which it is fixed as complementary provision serving to reinforce other admittedly valid provisions.

Having regard to the way in which the issue of validity came to this Court, I think the proper approach is to inquire whether s. 7(*e*), taken alone, can be supported as valid federal legislation, and, if not, whether it can be supported as part of a scheme of legislative control that Parliament may establish. In this connection I would not characterize the *Trade Marks Act* as the Federal Court of Appeal did in associating ss. 7 to 11 of the Act as representing "a set of general rules applicable to all trade and commerce in Canada, including a statutory version of the common law rule against passing off". I have already noted that ss. 8 to 11 belong to trade mark enforcement, and if we are left with s. 7 to represent *general* rules applicable to all trade and commerce in Canada, the generality resides only in the fact that s. 7 has no geographic limitation. This is the beginning of the problem not the end.

[...] I am quite prepared, in considering the scope of federal legislative power in relation to the regulation of trade and commerce, to look at the *Parsons* case in the widest aspects of its pronouncements on what that scope is. The attenuation of this broadly-phrased power cannot be attributed to the *Parsons* case but to a sequential course of decision which, in my view, failed to redeem the promise of what the *Parsons* case said. The *Parsons* case itself, on its facts, may even now be taken to have been correctly decided in so far as it concerned the validity of provincial legislation respecting contracts of insurance in the Province, and the prescription of statutory conditions for policies of fire insurance on property in the Province. [...]

I do not find anything in the case law on s. 91(2) that prevents this Court, even if it would retain a cautious concern for *stare decisis*, from taking the words of the Privy Council in the *Parsons* case, previously quoted, as providing the guide or lead to the issue of validity that arises here. I think the Federal Court of Appeal was correct in doing so, but I do not agree with its use of the *Parsons* criteria to sustain s. 7(*e*). I repeat the relevant sentence in the *Parsons* case [at p. 113 of 7 App. Cas.]:

> [...] the words "regulation of trade and commerce" [...] would include political arrangements in regard to trade requiring the sanction of Parliament, regulation of trade matters of interprovincial concern, and it may be that they would include general regulations of trade affecting the whole dominion.

It is the last-mentioned category that is to be considered here. I take it as it is phrased, or as paraphrased by Duff, C.J.C. in the *Natural Products Marketing Act* reference, [1936] 3 D.L.R. 622 at p. 631, 66 C.C.C. 180, [1936] S.C.R. 398 at p. 412, where he spoke of "general regulations of trade as a whole or regulations of general trade and commerce within the sense of the judgment in *Parsons's* case".

The plain fact is that s. 7(*e*) is not a regulation, nor is it concerned with trade as a whole nor with general trade and commerce. In a loose sense every legal prescription is regulatory, even the prescriptions of the *Criminal Code*, but I do not read s. 91(2) as in itself authorizing federal legislation that merely creates a statutory tort, enforceable by private action, and applicable, as here, to the entire range of business relationships in any activity, whether the activity be itself within or beyond federal legislative authority. If there have been cases which appeared to go too far in diminution of the federal trade and commerce power, an affirmative conclusion here would, in my opinion, go even farther in the opposite direction.

What is evident here is that the Parliament of Canada has simply extended or intensified existing common and civil law delictual liability by statute which at the same time has prescribed the usual civil remedies open to an aggrieved person. The Parliament of Canada can no more acquire legislative jurisdiction by supplementing existing tort liability, cognizable in provincial Courts as reflective of provincial competence, than the provincial Legislatures can acquire legislative jurisdiction by supplementing the federal criminal law: see *Johnson v. A.-G. Alta.*, [1954] 2 D.L.R. 625, 108 C.C.C. 1, [1954] S.C.R. 127.

One looks in vain for any regulatory scheme in s. 7, let alone s. 7(*e*). Its enforcement is left to the chance of private redress without public monitoring by the continuing oversight of a regulatory agency which would at least lend some colour to the alleged national or Canada-wide sweep of s. 7(*e*). The provision is not directed to trade but to the ethical conduct of persons engaged in trade or in business, and, in my view, such a detached provision cannot survive alone unconnected to a general regulatory scheme to govern trading relations going beyond merely local concern. Even on the footing of being concerned with practices in the conduct of trade, its private enforcement by civil action gives it a local cast because it is as applicable in its terms to local or intraprovincial competitors as it is to competitors in inter-provincial trade.

[The opinion of de Grandpré J. (Martland and Judson JJ. concurring) is omitted.]

GENERAL MOTORS OF CANADA LTD. v. CITY NATIONAL LEASING
[1989] 1 S.C.R. 641.

DICKSON C.J. [Beetz, McIntyre, Lamer, La Forest and L'Heureux-Dubé JJ. concurring]: — The principal issue in this appeal is the constitutional validity of s. 31.1 of the *Combines Investigation Act*, R.S.C. 1970, c. C-23. Section 31.1 creates a civil cause of action for certain infractions of the *Combines Investigation Act*. It is this fact which makes the section constitutionally suspect: a civil cause of action is within the domain of the provinces to create. The essential question raised by this appeal is whether s. 31.1 can, nevertheless, be upheld as constitutionally valid by virtue of its relationship with the *Combines Investigation Act*. Answering this question requires addressing two issues: first, is the Act valid under the federal trade and commerce power, expressed in s. 91(2) of the *Constitution Act, 1867*; and second, is s. 31.1 integrated with the Act in such a way that it too is *intra vires* under s. 91(2). [...]

THE GENERAL TRADE AND COMMERCE POWER

[C]ourts have been sensitive to the need to reconcile the general trade and commerce power of the federal government with the provincial power over property and civil rights. Balancing has not been easy. Following the initial articulation of the scope of the general trade and commerce power in *Parsons*, supra, the Privy Council briefly adopted what might be regarded as an overly inclusive interpretation of the power in *John Deere Plow Co. v. Wharton*, [[1915] A.C. 330] before retreating to an overly restrictive stance to its interpretation in the *Board of Commerce* [[1922] 1 A.C. 191] case. In *Wharton*, Viscount Haldane, at p. 340, speaking of federally-incorporated companies, sketched in broad terms the federal power to regulate trade and commerce under the second branch of *Parsons*:

> [...] if it be established that the Dominion Parliament can create such companies, then it becomes a *question of general interest throughout the Dominion* in what fashion they should be permitted to trade. (emphasis added)

In contrast, in the *Board of Commerce* case, the Privy Council rejected the trade and commerce power (without distinguishing between the two branches) as the basis for anti-combines legislation, holding that the trade and commerce power had no independent content and could only be invoked as ancillary to other federal powers. This view of the trade and commerce power was rejected some nine years later by the Privy Council in *Proprietary Articles Trade Association*, supra, in the passage quoted earlier.

With respect, in my view, neither the position articulated in *Wharton* nor that advanced in the *Board of Commerce* case correctly assesses the balance to be struck between s. 91(2) and s. 92(13). *Wharton* is clearly overly expansive, sweeping all general economic issues into the grasp of s. 91(2). On the other hand, the residual interpretation articulated in the *Board of Commerce* case fails to breathe life into the trade and commerce power and fails to recognize that provincial powers are a subtraction from the federal powers. The true balance between property and civil rights and the regulation of trade and commerce must lie somewhere between an all pervasive interpretation of s. 91(2) and an interpretation that renders the general trade and commerce power to all intents vapid and meaningless. *Vapour*

This Court took the first step towards delineating more specific principles of validity for legislation enacted under the general trade and commerce power in *Vapour Canada* [[1977] 2 S.C.R. 134]. [...]

Chief Justice Laskin, speaking for five members of the Court, proposed three hallmarks of validity for legislation under the second branch of the trade and commerce power. First, the impugned legislation must be part of a general regulatory scheme. Second, the scheme must be monitored by the continuing oversight of a regulatory agency. Third, the legislation must be concerned with trade as a whole rather than with a particular industry. Each of these requirements is evidence of a concern that federal authority under the second branch of the trade and commerce power does not encroach on provincial jurisdiction. By limiting the means which federal legislators may employ to that of a regulatory scheme overseen by a regulatory agency, and by limiting the object of federal legislation to trade as a whole, these requirements attempt to maintain a delicate balance between federal and provincial power.

[...] Three members of the Court affirmed the *Vapour Canada* criteria in *Canadian National Transportation*. [...] In reaching the conclusion that s. 32(1)(c) of the *Combines Investigation Act* was within the scope of the general trade and commerce power, and writing for the minority of the Court, I adopted Laskin C.J.'s three criteria in *Vapour Canada*, supra, but added two factors that I considered indicia of the valid exercise of the general trade and commerce power; (i) the legislation should be of a nature that the provinces jointly or severally would be constitutionally incapable of enacting; and (ii) the failure to include one or more provinces or localities in a legislative scheme would jeopardize the successful operation of the scheme in other parts of the country. These two requirements, like Laskin C.J.'s three criteria, serve to ensure that federal legislation does not upset the balance of power between federal and provincial governments. In total, the five factors provide a preliminary check-list of characteristics, the presence of which in legislation is an indication of validity under the trade and commerce power. These indicia do not, however, represent an exhaustive list of traits that will tend to characterize general trade and commerce legislation. Nor is the presence or absence of any of these five criteria necessarily determinative. [...]

On any occasion where the general trade and commerce power is advanced as a ground of constitutional validity, a careful case by case analysis remains appropriate. The five factors articulated in *Canadian National Transportation* merely represent a principled way to begin the difficult task of distinguishing between matters relating to trade and commerce and those of a more local nature. [...]

APPROACH TO DETERMINING CONSTITUTIONALITY

[...] In my view, in circumstances such as exist in the case at bar, it will normally be necessary to consider both the impugned provision and the Act as a whole (or a significant part of it) when undertaking a constitutional analysis. This approach coheres with that undertaken in *Canadian National Transportation*, supra, and *Vapour Canada*, supra. The first step should be to consider whether and to what extent the impugned provision can be characterized as intruding into provincial powers. If it cannot be characterized as intruding at all, i.e., if in its pith and substance the provision is federal law, and if the act to which it is attached is constitutionally valid (or if the provision is severable or if it is attached to a severable and constitutionally valid part of the act) then the investigation need go no further. In that situation both the provision and the act are constitutionally unimpeachable. If, as may occur in some instances, the impugned provision is found to be constitutionally unimpeachable while the act containing it is not, then the act must be assessed on its own. In these instances, it is clear that the claim of invalidity should originally have been made against the act and not against the particular provision. In most cases like the present, however, it will be concluded that the impugned provision can be characterized, *prima facie*, as intruding to some extent on provincial powers: the question is to what extent. I emphasize that in answering this initial question the court is considering the provision on its own and not assessing the act; thus the answer it reaches does not provide a conclusion with respect to the ultimate constitutional validity of the provision. The purpose is merely to ascertain the degree to which the provision could be said to intrude on provincial powers, so that this intrusion can be weighed in light of the possible justification for the section.

Such a justification will result from the impugned provision's relationship to valid legislation. Thus the next step in the process is to ascertain the existence of valid legislation. In considering cases argued under the general trade and commerce power, such as the present, this step involves ascertaining whether the act, or a severable part of the act which includes the impugned provision, contains a regulatory scheme. The presence of a scheme of legislation is one of the most basic characteristics, although not a *sine qua non*, of valid trade and commerce legislation. Most provisions upheld under the second branch of s. 91(2) will be connected to a regulatory scheme. In cases where a regulatory scheme is not found the court will then have to consider whether the legislation to which the provision is attached can nonetheless be supported by virtue of the existence of the other requirements for a valid exercise of the general trade and commerce power.

A regulatory scheme may be found in only a part of the act in question, if that part can stand alone, or it may be found in the entire act. The portion of the statute necessary to establish the existence of a regulatory scheme will not always be easy to discern. In those instances where a challenged provision, taken alone, comprehends a complete regulatory mechanism, the provision itself constitutes the appropriate starting point. In other cases, it will be necessary to examine the entire statute before a regulatory scheme may be identified. Once the presence of a regulatory scheme has been shown it will be necessary, using the factors outlined in *Vapour Canada*, supra and *Canadian National Transportation* (cites omitted), to determine its constitutional validity. Only after this has been done should the court turn to more careful consideration of the relationship between the particular impugned provision and the scheme.

The final question is whether the provision can be constitutionally justified by reason of its connection with valid legislation. As Laskin C.J. remarked in *Vapour Canada*, supra, inclusion of an invalid provision in a valid statute does not necessarily stamp the provision with validity. Here the court must focus on the relationship between the valid legislation and the impugned provision. Answering the question first requires deciding what test of "fit" is appropriate for such a determination. By "fit" I refer to how well the provision is integrated into the scheme of the legislation and how important it is for the efficacy of the legislation. The same test will not be appropriate in all circumstances. In arriving at the correct standard the court must consider the degree to which the provision intrudes on provincial powers. The case law, to which I turn below, shows that in certain circumstances a stricter requirement is in order, while in others, a looser test is acceptable. For example, if the impugned provision only encroaches marginally on provincial powers, then a "functional" relationship may be sufficient to justify the provision. Alternatively, if the impugned provision is highly intrusive *vis-à-vis* provincial powers then a stricter test is appropriate. A careful case by case assessment of the proper test is the best approach.

In determining the proper test it should be remembered that in a federal system it is inevitable that, in pursuing valid objectives, the legislation of each level of government will impact occasionally on the sphere of power of the other level of government; overlap of legislation is to be expected and accommodated in a federal state. Thus a certain degree of judicial restraint in proposing strict tests which will result in striking down such legislation is appropriate.

[...] In the present appeal, the appellant focuses its attack on a particular section of the Act. The issue is not whether the Act as a whole is rendered *ultra vires* because it reaches too far, but whether a particular provision is sufficiently integrated into the Act to sustain its constitutionality. In numerous cases courts have considered the nature of the relationship which is required, between a provision which encroaches on provincial jurisdiction and a valid statute, for the provision to be upheld. In different contexts courts have set down slightly different requirements, viz: "rational and functional connection" in *Papp v. Papp*, [1970] 1 O.R. 331, *R. v. Zelensky*, [1978] 2 S.C.R. 940 and *Multiple Access Ltd. v. McCutcheon*, [1982] 2 S.C.R. 161; "ancillary", "necessarily incidental" and "truly necessary" in the *Regional Municipality of Peel v. MacKenzie*, supra; "intimate connection" "an integral part" and "necessarily incidental" in *Northern Telecom Ltd. v. Communications Workers of Canada*, [1980] 1 S.C.R. 115; "integral part" in *Clark v. Canadian National Railway Co.*, [1988] 2 S.C.R. 680; "a valid constitutional cast by the context and association in which it is fixed as a complementary provision" in *Vapour Canada*, supra; and "truly necessary" in *R. v. Thomas Fuller Construction Co. (1958) Ltd.*, [1980] S.C.R. 695. I believe the approach I have outlined is consistent with the results of this jurisprudence. These cases are best understood as setting out the proper test for the particular context in issue, rather than attempting to articulate a test of general application with reference to all contexts. Thus the tests they set out are not identical. As the seriousness of the encroachment on provincial powers varies, so does the test required to ensure that an appropriate constitutional balance is maintained. In surveying past jurisprudence it is to be expected that some example of patterns between the appropriate test of fit, and the head of power under which the federal legislation is valid, will be found. Such patterns exist not only because of a possible degree of similarity between the federal legislation which falls under any one head of power, but also for the reason that certain federal heads of power, for example, s. 92(10), are narrow and distinct powers which relate to particular works and undertakings and are thus quite susceptible to having provisions "tacked-on" to legislation which is validated under them, while other federal heads of power, for example, trade and commerce, are broad and therefore less likely to give rise to highly intrusive provisions.

The steps in the analysis may be summarized as follows: First, the court must determine whether the impugned provision can be viewed as intruding on provincial powers, and if so to what extent (if it does not intrude, then the only possible issue is the validity of the act). Second, the court must establish whether the act (or a severable part of it) is valid; in cases under the second branch of s. 91(2) this will normally involve finding the presence of a regulatory scheme and then ascertaining whether that scheme meets the requirements articulated in *Vapour Canada,* supra, and in *Canadian National Transportation* (cites omitted). If the scheme is not valid, that is the end of the inquiry. If the scheme of regulation is declared valid, the Court must then determine whether the impugned provision is sufficiently integrated with the scheme that it can be upheld by virtue of that relationship. This requires considering the seriousness of the encroachment on provincial powers, in order to decide on the proper standard for such a relationship. If the provision passes this integration test, it is *intra vires* Parliament as an exercise of the general trade and commerce power. If the provision is not sufficiently integrated into the scheme of regulation, it cannot be sustained under the second branch of s. 91(2). I note that in certain cases it may be possible to dispense with some of the aforementioned steps if a clear answer to one of them will be dispositive of the issue. For example, if the provision in question has no relation to the regulatory scheme then the question of its validity may be quickly answered on that ground alone. The approach taken in a number of past cases is more easily understood if this possibility is recognized.

DOES S. 31.1 ENCROACH ON PROVINCIAL POWERS?

[...] As s. 31.1 creates a civil right of action it is not difficult to conclude that the provision does, on its face, appear to encroach on provincial power to some extent. The creation of civil actions is generally a matter within provincial jurisdiction under s. 92(13) of the *Constitution Act, 1867*. This provincial power over civil rights is a significant power and one that is not lightly encroached upon. In assessing the seriousness of this encroachment, however, three facts must be taken into consideration. The first is that s. 31.1 is only a remedial provision; its purpose is to help enforce the substantive aspects of the Act, but it is not in itself a substantive part of the Act. By their nature, remedial provisions are typically less intrusive *vis-à-vis* provincial powers. The second important fact is the limited scope of the action. Section 31.1 does not create a general cause of action; its application is carefully limited by the provisions of the Act. The third relevant fact is that it is well-established that the federal government is not constitutionally precluded from creating rights of civil action where such measures may be shown to be warranted. This Court has sustained federally-created civil actions in a variety of contexts. [...]

In sum, the impugned provision encroaches on an important provincial power; however, the provision is a remedial one; federal encroachment in this manner is not unprecedented and, in this case; encroachment has been limited by the restrictions of the Act.

THE PRESENCE OF A REGULATORY SCHEME IN THE COMBINES INVESTIGATION ACT

The second step in determining the validity of s. 31.1 is to establish whether the Act contains a regulatory scheme. The presence of a well-orchestrated scheme of economic regulation is immediately apparent on examination of the *Combines Investigation Act*. The existence of a regulatory scheme is in evidence throughout the entire Act. [...]

[A discussion of the contents of the *Combines Investigation Act* has been omitted]

From this overview of the *Combines Investigation Act* I have no difficulty in concluding that the Act as a whole embodies a complex scheme of economic regulation. The purpose of the Act is to eliminate activities that reduce competition in the market-place. The entire Act is geared to achieving this objective. The Act identifies and defines anti-competitive conduct. It establishes an investigatory mechanism for revealing prohibited activities and provides an extensive range of criminal and administrative redress against companies engaging in behaviour that tends to reduce competition. In my view, these three components, elucidation of prohibited conduct, creation of an investigatory procedure, and the establishment of a remedial mechanism, constitute a well-integrated scheme of regulation designed to discourage forms of commercial behaviour viewed as detrimental to Canada and the Canadian economy.

THE VALIDITY OF THE REGULATORY SCHEME

Having discerned the presence of a regulatory scheme in the *Combines Investigation Act*, it is necessary to consider the validity of the scheme under the general trade and commerce power in light of the criteria established in *Canadian National Transportation* (cites omitted). Four criteria remain to be examined: (1) whether the regulatory scheme operates under the oversight of an agency, (2) whether the Act is concerned with trade in general, (3) whether the provinces would be constitutionally capable of enacting combines legislation, and finally, (4) whether the failure to include one or more provinces or localities would jeopardize the successful operation of the *Combines Investigation Act*.

The foregoing review of the *Combines Investigation Act* leaves no doubt that the scheme regulating anti-competitive activities operates under the watchful gaze of a regulatory agency. The regulatory mechanism is carefully controlled by the Director of Investigation and Research and to a lesser degree by the Restrictive Trade Practices Commission. [...]

I am also of the view that the *Combines Investigation Act* meets the remaining three indicia of *Canadian National Transportation*. These criteria share a common theme; all three are indications that the scheme of regulation is national in scope and that local regulation would be inadequate. The Act is quite clearly concerned with the regulation of trade in general, rather than with the regulation of a particular industry or commodity. [...]

As I noted earlier, the purpose of the Act is to ensure the existence of a healthy level of competition in the Canadian economy. The deleterious effects of anti-competitive practices transcend provincial boundaries. Competition is not an issue of purely local concern but one of crucial importance for the national economy. [...]

It is evident [...] that competition cannot be effectively regulated unless it is regulated nationally. As I have said, in my view combines legislation fulfills the three indicia of national scope as described in *Canadian National Transportation*: it is legislation "aimed at the economy as a single integrated national unit rather than as a collection of separate local enterprises", it is legislation "that the provinces jointly or severally would be constitutionally incapable of passing" and "failure to include one or more provinces or localities would jeopardize successful operation" of the legislation "in other parts of the country".

The above arguments also answer the claim of the Attorney General of Quebec that the regulation of competition does not fall within federal jurisdiction in its intraprovincial dimension and thus the Act should be read down so that s. 31.1 only applies to interprovincial trade. Quebec relies on two points to support its position. First in the *Interim Report on Competition Policy* of the Canadian Economic Council, the Report which the federal government relies on to show that competition is exclusively federal, there is a passage at p. 108 that recognizes that the provinces have an important role to play in local competition laws:

> We would like to make it emphatically clear that in recommending such a test we intend no implication whatever that the federal government should seek exclusive occupancy of the field of competition policy under civil law, or that only the federal government is competent to manage competition policy in Canada. On the contrary, while it is clear that a considerable proportion of Canadian economic activity crosses provincial and international boundaries, and would be impossible to subject effectively to any provincial competition policy, we believe that the provinces could play a most useful role in respect of other lines of activity under their existing constitutional powers. Their assumption of such a role would be a most welcome development. If the recommendations of this

Report are largely framed in terms of federal legislation, this is because a federal presence is clearly indispensable and the federal government has hitherto been, to all intents and purposes, the sole active occupant of the field. But the door to provincial participation should be left widely ajar. Such activity by the provinces would be in many ways a natural extension of their already considerable activity in the field of consumer protection.

The second point is that provincial law, both *Civil Code* and common law, already provides some remedies for unfair competition, as in the *Quebec Ready Mix* case where the suit was brought under art. 1053 of the *Civil Code*, as well as s. 31.1 of the *Combines Investigation Act*. [...]

The arguments made above offer a response to these points. They make it clear that not only is the Act meant to cover intraprovincial trade, but that it must do so if it is to be effective. Because regulation of competition is so clearly of national interest and because competition cannot be successfully regulated by federal legislation which is restricted to interprovincial trade, the Quebec argument must fail. I also note that, contrary to the view of Marceau J. in the Trial Division of the Federal Court in *Quebec Ready Mix*, supra, at p. 208, that the presence of an already existing action in Quebec law does not argue for invalidating federal legislation. I would repeat what I said at p. 175 of *Multiple Access*, supra, (which words were also quoted by MacGuigan J. in the Court of Appeal's judgement in *Attorney General of Canada v. Quebec Ready Mix*, supra, at p. 78): "The validity of the federal legislation must be determined without heed to the [...] [provincial] legislation."

On the other hand, competition is not a single matter, any more than inflation or pollution. The provinces too, may deal with competition in the exercise of their legislative powers in such fields as consumer protection, labour relations, marketing and the like. The point is, however, that Parliament also has the constitutional power to regulate intraprovincial aspects of competition.

In sum, the *Combines Investigation Act* is a complex scheme of competition regulation aimed at improving the economic welfare of the nation as a whole. It operates under a regulatory agency. It is designed to control an aspect of the economy that must be regulated nationally if it is to be successfully regulated at all. [...]

I am therefore of the view that the *Combines Investigation Act* as a whole is *intra vires* Parliament as legislation in relation to general trade and commerce. [...]

THE VALIDITY OF S. 31.1 OF THE COMBINES INVESTIGATION ACT

[...] As I have already noted, mere inclusion in a valid legislative scheme does not *ipso facto* confer constitutional validity upon a particular provision. The provision must be sufficiently related to that scheme for it to be constitutionally justified. The degree of relationship that is required is a function of the extent of the provision's intrusion into provincial powers. I have already discussed this issue and concluded that s. 31.1 intrudes, though in a limited way, on the important provincial power over civil rights. In this light, I do not think that a strict test, such as "truly necessary" or "integral", is appropriate. On the other hand, it is not enough that the section be merely "tacked on" to admittedly valid legislation. The correct approach in this case is to ask whether the provision is functionally related to the general objective of the legislation, and to the structure and the content of the scheme. A similar test has been applied in other cases, as I have noted, and I think it is also the proper test for the circumstances of this appeal. [...]

I am of the opinion that the necessary link between s. 31.1 and the Act exists. Section 31.1 is an integral, well-conceived component of the economic regulation strategy found in the *Combines Investigation Act*. Even if a much stricter test of fit were applied – for instance, one of "necessarily incidental" – section 31.1 would still pass the test. Under the test of "functionally related" the section is clearly valid.

Section 31.1 is one of the arsenal of remedies created by the Act to discourage anti-competitive practices. Section 31.1 simply serves to reinforce other sanctions of the Act. The other remedial responses include orders of the Restrictive Trade Practices Commission (Part IV. 1), interim injunctions (Part IV), and criminal sanctions (Part V). Like the other remedies, s. 31.1 is intimately linked to the *Combines Investigation Act*. It takes on meaning only by reference to other provisions of the Act and has no independent content. As a result, the section is carefully bounded by the parameters of the *Combines Investigation Act*. It provides a private remedy only for particular violations of the Act and does not create a private right of action at large.

Section 31.1 of the *Combines Investigation Act* is also fundamentally integrated into the purpose and underlying philosophy of the *Combines Investigation Act*. There is a close congruence between the goal of enhancing healthy competition in the economy and s. 31.1 which creates a private remedy dependent for its effectiveness on individual initiative. The very exercise of the remedy in s. 31.1 by a company against a competitor whose behaviour has transgressed the code of conduct established by the Act may be said to reflect and promote the spirit of competition informing the *Combines Investigation Act*. In my view, the intimate tie between the purpose of the Act and a privately initiated and privately conducted enforcement mechanism is a strong indication that s. 31.1 is enmeshed in the fabric in the Act.

It is important to note that s. 31.1 does not create a general action for damages. [...] It seems to me that s. 31.1 is fully integrated into the Act, indeed, it is a core provision of the very pith and substance of the Act. As the Attorney General of Canada submits, the civil action for damages provided by s. 31.1 for an occurrence of the anti-competitive practices set out in s. 34(1)(*a*) is clearly as much a part of the legislative scheme regulating competition throughout Canada as is the criminal action for fines and imprisonment or the administrative action involving an inquiry or the reduction of customs duties. Together or apart, the civil, administrative, and criminal actions provide a deterrent against the breach of the competitive policies set out in the Act. In this respect s. 31.1 is part of a legislative scheme intended to create "a more complete and more effective system of enforcement in which public and private initiative can both operate to motivate and effectuate compliance." (per MacGuigan J. at p. 77 in *Quebec Ready Mix*, supra.)

[...] For all of the foregoing reasons I am of the view that s. 31.1 is *intra vires* Parliament by virtue of its relationship to the scheme of economic regulation found in the *Combines Investigation Act*. [...]

KIRKBI AG v. RITVIK HOLDINGS INC.
[2005] 3 S.C.R. 302.

The judgment of the Court was delivered by

LeBEL J.:—

¶ 1 For many years, Kirkbi AG ("Kirkbi") has been a well-known and successful manufacturer of construction sets for children, and at times, for their parents too....[I]t is engaged in a long-running dispute with the respondent ... "Ritvik", a Canadian toy manufacturer. After the expiry of the last LEGO patents in Canada, the respondent began manufacturing and selling similar bricks, using the same locking method.

¶ 2 Kirkbi is now relying on an unregistered trade-mark, the "LEGO indicia", which consists of the well-known geometrical pattern of raised studs on the top of the bricks as the basis for a claim of passing off under s. 7(b) of the Trade-marks Act, R.S.C. 1985, c. T-13. Kirkbi seeks to prevent Ritvik from marketing its competing products without a proper disclaimer that its building blocks are not LEGO bricks and are not supplied by Kirkbi. Absent such a warning to consumers, the appellant argues, confusion arises and there are grounds for a passing-off action under s. 7(b). [...]

¶ 8 Ritvik...denied that s. 7(b) of the *Trade-marks Act* had been breached and that the tort of passing off had been made out. [...] [and] raised the constitutionality of s. 7(b) of the *Trade-marks Act*. [...] because it is not linked or connected in any way to the trade-mark registration scheme in the Act.

[...]

(1) Trade and Commerce

¶ 15 The grant of legislative authority to the Parliament of Canada listed in s. 91 of the Constitution Act, 1867 does not specify that trade-marks are a component of the federal government's power to legislate. Patents and copyrights are explicitly allocated to federal legislative power (s. 91(22) and (23)). Pursuant to s. 91(2), the federal government has exclusive jurisdiction in relation to trade and commerce. In *Citizens Insurance Co. of Canada v. Parsons*, the Judicial Committee of the Privy Council distinguished two branches of federal power under s. 91(2): (1) the power over international and interprovincial trade and commerce, and (2) the power over general trade and commerce affecting Canada as a whole ("general trade and commerce"). This interpretation of s. 91(2), which limits the scope of the federal trade and commerce power to these two branches, is intended to ensure a proper constitutional balance between the otherwise overlapping federal power over trade and commerce (s. 91(2)) and the provincial power over property and civil rights in the province (s. 92(13)) [...]

¶ 16 The "general trade and commerce" category requires an assessment of the relative importance of an activity to the national economy as well as an inquiry into whether an activity should be regulated by Parliament as opposed to the provinces. To determine whether a particular issue requires national rather than local regulation, this Court has set out five criteria to be considered. These criteria are integrated into an assessment of whether federal legislation can be supported on the basis of Parliament's authority over general trade and commerce. They reflect principles which help distinguish the federal trade and commerce power from the provincial property and civil rights power. In two comprehensive decisions dealing with the second branch of s. 91(2) (*Attorney General of Canada v. Canadian National Transportation, Ltd.; General Motors of Canada Ltd. v. City National Leasing*, Dickson C.J. adopted and extended the three indicia initially set out by Laskin C.J. in *MacDonald v. Vapor Canada Ltd.*. These requirements "serve to ensure that federal legislation does not upset the balance of power between federal and provincial governments" (*City National Leasing*, at p. 662).

¶ 17 The jurisprudence of our Court now recognizes that the following factors are hallmarks of a valid exercise of Parliament's general trade and commerce power: (i) the impugned legislation must be part of a regulatory scheme; (ii) the scheme must be monitored by the continuing oversight of a regulatory agency; (iii) the legislation must be concerned with trade as a whole rather than with a particular industry; (iv) the legislation should be of a nature that provinces jointly or severally would be constitutionally incapable of enacting; and (v) the failure to include one or more provinces or localities in a legislative scheme would jeopardize the successful operation of the scheme in other parts of the country (*City National Leasing*, at pp. 662-63). These factors are not exhaustive and, to be valid, it is not necessary for federal legislation to satisfy all five criteria:

> In total, the five factors provide a preliminary check-list of characteristics, the presence of which in legislation is an indication of validity under the trade and commerce power. These indicia do not, however, represent an exhaustive list of traits that will tend to characterize general trade and commerce legislation. Nor is the presence or absence of any of these five criteria necessarily determinative. As noted in *Canadian National Transportation*, supra, at p. 268:
>
>> The above does not purport to be an exhaustive list, nor is the presence of any or all of these indicia necessarily decisive. The proper approach to the characterization is still the one suggested in Parsons, a careful case by case assessment. Nevertheless, the presence of such factors does at least make it far more probable that what is

> being addressed in a federal enactment is genuinely a national economic concern and not just a collection of local ones.
>
> On any occasion where the general trade and commerce power is advanced as a ground of constitutional validity, a careful case by case analysis remains appropriate. The five factors articulated in *Canadian National Transportation* merely represent a principled way to begin the difficult task of distinguishing between matters relating to trade and commerce and those of a more local nature.
>
> (*City National Leasing*, at pp. 662-63) [...]

¶ 19 The constitutionality of specific provisions of the *Trade-marks Act* has been challenged but the validity of the Act as a whole has never been conclusively determined. The courts have implicitly recognized the validity of this federal legislation in several decisions ...The constitutionality of the *Trade-marks Act* as a whole is not challenged on this appeal.

(2) Determining the Constitutionality of Section 7(b): the Test to be Applied

¶ 20 In *City National Leasing*, Dickson C.J. set out the proper framework for analysis to determine the characterization of an impugned provision for constitutional purposes. He stressed that the mere fact that a provision codifies a civil cause of action does not necessarily make it ultra vires the federal government. Although the creation of civil causes of action is generally a matter of property or civil rights in the province, a finding that a provision standing alone, in its pith and substance, intrudes on provincial powers does not determine its ultimate constitutional validity. At the same time, a provision will not be valid merely because the main provisions of an Act are valid. It is necessary to consider both the impugned provision and the Act as a whole when undertaking constitutional analysis. The nature of the relationship between a provision and the statute determines the extent to which the provision is integrated into otherwise valid legislation. If the legislation is valid and the provision is sufficiently integrated within the scheme, it can be upheld by virtue of that relationship: a provision may take on a valid constitutional cast by the context and association in which it is fixed as complementary provision serving to reinforce other admittedly valid provisions (*Vapor Canada*, at pp. 158-59, per Laskin C.J.).

¶ 21 The three-part test for determining whether the impugned provision is within the constitutional powers of the enacting legislature was restated by this Court in *Kitkatla Band v. British Columbia (Minister of Small Business, Tourism and Culture)*at para. 58, here paraphrased to reflect the facts of this case:

> 1. Does the impugned provision intrude into a provincial head of power, and to what extent?

2. If the impugned provision intrudes into a provincial head of power, is it nevertheless part of a valid federal legislative scheme?

3. If the impugned provision is part of a valid federal scheme, is it sufficiently integrated with that scheme?

(3) Application to the Facts of this Case

¶ 22 S. 7 of the *Trade-marks Act* [provides]:

7. No person shall...

(b) direct public attention to his wares, services or business in such a way as to cause or be likely to cause confusion in Canada, at the time he commenced so to direct attention to them, between his wares, services or business and the wares, services or business of another...

(a) *Characterization of the Impugned Provision: Does Section 7(b) Encroach on Provincial Powers?*

¶ 23 The first stage of the analysis requires a characterization of the impugned provision in isolation from the rest of the statute. We look to its purpose and its effect to determine whether the provision encroaches on provincial powers, and if so, to what extent ... Section 7(b) creates a civil cause of action that essentially codifies the common law tort of passing off ... Standing alone it appears to encroach on provincial power, namely property and civil rights in the province (s. 92(13)). As Dickson C.J. noted in *City National Leasing*: "This provincial power over civil rights is a significant power and one that is not lightly encroached upon" (pp. 672-73). As explained above, if s. 7(b) is sufficiently integrated into the scheme of the *Trade-marks Act* as a whole, then it will nonetheless be intra vires Parliament.

¶ 24 In *City National Leasing*, this Court found that the intrusion of s. 31.1 of the *Combines Investigation Act*, R.S.C. 1970, c. C-23, into provincial jurisdiction was minimal. In coming to this conclusion Dickson C.J. highlighted the following three factors: (i) the provision was remedial and was not in itself a substantive part of the Act; the provision did not create a general cause of action; (ii) its application was limited by the provisions of the Act; and (iii) Parliament was not constitutionally precluded from creating rights of civil action where such measures are shown to be warranted (p. 673).

¶ 25 These factors apply equally to s. 7(b) of the *Trade-marks Act*. First, s. 7(b) is remedial; its purpose is to enforce the substantive aspects of the *Trade-marks Act* relating to unregistered trade-marks [...]

¶ 26 Second, the passing-off action protects unregistered trade-marks and goodwill enjoyed by the trade-marks. Section 7(b) is therefore limited by the provisions of the *Trade-marks Act*: it does not expand the federal jurisdiction in relation to trade-marks and trade-names but merely rounds out an otherwise incomplete trade-mark scheme ... Unlike s. 7(e), which was found to be *ultra vires*

Parliament because it did not have any connection with the enforcement of trade-marks or trade-names ... and was significantly broader in application, the creation of a statutory action for passing off in s. 7(b) is limited in its application.

¶ 27 ... Not only has this Court sustained federally created civil causes of action in a number of cases, but the test developed by this Court in *City National Leasing* and in *Kitkatla* (outlined above) makes clear that civil causes of action are *intra vires* Parliament if sufficiently integrated into valid federal legislation. In sum, although the impugned provision encroaches on an important provincial power, the intrusion is minimal. [...]

(b) *The Validity of the Federal Trade-marks Act*

¶ 28 In the second stage of the analysis, the Court must determine whether the *Trade-marks Act* is a valid exercise of Parliament's general trade and commerce power. The analysis is guided by the five indicia of validity set out above. In *Asbjorn Horgard A/S*, MacGuigan J.A. of the Federal Court of Appeal noted that:

> All of the criteria of Chief Justice Dickson are verified in the Act: a national regulatory scheme, the oversight of the Registrar of Trade Marks, a concern with trade in general rather than with an aspect of a particular business, the incapability of the provinces to establish such a scheme and the necessity for national coverage. [p. 559]

The parties do not dispute Parliament's constitutional power to regulate registered trade-marks. Rather, it is Parliament's right to create a civil remedy in relation to an unregistered trade-mark that is in issue. The respondent's position is that the only regulatory scheme in the *Trade-marks Act* is the scheme governing registered trade-marks. In my view this is an incorrect characterization of the Act. The *Trade-marks Act* establishes a regulatory scheme for both registered and unregistered trade-marks.

¶ 29 The protection of unregistered trade-marks is integral to the legitimacy, legal standards and efficacy of registered trade-marks. The *Trade-marks Act* is clearly concerned with trade as a whole, as opposed to within a particular industry. There is no question that trade-marks apply across and between industries in different provinces. Divided provincial and federal jurisdiction could mean that the provincial law could be changed by each provincial legislature. This could result in unregistered trade-marks that were more strongly protected than registered trade-marks, undermining the efficacy and integrity of the federal Parliament's *Trade-marks Act*. The lack of a civil remedy integrated into the scheme of the Act, applicable to all marks, registered or unregistered, might also lead to duplicative or conflicting and hence inefficient enforcement procedures. [...]

¶ 31 The scheme set out in the *Trade-marks Act* regulates both registered and unregistered trade-marks. It regulates the adoption, use, transfer, and enforcement of rights in respect of all trade-marks. If trade-marks are intended to protect the goodwill or reputation associated with a particular business and to prevent confusion in the marketplace, then a comprehensive scheme dealing with both registered and unregistered trade-marks is necessary to ensure adequate protection. The inclusion of unregistered trade-marks in the regulatory scheme is necessary to ensure the protection of all trade-marks. The *Trade-marks Act* is more than simply a system of registration.

(c) *The Extent of Integration*

¶ 32 The final step in the analysis is to determine whether the provision is sufficiently integrated into the otherwise valid statute. The inquiry has two parts. First, it is necessary to determine the appropriate test of "fit", namely "how well the provision is integrated into the scheme of the legislation and how important it is for the efficacy of the legislation" (*City National Leasing*, at p. 668). Once the correct standard is determined, the test is applied on a case-by-case basis. If the provision passes this integration test, it is *intra vires* Parliament as an exercise of the general trade and commerce power. If the provision is not sufficiently integrated into the scheme of regulation, it cannot be sustained under the second branch of s. 91(2). To determine the degree of integration required, it is necessary to consider the extent to which the provision encroaches on provincial powers: "The degree of relationship that is required is a function of the extent of the provision's intrusion into provincial powers" (*City National Leasing*, at p. 683). If the encroachment is minimal, then a "functional relationship" is sufficient to sustain the constitutionality of the provision (p. 669). If the provision is highly intrusive, a stricter test is applied: the provision must be "truly necessary" or "integral" to the federal scheme (pp. 669 and 683). Consideration of the seriousness of the encroachment on provincial powers and of the proper standard for the relationship between a legislative provision and a valid federal scheme ensures that the balance of constitutional powers is maintained and focuses the analysis on the "pith and substance" of the provision.

¶ 33 As outlined above, s. 7(b) of the Act only minimally intrudes into provincial jurisdiction over property and civil rights. It is a remedial provision limited to trade-marks as defined in the Act (ss. 2 and 6). As this Court observed in *Vapor Canada* and the Federal Court of Appeal held in *Asbjorn Hogard A/S*, s. 7(b) "rounds out" the federal trade-marks scheme. In this regard s. 7(b) is, in its pith and substance, directly connected to the enforcement of trade-marks and trade-names in Canada because it is directed to avoiding confusion through use of trade-marks.

¶ 34 In *Vapor Canada*, this Court struck down s. 7(e) of the *Trade-marks Act* on the ground that it was unrelated to trade or to trade-marks, or other forms of intellectual property subject to federal legislative authority. Laskin C.J. concluded that s. 7(e) "is not directed to trade but to the ethical conduct of persons engaged in trade or in business, and ... such a detached provision cannot survive alone unconnected to a general regulatory scheme" (p. 165). [...]

¶ 35 The respondent submits that the civil action in s. 7(b) has no functional connection to the registered trade-mark scheme in the *Trade-marks Act*. Having concluded that the Act creates a scheme regulating both registered and unregistered trade-marks, the functional relation of s. 7(b) to the scheme in the *Trade-marks Act* is apparent. In its pith and substance, s. 7(b) is directly connected to the enforcement of trade-marks and trade-names in Canada: the civil remedy in

s. 7(b) protects the goodwill associated with trade-marks and is directed to avoiding consumer confusion through use of trade-marks. As Gill and Jolliffe note: "No provision of s. 7 is more inextricably linked to the overall scheme of the *Trade-marks Act* than is s. 7(b)" (p. 2-22).

¶ 36 ... [T]he passing-off action plays a clear role in the federal scheme. Without this provision there would be a gap in the legislative protection of trade-marks. This would create inconsistencies in the protection of registered and unregistered trade-marks and lead to uncertainty. Section 7(b) is sufficiently integrated into the federal scheme and, in this respect, is significantly different from s. 7(e). I conclude that s. 7(b) lies within the federal government's legislative competence. [...]

[Justice LeBel then discussed the trade-mark and passing-off issues, and concluded:]

¶ 69 Under the modern law of passing off, a passing-off action by the appellant was bound to fail. [...]

¶ 70 For these reasons, I would dismiss the appeal with costs.

(e)   The National Market and the Division of Powers

- Research Note -
THE INCREASED IMPORTANCE OF THE NATIONAL MARKET

The conceptual notion of the Canadian "national market" runs through various areas of constitutional law. When the Courts and the Judicial Committee of the Privy Council have invalidated provincial regulatory schemes as being in relation to trade and commerce, the theory running behind it is that of the national market.

The national market is partly the rationale for the Canadian union and is partly the genius of the Canadian union. The founding fathers of the Constitution intended that a common economic space would exist and be protected. This is the reason why the significant economic levers were given to the federal government: Public Debt and Property, Trade and Commerce, the borrowing of Money on the Public Credit, Currency and Coinage, Banking and Savings Banks, Weights and Measures, Bills of Exchange, Interest, Legal Tender, and Bankruptcy.

Additional provisions secure the national market: section 121 indicates a desire that the market not be segmented by provincial borders and that the provinces not be allowed to seal up their borders to the free circulation of national factors of production. Unfortunately, the wording is limited to 19th Century terms ("All the Articles of the Growth, Produce, or Manufacture of any one of the Provinces shall, from and after the Union, be admitted free into each of the other Provinces"), whereas a modern phrase would encompass the free movement of goods, services, people and capital.

The trade and commerce power is a central part of the constitutional foundation of the national market and should be read in this light. The successful operation of the "national market" implies the free movement of people, goods, and capital. To varying degrees, various instruments of the Constitution have recognized each.

One such instrument is section 121 of the *Constitution Act, 1867*, which provides "all articles of the Growth Produce or Manufacture of any one of the Provinces shall, from and after the Union, be admitted free into each of the other Provinces." The early cases read section 121 narrowly, as prohibiting only customs duties on the transitive goods across a provincial boundary. Subsequently, in *Murphy v. CPR*, [1958] S.C.R. 626, 642, Justice Rand stated that "What is forbidden is a trade regulation, that in its essence and purpose is related to a provincial boundary." The federal government proposed a more robust version of section 121 in the process leading to the 1982 constitutional renovation. Ottawa proposed:

> 121. (1) Neither Canada nor a province shall be law or practice discriminate in a manner that unduly impedes the operation of the Canadian economic union, directly or indirectly, on the basis of the province or territory of residence or former residence of a person, on the basis of the province or territory of origin or destination of goods, services or capital or on the basis of the province or territory into which or from which goods, services or capital are imported or exported.
>
> (2) Nothing in subsection (1) renders invalid a law of Parliament or of a legislature enacted in the interests of public safety, order, health or morals.
>
> (3) Nothing in subsection (1) renders invalid a law of Parliament enacted pursuant to the principles of equalization and regional development to which Parliament and the legislatures are committed or declared by Parliament to be in an overriding national interest or enacted pursuant to an international obligation undertaken by Canada.
>
> (4) Nothing in subsections (2) or (3) renders valid a law of Parliament or a legislature that impedes the admission free into any province of goods, services or capital originating in or imported into any other province or territory. (emphasis added.)

This proposal was rejected by nine of ten provinces.

The free movement of people is guaranteed by s. 6(2) of the *Canadian Charter of Rights and Freedoms*, which states:

> 6. (2) Every citizen of Canada and every person who has the status of a permanent resident of Canada has the right
>
> (a) to move to and take up residence in any province; and
> (b) to pursue the gaining of a livelihood in any province

In *Canadian Egg Marketing Agency v. Richardson*, [1998] 3 S.C.R. 157, the Supreme Court considered the failure to broaden section 121. A majority of the Court approached the failure of a revised section 121 to broaden constitutional protection for the Canadian common market as a reason to withhold these purposes from s. 6 of the *Charter*.

> [...] The jurisprudence and history of s. 121 suggests what s. 6 was not intended to accomplish. The objective of s. 6 should not be interpreted in terms of a right to engage in any specific type of economic activity. Entrenching mobility rights with regard to the specified factors of economic production was proposed and roundly rejected. By contrast, the inclusion of s. 6 in the *Charter* reflects a human rights objective: to ensure mobility of persons, and to that end the pursuit of a livelihood on an equal footing with others regardless of residence. It guarantees the mobility of persons, not as a feature of the economic unity of the country, but in order to further a human rights purpose. It is centered on the individual. Section 6 neither categorically guarantees nor excludes the right of an individual to move goods, services, or capital into a province without regulation operating to interfere with that movement.

This narrow approach to the common market drew a dissent from Madame Justice McLaughlin. She stated:

> Section 6 [...] has two purposes, one collective, one individual: (1) to promote economic union among the provinces; and (2) to ensure to all Canadians one of the fundamental incidents of citizenship: the right to travel throughout the country, to choose a place of residence anywhere within its borders and to pursue a livelihood, all without regard to provincial boundaries. These purposes are related.

Mr. Justice La Forest explained the importance of the "national market" in the context of s. 6(2) in *Law Society of Alberta v. Black*, [1989] 1 S.C.R. 591:

> The attainment of economic integration occupied a place of central importance in the scheme [of the drafters of the *B.N.A. Act 1867*]. [...] The concept of Canada as a single country comprising what one would now call a common market was basic to the Confederation arrangements and the drafters of the *British North America Act* attempted to pull down the existing internal barriers that restricted movement within the country. [...] During the constitutional exercise culminating in the enactment of the *Charter*, there was a wave of political and academic concern regarding the construction of numerous barriers to interprovincial economic activity. [...]

Mr. Justice La Forest further developed these concepts in *Morguard Investments v. De Savoye*, [1990] 3 S.C.R. 1077, which were summarized in *Hunt v. T&N plc.*, supra p. 428:

> [T]he traditional rules emphasizing sovereignty seem to "fly in the face of the obvious intention of the Constitution to create a single country". Among the factors I identified [in *Morguard Investments v. De Savoye*, [1990] 3 S.C.R. 1077] that would also support a more cooperative spirit in recognition and enforcement were (1) common citizenship (2) interprovincial mobility of citizens (3) the common market created by the union as reflected in ss. 91(2), 91(10), 121 and the peace, order and government clause, and (4) the essentially unitary structure of our judicial system with the Supreme Court of Canada at its apex to which I have earlier referred.

There are no similar provisions for the free movement of capital in the *Charter*. However, the free movement of capital is largely secured by various provisions of the *Constitution Act 1867*. In Securing the Canadian Economic Union in the Constitution (1980), Jean Chretien explained:

> The free movement of capital is assured to a large extent by virtue of Parliament's exclusive authority over currency and coinage (91[14]), banking, incorporation of banks and the issue of paper money (91[15]), savings banks (91[16]), legal tender (91[20]), and its authority to borrow money on the public credit (91[4]).

Barriers to the free movement of goods have persisted in Canada. In 1994, the provincial and federal governments attempted to remove these barriers with the Agreement on Internal Trade (AIT). The AIT contains free trade principles similar to those found in treaties such as the NAFTA and the GATT. The parties pledged that no new barriers would be introduced; the principle of non-discrimination would apply; rights of entry and exit were solidified; government procurement measures and the principle of transparency were introduced.

Critics have argued that the AIT is too weak (see Robert Howse, "Securing the Canadian Economic Union: Legal and Constitutional Options for the Federal Government," CD Howe Institute Commentary (June 1996)). It is a non-binding political accord. Parties may opt out of it. Findings of the dispute resolution panel are unenforceable, but costs awards by the panel are. The provincial implementing legislation has been weak and has made only minor adjustments to the existing legislative framework.

These are important criticisms. It is to be hoped that the federal and provincial governments can find means to strengthen the accord. While it is not necessary (or even perhaps desirable, see Prof. Swinton's commentary below)that additional strength come from supervision by the courts, court review is in theory possible. The AIT could be given "quasi-constitutional" status similar to the Diefenbaker Bill of Rights or the Human Rights Codes. The concept of the "national market" explained by Mr. Justice La Forest could be further elaborated in the jurisprudence. Given the constitutional significance of the national market, and its repeated recognition in the Supreme Court cases, there is certainly reason to think that appropriate federal supports additional to the AIT could be sustained under the trade and commerce power.

K. SWINTON, "COURTING OUR WAY TO ECONOMIC INTEGRATION: JUDICIAL REVIEW AND THE ECONOMIC UNION"
(1995), 25 CDN. BUS. I J 780.

Efforts to strenglhen the Canadian economic union have been an important part of the public policy agenda since the late 1970s, as evidenced by the many attempts at constitutional and consensual reform made by federal and provincial governments. Depending on one's perspective, the results have been hopeful, very modest or illusory — and, in any event, a long time coming. Constitutional amendments in 1982 included a guarantee of labour mobility in the *Canadian Charter of Rights and Freedoms* to supplement the limited "common market" clause found in s. 121 of the *Constitution Act, 1867*. More ambitious federal proposals to include a broad common market clause plus a mechanism for devising rules for the more efficient functioning of the economic union were quickly removed from the agenda in the Charlottetown round of constitutional negotiations through 1991 and 1992.

Nevertheless, federal, provincial and territorial negotiators finally reached an agreement on the reduction of internal trade barriers in July of 1994. The agreement contains a lengthy set of commitments for the removal of trade barriers and include a complex set of dispute settlement mechanisms, including a clear signal that the obligations are not subject to judicial oversight. Even without this commitment to further economic integration, the Canadian economy has been undergoing a dramatic restructuring in response to international economic forces, which include new obligations under international trade agreements such as the General Agreement on Tariffs and Trade (GATT) and the North American Free Trade Agreement (NAFTA). Inevitably, these rules are having an impact on internal economic policy as well as international trade.

Arguments are still made frequently, however, that this is not enough. Sometimes, the complaint is that international norms protect the citizens of other countries better than Canadians within the country. While the Internal Trade Agreement is designed to redress that problem, many are of the view that is needs more "muscle" and a binding enforcement mechanism.

[A discussion of the modern trade and commerce cases follows:]

[...]

[The] various strands of doctrine under the *Charter* and the distribution of powers suggest the possibility of further judicial constraints on provincial action and, even more likely, possible augmentation of federal legislative powers in a number of policy areas, including the environment, treaty power, regulation of reproductive technologies and trade regulation, at both the domestic and international levels. [...]

THE CANADIAN ECONOMIC UNION AND TRADE BARRIERS

While much has been written on the need to reduce barriers to the mobility of labour, goods, capital and services within Canada, a significant degree of confusion remains about what constitutes an unacceptable barrier. Critics of

617

the *status quo* are quick to point to government procurement practices that favour local suppliers over out-of-province suppliers, agricultural product marketing boards that impose production and marketing quotas for each province and regional development grants that favour production in one province over another. In each of these examples, and many others, the provincial affiliation of a product, service or supplier is an important consideration affecting government action. If these were the only types of action which gave rise to problems, we might describe the concept of a trade barrier as encompassing direct discrimination on the basis of residence. Thus, the goal of barrier elimination would be based on an equal treatment model that would forbid distinctions on the basis of provincial residence. This goal is sometimes described in the literature as "negative integration", that is, an end to arbitrary and purposeful discrimination.

This was said to be the objective of the federal proposals to strengthen s. 121 of the *Constitution Act, 1867* in the Charlottetown round of constitutional negotiations, when the federal government sought to include a guarantee of the free movement of labour, capital, services and goods in a revised s. 121. The proposal generated much hostility, in part because it became clear during subsequent debate that some of its supporters were wedded to a more ambitious definition of barriers that would encompass indirect forms of discrimination as well as direct, for example, the refusal of a province to recognize occupational qualifications obtained in another province or even different product, consumer protection or environmental standards in different provinces. Therefore, the goal seemed to be "positive integration" or the harmonization of policies across jurisdictions as well, but through a mechanism whereby the courts would invalidate laws that created added burdens. If this was indeed the purpose — to use the new s. 121 to attack varying regulatory responses by striking them down — the underlying philosophy seemed to be hostile to government intervention in the marketplace.

But even if overt discrimination had been the only issue and the section needed only to be interpreted in that way, the constitutional entrenchment of a guarantee of mobility for labour, goods, capital and services would remain a controversial statement of public policy without the addition of some notion of acceptable limitations, for example, limitations enabling a province to protect the health and safety of residents by preventing the entry of harmful products from other provinces. Even those committed to maximum mobility would concede that there can be some legitimate limitations on movement. Indeed, even when equal treatment is the goal, experience with equality law in other areas makes it clear that identical treatment for all is not the only nor even the primary underlying value; rather, we accept differential treatment of groups where such treatment is justifiable to achieve some further principle of justice. So too in our pursuit of equal treatment in the economic union, there may be persuasive reasons for treating provincial residents and non-residents differently in some circumstances.

The difficulty, of course, is in reaching a consensus on which limitations are reasonable and which are arbitrary. Some economists, emphasizing a goal of wealth maximization, would accept governmental intervention only to correct market failures. On the other hand most people would accept the legitimacy of other public policy objectives and a more interventionist role for the state, for example, to pursue the goal of preserving regions by providing business incentives to create local employment or by favouring residents in awarding government contracts in order to provide employment opportunities and to develop business expertise. In relation to the Charlottetown proposals, there was much discomfort about leaving the determination to the judiciary as to which values were relevant and, ultimately, what the appropriate role of the state is, without providing the courts with further guidance.

The need to develop a concept of acceptable barriers becomes even more compelling if the definition of trade barriers also incorporates indirect burdens on mobility. While different employment equity or consumer labeling schemes across the provinces may create burdens on companies that trade in a number of jurisdictions (because they require duplicative reporting or prevent economies of scale), the primary objective underlying these measures may be a rejection of market-based solutions and a concern for other values, such as greater justice for disadvantaged groups, or a different view of the appropriate level of state intervention and its benefits. Therefore, once we start to scrutinize indirect forms of discrimination, we need an even richer concept of reasonable limitations.

In addition, we need to think about ways to manage diversity or to promote harmony across jurisdictions without undermining important regulatory goals. As Douglas Purvis pointed out with respect to the Charlottetown proposals, the underlying desire for greater positive integration requires us to think about political implications. In his words,

> [...] it can be argued that increased economic integration implies increased political integration. Thus, in this sense, there is a trade-off between economic benefits and political sovereignty.

By now it should be clear that in relation to both the definition of barriers and the notion of acceptable justifications, consideration must be given to the values underlying federalism, since the inevitable result of moving towards greater economic integration is to curtail the freedom of action — indeed, the sovereignty — of governments, especially at the provincial level. There are a number of perspectives from which federalism can be evaluated, since federalism is not an end in itself but a means to promote other objectives. Even within economic rationales, there is no consensus on how a federal system should operate, with some stressing the need to curtail externalities associated with provincial jurisdiction and others emphasizing the value of diversity as a way to promote responsiveness to citizen's preferences. More importantly, an economic perspective is only one way of evaluating federalism. Others emphasize the importance of federalism in expressing different visions of community or citizenship or in promoting democratic values, for example, through a system of checks and balances on government. Indeed, Canadian federalism has long placed great value on provincial autonomy, in recognition of strong regional loyalties and Quebec's distinctive place in Canadian confederation.

Whether one operates from community models or certain economic models, federalism is valued because it theoretically provides a better opportunity for governments at the regional/provincial level to respond to citizens' preferences, because of the greater homogeneity that comes with smaller jurisdictions or because of the ensuing competition between jurisdictions. But, of course, that responsiveness and the diversity in policy which is likely to result brings us back to the debate about distortions or barriers within the larger economic union. If "barriers" are defined to include both direct and indirect burdens on mobility, a huge number of provincial (and federal) practices become suspect.

In considering which of these practices impose serious burdens that run afoul of the Constitution, decision makers must weigh a number of competing concerns that include not only the value of freedom of movement in the Canadian common market and the justifications for limiting mobility in such a market in general but also the particular values of federalism. This may well require a determination of important institutional questions as well. More precisely, in a federal system it is not enough to conclude that a practice is discriminatory or unduly burdensome; rather one must go on to ask how integration will most feasibly and legitimately result: through judicial prohibitions of the practice; through unilateral federal action; through intergovernmental cooperation and negotiations; through new institutional reforms; or through formal constitutional change.

In sum, the reduction of barriers to internal trade can only be accomplished after complex decisions rooted in economic and political theory and reality.

THE AGREEMENT ON INTERNAL TRADE

The complexity of the problem of internal trade barriers in a federal system is clearly recognized in the federal/provincial Agreement on Internal Trade (the Agreement). While the preamble notes that one objective is to "promote an open, efficient and stable domestic market" and to "reduce and eliminate, to the greatest extent possible, barriers to the free movement of persons, goods, services and investments within Canada", it also "recognize[s] the diverse social cultural and economic characteristics of the provinces". And while there is a commitment to "reciprocal non-discrimination" in Article 401 and to the harmonization of standards in a number of areas (Article 405), the Agreement nevertheless recognizes that legislatures can pursue "legitimate objectives", which include: public security and safety; public order; protection of human, animal or plant life or health; protection of the environment; consumer protection; protection of the health, safety and well-being of workers; and affirmative action programs for disadvantaged groups (Article 200). Such legitimate objectives cannot "impair unduly" access of goods, services, investments and persons from another province nor can they be "more trade restrictive than necessary" to achieve the objective (Article 404(b) and (c)).

What is most noticeable in the Agreement is the commitment to further processes, either to harmonize standards and regulations or to increase the frequency of recognition of another jurisdiction's standards, for example, in the area of occupational licensing. It is clear the negotiations saw the task of harmonization, in particular, as a long-term exercise that would in many cases require difficult policy decisions about the appropriate level and form of regulation weighed against the costs resulting from divergent responses in different jurisdictions. In part because of the policy tradeoffs implicit in the exercise, they chose not to confer on the courts the responsibility for overseeing the implementation of the Agreement. Instead, they chose to specify different mechanisms for particular areas, including provisions for monitoring and reporting, leading ultimately to a process of mediation and non-binding arbitration (Chapter 17) that can ultimately result in retaliatory sanctions against a non-compliant actor (Article 1710).

While the Agreement clearly acknowledges the difficulty of regulating trade barriers in a federal system and leaves much to be worked out in the future, this is one reason why critics worry about its effectiveness. In addition, the fact that the Agreement is enforced through a form of consensual arbitration rather than a binding form of adjudication is problematic for those who want sterner obligations imposed on governments. Finally, the uncertain legal status of the Agreement is cause for concern. Principles of parliamentary sovereignty dictate that the Agreement cannot bind a future legislature since it is the result of executive action. Even were it to be ratified by legislation, this could not stop a subsequent legislature from repealing it.

Thus, the question surfaces again whether there is an expanded role for the Supreme Court of Canada to play in the regulation of internal trade barriers to supplement the Agreement. In turning to this question, it is important to keep in mind the debate about trade barriers described earlier, for those who urge a more active role for the courts must not only show how the judges should weigh competing concerns about barriers but must also confront the magnitude of what they ask in terms of judicial activism. This necessarily requires an assessment of the legitimacy of the judicial role in this exercise. [...]

COURTING ECONOMIC INTEGRATION

1. Direct Discrimination

From the perspective of those seeking greater judicial activism to protect the economic union from direct discrimination, there are obvious deficiencies in the present jurisprudence. First, the doctrine developed to date does not adequately oversee government spending practices. While government contractual activity is subject to the *Charter*, policies implemented through the spending power, tax deductions or credits or ownership of resources have not been subject to the constitutional distribution of powers that constrain governmental use of legislative and regulatory instruments. The result is that provinces have been able to discriminate in such areas as government procurement, wine and beer pricing and investment incentives by using financial instruments even though direct regulation to achieve the same ends would have run afoul of the distribution of legislative powers.

A second concern about the existing jurisprudence is the narrow definition of "trade and commerce" within s. 91(2), which emphasizes trade in goods. This allows the provinces wide scope to regulate land ownership and use and labour policy since these have not been seen as elements of trade nor have they come within the scope of the common market clause in s. 121.

Judicial intervention to constrain direct discrimination through the exercise of the spending power would be a dramatic change in the judicial role, as the Canadian Supreme Court has never taken an active role in the supervision of the spending power. The result has been that financial initiatives have been an important instrument of flexibility in the federal system. Admittedly, numerous critics of the judges' hands-off attitude have argued that the courts should subject the spending power to the same constraints as the legislative powers in ss. 91 and 92 of the Constitution. However, the judicial response, such as it is, assumes that spending is of a different nature than legislating since there is normally less coercion associated with the expenditure of funds or the conferral of tax advantages than with regulation.

But what if the only constraint was to be non-discrimination, on the basis that this is consistent with the constitutional commitment to an economic union? Even here, judicial supervision of the spending power would be a very delicate exercise since the judges would have to engage in a highly political activity when determining which expenditures were acceptable. For example, what would be the legality of federal government expenditures that discriminated among provinces, for example, the allocation of a government contract to build aircraft that benefitted one province rather than another, lower bidder, perhaps for regional development reasons? Should a province be prevented from providing tax holidays to new investors in the province who create jobs? Even if discrimination in government procurement were the only concern, thought would still have to be given to acceptable justifications, such as the protection for regional development programmes.

2. Indirect Discrimination

Moving beyond direct discrimination and "protectionism", the doctrines developed under the federal trade and commerce power and the provincial power over property and civil rights have been criticized for the conceptual focus on whether the subject of regulation is in the interprovincial or international flow of commerce or intraprovincial in *situs*. If a province regulates a business within the province without trying to prevent cross-border flow of goods, the measure passes constitutional scrutiny. But this approach ignores the burdens that can be imposed on the national economy from diversity in provincial regulations of business activity. Thus, critics of the *status quo* call for greater sensitivity to the spillover effects of provincial jurisdiction on those in other jurisdictions and to their overall impact on the national economy.

One could meet these concerns by a shift to judicial oversight of indirect discrimination through a "burdens on commerce" approach to provincial jurisdiction. This approach would require the courts to assume a much more openly political role since judges would have to decide the magnitude of unacceptable burdens on commerce weighed against a wide array of policy justifications put forward by provincial governments. They would have to determine whether their concern was the overall economic burden or only control of externalities. They would also have to decide what is a significant burden when weighed against other values such as distributional concerns. These types of inquiry require detailed factual evidence to enable the court to reach a decision and this will often be a problem as such evidence may be lacking or there are conflicting views about the benefits and costs of the regulation. Indeed, a good indication of the empirical uncertainty which is bound to arise is seen in the debate about the extent and cost of current internal trade barriers.

However, even more important with a shift of burdens-on-commerce approach is the implication for both public policy and the balance of power in the federal system. The approach implies that provincial laws should be struck down if they impose an undue burden on commercial activity because, for example, there are diverse product or occupational standards in a number of provinces. But what then of the underlying policy objectives in the various jurisdictions? Obviously the provinces chose to regulate these areas because of concerns about the inefficacy of market-based solutions, yet the finding that a provincial law unduly burdens commerce will leave the area unregulated because of the impact on the provincial regulations. On the assumption that the underlying goal of this approach is not to enshrine a concept of minimal government and market primacy but to promote positive integration or harmonization, the obvious judicial solution the problem of the regulatory gap must be to allow the federal a government to step in to address the problem. Thus, in order to promote harmonization or positive integration under this scenario, as well as to reduce burdens on commerce, there must not only be constraints at the provincial level but also significant expansion of the federal power over trade and commerce. [...]

In Canada's last constitutional round, the proposal to expand s. 121 was accompanied by a companion proposal for a new section that would have established a new institutional mechanism to promote positive integration through a form of federal/provincial decision-making process to address matters important to the efficient function of the economic union. Nevertheless, this proposal, which required the consent of two-thirds of the provinces having 50% of the population to any such Act of Parliament, was seen as a federal power grab by many, especially those in Quebec, and the proposal was quickly shelved. [...]

Clearly, the kind of supervisory role contemplated for the courts as just described is precisely the role which government negotiators rejected, both in the Charlottetown round and in the more recent intergovernmental trade agreement. Before the courts take on a more active role in this area then, serious consideration must be given to the legitimacy of this kind of intervention. While some might argue that the failure to achieve results in the constitutional amendment process justifies judicial action to help adapt the existing Constitution to meet current policy needs, another reading of the outcome of that process is the general resistance to constitutional rules to govern the economic union, especially open-ended rules enforced by the courts that allow judges to work out the appropriate balance between the state and markets and between uniformity and diversity. The constitutional route engenders concerns about the legitimacy of judicial review in this area, the competence of the judges to deal with the problem and the danger of rigidity that comes with enshrining a particular vision of state and markets rather than allowing that vision to adapt over time.

4. Taxation and Spending Powers

(a) Overview

MAGNET, "THE CONSTITUTIONAL DISTRIBUTION OF TAXATION POWERS IN CANADA"
(1978), 10 OTTAWA L. REV. 473 [revised 2007].

Immediately prior to Confederation, British North America, though politically structured, was an economically decentralized cluster of small and scattered settlements. Only twenty per cent of its 3.5 million people lived in cities. Transportation difficulties were formidable and proved to be the main obstacle to development. This was intensified by a severe winter which annually closed all water routes for five months.

By 1866 the then province of Canada and the municipalities had extended loans totaling $40 million to railway companies. The investments soured. There was a substantial public debt and poor public credit. The railway network was conceived on a continental scale; it was ill-suited to the economic needs of the primarily agricultural province of Canada.

After the *Act of Union* in 1840, British opinion mounted for Canada to become responsible for her own defence. At the same time, American pressure on the western territories became severe. The Northern Pacific Railway, chartered by Americans in 1864, had the object of providing transcontinental service. American settlement was pushing ever northward. Without the protection of British troops, American expansionist claims to the west seemed impossible to resist.

John G. Diefenbaker, speaking
in the House of Commons.

The scheme of Confederation was principally designed to overcome these problems. It was thought that a larger, strongly centralized political unit would be capable of (a) re-establishing the public credit, (b) undertaking the considerable public expenditure on transport which was the condition precedent to development, and (c) offering a sufficient defence posture to resist American pressure.

Cultural and sectional rivalries proved insuperable obstacles to the legislative union foreseen by Sir John A. Macdonald. A federal state, characterized by strong cultural and regional guarantees, was the compromise. But there was to be no question of economic decentralization. By the *British North America Act, 1867* the Dominion government was granted legislative power over:

91(3) The raising of Money by any Mode or System of Taxation.

By section 122 of the Act customs and excise, which accounted for the vast bulk of public revenue immediately prior to Confederation, were brought within the central government's exclusive competence. Section 118 of the Act, since repealed, made provision for payment of subsidies by the central government to the province with the intent that they be "in full settlement of all future demands on Canada". In the early years of Confederation such subsidies accounted for some fifty per cent of all provincial revenues.

These provisions left no doubt in the minds of the founders that the Dominion would have the pre-eminent power of taxation. Both the Quebec and London Resolutions declared that payment of subsidies to the provinces was "in consideration of the transfer to the General Parliament of the powers of taxation".

The *B.N.A. Act* granted powers of taxation to the provincial legislatures too. These were not considered significant. It was thought that provincial activities would be limited and their revenue needs slight; the legislatures, accordingly, would have no need to resort to most tax pools. Therefore, by section 92 of the *B.N.A. Act*, the legislatures were restricted to

> 92(2) Direct Taxation within the Province in order to the raising of a Revenue for Provincial Purposes.

> 92(9) Shop, Saloon, Tavern, Auctioneer, and other Licences in order to the raising of a Revenue for Provincial, Local or Municipal Purposes.

One of the overriding ideas of the Confederation scheme was the creation of a large free trade area in which strong industry could develop and prosper. This fundamental principle was constitutionally expressed by section 121 of the *B.N.A. Act*, which read:

> 121. All Articles of Growth, Produce or Manufacture of any one of the Provinces shall from and after the Union, be admitted free into each of the other Provinces.

Section 125 is important. It contemplates restrictions of substance which grow out of the realization, noted by Chief Justice Marshall, that "a right to tax is a right to destroy". The restrictions ensure that taxing powers will not be used to upset the framework of Confederation. Section 125 provides:

> 125. No Lands or Property belonging to Canada or any Province shall be liable to Taxation.

Sections 53 and 54 impose requirements of form and, in the case of s. 53, a requirement of principle. By s. 53,

> 53. Bills for appropriating any Part of the Public Revenue, or for imposing any Tax or Impost, shall originate in the House of Commons.

This section confirms the primacy of the Lower Chamber over the Senate in measures for the imposition of taxes. It also imports a constitutional principle of "no taxation without representation," a principle interpreted by the Supreme Court as requiring that taxation can only be imposed by Parliament or Parliament's clearly authorized delegate.

Section 54 provides:

> 54. It shall not be lawful for the House of Commons to adopt or pass any Vote, Resolution, Address or Bill for the Appropriation of any Part of the Public Revenue, or of any Tax or Impost, to any Purpose that has not been first recommended to that House by Message of the Governor General in the Session in which such Vote, Resolution, Address, or Bill is proposed.

Sections 53 and 54 must be understood in light of the remarks of Pigeon J. in *Re Agricultural Products Marketing Act*, (reaffirmed in 2001 in *Ont. English Catholic Teachers Assoc. v. Ont.*) that the sections are "not entrenched provisions of the Constitution". They may be amended unilaterally.

Sections 53 and 54 are discussed at length in Magnet, *Modern Constitutionalism: Identity, Equality and Democracy* (Butterworths: 2004), chp. 7 "Taxation, Democracy and the Constitution".

- Research Note -
ANALYSING THE MODERN TAXING POWER

The taxing powers assigned to Canada's legislatures by the *Constitution Act, 1867* provoke more division of powers litigation than any other provisions in the *Constitution Act, 1867*. What are the critical questions that must be answered in these cases?

IS TAXATION INVOLVED?

The question that must first be asked is: does the legislation at issue impose a tax, or does it impose something else? Governments can charge money for many different reasons — when a law student pays $10.00 for a copy of a piece of legislation from Access Ontario, she is paying a charge, which raises revenue. But it would be difficult to characterize this as a tax — or even as a "regulatory charge". To be a tax, a charge must have some constitutionally-defined limits, form, and scope. The first part of this section considers the constitutional meaning of 'taxation' as distinct from other forms of charges imposed by law to support a variety of regulatory purposes.

IS THE TAXATION 'DIRECT OR INDIRECT'?

Central to the design of the federal distribution of taxation powers is a distinction between direct and indirect taxes. This distinction comes from John Stuart Mill's 19th century classic, *Principles of Political Economy* (Book V, ch. 3). Mill thought that distinguishing between direct and indirect taxes would enhance democracy because the electorate better perceives direct taxes. With greater scrutiny by the citizenry comes more resistance to public expenditure, more accountability from public authorities, and more control by the demos.

Canada's framers subscribed to this doctrine by restricting the provincial legislatures and their municipal subdivisions to "direct taxation".

IS THE TAXATION 'WITHIN THE PROVINCE'?

Constitutional law prohibits the "imposition by a Province of any tax upon citizens beyond its borders." (*CIGOL v. Saskatchewan*, at 584). This is a now a central explanation why provinces are limited to direct taxation.

In *Manitoba v. Air Canada*, [1980] 2 S.C.R. 303 at 316-319, Laskin C.J.C. voided a provincial taxing statute which taxed individuals in aircrafts that temporarily landed in Manitoba on route to another destination. The Chief Justice ruled:

> Merely going through the air space over Manitoba does not give the aircraft a situs there to support a tax which constitutionally must be "within the Province." In the case of aircraft operations, there must be a substantial, at least more than a nominal, presence in the Province to provide a basis for imposing a tax in respect of the entry of aircraft into the Province. [...] Moreover, there is, at best, merely a notional drawing into the taxation net of interprovincial and extraprovincial operations, and constitutional authority, which is limited to direct taxation within the Province, cannot be extended by self-serving definitions.

In *Air Canada v. Minister of Revenue et al.* (1996), 28 O.R. (3d) 97 [leave to appeal to SCC dismissed Sept. 26/96], the Ontario Court of Appeal considered whether the province could tax gasoline purchased and primarily consumed outside the province by Air Canada and Canadian Airlines. Morden A.C.J.O. held:

> The subject-matter of the tax in the present case is a transaction or event — not the use of an aircraft — but rather the transfer of aviation fuel into the fuel tank of an aircraft. Clearly, both the transaction and the aviation fuel, as well as the taxpayer, are "within the province" and I do not think that the fact that the aviation fuel was, initially, purchased outside the province, weakens the connection between the province and the transaction. [...] Notwithstanding that the aviation fuel in question has been purchased outside Ontario and is, substantially, consumed outside the province, there is no extraprovincial aspect to the subject-matter of the tax in this case in the way there was in the *Manitoba* case.

The notion of a physical presence within the province upon which these cases determine the constitutional meaning of "within the Province" is unsatisfactory. This difficulty mirrors similar problems in determining "within the Province" in the property and civil rights cases. As we saw *supra* in *Churchill Falls v. A. G. Nfld.*. searching for a physical *situs* in answer to the question 'where is taxation imposed or felt' leads to unprincipled and sometimes unjust results. Intellectual concepts like taxation have no physical *situs*.

"Within the Province" is a constitutional (or intellectual) notion, not a physical one. Accordingly, the appropriate analysis must be by constitutional method – not geography. The guiding value ought to be whether the province advances a sufficient "sphere of interest" to undergird the assertion of provincial legislative jurisdiction. To pour this concept into more familiar language of constitutional analysis: is the challenged taxing statute in object and purpose, pith and substance and effect in relation to direct taxation within the province?

LICENSES, LEVIES AND REGULATORY CHARGES

If the imposition is neither direct nor indirect taxation, it becomes relevant to ask: what kind of charge is it? Section 92(9) supports a power to impose licensing charges. There are other permissible charges as well. A probate fee, for example, is neither a tax nor a licensing charge. It is supportable as being a charge "ancillary or adhesive to a regulatory scheme." It is no objection to such charges that they possess a measure of indirectness.

The line between a "regulatory charge ancillary to a regulatory scheme" and an "indirect tax" is difficult to draw.

In *Ontario Home Builders* and *Allard Contractors*, the Supreme Court of Canada ruled that a charge can be levied to defray the costs of a regulatory scheme, notwithstanding that it is indirect in the sense of the constitutional cases. The term "regulatory scheme" is a term of art in constitutional law that is discussed in *Westbank First Nation v. B.C. Hydro, infra.* and *Kirkbi v. Ritvik Holdings, supra*.

TAXATION OF NATURAL RESOURCES

This issue became a focal point of provincial concern following the decision of the Supreme Court of Canada in *Canadian Industrial Gas and Oil Ltd. v. Government of Saskatchewan* (1977), infra at p. 637. This case considered a complex of Saskatchewan legislation and regulations by which Saskatchewan levied a "mineral income tax" at the wellhead on the price received by an oil producer, and a royalty surcharge imposed upon oil produced from existing crown lands or from newly expropriated lands. The mineral income tax and royalty surcharge were 100% of the difference between the new rising world price and the "basic wellhead price", a price received by oil producers prior to the first spectacular rise in oil prices in 1973. The majority of the Supreme Court of Canada held the tax and royalty surcharge to be beyond the powers of the province, since, as the Court found, they were indirect taxes designed to regulate the price of Saskatchewan oil in the export market.

Following the *CIGOL* decision, Saskatchewan and other provinces became determined to remove the "direct taxation" restriction on provincial taxing powers from Canada's Constitution. The provincial case received some support from the federal New Democratic Party in the Constitutional discussions of the late 1970s and early 1980s. As a result, new provincial taxation powers were included as section 92A(4) of the *Constitution Act, 1982*.

Section 92A(4) provides:

> 92A. (4) In each province, the legislature may make laws in relation to the raising of money by any mode or system of taxation in respect of
> (a) non-renewable natural resources and forestry resources in the province and the primary production therefrom, and
> (b) sites and facilities in the province for the generation of electrical energy and the production therefrom,
>
> whether or not such production is exported in whole or in part from the province, but such laws may not authorize or provide for taxation that differentiates between production exported to another part of Canada and production not exported from the province.

In *Moull*, "Section 92A of the *Constitution Act, 1867*" (1983), 61 *Can. Bar Rev.* 715 at p. 718 contends that "Subsection 92A(4) is a relatively straightforward attempt to give the provinces the power to levy indirect taxation in the resources field.... Under clause 92A(4)(a), the provinces will now be able to tax both the resource in place and its 'primary production', or in other words both the resource itself *in situ* and the product that results from its severance, by any system of taxation including indirect taxation".

(b)   Is it a Tax?

WESTBANK FIRST NATION v. BRITISH COLUMBIA HYDRO AND POWER AUTHORITY
[1999] 3 S.C.R. 134.

GONTHIER J. (for the Court): —

[...] Between 1951 and 1978, the respondent acquired eight permits from Her Majesty the Queen in Right of Canada to use and occupy various lands on the Tsinstikeptum Indian Reserves No. 9 and No. 10 in British Columbia. The permits were granted pursuant to s. 28(2) of the *Indian Act* with the consent of the appellant. The respondent held the permits in order to build electric transmission and distribution lines and to provide electrical energy to the residents of the Reserves. In 1990, the appellant passed the *Westbank Indian Band Assessment By-law ("1990 Assessment By-law") and the Westbank Indian Band Taxation By-law ("1990 Taxation By-law")*, pursuant to its authority under s. 83(1)(a) of the *Indian Act*. These by-laws were amended in subsequent years, but the relevant provisions remained the same. The appellant passed additional by-laws from

1991 to 1995, and under these by-laws the respondent was assessed $124,527.25 in taxes, penalties, and interest. The respondent refused to pay the assessed taxes, and did not appeal the assessment notices. [...]

The only issue to be determined in this appeal is whether s. 125 of the *Constitution Act, 1867*, precludes the Westbank First Nation from imposing its taxation and assessment by-laws on B.C. Hydro, an agent of the provincial Crown. [...]

[S]ection [125] is one of the tools found in the Constitution that ensures the proper functioning of Canada's federal system. It grants to each level of government sufficient operational space to govern without interference. It is founded upon the concept that imposing a tax on a level of government may significantly harm the ability of that government to exercise its constitutionally mandated governmental functions. In *McCulloch v. Maryland*, 17 U.S. (4 Wheat.) 316 (1819), at p. 431, Marshall C.J. explained this concept as follows:

> That the power to tax involves the power to destroy; that the power to destroy may defeat and render useless the power to create; that there is plain repugnance, in conferring on one government a power to control the constitutional measures of another, which other, with respect to those very measures, is declared to be supreme over that which exerts the control, are propositions not to be denied.

In *Re Exported Natural Gas Tax*, [1982] 1 S.C.R. 1004, the majority of this Court referred to these statements at p. 1056, explaining at p. 1065 that "s. 125 is plainly intended to prevent inroads, by way of taxation, upon the property of one level of government, by another level of government."

While Canadian federalism requires some separation between each level of government, this rule is not absolute. Canada's federal system is a flexible one, and the Constitution does not create "enclaves" around federal or provincial actors. As Dickson C.J. explained in *OPSEU v. Ontario (Attorney General)*, [1987] 2 S.C.R. 2, at p. 18, "[t]he history of Canadian constitutional law has been to allow for a fair amount of interplay and indeed overlap between federal and provincial powers" (see also Dickson C.J.'s comments in *General Motors of Canada Ltd. v. City National Leasing*, [1989] 1 S.C.R. 641, at p. 669). Flexible federalism demands protection from taxation, but not from all forms of charges, when the charges are levied in support of other regulatory objectives within the competence of the taxing authority.

While the primary constitutional value served by s. 125 is federalism, it also secondarily advances the constitutional value of democracy. As this Court recently explained in *Re Eurig Estate*, [1998] 2 S.C.R. 565, at para. 30, the Canadian Constitution (through the operation of s. 53 of the *Constitution Act, 1867*) demands that there should be no taxation without representation. In other words, individuals being taxed in a democracy have the right to have their elected representatives debate whether their money should be appropriated, and determine how it should be spent. Intergovernmental taxation is prohibited, in part, because one group of elected representatives should not be allowed to decide how taxes levied under and within the authority of another group of elected representatives should be spent. At the same time, governments are not immune from paying user fees, such as water rates, in part because the government can choose whether to use the service, and the money charged is spent solely on providing that service: *Attorney General of Canada v. City of Toronto* (1892), 23 S.C.R. 514; *Attorney General of Canada v. Registrar of Titles*, [1934] 4 D.L.R. 764 (B.C.C.A), at pp. 771-72. In this way, imposing a user fee is more like charging a fee for a merchantable commodity than imposing any form of taxation. [...]

B. Regulatory Charges Distinguished from Taxes

The natural starting point for characterizing a governmental levy is this Court's decision in *Lawson v. Interior Tree Fruit and Vegetable Committee of Direction*, [1930] S.C.R. 357, at pp. 362-63. In that case, Duff J., as he then was, explained that the impugned charges in that case were taxes because they were (1) enforceable by law, (2) imposed under the authority of the legislature, (3) imposed by a public body, and (4) intended for a public purpose. Duff J. also noted that the charges there were compulsory, and affected a large number of people.

These indicia of "taxation" were recently adopted by this Court in *Re Eurig Estate*, supra, at para. 15. Major J., writing for the majority of this Court, added another possible factor to consider when characterizing a governmental levy, stating at para. 21 that "[a]nother factor that generally distinguishes a fee from a tax is that a nexus must exist between the quantum charged and the cost of the service provided." This was a useful development, as it helps to distinguish between taxes and user fees, a subset of "regulatory charges".

A distinction is made between simple "taxation" and "regulation", or what has elsewhere been described as "regulatory charges": P. W. Hogg, *Constitutional Law of Canada*, (loose-leaf ed.), vol. 1, at p. 30-28; J. E. Magnet, *Constitutional Law of Canada*, (7th ed. 1998), vol. 1, at p. 481; G.V. La Forest, *The Allocation of Taxing Power Under the Canadian Constitution* (2nd ed. 1981). The distinction between taxes, on the one hand, and regulatory charges, on the other, was highlighted by the majority of this Court in *Re Exported Natural Gas Tax*, supra, at pp. 1055, 1070, 1072 and 1075. In that case, the majority explained at p. 1070 that a tax is to be distinguished from a "levy [imposed] primarily for regulatory purposes, or as necessarily incidental to a broader regulatory scheme."

It goes without saying that in order for charges to be imposed for regulatory purposes, or to otherwise be "necessarily incidental to a broader regulatory scheme", one must first identify a "regulatory scheme". Certain indicia have been present when this Court has found a "regulatory scheme". The factors to consider when identifying a regulatory scheme include the presence of: (1) a complete and detailed code of regulation; (2) a specific regulatory purpose which seeks to affect the behaviour of individuals; (3) actual or properly estimated costs of the regulation; and (4) a relationship between the regulation and the person being regulated, where the person being regulated either causes the need for the regulation, or benefits from it. This is only a list of factors to consider; not all of these factors must be present to find a regulatory scheme. Nor is this list of factors exhaustive.

The first factor to consider is the nature of the purported regulation itself. Regulatory schemes are usually characterized by their complexity and detail. In *Allard Contractors Ltd. v. Coquitlam (District)*, [1993] 4 S.C.R. 371, at p. 409, the regulatory scheme there was described as a "complete and detailed code for the regulation of the gravel and soil extraction and removal trade". In *Ontario Home Builders' Assn. v. The York Region Board of Education*, [1996] 2 S.C.R. 929, at p. 966, the charge was described as part of a "complex regulatory framework governing land development." And, in *General Motors of Canada Ltd. v. City National Leasing*, supra, at p. 676, the *Combines Investigation Act* was described as "a complex scheme of economic regulation."

A regulatory scheme will have a defined regulatory purpose. A purpose statement contained in the legislation may provide assistance to the court in this regard. Professor Magnet, supra, at p. 459, correctly explains that a regulatory scheme usually "delineates certain required or prohibited conduct". For example, in *Re Exported Natural Gas Tax*, supra, at p. 1075, the levy there was held to not be a regulatory charge because "the tax belies any purpose of modifying or directing the allocation of gas to particular markets. Nor does the tax purport to regulate who distributes gas, how the distribution may occur, or where the transactions may occur." In sum, a regulatory scheme must "regulate" in some specific way and for some specific purpose.

Regulatory schemes usually involve expenditures of funds on costs which are either known, or properly estimated. In the indirect tax cases, evidence was provided demonstrating how the revenues would be used and how the regulatory costs of the scheme were estimated. In *Ontario Home Builders'*, supra, at p. 982, the charge levied was "meticulous in its detail" and "clearly operate[d] so as to limit recoupment to the actual costs". In *Allard*, supra, evidence was led by city officials demonstrating the actual costs of annual road repair, based on estimates from similar repairs in the municipality. In both cases, there was a fairly close "nexus" between the estimated costs and the revenues raised through the regulatory scheme.

Finally, the individual subject to the regulatory charge will usually either benefit from the regulation, or cause the need for the regulation: Magnet, supra, at p. 459. In *Allard*, supra, the gravel trucks caused the need for the repair to the roads; in *Ontario Home Builders'*, supra, the developers and the new home owners caused the need for the new schools. In both cases the individuals being charged also benefitted from the regulation.

A regulatory charge may exist to defray the expenses of the regulatory scheme, as was the case in *Allard* or *Ontario Home Builders'*, or the regulatory charges themselves may be the means of advancing a regulatory purpose. [...] A per-tonne charge on landfill waste may be levied to discourage the production of waste [...] A deposit-refund charge on bottles may encourage recycling of glass or plastic bottles [...]

In all cases, a court should identify the primary aspect of the impugned levy. [...] Although in today's regulatory environment, many charges will have elements of taxation and elements of regulation, the central task for the court is to determine whether the levy's primary purpose is, in pith and substance: (1) to tax, i.e., to raise revenue for general purposes; (2) to finance or constitute a regulatory scheme, i.e., to be a regulatory charge or to be ancillary or adhesive to a regulatory scheme; or (3) to charge for services directly rendered, i.e., to be a user fee. [...]

Section 125 applies only to taxes properly enacted under s. 91(3) or 92(2) of the *Constitution Act, 1867*. As this Court explained in *Re Exported Natural Gas Tax*, at p. 1068, s. 125 does not purport to affect activities of government other than taxation. Consequently, the section will not usually apply to user fees, for they cannot be considered to be "taxation" in the constitutional meaning of the word, as developed above: *City of Toronto*, supra; *Minister of Justice v. City of Levis*, [1919] A.C. 505; *Registrar of Titles*, supra. In particular, it is difficult to say that payment of charges for such merchantable commodities are "compulsory" or are used for a "public purpose": *Registrar of Titles*, supra, at pp. 771-72; *Urban Outdoor Trans Ad v. Scarborough (City)* (1999), 43 O.R. (3d) 673 (Sup. Ct.), at p. 683. However, some services may be so essential that although in theory it is not compulsory to pay for the services, in reality it is: *City of Levis*, supra, at p. 513; *Re Eurig Estate*, supra, at para. 17.

Nor does s. 125 apply to other types of regulatory charges, as I have described them above. Where a charge itself is the mechanism for advancing a regulatory purpose, such as a charge that encourages or discourages certain types of behaviour, or where a charge is "ancillary or adhesive to a regulatory scheme" which may be used to defray the costs of that scheme, then they will usually be applicable to the other order of government. As the majority of the Court explained in *Re Exported Natural Gas Tax*, supra, at p. 1070:

> If the primary purpose is the raising of revenue for general federal purposes then the legislation falls under s. 91(3) and the limitation in s. 125 is engaged. If, on the other hand, the federal government imposes a levy primarily for regulatory purposes, or as necessarily incidental to a broader regulatory scheme, such as the "adjustment levies" considered in *Reference respecting the Agricultural Products Marketing Act, R.S.C. 1970, s. A-7 et al.,* [1978] 2 S.C.R. 1198 or the unemployment insurance premiums in *Attorney-General for Canada v. Attorney-General for Ontario,* [1937] A.C. 355, then the levy is not in pith and substance "taxation" and s. 125 does not apply.

By protecting each level of government from taxation, but not from other types of regulatory charges, the Constitution accords a degree of operational space to the governments in a manner which best advances the goals of Canada's flexible federalism. It is with these concepts in mind that I now turn to the governmental levy at issue in this case.

D. Characterization of the Westbank First Nation Taxation By-laws

[...] The charges imposed by Westbank bear all of the hallmarks of "taxation". The charges here are enforceable by law. [...] The taxes are as compulsory as any municipal tax on land or interests in land.

The impugned charges are imposed under the authority of the legislature and levied by a public body. The by-laws are imposed pursuant to the power conferred by n. 83 of the *Indian Act* [...]

The charges are levied for a public purpose. In this case, the public purpose is for general Band governance. [...] As Lamer C.J. explained in *Canadian Pacific Ltd. v. Matsqui Indian Band*, [1995] 1 S.C.R. 3, at p. 33, the purposes of these taxes are "to promote the interests of Aboriginal peoples and to further the aims of self-government." [...] Here, the specific purpose of these taxes is to simply raise revenue, to be brought into the discretionary spending accounts of the Band. No evidence has been brought demonstrating that these charges have a secondary purpose of discouraging or encouraging any behaviour of the respondent, nor have any other regulatory purposes been demonstrated.

The appellant has also not demonstrated that these charges form a nexus with any regulatory costs such as to bring it into the type of charge contemplated by *Allard*, supra, and *Ontario Home Builders'*, supra. The charge forms no part of a regulatory scheme. Although the *Indian Act* is legislation in relation to Indian land, this is insufficient to meet the requirements for a "regulatory scheme" in the constitutional sense. There is insufficient evidence demonstrating that the charge is attached to any "complete and detailed code"; nor can it be said that this forms part of a "complex regulatory framework". There are no costs of a regulatory scheme identified. Westbank does not seek to alter B.C. Hydro's behaviour in any way. B.C. Hydro has not caused the need for any regulation, to which the charges adhere. Nor does it benefit from any regulation provided. In summary, these charges do not "regulate" in any sense of the word, and they are not attached to any scheme which does.

[...] In *Re Eurig Estate*, supra, para. 20, the charge was directed to the "court administration in general", as opposed to the general expenses of the province, and yet this was still held to be a tax. As in *Re Eurig Estate*, supra, at paras. 18-23, here there is only a loose, if any, relationship between the charge and any costs. I agree with the Attorney General of British Columbia's submissions that the Constitution demands more precision in order to oust the operation of s. 125. [...]

VII - Summary

Section 125 of the *Constitution Act, 1867*, advances the goals of federalism and democracy by according a degree of operational space to each level of government, free from interference by the other. It prohibits one level of government from taxing the property of the other. However, it does not prohibit the levying of user fees or other regulatory charges properly enacted within the government's sphere of jurisdiction.

In order to determine whether the impugned charge is a "tax" or a "regulatory charge" for the purposes of s. 125, several key questions must be asked. Is the charge: (1) compulsory and enforceable by law; (2) imposed under the authority of the legislature; (3) levied by a public body; (4) intended for a public purpose; and (5) unconnected to any form of a regulatory scheme? If the answers to all of these questions are affirmative, then the levy in question will generally be described as a tax.

As is evident from the fifth inquiry described above, the Court must identify the presence of a regulatory scheme in order to find a "regulatory charge". To find a regulatory scheme, a court should look for the presence of some or all of the following indicia of a regulatory scheme: (1) a complete, complex and detailed code of regulation; (2) a regulatory purpose which seeks to affect some behaviour; (3) the presence of actual or properly estimated costs of the regulation; (4) a relationship between the person being regulated and the regulation, where the person being regulated either benefits from, or causes the need for, the regulation. This list is not exhaustive. In order for a charge to be "connected" or "adhesive" to this regulatory scheme, the court must establish a relationship between the charge and the scheme itself. This will exist when the revenues are tied to the costs of the regulatory scheme, or where the charges themselves have a regulatory purpose, such as the regulation of certain behaviour.

In the case at bar, the levies are properly described as being, in pith and substance, taxation enacted under s. 91(3) of the *Constitution Act, 1867*. They are enforceable by law, imposed under the authority of the legislature, and are levied by a public body for a public purpose. The appellant has not demonstrated that the levies are connected to a "regulatory scheme" which could preclude the application of s. 125. The charge does not form any part of a detailed code of regulation. No costs of the regulatory scheme have been identified, to which the revenues from these charges are tied. The appellant does not seek to influence the respondent's behaviour in any way with these charges. There is no relationship between B.C. Hydro and any regulation to which these charges adhere. Although the *Indian Act* is legislation in relation to "Indians and Lands reserved for the Indians", this does not, in itself, create a "regulatory scheme" in the sense required by the Constitution.

As these taxes are imposed on B.C. Hydro, which it is conceded is an agent of the provincial Crown, s. 125 is engaged. As such, the taxation and assessment by-laws are inapplicable to the respondent. [...]

(c)   Direct Taxation vs. Indirect Taxation

MAGNET, "THE CONSTITUTIONAL DISTRIBUTION OF TAXATION POWERS IN CANADA"
(1978), 10 OTTAWA L.R. 473 AT 485-7.

DIRECT TAXATION

The constitutional division of expenditure authority in Canada has remained largely unchanged since Confederation. The provincial governments still are responsible for such areas as education, health, welfare and other forms of social assistance, asylums, administration of justice in the province, local public works and municipalities. What has changed, and changed radically since 1867, is the substance of political economy and consensus respecting what is the proper role of government in discharging responsibility for precisely these areas of jurisdiction. In 1867, in accordance with *laissez-faire* economics, provincial expenditures in the above fields were negligible. The complete opposite obtains today. There is active and expanding governmental initiative in all the above-mentioned provincial areas of jurisdiction. The amounts account for the vast bulk of public expenditure. Very considerable sums, oftentimes half of the total expended, are recouped by the provincial governments from the federal government in the form of conditional and unconditional transfers. [...] The balance comes largely from the provincial treasury, which must be filled by means of provincial taxation. Of course, all of this would be impossible by the original inspiration, in respect of taxing and spending authority, of the *B.N.A. Act*.

In fact, the constitutional distribution of taxation powers proved unworkable from the start. The provinces found themselves without sufficient revenues to discharge their limited functions. Moreover, the transfer of revenues and responsibilities following Confederation put all provinces in a deficit position. When the Privy Council's interpretation of the *B.N.A. Act* enormously increased provincial jurisdiction, some means had to be found to finance expanding provincial responsibilities. Three mechanisms were tried to ameliorate this unsatisfactory constitutional arrangement. The first was dissolution of the Confederation. This was not conspicuously successful, [but in Quebec the idea remains current]. Nova Scotia was the only government to attempt it. Within two years after union, under the leadership of Joseph Howe, the Imperial Parliament was petitioned to release the province from Confederation. The second alternative involved an increase in the subsidies paid under the *B.N.A. Act*. Despite some early federal willingness to alter the subsidies stated by the *B.N.A. Act* to be in full settlement of all claims on the central government, several events intervened to make the Dominion government rely on the full settlement clause and refuse further increase. A global depression, beginning in 1873, placed a severe crimp in the central government's fiscal capacities. The railroads entailed vast expense, creating further federal monetary restraint. From 1873 until 1906 the subsidy payments stood unaltered. Lastly, resort by the provinces to their own powers of taxation was explored. Some means had to be developed to make these significant. The means found was a judicial stretching of the concept of "direct taxation" of to encompass modes of taxation which would have been quite unimaginable to the Fathers of Confederation.

THE LEGAL TEST

The terms "direct and indirect taxation" were first considered by the Privy Council in *Attorney-General for Quebec v. Reed*. In that case the Earl of Selborne L.C. took as the measure of these words, their use in Mill's *Principles of Political Economy*. Mill had said:

> Taxes are either direct or indirect. A direct tax is one which is demanded from the very person who, it is intended or desired, should pay it. Indirect taxes are those which are demanded from one person in the expectation and intention that he shall indemnify himself at the expense of another such as the excise or customs. The producer or importer of a commodity is called

upon to pay tax on it, not with the intention to levy a peculiar contribution upon him, but to tax through him the consumers of the commodity, from whom it is supposed that he will recover the amount by means of an advance in price.

In *Bank of Toronto v. Lambe*, a Quebec statute imposed a tax on every bank doing business in the province, varying with the paid-up capital of the bank. Lord Hobhouse, in considering the validity of the tax, applied Mill's test, but vastly changed the meaning and scope of the words used. First, it was said that the test was a legal and not an economic one; accordingly, the opinions of economists as to the ultimate incidence of the tax were of no relevance. Second, the question was what did the words mean as used in the statute. Accordingly, the court had to determine the general tendency of the tax and the common understanding of men as to those tendencies.

The general tendency of a tax is a question of substance and not of form; it does not depend on the particular words used in the statute. Moreover, the ultimate incidence of the tax in any particular case is not of significance in determining the legal validity of the tax within Lord Hobhouse's test.

It is all very well to distinguish general tendency from ultimate incidence. But the question has to be put squarely as to what meaning, if any, the concept "general tendency as commonly understood" has. In *Lambe's* case there could be no question that the taxation would work its way through the bank's operations and be passed on to the bank's customers in the form of increased charges for services. Does the test mean, therefore, that the court should pretend a total lack of sophistication in appreciating this?

A lot of learning can go into distinguishing direct and indirect taxation. But how useful is it? The original rationale for the distinction was that the provinces should be prevented from embarking on ambitious expenditures. It was thought the best way to do this was by subjecting the legislatures to the political resistance encountered in levying direct taxation. By archaic political economy, direct taxation was thought to be more perceived. It provided, therefore, for greater scrutiny of the actions of the legislature by the electorate.

No one now seriously believes that the provinces do not have very significant and expensive responsibilities. Nor does anyone seriously contend that direct taxation has any more or less advantages than indirect taxation from the viewpoint of political economy. A crucial question, to which I shall return, must be put: what purpose does the distinction between direct and indirect taxation serve at the present day and what constitutional value does it protect?

CANADIAN INDUSTRIAL GAS & OIL LTD. v. SASK.
[1978] 2 S.C.R. 545, 80 D.L.R. (3d) 449 at 451 et seq.

MARTLAND J. [Laskin C.J., Beetz, Judson, Ritchie, Spence and Pigeon, JJ. concurring]: — [The] validity [of certain Saskatchewan legislation] [...] was challenged [unsuccessfully at trial and on appeal] by the appellant, a corporation engaged in the exploration for, drilling for and production of oil and natural as in Saskatchewan and owning freehold leases, Crown leases and royalty interests in that Province. [...]

The legislation was enacted following the sharp rise in the price of oil on the world market which occurred in 1973. The effect of the legislation has been summarized in the reasons of my brother Dickson, which I have had the advantage of reading. For purposes of convenience I substantially repeat that summary here:

> First, production revenues from freehold lands were subjected to what was called a "mineral income tax". The tax was 100% of the difference between the price received at the well-head and the "basic well-head price", a statutory figure approximately equal to the price per barrel received by producers prior to the energy crisis. The owner's interest in oil and gas rights in producing tracts of less than 1,280 acres were exempted from tax. Deductions approved by the Minister of Mineral Resources were allowed in respect of increases in production costs and extraordinary transportation costs. Provision was made for the Minister to determine the well-head value of the oil where he was of the opinion that oil had been disposed of at less than its fair value.
>
> Secondly, all petroleum and natural gas in all producing tracts within the Province were expropriated and subjected to what was called a "royalty surcharge". Oil and gas rights owned by one person in producing tracts not exceeding 1,280 acres were exempted. Although introduced by Regulation rather than statute, the royalty surcharge is calculated in the same manner as the mineral income tax. For all practical purposes they are the same, save one exception. The well-head value for the purposes of royalty surcharge is the *higher* of the price received at the well-head and the price per barrel listed in the Minister's order. [...]

The practical consequence of the application of this legislation is that the Government of Saskatchewan will acquire the benefit of all increases in the value of oil produced in that province above the set basic well-head price fixed by the statute and regulations, which is approximately the same as that which existed in 1973 before the increase in world prices for oil. In this connection, there is the important fact that 98% of all crude oil produced in Saskatchewan is destined for export from the Province either to Eastern Canada or the United States of America. [...]

DIRECT OR INDIRECT TAXATION

My brother Dickson has reviewed the leading authorities dealing with the distinction between direct and indirect taxation. It is not necessary for me to repeat that review here. He has pointed out that it has been settled that:

> The dividing line between a direct and an indirect tax is referable to and ascertainable by the "general tendencies of the tax and the common understanding of men as to those tendencies" [...] The general tendency of a tax is the relevant criterion.

He has also pointed out that certain well understood categories of taxation have been generally established as falling within one or other of these classes.

Thus custom levies are recognized as being indirect taxes, whereas income and property taxes have been recognized as being direct taxes. Similarly, a commodity tax has, as a general rule, been regarded as an indirect tax. The appellant submits that the levies here in question are commodity taxes, and refers to the Privy Council decision in *The King v. Caledonian Collieries Ltd.*, [1928] A.C. 358 at p. 362.

In that case the tax was imposed upon the gross revenue of every mine owner, at a rate not to exceed 2%. The Privy Council considered that the general tendency of the tax would be for a mine owner to seek to recover the tax from his purchasers.

A sales tax, imposed upon vendors of goods, has been generally regarded as an indirect tax. On the other hand, where the tax, although collected through the vendor is actually paid by the ultimate consumer, the tax has been held to be direct: *Atlantic Smoke Shops Ltd. v. Conlon*, [1943] A.C. 550; *Cairns Construction Ltd. v. Government of Saskatchewan*, [1960] S.C.R. 619. However, in the present case the tax is imposed upon and payable by the producer in relation to the sale price of the oil which is produced. It is a sales tax, but the contention of the respondents is that it is not an indirect tax because the legislation does not contemplate and seeks to preclude the recovery of the tax from the purchaser.

The respondent contends that the mineral income tax is, as its name implies, an income tax, and so, a direct tax. I agree with the reasons of my brother Dickson for holding that that tax is not an income tax as that term is understood in the authorities which say that an income tax is a direct tax. The respondent submits, with respect to the royalty surcharge, that it is not a tax, but that it is a genuine royalty payable to the Crown, as the owner of mineral rights, by its lessees who have been authorized to extract minerals from Crown lands. To determine the validity of this contention it is necessary to consider the nature of the legal relationship between the Crown and the persons from whom payment of the royalty surcharge is demanded.

Some of these persons were the holders of petroleum and natural gas leases from the owners of the freehold interest in such minerals. Their obligations to pay royalties depended upon the terms of the lease from the freehold owner. The effect of Part IV of Bill 42 was to expropriate the rights of the freehold owners in the petroleum and natural gas in their lands, save in the case of freehold owners of producing tracts which had an aggregate total area of 1,280 acres or less.

Owners coming within this exemption would retain title of their petroleum and natural gas rights and the legal relationship between them and their lessees would continue. However, Bill 42 imposed on such lessees the obligation to pay mineral income tax in respect of their production.

With respect to lands not falling within the exemption, the owners were divested of their title, which was given, by the statute, to the Crown. This was accomplished by s-s. 28(1) of Bill 42, but the transfer to and vesting of title in the Crown was stated to be "subject to any lease affecting the same that may exist immediately preceding the tenth day of December, 1973".

The rights of leaseholders in this category were thus preserved. However, s-s. 33(2) subjected such lessees to the same royalty surcharge as was imposed upon lessees leasing directly from the Crown. It provided:

> 33(2) Any person having a lease of the oil and gas rights or any of them shall be subject to section 63 of *The Petroleum and Natural Gas Regulations, 1969*, when enacted pursuant to section 18 and shall be liable to pay the royalty surcharge provided for therein from the first day of January, 1974, as if the lease came within subsection (1) of section 63.

The levy thus imposed cannot, in my opinion, be a royalty. The royalty payable by the lessee was fixed by the terms of his lease, and that lease was preserved by the terms of s-s. 28(1). It was not expropriated by the Crown. The imposition upon the lessee of the royalty surcharge levy was, in my opinion, a tax upon the lessee's share of the production to which he was lawfully entitled. I agree with my brother Dickson that this levy fell within the criteria laid down by Duff, J., as he then was, in *Lawson v. Interior Tree Fruit & Vegetable Committee*, [1931] S.C.R. 357 at p. 363, for deciding whether a levy constituted a tax. [...]

In my opinion the royalty surcharge made applicable to these Crown leases was not a royalty for which provision was made in the lease agreement. It was imposed as a levy upon the share of production to which, under the lease, the lessee was entitled, and was a tax upon production.

I agree with the reasons of my brother Dickson for concluding that the royalty surcharge is a tax imposed upon Crown lessees of the same nature as the mineral income tax imposed upon lessees holding leases from freehold owners. It is significant that the royalty surcharge is computed in the same manner as the mineral income tax, and that the proceeds of both are to be paid into the same fund. [...]

Both the mineral income tax and the royalty surcharge are taxes upon the production of oil virtually all of which is produced for export from the Province of Saskatchewan.

[...] These taxing provisions, *i.e.*, both mineral income tax and royalty surcharge, have the following impact upon the Saskatchewan oil producer. In the first place he is effectively precluded from recovering in respect of the oil which he produces any return greater than the basic well-head price per barrel. He is subjected to an income freeze at that figure and can obtain no more than that. In the second place, he is compelled to sell his product at a price which will equal what the Minister determines to be the fair value of the oil which he produces. He must do this, because his production of oil is subject to a tax per barrel representing the difference between fair value and basic well-head price. If he is the lessee of mineral rights in lands in respect of which the mineral rights were expropriated by the Crown, he does not even have the option to discontinue production. Discontinuance of production without ministerial consent is subject to a heavy penalty.

The tax under consideration is essentially an export tax imposed upon oil production. In the past a tax of this nature has been considered to be an indirect tax. In *A.-G. B.C. v. Macdonald Murphy Lumber Co.*, [1930] A.C. 357, the Privy Council considered the validity of a timber tax imposed by s. 58 of the *Forest Act*, R.S.B.C. 1924, c. 93, upon all timber cut within the Province, except that upon which a royalty was payable, but which provided for a rebate or nearly all of the tax in the case of timber used or manufactured in the Province. In his reasons in that case Lord Macmillan, at pp. 364-5 A.C., said:

> Mr. Lawrence, however, contended that although the tax might accurately be described as an export duty, this did not necessarily negative its being a direct tax within the meaning of the Act. Without reviewing afresh the niceties of discrimination between direct and indirect taxation it is enough to point out that an export tax is normally collected on merchantable goods in course of transit in pursuance of commercial transactions. Whether the tax is ultimately borne by the exporting seller at home or by the importing buyer abroad depends on the terms of the contract between them. It may be borne by the one or by the other. It was said in the present case that the conditions of the competitive market in the United States compelled the exporter of timber from British Columbia to that country to bear the whole burden of the tax himself. That, however, is a matter of the exigencies of a particular market, and is really irrelevant in determining the inherent character of the tax. While it is no doubt true that a tax levied on personal property, no less than a tax levied on real property, may be a direct tax where the taxpayer's personal property is selected as the criterion of his ability to pay, a tax which, like the tax here in question, is levied on a commercial commodity on the occasion of its exportation in pursuance of trading transactions, cannot be described as a tax whose incidence is, by its nature, such that normally it is finally borne by the first payer, and is not susceptible of being passed on. On the contrary, the existence of an export tax is invariably an element in the fixing of prices, and the question whether it is to be borne by seller or purchaser in whole or in part is determined by the bargain made. The present tax thus exhibits the leading characteristic of an indirect tax as defined by authoritative decisions.

The mineral income tax and the royalty surcharge are taxes imposed in a somewhat unusual manner. The mineral income tax purports to be a direct tax upon income imposed upon the taxpayer, which he cannot pass on to his purchaser. The royalty surcharge, while carrying a different title, is the same in nature. What differentiates this legislation from other legislation imposing export taxes is that the true effect of the legislation is to impose a freeze upon the actual income which the producer exporter can derive from the sale of his product. All that he is permitted to retain on the sale of each barrel of oil is the basic well-head price. In addition to being subjected to an income freeze, he is compelled to sell his product at a price equivalent to what the Minister considers to be its fair value in order to obtain the funds necessary to meet the tax. This amount per barrel over and above the basic well-head price he must obtain from his purchaser as a part of the purchase price. In essence the producer is a conduit through which the increased value of each barrel of oil above the basic well-head price is channeled into the hands of the Crown by way of tax. The increase in value is itself the tax and it is paid by the purchaser of the oil.

It is contended that the imposition of these taxes will not result in an increase in the price paid by oil purchasers, who would have been required to pay the same market price even if the taxes had not been imposed, and so there could be no passing on of the tax by the Saskatchewan producer to his purchaser. On this premise it is argued that the tax is not indirect. This, however, overlooks the all important fact that the scheme of the legislation under consideration involves the fixing of the maximum return of the Saskatchewan producers at the basic well-head price per barrel, while at the same time compelling him to sell at a higher price. There are two components in the sale price, first the basic well-head price and second the tax imposed. Both are intended by the legislation to be incorporated into the price payable by the purchaser. The purchaser pays the amount of the tax as a part of the purchase price.

For these reasons it is my opinion that the taxation scheme comprising the mineral income tax and the royalty surcharge does not constitute direct taxation within the Province and is therefore outside the scope of the provincial power under s-s. 92(2) of the *British North America Act, 1867*. [...]

For these reasons, in my opinion, the statutory provisions, and the Regulations and orders enacted and made relating to the imposition of the mineral income tax and the royalty surcharge, are *ultra vires* of the Legislature of the Province of Saskatchewan. [...]

DICKSON J. [De Grandpré J. concurring]: — The question raised in this appeal is whether a complex of legislation, enacted by the Legislature of Saskatchewan, following the onset in late 1973 of what has been called the "energy crisis", is *intra vires* the Legislature of Saskatchewan. [...]

Virtually all of the crude oil produced in Saskatchewan is exported from the Province. In 1973, only 1.8% of Saskatchewan crude was used in Saskatchewan refineries; 43.9% was used in Provinces of Canada other than Saskatchewan; and 54.3% was exported to the United States. This is attributable in part to the fact that most of the oil produced in the Province is medium or heavy crude which, when refined, produces a heavy residue of bunker oil suitable only for use in heavy industry, which is not present in Saskatchewan. Another contributing factor is the fact that the flow of the pipeline through which the oil leaves the Province is from west to east. Light and medium crudes, suitable for use in Saskatchewan, are produced in the southeastern part of the Province, far from the refineries at Regina and Moose Jaw. These refineries are served by oil from the Province of Alberta. The appellant, Canadian Industrial Gas & Oil Ltd., is a producer of crude oil in Saskatchewan and sells its entire production at the well site. Virtually all of its product leaves the Province by pipeline for refining by others in more easterly Provinces of Canada or in the United States. [...] Prior to the enactment of the legislation, the validity of which is questioned in these proceedings, the appellant's weighted average receipt per barrel for the Province amounted to $3.10, with direct field costs of 58¢ per barrel, exclusive of administrative overhead, depreciation, depletion and taxes.

Since the legislation came into force there have been no significant changes in the marketing of Saskatchewan crude oil. The levels of production and exports of oil have continued at a constant or slightly increased tempo, close to production capacity. [...] I adjudge:

1. That the mineral income tax is not an income tax; it is, however, a direct tax, and therefore within provincial competence.

2. That the royalty surcharge is not a royalty; it too is a tax but also a direct tax.

3. That the entire legislative scheme is aimed at taxation and its effect, if any, upon extra-provincial trade and commerce is incidental and non-disabling. [...]

DIRECT OR INDIRECT TAXATION

The appellant claims that the mineral income tax and the royalty surcharge are indirect taxes and hence beyond the power of a provincial Legislature. The established guide for determining the validity of this submission is the classical formulation of John Stuart Mill (*Principles of Political Economy*, Book V, c. 3):

> Taxes are either direct or indirect. A direct tax is one which is demanded from the very person who it is intended or desired should pay it. Indirect taxes are those which are demanded from one person in the expectation and intention that he shall indemnify himself at the expense of another, such are the excise or customs.

> The producer or importer of a commodity is called upon to pay a tax on it not with the intention to levy a peculiar contribution upon him, but to tax through him the consumers of the commodity, from whom it is supposed that he will recover the amount by means of an advance in price.

Mill's well-known writings appeared not long before the drafting of the *British North America Act, 1867* and were presumed by the Privy Council to be familiar to the Fathers of Confederation. The definition was first applied in *A.-G. Quebec v. Reed* (1884), 10 App. Cas. 141. In that case it was held that the question whether a tax is a direct or an indirect tax cannot depend upon special events which may vary in particular cases; the best general rule is to look to the time of payment and if at that time the incidence of the tax is uncertain then it cannot be called direct taxation. Mill's test became firmly established in *Bank of Toronto v. Lambe* (1887), 12 App. Cas. 575. In that case Lord Hobhouse said that while it was proper and, indeed, necessary to have regard to the opinion of economists, the question is a legal one, *viz.*, what the words mean as used in the statute. The problem is primarily one of law rather than of refined economic analysis. The dividing line between a direct and an indirect tax is referable to and ascertainable by the "general tendencies of the tax and the common understanding of men as to those tendencies": *Lambe's* case.

The general tendency of a tax is the relevant criterion. This must be distinguished from the ultimate incidence of the tax in the circumstances of the particular case (cites omitted).

In *City of Charlottetown v. Foundation Maritime Ltd.*, [1932] S.C.R. 589, Rinfret, J., pointed out that Mill's canon is founded on the theory of the ultimate incidence of the tax, not the ultimate incidence depending on the special circumstances of individual cases.

The nature of the tax is a question of substance and does not turn on the language used by the Legislature: *The King v. Caledonian Collieries Ltd.*, [1928] A.C. 358.

There can be no doubt that by the words "direct and indirect taxation" the Fathers of Confederation contemplated certain distinct categories of taxation, as well as a general test of directness. Only certain of such categories, such as income and property taxes, were to be available to the Legislatures. There were two reasons for this. The first was based on arcane political economy. It was thought that a direct tax would be more perceived than an indirect tax. The effect was thought to provide for greater scrutiny and reticence by the electorate with a resulting parsimony in public expenditure. The second reason proved wrong from the start. It was thought that provincial activities would be limited and revenue needs would be slim; the Legislatures, therefore, would have no necessity to resort to most tax pools.

Clearly, direct and indirect taxation are terms of historical reference, and although there is no reason to believe that the *British North America Act, 1867* is not a document of evolving meaning, not limited to its original inspiration, jurisprudence, in so far as concerns particular forms of taxation like income or property taxes, has captured the historical spirit of "direct" and "indirect" taxation and preserved it. The effect of this was explained by Viscount Cave, L.C., in *City of Halifax v. Fairbanks*, [[1928] A.C. 117 at 125]:

What then is the effect to be given to Mill's formula above quoted? No doubt it is valuable as providing a logical basis for the distinction already established between direct and indirect taxes, and perhaps also as a guide for determining as to any new or unfamiliar tax which may be imposed in which of the two categories it is to be placed; but it cannot have the effect of disturbing the established classification of the old and well known species of taxation, and making it necessary to apply a new test to every particular member of those species. The imposition of taxes on property and income, of death duties and of municipal and local rates is, according to the common understanding of the term, direct taxation, just as the exaction of a customs or excise duty on commodities or of a percentage duty on services would ordinarily be regarded as indirect taxation; and although new forms of taxation may from time to time be added to one category or the other in accordance with Mill's formula, it would be wrong to use that formula as a ground for transferring a tax universally recognized as belonging to one class to a different class of taxation.

Historically well-understood categories of taxation have a known jurisprudential fate. Thus, a customs levy cannot be made by the Legislature whereas a property tax or income tax falls unquestionably within their competence. Careful constitutional analysis is required in respect of any unusual or hybrid form of taxation. A hybrid form of taxation may well have aspects which are direct and others which are indirect. By nineteenth century political economy, any element of indirectness was a stigma as tending to obfuscate the actions of the Legislature. That consideration is of minor importance today. In assessing the policy of a new form of taxation the jurisprudence offers no certain guide. One begins with the *British North America Act, 1867*, in which there are two additional criteria – (1) that the taxation be within the Province, and (2) that it be in order to the raising of a revenue for provincial purposes. Implicit in this, and more important than a vestige of indirectness, is the prohibition of the imposition by a Province of any tax upon citizens beyond its borders. Additionally, a Province cannot, through the ostensible use of its power to tax, invade prohibited fields. It cannot by way of taxation regulate trade and commerce or prohibit the free admission of produce or manufactured goods from other Provinces. It must confine itself to the raising of a revenue for provincial purposes.

Argument was directed to the Court to the effect that the tax here in question is a commodity tax and, as such, the general tendency would be for the tax to be passed on and therefore categorized as indirect. It is true that a tax on any one commodity whether laid on its production, its importation, its carriage from place to place, or its sale will, as a general rule, raise the value and price of the commodity by at least the amount of the tax: Mill, Vol. II (1893 ed.), at p. 435. That is very old doctrine and for that reason a commodity tax is traditionally conceived as an indirect tax. The Courts have taken that as one criterion in characterizing the tax (cites omitted). But there is a caveat. Taxes imposed on the consumers of particular commodities are often called, or seem to be, taxes on commodities but they are not. Consumer taxes are normally regarded as direct. See *A.-C. B.C. v. Kingcome Navigation Co. Ltd.*, supra, and *Atlantic Smoke Shops Ltd. v. Conlon*, [1943] A.C. 550, as related to consumption of non durable goods and *Cairns Construction Ltd. v. Government of Saskatchewan*, [1960] S.C.R. 619, related to durable goods.

This appeal cannot be decided simply on the basis that the mineral income tax is levied on a commercial commodity. The Court is obliged to examine the legislation and relevant facts for the purpose of determining, by the application of the test formulated by Mill, as developed in the authorities, whether the tax is direct or indirect. In *Atlantic Smoke Shops Ltd. v. Conlon*, Viscount Simon, L.C., asserted that two distinct categories of taxes should not be understood as relieving the Courts of the obligation of examining each particular tax, or as justifying the classification of a tax as indirect simply because it was associated with the purchase of a commodity. A similar approach was taken in *A.-G. B.C. v. Esquimalt & Nanaimo R. Co.*, [1950] A.C. 87.

It is hard to see that the mineral income tax fits snugly into the commodity tax category. There are several rough edges. First, the tax falls upon a holder of certain rights in respect of part of the amount received. Secondly, unlike a true commodity tax, *i.e.*, a fixed imposition or a percentage of the commodity – s. 6 of the Act contemplates an imposition varying with production costs. If production costs rise, the share of the Province by taxation falls. Thirdly, the tax is not an "add-to-the-price" impost but rather a "take-from-the-owner" levy.

Finally, the tax does not fall on the product but only on certain entitled holders. Owners of rights having an aggregate area of less than 1,280 acres in producing tracts are exempted. For these reasons, the tax resists classification as a commodity tax in so far as constitutional jurisprudence knows that term. It must be subject, therefore, to further constitutional scrutiny.

Counsel for the Province attempted to support the tax as constituting an income tax on the authority of *Forbes v. A.-G. Man.*, [1937] A.C. 260. The so-called "mineral income tax" is not an income tax in any generally recognized sense of the term. A true income tax means, for taxation purposes, a levy on gains and profits: *The King v. Caledonian Collieries Ltd.*, supra. The evidence of Professor Barber in the case at bar confirms that view. He defined income tax as being, according to generally accepted accounting principles and business practice, a tax imposed on net income and in determining such net income any expenses incurred in earning that income are inherently deductible.

In *Nickel Rim Mines Ltd. v. A.-G. Ont.*, [1966] 1 O.R. 345, cited by counsel for the Province, the tax was held to be a direct tax but it was levied upon annual profits, determined after taking into account a "long list of deductions". The tax was described by Wells, J., as one on "net profits ascertained or estimated". On appeal [*loc. cit.*], Porter, C.J.O., referred to the tax as a "profit tax". In my view, the *Nickel Rim* case does not assist the Province. The tax is not levied upon net income. It is more in the nature of a gross revenue tax – as above a certain statutory figure it becomes a 100% levy – that has generally in the past been regarded as an indirect tax. The tax is in essence a flat sum which will vary according to the sale price of the oil but is not necessarily reflective of *actual* expense experience. Expenses are discretionary and not inherently deductible so as to fall within the definition of an income tax. If s. 4A should ever come into play the tax would be levied not on the price received but on a ministerial figure. In sum, an income tax is a tax upon gross receipts less expenses. In the instant tax it is possible that these two figures will be subject to ministerial determination.

It should be clear from the foregoing that neat constitutional categories are of marginal assistance in the present case. The tax resists such classification; it is a hybrid. It must be assessed in the light of constitutional analysis, keeping in mind the *indicia* to which I have above referred.

Can it be said, then, that the tax is one which is demanded from the very person who it is intended or desired should pay it, or can it be said, rather, that it is demanded from the oil producer in the expectation and intention that he shall indemnify himself at the expense of another? The question is not easily answered. An example might assist. If we assume a basic well-head price of $3 per barrel and a sale at $7 per barrel, the tax would amount to $4 per barrel. If basic well-head price and production costs remain constant but the selling price increases to $11 per barrel, the tax would amount to $8 per barrel. It is quite obvious that the oil producer will not be in a position to bear the tax of $4 or $8 out of the basic well-head price of $3 per barrel which he retains. On this view it is arguable that the tax is passed on to the purchaser as a component of price. I do not think, however, that this can be said to be the true view. An indirect tax is an amount which is added to what would otherwise be the price of the commodity or service. This appears from Mill's formulation. He says that tax is indirect when the producer is called upon to pay a tax not with the intention of levying a contribution upon him, but to tax through him the consumers of the commodity, from whom it is supposed that he will recover the amount "by means of an advance in price", *i.e.*, as an "add-on". In *A.-G. B.C. v. Esquimalt & Nanaimo R. Co.*, supra, Lord Greene pointed out that in order to constitute an indirect tax the *tax itself* must have a general tendency to be passed on. If an article selling for $10 is subjected to a 10% customs duty, the general tendency would be simply to add the amount of the tax or more to the price of the commodity. The purchaser would then pay one dollar or more in excess of the amount he would have paid in the absence of the tax. In *Security Export Co. v. Hetherington*, [1923] S.C.R. 539 at p. 558, Duff, J., adopted the following definition of a direct tax, taken from the Oxford Dictionary:

> one levied immediately upon the persons who are to bear the burden, as opposed to *indirect* taxes levied upon commodities, of which *the price is thereby increased* so that the persons on whom the incidence ultimately falls pay indirectly a proportion of taxation included in the price of the article. (emphasis added.)

If the price is increased by reason of the tax, the tendency will be to have the consumer bear the increase. If the price is not increased, the tendency will be to have the producer bear the tax. For myself, I can find nothing in the language of the Act nor in the oral or documentary evidence to suggest that the price of Saskatchewan oil was increased by the addition of the "mineral income tax" levied, or that the purchaser of Saskatchewan crude paid more per barrel than he would have paid in the absence of the tax. Nor can I discover anything which leads me to conclude that the Legislature of Saskatchewan acted on any view other than that of collecting maximum tax from the persons who are by the statute made liable to pay it, namely, Saskatchewan oil producers.

There is a further consideration which should not be overlooked. If it had been intended that those subject to the tax would pass it on to others the inclusion of the "farmers' section", exempting tracts not exceeding 1,280 acres, would have been quite unnecessary.

The "farmers' section" highlights the essential axis on which the present litigation revolves. It is a dispute concerning who, as between the producers and the Government of Saskatchewan, will reap the benefit of a fortuitous rise in the price of oil. In the case of producers holding rights in producing tracts in excess of 1,280 acres, the Legislature has determined the benefit shall accrue to provincial coffers; in the case of a producer in a smaller tract, the Legislature has abstained from imposition leaving the benefit in the producer's pocket. The ultimate position of the final consumer is unaffected. It is also patent that any attempt by an oil producer to pass on an amount additional to the selling price would be self-defeating. Every increase in selling price will be reflected by an equal increase in tax as, according to the formula, tax equals well-head price received minus basic well-head price.

Reference was made in the Saskatchewan Courts, and in argument in this Court, to the international or "world" price of oil and the effect of such upon the pricing of Saskatchewan crude. It has been contended on behalf of the Province that the world price would place a ceiling on the price of Saskatchewan crude and, therefore, the Saskatchewan producer could not pass on the mineral income tax to the purchaser. Again, to take an example, if world price were $11 per barrel and basic well-head price $3 per barrel, the mineral income tax would amount to $8 per barrel. The producer could not recover this amount by increasing the price to $19 per barrel and for good reasons (i) his oil could not command that price in the market, and (ii) he would be deprived of the additional revenue by the mechanics of the Act.

If Saskatchewan oil is sold in the market at prevailing market prices, as I understand to be the case, then I do not think it can properly be said that the Eastern Canadian oil consumer pays more by reason of imposition of the tax. There is no added "burden" to "cling" to the commodity unit: see Rand, J., in C.P.R. Co. et al. v. A.-G. Sask. et al., [1952] 2 S.C.R. 231. [...]

I cannot stress too strongly the point that purchasers would be paying the same price whether the tax existed or not. This fact, to my mind, conclusively prevents the levy from being in the nature of an indirect tax or an export tax. It is not passed on to purchasers to augment the price they would otherwise pay. Instead, they pay exactly the price they would pay in the absence of the tax and the producers are taxed on the profits they would otherwise receive.

I would hold that, in its true nature and effect, the mineral income tax constitutes direct taxation within the Province in order to the raising of a revenue for provincial purposes.

The Province seeks to sustain the constitutionality of the royalty surcharge imposed by the *Oil and Natural Gas Regulations, 1969*, on the basis that it is a "variable" royalty. The right of the Crown, in respect of Crown lands, to impose contractually a royalty and to vary such royalty is undisputed. The validity of a variable royalty was considered and affirmed in *A.-G. Alta. et al. v. Huggard Assets Ltd.*, [1953] A.C. 420. Failing that, it is said that the royalty surcharge can be supported as direct taxation or as legislation in relation to property and civil rights in the Province.

The first question to be determined in respect of royalty surcharge, therefore, is whether the royalty surcharge is a royalty or a tax. The answer to that question turns on whether the Province, in imposing royalty surcharge, was acting *qua* lessor or *qua* taxing authority. In other words, was the relationship of the Legislature *vis-à-vis* the oil producer that of lessor-lessee or was the true character of the relationship that of sovereign taxing authority-taxpayer. [...]

The characteristics of a royalty were noted by Maclean, J., in *B. & B. Royalties Ltd. v. Minister of National Revenue*, [1940] Ex. C.R. 90. In that case "royalty" was defined as, p. 92 Ex. C.R., "an interest in production reserved by the original lessor by way of rent for the right or privilege of taking oil or gas out of a designated tract of land". Cameron, J., in *Ross v. Minister of National Revenue*, [1950] Ex. C.R. 411 at p. 418, referred to royalties as "periodical payments either in kind or money which depend upon and vary in amount according to the production and use of the mine or well, and are payable for the right to explore for, bring into production and dispose of the oils or minerals yielded up". In general terms, a royalty as applied to an oil and gas lease is a share, as provided in the lease, of the oil or gas produced, or the proceeds thereof, for the privilege of exploring for and recovering oil and gas. [...] A tax, on the other hand, is a compulsory contribution, imposed by the sovereign authority for public purposes or objects. Duff, J., made that point in *Lawson v. Interior Tree Fruit & Vegetable Committee*, [1931] S.C.R. 357 at p. 363. He identified certain levies as taxes and in so doing applied the following criteria: (i) enforceable by law; (ii) imposed under the authority of the Legislature; (iii) imposed by a public body; (iv) for a public purpose: see also *Lower Mainland Dairy Products Sales Adjustment Committee v. Crystal Dairy Ltd.*, [1933] A.C. 168. [...]

Section 63(1) of the Regulations imposes the royalty surcharge on "oil produced or deemed to be produced from Crown lands". That imposition touches persons who are not in any contractual relationship with the Crown such as those who assigned Crown leases but retained a gross override, or those persons who purchased royalty trust certificates under the terms of a royalty trust. It is hard to see that these people stand in a contractual relationship with the Crown. The obligation arises by legislative command, not by a process of negotiation between free wills, resulting in a meeting of minds. [...]

When oil and gas rights in the Province were expropriated, those rights would be subject in many instances to existing freehold oil and gas leases. Those leases would not contain the reddendum clause found in Crown leases, permitting the Crown to vary the rate of royalty from time to time. Section 33(2) subjected the lease holder, by statute, to the royalty surcharge but the point to note is that this was not pursuant to a negotiated and agreed reddendum clause in the lease. The only way the Crown could reach the persons holding freehold leases of expropriated oil and rights and obtain more than the royalty reserved in those leases would be by way of legislation amending the leases or by taxation. The obligation to pay the royalty surcharge arises *ex lege* and not *ex contractu*. Another distinguishing feature is that a conventional royalty is a percentage (normally fixed but which may, in the case of Crown leases, be varied by the lessor) of production. The royalty surcharge is the taking of everything in excess of a statutory figure.

Foreign also to any lessor-lessee relationship is the constraint imposed by s. 42 of Bill 42, which exposes to a fine of $1,000 per day any person who causes production to be stopped without ministerial consent.

In my view, although in name a royalty, the royalty surcharge is, in substance, a tax. Except as affecting lessees under pre-existing Crown leases, it is a levy compulsorily imposed on previously existing contractual rights by a public authority for public purposes. It is patent that the consensual agreement and mutuality ordinarily found in a lessor-lessee relationship is entirely absent in the relationship between the Crown and persons subjected to the royalty surcharge. Royalty surcharge is the same 100% levy as is imposed in other terms as mineral income tax. That it is a tax is not fatal. In object and purpose and mode of exaction it is congruent with mineral income tax. It is therefore direct and falls within provincial competence. [...]

I would dismiss the appeal with costs to the respondent as against the appellant but without costs to any of the intervenants.

REFERENCE RE QUEBEC G.S.T.
[1994] 2 S.C.R. 715

GONTHIER J. [for the Court]: — [...] In this reference, we are asked to consider the constitutional validity of proposed amendments to the Province of Quebec's sales tax ("QST"). These amendments are designed to transform the QST into a tax similar in all essential respects to the federal goods and services tax ("GST"). Pursuant to an agreement between the Province of Quebec and the Government of Canada on August 30, 1990, the tax bases of the federal and provincial consumption taxes were substantially harmonized and the Province of Quebec accepted responsibility for administering the GST in Quebec. The proposed amendments which form the subject of this reference would represent the final steps in harmonizing the QST and GST. The GST was the subject of an earlier reference to this Court and was held to be *intra vires* Parliament (*Reference Re Goods and Services Tax*, [1992] 2 S.C.R. 445 ("*GST Reference*")). The validity of the federal tax, however, is in no way determinative of the issues raised in this reference. Although the desire to harmonize federal and provincial consumption taxes is administratively and politically attractive, it remains to be determined whether the proposal is compatible with the Constitution.

The principal difference between the existing QST and the GST derives from the concept of "non-taxable supplies" present in the provincial regime. This concept ensures that the QST is a retail sales tax, that is, one which is collected at the retail level. The GST, in contrast, is a value-added tax which is collected and reimbursed at every stage along the production and marketing chain with the final consumer ultimately being the one to pay the tax. The net result of the two taxes is identical· the ultimate consumer pays the tax; however, the mechanism for achieving this end differs. [...]

The general operation of the proposed tax is clear from an examination of the concept of taxable supply. A taxable supply is defined in s. 1 of the draft Act as the provision of property or a service in any manner, including sale, transfer, barter, exchange, licence, lease, gift or alienation in the course of a commercial activity. Every purchaser of a taxable supply must pay a tax equal to 8 percent of the value of the consideration given for the supply (in certain cases reduced to 4 or 0 percent (zero-rated supplies); draft Act, s. 2). As with the GST, the purchaser of a taxable supply who uses that good or service in the production of other taxable supplies will be entitled to a refund from the government equal to the amount of tax initially paid on its inputs (the input tax refund or the input tax credit under the GST; draft Act, s. 13). To the extent that taxable supplies are not used by the purchaser to produce other taxable supplies, by definition they will be consumed by the purchaser for non-commercial purposes. In such a case, the purchaser will not be eligible for an input tax refund. The tax will thus be collected and refunded at each stage of the production and marketing process until the ultimate consumer is reached. The input tax refund mechanism, in the case of taxable supplies, thus ensures that the tax is paid by the ultimate consumer. [...]

The collection of the tax will be assured by every person engaged in commercial activities who makes a taxable supply. The persons collecting the tax are agents of the Minister of Revenue and are required to be registered with the Minister (draft Act, ss. 25 and 28). [...]

The central issue in this reference is whether the proposed tax, in its general operation as well as its specific details, is a tax within the provincial taxing power contained in s. 92(2) of the *Constitution Act, 1867*. Section 92(2) stipulates:

> **92.** In each Province the Legislature may exclusively make Laws in relation to Matters coming within the Classes of Subjects next herein-after enumerated; that is to say, — [...]
>
> 2. Direct Taxation within the Province in order to the raising of a Revenue for Provincial Purposes.

It is well established that whether a given tax is direct or indirect in terms of the *Constitution Act, 1867* is a question of law and not of economic incidence. The test predominately relied on in the jurisprudence to distinguish between the two types of taxes is the formulation employed by John Stuart Mill in his 1848 treatise, *Principles of Political Economy,* Book V, c. III, at p. 371:

> A direct tax is one which is demanded from the very persons who, it is intended or desired, should pay it. Indirect taxes are those which are demanded from one person in the expectation and intention that he shall indemnify himself at the expense of another; such as the excise or customs.

Though this formulation is no longer used by economists, it has served and continues to serve the legal purpose of providing a relatively clear bench mark for applying the division of taxation powers contained in ss. 91 and 92 of the *Constitution Act, 1867*. Definitively adopted for that purpose in *Bank of Toronto v. Lambe* (1887), 12 App. Cas. 575 (P.C.), the distinction has subsequently been applied in a number of cases including *Allard Contractors Ltd. v. Coquitlam (District)*, [1993] 4 S.C.R. 371.

The application of Mill's distinction during the last century allows us to predict the constitutional fate of some taxes with a measure of confidence. In analyzing a given tax, it should be remembered that the courts examine the general tendency of the tax, rejecting exceptional factual circumstances as legally irrelevant (*Lambe*, supra; *Brewers and Maltsters' Association of Ontario v. Attorney-General for Ontario*, [1897] A.C. 231). Customs duties and excise taxes, as Mill noted, are indirect taxes. The tax in these two cases is paid by the importer or manufacturer with, it has been said, "the expectation and intention" that it will generally be passed on to the purchaser as an element of the price. There is no intention in either case to place the burden of the tax on the manufacturer or importer, who simply act as conduits through which to pass on the burden to others. The tax is therefore not paid by the person who is intended to bear the burden. Property, income and consumption taxes, in contrast, have been historically held to be direct taxes since their general tendency is that the person intended to bear the burden of the tax is the one who pays it. The intention apparent in the case of customs duties and excise taxes that the tax be passed on with the good is absent from property, income and consumption taxes.

The case law interpreting s. 92(2) contains various indicia or propositions which serve to guide the courts. Five of these are of particular relevance in determining the constitutionality of the proposed provincial value-added tax.

As noted above, one indicium is whether the intention of the legislator as to who should bear the tax is clear. In the case of direct taxes, Viscount Simon recognized that "the taxing authority is not indifferent as to which of the parties to the transaction ultimately bears the burden, but intends it as a `peculiar contribution' on the particular party selected to pay the tax" (*Atlantic Smoke Shops, Ltd. v. Conlon*, [1943] A.C. 550, at p. 564). A related indicium of direct taxation is whether everyone knows how much tax they really pay (Mill, Book V, c. VI, cited with approval by Viscount Simon in *Atlantic Smoke Shops*; see also *Attorney-General for Quebec v. Reed* (1884), 10 App. Cas. 141 (P.C.)). At Confederation, the decision to limit the provincial legislatures to direct taxation was aimed at transparency and thought to enhance political accountability. Though the criterion of accountability may not be the central focus of the more recent jurisprudence pertaining to s. 92(2), transparency still serves to identify a tax as direct.

A third indicium, one of indirectness, was recognized by Rand J. in *Canadian Pacific Railway Co. v. Attorney General for Saskatchewan*, [1952] 2 S.C.R. 231. He pointed to the attachment of a tax to a good as a strong indication that the tax is indirect (at pp. 251-52):

> If the tax is related or relatable, directly or indirectly, to a unit of the commodity or its price, imposed when the commodity is in course of being manufactured or marketed, then the tax tends to cling as a burden to the unit or the transaction presented to the market.

Thus, where the tax "clings" to the product in the sense that its amount attaches to the good and moves together with the good through the chain of supply, an element of indirectness may be present. The validity of Rand J.'s indicator is demonstrated most vividly by customs duties and excise taxes. This test was recently applied in *Allard Contractors*, supra, at pp. 394-98, to identify a volumetric fee on soil removal as an indirect tax.

At first glance, provincial consumption taxes would appear to be taxes which attach to a good; however, the case law has unequivocally and correctly recognized such taxes as direct (see *Atlantic Smoke Shops*, supra, and *Cairns Construction Ltd. v. Government of Saskatchewan*, [1960] S.C.R. 619). In particular, a number of cases have held that consumption taxes will be direct even though they may be passed on when the good or service initially taxed is incorporated or transformed into a new good or service (see *Attorney-General for British Columbia v. Kingcome Navigation Co.*, [1934] A.C. 45; *Cairns*, supra). Thus where a tax is imposed on the consumption of fuel oil, the fact that the oil may be used in the manufacture of another good and thereby passed on as part of the cost of that good does not render the tax unconstitutional. The good is consumed and the tax therefore cannot be passed on with the good as is the case with an import duty.

The final proposition of relevance in determining the constitutional validity of the proposed value-added tax is that the nature of a tax is not affected by the system of collection (see *Kingcome*, supra; *Atlantic Smoke Shops*, supra, and *Cairns*, supra). The fact that a retailer collects the tax from a consumer on behalf of the government and then physically pays the money over to the government does not alter the characterization of such a tax as direct. The person intended to bear the burden of the tax, the consumer, is still the one who in reality pays it even though the retailer as agent for the government collects it. It is true that the retailer bears a burden in relation to the collection of the tax; however, this burden is part of the general cost of doing business and cannot be related to or passed on in a recognizable form with any particular good.

In approaching new taxes, the constitutional fate of which is unknown, it is not without interest to refer to an important effect of the s. 92(2) limitation to direct taxation. In addition to the historical desire to promote transparency and accountability, one finds a concern in the case law and literature regarding taxation of persons outside the province by indirect means or taxation which interferes with interprovincial or international trade. The prohibition against excise taxes and customs duties clearly achieves this latter purpose. As my colleague La Forest J. noted in his study of the taxation power under the Canadian Constitution, "the person who ultimately pays an excise tax may have no other connection with the province benefitting from the tax than that the product was originally produced or manufactured there" (G. V. La Forest, *The Allocation of Taxing Power Under the Canadian Constitution* (2nd ed. 1981), at p. 202).

My review of the jurisprudence interpreting s. 92(?) has revealed that apart from excise taxes, import duties, or taxes of a similar nature and the two more general limitations highlighted in the preceding paragraph, the provinces have come to enjoy considerable freedom in constructing their tax systems. Having examined the basic principles informing the interpretation and application of s. 92(2), I now turn to a detailed examination of the tax proposed in the draft Act.

THE GENERAL SCHEME OF THE PROPOSED TAX

A perusal of the economics literature reveals that value-added taxes are often seen as refined versions of consumption taxes (see, for example, Whalley and Fretz, *The Economics of the Goods and Services Tax* (1990)). Collection earlier in the production and marketing chain is thought to increase compliance by collecting the bulk of tax revenues from larger organizations believed to have more dependable accounting systems. Furthermore, until someone resells a good they have purchased, they can be assumed to be the consumer and therefore liable to pay the tax. To avoid the ultimate burden of paying the tax, they must prove that the good or service was used in the provision of another taxable supply. This "onus" is easily discharged by collecting the tax on behalf of the government when taxable supplies are made to other persons and by filing returns which detail the amount of tax collected and the amount "paid" in respect of inputs. Enforcement is thereby enhanced by the documentary record created.

As was noted above, consumption taxes have historically been held to be direct taxes. In *Cairns,* supra, this Court held that a tax on consumers of tangible personal property purchased at the retail level was direct. A similar conclusion was reached in *Atlantic Smoke Shops,* supra, where the tax was on tobacco purchased for consumption from a retail vendor. To the extent that the proposed value-added tax is in fact a consumption tax on the ultimate consumer, these cases provide some support for its validity. The real question in determining if the tax is direct, however, is not whether it is a consumption tax, but whether the person intended to bear the burden of the tax is the person paying the tax.

The unique feature of a value-added tax, its collection along the production and marketing chain, may be the chief attraction for governments. However, the collection mechanism, which provides for the tax as the good moves through the consumption chain, may at first sight appear to raise the spectre of an indirect tax.

It was maintained before us that value-added taxes are similar to excise taxes or customs duties in that the tax is in some sense passed on with the good and indemnification occurs when the good is sold. It will be remembered that Rand J. in *Canadian Pacific Railway Co. v. Attorney General for Saskatchewan,* supra, identified the fact that the tax tended to cling to a good as an indication of indirectness. The fact that the tax is recouped through a series of indemnifications before the good reaches the final consumer does not, however, make the value-added tax an indirect tax for constitutional purposes. Close examination of the proposed tax reveals that the person who ultimately pays the tax is the one intended to bear the burden, and, therefore, the tax is direct.

As noted above, the proposed tax will be paid and then reimbursed at each stage until final consumption. Imposing the tax at each level in the consumption chain is simply a method of tax collection by instalments. The persons who collect the tax along the chain and who are reimbursed are really tax collectors. The draft Act, it will be remembered, explicitly identifies these persons as agents of the Minister of Revenue in their capacity as tax collectors (draft Act, s. 28). Rather than putting forward a new and different type of tax, the essence of the proposed amendments is simply to substitute a new mechanism of collection.

The availability of the input tax refunds is the key to understanding what is truly going on prior to the stage of ultimate consumption. Eligibility for an input tax refund relieves the consumer turned supplier from the burden of the tax which is then charged to the person who purchases the good. The reimbursement of the tax initially "paid" through the mechanism of the input tax refund means that there is no tax to be passed on. The input tax refund thus guarantees that the person who ultimately pays the tax is the one who was intended should bear the burden and that therefore the proposed tax is a form of direct taxation. [...]

The *amicus curiae*, however, attacked the proposed tax by focusing on the input tax refund. The *amicus curiae* argued that the person who initially "pays" the tax is not the person whom the legislature has chosen to bear the burden. These persons, it was argued, pass the tax and the burden back to the government by the mechanism of the input tax refund. I cannot accept this argument. The registrants are not in any constitutionally significant sense the persons paying the tax when they resell the good or another good or service which the taxed good was used to produce. The input tax refund in such a case operates to ensure that any tax initially paid is fully reimbursed. Registrants therefore do not pay the tax or bear the burden, as stated above, they merely function as tax collectors transferring the revenues to the government as was the case in *Cairns,* supra, and *Kingcome,* supra. [...]

It is true that as tax collectors registrants bear hidden burdens in relation to the role assigned them under the scheme. These burdens consist of the administrative cost of keeping records and filing returns as well as the cost of transferring funds to the government prior to reimbursement. In the *GST Reference,* these costs were identified as administrative burdens and it was held that the obligation on a province to collect and remit the GST was not taxation of a province's property (supra, at pp. 483 and 481). It is likely that these burdens will be passed on to consumers; however, this fact does not alter the general tendency of the tax for the purposes of s. 92(2). These burdens are not taxes. These costs will not attach to any particular good, but rather will be part of the general cost of doing business. As a general cost of doing business, the burdens would often be transferred in one form or another, but they are not related to any particular good. It is not "the tax" that is passed on. The requirement that the tax be direct is satisfied. It is paid by the very person intended to bear its burden.

As to the concern that a value-added tax might result in taxation of persons outside the province by indirect means, it must be recognized that the collection of the bulk of tax revenues prior to the retail level creates the possibility that a good shipped to another province will carry with it the provincial tax as part of its price. This situation does not arise with the existing sales taxes because they are imposed exclusively at the retail level and not at the wholesale or manufacturing level. Absent provision for a refund in cases where the good is shipped outside the province, the manufacturer or wholesaler would clearly attempt to recoup the tax paid on the particular good from the consumers in the destination province.

The drafters of the proposed Act, however, have avoided this problem. Section 12 identifies "a supply shipped outside Québec" as a zero-rated supply. As a zero-rated supply, no tax is collected from the recipient and the registrant making the supply is eligible for an input tax refund corresponding to the tax initially paid. The refund thus ensures that the proposed tax has no extra-territorial effects. The fact that someone might not bother claiming the exemption and would thereby pass on the tax to consumers in other provinces would not alter the general tendency of the tax.

The preceding review of the general scheme of the proposed tax and my conclusion that the tax, through the mechanism of the input tax refund, operates as a direct tax leads to an affirmative answer in respect of the first constitutional question. [...]

(d)   Licenses and "Regulatory Charges"

MAGNET, "THE CONSTITUTIONAL DISTRIBUTION OF TAXATION POWERS IN CANADA"
(1978), 10 Ottawa L. Rev. 473 at 521-5.

THE PROVINCIAL LICENSING POWER

1. *Difficulties of Relating Sections 92(2) and 92(9)*

The provincial legislatures have a second source of revenue raising competence; the licensing power found in section 92(9) of the *B.N.A. Act*. Section 92(9) provides that:

> In each Province the Legislature may exclusively make Laws in relation to Matters coming within the Classes of Subjects next herein-after enumerated; that is to say, [...]

> 9. Shop, Saloon, Tavern, Auctioneer, and other Licences in order to the raising of a Revenue for Provincial, Local or Municipal Purposes.

This clause has been a source of difficulty. A plain reading of the text appears to confer a species of taxing power in respect of the enumerated categories of business. *Prima facie*, the clause contemplates indirect taxing power since the fees would be passed on as part of a higher price for goods and services. There are two difficulties obstructing this interpretation. First, the Privy Council has concluded that the enumerated businesses do not form a genus; the words "other licences" are thus unrestricted. Secondly, the Privy Council has found the source of provincial trade regulatory power to be elsewhere than in section 92(9); it has said, moreover, that section 92(9) cannot constitute an independent source of such power.

If the first point means that the provinces are competent to indirectly tax any type of business by means of a licensing scheme, section 92(2) is rendered substantially nugatory. If provinces are limited to direct license fees forming part of a licensing scheme, then section 92(9) has no independent force. Its revenue raising powers would be subsumed totally within section 92(2) and it has been held to confer no autonomous regulatory power either.

A possible means of overcoming these difficulties is in the suggestion that any fees levied by a province, pursuant to a licensing scheme, must be limited in amount to the expense of the scheme. In other words, the provinces are competent to regulate pursuant to heads of section 92 other than head 9; head 9 allows the costs of regulation to be defrayed by means of license fees. According to this line of argument, the provinces are incompetent to go further and levy license fees in excess of regulatory costs.

Insofar as the object of this suggestion is to revivify section 92(9) as a meaningful source of power, it is of dubious assistance. The Privy Council has found the source of regulatory power in respect of local businesses to be within sections 92(13) and 92(16). Since 1938, moreover, the power to impose expense levies for such schemes has been found in those sections as well. It has been unnecessary to resort to section 92(9) to support such legislation. The difficulty, therefore, remains one of logic. Either section 92(2) is rendered substantially meaningless, or section 92(9) suffers this fate.

2. Section 92(9): How Far a Source of Indirect Taxing Power?

The first comprehensive treatment of this problem was offered by Duff J. in Lawson v. Interior Tree Fruit and Vegetable Committee of Direction. Mr. Justice Duff agreed with earlier authorities that section 92(9) was not a separate source of regulatory power. He said:

> On the other hand, the last mentioned head authorizes licences for the purpose of raising a revenue, and does not, I think, contemplate licences which, in their primary function, are instrumentalities for the control of trade – even local or provincial trade.

Mr. Justice Duff considered that any source of provincial regulatory power must be found within other heads of section 92. This author suggests sections 92(8), 92(10), 92(13) or 92(16) as possible examples. Duff J. made it clear, however, that section 92(9) could not of itself constitute a source of regulatory power.

Did Mr. Justice Duff then consider that section 92(9) had no independent force? That proposition certainly does not emerge from his reasons. He considered that levies incidental to an otherwise valid regulatory scheme could be imposed in the form of license fees and that such levies need not meet the test of directness required by section 92(2). He stated:

> *Prima facie*, it would appear, from inspection of the language of the two several heads [s. 92(2) and s. 92(9)], that the taxes contemplated by no. 9 are not confined to taxes of the same character as those authorized by no. 2, and that accordingly imposts which would properly be classed under the general description "indirect taxation" are not for that reason alone excluded from those which may be exacted under head 9.

It might of course be said that this explanation of Mr. Justice Duff's words is no explanation at all. The point could be taken that he was contemplating only an expense levy to defray the administrative costs of an otherwise valid regulatory scheme. That may be so, but it must be recognized that Mr. Justice Duff was writing in 1931, before it was clear law that an expense levy was valid. Indeed, two years later, the Privy Council struck down an expense levy which was incidental to an equalization scheme.

In 1938 the Privy Council made it clear in *Shannon* that an expense levy was valid. But the Justices appear to have extended the words of Mr. Justice Duff. Lord Atkin said this:

> On this part of the case the Justices, with great respect, think that the present Chief Justice, then Duff J., took a somewhat narrow view of the Provincial powers under s. 92(9) in *Lawson v. Interior Tree Fruit Vegetable Committee of Direction*, where he says: "on the other hand, the last-mentioned head authorizes licences for the purpose of raising a revenue, and does not, I think, contemplate licences which, in their primary function, are instrumentalities for the control of trade – even local or provincial trade." It cannot, as the Justices think, be an objection to a licence plus a fee that it is directed both to the regulation of trade and to the provision of revenue. It would be difficult in the case of saloon and tavern licences to say that the regulation of the trade was not at least as important as the provision of revenue. And, if licences for the specified trades are valid, the Justices see no reason why the words "other licences" in s. 92(9) should not be sufficient to support the enactment in question.

I say that this is an extension of Mr. Justice Duff's words; however, it may be argued that the Justices, in *Shannon*, are in fact extending *Lawson* only by interpreting section 92(9) as a separate source of provincial regulatory power and not by extending provincial taxing competence. That argument presents this difficulty: if section 92(9) is indeed a separate source of regulatory power, then the provincial legislatures would have easy access to otherwise exclusively federal fields. If this conclusion be not admitted, then I fail to see any distinction between section 92(9) and sections 92(8), (10), (13) and (16) as sources of provincial regulatory power.

I would offer another interpretation of the *Shannon* case. My view is that Lord Atkin, in holding that Mr. Justice Duff took a narrow approach, was pointing to the narrowness of restricting provincial legislation under section 92(9) to the imposition of an expense levy only. Lord Atkin went a step further. He held, as I understand him, that section 92(9) was a source of revenue raising power for the provinces not restricted to the expenses of a regulatory scheme. The section could constitute a source of indirect taxation power ancillary to an otherwise valid regulatory scheme.

If this interpretation be correct, the crucial question which remains in the wake of *Shannon* is this: how far does section 92(9) allow the provinces to go in levying, incidental to an otherwise valid regulatory scheme, indirect taxation for the raising of a revenue for provincial purposes? In other words, the essential question at the present day is, to what extent does section 92(9) constitute an exception to section 92(2)?

When a province undertakes to regulate a trade pursuant to a valid source of provincial power, it may impose indirect taxes against that trade in the form of license fees. But there is a *caveat*. The whole legislative scheme must be *in relation to* the regulation of a trade pursuant to some source of legislative power other than section 92(9) of the *B.N.A. Act*. It must not be *in relation to* the raising of monies by indirect taxation. In sum, my submission, resting on *Shannon* and later cases, is that section 92(9) constitutes an independent source of provincial collateral indirect taxation power when used ancillary to a valid regulatory scheme. [...]

This view of section 92(9) means that the provinces have a power of collateral indirect taxation greater than anything hitherto recognized by legal writers of the courts. To take an example: suppose that ancillary to an equalization scheme such as the one considered in *Reference Re Agricultural Products Marketing Act*, levies were imposed beyond the expenses of the scheme and beyond those which would be rateably returned to producers. Would such levies be valid? As noted above, the *Reference Re Agricultural Products Marketing Act* itself is not of sufficient amplitude to support the levies. However, section 92(9), on this view, would support them. There is one requirement: the levies must be truly ancillary to the scheme. By ancillary, I mean that they must bear a rational functional connection to it. If they do, then no constitutional objection fairly ought to lie to the levies being brought into the general revenues of the province to be used for general provincial purposes.

ALLARD CONTRACTORS v. COQUITLAM
[1993] 4 S.C.R. 371.

[Certain roads in the municipality of Coquitlam and Maple Ridge were being damaged by gravel trucks hauling gravel material. To pay for the repair of the road, those municipalities passed by-laws which prohibited the removal of soil and other substances from land within the municipalities except as authorized by permit. To obtain a permit, the gravel operators had to pay a "volumetric fee": a permit fee that was dependent on the volume of material removed. The gravel operators challenged the by-laws on the ground that they were *ultra vires* the municipalities as being in relation to indirect taxation.]

IACOBUCCI J. [for the Court]: — Later in these reasons, I will conclude that the variable fees at issue in this case are referable to an overall scheme of gravel and road regulation, and that s. 92(9), in conjunction with ss. 92(13) and (16), of the *Constitution Act, 1867* validates those fees to the extent that they comprehend an element of indirect taxation. This final conclusion depends upon several layers of analysis. It rests most directly upon an analysis of whether the *Municipal Act* and by-laws create a regulatory scheme to which the fees can be related. That regulatory analysis, in turn, presupposes that s. 92(9) can support indirect licence fees as part of a regulatory scheme, in so far as such fees might otherwise be called indirect taxes. Finally, an allegation of indirect taxation is only relevant, and an analysis of s. 92(9) is only necessary, to the extent that the variable fees at issue can be considered indirect in their general tendency. I therefore begin by examining the general tendency of the variable licence fees. I will later proceed to examine case law on s. 92(9), to analyze the *Municipal Act* and by-laws for evidence of a regulatory scheme which is related to the variable fees, and to conclude in the manner indicated above.

THE GENERAL TENDENCY OF THE PERMIT FEES

By virtue of s. 92(2) of the *Constitution Act, 1867*, the provinces are given the power to raise revenue for provincial purposes only by means of direct taxation. The existence of this power means that in the typical case of a flat rate licence fee, very little division of powers analysis is required. This is true because it has been generally accepted, since the classic decision of *Bank of Toronto v. Lambe* (1887), 12 A.C. 575 (P.C.), that a flat fee constitutes a form of direct taxation.

It is when courts are presented with variable licence fees that the question of indirect taxation can arise. Whereas *Lambe*, supra, determined that the general tendency of a flat fee is direct, in the case of a variable fee, no automatic conclusion as to general tendency can be drawn. Each case must be examined to determine whether a variable fee calculated according to the number or value of a licensee's transactions is direct or indirect in its general tendency.

Loading gravel into trucks as part of a relief project (British Columbia, 1933).

On the facts of this case, I have no doubt that the volumetric fees at issue are indirect in their general tendency. Each of the respondent municipalities has created a fee which varies according to the volume of gravel removed by the appellants. For instance, Coquitlam By-law No. 1914, 1988, s. 13(a) establishes a fee of 26 cents per cubic meter of soil removed. That such a variable fee, imposed in relation to a commodity such as gravel which is intended for trade in the market, is legally indirect in its general tendency can be quickly demonstrated. [...]

Both *Lambe*, supra, and *Attorney-General for British Columbia*, supra, therefore appear to recognize that a tax measured with reference to a marketable commodity is usually indirect in its general tendency. It remained for Rand J. in *Canadian Pacific Railway Co. v. Attorney General for Saskatchewan*, [1952] 2 S.C.R. 231 ("*Saskatchewan*"), to explain clearly why this might be so. In commenting upon *Attorney-General for British Columbia v. Esquimalt and Nanaimo Railway Co.*, [1950] A.C. 87 (P.C.), Rand J. stated (at pp. 251-52):

> Lord Greene in the same case speaks of the "fundamental difference" between the "economic tendency" of an owner to try to shift the incidence of a tax and the "passing on" of the tax regarded as the hallmark of an indirect tax. In relation to commodities in commerce, I take this to lie in the agreed conceptions of economists of charges which fall into the category of accumulating items: and the question is, what taxes, through intention and expectation, are to be included in those items? If the tax is related or relatable, directly or indirectly, to a unit of the commodity or its price, imposed when the commodity is in course of being manufactured or marketed, then the tax tends to cling as a burden to the unit or the transaction presented to the market.

Although other approaches have been suggested (see the discussion in G. V. La Forest, *The Allocation of Taxing Power Under the Canadian Constitution* (2nd ed. 1981), at pp. 88-92), I am of the opinion that an appropriate test for indirect taxation exists within the above quotation from Rand J., namely: is the tax related or relatable, directly or indirectly, to a unit of the commodity or its price, imposed when the commodity is in the course of being manufactured or marketed? [...]

I cannot help but observe that the court in *Colpitts* seems to suggest that an indirect tax involves a perfect correlation between a tax and the increased cost of a commercial item. [...] While the tax imposed with reference to such units may indeed be absorbed into general "production costs", that does not prevent the tax from clinging as a burden to the vast majority of units which end up entering the market. To the extent that *Colpitts* denies this proposition, I would overrule it. [...]

The finding that the variable fees are indirect in their general tendency leads inevitably to the argument that such fees are *ultra vires* the province as being in relation to indirect taxation. I proceed, therefore, to consider those cases which have examined s. 92(9) and its capacity to embrace the concept of indirect taxation. [...]

My review of case law thus leads me to suppose that it has yet to be determined whether s. 92(9) comprehends a power to levy indirect taxes in order to raise revenue in excess of regulatory costs. Likewise, the cases reviewed tend generally to consider s. 92(9) in combination with other s. 92 powers. I agree with the following statement made by my colleague La Forest J. in his book on the subject, supra, at p. 159:

> A close reading of the cases, therefore, indicates that the courts look upon heads (9), (13) and (16) as together giving the provinces power to regulate intraprovincial trade by means of a licensing scheme and to permit the levy of fees for such licences to support the scheme even if the fees constitute indirect taxation. But they limit indirect taxation by licences to this purpose.

I note that the Attorneys General for Quebec, Ontario and British Columbia argued in favour of an interpretation for s. 92(9) which makes the licensing power clearly independent of other s. 92 heads: see also J. E. Magnet, "The Constitutional Distribution of Taxation Powers in Canada" (1978), 10 *Ottawa L. Rev.* 473, at pp. 522-27. In particular, it was said that the power to raise money to support a regulatory scheme through indirect taxation already resides in the heads of power noted by La Forest J., and that if licences are limited in this respect, s. 92(9) will be redundant. I am pressed, however, to mention that a power of indirect taxation in s. 92(9) extending substantially *beyond* regulatory costs could have the more serious consequence of rendering *s. 92(2)* meaningless. And, in any event, the facts of this case do not demand a final resolution of the point.

In my opinion, therefore, it is unnecessary to examine further the jurisprudence associated with s. 92(9). The authorities establish to my satisfaction that the following question frames the relevant inquiry: can the variable fees be supported as ancillary or adhesive to a valid provincial regulatory scheme? Bearing this question in mind, I will now consider several specific arguments of the appellants. [...]

[T]he appellants argued that the volumetric fees at issue had the potential to raise funds substantially in excess of the amounts required to cover the costs of regulation, including road repair. Although the point was again disputed in this Court, Trainor J. below suggested that there "is some evidence that considerably more moneys would be received from this volumetric levy than the amount actually required" (p. 318). Like Trainor J., however, I would state that it is not for this Court to undertake a rigorous analysis of a municipality's accounts. A surplus itself is not a problem so long as the municipalities made reasonable attempts to match the fee revenues with the administrative costs of the regulatory scheme, which is what occurred in this case. It is easy to imagine reasons for the existence of a so-called "surplus" at any given time. For example, changes in forecasted prices might lead to road repair being over-budgeted, or a municipality might choose not to repair a certain road in order to undertake more extensive repairs or reconstruction at a later date.

Although it might be possible to attack a fee structure demonstrably intended to raise revenue in excess of regulatory needs on constitutional grounds, in this case no evidence of such intention has been proved. On this point, therefore, the municipalities may be given reasonable leeway. In the result, I am of the view that the volumetric levy in this case was intended only to cover the costs of the regulatory scheme, including road repair. [...]

I conclude that in so far as the volumetric fee can be considered a form of indirect taxation, it is supportable as ancillary or adhesive to a valid regulatory scheme. The financial incidents of that scheme are supportable under the licensing power of s. 92(9) viewed in conjunction with other heads of regulatory power in s. 92, particularly ss. 92(13) and (16). On the facts of this case, it is unnecessary to decide whether s. 92(9) would support a power of indirect taxation independent of these other provisions, or whether it would support a similar power capable of raising funds in excess of regulatory expenses. The volumetric fees in s. 930(2) of the *Municipal Act* and the derivative by-laws are *intra vires* the province of British Columbia and the respondent municipalities, respectively.

ONTARIO HOME BUILDERS' ASSOCIATION v. YORK REGION BD. OF EDUCATION
[1996] 2 S.C.R. 929.

[The Region of York passed a by-law requiring builders and land developers to pay an "Educational Development Charge" (EDC) for the cost of new educational facilities in the new developments. The money raised by EDCs could only be used for new infrastructure and regulatory costs associated with the new development. The Ontario Home Builders' Association challenged the bylaw on the grounds that, *inter alia*, it was *ultra vires* the municipality as being in relation to indirect taxation.]

IACOBUCCI J. [Lamer C.J. and Sopinka, Cory and Major JJ. concurring]: — [...] I conclude that the education development charges constitute indirect taxation contrary to s. 92 of the *Constitution Act, 1867*. However, it is also my conclusion that Part III of the Act is *intra vires* the province as ancillary or adhesive to a valid regulatory scheme pursuant to ss. 92(9), (13) and (16). [...]

It is important to consider both the historical and legislative context within which the EDC scheme is situated in order to resolve the issues at hand. At the time of Confederation, responsibility for the financing of education was shared by the state, local authorities, and parents of pupils. From expert evidence in the record, apparently schools were historically supported through five sources of revenue: provincial and municipal grant revenue, local taxation, rates (i.e., fees charged to property owners), parental support for items like textbooks, and voluntary subscriptions. Currently, grants and taxation based on local assessment, apart from EDCs, constitute the major sources of school revenues.

Generally, in 1867, the operating expenses of school boards were funded both locally and through provincial grants. By contrast, the capital expenditures of school boards were in large part financed only locally, with provincial grants for capital expenditures being made only in rare and unusual circumstances. Today, capital expenditures are financed both provincially, through capital grants, and locally, through rates on property. EDCs are imposed on designated land undergoing development without regard to the school support of the land owner. As well, rates can be used for operating and capital expenses, while EDCs can only be used to fund the local share of approved capital expenditures required by the new development. [...]

Before the enactment of this legislation, municipalities financed infrastructure solely through the imposition of lot levies. However, the Act recognizes the principle that "new development should pay its own way", and should not impose further tax burdens on existing residents. The provision of adequate school facilities in a given residential development is an integral element of urban planning.

This is reflected in the *Planning Act* which explicitly states that the "adequate provision and distribution of educational [...] facilities" and the "adequacy of school sites" are important considerations that must be factored into land use plans (ss. 2(i), 51(24)(a) and (j), as am. by S.O. 1994, c. 23, ss. 5, 30). EDCs play a significant role in addressing this aspect of urban planning. The Act, including the EDC scheme, is one component of a complex regulatory framework governing land development in Ontario, comprised of at least nine different statutes. [...]

The purpose of the EDC scheme is to ensure that education capital costs made necessary by new residential development are borne by the new development itself, rather than imposing an additional burden on existing homeowners. Significantly, capital costs associated with existing schools, or the building of schools for existing pupils currently accommodated in portables or sent by bus to distant schools cannot be defrayed through revenues raised by EDCs. [...]

In the case at bar, an EDC may at first blush seem to bear the characteristics of a land tax in that it is, in the words of the enabling legislation, imposed on "land undergoing residential and commercial development". Further, the failure to pay the EDC results in the charge being placed on the tax roll in respect of a specific parcel of land. In many respects, the EDC scheme is a novel scheme of taxation which involves features of both direct and indirect taxation.

However, in my view, EDCs are not true land taxes in the traditional sense. The purpose of the EDC scheme is not taxation of land, but rather, taxation imposed in order to defray the costs of infrastructure necessitated by new residential development. [...]

In a sense, EDCs are imposed in the course of manufacture on the commodity to be sold, that is, the new house or building. Most of the charge payers, the majority of whom are developers, intend to trade in the commodity, that is to sell the newly constructed buildings. It follows, in my view, that EDCs cling as a burden to new buildings when they are brought to market. Accordingly, EDCs constitute indirect taxation and are *ultra vires* provincial competence under s. 92(2).

However, it is my opinion that the EDC scheme is ultimately *intra vires* the province as ancillary to a valid regulatory scheme for the provision of educational facilities as a component of land use planning, pursuant to ss. 92(9), (13) and (16) of the *Constitution Act, 1867*, as interpreted by *Allard*, supra. [...]

Further, EDC revenues are to be deposited in two accounts, one for revenue on account of residential development, and the second for revenue on account of commercial development (ss. 5(1)-(3)). Where two or more coterminous school boards generate EDC revenues, the proceeds are commingled in the two accounts (s. 5(4)). Significantly, funds can only be withdrawn when a specific project has been approved by the Minister of Education, and then only in an amount equal to the actual local share of the project. [...]

It is my opinion that the EDCs are indeed part of a comprehensive and integrated regulatory scheme, namely, the entirety of planning, zoning, subdivision and development of land in the province. [...]

Further, just as the gravel excavators in *Allard* benefitted from the regulatory scheme in terms of road improvements, so too do the developers receive a considerable benefit from the EDC scheme: a development with adequate amenities. The presence of adequate school facilities clearly contributes to the marketability of a new home. [...]

For the foregoing reasons, it is my opinion that EDCs are properly adhesive to the province's planning and development regime, and accordingly, are *intra vires* the province of Ontario pursuant to ss. 92(9), (13) and (16) of the *Constitution Act, 1867*. [...]

[In an addendum to his judgement, his Lordship responded to La Forest J.'s dissent.]

[I]t is my opinion that, while the jurisprudence reveals that land taxes are generally direct taxes, the cases do not prevent a tax on land by itself from being treated as an indirect tax. To repeat, the EDCs are simply not true land taxes in the traditional sense. Rather, the EDC scheme is indirect taxation which is ancillary to a constitutionally valid provincial regulatory regime. My colleague's contention, at para. 139, that I have attempted "by the use of the Mill's test to transform what in all other respects falls within the category of a land tax, and so converts a direct tax into an indirect tax" is, therefore, beside the point.

La FOREST J. [L'Heureux-Dubé, Gonthier and McLachlin JJ. concurring]: — The major issues upon which I shall focus are those concerning the interpretation of s. 92 of the *Constitution Act, 1867*. While I agree with my colleague's conclusion that the EDCs are *intra vires* the province, I do so for quite different reasons. I respectfully disagree with him that the EDC scheme is valid as a regulatory charge under the combined operation of ss. 92(9), (13) and (16) of the *Constitution Act, 1867*. Rather, in my view, the scheme is valid as being in pith and substance "Direct Taxation within the Province in order to the raising of a Revenue for Provincial Purposes" within the meaning of s. 92(2) of that Act. [...]

The bulk of the legislative powers assigned to Parliament and the provinces under the Constitution are essentially of a regulatory nature. It cannot be assumed that the grant of a power to regulate, *ipso facto*, carries with it the power to levy the financial resources necessary to give effect to a regulatory scheme. As in the case of other federations, a sharp division is made between the power to regulate and the power to raise revenue. Specific provisions exist respecting the raising of revenue. [...]

I do not think that the Constitution *specifically* contemplates a provincial power regarding "regulatory charges". Provinces can impose indirect levies if, in doing so, they are legislating under a different head of power than their s. 92(2) taxing power — for example, property and civil rights (s. 92(13)), the administration of justice (s. 92(14)) or matters of local or private nature (s. 92(16)) — and, consequently, outside the scope of the limitation to direct taxes imposed by that provision. Thus, the analysis is no different from the traditional analysis courts have undertaken when dealing with judicial review on federal grounds. Courts will identify the pith and substance of a given piece of legislation providing for the imposition of a levy; they will seek to find its dominant purpose or true character. Legislation aimed, in pith and substance, at raising revenue, will be subject to the requirement of directness provided for in s. 92(2). Legislation not relating, in pith and substance, to taxation as contemplated by s. 92(2) of the *Constitution Act, 1867*, will therefore not be subject to the directness requirement provided for in that section. [...]

The persons called upon to pay the EDCs are owners of land upon which construction, mostly housing, is to be undertaken, the levies to be used to build schools the local school board may consider necessary for the children who will live in the houses. An EDC seems to me to have all the earmarks of a tax as identified by previous decisions of this Court — a compulsory levy imposed by law by a public body for a public purpose. It is, as I earlier noted, in pith and substance, a tax. It is not aimed at regulating the construction of houses or other buildings. It is not an integral part of the activity in which those engaged are regulated. Rather it is expressly aimed at raising a revenue for another purpose, building schools. Regulatory charges have thus far been tied, as they must constitutionally be, to the regulation of particular activities. The levy certainly does not regulate those engaged in the construction of houses. Nor does it regulate the building of schools; it simply collects monies from those constructing houses for the purpose of building schools. [...]

To extend the concept of regulatory charges in the manner proposed would virtually deprive the distinction between taxation and regulation of all meaning. A skillful draftsman (or, in this case, counsel) could easily find ways to combine interrelated activities into global schemes and impose "regulatory charges" on a person engaged in any of these activities to pay for the costs of other activities. [...]

As I noted at the outset, I am of the view that the EDC scheme is *intra vires* the Legislature of Ontario as a direct tax within the meaning of the *Constitution Act, 1867*. I do so because it is a tax on land, a type of tax that has always been regarded as a quintessential example of a direct tax. It bears all the usual hallmarks of a land tax. It is imposed on the owner, and it is collectable against the land itself. [...]

(e)   Section 121

GOLD SEAL LTD. v. DOM. EXPRESS CO.
(1921), 62 S.C.R. 424.

ANGLIN J.: — The plaintiff company is incorporated under the *Dominion Companies' Act* and empowered to engage throughout Canada, in buying, selling, importing and exporting intoxicating liquors. The defendant company is a common carrier and operates between the points to and from which the liquors, of which the carriage is in question in this action, were consigned. The plaintiff sues to recover damages for alleged wrongful refusal by the defendant to accept for transport 4 consignments of intoxicating liquors, within the meaning of that term in the *Canada Temperance Act*, which were duly tendered to it. One of these shipments, tendered at Vancouver, B.C., was, to the knowledge of the defendant, intended for export by the plaintiff from its warehouse at the city of Calgary in the Province of Alberta. [...]

It is stated in the special case that the defendant justified its refusal to accept the tendered shipments solely on the ground that, having regard to the *Canada Temperance Act*, [...] it could not lawfully carry intoxicating liquors into the several Provinces for which the shipments were respectively destined, *viz.*, Alberta, Saskatchewan and Manitoba. [...]

The appellant urged the following grounds of appeal;

(I.) That s. 152 *et seq.*, added to the *Canada Temperance Act* in 1919 by 10 Geo. V., ch. 8, are *ultra vires* of the Dominion Parliament, because [...] [t]he legislation of 1919 when brought into force prohibits the importation of intoxicating liquor into those Provinces where its sale for beverage purposes is forbidden by provincial law. [...]

It is common ground that the prohibition of importation is beyond the legislative jurisdiction of the Province. It is not covered by any of the enumerated heads of sec. 92. It lies outside of the subject matters enumeratively entrusted to the Provinces under that section and upon it, therefore the Dominion Parliament can legislate effectively as regards a Province under its general power "to make laws for the peace, order and good government" of Canada. [...]

Neither is the legislation under consideration in my opinion obnoxious to sec. 121 of the *B.N.A. Act*. The purpose of that section is to ensure that articles of the growth, produce or manufacture of any Province shall not be subjected to any customs duty when carried into any other Province. Prohibition of import in aid of temperance legislation is not within the purview of the section.

DUFF J.: — The capacity of the Parliament of Canada to enact the amendment of 1919 is denied. With this I do not agree. And, first, I am unable to accept the contention founded upon sec. 121 of the *B.N.A. Act*; the phraseology adopted, when the context is considered in which this section is found, shews, I think, that the real object of the clause is to prohibit the establishment of customs duties affecting inter-provincial trade in the products of any Province of the Union.

667

MIGNAULT J.: — [...] Nor do I think that any argument can be based on sec. 121 of the B.N.A. Act which states that "All articles of the growth, produce or manufacture of any of the Provinces shall, from and after the Union, be admitted free in each of the other Provinces."

This section, which so far as I know has never been judicially construed, is in Part VIII. of the Act, bearing the heading "Revenues, Debts, Assets, Taxation," and is followed by two sections which deal with customs and excise laws and custom duties.

In the United States Constitution, to which reference may be made for purposes of comparison there [is] a somewhat similar provision (art. 1, sec. 9, paras. 5 and 6) the language of which, however, is much clearer than that of sec. 121. It says: "No tax or duty shall be laid on articles exported from any state.

No preference shall be given, by any regulation of commerce or revenue, to the ports of one state over those of another; nor shall vessels bound to or from one state be obliged to enter, clear or pay duties to another."

I think that, like the enactment I have just quoted the object of sec. 121 was not to decree that all articles of the growth, produce or manufacture of any of the Provinces should be admitted into the others, but merely to secure that they should be admitted "free," that is to say without any tax or duty imposed as a condition of their admission. The essential word here is "free" and what is prohibited is the levying of custom duties or other charges of a like nature in matters of interprovincial trade. My conclusion therefore is that in view of the provisions of the statute of 1921 judgment can no longer be rendered in favour of the appellant on the only point where, in my opinion, under the then state of the law, it was justified in attacking the proclamation and the Order in Council. The appeal must consequently be dismissed.

[The dissenting judgment of Idington J. has been omitted.]

MURPHY v. C.P.R.
[1958] S.C.R. 626.

LOCKE J. [Taschereau, Locke, Fauteux and Abbott JJ.]: — [...] The appellant is the president and the majority shareholder of a company named Mission Turkey Farms Ltd., incorporated under the laws of British Columbia and which carries on the business of raising turkeys at Mission City and Princeton in that province. On September 29, 1954, the appellant tendered to the respondent at Winnipeg one sack of wheat, one of oats and one of barley, requesting that the grain be conveyed to Princeton and at the time tendered the proper freight charges. It was admitted at the trial that this grain was grown in Manitoba. [...] [T]he respondent pleaded that it refused to accept the grain for transport and to accept the money tendered as freight since the appellant was prohibited from causing the grain to be so transported and the respondent was prohibited from transporting it by the provisions of the *Canadian Wheat Board Act* and particularly s. 32 and the regulations made pursuant to that Act.

The constitutional issue was raised by the reply by which it was alleged that the *Canadian Wheat Board Act* was *ultra vires* the Parliament of Canada and that the regulations referred to were, therefore, invalid. [...] The reference to the powers of Parliament under s. 91 was further amplified by contending that s. 32 of the Act exceeded the powers of Parliament in that s. 121 of the *British North America Act* provides that all articles of the growth, produce or manufacture of any of the provinces shall be admitted free into each of the other provinces and that the provisions of the impugned Act enabled the Wheat Board to exact a tax on all grain transported from one province to the other. [...]

There remains the question so to whether the legislation contravenes the provisions of s. 121 of the *British North America Act*. That section has been construed in the judgment delivered in this Court in *Gold Seal Limited v. The Attorney General of Alberta*, where Duff J., as he then was, said (p. 456):

> [...] that the real object of the clause was to prohibit the establishment of customs duties affecting interprovincial trade in the products of any province of the Union.

and Anglin J. as he then was, agreed (p. 466). This interpretation was accepted by the Judicial Committee in *Atlantic Smoke Shops Limited v. Conlon*. There is nothing of this nature authorized by the *Canadian Wheat Board Act*.

In my opinion, this appeal fails and should be dismissed with costs. There should be no order as to costs for or against the intervenant.

RAND J.: — This appeal impugns the validity of prohibitory and compulsory features of *The Canadian Wheat Board Act, 1935*, as amended. The appellant is a poultry farmer in British Columbia and the president and majority shareholder of a company organized to engage in the business of raising and marketing poultry. Sufficient quantities of feed in wheat, oats and barley to meet the requirements of business of that class are not available from local production and it has become necessary to import from the prairie provinces; and it is out of an attempted shipment by the appellant from Manitoba to British Columbia that the dispute arises. [...]

The main contention was that the legislation and regulations infringed s. 121 of the Act of 1867 that

> All articles of the Growth, Produce or Manufacture of any one of the Provinces shall, from and after the Union, be admitted free into each of the Provinces.

Assuming this section to be applicable equally to action by Dominion and province, is the charge exacted as a condition of the shipment an impediment to that free passage for which the section provides? Viewing it in isolation, as a hindrance to interprovincial trade detached from all other aspects, the demand bears the appearance of a violation. Apart from matters of purely local and private concern, this country is one economic unit; in freedom of movement its business interests are in an extra-provincial dimension, and, among other things, are deeply involved in trade and commerce between and beyond provinces.

But when the exaction is looked at in its true character, as an incident in the administration of a comprehensive extra-provincial marketing scheme, with its necessity of realizing its object in the returns to producers for all production except for local purposes, interference with the free current of trade across provincial lines disappears. The subjects of trade by their nature embody an accumulation of economic values within legislative jurisdiction, wages, taxes, insurance, licence fees, transportation and others, all going directly or indirectly to make up or bear upon the economic character of those subjects; and the charge here is within that category as one item in a scheme that regulates their distribution.

"Free", in s. 121, means without impediment related to the traversing of a provincial boundary. If, for example, Parliament attempted to equalize the competitive position of a local grower of grain in British Columbia with that of one in Saskatchewan by imposing a charge on the shipment from the latter representing the difference in production costs, its validity would call for critical examination. That result would seem also to follow if Parliament, for the same purpose, purported to fix the price at which grain grown in Saskatchewan could be sold in or for delivery in British Columbia. But burdens for equalizing competition in that manner differ basically from charges for services rendered in an administration of commodity distribution. The latter are items in selling costs and can be challenged only if the scheme itself is challengeable.

Section 121 has been considered in two cases, *Gold Seal Limited v. Attorney General of Alberta* and *Atlantic Smoke Shop Limited v. Conlon*. In the former a majority of this Court, Duff J., Anglin J. and Mignault J., held that prohibition by Parliament of the importation of intoxicating liquor manufactured in a province into another where its sale for consumption was illegal did not infringe the section; Duff J. at p. 456 said:

> The phraseology adopted, when the context is considered in which this section is found, shows, I think, that the real object of the clause is to prohibit the establishment of customs duties affecting interprovincial trade in the products of any province of the Union;

A similar view was expressed by Anglin J. at p. 466, and by Mignault J. at p. 470 who added to customs duties "other charges of a like nature". In *Atlantic Smoke Shop*, at p. 569, Viscount Simon remarked in part on the *Gold Seal* judgment:

> The meaning of section 121 cannot vary according as it is applied to dominion or to provincial legislation, and the Justices agree with the interpretation put on the section in the *Gold Seal* case.

What was being considered there was a provincial tax to be paid by a person purchasing tobacco at retail for consumption by himself or others. Included in the confirmation was s. 5 which required of residents payment of the tax on tobacco brought in for their personal consumption from other provinces. Infringement of s. 121 in that case would have been by a tax as distinguished from *Gold Seal*, by prohibition in support of valid provincial law; in neither was it necessary to explore s. 121 beyond those limits. [...]

[I]n constitutional theory, a new and paramount Dominion was created to which was attributed power to legislate for its peace, order and good government generally. This was subject to certain local and private powers exclusively vested in provinces then created; but those powers in turn were made subordinate to paramount and exclusive authority specifically defined and reserved to the Dominion. The organization was brought into existence as of an original creation. Expressly and by implication the existing structures, their laws, institutions and constitutional status, so far as compatible with the new order, were carried forward; but in the words of Viscount Haldane in *Attorney General, Commonwealth of Australia v. The Colonial Sugar Refining Company Limited,*

> [...] although it (the Canadian Constitution) was founded on the Quebec Resolutions and so must be accepted as a treaty of union among the then provinces, yet when once enacted by the Imperial Parliament it constituted a fresh departure, and established new Dominion and Provincial Governments with defined powers and duties both denied from the Act of the Imperial Parliament which was their legal source. [...]

This diversity in structure and the scope and character of power over interstate trade and commerce, although illuminating in its disclosure of variant constitutional arrangements, suffices to require an independent approach to and appraisal of the question before us. Section 91(2) of the Act of 1867, confides to Parliament, "Notwithstanding anything in this Act," the exclusive legislative authority to make laws in relation to "The Regulation of Trade and Commerce". By what has been considered the necessary corollary of the scheme of the Act as a whole, apart from general regulations applicable equally to all trade, and from incidental requirements, this authority has been curtailed so far but only so far as necessary to avoid the infringement, if not "the virtual extinction", of provincial jurisdiction over local and private matters including intraprovincial trade; but the paramount authority of Parliament is trenched upon expressly only as it may be affected by s. 121. Pertinent to this is the ruling in *Attorney General of British Columbia v. Attorney General of Canada*, affirmed, in which it was held that customs duties imposed on the import of liquor by British Columbia under s. 91(2) did not violate s. 125 exempting all property of the province from taxation.

I take s. 121, apart from customs duties, to be aimed against trade regulation which is designed to place fetters upon or raise impediments to or otherwise restrict or limit the free flow of commerce across the Dominion as if provincial boundaries did not exist. That it does not create a level of trade activity divested of all regulation I have no doubt; what is preserved is a free flow of trade regulated in subsidiary features which are or have come to be looked upon as incidents of trade. What is forbidden is a trade regulation that in its essence and purpose is related to a provincial boundary.

The scheme of the *Wheat Act* is primarily to benefit producers of wheat in areas to which that product can now be said to be indigenous. Its effect is not to reduce the quantity of either foreign or interprovincial trade; whatever the demands of the provinces for these goods, the Board, under its duty to market the production of the "regulated areas", is bound to supply those requirements. But it is concerned also to spread the furnishing of that supply equitably among the producers. The individual with grain on hand may, because of quota, be unable to sell at the particular moment to a buyer in another province but his neighbour can do so. If the demands, export and interprovincial, are sufficient, all production will move into trade; what may be delayed is the particular disposal by the individual of his excess over the initial quota, not the movement of grain. The Act operates on the individual by keeping him in effect in a queue but the orderly flow of products proceeds unabated. Section 121 does not extend to each producer in a province an individual right to ship freely regardless of his place in that order. Its object, as the opening language indicates, is to prohibit restraints on the movement of products. With no restriction on that movement, a scheme concerned with internal relations of producers, which, while benefitting them, maintains a price level burdened with no other than production and marketing charges, does not clash with the section. If it were so, what, in these days has become a social and economic necessity, would be beyond the total legislative power of the country, creating a constitutional hiatus. As the provinces are incompetent to deal with such a matter, the two jurisdictions could not complement each other by co-operative action: nothing of that nature by a province directed toward its own inhabitants could impose trade restrictions on their purchases from or sales of goods to other provinces. It has become a truism that the totality of effective legislative power is conferred by the Act of 1867, subject always to the express or necessarily implied limitations of the Act itself; and I find in s. 121 no obstacle to the operation of the scheme in any of the features challenged.

I would, therefore, dismiss the appeal with costs.

[The concurring judgment of Mr. Justice Cartwright has been omitted.]

(f)   Section 125

[**Note:** See *Westbank First Nations v. BC Hydro*, supra. at p. 629.]

REF. RE TAX PROPOSED BY PARLIAMENT OF CAN. ON EXPORTED NATURAL GAS
[1982] I S.C.R. 1004, (SUB NOM. REF. RE. ALTA. NATURAL GAS TAX).

MARTLAND, RITCHIE, DICKSON, BEETZ, ESTEY and CHOUINARD JJ.: — This appeal relates to a levy which the Crown in right of Canada seeks to impose upon certain natural gas owned, produced, and to be exported, by the Crown in right of Alberta. [...]

[O]nly one issue is raised: Does s. 125 protect the particular natural gas from the intended levy of the Parliament of Canada. Expressed in another way, is it within the legislative authority of the Parliament of Canada to impose a tax in respect of natural gas which, at all material times prior to its export, belongs to the Crown in Right of Alberta? [...]

[...] Section 125, supra, protected the lands and property of one level of government from incursion by way of taxation by the other level of government. This might seem, without more, to settle the present controversy in favour of the

Province of Alberta but, as we shall see, the matter is not that plain. Section 125 must be read within the context of the entire *B.N.A. Act* and, in particular s. 91 of the Act.

At Confederation each of the original confederating colonies received the entire beneficial interest of the Crown in Crown lands situate within its boundaries, with the limited exception of certain public works acquired by the Dominion under s. 108 or assumed for fortifications or defence under s. 117. See *St. Catharine's Milling and Lumber Company v. The Queen* (1888), 14 App. Cas. 46 (P.C.), *per* Lord Watson at p. 57.

The right of exploitation by the provinces of provincially-owned natural resources flows logically from that ownership. [...]

The relationship between sections 91 and 125 of the Act is revealed by the use in the latter provision of the expression "taxation". This is a specific reference to an action which might be taken by one legislature or the other in the course of its governmental functions. It is this action from which the lands and property of the other level of government are exempted. The section does not purport to exempt the lands or property of either the province or the Dominion from proper regulatory action taken by the other level of government within its allocated spheres in sections 91 and 92; but such lands or property are not subject to the taxation activities of the other level of government either under s. 91(3) or 92(2). [...] On this appeal it therefore falls to the Attorney General of Canada to demonstrate that the action undertaken by Parliament in Bill C-57 relates to legislative functions under s. 91 other that those confined purely and simply to taxation. [...]

The provisions of Bill C-57, the proposed federal *Excise Tax Act* are designed to ensure that all gas produced in Canada will be subject to tax. Section 25.13 is the charging section:

> 25.13(1) There shall be imposed, levied and collected on the receipt of marketable pipeline gas by a distributor in Canada a tax at the rate specified in subsection (5).

> (2) There shall be imposed, levied and collected on the receipt of marketable pipeline gas by a consumer in Canada from a gas producer or a broker, or from any person acting for or on behalf of a gas producer or a broker, a tax at the rate specified in subsection (5).

A "distributor" is defined generally in s. 25.1(1) as meaning a person who, in any year, carried on the business of selling marketable pipeline gas to consumers in Canada. No tax is imposed on the exportation of gas as such. The word "distributor", however, is given an extended meaning by a deeming provision s. 25.1(2) which reads:

> Where any marketable pipeline gas in respect of which no tax has been paid under this Part is exported from Canada for use outside Canada pursuant to a licence issued under Part VI of the

> *National Energy Board Act* or pursuant to any other authority under that Act, the exporter of that gas is, for the purposes of this Part, deemed to be the distributor of that gas and to have received that gas at the time he exports it.

The new Part has many other provisions but the only other one directly of interest in the present appeal is s. 25.12 which provides:

> 25.12 This Part binds Her Majesty in right of Canada or a province and every person acting for or on behalf of Her Majesty in right of Canada or a province.

It is the contention of the Attorney General of Canada that despite the fact that, (i) all Crown lands, mines and minerals in Alberta are owned by the province; (ii) the province produced its natural gas and transported the gas by pipeline for export sale to a purchaser in the United States of America; and (iii) the province maintains sole ownership of the said natural gas until it is delivered to the American purchaser on the American side of the border, the province falls within the "deeming" provision of s. 25.1(2) and is therefore liable to tax. [...]

The immunity conferred by s. 125 must override the express powers of taxation contained in ss. 91(3) and 92(2). The legislative powers conferred by Part VI (ss. 91 to 95) must be regarded as qualified by provisions elsewhere in the Act. Otherwise those other provisions are meaningless. The courts have consistently proceeded on the basis that s. 91 and s. 92 powers are so qualified even where the legislative power is fortified by a *non obstante* clause. The *Johnny Walker* case, to which much attention was paid during argument, is a good example. All courts proceeded on the basis that s. 125 would, in appropriate circumstances, limit Parliament's legislative powers under s. 91. The overriding nature of s. 125 and, indeed, of the whole of Part VIII, was endorsed by Duff, J., in the *Water-Powers* case, supra. "There is nothing more clearly settled", Duff wrote, "than the proposition that in construing section 91, its provisions must be read in light of the enactments of section 92, and of the other sections of the Act, and that, where necessary, the *prima facie* scope of the language may be modified to give effect to the Act as a whole" (at p. 216). After referring to the division of assets in Part VIII and the express limitation on the power of taxation expressed in s. 125, Duff, J., concluded: " [...] it cannot be maintained that it is competent to the Dominion in exercise of (section 91) powers to legislate in disregard of the provisions of sections 102-126" (at p. 217).

Section 125 raised to the rank of constitutional guarantee the immunity of provincial property from taxation. Section 125 is an exception to the general constitutional competence of the federal Parliament in the matter of taxation based on s. 91(3) and in this manner the section renders inapplicable to the property of the provinces federal fiscal legislation enacted pursuant to s. 91(3). While s. 125 restricts the federal taxing power, it does not limit the exercise of the other heads of power found in s. 91. Provincial Crown lands are not immune from the operation of Dominion laws made in exercise of competent authority affecting the use of such property. This proposition flows from the doctrine that laws "in relation to" a federal head of power may "affect" provincial jurisdiction or property.

Federal legislation which is in form taxation may yet be binding on a province if it is in substance and primarily enacted under another head of power. This was recognized in the *Johnny Walker* case. A majority of the judges in this court (and the Privy Council [1924] A.C. 222) held that customs duties and other duties imposed by the Dominion of Canada could be levied upon alcoholic liquors imported by the Government of British Columbia for the purpose of sale, notwithstanding s. 125 of the *B.N.A. Act*. [...]

Although the [chief judgment of Lord Buckmaster] is equivocal we think the better view is that customs duties on imported goods were viewed by their Lordships as primarily supportable under Parliament's constitutional authority to regulate trade and commerce. The fiscal immunity of the provincial Crown could not prevail with respect to federal legislation founded upon a head of constitutional competence other than s. 91(3). [...]

We agree with Professor Hogg who, referring to s. 125, states:

> This provides an intergovernmental immunity from taxation, but only from taxation upon 'lands or property belonging to Canada or any province'. The section was held inapplicable in the *Johnny Walker* case, apparently because the Privy Council held that the customs duties were designed to regulate trade and commerce as well as to raise revenue. Since most taxes are levied with a view to their effects on the economy as well as their revenue yield, this reasoning seems unsatisfactory. However, if their Lordships were regarding the customs legislation as primarily regulatory, then it is easier to understand not only why s. 125 did not apply, but also why the federal Parliament was held competent to tax the province (at p. 413).

La Forest, *ibid.* at p. 183, speaking of the *Johnny Walker* case, states: "section 125 was not meant to interfere with legislative authority other than the taxing power".

The essential question here is no different than in any other constitutional case: What is the "pith and substance" of the relevant legislation. If the primary purpose is the raising of revenue for general federal purposes then the legislation falls under section 91(3) and the limitation in s. 125 is engaged. If, on the other hand, the federal government imposes a levy primarily for regulatory purposes, or as necessarily incidental to a broader regulatory scheme, such as the "adjustment levies" considered in *Reference Re Agricultural Products Marketing Act*, [1978] 2 S.C.R. 1198; 19 N.R. 361, or the unemployment insurance premiums in *Attorney General of Canada v. Attorney General of Ontario*, [1937] A.C. 355, then the levy is not in pith and substance "taxation" and s. 125 does not apply.

CHARACTERIZING THE PROPOSED LEGISLATION

The first submission of the Attorney General of Canada is that the proposed tax is an export tax, analogous to the customs duties considered in the *Johnny Walker* case, and thus binding on the province. He argues that the tax is a tax on the export of natural gas from Canada; that a tax on export is a duty in the nature of a customs duty, and that a customs duty is not a tax on lands or property as those words are used in s. 125 of the B.N.A. Act. Accompanying this submission is the argument that the measure is supportable as being in relation to international trade. These arguments are allied since they can both be reduced to the assertion that the measure is not "taxation" and thus is not limited by s. 125.

In our view there is little, if anything, in the language of Bill C-57 to support the contention that the proposed tax is valid as being an export tax. The tax is not levied exclusively on exported gas. It is levied without differentiation, as to the rate of tax or otherwise, between exported gas and gas that is not exported. Section 25.1(2) does not, in terms, purport to impose a tax on gas that is exported from Canada. The proposed tax applies to the "receipt" of all marketable pipeline gas produced in Canada. It is the deemed receipt, and not export, that triggers liability.

A tax on the transit of goods from inside to outside the country may be imposed for the purpose of raising money or for the purpose of regulating trade or both. Even if the tax is aimed at export, provincial property is protected under s. 125 unless the federal legislation is regulatory. Thus, if the levy here in question were regarded as aimed at exports it would be necessary also, for the appeal to succeed, to conclude that it not be "taxation" in the sense of the foregoing discussion. There is to the proposed tax no aspect of the regulation of trade and commerce that would support its imposition under Head 2 of s. 91 of the B.N.A. Act. For the reasons which follow, Bill C-57 should be regarded, in our view, as purely and simply a taxing measure, imposed for revenue purposes.

The text of Bill C-57 contains no language to indicate that the tax is imposed as a regulatory device or to reduce or eliminate the export of natural gas. The tax is imposed in a uniform manner. It imposes a tax on all gas produced whether consumed outside or inside Alberta. It applies equally to distributors, local or national, to exporters, to consumers. It is recoverable from anyone who uses or sells natural gas.

It is urged upon this court by counsel for the Attorney General of Canada that the statute finds its constitutional base in s. 91(2) (Trade and Commerce) of the B.N.A. Act, as well as s. 91(3) (Taxation by any Mode). The importance of the distinction between the one constitutional base and the other lies in the ultimate problem of discerning the relationship between the federal legislative powers under s. 91 and their exercise, and the presence in the Act of s. 125. As will be seen, there is nothing in Part IV.1 added to the Excise Tax Act, supra, by Bill C-57 which in any way regulates the flow of natural gas produced in Canada through interprovincial or international channels. It is not a conservation statute nor is it indeed a price regulating statute. It has nothing to do with the channels of industry into which the gas should be routed, as, for example, in replacement of electricity, coal or other sources of energy. In short, it is purely, as announced in the budget and the National Energy Program 1980 a revenue raising measure. Even in this aspect, the tax is in no way aimed, as the expression was used by all parties before this court, at the export sector of the natural gas industry. The Act incidentally taxes exports, but only by the indirect device of a deeming process.

In cases considering tax measures, it may be difficult to find a single "pith and substance" of legislation. A fiscal instrument may be chosen precisely because it can kill two birds with one stone, regulating the industry while raising revenue. The legislation may [be] [...] supportable under two different heads of power. [...] It is seldom necessary to assign a particular head of power if a matter clearly falls within several heads of s. 91 or s. 92. In the present case, however, a specific assignment is necessary. This is because s. 125 is by its terms addressed only to s. 91(3), the power of taxation. It does not attenuate federal power to legislate under other heads in s. 91, such as "trade and commerce".

Such an analysis will not save a tax which is in pith and substance only a revenue-raising mechanism, but which may exhibit ancillary regulatory characteristics. This leads one to consider the intended or anticipated effect of the proposed tax, its place in the *National Energy Program 1980* and how it relates to other federal legislation affecting the natural gas industry.

The *Shorter Oxford English Dictionary*, 3rd ed., (1944 revised with corrections 1975) defines "to regulate" as "to control, govern, or direct by rule or regulations; to subject to guidance or restrictions [...] to adjust, in respect of time, quantity, etc., with reference to some standard or purpose". In relation to "regulation of trade and commerce", this definition and common sense would suggest a restraint upon or channeling of economic behaviour in pursuit of policy goals. The proposed tax in this case, when viewed in light of other legislation touching the natural gas industry, has no such regulatory effect on behaviour. By its very comprehensiveness, the tax belies any purpose of modifying or directing the allocation of gas to particular markets. Nor does the tax purport to regulate who distributes gas, how the distribution may occur, or where the transactions may occur.

It might be said that in a free market, a general tax touching all natural gas would either lead to an increase in the price charged for gas, or if that is impossible a shifting of money and effort out of a less profitable natural gas production industry into other industries. In a word, either the consumption or production of natural gas could be discouraged. There could be valid policy reasons for such discouragement, and excise taxes have often been justified on bases apart from revenue generation: see Broadway and Kitchen, *Canadian Tax Policy*, Canadian Tax Paper No. 63, (1980) at pp. 201 ff. The application of differential rates of taxation, for example, might reveal a regulatory or directive purpose. Yet in the present case, no such purpose or justification is advanced. Nor has the federal government expressed any desire to create disincentives to gas production or distribution. The proposed tax was not argued to be a conservation measure.

The quantity, movement and price of natural gas are carefully regulated under the present legislation and remain unaffected by the tax.

When viewed in the context of [the] all-embracing [federal legislative] scheme to control the natural gas industry, the present tax is clearly not a "regulatory tool" in itself. Every major aspect of the industry is already subject to licencing, prohibitions, orders and so on. On a plain reading of Bill C-57 it is manifest that the proposed tax adds nothing to the existing structure of regulation, save revenue. [...]

Although characterization must rest essentially upon the language of the proposed enactment and what can be drawn therefrom we have, in this instance, the complementary and explanatory materials which have been alluded to earlier. Even the most cursory reading of the *National Energy Program 1980* and in particular the passages quoted, leaves no doubt as to the thrust of the proposed new taxes. The language is clear, unambiguous, emphatic. Revenue sharing arrangements in Canada are "extraordinarily unfavourable to the national government" (No. 4); the "effort to support the economy has left the national government's fiscal position badly weakened" (No. 5); one provincial government enjoys most of windfall, "upside" appreciation accruing from the increase in price of domestic petroleum (No. 6); the Government of Canada must have a reasonable share of revenues from oil and gas production (No. 6); the national government must gain access to the funds it needs (No. 8); the Program "will create a framework for more balanced sharing between the producing provinces [...] and the Government of Canada, which has a national claim [...] to a share in the industry's revenues" (No. 9); "Another source of revenue is needed. The Government of Canada will, therefore, impose a new natural gas and gas liquids tax" (No. 13).

The *National Energy Program 1980* deplores the absence of any "legislatively-defined arrangements under this Act (the *British North America Act*), for the sharing of revenue arising from the exploitation of natural resources, including petroleum" (No. 3). It is this very absence that in our view renders the proposed tax invalid in respect of provincially-owned natural gas.

Section 125 provides, in broad terms, that no lands or property of the federal or provincial Crown shall be "liable to taxation" The purpose of this immunity, as we have seen, is to prevent one level of government from appropriating to its own use the property of the other, or the fruits of that property. This immunity would be illusory if it applied only to taxes "on property" but not to a tax on the Crown in respect of a transaction affecting its property or on the transaction itself. The immunity would be illusory since, by the simple device of framing a tax as "*in personam*" rather than "*in rem*" one level of government could with impunity tax away the fruits of property owned by the other. The fundamental constitutional protection framed by s. 125 cannot depend on subtle nuances of form.

In the present case the subject matter of the tax is the property of the provincial Crown, whether one speaks in terms of taxing property or taxing the Crown in respect of property or taxing a transaction relative to Crown property. If the exemption protects the "gas", the "receipt" of the gas does not fall outside the exemption. [...]

The Attorney General of Canada argues that the Province of Alberta voluntarily entered into the business of searching for and producing natural gas; tax is payable by the province as a result of having embarked on a commercial activity as an ordinary trader. In the court below the Attorney General of Canada conceded that while *in situ* natural gas belonging to the province is protected from taxation. His argument therefore amounts to this. So long as the gas remains in the ground it is free of tax but as soon as the Crown seeks to realize on the asset in the public interest, the federal Parliament may tax at will the proceeds of the disposition of the resource. We do not think s. 125 is to be so interpreted, nor the protection of the section so readily lost. [..]

The allocation in 1930, by agreement and constitutional amendment, of property to the Crown in the right of the Province of Alberta necessarily carries with it the right of the province to the proceeds of disposition – in the words of Duff, J., to "enjoy the fruits of that property". The resources were intended to be an important source of revenue, indeed the basis of the provincial financial integrity, and therefore must be capable of realization. Some activity must accompany any disposal. The immunity is not lost merely because the Province of Alberta was engaged in the simple removal and transportation of natural gas in its natural unprocessed state. Water and certain impurities were removed somewhere between the wellhead and the international boundary. It is clear that the natural gas was not processed or combined in any way with any other material. At the border the gas was delivered to the United States buyer. It can hardly be said that the province was in the 'business' of processing natural gas. It was simply selling its property in its natural and deliverable state and to which property the province undoubtedly has the sole and absolute title.

CONCLUSION

It is important to recognize and indeed to emphasize that we are here dealing with the taxation of natural gas, or were we to accept the Attorney General of Canada's characterization, the taxation of either the movement of natural gas or a transaction involving a specific resource, i.e. natural gas. Irrespective of the characterization given, the title to the natural gas is clearly in the province. We are not concerned with the taxation or regulation of the provision of a service by a province or with the conduct by a province of business which incidentally concerns the consumption of a resource property. Considerations which might concern a court in any or all of these other matters are of no application in the application of s. 125 to legislation in the form of the proposed Part IV.1 of the *Excise Tax Act*, supra.

The two questions posed in the Reference do not lend themselves to individual affirmative or negative answers but rather must be answered in substance:

1.	Bill C-57 is not an exercise of the trade and commerce function under s. 91(2) by the Parliament of Canada; it is in pith and substance taxation.
2.	Section 92(3) must be subordinated to the express provisions of s. 125;
3.	The *British North America Act, 1930*, places the ownership position of the Province of Alberta not lower than that enjoyed by the original provinces under s. 109 and therefore, where s. 125 is applicable, the province is fully entitled to the benefits of its protection;
4.	Therefore, s. 25.13(1) is *ultra vires* with respect to the interests of the Province of Alberta as the owner, and deemed distributor under s. 25.1(2), of the gas in question. [...]

LASKIN C.J.C., McINTYRE and LAMER JJ. (dissenting): — [...] Two points must initially be made. First, and this must not be forgotten, the federal powers above-mentioned [ss. 91(2) and (3)] operate and may be invoked notwithstanding anything in the *British North America Act* and, hence, notwithstanding s. 125 or any other provincial protection or provincial legislative authority. Second, this is not a case where provincial authority or provincial action under its competent legislation is posed against unexercised federal power. Parliament has (for the purposes of this case) legislated affirmatively, and we are consequently concerned with the substance of what it has (figuratively) enacted.

Moreover, there is no principle of provincial Crown immunity from federal legislative authority, whether regulatory authority or tax authority, once a provincial Crown purports to enter the export field and engage in international transactions. That is this case. Indeed, the national government would become hostage to Crowns in right of the Province if the latter could transcend general federal control of international trade simply by asserting that it was bringing Crown properties into the international market. [...]

There are some preliminary observations that must be made. It is, in our opinion, unreal to contend that the federal taxing power envisages only what might be called pure taxation. The definition of the power as directed to the raising of money by *any mode or system* of taxation (the underlining is ours) is enough to dispel such a notion. Of course, taxing measures may be designed to raise revenue without any other considerations, but many taxing measures have economic objectives, sometimes plainly stated, sometimes implicit. Moreover, when such measures are enacted in conjunction with measures under the trade and commerce power, as, for example, in customs legislation, they can hardly be considered as merely revenue-raising. This is certainly the case when export and import controls are put in place either alone under a licensing system or in conjunction with taxation so as to promote economic objectives which are open to Parliament.

We need hardly add that we know of no constitutional principle which precludes either Parliament or a provincial Legislature from basing legislation on an invocation of two or more assigned legislative powers. To strip challenged legislation of a basic support and then, on that footing, to find vulnerability in what is left is not an acceptable judicial approach to a policy as carefully structured as the comprehensive one which is before us.

Contrary to the view taken by the Alberta Court of Appeal, we find it impossible to characterize the proposed legislation in this case as imposing taxation unconnected with any regulatory scheme or regime. The conclusion reached by that Court was that the federal measure cannot constitutionally apply to a provincial Crown-owned resource, even upon its exportation, or, if it purports so to apply, it is an unconstitutional exaction. Moreover, we are unable to agree, and this for the reasons which follow, that the tax is imposed on Crown-owned property in the sense of s. 125. Once the property, here (to use the terms of the challenged legislation) marketable pipeline gas, is exported from Canada so as to attract the tax, we are no longer concerned with property *in situ*, or even with property of the Province enjoyed therein, whether by the Crown owner or by transferees, but rather with an international commercial transaction which is based upon an acknowledged requirement of federal approval for the intended exportation of the particular substance. [...]

[T]he National Energy Program [demonstrates], we think [...] that, in relation to the proposed legislation under challenge here, there is a blend of tax and regulatory policies aimed at realizing the three precepts stated by the responsible Minister, with emphasis on promoting the Canadianization of energy resources, the encouragement of energy conservation and the support of an allocation scheme under which tax money collected for natural gas and as well for oil as they go out will be used to help pay for oil as it comes in through importation. [...]

The *National Energy Board Act*, R.S.C. 1970, c. N-6, as amended, as a related statute, may even more confidently be regarded as giving character to the proposed legislation herein by reason of the acknowledgment of required subservience to the licensing provisions of that *Act*. Section 81 of the *Act*, found in Part VI, provides that "except as provided in the regulations, no person shall export any gas [...] or import any gas except under the authority of and in accordance with a licence issued under this Part." Conditions to be met for a licence to export or import gas are set out in succeeding provisions which it is unnecessary to examine in any detail.

We need only say here that the export licence cannot be seen as a mere yielding to a regulatory authority and, thereafter, as standing apart from the tax, leaving it as an independent and unconnected levy on gas produced in and by Alberta. This is to ignore the setting in which the levy is imposed, a matter which we have already canvassed. [...]

Only if federal power is exercised under s. 91 (as is the contemplation of the present reference) does it become necessary to consider the degree to which s. 125 immunizes provincial lands or property from the federal exercise. We readily agree with the submission of the Attorney-General of Alberta that the *non obstante* clause of s. 91 does not itself qualify whatever scope s. 125 has, but that is because s. 125, not being itself a grant of legislative power, is not brought into possible conflict with the grants of federal legislative power in s. 91, so as to make it necessary to find a mutual accommodation as is the case with the grants of provincial legislative power under s. 92.

The *non obstante* clause of s. 91 has, however, another office, another aspect, and that is to declare the paramountcy of valid federal legislation as against any incompatible provincial legislation and as against any other provisions of the *Act* of 1867 such as ss. 109 and 117, or s. 125. The question that arises on this score – and it is in truth the critical question in this case – is how far is it constitutionally proper to limit the exercise of federal power in the light of the protection given to provincial Crown property by s. 125.

We reject completely any contention or suggestion that the paramountcy exemplified in the plain and unambiguous language of s. 91 ("notwithstanding *anything* in this Act, the exclusive legislative authority of the Parliament of Canada extends," etc.) is subject to qualification and is subordinated either to s. 125 or to any other provincial protective provision or legislative authority. That does not mean, however, that an accommodation is excluded which would give rational scope to s. 125 or to other provincial matters without completely suppressing federal authority given in *non obstante* terms. [...]

In our opinion, a rational reconciliation of s. 125 with exercises of federal legislative power under s. 91 lies in recognizing the immunity of property and natural resources of the provincial Crown from federal taxation of such property and resources within the Province, or in respect of intraprovincial transactions. This would be to recognize the exclusive legislative authority of the Province in matters that do not extend beyond provincial territorial limits. We have as well, no reason to doubt that the Province may engage in extra-provincial transactions as a proprietor (in respect of its natural resources) so long as there is no inhibiting or regulating federal legislation. In short, it may do as a proprietor (absent federal legislation) what it might not be able to do as a legislator. [...]

These considerations do not apply to the present case either in terms of the facts, stated and assumed in the order of reference, or in terms of the proposed legislation to which those facts are addressed.

In the first place, even if the Province is acting only as proprietor, it confronts applicable federal legislation governing the export of natural gas, legislation under which an export licence is admittedly required. We construe the Province of Alberta's principal position to be that the Parliament of Canada may exercise its regulatory authority over provincial Crown property or resources in relation to export but not in relation to taxation; and we make the same assessment of the views expressed by the Alberta Court of Appeal. There is, hence, no challenge to the imposition of any obligation to obtain a licence for an international transaction in natural gas. What is challenged is any association of a tax with the regulated export of natural gas or, to put it another way, a rejection of any connection between the tax and the licence. The ground of the challenge is simply that the tax is not part of any regulatory scheme connected with the export licence. What this appears to mean is that unless the tax is interwoven in the licence requirement, as, for example, by being made a condition of securing permission to export, it stands apart as simply a superadded revenue measure unconnected with any regulation or control of export. On this basis, so the argument goes, it does not differ from a tax on the natural resource itself, something forbidden by s. 125.

We are guilty of repetition in asserting here, as we did earlier, that we have here not only no segregated elements but rather a situation in which both the export licence and the tax are pieces of the overall energy program embraced in the proposed federal legislation, a program which we have already examined. [...]

The charging section of the proposed legislation imposes the tax "on the receipt of marketable pipeline gas by a distributor" and the exporting Crown is made liable for the tax as a distributor and, therefore, by a statutorily deemed receipt of the gas in that character. It is the receipt of gas (the deemed receipt here) which is taxable, and the tax becomes payable by a distributor upon such receipt. [...]

It is a transaction tax, arising upon the movement of property across an international border. The prescription for its collection from the person, here the Crown provincial, does not affect its character. It is by that character taken out of the cocoon of s. 125. [...]

The central question here is thus reduced to the degree of refinement addressed to the proposed legislation; in short, whether it makes practical sense so to divorce the export tax from the overall energy policy as reflected in the National Energy Program and in the *National Energy Board Act* as to conclude that two unrelated matters are involved, one being a pure revenue measure and, even more, being a taxation of provincial Crown property, albeit that property has entered into the stream of commerce under an export licence. The plain fact is that the matters are very much related, as both the order of reference and the proposed legislation indicate. They are parts in a mosaic, a combination of elements in an integrated program. [...]

We have one other observation. The proposed federal legislation, as noted early in these reasons, is intended to be an addition to the federal *Excise Tax Act*. There is no doubt that the *Act* serves an important revenue purpose but it is equally true that it reflects economic objectives. This was noticed by the Quebec Court of Appeal in *Reader's Digest Association (Canada) Ltd. v. Attorney-General of Canada* (1965), 59 D.L.R. 2d 54, affirming (1962), 37 D.L.R. 2d 239, which sustained a federal excise tax on the value of advertising material in special editions (as defined) of non-Canadian periodicals published in Canada. The tax was designed to aid Canadian periodicals or had that effect. Both Hyde J.A. and Rinfret J.A. expressed the view that (in the words of Hyde J.A. at p. 58), the *Excise Tax Act* "contains several Parts where the *Act* is used to raise revenue and protect Canadian trade and commerce." In our opinion, the legislation being questioned here is of that character. It has a constitutional base in both those heads of federal power.

What seem to dominate the views of the Alberta Court of Appeal and the views of the majority in the present appeal are a preference for protecting the property interests of the provincial Crown and a subordination of federal legislation because of the form in which that legislation is cast. We mentioned this at the outset of these reasons, and we return to it to say emphatically that it is not for the Court to attempt to soften the stated effect of federal legislation. There is nothing in the reasons of the majority that deny the power of Parliament to legislate the tax in relation to export, whether in respect of the provincial Crown or any other person. We witness here the odd result that those other than the Crown provincial are subjected to federal controls from which the Crown provincial is relieved, although the legislation purports to apply in both instances.

We would allow the appeal, set aside the decision of the Alberta Court of Appeal and issue a declaration that the proposed tax would be validly exacted in respect of the export of natural gas produced by the Crown in right of Alberta.

REFERENCE RE G.S.T.
[1992] 2 S.C.R. 445.

THE CHIEF JUSTICE [Lamer, Gonthier, Cory, McLachlin and Iacobucci, JJ., concurring]: —

These appeals involve a challenge to the constitutionality of the federal Goods and Services Tax. [...]

The GST is designed to be a tax on consumption. To this end, the *GST Act* contemplates three classes of goods and services. Taxable supplies attract the tax of seven percent each time they are sold. To the extent that the purchaser of a taxable supply uses that good or service in the production of other taxable supplies, it is entitled to an "input tax credit" and can recover the tax it has paid from the government. [...]

Canada concedes, and I am of the same view, that the *GST Act* affects matters which fall within the provincial jurisdiction under s. 92(13) to pass legislation in relation to property and civil rights in the province. It is therefore necessary to answer two questions in order to determine whether this incursion into provincial jurisdiction is justified. First, it is necessary to decide whether the *GST Act* is a valid exercise of any federal head of jurisdiction under s. 91 of the *Constitution Act, 1867*. Secondly, it must be decided whether the effect the GST scheme has on matters traditionally within the province's jurisdiction can be said to be necessarily incidental to the exercise of this federal power. In my view, the answer to the first question is quite simple. The *GST Act* has no purpose other than to raise revenue for the federal government, and it does in fact raise revenue at the point of consumption of taxable supplies. As such, it would be hard to dispute that the Act itself is properly characterized as being in relation to a mode or system of taxation in the meaning of s. 91(3) of the *Constitution Act, 1867*. While the *GST Act* certainly affects matters falling under provincial jurisdiction, it cannot reasonably be said to be aimed at a provincial purpose. [...]

Section 125 of the *Constitution Act, 1867* provides as follows:

> 125. No Lands or Property belonging to Canada or any Province shall be liable to Taxation.

In *Reference Re Exported Natural Gas Tax,* supra, at p. 1081, the majority of this Court concluded that s. 91(3) of the *Constitution Act, 1867* must be subordinated to s. 125. Section 125, therefore, is an exception to the general taxation power of the federal Parliament under s. 91(3). The Attorney General for Alberta argues that the imposition upon the province of the obligation to collect and remit the GST when the province acts as a supplier runs afoul of this constitutional injunction and is therefore *ultra vires* Parliament.

Canada does not contend that a province is liable to pay the GST as a purchaser of taxable supplies. Instead, it claims simply that the province is under an obligation to collect and remit the GST from purchasers of taxable supplies when the province acts as supplier. The Attorney General for Alberta's position is that this amounts to taxation of the property of the province.

In *Reference Re Exported Natural Gas Tax,* supra, the majority of this Court said, at p. 1078 that

> Section 125 provides, in broad terms, that no lands or property of the federal or provincial Crown shall be "liable to taxation". The purpose of this immunity, as we have seen, is to prevent one level of government from appropriating to its own use the property of the other, or the fruits of that property. This immunity would be illusory if it applied only to taxes "on property" but not to a tax on the Crown in respect of a transaction affecting its property or on the transaction itself. The immunity would be illusory since, by the simple device of framing a tax as "in personam" rather than "in rem" one level of government could with impunity tax away the fruits of property owned by the other. The fundamental constitutional protection framed by s. 125 cannot depend on subtle nuances of form.

By analogy to this reasoning, the Attorney General for Alberta submits that the imposition of the GST on taxable supplies made by the province as vendor amounts to taxation of the "fruits" of provincial property. It is said that if provincial property is exempt from taxation, then it cannot be taxed indirectly by characterizing the subject matter of the tax as a "transaction" involving that property. The imposition of the GST on property sold by the province, it is argued, runs contrary to the protection of s. 125 of the *Constitution Act, 1867* and therefore is *ultra vires* Parliament.

In my opinion, with respect, the Attorney General for Alberta's analogy cannot withstand scrutiny. In *Reference Re Exported Natural Gas Tax,* this Court was considering federal legislation which purported to impose a tax upon the receipt by distributors of natural gas that was the property of the province of Alberta. By the operation of a deeming provision, where natural gas was exported, the exporter was treated as a "distributor" of the natural gas exported and was deemed to have "received" it at the time it was exported. In consequence, the province became liable to pay a tax upon natural gas that remained the property of Alberta at the moment of its export.

The GST, in contrast, does not apply to exports. It applies to the domestic provision of taxable supplies, and it is the purchaser, rather than the supplier, which is liable to pay the tax. Indeed, the tax only becomes payable by virtue of transactions in which some property interest has left the supplier and become vested in the purchaser. Clearly, therefore, it is the purchaser, not the vendor, which is taxed.

Nor can it plausibly be said that the imposition of the GST on sales of provincial property amounts to a tax on the fruits of provincial property in that, due to their liability to pay the GST, purchasers will purchase less of such property, resulting in lost sales and diminished revenues to the province. The fact that a federal tax renders provincial property less commercially attractive than it would be if the tax did not apply does not render that tax a tax upon provincial property. In *Phillips v. City of Sault Ste. Marie,* [1954] S.C.R. 404, this Court considered the case of a municipal tax levied on tenants of land owned by the Crown in right of Canada. The tax was assessed on the basis of the value of the premises occupied as assessed by the city. This Court found that the tax was not levied upon the land, but upon the occupants; the value of the land was simply the measure by which the liability of the occupants to pay the tax was to be assessed. Consequently, the tax did not violate s. 125 of the *Constitution Act, 1867*, notwithstanding that, *de facto*, its collection might lower the returns that the Crown in right of Canada could realize from rental of the land.

Clearly, a practical consequence of the collection and remittance responsibilities imposed by the *GST Act* may result in a cost to the province, but neither the true aim and purpose of the scheme nor its incidental effects runs contrary to the spirit of s. 125. As the majority of this Court clearly stated in *Reference Re Exported Natural Gas Tax*, supra, at pp. 1053-54, in order to violate s. 125 the impugned measure must in pith and substance constitute taxation. The possibility that the GST may have the effect of reducing provincial revenues from the sale of provincial property does not render the GST a "taxation" of provincial property. Nor does the calculation of the GST as a fraction of a price a portion of which is provincial tax amount to the federal taxation of provincial tax. Rather, the price paid for a taxable supply, including a component that is provincial tax, is the measure chosen by Parliament by which the liability of the purchaser to pay the GST is calculated.

Since the obligation of a province to collect and remit the GST when it acts as supplier does not amount to a taxation of the province's property, s. 125 of the *Constitution Act, 1867* has no application in these situations. Consequently, the fourth constitutional question must be answered in the negative.

[The concurring opinion of La Forest J. (L'Heureux-Dubé J. concurring) is omitted.]

(g)   The Spending Power

MAGNET, "THE CONSTITUTIONAL DISTRIBUTION OF TAXATION POWERS IN CANADA"
(1978), 10 OTTAWA L. REV. 473 AT 480-4.

The federal government has a plenary authority to spend or gift any monies in its possession as it sees fit. Section 91(1A) of the *B.N.A. Act*, The Public Debt and Property, is the constitutional source of such authority. If Parliament makes gifts, it may attach to them whatever conditions it desires. It can, by means of conditional gifts, make it exceedingly tempting for a province to follow a particular course of action. There is no constitutional objection to a gift to a provincial legislature, for example, of "$1 million per annum, but if it happens that seventy per cent of the province's students fail to pass certain health requirements set out hereinafter, the gift is to terminate". No province is obliged to accept such a gift.

Intergovernmental conditional transfers are of great, albeit declining importance in Canadian federalism. [...]

Although Parliament has a wide latitude to raise monies by taxation, and an equally wide latitude to spend monies thereby collected, it does not follow that the powers thus combined can be used to invade provincial heads of jurisdiction. There is still the requirement that the monies raised and/or spent be "in relation to" taxation or the public debt and property, or bear a "rational, functional connection" thereto. Provision for the gathering together of a fund, and the spending of it, must not be "in relation to" a matter of provincial power and thus a colourable attempt to usurp provincial jurisdiction. This point was made forcefully by Lord Atkin in *Attorney-General for Canada v. Attorney-General for Ontario (Unemployment Insurance Reference)* who, in striking down the *Employment and Social Insurance Act*, said:

> But assuming that the Dominion has collected by means of taxation a fund, it by no means follows that any legislation which disposes of it is necessarily within Dominion competence.

> It may still be legislation affecting the classes of subjects enumerated in s. 92, and, if so, would be *ultra vires*. In other words, Dominion legislation even though it deals with Dominion property, may still be so framed as to invade civil rights within the Province, or encroach upon the classes of subjects which are reserved to provincial competence.

All taxation ultimately involves regulation; "to some extent it [taxation] interposes an economic impediment to the activity taxed as compared with others not taxed". Lord Atkin's often repeated statement draws attention to that fact; it underlines that there must be a dividing line between regulatory effects created by taxation which are tolerable, and regulatory effects which are not tolerable.

What is that dividing line? Ultimately that question falls to be decided in this way: if a taxing statute effects, in addition to taxation, clearly discernible regulatory results, the validity of the statute depends on whether the subject matter of the regulation falls within, or is necessarily incidental to, the regulatory powers of the jurisdiction levying the tax. If it does, the taxing statute stands unimpeded; if it does not, the taxing statute is as incompetent to the jurisdiction as is the exercise of the regulatory power *simpliciter*. This point, gleaned from American, Canadian and Australian cases, was succinctly put by Professor MacKinnon in 1964:

> In other words, where a statute both taxes and regulates, its validity as a whole depends on whether the taxing authority has power to regulate the subject matter affected by the tax, and it is immaterial whether the tax is inoperative in respect of those who comply with the statute's regulations. The tax is in aid of the regulation: if the regulation be valid, then so also is the tax: if the regulation be invalid, the tax is invalid also.

The spending power draws attention to a rather nice question. Suppose Parliament raises monies by taxation, and launders those monies through the Consolidated Revenue Fund. It proceeds to return the monies to the provinces in the form of conditional grants directed to purposes under provincial jurisdiction. Is the prohibition in the *Unemployment Insurance Reference* thereby activated? It seems hard to believe that this means of subverting provincial jurisdiction would be tolerated were *Hansard* to disclose this intention in relation to the scheme as a whole. Yet the question remains as to how far conditional grants need go before they are viewed as a device subversive of Confederation. Professor Laskin (as he then was) suggested that perhaps Lord Atkin, in the *Unemployment Insurance Reference*, went too far. It is decidedly worth considering whether, on the contrary, he did not go far enough.

Objections to federal use of the spending power have been confined to the political and administrative levels; Canada's eleven governments have exhibited a clear reluctance to test the reach of the federal spending power by a court challenge. Nevertheless, intergovernmental transfers ultimately are subject to constitutional constraints. These cannot be fully appreciated without consideration of the policy issues involved.

At the outer limit of the spending power three heads of policy emerge. First, intergovernmental transfers blur electoral lines of responsibility. The electorate is confused as to which governmental body is responsible for what policy. Electoral accountability is diminished. Secondly, intergovernmental transfers interfere with the decision-making process of the recipient government. (This objection is limited to conditional transfers only.) The donee government finds it unacceptably difficult to refuse the conditional grants as it thereby subjects its electorate to taxation without benefit. The recipient government loses motive power in initiating programs. Its priorities are altered. Thirdly, intergovernmental transfers (limited to conditional transfers) allow the donor government to formulate policy in areas of jurisdiction incompetent to it and exclusively competent to the donee government. The transfers become a means of making watertight jurisdictions permeable to action by the incompetent government. They disturb the constitutional division of powers.

These objections are undoubtedly weighty, but they gather no strength in a vacuum. They must be tested against the constitutional design of a federal state, and the federal purposes that are nourished by the challenged procedure. Absent specific constitutional prohibition, allegations of implicitly obnoxious constitutional effects must be balanced against the special requirements of divided jurisdiction.

Intergovernmental transfers further three major policies. First, the transfers assure a minimum acceptable level of public services in different regions. This responds to the perceived consensus of the national constituency and to the inherent purpose of Confederation. National economic policies, such as the tariff, artificially force the economic growth of certain regions; intergovernmental transfers redress the balance by redistributing the benefits of federal union. This point has been succinctly summarized by Mr. Lynn:

> Some differences in service levels between regions of a federal
> state are acceptable as a logical consequence of the autonomy
> enjoyed by the regional governments, but if the differences
> become intolerable to those in the lower income regions, the
> federation may dissolve.

Secondly, public investment involves certain spillover effects which result from the lack of congruence between provincial jurisdictions and tax cost/benefit areas. When spillovers become great, as when the province paying for the program significantly benefits those who are not members of the tax region, provincial reluctance to undertake the program is considerable. To take the obvious example, if a province discovers that the graduates of a particular costly education program consistently migrate to other provinces, it will shrink from footing the bill for providing that particular educational opportunity. "In other words, underspending on services will result if a community is aware that some benefits generated by its spending spill over to individuals outside. [...] The upshot is simply that some important public services will be under supplied from the viewpoint of society as a whole." Only a government responding to a national constituency can compensate, constitutionally and politically, for regional spillover effects. Thirdly, an integrated common market, such as Canada strives to be, requires a high degree of mobility for labour and capital. If the quality of important social services and benefits differs sharply across different regions of the federation, an impermissible chill to mobility may be generated. Inefficient or lopsided economic development may result. Federal responsibility for the national economy and for the inherent rights of citizenship demands federal attention to such effects.

In the event a constitutional challenge is made to the machinery of conditional intergovernmental transfers, it is highly dubious that a *per se* ruling, *i.e.* that the grants are or are not permissible *per se*, would be warranted. The specific grant in question should be tested upon the policies outlined above and upon whatever additional constitutional support it obtains from the catalogue of constitutional powers to which it relates. It is clear that the use of taxation power alone to amass funds does not validate any subsequent use of those funds. But the precise range of objects and effects, and their mechanisms, to which the Constitution permits intergovernmental transfers to be addressed is not at present precisely discernible. It is a delicate matter of constitutional policy, to be worked out in the circumstances of each particular case, on a case by case basis, if judicial clarification should be sought. Narrow judicial rulings on highly charged political issues encourage compromise; if political compromise or restraint is not forthcoming, the court inevitably will have a second opportunity to consider the issue, and this time with the added experience of the effects judicial intervention has produced.

- Research Note -
THE SPENDING POWER AND ATTEMPTS TO LIMIT IT

Mr. Driedger disagrees sharply with the views expressed above in "The Spending Power" (1981), 7 *Queen's L.J.* 124. His point is that a grant of money by the government of Canada is not a "law" in relation to "public property" under s. 91(1A) of the *Constitution Act, 1867*. It is simply the making of a gift and, as such, is a purely political function. "It is well established under our system of government," Mr. Driedger writes (at p. 130), "that once Parliament grants money to the sovereign he is free to spend it as he pleases, subject only to such restrictions as Parliament imposes." Mr. Driedger continues (at 133-4):

The current complaints about Parliament's spending power arise largely out of shared welfare programmes, which contemplate expenditures by both federal and provincial governments. Parliament provides for grants to the provinces on condition they enact the kind of a law described in the federal statute. These are known as conditional grants. If Parliament can make an outright grant it follows that Parliament may make a conditional grant. The greater includes the less. The conditions set out in the federal granting statute are no more 'laws' in relation to the subject-matter of the grant than are conditions attached to a grant by a philanthropist. It is easy to see how the provinces can be irritated. The federal government takes the initiative by offering to share in the cost of a welfare scheme to be enacted and administered by the provinces. The provinces are virtually forced to join the scheme, for if they do not the provincial government would suffer politically; but if they come in they may not be able to afford the expenditure required, and in any case it upsets their budgets because they must now divert money they intended for roads, schools and hospitals. Having joined, they then must live under the threat that the federal government will pull out, leaving them holding the bag; they cannot pull themselves out for political reasons, and they may not be able to afford the increased expenditure. The Government of Canada, through its spending power, has at its disposal a powerful political weapon.

There is indeed a problem, but it is a political problem and not a constitutional or legal one. It can be settled only by agreement between governments under which the Government of Canada would agree not to impose new cost-sharing arrangements nor to withdraw any without first consulting the provinces, and perhaps also would require some degree of provincial consent. Such an agreement could then be ratified by statute.

The political resolution to which Mr. Driedger refers has been sought in the various proposals to amend the Constitution. The Meech Lake Accord, for example, would have added the following section to the *Constitution Act*:

106A.(1) The Government of Canada shall provide reasonable compensation to the government of a province that chooses not to participate in a national shared-cost program that is established by the Government of Canada after the coming into force of this section in an area of exclusive provincial jurisdiction, if the province carries on a program of initiative that is compatible with the national objectives.

(2) Nothing in this section extends the legislative powers of the Parliament of Canada or of the legislatures of the provinces."

The Charlottetown Accord also recommended the addition of a provision in the Constitution that would have provided compensation for provinces opting out of programs established by the federal government under the federal spending power.

These proposals have come as a result of numerous complaints by the provinces about the intrusiveness of the federal spending power. The provinces allege that the federal spending power blurs the lines established by the division of powers and distorts constitutional responsibilities. However, it is interesting to note that the provinces have also occasionally intruded into federal jurisdiction by exercising the *provincial* spending power. Most recently, in *Lovelace v. Ontario*, [1997] 33 O.R. (3d) 735, the Court upheld a provincial scheme that established a "Casinorama" on the Rama First Nation Reserve as a valid exercise of the provincial spending power. In considering a constitutional challenge to the scheme as an intrusion of federal power in relation to 91(24) (Indians and lands reserved to Indians), the Court held:

> [I]t cannot be said that the Casino Rama project impairs the status or capacity of Indians. Casino Rama is a straightforward exercise of the provincial spending power. The First Nations Fund is a vehicle for the distribution of government monies and the monetary benefits can target reserves or Indian communities without the province legislating in relation to "Indians or lands reserved for Indians." The province is entitled to spend money on matters that fall within federal jurisdiction. [...]

Is this also a 'distortion of constitutional responsibilities'?

WINTERHAVEN STABLES LTD. v. CANADA (ATTORNEY GENERAL)
(1988) 53 D.L.R. (4th) 413 (ALTA CA).

IRVING J.A. [for the Court]: — The main issue in this appeal is whether the appellant is liable to the payment of income tax if, as is argued, the *Income Tax Act*, R.S.C. 1952, c. 148, as amended, and certain "spending" statutes, being the Canada Assistance Plan, R.S.C. 1970, c. C-1, as amended, the *Canada Health Act*, S.C. 1984, c. 6 and the *Federal-Provincial Fiscal Arrangements and Federal Post-Secondary Education and Health Contributions Act, 1977*, R.S.C. 1976-77, c. 10, as amended, are *ultra vires* the Parliament of Canada because the *Income Tax Act* is said to offend section 92(2) of the *Constitution Act, 1867*, as being direct taxation within a province in order to raise revenue for provincial purposes, and because the other spending statutes are said to offend section 92 of the *Constitution Act, 1867*, as being legislation with respect to matters within the exclusive jurisdiction of the provinces.

Shortly put, the position of the appellants is that Canada, by the powers of its purse, has unconstitutionally coerced the provinces to participate in certain programs proposed by Canada, with standards and criteria established by Canada, although such programs lie exclusively within the jurisdiction of the provinces.

For the reasons set out hereunder, I agree with the conclusions of the trial judge that the impugned legislation is *intra vires* the Parliament of Canada. [...]

THE CONSTITUTIONALITY OF THE "SPENDING" STATUTES

The gist of the appellant's argument on this aspect is that Canada, through the power of the purse, can invade areas of jurisdiction reserved to the provinces and coerce the provinces to adopt schemes and programs devised by Canada. The appellant argues that in consequence, Canada through its funding, effectually usurps jurisdiction reserved exclusively to the provinces by section 92 of the *Constitution Act, 1867*. The programs under the spending statutes at issue in this case involve payments and contributions made by Canada to provinces in respect of health care pursuant to the *Canada Health Act*, payments and contributions by Canada to provinces in respect of welfare services under the *Canada Assistance Plan* (supra) and payments and contributions by Canada to the provinces in respect of post-secondary education pursuant to the *Federal-Provincial Fiscal Arrangement and Federal Post-Secondary Education and Health Contributions Act* (supra). Payments by Canada to the provinces for these programs totaled nearly 16 billion dollars for the 1985-86 fiscal year. [...]

The appellant says that these statutes are, in pith and substance, legislation in relation to matters exclusively within the legislative competence of the provinces. The respondent replies that while the statutes may ultimately have an effect on matters within exclusive provincial competence they are not legislation in relation to it. They are statutes authorizing the allocation of federal funds to assist the provinces in providing services. I acknowledge that the consequence is to impose considerable pressure on the provinces to pass complementary legislation or otherwise comply with the conditions of the allocation, but questions of constitutional validity under ss. 91 and 92 are not resolved by looking at the ultimate probable effect. The Act, as a whole, contemplates Canada providing financial assistance to the provinces. The argument is, essentially, that Parliament cannot attach "strings" to that assistance in the form of national standards. A province could, presumably, take federal assistance and use it unwisely, arbitrarily, irrationally, so long as it was used for a provincial purpose. To hold that conditions cannot be imposed would be an invitation to discontinue federal assistance to any region or province, destroying an important feature of Canadian federalism. In sum, the appellant's argument is that Parliament is indirectly legislating in respect of matters within provincial jurisdictions. It argues that Parliament cannot directly prohibit extra-billing (over and above health care payments) by doctors, so it cannot achieve the same end by the conditions attached to funding. The conclusion does not follow. Parliament has not by legislative force achieved the result. The Constitution does not proscribe those incentives or economic pressure. If, for example, all or a substantial number of provinces decided not to accept the conditions, there would be no effect on matters within provincial jurisdiction. Legislation prohibiting direct billing would be, in pith and substance, legislation in relation to a s. 92 head. The judge did not so characterize this legislation, nor would I. The question then becomes whether the conditions attached to this spending legislation are colourable, as distinct from setting legitimate national standards.

The pattern established over many years whereby Canada and the provinces have developed such shared-cost programs within areas within provincial legislative jurisdiction, was recognized in the *Constitution Act, 1867*, which provides:

> "36(1) Without altering the legislative authority of Parliament or of the provincial legislatures, or the rights of any of them with respect to the exercises of their legislative authority, Parliament and the legislatures, together with the government of Canada and the provincial governments, are committed to
>
> > (a) promoting equal opportunities for the well-being of Canadians;
> > (b) furthering economic development to reduce disparity in opportunities; and
> > (c) providing essential public services of reasonable quality to all Canadians.
>
> (2) Parliament and the government of Canada are committed to the principle of making equalization payments to ensure that provincial governments have sufficient revenues to provide reasonably comparable levels of public services at reasonably comparable levels of taxation."

This practice of developing such shared-cost programs is further reflected in the proposed 1987 Constitutional Accord (commonly referred to as the "Meech Lake Agreement") which proposes that the *Constitution Act 1867* be amended by adding:

Shared-cost program
"106A.(1) The Government of Canada shall provide reasonable compensation to the government of a province that chooses not to participate in a national shared-cost program that is established by the Government of Canada after the coming into force of this section in an area of exclusive provincial jurisdiction, if the province carries on a program of initiative that is compatible with the national objectives.

Legislative power not extended
(2) Nothing in this section extends the legislative powers of the Parliament of Canada or of the legislatures of the provinces."

With the background of a long-standing convention whereby Canada and the provinces have negotiated for the establishment of national shared-cost projects, can it be suggested that the "spending statutes" here in issue are *ultra vires*? In my view, such an argument cannot be sustained. I agree with the reasoning of the trial judge:

"(1) In my view the legislation under review is not legislation in relation to provincial matters of health, post-secondary education and welfare but is legislation to provide financial assistance to provinces to enable them to carry out their responsibilities.

(2) Parliament has the authority to legislate in relation to its own debt and its own property. It is entitled to spend the money that it raises through proper exercise of its taxing power in the manner that it chooses to authorize. It can impose conditions on such disposition so long as the conditions do not amount in fact to a regulation or control of a matter outside federal authority. The federal contributions are now made in such a way that they do not control or regulate provincial use of them. As well there are opting out arrangements that are available to those provinces who choose not to participate in certain shared-cost programs."

The appeal accordingly fails and must be dismissed.

- Research Note -
CUTS TO THE CANADA ASSISTANCE PLAN

In *Reference Re Canada Assistance Plan*, S.C.C., May 15, 1991 the Supreme Court considered a provincial challenge to the unilateral decision of Parliament under the *Government Expenditures Restraint Act* to cut payments to the provinces. In rejecting this challenge, the Court addressed one of the Provinces' arguments as follows:

> I turn to the second branch of this argument of the Attorney General of Manitoba. This was the argument that the "overriding principle of federalism" requires that Parliament be unable to interfere in areas of provincial jurisdiction. It was said that, in order to protect the autonomy of the provinces, the Court should supervise the federal government's exercise of its spending power, But supervision of the spending power is not a separate head of judicial review. If a statute is neither *ultra vires* nor contrary to the *Canadian Charter of Rights and Freedoms*, the courts have no jurisdiction to supervise the exercise of legislative power.

In this case, the Court was asked to consider the *Canada Assistance Plan* [CAP] and legislation which amended its terms. The *CAP* authorizes spending in areas of provincial jurisdiction and subjects the provinces to federal conditions in using the federal grants. Since the Court refused to discipline federal spending in areas of provincial jurisdiction when conditional grants were involved, it would seem that the *Reference Re Canada Assistance Plan* is conclusive as to the validity of the federal spending power when imposing conditions on provincial action. Of course, if it could be shown that the entire scheme were for a colourable purpose, different considerations might arise. Otherwise, the Alberta Court of Appeal seems to have truly stated the law as regards the federal spending power in *Winterhaven Stables*.

5. Criminal Law

(a) General

CONSTITUTION ACT, 1867
c. 3, ss. 91, 92.

91. It shall be lawful for the Queen, by and with the Advice and Consent of the Senate and House of Commons, to make Laws for the Peace, Order, and good Government of Canada, in relation to all Matters not coming within the Classes of Subjects by this Act assigned exclusively to the Legislatures of the Provinces; and for greater Certainty, but not so as to restrict the Generality of the foregoing Terms of this Section, it is hereby declared that (notwithstanding anything in this Act) the exclusive Legislative Authority of the Parliament of Canada extends to all Matters coming within the Classes of Subjects next herein-after enumerated; that is to say, – [...]

27.   The Criminal Law, except the Constitution of Courts of Criminal Jurisdiction, but including the Procedure in Criminal Matters. [...]

92. In each Province the Legislature may exclusively make Laws in relation to Matters coming within the Classes of Subject next herein-after enumerated; that is to say, – [...]

14.   The Administration of Justice in the Province, including the Constitution, Maintenance, and Organization of Provincial Courts, both of Civil and of Criminal Jurisdiction, and including Procedure in Civil Matters in those Courts.

15.   The Imposition of Punishment by Fine, Penalty, or Imprisonment for enforcing any Law of the Province made in relation to any Matter coming within any of the Classes of Subjects enumerated in this Section.

- Research Note -

THE CRIMINAL LAW POWER

By s. 91(27) of the *Constitution Act, 1867*, Parliament has exclusive legislative authority in relation to "The Criminal Law" and "the Procedure in Criminal Matters."

Parliament's criminal law power is wide. It is not limited to matters traditionally criminal; it includes the power to make new crimes. The criminal law power is "necessarily an expanding field" (*PEI v. Egan*).

Criminal Law Purposes

For legislation to be sustained under the criminal law power, there must be a relationship between the "legislative purpose" and the "nature of the prohibited conduct". So observed Professor Gerald Le Dain (as he then was) in an insightful article. The *Margarine* case, reproduced below, explicitly identified the common criminal law purposes that would sustain federal legislation under the criminal law power: "Public peace, order, security, health, morality: these are the ordinary though not exclusive ends served by that law ..." Prof. Le Dain commented that the *Margarine* court:

> emphasized that in determining whether legislation that is in criminal law form has a bona fide criminal law purpose one must look at the supposed "evil" to which it is directed. The conclusion against validity in the *Margarine* case was based on a combination of two factors: margarine was admitted not to constitute a hazard to health, and the legislation was clearly concerned with the protection of dairy farmers from competition.... [T]he issue is not whether particular conduct is appropriate for criminal law prohibition, but whether the criminal law form is being used to pursue an ultra vires legislative purpose.... [T]he nature of the prohibited conduct is necessarily an important consideration in reaching a conclusion on this issue. (*Duff and the Constitution* (1974), 12 O.H.L.J. 261.)

Prof. Le Dain's helpful analysis – that it is "the nature of the prohibited conduct" that determines whether the criminal law power can embrace it – leaves open an important question that still prompts debate in the cases. Must there be some degree of harm that the conduct risks causing to the public to activate Parliament's criminal law power? Justice Major held that the prohibited activity "must pose a significant, grave and serious risk of harm to public health, morality, safety or security before it can fall within the purview of the criminal law power;" *RJR-MacDonald*, infra, at paras. 199-202. Justice Arbour disagreed: "[t]here is, as such, no constitutional threshold of harm required for legislative action under the criminal law power;" *Malmo-Levine v. The Queen*, [2003] 3 S.C.R. 571, at para 202.

The debate as to whether, and if so, how much harm is required to nourish use of the federal criminal law power can never be concluded in these terms . If harm is required, attempts to quantify the minimum risk of harm necessary to engage the criminal law power are bound to flounder. The concepts of harm and benignity are simply too fleeting to provide a solid springboard to launch constitutional power.

The real question that must be answered is whether the dominant purpose of the challenged legislation is protection of vital public interests (notwithstanding ancillary impacts on private relationships). A positive answer to this question will sustain use of the criminal law power. By contrast, if the dominant purpose of the challenged legislation is to balance out private interests against each other, as is done by the private law of property, contract, tort and trusts, the legislation cannot be sustained under the criminal law power.

This form of analysis implies that legal provisions to balance private interests against each other will overlap considerably with protection of the public interest. This will give rise to much opportunity for concurrent federal and provincial action. The jurisprudence confirms the validity of this observation. The cases contain many examples of the concurrent use of criminal law and provincial regulatory powers. This is particularly true concerning risky behaviours that attract the criminal law sanction, including regulation of driving and dangerous products.

'Colourable' Legislation

One important limit on Parliament's criminal law power is the doctrine of colourability. Parliament obtains no authority to enact statutes under the criminal law power by casting statutes in the form of a prohibition and penalty for breach – legislation which says 'Thou shalt not, or else'. As we will see in the cases that follow, whether challenged legislation is validly enacted under the criminal law power is judged by reference to whether the object, purpose or effect of the legislation discloses a genuine criminal law purpose. Federal legislation that disguises a regulatory purpose behind the facade of prohibition and penalty will still be unconstitutional if the activities regulated fall within the provincial catalogue of powers.

This is the teaching of the *Insurance* and *Margarine* cases. These cases found in challenged federal statutes legislative purposes to regulate the insurance and dairy industries, and struck down the statutes for that reason.

In *A.G. Canada v. A.G. Alberta*, [1916] 1 A.C. 588 the Privy Council considered the *Dominion Insurance Act* which provided that no company or person should do insurance business unless they had received a Dominion insurance licence. The *Insurance Act* fortified the prohibition with a penalty for contravention. The Privy Council ruled the *Insurance Act* was *ultra vires* the powers of Parliament. Following that defeat Parliament amended the Act, strengthening its enforcement with new provisions in the *Criminal Code*. These created a criminal offence to do insurance business without a Dominion licence. Counsel for Canada defended the amended scheme on the ground that the earlier statute derived coercive force from the *Insurance Act*, whereas the new legislation created an indictable offence within the *Criminal Code* itself and was therefore a valid exercise of Parliament's criminal law power. Unpersuaded, the Court searched for the true nature and character" of the enactment This was determined to be "the regulation of the business of insurance within a province," a purpose which lay beyond federal jurisdiction. The *Criminal Code* amendments were struck down: *A. G. Ontario v. Reciprocal Insurers*, [1924] A.C. 328.

This theory was elaborated and applied in the *Margarine Reference*, which follows below. The theory is that despite the presence of a prohibition under penal sanction, statutes must have a true criminal law purpose to pass constitutional muster. Courts will strike down "colourable" statutes – federal legislation which tries to disguise regulatory purposes lying within provincial jurisdiction by casting the statute as a prohibition enforced by criminal sanction for breach.

Provincial Penalties

By section 92(15), the provinces have legislative authority to impose punishment by imprisonment, fine and other penalty. The provincial power to punish is essentially ancillary to the regulatory jurisdiction conferred by the catalogue of provincial powers in section 92. Section 92(15) provides for the imposition of penalties to enforce provincial prohibitions or provincial regulation of conduct. The power to regulate or prohibit the conduct to which the penalty attaches must be found elsewhere in the catalogue of powers s. 92 confers on provincial legislatures. Section 92(15) confers no power to regulate or prohibit conduct; it only confers power to enforce by penalty an otherwise valid provincial prohibition or regulation.

Civil Remedies

May Parliament enforce by civil remedy valid federal prohibitions or regulation of conduct? Generally speaking, Parliament may enforce by civil penalty any prohibition or regulation of conduct it enacts where the standard of conduct relates to a matter coming within Parliament's s. 91 powers, including the criminal law power. This is to be distinguished from prohibiting risk creating activities normally within provincial jurisdiction where enforcement of the prohibition is by civil remedy for damages caused.

Parliament may set standards of conduct pursuant to its catalogue of powers and enforce obedience by civil remedy. Parliament may not set standards of conduct relating to matters within provincial jurisdiction and enforce compliance by civil remedy (or even by criminal penalty for that matter).

While easy to state in the abstract, this principle causes difficulty in application. This is because tort law lies within the exclusive legislative authority of the provincial legislatures. The fundamental theory of tort law is to impose reasonable standards of conduct to prevent the creation of reasonably foreseeable risks of harm, and therefore to act as a disincentive to risk-creating behaviour (*Resurface Corp. v. Hanke*, [2007] S.C.J. No. 7, para 6).

It is sometimes difficult to disentangle the creation of a duty of care in tort (take care not to...) from a prohibition in criminal law (don't...). Distinguishing between the two is complex because the difference goes beyond form and language. As we have seen, the difference lies in the subtle distinction between the intention to balance out private relationships from the intention to protect the public interest. Therein lies the difficulty: if the federal prohibition has a valid criminal law purpose relating to protecting the public, enforcement may be by civil action for damages caused or by criminal sanction. If the federal regulation in essence balances out private relationships, it cannot be saved by the addition of a criminal penalty, nor would civil enforcement be valid either.

A related analytical problem is to distinguish criminal prohibitions aimed at protecting the public from risk creating behaviour, from civil duties of care that discourage risk creating behaviour by making the originator of the risk pay.

The criminal law paradigm essentially prohibits or regulates risky behaviours. The private law paradigm essentially compensates for damages caused by risky behaviours. Though the two paradigms run at tangents to each other, it remains true that both criminal and private law systems intend to discourage risky behaviours. Therein lies the difficulty for constitutional analysis. The criminal law and private law systems are not congruent, but they overlap in purpose. It is why risky behaviours may be validly and concurrently embraced by both civil and criminal law systems, each system authorized by separate constitutional provisions

Parliament may impose civil remedies in damages for purposes other than enforcing regulation of conduct deemed offensive to the public interest. Parliament may provide for restitution of property stolen, or payment of damages *in lieu*. In this example, the criminal law power extends to novel methods of enforcement, sentencing and punishment, notwithstanding that these might overlap with civil damages in private law.

The essential requirement for enactment of civil remedies pursuant to the criminal law power is integration of the remedy into a valid federal regulatory scheme, the central thrust of which is an intention to protect the public interest. This is the fundamental inspiration of *MacDonald v. Vapour Canada, supra.* and *R. v. Zelensky*, [1978] 2 S.C.R. 940. The integration may occur by the remedy being a rational, functional means of enforcing the regulation of conduct; it may occur by elaboration of sentencing theory or otherwise. The crucial point is that civil remedies may be part of regulatory schemes authorized under the criminal law power so long as the object, purpose and effect of the scheme as a whole relates to a valid criminal law purpose.

Administration of Justice in the Province

By s. 92:14 of the *Constitution Act, 1867* provincial legislatures have exclusive legislative authority in relation to "The Administration of Justice in the Province". This power entitles the provinces to establish police forces, prosecution services, penitentiaries, parole services, and ancillary agencies associated with the administration of criminal justice in the province. This power is elaborated in the cases that follow.

(b) Federal Jurisdiction

PROPRIETARY ARTICLES TRADE ASSN. v. A.G. CAN.
(RE COMBINES INVESTIGATION ACT AND S. 498 CRIMINAL CODE)
[1931] A.C. 310 (P.C.).

LORD ATKIN [for the Court]: - The questions submitted to the Court were: -

1. Is the *Combines Investigation Act*, R.S. Can., 1927, c. 26, *ultra vires* the Parliament of Canada either in whole or in part, and if so, in what particular or particulars or to what extent?

2. Is s. 498 of the *Criminal Code ultra vires* the Parliament of Canada, and if so, in what particular or particulars or to what extent?

The Supreme Court answered both questions in the negative. [...]

By this Act "combines" are defined as combines "which have operated or are likely to operate to the detriment or against the interest of the public, [...] and which result from any agreement which has the effect of [...] lessening competition in [...] production or manufacture, or "otherwise restraining or injuring trade or commerce. By the Act the Governor in Council may name a Minister of the Crown to be charged with the administration of the Act, and must appoint a registrar of the *Combines Investigation Act*. The registrar is charged with the duty to inquire whether a combine exists, whenever an application is made for that purpose by six persons supported by evidence, or whenever he has reason to believe that a combine exists, or whenever he is directed by the Minister so to inquire. [...]

[...] By s. 32 "Every one is guilty of an indictable offence and liable to a penalty not exceeding ten thousand dollars or to two years' imprisonment, [...]

Under a group of ss. 29 to 31, entitled "Remedies" powers are given as in previous Acts for the Governor in Council to reduce customs duties, and for the Exchequer Court to revoke licences where the duties are used to facilitate a combine or when the holder of a patent uses it so as unduly to limit the manufacture, or enhance the price of any article.

In their Lordships' opinion s. 498 of the *Criminal Code* and the greater part of the provisions of the *Combines Investigation Act* fall within the power of the Dominion Parliament to legislate as to matters falling within the class of subjects, "the criminal law including the procedure in criminal matters" (s. 91, head 27). The substance of the Act is by s. 2 to define, and by s. 32 to make criminal, combines which the legislature in the public interest intends to prohibit. The definition is wide, and may cover activities which have not hitherto been considered to be criminal. But only those combines are affected "which have operated or are likely to operate to the detriment or against the interest of the public, whether consumers producers, or others"; and if Parliament genuinely determines that commercial activities which can be so described are to be suppressed in the public interest, their Lordships see no reason why Parliament should not make them crimes. "Criminal law" means "the criminal law in its widest sense": *Attorney-General for Ontario v. Hamilton Street Ry. Co.* It certainly is not confined to what was criminal by the law of England or of any Province in 1867. The power must extend to legislation to make new crimes. Criminal law connotes only the quality of such acts or omissions as are prohibited under appropriate penal provisions by authority of the State. The criminal quality of an act cannot be discerned by intuition; nor can it be discovered by reference to any standard but one: Is the act prohibited with penal consequences? Morality and criminality are far from co-extensive; nor is the sphere of criminality necessarily part of a more extensive field covered by morality – unless the moral code necessarily disapproves all acts prohibited by the State, in which case the argument moves in a circle. It appears to their Lordships to be of little value to seek to confine crimes to a category of acts which by their very nature belong to the domain of "criminal jurisprudence"; for the domain of criminal jurisprudence can only be ascertained by examining what acts at any particular period are declared by the State to be crimes, and the only common nature they will be found to possess is that they are prohibited by the State and that those who commit them are punished. Their Lordships agree with the view expressed in the judgment of Newcombe J. that the passage in the judgment of the Board in the *Board of Commerce* case to which allusion has been made, was not intended as a definition. In that case their Lordships appear to have been contrasting two matters "one obviously within the line, the other obviously outside it". For this purpose it was clearly legitimate to point to matters which are such serious breaches of any accepted code of morality as to be obviously crimes when they are prohibited under penalties. The contrast is with matters which are merely attempts to interfere with Provincial rights, and are sought to be justified under the head of "criminal law" colourably and merely in aid of what is in substance an encroachment. The Board considered that the *Combines and Fair Prices Act* of 1919 came within the latter class, and was in substance an encroachment on the exclusive power of the Provinces to legislate on property and civil rights. The judgment of the Board arose in respect of an order under Part II, of the Act. Their Lordships pointed out five respects in which the Act was subject to criticism. It empowered the Board of Commerce to prohibit accumulations in the case of non-traders; to compel surplus articles to be sold at prices fixed by the Board; to regulate profits; to exercise their powers over articles produced for his own use by the householder himself; to inquire into individual cases without applying any principles of general application. None of these powers exists in the provisions now under discussion. There is a general definition, and a general condemnation; and if penal consequences follow, they can only follow from the determination by existing courts of an issue of fact defined in express words by the statute. The greater part of the statute is occupied in setting up and directing machinery for making preliminary inquiries whether the alleged offence has been committed. It is noteworthy that no penal consequences follow directly from a report of either commissioner or registrar that a combine exists. It is not even made evidence. The offender, if he is to be punished, must be tried on indictment, and the offence proved in due course of law. Penal consequences, no doubt, follow the breach of orders made for the discovery of evidence; but if the main object be intra vires, the enforcement of orders genuinely authorized and genuinely made to secure that object are not open to attack.

It is, however, not enough for Parliament to rely solely on the powers to legislate as by the criminal law for support of the whole Act. The remedies given under ss. 25 and 30 enforcing maximum duty and revoking patents have no necessary connection with the criminal law and must be justified on other grounds. Their Lordships have no doubt that they can both be supported as being reasonably ancillary to the powers given respectively under s. 91, head 3, and affirmed by s. 122, "the raising of money by any mode or system of taxation," and under s. 91, head 22, "patents of invention and discovery." It is unfortunately beyond dispute that in a country where a general protective tariff exists persons may be found to take advantage of the protection, and within its walls form combinations that may work to the public disadvantage. It is an elementary point of self-preservation that the legislature which creates the protection should arm the executive with powers of withdrawing or relaxing the protection if abused. The same reasoning applies to grants of monopolies under any system of patents. The view that their Lordships have expressed makes it unnecessary to discuss the further ground upon which the legislation has been supported by reference to the power to legislate under s. 91, head 2, for "The regulation of trade and commerce." [...]

Their Lordships are of opinion that the Supreme Court of Canada were right in answering both questions in the negative, and that this appeal should be dismissed, and they will humbly advise His Majesty accordingly.

REFERENCE RE S. 5(a) OF THE DAIRY INDUSTRY ACT (MARGARINE CASE)
[1949] S.C.R. 1.

RAND J.: — His Excellency in Council has referred to this Court the following question: —

> Is section 5(a) of the *Dairy Industry Act*, R.S.C. 1927, Chapter 45, *ultra vires* of the Parliament of Canada either in whole or in part and if so in what particular or particulars and to what extent?

The section is as follows: –

> 5. No person shall
> (a) manufacture, import into Canada, or offer, sell or have in his possession for sale, any oleomargarine, margarine, butterine, or other substitute for butter, manufactured wholly or in part from any fat other than that of milk or cream; [...]

[The Justice reviewed the history of the legislation, noting that when first enacted, the legislation's Preamble recited that butter substitutes were "injurious to health."]

But whatever might have been the case of the 1886 legislation, the situation now is that not only has the preamble disappeared, but its recital of fact is admittedly no longer true of either margarine or oleomargarine. It is conceded that both of them "the latter containing animal fat other than milk added to the ingredients, chiefly vegetable oils, of the former" are substantially as nutritious, possess as much energy value and are as free from deleterious effects as butter itself; [...]

The appearance of the provision in a statute dealing comprehensively with the dairy industry and the inclusion of prohibition of importation, the ordinary mode of protection of industry in its ultimate form, are, for this initial purpose, of considerable significance. On the other hand, the scope and importance of agriculture in the economy of this country, the part played by the dairy industry as an essential branch of it, and the desirability of maintaining a market demand for butter to meet the seasonal exigencies of that industry, are beyond controversy. What, then, in that whole background is the true nature of the enactment?

Mr. Varcoe argues that it is simply a provision of criminal law, a field exclusively Dominion, and the issue I think, depends upon the validity of that contention. In *The Proprietary Articles Trade Association v. Attorney-General of Canada*, (1), Lord Atkin rejected the notion that the acts against which criminal law is directed must carry some moral taint. A crime is an act which the law, with appropriate penal sanctions, forbids; but as prohibitions are not enacted in a vacuum, we can properly look for some evil or injurious or undesirable effect upon the public against which the law is directed. That effect may be in relation to social, economic or political interests; and the legislature has had in mind to suppress the evil or to safeguard the interest threatened. [...]

Criminal law is a body of prohibitions; but that prohibition can be used legislatively as a device to effect a positive result is obvious; we have only to refer to Adam Smith's Wealth of Nations, Vol. II, chapters 2 and 3 to discover how extensively it has been used not only to keep foreign goods from the domestic market but to prevent manufactures in the colonies for the benefit of home industries; [...]

Is the prohibition then enacted with a view to a public purpose or purpose which can support it as being in relation to criminal law? Public peace, order, security, health, morality: these are the ordinary though not exclusive ends served by that law, but they do not appear to be the object of the parliamentary action here. That object, as I must find it, is economic and the legislative purpose, to give trade protection to the dairy industry in the production and sale of butter; to benefit one group of persons as against competitors in business in which, in the absence of the legislation, the latter would be free to engage in the provinces. To forbid manufacture and sale for such an end is *prima facie* to deal directly with the civil rights of individuals in relation to particular trade within the provinces: *Shannon v. Lower Mainland Dairy Board*.

The public interest in this regulation lies obviously in the trade effects: it is annexed to the legislative subject matter and follows the latter in its allocation to the one or other legislature. But to use it as a support for the legislation in the aspect of criminal law would mean that the Dominion under its authority in that field, by forbidding the manufacture or sale of particular products, could, in what it considered a sound trade policy, not only interdict a substantial part of the economic life of one section of Canada but do so for the benefit of that of another. Whatever the scope of the regulation of interprovincial trade, it is hard to conceive a more insidious form of encroachment on a complementary jurisdiction.

This conclusion is not in conflict with *Attorney-General of British Columbia v. Attorney General of Canada*, (Section 498(a) of the *Criminal Code*). There, the essential nature of the legislation was not the equalization of civil rights between competitors or promoting the interest of one trade as against another; it was the safeguarding of the public against the evil consequences of certain fetters upon free and equal competition. There is no like purpose here; there is nothing of a general or injurious nature to be abolished or removed: it is a matter of preferring certain local trade to others.

[The judgments of Rinfret C.J. and Kerwin J. (dissenting) are omitted. The judgments of Taschereau, Kellock, Estey, and Locke JJ. are omitted.]

An appeal was dismissed by the *Privy Council (sub nom. Can. Federation of Agriculture v. A.G. Que.)* [1951] A.C. 179, [1950] 4 D.L.R. 689. Lord Morton quoted the last three paragraphs of Mr. Justice Rand's judgment and continued:

> With these observations the Justices entirely agree, and they are fatal to counsel's second argument in support of the appeal. That argument would have had more weight if it had been possible to contend that the object of the prohibition was to exclude from Canada substances injurious to health.]

MORGENTALER v. THE QUEEN
[1976] 1 S.C.R. 616.

[Morgentaler was acquitted at trial of unlawfully procuring a miscarriage of a female person, contrary to s. 251 C.C.C. A Crown appeal to the Court of Appeal set aside the acquittal and substituted a conviction. A majority of the Supreme Court of Canada dismissed a further appeal. The majority did not discuss whether s. 251 was constitutionally defective. That issue, however, was canvassed by Laskin, C.J. in dissenting reasons.]

LASKIN C.J.C. [Judson and Spence JJ. concurring] (dissenting): — Section 251 of the *Criminal Code*, in its present form, which is as it was when the charge against Dr. Morgentaler was laid, reads as follows:

> 251.(1) Every one who, with intent to procure the miscarriage of a female person, whether or not she is pregnant, uses any means for the purpose or carrying out his intention is guilty of an indictable offence and is liable to imprisonment for life.

> (2) Every female person who, being pregnant, with intent to procure her own miscarriage, uses any means or permits any means to be used for the purpose of carrying out her intention is guilty of an indictable offence and is liable to imprisonment for two years. [...]

> (4) Subsections (1) and (2) do not apply to
>> (a) a qualified medical practitioner, other than a member of a therapeutic abortion committee for any hospital, who in good faith uses is an accredited or approved hospital any

means for the purpose of carrying out his intention to procure the miscarriage of a female person, or

(b) a female person who, being pregnant, permits a qualified medical practitioner to use in an accredited or approved hospital any means described in paragraph (a) for the purpose of carrying out her intention to procure her own miscarriage, if, before the use of those means, the therapeutic abortion committee for that accredited or approved hospital, by a majority of the members of the committee and at a meeting of the committee at which the case of such female person has been reviewed,

(c) has by certificate in writing stated that in its opinion the continuation of the pregnancy of such female person would or would be likely to endanger her life or health, and [...]

First, as to the attack on validity. The contention that s. 251 was invalid as being an encroachment on provincial legislative power in relation to hospitals and to the regulation of the profession of medicine and the practice of medicine was made by the appellant alone. It was founded on the position that s. 251 did not meet the test of valid criminal law set out by Rand J. in the *Margarine Reference*, *Reference Re Validity of Section 5(a) of the Dairy Industry Act*, [1949] S.C.R. 1, where that learned judge stated it as follows (at 49-50):

> A crime is an act which the law, with appropriate penal sanctions, forbids; but as prohibitions are not enacted in a vacuum, we can properly look for some evil or injurious or undesirable effect upon the public against which the law is directed. That effect may be in relation to social, economic or political interests; and the legislature has had in mind to suppress the evil or to safeguard the interest threatened. [...]
>
> Is the prohibition then enacted with a view to a public purpose which can support it as being in relation to criminal law? Public peace, order, security, health, morality: these are the ordinary though not exclusive ends served by that law. [...]

In my opinion, the provisions of s. 251 as it stood after the amendment in 1969 are well within the scope of the tests by which the late Justice Rand would measure a valid exercise of the federal criminal law power.

The wide scope of the exclusive federal criminal law power has been consistently asserted in the relevant case law in both the Privy Council, when it was Canada's ultimate appellate court, and in this Court. Parliament, in fastening upon certain behaviour or conduct or activity as criminal by proscribing it with penal sanctions, exercises a judgment which is not constitutionally impeachable simply because it may attract the opposition of a section of the population. The remedy or relief, as the case may be, lies with Parliament and not with this Court unless it is made plain to the Court that the use of the penal sanction was a colourable or evasive means of drawing into the orbit of the federal criminal law measures that did not belong there, either because they were essentially regulatory of matters within exclusive provincial competence or were otherwise within such exclusive competence. Counsel for the appellant invoked history to support the submission that whatever the basis of prohibitory abortion legislation when first enacted in England by *Lord Ellenborough's Act*, 1803 (U.K.), c. 58, the evil aimed at had substantially abated because of improved medical and surgical procedures now known and practised, and especially because of the widely-used surgical suction procedure practised by the appellant to terminate a pregnancy. Counsel relied on the recent judgments of the Supreme Court of the United States in *Roe v. Wade* (1973), 410 U.S. 113 and *Doe v. Bolton* (1973), 410 U.S. 179. [...]

What counsel sought to draw from *Roe v. Wade* and *Doe v. Bolton* was that the present s. 251 of the *Criminal Code* could no longer be supported as legislation for the protection of a pregnant woman's health, and hence that rationale could no longer justify the presence of s. 251 in the *Criminal Code*. This, however, is to attribute to Parliament a particular, indeed exclusive concern under s. 251 with health, to the exclusion of any other purpose that would make it a valid exercise of the criminal law power. I am unable to accept this assessment of the basis of s. 251. Perhaps the matter would have a different face if there was here the kind of material that moved the courts in the *Margarine Reference* (*Reference Re Validity of Section 5(a) of the Dairy Industry Act*, [1949] S.C.R. 1, aff'd [1951] A.C. 179) to hold that the challenged s. 5(a) could no longer be supported as for the protection of health. Moreover, in the case there was no other supporting purpose open (apart from Parliament's power to control exports and imports of margarine). What is patent on the face of the prohibitory portion of s. 251 is that Parliament has in its judgment decreed that interference by another, or even by the pregnant woman herself, with the ordinary course of conception is socially undesirable conduct subject to punishment. That was a judgment open to Parliament in the exercise of its plenary criminal law power, and the fact that there may be safe ways of terminating a pregnancy or that any woman or women claim a personal privilege to that end, becomes immaterial. I need cite no authority for the proposition that Parliament may determine what is not criminal as well as what is, and may hence introduce dispensations or exemptions in its criminal legislation. It has done this in respect of gaming and betting by prescribing for lawful operation of pari-mutuel systems (s. 188), by exempting agricultural fairs or exhibitions from certain of the prohibitions against lotteries and games of chance (s. 18Y(3)) and by expressly permitting lotteries under stated conditions (s. 190). I point also to the *Lord's Day Act*, R.S.C. 1970, c. L-13 as an illustration of a federal statute drawing its validity from the criminal law power which contains various exemptions.

Thus, I see nothing in s. 251(4)(5) that, either alone or in relation to s. 251 as a whole, casts any doubt on its validity. There is, finally, the very relevant point that having regard to the residuary feature of federal legislative power, s. 251 cannot be invalidated unless it be shown that it is in relation to a head of exclusive provincial legislative power. The only suggested bases of invalidation put forward by the appellant were the exclusive provincial powers under s. 92(7)(13) and (16). The short answer to these assertions is that in so far as s. 251 has any relationship to the establishment of hospitals or the regulation of the medical profession or the practice thereof, the relationship is so incidental as be little short of ephemeral. [...] *Appeal dismissed.*

[Note: See *R. v. Morgantaler* (1993) which is reproduced in Part II(1)(b), "Judicial Tools for Resolving Federalism Disputes", supra, for a detailed discussion of this topic.]

RJR-MACDONALD INC. v. CANADA (ATTORNEY GENERAL)
[1995] 3 S.C.R. 199.

[Sections 4 and 5 of the *Tobacco Products Control Act* prohibited the advertisement of tobacco products offered for sale in Canada, but does not extend to foreign advertising. Sections 6 to 8 dealt with promotion by permitting the advertisement of the full name of the tobacco manufacturer in a cultural or sporting event but prohibiting the promotion of brand names at these events. Tobacco trade marks were also prohibited from being used on any article other than tobacco products. Sections 9 through 11 demanded that certain cautionary messages be contained on all tobacco packages, such as "Cigarettes are addictive" and "Smoking can kill you". Sections 11 through 16 enforced these prohibitions by creating indictable offences and offences punishable on summary conviction. The penalties included fines and/or imprisonment.

The appellants, *RJR-MacDonald Inc.* and *Imperial Tobacco Ltd.* sought a declaration that the Act was wholly *ultra vires* Parliament and invalid as failing to come within Parliament's criminal law power at s. 91(24) and also as an unjustified infringement of freedom of expression guaranteed by s. 2(*b*) of the *Canadian Charter of Rights and Freedoms*. The Quebec Superior Court declared the whole of the Act *ultra vires* the Parliament of Canada and as well found it to be of no force or effect as an unjustified infringement of s. 2(*b*) of the *Charter*. The Quebec Court of Appeal reversed this judgment.]

La **FOREST J.** [Lamer C.J. and L'Heureux-Dubé, Gonthier, Cory, McLachlin and Iacobucci JJ. concurring on this issue]: — The purpose of the Act is set out in s. 3, which reads:

> **3.** The purpose of this Act is to provide a legislative response to a national public health problem of substantial and pressing concern and, in particular,
>
> (*a*) to protect the health of Canadians in the light of conclusive evidence implicating tobacco use in the incidence of numerous debilitating and fatal diseases;
>
> (*b*) to protect young persons and others, to the extent that is reasonable in a free and democratic society, from inducements to use tobacco products and consequent dependence on them; and
>
> (*c*) to enhance public awareness of the hazards of tobacco use by ensuring the effective communication of pertinent information to consumers of tobacco products. [...]

[T]he Act does not purport to proscribe the sale, distribution or use of tobacco products. Rather, as its long title indicates, the Act seeks to attain its purpose through the institution of a prohibition on the advertising and promotion of tobacco products offered for sale in Canada and through the institution of a requirement that manufacturers of tobacco products display health warnings on tobacco product packages. [...]

The first question arising on these appeals is whether the Act constitutes a valid exercise of the federal criminal law power and is therefore *intra vires* the federal Parliament. Section 91(27) of the *Constitution Act, 1867* confers on the federal Parliament the exclusive power to legislate in relation to the criminal law. The criminal law power is plenary in nature and this Court has always defined its scope broadly. As Estey J. observed in *Scowby v. Glendinning*, [1986] 2 S.C.R. 226, at p. 238, "[t]he terms of s. 91(27) of the Constitution must be read as assigning to Parliament exclusive jurisdiction over criminal law in the widest sense of the term"; see also *Attorney-General for Ontario v. Hamilton Street Railway Co.*, [1903] A.C. 524 (P.C.), at pp. 528-29. In developing a definition of the criminal law, this Court has been careful not to freeze the definition in time or confine it to a fixed domain of activity [...] In *Proprietary Articles Trade Association v. Attorney-General for Canada*, [1931] A.C. 310 (*PATA*), at p. 324, the Privy Council defined the federal criminal law power in the widest possible terms to include any prohibited act with penal consequences. Subsequent to that decision, this Court recognized that the Privy Council's definition was too broad in that it would allow Parliament to invade areas of provincial legislative competence colourably simply by legislating in the proper form; see *Scowby, supra*, at p. 237. So, as Estey J. put it in *Scowby*, at p. 237, "it was accepted that some legitimate public purpose must underlie the prohibition". This necessary adjustment was introduced in *Reference Re Validity of Section 5(a) of the Dairy Industry Act*, [1949] S.C.R. 1 (the *Margarine Reference*). [...]

Taking into account the broad definition of the criminal law developed by this Court, I am satisfied that the Act is, in pith and substance, criminal law. A law's pith and substance, or "matter", is best described as its dominant purpose or true character; see *Morgentaler, supra*, at pp. 481-82. From a plain reading of the Act, it seems clear that Parliament's purpose in enacting this legislation was to prohibit three categories of acts: advertisement of tobacco products (ss. 4 and 5), promotion of tobacco products (ss. 6 to 8) and sale of tobacco products without printed health warnings (s. 9). These prohibitions are accompanied by penal sanctions under s. 18 of the Act, which, as Lord Atkin noted in *PATA, supra*, at p. 324, creates at least a *prima facie* indication that the Act is criminal law. However, the crucial further question is whether the Act also has an underlying criminal public purpose in the sense described by Rand J. in the *Margarine Reference, supra*. The question, as Rand J. framed it, is whether the prohibition with penal consequences is directed at an "evil" or injurious effect upon the public.

In these cases, the evil targeted by Parliament is the detrimental health effects caused by tobacco consumption. This is apparent from s. 3, the Act's "purpose" clause. [...]

Quite clearly, the common thread running throughout the three enumerated purposes in paras. 3(*a*) to (*c*) is a concern for public health and, more specifically, a concern with protecting Canadians from the hazards of tobacco consumption. This is a valid concern. A copious body of evidence was introduced at trial demonstrating convincingly, and this was not disputed by the appellants, that tobacco consumption is widespread in Canadian society and that it poses serious risks to the health of a great number of Canadians. I note in passing the well-established principle that a court is entitled, in a pith and substance analysis, to refer to extrinsic materials, such as related legislation, Parliamentary debates and evidence of the "mischief" at which the legislation is directed. [...]

Statistics show that approximately 6.7 million Canadians, or 28 percent of Canadians over the age of 15, consume tobacco products. [...] Indeed, it has been estimated that smoking causes the premature death of over 30,000 Canadians annually. [...] Overwhelming evidence was introduced at trial that tobacco use is a principal cause of deadly cancers, heart disease and lung disease. [...]

It appears, then, that the detrimental health effects of tobacco consumption are both dramatic and substantial. Put bluntly, tobacco kills. Given this fact, can Parliament validly employ the criminal law to prohibit tobacco manufacturers from inducing Canadians to consume these products, and to increase public awareness concerning the hazards of their use? In my view, there is no question that it can. "Health", of course, is not an enumerated head under the *Constitution Act, 1867*. As Estey J. observed in *Schneider v. The Queen*, [1982] 2 S.C.R. 112, at p. 142:

> [...] "health" is not a matter which is subject to specific constitutional assignment but instead is an amorphous topic which can be addressed by valid federal or provincial legislation, depending in the circumstances of each case on the nature or scope of the health problem in question.

Given the "amorphous" nature of health as a constitutional matter, and the resulting fact that Parliament and the provincial legislatures may both validly legislate in this area, it is important to emphasize once again the plenary nature of the criminal law power. In the *Margarine Reference, supra*, at pp. 49-50, Rand J. made it clear that the protection of "health" is one of the "ordinary ends" served by the criminal law, and that the criminal law power may validly be used to safeguard the public from any "injurious or undesirable effect". The scope of the federal power to create criminal legislation with respect to health matters is broad, and is circumscribed only by the requirements that the legislation must contain a prohibition accompanied by a penal sanction and must be directed at a legitimate public health evil. If a given piece of federal legislation contains these features, and if that legislation is not otherwise a "colourable" intrusion upon provincial jurisdiction, then it is valid as criminal law; see *Scowby, supra*, at pp. 237-38. [...]

[T]here is no evidence in the present cases that Parliament had an ulterior motive in enacting this legislation, or that it was attempting to intrude unjustifiably upon provincial powers under ss. 92(13) and (16). They thus differ from the *Margarine Reference, supra*, where the prohibition was not really directed at curtailing a public evil, but was in reality, in pith and substance, aimed at regulating the dairy industry. [...]

Given the addictive nature of tobacco products, and the fact that over one-third of Canadians smoke, it is clear that a legislative prohibition on the sale and use of tobacco products would be highly impractical. Indeed a prohibition on the manufacture and sale of tobacco products would likely lead many smokers to resort to alternative, and illegal, sources of supply. As legislators in this country discovered earlier in the century, the prohibition of a social drug such as tobacco or alcohol leads almost inevitably to an increase in smuggling and crime.

However, the mere fact that it is not practical or realistic to implement a prohibition on the use or manufacture of tobacco products does not mean that Parliament cannot, or should not, resort to other intermediate policy options. [...]

This Court has long recognized that Parliament may validly employ the criminal law power to prohibit or control the manufacture, sale and distribution of products that present a danger to public health, and that Parliament may also validly impose labeling and packaging requirements on dangerous products with a view to protecting public health. This was recognized as early as the *Margarine Reference, supra.* [...]

It is clear from Laskin C.J.'s analysis [in *R. v. Wetmore*, [1983] 2 S.C.R. 284] that legislation with respect to food and drugs that is aimed at protecting the "physical health and safety of the public" is a valid exercise of the federal criminal law power. [...]

[T]he necessary implication of the reasoning in *Wetmore* and the *Margarine Reference* is that the federal criminal law power to legislate with respect to dangerous goods also encompasses the power to legislate with respect to health warnings on dangerous goods. Since health warnings serve to alert Canadians to the potentially harmful consequences of the use of dangerous products, the power to prohibit sales without these warnings is simply a logical extension of the federal power to protect public health by prohibiting the sale of the products themselves. As noted by Lamer C.J. in *R. v. Swain*, [1991] 1 S.C.R. 933, at p. 999, "it has long been recognized that there also exists a preventative branch of the criminal law power". [...]

From the foregoing, it is clear that Parliament could, if it chose, validly prohibit the manufacture and sale of tobacco products under the criminal law power on the ground that these products constitute a danger to public health. Such a prohibition would be directly analogous to the prohibitions on dangerous drugs and unsanitary foods or poisons mentioned earlier, which quite clearly fall within the federal criminal law power. In my view, once it is accepted that Parliament may validly legislate under the criminal law power with respect to the manufacture and sale of tobacco products, it logically follows that Parliament may also validly legislate under that power to prohibit the advertisement of tobacco products and sales of products without health warnings. In either case, Parliament is legislating to effect the same underlying criminal public purpose: protecting Canadians from harmful and dangerous products. [...]

I think it right to address directly the three principal arguments raised by the appellants in support of their submission that the Act is not valid as criminal law. [...]

The appellants' first argument is that the Act is not a valid exercise of the criminal law power because it does not involve conduct having an affinity with a traditional criminal law concern. The appellants observe that both tobacco consumption and tobacco advertising have always been legal in this country and, on this basis, argue that this legislation does not serve a "public purpose commonly recognized as being criminal in nature"; see *Swain, supra*, at p. 998.

In my view, this argument fails because it neglects the well-established principle that the definition of the criminal law is not "frozen as of some particular time"; see *Zelensky, supra,* at p. 951 (*per* Laskin C.J.). It has long been recognized that Parliament's power to legislate with respect to the criminal law must, of necessity, include the power to create new crimes. [...]

In my view, the reasoning in *PATA* and *Goodyear Tire* is directly applicable here. The simple fact that neither tobacco consumption nor tobacco advertising have been illegal in the past in no way precludes Parliament from criminalizing either of those activities today. Indeed, given the fact that the first medical reports linking cigarette smoking to disease did not emerge until the 1950s, and that governments have only recently been made aware of the truly devastating health consequences of tobacco consumption, it is clear that Parliament had no reason, before that time, to criminalize this activity. [...] It would be artificial, if not absurd, to limit Parliament's power to legislate in this emerging area of public health concern simply because it did not, and logically could not, legislate at an earlier time. [...]

The appellants' second argument is that the Act lacks the requisite "criminal public purpose" because Parliament cannot criminalize an activity ancillary to an "evil" (the advertisement and promotion of tobacco), when the underlying activity the legislation is designed to combat (the manufacture, sale and consumption of tobacco) is itself legal.

In my view, this argument fails because it cannot be reconciled with the recent jurisprudence of this Court. In both *Reference Re ss. 193 and 195.1(1)(c) of the Criminal Code (Man.)*, [1990] 1 S.C.R. 1123 (the *Prostitution Reference*), and *Rodriguez v. British Columbia (Attorney General)*, [1993] 3 S.C.R. 519, this Court upheld the constitutionality of legislation that criminalized an ancillary activity without also criminalizing the underlying activity or "evil". [...]

In my view, the reasoning in the *Prostitution Reference* and *Rodriguez* is directly applicable to the present cases. Although the manufacture, sale and consumption of tobacco has not been criminalized under the Act, it is clear that Parliament's underlying purpose in criminalizing tobacco advertising and promotion is to eradicate the practice. The fact that Parliament has chosen a "circuitous path" to accomplish this goal does not in any way lessen the constitutional validity of the goal. I emphasize once again that it is the pith and substance of the legislation, not Parliament's wisdom in choosing the legislative method, that is the touchstone in a division of powers analysis.

The appellants' third argument is that the Act is fundamentally regulatory, not criminal, in nature. In support of this argument, they observe that the Act contains exemptions for publications and broadcasts originating outside Canada (s. 4(3)), for the Dunhill trademark (s. 8(3)), and for tobacco product substitutes exempted by the Governor in Council on the ground that they pose less risk to the health of users (s. 17(*a*)). The practical effect of these exemptions, the appellants argue, is that the very same act can be legal when committed by one party in Canada but illegal when committed by another.

In my view, this argument fails because it disregards the long-established principle that the criminal law may validly contain exemptions for certain conduct without losing its status as criminal law. As early as 1959, in *Lord's Day Alliance of Canada v. Attorney General of British Columbia*, [1959] S.C.R. 497, this Court held that the *Lord's Day Act*, R.S.C. 1952, c. 171, which prohibited gambling on Sunday, was a valid exercise of the criminal law power despite the fact that s. 6 of that Act created an exemption for provinces which had passed legislation to the contrary. [...]

This principle was reiterated in *Morgentaler v. The Queen*, [1976] 1 S.C.R. 616, where this Court addressed the constitutionality of s. 251 of the *Criminal Code* [...] Laskin C.J., dissenting in the result but not on this issue, made it clear that the creation of such an exemption did not detract from the validity of the provision as criminal law, at p. 627:

> I need cite no authority for the proposition that Parliament may determine what is not criminal as well as what is, and may hence introduce dispensations or exemptions in its criminal legislation. It has done this in respect of gaming and betting by prescribing for lawful operation of pari-mutuel systems, [...] by exempting agricultural fairs or exhibitions from certain of the prohibitions against lotteries and games of chance [...] and by expressly permitting lotteries under stated conditions. [...]

Most recently, in *R. v. Furtney*, [1991] 3 S.C.R. 89, this Court reaffirmed Laskin C.J.'s conclusion. In *Furtney*, the Court addressed a challenge to s. 207 of the *Criminal Code*, R.S.C., 1985, c. C-46, which prohibited lotteries but created an exemption for provincial lotteries conducted in accordance with terms and conditions of licences issued by the Lieutenant Governor. The Court held that the *Code* provision was valid criminal law, even though it delegated regulatory power to the provincial Lieutenant Governors in Council to create exemptions. [...]

The clear implication of this Court's decisions in *Lord's Day Alliance*, *Morgentaler* and *Furtney*, is that the creation of a broad status-based exemption to criminal legislation does not detract from the criminal nature of the legislation. On the contrary, the exemption helps to define the crime by clarifying its contours. In my view, this is precisely what Parliament has done in creating exemptions under the Act. The crime created by Parliament is the advertisement and promotion of tobacco products offered for sale in Canada. Rather than diluting the criminality of these acts, the exemptions to which the appellants refer serve merely to delineate the logical and practical limits to Parliament's exercise of the criminal law power in this context. [...]

For all the foregoing reasons, I am of the view that the Act is a valid exercise of the federal criminal law power. Having reached this conclusion, I do not find it necessary to address the Attorney General's further submission that the Act falls under the federal power to legislate for the peace, order and good government of Canada. [...]

MAJOR J. [Sopinka J. concurring on this issue] (dissenting on this issue): — [...] I agree with Justice La Forest that Parliament could prohibit the sale of tobacco products without printed health warnings under its criminal law power but that is not the issue in these appeals.

It is undisputed that Parliament may legislate with respect to hazardous, unsanitary, adulterated and otherwise dangerous foods and drugs pursuant to its power to legislate in the field of criminal law.

It follows that Parliament can require manufacturers to place warnings on tobacco products which are known to have harmful effects on health. Manufacturers of tobacco products are under a duty to disclose and warn of the dangers inherent in the consumption of tobacco products. Failure to place warnings on tobacco products can validly constitute a crime, a "public wrong" which merits proscription and punishment and ought to be suppressed as "socially undesirable conduct". [...]

However, I do not agree that Parliament under its criminal law power is entitled to prohibit *all* advertising and promotion of tobacco products and restrict the use of tobacco trademarks as provided for in ss. 4, 5, 6, 8 and 9 of the Act. [...] Although Parliament's power to legislate in the field of criminal law is broad, it is subject to constitutional limits.

A definitive and all-encompassing test to determine what constitutes a "criminal offence" remains elusive but the activity which Parliament wishes to suppress through criminal sanction must pose a significant, grave and serious risk of harm to public health, morality, safety or security before it can fall within the purview of the criminal law power. While there is a range of conduct between the most and less serious, not every harm or risk to society is sufficiently grave or serious to warrant the application of the criminal law.

The heart of criminal law is the prohibition of conduct which interferes with the proper functioning of society or which undermines the safety and security of society as a whole. *Reference Re Alberta Statutes*, [1938] S.C.R. 100, held that a crime is a public wrong involving a violation of the public rights and duties to the whole community, considered as a community, in its social aggregate capacity. Matters which pose a significant and serious risk of harm or which cause significant and serious harm to public health, safety or security can be proscribed by Parliament as criminal.

Consequently, lesser threats to society and its functioning do not fall within the criminal law, but are addressed through non-criminal regulation, either by Parliament or provincial legislatures, depending on the subject matter of the regulation. [...]

Sopinka J. in *Morgentaler, supra*, stated that to find a valid exercise of Parliament's criminal law power, the presence of a criminal public purpose or object is pivotal. I agree that criminal law is not frozen in time. Parliament can decriminalize what once was thought criminal, and can also criminalize conduct which was not part of the criminal law at the time of Confederation. I disagree that affinity with a traditional criminal law concern has no part to play in the analysis, whether the conduct proscribed by Parliament has an affinity with a traditional criminal law concern is a starting point in determining whether a particular matter comes within federal criminal competence. [...]

The objective of the advertising ban and trade mark usage restrictions, as stated by McLachlin J., is to prevent Canadians from being persuaded by advertising and promotion to use tobacco products. I respectfully disagree with La Forest J. that this type of persuasion constitutes criminal conduct.

Tobacco advertising and promotion may encourage some people to start or to continue to smoke. For that reason, it is viewed by many as an undesirable form of commercial expression. I do not disagree that it may be an undesirable form of expression, but is this undesirability sufficient to make such expression criminal? Does tobacco advertising pose a significant, grave and serious danger to public health? Or does it simply encourage people to consume a legal but harmful product? I cannot agree that the commercial speech at issue poses such a significant, grave and serious danger to public health to fall within the purview of the federal criminal law power. In my opinion, the Act is too far removed from the injurious or undesirable effects of tobacco use to constitute a valid exercise of Parliament's criminal law power. [...]

Parliament could have criminalized tobacco use, but has chosen not [to] do so for a variety of reasons. The Act does not directly address the injurious or undesirable effects of tobacco use. La Forest J., in response to this concern, notes that in some circumstances Parliament has criminalized ancillary activities without criminalizing the core activity itself, and that this Court has upheld such measures as a valid exercise of the criminal law power. With respect, the cases cited by La Forest J. — *Reference Re ss. 193 and 195.1(1)(c) of the Criminal Code (Man.)*, [1990] 1 S.C.R. 1123 (solicitation for the purposes of prostitution and the operation of bawdy houses) and *Rodriguez v. British Columbia (Attorney General)*, [1993] 3 S.C.R. 519 (prohibition on assisted suicide) — concern matters which have traditionally been subject to criminal sanctions. Moreover, the "ancillary" activities proscribed in the above two examples pose significant and serious dangers in and of themselves.

It is well known that crime often follows in the wake of prostitution and its related activities. It is also well known that assisted suicide can engender all manner of evils, not the least of which is involuntary euthanasia. Hence the criminalization of solicitation of prostitution where prostitution itself is legal, or the criminalization of assisted suicide where suicide itself is legal does not provide a useful analogy to the criminalization of tobacco advertising where tobacco consumption is legal. The fact that the "ancillary" activities in the *Prostitution Reference* and in *Rodriguez* of themselves pose serious risks of harm to society makes the analogy less than compelling.

Since Parliament has chosen not to criminalize tobacco use, it is difficult to understand how tobacco advertising can somehow take on the character of criminal activity. The Act does not deal in any way with the regulation or prohibition of dangerous products or drugs. The underlying "evil" of tobacco use which the Act is designed to combat remains perfectly legal. Tobacco advertising is in itself not sufficiently dangerous or harmful to justify criminal sanctions. In my view, it is beyond Parliament's competence to criminalize this type of speech where Parliament has declined to criminalize the underlying activity of tobacco use. [...]

In these appeals, McLachlin J. notes that despite the advertising ban, 65 percent of the Canadian magazine market will contain tobacco advertisements, given that the ban applies only to Canadian media and not to imported publications. The exemptions for advertising cannot be seen as being limited in nature because most Canadians will be exposed to advertising for tobacco products in newspapers, magazines and so forth. It is hard to understand how the respondent on the one hand claims that nothing short of a total ban will accomplish the goal of reducing tobacco consumption while at the same time the Act allows a very significant amount of advertising to enter the country. It is difficult to imagine how tobacco advertising produced by the United States or other countries and distributed in Canada through publications somehow becomes criminal when produced and distributed by Canadians. The broadly based exemptions contained in the Act, combined with the fact that the Act does not engage a typically criminal public purpose, leads to the conclusion that the prohibitions on advertising cannot be upheld as a valid exercise of Parliament's criminal law power.

The Act, except for s. 9 and its associated provisions relating to mandatory health warnings on tobacco packaging, cannot be upheld as valid criminal legislation. The Act is a regulatory measure aimed at decreasing tobacco consumption. While Parliament's desire to limit tobacco advertising may be desirable, its power to do so cannot be found in s. 91(27) of the *Constitution Act, 1867*. [...]

REFERENCE RE FIREARMS ACT (CAN.),
[2000] 1 S.C.R. 783.

BY THE COURT —

¶ 1 In 1995, Parliament amended the *Criminal Code*, R.S.C., 1985, c. C-46, by enacting the *Firearms Act*, S.C. 1995, c. 39, commonly referred to as the gun control law, to require the holders of all firearms to obtain licences and register their guns. In 1996, the Province of Alberta challenged Parliament's power to pass the gun control law by a reference to the Alberta Court of Appeal. The Court of Appeal by a 3:2 majority upheld Parliament's power to pass the law. The Province of Alberta now appeals that decision to this Court. [...]

¶ 6 For many years, the *Criminal Code* has restricted access to firearms, mainly automatic weapons and handguns, by classifying some as prohibited and some as restricted. The *Firearms Act* amendments extended this regulation to all firearms, including rifles and shotguns. As a result, s. 84 of the *Criminal Code* now controls three classes of firearms: (1) prohibited firearms (generally automatic weapons); (2) restricted firearms (generally handguns); and (3) all other firearms (generally rifles and shotguns). The third class of guns is variously referred to as "ordinary firearms", "long guns", and "unrestricted firearms". We will refer to this class as "ordinary firearms".

¶ 7 The reference questions focus on the validity of the licensing and registration provisions for ordinary firearms introduced by the *Firearms Act*. The licensing sections of the Act provide that a person must be licensed in order to possess a firearm. Eligibility for a licence reflects safety interests. An applicant with a criminal record involving drug offences or violence, or a history of mental illness, may be denied a licence. An applicant who seeks to acquire a firearm must pass a safety course which requires a basic understanding of firearm safety and the legal responsibilities of firearm ownership. The chief firearms officer, who issues licences, may conduct a background check on the applicant in order to determine eligibility, and may attach conditions to a licence. Once issued, a licence is valid for five years, but it may be revoked for contravention of its conditions or for certain criminal convictions. A licence refusal or revocation may be appealed to a court.

¶ 8 The registration provisions of the Act are more limited. A firearm cannot be registered unless the applicant is licensed to possess that type of firearm. Registration is generally done by reference to the serial number on the firearm. A registration certificate is valid as long as its holder owns the weapon. If ownership of a registered weapon is transferred, the new owner must register the weapon. In order to give gun owners time to register their weapons, people who owned ordinary firearms as of January 1, 1998 are deemed to hold registration certificates that are valid until January 1, 2003. Possession of an unregistered firearm of any type is an offence. All licences and registration certificates, along with imported, exported, lost and stolen guns, are recorded in the Canadian Firearms Registry, which is operated by a federal appointee. [...]

¶ 15 The issue before us is whether the licensing and registration provisions of the *Firearms Act* constitute a valid federal enactment pursuant to Parliament's jurisdiction over criminal law or its peace, order and good government power. In order to answer this question, we must engage in the division of powers analysis used so often by this Court [...]. There are two stages to this analysis. The first step is to determine the "pith and substance" or essential character of the law. The second step is to classify that essential character by reference to the heads of power under the *Constitution Act, 1867* in order to determine whether the law comes within the jurisdiction of the enacting government. If it does, then the law is valid.

A. Characterization: What Is the Pith and Substance of the Law?

¶ 16 The first task is to determine the "pith and substance" of the legislation. To use the wording of ss. 91 and 92, what is the "matter" of the law? What is its true meaning or essential character, its core? To determine the pith and substance, two aspects of the law must be examined: the purpose of the enacting body, and the legal effect of the law.

¶ 17 A law's purpose is often stated in the legislation, but it may also be ascertained by reference to extrinsic material such as Hansard and government publications: see *Morgentaler supra*, at pp. 483-84. While such extrinsic material was at one time inadmissible to facilitate the determination of Parliament's purpose, it is now well accepted that the legislative history, Parliamentary debates, and similar material may be quite properly considered as long as it is relevant and reliable and is not assigned undue weight. [...] Purpose may also be ascertained by considering the "mischief" of the legislation — the problem which Parliament sought to remedy. [...]

¶ 18 Determining the legal effects of a law involves considering how the law will operate and how it will affect Canadians. The Attorney General of Alberta states that the law will not actually achieve its purpose. Where the legislative scheme is relevant to a criminal law purpose, he says, it will be ineffective (e.g. criminals will not register their guns); where it is effective it will not advance the fight against crime (e.g. burdening rural farmers with pointless red tape). These are concerns that were properly directed to and considered by Parliament. Within its constitutional sphere, Parliament is the judge of whether a measure is likely to achieve its intended purposes; efficaciousness is not relevant to the Court's division of powers analysis. [...] Rather, the inquiry is directed to how the law sets out to achieve its purpose in order to better understand its "total meaning". [...] In some cases, the effects of the law may suggest a purpose other than that which is stated in the law: see *Morgentaler, supra*, at pp. 482-83; *Attorney-General for Alberta v. Attorney-General for Canada*, [1939] A.C. 117 (P.C.) (*Alberta Bank Taxation Reference*). [...] In other words, a law may say that it intends to do one thing and actually do something else. Where the effects of the law diverge substantially from the stated aim, it is sometimes said to be "colourable".

¶ 19 Against this background, we turn to the purpose of the *Firearms Act*. Section 4 states that the purpose of the Act is "to provide [...] for the issuance of licences, registration certificates and authorizations under which persons may possess firearms" and "to authorize [...] the manufacture of" and "transfer of" ordinary firearms. This is the language of property regulation. However, this regulatory language is directly tied to a purpose cast in the language of the criminal law. The licensing, registration and authorization provisions delineate the means by which people can own and transfer ordinary firearms "in circumstances that would otherwise constitute [a criminal] offence". Those who challenge the legislation point to the first part of the section and its regulatory focus. Those who seek to uphold the law point to the second part of the section and its criminal focus.

¶ 20 The statements of the Honourable Allan Rock, Minister of Justice at the time, in his second-reading speech in the House of Commons, reveal that the federal government's purpose in proposing the law was to promote public safety. He stated: "The government suggests that the object of the regulation of firearms should be the preservation of the safe, civilized and peaceful nature of Canada" (*House of Commons Debates*, vol. 133, No. 154, 1st Sess., 35th Parl., February 16, 1995, at p. 9706). Mr. Rock went on to describe the contents of the bill in more detail:

First, tough measures to deal with the criminal misuse of firearms; second, specific penalties to punish those who would smuggle illegal firearms; and third, measures overall to provide a context in which the legitimate use of firearms can be carried on in a manner consistent with public safety. (emphasis added.)

(*House of Commons Debates, supra*, at p. 9707. See also the judgment of Fraser C.J.A., at paras.169-72.)

Later, the Minister referred to the problems of suicide, accidental shootings, and the use of guns in domestic violence, and detailed some of the shooting tragedies that had spurred public calls for gun control. Russell MacLellan, the Parliamentary Secretary of Justice at the time, underscored the government's concerns, noting that the Act pursues "three fundamental policies: the deterrence of the misuse of firearms, general controls on persons given access to firearms, and controls placed on specific types of firearms" ("Canada's firearms proposals" (1995), 37 *Can. J. Crim.* 163).

¶ 21 Another way to determine the purpose of legislation is to look at the problems it is intended to address – the so-called "mischief" approach. The *Firearms Act* is aimed at a number of evils or "mischiefs". One is the illegal trade in guns, both within Canada and across the border with the United States: see *The Government's Action Plan on Firearms Control*, tabled in the House of Commons in 1994. Another is the link between guns and violent crime, suicide, and accidental deaths. In a paper commissioned by the Department of Justice in 1994, "The impact of the availability of firearms on violent crime, suicide, and accidental death: A review of the literature with special reference to the Canadian situation", Thomas Gabor found that all three causes of death may increase in jurisdictions where there are the fewest restrictions on guns. Whether or not one accepts Gabor's conclusions, his study indicates the problem which Parliament sought to address by enacting the legislation: the problem of the misuse of firearms and the threat it poses to public safety.

¶ 22 Finally, there is a strong argument that the purpose of this legislation conforms with the historical public safety focus of all gun control laws. This reference challenges the licensing and registration provisions of the Act only as they relate to ordinary firearms. Alberta does not question the licensing and registration of restricted and prohibited weapons. It freely admits that the restrictions on those categories of weapons are constitutional. Indeed, Alberta would have difficulty alleging otherwise, as numerous courts have upheld the validity of different aspects of the federal gun control legislation that existed prior to the enactment of this Act. [...]

¶ 23 [...] These cases upheld the previous gun control legislation on the basis that Parliament's purpose was to promote public safety. The *Firearms Act* extends that legislation in two respects: (1) it requires all guns to be registered, not just restricted and prohibited firearms; and (2) eventually all gun owners will be required to be licensed, not just those who wish to acquire a firearm. These changes represent a continuation of Parliament's focus on safety concerns, and constitute a limited expansion of the pre-existing legislation. Given the general acceptance of the gun control legislation that has existed for the past hundred years, the constitutional validity of which has always been predicated on Parliament's concern for public safety, it is difficult to now impute a different purpose to Parliament. This supports the view that the law in pith and substance is about public safety.

¶ 24 The effects of the scheme – how it impacts on the legal rights of Canadians – also support the conclusion that the 1995 gun control law is in pith and substance a public safety measure. The criteria for acquiring a licence are concerned with safety rather than the regulation of property. Criminal record checks and background investigations are designed to keep guns out of the hands of those incapable of using them safely. Safety courses ensure that gun owners are qualified. What the law does not require also shows that the operation of the scheme is limited to ensuring safety. For instance, the Act does not regulate the legitimate commercial market for guns. It makes no attempt to set labour standards or the price of weapons. There is no attempt to protect or regulate industries or businesses associated with guns. [...] Unlike provincial property registries, the registry established under the Act is not concerned with prior interests, and unlike some provincial motor vehicle schemes, the Act does not address insurance. In short, the effects of the law suggest that its essence is the promotion of public safety through the reduction of the misuse of firearms, and negate the proposition that Parliament was in fact attempting to achieve a different goal such as the total regulation of firearms production, trade, and ownership. We therefore conclude that, viewed from its purpose and effects, the *Firearms Act* is in "pith and substance" directed to public safety.

B. Classification: Does Parliament Have Jurisdiction to Enact the Law?

¶ 25 Having assessed the pith and substance or matter of the law, the second step is to determine whether that matter comes within the jurisdiction of the enacting legislature. We must examine the heads of power under ss. 91 and 92 of the *Constitution Act, 1867* and determine what the matter is "in relation to". In this case, the question is whether the law falls under federal jurisdiction over criminal law or its peace, order and good government power; or under provincial jurisdiction over property and civil rights. The presumption of constitutionality means that Alberta, as the party challenging the legislation, is required to show that the Act does not fall within the jurisdiction of Parliament. [...]

¶ 26 The determination of which head of power a particular law falls under is not an exact science. In a federal system, each level of government can expect to have its jurisdiction affected by the other to a certain degree. As Dickson C.J. stated in *General Motors of Canada Ltd. v. City National Leasing*, [1989] 1 S.C.R. 641, at p. 669, "overlap of legislation is to be expected and accommodated in a federal state". Laws mainly in relation to the jurisdiction of one level of government may overflow into, or have "incidental effects" upon, the jurisdiction of the other level of government. It is a matter of balance and of federalism: no one level of government is isolated from the other, nor can it usurp the functions of the other.

¶ 27 As a general rule, legislation may be classified as criminal law if it possesses three prerequisites: a valid criminal law purpose backed by a prohibition and a penalty. [...]

¶ 28 Before determining whether the three criminal law criteria are met by this legislation, some general observations on the criminal law power may be apposite. Criminal law, as this Court has stated in numerous cases, constitutes a broad area of federal jurisdiction. [...] The criminal law stands on its own as federal jurisdiction. Although it often overlaps with provincial jurisdiction over property and civil rights, it is not "carved out" from provincial jurisdiction, contrary to the view of Conrad J.A. It also includes the law of criminal procedure, which regulates many aspects of criminal law enforcement, such as arrest, search and seizure of evidence, the regulation of electronic surveillance and the forfeiture of stolen property.

¶ 29 Not only is the criminal law a "stand-alone" jurisdiction, it also finds its expression in a broad range of legislation. The *Criminal Code* is the quintessential federal enactment under its criminal jurisdiction, but it is not the only one. The *Food and Drugs Act*, the *Hazardous Products Act*, the *Lord's Day Act*, and the *Tobacco Products Control Act* have all been held to be valid exercises of the criminal law power. [...] Thus the fact that some of the provisions of the *Firearms Act* are not contained within the *Criminal Code* has no significance for the purposes of constitutional classification.

¶ 30 Although the criminal law power is broad, it is not unlimited. [...]

¶ 31 Within this context, we return to the three criteria that a law must satisfy in order to be classified as criminal. The first step is to consider whether the law has a valid criminal law purpose. Rand J. listed some examples of valid purposes in the *Margarine Reference* at p. 50: "Public peace, order, security, health, morality: these are the ordinary though not exclusive ends served by [criminal] law". Earlier, we concluded that the gun control law in pith and substance is directed at public safety. This brings it clearly within the criminal law purposes of protecting public peace, order, security and health.

¶ 32 In determining whether the purpose of a law constitutes a valid criminal law purpose, courts look at whether laws of this type have traditionally been held to be criminal law: see *Morgentaler,* supra, at p. 491, and *RJR-MacDonald,* supra, at para. 204. [...] Courts have repeatedly held that gun control comes within the criminal law sphere. [G]un control has been a matter of criminal law since before the enactment of the *Criminal Code* in 1892, and has continued since that date. [...]

¶ 33 Gun control has traditionally been considered valid criminal law because guns are dangerous and pose a risk to public safety. Section 2 of the *Criminal Code* (as amended by s. 138(2) of the *Firearms Act*) defines a "firearm" as "a barreled weapon from which any shot, bullet or other projectile can be discharged and <u>that is capable of causing serious bodily injury or death to a person</u>" (emphasis added). This demonstrates that Parliament views firearms as dangerous and regulates their possession and use on that ground. The law is limited to restrictions which are directed at safety purposes. As such, the regulation of guns as dangerous products is a valid purpose within the criminal law power. [...]

¶ 34 The finding of a valid criminal law purpose does not end the inquiry, however. In order to be classified as a valid criminal law, that purpose must be connected to a prohibition backed by a penalty. The 1995 gun control law satisfies these requirements. Section 112 of the *Firearms Act* prohibits the possession of a firearm without a registration certificate. Section 91 of the *Criminal Code* (as amended by s. 139 of the *Firearms Act*) prohibits the possession of a firearm without a licence and a registration certificate. These prohibitions are backed by penalties: see s. 115 of the *Firearms Act* and s. 91 of the *Code*.

¶ 35 It thus appears that the 1995 gun control law possesses all three criteria required for a criminal law. However, Alberta and the provinces raised a number of objections to this classification which must be considered.

(1) Regulation or Criminal Prohibition?

[...]

¶ 38 [T]he law's prohibitions and penalties are not regulatory in nature. They are not confined to ensuring compliance with the scheme, as was the case in *Boggs v. The Queen*, [1981] 1 S.C.R. 49, but stand on their own, independently serving the purpose of public safety. Nor are the prohibitions and penalties directed to the object of revenue generation. Parliament's intention was not to regulate property, but to ensure that only those who prove themselves qualified to hold a licence are permitted to possess firearms of any sort.

¶ 39 Alberta and the supporting interveners argued that the only way Parliament could address gun control would be to prohibit ordinary firearms outright. With respect, this suggestion is not supported by either logic or jurisprudence. First, the jurisprudence establishes that Parliament may use indirect means to achieve its ends. A direct and total prohibition is not required: see *Reference Re ss. 193 and 195.1(1)(c) of the Criminal Code (Man.)*, [1990] 1 S.C.R. 1123; and *RJR-MacDonald, supra*. Second, exemptions from a law do not preclude it from being prohibitive and therefore criminal in nature: see *R. v. Furtney*, [1991] 3 S.C.R. 89, *Morgentaler v. The Queen*, [1976] 1 S.C.R. 616, and *Lord's Day Alliance of Canada v. Attorney General of British Columbia*, [1959] S.C.R. 497. Third, as noted above, the prohibition in this case is not merely designed to enforce a fee payment or regulatory scheme separate from the essential safety focus of the law: by way of contrast, see *Boggs, supra*. Finally, if prohibition is not required to make handgun control constitutional, which no one suggests, why should it be required for ordinary firearms?

¶ 40 In a related argument, some provincial interveners contended that if the purpose of the legislation is to reduce misuse, then the legislation should deal with misuse directly. On this view, Parliament could prohibit the careless or intentional misuse of guns, as it has in ss. 85-87 of the *Criminal Code*, but could not prohibit people from owning guns if they present risks to public safety or regulate how people store their guns. Again, the answer is that Parliament may use indirect means to further the end of public safety. [...] A prohibition on misuse is unlikely to deter a potential suicide; a prohibition on gun ownership may do so. [...] A prohibition on misuse is unlikely to prevent the death of a child who plays with a gun; a prohibition on irresponsible ownership or careless storage may do so. [...] Whether the 1995 gun law actually achieves these ends is not at issue before us; what is at issue is whether Parliament, in targeting these dangers, strayed outside its criminal law power. In our view, it did not.

(2) Property and Civil Rights or Criminal Law?

¶ 41 Alberta's second major objection to classifying the 1995 gun control scheme as criminal law is that it is indistinguishable from existing provincial property regulation schemes such as automobile and land title registries.

¶ 42 This argument overlooks the different purposes behind the federal restrictions on firearms and the provincial regulation of other forms of property. Guns are restricted because they are dangerous. While cars are also dangerous, provincial legislatures regulate the possession and use of automobiles not as dangerous products but rather as items of property and as an exercise of civil rights, pursuant to the provinces' s. 92(13) jurisdiction.

[...]

¶ 43 The argument that the federal gun control scheme is no different from the provincial regulation of motor vehicles ignores the fact that there are significant distinctions between the roles of guns and cars in Canadian society. Both firearms and automobiles can be used for socially approved purposes. Likewise, both may cause death and injury. Yet their primary uses are fundamentally different. Cars are used mainly as means of transportation. Danger to the public is ordinarily unintended and incidental to that use. Guns, by contrast, pose a pressing safety risk in many if not all of their functions. [...] [T]he Act addresses those aspects of gun control which relate to the dangerous nature of firearms and the need to reduce misuse.

[...]

¶ 46 In a further variation on this argument, the provinces of Ontario and Saskatchewan submitted that even if the licensing provisions of the law were valid criminal legislation, the registration provisions are mainly provincial property legislation and should be severed and struck out. The argument is that the registration portions of the Act simply amount to regulation, with little connection to the public safety purpose advanced by the federal government to justify the Act as a whole. [...]

¶ 47 We are not persuaded that the registration provisions can be severed from the rest of the Act, nor that they fail to serve Parliament's purpose in promoting public safety. The licensing provisions require everyone who possesses a gun to be licensed. The registration provisions require all guns to be registered. The combination of the two parts of the scheme is intended to ensure that when a firearm is transferred from one person to another, the recipient is licensed. Absent a registration system, this would be impossible to ascertain. If a gun is found in the possession of an unlicensed person, the registration system permits the government to determine where the gun originated. With a registration scheme in place, licensed owners can be held responsible for the transfer of their weapons. The registration system is also part of the general scheme of the law in reducing misuse. If someone is found guilty of a crime involving violence, or is prohibited from possessing a weapon, the registration scheme is expected to assist the police in determining whether the offender actually owns any guns and in confiscating them. The registration scheme is also intended to reduce smuggling and the illegal trade in guns. These interconnections demonstrate that the registration and licensing portions of the *Firearms Act* are both tightly linked to Parliament's goal in promoting safety by reducing the misuse of any and all firearms. Both portions are integral and necessary to the operation of the scheme. [...] [N]o improper purpose in including registration in the scheme has been demonstrated.

(3) <u>Undue Intrusion into Provincial Powers?</u>

¶ 48 [...] [A]n appropriate balance must be maintained between the federal and provincial heads of power. A federal state depends for its very existence on a just and workable balance between the central and provincial levels of government, as this Court affirmed in *Reference Re Secession of Québec*, [1998] 2 S.C.R. 217; see also *General Motors of Canada Ltd. v. City National Leasing, supra*. The courts, critically aware of the need to maintain this balance, have not hesitated to strike down legislation that does not conform with the requirements of the criminal law: see *Boggs, supra*, and the *Margarine Reference, supra*. [...]

¶ 49 The argument that the 1995 gun control law upsets the balance of Confederation may be seen as an argument that, viewed in terms of its effects, the law does not in pith and substance relate to public safety under the federal criminal law power but rather to the provincial power over property and civil rights. Put simply, the issue is whether the law is mainly in relation to criminal law. If it is, incidental effects in the provincial sphere are constitutionally irrelevant. [...] On the other hand, if the effects of the law, considered with its purpose, go so far as to establish that it is mainly a law in relation to property and civil rights, then the law is *ultra vires* the federal government. In summary, the question is whether the "provincial" effects are incidental, in which case they are constitutionally irrelevant, or whether they are so substantial that they show that the law is mainly, or "in pith and substance", the regulation of property and civil rights.

¶ 50 In our view, Alberta and the provinces have not established that the effects of the law on provincial matters are more than incidental. First, the mere fact that guns are property does not suffice to show that a gun control law is in pith and substance a provincial matter. Exercises of the criminal law power often affect property and civil rights to some degree. [...] Food, drugs and obscene materials are all items of property and are all legitimate subjects of criminal laws. [...]

¶ 51 Second, the Act does not significantly hinder the ability of the provinces to regulate the property and civil rights aspects of guns. Most provinces already have regulations dealing with hunting, discharge within municipal boundaries, and other aspects of firearm use, and these are legitimate subjects of provincial regulation: see *R. v. Chiasson* (1982), 66 C.C.C. (2d) 195 (N.B.C.A.), *aff'd* [1984] 1 S.C.R. 266. The Act does not affect these laws.

¶ 52 Third, the most important jurisdictional effect of this law is its elimination of the ability of the provinces to <u>not</u> have any regulations on the ownership of ordinary firearms. The provinces argue that it is in their power to choose whether or not to have such a law. By taking over the field, the federal government has deprived the provinces of that choice. Assuming (without deciding) that the provincial legislatures would have the jurisdiction to enact a law in relation to the property aspects of ordinary firearms, this does not prevent Parliament from addressing the safety aspects of ordinary firearms. The double aspect doctrine permits both levels of government to legislate in one jurisdictional field for two different purposes: *Egan, supra.*

¶ 53 [...] While we are sensitive to the concern of the provincial governments that the federal jurisdiction over criminal law not be permitted such an unlimited scope that it erodes the constitutional balance of powers, we do not believe that this legislation poses such a threat.

(4) Is Moral Content Required?

¶ 54 Yet another argument is that the ownership of guns is not criminal law because it is not immoral to own an ordinary firearm. There are two difficulties with this argument. The first is that while the ownership of ordinary firearms is not in itself regarded by most Canadians as immoral, the problems associated with the misuse of firearms are firmly grounded in morality. Firearms may be misused to take human life and to assist in other immoral acts, like theft and terrorism. Preventing such misuse can be seen as an attempt to curb immoral acts. Viewed thus, gun control is directed at a moral evil.

¶ 55 The second difficulty with the argument is that the criminal law is not confined to prohibiting immoral acts: see *Proprietary Articles Trade Association v. Attorney-General for Canada*, [1931] A.C. 310 (P.C.) While most criminal conduct is also regarded as immoral, Parliament can use the criminal law to prohibit activities which have little relation to public morality. For instance, the criminal law has been used to prohibit certain restrictions on market competition: see *Attorney-General for British Columbia v. Attorney-General for Canada* (cites omitted). Therefore, even if gun control did not involve morality, it could still fall under the federal criminal law power. [...]

¶ 58 We conclude that the [...] legislation is in relation to criminal law pursuant to s. 91(27) of the *Constitution Act, 1867* and hence *intra vires* Parliament. It is not regulatory legislation and it does not take the federal government so far into provincial territory that the balance of federalism is threatened or the jurisdictional powers of the provinces are unduly impaired.

¶ 59 Having determined that the legislation constitutes a valid exercise of Parliament's jurisdiction over criminal law, it is unnecessary to consider whether the legislation can also be justified as an exercise of its peace, order and good government power.

¶ 60 We would dismiss the appeal. [...]

R. v. MALMO-LEVINE
[2003] 3 S.C.R. 571

The judgment of McLachlin C.J. and Gonthier, Iacobucci, Major, Bastarache and Binnie JJ. was delivered by

¶ 1 **GONTHIER and BINNIE JJ.:**— In these appeals, the Court is required to consider whether Parliament has the legislative authority to criminalize simple possession of marihuana and, if so, whether that power has been exercised in a manner that is contrary to the Canadian Charter of Rights and Freedoms. [...]

¶ 7 The appellant describes himself as a "marihuana / freedom activist". Self-represented in these proceedings, his primary concern is with interference by the state in what he believes to be the personal autonomy of its citizens. He stated in his oral argument:

> I'm part of a growing number of such activists, who view cannabis re-legalization as a key part of protecting human rights and our Mother Earth, while, at the same time, helping to end [the] war on poverty.

> As you can see, I'm not a lawyer. I am, however, a cannabis user and a researcher, and I would like very much to be a cannabis retailer and perhaps grow a few plants.

¶ 8 Malmo-Levine does not deny that marihuana use can have harmful effects. On the contrary, since October 1996, he has helped operate an organization in East Vancouver known as the Harm Reduction Club, a co-operative, non-profit association which recognizes some potential harm associated with the use of marihuana and seeks to reduce it. The stated object of the Club is to educate its users and the general public about marihuana and provide unadulterated marihuana at cost. It provides instruction about safe smoking habits "to minimize any harm from the use of marihuana", and requires its members to pledge not to operate motor vehicles or heavy equipment while under its influence.

¶ 9 On December 4, 1996, police entered the premises of the Harm Reduction Club and seized 316 grams of marihuana, much of it in the form of "joints". The appellant was charged both with simple possession of marihuana and with possession for the purpose of trafficking. [...]

¶ 22 The trial judge in Caine estimated that over 600,000 Canadians now have criminal records for cannabis-related offences, and that widespread use despite the criminal prohibition encourages disrespect for the law. [...]

¶ 40 The evidentiary issue at the core of the appellants' constitutional challenge is the "harm principle", and the contention that possession of marihuana for personal use is a "victimless crime". The appellants say that even with respect to the user himself or herself there is no cogent evidence of "significant" or "non-trivial" harm.

[Review of the Evidence omitted]

¶ 63 We have been shown no reason to interfere with these findings of fact. It seems clear that the use of marihuana has less serious and permanent effects than was once claimed, but its psychoactive and health effects can be harmful, and in the case of members of vulnerable groups the harm may be serious and substantial. [...]

1. The Purpose of the NCA

¶ 65 Braidwood J.A., ... reviewed the legislative history in detail and concluded that the prohibition on simple possession of marihuana always "had more than one rationale. It was always meant to prevent the harm to society caused by drug addiction, such as the petty thefts that occur to raise funds to buy drugs".... We accept this analysis. ... the evidence supports the conclusion of Braidwood J.A. that a major purpose of the prohibition has been, since its enactment and continued thereafter, to be to protect health and public safety. [...]

2. Legislative Jurisdiction with Respect to Narcotics

(a) *Peace, Order and Good Government*

¶ 67 ... Almost 25 years ago, a majority of this Court upheld the constitutional validity of the NCA under Parliament's residual authority to legislate for POGG: *R. v. Hauser*, [1979] 1 S.C.R. 984. Pigeon J., for the majority, took the view that the NCA "is essentially legislation adopted to deal with a genuinely new problem which did not exist at the time of Confederation and clearly cannot be put in the class of 'Matters of a merely local or private nature'" (p. 1000). Accordingly, Pigeon J. reasoned, the subject matter of the NCA is similar to other new developments such as aviation and radio communication. Dickson J., as he then was, dissented on this point, finding that the NCA should be considered as a matter of federal criminal power. [...]

¶ 69 In *Labatt Breweries of Canada Ltd. v. Attorney General of Canada*, [1980] 1 S.C.R. 914, at pp. 944-45, the Court outlined three instances in which the federal residual power applies:

(i) the existence of a national emergency;

(ii) with respect to a subject matter which did not exist at the time of Confederation and is clearly not in a class of matters of a merely local or private nature;

(iii) where the subject matter "goes beyond local or provincial concern and must, from its inherent nature, be the concern of the Dominion as a whole".

¶ 70 It is not contended that the use of marihuana rises to the level of a national emergency. As to the second category, if, as we conclude infra, the NCA is a valid exercise of the criminal law power, it would not be consistent with that conclusion to uphold it under the branch of POGG that deals with "new" legislative subject matter not otherwise allocated. To that extent we disagree with the view taken by the majority in *Hauser*, supra.

¶ 71 These observations leave only the third category as a potential source of authority under POGG. The Attorney General of Canada contends that the control of narcotics is a legislative subject matter that "goes beyond local or provincial concern and must, from its inherent nature, be the concern of the Dominion as a whole". He puts his position as follows:

> The importation, manufacture, distribution, and use of psychoactive substances are matters having an impact on the country as a whole, and which can only be dealt with on an integrated national basis. Additionally, the international aspects are such that these matters cannot be effectively addressed at the local level.

¶ 72 We do not exclude the possibility that the NCA might be justifiable under the "national concern" branch on the rationale adopted in *R. v. Crown Zellerbach Canada Ltd.*, [1988] 1 S.C.R. 401, at p. 432, where we held that concerted action amongst provincial and federal entities, each acting within their respective spheres of legislative jurisdiction, was essential to deal with Canada's international obligations regarding the environment. In our view, however, the Court should decline in this case to revisit Parliament's residual authority to deal with drugs in general (or marihuana in particular) under the POGG power. If, as is presently one of the options under consideration, Parliament removes marihuana entirely from the criminal law framework, Parliament's continuing legislative authority to deal with marihuana use on a purely regulatory basis might well be questioned. The Court would undoubtedly have more ample legislative facts and submissions in such a case than we have in this appeal. Our conclusion that the present prohibition against the use of marihuana can be supported under the criminal law power makes it unnecessary to deal with the Attorney General's alternative position under the POGG power, and we leave this question open for another day.

(b) The Criminal Law Power

¶ 73 The federal criminal law power is "plenary in nature" and has been broadly construed:

> A crime is an act which the law, with appropriate penal sanctions, forbids; but as prohibitions are not enacted in a vacuum, we can properly look for some evil or injurious or undesirable effect upon the public against which the law is directed. That effect may be in relation to social, economic or political interests; and the legislature has had in mind to suppress the evil or to safeguard the interest threatened.

> (*Reference re Validity of Section 5(a) of the Dairy Industry Act*, [1949] S.C.R. 1 (the "*Margarine Reference*"), at p. 49)

In the present case the "evil or injurious or undesirable effect" is the harm attributed to the non-medical use of marihuana.

¶ 74 For a law to be classified as a criminal law, it must possess three prerequisites. a valid criminal law purpose backed by a prohibition and a penalty: *Reference re Firearms Act,* [2000] 1 S.C.R. 783, 2000 DCC 31, at para. 27. The criminal power extends to those laws that are designed to promote public peace, safety, order, health or other legitimate public purpose. In *RJR-MacDonald Inc. v. Canada (Attorney General)*, [1995] 3 S.C.R. 199, it was held that some legitimate public purpose must underlie the prohibition. In *Labatt Breweries, supra,* in holding that a health hazard may ground a criminal prohibition, Estey J. stated the potential purposes of the criminal law rather broadly as including "public peace, order, security, health and morality" (p. 933). Of course Parliament cannot use its authority improperly, e.g. colourably, to invade areas of provincial competence: *Scowby v. Glendinning,* [1986] 2 S.C.R. 226, at p. 237. [...]

¶ 76 The purpose of the NCA fits within the criminal law power, which includes the protection of vulnerable groups [...]

¶ 77 The protection of vulnerable groups from self-inflicted harms does not, as Caine argues, amount to no more than "legal moralism". Morality has traditionally been identified as a legitimate concern of the criminal law ... although today this does not include mere "conventional standards of propriety" but must be understood as referring to societal values beyond the simply prurient or prudish.... The protection of the chronic users identified by the trial judge, and adolescents who may not yet have become chronic users, but who have the potential to do so, is a valid criminal law objective.... In our view, the control of a "psychoactive drug" that "causes alteration of mental function" clearly raises issues of public health and safety, both for the user as well as for those in the broader society affected by his or her conduct.

¶ 78 The use of marihuana is therefore a proper subject matter for the exercise of the criminal law power. *Butler* held, at p. 485, that if there is a reasoned apprehension of harm Parliament is entitled to act, and in our view Parliament is also entitled to act on reasoned apprehension of harm even if on some points "the jury is still out". In light of the concurrent findings of "harm" in the courts below, we therefore confirm that the *Narcotic Control Act* in general, and the scheduling of marihuana in particular, properly fall within Parliament's legislative competence under s. 91(27) of the Constitution Act, 1867. [...]

ARBOUR J: —

A. The Division of Powers Issue

[...] My colleagues Gonthier and Binnie JJ. have concluded that the impugned provisions fall under the criminal law head of power. For that reason, they conclude that it is not necessary to revisit the correctness of the conclusion in *R. v. Hauser,* [1979] 1 S.C.R. 984, with respect to Parliament's residual authority to deal with drugs in general or marihuana in particular under the peace, order and good government power. I am in general agreement with the conclusion reached by my colleagues [...]

¶ 206 As mentioned above, legislation which properly falls under one of the federal heads of power will pass the division of powers challenge, but may still be found to infringe on a right or freedom protected by the Charter. With regard to the federal criminal law power, under s. 91(27) of the *Constitution Act, 1867*, Parliament has been accorded the power to make criminal law in the widest sense [...] It is entirely within Parliament's discretion to determine what evil it wishes to suppress by penal prohibition and what threatened interest it thereby wishes to safeguard. Apart from the Charter, the only qualification attached to Parliament's plenary power over criminal law is that it cannot be employed colourably. Like other legislative powers, the criminal law power does not permit Parliament, simply by legislating in the proper form, colourably to invade areas of exclusively provincial legislative competence. To determine whether such a colourable attempt is made, we must determine whether a legitimate public purpose underlies the criminal prohibition. [...]

¶ 207 In the *Margarine Reference*, supra, Rand J. drew attention, at pp. 49-50, to the need to identify the evil or injurious effect at which a penal prohibition was directed and explained that a prohibition is not criminal unless it serves "a public purpose which can support it as being in relation to criminal law". Further, he explained that the "ordinary though not exclusive ends" served by the criminal law are "[p]ublic peace, order, security, <u>health</u>, [and] morality" (emphasis added).

¶ 208 The main objective of the impugned legislation here is protection from the possible adverse health consequences of marihuana use. The objective of the state in prohibiting marihuana has been summarized by Rosenberg J.A. in Clay's companion case *R. v. Parker* (2000), 146 C.C.C. (3d) 193, at para. 143:

> First, the state has an interest in protecting against the harmful effects of use of that drug. Those include bronchial pulmonary harm to humans; psychomotor impairment from marihuana use leading to a risk of automobile accidents and no simple screening device for detection; possible precipitation of relapse in persons with schizophrenia; possible negative effects on immune system; possible long-term negative cognitive effects in children whose mothers used marihuana while pregnant; possible long-term negative cognitive effects in long-term users; and some evidence that some heavy users may develop a dependency. The other objectives are: to satisfy Canada's international treaty obligations and to control the domestic and international trade in illicit drugs.

¶ 208 Jurisdiction over health is shared between Parliament and the provincial legislatures; their respective competence depends on the pith and substance of the particular measure at issue. [...]

Given the "amorphous" nature of health as a constitutional matter, and the resulting fact that Parliament and the provincial legislatures may both validly legislate in this area, it is important to emphasize once again the plenary nature of the criminal law power. In the *Margarine Reference*, supra, at pp. 49-50, Rand J. made it clear that the protection of "health" is one of the "ordinary ends" served by the criminal law, and that the criminal law power may validly be used to safeguard the public from any "injurious or undesirable effect". The scope of the federal power to create criminal legislation with respect to health matters is broad, and is circumscribed only by the requirements that the legislation must contain a prohibition accompanied by a penal sanction and must be directed at a legitimate public health evil. If a given piece of federal legislation contains these features, and if that legislation is not otherwise a "colourable" intrusion upon provincial jurisdiction, then it is valid as criminal law [...]

¶ 210 There is, as such, no constitutional threshold of harm required for legislative action under the criminal law power. There had been uncertainties in the past in this regard, as some would have required "significant, grave and serious risk of harm to public health, morality, safety or security" before a prohibition could fall within the purview of the criminal law power (see, e.g., *RJR-MacDonald, supra*, at paras. 199-202, per Major J.). It is now established that as long as the legislation is directed at a legitimate public health evil and contains a prohibition accompanied by a penal sanction, and provided that it is not otherwise a "colourable" intrusion upon provincial jurisdiction, Parliament has, under s. 91(27) of the *Constitution Act, 1867*, discretion to determine the extent of the harm it considers sufficient for legislative action (*RJR-MacDonald, supra*, at para. 32; *Reference re Firearms Act (Can.), supra*, at para. 27). Obviously, however, where Parliament relies on the protection of health as its legitimate public purpose, it has to demonstrate the "injurious or undesirable effect" from which it seeks to safeguard the public. This will likely be done by demonstrating the harm to the health of individuals or the public associated with the prohibited conduct. While there is no constitutional threshold level of harm required before Parliament may use its broad criminal law power, conduct with little or no threat of harm is unlikely to qualify as a "public health evil".

[Dissenting opinions of Lebel J and Deschamps J omitted. Both agreed with the majority on the division of powers issues.]

R. v. DEMERS
[2004] 2 S.C.R. 489

The judgment of McLachlin C.J. and Iacobucci, Major, Bastarache, Binnie, Arbour, Deschamps and Fish JJ. was delivered by

IACOBUCCI and BASTARACHE JJ.: —

I. Introduction

¶ 1 This appeal raises the issue of ... whether the regime set out by Parliament in Part XX.1 Cr. C. is unconstitutional under the division of powers analysis or under [...] the *Canadian Charter of Rights and Freedoms* when applied to persons who have been found permanently unfit to stand trial.

¶ 2 We have found that the application of the impugned provisions to persons found unfit to stand trial, on account of permanent or temporary mental disorder, falls within the legislative jurisdiction of the Parliament of Canada. However, we have also found that persons who are permanently unfit to stand trial and do not pose a significant threat to public safety suffer a breach of their liberty interest under s. 7 of the *Charter* because they are subject to indefinite appearances before the Review Board and to the exercise of its powers over them. The limitation of their liberty interest does not accord with the principles of fundamental justice and cannot be saved under s. 1 of the *Charter*. [...]

II. Background

¶ 3 The appellant suffers from Trisomy 21, more commonly known as Down Syndrome, which causes him to be moderately intellectually handicapped. On January 23, 1997, he appeared before the Court of Quebec in relation to charges of sexual assault under s. 271(1)(a) Cr. C.... [T]he appellant was declared unfit to stand trial, following which he remained in hospital until he was discharged three months later, on May 5, 1997, by a Review Board acting under ss. 672.47 and 672.54 Cr. C. His discharge was subject to the condition that he live with his family, keep the peace and establish a consensual treatment regime together with his parents and medical professionals. [...]

¶ 8 In the wake of this Court's decision in *R. v. Swain*, [1991] 1 S.C.R. 933, Parliament introduced Part XX.1 Cr. C. The provisions in Part XX.1 establish a regime for dealing with accused persons who suffer from mental disorders ... [including] individuals declared unfit to stand trial.

¶ 9 Under s. 672.23(1) Cr. C., where a court has reasonable grounds to believe that the accused is unfit to stand trial, it may direct, on its own motion or on the application of one of the parties, that the issue of fitness of the accused be tried. The court has the power under s. 672.11 to order an assessment of the accused, which constitutes an examination by a medical practitioner on the mental condition of the accused, and any incidental observation or examination of the accused. During a trial on the fitness of the accused, an unrepresented accused is provided with legal representation under s. 672.24(1). He or she is presumed fit to stand trial (s. 672.22). The party requesting that the issue of fitness be tried bears the burden of proving on a balance of probabilities that the accused is unfit to stand trial (ss. 672.22 and 672.23(2)). Although expert evidence is relied on heavily, the ultimate issue of fitness is decided by the trier of fact (s. 672.26).

¶ 10 If the accused is found unfit to stand trial, the court may order the forcible treatment of the accused for up to 60 days if (i) the Crown requests forcible treatment and (ii) according to a medical practitioner, specific treatment should be administered for the purpose of making the accused fit to stand trial (ss. 672.58 and 672.59). Immediately following such treatment or a finding that the accused is unfit to stand trial (in the event that no treatment of the accused is ordered), a disposition hearing is held, either by the court (s. 672.45) or alternatively by a Review Board (s. 672.47) to determine whether, and subject to what conditions, if any, the accused should be released or detained. The body conducting the disposition hearing must take into consideration the factors set out in s. 672.54: the need to protect the public from dangerous persons, the mental condition of the accused, the reintegration of the accused into society and the other needs of the accused. It must be pointed out that under s. 672.54, the Review Board is not authorized to grant an absolute or unconditional discharge to persons who are unfit to stand trial (although it does allow for the absolute discharge of individuals declared NCR).

¶ 11 Following its initial disposition in respect of an accused, the Review Board must conduct a hearing every year to determine whether the circumstances warrant a modification of its disposition (s. 672.01(1)). If the accused is fit to stand trial, he is sent to trial under s. 672.48, and the jurisdiction of the Review Board ceases to operate. Otherwise, and subject to what will be said immediately below, another review hearing is held the following year.

¶ 12 In addition to the proceedings conducted by the Review Board, under s. 672.33, every two years, the Crown must appear before a court to show that there still exists a prima facie case against the accused. This is the only way the Crown can justify maintaining the outstanding criminal charge against the accused. In the event that the Crown cannot make out a prima facie case against the accused, the court is required to acquit the accused.

¶ 13 The result of the combined operation of ss. 672.33, 672.54 and 672.81(1) is that an accused found unfit to stand trial remains in the "system" established under Part XX.1 until either (a) he or she becomes fit to stand trial or (b) the Crown fails to establish a *prima facie* case against him or her.

B. *Division of Powers*

¶ 14 We will first examine the issue as to whether the impugned provisions fall within Parliament's criminal law power under s. 91(27) of the *Constitution Act, 1867*, or whether, as the appellant contends, it is *ultra vires*.

¶ 15 Whenever an issue of division of powers arises, the first step in the analysis is to characterize the "pith and substance" of the impugned legislation. In order to determine the pith and substance of any particular legislative provision, it is necessary to examine that provision in its overall legislative context: *Swain, supra*, at p. 998. [...]

¶ 16 Parliament's jurisdiction over criminal law was recently examined by this Court in *R. v. Malmo-Levine*, at paras. 73-74 [...]

¶ 17 In determining whether the purpose of a law constitutes a valid criminal law purpose, courts also look at whether laws of this type have traditionally been held to be criminal law. [...]

¶ 18 The pith and substance of Part XX.1 Cr. C. is revealed by its twin goals of protecting the public and treating the mentally ill accused fairly and appropriately...

¶ 19 The appellant contends that once it has been established that a person will not be tried because of permanent unfitness to stand trial, the circumstances no longer constitute a matter within Parliament's criminal law power. Instead, he claims that persons who represent a danger to themselves or others fall under the exclusive provincial jurisdiction of property and civil rights pursuant to s. 92(13) of the *Constitution Act, 1867*. The appellant also argues that the impugned provisions are not within Parliament's criminal law powers because their pith and substance is the protection of society from persons with dangerous mental states, not persons who have engaged in conduct proscribed by the *Criminal Code*.

¶ 21 [T]o say that the[se] ... considerations apply to the accused person found unfit to stand trial is to ignore fundamental differences between persons who are found to be [not criminally responsible [NCR] and persons who are found unfit to stand trial. The difference in legal status between the NCR and the unfit accused has been discussed by R. D. Schneider in "Mental Disorder in the Courts: Absolute Discharge for Unfits?" (2000), 21 *For the Defence* 36, at p. 38:

> The NCR accused has not been convicted of a crime, but the criminal proceedings have been fully concluded and a final verdict obtained. Therefore, society's residual hold on the accused can only be justified if the accused is shown to be a significant threat to the safety of the public. <u>On the other hand, the unfit accused has yet to be tried. So long as the information or indictment is outstanding the court and/or the Review Board maintain jurisdiction over the accused</u>. Jurisdiction over the unfit has nothing to do with dangerousness. The fitness rules were established to ensure that a prosecution not proceed where an accused is not able to adequately respond to the state. The rules are in place to protect the accused. While it is true that an accused may be "permanently unfit", surely that status accompanied by the presumption of innocence [*Charter*, s. 11(*d*)] is preferable to either proceeding against the unfit accused or terminating the outstanding charges. [Emphasis added.]

¶ 22 Thus, when a verdict of NCR has been rendered, the criminal process has ended and the exercise of criminal state power over NCR offenders can only be justified under the protective branch of the criminal law, when it is proven that the NCR offender presents a significant threat to the public. However, the situation is different with respect to accused found unfit to stand trial: the criminal law's jurisdiction over the unfit accused does not stem from the protective branch of the criminal law, unless he or she is found to be dangerous. Rather, the criminal justice system maintains jurisdictional control over the accused found unfit to stand trial because that person is subject to a criminal accusation and pending proceedings. As long as this accusation is maintained, it is not necessary to consider the dangerousness of the accused or the protection of the public because other considerations justify Parliament's jurisdiction in regards to accused found unfit to stand trial, namely its jurisdiction over criminal procedure.

¶ 23 Parliament's power in matters of criminal law, under s. 91(27) of the *Constitution Act, 1867*, expressly includes "the [p]rocedure in [c]riminal [m]atters".... From the time a person is accused of a crime under the *Criminal Code*, the criminal process is validly engaged and its hold on the accused found unfit to stand trial is established. Therefore, the authority to establish a scheme to administer the rights of the accused found unfit to stand trial flows from Parliament's jurisdiction on criminal law, including criminal procedure.

¶ 24 The system of Crown pre-charge screening in Quebec was described by this Court in *R. v. Regan* [...]

[TRANSLATION] The prosecutor's decision to authorize the laying of criminal charges presupposes that the conduct complained of constitutes an offence in law, that there are reasonable grounds to believe that the person under investigation is the perpetrator, that it is legally possible to prove it, and that it is appropriate to prosecute. In exercising prosecutorial discretion, the prosecutor must take into account various policy and social considerations.

Consequently, when the Crown has reasonable grounds to believe that the person under investigation is the perpetrator, that it is legally possible to prove it and that it is appropriate to prosecute, it will lay criminal charges and the person falls within Parliament's criminal law jurisdiction. Such a finding reinforces the government's fundamental interest in bringing to trial an individual accused of a serious crime.

¶ 25 As mentioned above, Part XX.1 Cr. C. was enacted as a balanced response to this Court's decision in *Swain*. This new scheme reflects both the public's needs (protection from dangerous individuals and bringing to trial an individual accused of a serious crime) and the needs of the accused (right to a fair trial, assessment and treatment of persons with mental disorders). The pith and substance of the impugned provisions falls within both the preventive and criminal procedure branches of the criminal law, all within well-accepted criminal law purposes (*Margarine Reference, supra*).

¶ 26 In *Swain, supra*, this Court found that the predecessor legislation to Part XX.1 was a valid exercise of Parliament's criminal law power under s. 91(27) of the *Constitution Act, 1867*. After citing *MacDonald v. Vapor Canada Ltd.*, [1977] 2 S.C.R. 134, at p. 146, as an authority for the proposition that "legislation under the preventative branch of the criminal law power must relate in some way to criminal proceedings" but does not require an actual conviction, Lamer C.J. explained, at p. 1001:

> Since the insanity provisions only relate to persons whose actions are proscribed by the *Criminal Code*, the required connection with criminal law is present. The system of Lieutenant Governor warrants, through the supervision of persons acquitted by reason of insanity, serves to prevent further dangerous conduct proscribed by the *Criminal Code* and thereby protects society. The protection of society is clearly one of the aims of the criminal law.

> While I am aware of the potential danger of eroding provincial power if "protection of society" is characterized too broadly, I would emphasize that in this case Parliament is protecting society from individuals whose behaviour is proscribed by the *Criminal Code*. The provisions do not relate to all insane persons, but only those who, through their actions, have brought themselves within the criminal law sphere.

¶ 27 It is also important to note that laws dealing with the unfit accused have long been accepted as valid criminal law. Until 1990, where an accused was "acquitted on the basis of mental illness, he or she was not released, but was automatically detained at the pleasure of the Lieutenant Governor in Council: *Criminal Code*, s. 614(2) (formerly s. 542(2)) (repealed S.C. 1991, c. 43, s. 3)": *Winko, supra*, at para. 18.

¶ 28 Finally, as stated by Dickson C.J. in *OPSEU v. Ontario (Attorney General)* ... where one level of government supports the constitutionality of another level's legislation, the Court should be cautious before finding the impugned provision *ultra vires* [...]

In the case at bar, the Attorney General of Canada, as well as the Attorney General of Ontario, have intervened to support the constitutionality of the impugned provisions of the *Criminal Code*.

¶ 29 Thus, for all the aforementioned reasons, we are of the view that the application of ss. 672.33, 672.54 and 672.81(1) Cr. C. to persons found unfit to stand trial, on account of permanent or temporary mental disorder, falls within the legislative jurisdiction of the Parliament of Canada under s. 91(27) of the *Constitution Act, 1867*. [...]

[Justices Iacobucci and Bastarache then considered whether the impugned provisions violated s. 7 of the Charter. They concluded as follows:]

¶ 66 For the above reasons, we would allow the appeal, set aside the judgment of the Superior Court, and declare that ss. 672.33, 672.54 and 672.81(1) Cr. C. are overbroad, thus violating the s. 7 rights of permanently unfit accused who do not pose a significant threat to society. [...] The most appropriate remedy in this case is a suspended declaration of invalidity for a period of twelve months. If after twelve months Parliament does not cure the unconstitutionality of the regime, accused who qualify can ask for a stay of proceedings [...]

The following are the reasons delivered by

LeBEL J.: —

¶ 68 ... I agree with my colleagues' conclusion regarding the breach of s. 7 of the *Charter*, but I disagree with respect to the division of powers issue. [...]

¶ 69 In my view, the criminal procedure power under s. 91(27) of the *Constitution Act, 1867* does not grant Parliament the authority to supervise and detain accused who are permanently unfit to stand trial. Although Parliament is competent to legislate procedures for unfit accused at the outset of proceedings, once a court has determined that the accused is in fact permanently unfit to stand trial, the jurisdiction shifts to the provincial governments under their health power. [...]

¶ 71 Justices Iacobucci and Bastarache conclude that, with respect to permanently unfit accused, ss. 672.33, 672.54 and 672.81(1) of the *Criminal Code* are a valid exercise of Parliament's criminal procedure power under s. 91(27) of the *Constitution Act, 1867*. I disagree. The supervision and treatment of permanently unfit accused and the protection of the public from potentially violent permanently unfit accused are matters exclusively within the health jurisdiction of the provinces under ss. 92(7), 92(13), and 92(16).

A. Historical Scope of the Criminal Law Power

¶ 72 This appeal raises fundamental questions regarding our constitutional structure, including the proper relationship between the *Constitution Act, 1867* and the *Charter*. Historically, the federal criminal law power and the contingent criminal procedure power have been construed broadly. The classic definition of the scope of the criminal law was provided by Rand J. in *Reference re Validity of Section 5(a) of the Dairy Industry Act* ... This wide scope has been consistently affirmed by the Court [...]

¶ 73 Similarly, as a corollary of this plenary criminal law power, Parliament's jurisdiction over criminal procedure under s. 91(27) has also been construed broadly. A precise definition of "procedure in criminal matters", however, has been difficult to formulate:

> It is not necessary and perhaps impossible, to find a satisfactory definition of "criminal procedure." Although I would reject the view which would confine criminal procedure to that which takes place within the courtroom on a prosecution, I am equally of the opinion that "criminal procedure" is not co-extensive with "criminal justice" or that the phrase "criminal procedure" as used in the *B.N.A. Act* can drain from the words "administration of justice" in s. 92(14) that which gives those words much of their substance — the element of "criminal justice."*Di Iorio v. Warden of the Common Jail of the City of Montreal*, at pp. 209-10 [...]

Based on the apparent elasticity of the concept, the Court held that the preventative branch of criminal procedure under s. 91(27) gave Parliament jurisdiction over the detention of accused who have been found not criminally responsible ("NCR") [...]

¶ 74 In *Swain, supra*, Lamer C.J....held that the provisions dealing with the detention of persons who had been acquitted by reason of mental disorder were founded on the "preventative" branch of the criminal procedure power.

¶ 75 ... While Lamer C.J. held, at p. 1000, that "a conviction is not necessary before Parliament can legislate pursuant to this particular aspect of s. 91(27)", he qualified the scope of the preventative aspect such that it must relate in some way to criminal proceedings (p. 1001). Lamer C.J. concluded that the provisions only apply to those insane individuals who have committed acts (i.e. the *actus reus*) proscribed by the *Criminal Code* (at p. 1001) [...]

¶ 76 The conclusions reached regarding the scope of the criminal procedure power in *Swain* and *Winko* do not apply to accused who are unfit by reason of a mental disorder; they only apply to NCR accused. Unlike NCR accused, the Crown has not proved beyond a reasonable doubt that an accused found unfit to stand trial has committed an offence. Rather, an accused found unfit to stand trial only stands charged with a criminal offence; in order to maintain its hold over the accused under Part XX.1, the Crown need only demonstrate a *prima facie* case. [...]

¶ 77 Because the conclusions in *Swain* and *Winko* only apply to NCR accused, we must consider the reach of s. 91(27) in respect of temporarily and permanently unfit accused with fresh eyes. In my view, the criminal procedure power applies to temporarily but not permanently unfit accused. I will discuss the reasons for my conclusion below. [...]

¶ 87 Lamer C.J. in *Swain, supra,* held that the preventative aspect of the criminal procedure power must relate in some way to criminal proceedings. Following intervention by the police, an accused typically has his or her initial brush with criminal proceedings when he or she is charged with an offence, and is thereafter firmly within the grasp of the federal criminal procedure power. At any time once proceedings against an accused have been commenced, but prior to a verdict, the court may of its own motion, or on an application by the accused or the prosecution, direct that the fitness of the accused be tried (s. 672.23(1)). Where the verdict is that the accused is unfit to stand trial, proceedings are suspended pending the accused's return to fitness.

¶ 88 Like my colleagues, I conclude that the pith and substance of Part XX.1 in relation to accused found unfit to stand trial is the treatment and supervision of these accused as well as the protection of the public while they remain unfit and subject to an outstanding criminal charge . Part XX.1 is predicated on an accused found unfit to stand trial becoming fit for trial. [...]

¶ 89 Insofar as the aim of Part XX.1 is concerned with the treatment and supervision of a temporarily unfit accused and the protection of the public during the accused's limited period of unfitness, its ultimate aim is to try the accused once he or she becomes fit. In my opinion, this falls squarely within the ambit of the criminal procedure power because it "relate[s] in some way to criminal proceedings" -- i.e., the trial: *Swain, supra,* at p. 1001. The continued subjection of an unfit accused to Part XX.1 is justified under the goal of trying him or her for the offence charged. However, where the accused is <u>permanently</u> unfit to stand trial, the overriding goal of Part XX.1 is absent and Parliament loses jurisdiction.

¶ 90 As I discussed above, the scope of the criminal procedure power under s. 91(27) needs to be re-evaluated in light of the evolution in our constitutional culture since the entrenchment of the *Charter*. In choosing one of several possible interpretations of the criminal procedure power that implicate human rights, the interpretation that best accords with the imperatives of human rights and freedoms should be adopted. Under the existing scheme, an accused who is permanently unfit will forever be within the grip of the state's machinery for criminal justice. He or she will always have the weight of a criminal accusation hanging overhead, but the day of judgment is permanently postponed. Meanwhile, without the final adjudication of his or her culpability, a permanently unfit accused is subject to the ongoing control of the state through <u>criminal</u> proceedings set out in Part XX.1. His or her continued detention or conditional liberty cannot be justified by progress towards a trial.

¶ 91 In my opinion, a person cannot be subject to state control and have limits imposed on his or her liberty based on the criminal procedure power absent progress towards the adjudication of his or her legal culpability. This is a fundamental human right. The principle is affirmed in ss. 7 and 11(b) of the *Charter*. In construing the scope of the criminal procedure power, an interpretation at odds with this principle should be eschewed. The continued control over a permanently unfit accused and the resulting protection of the public based on a *prima facie* case do not "relate in some way to criminal proceedings". The continued supervision, detention or conditional liberty of a permanently unfit accused can only relate to the mental health of the individual, and this is considered to be within the provincial jurisdiction under ss. 92(7), 92(13) and 92(16) of the *Constitution Act, 1867*: see *Schneider v. The Queen*, [1982] 2 S.C.R. 112, at pp. 135-36.

¶ 92 Further, this approach has the salutary effect of respecting and enhancing the permanently unfit accused's human dignity: rather than being stigmatized by criminal proceedings, his or her needs and those of society can be addressed through mental health legislation. Persons with a mental disorder are a historically disadvantaged group and have been, and continue to be, subjected to social prejudice. We should adopt an interpretation of s. 91(27) that does not perpetuate that disadvantage and prejudice. The potential danger a permanently unfit accused may present is more properly attributable to his or her mental illness and is a matter of health and not criminal procedure. The need to protect the community from permanently unfit accused who pose a significant threat to public safety can be answered through the exercise of the provincial health power.

¶ 93 Consequently, I find that Parliament is not competent under its criminal procedure jurisdiction to legislate for the supervision, treatment, detention or control of permanently unfit accused. Once a court has found that an accused is permanently unfit to stand trial, the criminal procedure jurisdiction is exhausted. Administrative supervision or control is then a matter falling within the jurisdiction of the provincial health power. The present scheme does not provide for a finding of permanent or temporary fitness; it will have to be amended accordingly. On the facts of this case, it is clear that Mr. Demers will never become fit for trial. [...]

¶ 108 Consequently, I would allow the appeal, order that the impugned provisions be declared invalid under s. 52 of the *Constitution Act, 1982* insofar as they violate the division of powers and the *Charter*, and suspend the declaration for one year. I would also order that Mr. Demers be granted a stay within 30 days under s. 24(1) of the *Charter* for the violation of his s. 7 rights. All other permanently unfit accused who do not pose a significant threat to public safety should be given a stay within 30 days.

(c)   Provincial Jurisdiction

(i)   Regulatory Offences

N.S. BD. OF CENSORS v. MCNEIL
[1978] 2 S.C.R. 662.

[The facts of this case are reported at p. 399]

THE CHIEF JUSTICE [Judson, Spence and Dickson JJ., concurring] (*dissenting*): — What is involved, as I have already noted, is an unqualified power in the Nova Scotia Board to determine the fitness of films for public viewing on considerations that may extend beyond the moral and may include the political, the social and the religious. Giving its assertion of power the narrowest compass, related to the film in the present case, the Board is asserting authority to protect public morals, to safeguard the public from exposure to films, to ideas and images in films, that it regards as morally offensive, as indecent, probably as obscene.

The determination of what is decent or indecent or obscene in conduct or in a publication, what is morally fit for public viewing, whether in films, in art or in a live performance is, as such, within the exclusive power of the Parliament of Canada under its enumerated authority to legislate in relation to the criminal law. This has been recognized in a line of cases in which, beginning with the seminal case of *Attorney-General of Ontario v. Hamilton Street Rwy.*, (where it was said that it is the criminal law in the widest sense that falls within exclusive federal authority), the criminal law power has been held to be as much a brake on provincial legislation as a source of federal legislation. For example, in *Switzman v. Elbling*, the Supreme Court invalidated a provincial statute which not only made it illegal for the possessor or occupier of a house to use or permit it to be used to propagate communism or bolshevism (which were not defined), but also made it unlawful to print, publish or distribute any newspaper or writing propagating or tending to propagate communism or bolshevism. Fauteux J., as he then was, said this, in a passage of his reasons, at p. 320, which can equally be applied here:

> [...] In this specific instance, the subject-matter of the main provision – the prohibition of Communistic propaganda – is certainly one not coming, by itself, within the class of subjects enumerated in s. 92 as being within the competence of the Legislature. Parliament alone, legislating in criminal matters, is competent to enact, define, prohibit and punish these matters of a writing or of a speech that, on account of their nature, injuriously affect the social order or the safety of the state. Such are, for example, defamatory, obscene, blasphemous or seditious libels. In such cases, the rights being encroached upon are not those of an individual entitling him to a monetary compensation. The rights encroached upon are those of society itself, involving punishment. [...]

Similarly apt here is *Harrell v. Montreal*, where a by-law which forbade the display of pictures of nudes or semi-nudes on news stands without the prior approval of the Chief of Police was held invalid, especially in the light of the obscenity provisions of the *Criminal Code*.

It is beside the point to urge that morality is not co-extensive with the criminal law. Such a contention cannot of itself bring legislation respecting public morals within provincial competence. Moreover, the federal power in relation to the criminal law extends beyond control of morality, and is wide enough to embrace anti-social conduct or behaviour and has, indeed, been exercised in those respects.

This is not a case where civil consequences are attached to conduct defined and punished as criminal under federal legislation, as in *McDonald v. Down*, but rather a case where a provincially authorized tribunal itself defines and determines legality, what is permissible and what is not. This, in my view, is a direct intrusion into the field of criminal law. At best, what the challenged Nova Scotia legislation is doing is seeking to supplement the criminal law enacted by Parliament, and this is forbidden: see *Johnson v. Attorney-General of Alberta*, per Rand J. at p. 138 (see also *St. Leonard v. Fournier* at p. 320 (cites omitted)).

It was contended, however, by the appellant and by supporting intervenants that the Nova Scotia Board was merely exercising a preventive power, no penalty or punishment being involved, no offence having been created. It is true, of course, that no penalty or punishment is involved in the making of an order prohibiting the exhibition of a film, but it is ingenuous to say that no offence is created when a licensee who disobeyed the order would be at risk of a cancellation of his licence and at risk of a penalty and any one else who proposed to exhibit the film publicly would likewise be liable to a penalty. Indeed, the contention invites this Court to allow form to mask substance and amounts to an assertion that the provincial legislature may use the injunction or prohibitory order as a means of controlling conduct or performances or exhibitions, doing by prior restraint what it could not do by defining an offence and prescribing *post facto* punishment. [...] The short answer, in any event, to the provincial contention is that given by the Privy Council in *Attorney-General of Ontario v. Canada Temperance Federation*, at p. 207 where Viscount Simon noted that "to legislate for prevention appears to be on the same basis as legislation for cure", a proposition that was applied by this Court in *Goodyear Tire & Rubber Co. of Canada Ltd. v. The Queen*, at p. 309.

It does not follow from all of the foregoing that provincial legislative authority may not extend to objects where moral considerations are involved, but those objects must in themselves be anchored in the provincial catalogue of powers and must, moreover, not be in conflict with valid federal legislation. It is impossible in the present case to find any such anchorage in the provisions of the Nova Scotia Statute that are challenged, and this apart from the issue of conflict which, I think, arises in relation to ss. 159 and 163 of the *Criminal Code*. What is asserted, by way of tying the challenged provisions to valid provincial regulatory control, is that the Province is competent to licence the use of premises, and entry into occupations, and may in that connection determine what shall be exhibited in those premises. This hardly touches the important issue raised by the present case and would, if correct, equally justify control by the Province of any conduct and activity in licensed premises even if not related to the property aspect of licensing, and this is patently indefensible. Moreover, what is missing from this assertion by the appellant is a failure to recognize that the censorship of films takes place without relation to any premises and is a direct prior control of public taste. *Bédard v. Dawson*, which was heavily relied on by the appellant, does not assist the provincial contention because there, in the view of this Court at the time, the challenged provincial legislation related to the occupation and enjoyment of premises, and it was distinguished on that account from the wider legislation that was invalidated by this Court in *Switzman v. Elbling*, supra. [...]

Much more relevant here than the principle sought to be applied on the basis of *Bédard v. Dawson*, supra, is that which is reflected in *Henry Birks and Sons (Montreal) Ltd. v. Montreal*. In invalidating provincial prohibitory legislation directed to compulsory observance of certain religious or feast days this Court made it clear that a tenuous connection with property (the operation of shops and businesses) will not save provincial legislation which is paramountly directed to religious or moral observance. Even the tenuous connection with property in the *Birks* case is absent here. Similarly relevant is *R. v. Hayduck* where provincial legislation making it an offence for a man to register at a hotel with a woman falsely held out to be his wife was struck down, nothing in the legislation touching the hotel operator. [...]

For all the foregoing reasons I would dismiss this appeal and answer the constitutional question in the negative. [...]

RITCHIE J. [Martland, Pigeon, Beetz and de Grandpré JJ. concurring]: — [...] Simply put, the issue raised by the majority opinion in the Appeal Division is whether the Province is clothed with authority under s. 92 of the *British North America Act* to regulate the exhibition and distribution of films within its own boundaries which are considered unsuitable for local viewing by a local Board on grounds of morality or whether this is a matter of criminal law reserved to Parliament under s. 91(27).

In the present context, the question of whether or not the impugned legislation encroaches on the criminal law authority is, in my opinion, best approached in light of the statement made by Kerwin, C.J., in the course of his reasons for judgment in the *Lord's Day Alliance*, at p. 503, where he said:

> In constitutional matters there is no general area of criminal law and in every case the pith and substance of the legislation in question must be looked at.

Under the authority assigned to it by s. 91(27), the Parliament of Canada has enacted the *Criminal Code*, a penal statute the end purpose of which is the definition and punishment of crime when it has been proved to have been committed.

On the other hand, the *Theatres and Amusements Act* is not concerned with creating a criminal offence or providing for its punishment, but rather in so regulating a business within the Province as to prevent the exhibition in its theatres of performances which do not comply with the standards of propriety established by the Board.

The areas of operation of the two statutes are therefore fundamentally different on dual grounds. In the first place, one is directed to regulating a trade or business where the other is concerned with the definition and punishment of crime; and in the second place, one is preventive while the other is penal.

As the decision of the Appellate Division depends upon equating morality with criminality, I think it desirable at this stage to refer to the definitive statement made by Lord Atkin in this regard in the course of his reasons for judgment in *Proprietary Articles Trade Association v. Attorney-General of Canada,* where he said, at p. 324:

> Morality and criminality are far from coextensive; nor is the sphere of criminality necessarily part of a more extensive field covered by morality – unless the moral code necessarily disapproves all acts prohibited by the State, in which case the argument moves in a circle. It appears to the Justices to be of little value to seek to confine crimes to a category of acts which by their very nature belong to the domain of 'criminal jurisprudence'; [...]

I share the opinion expressed in this passage that morality and criminality are far from coextensive and it follows in my view that legislation which authorizes the establishment and enforcement of a local standard of morality in the exhibition of films is not necessarily "an invasion of the federal criminal field" as Chief Justice MacKeigan thought it to be in this case.

Even if I accepted the view that the impugned legislation is concerned with criminal morality, it would still have to be noted that it is preventive rather than penal and the authority of the Province to pass legislation directed towards prevention of crime is illustrated by the case of *Bédard v. Dawson,* which was concerned with the validity of a statute of the Province of Quebec entitled "An Act respecting the owners of houses used as disorderly houses", by which the judge was authorized to order the closing of a disorderly house. The legislation was held to be *intra vires* on the ground that it was concerned with property within the Province and Mr. Justice Anglin said, at p. 685:

> [...] I am of the opinion that this statute in no wise impinges on the domain of criminal law but is concerned exclusively with the control and enjoyment of property and the safeguarding of the community from the consequences of an illegal and injurious use being made of it – a pure matter of civil right. In my opinion in enacting the statute now under consideration the legislature exercised the power which it undoubtedly possesses to provide for the suppression of a nuisance and the prevention of its recurrence by civil process.

The law of nuisance was undoubtedly a factor in the reasoning of some of the judges in this Court and in the Court of King's Bench of Quebec, but in my view the matter was not too broadly stated by Duff, J., as he then was, at p. 684, where he said:

The legislation impugned seems to be aimed at suppressing conditions calculated to favour the development of crime rather than at the punishment of crime. This is an aspect of the subject in respect of which the provinces seem to be free to legislate. I think the legislation is not invalid.

As I have already said, however, I take the view that the impugned legislation is not concerned with criminality. The rejection of films by the Board is based on a failure to conform to the standards of propriety which it has itself adopted and this failure cannot be said to be "an act prohibited with penal consequences" by the Parliament of Canada either in enacting the *Criminal Code* or otherwise. This is not to say that Parliament is in any way restricted in its authority to pass laws penalizing immoral acts or conduct, but simply that the provincial government in regulating a local trade may set its own standards which in no sense exclude the operation of the federal law.

There is, in my view, no constitutional barrier preventing the Board from rejecting a film for exhibition in Nova Scotia on the sole ground that it fails to conform to standards of morality which the Board itself has fixed notwithstanding the fact that the film is not offensive to any provision of the *Criminal Code*; and, equally, there is no constitutional reason why a prosecution cannot be brought under s. 163 of the *Criminal Code* in respect of the exhibition of a film which the Board of Censors has approved as conforming to its standards of propriety. [...]

It will be seen that in my view the impugned legislation "has for its true object, purpose, nature and character" the regulation and control of a local trade and that it is therefore valid provincial legislation.

RIO HOTEL LTD. v. LIQUOR LICENSING BD.
[1987] 2 S.C.R. 59.

[*New Brunswick's Liquor Control Act* required that liquor licence holders also hold an entertainment licence to which the Board could attach conditions with respect to live entertainment and contests held on the licensed premises. The conditions attaching to appellant's entertainment licence specified the degree of nudity acceptable and rules for staging events presupposing the removal of clothing. The *Criminal Code*, however, includes provisions dealing with nudity (s. 170), indecent acts (s. 169), immoral, indecent or obscene performances in a theatre (s. 163), indecent shows in public (s. 159(2)(*b*)), and causing a disturbance in or near a public place (s. 171).

At issue was whether or not the entertainment licence conditions imposed by the Board were an infringement upon the federal criminal power or whether these conditions could be appended to or enacted in support of a valid provincial legislative scheme.]

DICKSON C.J.C. [McIntyre, Wilson and LeDain JJ. concurring]: — The issue in this appeal is whether a province has legislative authority to prevent "nude entertainment" as one aspect of a legislative scheme regulating the sale of liquor in the province. [...]

It has long been settled that under s. 92(13) and (16) of the *Constitution Act, 1867*, the provinces are vested with legislative authority to regulate the conditions for the sale and consumption of alcohol within the province. [...] It is also well settled that in regulating the distribution of alcohol, a province may attach conditions to any licence with a view to providing for the "good government" of liquor traffic [ ]

It seems clear therefore that s. 63.01(5) of the *Liquor Control Act*, R.S.N.B. 1973, c. L-10, as am., which permits the provincial Liquor Licensing Board to attach conditions to a liquor licence prohibiting "specified kinds of live entertainment" in licensed premises, is *prima facie* within the legislative competence of the New Brunswick Legislature. [...]

The dispute therefore resolves itself into the following question: Can a provincial prohibition of nude entertainment attached to a liquor licensing scheme operate notwithstanding the more general but related prohibitions contained in the Code? [...]

I conclude that the provincial legislation which authorizes the impugned licence condition is *intra vires* the Legislature of New Brunswick. The legislation is, as I have stated, *prima facie* related to property and civil rights within the Province and to matters of a purely local nature. The Legislature seeks only to regulate the forms of entertainment that may be used as marketing tools by the owners of licensed premises to boost sales of alcohol. Although there is some overlap between the licence condition precluding nude entertainment and various provisions of the *Code*, there is no direct conflict. It is perfectly possible to comply with both the provincial and the federal legislation. Moreover, the sanction for breach of the provincially-imposed licence conditions is suspension or cancellation of the liquor licence. No penal consequences ensue for the nude entertainer or for the holder of the licence. Under the relevant *Code* provisions, the primary object is obviously to punish entertainers and proprietors who breach the prohibitions on public nudity. I cannot say that the federal characteristics of this subject matter are palpably more important than the provincial characteristics. The provincial regulatory scheme relating to the sale of liquor in the Province can, without difficulty, operate concurrently with the federal *Criminal Code* provisions.

I should point out that the instant case is distinguishable from the situation discussed in *Westendorp v. The Queen*, [1983] 1 S.C.R. 43. In that case, the City of Calgary enacted a by-law purportedly in relation to the use of city streets. In fact, one section of the by-law was a blatant and colourable attempt to punish prostitution. That section was held by this Court to be an "intruded provision" that bore no relation, either in subject-matter or in the scale of penalties, to the remainder of the by-law. In other words, the prostitution provision could not be said to relate to any head of provincial jurisdiction; it was not truly part of a regulatory scheme authorized under s. 92(13) or (16) of the *Constitution Act, 1867*. The licence conditions in the instant case are only part of a comprehensive scheme regulating the sale of liquor in New Brunswick. There is no colourable intrusion upon a federal head of jurisdiction. [...]

ESTEY J. [Lamer J. concurring]: — It need hardly be observed that a province could provide in its liquor control legislation a condition that a conviction of the licensee under the *Code* would be grounds for cancellation of the licence. It does not follow, however, that it is open to the province to reenact the criminal provision and accomplish the same result by effectively "convicting" the licensee of a criminal offence already existing in federal law, under its own process and in its own forum.

As already noted there have been several cases where the provincial regulation of conduct within licensed premises has been held valid. In *Hodge v. The Queen,* supra, the Privy Council held that a regulation of the provincial Liquor Licence Commissioners, which prohibited the use of a billiard table during any time when the sale of liquor was prohibited by the *Liquor Licence Act,* was *intra vires* the province under s. 92(16). the Justices held at p. 131 that "the powers intended to be conferred by the Act in question, when properly understood, are to make regulations in the nature of police or municipal regulations of a merely local character for the good government of taverns [...] and such as are calculated to preserve, in the municipality, peace and public decency, and repress drunkenness and disorderly and riotous conduct". [...]

The segregation of the federal and the provincial powers [...] relates to two different situations. The first situation concerns the regulation of licensed premises, and the provincial enactment in question goes to the imposition of conditions to be maintained by the licensee in order to maintain his licence. The second situation occurs where a province purports to append penalties to a valid provincial undertaking such as the regulation of streets in a municipality. In the former case, it is much easier to determine provincial validity because the reference to conduct is only in relation to the operation of an activity which properly falls within provincial competence. Thus the licensing program is part of a general provincial regulatory program. Consequently, the provincial legitimacy is found in s. 92(13) and/or (16). In the second category the problem is rendered more difficult by the fact that the provincial regulation reaches outside premises owned or controlled by a provincial licensee. In that circumstance, the province again must find a valid provincial regulatory program and must confine the offences created in support of that program to those which are reasonably necessary for that purpose.

The longer the penalty and the closer the terminology comes to describing conduct traditionally criminal, the more doubtful the validity of the provincial enactment. The exclusive right in Parliament to legislate with reference to criminal law and criminal procedure may not be eroded by provincial legislation disguised as that which is necessary to give effect to an otherwise valid provincial program. [...]

[I]n this appeal there is to be found a provincial legislative program relating to the licensing of premises for the sale of alcoholic beverages and for the employment of entertainment as an aid to the marketing of those services. [...]

The impugned legislation now before this Court does not touch upon the forbidden field of criminal law is a regulation enacted in relation to a valid provincial licensing scheme. [...]

I therefore would dismiss the appeal with costs.

[The concurring judgment of Beetz J. is omitted.]

A.G. CAN. v. MONTREAL
[1978] 2 S.C.R. 770

BEETZ J. [Martland, Judson, Ritchie, Pigeon and de Grandpré JJ. concurring]: — Appellant Claire Dupond has attacked the constitutional validity of the City of Montreal By-law 3926 and of Ordinance no. 1 passed by the Executive Committee of the City pursuant to s. 5 of that By-law. [...]

By-law 3926 reads as follows: [...]

> 1. – Anyone is entitled to the use and enjoyment of the streets, public places and public domain of the City of Montreal untroubled and in peace and public order.

> 2. – Assemblies, parades or other gatherings that endanger tranquility, safety, peace or public order are prohibited in public places and thoroughfares, parks or other areas of the City's public domain. [...]

> 3. – No person participating in or present at an assembly, parade or other gathering on the public domain of the City shall molest or jostle anyone, or act in any way so as to hamper the movement, progress or presence of other citizens also using the public domain of the City on that occasion. [...]

> 5. – When there are reasonable grounds to believe that the holding of assemblies, parades or gatherings will cause tumult, endanger safety, peace or public order [...] the Executive Committee may, by ordinance, [prohibit] [...] the holding of any or all assemblies, parades or gatherings.

> 7. – Whoever participates in an assembly, parade or gathering held in violation of this by-law [...] shall be liable to either imprisonment or a fine, [...]

The Ordinance passed by the Executive Committee of the City pursuant to s. 5 of the By-law reads as follows: [...]

> The holding of any assembly, parade or gathering anywhere and at any time on the public domain of the City is prohibited for a time-period of thirty (30) days to end the thirteenth (13th) day of December 1969 at midnight, [...]

In *Hodge v. The Queen*, the Judicial Committee of the Privy Council upheld the constitutional validity of the *Ontario Liquor License Act* of 1877 and of regulations enacted pursuant to that Act. At page 131, the Judicial Committee referred to those regulations as

> regulations in the nature of police or municipal regulations of a merely local character [...] and such as are calculated to preserve in the municipality, peace [...] and repress [...] disorderly and riotous conduct.

I could not find a better description to characterize s. 5 of the By-law and the Ordinance. They are on their face regulations of a merely local character. The Ordinance was passed for reasons peculiar to the City of Montreal at the relevant time. Both s. 5 and the Ordinance relate to the use of the municipal public domain in exceptional circumstances when there are reasonable grounds to believe that the holding of assemblies, parades or gatherings in the streets, parks and other parts of the public domain will endanger safety, peace or public order. These are not punitive but essentially preventive measures, the purpose and effect of which is the prevention of conditions conducive to breaches of the peace and detrimental to the administration of justice. This preventive character is illustrated by the fact that the Ordinance prohibits the holding on the public domain of and assembly, parade or gathering, including those of the most innocent and innocuous kind. The temporary nature of the Ordinance and of any ordinance which could be passed pursuant to s. 5 is also indicative of the preventive aspect of this legislative scheme.

In *Reference Re the Adoption Act*, Sir Lyman Duff wrote, at p. 403:

> [...] while as subject matter of legislation, the criminal law is entrusted to the Dominion Parliament, responsibility for the administration of justice and, broadly speaking, for the policing of the country, the execution of the criminal law, the suppression of crime and disorder, has from the beginning of Confederation been recognized as the responsibility of the provinces and has been discharged at great cost to the people; so also, the provinces, sometimes acting directly, sometimes through the municipalities, have assumed responsibility for controlling social conditions having a tendency to encourage vice and crime.

It is now well established that the suppression of conditions likely to favour the commission of crimes falls within provincial competence: *Bédard v. Dawson, Di Iorio v. Warden of the Montreal Jail*.

It would be an over-simplification to say that ordinances which may be passed under s. 5 are purely prohibitory: demonstrations can be restricted to certain areas of the municipal public domain, to certain times of the day or the night, to certain types of assemblies, parades or gatherings; that is why, in spite of the prohibitory form of the ordinances, s. 5 can be said to be, in substances, regulatory of the use of the public domain as the by-law held *intra vires* by McRuer C.J.H.C. in *R. v. Campbell*.

However, I would not hesitate to uphold the validity of ordinances contemplated by s. 5 even if they were strictly prohibitory:

> A provincial enactment does not become a matter of criminal law merely because it consists of a prohibition and makes it an offense for failure to observe the prohibition; [...]

(per Judson J. in *O'Grady v. Sparling*, at p. 810).

In my view, the impugned enactments relate to a matter of a merely local nature in the Province within the meaning of s. 92(16) of the Constitution. Bearing in mind that the other heads of power enumerated in s. 92 are illustrative of the general power of the Province to make laws in relation to all matters of a merely local or private nature in the Province, I am of the opinion that the impugned enactments also derive constitutional validity from heads (8), (13), (14) and (15) of s. 92.

[...] One line of argument was that the impugned enactments are anti-riot measures dealing with a field already covered by ss. 64 to 70 of the *Criminal Code* and that their essential purpose is to supplement what was thought to be a lacuna in the Code.

I do not agree that s. 5 and the Ordinance deal with the same subject matter as the Code, under the same aspect and for the same purpose. They differ in more than one way but the main difference is as follows: the *Criminal Code* forbids unlawful assemblies and riots and provides for the punishment of these offenses once they have been committed; it also compels a justice, mayor or sheriff to command, in Her Majesty's name, the dispersion of an unlawful assembly which has already begun to disturb the peace tumultuously; s. 5 and the Ordinance on the other hand are aimed at preventing assemblies, parades and gatherings which have not yet taken place. There are in the Code no preventive measures similar to s. 5 of the By-law. Counsel for the Attorney General for Canada readily conceded this; his point was that Parliament could enact a measure such as s. 5 of the By-law, and moreover, that only Parliament could do so.

It may be that Parliament could enact measures of a preventive nature under its ancillary powers. But we are not concerned in this case with the outer limits of federal jurisdiction over criminal law and I fail to see how the fact that Parliament has not exercised a possible incidental power should sterilize provincial legislative competence and prevent a province or a city from exercising their own powers. And, in the exercise of their own powers, the provinces may constitutionally complement federal legislation. The reports are replete with cases where provincial legislation complementary to federal legislation was upheld as long as it did not collide with the latter: *Provincial Secretary of Prince Edward Island v. Egan; Validity of Section 92(4) of the Vehicles Act, 1957 (Sask.); Smith v. The Queen; O'Grady v. Sparling, (supra); Stephens v. The Queen; Lieberman v. The Queen; Fawcett v. Attorney General for Ontario; Mann v. The Queen.* [...]

I cannot see anything in the Ordinance which interferes with freedom of religion, of the press or of speech, or which imposes religious observances, in such a way as to bring the matter within the criminal law power of Parliament. The Ordinance prohibits the holding of *all* assemblies, parades or gatherings for a time period of thirty days, irrespective of religion, ideology or political views. It does so for the reasons given in the reports of the Director of the Police Department and of the Chief Attorney of the City; the reasons have nothing to do with those for which provincial enactments were invalidated in the *Saumur, Birks* and *Switzman* cases.

Furthermore, the discretionary power to pass an Ordinance under s. 5 of the By-law is not an uncontrollable discretion given to a municipal officer, as was the case in *Saumur*: it is vested in the Executive Committee of the City; it cannot be exercised except on report of the Directors of the Police Department and of the Law Department of the City; this report must give reasons why an ordinance should be passed; these reasons must be up to the standard contemplated in the preamble of the By-law and in s. 5, that is, an exceptional emergency situation must have arisen which warrants the enactment of preventive measures; finally, the prohibition must be limited in time to the period determined by the Executive Committee; it must be temporary for by their very nature exceptional emergency measures cannot be permanent. [...]

LASKIN C.J.C. [Spence and Dickson JJ. concurring] (*dissenting*):— The terms of the impugned By-law and of the Ordinance, passed pursuant to s. 5 thereof, are set out in the reasons of my brother Beetz which I have had the advantage of reading, and I shall not repeat them. It is obvious from the recitals as well as from the terms of the key s. 5 that the City of Montreal has enacted a mini-Criminal Code, dealing with apprehended breach of the peace, apprehended violence and the maintenance of public order, and we are urged to sustain this incursion into the field of criminal law – a matter exclusively for the Parliament of Canada – because it is a matter of a local or private nature in the Province.

The only local or private aspect is, in my opinion, the territorial ambit of the By-law and of the Ordinance, and this has never been a test of constitutional validity. My brother Beetz has referred to the challenged provisions as regulatory of the public domain, the reference being to public streets and parks. It is not, however, directed to that end as the recitals and central terms clearly indicate. What it does, plainly and without reference to any regulatory consideration, is to make it a punishable offence – a crime – to breach s. 5 of the By-law and the Ordinance. Sections 1 and 3 of the By-law do have a relationship to traffic regulation and may be justified in themselves on that basis as provisions which may competently be authorized by provincial legislation. They are, however, integrated in other provisions which are in no sense directed to traffic considerations or to any regulatory use of public parks and, indeed, as my brother Beetz has noted, the focus is on s. 5 of the By-law and on the Ordinance passed in implementation thereof. That provision is so explicitly directed to breach of the peace and to the maintenance of public order as to fall squarely within exclusive federal authority in relation to the criminal law.

The very title of the By-law, as one "relating to exceptional measures to safeguard the free exercise of civil liberties, to regulate the use of the public domain and to prevent riots and other violations of order, peace and public safety" shows its character. The references to safeguarding the free exercise of civil liberties and to regulation of the use of the public domain are hollow references, not in any way fulfilled by the substantive terms of the By-law as are the references to riots, breach of the peace and public order. Moreover, the enactment of the By-law as an exceptional measure is itself an indicator of how far removed it is from any concern, except a consequential one, with regulation of the use of streets and public parks. The enactment of the By-law smacks of an assertion of municipal authority to legislate for the "peace, order and good government" of the City of Montreal, an authority which I do not find in the catalogue of provincial powers under the *British North America Act*. [...]

No doubt a prohibition, as a matter of its impact, is regulatory but, for constitutional purposes, provincial prohibitions to be valid have to be associated with a valid scheme of regulation as enforcements or reinforcements thereof, and are not sustainable as peremptory directions against forbidden conduct or behaviour. [...] There is no substratum of regulation upon which a sanction has been mounted.

Two other points are made by the proponents of the By-law. One is that it was called forth by exceptional conditions in Montreal, an assertion which in itself makes the By-law suspect. There is no accretion to provincial legislative authority to enable it to deal with apprehended riots or public disorder merely because the provincial government or delegated municipal authorities are of the opinion that preventive measures must be taken. They may be taken under ordinary police powers and in accordance with the federal *Criminal Code*, to which I will refer later in these reasons. The second point is that there is no constitutional bar to provincial (or validly authorized municipal) legislation which complements the federal *Criminal Code*. This is a proposition which flies in the face of the scheme of distribution of legislative power; it is destructive of the principle of exclusiveness as expressed in *Union Colliery Co. v. Bryden*, at p. 588; and it is not supported by any authorities. Cases such as *O'Grady v. Sparling* and *Mann v. The Queen*, to take two of those relied upon by the proponents of the By-law, turn on a conclusion that the enactments challenged therein were independently valid as being in relation to a matter within provincial competence. Judson J., speaking for the majority in *O'Grady v. Sparling*, at p. 810, said that "The power of a provincial legislature to enact legislation for the regulation of highway traffic is undoubted [...] [and] the legislation under attack here is part and parcel of this regulation". It cannot be said of the challenged s. 5 of the By-law in this case that it has any such anchorage.

Whether the apt term be "complementary" or "supplementary", it has hitherto been a mark of our constitutional jurisprudence that a Province cannot legislate to reinforce the federal criminal law: *Johnson v. Attorney General of Alberta*. The fact that it might seek to foreclose a breach of the criminal law by preventive measures did not relieve against this provincial disability: see *Attorney General for Ontario v. Koynok*. There may, of course, be differences as to the appropriateness of the application of this principle in particular cases but the principle itself has not, as I read the case law, been heretofore doubted. [...]

There is a distasteful part of the challenged By-law and Ordinance which, surprisingly, appears to be relied on to support their validity. The prohibition of assemblies or gatherings is not limited to those from which disorder or violence is anticipated but extends to all assemblies, all gatherings for the prescribed thirty-day period. I am unable to appreciate how this gives credence to the By-law as a local measure. We are left in no doubt here as to the scope of operation of the By-law. In *Saumur v. City of Québec*, Kellock J. noted that the challenged by-law there was "not to be judged from the standpoint of matters to which it might be limited but upon the completely general terms in which it in fact is couched" (at p. 339). Here, persons who might seek to associate or gather for innocent purposes are to be barred, not because of any problem as to whether certain public areas should be open at certain times or on certain days or occasions – all of which go to their ordinary regulation – but because of a desire to forestall the violent or the likely violent. This is the invocation of a doctrine which should alarm free citizens even if it were invoked and applied under the authority of the Parliament of Canada, which has very wide power to enact criminal law. To find it invoked by a delegated authority like a municipality, which is limited at the outside to those powers that are open to a Province, appears to me to be an aggravation of its intrusion into the field of criminal law.

Certainly, enforcement of the criminal law is often difficult, and where large numbers of persons may be involved the difficulties are compounded. Yet it has always been central to our criminal law that the police are expected to enforce it against violators and not against innocents, and to exercise a reasonable and honest judgment as to those who are in each of these classifications. What can be more draconian than for a municipality to ignore the distinction and then to insist that it is not legislating in relation to crime or criminal law when its prime purpose is to forestall anticipated breaches of the peace and to deal with unlawful assemblies and riots! [...]

I would allow the appeal, set aside the judgment below and restore the order at trial declaring the By-law and the Ordinance *ultra vires*. It is clear that if s. 5 goes, ss. 6 and 7 of the By-law must also fall, and so too must s. 4. This effectively denudes the By-law of any substance. [...]

ALLAN SINGER LTD. v. A.G. QUE.
[1988] 2 S.C.R. 790.

[Appellant challenged certain sections of the *Charter of the French language*, R.S.Q., c. C-11 [Bill 101] which prohibited the erection of signs in languages other than French. Appellant argued, *inter alia*, that s. 58 of the impugned statute was a prohibition with penal consequences with an insufficient nexus to a legitimate provincial regulatory scheme. One contention of the appellant was that the legislation was *ultra vires* as legislation in relation to criminal law. Section 58 reads:

58. Public signs and posters and commercial advertising shall be solely in the official language.

Notwithstanding the foregoing, in the cases and under the conditions or circumstances prescribed by regulation of the Office de la langue française, public signs and posters and commercial advertising may be both in French and in another language or solely in another language.]

THE COURT: — [...] It appears to have been accepted by all the members of the Court of Appeal, whether expressly or impliedly, that provincial legislative jurisdiction with respect to language is not an independent one but is rather "ancillary" to the exercise of jurisdiction with respect to some class of subject matter assigned to the province by s. 92 of the *Constitution Act, 1867*. That conclusion was based primarily on what was said by this Court in *Jones v. Attorney General of New Brunswick*, [1975] 2 S.C.R. 182, and on the opinion of Professor Hogg in *Constitutional Law of Canada* (2nd ed. 1985), at pp. 804-6, which in turn is based on what was said in *Jones*. [...] [T]his Court agrees with that conclusion. [...]

We adopt the following passages of the opinion of Professor Hogg as a statement of the law on this question, *i.e.* that:

> [...] language is not an independent matter of legislation (or constitutional value); that there is therefore no single plenary power to enact laws in relation to language; and that the power to enact a law affecting language is divided between the two levels of government by reference to criteria other than the impact of law upon language. On this basis, a law prescribing that a particular language or languages must or may be used in certain situations will be classified for constitutional purposes not as a law in relation to language, but as a law in relation to the institutions or activities that the provision covers. [...]

> [...] for constitutional purposes language is ancillary to the purpose for which it is used, and a language law is for constitutional purposes a law in relation to the institutions or activities to which the law applies.

In order to be valid, provincial legislation with respect to language must be truly in relation to an institution or activity that is otherwise within provincial legislative jurisdiction.

[...]

The majority in the Court of Appeal held that the challenged provisions were in relation to commerce within the province. The minority opinion, as expressed by Paré J.A., with whom Montgomery J.A. concurred in separate dissenting reasons, was that while the provisions requiring the "joint use" of French, to use the terms of the constitutional questions, could be said to be in relation to commerce within the province, those requiring the "exclusive use" of French could not. Paré J. based this distinction on the premise that in order to be in relation to commerce within the province a language provision must be calculated to favour such commerce or at least be of some remedial nature in relation to it. He reasoned that while the requirement of the "joint use" of French obviously conferred certain benefits on the francophone population in commercial dealings which would enure to the over-all benefit of commerce within the province, the requirement of the exclusive use of French while perhaps conferring some advantage on francophones could not conceivably have any over-all beneficial effect on commerce within the province. He concluded that the purpose of the requirement of the "exclusive use" of French was the purely ideological one, unrelated to commerce within the province, of enhancing the status of French.

On this issue we are in agreement with the majority in the Court of Appeal. It is true, as the preamble of the *Charter of the French Language* indicates, that one of its objects is "to make of French the language of [...] commerce and business" but that object necessarily involves the regulation of an aspect of commerce and business within the province, whatever the nature of the effect of such regulation may be. The purpose and effect of the challenged provisions of Chapter VII of the *Charter of the French Language* entitled "The Language of Commerce and Business" is to regulate an aspect of the manner in which commerce and business in the province may be carried on and as such they are in relation to such commerce and business. That the over-all object of the *Charter of the French Language* is the enhancement of the status of the French language in Quebec does not make the challenged provisions any less an intended regulation of an aspect of commerce within the province. As such, they fall within provincial legislative jurisdiction under the *Constitution Act, 1867*. [...]

The appellant made elaborate submissions in support of the contention that s. 58, as a prohibition with penal consequences of the use of any language other than French, was criminal law. The appellant referred to the many decisions of this Court, including its most recent judgment in *Rio Hotel Ltd. v. New Brunswick (Liquor Licensing Board)*, [1987] 2 S.C.R. 59, which have considered the criteria for distinguishing between criminal law and provincial penal provisions in the exercise of a valid provincial regulatory jurisdiction. The essential premise underlying the contention that s. 58 is criminal law is that it is not sufficiently related to a provincial regulatory scheme to meet the test reflected in the cases. This is, in effect, the premise that has been rejected in holding that s. 58 and the other challenged provisions of the *Charter of the French Language* and the *Regulation respecting the language of commerce and business* constitute the regulation of an aspect of commerce within the province – the linguistic basis on which certain commercial activity may be carried on. Section 58 cannot be viewed in isolation from the other provisions of the *Charter of the French Language* and the *Regulation respecting the language of commerce and business*. Together they constitute a regulatory scheme directed to certain aspects of commercial activity. The regulatory concern is avowedly the relationship between language status and such commercial activity but it is nevertheless a valid provincial regulatory purpose in relation to commerce within the province. This is not the prohibition of the use of language in and for itself as constituting conduct having affinity with some traditional criminal law concern such as morality or public order. We are therefore of the opinion that s. 58 of the *Charter of the French Language* is not *ultra vires* the provincial legislature as constituting criminal law.

WESTENDORP v. R.
[1983] I S.C.R. 43.

THE CHIEF JUSTICE [for the Court]: — This appeal which is here by leave of this Court, arises out of a charge against the appellant of being on a street for the purpose of prostitution in contravention of s. 6.1(2) of By-law 9022 of the City of Calgary, as enacted by amending By-law 25M81. The accused was acquitted at her trial on the ground, *inter alia*, that the impugned by-law was unconstitutional as invading federal authority in relation to the criminal law as well as federal legislation in that area. The acquittal was set aside by the Alberta Court of Appeal, speaking through Kerans J.A., who held that there was no invasion of the federal criminal law power. [...]

The facts are not in dispute. There is no question but that the accused and a female friend approached a plain clothes officer on a city street and solicited his interest to engage in intercourse or fellatio for stated payments. They moved with him to a car on a parking lot where another plain clothes officer was waiting and both women were then arrested. The charge followed, reading that the accused Westendorp was on the street for the purpose of prostitution. [...]

THE CALGARY BY-LAW AND SECTION 6.1 THEREOF

[...] Section 6.1 was included as the last section in group of provisions under the heading "Use of Streets". [...] Section 6.1 as found in by-law 9022 reads:

> 6.1 (1) In this section [...]
>
> (b) "prostitution" means the sale or offering for sale of sexual services and includes the purchase or offering to purchase sexual services;
>
> (2) No person shall be or remain on a street for the purpose of prostitution.
>
> (3) No person shall approach another person on a street for the purposes of prostitution.
>
> (4) Any person contravening the provisions of this section is guilty of an offence and is liable on summary conviction: [to fine or imprisonment for default in payment. ...]

TERMS OF SECTION 6.1: ITS PITH AND SUBSTANCE

It is patent, from a comparison of s. 6.1 with sections 3, 4 and 5 of the by-law, that s. 6.1 is of a completely different order from its preceding sections and, certainly, from all those succeeding it. It is specious to regard s. 6.1 as relating to control of the streets. If that were its purpose, it would have dealt with congregation of persons on the streets or with obstruction, unrelated to what the congregating or obstructing persons say or otherwise do. As the by-law stands and reads, it is activated only by what is said by a person, referable to the offer of sexual services. For persons to converse together on a street, as did the two women and the police officer here, and to discuss a recent or upcoming sporting event or a concert or some similar event would not attract liability. It is triggered only by an offer of sexual services or a solicitation to that end. There is no violation of s. 6.1 by congregation or obstruction *per se*; the offence arises only by proposing or soliciting another for prostitution. To remain on a street for the purpose of prostitution or to approach another for that purpose is so patently an attempt to control or punish prostitution as to be beyond question. The matter goes beyond the provincial legislation held by this Court to be invalid in *Switzman v. Elbling*, [1957] S.C.R. 285 which prohibited any person to possess or occupy a house in the Province to propagate communism or bolshevism. It is clearly distinguishable from *Bédard v. Bédard*, [1923] S.C.R. 681, where the provincial legislation under attack there was justified as concerned with the control and enjoyment of property. There is no property question here, no question even of interference with the enjoyment of public property let alone private property.

CRIMINAL LAW: PROVINCIAL JURISDICTION

Nor can any comparison be made between this case and the judgment of this Court in *Dupond v. Montreal*, [1978] 2 S.C.R. 770, which related to a municipal antidemonstration by-law which was also emphasized as being of a temporary nature. That by-law related plainly to parades and assemblies on the streets, different from s. 6.1 of the present case.

The question remains, however, whether, recognizing the differences in principle between the present case and the three cases in this Court mentioned above, there is nonetheless constitutional scope for the valid enactment of the challenged by-law. This brings me to consider the reasons given by Kerans J.A. for upholding the by-law. He construed it as an attempt to deal with a public nuisance. This is not how the offence under the by-law is either defined or charged. The recitals in the by-law as enacted by By-law 25M81 cannot be used to justify substantive charging sections when those sections contain a different formulation and their own definition of an offence. It is these aspects that present the constitutional issue.

In examining the submission of counsel for the accused that the by-law was a colourable attempt to deal, not with a public nuisance but with the evil of prostitution, Kerans J.A. observed that the evil of prostitution is a matter of public morality and, if the pith and substance of this legislation were an attack on this evil, it might well be a matter beyond the competence of the Legislature of Alberta. He then went on to say that "the by-law does not strike at prostitution as such; it does not seek to suppress the market for sexual favours; it seeks only to protect the citizens who use the streets from the irritation and embarrassment of being unwilling participants in that market".

This assessment of "pith and substance" is to me baffling when regard is had to the terms of s. 6.1. It becomes doubly baffling when Kerans J.A. says this:

> I concede that the Calgary legislation makes it an offence for a prostitute simply to enter upon a street for the purpose of prostitution, i.e. without yet doing anything. But this is not an attack on prostitution as such. This is an attempt, by preventative measure, to regulate the activities of the prostitutes and their customers on the streets. It is, as it were, a pre-emptive strike. And as such is troubling. But it is insufficiently troubling to change the pith and substance of the legislation.

What appears to me to emerge from Kerans J.A.'s consideration of the by-law is to establish a concurrency of legislative power, going beyond any double aspect principle and leaving it open to a Province or to a municipality authorized by a Province to usurp exclusive federal legislative power. If a Province or municipality may translate a direct attack on prostitution into street control through reliance on public nuisance, it may do the same with respect to trafficking in drugs. And, may it not, on the same view, seek to punish assaults that take place on city streets as an aspect of street control!

However desirable it may be for the municipality to control or prohibit prostitution, there has been an over-reaching in the present case which offends the division of legislative powers. I would, accordingly, allow the appeal, set aside the judgment of the Alberta Court of Appeal and restore the acquittal directed by the Provincial Court Judge.

- Research Note -

PROVINCIAL REGULATORY "CRIMES"

The jurisprudence of the Privy Council and the Supreme Court of Canada invites intense scrutiny of provincial regulatory prohibitions that entail penal consequences, particularly where the prohibition is only loosely or tenuously connected to a provincial regulatory scheme. Provincial prohibitions cannot stand on their own, in the sense of criminalizing conduct, without some further regulatory objective. Provincial prohibitions must be anchored in the catalogue of provincial legislative powers and they must serve valid provincial regulatory purposes.

In *Schneider v. The Queen*, [1982] 2 S.C.R. 112 at pp. 142-143, Estey J., in a concurring judgment, wrote:

> Without the existence of the prerequisite provincial authority independent of the offence creating provisions, [provincial] legislation would be invalid as trenching upon the exclusive federal jurisdiction in criminal law.

In *Edwards Books v. The Queen*, [1986] 2 S.C.R. 713 at p. 741, the Court recognized that the task of defining the boundary between prohibitions in pursuit of provincial regulatory objectives and criminal law is "difficult". It is suggested that the true principle which delineates this boundary is as follows: Where provincial prohibitory legislation exhibits a sufficient nexus or connection to provincial regulatory powers, such legislation will not offend exclusive federal jurisdiction in relation to the criminal law. Where, however, the nexus between the prohibition and provincial regulatory power is tenuous, or absent, provincial prohibitions are *ultra vires* [see: *A.-G. Canada v. Dupond*, [1978] 2 S.C.R. 770 at p. 781 and *McNeil v. N.S. Bd. of Censors*, [1978] 2 S.C.R. 662 at p. 685].

There are several factors which indicate that a sufficient nexus exists in order to support provincial prohibitions in aid of regulatory objectives. They include:

(a)   Whether the prohibition enforces standards created as part of a *comprehensive* provincial regulatory scheme. The standards should be reasonably related to provincial regulatory purposes such as business ethics, rather than moral objectives in and of themselves, such as the elimination of pornography [see: *Rio Hotel v. Liquor Licencing Bd.*, [1987] 2 S.C.R. 59, per Dickson C.J.C. at p. 63; *McNeil v. N.S. Bd. of Censors*, supra, at pp. 691, 693; *Edwards Books v. The Queen*, supra, at p. 741].

(b)   Whether the provincial legislation, in pith and substance, relates to provincial legislative powers such as highway control, zoning or health, the prohibition being but a means of enforcement [see: *O'Grady v. Sparling*, [1960] S.C.R. 804; *Bédard v. Dawson*, [1923] S.C.R. 681].

(c)   Whether the prohibition is an enforcement mechanism in aid of a scheme that aims at regulatory control of property, such as zoning; as contrasted with prohibition of offensive conduct which may happen to occur on provincial property. Estey J. (Lamer J. concurring) in *Rio Hotel v. Liquor Licencing Bd.*, supra, at pp. 79-80, wrote:

> The second situation occurs where a province purports to append penalties to a valid provincial undertaking such as the regulation of streets in a municipality. [...] In the second category the problem is rendered more difficult by the fact that the provincial regulation reaches outside premises owned or controlled by a provincial licensee. In that circumstance, the province again must find a valid provincial regulatory program and must confine the offences created in support of that program to those which are *reasonably necessary* for that purpose. (emphasis added)

(d)   Whether the regulatory scheme is occasioned by some compelling, temporary local circumstance or emergency, which requires stern control at the local level, either in anticipation of crisis, or to deal effectively with the crisis. In these circumstances, a concurrent jurisdiction to prohibit *temporarily* will be recognized in the Province, where necessary to maintain order in the face of exigent circumstances [see: *A.G. Can. v. Montreal*, [1978] 2 S.C.R. 770].

Several factors indicate the absence of a sufficient nexus to provincial regulatory power to support a provincial prohibition. These include:

(a)   The prohibition is an end in itself, the purpose of which is to enforce compliance with the legislature's view of morality or sanctity [see: *Henry Birks v. Montreal*, [1955] S.C.R. 799 at pp. 810-811; *Lieberman v. The Queen*, [1963] S.C.R. 643 and *Westendorp v. The Queen*, [1983] 1 S.C.R. 43].

(b)   The prohibition is directed to standards of public order or safety through the criminalizing of activity perceived as a public wrong. The prohibition in object and purpose aims at the maintenance of public order, as contrasted with protecting the safety or rights of individuals from the consequences of harmful conduct (see: *Russel v. The Queen* (1881-1882), 7 A.C. 829 at p. 839; *In re McNutt* (1912), 47 S.C.R. 256 at pp. 266-267; *Switzman v. Elbling*, [1957] S.C.R. 285].

(c)   Finally, provincial prohibitions become suspect when they intrude into areas traditionally associated with federal criminal jurisdiction. In *Rio Hotel v. Liquor Licensing Bd.*, supra, at p. 80, Estey J. wrote:

> The longer the penalty and the closer the terminology comes to describing conduct traditionally criminal, the more doubtful the validity of the provincial enactment.

Provincial legislation that unduly interferes with fundamental freedoms of religion, speech, expression, assembly or association requires extraordinary justification in local circumstance in order to be upheld as a concurrent exercise of provincial regulatory power [see: *A.G. Can. v. Montreal*, supra; *Henry Birks v. Montreal*, supra; *Switzman v. Elbling*, supra].

(ii) Administration of Justice in the Province: s. 92(14)

DI IORIO V. MONTREAL JAIL WARDEN
[1978] 1 S.C.R. 152.

[Nicola Di Iorio and Gerard Fontaine were found guilty of contempt for refusing to testify at an inquiry before the Quebec Police Commission and were sentence to one year in jail. The appellants petitioned for writs of *habeas corpus* and challenged the validity of the Order-in-Council and s. 19 of the *Police Act*, which combined to create the police inquiry. They asserted that this was legislation in relation to criminal law, *ultra vires* the provincial legislatures.]

LASKIN C.J.C. [De Grandpré J. concurring] (dissenting): — [...] The issue, in short, is this. Since the Parliament of Canada has exclusive legislative authority in relation to the criminal law including procedure in criminal matters [...] is it open to a Province to authorize a provincially-established tribunal to conduct an inquiry, with supporting sanctions to compel appearance and testimony, into crime and into crime in all its ramifications, including the organizations and persons involved? [...]

The provincial case [...] is founded on the legislative power conferred on the provincial Legislatures by s. 92(14) of the *British North America Act, 1867*, [...]

92. [...]

14.   The Administration of Justice in the Province, including the Constitution, Maintenance, and Organization of Provincial Courts, both of Civil and of Criminal Jurisdiction, and including Procedure in Civil Matters in those Courts. [...]

"Administration of Justice in the Province" within s. 92(14) is not a head of power which has hitherto been closely examined in the case law. It has been regarded, and properly so, as supporting provincial appointment of judicial officers and Judges other than those covered by s. 96: see, for example, *R. v. Bush* (1888), 15 O.R. 398. It certainly envisages the provision of facilities through which Courts and like tribunals can carry out their functions, and also, I would say, the appointment of support staff and enforcement officials necessary to assist in the judicial process. In *Valin v. Langlois* (1879), 3 S.C.R. 1, the Supreme Court of Canada took s. 92(14) to relate to the organization of Courts of justice for the Province and Henry, J., expanded on this to say (at p. 67) that "administration of justice *in the Province*" means "the power of legislating for the administration of justice in the Province in regard to the subjects given by the [*British North America*] *Act* and, to that extent only, to provide for 'the Constitution, maintenance and organization of Provincial Courts,' including the procedure necessary for the administration of justice in reference to those and kindred subjects" [...] *Valin v. Langlois* [...] is [...] indicative of a view of s. 92(14) which, in my opinion, pays due regard to the scheme of distribution of legislative power and to the limitations on provincial competence that arise out of the catalogue of exclusive federal powers. [...]

It is unnecessary for a Province to rely on s. 92(14) if it would authorize an inquiry into an industry or an activity that is within provincial competence. The Province can rely for this on other heads of power in s. 92 which embrace the industry or the activity within their scope. It would, of course, rely on s. 92(14) if the inquiry was directed to the operation of provincial Courts or of other tribunals that determine rights and liabilities. What is involved here, however, is not of that order. [...]

If the inquiry or investigation were put on foot by the Province with a view to possible prosecution, is there any doubt but that it would amount to an invasion of the federal criminal law power? What we have here is an inquisitorial process, more draconian than what Parliament has prescribed in relation to the investigation, detection and prosecution of crime; and yet it is contended that by stopping at investigation and detection (under the inquiry) and avoiding entry or possible entry into prosecution, the Province may constitutionally take over this large area of the criminal law, save for the minimal restraint of s. 5 of the *Canada Evidence Act*. This, to me, is not only a colourable invasion but a direct invasion of exclusive federal competence. An administrative, *quasi*-judicial coercive investigation at large into crime has nothing to do with the "Administration of Justice in the Province". [...]

What is presented here under s. 19 of the *Police Act* is a provincial adoption of a new form of procedure for inquiring into crime, a procedure in a criminal matter, within s. 91(27), and although there is no direct attempt under s. 19 and under the implementing Order in Council to change the existing criminal law, a different method of examining its operation is prescribed from the method laid out in the *Criminal Code* and in allied federal legislation. As I have already noted, Parliament could authorize a wholesale inquiry of that kind in addition to the individualized enforcement that has been traditional with us. For the Province to do it, however, is for it to provide a type of supplementary administration which, in my opinion, is beyond its powers. I borrow and adapt the words of Rand, J., in *Johnson v. A.-G. Alta.* (1954), 108 C.C.C. 1 at p. 12, [1954] 2 D.L.R. 625 at p. 636, [1954] S.C.R. 127 at p. 138, where, speaking it is true in another context, he said that "any local legislation of a supplementary nature that would tend to weaken or confuse [the] enforcement [of the criminal law] would be an interference with the exclusive power of Parliament".

It is evident from the submissions of the Provinces that they would read s. 92(14) as if the words in it were "administration of criminal justice as well as of civil justice". I am satisfied on such authorities as there are, as well as on the scheme of the *British North America Act, 1867*, that administration of criminal justice, whatever be the form that it takes, is for Parliament alone to prescribe. [...]

For the reasons I have given, I would allow the appeal and declare that s. 19 of the *Police Act* is *ultra vires* the Legislature of Quebec. [...]

DICKSON J. [Martland, Judson, Ritchie and Spence JJ., concurring]: This appeal, in my opinion, must be dismissed, essentially for two reasons. First I cannot subscribe to the view that administration of criminal justice is for Parliament alone to prescribe. Section 92(14) of the *British North America Act, 1867*, gives the Provinces power over "Administration of Justice within the Province". To confine the meaning of "Justice" to civil justice alone is to give to s. 92(14) a strained and truncated effect at war with the plain words of the section and with what would appear to have been the clear intent of the Fathers of Confederation. Secondly, as to the contempt power, from earliest times coroners inquiring into deaths occurring from other than natural causes, fire marshals inquiring into mysterious fires and countless commissioners holding public inquiries pursuant to federal or provincial Public Inquiries Acts have had power to summon witnesses, to require them to give evidence on oath and to punish them for contempt for refusal to be sworn. The Quebec Inquiry Commission into Organized Crime has the same powers, no more and no less. There is nothing in the record to sustain the view that in the exercise of those powers the Inquiry Commission has acted in any way differently from coroners, fire marshals or commissioners holding public inquiries in the past.

This case arises out of the Quebec Inquiry into Organized Crime established in 1972 pursuant to the *Police Act*, 1968 (Que.), c. 17. Section 19 [am. 1971, c. 16, s. 4; 1972, c. 16, s. 1] of that Act requires the Quebec Police Commission to make an inquiry, whenever requested to do so by the Lieutenant-Governor in Council, respecting any aspect of crime. The section also makes provision for an inquiry into the activities of an organization or system, its ramifications and the persons involved, to the extent prescribed, whenever there is reason to believe that in the fight against organized crime or terrorism and subversion it is in the public interest to order such an inquiry. [...]

The immediate question is whether s. 19 of the *Police Act* and the Order in Council are beyond the constitutional competence of the Province of Quebec to enact. At issue also is a question of more profound implication, namely, whether the conduct of inquiries, unconnected with specific criminal proceedings, into the state of public order within a Province is beyond the competence of provincial authority.

In each Province, the Legislature may "exclusively" make laws in relation to the "Administration of Justice in the Province". Section 92(14) of the *British North America Act, 1867*, in part so provides. This plenary power is plainly very wide, but subtracted therefrom, by s. 91(27), in favour of federal authority, is "The Criminal Law, except the Constitution of the Courts of Criminal Jurisdiction, but including the Procedure in Criminal Matters."

The scheme of the Act under ss. 91(27) and 92(14) contemplates that jurisdiction over the administration of justice in a Province will remain with the Provinces; the Provinces are invested with a plenitude of powers in this area but subject to the reservation of criminal law and procedure as an exception to the general principle.

Establishment of provincial superior, District or County Courts is a co-operative matter between federal and provincial authority. Section 92(14), which gives the Provinces exclusive legislative power over "the Administration of Justice in the Province", continues "including the Constitution, Maintenance and Organization of Provincial Courts, both of Civil and of Criminal Jurisdiction, and including Procedure in Civil Matters in those Courts." Section 96 provides for the appointment by the Governor-General of the Judges of the Superior, District and County Courts in each Province. Thus, procedure in criminal matters rests with the federal authority whereas, generally speaking, procedure in civil matters in provincial Courts, as well as the Constitution, maintenance and organization of these Courts, falls under provincial jurisdiction.

The question in the present case is whether the words "the Administration of Justice in the Province" are to be given a fair, large and liberal construction or, whether by reason of the abstraction of criminal law and criminal procedure, they must receive such attenuated interpretation as would confine "administration of justice" to nothing more than "administration of civil justice". In my opinion, Canadian legislative history, as well as the development of legal institutions within the Provinces since Confederation, favour the broader construction as do, by and large, the authorities, admittedly few in number, which touch upon the subject under consideration. [...]

The fight against organized crime has been a responsibility of the law enforcement agencies of the Province of Quebec. Although the tentacles of organized crime reach far beyond provincial or even national boundaries, the Inquiry is *bona fide* directed against acts done within the Province of Quebec where escalating levels of crime and violence have taken an increasing toll of lives and property.

The Inquiry by its terms is directed into the activities of organizations and systems and to the ramifications of those organizations and systems and the persons involved, to the extent that those organizations or systems operate in areas notoriously inviting to organized crime, such as illegal gambling, extortion, shylocking, drug traffic, prostitution and corruption.

The Inquiry does not act as a criminal Court or exercise criminal jurisdiction. The conduct of the Inquiry is not part of a criminal prosecution under the *Criminal Code* nor is it an investigation into a particular crime or transaction which later might be the subject of a criminal charge. We are not here concerned with a criminal trial, structured as a dispute between two sides, the Crown and the accused. The function of the Inquiry is merely to investigate and report; no person is accused; those who appear do so as witnesses; there is no *lis*; there is no attempt to alter criminal procedure. The proceedings of the commission are not criminal proceedings in the sense that punishment is their aim. The legislation under attack establishes an inquiry into the nature and prevalence of certain types of illegal conduct within the Province of Quebec but does not seek to create new crimes or to alter old ones. [...]

The words "Administration of Justice" in s. 92(14) are intended to have wide meaning. They *include*, but are not limited to, the Constitution, maintenance and organization of provincial Courts of civil and criminal jurisdiction and they *include* procedure in civil matters. Any interpretation which would limit s. 92(14) to the setting up of the Courts ignores the plain meaning of the words in the section and the plain meaning of the order in which those words appear as well as history and legislative intent. The use of the word "including" in s. 92(14) is no more intended to confine the "administration of justice" to "the Constitution, maintenance and organization of the Courts" than the use of the same word "including" in s. 91(27) is intended to limit "the Criminal Law" to "Procedure in Criminal Matters". As Mr. Justice Estey observed in *R. v. Pelletier* at p. 524 C.C.C., p. 685 O.R. (cites omitted), the words following "including" in s. 92(14) seek to amplify rather than restrict.

Both the federal and provincial Governments have accepted for over a century the status of the provincial Governments to administer criminal justice within their respective boundaries. The provincial mandate in that field has consistently been recognized as part and parcel of the responsibility of a provincial Government for public order within the Province.

Under head 92(14) of our Constitution, as I understand it, law enforcement is primarily the responsibility of the Province and in all Provinces the Attorney-General is the chief law enforcement officer of the Crown. He has broad responsibilities for most aspects of the administration of justice. Among these within the field of criminal justice, are the Court system, the police, criminal investigation and prosecutions, and corrections. The provincial police are answerable only to the Attorney-General as are the provincial Crown Attorneys who conduct the great majority of criminal prosecutions in Canada. [...]

It seems late in the day to strip the Provinces of jurisdiction in respect of criminal justice which they have exercised without challenge for well over 100 years. That is not to say that jurisdiction in the strict sense can come through consent or laches; however, history and governmental attitudes can be helpful guides to interpretation. [...]

The Order in Council establishing the Commission of Inquiry requires the Commission only to inquire and report to the Attorney-General. The action taken will rest with the Attorney-General. It could take the form of establishing new and different techniques or organization within the bodies charged with law enforcement. It could take the form of prosecutions, subject to the protection afforded witnesses by the *Canada Evidence Act*, R.S.C. 1970, c. E-10. Changes to the *Police Act* or other provincial legislation might be required in which the provincial Government could act within its constitutional capacity. A provincial commission of inquiry, inquiring into *any* subject, might submit a report in which it appeared that changes in federal laws would be desirable. There is nothing novel in this. Changes to the *Criminal Code* might seem warranted in which event one would expect the Attorney-General to act in liaison with the federal Government, as is done daily. [...]

The phrase "criminal procedure" does not lend itself to precise definition. In one sense, it is concerned with proceedings in the criminal Courts and such matters as conduct within the courtroom, the competency of witnesses, oaths and affirmations, and the presentation of evidence. Some cases have defined procedure even more narrowly in finding that it embraces the three technical terms – pleading, evidence and practice. In a broad sense, it encompasses such things as the rules by which, according to the *Criminal Code*, police powers are exercised, the right to counsel, search warrants, interim release, procuring attendance of witnesses.

The words of Mr. Justice Taschereau, as he then was, in *A.G. Qué. v. A.-G. Can.* (1945), 84 C.C.C. 369 at p. 394, [1945] 4 D.L.R. 305 at p. 328, [1945] S.C.R. 600 at p. 603, would suggest that the narrow construction is the more appropriate:

> The power given to the Federal Parliament to legislate in criminal law and criminal procedure, is the power to determine what shall or what shall not be "criminal", and to determine the steps to be taken in prosecutions and other criminal proceedings before the Courts.

Macdonald, C.J.A., in *Re Clement* (1919), 33 C.C.C. 119 at p. 120, 48 D.L.R. 237, at p. 238 *sub nom. Re Public Inquiries Act*, [1919] 3 W.W.R. 115 at p. 117, wrote to the same effect:

> The making of the criminal laws of Canada is assigned exclusively to the Dominion, so is the regulation of procedure in criminal matters. "Criminal matters are, in my opinion, proceedings in the criminal Courts, and "procedure" means the steps to be taken in prosecutions or other criminal proceedings in such Courts.

It is not necessary and perhaps impossible, to find a satisfactory definition of "criminal procedure". Although I would reject the view which could confine criminal procedure to that which takes place within the court-room on a prosecution, I am equally of the opinion that "criminal procedure" is not co-extensive with "criminal justice" or that the phrase "criminal procedure" as used in the *British North America Act, 1867*, can drain from the words "administration of justice" in s. 92(14) that which gives those words much of their substance – the element of "criminal justice".

The Courts have long distinguished between procedure and substantive law, and it would be wrong to take the form for the substance.

It would also seem that a valid distinction can be made between criminal procedure and an inquiry into criminal acts. What is in issue here is an inquiry into specific matters encompassed by the term, administration of justice in the Province. The Inquiry possesses purposes and functions which are separate and distinct from the procedures which accompany the investigation and prosecution in a criminal matter. Accepting that police investigation of an individual must comply with federal standards of criminal procedure, it is not immediately apparent why an investigative overview of crime on a collective basis should be open to constitutional attack.

It has been argued that "administration of justice" relates only to administration in respect of heads of exclusive provincial power. I cannot accept that view. The phrase "administration of justice" is free standing and an independent source of provincial power which would be shorn of meaning if reliance had to be placed always on some other head of power to give it effect. [...]

I would answer the question in the negative and dismiss the appeals.

[The concurring opinion of Beetz J. is omitted, as is the concurring opinion of Pigeon J. (with whom Martland, and Ritchie JJ. concurred).]

A.-G. QUE. V. A.-G. CAN.
[1979] 1 S.C.R. 218.

[The Keable Commission was established by the Quebec government to inquire into alleged wrongdoings by various police forces, including the R.C.M.P. The mandate of the Commission included investigation and report on circumstances surrounding searches carried on in the Montreal area in 1972, and specifically: the closing of investigation files following complaints regarding the searches; investigation report discrepancies; the destruction of documents; the collaboration between the RCMP, Quebec, and Montreal Urban Police forces; and the search methods used. The Commission was to investigate and report on circumstances of events relevant to other activity, including: an illegal entry made in 1973, the burning of a farm in 1972, and the theft of dynamite. Finally, the Commission was to report on these activities and make recommendations regarding measures to be taken to prevent future repetition of such activity.

On September 28, 1977, the Solicitor-General of Canada was served with a subpoena demanding documents concerning RCMP searches of the offices of the Agence de presse libre du Québec. The documents called for included: the originals of all files prepared by the RCMP or other forces regarding the search; operation reports; analysis reports on documents seized; notebooks and records of all RCMP members taking part in the search; and all written correspondence or reports of oral communication between 1972 and 1977 among the various police forces, within the same police forces, within the Quebec Department of Justice, or with the Solicitor General of Canada. Subsequent subpoenas demanded further documents. The Solicitor-General refused to comply.

The Attorney-General for Canada challenged the scope of the Commission's power, alleging that the Commission's interpretation of its mandate was *ultra vires* the powers of the Quebec legislature.]

PIGEON J. [Martland, Ritchie, Dickson and Beetz JJ. concurring]: — [...] It was contended that there was nothing to prevent a provincial government from ordering, in the public interest, an investigation into any subject whatever, just as any university or private institution can. The short answer to this contention is that this is not an inquiry of the same kind; it is being made, not by resorting only to generally available sources of information, but by compelling the attendance of witnesses to testify under oath and to produce documents. Such powers are not available to a commission set up by virtue of the royal prerogative, they depend on statutory authority, in the present case, on the *Public Inquiry Commission Act* under which this Commission was established. A provincial statute cannot be effective beyond the constitutional limits of a provincial legislature's authority. [...]

AG / Canada

On the other hand, it appears to me that the majority opinion in *Di Iorio v. Warden of the Montreal Jail*, is conclusive of the validity of the Commission's mandate to the extent that it is for an inquiry into specific criminal activities. I can see no basis for a distinction between such an inquiry and an inquiry into "organized crime" as in *Di Iorio*, or a coroner's inquiry into a criminal homicide as in *Faber v. The Queen* (cites omitted), or a fire marshal's inquiry into arson as in *Regina v. Coote*. Notwithstanding all the arguments submitted by counsel for the Solicitor General of Canada, I find myself bound by authority to hold that such inquiries come within the scope of "The Administration of Justice in the Province". [...]

Great stress was laid by the appellants as well as by intervenants on Dickson's J. statement in *Di Iorio*, at p. 208, that "A provincial commission of inquiry, inquiring into *any* subject, might submit a report in which it appeared that changes in federal laws would be desirable". This was said *obiter* in a case concerning an inquiry into organized crime. As previously noted, the basis of the decision was that such an inquiry into criminal activities is within the proper scope of "The Administration of Justice in the Province". The intended meaning of the sentence quoted is not that a provincial commission may validly inquire into any subject, but that any inquiry into a matter within provincial competence may reveal the desirability of changes in federal laws. The commission might therefore, whatever may be the subject into which it is validly inquiring, submit a report in which it appeared that changes in federal laws would be desirable. This does not mean that the gathering of information for the purpose of making such a report may be a proper subject of inquiry by a provincial commission.

I thus must hold that an inquiry into criminal acts allegedly committed by members of the R.C.M.P. was validly ordered, but that consideration must be given to the extent to which such inquiry may be carried into the administration of this police force. It is operating under the authority of a federal statute, the *Royal Canadian Mounted Police Act*, (R.S.C. 1970, c. R-9). It is a branch of the Department of the Solicitor General, (*Department of the Solicitor General Act*, R.S.C. 1970, c. S-12, s. 4). Parliament's authority for the establishment of this force and its management as part of the Government of Canada is unquestioned. It is therefore clear that no provincial authority may intrude into its management. While members of the force enjoy no immunity from the criminal law and the jurisdiction of the proper provincial authorities to investigate and prosecute criminal acts committed by any of them as by any other person, these authorities cannot, under the guise of carrying on such investigations, pursue the inquiry into the administration and management of the force. The doctrine of colourability is just as applicable in adjudicating on the validity of a commission's term of reference or decisions as in deciding on the constitutional validity of legislation. As Viscount Simon said in *Attorney General for Saskatchewan v. Attorney General for Canada*, (at p. 124) "you cannot do that indirectly which you are prohibited from doing directly".

The words [in] [...] the Commissioner's mandate, do not contemplate an inquiry into criminal acts but into the methods [regulations and practices] used by the police forces. Those are essential aspects of their administration and therefore, to the extent that those words relate to the R.C.M.P., what they purport to authorize is beyond provincial jurisdiction to inquire into. That this is the intended scope of the inquiry is apparent from the subpoenas which call for the production of all operating rules and manuals. [...]

THE SOLICITOR GENERAL NOT A COMPELLABLE WITNESS

I do not find it necessary to review at great length the numerous authorities cited on the fourth constitutional question. Because, at common law, a commission of inquiry has no power to compel the attendance of witnesses and to require the production of documents, any jurisdiction for such purposes depends on statutory authority, and it seems clear that provincial legislation cannot be effective by itself to confer such jurisdiction as against the Crown in right of Canada. In the recent case of *Her Majesty in right of Alberta v. C.T.C.*, Laskin C.J., said with the concurrence of all but two of the other members of the Court (at p. 72):

> [...] a Provincial Legislature cannot in the valid exercise of its legislative power, embrace the Crown in right of Canada in any compulsory regulation. [...]

Appellants submit that the decision of this Court in *Regina v. Snider* means that a minister of the Crown is a compellable witness at a trial and they point out that under s. 7 of the provincial Act a commissioner has "all the powers of a judge of the Superior Court in term". This enactment cannot, at least towards federal authorities, have the effect of making an inquiry the legal equivalent of a trial. [...] I would therefore answer question 4 in the negative.

ESTEY J. [Spence J. concurring]: — I have had the opportunity of reading the judgment of my brother, Pigeon J., and with his disposition of this appeal I am respectfully in complete agreement. [...]

In my view, the "administration of justice" authorizes and indeed requires a province to establish, maintain and operate such facilities as may from time to time be necessary and advisable for the proper and effective enforcement of the criminal law. That is not to say that only these activities are embraced in the expression "administration of justice". On the other hand, it is not only the Province and its agencies which may be concerned with the enforcement of the criminal law. It is equally clear that s. 92(14) does not authorize the Province to legislate with respect to criminal procedure directly or indirectly. It is the *Criminal Code* which sets forth the procedure prescribed by the sovereign authority, the Parliament of Canada, and which is to be followed in the investigation of crime and in the prosecution of ensuing charges. The Province, in the discharge of its role under s. 92(14) of The *British North America Act* may be required, or may find it convenient, to examine by the usual executive agencies or by a commission of enquiry, the operation of its policing facilities and personnel, and the prevalence of crime and its nature in the Province. Such was the case before the Court in *Di Iorio*, supra. At the other end of the scale, the enforcement agencies of the Province may of course investigate allegations or suspicions of specific crime with a view to the enforcement of the criminal law by prosecution. This investigation must be in accordance with federally prescribed criminal procedure and not otherwise, as for example, by coercive enquiry under general enquiry legislation of the Province.

In the middle of the scale is the situation facing the Court in this proceeding. The Province has set out to investigate the operations of provincial and municipal police apparatus in relation to certain specific events which have obvious criminal connotations. [...] Where, as I believe the case to be here, the substance of the provincial action is predominantly and essentially an enquiry into some aspects of the criminal law and the operations of provincial and municipal police forces in the Province, and not a mere prelude to prosecution by the Province of specific criminal activities, the provincial action is authorized under s. 92(14). [...]

[T]o strip a province of the right to investigate the operations of provincial and municipal police in the detection of crime and the enforcement of the criminal law would be to put a serious impediment in the path of those authorities charged with "the administration of justice" within the Province and I would not readily find such an interpretation to be appropriate in the application of these competing subsections of ss. 91 and 92. This right or authority on the part of the Province in relation to s. 92(14) does not by a back door, as it were, lead to a right to investigate a validly established federal organization, including a federal police organization. That is not to say that where members of such a federally organized force offend the criminal law, the ordinary agencies of criminal investigation and law enforcement within the Province would not operate as in the case of any other individuals. There may be circumstances in those Provinces which have contractual or other arrangements with the federal government with reference to the maintenance of police forces which will call into question different principles, but with which we are not here concerned.

It is my view, therefore, that a province may investigate an identified crime in the manner and through the procedures prescribed by Parliament, remaining free in the directing of its forces engaged in the administration of justice within the Province to investigate crimes and criminal activities generally and the operations of provincially organized agencies engaged in law enforcement; but neither plenary authority may investigate the undertaking of an agency validly established by the other plenary authority. The dividing line will at all times be difficult to establish. This is an unhappy characteristic of constitutional law and its application. Difficulty in ascertaining the precise boundary in specific circumstances is no reason to withdraw from the responsibility of enunciating a constitutional doctrine which recognizes the validity of the exclusive authorities in the subsections of ss. 91 and 92 respectively.

I add these few words in these proceedings because of the tendency which may develop to construe the aforementioned judgments of this Court as necessarily indicating a hardening into what might be construed as an arbitrary principle available in a slide rule sense for the determination of appropriate provincial or federal actions in related but not necessarily parallel circumstances.

[The concurring judgment of Pratte J. is omitted.]

STARR v. HOULDEN
[1990] 1 S C R 1366

[Allegations were made in the press that Starr, the President of a section of a registered charity, had made contributions from the charity's funds to political parties and that there was an association between her and Tridel Corporation Inc. Allegations about the relationship between Starr and various public officials, elected and unelected, mounted in the media and in the Legislative Assembly. Ashworth, the Executive Director of the Premier's Office, resigned his position after revealing that Starr had arranged for his family to receive personal benefits at no cost to himself. The province instituted a number of investigations.

A commission of inquiry was appointed pursuant to the *Public Inquiries Act* to inquire into the facts surrounding the relationships between Starr, any person or a corporation she may have acted for, including Tridel Corporation Inc., and any elected and appointed officials, including Ashworth. The appellants' requested the Commissioner to state a case dealing with the competence of the province to establish the inquiry and its potential effects on individual rights at common law and under the *Canadian Charter of Rights and Freedoms*. Three constitutional questions queried: (1) whether the inquiry's terms of reference fell within Parliament's criminal law power; ...]

LAMER J. — [Dickson C.J.C., La Forest, Sopinka, Gonthier and Cory JJ., concurring]: — The reasons of Pigeon J. [in *Di Iorio*] seem to suggest that [...] the provinces have the jurisdiction to set up an inquiry solely for the purpose of investigating whether a particular crime was committed. That position is, with respect, a broader reading of *Faber* (cites omitted) than is necessary, and one that is strictly speaking *obiter* since, on the facts of *Di Iorio*, the commission of inquiry was concerned with organized crime generally and not whether a specific crime was committed.

Dickson J. [in *Di Iorio*] explicitly addressed the central issue of the limits of provincial competence to establish commissions of inquiry with specific regard for the inquiry into organized crime before the Court. At page 201 he stated:

> The Inquiry by its terms is directed into the activities of organizations and systems and to the ramifications of those organizations and systems and the persons involved, to the extent that those organizations or systems operate in areas notoriously inviting to organized crime. [...]
>
> The Inquiry does not act as a criminal court or exercise criminal jurisdiction. The conduct of the Inquiry is not part of a criminal prosecution under the *Criminal Code nor is it an investigation into a particular crime or transaction which later might be the subject of a criminal charge*. We are not here concerned with a criminal trial, structured as a dispute between two sides, the Crown and the accused. The function of the Inquiry is merely to investigate and report: no person is accused; those who appear do so as witnesses; there is no *lis*; there is no attempt to alter criminal procedure. The proceedings of the Commission are not criminal proceedings in the sense that punishment is their aim. The legislation under attack establishes an inquiry into the nature and prevalence of certain types of illegal conduct within the Province of Quebec. [...] (emphasis added.)

[...] a valid distinction can be made between criminal procedure and an inquiry into criminal acts. What is in issue here is an inquiry into specific matters encompassed by the term, Administration of Justice in the Province. The Inquiry possesses purposes and functions which are separate and distinct from the procedures which accompany the investigation and prosecution in a criminal matter. *Accepting that police investigation of an individual must comply with federal standards of criminal procedure, it is not immediately apparent why an investigative overview of crime on a collective basis should be open to constitutional attack.* (emphasis added.) [...]

This leads me to a consideration of the decision of this Court in *Attorney General (Que.) and Keable v. Attorney General (Can.), supra.* [...] In my view, having regard for my interpretation of *Faber* (cites omitted) and *Di Iorio*, [...] the decision of Pigeon J. should not be taken to mean that it is within provincial jurisdiction to directly investigate particular individuals in respect of their alleged commission of specific criminal offences. [...]

While *Keable* dealt with specific allegations of illegal acts by members of the R.C.M.P., there were no individuals named in the terms of reference and nor was the inquiry empowered to examine one specific crime allegedly committed by particular persons. I also note that in *Keable* the terms of reference of the Commission empowered it to investigate certain specific "illegal or reprehensible acts" so that it could make recommendations to ensure that those acts would not be repeated by the R.C.M.P. in the future. In that light, while the Commission no doubt was empowered to inquire into certain potentially illegal activity, the inquiry's focus was on the more general issue of R.C.M.P. methods of investigation and wrongdoing in that context, a matter within provincial jurisdiction. [...]

The case of *R. v. Hoffmann-La Roche Ltd.* (1981), 33 O.R. (2d) 694, concerned a prosecution for predatory pricing under the *Combines Investigation Act*, R.S.C. 1970, c. C-23. Martin J.A. [...] stated the following at p. 724:

It is well established that a Province may create provincial agencies such as coroners, fire marshals, securities commissions and commissions of inquiry and endow them with the power to summon witnesses and compel them to give evidence under oath in an inquiry conducted for a valid provincial purpose, notwithstanding that any witness required to give evidence may potentially be a defendant in a subsequent criminal proceeding. [...]

The investigation of most crime is, however, conducted by the police acting principally under their common law powers and statutory powers of search and seizure and electronic surveillance, occasionally assisted in their investigation by the fruits of inquiries such as those mentioned above. The police are entitled to question any person, whether suspected or not, in order to ascertain whether a crime has been committed, and if so, to discover the person who committed it. The police, while they are entitled to question suspects have, in general, no power however, to compel answers.

Notwithstanding the overlapping between s. 91(27) and s. 92(14), manifestly it would not be within provincial competence to enact legislation enabling a police officer to summon a suspect before an official and submit the suspect to compulsory examination under oath with respect to his involvement in a crime. Even though such legislation might be described as legislation in relation to the investigation of offences and thus appear to fall within the category of the administration of justice, such legislation in pith and substance would be legislation in relation to criminal procedure and thus within the *exclusive* competence of Parliament. (emphasis added.)

Significantly, this overview by Martin J.A. was expressly endorsed by a majority of this Court in *Attorney General of Canada v. Canadian National Transportation, Ltd.*, [1983] 2 S.C.R. 206, at p. 242. In my view, the interpretation given by Martin J.A. to the trilogy of cases I have analyzed thus far is consistent with the thread flowing throughout all of them: the inquiry process cannot be used by a province to investigate the alleged commission of specific criminal offences by named persons. The use of the inquiry process in that way, having regard for the ability to coerce those named individuals to testify, would in effect be circumventing the criminal procedure which is within the exclusive jurisdiction of Parliament.

My interpretation of the interplay between provincial inquiries and investigation of specific crimes has more recently been supported by the Ontario Court of Appeal in *Re Nelles* and *Grange* (cites omitted). This case concerned a provincial inquiry into certain baby deaths at a Toronto hospital. While the effect of this decision has been raised as a separate ground of appeal by the appellants in the case at bar, I believe that it is of some note as regards the first constitutional question stated by this Court. The issue, on a stated case, was whether the Commissioner, Grange J., could express an opinion on who was responsible, whether by intent or by accident, for the baby deaths. In other words, to use the compendious expression, could he "name names"? The court held that he could not.

A public inquiry is not the means by which investigations are carried out with respect to the commission of particular crimes [...] Such an inquiry is a coercive procedure and is quite incompatible with our notion of justice in the investigation of a particular crime and the determination of actual or probable criminal or civil responsibility.

What is important is that a finding or conclusion stated by the commissioner would be considered by the public as a determination and might well be seriously prejudicial if a person named by the commissioner as responsible for the

> deaths in the circumstances were to face such accusations in further proceedings. Of equal importance, if no charge is subsequently laid, a person found responsible by the commissioner would have no recourse to clear his or her name. [...]

> Further, it is a reasonable inference that a person intends the natural consequences of his acts and such a finding as that referred to against a nurse in this case would leave nothing further to be said to amount to a conclusion forbidden by the Order in Council.

Although the constitutional validity of the Order in Council was not in issue, the interpretative limitations which were imposed by the court were designed to ensure that it stayed within provincial jurisdiction.

Finally, my analysis of judicial precedent ends with a review of the most recent decision of this Court in this area, *O'Hara v. British Columbia* (cites omitted). This case concerned a provincial inquiry investigating alleged injuries sustained by a prisoner while in custody at a police station. A hearing under the provincial *Police Act*, R.S.B.C. 1979, c. 331, had cleared the police of any wrongdoing, and therefore the inquiry was established to investigate and report on, among other things, the factors surrounding the detention of the prisoner, how he sustained the injuries, who inflicted them and whether there were any irregularities or wrongdoing in respect of the hearing under the *Police Act*. The only person named in the terms of reference was the prisoner. The Chief Justice delivered the majority judgment of this Court upholding the constitutionality of the inquiry. In so doing, he explicitly recognized, at p. 607, that "A province must respect federal jurisdiction over criminal law and criminal procedure". [...]

> A province has a valid and legitimate constitutional interest in determining the nature, source and reasons for inappropriate and possibly criminal activities engaged in by members of police forces under its jurisdiction. At stake is the management of the means by which justice is administered in the province. That such activity may later form the basis of a criminal charge and thus engage federal interests in criminal law and criminal procedure, does not, in my view, undermine this basic principle [...] the present inquiry is aimed at getting to the bottom of an incident of police misconduct which has undermined the proper administration of justice. The federal authorities have no jurisdiction over the discipline of the police officers who are the subject of the inquiry. [...] The inquiry is mandated to investigate alleged acts of wrongdoing for purposes different from those which underlie criminal law and criminal procedure. The purpose of the inquiry is not to determine criminal responsibility. As such, it is no different from a coroner's inquiry, the constitutionality of which was affirmed by this Court in *Faber* (cites omitted).

In my view, this passage from the judgment of the Chief Justice reconciles to a large extent the cases that have gone before in this area, while adhering to well established principles of adjudication in the context of division of powers. The comments of the Chief Justice recognize that there may be a "double aspect" to a commission of inquiry. There will be cases, however, where the Court is able to identify a predominant feature that outweighs the competing, incidental aspect. In *Keable* for example, while the Commission was empowered to investigate certain alleged criminal acts committed by police forces, its focus was on methods of police investigation, improprieties in relation thereto and recommendations for ensuring that the reprehensible acts were not repeated. Similarly, in *O'Hara* (cites omitted) the Chief Justice identified, at p. 610, the "management of the means by which justice is administered in the province" as the predominant feature of the inquiry.

Additionally, the Chief Justice in *O'Hara*, while upholding an inquiry into a specific incident, the conclusions of which may have led to criminal charges, explicitly made clear that the inquiry was *intra vires* the province because it did not serve to affix criminal responsibility to a particular individual. Rather, it was more generally concerned with police misconduct. Of some note is the fact that in *O'Hara* a hearing under the *Police Act* in relation to the incident at issue exonerated the police of any wrongdoing. There was no ongoing independent police investigation into possible criminal charges. Finally, and in my view an element of the decision that is of great importance, is the following *caveat* found at pp. 611-12:

> [...] a province may not interfere with federal interests in the enactment of and provision for a uniform system of criminal justice in the country as embodied in the *Criminal Code*. An inquiry enacted solely to determine criminal liability and to bypass the protection accorded to an accused by the *Criminal Code* would be *ultra vires* of a province, being a matter relating to criminal law and criminal procedure. This limitation on provincial jurisdiction is an acknowledgment of the federal nature of our system of self-government. (emphasis added.) [...]

In sum then, the decision in *O'Hara* speaks as much to the limitations on provincial commissions of inquiry as it does to their breadth. The judgment is a clear affirmation of the view that the pith and substance of a commission must be firmly anchored to a provincial head of power, and that it cannot be used either purposely or through its effect, as a means to investigate and determine the criminal responsibility of specific individuals for specific offences.

APPLICATION OF THE PRINCIPLES TO THE CASE AT BAR

Despite the length of the preceding analysis of jurisprudence, the applications of the principles to the present case are, in my view, quite straightforward. I prefer at the outset to state my general conclusions. In my view the commission of inquiry before this Court is, in pith and substance, a substitute police investigation and preliminary inquiry into a specific offence defined in s. 121 of the *Criminal Code*, alleged to have been committed by one or both of the named individuals, Patricia Starr and Tridel Corporation Inc. This is not to say that an inquiry's terms of reference may never contain the names of specific individuals. Rather, it is the combined and cumulative effect of the names together with the incorporation of the *Criminal Code* offence that renders this inquiry *ultra vires* the province. The terms of reference name private individuals and do so in reference to language that is virtually indistinguishable from the parallel *Criminal Code* provision. Those same terms of reference require the Commissioner to investigate and make findings of fact that would in effect establish a *prima facie* case against the named individuals sufficient to commit those individuals to trial for the offence in s. 121 of the *Code*. The net effect of the inquiry, although perhaps not intended by the province, is that it acts as a substitute for a proper police investigation, and for a preliminary inquiry governed by Part XVIII of the *Code*, into allegations of specific criminal acts by Starr and Tridel Corporation Inc. While public officials are involved within the scope of the inquiry, the investigation of them is defined in terms of whether they had dealings with Ms. Starr or Tridel Corporation Inc., and is therefore incidental to the main focus of the Commissioner's mandate. [...]

In my view, there are two key facts, whose combined and cumulative effect, lead me to the conclusion that this inquiry is in effect a substitute criminal investigation and preliminary inquiry. First, the only named parties are two private individuals, one being a corporation, who have been singled out for investigation. Unlike *O'Hara*, where the named individual was the victim of alleged misconduct, the present inquiry names individuals who are the alleged perpetrators of the misconduct. Second, the investigation of these two named individuals is in the context of a mandate that, as recognized by the Court of Appeal for Ontario, bears a "striking resemblance" to s. 121(1)(*b*) of the *Criminal Code*. [...]

A plain reading of the terms of reference, in my view, clearly establishes that the conclusions drawn by the Commissioner will necessarily include a finding of a *nexus* between the dealings identified and any benefits that he finds were conferred to public officials. That is, essentially, the offence defined by s. 121(1)(*b*). [...]

[I]t is not necessary for the Commissioner to make findings of guilt in the true sense of the word for the inquiry to be *ultra vires* the province. It suffices if the inquiry is in effect a substitute police investigation and preliminary inquiry into a specific allegation of criminal conduct by named, private citizens. In my view, the investigation the Commissioner is asked to undertake, and the findings of fact he will make as a result of his investigation, place him in a similar position as a judge conducting a preliminary inquiry under s. 535 of the *Criminal Code*. [...]

To allow this inquiry to continue as it is formulated, would result in the Commissioner's assimilating his role to that of judge presiding at a preliminary inquiry. In essence the inquiry is entering into the preliminary stages of the judicial criminal process by taking evidence, determining its sufficiency and ultimately deciding whether a *prima facie* case exists against either or both Starr and Tridel Corporation Inc. There is no doubt that a number of cases have held that inquiries whose predominant role it is to elucidate facts and not conduct a criminal trial are validly constituted even though there may be some overlap between the subject-matter of the inquiry and criminal activity. Indeed, it is clear that the fact that a witness before a commission may subsequently be a defendant in a criminal trial does not render the commission *ultra vires* the province. But in no case before this Court has there ever been a provincial inquiry that combines the virtual replication of an existing *Criminal Code* offence with the naming of private individuals while ongoing police investigations exist in respect of those same individuals. One of the implications for allowing the inquiry to go on in its present form is that the inquiry can compel a "witness" who is really one of the named "suspects" to answer questions under oath even though that person could not have been compelled to provide incriminating evidence against herself in the course of a regular police investigation, during the course of a preliminary inquiry under the *Code* (see s. 541) or during the course of a trial in which she is an accused. [...]

[T]he inquiry before this Court is *ultra vires* the province because it is in pith and substance a substitute investigation and preliminary inquiry of named individuals for a specific criminal offence. [...]

[P]rovinces should be given ample room within their constitutional competence to establish public inquiries aimed at investigating, studying and recommending changes for the better government of their citizens. What a province may not do, and what it has done in this case, is enact a public inquiry, with all its coercive powers, as a substitute for an investigation and preliminary inquiry into specific individuals in respect of specific criminal offences. This is an interference with federal interests in the enactment of and provision for a system of criminal justice as embodied in the *Criminal Code*. The net effect of such an inquiry is to bypass the protection accorded to an individual by the *Criminal Code* and is accordingly *ultra vires* the province as being a matter relating to s. 91(27) of the *Constitution Act, 1867*. This limitation on provincial competence has consistently been reiterated in decisions emanating from this Court that have upheld the constitutionality of other provincial public inquiries. In substance, the present inquiry offends the principle that a province cannot compel a person to submit to questioning under oath with respect to her involvement in a suspected criminal offence for the purpose of gathering sufficient evidence to lay charges or to gather sufficient evidence to establish a *prima facie* case. [...]

CANADIAN RED CROSS ET AL. v. KREVER
[1997] 3 S.C.R. 440.

CORY J. [for the Court]: — More than 1,000 Canadians became directly infected with Human Immunodeficiency Virus (HIV) from blood and blood products in the early 1980s. Approximately 12,000 Canadians became infected with Hepatitis C from blood and blood products during the same time period. This tragedy prompted the federal, provincial and territorial ministers of health to agree in September of 1993 to convene an inquiry which would examine the blood system.

On October 4, 1993, pursuant to Part I of the *Inquiries Act*, R.S.C., 1985, c. I-11 (the Act), the Government of Canada appointed Krever J.A. of the Ontario Court of Appeal (the Commissioner) to review and report on the blood system in

Canada.[...] Twenty-five interested parties were granted standing, including the appellants, The Canadian Red Cross Society and Bayer Inc., the federal government and each of the provincial governments except for Quebec. [...]

On October 26, 1995, Commission counsel delivered a memorandum to all parties inviting them to inform the Commission of the findings of misconduct they felt should be made by the Commission. The memorandum explained that under s. 13 of the Act, the Commissioner is required to give notice to any person against whom he intends to make findings of misconduct. The parties' submissions would help ensure that the notices gave warning of all the possible findings of misconduct which might be made by the Commission. These confidential submissions would be read only by Commission counsel, and would be considered for inclusion in notices issued by the Commissioner. Only those possible findings which were supported by evidence adduced in the public hearings and which were anticipated to be within the scope of the Commissioner's final report were included in the notices.

On December 21, 1995, the final day of scheduled hearings, 45 confidential notices naming 95 individuals, corporations and governments, each containing between one and 100 allegations, were delivered pursuant to s. 13 of the Act. The notices advised that the Commission might reach certain conclusions based on the evidence before it, that these conclusions may amount to misconduct within the meaning of s. 13, and that the recipients had the right to respond as to whether the Commissioner ought to reach these conclusions. The recipients were given until January 10, 1996 to announce whether and how they would respond to the notices in their final submissions.

A number of the recipients of notices brought applications for judicial review in the Federal Court. [...]

Inquiries Act, R.S.C., 1985, c. I-11

2. The Governor in Council may, whenever the Governor in Council deems it expedient, cause inquiry to be made into and concerning any matter connected with the good government of Canada or the conduct of any part of the public business thereof. [...]

12. The commissioners may allow any person whose conduct is being investigated under this Act, and shall allow any person against whom any charge is made in the course of an investigation, to be represented by counsel.

13. No report shall be made against any person until reasonable notice has been given to the person of the charge of misconduct alleged against him and the person has been allowed full opportunity to be heard in person or by counsel.

[In *Phillips v. Nova Scotia*, [1995] 2 S.C.R. 97, this court described] the history and role of commissions of inquiry: [...]

As *ad hoc* bodies, commissions of inquiry are free of many of the institutional impediments which at times constrain the operation of the various branches of government. They are created as needed, although it is an unfortunate reality that their establishment is often prompted by tragedies such as industrial disasters, plane crashes, unexplained infant deaths, allegations of widespread child sexual abuse, or grave miscarriages of justice.

At least three major studies on the topic have stressed the utility of public inquiries and recommended their retention: Law Reform Commission of Canada, Working Paper 17, *Administrative Law: Commissions of Inquiry* (1977); Ontario Law Reform Commission, *Report on Public Inquiries* (1992); and Alberta Law Reform Institute, Report No. 62, *Proposals for the Reform of the Public Inquiries Act* (1992). They have identified many benefits flowing from commissions of inquiry. Although the particular advantages of any given inquiry will depend upon the circumstances in which it is created and the powers it is given, it may be helpful to review some of the most common functions of commissions of inquiry.

One of the primary functions of public inquiries is fact-finding. They are often convened, in the wake of public shock, horror, disillusionment, or scepticism, in order to uncover "the truth". Inquiries are, like the judiciary, independent; unlike the judiciary, they are often endowed with wide-ranging investigative powers. In following their mandates, commissions of inquiry are, ideally, free from partisan loyalties and better able than Parliament or the legislatures to take a long-term view of the problem presented. Cynics decry public inquiries as a means used by the government to postpone acting in circumstances which often call for speedy action. Yet, these inquiries can and do fulfil an important function in Canadian society. In times of public questioning, stress and concern they provide the means for Canadians to be apprised of the conditions pertaining to a worrisome community problem and to be a part of the recommendations that are aimed at resolving the problem. Both the status and high public respect for the commissioner and the open and public nature of the hearing help to restore public confidence not only in the institution or situation investigated but also in the process of government as a whole. They are an excellent means of informing and educating concerned members of the public.

Undoubtedly, the ability of an inquiry to investigate, educate and inform Canadians benefits our society. A public inquiry before an impartial and independent commissioner which investigates the cause of tragedy and makes recommendations for change can help to prevent a recurrence of such tragedies in the future, and to restore public confidence in the industry or process being reviewed. [...]

A commission of inquiry is neither a criminal trial nor a civil action for the determination of liability. It cannot establish either criminal culpability or civil responsibility for damages. Rather, an inquiry is an investigation into an issue, event or series of events. The findings of a commissioner relating to that investigation are simply findings of fact and statements of opinion reached by the commissioner at the end of the inquiry. They are unconnected to normal legal criteria. They are based upon and flow from a procedure which is not bound by the evidentiary or procedural rules of a courtroom. There are no legal consequences attached to the determinations of a commissioner. They are not enforceable and do not bind courts considering the same subject matter. [...]

What then should be the result of the appellants' submission that a commissioner conducting a public inquiry does not have the jurisdiction to make findings that would be considered by reasonably informed members of the public to be a determination of criminal or civil liability? Since it is clear that a commissioner's findings cannot constitute findings of legal liability, it would appear that the appellants are asserting that in light of the potential harm to the reputations of parties or witnesses, a commissioner should not be permitted to allocate blame or assign responsibility for the events under scrutiny. While they acknowledge that a commissioner does have the authority to make findings of fact, they appear to challenge his ability to assess those facts or to evaluate what happened according to a standard of conduct. [...]

Section 13 of the Act makes it clear that commissioners have the power to make findings of misconduct. In order to do so, commissioners must also have the necessary authority to set out the facts upon which the findings of misconduct are based, even if those facts reflect adversely on some parties. If this were not so, the inquiry process would be essentially pointless. Inquiries would produce reports composed solely of recommendations for change, but there could be no factual findings to demonstrate why the changes were necessary. If an inquiry is to be useful in its roles of investigation, education and the making of recommendations, it must make findings of fact. It is these findings which will eventually lead to the recommendations which will seek to prevent the recurrence of future tragedies.

These findings of fact may well indicate those individuals and organizations which were at fault. Obviously, reputations will be affected. But damaged reputations may be the price which must be paid to ensure that if a tragedy such as that presented to the Commission in this case can be prevented, it will be. [...]

The appellants do not appear to challenge the power of a commissioner to make findings of fact; their objection is to the commissioner's assessment of those facts. However, in my view, the power of commissioners to make findings of misconduct must encompass not only finding the facts, but also evaluating and interpreting them. This means that commissioners must be able to weigh the testimony of witnesses appearing before them and to make findings of credibility. This authority flows from the wording of s. 13 of the Act, which refers to a commissioner's jurisdiction to make findings of "misconduct". According to the *Concise Oxford Dictionary* (8th ed. 1990), misconduct is "improper or unprofessional behaviour" or "bad management". Without the power to evaluate and weigh testimony, it would be impossible for a commissioner to determine whether behaviour was "improper" as opposed to "proper", or what constituted "bad management" as opposed to "good management". [...]

The principal argument presented to prohibit commissioners from making findings which include evaluations of the conduct of individuals is that those findings may harm the reputations of the named parties. However, I am not convinced that a commissioner's evaluation of facts found to be unfavourable to a party will necessarily aggravate the damage caused to the reputation of the party by the unfavourable findings of fact standing by themselves. For example, suppose an inquiry made the following unfavourable factual findings:

Company X learned by late summer or early fall 1984 that its manufacturing process for producing untreated factor concentrates was ineffective in destroying the causative agent of AIDS. A safer, viable process for producing heat-treated factor concentrates was available and in use. Company X did not withdraw its products produced by the ineffective and unsafe process.

Is the damage to the reputation of the party caused by these findings increased if the commissioner's evaluation of them is included, as in the following example?

Company X learned by late summer or early fall 1984 that its manufacturing process for producing untreated factor concentrates was ineffective in destroying the causative agent of AIDS, and that a safer, viable process for producing heat-treated factor concentrates was available and in use. Despite its knowledge of the grave dangers to the public, Company X failed to withdraw those products produced by what it knew to be an ineffective and unsafe process. This was unacceptable conduct.

It cannot be said that there would be any real difference between the public's impression of Company X's conduct if the findings were phrased in the second manner rather than the first. The harm to the company's reputation must result from setting out the factual findings. Since this is clearly within the commissioner's jurisdiction, I see no reason why the commissioner should be prevented from drawing the appropriate evaluations or conclusions which flow from those facts.

In addition, to limit a commissioner solely to findings of fact would require first the commissioner and, subsequently, the courts to wrestle with the difficult issue of distinguishing between fact and opinion. On my interpretation of the statute it is not necessary to consider that question. The wording of s. 13 by necessary inference authorizes a commissioner to make findings of fact and to reach conclusions based upon those facts, even if the findings and conclusions may adversely affect the reputation of individuals or corporations. [...]

The appellants contend that even if findings of misconduct are authorized by the Act, this power has been restricted by decisions of the courts. They argue that the judicial restriction is such that the authority cannot be exercised if the findings would appear in the eyes of the public to be determinations of liability. In support of their position, they rely on comments made by the Ontario Court of Appeal in *Nelles* (cites omitted), which were favourably referred to by this Court in *Starr v. Houlden*, supra, at p. 1398. In *Nelles*, the court prohibited a provincially appointed commissioner from expressing his opinion as to whether the death of any child was the result of the action, accidental or otherwise, of any named persons. This restriction, the court held, flowed from the terms of the inquiry's authorizing order, which forbade the commissioner from expressing "any conclusion of law regarding civil or criminal responsibility". That provision stemmed from the concern that, in its absence, the inquiry would intrude upon the federal criminal law power. The Court of Appeal described this concern in these words at p. 220:

> [...] the fact that the findings or conclusions made by the commissioner are not binding or final in future proceedings is not determinative of what he will decide. What is important is that a finding or conclusion stated by the commissioner would be considered by the public as a determination and might well be seriously prejudicial if a person named by the commissioner as responsible for the deaths in the circumstances were to face such accusations in further proceedings. Of equal importance, if no charge is subsequently laid, a person found responsible by the commissioner would have no recourse to clear his or her name.

The appellants rely upon this statement to support their position that a commissioner cannot make findings which would appear in the eyes of the public to be determinations of legal liability.

I cannot accept this position. The test set out above is appropriate when dealing with commissions investigating a particular crime. However, it should not be applied to inquiries which are engaged in a wider investigation, such as that of the tragedy presented in this case. I agree with the Federal Court of Appeal that if the comments made in *Nelles* were taken as a legal principle of law applicable to every inquiry, the task of many if not most commissions of inquiry would be rendered impossible.

The decisions in *Nelles* and *Starr* are distinguishable from the case at bar. In *Nelles*, the court found that the purpose of the inquiry was to discover who had committed the specific crime of killing several babies at the Hospital for Sick Children in Toronto. By the time the case reached the Court of Appeal, one criminal prosecution for the deaths had failed and an extensive police investigation into the deaths was still continuing. When it established the commission, the government described it as an inquiry into deaths thought to have been the result of deliberate criminal acts. Further, the Attorney General had stated that if further evidence became available which would warrant the laying of additional charges, they would be laid and the parties vigorously prosecuted. The court clearly viewed the proceedings as tantamount to a preliminary inquiry into a specific crime. For the commissioner to have named the persons he considered responsible would, in those circumstances, have amounted to a clear attribution of criminal responsibility.

Starr can be similarly distinguished. The public inquiry in that case arose out of widely publicized allegations of conflict of interest and possible criminal activity by Patricia Starr and Tridel Corporation. The Order in Council establishing the inquiry named both Starr and Tridel and, without providing any requirement for making recommendations, mandated an investigation into their conduct in language virtually indistinguishable from the pertinent *Criminal Code* provisions. This Court concluded that the purpose of the inquiry was to conduct an investigation solely for the purpose of obtaining evidence, determining its sufficiency and deciding whether a *prima facie* criminal case had been established against either of the named parties. In the reasons, this observation was made at p. 1403:

> [...] there seems to be a complete absence of any broad, policy basis for the inquiry. This is not, for example, a commission of inquiry into the relationship of charities and public officials. There is no express mandate for the Commissioner to inquire into anything other than the specific allegations of the relationship between dealings by public officials with the two named individuals and any benefits that may have been conferred to the officials.

At page 1405, this conclusion was reached regarding the aim of the commission:

> There is nothing on the surface of the terms of reference or in the background facts leading up to the inquiry to convince me that it is designed to restore confidence in the integrity and institutions of government or to review the regime governing the conduct of public officials. Any such objectives are clearly incidental to the central feature of the inquiry, which is the investigation and the making of findings of fact in respect of named individuals in relation to a specific criminal offence.

The Court concluded that the inquiry was *ultra vires* the province.

Clearly, those two inquiries were unique. They dealt with specific incidents and specific individuals, during the course of criminal investigations. Their findings would inevitably reflect adversely on individuals or parties and could well be interpreted as findings of liability by some members of the public. In those circumstances, it was appropriate to adopt a strict test to protect those who might be the subject of criminal investigations. However, those commissions were very different from broad inquiries such as an investigation into the contamination of Canada's blood system, as presented in this case.

The strict test set out in *Nelles* has not been followed in other cases dealing with commissions of inquiry. In *Phillips*, supra, the Court refused, at para. 19, to suspend an inquiry which had the stated purpose of investigating the explosion at the Westray mine, including " [...] (b) whether the occurrence was or was not preventable; (c) whether any neglect caused or contributed to the occurrence; [...] (f) whether there was compliance with applicable statutes, regulations, orders, rules, or directions. [...]"

In *O'Hara*, (cites omitted) an inquiry was upheld in circumstances where the commissioner was to report on whether a prisoner sustained injuries while detained in police custody, and if so, the extent of the injuries, the person or persons who inflicted them, and the reason they were inflicted. The court made a distinction between inquiries aimed at answering broad policy questions and those with a predominantly criminal law purpose. The inquiry was upheld, despite the fact that it would inevitably lead to findings of misconduct against particular individuals, because it was not aimed at investigating a specific crime, but rather at the broad goal of ensuring the proper treatment by police officers of persons in custody.

Nor was a strict approach taken in the earlier case of *Attorney General (Qué.) and Keable v. Attorney General (Can.)*, [1979] 1 S.C.R. 218, at pp. 226-27, where this Court upheld an inquiry into "the conduct of all persons involved in [...] [an] illegal entry made during January 1973 [...] setting fire to a farm [...] [and] theft of dynamite".

Clearly, the findings that may be made in *Phillips* and that were made in *O'Hara* and *Keable* would fail the strict test set out in *Nelles* and referred to in *Starr*. Yet each of these commissioners has made or may make findings of misconduct, as authorized by the Act. This they could not and cannot do without stating findings of fact that are likely to have an adverse effect on the reputation of individuals. Nonetheless, the inquiries were upheld by this Court. It follows that the strict test advanced by the appellants cannot be of general application. A more flexible approach must be taken in cases where inquiries are general in nature, and are established for a valid public purpose and not as a means of furthering a criminal investigation.

What Can be Included in a Commissioner's Report?

What then can commissioners include in their reports? The primary role, indeed the *raison d'être*, of an inquiry investigating a matter is to make findings of fact. In order to do so, the commissioner may have to assess and make findings as to the credibility of witnesses. From the findings of fact the commissioner may draw appropriate conclusions as to whether there has been misconduct and who appears to be responsible for it. However, the conclusions of a commissioner should not duplicate the wording of the *Code* defining a specific offence. If this were done it could be taken that a commissioner was finding a person guilty of a crime. This might well indicate that the commission was, in reality, a criminal investigation carried out under the guise of a commission of inquiry. Similarly, commissioners should endeavour to avoid making evaluations of their findings of fact in terms that are the same as those used by courts to express findings of civil liability. As well, efforts should be made to avoid language that is so equivocal that it appears to be a finding of civil or criminal liability. Despite these words of caution, however, commissioners should not be expected to perform linguistic contortions to avoid language that might conceivably be interpreted as importing a legal finding.

Findings of misconduct should not be the principal focus of this kind of public inquiry. Rather, they should be made only in those circumstances where they are required to carry out the mandate of the inquiry. A public inquiry was never intended to be used as a means of finding criminal or civil liability. No matter how carefully the inquiry hearings are conducted they cannot provide the evidentiary or procedural safeguards which prevail at a trial. Indeed, the very relaxation of the evidentiary rules which is so common to inquiries makes it readily apparent that findings of criminal or civil liability not only should not be made, they cannot be made.

Perhaps commissions of inquiry should preface their reports with the notice that the findings of fact and conclusions they contain cannot be taken as findings of criminal or civil liability. A commissioner could emphasize that the rules of evidence and the procedure adopted at the inquiry are very different from those of the courts. Therefore, findings of fact reached in an inquiry may not necessarily be the same as those which would be reached in a court. This may help ensure that the public understands what the findings of a commissioner are – and what they are not. [...]

[The Justice then considered whether the s.13 notices delivered to the appellants were unfair or beyond the Commissioner's jurisdiction (in the administrative law sense) and concluded they were not.]

A.G. CAN. v. C.N. TPT. LTD.; A.G. CAN. v. C.P. TPT. CO.
[1983] 2 S.C.R. 206.

LASKIN C.J.C. [Ritchie, Estey and McIntyre JJ. concurring]: — [...] [T]he particular questions raised in this appeal [...] read as follows:

> 1. Does the constitutional validity of s. 32(1)(*c*) [reen. 1974-75-76, c. 76, s. 14] of the *Combines Investigation Act*, R.S.C. 1970, c. C-23, depend upon s. 91(27) of the *British North America Act*?

> 2. If so, is it within the competence of the Parliament of Canada to enact legislation as in s. 2 of the *Criminal Code*, [R.S.C. 1970, c. C-34] and s. 15(2) of the *Combines Investigation Act*, to authorize the Attorney General of Canada or his agents to prefer indictments and conduct proceedings in respect of alleged violations of the aforementioned provision?

They require fleshing out to show how they arose and I turn to the relevant facts.

An officer under the federal *Combines Investigation Act* swore an information against the respondents, charging them and other corporations and individuals with unlawful conspiracy to prevent or lessen unduly competition in the interprovincial transportation of general merchandise in shipments weighing up to and including 10,000 pounds from points in Alberta to points in British Columbia, Saskatchewan and Manitoba to points in Alberta [contrary to s. 32 of the *Combines Investigation Act*.]

The conduct of the proceedings was put in the hands of counsel authorized by the Attorney General of Canada. Prohibition was thereupon sought by various of those charged with the offence to restrain the Alberta Provincial Court, before which the information was brought, from proceeding thereon so long as the prosecution was to be conducted by counsel for the federal Attorney General. [...]

Section 15(2) of the *Combines Investigation Act* reads as follows:

> (2) The Attorney General of Canada may institute and conduct any prosecution or other proceedings under this Act, and for such purposes he may exercise all the powers and functions conferred by the *Criminal Code* on the attorney general of a province.

The definition of s. 2 of "Attorney General" in the *Criminal Code* embraces the Attorney General or Solicitor General of a province and as well federal prosecuting authorities in the following specification:

> 2. In this Act [...]

> "Attorney General" means the Attorney General or Solicitor General of a province in which proceedings to which this Act applies are taken and, with respect to
> (a)   the Northwest Territories and the Yukon Territory, and
> (b)   proceedings instituted at the instance of the Government of Canada and conducted by or on behalf of that Government in respect of a violation of or conspiracy to violate any Act of the Parliament of Canada or a regulation made thereunder other than this Act,
> means the Attorney General of Canada and, except for the purposes of subsections 505(4) and 507(3), includes the lawful deputy of the said Attorney General, Solicitor General and Attorney General of Canada. [...]

It was the federal parliament's decision to give general prosecuting authority under the *Criminal Code* to the provincial Attorneys General or Solicitors General and to limit federal prosecutors to the prosecution of proceedings instituted at the suit of the government of Canada in respect of a violation or conspiracy to violate any federal Act or regulation thereunder other than the *Criminal Code*. [...]

Language and logic inform constitutional interpretation, and they are applicable in considering the alleged reach of s. 92(14) and the allegedly correlative limitation of criminal procedure in s. 91(27). I find it difficult, indeed impossible, to read s. 92(14) as not only embracing prosecutorial authority respecting the enforcement of federal criminal law but diminishing the *ex facie* impact of s. 91(27) which includes procedure in criminal matters. As a matter of language, there is nothing in s. 92(14) which embraces prosecutorial authority in respect of federal criminal matters. Section 92(14) grants jurisdiction over the administration of justice, including procedure in civil matters and including also the Constitution, maintenance and organization of civil and criminal provincial courts.

The section thus narrows the scope of the criminal law power under s. 91, but only with respect to what is embraced within "the Constitution, Maintenance and Organization of Provincial Courts [ ] of Criminal Jurisdiction". By no stretch of language can these words be construed to include jurisdiction over the conduct of criminal prosecutions. Moreover, as a matter of conjunctive assessment of the two constitutional provisions, the express inclusion of procedure in civil matters in provincial courts points to an express provincial exclusion of procedure in criminal matters specified in s. 91(27).

There is, in addition, an attempt here to prefer the general administration of justice over the special criminal law and procedure, when there is no language in the former to override or even suggest the latter. The respondents and the supporting intervenors submit that because s. 92(14) includes the Constitution of courts of "criminal jurisdiction" the word "criminal" must be imported into the opening words of the section, which must be construed as if they said "the Administration of Civil and Criminal Justice in the Province". However, this is not how the section was drafted; neither logic nor grammar support this construction. [...]

It must be remembered, at the risk of undue repetition, that the practice of provincial prosecution was continued after 1867 into post-1867 by virtue of s. 129 [of the *British North America Act*].

It was a practical accommodation to allow this to continue, and the affirmation of this practice under the 1892 *Criminal Code* and in ensuing years did not, as I read the authorities, cast any doubt on federal authority to invest and regulate provincial prosecutorial power to enforce the federal criminal law. [...]

It must be remembered that s. 92(14) is a grant of legislative power and if it gave the provinces legislative authority over the conduct of criminal prosecutions, then federal legislation conferring prosecutorial authority on either provincial or federal Attorneys General would be *ultra vires*. It cannot be argued that Parliament confers prosecutorial authority only with the consent of the provinces, for this would involve all unconstitutional delegation of legislative power: see *A.-G. N.S. v. A.-G. Can.* (the "*N.S. Interdelegation*" case), [1951] S.C.R. 31, [1950] 4 D.L.R. 369. The provincial position appears to blur legislative and executive power and to treat s. 92(14) as if it were a grant of executive power to which the legislative power of Parliament under s. 91(27) was subordinate.

[The respondents and the supporting intervenors submitted that because s. 92(14) includes the Constitution of courts of "criminal jurisdiction", the word "criminal" must be injected into the opening words of the section, which must be construed as if they said "the Administration of Civil and Criminal Justice in the Province"].

I have examined the pre-Confederation debates in the then provincial Parliament of Canada. Nothing in these [debates] touches the issue now before us, nor is there any basis for any special reading of the Charlottetown or the subsequent London Palace Hotel resolutions to gloss the present s. 92(14) and s. 91(27) in the way proposed by the respondents and their supporting intervenors.

It is patent that neither the respondents nor their supporting intervenors view the present case as pointing to possible concurrency. Since Parliament has in fact legislated, that would defeat their contention without more. Yet there is good reason to say that even if there is merit in the respondents' position, there is at least equal merit in the assertion of parliamentary authority to control prosecution for violation of the federal criminal law. The issue, put in these terms, is not a new one. The Privy Council explained the matter in terms of the so-called trenching doctrine in *Tennant v. Union Bank of Can.*, [1894] A.C. 31, 5 Cart. B.N.A. 244, as supporting a privileged encroachment on provincial legislative authority to give effect to exclusive and paramount federal power in relation to the classes of subjects assigned to Parliament under the enumerated heads of s. 91. The obverse view arises, as shown in the *Assignments and Preferences* case, *A.G. Ont. v. A.G. Can.*, [1894] A.C. 189 (P.C.), when there is an absence of federal legislation to supersede the lawful enactment of provincial legislation within one of its assigned powers.

Two observations, one by former Justice Rand and the second by former Justice Judson, are, in my opinion, a more reasonable approach to the so-called trenching doctrine and its associated "ancillary" or necessarily incidental doctrines than those expressed by the Privy Council in *Tennant v. Union Bank of Can.*, supra. In *A.G. Can. v. C.P.R.*, [1958] S.C.R. 285 at 290, 76 C.R.T.C. 241, 12 D.L.R. (2d) 625, Rand J. said this:

> Powers in relation to matters normally within the provincial field, especially of property and civil rights, are inseparable from a number of the specific heads of s. 91 [...] under which scarcely a step could be taken that did not involve them. In each such case the question is primarily not how far Parliament can trench on s. 92 but rather to what extent are property and civil rights within the scope of the paramount power of Parliament. *Tennant v. Union Bank* [supra] in which a provision under the *Bank Act* for taking security for loans made by a bank in disregard of provincial forms of security and registration was upheld in a characteristic example. [...]

Those two references exhibit the strength of the force residing in an enumerated class of subject in s. 91 when all those classes are expressed to repose legislative authority in Parliament, both exclusively and notwithstanding anything in s. 92. The effect so given resides in s. 91(27) no less than in other enumerations in s. 91.

Spence J. [noted at pp. 1002-1004 of *R. v. Hauser*, [1979] 1 S.C.R. 984] [...]

> [...] Parliament has, throughout the *Criminal Code*, granted jurisdiction to various provincial courts and has imposed duties and has conferred powers on various provincial officials including of course the Attorneys General of the provinces. Those provincial courts in exercising such jurisdiction and those Attorneys General and other provincial officials in discharging their duties so imposed and exercising their powers so conferred do so by virtue of the federal legislation enacted under the enumerated head no. 27 of s. 91 of the *British North America Act*. [...]

I can see no bar to Parliament, in the discharge of its valid legislative power, providing that as to certain duties or procedures the provincial officials shall not be used exclusively but the power may also be exercised by a federal official who may be the Attorney General of Canada or any investigating or prosecuting agency designated by Parliament.

Indeed it is difficult to understand how much of the federal legislative field could be dealt with efficiently by other methods. Much of the legislation in such fields is in essence regulatory and concerns such typically federal matters as trade and commerce, importation and exportation and other like matters. The administration of such fields requires decisions of policy and certainly would include the establishment of a policy as to the means of and methods of enforcement. It would be a denial of the basic concept of federalism to permit the provincial authorities to have exclusive control of the enforcement of such legislation and the sole determination as to how and when the legislation should be enforced by institution of prosecution or against whom such prosecution should be instituted. If the legislative field is within the enumerated heads in s. 91, then the final decision as to administrative policy, investigation and prosecution must be in federal hands. [...]

It first must be noted that s. 91(27) grants to the federal Parliament jurisdiction in "the Procedure in Criminal Matters" and that power is, by virtue of the concluding sentence of s. 91, exclusive to Parliament. Secondly and most important, s. 92(14) is by its very words limited to administration of justice "in the Province". I do not contend that those words mean the administration of justice in civil matters only for, in the same enumerated head, both "civil" and "criminal" are expressly mentioned and contrasted and it would have been inevitable that the draftsman would have inserted the word "civil" in the phrase "in the Province" if such a limitation were intended. But I am of the opinion that the words "in the Province" indicate that the legislator was concerned with the operation of the judicial machinery within the confines of the province and not with the vital matter of who should enforce and prosecute breaches of federal statutes. [...]

Duff C.J. said in *Reference Re Dom. Trade and Indust. Comm. Act*, [1936] S.C.R. 379 at p. 383:

We do not think it can be said that the authority to provide for the prosecution of criminal offences falls "strictly" within the subject "Criminal law and criminal procedure." – head 27 of the enumerated heads of section 91; but our view is that the authority to make such provision, and the authority to enact conditions in respect of the institution and the conduct of criminal proceedings is necessarily incidental to the powers given to the Parliament of Canada under head no. 27 (*Proprietary Articles Trade Assn. v. A.G. Can.*, [1931] A.C. 310 (P.C.) at 326-7)

> It is this view which I have attempted to express above. In the judgment of the Judicial Committee reported as *A.G. Ont. v. A.G. Can.; Reference Re Dom. Trade and Indust. Comm. Act* (1937), 67 C.C.C. 342, [1937] 1 D.L.R. 702, [1937] A.C. 405, it would appear, as a result of submissions by counsel representing the Attorney General of Canada, Lord Atkin took a much narrower view of the provision. [...]

He concluded by preferring the reasons above-quoted by Duff C.J. and in the result answered both questions in the affirmative.

I turn now to say a word about the recent judgment of the Ontario Court of Appeal in *Hoffmann-La Roche,* supra. Martin J.A., speaking for the court in that case, found himself substantially in agreement with Spence J. in *Hauser.* [...] Thus, he said (at p. 225):

> I am satisfied that, *at the least,* Parliament has concurrent jurisdiction with the provinces to enforce federal legislation validly enacted under head 27 of s. 91 which, like the *Combines Investigation Act,* is mainly directed at suppressing in the national interest, conduct which is essentially trans-provincial in its nature, operation and effects, and in respect of which the investigative function is performed by federal officials pursuant to powers validly conferred on them and using procedure which only Parliament can constitutionally provide.

And, again (at p. 228):

> In my view, the special investigative powers which have since its enactment been an integral part of the *Combines Investigation Act* place beyond question the authority of federal officers to enforce its provisions. I am also of the view that the conferring of those investigative powers falls within criminal procedure under s. 91(27). As Mr. Robinette aptly put it, it would be startling if the Attorney General of Canada can have the conduct of prosecutions under the *Narcotic Control Act* because that Act is not criminal law and cannot have the conduct of prosecutions under the *Combines Investigation Act* because it is criminal law.

Martin J.A. discussed *Di Iorio* at some length and pointed out the distinction which exists in the case before him. He said this (at pp. 228-9):

In *Di Iorio v. Montreal Jail Warden*, [1978] 1 S.C.R. 152 [...] the Supreme Court of Canada accepted that there is a degree of overlapping between the powers assigned to Parliament under s. 91(27) and those assigned to the provinces under s. 92(14) and that a matter which for some purpose may fall within the scope of the federal power over criminal law and procedure may also fall within the legitimate concern of the provinces as pertaining to the administration of justice (per Dickson J. at p. 207). [...]

Notwithstanding the overlapping between s. 91(27) and s. 92(14), manifestly it would not be within provincial competence to enact legislation enabling a police officer to summon a suspect before an official and submit the suspect to compulsory examination under oath with respect to his involvement in a crime. Even though such legislation might be described as legislation in relation to the investigation of offences and thus appear to fall within the category of the administration of justice, such legislation in pith and substance would be legislation in relation to criminal procedure and thus within the *exclusive* competence of Parliament.

Finally, returning to the *Combines Investigation Act*, he observed (at p. 230):

The provisions of the *Combines Investigation Act* empowering federal officials charged with the enforcement of the Act to compel any person resident or present in Canada to give evidence under oath has, as I have previously mentioned, been a characteristic feature of the Act since its enactment. Two things are obvious: the first is that Parliament evidently considered that ordinary police investigation by the province would not be effective to investigate the kinds of conduct at which the *Combines Investigation Act* strikes, and which seldom respects provincial boundaries. The second is that it would not be competent for a provincial legislature to vest these powers in provincial or federal officials for the purpose of investigating offences under the Act.

The subject matter of the investigation provided for in the Act and with respect to which witnesses may be compelled to give evidence, is not general conditions in a province with respect to the existence of combines or predatory pricing practices or the conditions favourable to their formation or operation. Rather, the investigation contemplated is the investigation of specific transactions in relation to specified offences under the Act, including offences under s. 34, to determine whether a prosecution is warranted. Frequently, the persons required to submit to compulsory examination under oath are suspected of having committed certain offences under the Act or are the officers of corporations suspected of having committed such offences and who as a result are potentially defendants in a subsequent prosecution. The investigative provisions of the *Combines Investigation Act* have never been successfully challenged, and indeed neither counsel for the appellant nor counsel for the Attorney General of Ontario before us challenged their validity. In *Reference Re Validity of Combines Investigation Act, supra*, Duff J., after pointing out that the Act, as its name imported, provided for the investigation of matter touching the existence of a combine or a pending combine, said [[1929] S.C.R. 409] and p. 418:

> The other point of view is that of responsibility of the Dominion with regard to the Criminal Law. The authority in relation to the Criminal Law and Criminal procedure given by s. 91(27) would appear to confer upon the Dominion, not as an incidental power merely, but as an essential part of it, the power to *provide for investigation into crime, actual and potential*. (The italics are Martin J.A.'s.)

> On appeal from the judgment of the Supreme Court of Canada the Judicial Committee of the Privy Council agreed with the opinion of the Supreme Court of Canada that no part of the *Combines Investigation Act* was *ultra vires*.

He concluded as follows (at p. 233):

> The validity of the provisions of the *Combines Investigation Act* vesting investigative powers in federal officers is, in my view, beyond question. The discharge of the investigative function by federal officials, and the vesting of the prosecutorial function *exclusively* in the Attorney General of the province would result in the very disunity which Dickson J. found unacceptable. Since the investigative function is validly vested in federal officers, the authority of Parliament to empower the Attorney General of Canada to initiate and conduct prosecutions under the Act is necessarily incident or ancillary to the scheme of the legislation, or to use the language of Laskin J.A. (as he then was) in *Papp v. Papp*, [1970] 1 O.R. 331 at 335-36, 8 D.L.R. (3d) 389 (C.A.), "there is a rational, functional connection" between the investigative procedures provided for in the Act and the vesting of prosecutorial power in the Attorney General of Canada under s. 15(2) of the Act.

> In my view, the vesting of prosecutorial powers in the Attorney General of Canada in respect of violations of the *Combines Investigation Act* does not offend any constitutional principle or any understanding that may have existed at the time of Confederation with respect to the enforcement of the criminal law.

Accordingly, I agree with the trial judge that even if the constitutional validity of the *Combines Investigation Act* depends on head 27 of s. 91 of the *B.N.A. Act*, it is within the legislative competence of Parliament as in s. 2 "Attorney General" (b) of the Code and s. 15(2) of the *Combines Investigation Act* to authorize the Attorney General of Canada to prefer indictments and have the conduct of prosecutions in respect of violations of that Act. [...]

Apart from the reasons in this court which I have produced, it is sufficient in my view to rely on the *Pelletier* case, the reasons of Spence J. in *Hauser* and the reasons of the Ontario Court of Appeal in the *Hoffman-La Roche* case. The reasons and decisions to which I refer lead to the conclusion that this appeal should be allowed, the judgment of the Alberta Court of Appeal set aside and the questions posed for decisions should be answered in the affirmative. I would add that the reasons of Martin J.A. in *Hoffman-La Roche* are in my view unassailable and, in themselves, would justify responding affirmatively to the federal claim of prosecutorial authority.

[Concurring reasons of Dickson J. are reproduced supra, p. 587. The concurring reasons of Beetz and Lamer JJ. are also omitted. In *R. v. Wetmore*, [1983] 2 S.C.R. 284 a six-person majority of the Court reaffirmed the reasons of Laskin, C.J.C. in *A.G. Canada v. C.N. Transport*, supra.]

6. Transportation and Communication

(a) General

ELIZABETH F. JUDGE, "THE INTERNET AND THE DIVISION OF POWERS"
[Original Contribution]

"Internet regulation" is an umbrella term that covers a wide range of potential legislative areas. A statute might regulate internet actors, such as internet service providers or content providers, internet infrastructure, internet content, or the application of traditional rights or causes of action in the internet context.

Jurisdiction issues preoccupy many discussions about internet regulation. When the internet was a relatively new communication medium, many observers thought that the internet was "borderless" and, as such, impervious to legal regulation, or at least extremely difficult to regulate. Since concepts of personal and adjudicative jurisdiction rely on geographical location and physical contacts, the argument was that jurisdiction concepts could not easily be applied to cyberspace. The characterization of the internet has evolved, so it is now viewed by many as a "cross-border" communication activity, which crosses both provincial and national borders, rather than as a "borderless" communication activity. It is true that the internet presents challenging issues for jurisdiction because of its "cross-border" nature, but general jurisdiction principles can and should be applied to the internet.

Legislative jurisdiction (or the division of legislative powers) determines whether Parliament or the provincial legislatures are constitutionally authorized to regulate the internet and whether the legislative power is exclusive or shared. Legislative jurisdiction relies on geographical location and physical contacts to a lesser extent than does personal and adjudicative jurisdiction. Determining whether Parliament or the provincial legislatures have power to regulate an aspect of the internet depends on classical constitutional analysis. A reviewing court must determine whether the pith and substance of the regulatory statute in question relates to a matter that comes within an enumerated head of power in sections 91 and 92 of the *Constitution Act, 1867*.[1]

The potential sources of federal jurisdiction for internet regulation include section 91 (29), interprovincial and international works and undertakings; section 91(2), trade and commerce; and the national concern branch of the residuary power inherent in the "peace, order and good government" clause that begins section 91. The potential sources of provincial jurisdiction include section 92 (10), "Local Works and Undertakings"; section 92(13), "Property and Civil Rights in the Province"; and section 92 (16), "Generally all Matters of a merely local or private Nature in the Province."

Section 92 (10) works together with section 91(29) to divide legislative power over communication and transportation between Parliament and the provincial legislatures. Section 92 (10) provides that the provinces have exclusive power to legislate in relation to "Local Works and Undertakings." Section 92 (10)(a) excepts from this grant of power shipping, railways, canals, and also "Telegraphs, and other Works and Undertakings connecting the Province with any other or others of the Provinces, or extending beyond the Limits of the Province." By a series of court decisions, the exception in section 92 (10)(a), read together with s. 91 (29), has come to mean that Parliament has exclusive legislative jurisdiction over interprovincial and international works and undertakings that relate to communication. The distinction between "works" and "undertakings" is not always rigorously maintained. Generally, a "work" is a physical thing and not a service; an "undertaking" is the arrangement in the course of which physical things are used rather than the physical thing itself. Undertakings are "organizations", "enterprises", or, more broadly, the communicative activity itself.

Section 92 (10) mentions specifically only "Telegraphs" as a mode of communication that is excepted from provincial legislative authority and transferred to Parliament. As mentioned, court decisions have extended this constitutional reference to telegraphs, so that s. 92 (10) now includes telephone,

---

1   See *Ward v. Canada (Attorney General)*, [2002] 1 S.C.R. 569; *Global Securities Corp. v. British Columbia (Securities Commission)*, [2000] 1 S.C.R. 494; *General Motors of Canada Ltd v. City National Leasing*, [1989] 1 S.C.R. 641 [*City National Leasing*].

radio, broadcast television and cable television within federal jurisdiction.[1] The legislative authority created by sections 92 (10)(a) and 91 (29) is "exclusive." This means that the initial classification of an undertaking as "interprovincial" or "local" is critical because the classification determines whether the undertaking is subject to regulation by Parliament or by the provincial legislatures. If an undertaking is classified as "interprovincial," Parliament has exclusive jurisdiction that extends broadly to cover regulation of content, operations, labour, equipment, facilities, and even activity which is entirely intraprovincial. The test looks at the nature of the service and asks whether the interprovincial service is "continuous and regular." The percentage of interprovincial activity, the location of the physical facilities, and the identification of the owners are not determinative.

For example, in *Alberta Government Telephones v. Canadian Radio-television and Telecommunications Commission*, the physical facilities of Alberta Government Telephones (AGT) were entirely within the province of Alberta.[2] Additionally, AGT carried telephone messages only within the borders of Alberta. However, AGT had cooperative arrangements with telephone companies outside Alberta so that its subscribers could make telephone calls to, and receive calls from, those who lived outside the province. Emphasizing the interprovincial cooperative agreements and telecommunications network, the Supreme Court of Canada held that AGT was an interprovincial undertaking, and thus subject to the exclusive legislative authority of Parliament.

Although there is little jurisprudence thus far to indicate how the courts will apply section 92(10)(a) to the internet, *AGT* has been used as a precedent to support federal jurisdiction. In *Island Telecom*,[3] the Canadian Industrial Relations Board concluded that an ISP met the definition of a federal work because the nature of its service is to give telecommunication access to an international network. Consistent with section 92 (10)(a) principles, the Board focused on the nature of the services offered by the ISP rather than the location of the physical infrastructure. The global character of the internet was critical to the Board's decision that the ISP's services were "interprovincial."

---

1   With respect to broadcasting, the CRTC in its 1999 "New Media" decision ruled that all services delivered over the internet would fall within the definition of "broadcasting" under the *Broadcasting Act*, and therefore within the CRTC's regulatory jurisdiction, with the exception of material that is predominantly alphanumeric text or which is significantly customizable by the individual user. *Report on New Media*, Broadcasting Public Notice CRTC 1999 -84 / Telecom Public Notice CRTC 99-14 (17 May 1999). Although the CRTC concluded that it had jurisdiction to regulate this new media material under the *Broadcasting Act*, it issued an order exempting from regulation "all new media broadcasting undertakings," which are defined as providing broadcasting services delivered and accessed over the internet. *Exemption order for new media broadcasting undertakings*, Public Notice CRTC 1999-197 (17 December 1999).

2   [1989] 2 S.C.R. 225.

3   [2000] C.I.R.B.D. No. 12.

Likewise in *City-TV*, the Board determined that webcasting and interactive services were equivalent to a section 92(10)(a) interprovincial communication activity.[1] A company that performed these services on a "continuous and regular" basis was held to be subject to the *Canada Labour Code*. This conclusion followed even though the company's primary activity was designing and marketing websites, an activity which, but for the interprovincial communications issue, would have fallen within the province's legislative authority under section 92 (13), property and civil rights. The Board emphasized the internet's "scope and complexity" and the "ubiquitous" nature of internet communications. The principle of exclusivity of jurisdiction that was entailed in finding an interprovincial communications undertaking brought all aspects of the undertaking, including labour relations, under federal jurisdiction.

Another source of federal jurisdiction is the trade and commerce power at section 91(2). Based on the criteria in *MacDonald v. Vapor Canada, Attorney General of Canada v. Canadian National Transportation,* and *General Motors of Canada v. City National Leasing,* federal jurisdiction of the internet could be defended by arguing that, given the internet's cross-border nature, the provinces were incapable of enacting effective legislation to regulate the internet. Any legislative scheme would be jeopardized if one of the provinces failed to enact an appropriate statute.[2]

The national concern branch of the "peace, order and good government" clause might also sustain federal jurisdiction in relation to internet regulation. This power has been used to sustain federal jurisdiction in relation to radio and television communication. One factor used to justify invocation of the "national concern" doctrine is that the matter be a "genuinely new problem" which did not

---

1   *Communications, Energy and Paperworkers Union of Canada,* applicant, and CITY-TV, CHUM City Prod. Ltd., MuchMusic Network and BRAVO!, Division of CHUM Ltd., employer, [1999] C.I.R.B.D. No. 22.

2   *MacDonald v. Vapour Can. Ltd.,* [1977] 2 S.C.R. 134; *Attorney General of Canada v. Canadian National Transportation, Ltd.,* [1983] 2 S.C.R. 693; *City National Leasing, supra* note 1 at 661-662. A unanimous Supreme Court recently applied and affirmed the *City National Leasing* test in *Kirkbi AG v. Ritvik Holdings Inc.,* [2005] 3 S.C.R. 302. *Kirkbi* involved a division of powers issue with respect to Parliament's codification of the common law tort of passing off as s. 7(b) of the *Trade-marks Act.* The Court upheld section 7(b) as a proper exercise of the general trade and commerce power. Even though section 7(b) standing alone encroached on the province's jurisdiction over property and civil rights, it was *intra vires* Parliament. The intrusion on provincial power over property and civil rights was minimal and the section rounded out the otherwise incomplete federal regulatory scheme for trade-marks, which is a valid exercise of Parliament's general trade and commerce power.

exist at the time of Confederation.[1] The newness requirement is met in the case of the internet. Indeed, Bastarache J. has remarked that cyberspace is "perhaps the most stunning example of a technological innovation which defies traditional legal models" and that it is "hardly an exaggeration to say that cyberspace is sufficiently distinct from any other model of communication and human interaction that almost every important issue in civil law, and many in the criminal context, may need to be reviewed according to the particular circumstances of this new technology."[2] One caveat here is that while the internet is itself a new legal problem, legislation that regulates the internet may be classified in relation to some other matter, such as crime, and that other matter may not be "novel." A second caution relates to whether, in the relevant sense, regulation of the internet is a "Matter" at all.[3] As a subject matter of constitutional jurisdiction the internet may simply lack the required singleness and indivisibility required by the constitutional cases. It is possible, perhaps likely, that the internet is "an aggregate of several subjects [of constitutional jurisdiction] some of which form a substantial part of provincial jurisdiction."[4]

As long as the internet is a global medium, provincial jurisdiction will be difficult to defend because the grants of exclusive jurisdiction are limited to subjects "in the province." Section 92(13) covers property and civil rights in the province, section 92(16) covers matters of a "local or private nature in the province" and section 92(10) covers intraprovincial local works and undertakings. Moreover, although the 92(10)(c) declaratory power has been used sparingly, Parliament could bring a local work involving the internet under federal jurisdiction by declaring the work to be for the "general advantage of Canada."

A significant area where division of powers issues have been debated in the context of internet regulation is with respect to whether the provinces or the federal government has jurisdiction to regulate internet privacy. Privacy is a complicated division of powers subject because, depending on the context and the purpose of the legislation, privacy can fall within the provincial power under

---

1 *R. v. Hauser*, [1979] 1 S.C.R. 984 at 1000-1001; *R. v. Crown Zellerbach Can. Ltd.*, [1988] 1 S.C.R. 401, *per* Le Dain, J. ("The National concern doctrine applies to both new matters which did not exist at Confederation and to matters which [...] have since [...] become matters of national concern." Of course, to qualify under this doctrine, the subject regulated must be a "Matter" in the constitutionally relevant sense (see fn. 7). It may be questioned whether, in this sense, the internet qualifies.

2 *The Challenge of the Law in the New Millennium* (1997-1998), 25 Man. L.J. Paras. 11 and 13.

3 For a matter to qualify as a matter of national concern, "[i]t must have a singleness, distinctiveness and indivisibility that clearly distinguishes it from matters of provincial concern and a scale of impact on provincial jurisdiction that is reconcilable with the fundamental distribution of legislative power under the Constitution," *R. v. Crown Zellerbach Can. Ltd.*, [1988] 1 S.C.R. 401, *per* Le Dain, J.

4 *Re Anti-Inflation Act*, [1976] 2 S.C.R. 373 *per* Beetz J.

property and civil rights or within the federal power. Parliament exercised authority to regulate privacy in the *Personal Information Protection and Electronic Documents Act* (PIPEDA), a federal statute enacted in 2000, which protects information privacy on the internet by regulating private actors.[1] The statute applied immediately to any "federal work, undertaking or business". This language appears to connect Parliament's authority to section 92(10)(a) concepts, which, as we have seen, extend federal authority to all aspects of an interprovincial work or undertaking in communication. After a phase-in period of three years, PIPEDA also applied to intraprovincial activities if the province had failed to enact its own substantially similar privacy legislation within that time period. Parliament thus used a model of conditional legislation with an opt-out provision that provided for concurrent constitutional jurisdiction. Under PIPEDA, a single set of rules applies to protect personal information which is collected, used, or disclosed in commercial activity, including activity that take places on the internet.

The expansion of PIPEDA's application from federal works, undertakings and businesses to encompass intraprovincial activities has been defended by the federal government based on the general federal trade and commerce power under section 91(2). The arguments in support of this exercise of federal power are that the protection of personal information in electronic commerce is a matter of national concern, that legislation limited to international and interprovincial trade would not be effective, and that it is important to have a single standard and a single level of protection which apply across Canada.

In 2003, the province of Quebec challenged the constitutionality of PIPEDA based on federalism grounds.[2] It referred a question to the Quebec Court of Appeal, asking whether the privacy provisions of PIPEDA exceeded Parliament's legislative authority. Quebec has its own statute to protect personal information which has been found to be "substantially similar" to PIPEDA, and therefore the intraprovincial activity of Quebec businesses and organizations are exempted from PIPEDA.[3] However, Quebec is arguing that the federal government's right to review the provincial privacy statutes to determine if they are "substantially similar" to PIPEDA is incompatible with federalism principles. This case is pending at this writing in 2007.

Technological developments have already affected theories about jurisdiction to regulate the internet which rest on the assumption that the internet is borderless. As digital communications have evolved, it is often possible to

---

1   S.C. 2000, c. 5.

2   *Government of Quebec, Order-in-Council 1368-2003-12-30* (17 December 2003), *Concerning a reference to the Court of Appeal relating to the* Personal Information Protection and Electronic Documents Act (S.C. 2000, c. 5).

3   *Organizations in the Province of Quebec Exemption Order*, SOR/2003-374 (19 November 2003), P.C. 2003-1842, online: *Canada Gazette* 137: 25 (3 December 2003), http://canadagazette.gc.ca/partII/2003/20031203/html/sor374-e.html.

locate geographically where internet activity is taking place, as for example, to identify the place where internet communications originate and are received; this fact is already relevant to the prosecution of child pornography and hate crime offenses. The initial view of the internet as a borderless network is being revised toward a view of the internet as a cross-border network, with aspects that implicate provincial jurisdiction and aspects that implicate federal jurisdiction. As technological developments continue to erode the borderless character of internet communications, courts may become increasingly confident in the application of classical methods of constitutional analysis to federalism challenges to internet regulatory statutes.

CONSTITUTION ACT, 1867 (U.K.)
c. 3, ss. 91-2

91. It shall be lawful for the Queen, by and with the Advice and Content of the Senate and House of Commons, to make Laws for the Peace, Order, and good Government of Canada, in relation to all Matters not coming within the Classes of Subjects by this Act assigned exclusively to the Legislatures of the Provinces; and for greater Certainty, but not so as to restrict the Generality of the foregoing Terms of this Section, it is hereby declared that (notwithstanding anything in this Act) the exclusive   Legislative

Authority of the Parliament of Canada extends to all Matters coming within the Classes of Subjects next hereinafter enumerated; that is to say,– [...]

9. Beacons, Buoys, Lighthouses, and Sable Island.
10. Navigation and Shipping. [...]
13. Ferries between a Province and any British or Foreign Country or between Two Provinces....
29. Such Classes of Subjects as are expressly excepted in the Enumeration of the Classes of Subjects by this Act assigned exclusively to the Legislatures of the Provinces.

92. In each Province the Legislature may exclusively make Laws in relation to Matters coming within the Classes of Subject next herein-after enumerated; that is to say,– [...]

> 10. Local Works and Undertakings other than such as are of the following Classes:–
> (a) Lines of Steam or other Ships, Railways, Canals, Telegraphs, and other Works and Undertakings connecting the Province with any other or others of the Provinces, or extending beyond the Limits of the Province;
> (b) Lines of Steam Ships between the Province and any British or Foreign Country;
> (c) Such Works as, although wholly situate within the Province, are before or after their Execution declared by the Parliament of Canada to be for the general Advantage of Canada or for the Advantage of Two or more of the Provinces.

(b)   Federal Jurisdiction

(i)   Introduction

A.G. ONT. v. WINNER
[1954] A.C. 541(P.C.).

[The problem with which the Board were confronted in the present appeal was concerned with the conflicting jurisdiction of the Parliament of Canada on the one part, and on the other part of the legislation and regulations of the province of New Brunswick made under its local Acts.

The parties immediately concerned were originally (1), as defendant, one Winner who resided in the United States of America and was in the business (inter alia) of operating motor buses for the carriage of passengers and goods for hire or payment from Boston through the State of Maine and the province of New Brunswick to Glace Bay in the province of Nova Scotia and intermediately, and (2) as plaintiff, the respondent S.M.T. (Eastern) Ltd., which held licences granted by the Motor Carrier Board of the province of New Brunswick to operate motor buses for hire or payment over certain highways, which need not be further specified, between St. Stephen and the City of St. John, both in New Brunswick.

In substance the plaintiff's claim was for an injunction against the defendant restraining him from embussing and debussing (taking up or setting down) passengers within the province of New Brunswick, and a declaration that he had no right to do so. In his defence the defendant stated that he had in fact embussed and debussed passengers in the province and that he intended to continue doing so unless and until some court of competent jurisdiction should declare that he was legally debarred therefrom.]

LORD PORTER [for the Court]: — [...] [T]here was an appeal, by special leave, to their Lordships' Board by the Attorney-General for Ontario and others against that part of the judgment [of the S.C.C.] which permitted any kind of picking up or setting down within the province of New Brunswick whether in the course of a journey beginning outside the province and ending within it or in the course of a journey beginning with it and ending without the province. There was also a cross-appeal by Mr. Winner and others against the prohibition of purely intra-state traffic, that is, carriage from one point within the province to another point also within it.

Before their Lordships when dealing with the matter of the appeal it was urged (1) that Mr. Winner's business did not come within the exception contained in section 92(10)(a), and (2) that in any case the province as owner of, or as being in control of, its highways had jurisdiction over them not only to licence operations upon them but to regulate them in all respects. By virtue, it was said, of the powers of the province to control provincial highways and traffic, the Motor Carrier Board had power to grant or refuse a licence to Mr. Winner at their discretion. It was acknowledged that it had in fact granted him a licence, but asserted that the condition attached to the licence was merely a condition upon which he became entitled to operate upon the highways of the province, not a regulation of his business or undertaking.

The first proposition involves a close and careful consideration of the terms and effect of section 92(10)(a). The argument was put in a number of ways. In the first place it was said that works and undertakings must be read conjunctively, that the subsection has no operation unless the undertaking is both a work and an undertaking – the former a physical thing and the latter its use. There was, it was maintained, in the present instance no work, and the existence of a work was an essential element in order to make the subsection applicable. The necessity for the existence of both elements might, it was said, be illustrated by considering the case of a railway, where there was both a track and the carriage of goods and passengers over it, and in construing the words "works and undertaking" regard must be paid to the words associated with them in the subsection.

Their Lordships do not accept the argument that the combination of a work and an undertaking is essential if the subsection is to apply. Perhaps the simplest method of controverting it is to point out that the section begins by giving jurisdiction to the provinces over local works and undertakings. If, then, the argument were to prevail, the province would have no jurisdiction except in a case where the subject-matter was both a work and an undertaking. If it were not both, but only one or the other, the province would have no authority to deal with it, and at any rate under this section local works which were not also undertakings and local undertakings which were not works would not be subject to the jurisdiction of the province – a result which, so far as the Justices are aware, has never yet been contemplated. Moreover, in subsection (10)(c) the word "works" is found uncombined with the word "undertakings," a circumstance which leads to the inference that the words are to be read disjunctively so that if either works or undertakings connect the province with others or extend beyond its limits, the Dominion, and the Dominion alone, is empowered to deal with them. The case of steamships is an even more potent example of the difficulty of reconciling the suggested construction with the wording of the section. Lines of steamships between the province and any British or foreign country can carry on their operations without the existence of any works. The only connecting link which they provide is by passing to and fro from the one to the other. Their Lordships must accordingly reject the suggestion that the existence of some material work is of the essence of the exception. As in ships so in buses it is enough that there is a connecting undertaking.

It is true, and was contended, that it is possible to postulate that section 92(10) has a limited scope and deals only with matters which are both works and undertakings. Works alone and undertakings alone are in this aspect entrusted to the province under subsection (13) as being property and civil rights, or under (16) as being matters of a merely local or private nature in the province. It was argued, accordingly, that jurisdiction over inter-connecting works and undertakings is given to the Dominion under the general words inserted at the beginning and end of section 91 but not under section 92(10). In terms, however, the language of section 92(10)(*c*) embraces a wider subject-matter and, in their Lordships' view, is not confined to so limited a construction. All local works and all local undertakings are included under the phraseology used, and it is in their Lordships' opinion immaterial that *ex abundante cautela* they are again covered by subsection (13).

If the province is given authority over both local works and local undertakings it follows that the exceptional works and undertakings in subsection (10)(*a*) likewise comprise both matters.

Some illumination is, as their Lordships think, given by a consideration of the decision in the *Radio* case. [...]

The *Radio* case [...] expressly applies the provisions of section 92(10): "Their Lordships," it is said, draw special attention to the provisions of head (10) of section 92. These provisions, as has been explained in several judgments of the Board, have the effect of reading the excepted matters into the preferential place enjoyed by the enumerated subjects of section 91." After quoting the words of this subsection, the judgment continues: "Now, does broadcasting fall within the excepted matters? Their Lordships are of opinion that it does, falling in (a) within both the word `telegraphs' and the general words `undertakings connecting the province with any other or others of the provinces or extending beyond the limits of the province.'" Later the judgment proceeds to say "undertaking is not a physical thing but is an arrangement under which of course physical things are used."

In their Lordships' view, these expressions are directly applicable to the present case. In the *Radio* case there was no connecting work, only a connecting undertaking, unless the somewhat fanciful suggestion were to be adopted that the flow of an electric discharge across the frontier of a province is to be regarded as a physical connexion.

It is argued that the provinces are entrusted with local works and undertakings subject, however, to the exception that they must be "other than such as are in the following classes," and that on its true construction the section must mean "other than such *local* works and undertakings as are within those exceptions." The submission goes on to maintain that ex concessus Mr. Winner's work or undertaking is not local, having no anchorage, as it were, within the province, and for that reason is not within the exception. Their Lordships' Board does not so read the subsection. In their opinion "other than such" merely means such works and such undertakings as are within the categories thereafter set out.

The argument can be tested by considering its effect upon one of the specific subjects mentioned, e.g., railways. A railway is an exception to local works and undertakings because it is included in the words "other than such," etc. But if the appellants' argument is sound the section must mean local works and undertakings other than such local works and undertakings as are in the category of railways; and, as the exception only includes *local* works, it would take local railways out of the jurisdiction of the province, which it does not, and would not comprehend interconnecting railways, which have always been held to be included, and the inclusion of which is obviously one of the objects of the subsection.

One further point was put forward upon this aspect of the case. It was suggested that, whatever view be taken of the matters with which their Lordships have dealt, yet Mr. Winner's activity never became an undertaking until he received a licence; until then it was but a project; he could not get to work before he had a licence. It was true, the argument went on, that he had obtained a licence, but his licence only permitted him to run through New Brunswick without embarking or disembarking passengers. That was his undertaking and, so far as New Brunswick was concerned, it could not be enlarged by a claim that it was an inter-provincial or inter-national undertaking.

Their Lordships are not prepared to accept the contention that an undertaking has no existence until it is carried into effect or is capable of being lawfully carried out. It may be an undertaking at any rate if the promoter has done everything which was necessary on his part to put it in motion, and has made all the essential arrangements. Indeed, the argument that the undertaking did not come into existence until a licence was granted and the transporting actually began is, in their Lordships' view, inconsistent with the opinion expressed by the Board in *Toronto Corporation v. Bell Telephone Company of Canada.* [...]

In any case Mr. Winner had obtained a licence and has been exercising a business of transportation under it and has not limited his undertaking to the terms of his licence.

[...] The second contention put forward on behalf of the appellants was that whatever their exact legal position with regard to the roads, they admittedly make, maintain and control them; the roads are local works and undertakings constructed and maintained by the province; in that capacity it is entitled to regulate their use in any way it pleases and, indeed, to prohibit their use if it so wishes. The contention is an important one because, if it is true, interprovincial undertakings connecting one province with another are within the jurisdiction of the Dominion, but can be totally sterilized by Acts and regulations of the province curtailing or preventing the use of its roads. It was alleged that the roads are property in the province – as indeed they are – that roads of one province are divided by an imaginary line from those of another province or another nation at the point of meeting: there is therefore no connecting work and, their roads being local, the province has absolute power over their uses, i.e., both the method of use and whether they may or not be used at all.

Their Lordships are not concerned to dispute either the provincial control of the roads or that it has the right of regulation, but there nevertheless remains the question of the limit of control in any individual instance and the extent of the powers of regulation.

It would not be desirable, nor do their Lordships think that it would be possible, to lay down the precise limits within which the use of provincial highways may be regulated. Such matters as speed, the side of the road upon which to drive, the weight and lights of vehicles are obvious examples, but in the present case their Lordships are not faced with considerations of this kind, nor are they concerned with the further question which was mooted before them, viz., whether a province had it in its power to plough up its roads and so make interprovincial connections impossible. So isolationist a policy is indeed unthinkable. The roads exist and in fact form a connexion with other provinces and also, in this case, with another country. Since in their Lordships' opinion Mr. Winner is carrying on an undertaking connecting New Brunswick both with Nova Scotia and the State of Maine there exists an undertaking connecting province with province and extending beyond the limits of the province.

Prima facie at any rate, such an undertaking is entrusted to the control of the Dominion and taken out of that of the province. No doubt if it were not for section 92(10)(*a*) of the *British North America Act* the province, having jurisdiction over local works and undertakings and over property and civil rights within the province, could have prohibited the use of, or exercised complete autocratic control over, its highways, but the subsection in question withdraws this absolute right where the undertaking is a connecting one. To this limitation some meaning must be given, and their Lordships cannot accept the view that the jurisdiction of the Dominion is impaired by the province's general right of control over its own roads. So to construe this subsection would, in their Lordships' opinion, destroy the efficacy of the exception.

The limitation of the jurisdiction of Dominion and province has been many times canvassed and litigated both in the Canadian courts and in the Privy Council. Undoubtedly the province has wide powers of regulation. Many instances were adduced in the course of argument and their Lordships may refer to certain of those most relied upon. [...]

[In] *Great West Saddlery Co. Ltd. v. The King,* where the gist of the decision may be taken from the headnote where it says:

> A company incorporated by the Dominion under the *Companies Act of Canada* [...] with power to trade in any province may, consistently with sections 91 and 92 of the *British North America Act, 1867,* be subject to provincial laws of general application, such as laws imposing taxes, or relating to mortmain or requiring licences for certain purposes, or as to the form of contracts.

For the same reasons it was held in *Lymburn v. Mayland* that a provision prohibiting the selling of the shares of Dominion companies was not ultra vires provincial legislation inasmuch as it did not preclude them from selling their shares unless they were registered but merely subjected them to competent provisions applying to all persons trading in securities.

Both the latter cases, however, are careful to point out that legislation will be invalid if a Dominion company is sterilized in all its functions and activities or its status and essential capacities are impaired in a substantial degree. What provisions have the effect of sterilizing all the functions and activities of a company or impair its status and capacities in an essential degree will, of course, depend on the circumstances of each case, but in the present instance their Lordships cannot have any doubt but that the Act or the licence or both combined do have such an effect on Mr. Winner's undertaking in its task of connecting New Brunswick with both the United States of America and with the province of Nova Scotia.

Nor indeed, whatever may be said of the Act, is the licence a provision applying to all persons. It is a particular provision aimed at preventing Mr. Winner from competing with local transport companies in New Brunswick.

But, it is contended, there are two rights – that of the Dominion and that of the province – one giving power to the one body and the other to the other, and enabling Dominion or province to pass legislation dealing with its own topic: the province with its roads and the Dominion with connecting undertakings. So long as the Dominion has not, as it has not, passed legislation dealing with the matter, the powers overlap and the province is entitled to enact its own provisions which, unless and until the Dominion deals with the matter, are valid and enforceable. This argument does not appear to have been presented to the courts in Canada and their Lordships do not agree with it.

The province has indeed authority over its own roads, but that authority is a limited one and does not entitle it to interfere with connecting undertakings. It must be remembered that it is the undertaking, not the roads, which comes within the jurisdiction of the Dominion, but legislation which denies the use of provincial roads to such an undertaking or sterilizes the undertaking itself is an interference with the prerogative of the Dominion.

Whatever provisions or regulations a province may prescribe with regard to its roads it must not prevent or restrict inter-provincial traffic. As their Lordships have indicated, this does not in any way prevent what is in essence traffic regulation, but the provisions contained in local statutes and regulations must be confined to such matters.

In the present case they are not so confined. They do not contain provisions as to the use of the highways – they are not even general regulations affecting all users of them. They deal with a particular undertaking in a particular way and prohibit Mr. Winner from using the highways except as a means of passage from another country to another State. It does not indeed follow that a regulation of universal application is necessarily unobjectionable – each case must depend upon its own facts – but such a regulation is less likely to offend against the limitation imposed on the jurisdiction of the province inasmuch as it will deal with all traffic and not with that connecting province and province. The question as their Lordships see it, and indeed as it was argued, raises the hackneyed consideration what is the pith and substance of the provision under consideration. Is it in substance traffic regulation or is it an interference with an undertaking connecting province and province? Their Lordships cannot doubt but that it was the latter. It obviously sought to limit activities of an undertaking connecting the State of Maine with New Brunswick and New Brunswick with Nova Scotia. It was not mere regulation of road traffic. [...]

In their Lordships' opinion the action of the province was an incursion into the field reserved by the *British North America Act* to the Dominion. In coming to this conclusion their Lordships refrain from deciding whether the Act or the regulations or both are beyond the powers of the province. It may be that the Act can be so read as to apply to provincial matters only. If this be so, the licence given to Mr. Winner is an unauthorized limitation of his rights, because it is for the Dominion alone to exercise either by Act or by regulation control over connecting undertakings. On the other hand, it may be that the Act itself must be construed as interfering with undertakings connecting province with province or with another country. In either case the province, either through the Act itself or through the licence issued in pursuance of regulations made under the Act, has exceeded its jurisdiction. The licence, indeed, may be good as a licence, but the limitation imposed in it is *ultra vires and of no effect*.

There remains, however, the further question whether, although the licence cannot be limited in the manner imposed by the board, Mr. Winner can, nevertheless, as the Supreme Court adjudged, be prohibited from taking up and setting down purely provincial passengers, i.e., those whose journey both begins and ends within the province. So far as the Justices are able to judge, none of the parties and none of the interveners suggested such a compromise in any of the courts in Canada.

Their Lordships might, however, accede to the argument if there were evidence that Mr. Winner was engaged in two enterprises, one within the province and the other of a connecting nature. Their Lordships, however, cannot see any evidence of such a dual enterprise. The same buses carried both types of passenger along the same routes; the journeys may have been different, in that one was partly outside the province and the other wholly within, but it was the same undertaking which was engaged in both activities.

The Supreme Court, however, approached the question from a different angle. To them a distinction should be drawn between what was an essential and what an incidental portion of the enterprise. In their view the portion which could be shed without putting an end to it did not constitute an essential part of the undertaking and, therefore, could be dealt with by the province, leaving only the essential part for the Dominion's jurisdiction.

Their Lordships are of opinion that this method of approach results from a misapprehension of the true construction of section 92(10)(*a*) of the *British North America Act*. The question is not what portions of the undertaking can be stripped from it without interfering with the activity altogether; it is rather what is the undertaking which is in fact being carried on. Is there one undertaking, and as part of that one undertaking does the respondent carry passengers between two points both within the province, or are there two?

[...]

No doubt the taking up and setting down of passengers journeying wholly within the province could be severed from the rest of Mr. Winner's undertaking, but so to treat the question is not to ask is there an undertaking and does it form a connexion with other countries or other provinces, but can you emasculate the actual undertaking and yet leave it the same undertaking or so divide it that part of it can be regarded as inter-provincial and the other part as provincial.

The undertaking in question is in fact one and indivisible. It is true that it might have been carried on differently and might have been limited to activities within or without the province, but it is not, and their Lordships do not agree that the fact that it might be carried on otherwise than it is makes it or any part of it any the less an interconnecting undertaking.

[...] In coming to this conclusion their Lordships must not be supposed to lend any countenance to the suggestion that a carrier who is substantially an internal carrier can put himself outside provincial jurisdiction by starting his activities a few miles over the border. Such a subterfuge would not avail him. The question is whether in truth and in fact there is an internal activity prolonged over the border in order to enable the owner to evade provincial jurisdiction or whether in pith and substance it is interprovincial. Just as the question whether there is an inter-connecting undertaking is one depending on all the circumstances of the case, so the question whether it is a camouflaged local undertaking masquerading as an interconnecting one must also depend on the facts of each case and on a determination of what is the pith and substance of an Act or regulation.

Of course, as has so often been pointed out, whether upon the evidence adduced an activity can be adjudged to be local is a matter of law, but once it is decided that it can be local the question whether it is so is one of fact for the relevant tribunal to determine. In the case under consideration no such question arises, the undertaking is one connecting the province with another and extending beyond the limits of the province and therefore comes within the provisions of section 92(10)(a) and is solely within the jurisdiction of the Dominion.

The appeal was dismissed.

- Research Note -
INTERPROVINCIAL UNDERTAKINGS IN TRANSPORTATION AND COMMUNICATIONS

In *Re Tank Truck Tpt.*, [1960] O.R. 497, 25 D.L.R. (2d) 161, the Ontario High Court had to determine whether a trucking operation that conducted only 6 per cent of its activity beyond the province properly fell within the exclusive jurisdiction of Parliament under s. 92(10)(a). The Court determined that it did. McLennan J. rejected the argument of the respondent that the determination of whether an undertaking was interprovincial should be made on the basis of main or primary function, and that to ignore relative volume of activity would mean that any extraprovincial transportation would bring the undertaking under Dominion Jurisdiction. He stated at p. 170 (D.L.R.):

> In my opinion the *Winner* case does not support the contention of counsel for the respondent that the interconnecting operation must be the main function of the undertaking to come within s. 92(10)(*a*).
>
> The inference seems to be the other way and to paraphrase Lord Porter's words at p. 679 D.L.R., p. 581 A.C., p. 248 C.R.T.C., the only question, apart from a camouflaged local undertaking, is whether there is one undertaking and as a part of that undertaking does the applicant carry goods beyond the Province so as to connect Ontario and Quebec or extend beyond the limits of Ontario into the United States. [...]
>
> I agree with counsel for the respondent that not every undertaking capable of connecting Provinces or capable of extending beyond the limits of a Province does so in fact. The words "connecting" and "extending" in s. 92(10)(*a*) must be given some significance. For example a trucking company or a taxicab company taking goods or passengers occasionally and at irregular intervals from one Province to another could hardly be said to be an undertaking falling within s. 92(10)(*a*). As appears from the *Winner* case and the *Underwater Gas Developers* case "undertaking" involves activity and I think that to connect or extend, that activity must be continuous and regular, but if the facts show that a particular undertaking is continuous and regular, as the undertaking is in this case, then it does in fact connect or extend and falls within the exception in s. 10(*a*) regardless of whether it is of greater or less in extent than that which is carried on within the Province. The theory put forward by counsel for the respondent that the main and primary function of an undertaking, determined by volume, is a test to be applied to decide whether undertakings fall within s. 92(10)(*a*) must inevitably be a question of percentages. There is no sound principle upon which the line can be drawn. Should it be 60%, 70% or 80%? [...]

An appeal to the Ontario Court of Appeal, [1963]1 O.R. 272, 36 D.L.R. (2d) 636 was dismissed without reasons. See also: *R. v. Cooksville Magistrate's Court, ex parte Liquid Cargo Lines Ltd.*, [1965] 1 O.R. 84, 46 D.L.R. (2d) 700 wherein Haines J. held that interprovincial transport activity amounting to only 1.6% of applicants' service satisfied the requirement of "continuous and regular". He stated at p. 88 (O.R.):

> In my view, the fact that many of the applicant's extraprovincial trips are not made at fixed times in accordance with a predetermined schedule does not compel the conclusion that its

activity in that regard is not continuous and regular. Viewed from the point of view of the applicant company, it is clear that its customers are provided with extra-provincial service consistently and without interruption whenever they apply to the applicant for such service. The applicant stands ready at any time to engage in hauls outside the boundaries of the Province of Ontario at the instance of any of its customers, and for that purpose has gone to the pains and expense of acquiring transport permits and licences from a number of jurisdictions. Further, the evidence is clear that it has made such trips frequently during the period for which figures have been provided.

This case, however, should be contrasted with *Invictus Ltd. v. Man. Lab. Bd.* (1967), 62 W.W.R. 150, 65 D.L.R. (2d) 517 (*sub nom. R. v. Man. Lab. Bd., Ex parte Invictus Ltd.*) (Man.) in which Matas, J. rejected the view that the applicant's business fell under federal jurisdiction. The conclusion was reached notwithstanding that 5.5% of the company's gross revenues resulted from extraprovincial transport. While he agreed with the view expressed in *Re Tank Truck Tpt.*, above, Matas J. considered it to be stretching the meaning of the words "regular and continuous" to so categorize the applicant's extraprovincial activity. After noting that the company's intraprovincial business was conducted on a regular basis and the extraprovincial business was casual – trips undertaken in response to requests for the transport of horses – he concluded by stating at 529 (D.L.R.):

> In constitutional cases, no less than in other cases coming before the Court, it is necessary that the realities of the situation be assessed. The operations of the applicant, when examined from a practical aspect, are in pith and substance provincial in character. The applicant's extraprovincial transport of horses is incidental to what is essentially and basically an intraprovincial business.

> I am of the opinion that the extraprovincial traffic conducted by the applicant does not form part of an "extending or connecting" link as envisaged by s. 92(10)(*a*) of the *B.N.A. Act* and s. 53(*b*) of the *Industrial Relations and Disputes Investigation Act*. I conclude that, under the circumstances, the applicant's business falls within the jurisdiction of the provincial legislation. The application is dismissed with costs.

R. v. Man. Lab. Bd., Ex parte Invictus, above, reflects a more realistic judicial approach. The decision reflects the view that in order to characterize properly a work or undertaking as inter or intraprovincial, the operation must be examined from a "practical aspect". The court must determine whether, in pith and substance, the activity of *this* undertaking can be properly categorized as interprovincial in character. This is to be contrasted with comparing the features of the activity with a "test of general application" to be elicited from previous decisions, and making the determination on that basis. "Regular and continuous" is such a test. The problem with employing such a test is that it simply may not be suitable having regard to the nature of the service under examination.

In *Re Windsor Airline Limousine Services Ltd. and Ont. Taxi Assn. 1688* (1980), 30 O.R. (2d) 732, 117 D.L.R. (3d) 400 the Ontario Divisional Court had to determine whether a taxi service receiving 1 or 2 per cent of its business from trans-border business would be properly categorized as operating an interprovincial undertaking. It had been argued by counsel that the authorities suggested a test of general application against which the particular determination could be made. Concluding that the activity of the company was clearly intraprovincial in character, Reid. J., for the court, stated at p. 735 (O.R.):

> [...] [T]here does seem to be a spirit common to the language of both *Winner* and *Montcalm*. I think that together they provide a guideline that is applicable to cases of the type before us when they now arise.
>
> I find no essential difference between the concept expressed in *Winner* in terms of the "pith and substance" of a commercial undertaking from that expressed in *Montcalm* where the nature of the operation is, as I read that case, to be elicited from the ordinary activity of the undertaking. As I read *Montcalm* it requires that on the facts before us we consider the main or predominant business of the undertaking: what in *Montcalm* is described as its "ordinary" as opposed to its "exceptional" activity. That, in my opinion, satisfies as well the search for the pith and substance of the enterprise.

In *Re Ottawa-Carleton Regional Transit Commission and Amalgamated Transit Union, Local 279 et al.* (1983), 44 O.R. (2d) 560, 4 D.L.R. (4th) 452, the Ontario Court of Appeal had to consider whether a bus passenger service that serves both Ottawa and Hull should be classified as a provincial undertaking. Less than one-half of 1% of the total distance traveled by the transit commission was on the interprovincial routes. Cory J.A., writing for the court, held that because buses connected Ontario and Quebec on a regularly scheduled basis, the undertaking was properly classified as federal. In his reasons, Cory J.A. explicitly rejected the test outlined by Reid J. in *Windsor Airline Limousine Service Ltd.,* supra. At p. 570 (O.R.), Cory J.A. wrote:

> I believe the wrong test was applied in that case. A percentage of business test should not govern the determination.
>
> There are difficulties inherent in a quantitative approach. For example, the question must always arise, where should the line be drawn in any particular case? Should the crucial ratio be 80-20, 90-10, 95-5 or 60-40? If a quantitative approach is to be taken, then should a very large corporation with a small but regular extraprovincial business representing 4% of its operations be in a different category from a small concern with the same amount of extraprovincial business but, because of its smaller total operation, the extraprovincial work amounting to 50% of its total? Should the labour relations of the smaller concern be regulated by a different body than those of the larger

business? In my view, the quantitative approach should not be adopted. Rather, the determination of the essential issue as to whether the undertaking constitutes interprovincial should be based upon the continuity and regularity of the connecting operation or extraprovincial business.

In *Re R. and Cottrell Forwarding Co.* (1981), 33 O.R. (2d) 486, 12 M.V.R. 277, 124 D.L.R. (3d) 674 (Div. Ct.), the appellant shipping company did not perform an interprovincial transportation service itself. Rather, it assembled freight at three locations in Ontario and arranged for transportation of the goods to western Canada. The actual transportation was carried out by its own subsidiary companies, by independent truckers, or by one of the national railways. Cottrell did not possess or operate any of the equipment that transported the goods, nor did it lease or have exclusive dominion and control over railway cars that were used.

Cottrell was charged pursuant to the *Public Commercial Vehicles Act*, R.S.O. 1970, c. 375 with operating as an unlicensed freight forwarder. An acquittal was entered in the Provincial Court on the grounds that the business operations of Cottrell constituted an extraprovincial undertaking and therefore were not subject to provincial legislation. Henry J. subsequently allowed an appeal from that decision and convicted Cottrell. On further appeal to the Divisional Court, it was necessary to determine whether the appellant company fell within the meaning of "interprovincial undertaking". Steele J. speaking for the Court dismissed the appeal. He stated at p. 490 (O.R.):

> The Courts have consistently resisted attempts to divide business enterprises into distinct undertakings: see *Capital Cities Communications Inc. et al. v. Canadian Radio-Television Com'n et al.*, [1978] 2 S.C.R. 141. It is also clear that it is the pith and substance of the undertaking as a whole that must be considered to determine whether or not it is extraprovincial within the meaning of the Act. The term "undertaking" has been equated with the words "organization" (see *C.P.R. v. A.-G. B.C. et al.*, [1950] A.C. 122), and "enterprise" (see *A.-G. Ont. v. Winner*, supra). However, all of the enterprises or organizations or undertakings that have been held to be interprovincial undertakings within the meaning of the Act have themselves performed the carriage service or have operated the communications system under their own direct control: see *A.-G. Ont. v. Winner*, supra; *R. v. Borisko Bros. Quebec Ltd.* (1969), 29 D.L.R. (3d) 754 (Que. Sess. of Peace); *R. v. Toronto Magistrates, Ex p. Tank Truck Transport Ltd.*, [1960] O.R. 497 (H.C.); *affirmed* [1963] 1 O.R. 272 (C.A.); *Capital Cities Communications Inc. v. C.R.T.C.*, supra; *City of Toronto v. Bell Telephone Co. of Canada*, [1905] A.C. 52 (P.C.); *R. v. Cooksville Magistrate's Court, Ex p. Liquid Cargo Lines Ltd.*, [1965] 1 O.R. 84 (H.C.); *Re Pacific Produce Delivery & Warehouses Ltd. and Retail, Wholesale & Department Store Union, Local No. 580*, 44 D.L.R. (3d) 130, [1974] 3 W.W.R.

389 *sub nom. Pacific Produce Delivery & Warehouses Ltd. v. Labour Relations Board* (B.C.C.A.); *R. v. Letco Bulk Carriers Ltd.* (1978), 18 O.R. (2d) 562 (Ont. Co. Ct.); *Re Kleysen's Cartage Co. Ltd. and Motor Carrier Board of Manitoba* (1965), 51 W.W.R. 218 (Man. C.A.).

The instant case is distinguishable from all of these cases in that Cottrell is not involved in any of the tangible or physical aspects of the actual carriage of the goods. Its business is entirely contractual in that it arranges and co-ordinates the interprovincial transportation of its customers' goods. For this purpose it enters into a series of contracts with other carriers to perform the actual carriage.

In *Re Cannet Freight Cartage Ltd. and Teamsters Local 419*, supra, the Federal Court of Appeal dealt with the issue of whether or not the employees of Cannet were subject to federal jurisdiction as opposed to provincial jurisdiction. Cannet is an Ontario subsidiary of Cottrell and the Canada Labour Relations Board had certified its employees under the Canada legislation. Before the Court, the union and the Canada Labour Relations Board supported the Board's jurisdiction on the basis that the employees in question were employed upon or in connection with the operation of an interprovincial railway and, alternatively, on the basis that they were employed in an undertaking (the freight-forwarding operation of Cottrell) and extending beyond the limits of the Province. After holding that the employees were not employees upon or in connection with a railway but were employees of Cannet who were loading freight cars on behalf of the shipper and not for the railway, the Court considered the very issue that is before this Court, although in a somewhat different form, and Jackett C.J., at p. 475, stated as follows:

> I have even less trouble with the submission that the freight-forwarding operation was an undertaking connecting one Province with another or extending beyond the limits of a Province. Even if the applicant's activities and those of the Cottrell Company are viewed as integral parts of a whole, in my view they do not constitute an "undertaking" that falls within s. 92(10)(a) of the *British North America Act, 1867* or within the definition of "federal work, undertaking or business" in the *Canada Labour Code*. In my view, the only interprovincial undertaking involved here is the Canadian National interprovincial railway. Clearly, a shipper on that railway from one Province to another does not, by virtue of being such a shipper, become the operator of an interprovincial undertaking. If that is so, as it seems to me, the mere fact that a person makes a

> business of collecting freight in a Province for the
> purpose of shipping it in volume outside the Province
> by public carrier, does not make such a person the
> operator of an interprovincial undertaking.

In the same case, at p. 479, Heald J. stated as follows:

> I agree with the view expressed by the Chief Justice that
> the only interprovincial undertaking involved in this
> case is that of the C.N.R. and that a shipper on that
> railway from one Province to another does not, by such
> activity, become the operator of an interprovincial
> undertaking.

It is my opinion that these statements were not *obiter dicta* but
were part of the *ratio decidendi* of the case. While the decision of
the Federal Court of Appeal is not binding upon this Court it is
certainly persuasive. In any event, I agree with the decision with
certain amplifications. The railway company is the only body
carrying on the interprovincial undertaking and it has the
physical works as well. Clearly, if an individual customer of
Cottrell wished to ship goods to the west, it could contract with
the railway company to ship such goods. The mere fact that by
contract Cottrell agrees with that individual customer to enter
into the contract with the railway company and become the
shipper itself, does not make Cottrell anything other than a
shipper. The shipment is merely part of an over-all contract and
a person who has no tangible or physical property under its
control to operate an undertaking cannot, by contract, make
himself a person carrying on an undertaking within the
meaning of s. 92(10)(*a*) of the *British North America Act, 1867*.
Cottrell is not carrying on an undertaking or operation but is
merely providing a service by contract. To hold otherwise
would mean that any travel broker or other person engaged in
general commerce could, by contract, provide interprovincial
undertakings, even though he had no facilities whatsoever, and
thereby claim that he was not subject to provincial jurisdiction.
This would be unreasonable interpretation of the section in
question.

Finally, consideration should be given to *Northern Telecom Canada Limited
v. Communications Workers of Canada*, [1983] 1 S.C.R. 733. The issue in this case was
whether constitutional jurisdiction over labour relations of installers employed by
Northern Telecom – an affiliate of Bell Canada – belonged to the federal
Parliament or provincial governments. The bulk of the installer's work was
physical installation of sophisticated telecommunications equipment into Bell
Canada's communication network. Bell Canada, itself a federal undertaking,
bought most of its equipment from Northern Telecom. The installation process
required a high degree of cooperation between the two companies.

On appeal from a decision by the Federal Court of Appeal, the Supreme Court of Canada found the Canada Labour Relations Board had jurisdiction to grant certification. Mr. Justice Estey, at 765 ff. stated:

> Bell operates the core federal undertaking, a telecommunications system, interprovincially. Telecom installs integral equipment in that system. The steps to be taken in determining the appropriate constitutional jurisdiction are those prescribed by Dickson J. in the *Telecom* 1980 judgment, supra, at p. 133:
>
>> In the case at bar, the first step is to determine whether a core federal undertaking is present and the extent of that core undertaking. Once that is settled, it is necessary to look at the particular subsidiary operation, *i.e.*, the installation department of Telecom, to look at the "normal or habitual activities" of that department as "a going concern", and the practical and functional relationship of those activities to the core federal undertaking.
>
> In 1970 Lacourcière J. in *Northern Electric*, supra, reviewed an extensive record, applied the *Stevedores'* test (cites omitted), and concluded that the federal Board had jurisdiction. The Board in the present proceedings stated [at p. 89]:
>
>> What is different in the situation today from the way it was in 1970? Very little.
>
> The corporate interrelationship and degree of ownership integration between the customer and the supplier (Bell and Telecom) was reduced in the early 1970's as noted above. Corporate interrelationship is not, without more, a controlling factor, and in any case is reduced in significance somewhat by the post-1973 reduction of Bell's indirect interest in Telecom. In some circumstances it may well be a conclusive element in determining whether the evidence in question described form or reality in the relationship between employer and employees or between employer and customer. In the light of all the evidence and circumstances in these proceedings, I cannot conclude that the corporate relationship of Bell and Telecom is a factor bearing on the outcome here.
>
> We are not here concerned with micro-differences between the function of the installers and that of comparable Bell employees but rather with the macro-relationship between the work of the installers in the subsidiary operation and the functioning of the core undertaking. It is, with all respect to those who have down through the long years of this process otherwise concluded, my view on an examination of the record now before this Court,

that an application of the *ratio decidendi* of the *Stevedores'* case (cites omitted), and the tests for the determination of the appropriate constitutional classification prescribed in this Court in *Telecom 1980, supra,* lead inexorably to the assignment of the labour relations of these employees of Telecom to the federal jurisdiction. In the words of Beetz J. in *Montcalm,* supra, at p. 768:

> [...] but only if it is demonstrated that federal authority over these matters is an integral element of such federal competence. [...]

The facts I have already set out either by excerpts from testimony or from the Board award or the reasons for judgments below. The almost complete integration of the installers' daily work routines with the task of establishing and operating the telecommunications network makes the installation work an integral element in the federal works. The installation teams work the great bulk of their time on the premises of the telecommunications network. The broadening, expansion and refurbishment of the network is a joint operation of the staffs of Bell and Telecom. The expansion or replacement of the switching and transmission equipment, vital in itself to the continuous operation of the network, is closely integrated with the communications delivery systems of the network. All of this work consumes a very high percentage of the work done by the installers.

While it undoubtedly simplifies and clarifies the debate to attempt to define the work of the installers as being either the last step in manufacture or the first step in the operation of the telecommunications network, it is in part misleading to do so. Where the product loses its functional identity upon installation in a large system, it perhaps is not completely accurate to describe its integration as related to its manufacture. Manufacturing in its ordinary connotation refers to the fabrication of a product either from raw material to the complete finished state or the assembly of components and sub-assemblies into a finished product. Here the transmission and switching equipment as such are complete either on delivery to Bell or prior to its connection to the network. The connection to the network is simply putting the product, when finished, to work. The network is not complete without the product but the product is complete without the network. Thus it can be said with accuracy and logic that the installation is a step in the expansion or reconstitution of the federal works, the operating telecommunications network.

The characterization of the nature of the service rendered by the installer is not a clear-cut and simple process which can produce but one answer. Other tribunals have reached the opposite result from my conclusion, which I have reached with much hesitation and after much consideration of the views advanced by others in support of their conclusions. Several factors, however, seem to me to be overpowering. It seems to me that the assignment of these labour relations to the federal sphere reflects the nature of the work of the employees in question, the relationship between their services and the federal works, the geographic realities of the interprovincial scope of the work of these employees transcending as they do several provincial boundaries, and the close and complete integration of the work of these employees and the daily expansion, refurbishment and modernization of this extensive telecommunication facility.

Mr. Justice Dickson, in a concurring decision, further stated, at 772-774:

The appellants argue that the installers' work is merely the end of the manufacturing process; installation is simply effective delivery. The fact that installation of sophisticated equipment is no simple task and involves a significant amount of on-site testing makes no difference. It should be noted that the testing is primarily internal to the system just installed and does not normally involve testing along Bell's full network. It is also conceded that once installation is completed, the equipment is turned over to Bell Canada and it is Bell Canada's employees who are responsible for ordinary maintenance. It is argued that installers essentially do construction work as was found to be under provincial jurisdiction in *Montcalm*, supra.

This is not construction in the sense in which construction was held to be under provincial jurisdiction in *Montcalm*. In *Montcalm*, once the airport was completed, the construction workers would have nothing more to do with the federal undertaking. Bell Canada's operations are much different. The nature of Bell Canada's telecommunications system is that it continually is being renewed, updated, and expanded. Bell's system is highly automated, constantly being improved. It is the installers who perform this task. Although their job is not "maintenance" in the strict sense of the word, I think it is analytically much closer to maintenance than to ordinary construction of a federal undertaking. The installers' work is not preliminary to the operation of Bell Canada's undertaking; the work is an integral part of Bell Canada's operation as a going concern. It was earlier noted the installers have no contact with the rest of Telecom employees. In contrast, they do have contact with, and must closely co-ordinate their work with, Bell Canada employees. In this overall context, installation is not the end of the manufacturing process. It is not even properly described as the *beginning* of the operation of the federal undertaking. It is simply an essential part of the operations process. The installers' work is not the same kind of participation in the day-to-day operations of the federal undertaking as was present in the *Stevedoring* case or the *Letter Carriers* case (cites omitted), in the sense that Telecom installers ordinarily do not directly service users of the federal undertaking. That does not, however, render the installers' work any less vital to the federal undertaking.

I agree with the conclusion expressed by Chief Justice Thurlow in the Federal Court of Appeal [at p. 202]:

> But the feature of the case that appears to me to be of the greatest importance and to point with telling effect to the conclusion that the jurisdiction is federal is the fact, as I see it, that what the installers are doing, day in day out, during 80% of their working time, is participating in the carrying on of the federal undertaking itself which by reason of its nature requires a constant program of rearrangement, renewal, updating and expansion of its switching and transmission system and the installation of telecommunications equipment designed to carry out that need. With 80% of the work these installers are doing on a continuing basis being work done in Bell's undertaking, I am of the opinion that there is a foundation for the assertion of federal jurisdiction over their labour relations and that the Board should assume and exercise it in accordance with the *Canada Labour Code*. Further, in my view, the fact that 20% of the installers' work is not done for Bell does not change the conclusion.

Although I think this case is very close to the boundary line between federal and provincial jurisdiction, I am persuaded that the installers fall under federal jurisdiction.

(ii) Basis of Federal Jurisdiction:
"Interprovincial Workings and Undertakings"

TORONTO v. BELL TELEPHONE
[1905] A.C. 52 (P.C.).

LORD MACNAGHTEN [for the Court]: — This is an appeal from a judgment of the Court of Appeal for Ontario on a special case stated by agreement in two separate actions, in each of which the appellants, the corporation of the city of Toronto, claimed an injunction against the Bell Telephone Company of Canada.

The claim was founded upon the contention that the Telephone Company was not entitled to enter upon the streets and highways of the city and to construct conduits or lay cables thereunder, or to erect poles with wires affixed thereto upon or along such streets or highways without the consent of the corporation.

The company had been incorporated by a Dominion statute of April 29, 1880 (43 Vict. c. 67), for the purpose of carrying on the business of a telephone company. The scope of its business was not confined within the limits of any one province. It was authorized to acquire any lines for the transmission of telephone messages "in Canada or elsewhere," and to construct and maintain its lines along, across, or under any public highways, streets, bridges, watercourses, or other such places, or across or under any navigable waters, "either wholly in Canada or dividing Canada from any other country," subject to certain conditions and restrictions mentioned in the Act, which are not material for the present purpose.

The *British North America Act, 1867*, in the distribution of legislative powers between the Dominion Parliament and provincial legislatures, expressly excepts from the class of "local works and undertakings" assigned to provincial legislatures "lines of steam or other ships, railways, canals, telegraphs, and other works and undertakings connecting the province with any other or others of the provinces or extending beyond the limits of the province": sect. 92, sub-s. 10(*a*). Sect. 91 confers on the Parliament of Canada exclusive legislative authority over all classes of subjects so expressly excepted. It can hardly be disputed that a telephone company the objects of which as defined by its Act of incorporation contemplate

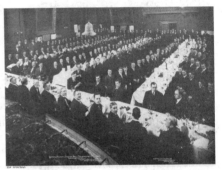

Bell Telephone Co.'s Second Annual Toronto Division Dinner (March, 1911)

extension beyond the limits of one province is just as much within the express exception as a telegraph company with like powers of extension. It would seem to follow that the Bell Telephone Company acquired from the legislature of Canada all that was necessary to enable it to carry on its business in every province of the Dominion, and that no provincial legislature was or is competent to interfere with its operations, as authorized by the Parliament of Canada. It appears, however, that shortly after the incorporation of the company doubts arose as to its right to carry on local business. The question was raised in the province of Quebec, and decided adversely to the company in the case of *Reg. v. Mohr*. In consequence of this decision, with which their Lordships are unable to agree, the company applied for and obtained from the legislature of Ontario an Act of March 10, 1882 (45 Vict. c. 71, Ontario), authorizing it to exercise within that province the powers which the *Dominion Act* had purported to confer upon it. This Act, however, according to the construction placed upon it by the corporation (which, for the present purpose, the Justices assume to be correct), makes the consent of the municipal council a condition precedent to the exercise of the company's powers in cities, towns, and incorporated villages.

The company was proceeding to construct its lines in the city of Toronto without having obtained the consent of the corporation, when the corporation brought the two actions which resulted in the special case the subject of the present appeal.

The case was heard in the first instance by Street J., who decided in favour of the corporation; but his decision was reversed by the Court of Appeal for Ontario, Maclennan J.A. dissenting.

The view of Street J. apparently was that, inasmuch as the Act of incorporation did not expressly require a connection between the different provinces, the exclusive jurisdiction of the Parliament of Canada over the undertaking did not arise on the passing of the Act, and would not arise unless and until such a connection was actually made. In the meantime, in his opinion, the connection was a mere paper one, and nothing could be done under the *Dominion Act* without the authority of the legislature of the province. This view, however, did not find favour with any of the learned Judges of Appeal. In the words of Moss C.J.O., "the question of the legislative jurisdiction must be judged of by the terms of the enactment, and not by what may or may not be thereafter done under it. The failure or neglect to put into effect all the powers given by the legislative authority affords no ground for questioning the original jurisdiction." If authority be wanted in support of this proposition, it will be found in the case of *Colonial Building and Investment Association v. Attorney-General of Quebec*, to which the learned Judges of Appeal refer.

[...] Their Lordships [...] agree with the Chief Justice.
[...] There are two minor points which ought perhaps to be noticed.

(1.) It was argued that the company was formed to carry on, and was carrying on, two separate and distinct businesses – a local business and a long-distance business. And it was contended that the local business and the undertaking of the company so far as it dealt with local business fell within the jurisdiction of the provincial legislature. But there, again, the facts do not support the contention of the appellants. The undertaking authorized by the Act of 1880 was one single undertaking, though for certain purposes its business may be regarded as falling under different branches or heads. The undertaking of the Bell Telephone Company was no more a collection of separate and distinct businesses than the undertaking of a telegraph company which has a long-distance line combined with local business, or the undertaking of a railway company which may have a large suburban traffic and miles of railway communicating with distant places. [...]

In the result, their Lordships will humbly advise His Majesty that the appeal ought to be dismissed.

ALBERTA GOVERNMENT TELEPHONES V. C.R.T.C.
[1989] 2 S.C.R. 225.

[Alberta Government Telephones (AGT) was created by statute by the province of Alberta to provide telephone and telecommunications services within the province. Its activities were subject to regulation by a provincial commission. AGT's physical equipment connected with the cable and microwave equipment of other companies at the Alberta border. AGT was also a member of Telecom Canada, an unincorporated group composed of telecommunications companies providing a network for telecommunications services throughout Canada. The agreements to which AGT was a party were subject to federal regulation by the Canadian Radio-television and Telecommunications Commission (CRTC) but the applications for approval of these agreements had been made by Telecom Canada and never by AGT. CNCP was not a member of Telecom Canada and was not a party to the agreements to which AGT was a party.

On September 17, 1982, CNCP brought an application to the CRTC seeking various orders under the *Railway Act* requiring AGT to provide facilities for the interchange of telecommunications traffic between the system operated by CNCP and the system operated by AGT. AGT, however, sought and was granted a writ of prohibition in the Federal Court, Trial Division on the ground that, although AGT was a federal undertaking within s. 92(10)(*a*), it was entitled to assert Crown immunity as an agent of the provincial Crown. The Federal Court of Appeal agreed that AGT was a federal undertaking, but held that AGT had exceeded its statutory mandate and was therefore not entitled to assert Crown immunity. The order of prohibition was set aside.

The constitutional questions before this Court queried (1) if AGT was a work or undertaking within federal legislative authority by virtue of s. 92(10)(*a*) or otherwise of the *Constitution Act, 1867*, and (2) if so, was AGT bound by the relevant provisions of the *Railway Act*. ...]

DICKSON C.J.C. [McIntyre, Lamer, La Forest and L'Heureux-Dubé JJ. concurring]: — The case law clearly establishes that if a work or undertaking falls within s. 92(10)(*a*) it is removed from the jurisdiction of the provinces and exclusive jurisdiction lies with the federal Parliament. [...]

In *Northern Telecom Ltd. v. Communications Workers of Canada*, [1980] 1 S.C.R. 115 (hereinafter *Northern Telecom, 1980*), this Court outlined the appropriate constitutional principles for determining whether legislative authority over the labour relations of employees lies in the federal or provincial sphere. [...] The Court adopted and summarized an earlier discussion on this point by Beetz J. in *Construction Montcalm Inc. v. Minimum Wage Commission*, [1979] 1 S.C.R. 754. Two of the six principles outlined in *Northern Telecom, 1980* at p. 132 are relevant here:

(5) The question whether an undertaking, service or business is a federal one depends on the nature of its operation.

(6) In order to determine the nature of the operation, one must look at the normal or habitual activities of the business as those of "a going concern", without regard for exceptional or casual factors; otherwise, the Constitution could not be applied with any degree of continuity and regularity.

There is ample authority for the proposition that the crucial issue in any particular case is the nature or character of the undertaking that is in fact being carried on:

[...] It is impossible, in my view, to formulate in the abstract a single comprehensive test which will be useful in all of the cases involving s. 92(10)(a). The common theme in the cases is simply that the court must be guided by the particular facts in each situation, an approach mandated by this Court's decision in *Northern Telecom, 1980*, supra. Useful analogies may be found in the decided cases, but in each case the determination of this constitutional issue will depend on the facts which must be carefully reviewed as was done by the trial judge in the present appeal.

[...] This Court has clearly stated that the location of the physical apparatus in one province and the fact that all the recipients of a service are within a single province will not preclude a finding that an undertaking is interprovincial in scope. In *Capital Cities Communications Inc. v. Canadian Radio-Television Commission*, [1978] 2 S.C.R. 141 (hereinafter *Capital Cities*), Laskin C.J. on behalf of the majority, rejected a similar argument made with respect to cable television companies (at p. 159):

> *The systems are clearly undertakings which reach out beyond the Province in which their physical apparatus is located;* and, even more than in the *Winner* case, they each constitute a single undertaking which deals with the very signals which come to each of them from across the border and transmit those signals, albeit through a conversion process, through its cable system to subscribers. (emphasis added.)

The point was made in *Public Service Board v. Dionne*, [1978] 2 S.C.R. 191 (hereinafter *Dionne*), that to focus the analysis on the location of the subscribers or the separate entity of the operating company of the service was to confuse the question. Laskin C.J. stated on behalf of the majority at p. 197:

> The fundamental question is not whether the service involved in cable distribution is limited to intraprovincial subscribers or that it is operated by a local concern but rather what the service consists of. [...] In all these cases, the inquiry must be as to the service that is provided and not simply as to the means through which it is carried on.

[...] The involvement of AGT in the transmission and reception of electronic signals at the borders of Alberta indicate that AGT is operating an interprovincial undertaking. I find the comment of Laskin C.J. in *Capital Cities*, cited earlier, to be fully applicable here. In that case, with reference to the cable television systems the Chief Justice stated that the systems were "clearly undertakings which reach out beyond the Province in which their physical apparatus is located" (supra, at p. 159). The analogy is apt as AGT's telecommunications system, taken as a whole, connects Alberta with the rest of Canada and with the United States, and other parts of the world. It undoubtedly extends beyond the province of Alberta.

[...] the jurisprudence shows therefore that mere interconnection of physical facilities in one province with those in a neighbouring province, territory or state may not be sufficient to attract the characterization of the undertaking involved as interprovincial in nature.

It is clear, however, that in the instant case the facts demonstrate much more than mere physical interconnection of AGT's system at provincial borders. It has been demonstrated that AGT is, through various commercial arrangements of a bilateral and multilateral nature, organized in a manner which enables it to play a crucial role in the national telecommunications system. It is through the organizational mechanisms described earlier that AGT is able to provide to its local subscribers services of an interprovincial and international nature.

[...] Reed J. found that AGT *itself* is operating an interprovincial undertaking and that it does so primarily through bilateral contracts, its role in Telecom Canada, and the physical interconnection of its system at the borders of Alberta. I agree with that conclusion.

[...] Underlying many of the arguments is an unjustified assumption that by choosing a particular corporate form the various players can control the determination of the constitutional issue. This Court has made it clear in this area of constitutional law that the reality of the situation is determinative, not the commercial costume worn by the entities involved.

[...] I have reached the conclusion that AGT's role and relationship with Telecom Canada is relevant to the decision on AGT's own constitutional character. The facts are unequivocal that AGT is the mechanism through which the residents of Alberta send and receive interprovincial and international telecommunications services. The services are provided through both corporate and physical arrangements which are marked by a high degree of cooperation.

One essential vehicle employed by AGT to interprovincialize and internationalize its services is the Telecom Canada organization. It is not necessary to attach a particular label to the legal relationship that exists between the members of Telecom Canada. It is a form of a joint venture and is a necessary feature of AGT's overall undertaking. I agree with Reed J. that AGT could not separate itself from Telecom Canada without significantly altering the fundamental nature of AGT's enterprise. AGT's relationship with Telecom also illustrates the role AGT plays in the provision of telecommunications services to Canadians as a whole. The national telephone system exists in its present form largely as a result of the Telecom Canada arrangements. AGT is a cooperative partner in this national system and this reinforces the conclusion that AGT is not operating a wholly local enterprise.

I do not find the fact that the members of Telecom Canada own their respective "works" to be significant. The separate ownership of works does not, in this case, take away from the degree of integration which exists between the member system and the level of cooperation and coordination which exists in the national telephone system; it does not make AGT's system less interprovincial and it does not make Telecom Canada enterprise a mere loose association of interested parties. Ownership itself is not conclusive.

[...]To ignore the interdependence of the various members of Telecom Canada because of the separate corporate structures involved would be a sacrifice of substance to form and would advance no constitutional value. I find no merit in the argument that AGT's involvement in the interprovincial flow of signals begins and ends at Alberta's border. This is unrealistic in the same way that it was unrealistic to see cable television stations as distinct entities once the broadcast signal was received at their antennae. AGT, in conjunction with the other members of Telecom, provides a physical framework for the provision of interprovincial and international telecommunications services. It is AGT itself that provides the critical interconnection at Alberta's borders.

[...] I would accordingly affirm the conclusion of Reed J. that, on the basis of the facts as found by her, AGT is an interprovincial undertaking within the meaning of s. 92(10)(*a*) of the *Constitution Act, 1867*.

[His Lordship went on to hold that AGT was entitled to Provincial Crown Immunity as against the federal *Railway* Act. The judgment of Wilson J., who agreed with Dickson C.J.C. on the jurisdiction issue, is omitted. This wide ruling was confirmed in *Téléphone Guèveremont v. Quebec*, [1994] 1 S.C.R. 878, where the Court made it clear that all telephone companies were under federal jurisdiction. Speaking for the Court, Lamer C.J.C. said:

> We are all of the view that Téléphone Guèveremont Inc. is an interprovincial work and undertaking within the legislative authority of the Parliament of Canada by virtue of ss. 92(10(a) and 91(29) of the *Constitution Act, 1867* by reason of the nature of the services provided and the mode of operation of the undertaking, which provides a telecommunication signal carrier service whereby its subscribes send and receive interprovincial and international communications as set out in the reasons of Rousseau-Houle J.A.]

S.M.T. (EASTERN) LTD. v. RUCH
14 M.P.R. 206, 50 C.R.T.C. 369, [1940] 1 D.L.R. 190 at 914 et seq. (N.B.).

HARRISON J.: — Section 11 of the *Motor Carrier Act* prohibits the operation of unlicensed motor vehicles to transport freight or passengers for hire within the Province. The defendants held no license from the Motor Carrier Board to operate their motor trucks and were operating in contravention of the *Motor Carrier Act*. The plaintiff asks to be protected in its franchise by restraining the defendants from carrying on a freight service between St. John and Moncton while unlicensed. It was objected that the proper procedure had not been followed to obtain the plaintiff's franchise from the Motor Carrier Board. The license, however, is regular on its face and I refuse to consider such objection. The action of the Board in granting the license cannot be attacked in a collateral proceeding such as the present case.

But the defendants claim that the plaintiff's franchise is void because the *Motor Carrier Act* or that portion of it which authorized the franchise to the plaintiff, and also that portion making it an offence for any person to operate a public motor truck without license from the Board, are *ultra vires* of the Legislature of New

Brunswick for the following reasons, which I am stating in my own words: [...] 4. Because the road from St. John to Moncton is a portion of an undertaking connecting one Province with another

[...]To say that any Province cannot legislate regarding a highway wholly within its own boundaries because such highway abuts upon a highway in another Province is a novel proposition. So far as I know no such claim has ever been made by the Dominion Government.

Two highways, one in New Brunswick and one in Nova Scotia which meet, do in a sense connect the two Provinces, but it cannot be said of such highway separately that it is a work or undertaking connecting one Province with the other.

In *Luscar Collieries v. McDonald*, [1927] 4 D.L.R. 85, 33 C.R.C. 399, it was held that a railway forming part of a continuous system of railways operated together by the Canadian National Ry. Co. and connecting the Province of Alberta with other Provinces is a work or undertaking connecting one Province with another, within the meaning of s. 92(10)(*a*).

The point of the case is contained in the words of the judgment "having regard to the way in which the railway is operated", *i.e.*, one management of a railway line running between two Provinces. On the other hand the highways in the Provinces of Nova Scotia and New Brunswick are operated under separate management. They are built separately and paid for by the Province in which they run. There is no central control of any kind over these highways. There is not even any agreement between the Provinces regarding them. The New Brunswick statutes dealing with the highway running from St. John to the Nova Scotia boundary do not contemplate its extension beyond the limits of the Province of New Brunswick. That the Nova Scotia road meets this New Brunswick road is a matter over which the New Brunswick Legislature has no control. The soil under the highways in New Brunswick is held under grants from the Province of New Brunswick and if such roads were at any time abandoned the land over which they run would be available to the owners, relieved of the public easement of passage over it. Grants of land bordering on a highway carry with them the soil under the highway to the middle line thereof.

I am of the opinion, therefore, that the highway between St. John and Moncton is a local work or undertaking in relation to which the New Brunswick Legislature has the exclusive right to make laws, and that it is not part of a work or undertaking connecting this Province with any other, within the meaning of the exception in s. 92(10)(*a*). [...]

Judgment for plaintiff.

WESTCOAST ENERGY INC. v. CANADA (NATIONAL ENERGY BOARD)
[1998] 1 S.C.R. 322.

IACOBUCCI and MAJOR JJ. [L'Heureux-Dube, Gonthier, Cory and Bastarache, JJ. concurring]: — The principal issue in this appeal is whether certain proposed natural gas gathering pipeline and processing plant facilities form part of a federal natural gas pipeline transportation undertaking under s. 92(10)(*a*) of the *Constitution Act, 1867*. [...]

The respondent, Westcoast Energy Inc. ("Westcoast"), owns and operates an integrated natural gas pipeline system. Raw natural gas is received from production fields located in the Yukon, the Northwest Territories, Alberta and British Columbia and transported through gathering pipelines to gas processing plants where it is processed to remove impurities. The processed gas is transported through Westcoast's mainline gas transmission pipeline to delivery points within British Columbia, Alberta and the United States.

This appeal arises out of two separate applications by Westcoast to the National Energy Board (the "Board") for certain exemption orders and certificates pursuant to the *National Energy Board Act* in respect of proposed expansions of Westcoast's gathering pipeline and processing plant facilities in the Fort St. John and Grizzly Valley resource areas, respectively. [...]

The Westcoast natural gas pipeline system is essentially a network of gathering pipelines which feed gas into four gas processing plants, which in turn feed processed gas into an interprovincial mainline transmission pipeline. Natural gas is extracted by independent producers at production fields in the Yukon, the Northwest Territories, British Columbia and Alberta. The extracted gas is called "raw gas" and contains a mixture of both gaseous and liquid hydrocarbons consisting primarily of methane, as well as other substances such as water, hydrogen sulphide and carbon dioxide. Water is removed from the raw gas by the producers before it is delivered into the Westcoast gathering pipelines to avoid corrosion and the formation of hydrates which can obstruct the flow of gas.

The raw gas is transported through the Westcoast gathering pipelines by means of compression to one of four Westcoast processing plants, where it is processed to remove impurities, including hydrogen sulphide, carbon dioxide and liquid hydrocarbons. These impurities must be removed from the raw gas before it can be used by the ultimate consumers. The processed gas is called "residue gas" or "sales gas" and is delivered into the Westcoast mainline transmission pipeline for transportation by means of compression to markets in British Columbia, Alberta and the United States. The processing of the raw gas produces several byproducts which are also commercially valuable. [...]

The Fort St. John application concerned a proposal by Westcoast to expand its facilities in the vicinity of the Fort St. John Processing Plant through: (1) the construction of four loops and one extension of existing gathering pipelines; (2) the addition of three new compressor facilities; (3) the construction of the new Aitken Creek Plant, which is to be connected on the upstream side to the gathering pipelines and on the downstream side to Westcoast's main transmission pipeline through an expanded Aitken Creek Pipeline; and (4) the construction of a loop of the Aitken Creek Pipeline connecting the new Aitken Creek Plant with the mainline transmission pipeline. The estimated cost of the proposed project was estimated to be approximately $397,000,000 at the time of the application, of which approximately $265,000,000 was for the construction of the processing plant. Westcoast applied to the Board for: (1) a certificate of public convenience and necessity pursuant to s. 52 of the *National Energy Board Act* authorizing the construction and operation of pipeline facilities; (2) an order pursuant to s. 58 to exempt the new Aitken Creek Plant, additional compressor facilities and certain additional pipeline facilities from the provisions of ss. 30, 31, 33 and 47; and (3) an order pursuant to s. 59 confirming that the tolls for services to be provided through the proposed facilities would be determined on a "rolled-in" basis.

The Grizzly Valley application concerned a proposal by Westcoast to expand its facilities in the vicinity of the Grizzly Valley area through: (1) the construction of a loop of the existing Grizzly Pipeline to increase its capacity to transport raw gas to the Pine River Plant; (2) the construction of several gathering pipelines; (3) an expansion of the Pine River Plant to increase its capacity; (4) the construction of a fuel gas pipeline connected to the existing Sukunka Fuel Gas Pipeline to deliver fuel gas to the producers in the Highhat supply area; (5) the construction of a loop of the Pine River mainline transmission pipeline to increase its capacity; and (6) an upgrade of an existing compressor unit at Compressor Station No. 2. The total cost of the proposed Grizzly Valley facilities was estimated to be approximately $400,000,000 at the time of the application, of which approximately $348,800,000 was for the Pine River Plant expansion facilities, $29,500,000 was for the Grizzly Valley gathering facilities and $21,700,000 was for the mainline transmission facilities. Westcoast applied to the Board for: (1) an order pursuant to s. 58 to exempt the proposed processing, compressor, and pipeline facilities from the provisions of ss. 30, 31 and 47; and (2) an order pursuant to s. 59 confirming that the tolls for services to be provided at the proposed facilities would be determined on a "rolled-in" basis. [...]

Subsection 92(10) of the *Constitution Act, 1867* provides generally that local works and undertakings within a province come within provincial jurisdiction. However, the combined effect of ss. 91(29) and 92(10)(*a*) creates an exception whereby Parliament has exclusive jurisdiction over works and undertakings that come within the phrase "Lines of Steam or other Ships, Railways, Canals, Telegraphs, and other Works and Undertakings connecting the Province with any other or others of the Provinces, or extending beyond the Limits of the Province" in s. 92(10)(*a*). The effect of s. 92(10)(*a*) is that interprovincial transportation and communications works and undertakings fall within federal jurisdiction. See the discussion by Professor Hogg in *Constitutional Law of Canada* (3rd ed. 1992) (loose-leaf), Vol. 1, at pp. 22-2 and 22-3.

Campbell-Bennett Ltd. v. Comstock Midwestern Ltd. [1954] S.C.R. 207, [c]onfirmed that a pipeline which extends beyond the boundaries of a province, such as the Westcoast mainline transmission pipeline, is a federal transportation undertaking under s. 92(10)(*a*). It is apparent that whether the Board has jurisdiction over the construction and operation of the proposed Fort St. John and

Grizzly Valley gathering pipeline and gas processing plant facilities under the *National Energy Board Act* depends on whether these facilities also come within federal jurisdiction under s. 92(10)(*a*).

It is well settled that the proposed facilities may come within federal jurisdiction under s. 92(10)(*a*) in one of two ways. First, they are subject to federal jurisdiction if the Westcoast mainline transmission pipeline, gathering pipelines and processing plants, including the proposed facilities, together constitute a single federal work or undertaking. Second, if the proposed facilities do not form part of a single federal work or undertaking, they come within federal jurisdiction if they are integral to the mainline transmission pipeline. See *Central Western, per* Dickson C.J., at pp. 1124-25 (cites omitted):

> There are two ways in which Central Western may be found to fall within federal jurisdiction and thus be subject to the *Canada Labour Code*. First, it may be seen as an interprovincial railway and therefore come under s. 92(10)(*a*) of the *Constitution Act, 1867* as a federal work or undertaking. Second, if the appellant can be properly viewed as integral to an existing federal work or undertaking it would be subject to federal jurisdiction under s. 92(10)(*a*). For clarity, I should point out that these two approaches, though not unrelated, are distinct from one another. For the former, the emphasis must be on determining whether the railway is <u>itself</u> an interprovincial work or undertaking. Under the latter, however, jurisdiction is dependent upon a finding that regulation of the subject matter in question is integral to a core federal work or undertaking. (emphasis in the original.)

Thus, the first issue is whether the Westcoast mainline transmission pipeline, gathering pipelines and processing plants, including the proposed facilities, together constitute a single federal work or undertaking. If not, we must consider whether the gathering pipeline and processing plant facilities are essential, vital and integral to the mainline transmission pipeline undertaking.

Do the Westcoast mainline transmission pipeline, gathering pipelines and processing plants together constitute a single federal work or undertaking?

(a)   The Features of a Single Federal Undertaking

Section 92(10)(*a*) refers to both "works" and "undertakings". "Works" were defined in *City of Montreal v. Montreal Street Railway*, [1912] A.C. 333 (P.C.), at p. 342, as "physical things, not services". Since the proposed gathering pipeline and processing plant facilities will be located entirely within the province of British Columbia, it seems clear that they would constitute local works. As a result, the submissions of the parties concentrated on whether Westcoast operated a single federal undertaking. "Undertaking" was defined in *Re Regulation & Control of Radio Communication*, [1932] 2 D.L.R. 81 (P.C.), at p. 86, as "not a physical thing, but [...] an arrangement under which [...] physical things are used." Professor Hogg concludes in *Constitutional Law of Canada, supra*, at p. 22-4, that the term "undertaking" appears to be equivalent to "organization" or "enterprise".

In *Alberta Government Telephones v. Canada (Canadian Radio-television and Telecommunications Commission)*, [1989] 2 S.C.R. 225 (*A.G.T.*), Dickson C.J. stated at p. 259 that "[t]he primary concern is not the physical structures or their geographical location, but rather the service which is provided by the undertaking through the use of its physical equipment."

The cases grouped under what has become known as the first test in *Central Western* (cites omitted), demonstrate that whether a single federal undertaking exists for the purposes of s. 92(10)(*a*) depends on a number of factors. It is clear that the mere fact that a local work or undertaking is physically connected to an interprovincial undertaking is insufficient to render the former a part of the latter. See *Central Western*, supra, at pp. 1128-29. The fact that both operations are owned by the same entity is also insufficient. In *A.G.T.*, supra, Dickson C.J. stated at p. 263 that "[t]his Court has made it clear in this area of constitutional law that the reality of the situation is determinative, not the commercial costume worn by the entities involved" and, at p. 265, that "[o]wnership itself is not conclusive". A single entity may own more than one undertaking. See *Canadian Pacific Railway Co. v. Attorney-General for British Columbia*, [1950] A.C. 122 (P.C.) (the *Empress Hotel* case), at p. 143 (cites omitted).

In order for several operations to be considered a single federal undertaking for the purposes of s. 92(10)(*a*), they must be functionally integrated and subject to common management, control and direction. Professor Hogg states, at p. 22-10, that "[i]t is the degree to which the [various business] operations are integrated in a functional or business sense that will determine whether they constitute one undertaking or not." He adds, at p. 22-11, that the various operations will form a single undertaking if they are "actually operated in common as a single enterprise." In other words, common ownership must be coupled with functional integration and common management. A physical connection must be coupled with an operational connection. A close commercial relationship is insufficient. See *Central Western* at p. 1132 (cites omitted).

Common management and operational control was determinative in *Luscar Collieries, Limited v. McDonald*, [1927] A.C. 925 (P.C.), and their absence was determinative in *Central Western* (cites omitted). In *Luscar, supra*, the Privy Council held that a short line of railway located entirely within Alberta formed part of the Canadian National Railway Company ("CN") federal railway undertaking. Although the line was owned by the appellant Luscar, Lord Warrington focused at pp. 932-33 on the fact that it was operated by CN pursuant to several agreements:

> The Justices agree with the opinion of Duff J. that the Mountain Park Railway and the Luscar Branch are, under the circumstances hereinbefore set forth, a part of a continuous system of railways operated together by the Canadian National Railway Company and connecting the Province of Alberta with other Provinces in the Dominion. [...]
>
> In the present case, <u>having regard to the way in which the railway is operated</u>, the Justices are of the opinion that it is in fact a railway connecting the Province of Alberta with others of

the Provinces, and therefore falls within s. 92, head 10 (*a*), of the Act of 1867. There is a continuous connection by railway between the point of the Luscar Branch farthest from its junction with the Mountain Park Branch and parts of Canada outside the Province of Alberta. <u>If under the agreements hereinbefore mentioned the Canadian National Railway Company should cease to operate the Luscar Branch</u>, the question whether under such altered circumstances the railway ceases to be within s. 92, head 10 (*a*), may have to be determined, but that question does not now arise. (emphasis added.)

The question left open by the Privy Council in the concluding sentence of this passage arose in *Central Western* (cites omitted), which also involved a short line of railway located entirely within Alberta. The appellant Central Western Railway Corporation had purchased the line from CN but, unlike the situation in *Luscar,* supra, CN did not operate the line. Dickson C.J. distinguished *Luscar,* supra, on this basis and held that the absence of a close operational connection in the case before the Court meant that the Central Western line did not form part of the CN federal railway undertaking for the purposes of s. 92(10)(*a*). The close commercial relationship between Central Western and CN was insufficient. He summarized his position at p. 1132:

> In my view, while the factors mentioned by the respondents indicate a close commercial relationship between the two railways they do not show that CN operates Central Western. Rather, the sale of Central Western has resulted in a fundamental change in the management of the rail line. Most notably, the difference is manifested in the daily control of the business of the rail line. The distribution of the grain cars along the rail line is handled by the appellant, and CN rail cars do not travel on Central Western, nor does the federal rail company participate in the management of any of the leases connected to the property. Basically, CN exercises no control over the running of the rail line, making it difficult to view Central Western as a federal work or undertaking.

This inquiry into whether various operations are functionally integrated and managed in common requires a careful examination of the factual circumstances of any given case. In *Northern Telecom Ltd. v. Communications Workers of Canada (No. 1),* [1980] 1 S.C.R. 115, at p. 132, it was stated that "one must look at the normal or habitual activities of the business as those of 'a going concern', without regard for exceptional or causal factors." As was stressed by Dickson C.J. in *A.G.T.,* supra, at pp. 257-58, the court must focus on "the nature or character of the undertaking that is in fact being carried on". He went on to state, at p. 258:

> It is impossible, in my view, to formulate in the abstract a single comprehensive test which will be useful in all of the cases involving s. 92(10)(*a*). The common theme in the cases is simply that the court must be guided by the particular facts in each

situation. [...] Useful analogies may be found in the decided cases, but in each case the determination of this constitutional issue will depend on the facts which must be carefully reviewed as was done by the trial judge in the present appeal.

The manner in which the undertaking might have been structured or the manner in which other similar undertakings are carried on is irrelevant. This principle was emphasized by Lord Porter in *Attorney-General for Ontario v. Winner*, [1954] A.C. 541 (P.C.), at pp. 581-82:

> The question is not what portions of the undertaking can be stripped from it without interfering with the activity altogether; it is rather what is the undertaking which is in fact being carried on. Is there one undertaking, and as part of that one undertaking does the respondent carry passengers between two points both within the province, or are there two? [...]

> The undertaking in question is in fact one and indivisible. It is true that it might have been carried on differently and might have been limited to activities within or without the province, but it is not, and the Justices do not agree that the fact that it might be carried on otherwise than it is makes it or any part of it any the less an interconnecting undertaking.

The fact that one aspect of a business is dedicated exclusively or even primarily to the operation of the core interprovincial undertaking is an indication of the type of functional integration that is necessary for a single undertaking to exist. See *Empress Hotel* (cites omitted), where the Privy Council held that the Empress Hotel in Victoria, British Columbia did not form part of the appellant's federal railway undertaking, but suggested in *obiter dicta* at p. 144 that a hotel built by the railway exclusively to serve its passengers could:

> It appears from the facts stated in the order of reference that the appellant has so interpreted its powers and that in the Empress Hotel it does carry on general hotel business. <u>It may be that, if the appellant chose to conduct a hotel solely or even principally for the benefit of travelers on its system, that hotel would be a part of its railway undertaking.</u> The Justices do not doubt that the provision of meals and rest for travelers on the appellant's system may be a part of its railway undertaking whether that provision is made in trains or at stations, and such provision might be made in a hotel. But the Empress Hotel differs markedly from such a hotel. Indeed, there is little, if anything, in the facts stated to distinguish it from an independently owned hotel in a similar position. No doubt the fact that there is a large and well-managed hotel at Victoria tends to increase the traffic on the appellant's system; it may be that the appellant's railway business and hotel business help each other, but that does not prevent them from being separate businesses or undertakings. (emphasis added.) [...]

In our opinion, the fact that an activity or service is not of a transportation or communications character does not preclude a finding that it forms part of a single federal undertaking for the purposes of s. 92(10)(*a*) under the first test in *Central Western* (cites omitted). The test remains a fact based one. As Dickson C.J. made clear in *Alberta Government Telephones*, supra, at p. 258:

> It is impossible, in my view, to formulate in the abstract a single comprehensive test which will be useful in all of the cases involving s. 92(10)(*a*). The common theme in the cases is simply that the court must be guided by the particular facts in each situation. [...] Useful analogies may be found in the decided cases, but in each case the determination of this constitutional issue will depend on the facts which must be carefully reviewed. [...]

That is not to say, however, that it is impossible to identify certain *indicia* which will assist in the s. 92(10)(*a*) analysis. In our view, the primary factor to consider is whether the various operations are functionally integrated and subject to common management, control and direction. The absence of these factors will, in all likelihood, determine that the operations are not part of the same interprovincial undertaking, although the converse will not necessarily be true. Other relevant questions, though not determinative, will include whether the operations are under common ownership (perhaps as an indicator of common management and control), and whether the goods or services provided by one operation are for the sole benefit of the other operation and/or its customers, or whether they are generally available.

Because of the factual nature of this determination, evidence of the ordinary way in which business is conducted within a particular industry will not be particularly relevant. Thus, the reliance by BC Gas on the expert evidence adduced before the Board as to the typical characterization of the natural gas industry is perhaps misplaced. Although it was accepted by the Federal Court of Appeal in *The Queen v. Nova, An Alberta Corporation*, [1988] 2 C.T.C. 167 (F.C.A.), that the industry is generally divided into four distinct stages — exploration, production and development (including extraction, dehydration, and transportation through gathering lines to processing plants), transportation from processing plants to regions of consumption, and distribution to the ultimate consumer — and although the Board characterized gas processing and gas transmission as "fundamentally different activities", this does not preclude the two operations from being part of the same interprovincial undertaking for the purposes of s. 92(10)(*a*). While this division may be convenient for industrial purposes, it has no bearing on the constitutional division of powers between the federal and provincial legislatures.

Whether the Westcoast gathering pipelines, processing plants and mainline transmission pipeline constitute a single undertaking depends on the degree to which they are in fact functionally integrated and managed in common as a single enterprise. What is important is how Westcoast actually operates its business, not how it might otherwise operate it or how others in the natural gas industry operate their businesses: see *Winner*, supra, at pp. 581-82. The fact that the natural gas industry is typically divided into the four sectors described above is beside the point, as is the fact that producers typically own gathering pipelines and processing plants. As discussed below, it is precisely because Westcoast's business is exceptional that we conclude that it comprises a single federal undertaking. We also emphasize that the manner in which participants in the natural gas industry typically describe the industry cannot dictate the characterization for constitutional purposes. Finally, the fact that this description of the industry was adopted in *Nova,* supra is irrelevant for the purposes of this appeal since that case dealt with the unrelated matter of the appropriate capital cost allowance classification of certain pieces of yard pipe, metering pipe and valves for income tax purposes.

(b)   Application of these principles to the business of Westcoast

Turning to the application of the principles discussed above, the fact that the Westcoast gathering pipelines and processing plants are physically connected to the mainline transmission pipeline is insufficient by itself to conclude that they constitute a single federal undertaking. Further, the fact that Westcoast owns all of these facilities is insufficient. However, we agree with Hugessen J.A. that the description of the business and facilities of Westcoast by the Board in its Fort St. John reasons and Order No. MO-21-95 concerning the Grizzly Valley reference demonstrate that Westcoast manages them in common as a single enterprise which is functionally integrated.

It is apparent that the Westcoast facilities and personnel are subject to common control, direction and management, and are operated in a coordinated and integrated manner. Westcoast management personnel in Vancouver control and direct the field personnel who operate the gathering pipeline, processing plant and mainline transmission pipeline facilities. The gathering pipeline facilities and the mainline transmission pipeline facilities, and the associated compressor facilities, are operated by the same field personnel. Both sets of pipeline facilities are serviced by common field offices, pipe storage yards, warehouses, compression repair facilities and measurement and pipeline maintenance shops. Employees in Vancouver are responsible for monitoring and controlling the flow of gas through both the gathering pipelines and the mainline transmission pipeline. Although the operation of the processing plants is carried out by different persons at each plant, this is done under the direction and supervision of management located in Vancouver. Finally, the gathering, processing and transmission facilities are connected by a sophisticated telecommunications system.

This functional integration is underscored by the fact that the primary purpose of processing the raw gas at the Westcoast processing plants is to facilitate its transmission through the Westcoast mainline transmission pipeline. As discussed above, the raw gas that is extracted at the production fields often contains impurities, including hydrogen sulphide and carbon dioxide. These impurities must be removed from the gas before it is delivered into the mainline transmission pipeline for two reasons. First, the combination of sulphur dioxide and carbon dioxide is corrosive. While steel used in the gathering pipelines is designed to withstand this corrosion, the steel used in the mainline transmission pipeline is not. Second, hydrogen sulphide is toxic and poses unacceptable safety and environmental risks. As such, gas which contains hydrogen sulphide cannot be transported through the heavily populated areas through which the mainline transmission pipeline runs.

BC Gas argued that these concerns are incidental to the primary purpose of processing, which it characterized as the transformation of the raw gas into commercially useful products, including residue gas and other useful byproducts like sulphur. In our opinion, this purpose is irrelevant to Westcoast's business. It is true that the raw gas must be processed to remove impurities before it can be used by the ultimate consumer. However, what is important from the perspective of Westcoast is that this processing occur <u>before</u> the gas is delivered into its mainline transmission pipeline because of the design, safety and environmental concerns set out above.

In addition, processing is provided by Westcoast almost exclusively in respect of gas which is subsequently delivered into the Westcoast mainline transmission pipeline. While some raw gas is delivered to Westcoast's processing plants by means of gathering lines owned and operated by others, virtually all of the residue gas that is processed at the Westcoast processing plants is delivered into the Westcoast mainline transmission pipeline for transportation onward. This residue gas consists primarily of methane, which comprises approximately 80 per cent of the raw gas prior to processing. Westcoast does not offer processing as an independent service in respect of gas that it does not transport in its mainline transmission pipeline. [...]

It is significant that, except for some small quantities, Westcoast does not own or deal in the natural gas that it transports. The fact that processing the gas transforms it into a commercially useful state and produces byproducts which are also commercially valuable may be relevant to the owners of these substances, but it is irrelevant to Westcoast. Its only interest is in providing transportation and processing services to the owners of the gas and its byproducts. [...]

The facts demonstrate that, above and beyond the coordination described above, Westcoast also operates the gathering pipelines, processing plants and mainline transmission pipeline in common as a single enterprise. Simply put, the facilities are subject to common control, direction and management by Westcoast. This is what distinguishes the Westcoast undertaking from others in the natural gas industry. The coordination exhibited by the Westcoast facilities may be a necessary feature of the natural gas industry, but the common management of these facilities by Westcoast as a single business is not. It is obviously not a feature of those independently owned gathering pipelines which feed into the Westcoast processing plants and those independently owned processing plants which feed into the Westcoast mainline transmission pipeline. Westcoast has no control over these facilities. [...]

Are the Westcoast gathering pipeline and processing plant facilities integral to the mainline transmission pipeline?

In light of the above conclusion, it is unnecessary for us to consider whether the proposed facilities would be essential, vital and integral to the mainline transmission pipeline under the second test in *Central Western* (cites omitted), and accordingly we express no opinion on this issue. [...]

Conclusion

We conclude that the Westcoast gathering pipelines, processing plants and mainline transmission pipeline, of which the proposed Fort St. John and Grizzly Valley facilities would form part, constitute a single federal transportation undertaking which is engaged in the transportation of natural gas from production fields located in the Yukon, the Northwest Territories, Alberta and British Columbia to delivery points within Alberta and British Columbia and the international boundary with the United States. As such, the proposed facilities come within the exclusive jurisdiction of Parliament under s. 92(10)(*a*) of the *Constitution Act, 1867*. [...]

[The dissenting reasons of cLachlin J. are omitted.]

(iii) Scope of Federal Jurisdiction

CAPITAL CITIES COMMUNICATIONS INC. v. C.R.T.C.
[1978] 2 S.C.R. 141.

LASKIN C.J.C. [Martland, Judson, Ritchie, Spence and Dickson JJ. concurring]: — The issues in this appeal arise out of three decisions of the Canadian Radio-Television Commission (now the *Canadian Radio-television and Telecommunications Commission*: see 1975 (Can.), c. 49) issued on May 1, 1974, made in pursuance of applications by Rogers Cable TV Limited, Coaxial Colourview Limited and Bramalea Telecable Limited for amendment of their respective cable television licences "to permit commercial deletion and substitution on a random basis on all United States television stations carried from time to time on the basic service which presently includes channels 2, 4 and 7 Buffalo".

[...] Rogers' licence, which is formally a licence to carry on a "broadcasting receiving undertaking", as defined in the *Broadcasting Act, 1967-68* (Can.), c. 25, now R.S.C. 1970, c. B-11 (to which reference will be made later in these reasons) authorized it to serve certain areas of Metropolitan Toronto with an off-air broadcasting receiving antenna at a specified location.

[...]The appellants were not and were not required to be licensed by the respondent CRTC. Their programmes reached Canadian viewers in areas adjacent to Buffalo, including Toronto, and were freely available to those whose television sets could directly receive those programmes. They could however receive them, and other programmes too which their sets could not attract, by becoming subscribers of Rogers through the latter's cable operation. [...]

What precipitated the matters now before this Court was Rogers' decision, made and carried out some time prior to October, 1973, to delete commercial messages from the programmes received from the appellants' stations and to transmit those programmes to its subscribers without those messages but with substituted announcements of its own. The appellants threatened and, indeed, took legal action against Rogers, and this litigation is pending in lower Courts. Rogers thereupon applied for amendment of its licence in terms already noted.

The appellants intervened, apparently without objection, in the public hearings held by CRTC to consider the applications of Rogers and the two other applicants. Among the grounds advanced by the appellants in opposition to the licence amendment sought by the applicants was a challenge to the jurisdiction of CRTC. The respondent Commission granted the applications in part in a decision dated May 1, 1974. [...]

Following the granting of leave to appeal [to this Court] the constitutional question raised in the appeal [...] [was] reformulated [...] as follows:

> Whether the *Broadcasting Act*, RSC 1970, Chapter B-11 and regulations made thereunder, are ultra vires the Parliament of Canada insofar as they purport to regulate, or to authorize the

"...the Canada Council and the CRTC are there to make us cultured Canadians, and we've always gone along with it..."

Canadian Radio-Television Commission to licence and to regulate the content of programs carried by CATV systems situated wholly within Provincial boundaries.

[...]The main argument of the appellants and of those in support of their position is that legislative jurisdiction is divided in respect of regulation of television signals received by cablevision companies. Exclusive federal jurisdiction is conceded so far as concerns the reception of foreign or domestic television signals at the antennae of the cablevision companies. It is contended, however, that once received at those antennae federal legislative power is exhausted, and any subsequent distribution of those signals, whether in the same or modified form, within a particular Province is a matter exclusively for that Province.

[...] I am unable to accept the submission of the appellants and of the Attorneys-General supporting them that a demarcation can be made for legislative purposes at the point where the cable distribution systems receive the Hertzian waves. The systems are clearly undertakings which reach out beyond the Province in which their physical apparatus is located; and, even more than in the *Winner* case, they each constitute a single undertaking which deals with the very signals which come to each of them from across the border and transmit those signals, albeit through a conversion process, through its cable system to subscribers. The common sense of which the Privy Council spoke in the *Radio* case seems to me even more applicable here to prevent a situation of a divided jurisdiction in respect of the same signals or programmes according to whether they reach home television sets and the ultimate viewers through Hertzian waves or through coaxial cable.

The fallacy in the contention on behalf of the Attorney-General of Ontario and of the Attorneys-General of Quebec and of British Columbia, and, indeed, of the appellants, is in their reliance on the technology of transmission as a ground for shifting constitutional competence when the entire undertaking relates to and is dependent on extra-provincial signals which the cable system receives and sends on to subscribers. It does not advance their contentions to urge that a cable distribution system is not engaged in broadcasting. The system depends upon a telecast for its operation, and is no more than a conduit for signals from the telecast, interposing itself through a different technology to bring the telecast to paying subscribers.

[...] [Quebec's] contention appears to be that since there is a local character to the cable distribution system in its physical aspect, and it may be receiving signals intraprovincially, it does not fall under total federal legislative authority. I understood, however, that it was conceded that federal jurisdiction was exclusive in respect of the receipt of signals at the antenna of the cable distribution system, wherever be their point of emanation. If that be the case, I do not see how legislative competence ceases in respect of those signals merely because the undertaking which receives them and sends them on to its local subscribers does so through a different technology.

In addition to the foregoing submissions, which do not differ from those made by others opposing federal jurisdiction, counsel for the Attorney-General of Quebec denied federal authority over the content of cable television, at least at the point of distribution through the coaxial cables. This, however, simply rephrases the issue in the present case without changing its substance. What the reformulation suggests, however, is that the Parliament of Canada may regulate, perhaps by a licensing system, the equipment or machinery through which signals are received in international or interprovincial transmission but that is all. There was a time when licensing of receiving sets was prescribed by federal legislation; but if, as is alleged, there is no authority to regulate content, it is difficult to understand how there can be a constitutional basis for federal licensing of receiving sets in a Province, or even of transmitting apparatus which sends signals by way of international and interprovincial transmission. To put the matter in another perspective, it would be as if an interprovincial or international carrier of goods could be licensed for such carriage but without federal control of what may be carried or of the conditions of carriage.

This submission amounts to a denial of any effective federal legislative jurisdiction of what passes in interprovincial or international communication, whether by radio or television, and is in truth an invitation to this Court to recant from the *Radio* case. It would, presumably, leave federal authority in relation to "telegraphs" intact, though reducing the meaning of that head of power from the meaning attributed to it by the Privy Council in the *Radio* case.

[...] The Privy Council remarked in the *Radio* case that "`undertaking' is not a physical thing but is an arrangement under which of course physical things are used" ([1932] A.C. 304, at p. 315). It returned to the matter in the *Winner* case where it distinguished a connecting work and a connecting undertaking, saying that "in the *Radio* case there was no connecting work only a connecting undertaking unless the somewhat fanciful suggestion were to be adopted that the flow of an electrical discharge across the frontier of a Province is to be regarded as a physical connection" ([1954] A.C. 541, at p. 574). The technology of cable television does not make the operation of a cable distribution system which draws on signals emanating from outside Canada any less an "undertaking" than the radio operations which were the subject of enquiry in the *Radio* case. The word has been given a large meaning, as indicated by the references by Kellock J. in the *Stevedoring* case, at p. 556 (cites omitted) to the broad view taken in both the *Winner* case, where the word "undertaking" was used interchangeably with "enterprise" and in the *Empress Hotel* case (cites omitted), where it was equated with "organization".

I am therefore in no doubt that federal legislative authority extends to the regulation of the reception of television signals emanating from a source outside of Canada and to the regulation of the transmission of such signals within Canada. Those signals carry the programmes which are ultimately viewed on home television sets; and it would be incongruous, indeed, to admit federal legislative jurisdiction to the extent conceded but to deny the continuation of regulatory authority because the signals are intercepted and sent on to ultimate viewers through a different technology. Programme content regulation is inseparable from regulating the undertaking through which programmes are received and sent on as part of the total enterprise.

[Pigeon, Beetz and de Grandpré JJ. dissented. In result, the appeal was dismissed.]

DIONNE v. PUBLIC SERVICES BD. (QUE.)
[1978] 2 S.C.R. 191.

LASKIN C.J.C. [Martland, Judson, Ritchie, Spence and Dickson JJ. concurring]: — This appeal raises a constitutional question which, by an order of March 16, 1977 was formulated as follows:

> Are section 23 of the *Public Service Board Act* (R.S.Q. 1964, c. 229) and the ordinances rendered pursuant thereto unconstitutional, *ultra vires* or inoperative to the extent that they apply to a cable distribution public service as defined in the Regulation respecting cable distribution public services (O.C. 3565-73 of the 25th of September, 1973) adopted pursuant to section 3a of the *Communications Department Act* (L.Q. 1969, c. 65).

The Quebec Court of Appeal in dealing with the issues raised by this question concluded unanimously, in reasons delivered by Tremblay C.J.Q., that it was beyond the competence of the Province of Quebec to regulate the operation of cable distribution systems through which television signals were captured and transmitted to subscribers. In the result, the Quebec Court of Appeal set aside three decisions of the Quebec Public Service Board which had authorized François Dionne, a respondent in this Court, and Raymond d'Auteuil, one of the appellants herein, to operate cable distribution enterprises in certain defined areas in the Province and which had settled certain questions touching the carrying out of the authorizations.

[...] This Court concluded, on the facts established in the *Capital Cities* case, that exclusive legislative authority in relation to the regulation of cablevision stations and their programming, at least where such programming involved the interception of television signals and their retransmission to cablevision subscribers, rested in the Parliament of Canada.

Since the matter was argued anew in the present case, and since other Provinces intervened in support of the Quebec Attorney-General's challenge to exclusive federal competence (they having also intervened in the *Capital Cities* case), I think it desirable that something more be said here, notwithstanding the extensive canvass that was made in the *Capital Cities* case. The two central strands of what I may call the provincial submissions were that (1) two enterprises, having no necessary connection with each other, were involved in television operations and in cablevision operations and (2) the fact that different controlling entities were involved in those operations emphasized the separateness of the enterprises, and since the cable distribution operation was locally situate and limited in its subscriber relations to persons in Quebec it was essentially a local work or undertaking within provincial competence under s. 92(10) of the *British North America Act*.

The fundamental question is not whether the service involved in cable distribution is limited to intraprovincial subscribers or that it is operated by a local concern but rather what the service consists of. This is the very question that was faced by the Privy Council in the *Radio* case, supra, (in a different context, it is true) and which was also before that body in *Attorney General of Ontario v. Winner*. There is another element that must be noticed, and that is that where television broadcasting and receiving is concerned there can no more be a separation for constitutional purposes between the carrier system, the physical apparatus, and the signals that are received and carried over the system than there can be between railway tracks and the transportation service provided over them or between the roads and transport vehicles and the transportation service that they provide. In all these cases, the inquiry must be as to the service that is provided and not simply as to the means through which it is carried on. Divided constitutional control of what is functionally an interrelated system of transmitting and receiving television signals, whether directly through air waves or through intermediate cable line operations, not only invites confusion but is alien to the principle of exclusiveness of legislative authority, a principle which is as much fed by a sense of the Constitution as a working and workable instrument as by a literal reading of its words. In the present case, both the relevant words and the view of the Constitution as a pragmatic instrument come together to support the decision of the Quebec Court of Appeal.

I should emphasize that this is not a case where the cable distribution enterprises limit their operations to programmes locally produced by them for transmission over their lines to their local subscribers. Admittedly, they make use of television signals received at their antennae, both from within and without the Province; and the fact that they may make changes or deletions in transmitting the off-air programmes to their subscribers does not affect their liability to federal regulatory control. The suggested analogy with a local telephone system fails on the facts because the very technology employed by the cable distribution enterprises in the present case establishes clearly their reliance on television signals and on their ability to receive and transmit such signals to their subscribers. In short, they rely on broadcasting stations, and their operations are merely a link in a chain which extends to subscribers who receive the programmes through their private receiving sets. I do not think that any argument based on relative percentages of original programming and of programmes received from broadcasting stations can be of any more avail here than it was in *Re Tank Truck Transport Ltd.*

For these reasons, as well as for those in the *Capital Cities* case, in which judgment is being given concurrently with the judgment herein, I would dismiss the appeal with costs. There will be no costs to the Attorney General of Canada nor to or against any of the intervenors. [...]

PIGEON J. (dissenting): — [...] In my view, the question in this case is whether the unchallengeable federal jurisdiction over radiocommunication involves exclusive legislative authority over all cable distribution systems making use of signals received by radiocommunication or whether such exclusive authority extends only to what I will call the radiocommunication aspect.

It is important at the outset to observe that federal jurisdiction over some activities or operations does not necessarily mean that any undertaking involved in such activities or operations automatically comes under federal jurisdiction.

[...] It must be stressed that by virtue of [s. 92 (10),] provincial jurisdiction over all undertakings is the rule, federal jurisdiction being the exception. With reference to undertakings of the kind with which we are presently concerned, it is to be noted that telegraph lines are specially included among the undertakings under provincial jurisdiction because exception is made only of those which connect the province with another or extend beyond its limits. At the time of Confederation, telegraph lines were the only known kind of lines used for communication at a distance by means of electrical impulses carried over wires. However, in *Toronto v. Bell Telephone Co.*, the Privy Council had no difficulty in coming to the conclusion that telephone lines should be considered as telegraph lines for constitutional purposes.

[...] Coaxial cables are nothing but a further development in the technology of using wires for the transmission of signals by means of electrical impulses.

[...] In support of federal jurisdiction over coaxial cable networks it is contended that the change of technology in transmission should make no difference. The fallacy of this argument is that it is inconsistent with the very basis of federal jurisdiction which is the use of hertzian waves. Let us not forget that the basic constitutional rule is provincial jurisdiction over local undertakings. Telegraph systems are specifically included in local undertakings. It is clear that these include all communication systems by electrical signals transmitted over wires as appears from the *Bell Telephone Co.* case. In the *Radio* case, the judgments of the majority in this Court which were affirmed by the Privy Council, make it abundantly clear that the very basis of federal jurisdiction was that hertzian waves, by their very nature, could not be confined within a province.

With respect to what was said by the Privy Council, it is important to bear in mind that the case was a reference dealing solely with "radio communications" that is transmissions by means of hertzian waves. The language used should be construed in the light of the question which was under consideration and should not be treated as applicable to an entirely different question.

I think it is of the utmost importance in this matter, to consider the tremendous extent to which communications transmitted by hertzian waves at one point or another are used by undertakings under provincial jurisdiction or conveyed by such undertakings. With the exception of the Bell Telephone Co. system which was established as an interprovincial undertaking and declared by Parliament to be a work for the general advantage of Canada, telephone companies generally come under provincial jurisdiction. It is a well-known fact, of which we are entitled to take judicial notice, that they carry on their wires or cables not only telephone conversations but communications of all kinds, including radio network programs. No one has ever contended that, on that account, they have become undertakings subject to federal jurisdiction. [...]

It will thus be seen that from a physical point of view, with respect to the material set-up which is the essential feature of a cable system, the provincial aspect is by far predominant. The distinctive feature of a cable system, as opposed to radio broadcasting, is that its channels of communication are carried over metal cables strung on poles throughout the area served instead of being carried over what is commonly called "airwaves". The importance of the provincial aspect is therefore undeniable. However, when an aerial is the sole source of signals to be distributed over the cable network, it cannot be denied that this part is also essential. Nevertheless, in view of the considerations previously developed, I cannot agree that "common sense" dictates that on that account the whole undertaking should be under federal jurisdiction.

[...] I cannot agree that the federal authority over radio broadcasting must extend to all undertakings receiving radio broadcasts. In the *Radio* case it was held that federal authority must extend to radio receivers but this does not mean or imply that it must extend to all undertakings operating receivers. Hotels often have aerials and cable distribution networks feeding more receiving sets than many cable distribution undertakings, could this put them under federal control? It is true that for them it is accessory to their principal business. But cable distribution is a developing technology which may, in time, not only complement but even supplant radio broadcasting as a means of bringing television and some other programs to the public. Those undertakings are essentially localized and as is properly stressed in the Public Service Board decisions, they should be specially controlled for the purpose of serving the local needs of the particular area for which they are licensed and must, on account of practical consideration enjoy an exclusive franchise.

[...] I would therefore allow the appeal [...]

[Beetz and de Grandpré JJ. concurred with Pigeon J.]

(c)   Provincial Power to Interfere Collaterally

BELL CANADA v. QUÉBEC (LA COMMISSION DE LA SANTÉ ET DE LA SÉCURITÉ DU TRAVAIL)
[1988] 1 S.C.R. 749.

BEETZ J. [for the Court]: —

I- INTRODUCTION

This appeal is the third of a trilogy. All three appeals raise similar questions which may be stated as one: is a provincial statute regulating health and safety in the workplace, like the statutes at issue, constitutionally applicable to a federal undertaking?

The first appeal is that of *Alltrans Express Ltd. v. British Columbia (Workers' Compensation Board)*, [1988] 1 S.C.R. 897 ("*Alltrans*"). The federal undertaking in question is a trucking business with exclusively interprovincial and international operations. The orders challenged by the undertaking are those of a report by an inspector of the Workers' Compensation Board (the "*Board*"). That report found certain breaches of the *Industrial Health and Safety Regulations*, B.C. Reg. 585/77 (the "*Regulations*"), and noted in particular that, in the maintenance and repair workshops of Alltrans Express Ltd., workers employed by Alltrans wore running

shoes instead of the safety boots prescribed by the *Regulations*. The report ordered
Alltrans Express Ltd. to ensure that its workers wore the regulation safety boots. It
further ordered the business to establish and maintain a safety committee, in
accordance with the *Regulations*. The *Regulations* were promulgated by the *Board*
under the *Workers Compensation Act*, R.S.B.C. 1979, c. 437, and the inspector's
report was made in accordance with that Act and the regulations adopted
pursuant to it. Alltrans Express Ltd. by a petition asked the Court to declare the
orders contained in the inspection report invalid on the ground that they fell
within the exclusive legislative jurisdiction of the Parliament of Canada.

The second appeal is that of *Canadian National Railway Co. v. Courtois*,
[1988] 1 S.C.R. 868 (*"Canadian National"*). A collision between two trains owned by
Canadian National Railway Co. cost the lives of three employees of that federal
undertaking and injured a fourth. An inspector, Christiane Courtois, initiated an
investigation into the railway accident and sent subpoenas to Canadian National
employees. In doing so, she was acting pursuant to ss. 62 and 177 to 193 of the *Act
Respecting occupational health and safety*, S.Q. 1979, c. 63 (the *"Act"*), which require
an employer to prepare an accident report and empower an inspector appointed
by the Commission de la santé et de la sécurité du travail (the *"C.S.S.T."*) to
investigate and issue remedial orders requiring any person to comply with the *Act*
or regulations and fixing a time within which such person must comply. Canadian
National sought by evocation to halt the holding of this investigation on the
ground, *inter alia*, that the *Act* does not constitutionally apply to them and that the
inspector had no jurisdiction to hold the investigation.

Finally, in the appeal at bar (*"Bell Canada"*), the question is whether the
Act, and in particular its ss. 33, 36, 37 and 40 to 45, regarding the protective
reassignment of a pregnant worker, are constitutionally applicable to respondent
Bell Canada, another federal undertaking.

If it is found that the *Act* is constitutionally applicable to Canadian
National and to Bell Canada, it will also be necessary to decide whether the
provisions of this provincial *Act* are rendered inoperative on account of their
inconsistency with the valid provisions of a federal statute. [...]

II- FACTS

[...] At all relevant times Joanne Carrière-Laniel was employed by Bell
Canada in Valleyfield as a telephone operator. The telephone exchange in which
she worked handled, *inter alia*, long distance calls requiring operator assistance
and the directory assistance service. [...]

Bell Canada planned to convert the Valleyfield telephone exchange to
VDT units on May 23, 1981. When Mrs. Carrière-Laniel learned of her employer's
intention in this regard, knowing she was pregnant, she expressed certain
reservations to her immediate superior on May 5, 1981 about working with VDT
units. On May 11, her superior offered her another position. Mrs. Carrière-Laniel
refused.

On May 23, 1981 the Valleyfield office was equipped with VDT units. Mrs. Carrière-Laniel was then on leave until June 7. By various applications, the first of which was made on June 8, 1981, Mrs. Carrière-Laniel obtained unpaid maternity leave for the period from June 8, 1981 to July 19, 1982. Mrs. Carrière-Laniel has not been back to work for Bell Canada since May 23, 1981. She finally resigned on July 9, 1982.

In the meantime, on June 9, 1981 Mrs. Carrière-Laniel gave her immediate superior a letter from a physician confirming that she was pregnant. On the same day she gave her superior a protective re-assignment certificate (ss. 40 and 33 of the *Act*). On July 7, 1981, Bell Canada challenged this protective re-assignment application on the form provided for the purpose.

Ginette Bilodeau had the responsibility of deciding on the application for protective re-assignment by Mrs. Carrière-Laniel. In an undated decision she allowed the application and proceeded to have the *C.S.S.T.* pay Mrs. Carrière-Laniel the compensation provided for in s. 36 of the *Act*, in this case, the sum of $5,535.81.

By its motion in evocation Bell Canada is asking the Court to declare that the undated decision by Ginette Bilodeau, apparently already put into effect, was *ultra vires* the *C.S.S.T.* and cannot be set up against applicant, and if necessary to quash and set aside that decision. It is also asking the Court to declare that ss. 33, 36, 37 and 40 to 45 of the *Act* do not apply to it. [...]

III- SUMMARY OF APPLICABLE PRINCIPLES

Proposition One

General legislative jurisdiction over health belongs to the provinces, subject to the limited jurisdiction of Parliament ancillary to the powers expressly conferred by s. 91 of the *Constitution Act, 1867* or the emergency power relating to the peace, order and good government of Canada: *Schneider v. The Queen*, [1982] 2 S.C.R. 112, at p. 137, reasons of Dickson J. – as he then was – writing for seven judges of this Court. This jurisdiction has historically been seen as resting with the provinces under s. 92(16) of the *Constitution Act, 1867*, "Generally all Matters of a merely local or private Nature in the Province", although the considerable dimensions of this jurisdiction were probably not foreseen in 1867.

Proposition Two

In principle, labour relations and working conditions fall within the exclusive jurisdiction of the provincial legislatures: these matters fall into the class of subjects mentioned in s. 92(13) of the *Constitution Act, 1867*, "Property and Civil Rights in the Province": *Toronto Electric Commissioners v. Snider*, [1925] A.C. 396 ("*Snider*").

Proposition Three

Notwithstanding the rule stated in proposition two, Parliament is vested with exclusive legislative jurisdiction over labour relations and working conditions when that jurisdiction is an integral part of its primary and exclusive jurisdiction over another class of subjects, as is the case with labour relations and working conditions in the federal undertakings covered by ss. 91(29) and 92(10)*a.*, *b.* and *c.* of the *Constitution Act, 1867*, that is undertakings such as Alltrans Express Ltd., Canadian National and Bell Canada. It follows that this primary and exclusive jurisdiction precludes the application to those undertakings of provincial statutes relating to labour relations and working conditions, since such matters are an essential part of the very management and operation of such undertakings, as with any commercial or industrial undertaking[.] [...]

Proposition Four

Several years before the exclusive legislative jurisdiction of Parliament over the working conditions and management of federal undertakings was recognized and established, the Judicial Committee of the Privy Council had held that provincial workmen's compensation schemes were applicable to federal undertakings: *Workmen's Compensation Board v. Canadian Pacific Railway Co.*, [1920] A.C. 184 ("*Workmen's Compensation Board*").

[...] It should be noted that, side by side with workmen's compensation statutes which have a compensatory purpose, legislators have in recent decades gradually adopted other legislation with a preventive purpose.

[...] What was held by the Judicial Committee in *Workmen's Compensation Board* to be applicable to a federal undertaking was the compensatory scheme established by the statute at issue in that case. [...]

V- CONSTITUTIONAL QUESTIONS

The constitutional questions served upon the Attorney General of Canada and the Attorneys General of all provinces in the case at bar are as follows:

Whether ss. 33, 36, 37 and 40 to 45 of an *Act respecting occupational health and safety* (R.S.Q., c. S-2.1) are constitutionally applicable to Bell Canada?

If so, whether these sections are inoperative in respect of Bell Canada as being incompatible or conflicting with federal legislation in the same area applicable to Bell Canada? [...]

VII- CHARACTERIZATION OF THE ACT RESPECTING OCCUPATIONAL HEALTH AND SAFETY

[His Lordship considered the provisions of the act in detail and concluded:]

In view of such a large number of express provisions, one cannot help being struck by the fact that the legislator intended to enact rules regulating the very management and operations of all undertakings it sought to make subject to

841

the *Act*, and appears to have been primarily motivated by a desire not to leave any
aspect of the management and operation out.

Furthermore, the White Paper makes no secret of this intention, which it
expressly confirms at p. 201, *inter alia*:

> [TRANSLATION] As the government's objective is to protect
> the health and safety of workers, it is understandable that the
> definition of workers' rights is regarded as of great importance.
> It is also understandable that employers appear more bound by
> obligations than profiting from rights. *Their obligations in the
> occupational health and safety field result from the rights they possess
> initially over the organization and layout of the workplace as owners
> and managers of their undertakings.* (emphasis added.) [...]

VIII- CLASSIFICATION OF THE ACT RESPECTING OCCUPATIONAL HEALTH AND SAFETY

[...] As we saw under the previous heading, the *Act* is not related to the
subject-matter of health. It accordingly does not fall into the class of subjects
mentioned in subs. 16 of s. 92 of the *Constitution Act, 1867*: "Generally all Matters
of a merely local or private Nature in the Province". Proposition one stated at the
start of these reasons is thus inapplicable. [...]

I will now consider propositions two and three.

The *Act* deals with the following matters: working conditions, labour
relations and the management of undertakings. Under proposition two, these
subjects in principle fall into the class of subject mentioned in s. 92(13) of the
Constitution Act, 1867: "Property and Civil Rights in the Province". The *Act* is
therefore *intra vires*, valid and applicable to undertakings which it may
constitutionally cover.

However, consistent with proposition three and by exception to
proposition two, the *Act* characterized as above cannot be applied to the federal
undertakings mentioned in s. 91(29) and s. 92(10)*a.*, *b.* and *c.* of the *Constitution Act,
1867*, without regulating essential parts of those undertakings and without
making the *Act*, as a consequence of such an application, a statute dealing with
matters that fall within the classes of subjects mentioned in those subsections. The
Act is therefore not applicable to undertakings such as Bell Canada and Canadian
National.

However, it will be necessary to look further at proposition three and the cases
on which it is based. [His Lordship reviewed the cases.]

The power to make laws regarding matters falling within the class of
subject of the postal service mentioned in s. 91 of the *Constitution Act, 1867* is no
more or less exclusive than the power to make laws regarding matters falling
within the class of subject of federal undertakings covered by ss. 91(29) and
92(10)*a.*, *b.* and *c.*, quite apart from the question of whether Parliament has

exercised its primary powers. If this exclusivity suffices to remove the postal service from the scope of an Act like the Saskatchewan minimum wage statute, it also suffices, and in the same way, to remove federal undertakings from the scope of a statute of the same type, as was held in *Bell Canada 1966* and as the Court must now find.

[...] In the *Postal Service Case 1948* and the *Stevedoring* case (cites omitted), the Court had already indicated the outline of an answer to this crucial question: does Parliament's power to legislate on working conditions and labour relations in federal undertakings and on the management of those undertakings derive from its primary, elementary or unassailable jurisdiction over them? – or on the contrary does it derive from the power which is incidental and ancillary to its primary jurisdiction, and which it is recognized as having by Lord Tomlin's third proposition in *Attorney-General for Canada v. Attorney-General for British Columbia*, [1930] A.C. 111, at p. 118:

> (3.) It is within the competence of the Dominion Parliament to provide for matters which, though otherwise within the legislative competence of the provincial legislature, are necessarily incidental to effective legislation by the Parliament of the Dominion upon a subject of legislation expressly enumerated in s. 91.

The answer to this crucial question dictates the answer to the question of whether provincial statutes apply to federal undertakings in the area of working conditions and labour relations and the management of undertakings. Such provincial legislation is inapplicable to federal undertakings when it has the effect of regulating matters which fall within the primary jurisdiction of Parliament. The question was to be finally resolved by *Bell Canada 1966*.

This was an action brought in the Superior Court by which the Quebec Minimum Wage Commission claimed some $50,000 from Bell Canada as a levy for 1959 under regulations adopted pursuant to the *Minimum Wage Act*, R.S.Q. 1941, c. 164, s. 8e. [...]

Bell Canada admitted that the *Minimum Wage Act* was constitutionally valid but argued that the Act was not applicable to it.

[...] At page 771 Martland J. wrote:

> The appellant's submission is that the legislation in question did apply to the respondent until the federal parliament occupied the field and that this was not done until the enactment, on March 18, 1965, of the *Canada Labour Standards Code*, Statutes of Canada 1964-65, c. 38.

[...] [Martland J. cited ss. 91(29) and 92(10) of the *Constitution Act, 1867* and continued at pp. 771-772 S.C.R.:]

I have quoted these well known provisions of the Act in full because I think it is of assistance to refer back to their actual wording in defining the issue in the present case. The *Minimum Wage Act* is a statute which, *inter alia*, purports to regulate to an extent the wages to be paid by the respondent to its employees. If the regulation of the wages paid to its employees by an undertaking within the excepted classes in s. 92(10) is a *"matter"* coming within those classes of subject, then, by virtue of s. 91(29), it is within the exclusive legislative authority of the Canadian Parliament.

The question is, therefore, as to what "matters" are within the classes of legislative subjects defined in that paragraph. Clearly they extend beyond the mere physical structure of, e.g., a railway or a telegraph system. The words "works" and "undertakings" are to be read disjunctively (*Attorney-General for Ontario v. Winner*, [1954] A.C. 541) and the word "undertaking" has been defined in *re Regulation and Control of Radio Communication in Canada*, [1932] A.C. 304 at 315.

[...] In my opinion all matters which are a vital part of the operation of an interprovincial undertaking as a going concern are matters which are subject to the exclusive legislative control of the federal parliament within s. 91(29). It was not disputed in argument that the regulation of the rates to be paid by the respondent's customers is a matter for federal legislation. In the *Winner* case, supra, the regulation of those places at which passengers of an interprovincial bus line might be picked up or to which they might be carried was held not to be subject to provincial control. Similarly, I feel that the regulation and control of the scale of wages to be paid by an interprovincial undertaking, such as that of the respondent, is a matter for exclusive federal control.

I would adopt the statement of Abbott J. in this Court, in the *Reference as to the Validity of the Industrial Relations and Disputes Investigation Act*:

> The right to strike and the right to bargain collectively are now generally recognized, and the determination of such matters as hours of work, rates of wages, working conditions and the like, is in my opinion *a vital part of the management and operation of any commercial or any industrial undertaking*. This being so, the power to regulate such matters, in the case of undertakings which fall within the legislative authority of Parliament lies with Parliament and not with the Provincial Legislatures. (emphasis added.)

[...] I think it is quite impossible to distinguish the circumstances of the case at bar from those of *Bell Canada 1966*. The working conditions and labour relations as well as the management of federal undertakings such as Bell Canada, are matters falling within the classes of subject mentioned in s. 91(29) of the *Constitution Act, 1867*, and consequently fall within the exclusive legislative jurisdiction of the Parliament of Canada.

Moreover, as I indicated at the start of these reasons, the exclusivity rule approved by *Bell Canada 1966* does not apply only to labour relations or to federal undertakings. It is one facet of a more general rule against making works, things or persons under the special and exclusive jurisdiction of Parliament subject to provincial legislation, when such application would bear on the specifically federal nature of the jurisdiction to which such works, things or persons are subject. [...]

4. IMPAIRMENT OF FEDERAL UNDERTAKINGS

[...] I think it is worth making certain clarifications regarding the concept of impairment. If the application of a provincial statute to a federal undertaking has the effect of impairing or paralyzing it, that *a fortiori* is an almost certain sign that such application bears upon the specifically federal nature of the undertaking and constitutes an encroachment on the exclusive legislative authority of Parliament. It is for this reason that it would appear to me to be useful to show how various provisions of the *Act* are in fact likely to impair the operations and functioning of federal undertakings; which is an additional reason for regarding it as inapplicable to those undertakings, regardless of any conflict between federal and provincial legislation.

The concept of impairment apparently originated in decisions of the Judicial Committee when it had to be decided the extent to which federally incorporated companies are subject to provincial statutes which are general in application, and in particular to the general companies legislation in effect in a province. Laskin C.J. summarized the question in *Natural Parents*, at pp. 761-62, and I can do no better than to quote him:

> If the phrase "provincial laws of general application" has any source, it is in the "federal company" cases, involving the relationship of general companies legislation of a province to federally incorporated companies. Thus, in *John Deere Plow Co. v. Wharton*, [1915] A.C. 330, at pp. 342-3, Lord Haldane commented as follows:

> It is true that even when a company has been incorporated by the Dominion Government with powers to trade, it is not the less subject to provincial laws of general application enacted under the powers conferred by s. 92.

> The history of this matter is well known because from the very beginning of its concern with the *British North America Act* the Privy Council drew a distinction between authority to

incorporate companies and to prescribe their powers and their corporate structure and the internal relationship of shareholders and directors and authority to regulate the activities or enterprises in which the companies are engaged. It was in this connection that Lord Haldane made the observation above quoted. Yet in the very case in which he made it, the Privy Council concluded that it was not open to a province under its general companies legislation to require a licence of a federally incorporated company as a condition of carrying on business *qua* company because this would in effect prevent it from exercising the powers with which it was endowed by federal authority.

> *Attorney-General of Manitoba v. Attorney-General of Canada*, [1929] A.C. 260, and *Lymburn v. Mayland*, [1932] A.C. 318, are two contrasting cases in which the principle of *John Deere Plow*, seen in later cases like *Great West Saddlery Co. v. The King*, [1921] 2 A.C. 91, was applied to provincial legislation which was alleged to put federally incorporated companies at the mercy of the province in respect of the sale of their shares.

[...] While it is not necessary for the purpose of concluding as to the inapplicability of a provincial statute, the transposition of the concept of impairment from the field of federally incorporated companies to that of federal undertakings may be valid in cases in which the application of provincial legislation to federal undertakings in fact impairs the latter, paralyzes them or destroys them. Indeed, many provisions which are fundamental to the *Act* are clearly likely to impair the undertaking to which it applies.

In deciding what constitutes impairment the Court cannot disregard potential impairment or effects, especially when, as here, far-reaching provincial statutes are at issue here designed to be accompanied by a large number of regulations, ordinances or remedial orders, or which can have major as well as minor effects on the undertaking, effects which cannot be foreseen at the time the Court must rule on whether the statute is applicable, as is true for example with exercise of the right of refusal. Furthermore, though the constitutional questions presented in the cases which make up this trilogy only make reference to certain provisions of the *Act*, these provisions must be placed in the context of the *Act* taken as a whole, as counsel did in their factums and oral argument. In my view, many of the fundamental provisions of the *Act* have the effect of impairing the undertakings to which they apply. [...]

X- CONCLUSION

I would answer the first constitutional question in the negative. In view of my answer to the first question, it is not necessary to answer the second. [...]

C.N.R. v. CLARK
[1988] 2 S.C.R. 680.

[Respondent, who was then two years old, was seriously injured when he was struck by a C.N. train after he had wandered onto unfenced C.N. lands and railway tracks. The accident was alleged to have been caused by the negligence of the appellant and its employees, and in particular by a breach of common law duty of care, as well as breaches of provisions of the *Railway Act* and the Uniform Code of Operating Rules. The action was instituted more than three years after the cause of action arose. In its defence the appellant denied the allegations of negligence and pleaded in the alternative that the respondent's action was barred by the two-year limitation period in s. 342(1) of the *Railway Act*. Respondent, however, argued that the applicable limitations of actions provision was s. 18 of the provincial *Limitations of Actions Act*, which would permit the action to be commenced within six years of the infant's attaining the age of majority. On an application for the determination before trial of a question of law, the Court of Queen's Bench held that the limitation period in s. 342(1) of the *Railway Act* was not applicable to the respondent's action against the appellant. The Court of Appeal upheld that decision. At issue here is whether s. 342(1) is applicable as a matter of construction and constitutional validity. The constitutional questions queried (1) whether s. 342(1) of the *Railway Act* was constitutionally valid or constitutionally applicable to this action, and (2) if so, whether it conflicted with and rendered inoperative s. 18 of the provincial *Limitation of Actions Act*.

The Court held that sec. 342(1) of the *Railway Act* applied to the infant plaintiff as a matter of statutory construction and then considered the constitutional questions:]

APPLICATION OF PROVINCIAL LAW TO S. 92(10) UNDERTAKINGS

The first principle is that of the general applicability of provincial legislation of general application. It is well established that undertakings falling within federal competence by virtue of s. 92(10) are subject to provincial laws of general application: see the recent judgment of this Court in *Bell Canada v. Quebec (Commission de la santé et de la sécurité du travail)*, [1988] 1 S.C.R. 749, at pp. 762-3, per Beetz J., describing the "general rule" in the following way:

> [...] works, such as federal railways, things, such as land reserved for Indians, and persons, such as Indians, who are within the special and exclusive jurisdiction of Parliament, are still subject to provincial statutes that are general in their application, whether municipal legislation, legislation on adoption, hunting or the distribution of family property, provided however that the application of these provincial laws does not bear upon those subjects in what makes them specifically of federal jurisdiction:

THE "INTEGRAL ELEMENT" TEST FOR FEDERAL LEGISLATIVE COMPETENCE

The second important principle is that the constitutionality and application of federal legislation pursuant to s. 92(10) is governed by what has been described as the "integral element" approach. The term "integral element" is from the opinion of Beetz J. in *Construction Montcalm Inc. v. Minimum Wage Commission*, [1979] 1 S.C.R. 754. The question arose in that case whether provincial

847

wage control legislation was applicable to a contractor working on the
construction of an airport on land belonging to the federal government. Beetz J.,
writing for the majority, held the provincial laws were applicable (at pp. 768-9):

> The issue must be resolved in the light of established principles
> the first of which is that Parliament has no authority over labour
> relations as such nor over the terms of a contract of
> employment; exclusive provincial competence is the rule:
> *Toronto Electric Commissioners v. Snider*, [1925] A.C. 396. By way
> of exception however, Parliament may assert exclusive
> jurisdiction over these matters if it is shown that such
> jurisdiction is an integral part of its primary competence over
> some other single federal subject: In *re the validity of the Industrial
> Relations and Disputes Investigation Act* [1955] S.C.R. 529 (the
> *Stevedoring* case (cites omitted)). It follows that primary federal
> competence over a given subject can prevent the application of
> provincial law relating to labour relations and the conditions of
> employment but only if it is demonstrated that federal authority
> over these matters is an integral element of such federal
> competence; thus, the regulation of wages to be paid by an
> undertaking, service or business, and the regulation of its
> labour relations, being related to an integral part of the
> operation of the undertaking, service or business, are removed
> from provincial jurisdiction and immune from the effect of
> provincial law if the undertaking, service or business is a federal
> one. [...]

The majority of the Court was of the view that the construction of an
airport is not in every respect an integral part of aeronautics. A contrast was made
between the design of an airport, which would be something of exclusive federal
interest, and a requirement that a protective helmet be worn, a matter which
would relate to provincial safety regulations and have nothing to do with
aeronautics. The *Construction Montcalm Inc.* approach was affirmed the following
year in *Northern Telecom Ltd. v. Communication Workers of Canada*, [1980] 1 S.C.R.
115. In that case the issue was whether employees of Northern Telecom were
employed upon or in connection with the operation of any federal work,
undertaking or business so as to come within the jurisdiction of the Canada
Labour Relations Board. *Construction Montcalm* was summarized as follows, at pp.
131-2:

> In an elaboration of the foregoing, Mr. Justice Beetz in
> *Construction Montcalm Inc. v. Minimum Wage Commission* set out
> certain principles which I venture to summarize:
>
> (1) Parliament has no authority over labour relations as such nor
> over the terms of a contract of employment: exclusive provincial
> competence is the rule;
>
> (2) By way of exception, however, Parliament may assert
> exclusive jurisdiction over these matters if it is shown that such
> jurisdiction is an integral part of its primary competence over
> some other single federal subject;

(3) Primary federal competence over a given subject can prevent the application of provincial law relating to labour relations and the conditions of employment but only if it is demonstrated that federal authority over these matters is an integral element of such federal competence;

(4) Thus, the regulation of wages to be paid by an undertaking, service or business, and the regulation of its labour relations, being related to an integral part of the operation of the undertaking, service or business, are removed from provincial jurisdiction and immune from the effect of provincial law if the undertaking, service or business is a federal one;

(5) The question whether an undertaking, service or business is a federal one depends on the nature of its operation;

(6) In order to determine the nature of the operation, one must look at the normal or habitual activities of the business as those of "a going concern", without regard for exceptional or casual factors; otherwise, the Constitution could not be applied with any degree of continuity and regularity.

A recent decision of the British Columbia Labour Relations Board, *Arrow Transfer Co. Ltd.*, [1974] 1 Can. L.R.B.R. 29, provides a useful statement of the method adopted by the courts in determining constitutional jurisdiction in labour matters. First, one must begin with the operation which is at the core of the federal undertaking. Then the courts look at the particular subsidiary operation engaged in by the employees in question. The court must then arrive at a judgment as to the relationship of that operation to the core federal undertaking, the necessary relationship being variously characterized as "vital", "essen- tial" or "integral".

While tailored to meet the particular issue of constitutional competence in the field of labour relations, this summary provides a guide for the analysis required in the case at bar.

These principles were recently reiterated in *Bell Canada v. Quebec (Commission de la santé et de la sécurité du travail)*, supra. There, provincial occupational health and safety legislation was held inapplicable to a s. 92(10) undertaking on the ground that the provincial measures entered (at p. 748) "directly and massively into the field of working conditions and labour relations on the one hand and, on the other [...] into the field of the management and operation of undertakings". A similar result was reached in the companion cases, *Canadian National Railway Co. v. Courtois*, [1988] 1 S.C.R. 868, and *Alltrans Express Ltd. v. British Columbia (Workers' Compensation Board)*, [1988] 1 S.C.R. 897. Provincial limitation of action legislation plainly does not impinge upon the management or operation of the railway in the manner of the legislation at issue in those cases. Moreover, as noted earlier, Beetz J. specifically adverted to the first general constitutional principle which prevails with reference to s. 92(10) undertakings: they are subject to provincial laws of general application that do not bear upon their specifically federal aspects.

APPLICATION OF PRINCIPLES

There can be no doubt that the New Brunswick legislature is constitutionally competent to legislate, as it did, in respect of general limitation periods by virtue of ss. 92(13) and 92(14) of the Constitution.

It is clear from the authorities just discussed that undertakings which fall under federal legislative competence by virtue of s. 92(10) are not thereby removed from the ambit of provincial legislative competence, and equally, that they are not entirely embraced by the legislative authority of Parliament. While s. 342(1) of the *Railway Act* is plainly legislation in relation to railways, a limitation provision relating to an action for personal injury caused by a railway cannot be said to be an integral part of federal jurisdiction. The core federal responsibility regarding railways is to plan, establish, supervise and maintain the construction and operation of rail lines, railroad companies, and related operations. The establishment of general limitation periods which affect those injured by the negligence of the railway is not, to our mind, part of that core federal responsibility or of any penumbra sufficiently proximate to satisfy the test articulated in the cases just referred to. Such limitation periods are not an integral part of jurisdiction over railways, but rather, as La Forest J.A. put it in the Court of Appeal, at p. 70, "an attempt to reframe for the benefit of railway undertakings the general legal environment of property and civil rights in which these undertakings function in common with other individuals and enterprises". The analogy drawn by La Forest J.A. to the operation of interprovincial truck and bus lines serves to illustrate the point. There can be no doubt that such undertakings fall within federal competence pursuant to s. 92(10), yet it would seem extraordinary to suggest that Parliament could impose a special limitation period to govern actions for injuries caused by undertakings and thereby massively disrupt and interfere with the course of personal injury litigation within the province where an accident occurred. We conclude, therefore, that the assumption made in *Pszenicnz* regarding the constitutionality of the limitation period in the *Railway Act* is no longer valid. We would hold that s. 342(1) is *ultra vires* in so far as it applies to an action such as the present one.

7.   Treaty-Making Power

- Research Note -
THE LABOUR CONVENTIONS CASE

In the *Labour Conventions* case (*A.G. Can. v. A.G. Ont.*, [1937] A.C. 326, [1937] 1 W.W.R. 299, [1937] 1 D.L.R. 673 (P.C.)), the Privy Council was asked to decide on the constitutionality of three statutes, passed by the Parliament of Canada, that gave effect to conventions adopted by the International Labour

Organization of the League of Nations in accordance with the Labour Part of the Treaty of Versailles, Canada being a signatory to the Treaty and the conventions. The statutes dealt with "Hours of Work," "Weekly Rest" and "Minimum Wage."

The Privy Council acknowledged "that the creation of the obligations undertaken in treaties and the assent to their form and quality are the function of the executive alone" ([1937] A.C. 348). The question remained however as to whether this ability of the executive to create the obligations for Canada also conferred upon Parliament the power to pass the laws necessary for the performance of the obligations, "even where these laws dealt with matters within the apparent jurisdiction of the Provinces."

The Attorney General for Canada sought to support Parliament's jurisdiction through s. 132 of the *Constitution Act, 1867* (U.K.), c. 3. The Privy Council rejected the argument, [at 349]:

> The first ground upon which counsel for the Dominion sought to base the validity of the legislation was s. 132. So far as it is sought to apply this section to the conventions when ratified the answer is plain. The obligations are not obligations of Canada as part of the British Empire, but of Canada, by virtue of her new status as an international person, and do not arise under a treaty between the British Empire and foreign countries. This was clearly established by the decision in the *Radio* case, and their Lordships do not think that the proposition admits of any doubt.

It was then argued that Parliament's jurisdiction could be found in the distribution of powers. Lord Atkin stated [at 350]:

> If, therefore, s. 132 is out of the way, the validity of the legislation can only depend upon ss. 91 and 92. Now it had to be admitted that normally this legislation came within the classes of subjects by s. 92 assigned exclusively to the Legislatures of the Provinces, namely – property and civil rights in the Province. This was in fact expressly decided in respect of these same conventions by the Supreme Court in 1925. How, then, can the legislation be within the legislative powers given by s. 91 to the Dominion Parliament? It is not within the enumerated classes of subjects in s. 91: and it appears to be expressly excluded from the general powers given by the first words of the section. It appears highly probable that none of the members of the Supreme Court would have departed from their decision in 1925 had it not been for the opinion of the Chief Justice that the judgments of the Judicial Committee in the *Aeronautics* case and the *Radio* case constrained them to hold that jurisdiction to legislate for the purpose of performing the obligation of a treaty resides exclusively in the Parliament of Canada. Their Lordships cannot take this view of those decisions. The *Aeronautic* case concerned legislation to perform obligations imposed by a treaty between the Empire and foreign countries.

Sect. 132, therefore, clearly applied, and but for a remark at the end of the judgment which in view of the stated ground of the decision was clearly obiter, the case could not be said to be an authority on the matter now under discussion. The judgment in the *Radio* case appears to present more difficulty. But when that case is examined it will be found that the true ground of the decision was that the convention in that case dealt with classes of matters which did not fall within the enumerated classes of subjects in s. 92, or even within the enumerated classes in s. 91. Part of the subject-matter of the convention, namely – broadcasting, might come under an enumerated class, but if so it was under a heading "Interprovincial Telegraphs," expressly excluded from s. 92. Their Lordships are satisfied that neither case affords a warrant for holding that legislation to perform a Canadian treaty is exclusively within the Dominion legislative power.

For the purposes of ss. 91 and 92, i.e., the distribution of legislative powers between the Dominion and the Provinces, there is no such thing as treaty legislation as such. The distribution is based on classes of subjects; and as a treaty deals with a particular class of subjects so will the legislative power of performing it be ascertained.

The Privy Council went on to reject arguments based on Lord Watson's dicta in the *Local Prohibitions* case (*A.G. Ont. v. A.G. Can.*, [1896] A.C. 348 (P.C.)). They could not find that the legislation was a matter of "national concern" or one affecting the "body politic" of the land.

The conclusion, then, is that ([1937] A.C. 352):

It follows from what has been said that no further legislative competence is obtained by the Dominion from its accession to international status, and the consequent increase in the scope of its executive functions. It is true, as pointed out in the judgment of the Chief Justice, that as the executive is now clothed with the powers of making treaties so the Parliament of Canada, to which the executive is responsible, has imposed upon it responsibilities in connection with such treaties, for if it were to disapprove of them they would either not be made or the Ministers would meet their constitutional fate. But this is true of all executive functions in their relation to Parliament. There is no existing constitutional ground for stretching the competence of the Dominion Parliament so that it becomes enlarged to keep pace with enlarged functions of the Dominion executive.

MELANIE MALLET, "A PRIMER ON TREATY MAKING AND TREATY IMPLEMENTATION IN CANADA"
(Original Contribution)

Contemporary problems increasingly transcend national boundaries and require the remedial efforts of multiple state parties. Environmental pollution and child abduction are good examples. International treaties are increasingly important as an instrument of domestic public policy. Today, 40% of domestic legislation is enacted as a result of international commitments.[1]

1. Forming the Treaty Obligation

At the outset, it helps to be clear about "who does what" in terms of treaty making and implementation. Ratifying a treaty[2] creates an obligation at international law; this act is a prerogative of the Crown in right of Canada, rough shorthand for the federal executive.

Several elements of this last statement require further explanation. Prerogative powers are "residual" powers - the remnant of the powers once personally held and exercised by the Sovereign. Under the conventions of responsible government, prerogative powers are exercised by the executive branch of government on the advice of the responsible Minister of the Crown. The prerogative is "personal" to the Crown. The exercise of the Crown's prerogative to make treaties requires no permission from or collaboration with either of the remaining branches of government.

Why is treaty making an exclusively federal prerogative with no parallel capacity for the Crown in Right of the provinces? Professor Ruth Sullivan provides the answer.[3] Only entities with external sovereignty can receive and exercise the rights conferred by international law. This premise, she explained, emanates from Canada's constitutional arrangements, not from the rules of international law. The capacity to act extraterritorially equates to external sovereignty. Rights and powers flowing from external sovereignty are collectively referred to as the foreign affairs power, which includes the power to make treaties.

---

1 A. de Mestral and E. Fox-Decent, "Implementation and Reception: The Congeniality of Canada's Legal Order to International Law" in *The Globalized Rule of Law: Relationships Between International and Domestic Law*, O. Fitzgerald, ed. (Toronto: Irwin Law, 2006) at 34.

2 Signing the agreement does not always crystallize the obligation. Some treaties will not bind their signatories until ratified by the requisite number of states.

3 R. Sullivan "Jurisdiction to Negotiate and Implement Free Trade Agreements in Canada" in Magnet, Constitutional Law of Canada (8th ed. 2001), p. 772 ff.

Canada's constitution does not endow the provinces with capacity to legislate extraterritorially. This withholds external sovereignty from Canada's provinces. An implication of this extraterritorial incapacity is that provinces are incapable of exercising or receiving the rights conferred at international law, including treaty making.

The characterization of treaty making as the sole prerogative of the Crown in right of Canada has one consequence which bears repeating. The Governor General, as a representative of the Sovereign, acts on the advice of the federal foreign affairs minister in exercising the treaty making power but not on the counsel of Parliament. The Governor General can therefore ratify a treaty binding Canada at international law without the prior sanction of the legislative branch of government.

2. Implementing the Treaty Obligation

Under Canada's constitutional arrangements, creating a treaty obligation and implementing that obligation require separate constitutional warrant. Implementation raises issues relating to both the separation of powers and to the division of legislative powers between federal and provincial governments.

With regard to the separation of powers and treaty making, the federal executive can bind the country at international law but generally cannot ensure that the treaty obligation will be honoured at home. The prerogative is the source of the Crown's ability to enter the treaty, but it confers no power to legislate.

This divide between executive and legislative functions with regard to treaty obligations is important because of Canada's dualist system. Dualism means that Canada - like the United Kingdom - distinguishes between obligations at international law and those at domestic law. International obligations do not automatically form part of the domestic legal system. Rather, most of these obligations must be transformed into Canada's legal system by a separate act of the legislative branch.[1] This system ensures some balance of power between executive and legislative branches of government, preventing the executive from overriding Parliament's powers simply by entering into international agreements. In theory, Parliament could refuse to pass the legislation required to domesticate international obligations, although this possibility is remote where the government has a commanding majority in Parliament.

Further difficulties in treaty implementation are created by Canada's distribution of legislative powers between federal and provincial legislatures. In Canada, legislative power is divided between federal and provincial legislatures by sections 91 to 95 of the *Constitution Act, 1867*. The federal executive can ratify an agreement dealing with almost any conceivable subject matter. It does not

---

1   Only those treaty obligations which necessitate changes to the domestic legal system require legislation. (*Labour Conventions, infra*). de Mestral and Fox-Decent point out that this might not be true of treaties representing customary international law, supra note 1 at p. 853.

follow that Parliament will have the jurisdiction to implement the agreement. Treaty implementation must respect the federal division of powers. This idea is set out in a trilogy of cases from the Privy Council era.[1]

The first of these cases, the *Aeronautics Reference*,[2] concerned an agreement regulating aeronautics that Canada ratified after the Great War. At issue was federal jurisdiction to enact a far-reaching range of legislative measures to transform the treaty obligations. Some of the measures governed by the treaty, such as licencing, normally fall within provincial jurisdiction under section 92(13). The Privy Council found that Parliament could enact the legislation. Crucial to this decision, however, was the nature of the agreement signed. The treaty was ratified by Canada on behalf of the British Empire, placing it within section 132 of the *British North America Act, 1867*. That section gave Parliament the power it needed to fulfill its responsibilities arising under Empire treaties.

Following the Statute of Westminister, Canada acquired external sovereignty, and with it the capacity to enter into international agreements on its own. This ended the relevance of section 132.

Subsequently, the *Radio Reference*[3] considered Parliament's authority to implement treaties governing radio communications. In contrast to the earlier aeronautics treaty, these obligations arose from Canada's independent ratification of several treaties. On this basis, the Privy Council determined that Parliament could not use section 132 as a basis for its legislation. However, federal jurisdiction to implement the treaty obligations was found on the basis of the residual POGG power, because radio communications had not been distributed to either order of government under section 91 or section 92.

In 1937, the *Labour Conventions Case* finally settled the question of which order of government had legislative power to implement treaties.[4] The federal government ratified a series of agreements regulating labour conditions. Parliament then attempted to implement these obligations. The Privy Council found the federal legislation *ultra vires* Parliament, as it concerned matters coming within section 92(13). The Privy Council denied that Parliament could always rely on section 132 or the POGG power as bases for implementing treaty obligations. Lord Atkin offered several important comments about Canada's system of treaty making and implementation in the decision. These propositions remain authoritative and some of his conclusions regarding the overlay of Canada's federal system on treaty arrangements should be emphasized.

---

1   Professor Sullivan, *supra* note 3, at p. 853, also treats these cases in her discussion.
2   *Reference re the Regulation and Control of Aeronautics in Canada*, [1932] AC 54 (P.C.).
3   *Reference re Regulation and Control of Radio Communication in Canada*, [1932] AC 304 (P.C.).
4   *A.G. Canada v. A.G. Ontario*, [1937] AC 326 (P.C.).

First, Lord Atkin established that the Constitution contains no freestanding grant of power to implement treaties apart from section 132. Rather, the jurisdiction to implement treaties is divided along the line drawn by sections 91 and 92. Therefore, if a treaty regulates a subject matter falling to section 91(27), for instance, the federal government has the constitutional authority to implement the obligation. However, the federal government does not have the authority to transform treaty obligations that regulate provincial subjects, such as property and civil rights. Lord Atkin cautioned that Parliament must not be allowed to absorb provincial legislative authority by ratifying international agreements treating provincial subject matters. Concern that the federal government might use its treaty making power to get around the formal division of powers is evident throughout the judgment.

3. After *Labour Conventions*

The consequence of *Labour Conventions* is that Canada might find itself unable to comply with its international obligations if the provinces are uncooperative. A recent example will help illustrate. Implementing Canada's obligations to reduce emissions of "greenhouse gases" under the Kyoto Protocol requires the exercise of provincial legislative power in relation to energy and manufacturing. While the federal executive incurred the obligations under Kyoto, implementation of some of the treaty obligations requires legislative action in areas falling outside of Parliament's jurisdiction. The former Liberal government was prepared to proceed with implementation in spite of provincial protests that this would encroach on their jurisdiction. In the face of an almost certain constitutional challenge by the provinces, the validity of federal implementing legislation would have depended on whether the government could have found an appropriate anchor in section 91. If not, the former government would have been unable to honour its commitments.

Lord Atkin pointed out in *Labour Conventions* that the federal government might avoid these impasses by consulting with affected provinces before ratifying a treaty. Often, the federal government does engage in provincial consultation, but there are no rules requiring this or setting out what level of consent is needed before ratification can occur. As a result, there have been periodic calls to formalize the practice. Bloc Québecois MP Jean-Yves Roy tabled a private member's bill in 2004 that would have prevented the federal executive government from ratifying treaties touching areas of provincial jurisdiction without prior consultation. The bill was unsuccessful.

While it is true that prior consultation with the provinces might avoid some of the problems of implementation, requiring provincial permission is not desirable in every instance. As the Kyoto example illustrates, Canada's ability to "pull its weight" in agreements beneficial to the world community can be compromised where federal and provincial priorities are not aligned. Canada's participation in remedying a global harm has been jeopardized by provinces' economic self-interest, a distasteful reality for many.

The provinces' ability to hamstring treaty implementation has been criticized since 1937. Various suggestions for change have been presented. As a scholar, Bora Laskin lamented the state of affairs established in *Labour*

Conventions. Sitting as Chief Justice of Canada in *Vapour Canada*,[1] Laskin revisited the idea that a general federal power to implement treaty obligations could be based in the POGG power. This suggestion has roundly been dismissed as obiter and has yet to take root.

Others suggest formal constitutional modification to bring Canada's treaty implementation regime in line with that of Australia. Australia's constitution explicitly gives the federal legislature power to legislate in respect of all treaty obligations, even those that touch areas of sub-national jurisdiction. While this idea might be appealing, the chances of such a dramatic constitutional change ever passing through Canada's complex amending formulae are remote.

Professor Sullivan[2] noted that moderate amendments to the status quo might be the most feasible. She referred to Professor LaForest's proposals which rely on judicial interpretation to get around the *Labour Conventions* problem. First, constitutional analyses of implementing legislation might recognize an international aspect to subject matters normally coming within provincial jurisdiction. This international aspect would support federal legislation. LaForest's second suggestion was a restatement of the "necessarily incidental" doctrine.

This suggestion would save provisions that encroach on provincial jurisdiction if they are part of a broader valid statute implementing treaty obligations.

At times, the federal government tries to avoid jurisdictional squabbles by exercising caution in implementing treaty commitments that would otherwise encroach on areas of provincial jurisdiction. Results are varied. The *Species at Risk Act* (SARA), for instance, is federal legislation implementing some of Canada's commitments under the *Convention on Biological Diversity*. The legislation's ability to combat species extinction is undermined by its limited application to federal lands. David Boyd[3] pointed out that animals found on provincial land might be subject to different regulations than animals located on federal lands. Animals, of course, move about without regard for political boundaries. These factors point to the shortcomings of a fragmented approach to species protection. To be fair, federal tactics on the issue also include intergovernmental agreements to harmonize legislation, as well as methods to address provincial inaction. To the extent that these measures are not enforceable, however, SARA highlights the deficiencies of federal restraint.

Negotiating federal and provincial dynamics will become more pressing as international obligations touch on increasingly complex issues that do not respect Canada's neat constitutional allocation of responsibilities. Changing the formal rules of treaty implementation would involve significant and difficult amendment to Canada's legal system. For that reason, governments have reconciled themselves to working within the rules set out in *Labour Conventions*, aware that the rise of global problem-solving remains entangled in the realities of Canadian federalism.

---

1 *MacDonald v. Vapor Canada*, [1977] 2 S.C.R. 134.
2 *Supra* note 3, p. 853.
3 *Unnatural Law: Rethinking Canada's Environmental Law and Policy* (Vancouver: UBC Press, 2003).

PART IV

ABORIGINAL PEOPLES

1. Introduction

CONSTITUTION ACT, 1867

91. [...] it is hereby declared that (notwithstanding anything in this Act) the exclusive Legislative Authority of the Parliament of Canada extends to all Matters coming within the Classes of Subjects next hereinafter enumerated; that is to say, –

24. Indians, and Lands reserved for the Indians.

Minister Jane Stewart Apologizing to Chief Phil Fontaine for Residential School Abuse, 1998

CONSTITUTION ACT, 1982

CANADIAN CHARTER OF RIGHTS AND FREEDOMS

25. The guarantee in this *Charter* of certain rights and freedoms shall not be construed so as to abrogate or derogate from any aboriginal, treaty or other rights or freedoms that pertain to the aboriginal peoples of Canada including

(*a*) any rights or freedoms that have been recognized by the *Royal Proclamation* of October 7, 1763; and

(*b*) any rights or freedoms that now exist by way of land claims agreements or may be so acquired.

CONSTITUTION ACT, 1982

RIGHTS OF THE ABORIGINAL PEOPLES OF CANADA

35. (1) The existing aboriginal and treaty rights of the aboriginal peoples of Canada are hereby recognized and affirmed.

(2) In this Act, "aboriginal peoples of Canada" includes the Indian, Inuit and Métis peoples of Canada.

(3) For greater certainty, in subsection (1) "treaty rights" includes rights that now exist by way of land claims agreements or may be so acquired.

(4) Notwithstanding any other provision of this Act, the aboriginal and treaty rights referred to in subsection (1) are guaranteed equally to male and female persons.

35.1 The government of Canada and the provincial governments are committed to the principle that, before any amendment is made to Class 24 of section 91 of the *"Constitution Act 1867"*, to section 25 of this Act or to this Part,

(*a*) a constitutional conference that includes in its agenda an item relating to the proposed amendment, composed of the Prime Minister of Canada and the first ministers of the provinces, will be convened by the Prime Minister of Canada; and

(*b*) the Prime Minister of Canada will invite representatives of the aboriginal peoples of Canada to participate in the discussion on that item.

THE ROYAL PROCLAMATION

October 7, 1763.

[...] And whereas it is just and reasonable, and essential to our Interest, and the Security of our Colonies, that the several Nations or Tribes of Indians with whom We are connected, and who live under our Protection, should not be molested or disturbed in the Possession of such Parts of Our Dominions and Territories as, not having been ceded to or purchased by Us, are reserved to them, or any of them, as their Hunting Grounds. – We do therefore, with the Advice of our Privy Council, declare it to be our Royal Will and Pleasure, that no Governor or Commander in Chief in any of our Colonies of Quebec, East Florida, or West Florida, do presume, upon any Pretence whatever, to grant Warrants of Survey, or pass any Patents for Lands beyond the Bounds of their respective Governments, as described in their Commissions; as also that no Governor or Commander in Chief in any of our other Colonies or Plantations in America do presume for the present, and until our further Pleasure be known, to grant Warrants of Survey, or pass Patents for any Lands beyond the Heads or Sources of any of the Rivers which fall into the Atlantic Ocean from the West and North West, or upon any Lands whatever, which, not having been ceded to or purchased by Us as aforesaid, are reserved to the said Indians, or any of them.

And We do further declare it to be Our Royal Will and Pleasure, for the present as aforesaid, to reserve under our Sovereignty, Protection, and Dominion, for the use of the said Indians, all the Lands and Territories not included within the Limits of Our said Three new Governments, or within the Limits of the Territory granted to the Hudson's Bay Company, as also all the Lands and Territories lying to the Westward of the Sources of the Rivers which fall into the Sea from the West and North West as aforesaid.

And We do hereby strictly forbid, on Pain of our Displeasure, all our loving Subjects from making any Purchases or Settlements whatever, or taking Possession of any of the Lands above reserved, without our especial leave and Licence for that Purpose first obtained.

And, We do further strictly enjoin and require all Persons whatever who have either wilfully or inadvertently seated themselves upon any Lands within the Countries above described, or upon any other Lands which, not having been ceded to or purchased by Us, are still reserved to the said Indians as aforesaid, forthwith to remove themselves from such Settlements.

And whereas great Frauds and Abuses have been committed in purchasing Lands of the Indians, to the great Prejudice of our Interests, and to the great Dissatisfaction of the said Indians; In order, therefore, to prevent such Irregularities for the future, and to the end that the Indians may be convinced of our Justice and determined Resolution to remove all reasonable Cause of Discontent, We do, with the Advice of our Privy Council strictly enjoin and require, that no private Person do presume to make any purchase from the said Indians of any Lands reserved to the said Indians, within those parts of our Colonies where, We have thought proper to allow Settlement; but that, if at any Time any of the Said Indians should be inclined to dispose of the said Lands, the same shall be Purchased only for Us, in our Name, at some public Meeting or Assembly of the said Indians, to be held for that Purpose by the Governor or Commander in Chief of our Colony respectively within which they shall lie; and in case they shall lie within the limits of any Proprietary Government, they shall be purchased only for the Use and in the name of such Proprietaries, conformable to such Directions and Instructions as We or they shall think proper to give for that Purpose; And we do, by the Advice of our Privy Council, declare and enjoin, that the Trade with the said Indians shall be free and open to all our Subjects whatever, provided that every Person who may incline to Trade with the said Indians do take out a Licence for carrying on such Trade from the Governor or Commander in Chief of any of our Colonies respectively where such Person shall reside, and also give Security to observe such Regulations as We shall at any Time think fit, by ourselves or by our Commissaries to be appointed for this Purpose, to direct and appoint for the Benefit of the said Trade:

And we do hereby authorize, enjoin, and require the Governors and Commanders in Chief of all our Colonies respectively, as well those under Our immediate Government as those under the Government and Direction of Proprietaries, to grant such Licences without Fee or Reward, taking especial Care to insert therein a Condition, that such Licence shall be void, and the Security forfeited in case the Person to whom the same is granted shall refuse or neglect to observe such Regulations as We shall think proper to prescribe as aforesaid.

And we do further expressly enjoin and require all Officers whatever, as well Military as those Employed in the Management and Direction of Indian Affairs, within the Territories reserved as aforesaid for the use of the said Indians, to seize and apprehend all Persons whatever, who standing charged with Treason, Misprisions of Treason, Murders, or other Felonies or Misdemeanors, shall fly from Justice and take Refuge in the said Territory, and to send them under a proper guard to the Colony where the Crime was committed of which they stand accused, in order to take their Trial for the same.

Given at our Court at St. James's the 7th Day of October 1763, in the Third Year of our Reign.

GOD SAVE THE KING

George R.

FIRST NATIONS IN CANADA
DEPARTMENT OF INDIAN AFFAIRS AND NORTHERN DEVELOPMENT (1997)

General Introduction

Aboriginal peoples have occupied the territory now called Canada for several thousands of years. Many diverse and autonomous First Nations lived in the territory as hunters and gatherers for most of that period of time. The term "Indian," which outsiders long used to refer to First Nations peoples, is now considered a misnomer (an error in naming). "Indian" peoples in Canada today prefer to be known as First Nations. Canada's two other Aboriginal peoples are the Inuit and the Métis. Inuit are Arctic people. They have lived along the coastal edge and the islands of Canada's far North for thousands of years. Métis are people of mixed ancestry, the descendants of Aboriginal peoples who intermarried with European fur traders and settlers.

First Nations varied as widely as the terrain of Canada itself. In the wide Prairie interior, small groups of families co-operated in hunting the migratory buffalo which provided the meat and skins necessary for their survival. These people designed shelters to suit their nomadic existence. The tipi - a conical pole structure covered with skins - was portable, easily erected, warm, well ventilated and sound enough to weather strong winds.

The Pacific Coast First Nations, on the other hand, evolved a very different culture. The bounty of the sea - salmon, shellfish and the great whale - made possible the creation of permanent villages and leisure time to carve from cedar and stone magnificent art objects now housed in museums throughout the world.

Equally distinct and unique were the cultures of the nomadic Woodland people, the tribes of the British Columbia interior plateau, the Iroquoian farmers of southeastern Ontario and the hunters of the northern barren lands. [...]

Pre-history

The first inhabitants of a largely glacier-covered North America were hunters. They hunted big game animals like the giant sloth and the mammoth, both of which were much larger than any land mammal of the 20th century. The weapons hunters used were wooden lances with sharp stone heads, made by painstakingly chipping pieces from flint rock. Historians studying the prehistoric era speculate that hunters made their attacks at very close range, probably when the animal was mired in a bog.

The Big Game Hunting Culture flourished in Canada's plains and eastern woodlands until about 8000 B.C. In Canada's far West there developed a similar ancient hunting and fishing culture known as Old Cordilleran.

When the glaciers began to melt, the gradually warming climate changed the face of the land and dramatically affected the wildlife. The mammoth soon became extinct. In the forests surrounding the lakes left by retreating glaciers, the people hunted deer, bear, elk and smaller game.

The culture that originated in this moist, forested region has come to be known as Boreal Archaic. Lasting until about 6000 B.C., it was marked by the use of various wood-working tools, including axes, gouges and adzes (an axe with an inward-turning blade). With these, the Boreal Archaic peoples were able to make dugout canoes.

By 1000 B.C., the Early Woodland Culture had developed in eastern North America. During this period, the population became more stable and individual cultures began to crystallize. New features such as pottery and ceremonial burials were gradually incorporated into the cultures of prehistoric tribes in Canada.

First Encounters [...] Religious Missions

Jesuit missionaries followed Champlain to the New World where they lived among various tribes, seeking Christian converts and recording their experiences and impressions. The Jesuits compiled these records into reports which they sent periodically to their superiors in France. These reports were eventually consolidated in 73 volumes (called the Jesuit Relations), which have become a primary source for researchers examining the early history of Aboriginal peoples in Canada.

Besides seeking converts, Jesuits and Sulpicians (another religious order) also undertook the first attempts at full-scale assimilation of First Nations into French culture. The plan was to remove children from their home environment and educate them in live-in schools, either in France or in one of the new settlements. This scheme was not very successful, however, as all the students eventually returned to their people. The Ursuline nuns made similar attempts with girls from First Nations communities, but their efforts were likewise abandoned when the nuns observed the girls becoming ill and depressed in their new surroundings. In the late 17th and mid-18th centuries the Jesuits successfully established Christian villages among First Nations. The present-day Quebec First Nations of Kahnawake, Akwesasne and Huron-Wendat all had their origins in this tutelary system of the Jesuit missionaries.

The Ravages of Disease

The spiritual and material impact of the Europeans was reinforced by the devastating effects of disease. Unsanitary conditions and rotten food on European ships hastened the spread of [...] contagious disease among the passengers. Explorers, traders, settlers and missionaries brought a host of diseases to which First Nations had no immunity.

By the end of the 16th century many communities were destroyed by disease. Some historians have estimated that within a 200-year period, First Nations populations were reduced by as much as 95 percent. Typhoid, diphtheria, plague, influenza, measles, tuberculosis, venereal disease and scarlet fever killed thousands. Smallpox was particularly virulent among the Montagnais, and by 1640 it had reduced the Huron population in southern Ontario by half. [...]

Intertribal Conflict

The fur trade aggravated the long-standing enmity between the Huron and the Iroquois. The desire for blood revenge was replaced by the desire to dominate territory for lucrative trapping and a concerted effort to monopolize trade with Europeans. Through their established trade connections with the Algonquin along the Ottawa River, the Huron managed to establish a monopoly on furs sold to the French. This gave them great power and influence.

By the 1630s the five tribes of the Iroquois confederacy found themselves in not nearly so fortunate a situation, having exhausted most of the supply of fur-bearing animals in their own territory. Thus they began to look enviously on the more productive lands of the Huron.

Devastated by the smallpox epidemics of 1637-1641, the Huron lost many of their experienced leaders, leaving them more vulnerable to Iroquois attack. In 1644, the Iroquois captured three canoe flotillas transporting furs to the French. A subsequent attack in March of 1649 effectively shattered the Huron Nation. Many Huron fled west and were absorbed by other tribes. But essentially, the power of the Huron was ended for all time. The Iroquois did not stop with the destruction of the Huron Nation. Six months later they moved against the Tobacco Nation and in 1650 dispersed the Neutral and cleared the Ottawa River of the Algonquin. The Iroquois did not confine their hostilities to First Nations tribes. Their hatred of the French dated back to 1609 when Champlain, assisting the Algonquin and their Huron allies, had defeated a group of 200 warriors. The enmity engendered by that single incident was to have historical consequences lasting nearly 100 years. Not the least of these was the Iroquois tribe's continual harassment of the French settlements at Montréal, Trois-Rivières and Québec.

French Versus English

For more than 150 years the French and English competed for control of land and trade in Canada. French "coureurs de bois," many of them part Native, penetrated Northern Ontario to the Great Lakes and beyond, seeking new sources of furs.

In 1670 the King of England granted the Hudson's Bay Company control of all lands draining into the great bay for which the company was named. From that point, competition between the two nations for furs became vigorous. Traders representing the two powers advanced through the continent, everywhere repeating the tragic scenario that had been enacted in Eastern Canada and along the St. Lawrence. First Nations who engaged in trade became increasingly dependent on manufactured goods, while firearms and disease took their toll on human and animal life. Intertribal rivalries flared. The Cree and Assiniboine, for example, gradually moved west and north in search of more furs, displacing other tribes in the process. When Montréal fell to the British in 1760, ending French rule in Canada, the terms of surrender stated that the former First Nations allies of the French should be neither penalized nor disturbed in their possession of lands.

Three years later, in the *Royal Proclamation* setting out the boundaries of the newly acquired province of Quebec and those of the American colonies, First Nations' rights were more clearly defined. The proclamation specifically declared a huge area of the country between the Mississippi and the Appalachians to be "Indian territory." Purchases or settlements of that land were strictly forbidden without special "leave and licence" obtained from the Crown. [...]

First Nations' Right

After the American Revolution, the *Royal Proclamation of 1763* ceased to have any bearing on relations between First Nations and Americans. In Canada, however, the proclamation had established a framework for undertaking any future settlements of First Nations lands. Thereafter, it was accepted policy that while title to the land mass of Canada was vested in the Crown, the Aboriginal peoples maintained an underlying title to use and occupy the land. No settlement of land could be undertaken, therefore, until the First Nations' rights had been surrendered in negotiation between the Crown and First Nations occupants.

Between 1763 and 1800, 24 treaties were signed with different groups of First Nations, most of them covering the fertile agricultural lands along the north shore of Lake Ontario. The First Nations involved did not initiate these treaties, nor did they greatly influence the terms. The objective was simply to clear the land of the First Nations' title acknowledged in the *Royal Proclamation.*

At first, lump sum cash payments were made for these land surrenders. Later, however, the Crown undertook to set aside reserves and provide annuities and other benefits for First Nations surrendering title to their land. [...]

Experiments in Acculturation

The year 1830 is generally considered to be the beginning of the modern system of administration for First Nations in Canada. From that date, First Nations settlement on reserves began under government guardianship. [...]

Various methods of achieving assimilation were considered. Some believed that First Nations members should be placed among the settlers to learn through imitation. Others felt that they should be isolated on reserves where teachers, government agents and missionaries would serve as instructors. [...]

During the 1840s various royal commissions looked into the plight of the First Nations in Canada. Many First Nations members continued to lose land held on their behalf to squatters, loggers and poachers. To help combat this kind of intrusion, the Royal Commission of 1844 recommended various improvements in the administration of First Nations lands. In 1850 it was decided that stronger measures were required to protect First Nations and their lands. Acts were passed to achieve this in both Lower Canada (Quebec) and Upper Canada (Ontario). In Lower Canada all First Nations lands and property were vested in a commissioner of Crown lands and 93,000 hectares were set aside, which eventually permitted the creation of nine new reserves. One of the acts passed in Upper Canada made it an offence for anyone to deal with First Nations concerning their lands, or "to enter on, take possession of, or settle on any such lands, by pretext of any right or interest in the same."

The Robinson Treaties

In the 1850s attention turned for the first time to northern areas still occupied by groups of First Nations hunters. The attraction was minerals discovered along the shores of Lake Superior and Lake Huron. A commissioner, W.B. Robinson, was sent to negotiate with the Ojibway for surrender of their title to the land in question.

The treaties he negotiated were called the Robinson-Huron and Robinson-Superior treaties. Through them, the First Nations agreed "to surrender, cede, grant and convey unto Her Majesty, her heirs and successors forever, all their rights, title and interest to the land, and the right to fish and hunt in the lands they surrendered, until these lands are sold or leased to individuals or companies."

An Act for "Gradual Civilization"

In 1857 an act was passed aimed specifically at assimilating First Nations into the mainstream of colonial life. The essence of this act was the concept of "enfranchisement." By forsaking his First Nations heritage, a First Nations man with the appropriate qualifications could become a full citizen. Any First Nations male over the age of 21, literate in English or French, educated to an elementary level, of good moral character and free of debt could be declared to be enfranchised or "no longer deemed to be an Indian."

There would then be no distinction between him and other non-Native citizens. To encourage such a move, "enfranchised Indians would be granted fee simple title" to as much as 20 hectares of reserve land, plus an amount of money equal to the annuities the group he belonged to received on his behalf.

During the next decade a whole range of acts was passed relating to First Nations. These encouraged First Nations to move toward the social and political world of their non-Native neighbours. The acts also protected First Nations lands from alienation, guarded First Nations against the effects of alcohol, and provided for the management of Aboriginal schools and monies earned from First Nations lands. All this legislation was to be inherited by the new nation of Canada when it gained its independence from Britain in 1867. [...]

The Major Treaties

In 1871 the far western colony of British Columbia agreed to join Canada on condition that a rail link be built to the rest of the country within 10 years. At that time, First Nations members numbered perhaps 25,000 across the Prairies. But non-Native people now began to enter their territory in vast numbers. In 1871, to prepare the way, Canada began to obtain surrender of title to all lands that the new settlers would require. Geographical unity was thus the driving force behind a series of "numbered" treaties concluded in rapid succession throughout the fertile belt - the area of prime agricultural land north of the American border between Lake Superior and the Rocky Mountains.

For the most part, Treaty Nos. 1 to 11 featured similar provisions. With a few subtle differences, all the Western treaties provided for reserve lands, monetary payments, suits of clothing every three years to chiefs and headmen, yearly ammunition and twine payments (Treaty Nos. 1, 2 and 9 excepted) and some allowances for schooling. Treaty No. 6 was the only agreement providing for medical treatment and for "assistance in the case of pestilence or famine." [...]

Many historians speculate that while the commissioners saw the treaties in one way, First Nations had a different perspective. Often the two groups came together with vastly different expectations. First Nations sought protection from invading land-hungry settlers and the disruptions they sensed would follow these newcomers. They sought wide ranges which they could call their own and where they could live as they had in the past. The commissioners, on the other hand, saw reserves as places where Aboriginal peoples could learn to be settlers and farmers. For this and other reasons, the treaties left hanging many questions that are yet to be resolved.

The First Indian Act

In 1876 the Canadian Parliament passed its first consolidated *Indian Act*. Although there have been several major revisions, many of its provisions remain to this day. Consolidating all previous legislation with a host of new regulations, the *Indian Act* gave great powers to government to control First Nations living on reserves. It was during this period that the distinction between "Status" and "non-Status Indians" was first formulated. (Status Indians are those who are registered with the federal government as Indians according to the terms of the *Indian Act*. Non-Status Indians are those who are not registered.) [...]

Government control extended to First Nations reserve lands. The act of 1876 explicitly forbade the selling, alienation or leasing of any reserve land unless it was first surrendered or leased to the Crown. By an 1889 amendment, the government assumed greater control over land. This amendment was drafted specifically to permit the federal government to override any Aboriginal group's reluctance to have its land leased.

The *Indian Act* of 1876 also made provision for the election of First Nations chiefs, giving them limited authority over matters such as the allocation of land within reserves and the maintenance of roads. Essentially, these chiefs functioned as agents of the federal government, exercising limited power within federal supervision. Nor did this uniform system take into account the great diversity of First Nations and their cultures, particularly those accustomed to hereditary chieftainship. The concept of enfranchisement was a key provision of the act, the government's ultimate aim still being the total assimilation of the First Nations population in Canada. Very few opted to become enfranchised, however, and an 1880 amendment declared that any First Nations person obtaining a university degree would be automatically enfranchised. A 1933 amendment took enforced enfranchisement even further. By that amendment the government was empowered to order the enfranchisement of First Nations members meeting the qualifications set out in the act, even without the request of the individuals concerned. [...]

The Age of Resurgence

[...] The late 1940s [...] marked the beginning of a new era for First Nations in Canada. Aboriginal leaders emerged, forcefully expressing their people's desire to gain their rightful position of equality with other Canadians, and at the same time, maintain their cultural heritage. In British Columbia, Alberta, Saskatchewan and Ontario, First Nations formed provincially based organizations to protect and advance their interests. Many Aboriginal leaders drew attention to the fact that thousands of First Nations members had fought for their country in both world wars. Although considered good enough to fight, First Nations veterans were nevertheless treated as government wards on their return home. This obvious injustice helped increase the public's awareness of Aboriginal peoples' disadvantaged situation.

The Joint Committee hearings (1946-1948)

As a result of Aboriginal efforts and public concern, in 1946 Parliament established a special joint committee of the Senate and the House of Commons to consider revisions to the *Indian Act*. During the following three summers the committee received briefs and representations from First Nations, missionaries, schoolteachers and federal government administrators.

From these hearings the Canadian public learned just how far Aboriginal peoples had fallen behind all other groups of citizens in terms of living standards, health and education. Malnutrition and diseases caused by poor living conditions were widespread. Evidence also revealed that over 8,000 First Nations children had no access whatever to any kind of schooling. Many First Nations members addressing the committee rejected the idea of cultural assimilation into non-Native society. In particular, they spoke out against the enforced enfranchisement provisions of the *Indian Act*. First Nations also strongly criticized the extent of powers exercised by the government over their affairs. Many groups asked that these "wide and discretionary" powers be vested in the chiefs and councillors on reserves so that they in turn could determine questions of band membership and manage their own funds and reserve lands.

In addition, Aboriginal groups asked that the government adhere more strictly to provisions set out in the various treaties.

The 1951 Indian Act

Despite the extensive hearings, when the *Indian Act* was revised in 1951, it did not greatly differ from any previous legislation. The involuntary enfranchisement clause was retained, as were the provisions that determined Indian status. The *Indian Act* of 1951 therefore left unchanged those provisions that discriminated against Indian women on the basis of their sex. Indian women who married non-Indian men continued to lose their Indian status automatically.

The act, however, did introduce some changes. Laws banning the potlatch and other ceremonies were rescinded and First Nations members were given the freedom to enter public bars to consume alcohol. On the whole, however, government powers over First Nations life remained formidable. Moreover, Parliament did not act on the joint committee's recommendation that a claims commission be established to hear problems arising from the fulfilment of the treaties.

Although the *Indian Act* continued to block First Nations' desire for self-determination, by 1960 some definite improvements had been made in their social and economic conditions. It was in 1960 that the right to vote in federal elections was at long last extended to First Nations members. Aboriginal veterans played a big role in this change. They pointed out that they had fought for Canada in two world wars, yet were unfairly deprived of the right to vote.

With the provision of better health services in the mid-1950s, the Status Indian population increased rapidly. In addition, many more First Nations children had access to schooling, including secondary and post-secondary education. In general, however, the living conditions of Aboriginal peoples still fell far short of the standards other Canadians had come to expect as the norm.

The 1969 White Paper

In a further effort to help First Nations achieve equality with other Canadians, the federal government consulted with them extensively during 1968-1969 on proposed changes to the *Indian Act*. The 1969 White Paper on Indian Policy which the government then proposed, however, was overwhelmingly rejected by First Nations.

Essentially, the policy called for a repeal of the *Indian Act*, thus ending the federal responsibility for First Nations and terminating their special status. The policy also recommended that an equitable way be found for bringing the treaties to an end. In this way, the government hoped to abolish what it saw as the false separation between First Nations and the rest of Canadian society.

What the government had not fully understood was the value First Nations placed on their special status within confederation and on their treaty rights. The *Indian Act* thus revealed itself to be a paradox for First Nations. While it could be viewed as a mechanism for social control and assimilation, it was also the vehicle that confirmed the special status of First Nations members in Canada.

So strong was the negative reaction of First Nations and the general public that the government withdrew the White Paper. Ironically, the new policy had served to fan sparks of Aboriginal nationalism. First Nations leaders from across the country united in a reaffirmation of their separateness. The Indian Association of Alberta, for example, entitled their paper of counter proposals Citizens Plus. In other words, First Nations wanted all the benefits of Canadian citizenship in addition to their special rights deriving from their unique trust relationship with the Crown. The White Paper had the positive effect of clearing the air. The government sought new measures to help Aboriginal peoples gain from the benefits enjoyed by Canadian society as a whole, while preserving and encouraging their unique cultural heritage.

In 1969 all Indian agents were withdrawn from reserves across the country, ending the government's paternalistic presence on First Nations lands. At this time, the government also began to fund Aboriginal political organizations. Increasingly, these organizations focused on the need for full recognition of their Aboriginal rights and renegotiation of the treaties. They believed that only in this way could they rise above their disadvantaged position in Canadian society. Accordingly, in 1970 the government began funding Aboriginal groups and associations specifically for research into treaties and Aboriginal rights. [...]

Aboriginal Rights Confirmed

[...] [I]t was the court case of the Nisga'a of British Columbia, [...] heard in 1973, that brought the whole issue of Native claims into focus.

The province of British Columbia had consistently denied the existence of an Aboriginal interest in the land. After many years of persistence, the Nisga'a succeeded in bringing their fight for recognition of Aboriginal title to the Supreme Court of Canada. The issue at stake was whether or not such title existed in law.

Although the case was dismissed on a technicality, six of the seven judges acknowledged the existence of Aboriginal title in Canadian law. But the six split evenly on the issue of whether Aboriginal title continued to exist in British Columbia. The seventh judge ruled against the Nisga'a on a technical point of law. A review of this decision in August 1973 led the federal government to announce its willingness to negotiate land claims based on outstanding Aboriginal title.

The government's objective in settling these land claims was to exchange undefined Aboriginal rights for a clearly defined package of rights and benefits set out in a settlement agreement.

Native Claims

In 1973, the federal government recognized two broad classes of claims - comprehensive and specific.

Comprehensive claims are based on the recognition that there are continuing Aboriginal rights to lands and natural resources. Such claims arise in those parts of Canada where Aboriginal title has not previously been dealt with by treaty and other legal means. Comprehensive land claims are currently under negotiation in the Yukon, Labrador, most of British Columbia, Northern Quebec, Ontario and the Northwest Territories. The claims are termed "comprehensive" because of their wide scope. Comprehensive claims include such things as land title, fishing and trapping rights, financial compensation and other social and economic benefits.

Specific claims, on the other hand, deal with specific grievances that First Nations may have regarding the fulfilment of treaties. Specific claims also cover grievances relating to the administration of First Nations lands and other assets under the *Indian Act*.

From the early 1970s to March 1996, the government provided Aboriginal groups with approximately $380 million for work on their claims. This money enabled Aboriginal peoples to conduct research into treaties and Aboriginal rights and to research, develop and negotiate their claims. In 1986 the federal government announced a new comprehensive claims policy in answer to Aboriginal groups' concerns. One of Aboriginal peoples' main concerns had to do with the abolition of their rights and title to land. Historically, this was a problem with the treaty-making process. In the past, the federal government would only negotiate treaties if Aboriginal peoples accepted "extinguishment" of their Aboriginal rights and title. The new claims policy provided other options to this total extinguishment of rights and title. It also widened the scope of comprehensive claims negotiations to include crucial issues raised by Aboriginal peoples. Negotiations could now include offshore wildlife harvesting rights, the sharing of resource revenues and Aboriginal peoples' participation in environmental decision making. Negotiations could also include a federal government commitment to negotiate self-government with the First Nation. Another big change in the process of negotiating comprehensive claims came in 1990. Up until then, the federal government would negotiate no more than six claims at one time. After the new 1990 policy, there was no longer any limit on the number of claims the federal government was willing to negotiate with First Nations. [...]

Treaty Land Entitlement

Treaty land entitlements are a special type of specific claim. They involve claims for land under existing treaties.

In the late 19th and early 20th centuries, the Canadian government made treaties with First Nations in Manitoba, Saskatchewan, Alberta and parts of the Northwest Territories so that land could be occupied peacefully by incoming settlers and resource development take place. One of the federal government commitments under these treaties was to confirm reserves for First Nations peoples. However, some First Nations did not receive enough land because there was no accurate count made of their community members. Today, First Nations are settling the unfulfilled commitments under these existing treaties through the Treaty Land Entitlement process. Through one recent settlement - the Saskatchewan Treaty Land Entitlement Agreement - 25 First Nations will be able to buy land to add to their reserves. The First Nations will receive $450 million in federal and provincial funds over 12 years to purchase land and mineral rights from private owners who are willing to sell their land.

Economic Development

First Nations see community-based economic development as the key to self-determination. Aboriginal people closely link economic development with the settlement of land claims. They see promising economic opportunities based on their lands' natural resources. These opportunities include mining, fishing, logging and trapping.

In 1995 there were an estimated 18,000 Aboriginal-owned businesses across Canada. About 66 percent of Aboriginal businesses were in the service sector; 13 percent were in construction and related sectors. Another 12 percent were in the primary industries such as mining and forestry and 9 percent were businesses related to food processing, clothing, furniture, publishing and other manufacturing. One fast-growing area is Aboriginal tourism, where First Nations share their environment and cultural heritage with visitors from across North America and abroad.

Working in partnership with First Nations, the department's Economic Development Directorate provides information and advice to help Aboriginal peoples access economic opportunities. In 1994-1995, First Nations and Inuit communities managed $47.6 million from the department's economic development programs to support development of their businesses. First Nations in Western Canada who have oil and gas on their reserves are using these resources to build a sound economy for their members. Several First Nations in Saskatchewan and Alberta are taking part in an initiative which will give them full management and control of these resources on their reserve lands. [...]

2. Distribution of Legislative Powers

(a) Federal Legislative Power

R. v. MORRIS
[2006] S.C.C. 59.

[The accused, M and O, both members of the Tsartlip Indian Band of the Saanich Nation, were hunting at night when they shot at a decoy deer set up by provincial conservation officers to trap illegal hunters. They were arrested and charged with offences under British Columbia's Wildlife Act. At trial, the accused raised their right "to hunt over the unoccupied lands . . . as formerly" under the North Saanich Treaty of 1852 and introduced evidence that the particular night hunt for which they were charged was not dangerous. The trial judge found that "[n]ight hunting with illumination was one of the various methods employed by the Tsartlip [people] from time immemorial". However, despite the evidence that night hunting by Tsartlip hunters had yet to result in an accident, he nonetheless concluded that the accused did not have a treaty right to hunt at night because hunting at night with an illuminating device was "inherently unsafe."

Justices Deschamps and Abella ruled that the treaty guarantee to hunt "as formerly" includes the right to hunt according to the methods used by the Tsartlip before the treaty. They reasoned that this included a right to hunt at night, with illumination, but it did not include a right to hunt dangerously. Because British Columbia is big, they reasoned, a night hunt with illumination is not unsafe everywhere and in all circumstances.

Deschamps and Abella JJ. then considered issues relating to the division of powers and the implications of s. 88 of the *Indian Act*. This aspect of their opinion follows below.]

The judgment of Binnie, Deschamps, Abella and Charron JJ. was delivered by

DESCHAMPS AND ABELLA JJ. —

2.2 *Constitutional Division of Powers*

¶ 41 Having found that the Tsartlip's treaty rights include the right to hunt at night and with illumination, we must now determine whether the impugned provisions of the *Wildlife Act* are nevertheless applicable from the perspective of the constitutional division of powers in ss. 91 and 92 of the *Constitution Act, 1867*. By virtue of s. 91(24), Parliament has exclusive power to make laws in relation to "Indians, and Lands reserved for the Indians". Provincial laws whose "pith and substance" relates to this head of power are *ultra vires* and invalid [cites omitted]. However, provincial laws of general application that affect Indians only incidentally and are enacted under a provincial head of power will be found to be *intra vires* and valid.

¶ 42 In this case, there is no question that the relevant provisions of the *Wildlife Act* are valid provincial legislation under s. 92(13) of the *Constitution Act, 1867*, which refers to Property and Civil Rights in the Province. However, where a valid provincial law impairs "an integral part of primary federal jurisdiction over Indians or Lands reserved for the Indians" [cites omitted], it will be inapplicable to the extent of the impairment. Thus, provincial laws of general application are precluded from impairing "Indianness".[cites omitted]

¶ 43 Treaty rights to hunt lie squarely within federal jurisdiction over "Indians, and Lands reserved for the Indians". As noted by Dickson C.J. in *Simon*, at p. 411:

> It has been held to be within the exclusive power of Parliament under s. 91(24) of the *Constitution Act, 1867* to derogate from rights recognized in a treaty agreement made with the Indians.

This Court has previously found that provincial laws of general application that interfere with treaty rights to hunt are inapplicable to particular Aboriginal [cites omitted]. Where such laws are inapplicable because they impair "Indianness", however, they may nonetheless be found to be applicable by incorporation under s. 88 of the *Indian Act*.

2.3 *Section 88 of the Indian Act*

¶ 44 Section 88 reflects Parliament's intention to avoid the effects of the immunity imposed by s. 91(24) by incorporating certain provincial laws of general application into federal law. Section 88 reads as follows:

88. <u>Subject to the terms of any treaty</u> and any other Act of Parliament, all laws of general application from time to time in force in any province are applicable to and in respect of Indians in the province, except to the extent that those laws are inconsistent with this Act or any order, rule, regulation or by-law made thereunder, and except to the extent that those laws make provision for any matter for which provision is made by or under this Act.

¶ 45 But as the opening words of this provision demonstrate, Parliament has expressly declined to use s. 88 to incorporate provincial laws where the effect would be to infringe treaty rights. [...] [O]ne of the purposes of s. 88 is to accord "federal statutory protection to aboriginal treaty rights". Thus, on its face, s. 88 cannot be used to incorporate into federal law provincial laws that conflict with the terms of any treaty.

¶ 46 The clear language of this treaty exception in s. 88 is qualified by statements in this Court's jurisprudence that the provinces may regulate treaty rights under certain circumstances... After Confederation, some of the resources came to be regulated federally (e.g. the fishery), while others were regulated provincially (e.g. those harvested by trapping). In the case of the provincially regulated resources, the Court was not prepared to read the treaty right as requiring that access to them for purposes of *commercial* exploitation be subject to parallel and potentially conflicting federal and provincial oversight. That is not this case, which requires us to consider the more general question of what degree of provincial legislative interference with a non-commercial treaty right will trigger the s. 88 protection of treaty rights. Further consideration of the Court's position with respect to treaty rights of a commercial nature should be left for a case where it is directly in issue.

¶ 47 Where, as in this case, non-commercial rights are in issue, a distinction must be drawn between insignificant interference with the exercise of the treaty right and *prima facie* infringement of the right.

¶ 48 Regarding insignificant interference, this Court considered in *Côté* whether a provincial regulation requiring the payment of a small access fee for entry into a controlled harvest zone infringed a treaty right to fish. The fee was not revenue generating, but was intended to pay for the ongoing maintenance of roads and facilities within the controlled zone. Lamer C.J. held that this provincial regulation "impose[d] a modest financial burden on the exercise of th[e] alleged treaty right" (para. 88), thereby representing an insignificant interference with a treaty right, and consequently did not infringe that right.

¶ 49 In contrast in *Badger* this Court considered that a licensing scheme that imposed conditions as to the "hunting method, the kind and numbers of game, the season and the permissible hunting area" (para. 92) infringed the appellants' treaty right to hunt. Cory J., writing for the majority, held that this licensing scheme constituted a *prima facie* infringement of the appellants' treaty right to hunt, since it "denie[d] to holders of treaty rights ... the very means of exercising those rights" and was found to be "in direct conflict with the treaty right" (para. 94).

¶ 50 Insignificant interference with a treaty right will not engage the protection afforded by s. 88 of the *Indian Act* . [...] Therefore, provincial laws or regulations that place a modest burden on a person exercising a treaty right or that interfere in an insignificant way with the exercise of that right do not infringe the right.

¶ 51 A *prima facie* infringement, however, will trigger the s. 88 treaty right protection. In determining what constitutes a *prima facie* infringement of a treaty right, it is helpful to consider the Court's jurisprudence on this point. In *R. v. Sparrow*, [1999] 1 S.C.R. 1075, at p. 1112, Lamer C.J. and La Forest J. listed three questions that may assist in this determination:

> First, is the limitation unreasonable? Second, does the regulation impose undue hardship? Third, does the regulation deny to the holders of the right their preferred means of exercising that right?

¶ 52 [...] [C]are should be taken, in considering these questions, not to import an element of justification when attempting to identify an infringement [...]

¶ 53 Essentially, therefore, a *prima facie* infringement requires a "meaningful diminution" of a treaty right. This includes anything but an insignificant interference with that right. If provincial laws or regulations interfere insignificantly with the exercise of treaty rights, they will not be found to infringe them and can apply *ex proprio vigore* or by incorporation under s. 88.

¶ 54 The protection of treaty rights in s. 88 of the *Indian Act* applies where a conflict between a provincial law of general application and a treaty is such that it amounts to a *prima facie* infringement. Where a provincial law of general application is found to conflict with a treaty in a way that constitutes a *prima facie* infringement, the protection of treaty rights prevails and the provincial law cannot be incorporated under s. 88.

¶ 55 Where a *prima facie* infringement of a treaty right is found, a province cannot rely on s. 88 by using the justification test from *Sparrow* and *Badger* in the context of s. 35(1) of the *Constitution Act, 1982* ... The purpose of the *Sparrow/Badger* analysis is to determine whether an infringement by a government acting within its constitutionally mandated powers can be justified. This justification analysis does not alter the division of powers, which is dealt with in s. 88. Therefore, while the *Sparrow/Badger* test for infringement may be useful, the framework set out in those cases for determining whether an infringement is justified does not offer any guidance for the question at issue here.

3. *Application to this Case*

¶ 56 There is no treaty right to hunt dangerously. Thus, the prohibition against hunting "without reasonable consideration for the lives, safety or property of other persons" set out in s. 29 of the *Wildlife Act* is a limit that does not infringe the Tsartlip's treaty right to hunt. As stated earlier, the requirement to hunt safely was clearly within the common intention of the parties to the Treaty, as reflected by the language of the Treaty itself, which restricts hunting to "unoccupied lands". Where a treaty beneficiary is proven to have hunted dangerously, the Treaty does not provide a defence to charges brought under s. 29.

¶ 57 However, based on an understanding of the common intention of the parties to the Treaty, the Tsartlip's treaty right includes the right to hunt at night with illumination, with the modern incorporation of their ancestral method, namely the use of firearms.

¶ 58 The legislative prohibition set out in ... the *Wildlife Act* is absolute, and it applies without exception to the whole province, including the most northern regions where hours of daylight are limited in the winter months and populated areas are few and far between. The Legislature has made no attempt to prohibit only those specific aspects or geographic areas of night hunting that are unsafe by, for example, banning hunting within a specified distance from a highway or from residences. The impugned provisions are overbroad, inconsistent with the common intention of the parties to the treaties, and completely eliminate a chosen method of exercising their treaty right.

¶ 59 We respectfully disagree with our colleagues the Chief Justice and Fish J. that nothing short of a total ban on night hunting can address safety concerns. We believe that it would be possible to identify uninhabited areas where hunting at night would not jeopardize safety. This finding is supported by the evidence in this case that the Tsartlip's practice of night hunting with illuminating devices has never been known to have resulted in an accident, and that the conservation officers, in setting up the location for their mechanical decoy, were easily able to locate an area where night hunting could be practised safely. These facts amply demonstrate how something less than an absolute prohibition on night hunting can address the concern for safety.

¶ 60 We have no difficulty concluding, therefore, that the categorical ban on night hunting and hunting with illumination constitutes a *prima facie* infringement of a treaty right. A categorical prohibition clearly constitutes more than an insignificant interference with a treaty right. Although provincial laws of general application that are inapplicable to aboriginal people can be incorporated into federal law under s. 88 of the *Indian Act*, this cannot happen where the effect would be to infringe treaty rights. Because paras. (d) and (e) of s. 27(1) of the *Wildlife Act* constitute a *prima facie* infringement, they cannot be incorporated under s. 88 of the *Indian Act*.

¶ 61 For these reasons, we would allow the appeal, set aside the convictions and enter acquittals.

The reasons of McLachlin C.J. and Bastarache and Fish JJ. were delivered by

THE CHIEF JUSTICE AND FISH J. —

¶ 64 We conclude that the treaty right to hunt is subject to an internal limitation which excludes dangerous hunting. We further conclude that hunting at night with a firearm, as trial courts across the country have held, is hazardous and validly prohibited on that ground by provincial legislation of general application. In the result, we find that a provincial ban on night hunting with a firearm does not affect the appellants' treaty right to hunt.

¶ 65 With respect to those who are of a different view, we would therefore dismiss the appeal and affirm the convictions of both appellants.

(b)   Fiduciary Nature of the Crown's Authority

- Research Note -
FIDUCIARY DUTY

Fiduciary Relationship

In *R. v. Sparrow* the Supreme Court of Canada made these important observations:

> The words "recognition and affirmation", [in section 35(1) of the *Constitution Act, 1982*] incorporate the government's responsibility to act in a fiduciary capacity with respect to aboriginal peoples and so import some restraint on the exercise of sovereign power. Federal legislative powers continue, including the right to legislate with respect to Indians pursuant to s. 91(24) of the *Constitution Act, 1867*, but must be read together with s. 35(1). Federal power must be reconciled with federal duty and the best way to achieve that reconciliation is to demand the justification of any government regulation that infringes upon or denies aboriginal rights. [...]

> In *Guerin* ... this Court found that the Crown owed a fiduciary obligation to the Indians with respect to the lands. The *sui generis* nature of Indian title, and the historic powers and responsibility assumed by the Crown constituted the source of such a fiduciary obligation. In our opinion, Guerin, together with *R. v. Taylor and Williams* (1981), 34 O.R. (2d) 360, ground a general guiding principle for s. 35(1). That is, the Government has the responsibility to act in a fiduciary capacity with respect to aboriginal peoples. The relationship between the Government and aboriginals is trust-like, rather than adversarial, and contemporary recognition and affirmation of aboriginal rights must be defined in light of this historic relationship.

Fiduciary Liability

Guerin v. R. established a second point in addition to the pregnant observation that "the Government has the responsibility to act in a fiduciary capacity with respect to Aboriginal peoples.   The relationship between the Government and Aboriginals is trust-like...". *Guerin* established also that the Crown can be liable in damages to Aboriginal peoples for breach of its duties as a fiduciary.[1] This ruling has been repeatedly affirmed.[2]

---

1   *Guerin v. Canada*, [1984] 2 S.C.R. 335.
2   *R. v. Sparrow*, [1990] 1 S.C.R. 1075 at 1108; *Quebec (Attorney-General) v. Canada (National Energy Board)*, [1994] 1 S.C.R. 159 at 183: "It is now well settled that there is a fiduciary relationship between the federal Crown

Fiduciary duties in this second sense - fiduciary duties that give rise to liability in damages - do not exist at large. There must be a "cognizable Indian interest," over which the Crown has assumed discretionary control, to create a Crown fiduciary duty which is enforceable by an action in damages.[1]

While other interests can give rise to fiduciary obligations,[2] reserve land is the quintessence of the "cognizable Indian interests" fiduciary law will protect.

The Supreme Court explained why:

> The fiduciary relationship between the Crown and the Indians has its roots in the concept of aboriginal, native or Indian title. The fact that Indian bands have a certain interest in lands does not, however, in itself give rise to a fiduciary relationship between the Indians and the Crown. The conclusion that the Crown is a fiduciary depends upon the further proposition that the Indian interest in the land is inalienable except upon surrender to the Crown.

> An Indian Band is prohibited from directly transferring its interest to a third party. Any sale or lease of land can only be carried out after a surrender has taken place, with the Crown then acting on the Band's behalf. The Crown first took this responsibility upon itself in the Royal Proclamation of 1763. It is still recognized in the surrender provisions of the Indian Act. The surrender requirement, and the responsibility it entails, are the source of a distinct fiduciary obligation owed by the Crown to the Indians.[3]

The Crown's fiduciary obligations are at their highest when the Crown holds reserve land guaranteed by treaty for the benefit of the First Nation. This is because:

> The historical record leaves no doubt that native peoples acknowledged the ultimate sovereignty of the British Crown and agreed to cede their traditional homelands on the

---

[Footnote 2 continued from prior page]

and the aboriginal peoples of Canada..."; *Lac La Ronge Indian Band v. Canada*, [2000] 1 C.N.L.R. 245 at 344-45.

1   *Wewaykum Indian Band v. Canada*, [2002] 4 S.C.R. 245 at 85.

2   *Ibid.* at 85: "I do not suggest that the existence of a public law duty necessarily excludes the creation of a fiduciary relationship. The latter, however, depends on identification of a cognizable Indian interest, and the Crown's undertaking of discretionary control in relation thereto in a way that invokes responsibility 'in the nature of a private law duty', as discussed below."

3   *Guerin v. Canada*, [1984] 2 S.C.R. 335 at page 375-6.

understanding that the Crown would thereafter protect them in the possession and use of such lands as were reserved for their use ...The sections of the Indian Act relating to the inalienability of Indian lands seek to give effect to this protection by interposing the Crown between the Indians and the market forces which, if left unchecked, had the potential to erode Indian ownership of these reserves.[1]

Fiduciary obligations do not govern all aspects of the Crown-First Nation relationship and "do not provide a general indemnity."[2]

Identifying fiduciary obligations capable of giving rise to damages for breach is a fact-driven process:

> ... it is necessary ... to focus on the particular obligation or interest that is the subject matter of the particular dispute and whether or not the Crown has assumed discretionary control in relation thereto sufficient to ground a fiduciary obligation.[3]

The facts must show that the Crown has control of and discretion to deal with a cognizable Indian interest to create a fiduciary breach of which gives rise to damages. Discretionary control of another's interest is the classic situation giving rise to fiduciary obligation.

> where by statute, agreement, or perhaps by unilateral undertaking, one party has an obligation to act for the benefit of another, and that obligation carries with it discretionary power, the party thus empowered becomes a fiduciary. Equity will then supervise the relationship by holding him to the fiduciary's strict standard of conduct.[4]

Fiduciary obligations may also arise when:

> given all the surrounding circumstances, one party could reasonably have expected that the other party would act in the former's best interests with respect to the subject matter at issue.

> ... Elements such as trust, confidentiality, and the complexity and importance of the subject matter ... will determine whether it was reasonable for the advisee to expect that the advisor was in fact exercising his or her special skills in the other party's best interests.[5]

---

1   *Mitchell v. Peguis Indian Band*, [1990] 2 S.C.R. 85, 71 D.L.R. (4th) 193 at 225.
2   *Wewaykum Indian Band v. Canada*, [2002] 4 S.C.R. 245 at 87.
3   *Ibid.* at 83.
4   *Guerin v. Canada*, [1984] 2 S.C.R. 335 at 383-4.
5   *Hodgkinson v. Simms*, [1994] 3 S.C.R. 377 at 410, *per* La Forest for the majority.

Where a reserve exists at law, the Crown has fiduciary obligations. To discharge its fiduciary obligations respecting reserve land, the Crown must always fulfill

> basic obligations of loyalty, good faith in the discharge ... of its mandate, providing full disclosure appropriate to the subject matter, and acting with ordinary prudence with a view to the best interest of the aboriginal beneficiaries.[1]

Where a possible disposition of reserve land is at issue, the Crown's fiduciary duties expand to include:

> a fiduciary obligation to protect and preserve the Bands' interests from invasion or destruction... ordinary diligence must be used by the Crown to avoid invasion or destruction of the band's quasi-property interest by an exploitative bargain with third parties or, indeed, exploitation by the Crown itself.[2]

Expropriation of reserve land gives rise to an enforceable Crown fiduciary duty.[3,4]

In an expropriation situation, the Crown is bound by its fiduciary obligations to impair the First Nation's legal interests as little as possible:

> once it has been determined that an expropriation of Indian lands is in the public interest, a fiduciary duty arises on the part of the Crown to expropriate or grant only the minimum interest required in order to fulfill that public purpose, thus ensuring a minimal impairment of the use and enjoyment of Indian lands by the band."[5]

Fiduciary Duties and Public Law Duties

In certain circumstances the Crown has to manage other responsibilities it has as a government, which compete with its fiduciary duties.[6] An example is where the Crown expropriates reserve land for public works.

---

1   *Wewaykum Indian Band v. Canada*, [2002] 4 S.C.R. 245 at 86.
2   *Ibid*. at 100.
3   *Wewaykum Indian Band v. Canada*, [2002] 4 S.C.R. 245 at 98. In *Osoyoos Indian Band v. Oliver (Town)*, [2001] 3 S.C.R. 746 at 47, 52 the Supreme Court ruled: "Land may be removed from a reserve with the participation of the Crown, which owes a fiduciary duty to the band ... Fiduciaries are held to a high standard of diligence." See also *Kruger v. R.*, [1986] 1 F.C. 3 (F.C.A.).
4   *Osoyoos Indian Band v. Oliver (Town)*, [2001] 3 S.C.R. 746 at 47.
5   *Ibid*. at 52.
6   See *Wewaykum Indian Band v. Canada*, [2002] 4 S.C.R. 245 at 96: "When exercising ordinary government powers in matters involving disputes between Indians and non-Indians, the Crown was (and is) obliged to have

To manage this situation, the Crown must fairly and diligently balance the fiduciary duties it owes to a First Nation with the duties it owes to the public. In the balancing process the Crown must ensure that the First Nation's interests are impaired as little as possible.[1]

Because the Crown must "balance" interests does not mean that the Crown's fiduciary obligations are diminished or disappear: "[t]he Crown could not, merely by invoking competing interests, shirk its fiduciary duty."[2] The Crown can still pursue its competing public purposes, but because it is in a conflict of interest position, the Crown "bears the onus of demonstrating that its personal interest did not benefit from its fiduciary powers."[3]

Provincial Fiduciary Duties

Fiduciary duties can apply equally to the Crown in right of Canada and the Crown in right of the Province.[4]

Professor Leonard Rotman wrote:[5]

> [I]n *Cree Regional Authority v. Robinson (Federal Administrator)*, [1991] 4 CNLR 84 (Fed T.D.), it was correctly said that the Supreme Court's judgment in *Sparrow* did not distinguish between the federal and provincial Crowns in its discussion of fiduciary duties owed to Aboriginal peoples. Consequently, the

---

[Footnote 6 continued from prior page]

regard to the interest of all affected parties, not just the Indian interest. The Crown can be no ordinary fiduciary; it wears many hats and represents many interests, some of which cannot help but be conflicting..." See also *Fairford First Nation v. Canada (Attorney General)*, [1999] 2 F.C. 48 (T.D.) at 170: "Canada's necessary involvement under section 35 of the Indian Act in the taking of land from the Fairford Reserve for highway purposes by Manitoba gave rise to a fiduciary duty upon Canada to ensure that the best interests of the Band were protected in so far as Canada's unilateral discretion with respect to the transaction was concerned." See also *Kruger v. The Queen*, (C.A.), at page 13, per Heald J.A. and at page 45, *per* Urie J.A).

1   *Osoyoos Indian Band v. Oliver (Town)*, [2001] 3 S.C.R. 746 at 52, 54: "The duty to impair minimally Indian interests in reserve land not only serves to balance the public interest and the Indian interest, it is also consistent with the policy behind the rule of general inalienability in the Indian Act which is to prevent the erosion of the native land base."

2   *Wewaykum Indian Band v. Canada*, [2002] 4 S.C.R. 245 at 104.

3   *Blueberry River Indian Band v. Canada*, [1995] 4 S.C.R. 344 at 53.

4   *Halfway River First Nation v. British Columbia (Minister of Forests)*, [1997] 4 C.N.L.R. 45; *Gitanyow First Nation v. Canada*, [1999] 3 C.N.L.R. 89.

5   L.J. Rotman, Fiduciary Law (Toronto: Carswell, 2005) at 586.

Federal Court, Trial Division states that "the provincial authorities are also responsible for protecting the rights of the Native population.[1]

In *Makivik Corp. v. Canada (Minister of Canadian Heritage)*,[2] the Federal Court held that in some instances the provincial Crown has positive duties to protect aboriginal rights and interests.[3]

One instance in which positive provincial duties to First Nations exist is in the context of treaties. "[T]he equitable basis of finding a provincial fiduciary duty is concerned primarily with whether the province reaped benefits under the treaty."[4] When a province receives the benefit of tracts of First Nation land surrendered pursuant to a treaty, the province is imposed with a fiduciary obligation to faithfully implement those portions of the treaty that come within its constitutional jurisdiction. The province "cannot take the benefit of the surrender without incurring corresponding fiduciary obligations."[5]

The Judicial Committee of the Privy Council endorsed this line of reasoning in *Ontario Mining Company Ltd. v. Seybold*:

> [T]he Government of the province, taking advantage of the surrender of 1873, came at least under an honourable engagement to fulfill the terms on the faith of which the surrender was made, and, therefore, to concur with the Dominion Government in appropriating certain undefined portions of the surrendered lands as Indian reserves.[6]

The 'honourable engagement' referred to by the Privy Council in *Seybold* has developed into the modern equitable doctrine of a fiduciary obligation.[7]

---

1   *Ibid*. at 106.
2   *Makivik Corp. v. Canada (Minister of Canadian Heritage)*, [1999] 1 F.C. 38 (T.D.).
3   *Ibid*. at para. 83-84.
4   Leonard I. Rotman, "Provincial Fiduciary Obligations to First Nations: The Nexus Between Governmental Power and Responsibility," (1995) 32 Osgoode Hall L.J. 735 at 768.
5   B. Slattery, First Nations and the Constitution: A Question of Trust" (1992) 71 Can. Bar Rev. 261 at 275.
6   *Ontario Mining Company Ltd. v. Seybold* , [1903] A.C. 73 (P.C.) at 82-83.
7   Professor Rotman argues that the "honourable engagement" referred to by the Privy Council in 1902 has been developed by the judiciary into the modern equitable notion of a fiduciary obligation: L.J. Rotman, Fiduciary Law (Toronto: Carswell, 2005) at 768. In *Fiduciary Law* at p. 585, he also explains that: "The Crown's fiduciary duty to Aboriginal peoples necessitates, *inter alia*, that the honour of the Crown be maintained. Consequently, a greater legal obligation is certainly warranted than was recognized in *Seybold*, where the Judicial Committee of the Privy Council held that the province of Ontario/provincial Crown was only under

The B.C. Court of Appeal explained that treaty promises can form the basis of the provincial Crown's fiduciary duty to First Nations in *Halfway River*, The Court held that the provincial Crown's "fiduciary duty to the petitioners aris[es] from the treaty in issue ..."[1]

In *Huida Nation* the Supreme Court observed that the Crown's fiduciary duty to First Nations is rooted in the honour of the Crown. The honour of the Crown requires that the Crown fulfills its duties to First Nations through "concrete practices," not merely empty legislative gestures.[2]

GUERIN v. CANADA
[1984] 2 S.C.R. 335.

[In 1957, the Musqueam Indian Band surrendered valuable surplus reserve lands to the Crown for lease to a golf club. The terms obtained by the Crown were much less favourable than those presented to and agreed upon by the Band council. Indian Affairs Branch officials did not return to the Band for its approval of the less favourable, revised terms, nor would it disclose the terms to the Band or an appraiser assessing the adequacy of the proposed rent. The Band was unable to obtain a copy of the lease until March 1970. The Band commenced an action for damages against the Crown in 1975.

At trial, the judge found the Crown in breach of trust in entering the lease and awarded damages as of the date of the trial on the basis of the loss of income which might have been reasonable anticipated from other possible uses of the land. The Federal Court of Appeal set aside that judgment and dismissed a cross-appeal seeking more damages.

The Band appealed to the Supreme Court of Canada. (Note: s. 35 of the *Constitution Act, 1982* was not in force at the time of surrender, and was therefore not relied upon by the Court.)]

[Footnote 7 continued from prior page]

an honourable engagement to cooperate with the federal Crown in fulfilling treaty promises of establishing reserves from surrendered lands. Of course, the *Seybold* judgment may be said to no longer constitute good law, insofar as it was decided at a time when the Crown's fiduciary duty had yet to be explicitly recognized by Canadian courts and that duty is necessarily implicated in the scenario contemplated in *Seybold*. Thus, if a provincial Crown obtains exclusive proprietary and administrative rights over Indian lands surrendered by treaty, then it must, by necessity or logical implication, also obtain a portion of the fiduciary duty owed to the Aboriginal signatories to the treaty."

1   *Halfway River First Nation v. British Columbia (Ministry of Forests)*, [1999] B.C.J. No. 1880 at para. 86.
2   2004 S.C.C. 73 at paras. 16, 18.

DICKSON J. [Beetz, Chouinard and Lamer JJ. concurring]: —

IV Fiduciary Relationship

The issue or the Crown's liability was dealt with in the courts below on the basis of the existence or non-existence of a trust. In dealing with the different consequences of a "true" trust, as opposed to a "political" trust, Le Dain J. noted that the Crown could be liable only if it were subject to an "equitable obligation enforceable in a court of law". I have some doubt as to the cogency of the terminology of "higher" and "lower" trusts, but I do agree that the existence of an equitable obligation is the *sine qua non* for liability. Such an obligation is not, however, limited to relationships which can be strictly defined as "trusts". As will presently appear, it is my view that the Crown's obligations *vis-à-vis* the Indians cannot be defined as a trust. That does not, however, mean that the Crown owes no enforceable duty to the Indians in the way in which it deals with Indian land.

In my view, the nature of Indian title and the framework of the statutory scheme established for disposing of Indian land places upon the Crown an equitable obligation, enforceable by the courts, to deal with the land for the benefit of the Indians. This obligation does not amount to a trust in the private law sense. It is rather a fiduciary duty. If, however, the Crown breaches this fiduciary duty it will be liable to the Indians in the same way and to the same extent as if such a trust were in effect.

The fiduciary relationship between the Crown and the Indians has its roots in the concept of aboriginal, native or Indian title. The fact that Indian Bands have a certain interest in lands does not, however, in itself give rise to a fiduciary relationship between the Indians and the Crown. The conclusion that the Crown is a fiduciary depends upon the further proposition that the Indian interest in the land is inalienable except upon surrender to the Crown.

An Indian Band is prohibited from directly transferring its interest to a third party. Any sale or lease of land can only be carried out after a surrender has taken place, with the Crown then acting on the Band's behalf. The Crown first took this responsibility upon itself in the *Royal Proclamation of 1763*. It is still recognized in the surrender provisions of the *Indian Act*. The surrender requirement, and the responsibility it entails, are the source of a distinct fiduciary obligation owed by the Crown to the Indians. In order to explore the character of this obligation, however, it is first necessary to consider the basis of aboriginal title and the nature of the interest in land which it represents.

(a) *The Existence of Indian Title*

In *Calder v. Attorney General of British Columbia*, [1973] S.C.R. 313, this Court recognized aboriginal title as a legal right derived from the Indians' historic occupation and possession of their tribal lands. With Judson and Hall JJ. writing the principal judgments, the Court split three-three on the major issue of whether the Nishga Indians' aboriginal title to their ancient tribal territory had been extinguished by general land enactments in British Columbia. The Court also split on the issue of whether the *Royal Proclamation of 1763* was applicable to Indian lands in that province. Judson and Hall JJ. were in agreement, however, that aboriginal title existed in Canada (at least where it had not been extinguished by appropriate legislative action) independently of the *Royal Proclamation*. Judson J. stated expressly that the *Proclamation* was not the "exclusive" source of Indian title (pp. 322-23, 328). Hall J. said (at p. 390) that "aboriginal Indian title does not depend on treaty, executive order or legislative enactment".

The *Royal Proclamation of 1763* reserved "under our Sovereignty, Protection, and Dominion, for the use of the said Indians, all the Lands and Territories not included within the Limits of Our said Three new Governments, or within the Limits of the Territory granted to the Hudson's Bay Company, as also all the Lands and Territories lying to the Westward of the Sources of the Rivers which fall into the Sea from the West and North West as aforesaid" (R.S.C. 1970, Appendices, p. 123, at p. 127). In recognizing that the *Proclamation* is not the sole source of Indian title the *Calder* decision went beyond the judgment of the Privy Council in *St. Catherine's Milling and Lumber Co. v. The Queen* (1888), 14 App. Cas. 46. In that case Lord Watson acknowledged the existence of aboriginal title but said it had its origin in the *Royal Proclamation*. In this respect *Calder* is consistent with the position of Chief Justice Marshall in the leading American cases of *Johnson v. McIntosh*, 8 Wheaton 543 (1823), and *Worcester v. State of Georgia*, 6 Peters 515 (1832), cited by Judson and Hall JJ. in their respective judgments. [...]

It does not matter, in my opinion, that the present case is concerned with the interest of an Indian Band in a reserve rather than with unrecognized aboriginal title in traditional tribal lands. The Indian interest in the land is the same in both cases: see *Attorney-General for Quebec v. Attorney-General for Canada*, [1921] 1 A.C. 401, at pp. 410-11 (the *Star Chrome* case). It is worth noting, however, that the reserve in question here was created out of the ancient tribal territory of the Musqueam Band by the unilateral action of the Colony of British Columbia, prior to Confederation.

(b) *The Nature of Indian Title*

In the *St. Catherine's Milling* case, supra, the Privy Council held that the Indians had a "personal and usufructuary right" in the lands which they had traditionally occupied. Lord Watson said that "there has been all along vested in the Crown a substantial and paramount estate, underlying the Indian title, which became a plenum dominium whenever the title was surrendered or otherwise extinguished" (at p. 55). He reiterated this idea, stating that the Crown "has all along had a present proprietary estate in the land, upon which the Indian title was a mere burden" (at p. 58). This view of aboriginal title was affirmed by the Privy Council in the *Star Chrome* case. In *Amodu Tijani* (cites omitted), Viscount Haldane, adverting to the *St. Catherine's Milling* and *Star Chrome* decisions, explained the concept of a usufructuary right as "a mere qualification of or burden on the radical or final title of the Sovereign [...]" (p. 403). He described the title of the Sovereign as a pure legal estate, but one which could be qualified by a right of "beneficial user" that did not necessarily take the form of an estate in land. Indian title in Canada was said to be one illustration "of the necessity for getting rid of the assumption that the ownership of land naturally breaks itself up into estates, conceived as creatures of inherent legal principle." Chief Justice Marshall took a similar view in *Johnson v. McIntosh,* supra, saying, "All our institutions recognize the absolute title of the crown, subject only to the Indian right of occupancy [...]" (p. 588).

It should be noted that the Privy Council's emphasis on the personal nature of aboriginal title stemmed in part from constitutional arrangements peculiar to Canada. The Indian territory at issue in *St. Catherine's Milling* was land which in 1867 had been vested in the Crown subject to the interest of the Indians. The Indians' interest was "an interest other than that of the Province", within the meaning of s. 109 of the *Constitution Act, 1867.* Section 109 provides:

> **109.** All Lands, Mines, Minerals, and Royalties belonging to the several Provinces of Canada, Nova Scotia, and New Brunswick at the Union, and all Sums then due or payable for such Lands, Mines, Minerals, or Royalties, shall belong to the several Provinces of Ontario, Quebec, Nova Scotia, and New Brunswick in which the same are situate or arise, subject to any Trusts existing in respect thereof, and to any Interest other than that of the Province in the same.

When the land in question in *St. Catherine's Milling* was subsequently disencumbered of the native title upon its surrender to the federal government by the Indian occupants in 1873, the entire beneficial interest in the land was held to have passed, because of the personal and usufructuary nature of the Indians' right, to the Province of Ontario under s. 109 rather than to Canada. The same constitutional issue arose recently in this Court in *Smith v. The Queen,* [1983] 1 S.C.R. 554, in which the Court held that the Indian right in a reserve, being personal, could not be transferred to a grantee, whether an individual or the Crown. Upon surrender the right disappeared "in the process of release".

No such constitutional problem arises in the present case, since in 1938 the title to all Indian reserves in British Columbia was transferred by the provincial government to the Crown in right of Canada.

It is true that in contexts other than constitutional the characterization of Indian title as "a personal and usufructuary right" has sometimes been questioned. In *Calder,* supra, for example, Judson J. intimated at p. 328 that this characterization was not helpful in determining the nature of Indian title. In *Attorney-General for Canada v. Giroux* (1916), 53 S.C.R. 172, Duff J., speaking for himself and Anglin J., distinguished *St. Catherine's Milling* on the ground that the statutory provisions in accordance with which the reserve in question in *Giroux* had been created conferred beneficial ownership on the Indian Band which occupied the reserve. In *Cardinal v. Attorney General of Alberta,* [1974] S.C.R. 695, Laskin J., dissenting on another point, accepted the possibility that Indians may have a beneficial interest in a reserve. The Alberta Court of Appeal in *Western International Contractors Ltd. v. Sarcee Developments Ltd.,* [1979] 3 W.W.R. 631, accepted the proposition that an Indian Band does indeed have a beneficial interest in its reserve. In the present case this was the view as well of Le Dain J. in the Federal Court of Appeal. See also the judgment of Kellock J. in *Miller v. The King,* [1950] S.C.R. 168, in which he seems implicitly to adopt a similar position.

None of these judgments mentioned the *Star Chrome* case, however, in which the Indian interest in land specifically set aside as a reserve was held to be the same as the "personal and usufructuary right" which was discussed in *St. Catherine's Milling*.

It appears to me that there is no real conflict between the cases which characterize Indian title as a beneficial interest of some sort, and those which characterize it a personal, usufructuary right. Any apparent inconsistency derives from the fact that in describing what constitutes a unique interest in land the courts have almost inevitably found themselves applying a somewhat inappropriate terminology drawn from general property law. There is a core of truth in the way that each of the two lines of authority has described native title, but an appearance or conflict has nonetheless arisen because in neither case is the categorization quite accurate.

Indians have a legal right to occupy and possess certain lands, the ultimate title to which is in the Crown. While their interest does not, strictly speaking, amount to beneficial ownership, neither is its nature completely exhausted by the concept of a personal right. It is true that the *sui generis* interest which the Indians have in the land is personal in the sense that it cannot be transferred to a grantee, but it is also true, as will presently appear, that the interest gives rise upon surrender to a distinctive fiduciary obligation on the part of the Crown to deal with the land for the benefit of the surrendering Indians. These two aspects of Indian title go together, since the Crown's original purpose in declaring the Indians' interest to be inalienable otherwise than to the Crown was to facilitate the Crown's ability to represent the Indians in dealings with third parties. The nature of the Indians' interest is therefore best characterized by its general inalienability, coupled with the fact that the Crown is under an obligation to deal with the land on the Indians' behalf when the interest is surrendered. Any description of Indian title which goes beyond those two features is both unnecessary and potentially misleading.

(c) *The Crown's Fiduciary Obligation*

The concept of fiduciary obligation originated long ago in the notion of breach of confidence, one of the original heads of jurisdiction in Chancery. In the present appeal its relevance is based on the requirement of a "surrender" before Indian land can be alienated.

The *Royal Proclamation of 1763* provided that no private person could purchase from the Indians any lands that the *Proclamation* had reserved to them, and provided further that all purchases had to be by and in the name of the Crown, in a public assembly of the Indians held by the governor or commander-in-chief of the colony in which the lands in question lay. As Lord Watson pointed out in *St. Catherine's Milling*, supra, at p. 54, this policy with respect to the sale or transfer of the Indians' interest in land has been continuously maintained by the British Crown, by the governments of the colonies when they became responsible for the administration of Indian affairs, and, after 1867, by the federal government of Canada. Successive federal statutes, predecessors to the present *Indian Act*, have all provided for the general inalienability of Indian reserve land except upon surrender to the Crown, the relevant provisions is the present Act being ss. 37-41.

The purpose of this surrender requirement is clearly to interpose the Crown between the Indians and prospective purchasers or lessees of their land, so as to prevent the Indians from being exploited. This is made clear in the *Royal Proclamation* itself, which prefaces the provision making the Crown an intermediary with a declaration that "great Frauds and Abuses have been committed in purchasing Lands of the Indians, to the great Prejudice of our Interests, and to the great Dissatisfaction of the said Indians. [...]" Through the confirmation in the *Indian Act* of the historic responsibility which the Crown has undertaken, to act on behalf of the Indians so as to protect their interests in transactions with third parties, Parliament has conferred upon the Crown a discretion to decide for itself where the Indians' best interests really lie. This is the effect of s. 18(1) of the Act.

This discretion on the part of the Crown, far from ousting, as the Crown contends, the jurisdiction of the courts to regulate the relationship between the Crown and the Indians, has the effect of transforming the Crown's obligation into a fiduciary one. Professor Ernest Weinrib maintains in his article *The Fiduciary Obligation* (1975), 25 U.T.L.J. 1, at p. 7, that "the hallmark of a fiduciary relation is that the relative legal positions are such that one party is at the mercy of the other's discretion." Earlier, at p. 4, he puts the point in the following way:

> [Where there is a fiduciary obligation] there is a relation in which the principal's interests can be affected by, and are therefore dependent on, the manner in which the fiduciary uses the discretion which has been delegated to him. The fiduciary obligation is the law's blunt tool for the control of this discretion.

I make no comment upon whether this description is broad enough to embrace all fiduciary obligations. I do agree, however, that where by statute, agreement, or perhaps by unilateral undertaking, one party has an obligation to act for the benefit of another, and that obligation carries with it a discretionary power, the party thus empowered becomes a fiduciary. Equity will then supervise the relationship by holding him to the fiduciary's strict standard of conduct.

It is sometimes said that the nature of fiduciary relationships is both established and exhausted by the standard categories of agent, trustee, partner, director, and the like. I do not agree. It is the nature of the relationship, not the specific category of actor involved that gives rise to the fiduciary duty. The categories of fiduciary, like those of negligence, should not be considered closed. See, *e.g. Laskin v. Bache & Co. Inc.* (1971), 23 D.L.R. (3d) 385 (Ont. C.A.), at p. 392: *Goldex Mines Ltd. v. Revill* (1974), 7 O.R. 216 (Ont. C.A.), at p. 224.

It should be noted that fiduciary duties generally arise only with regard to obligations originating in a private law context. Public law duties, the performance of which requires the exercise of discretion, do not typically give rise to a fiduciary relationship. As the "political trust" cases indicate the Crown is not normally viewed as a fiduciary in the exercise of its legislative or administrative function. The mere fact, however, that it is the Crown which is obligated to act on the Indians' behalf does not of itself remove the Crown's obligation from the scope of the fiduciary principle. As was pointed out earlier, the Indians' interest in land is an independent legal interest. It is not a creation of either the legislative or executive branches of government. The Crown's obligation to the Indians with respect to that interest is therefore not a public law duty. While it is not a private law duty in the strict sense either, it is nonetheless in the nature of a private law duty. Therefore, in this *sui generis* relationship, it is not improper to regard the Crown as a fiduciary.

Section 18(1) of the *Indian Act* confers upon the Crown a broad discretion in dealing with surrendered land. In the present case, the document of surrender, set out in part earlier in these reasons, by which the Musqueam Band surrendered the land at issue, confirms this discretion in the clause conveying the land to the Crown "in trust to lease [...] upon such terms as the Government of Canada may deem most conducive to our Welfare and that of our people". When, as here, an Indian Band surrenders its interest to the Crown, a fiduciary obligation takes hold to regulate the manner in which the Crown exercises its discretion in dealing with the land on the Indians' behalf. [...]

The discretion which is the hallmark of any fiduciary relationship is capable of being considerably narrowed in a particular case. This is as true of the Crown's discretion vis-à-vis the Indians as it is of the discretion of trustees, agents, and other traditional categories of fiduciary. The *Indian Act* makes specific provision for such narrowing in ss. 18(1) and 38(2). A fiduciary obligation will not, of course, be eliminated by the imposition of conditions that have the effect of restricting the fiduciary's discretion. A failure to adhere to the imposed conditions will simply itself be a *prima facie* breach of the obligation. In the present case both the surrender and the Order in Council accepting the surrender referred to the Crown's leasing the land on the Band's behalf. Prior to the surrender the Band had also been given to understand that a lease was to be entered into with the Shaughnessy Heights Golf Club upon certain terms, but this understanding was not incorporated into the surrender document itself. The effect of these so-called oral terms will be considered in the next section.

(d) *Breach of the Fiduciary Obligation*

The trial judge found that the Crown's agents promised the Band to lease the land in question on certain specified terms and then, after surrender obtained a lease on different terms. The lease obtained was much less valuable. As already mentioned, the surrender document did not make reference to the "oral" terms. I would not wish to say that those terms had nonetheless somehow been incorporated as conditions into the surrender. They were not formally assented to by a majority of the electors of the Band, nor were they accepted by the Governor in Council, as required by subss. 39(1)(*b*) and (*c*). I agree with Le Dain J. that there is no merit in the appellants' submission that for purposes of s. 39 a surrender can be considered independently of its terms. This makes no more sense than would a claim that a contract can have an existence which in no way depends on the terms and conditions that comprise it.

Nonetheless, the Crown, in my view, was not empowered by the surrender document to ignore the oral terms which the Band understood would be embodied in the lease. The oral representations form the backdrop against which the Crown's conduct in discharging its fiduciary obligation must be measured. They inform and confine the field of discretion within which the Crown was free to act. After the Crown's agents had induced the Band to surrender its land on the understanding that the land would be leased on certain terms, it would be unconscionable to permit the Crown simply to ignore those terms. When the promised lease proved impossible to obtain, the Crown, instead of proceeding to lease the land on different, unfavourable terms, should have returned to the Band to explain what had occurred and seek the Band's counsel on how to proceed. The existence of such unconscionability is the key to a conclusion that the Crown breached its fiduciary duty. Equity will not countenance unconscionable behaviour in a fiduciary, whose duty is that of utmost loyalty to his principal.

While the existence of the fiduciary obligation which the Crown owes to the Indians is dependent on the nature of the surrender process, the standard of conduct which the obligation imports is both more general and more exacting than the terms of any particular surrender. In the present case the relevant aspect of the required standard of conduct is defined by a principle analogous to that which underlies the doctrine of promissory or equitable estoppel. The Crown cannot promise the Band that it will obtain a lease of the latter's land on certain stated terms, thereby inducing the Band to alter its legal position by surrendering the land, and then simply ignore that promise to the Band's detriment. See *e.g. Central London Property Trust Ltd. v. High Trees House Ltd.*, [1947] 1 K.B. 130; *Robertson v. Minister of Pensions*, [1949] 1 K.B. 227 (C.A.).

In obtaining without consultation a much less valuable lease than that promised, the Crown breached the fiduciary obligation it owed the Band. It must make good the loss suffered in consequence. [...]

[Dickson J. went on to adopt the quantum of damages awarded by the trial judge, $10M. The judgments of Wilson J. and Estey J., concurring in the result, are omitted.]

WEWAYKUM INDIAN BAND v. CANADA
[2002] 4 S.C.R. 245.

[The Cape Mudge Band, the Wewaikai, claims Reserve 11 and the Campbell River Band, the Wewaykum, claims Reserve 12. An 1888 report of a federal government surveyor recommended the creation of Reserves 11 and 12. These reserves were not identified as allocated to a particular band, but rather to the "Laich-kwil-tach (Euclataw) Indians". In 1900 Reserves 11 and 12 were shown on a schedule as allocated to the "Wewayakai [Cape Mudge] Band". The Cape Mudge Band on that basis claims both reserves although it was not, and never had been, in occupation of Reserve 11.

The Cape Mudge Band had a dispute about fishing rights with the Campbell River Band. This was resolved in 1907. The Resolution provided that the Cape Mudge Band ceded any claim over Reserve 11 to the Campbell River Band. This was recorded in a change to the departmental schedule of reserves. The name of the "We-way-akum band" was entered opposite Reserve 11, but, by error, the ditto marks against Reserve 12, directly beneath it, remained unchanged. The Campbell River Band relies on the departmental schedule, as changed, as evidence of its right to both Reserve 11 and Reserve 12.

In 1912, the McKenna McBride Commission visited the proposed reserves in the Campbell River area. It acknowledged that Reserve 11 was properly allocated to the Campbell River Band and noted the error with respect to Reserve 12 which, because of the ditto marks, appeared in the schedule as being also allocated to that band. In their respective submissions to the Commission, in accordance with actual incumbency, the Campbell River Band made no claim to Reserve 12 and the Cape Mudge Band made no claim to Reserve 11. However, the "ditto mark error" on the schedule was not corrected.

In 1938, British Columbia transferred administration and control of the lands to Canada. In 1943, Indian Affairs published a corrected schedule of reserves listing Reserve 11 for the Campbell River Band and Reserve 12 for the Cape Mudge Band. No formal amendments were made to orders-in-council that had appended the previous faulty schedules.

Each band says it would possess *both* reserves but for breaches of fiduciary duty by the federal Crown. The Federal Court, Trial Division dismissed both bands' claims and the Federal Court of Appeal upheld that decision.]

The judgment of the Court was delivered by

¶ 1 **BINNIE J.** — [...]

The Sui Generis Fiduciary Duty

¶ 72 If, as we affirm, neither band emerged from the reserve-creation process with both reserves, the issue arises whether this outcome establishes in the case of either appellant band a breach of fiduciary duty on the part of the federal Crown.

¶ 73 Prior to its watershed decision in *Guerin, supra*, this Court had generally characterized the relationship between the Crown and Indian peoples as a "political trust" or "trust in the higher sense". In *St. Catherines Milling and Lumber Co. v. The Queen* (1887), 13 S.C.R. 577 [...]

Taschereau J. of this Court described the Crown's obligation towards aboriginal people as a "sacred political obligation, <u>in the execution of which the state must be free from judicial control</u>" (p. 649 (emphasis added)). Over 60 years later, in *St. Ann's Island Shooting and Fishing Club Ltd. v. The King*, [1950] S.C.R. 211, Rand J. stated at p. 219:

> The language of the statute [*Indian Act*] embodies the accepted view that these aborigines are, in effect, wards of the State, whose care and welfare are a <u>political trust</u> of the highest obligation. [Emphasis added.]

¶ 74 The enduring contribution of *Guerin* was to recognize that the concept of political trust did not exhaust the potential legal character of the multitude of relationships between the Crown and aboriginal people. A quasi-proprietary interest (e.g., reserve land) could not be put on the same footing as a government benefits program. The latter will generally give rise to public law remedies only. The former raises considerations "in the nature of a private law duty" (*Guerin*, at p. 385). Put another way, the existence of a public law duty does not exclude the possibility that the Crown undertook, in the discharge of that public law duty, obligations "in the nature of a private law duty" towards aboriginal peoples. [...]

891

¶ 76 Thus in *Guerin* itself, where the Crown failed to carry out its mandate to negotiate on particular terms a lease of 162 acres of an existing Indian reserve to the Shaugnessy Heights Golf Club in suburban Vancouver, Dickson J. (as he then was) was able to distinguish the "political trust" cases as inapplicable in a passage that should be set out in its entirety (at pp. 378-79):

> . . . Indian title is an <u>independent legal right</u> which, although recognized by the Royal Proclamation of 1763, nonetheless predates it. For this reason ... "political trust" decisions are inapplicable to the present case. The "political trust" cases concerned essentially the distribution of public funds or other property held by the government. In each case the party claiming to be beneficiary under a trust depended entirely on statute, ordinance or treaty as the basis for its claim to an interest in the funds in question. <u>The situation of the Indians is entirely different. Their interest in their lands is a pre-existing legal right not created by Royal Proclamation, by s. 18(1) of the *Indian Act*, or by any other executive order or legislative provision</u>. [Emphasis added.]

Later in his reasons, Dickson J. further pointed out that fiduciary duty was imposed on the Crown *despite* rather than *because* of its government functions, at p. 385:

> As the "political trust" cases indicate, the Crown is not normally viewed as a fiduciary in the exercise of its legislative or administrative function. The mere fact, however, that it is the Crown which is obligated to act on the Indians' behalf does not of itself remove the Crown's obligation from the scope of the fiduciary principle. As was pointed out earlier, the Indians' interest in land is an independent legal interest. It is not a creation of either the legislative or executive branches of government. The Crown's obligation to the Indians with respect to that interest is therefore not a public law duty. While it is not a private law duty in the strict sense either, it is nonetheless in the nature of a private law duty. Therefore, in this *sui generis* relationship, it is not improper to regard the Crown as a fiduciary.

Wilson J., in a concurring opinion, made similar comments, at p. 352:

> It seems to me that the "political trust" line of authorities is clearly distinguishable from the present case because Indian title has an existence apart altogether from s. 18(1) of the *Indian Act*. It would fly in the face of the clear wording of the section to treat that interest as terminable at will by the Crown without recourse by the Band. [...]

¶ 78 The *Guerin* concept of a *sui generis* fiduciary duty was expanded in *R. v. Sparrow*, [1990] 1 S.C.R. 1075, to include protection of the aboriginal people's pre-existing and still existing aboriginal and treaty rights within s. 35 of the *Constitution Act, 1982*. In that regard, it was said at p. 1108.

> The *sui generis* nature of Indian title, and the <u>historic powers and responsibility assumed by the Crown</u> constituted the source of such a fiduciary obligation. In our opinion, *Guerin*, together with *R. v. Taylor and Williams* (1981), 34 O.R. (2d) 360, ground a general guiding principle for s. 35(1). That is, the Government has the responsibility to act in a fiduciary capacity with respect to aboriginal peoples. The relationship between the Government and aboriginals is trust-like, rather than adversarial, and contemporary recognition and affirmation of aboriginal rights must be defined in light of this historic relationship. [Emphasis added.] [...]

¶ 79 The "historic powers and responsibility assumed by the Crown" in relation to Indian rights, although spoken of in *Sparrow*, at p. 1108, as a "general guiding principle for s. 35(1)", is of broader importance.... [P]otential relief by way of fiduciary remedies is not limited to the s. 35 rights (*Sparrow*) or existing reserves (*Guerin*). The fiduciary duty, where it exists, is called into existence to facilitate supervision of the high degree of discretionary control gradually assumed by the Crown over the lives of aboriginal peoples. As Professor Slattery commented:

> The sources of the general fiduciary duty do not lie, then, in a paternalistic concern to protect a "weaker" or "primitive" people, as has sometimes been suggested, but rather in the necessity of persuading native peoples, at a time when they still had considerable military capacities, that their rights would be better protected by reliance on the Crown than by self-help.

> (B. Slattery, "Understanding Aboriginal Rights" (1987), 66 *Can. Bar Rev.* 727, at p. 753) [...]

¶ 80 This *sui generis* relationship had its positive aspects in protecting the interests of aboriginal peoples historically (recall, e.g., the reference in *Royal Proclamation, 1763*, R.S.C. 1985, App. II, No. 1, to the "great Frauds and Abuses [that] have been committed in purchasing Lands of the Indians"), but the degree of economic, social and proprietary control and discretion asserted by the Crown also left aboriginal populations vulnerable to the risks of government misconduct or ineptitude. The importance of such discretionary control as a basic ingredient in a fiduciary relationship was underscored in Professor E. J. Weinrib's statement, quoted in *Guerin*, *supra*, at p. 384, that: "the hallmark of a fiduciary relation is that the relative legal positions are such that one party is at the mercy of the other's discretion." .... Somewhat associated with the ethical standards required of a fiduciary in the context of the Crown and Aboriginal peoples is the need to uphold the "honour of the Crown". [...]

¶ 81 But there are limits. The appellants seemed at times to invoke the "fiduciary duty" as a source of plenary Crown liability covering all aspects of the Crown-Indian band relationship. This overshoots the mark. The fiduciary duty imposed on the Crown does not exist at large but in relation to specific Indian interests. In this case we are dealing with land, which has generally played a central role in aboriginal economies and cultures. [...] Fiduciary protection accorded to Crown dealings with aboriginal interests in land (including reserve creation) has not to date been recognized by this Court in relation to Indian interests other than land outside the framework of s. 35(1) of the *Constitution Act, 1982*.

¶ 82 Since *Guerin*, Canadian courts have experienced a flood of "fiduciary duty" claims by Indian bands across a whole spectrum of possible complaints [...]

¶ 83 I think it desirable for the Court to affirm the principle, already mentioned, that not all obligations existing between the parties to a fiduciary relationship are themselves fiduciary in nature ... and that this principle applies to the relationship between the Crown and aboriginal peoples. It is necessary, then, to focus on the particular obligation or interest that is the subject matter of the particular dispute and whether or not the Crown had assumed discretionary control in relation thereto sufficient to ground a fiduciary obligation. [...]

¶ 85 I do not suggest that the existence of a public law duty necessarily excludes the creation of a fiduciary relationship. The latter, however, depends on identification of a cognizable Indian interest, and the Crown's undertaking of discretionary control in relation thereto in a way that invokes responsibility "in the nature of a private law duty", as discussed below.

N. *Application of Fiduciary Principles to Indian Lands*

¶ 86 For the reasons which follow, it is my view that the appellant bands' submissions in these appeals with respect to the existence and breach of a fiduciary duty cannot succeed:

> 1. The content of the Crown's fiduciary duty towards aboriginal peoples varies with the nature and importance of the interest sought to be protected. It does not provide a general indemnity.

> 2. Prior to reserve creation, the Crown exercises a public law function under the Indian Act — which is subject to supervision by the courts exercising public law remedies. At that stage a fiduciary relationship may also arise but, in that respect, the Crown's duty is limited to the basic obligations of loyalty, good faith in the discharge of its mandate, providing full disclosure appropriate to the subject matter, and acting with ordinary prudence with a view to the best interest of the aboriginal beneficiaries.

> 3. Once a reserve is created, the content of the Crown's fiduciary duty expands to include the protection and preservation of the band's quasi-proprietary interest in the reserve from exploitation.

4. In this case, as the appellant bands have rightly been held to lack any beneficial interest in the other band's reserve, equitable remedies are not available either to dispossess an incumbent band that is entitled to the beneficial interest, or to require the Crown to pay "equitable" compensation for its refusal to bring about such a dispossession.

5. Enforcement of equitable duties by equitable remedies is subject to the usual equitable defences, including laches and acquiescence.

¶ 87 I propose to discuss each of these propositions in turn.

1. <u>The content of the Crown's fiduciary duty towards aboriginal peoples varies with the nature and importance of the interest sought to be protected. It does not provide a general indemnity.</u>

¶ 89 ... In the present case the reserve-creation process dragged on from about 1878 to 1928, a period of 50 years. From at least 1907 onwards, the Department treated the reserves as having come into existence, which, in terms of actual occupation, they had. It cannot reasonably be considered that the Crown owed no fiduciary duty during this period to bands which had not only gone into occupation of provisional reserves, but were also entirely dependent on the Crown to see the reserve-creation process through to completion.

¶ 90 The issue, for present purposes, is to define the content of the fiduciary duty "with respect to the lands occupied by the Band" ... at the reserve-creation stage insofar as is necessary for the disposition of these appeals.

¶ 91 The situation here, unlike *Guerin*, does not involve the Crown interposing itself between an Indian band and non-Indians with respect to an existing Indian interest in lands. Nor does it involve the Crown as "faithless fiduciary" failing to carry out a mandate conferred by a band with respect to disposition of a band asset. The federal Crown in this case was carrying out various functions imposed by statute or undertaken pursuant to federal-provincial agreements. Its mandate was not the *disposition* of an existing Indian interest in the subject lands, but the *creation* of an altogether new interest in lands to which the Indians made no prior claim by way of treaty or aboriginal right.

¶ 92 This is not to suggest that a fiduciary duty has no role to play in these circumstances. It is to say, however, that caution must be exercised. As stated, even in the traditional trust context not all obligations existing between the parties to a well-recognized fiduciary relationship are themselves fiduciary in nature ... Moreover ... not all fiduciary relationships and not all fiduciary obligations are the same: "[T]hese are shaped by the demands of the situation" ... Thus, for example, the singular demands of the administration of justice drive and "shape" the content of the fiduciary relationship between solicitor and client: *R. v. Neil*, [2002] 3 S.C.R. 631, 2002 SCC 70. These observations are of particular importance in a case where the fiduciary is also the government, as the Court in *Guerin* fully recognized [...]

¶ 93 The starting point in this analysis, therefore, is the Indian bands' interest in specific lands that were subject to the reserve-creation process for their benefit, and in relation to which the Crown constituted itself the exclusive intermediary with the province. The task is to ascertain the content of the fiduciary duty in relation to those specific circumstances.

2. Prior to reserve creation, the Crown exercises a public law function under the _Indian Act_ — which is subject to supervision by the courts exercising public law remedies. At that stage a fiduciary relationship may also arise but, in that respect, the Crown's duty is limited to the basic obligations of loyalty, good faith in the discharge of its mandate, providing full disclosure appropriate to the subject matter, and acting with ordinary prudence with a view to the best interest of the aboriginal beneficiaries.

¶ 94 Insofar as the appellant bands contend for a broad application of a fiduciary duty at the stage of reserve creation in non-s. 35(1) lands (as distinguished from their other arguments concerning existing reserves and reserve disposition), it is necessary to determine what the imposition of a fiduciary duty adds at that stage to the remedies already available at public law. The answer, I think, is twofold. In a substantive sense the imposition of a fiduciary duty attaches to the Crown's intervention the additional obligations of loyalty, good faith, full disclosure appropriate to the matter at hand and acting in what it reasonably and with diligence regards as the best interest of the beneficiary. In _Blueberry River_ McLachlin J. (as she then was), at para. 104, said that "[t]he duty on the Crown as fiduciary was 'that of a man of ordinary prudence in managing his own affairs'".... Secondly, and perhaps more importantly, the imposition of a fiduciary duty opens access to an array of equitable remedies [...]

¶ 95 In this case the intervention of the Crown was positive, in that the federal government sought to create reserves for the appellant bands out of provincial Crown lands to which these particular bands had no aboriginal or treaty right. As explained, the people of the Laich-kwil-tach First Nation arrived in the Campbell River area at about the same time as the early Europeans (1840-1853). Government intervention from 1871 onwards was designed to protect members of the appellant bands from displacement by the other newcomers.

¶ 96 When exercising ordinary government powers in matters involving disputes between Indians and non-Indians, the Crown was (and is) obliged to have regard to the interest of all affected parties, not just the Indian interest. The Crown can be no ordinary fiduciary; it wears many hats and represents many interests, some of which cannot help but be conflicting ... As the Campbell River Band acknowledged in its factum, "[t]he Crown's position as fiduciary is necessarily unique" (para. 96). In resolving the dispute between Campbell River Band members and the non-Indian settlers named Nunns, for example, the Crown was not solely concerned with the band interest, nor should it have been. The Indians were "vulnerable" to the adverse exercise of the government's discretion, but so too were the settlers, and each looked to the Crown for a fair resolution of their dispute. At that stage, prior to reserve creation, the Court cannot ignore the reality of the conflicting demands confronting the government, asserted both by the competing bands themselves and by non-Indians. As Dickson J. said in _Guerin_, _supra_, at p. 385:

It should be noted that fiduciary duties generally arise only with regard to obligations originating in a private law context. Public law duties, the performance of which requires the exercise of discretion, do not typically give rise to a fiduciary relationship. [Emphasis added.]

¶ 97 Here, as in *Ross River*, the nature and importance of the appellant bands' interest in these lands prior to 1938, and the Crown's intervention as the exclusive intermediary to deal with others (including the province) on their behalf, imposed on the Crown a fiduciary duty to act with respect to the interest of the aboriginal peoples with loyalty, good faith, full disclosure appropriate to the subject matter and with "ordinary" diligence in what it reasonably regarded as the best interest of the beneficiaries. As the dispute evolved into conflicting demands between the appellant bands themselves, the Crown continued to exercise public law duties in its attempt to ascertain "the places they wish to have" (as stated at para. 24), and, as a fiduciary, it was the Crown's duty to be even-handed towards and among the various beneficiaries. An assessment of the Crown's discharge of its fiduciary obligations at the reserve-creation stage must have regard to the context of the times. The trial judge concluded that each of these obligations was fulfilled, and we have been given no persuasive reason to hold otherwise.

3. Once a reserve is created, the content of the Crown's fiduciary duty expands to include the protection and preservation of the band's quasi-proprietary interest in the reserve from exploitation.

¶ 98 The content of the fiduciary duty changes somewhat after reserve creation, at which the time the band has acquired a "legal interest" in its reserve, even if the reserve is created on non-s. 35(1) lands. In *Guerin*, Dickson J. said the fiduciary "interest gives rise upon surrender to a distinctive fiduciary obligation on the part of the Crown" (p. 382). These dicta should not be read too narrowly. Dickson J. spoke of surrender because those were the facts of the *Guerin* case. As this Court recently held, expropriation of an existing reserve equally gives rise to a fiduciary duty [...]

¶ 99 At the time of reserve *disposition* the content of the fiduciary duty may change (e.g. to include the implementation of the wishes of the band members). In *Blueberry River*, McLachlin J. observed at para. 35:

It follows that under the *Indian Act*, the Band had the right to decide whether to surrender the reserve, and its decision was to be respected. At the same time, if the Band's decision was foolish or improvident — a decision that constituted exploitation — the Crown could refuse to consent. In short, the Crown's obligation was limited to preventing exploitative bargains. [...]

¶ 100 It is in the sense of "exploitative bargain", I think, that the approach of Wilson J. in *Guerin* should be understood. Speaking for herself, Ritchie and McIntyre JJ., Wilson J. stated that prior to any disposition the Crown has "a fiduciary obligation to protect and preserve the Bands' interests from invasion or destruction" (p. 350). The "interests" to be protected from invasion or destruction, it should be emphasized, are legal interests, and the threat to their existence, as in *Guerin* itself, is the exploitative bargain (e.g. the lease with the Shaughnessy Heights Golf Club that in *Guerin* was found to be "unconscionable"). This is consistent with *Blueberry River* and *Lewis*. Wilson J.'s comments should be taken to mean that ordinary diligence must be used by the Crown to avoid invasion or destruction of the band's quasi-property interest by an exploitative bargain with third parties or, indeed, exploitation by the Crown itself. (Of course, there will also be cases dealing with the ordinary accountability by the Crown, as fiduciary, for its administrative control over the reserve and band assets.)

¶ 101 The Cape Mudge appellants contend that the Crown breached its fiduciary duty with respect to its two reserves (while attacking the trial judge's rejection of this factual premise) by permitting (or even encouraging) the *1907 Resolution*. They have been deprived of their legal interest in Reserve No. 11, they say, by an "exploitative bargain". They gave away 350 acres for nothing.

¶ 102 While the reserves were not constituted, as a matter of law, until 1938, I would be prepared to assume that, for purposes of this argument, the fiduciary duty was in effect in 1907. The Cape Mudge Band argument is nevertheless unconvincing. I do not accept what, with respect, is its shaky factual premise, i.e., that the band "gave away" Reserve No. 11 as opposed to entering a quit claim in favour of a sister band with a superior interest. More importantly, this argument rests on a misconception of the Crown's fiduciary duty. The Cape Mudge forbears, whose conduct is now complained of, were autonomous actors, apparently fully informed, who intended in good faith to resolve a "difference of opinion" with a sister band. They were not dealing with non-Indian third parties (*Guerin*, at p. 382). It is patronizing to suggest, on the basis of the evidentiary record, that they did not know what they were doing, or to reject their evaluation of a fair outcome. Taken in context, and looking at the substance rather than the form of what was intended, the *1907 Resolution* was not in the least exploitative.

¶ 103 While courts applying principles of equity rightly insist on flexibility to deal with the unforeseeable and infinite variety of circumstances and interests that may arise, and which will fall to be decided under equitable rules, it must be said that the bold attempt of the appellant bands to extend their claim to fiduciary relief on the present facts is overly ambitious.

¶ 104 On the other hand, the trial judge and the Federal Court of Appeal adopted, with respect, too restricted a view of the content of the fiduciary duty owed by the Crown to the Indian bands with respect to their existing quasi-proprietary interest in their respective reserves. In their view, the Crown discharged its fiduciary duty with respect to <u>existing</u> reserves by balancing "the interests of both the Cape Mudge Indians and the Campbell River Indians and to resolve their conflict regarding the use and occupation of the [Laich-kwil-tach] reserves ... [without favouring] the interests of one band over the interest of the other". [...] With respect, the role of honest referee does not exhaust the Crown's fiduciary obligation here. The Crown could not, merely by invoking competing interests, shirk its fiduciary duty. The Crown was obliged to preserve and protect each band's legal interest in the reserve which, on a true interpretation of events, had been allocated to it. In my view it did so. [...]

Disposition

¶ 138 I would therefore dismiss the appeals with costs.

(c)   The Honour of the Crown

- Research Note -
HAIDA NATION v. BRITISH COLUMBIA

In *Haida Nation v. British Columbia (Minister of Forests)*, [2004] 3 S.C.R. 511 the Haida Nation challenged British Columbia's unilateral replacements and transfers of tree farming licenses over lands to which the Haida claimed Aboriginal title. Haida Nation claimed that government has a duty to consult with Aboriginal people whenever government decision-making could adversely affect an Aboriginal right or Aboriginal title, even in cases, as here, where the Aboriginal claim had merely been asserted, but not yet litigated successfully in court. Haida Nation alleged that the transfers were made without adequate consultation.

The Supreme Court of Canada agreed.

[16] The government's duty to consult with Aboriginal peoples and accommodate their interests is grounded in the honour of the Crown. The honour of the Crown is always at stake in its dealings with Aboriginal peoples [...]

[17] The historical roots of the principle of the honour of the Crown suggest that it must be understood generously in order to reflect the underlying realities from which it stems. In all its dealings with Aboriginal peoples, from the assertion of sovereignty to the resolution of claims and the implementation of treaties, the Crown must act honourably. Nothing less is required if we are to achieve "the reconciliation of the pre-existence of aboriginal societies with the sovereignty of the Crown" [...]

[25] Put simply, Canada's Aboriginal peoples were here when Europeans came, and were never conquered. Many bands reconciled their claims with the sovereignty of the Crown through negotiated treaties. Others, notably in British Columbia, have yet to do so. The potential rights embedded in these claims are protected by s. 35 of the *Constitution Act, 1982*. The honour of the Crown requires that these rights be determined, recognized and respected. This, in turn, requires the Crown, acting honourably, to participate in processes of negotiation. While this process continues, the honour of the Crown may require it to consult and, where indicated, accommodate Aboriginal interests.

[26] Honourable negotiation implies a duty to consult with Aboriginal claimants and conclude an honourable agreement reflecting the claimants' inherent rights. But proving rights may take time, sometimes a very long time. In the meantime, how are the interests under discussion to be treated? Underlying this question is the need to reconcile prior Aboriginal occupation of the land with the reality of Crown sovereignty. Is the Crown, under the aegis of its asserted sovereignty, entitled to use the resources at issue as it chooses, pending proof and resolution of the Aboriginal claim? Or must it adjust its conduct to reflect the as yet unresolved rights claimed by the Aboriginal claimants?

[27] The answer, once again, lies in the honour of the Crown. The Crown, acting honourably, cannot cavalierly run roughshod over Aboriginal interests where claims affecting these interests are being seriously pursued in the process of treaty negotiation and proof. It must respect these potential, but yet unproven, interests. The Crown is not rendered impotent. It may continue to manage the resource in question pending claims resolution. But, depending on the circumstances, discussed more fully below, the honour of the Crown may require it to consult with and reasonably accommodate Aboriginal interests pending resolution of the claim. To unilaterally exploit a claimed resource during the process of proving and resolving the Aboriginal claim to that resource, may be to deprive the Aboriginal claimants of some or all of the benefit of the resource. That is not honourable. [...]

[32] The jurisprudence of this Court supports the view that the duty to consult and accommodate is part of a process of fair dealing and reconciliation that begins with the assertion of sovereignty and continues beyond formal claims resolution. Reconciliation is not a final legal remedy in the usual sense. Rather, it is a process flowing from rights guaranteed by s. 35(1) of the *Constitution Act, 1982*. This process of reconciliation flows from the Crown's duty of honourable dealing toward Aboriginal peoples, which arises in turn from the Crown's assertion of sovereignty over an Aboriginal people and *de facto* control of land and resources that were formerly in the control of that people. [...]

[33] To limit reconciliation to the post-proof sphere risks treating reconciliation as a distant legalistic goal, devoid of the "meaningful content" mandated by the "solemn commitment" made by the Crown in recognizing and affirming Aboriginal rights and title: *Sparrow, supra*, at p. 1108. It also risks unfortunate consequences. When the distant goal of proof is finally reached, the Aboriginal peoples may find their land and resources changed and denuded. This is not reconciliation. Nor is it honourable.

[35] But, when precisely does a duty to consult arise? The foundation of the duty in the Crown's honour and the goal of reconciliation suggest that the duty arises when the Crown has knowledge, real or constructive, of the potential existence of the Aboriginal right or title and contemplates conduct that might adversely affect it: see *Halfway River First Nation v. British Columbia (Ministry of Forests)*, [1997] 4 C.N.L.R. 45 (B.C.S.C.), at p. 71, per Dorgan J.

[36] This leaves the practical argument. It is said that before claims are resolved, the Crown cannot know that the rights exist, and hence can have no duty to consult or accommodate. This difficulty should not be denied or minimized. As I stated (dissenting) in Marshall, supra, at para. 112, one cannot "meaningfully discuss accommodation or justification of a right unless one has some idea of the core of that right and its modern scope". However, it will frequently be possible to reach an idea of the asserted rights and of their strength sufficient to trigger an obligation to consult and accommodate, short of final judicial determination or settlement. To facilitate this determination, claimants should outline their claims with clarity, focussing on the scope and nature of the Aboriginal rights they assert and on the alleged infringements. This is what happened here, where the chambers judge made a preliminary evidence-based assessment of the strength of the Haida claims to the lands and resources of Haida Gwaii, particularly Block 6.

[37] There is a distinction between knowledge sufficient to trigger a duty to consult and, if appropriate, accommodate, and the content or scope of the duty in a particular case. Knowledge of a credible but unproven claim suffices to trigger a duty to consult and accommodate. The content of the duty, however, varies with the circumstances, as discussed more fully below. A dubious or peripheral claim may attract a mere duty of notice, while a stronger claim may attract more stringent duties. The law is capable of differentiating between tenuous claims, claims possessing a strong prima facie case, and established claims. Parties can assess these matters, and if they cannot agree, tribunals and courts can assist. Difficulties associated with the absence of proof and definition of claims are addressed by assigning appropriate content to the duty, not by denying the existence of a duty.

[38] I conclude that consultation and accommodation before final claims resolution, while challenging, is not impossible, and indeed is an essential corollary to the honourable process of reconciliation that s. 35 demands. It preserves the Aboriginal interest pending claims resolution and fosters a relationship between the parties that makes possible

negotiations, the preferred process for achieving ultimate reconciliation: see S. Lawrence and P. Macklem, "From Consultation to Reconciliation: Aboriginal Rights and the Crown's Duty to Consult" (2000), 79 Can. Bar Rev. 252, at p. 262. Precisely what is required of the government may vary with the strength of the claim and the circumstances. But at a minimum, it must be consistent with the honour of the Crown.

D. The Scope and Content of the Duty to Consult and Accommodate

[39] The content of the duty to consult and accommodate varies with the circumstances. Precisely what duties arise in different situations will be defined as the case law in this emerging area develops. In general terms, however, it may be asserted that the scope of the duty is proportionate to a preliminary assessment of the strength of the case supporting the existence of the right or title, and to the seriousness of the potentially adverse effect upon the right or title claimed. [...]

[40] In *Delgamuukw, supra*, at para. 168, the Court considered the duty to consult and accommodate in the context of established claims. Lamer C.J. wrote:

> The nature and scope of the duty of consultation will vary with the circumstances. In occasional cases, when the breach is less serious or relatively minor, it will be no more than a duty to discuss important decisions that will be taken with respect to lands held pursuant to aboriginal title. Of course, even in these rare cases when the minimum acceptable standard is consultation, this consultation must be in good faith, and with the intention of substantially addressing the concerns of the aboriginal peoples whose lands are at issue. In most cases, it will be significantly deeper than mere consultation. Some cases may even require the full consent of an aboriginal nation, particularly when provinces enact hunting and fishing regulations in relation to aboriginal lands [...]

> [42] At all stages, good faith on both sides is required. The common thread on the Crown's part must be "the intention of substantially addressing [Aboriginal] concerns" as they are raised (*Delgamuukw*, [1997] 3 S.C.R. 1010; 153 D.L.R. (4th) 193, at para. 168), through a meaningful process of consultation. Sharp dealing is not permitted. However, there is no duty to agree; rather, the commitment is to a meaningful process of consultation. As for Aboriginal claimants, they must not frustrate the Crown's reasonable good faith attempts, nor should they take unreasonable positions to thwart government from making decisions or acting in cases where, despite meaningful consultation, agreement is not reached. [...]

[47] When the consultation process suggests amendment of Crown policy, we arrive at the stage of accommodation. Thus the effect of good faith consultation may be to reveal a duty to accommodate. Where a strong prima facie case exists for the claim, and the consequences of the government's proposed decision may adversely affect it in a significant way, addressing the Aboriginal concerns may require taking steps to avoid irreparable harm or to minimize the effects of infringement, pending final resolution of the underlying claim. Accommodation is achieved through consultation, as this Court recognized in *R. v. Marshall*, [1999] 3 S.C.R. 533, at para. 22: "... the process of accommodation of the treaty right may best be resolved by consultation and negotiation".

The Supreme Court ruled that the Crown's obligation to consult the Haida was triggered. Haida Nation's claims to title and Aboriginal rights to harvest trees were long standing, strong and subject to significant injury by British Columbia's decision to replace the tree farming licence. The Court concluded that the strength of the Haida case for aboriginal title and the aboriginal right to harvest, together with the serious impact of transfer decision on those asserted rights, required significant accommodation to preserve the Haida's interest pending resolution of the Haida claims.

In *Taku River Tlingit First Nation v. British Columbia (Project Assessment Director)*, [2004] 3 S.C.R. 550 the Supreme Court considered the First Nation's objection to the construction of a 160 km road through the First Nation's traditional territory. The Court ruled that British Columbia had a duty to consult with the First Nation because the road could have significant adverse impacts. On assessment of the facts, the Court ruled British Columbia had consulted and fulfilled its duty to accommodate. Importantly, the Court stated that "[t]he Province was not under a duty to reach agreement with the TRTFN, and its failure to do so did not breach the obligations of good faith that it owed the TRTFN;" (para. 22). The Court continued:

[42] As discussed in *Haida*, the process of consultation may lead to a duty to accommodate Aboriginal concerns by adapting decisions or policies in response. The purpose of s. 35(1) of the *Constitution Act, 1982* is to facilitate the ultimate reconciliation of prior Aboriginal occupation with *de facto* Crown sovereignty. Pending settlement, the Crown is bound by its honour to balance societal and Aboriginal interests in making decisions that may affect Aboriginal claims. The Crown may be required to make decisions in the face of disagreement as to the adequacy of its response to Aboriginal concerns. Balance and compromise will then be necessary.

MIKISEW CREE FIRST NATION v. CANADA (MINISTER OF CANADIAN HERITAGE)
2005 S.C.C. 69.

The judgment of the Court was delivered by

¶ 1 **BINNIE J.**:— The fundamental objective of the modern law of aboriginal and treaty rights is the reconciliation of aboriginal peoples and non-aboriginal peoples and their respective claims, interests and ambitions. The management of these relationships takes place in the shadow of a long history of grievances and misunderstanding. The multitude of smaller grievances created by the indifference of some government officials to aboriginal people's concerns, and the lack of respect inherent in that indifference has been as destructive of the process of reconciliation as some of the larger and more explosive controversies. And so it is in this case.

¶ 2 Treaty 8 is one of the most important of the post-Confederation treaties. Made in 1899, the First Nations who lived in the area surrendered to the Crown 840,000 square kilometres of what is now northern Alberta, northeastern British Columbia, northwestern Saskatchewan and the southern portion of the Northwest Territories. Some idea of the size of this surrender is given by the fact that it dwarfs France (543,998 square kilometres) [...] In exchange for this surrender, the First Nations were promised reserves and some other benefits including, most importantly to them, the following rights of hunting, trapping, and fishing:

> And Her Majesty the Queen hereby agrees with the said Indians that they shall have right to pursue their usual vocations of hunting, trapping and fishing <u>throughout the tract surrendered</u> as before described, <u>subject to such regulations</u> as may from time to time be made by the Government of the country, acting under the authority of Her Majesty, <u>and saving and excepting such tracts as may be required or taken up</u> from time to time for settlement, mining, lumbering, trading or other purposes. [Emphasis added.]

(Report of Commissioners for Treaty No. 8 (1899), at p. 12)

¶ 3 In fact, for various reasons (including lack of interest on the part of First Nations), sufficient land was not set aside for reserves for the Mikisew Cree First Nation (the "Mikisew") until the *Indian Lands Agreement (1986) Act*, S.C. 1988, c. 39, 87 years after Treaty 8 was made. Less than 15 years later, the federal government approved a 118-kilometre winter road that, as originally conceived, ran through the new Mikisew First Nation Reserve at Peace Point. The government did not think it necessary to engage in consultation directly with the Mikisew before making this decision. After the Mikisew protested, the winter road alignment was changed to track the boundary of the Peace Point reserve instead of running through it, again without consultation with the Mikisew. The modified road alignment traversed the traplines of approximately 14 Mikisew families who reside in the area near the proposed road, and others who may trap in that area although they do not live there, and the hunting grounds of as many as 100 Mikisew people whose hunt (mainly of moose), the Mikisew say, would be adversely affected. The fact the proposed winter road directly affects only about 14 Mikisew trappers and perhaps 100 hunters may not seem very dramatic (unless you happen to be one of the trappers or hunters in question) but, in the context of a remote northern community of relatively few families, it is significant. Beyond that, however, the principle of consultation in advance of interference with existing treaty rights is a matter of broad general importance to the relations between aboriginal and non-aboriginal peoples. It goes to the heart of the relationship and concerns not only the Mikisew but other First Nations and non-aboriginal governments as well. [...]

¶ 5 About 5 percent of the territory surrendered under Treaty 8 was set aside in 1922 as Wood Buffalo National Park. The Park was created principally to protect the last remaining herds of wood bison (or buffalo) in northern Canada and covers 44,807 square kilometres of land straddling the boundary between northern Alberta and southerly parts of the Northwest Territories. It is designated a UNESCO World Heritage Site. The Park itself is larger than Switzerland.

¶ 6 At present, it contains the largest free-roaming, self-regulating bison herd in the world, the last remaining natural nesting area for the endangered whooping crane, and vast undisturbed natural boreal forests. More to the point, it was been inhabited by First Nation peoples for more than over 8,000 years, some of whom still earn a subsistence living hunting, fishing and commercial trapping within the Park boundaries. The Park includes the traditional lands of the Mikisew. As a result of the Indian *Treaty Lands Agreement (1986) Act*, the Peace Point Reserve was formally excluded from the Park in 1988 but of course is surrounded by it. [...]

A. *The Winter Road Project*

¶ 8 The proponent of the winter road is the respondent Thebacha Road Society, whose members include the Town of Fort Smith (located in the Northwest Territories on the northeastern boundary of Wood Buffalo National Park, where the Park headquarters is located), the Fort Smith Métis Council, the Salt River First Nation, and Little Red River Cree First Nation. The advantage of the winter road for these people is that it would provide direct winter access among a number of isolated northern communities and to the Alberta highway system to the south. The trial judge accepted that the government's objective was to meet "regional transportation needs" [...]

B. *The Consultation Process*

¶ 9 According to the trial judge, most of the communications relied on by the Minister to demonstrate appropriate consultation were instances of the Mikisew's being provided with standard information about the proposed road in the same form and substance as the communications being distributed to the general public of interested stakeholders. [...] Chief Poitras stated that the Mikisew did not formally participate in the open houses, because "... an open house is not a forum for us to be consulted adequately".

¶ 10 Apparently, Parks Canada left the proponent Thebacha Road Society out of the information loop as well. At the end of January 2001, it advised Chief Poitras that it had just been informed that the Mikisew did not support the road. [...] Chief

Poitras wrote a further letter to the Minister on January 29, 2001 and received a standard-form response letter from the Minister's office stating that the correspondence "will be given every consideration".

¶ 11 Eventually, after several more miscommunications, Parks Canada wrote Chief Poitras on April 30, 2001, stating in part: "I apologize to you and your people for the way in which the consultation process unfolded concerning the proposed winter road and any resulting negative public perception of the [Mikisew Cree First Nation]". At that point, in fact, the decision to approve the road with a modified alignment had already been taken.

¶ 12 On May 25, 2001, the Minister announced on the Parks Canada website that the Thebacha Road Society was authorised to build a winter road 10 metres wide with posted speed limits ranging from 10 to 40 kilometres per hour. The approval was said to be in accordance with "Parks Canada plans and policy" and "other federal laws and regulations". No reference was made to any obligations to the Mikisew.

¶ 13 The Minister now says the Mikisew ought not to be heard to complain, about the process of consultation because they declined to participate in the public process that took place. Consultation is a two-way street, she says. It was up to the Mikisew to take advantage of what was on offer. They failed to do so. In the Minister's view, she did her duty.

¶ 14 The proposed winter road is wide enough to allow two vehicles to pass. Pursuant to s. 36(5) of the *Wood Buffalo National Park Game Regulations*, SOR/78-830, creation of the road would trigger a 200-metre wide corridor within which the use of firearms would be prohibited. The total area of this corridor would be approximately 23 square kilometres.

¶ 15 The Mikisew objection goes beyond the direct impact of closure of the area covered by the winter road to hunting and trapping. The surrounding area would be, the trial judge found, injuriously affected. Maintaining a traditional lifestyle, which the Mikisew say is central to their culture, depends on keeping the land around the Peace Point reserve in its natural condition and this, they contend, is essential to allow them to pass their culture and skills onto the next generation of Mikisew. The detrimental impact of the road on hunting and trapping, they argue, may simply prove to be one more incentive for their young people to abandon a traditional lifestyle and turn to other modes of living in the south.

¶ 16 The Mikisew applied to the Federal Court to set aside the Minister's approval based on their view of the Crown's fiduciary duty, claiming that the Minister owes "a fiduciary and constitutional duty to adequately consult with Mikisew Cree First Nation with regard to the construction of the road" (trial judge, para. 26).

¶ 17 An interlocutory injunction against construction of the winter road was issued by the Federal Court, Trial Division on August 27, 2001. [...]

¶ 24 The post-Confederation numbered treaties were designed to open up the Canadian west and northwest to settlement and development. Treaty 8 itself recites that "the said Indians have been notified and informed by Her Majesty's said Commission that it is Her desire to open for settlement, immigration, trade, travel, mining, lumbering and such other purposes as to Her Majesty may seem meet". This stated purpose is reflected in a corresponding limitation on the Treaty 8 hunting, fishing and trapping rights to exclude such "tracts as may be required or taken up from time to time for settlement, mining, lumbering, trading or other purposes". The "other purposes" would be at least as broad as the purposes listed in the recital, mentioned above, including "travel".

¶ 25 There was thus from the outset an uneasy tension between the First Nations' essential demand that they continue to be as free to live off the land after the treaty as before and the Crown's expectation of increasing numbers of non-aboriginal people moving into the surrendered territory. It was seen from the beginning as an ongoing relationship that would be difficult to manage ... As Cory J. explained in *Badger*, at para. 57, "[t]he Indians understood that land would be taken up for homesteads, farming, prospecting and mining and that they would not be able to hunt in these areas or to shoot at the settlers' farm animals or buildings". [...]

¶ 27 Thus none of the parties in 1899 expected that Treaty 8 constituted a finished land use blueprint. Treaty 8 signalled the advancing dawn of a period of transition. The key, as the Commissioners pointed out, was to "explain the relations" that would govern future interaction "and thus to prevent any trouble" (Mair, at p. 61). [...]

A. *Interpretation of the Treaty*

¶ 30 In the case of Treaty 8, it was contemplated by all parties that "from time to time" portions of the surrendered land would be "taken up" and transferred from the inventory of lands over which the First Nations had treaty rights to hunt, fish and trap, and placed in the inventory of lands where they did not. Treaty 8 lands lie to the north of Canada and are largely unsuitable for agriculture. The Commissioners who negotiated Treaty 8 could therefore express confidence to the First Nations that, as previously mentioned, "the same means of earning a livelihood would continue after the treaty as existed before it" (p. 5).

¶ 31 I agree with Rothstein J.A. that not every subsequent "taking up" by the Crown constituted an infringement of Treaty 8 that must be justified according to the test set out in *Sparrow*. In *Sparrow*, it will be remembered, the federal government's fisheries regulations infringed the aboriginal fishing right, and had to be strictly justified. This is not the same situation as we have here, where the aboriginal rights have been surrendered and extinguished, and the Treaty 8 rights are expressly limited to lands not "required or taken up <u>from time to time</u> for settlement, mining, lumbering, trading or other purposes". (Emphasis added.) The language of the treaty could not be clearer in foreshadowing change. Nevertheless the Crown was and is expected to manage the change honourably.

¶ 32 It follows that I do not accept the *Sparrow*-oriented approach adopted in this case by the trial judge, who relied in this respect on *Halfway River First Nation v. British Columbia (Ministry of Forests)* ... [which] held that the government's right to take up land was "by its very nature limited" (para. 138) and "that *any* interference with the right to hunt is a *prima facie* infringement of the Indians' treaty right as protected by s. 35 of the *Constitution Act, 1982*" (para. 144 (emphasis in original)) which must be justified under the *Sparrow* test. [...] I cannot agree. The Mikisew argument presupposes that Treaty 8 promised continuity of nineteenth century patterns of land use. It did not, as is made clear both by the historical context in which Treaty 8 was concluded and the period of transition it foreshadowed.

B. *The Process of Treaty Implementation*

¶ 33 Both the historical context and the inevitable tensions underlying implementation of Treaty 8 demand a *process* by which lands may be transferred from the one category (where the First Nations retain rights to hunt, fish and trap) to the other category (where they do not). The content of the process is dictated by the duty of the Crown to act honourably. Although *Haida Nation* was not a treaty case, McLachlin C.J. pointed out, at paras. 19 and 35:

> The honour of the Crown also infuses the processes of treaty making and treaty interpretation. In making and applying treaties, the Crown must act with honour and integrity, avoiding even the appearance of "sharp dealing" (*Badger*, at para. 41). Thus in *Marshall, supra,* at para. 4, the majority of this Court supported its interpretation of a treaty by stating that "nothing less would uphold the honour and integrity of the Crown in its dealings with the Mi'kmaq people to secure their peace and friendship".

> But, when precisely does a duty to consult arise? The foundation of the duty in the Crown's honour and the goal of reconciliation suggest that the duty arises when the Crown has knowledge, real or constructive, of the potential existence of the Aboriginal right or title and contemplates conduct that might adversely affect it.

¶ 34 In the case of a treaty the Crown, as a party, will always have notice of its contents. The question in each case will therefore be to determine the degree to which conduct contemplated by the Crown would adversely affect those rights so as to trigger the duty to consult. *Haida Nation* and *Taku River* set a low threshold. The flexibility lies not in the trigger ("might adversely affect it") but in the variable content of the duty once triggered. At the low end, "the only duty on the Crown may be to give notice, disclose information, and discuss any issues raised in response to the notice" (*Haida Nation*, at para. 43). The Mikisew say that even the low end content was not satisfied in this case.

C. *The Mikisew Legal Submission*

¶ 35 The appellant, the Mikisew, essentially reminded the Court of what was said in *Haida Nation* and *Taku River*. This case, the Mikisew say, is stronger. In those cases, unlike here, the aboriginal interest to the lands was asserted but not yet proven. In this case, the aboriginal interests are protected by Treaty 8. They are established legal facts. As in *Haida Nation*, the trial judge found the aboriginal interest was threatened by the proposed development. If a duty to consult was found to exist in *Haida Nation* and *Taku River* then a fortiori, the Mikisew argue, it must arise here and the majority judgment of the Federal Court of Appeal was quite wrong to characterise consultation between governments and aboriginal peoples as nothing more than a "good practice" (para. 24).

The Content of Treaty 8

¶ 42 ... The "hunting, trapping and fishing clause" of Treaty 8 was extensively reviewed by this Court in *Badger*. In that case Cory J. pointed out that "even by the terms of Treaty No. 8 the Indians' right to hunt for food was circumscribed by both geographical limitations and by specific forms of government regulation" (para. 37). The members of the First Nations, he continued, "would have understood that land had been 'required or taken up' when it was being put to a [visible] use which was incompatible with the exercise of the right to hunt" (para. 53). [...]

¶ 44 The Federal Court of Appeal purported to follow *Badger* in holding that the hunting, fishing and trapping rights would be infringed only "where the Crown has taken up land in bad faith or has taken up so much land that no meaningful right to hunt remains" (para. 18). With respect, I cannot agree with this implied rejection of the Mikisew procedural rights. At this stage the winter road is no more than a contemplated change of use. The proposed use would, if carried into execution, reduce the territory over which the Mikisew would be entitled to exercise their Treaty 8 rights. Apart from everything else, there would be no hunting at all within the 200-metre road corridor. More broadly, as found by the trial judge, the road would injuriously affect the exercise of these rights in the surrounding bush. [...]

The Draft Environmental Assessment Report acknowledged the road could potentially result in a diminution in quantity of the Mikisew harvest of wildlife, as fewer furbearers (including fisher, muskrat, marten, wolverine and lynx) will be caught in their traps. [...] [I]t is apparent that the proposed road will adversely affect the existing Mikisew hunting and trapping rights, and therefore that the "trigger" to the duty to consult identified in *Haida Nation* is satisfied. [...]

(d) *Honour of the Crown*

¶ 51 The duty to consult is grounded in the honour of the Crown, and it is not necessary for present purposes to invoke fiduciary duties. The honour of the Crown is itself a fundamental concept governing treaty interpretation and application ... The honour of the Crown exists as a source of obligation independently of treaties as well, of course [...]

¶ 52 It is not as though the Treaty 8 First Nations did not pay dearly for their entitlement to honourable conduct on the part of the Crown; surrender of the aboriginal interest in an area larger than France is a hefty purchase price.

(2) Did the Extensive Consultations with First Nations Undertaken in 1899 at the Time Treaty 8 Was Negotiated Discharge the Crown's Duty of Consultation and Accommodation?

¶ 53 The Crown's second broad answer to the Mikisew claim is that whatever had to be done was done in 1899. The Minister contends:

While the government should consider the impact on the treaty right, there is no duty to accommodate in this context. <u>The treaty itself constitutes the accommodation of the aboriginal interest; taking up lands, as defined above, leaves intact the essential</u> ability of the Indians to continue to hunt, fish and trap. As long as that promise is honoured, the treaty is not breached and no separate duty to accommodate arises. [Emphasis added.]

¶ 54 This is not correct. Consultation that excludes from the outset any form of accommodation would be meaningless. The contemplated process is not simply one of giving the Mikisew an opportunity to blow off steam before the Minister proceeds to do what she intended to do all along. Treaty making is an important stage in the long process of reconciliation, but it is only a stage. What occurred at Fort Chipewyan in 1899 was not the complete discharge of the duty arising from the honour of the Crown, but a rededication of it.

¶ 55 The Crown has a treaty right to "take up" surrendered lands for regional transportation purposes, but the Crown is nevertheless under an obligation to inform itself of the impact its project will have on the exercise by the Mikisew of their hunting and trapping rights, and to communicate its findings to the Mikisew. The Crown must then attempt to deal with the Mikisew "in good faith, and with the intention of substantially addressing" Mikisew concerns (*Delgamuukw*, at para. 168). This does not mean that whenever a government proposes to do anything in the Treaty 8 surrendered lands it must consult with all signatory First Nations, no matter how remote or unsubstantial the impact. The duty to consult is, as stated in *Haida Nation*, triggered at a low threshold, but adverse impact is a matter of degree, as is the extent of the Crown's duty. Here the impacts were clear, established and demonstrably adverse to the continued exercise of the Mikisew hunting and trapping rights over the lands in question.

¶ 56 In summary, the 1899 negotiations were the first step in a long journey that is unlikely to end any time soon. [...] [T]he Crown's right to take up lands under the treaty ... is subject to its duty to consult and, if appropriate, accommodate First Nations' interests before reducing the area over which their members may continue to pursue their hunting, trapping and fishing rights. [...]

¶ 57 As stated at the outset, the honour of the Crown infuses every treaty and the performance of every treaty obligation. Treaty 8 therefore gives rise to Mikisew procedural rights (e.g. consultation) as well as substantive rights (e.g. hunting, fishing and trapping rights). Were the Crown to have barrelled ahead with implementation of the winter road without adequate consultation, it would have been in violation of its *procedural* obligations, quite apart from whether or not the Mikisew could have established that the winter road breached the Crown's *substantive* treaty obligations as well.

¶ 58 *Sparrow* holds not only that rights protected by s. 35 of the *Constitution Act, 1982* are not absolute, but also that their breach may be justified by the Crown in certain defined circumstances. The Mikisew rights under Treaty 8 are protected by s. 35. The Crown does not seek to justify in *Sparrow*-terms shortcomings in its consultation in this case. The question that remains, therefore, is whether what the Crown did here complied with its obligation to consult honourably with the Mikisew First Nation.

(3) Was the Process Followed by the Minister Through Parks Canada in this Case Sufficient?

¶ 59 Where, as here, the Court is dealing with a *proposed* "taking up" it is not correct (even if it is concluded that the proposed measure *if implemented* would infringe the treaty hunting and trapping rights) to move directly to a *Sparrow* analysis. The Court must first consider the *process* by which the "taking up" is planned to go ahead, and whether that process is compatible with the honour of the Crown. If not, the First Nation may be entitled to succeed in setting aside the Minister's order on the process ground whether or not the facts of the case would otherwise support a finding of infringement of the hunting, fishing and trapping rights.

¶ 60 I should state at the outset that the winter road proposed by the Minister was a permissible purpose for "taking up" lands under Treaty 8. [...]

¶ 61 The question is whether the Minister and her staff pursued the permitted purpose of regional transportation needs in accordance with the Crown's duty to consult. The answer turns on the particulars of that duty shaped by the circumstances here. In *Delgamuukw*, the Court considered the duty to consult and accommodate in the context of an infringement of aboriginal title (at para. 168):

> In occasional cases, when the breach is less serious or relatively minor, it will be no more than a duty to discuss important decisions that will be taken with respect to lands held pursuant to aboriginal title. Of course, even in these rare cases when the minimum acceptable standard is consultation, this consultation must be in good faith, and <u>with the intention of substantially addressing the concerns of the aboriginal peoples whose lands are at issue</u>. In most cases, it will be significantly deeper than mere consultation. Some cases may even require the full consent of an aboriginal nation, particularly when provinces enact hunting and fishing regulations in relation to aboriginal lands. [Emphasis added.]

¶ 62 In *Haida Nation*, the Court pursued the kinds of duties that may arise in pre-proof claim situations, and McLachlin C.J. used the concept of a spectrum to frame her analysis (at paras. 43-45):

> At one end of the spectrum lie cases where the claim to title is weak, the Aboriginal right limited, or the potential for infringement minor. <u>In such cases, the only duty on the Crown may be to give notice, disclose information, and discuss any issues raised in response to the notice</u>. [...]
>
> At the other end of the spectrum lie cases where a strong *prima facie* case for the claim is established, the right and potential infringement is of high significance to the Aboriginal peoples, and the risk of non-compensable damage is high. <u>In such cases deep consultation, aimed at finding a satisfactory interim solution, may be required</u>. While precise requirements will vary with the circumstances, the consultation required at this stage

may entail the opportunity to make submissions for consideration, formal participation in the decision-making process, and provision of written reasons to show that Aboriginal concerns were considered and to reveal the impact they had on the decision. This list is neither exhaustive, nor mandatory for every case. [...]

Between these two extremes of the spectrum just described, will lie other situations. Every case must be approached individually. Each must also be approached flexibly, since the level of consultation required may change as the process goes on and new information comes to light. <u>The controlling question in all situations is what is required to maintain the honour of the Crown and to effect reconciliation between the Crown and the Aboriginal peoples with respect to the interests at stake</u>. [...] [Emphasis added.]

¶ 63 The determination of the content of the duty to consult will, as *Haida* suggests, be governed by the context. One variable will be the specificity of the promises made. Where, for example, a treaty calls for certain supplies, or Crown payment of treaty monies, or a modern land claims settlement imposes specific obligations on aboriginal peoples with respect to identified resources, the role of consultation may be quite limited. If the respective obligations are clear the parties should get on with performance. Another contextual factor will be the seriousness of the impact on the aboriginal people of the Crown's proposed course of action. The more serious the impact the more important will be the role of consultation. Another factor in a non-treaty case, as *Haida* points out, will be the strength of the aboriginal claim. The history of dealings between the Crown and a particular First Nation may also be significant. Here, the most important contextual factor is that Treaty 8 provides a framework within which to manage the continuing changes in land use already foreseen in 1899 and expected, even now, to continue well into the future. In that context, consultation is key to achievement of the overall objective of the modern law of treaty and aboriginal rights, namely reconciliation.

¶ 64 The duty here has both informational and response components. In this case, given that the Crown is proposing to build a fairly minor winter road on *surrendered* lands where the Mikisew hunting, fishing and trapping rights are expressly subject to the "taking up" limitation, I believe the Crown's duty lies at the lower end of the spectrum. The Crown was required to provide notice to the Mikisew and to engage directly with them (and not, as seems to have been the case here, as an afterthought to a general public consultation with Park users). This engagement ought to have included the provision of information about the project addressing what the Crown knew to be Mikisew interests and what the Crown anticipated might be the potential adverse impact on those interests. The Crown was required to solicit and to listen carefully to the Mikisew concerns, and to attempt to minimize adverse impacts on the Mikisew hunting, fishing and trapping rights. The Crown did not discharge this obligation when it unilaterally declared the road realignment would be shifted from the reserve itself to a track along its boundary. I agree on this point with what Finch J.A. (now C.J.B.C.) said in *Halfway River First Nation* at paras. 159-160.

> The fact that adequate notice of an intended decision may have been given does not mean that the requirement for adequate consultation has also been met.
>
> The Crown's duty to consult imposes on it a positive obligation to reasonably ensure that aboriginal peoples are provided with all necessary information in a timely way so that they have an opportunity to express their interests and concerns, <u>and to ensure that their representations are seriously considered and, wherever possible, demonstrably integrated into the proposed plan of action</u>. [Emphasis added.]

¶ 65 It is true, as the Minister argues, that there is some reciprocal onus on the Mikisew to carry their end of the consultation, to make their concerns known, to respond to the government's attempt to meet their concerns and suggestions, and to try to reach some mutually satisfactory solution. In this case, however, consultation never reached that stage. It never got off the ground.

¶ 66 Had the consultation process gone ahead, it would not have given the Mikisew a veto over the alignment of the road. As emphasized in *Haida Nation*, consultation will not always lead to accommodation, and accommodation may or may not result in an agreement. There could, however, be changes in the road alignment or construction that would go a long way towards satisfying the Mikisew objections. We do not know, and the Minister cannot know in the absence of consultation, what such changes might be.

¶ 67 The trial judge's findings of fact make it clear that the Crown failed to demonstrate an "'intention of substantially addressing [Aboriginal] concerns' ... through a meaningful process of consultation" (*Haida Nation*, para 42). On the contrary, the trial judge held that

> [i]n the present case, at the very least, this [duty to consult] would have entailed a response to Mikisew's October 10, 2000 letter, and a meeting with them to ensure that their concerns were addressed early in the planning stages of the project. At the meetings that were finally held between Parks Canada and Mikisew, a decision had essentially been made, therefore, the meeting could not have been conducted with the genuine intention of allowing Mikisew's concerns to be integrated with the proposal. [para. 154]

The trial judge also wrote (at para. 157):

> it is not consistent with the honour of the Crown, in its capacity as fiduciary, for it to fail to consult with a First Nation prior to making a decision that infringes on constitutionally protected treaty rights.

¶ 68 I agree, as did Sharlow J.A., dissenting in the Federal Court of Appeal. She declared that the mitigation measures were adopted through a process that was "fundamentally flawed" (para. 153).

¶ 69 In the result I would allow the appeal, quash the Minister's approval order, and remit the winter road project to the Minister to be dealt with in accordance with these reasons. [...]

3. Section 35

(a) General Concepts

R. v. SPARROW

[1990] 1 S.C.R. 1075.

[Appellant was charged in 1984 under the *Fisheries Act* with fishing with a drift net longer than that permitted by the terms of his Band's Indian food fishing licence. He admitted that the facts alleged constitute the offence, but defended the charge on the basis that he was exercising an existing aboriginal right to fish and that the net length restriction contained in the Band's licence was invalid in that it was inconsistent with s. 35(1) of the *Constitution Act, 1982*.

Appellant was convicted. The trial judge found that an aboriginal right could not be claimed unless it was supported by a special treaty and that s. 35(1) of the *Constitution Act, 1982* accordingly had no application.

An appeal to County Court was dismissed for similar reasons. The Court of Appeal found that the trial judge's findings of facts were insufficient to lead to an acquittal. Its decision was appealed and cross-appealed. The constitutional question before the Supreme Court queried whether the net length restriction contained in the Band's fishing licence was inconsistent with s. 35(1) of the *Constitution Act 1982*.]

THE CHIEF JUSTICE AND La FOREST J. [for the Court]: — This appeal requires this Court to explore for the first time the scope of s. 35(1) of the *Constitution Act, 1982*, and to indicate its strength as a promise to the aboriginal peoples of Canada. Section 35(1) is found in Part II of that Act, entitled "Rights of the Aboriginal Peoples of Canada", and provides as follows:

> 35. (1) The existing aboriginal and treaty rights of the aboriginal peoples of Canada are hereby recognized and affirmed.

The context of this appeal is the alleged violation of the terms of the Musqueam food fishing licence which are dictated by the *Fisheries Act*, R.S.C. 1970, c. F-14, and the regulations under that Act. The issue is whether Parliament's power to regulate fishing is now limited by s. 35(1) of the *Constitution Act, 1982*, and, more specifically, whether the net length restriction in the licence is inconsistent with that provision.

Facts

The appellant, a member of the Musqueam Indian Band, was charged under s. 61(1) of the *Fisheries Act* of the offence of fishing with a drift net longer than that permitted by the terms of the Band's Indian food fishing licence. The fishing which gave rise to the charge took place on May 25, 1984 in Canoe Passage which is part of the area subject to the Band's licence. The licence, which had been issued for a one-year period beginning March 31, 1984, set out a number of restrictions including one that drift nets were to be limited to 25 fathoms in length. The appellant was caught with a net which was 45 fathoms in length. He has throughout admitted the facts alleged to constitute the offence, but has defended the charge on the basis that he was exercising an existing aboriginal right to fish and that the net length restriction contained in the Band's licence is inconsistent with s. 35(1) of the *Constitution Act, 1982* and therefore invalid. [...]

Analysis

We will address first the meaning of "existing" aboriginal rights and the content and scope of the Musqueam right to fish. We will then turn to the meaning of "recognized and affirmed", and the impact of s. 35(1) on the regulatory power of Parliament.

"Existing"

The word "existing" makes it clear that the rights to which s. 35(1) applies are those that were in existence when the *Constitution Act, 1982* came into effect. This means that extinguished rights are not revived by the *Constitution Act, 1982*. A number of courts have taken the position that "existing" means "being in actuality in 1982": *R. v. Eninew* (1983), 7 C.C.C. (3d) 443 (Sask. Q.B.), at p. 446, aff'd (1984), 12 C.C.C. (3d) 365 (Sask. C.A.). See also *Attorney-General for Ontario v. Bear Island Foundation* (1984), 49 O.R. (2d) 353 (H.C.); *R. v. Hare and Debassige* (1985), 20 C.C.C. (3d) 1 (Ont. C.A.); *Re Steinhauer and The Queen* (1985), 15 C.R.R. 175 (Alta. Q.B.); *Martin v. The Queen* (1985), 17 C.R.R. 375 (N.B.Q.B.); *R. v. Agawa* (1988), 28 O.A.C. 201.

Further, an existing aboriginal right cannot be read so as to incorporate the specific manner in which it was regulated before 1982. The notion of freezing existing rights would incorporate into the Constitution a crazy patchwork of regulations. Blair J.A. in *Agawa*, supra, had this to say about the matter, at p. 214:

> Some academic commentators have raised a further problem which cannot be ignored. The *Ontario Fishery Regulations* contained detailed rules which vary for different regions in the province. Among other things, the *Regulations* specify seasons and methods of fishing, species of fish which can be caught and catch limits. Similar detailed provisions apply under the comparable fisheries *Regulations* in force in other provinces. These detailed provisions might be constitutionalized if it were decided that the existing treaty rights referred to in s. 35(1) were those remaining after regulation at the time of the proclamation of the *Constitution Act, 1982*.

As noted by Blair J.A., academic commentary lends support to the conclusion that "existing" means "unextinguished" rather than exercisable at a certain time in history. Professor Slattery, "Understanding Aboriginal Rights" (1987), 66 *Can. Bar Rev.* 727, at pp. 781-82, has observed the following about reading regulations into the rights:

This approach reads into the Constitution the myriad of regulations affecting the exercise of aboriginal rights, regulations that differ considerably from place to place across the country. It does not permit differentiation between regulations or long-term significance and those enacted to deal with temporary conditions, or between reasonable and unreasonable restrictions. Moreover, it might require that a constitutional amendment be enacted to implement regulations more stringent than those in existence on 17 April 1982. This solution seems unsatisfactory.

See also Professor McNeil, "The Constitutional Rights of the Aboriginal People of Canada" (1982), 4 *Supreme Court L.R.* 255 at p. 258 (*q.v.*); Pentney, "The Rights of the Aboriginal Peoples of Canada in the *Constitution Act, 1982*, Part II, Section 35: The Substantive Guarantee" (1988), 22 *U.B.C.L. Rev.* 207.

The arbitrariness of such an approach can be seen if one considers the recent history of the federal regulation in the context of the present case and the fishing industry. If the *Constitution Act, 1982* had been enacted a few years earlier, any right held by the Musqueam Band, on this approach, would have been constitutionally subjected to the restrictive regime of personal licences that had existed since 1917. Under that regime, the Musqueam catch had by 1969 become minor or non-existent. In 1978 a system of band licences was introduced on an experimental basis which permitted the Musqueam to fish with a 75 fathom net for a greater number of days than other people. Under this regime, from 1977 to 1984, the number of Band members who fished for food increased from 19 persons using 15 boats, to 64 persons using 38 boats, while 10 other members of the Band fished under commercial licences. Before this regime, the Band's food fish requirement had basically been provided by Band members who were licensed for commercial fishing. Since the regime introduced in 1978 was in force in 1982, then, under this approach, the scope and content of an aboriginal right to fish would be determined by the details of the Band's 1978 licence.

The unsuitability of the approach can also be seen from another perspective. Ninety-one other tribes of Indians, comprising over 20,000 people (compared with 540 Musqueam on the reserve and 100 others off the reserve) obtain their food fish from the Fraser River. Some or all of these bands may have an aboriginal right to fish there. A constitutional patchwork quilt would be created if the constitutional right of these bands were to be determined by the specific regime available to each of those bands in 1982.

Far from being defined according to the regulatory scheme in place in 1982, the phrase "existing aboriginal rights" must be interpreted flexibly so as to permit their evolution over time. To use Professor Slattery's expression, in "Understanding Aboriginal Rights," supra, at p. 782, the word "existing" suggests that those rights are "affirmed in a contemporary form rather than in their primeval simplicity and vigour". Clearly, then, an approach to the constitutional guarantee embodied in s. 35(1) which would incorporate "frozen rights" must be rejected.

The Aboriginal Right

[...] The evidence reveals that the Musqueam have lived in the area as an organized society long before the coming of European settlers, and that the taking of salmon was an integral part of their lives and remains so to this day. [...] What the Crown really insisted on, both in this Court and the courts below, was that the Musqueam Band's aboriginal right to fish had been extinguished by regulations under the *Fisheries Act*.

The history of the regulation of fisheries in British Columbia is set out in *Jack v. The Queen*, [1980] 1 S.C.R. 294, especially at pp. 308 *et seq.* and we need only summarize it here. Before the province's entry into Confederation in 1871 the fisheries were not regulated in any significant way, whether in respect of Indians or other people. The Indians were not only permitted but encouraged to continue fishing for their own food requirements. Commercial and sport fishing were not then of any great importance. The federal *Fisheries Act* was only proclaimed in force in the province in 1876 and the first *Salmon Fishery Regulations for British Columbia* were adopted in 1878 and were minimal.

The 1878 regulations were the first to mention Indians. They simply provided that the Indians were at all times at liberty, by any means other than drift nets or spearing, to fish for food for themselves, but not for sale or barter. The Indian right or liberty to fish was thereby restricted, and more stringent restrictions were added over the years. As noted in *Jack v. The Queen, supra,* at p. 310:

> The federal Regulations became increasingly strict in regard to the Indian fishery over time, as first the commercial fishery developed and then sport fishing became common. What we can see is an increasing subjection of the Indian fishery to regulatory control. First, the regulation of the use of drift nets, then the restriction of fishing to food purposes, then the requirement of permission from the Inspector and, ultimately, in 1917, the power to regulate even food fishing by means of conditions attached to the permit.

The 1917 regulations were intended to make still stronger the provisions against commercial fishing in the exercise or the Indian right to fish for food; see P.C. 2539 of Sept. 11, 1917. The Indian food fishing provisions remained essentially the same from 1917 to 1977. The regulations of 1977 retained the general principles of the previous sixty years. An Indian could fish for food under a "special licence" specifying method, locale and times of fishing. Following an experimental program to be discussed later, the 1981 regulations provided for the entirely new concept of a Band food fishing licence, while retaining comprehensive specification of conditions for the exercise of licences.

It is this progressive restriction and detailed regulation of the fisheries which, respondent's counsel maintained, have had the effect of extinguishing any aboriginal right to fish. The extinguishment need not be express, he argued, but may take place where the sovereign authority is exercised in a manner "necessarily inconsistent" with the continued enjoyment of aboriginal rights. For this proposition, he particularly relied on *St. Catherine's Milling and Lumber Co. v. The Queen* (1888), 14 App. Cas. 46 (P.C.); *Calder v. Attorney-General of British Columbia, supra; Baker Lake (Hamlet) v. Minister of Indian Affairs and Northern Development*, [1980] 1 F.C. 518 (T.D.); and *Attorney-General for Ontario v. Bear Island Foundation, supra*. The consent to its extinguishment before the *Constitution Act, 1982* was not required; the intent of the Sovereign could be effected not only by statute but by valid regulations. Here, in his view, the regulations had entirely displaced any aboriginal right. There is, he submitted, a fundamental inconsistency between the communal right to fish embodied in the aboriginal right, and fishing under a special licence or permit issued to individual Indians (as was the case until 1977) in the discretion of the Minister and subject to terms and conditions which, if breached, may result in cancellation of the licence. The *Fisheries Act* and its regulations were, he argued, intended to constitute a complete code inconsistent with the continued existence of an aboriginal right.

At bottom, the respondent's argument confuses regulation with extinguishment. That the right is controlled in great detail by the regulations does not mean that the right is thereby extinguished. The distinction to be drawn was carefully explained, in the context of federalism, in the first fisheries case, *Attorney-General for Canada v. Attorney-General for Ontario*, [1898] A.C. 700. There, the Privy Council had to deal with the interrelationship between, on the one hand, provincial property, which by s. 109 of the *Constitution Act, 1867* is vested in the provinces (and so falls to be regulated *qua* property exclusively by the provinces) and, on the other hand, the federal power to legislate respecting the fisheries thereon under s. 91(12) of that Act. The Privy Council said the following in relation to the federal regulation (at pp. 712-13):

> [...] the power to legislate in relation to fisheries does necessarily to a certain extent enable the Legislature so empowered to affect proprietary rights. An enactment, for example, prescribing the times of the year during which fishing is to be allowed, or the instruments which may be employed for the purpose (which it was admitted the Dominion Legislature was empowered to pass) might very seriously touch the exercise or proprietary rights, and the extent, character, and scope of such legislation is left entirely to the Dominion Legislature. The suggestion that the power might be abused so as to amount to a practical confiscation of property does not warrant the imposition by the Courts of any limit upon the absolute power of legislation conferred. The supreme legislative power in relation to any subject-matter is always capable of abuse, but it is not to be assumed that it will be improperly used: if it is, the only remedy is an appeal to those by whom the Legislature is elected.

In the context of aboriginal rights, it could be argued that, before 1982, an aboriginal right was automatically extinguished to the extent that it was inconsistent with a statute. As Mahoney J. stated in *Baker Lake, supra*, at p. 568:

> Once a statute has been validly enacted, it must be given effect. If its necessary effect is to abridge or entirely abrogate a common law right, then that is the effect that the courts must give it. That is as true of an aboriginal title as of any other common law right.

See also *Attorney-General for Ontario v. Bear Island Foundation,* supra, at pp. 439-40. That in Judson J.'s view was what had occurred in *Calder,* supra, where, as he saw it, a series of statutes evinced a unity of intention to exercise a sovereignty inconsistent with any conflicting interest, including aboriginal title. But Hall J. in that case stated (at p. 404) that "the onus of proving that the Sovereign intended to extinguish the Indian title lies on the respondent and *that intention must be `clear and plain' ".* (emphasis added.) The test of extinguishment to be adopted, in our opinion, is that the Sovereign's intention must be clear and plain if it is to extinguish an aboriginal right.

There is nothing in the *Fisheries Act* or its detailed regulations that demonstrates a clear and plain intention to extinguish the Indian aboriginal right to fish. The fact that express provision permitting the Indians to fish for food may have applied to all Indians and that for an extended period permits were discretionary and issued on an individual rather than a communal basis in no way shows a clear intention to extinguish. These permits were simply a manner of controlling the fisheries, not defining underlying rights.

We would conclude then that the Crown has failed to discharge its burden of proving extinguishment. In our opinion, the Court of Appeal made no mistake in holding that the Indians have an existing aboriginal right to fish in the area where Mr. Sparrow was fishing at the time of the charge. This approach is consistent with ensuring that an aboriginal right should not be defined by incorporating the ways in which it has been regulated in the past.

The scope of the existing Musqueam right to fish must now be delineated. The anthropological evidence relied on to establish the existence of the right suggests that, for the Musqueam, the salmon fishery has always constituted an integral part of their distinctive culture. Its significant role involved not only consumption for subsistence purposes, but also consumption of salmon on ceremonial and social occasions. The Musqueam have always fished for reasons connected to their cultural and physical survival. As we stated earlier, the right to do so may be exercised in a contemporary manner. [...] In relation to this submission, it was contended before this Court that the aboriginal right extends to commercial fishing. While no commercial fishery existed prior to the arrival of European settlers, it is contended that the Musqueam practice of bartering in early society may be revived as a modern right to fish for commercial purposes. The presence of numerous interveners representing commercial fishing interests, and the suggestion on the facts that the net length restriction is at least in part related to the probable commercial use of fish caught under the Musqueam food fishing licence, indicate the possibility of conflict between aboriginal fishing and the competitive commercial fishery with respect to economically valuable fish such as salmon. We recognize the existence or this conflict and the probability of its intensification as fish availability drops, demand rises and tensions increase.

Government regulations governing the exercise of the Musqueam right to fish, as described above, have only recognized the right to fish for food for over a hundred years. This may have reflected the existing position. However, historical policy on the part of the Crown is not only incapable of extinguishing the existing aboriginal right without clear intention, but is also incapable of, in itself, delineating that right. The nature or government regulations cannot be determinative of the content and scope of an existing aboriginal right. Government policy can however regulate the exercise of that right, but such regulation must be in keeping with s. 35(1).

In the courts below, the case at bar was not presented on the footing of an aboriginal right to fish for commercial or livelihood purposes. Rather, the focus was and continues to be on the validity of a net length restriction affecting the appellant's food fishing licence. We therefore adopt the Court of Appeal's characterization of the right for the purpose of this appeal, and confine our reasons to the meaning of the constitutional recognition and affirmation of the existing aboriginal right to fish for food and social and ceremonial purposes.

"Recognized and Affirmed"

We now turn to the impact of s. 35(1) of the *Constitution Act, 1982* on the regulatory power of Parliament and on the outcome of this appeal specifically.[...] The approach to be taken with respect to interpreting the meaning of s. 35(1) is derived from general principles of constitutional interpretation, principles relating to aboriginal rights, and the purposes behind the constitutional provision itself. Here, we will sketch the framework for an interpretation of "recognized and affirmed" that, in our opinion, gives appropriate weight to the constitutional nature of these words.

In *Reference Re Manitoba Language Rights*, [1985] 1 S.C.R. 721, this Court said the following about the perspective to be adopted when interpreting a constitution, at p. 745:

> The Constitution of a country is a statement of the will of the
> people to be governed in accordance with certain principles
> held as fundamental and certain prescriptions restrictive of the
> powers of the legislature and government. It is, as s. 52 of the
> *Constitution Act, 1982* declares, the "supreme law" of the nation,
> unalterable by the normal legislative process, and unsuffering
> of laws inconsistent with it. The duty of the judiciary is to
> interpret and apply the laws of Canada and each of the
> provinces, and it is thus our duty to ensure that the
> constitutional law prevails.

The nature of s. 35(1) itself suggests that it be construed in a purposive way. When the purposes of the affirmation of aboriginal rights are considered, it is clear that a generous, liberal interpretation of the words in the constitutional provision is demanded. When the Court of Appeal below was confronted with the submission that s. 35 has no effect on aboriginal or treaty rights and that it is merely a preamble to the parts of the *Constitution Act, 1982*, which deal with aboriginal rights, it said the following, at p. 322:

> This submission gives no meaning to s. 35. If accepted, it would
> result in denying its clear statement that existing rights are
> hereby recognized and affirmed, and would turn that into a
> mere promise to recognize and affirm those rights sometime in

the future. [...] To so construe s. 35(1) would be to ignore its language and the principle that the Constitution should be interpreted in a liberal and remedial way. We cannot accept that that principle applies less strongly to aboriginal rights than to the rights guaranteed by the *Charter*, particularly having regard to the history and to the approach to interpreting treaties and statutes relating to Indians required by such cases as *Nowegijick v. R.*, [1983] 1 S.C.R. 29. [...]

In *Nowegijick v. R*, at p. 36 the following principle that should govern the interpretation of Indian treaties and statutes was set out:

[...] treaties and statutes relating to Indians should be liberally construed and doubtful expressions resolved in favour of the Indians.

In *R. v. Agawa,* supra, Blair J.A. stated that the above principle should apply to the interpretation of s. 35(1). He added the following principle to be equally applied, at pp. 215-16:

The second principle was enunciated by the late Associate Chief Justice MacKinnon in *R. v. Taylor and Williams* (1981), 34 O.R. (2d) 360. He emphasized the importance of Indian history and traditions as well as the perceived effect of a treaty at the time of its execution. He also cautioned against determining Indian rights "in a vacuum". The honour of the Crown is involved in the interpretation of Indian treaties and, as a consequence, fairness to the Indians is a governing consideration. He said at p. 367:

The principles to be applied to the interpretation of Indian treaties have been much canvassed over the years. In approaching the terms of a treaty quite apart from the other considerations already noted, the honour of the Crown is always involved and no appearance of 'sharp dealing' should be sanctioned.

This view is reflected in recent judicial decisions which have emphasized the responsibility of Government to protect the rights of Indians arising from the special trust relationship created by history, treaties and legislation: see *Guerin v. The Queen,* [1984] 2 S.C.R. 335, 55 N.R. 161, 13 D.L.R. (4th) 321.

In *Guerin,* supra, the Musqueam Band surrendered reserve lands to the Crown for lease to a golf club. The terms obtained by the Crown were much less favourable than those approved by the Band at the surrender meeting. This Court found that the Crown owed a fiduciary obligation to the Indians with respect to the lands. The *sui generis* nature of Indian title, and the historic powers and responsibility assumed by the Crown constituted the source of such a fiduciary obligation. In our opinion, Guerin together with *R. v. Taylor and Williams* (1981), 34

O.R. (2d) 360, ground a general guiding principle for s. 35(1). That is, the Government has the responsibility to act in a fiduciary capacity with respect to aboriginal peoples. The relationship between the Government and aboriginals is trust-like, rather than adversarial, and contemporary recognition and affirmation of aboriginal rights must be defined in light of this historic relationship.

We agree with both the British Columbia Court of Appeal below and the Ontario Court of Appeal that the principles outlined above, derived from *Nowegijick, Taylor and Williams* and *Guerin* should guide the interpretation of s. 35(1). As commentators have noted, s. 35(1) is a solemn commitment that must be given meaningful content (Lyon, *op. cit.*; Pentney, *op. cit.*; Schwartz, "Unstarted Business: Two Approaches to Defining s. 35 – 'What's in the Box?' and 'What Kind of Box?' ", Chapter XXIV, in *First Principles Second Thoughts: Aboriginal Peoples Constitutional Reform and Canadian Statecraft*; Slattery, *op. cit.*; and Slattery, "The Hidden Constitution: Aboriginal Rights in Canada" (1984), 32 *Am. J. of Comp. Law* 361).

In response to the appellant's submission that s. 35(1) rights are more securely protected than the rights guaranteed by the *Charter*, it is true that s. 35(1) is not subject to s. 1 of the *Charter*. In our opinion, this does not mean that any law or regulation affecting aboriginal rights will automatically be of no force or effect by the operation of s. 52 of the *Constitution Act, 1982*. Legislation that affects the exercise of aboriginal rights will nonetheless be valid, if it meets the test for justifying an interference with a right recognized and affirmed under s. 35(1).

There is no explicit language in the provision that authorizes this Court or any court to assess the legitimacy of any government legislation that restricts aboriginal rights. Yet, we find that the words "recognition and affirmation" incorporate the fiduciary relationship referred to earlier and so import some restraint on the exercise of sovereign power. Rights that are recognized and affirmed are not absolute. Federal legislative powers continue, including, of course, the right to legislate with respect to Indians pursuant to s. 91(24) of the *Constitution Act, 1867*. These powers must, however, now be read together with s. 35(1). In other words, federal power must be reconciled with federal duty and the best way to achieve that reconciliation is to demand the justification of any government regulation that infringes upon or denies aboriginal rights. Such scrutiny is in keeping with the liberal interpretive principle enunciated in *Nowegijick*, supra, and the concept of holding the Crown to a high standard of honourable dealing with respect to the aboriginal peoples of Canada as suggested by *Guerin v. The Queen*, supra. [...]

Section 35(1) suggests that while regulation affecting aboriginal rights is not precluded, such regulation must be enacted according to a valid objective. Our history has shown, unfortunately all too well, that Canada's aboriginal peoples are justified in worrying about government objectives that may be superficially neutral but which constitute *de facto* threats to the existence of aboriginal rights and interests. By giving aboriginal rights constitutional status and priority, Parliament and the provinces have sanctioned challenges to social and economic policy objectives embodied in legislation to the extent that aboriginal rights are affected. Implicit in this constitutional scheme is the obligation of the legislature to satisfy the test of justification. The way in which a legislative objective is to be attained must uphold the honour of the Crown and must be in keeping with the unique contemporary relationship, grounded in history and policy, between the Crown and Canada's aboriginal peoples. The extent of legislative or regulatory impact on an existing aboriginal right may be scrutinized so as to ensure recognition and affirmation.

The constitutional recognition afforded by the provision therefore gives a measure of control over government conduct and a strong check on legislative power. While it does not promise immunity from government regulation in a society that, in the twentieth century, is increasingly more complex, interdependent and sophisticated, and where exhaustible resources need protection and management, it does hold the Crown to a substantive promise. The government is required to bear the burden of justifying any legislation that has some negative effect on any aboriginal right protected under s. 35(1).

In these reasons, we will outline the appropriate analysis under s. 35(1) in the context of a regulation made pursuant to the *Fisheries Act*. We wish to emphasize the importance of context and a case-by-case approach to s. 35(1). Given the generality of the text of the constitutional provision and especially in light of the complexities of aboriginal history, society and rights, the contours of a justificatory standard must be defined in the specific factual context of each case.

Section 35(1) and the Regulation of the Fisheries

Taking the above framework as guidance we propose to set out the test for *prima facie* interference with an existing aboriginal right and for the justification of such an interference. [...] The first question to be asked is whether the legislation in question has the effect of interfering with an existing aboriginal right. If it does have such an effect, it represents a *prima facie* infringement of s. 35(1). Parliament is not expected to act in a manner contrary to the rights and interests of aboriginals, and, indeed, may be barred from doing so by the second stage of s. 35(1) analysis. The inquiry with respect to interference begins with a reference to the characteristics or incidents of the right at stake. Our earlier observations regarding the scope of the aboriginal right to fish are relevant here. Fishing rights are not traditional property rights. They are rights held by a collective and are in keeping with the culture and existence of that group. Courts must be careful, then, to avoid the application of traditional common law concepts of property as they develop their understanding of what the reasons for judgment in *Guerin,* supra, at p. 382, referred to as the "sui generis" nature of aboriginal rights. (See also Little Bear, "A Concept of Native Title," [1982] 5 *Can. Legal Aid Bul.* 99.)

While it is impossible to give an easy definition of fishing rights, it is possible, and, indeed, crucial, to be sensitive to the aboriginal perspective itself on the meaning of the rights at stake. For example, it would be artificial to try to create a hard distinction between the right to fish and the particular manner in which that right is exercised.

To determine whether the fishing rights have been interfered with such as to constitute a *prima facie* infringement of s. 35(1), certain questions must be asked. First, is the limitation unreasonable? Second, does the regulation impose undue hardship? Third, does the regulation deny to the holders of the right their preferred means of exercising that right? The onus of proving a *prima facie* infringement lies on the individual or group challenging the legislation. In relation to the facts of this appeal, the regulation would be found to be a *prima facie* interference if it were found to be an undue restriction on the Musqueam exercise of their right to fish for food. We wish to note here that the analysis does not merely require looking at whether the fish catch has been reduced below that needed for the reasonable food and ceremonial needs of the Musqueam Indians. Rather the test involves asking whether either the purpose or the effect of the restriction on net length unnecessarily infringes the interests protected by the fishing right. If, for example, the Musqueam were forced to spend undue time and money per fish caught or if the net length reduction resulted in a hardship to the Musqueam in catching fish, then the first branch of the s. 35(1) analysis would be met.

If a *prima facie* interference is found, the analysis moves to the issue of justification. This is the test that addresses the question of what constitutes legitimate regulation of a constitutional aboriginal right. The justification analysis would proceed as follows. First, is there a valid legislative objective? Here the court would inquire into whether the objective of Parliament in authorizing the department to enact regulations regarding fisheries is valid. The objective of the department in setting out the particular regulations would also be scrutinized. An objective aimed at preserving s. 35(1) rights by conserving and managing a natural resource, for example, would be valid. Also valid would be objectives purporting to prevent the exercise of s. 35(1) rights that would cause harm to the general populace or to aboriginal peoples themselves, or other objectives found to be compelling and substantial.

The Court of Appeal below held, at p. 331, that regulations could be valid if reasonably justified as "necessary for the proper management and conservation of the resource *or in the public interest*". (Emphasis added.) We find the "public interest" justification to be so vague as to provide no meaningful guidance and so broad as to be unworkable as a test for the justification of a limitation on constitutional rights. [...]

If a valid legislative objective is found, the analysis proceeds to the second part of the justification issue. Here, we refer back to the guiding interpretive principle derived from *Taylor and Williams* and *Guerin*, supra. That is, the honour of the Crown is at stake in dealings with aboriginal peoples. The special trust relationship and the responsibility of the government vis-à-vis aboriginals must be the first consideration in determining whether the legislation or action in question can be justified. [...]

In *Eninew*, Hall J.A. found, at p. 368, that "the treaty rights can be limited by such regulations as are reasonable". As we have pointed out, management and conservation of resources is indeed an important and valid legislative objective. Yet, the fact that the objective is of a "reasonable" nature cannot suffice as constitutional recognition and affirmation of aboriginal rights. Rather, the regulations enforced pursuant to a conservation or management objective may be scrutinized according to the justificatory standard outlined above.

We acknowledge the fact that the justificatory standard to be met may place a heavy burden on the Crown. However, government policy with respect to the British Columbia fishery, regardless of s. 35(1), already dictates that, in allocating the right to take fish, Indian food fishing is to be given priority over the interests of other user groups. The constitutional entitlement embodied in s. 35(1) requires the Crown to ensure that its regulations are in keeping with that allocation of priority. The objective of this requirement is not to undermine Parliament's ability and responsibility with respect to creating and administering overall conservation and management plans regarding the salmon fishery. The objective is rather to guarantee that those plans treat aboriginal peoples in a way ensuring that their rights are taken seriously.

Within the analysis of justification, there are further questions to be addressed, depending on the circumstances of the inquiry. These include the questions of whether there has been as little infringement as possible in order to effect the desired result; whether, in a situation of expropriation, fair compensation is available; and, whether the aboriginal group in question has been consulted with respect to the conservation measures being implement. The aboriginal peoples, with their history of conservation-consciousness and inter-dependence with natural resources, would surely be expected, at the least, to be informed regarding the determination of an appropriate scheme for the regulation of the fisheries.

We would not wish to set out an exhaustive list of the factors to be considered in the assessment of justification. Suffice it to say that recognition and affirmation requires sensitivity to and respect for the rights of aboriginal peoples on behalf of the government, courts and indeed all Canadians.

Application to this Case – Net Length Restriction Valid?

The Court of Appeal below found that there was not sufficient evidence in this case to proceed with an analysis of s. 35(1) with respect to the right to fish for food. In reviewing the competing expert evidence, and recognizing that fish stock management is an uncertain science, it decided that the issues at stake in this appeal were not well adapted to being resolved at the appellate court level.

Before the trial, defence counsel advised the Crown of the intended aboriginal rights defence and that the defence would take the position that the Crown was required to prove, as part of its case, that the net length restriction was justifiable as a necessary and reasonable conservation measure. The trial judge found s. 35(1) to be inapplicable to the appellant's defence, based on his finding that no aboriginal right had been established. He therefore found it inappropriate to make findings of fact with respect to either an infringement of the aboriginal right to fish or the justification of such an infringement. He did, however, find that the evidence called by the appellant "[c]asts some doubt as to whether the restriction was necessary as a conservation measure. More particularly, it suggests that there were more appropriate measures that could have been taken if necessary; measures that would not impose such a hardship on the Indians fishing for food. That case was not fully met by the Crown."

According to the Court of Appeal, the findings of fact were insufficient to lead to an acquittal. There was no more evidence before this Court. We also would order a re-trial which would allow findings of fact according to the tests set out in these reasons.

The appellant would bear the burden of showing that the net length restriction constituted a *prima facie* infringement of the collective aboriginal right to fish for food. If an infringement were found, the onus would shift to the Crown which would have to demonstrate that the regulation is justifiable. To that end, the Crown would have to show that there is no underlying unconstitutional objective such as shifting more of the resource to a user group that ranks below the Musqueam. Further, it would have to show that the regulation sought to be imposed is required to accomplish the needed limitation. In trying to show that the restriction is necessary in the circumstances of the Fraser River fishery, the Crown could use facts pertaining to fishing by other Fraser River Indians.

In conclusion, we would dismiss the appeal and the cross-appeal and affirm the Court of Appeal's setting aside of the conviction. We would accordingly affirm the order for a new trial on the questions of infringement and whether any infringement is nonetheless consistent with s. 35(1), in accordance with the interpretation set out here.

For the reasons given above, the constitutional question must be answered as follows:

Question   Is the net length restriction contained in the Musqueam Indian Band Indian Food Fishing Licence dated March 30, 1984 issued pursuant to the *British Columbia Fishery (General) Regulations* and the *Fisheries Act*, R.S.C. 1970, c. F-14 inconsistent with s. 35(1) of the *Constitution Act, 1982*?

Answer   This question will have to be sent back to trial to be answered according to the analysis set out in these reasons.

(b)   Aboriginal Rights

- Research Note -
ABORIGINAL RIGHTS

The law of Aboriginal rights can be synthesized from twelve decisions of the Supreme Court of Canada.[1] Taken together, these decisions lay out a five step test for determining the existence and scope of any claimed Aboriginal right.

---

1   *R. v. Sparrow*, [1990] 1 S.C.R. 1075; *R. v. Van der Peet*, [1996] 2 S.C.R. 507; *R. v. N.T.C. Smokehouse Ltd.*, [1996] 2 S.C.R. 672; *R. v. Gladstone*, [1996] 2 S.C.R. 723; *R. v. Nikal*, [1996] 1 S.C.R. 1013; *R. v. Pamajewon*, [1996] 2 S.C.R.

Aboriginal rights are those "practices, traditions and customs central to the aboriginal societies that existed in North America prior to contact with the Europeans."[1] Ancestral practices, traditions and customs are understood in light of their corresponding modern common law right. Courts asked to identify an aboriginal right will "examine the pre-sovereignty aboriginal practice and translate that practice ... into a modern legal right."[2]

To analyze claims of Aboriginal rights, the Court must consider 5 elements: (1) characterization, (2) location, (3) time, (4) "integral to distinctive culture" and (5) continuity.

Characterization

only after counsel has proposed it first ✗

The Court first must characterize the Aboriginal right being claimed.

Roadmap

Characterization of the right claimed is guided by 3 factors:
* the nature of the action which the applicant is claiming was done pursuant to an aboriginal right;
* the nature of the governmental regulation, statute or action being impugned;
* the pre-contact practice, custom or tradition being relied upon to establish the right.[3]

"The correct characterization of the ... claim is of importance because whether or not the evidence supports the appellant's claim will depend, in significant part, on what, exactly, that evidence is being called to support."[4]

The characterization of the right must be specific. The Supreme Court has consistently rejected characterizing claims for aboriginal rights on a general basis.[5]

• fail if too general

[Footnote 1 continued from prior page]

821; *R. v. Adams*, [1996] 3 S.C.R. 101; *R. v. Côté*, [1996] 3 S.C.R. 139; *Mitchell v. M.N.R.*, [2001] 1 S.C.R. 911; *R. v. Powley*, [2003] 2 S.C.R. 207, *R. v. Marshall; R. v. Bernard* [2005] 2 S.C.R. 220; *R. v. Sappier*, 2006 S.C.C. 54.

1   *R. v. Van der Peet*, [1996] 2 S.C.R. 507 at para 44; *Mitchell v. M.N.R.*, [2001] 1 S.C.R. 911 at para 15.

2   *R. v. Marshall; R. v. Bernard* [2005] 2 S.C.R. 220 at para 51 ("the court must examine the pre-sovereignty aboriginal practice and translate that practice into a modern right. The process begins by examining the nature and extent of the pre-sovereignty aboriginal practice in question. It goes on to seek a corresponding common law right".).

3   *R. v. Van der Peet*, para 53; *R. v. Sappier*, 2006 S.C.C. 54, para 20.

4   *R. v. Van der Peet*, [1996] 2 S.C.R. 507 at para 51.

5   *R. v. Van der Peet*, [1996] 2 S.C.R. 507 at para 69; *R. v. Sappier*, 2006 S.C.C. 54, para 24.

The Supreme Court's twelve cases lay down that "the existence of an aboriginal right will depend entirely on the practices, customs and traditions of the particular aboriginal community claiming the right."[1]

"The right must be identified and proven in the 'practices, traditions and customs' central to the particular community asserting the right."[2]

In *Pamajewon*, the Supreme Court ruled that the characterization of the appellant's claim as 'a broad right to manage the use of reserve lands' was overly general:

> Aboriginal rights, including any asserted right to self-government, must be looked at in light of the specific circumstances of each case and, in particular, in light of the specific history and culture of the aboriginal group claiming the right. The factors laid out in *Van der Peet*, and applied, *supra*, allow the Court to consider the appellants' claim at the appropriate level of specificity; the characterization put forward by the appellants would not allow the Court to do so.[3]

In *Mitchell*, the Supreme Court observed that "an overly broad characterization [of the Aboriginal right] risks distorting the right by neglecting the specific culture and history of the claimant's society."[4]

The Plaintiffs carry an onus to prove their claim with specific, relevant evidence.

> Evidence advanced in support of aboriginal claims, like the evidence offered in any case, can run the gamut of cogency from the highly compelling to the highly dubious. Claims must still be established on the basis of persuasive evidence demonstrating their validity on the balance of probabilities.[5]

---

1   *R. v. Van der Peet*, [1996] 2 S.C.R. 507 at para 69.
2   *Sawridge Band v. Canada* [2005] F.C.J. No. 1857 at para 283.
3   *R. v. Pamajewon*, [1996] 2 S.C.R. 821 at para 27; Re-affirmed *Mitchell v. M.N.R.*, [2001] 1 S.C.R. 911 at para 15.
4   *Mitchell v. M.N.R.*, [2001] 1 S.C.R. 911 at para 15.
5   *Mitchell v. M.N.R.*, [2001] 1 S.C.R. 911 at para 39.

Location

The Court must determine whether the claimed aboriginal right has a geographic character - whether it is site specific.[1]

Plaintiffs must lead evidence not only of the traditional practices that give rise to their claimed aboriginal right, but also where and how these traditions were practiced

In *Sawridge Band v. Canada* the Federal Court refused to allow the Plaintiffs to lead general evidence which:

> do[es] not assist the Court in deciding whether there are traditions, customs and practices internal to the Plaintiffs that support a right to decide membership in a way that has been unjustifiably abrogated by specific Amendments to the *Indian Act*.[2]

General evidence is inconsistent with the direction that "the existence of an aboriginal right will depend entirely on the practices, customs and traditions of the particular aboriginal community claiming the right."[3]

Time

Aboriginal claimants must prove that the traditional practices relied on were in existence prior to contact with the Europeans.

"Integral to Distinctive Culture"

Aboriginal claimants must prove that the asserted practice relied on was "integral to the distinctive culture" of their pre-contact Aboriginal community.

In *Van der Peet*, the Supreme Court explained that

> To satisfy the integral to a distinctive culture test the Aboriginal claimant must do more than demonstrate that a practice, tradition or custom was an aspect of, or took place in, the Aboriginal society of which he or she is a part. The claimant must demonstrate that the practice, tradition or custom was a central and significant part of the society's distinctive culture.

---

1 *R. v. Côté*, [1996] 3 S.C.R. 139 at para 39. Note that an Aboriginal right is not *required* to be site specific. Rather, this is an inquiry that the Court will make. In other words, the Plaintiffs must lead evidence of where and how the right was exercised. If it was only exercised in a specific area then the right will be limited to that area.

2 *Sawridge Band v. Canada* ,[2005] F.C.J. No. 1860, at para 76.

3 *R. v. Van der Peet*, [1996] 2 S.C.R. 507 at para 69.

He or she must demonstrate ... that the practice, tradition or custom with one of the things which made the culture of the society distinctive   that it was one of the things that really made the society what it was.[1]

In *Sawridge Band v. Canada* the Federal Court interpreted 'integral to the distinctive culture' to mean that the Plaintiff Bands asserted right to control their own membership "must be grounded in specific governance practices, laws and customs, *internal and integral to these particular Plaintiffs* [...]"[2]

Continuity

Aboriginal rights are communal rights. They are grounded in the existence of a historic aboriginal community and a present aboriginal community. Individuals may exercise aboriginal rights only by virtue of an ancestrally based membership in the present aboriginal community.[3]

Claimants must demonstrate continuity between the Aboriginal practice exercised by the historically based community that existed prior to contact with Europeans and the practice as it is exercised by their modern community today. The whole point is that the doctrine of aboriginal rights expresses a "commitment to protecting practices that were historically important features of particular aboriginal communities."[4]

In *Bernard/Marshall*, the Supreme Court added a new twist.

> [T]he court must examine the pre-sovereignty aboriginal practice and translate that practice into a modern right. The process begins by examining the nature and extent of the pre-sovereignty aboriginal practice in question. It goes on to seek a corresponding common law right. In this way, the process determines the nature and extent of the modern right and reconciles the aboriginal and European perspectives.[5]

This emphasis on the common law requires the Plaintiffs to show not only that the traditional practice existed, and was integral to the community, but also that the practice corresponds with a modern right being asserted, a right described or describable by common law concepts.

---

1   *R. v. Van der Peet*, [1996] 2 S.C.R. 507 at para 55.
2   *Sawridge Band v. Canada*, [2005] F.C.J. No. 1860 at para 76.
3   *R. v. Powley*, [2003] 2 S.C.R. 207, para 24.
4   *Ibid.* at para 45.
5   *R. v. Marshall; R. v. Bernard* [2005] 2 S.C.R. 220 at para 51.

Plaintiffs are required to characterize the asserted aboriginal right in terms of a modern common law analogue. The correspondence between ancestral practice relied on and modern right asserted must have integrity. "A pre-sovereignty aboriginal practice cannot be transformed into a different modern right."[1] Failure to make this link with care could prove fatal to the aboriginal rights claim.

R. v. VAN DER PEET
[1996] 2 S.C.R. 507.

[On September 11, 1987, the appellant, Dorothy Van der Peet, sold ten salmon caught by Steven and Charles Jimmy. The salmon were caught under the authority of an Indian food fish licence. The appellant was subsequently charged under s. 61(1) of the *Fisheries Act*, R.S.C. 1970, c. F-14, with the offence of selling fish caught under the authority of an Indian food fish licence, contrary to section 27(5) of the *British Columbia Fishery (General) Regulations*. The appellant, a member of the Sto:lo, did not contest these facts. Rather she defended the charges against her on the basis that she was exercising an Aboriginal right to sell fish. She argued that the Regulations infringed her existing Aboriginal right to sell fish, protected under section 35(1) of the *Constitution Act, 1982*. In that the Regulations violated s. 35(1), Van der Peet argued they were invalid.]

LAMER C.J. [La Forest, Sopinka, Gonthier, Cory, Iacobucci and Major JJ. Concurring]: —

[...] I now turn to the question which, as I have already suggested, lies at the heart of this appeal: How should the aboriginal rights recognized and affirmed by s. 35(1) of the *Constitution Act, 1982* be defined?

In her factum the appellant argued that the majority of the Court of Appeal erred because it defined the rights in s. 35(1) in a fashion which "converted a Right into a Relic"; such an approach, the appellant argued, is inconsistent with the fact that the aboriginal rights recognized and affirmed by s. 35(1) are <u>rights</u> and not simply aboriginal practices. The appellant acknowledged that aboriginal rights are based in aboriginal societies and cultures, but argued that the majority of the Court of Appeal erred because it defined aboriginal rights through the identification of pre-contact activities instead of as pre-existing legal rights.

While the appellant is correct to suggest that the mere existence of an activity in a particular aboriginal community prior to contact with Europeans is not, in itself, sufficient foundation for the definition of aboriginal rights, the position she would have this Court adopt takes s. 35(1) too far from that which the provision is intended to protect. Section 35(1), it is true, recognizes and affirms existing aboriginal <u>rights</u>, but it must not be forgotten that the rights it recognizes and affirms are <u>aboriginal</u>.

---

1   *R. v. Marshall; R. v. Bernard* [2005] 2 S.C.R. 220 at para 50.

In the liberal enlightenment view, reflected in the American Bill of Rights and, more indirectly, in the *Charter*, rights are held by all people in society because each person is entitled to dignity and respect. Rights are general and universal; they are the way in which the "inherent dignity" of each individual in society is respected: *R. v. Oakes*, [1986] 1 S.C.R. 103, at p. 136; *R. v. Big M Drug Mart Ltd.*, supra, at p. 336.

<u>Aboriginal</u> rights cannot, however, be defined on the basis of the philosophical precepts of the liberal enlightenment. Although equal in importance and significance to the rights enshrined in the *Charter*, aboriginal rights must be viewed differently from *Charter* rights because they are rights held only by aboriginal members of Canadian society. They arise from the fact that aboriginal people are <u>aboriginal</u>. As academic commentators have noted, aboriginal rights "inhere in the very meaning of aboriginality", Michael Asch and Patrick Macklem, "Aboriginal Rights and Canadian Sovereignty: An Essay on *R. v. Sparrow*" (1991), 29 Alta. L. Rev. 498, at p. 502; they are the rights held by Indians *qua* Indians", Brian Slattery, "Understanding Aboriginal Rights" (1987), 66 *Can. Bar Rev.* 727, at p. 776.

The task of this Court is to define aboriginal rights in a manner which recognizes that aboriginal rights are <u>rights</u> but which does so without losing sight of the fact that they are rights held by aboriginal people because they are <u>aboriginal</u>. The Court must neither lose sight of the generalized constitutional status of what s. 35(1) protects, nor can it ignore the necessary specificity which comes from granting special constitutional protection to one part of Canadian society. The Court must define the scope of s. 35(1) in a way which captures <u>both</u> the aboriginal and the rights in aboriginal rights.

The way to accomplish this task is, as was noted at the outset, through a purposive approach to s. 35(1). It is through identifying the interests that s. 35(1) was intended to protect that the dual nature of aboriginal rights will be comprehended. [...] A purposive approach to s. 35(1), because ensuring that the provision is not viewed as static and only relevant to current circumstances, will ensure that the recognition and affirmation it offers are consistent with the fact that what it is recognizing and affirming are "rights". Further, because it requires the court to analyze a given constitutional provision "in the light of the interests it was meant to protect"(*Big M Drug Mart Ltd.*, supra, at p. 344), a purposive approach to s. 35(1) will ensure that that which is found to fall within the provision is related to the provision's intended focus: aboriginal people and their rights in relation to Canadian society as a whole. [...]

General Principles Applicable to Legal Disputes Between Aboriginal Peoples and the Crown

Before turning to a purposive analysis of s. 35(1), however, it should be noted that such analysis must take place in light of the general principles which apply to the legal relationship between the Crown and aboriginal peoples. [...]

This interpretive principle, articulated first in the context of treaty rights [...] arises from the nature of the relationship between the Crown and aboriginal peoples. The Crown has a fiduciary obligation to aboriginal peoples with the result that in dealings between the government and aboriginals the honour of the Crown is at stake. Because of this fiduciary relationship, and its implication of the honour of the Crown, treaties, s. 35(1), and other statutory and constitutional provisions protecting the interests of aboriginal peoples, must be given a generous and liberal interpretation. [...] This general principle must inform the Court's analysis of the purposes underlying s. 35(1), and of that provision's definition and scope.

The fiduciary relationship of the Crown and aboriginal peoples also means that where there is any doubt or ambiguity with regards to what falls within the scope and definition of s. 35(1), such doubt or ambiguity must be resolved in favour of aboriginal peoples. In *R. v. Sutherland*, [1980] 2 S.C.R. 451, at p. 464, Dickson J. held that paragraph 13 of the Memorandum of Agreement between Manitoba and Canada, a constitutional document, "should be interpreted so as to resolve any doubts in favour of the Indians, the beneficiaries of the rights assured by the paragraph". This interpretive principle applies equally to s. 35(1) of the *Constitution Act, 1982* and should, again, inform the Court's purposive analysis of that provision.

Purposive Analysis of Section 35(1)

[...] When the court identifies a constitutional provision's purposes, or the interests the provision is intended to protect, what it is doing in essence is explaining the rationale of the provision; it is articulating the reasons underlying the protection that the provision gives. With regards to s. 35(1), then, what the court must do is explain the rationale and foundation of the recognition and affirmation of the special rights of aboriginal peoples; it must identify the basis for the special status that aboriginal peoples have within Canadian society as a whole. [...]

In my view, the doctrine of aboriginal rights exists, and is recognized and affirmed by s. 35(1), because of one simple fact: when Europeans arrived in North America, aboriginal peoples were already here, living in communities on the land, and participating in distinctive cultures, as they had done for centuries. It is this fact, and this fact above all others, which separates aboriginal peoples from all other minority groups in Canadian society and which mandates their special legal, and now constitutional, status.

More specifically, what s. 35(1) does is provide the constitutional framework through which the fact that aboriginals lived on the land in distinctive societies, with their own practices, traditions and cultures, is acknowledged and reconciled with the sovereignty of the Crown. The substantive rights which fall within the provision must be defined in light of this purpose; the aboriginal rights recognized and affirmed by s. 35(1) must be directed towards the reconciliation of the pre-existence of aboriginal societies with the sovereignty of the Crown. [...]

The Test for Identifying Aboriginal Rights in Section 35(1)

In order to fulfil the purpose underlying s. 35(1) — i e, the protection and reconciliation of the interests which arise from the fact that prior to the arrival of Europeans in North America aboriginal peoples lived on the land in distinctive societies, with their own practices, customs and traditions — the test for identifying the aboriginal rights recognized and affirmed by s. 35(1) must be directed at identifying the crucial elements of those pre-existing distinctive societies. It must, in other words, aim at identifying the practices, traditions and customs central to the aboriginal societies that existed in North America prior to contact with the Europeans.

In *Sparrow*, supra, this Court did not have to address the scope of the aboriginal rights protected by s. 35(1); however, in their judgment at p. 1099 Dickson C.J. and La Forest J. identified the Musqueam right to fish for food in the fact that:

> The anthropological evidence relied on to establish the existence of the right suggests that, for the Musqueam, the salmon fishery has always constituted an <u>integral part of their distinctive culture</u>. Its significant role involved not only consumption for subsistence purposes, but also consumption of salmon on ceremonial and social occasions. The Musqueam have always fished for reasons connected to their cultural and physical survival. (emphasis added.)

The suggestion of this passage is that participation in the salmon fishery is an aboriginal right because it is an "integral part" of the "distinctive culture" of the Musqueam. This suggestion is consistent with the position just adopted; identifying those practices, customs and traditions that are integral to distinctive aboriginal cultures will serve to identify the crucial elements of the distinctive aboriginal societies that occupied North America prior to the arrival of Europeans.

In light of the suggestion of *Sparrow*, supra, and the purposes underlying s. 35(1), the following test should be used to identify whether an applicant has established an aboriginal right protected by s. 35(1): in order to be an aboriginal right an activity must be an element of a practice, custom or tradition integral to the distinctive culture of the aboriginal group claiming the right. [...]

<u>Courts must take into account the perspective of aboriginal peoples themselves</u>

In assessing a claim for the existence of an aboriginal right, a court must take into account the perspective of the aboriginal people claiming the right. In *Sparrow*, supra, Dickson C.J. and La Forest J. held, at p. 1112, that it is "crucial to be sensitive to the aboriginal perspective itself on the meaning of the rights at stake". It must also be recognized, however, that that perspective must be framed in terms cognizable to the Canadian legal and constitutional structure. As has already been noted, one of the fundamental purposes of s. 35(1) is the reconciliation of the pre-existence of distinctive aboriginal societies with the assertion of Crown sovereignty. Courts adjudicating aboriginal rights claims must, therefore, be sensitive to the aboriginal perspective, but they must also be aware that aboriginal rights exist within the general legal system of Canada. [...]

Courts must identify precisely the nature of the claim being made in determining whether an aboriginal claimant has demonstrated the existence of an aboriginal right

Related to this is the fact that in assessing a claim to an aboriginal right a court must first identify the nature of the right being claimed; in order to determine whether a claim meets the test of being integral to the distinctive culture of the aboriginal group claiming the right, the court must first correctly determine what it is that is being claimed. [...]

The nature of an applicant's claim must be delineated in terms of the particular practice, custom or tradition under which it is claimed; the significance of the practice, custom or tradition to the aboriginal community is a factor to be considered in determining whether the practice, custom or tradition is integral to the distinctive culture, but the significance of a practice, custom or tradition cannot, itself, constitute an aboriginal right.

To characterize an applicant's claim correctly, a court should consider such factors as the nature of the action which the applicant is claiming was done pursuant to an aboriginal right, the nature of the governmental regulation, statute or action being impugned, and the practice, custom or tradition being relied upon to establish the right. In this case, therefore, the Court will consider the actions which led to the appellant's being charged, the fishery regulation under which she was charged and the practices, customs and traditions she invokes in support of her claim.

It should be acknowledged that a characterization of the nature of the appellant's claim from the actions which led to her being charged must be undertaken with some caution. In order to inform the court's analysis the activities must be considered at a general rather than at a specific level. Moreover, the court must bear in mind that the activities may be the exercise in a modern form of a practice, custom or tradition that existed prior to contact, and should vary its characterization of the claim accordingly.

In order to be integral a practice, custom or tradition must be of central significance to the aboriginal society in question

To satisfy the integral to a distinctive culture test the aboriginal claimant must do more than demonstrate that a practice, custom or tradition was an aspect of, or took place in, the aboriginal society of which he or she is a part. The claimant must demonstrate that the practice, custom or tradition was a central and significant part of the society's distinctive culture. He or she must demonstrate, in other words, that the practice, custom or tradition was one of the things which made the culture of the society distinctive — that it was one of the things that truly made the society what it was.

This aspect of the integral to a distinctive culture test arises from fact that aboriginal rights have their basis in the prior occupation of Canada by distinctive aboriginal societies. To recognize and affirm the prior occupation of Canada by distinctive aboriginal societies it is to what makes those societies distinctive that the court must look in identifying aboriginal rights. The court cannot look at those aspects of the aboriginal society that are true of every human society (e.g., eating to survive), nor can it look at those aspects of the aboriginal society that are only incidental or occasional to that society; the court must look instead to the defining and central attributes of the aboriginal society in question. It is only by focusing on the aspects of the aboriginal society that make that society distinctive that the definition of aboriginal rights will accomplish the purpose underlying s. 35(1). [...]

A practical way of thinking about this problem is to ask whether, without this practice, custom or tradition, the culture in question would be fundamentally altered or other than what it is. One must ask, to put the question affirmatively, whether or not a practice, custom or tradition is a defining feature of the culture in question.

The practices, customs and traditions which constitute aboriginal rights are those which have continuity with the practices, customs and traditions that existed prior to contact

The time period that a court should consider in identifying whether the right claimed meets the standard of being integral to the aboriginal community claiming the right is the period prior to contact between aboriginal and European societies. Because it is the fact that distinctive aboriginal societies lived on the land prior to the arrival of Europeans that underlies the aboriginal rights protected by s. 35(1), it is to that pre-contact period that the courts must look in identifying aboriginal rights.

The fact that the doctrine of aboriginal rights functions to reconcile the existence of pre-existing aboriginal societies with the sovereignty of the Crown does not alter this position. Although it is the sovereignty of the Crown that the pre-existing aboriginal societies are being reconciled with, it is to those pre-existing societies that the court must look in defining aboriginal rights. It is not the fact that aboriginal societies existed prior to Crown sovereignty that is relevant; it is the fact that they existed prior to the arrival of Europeans in North America. As such, the relevant time period is the period prior to the arrival of Europeans, not the period prior to the assertion of sovereignty by the Crown.

That this is the relevant time should not suggest, however, that the aboriginal group claiming the right must accomplish the next to impossible task of producing conclusive evidence from pre-contact times about the practices, customs and traditions of their community. It would be entirely contrary to the spirit and intent of s. 35(1) to define aboriginal rights in such a fashion so as to preclude in practice any successful claim for the existence of such a right. The evidence relied upon by the applicant and the courts may relate to aboriginal practices, customs and traditions post-contact; it simply needs to be directed at demonstrating which aspects of the aboriginal community and society have their origins pre-contact. It is those practices, customs and traditions that can be rooted in the pre contact societies of the aboriginal community in question that will constitute aboriginal rights. [...]

Where an aboriginal community can demonstrate that a particular practice, custom or tradition is integral to its distinctive culture today, and that this practice, custom or tradition has continuity with the practices, customs and traditions of pre-contact times, that community will have demonstrated that the practice, custom or tradition is an aboriginal right for the purposes of s. 35(1).

The concept of continuity is also the primary means through which the definition and identification of aboriginal rights will be consistent with the admonition in *Sparrow,* supra, at p. 1093, that "the phrase 'existing aboriginal rights' must be interpreted flexibly so as to permit their evolution over time". The concept of continuity is, in other words, the means by which a "frozen rights" approach to s. 35(1) will be avoided. Because the practices, customs and traditions protected by s. 35(1) are ones that exist today, subject only to the requirement that they be demonstrated to have continuity with the practices, customs and traditions which existed pre-contact, the definition of aboriginal rights will be one that, on its own terms, prevents those rights from being frozen in pre-contact times. The evolution of practices, customs and traditions into modern forms will not, provided that continuity with pre-contact practices, customs and traditions is demonstrated, prevent their protection as aboriginal rights.

I would note that the concept of continuity does not require aboriginal groups to provide evidence of an unbroken chain of continuity between their current practices, customs and traditions, and those which existed prior to contact. It may be that for a period of time an aboriginal group, for some reason, ceased to engage in a practice, custom or tradition which existed prior to contact, but then resumed the practice, custom or tradition at a later date. Such an interruption will not preclude the establishment of an aboriginal right. Trial judges should adopt the same flexibility regarding the establishment of continuity that, as is discussed, infra, they are to adopt with regards to the evidence presented to establish the prior-to-contact practices, customs and traditions of the aboriginal group making the claim to an aboriginal right.

Further, I would note that basing the identification of aboriginal rights in the period prior to contact is not inconsistent with the fact that s. 35(2) of the *Constitution Act, 1982* includes within the definition of "aboriginal peoples of Canada" the Métis people of Canada.

Although s. 35 includes the Métis within its definition of "aboriginal peoples of Canada", and thus seems to link their claims to those of other aboriginal peoples under the general heading of "aboriginal rights", the history of the Métis, and the reasons underlying their inclusion in the protection given by s. 35, are quite distinct from those of other aboriginal peoples in Canada. As such, the manner in which the aboriginal rights of other aboriginal peoples are defined is not necessarily determinative of the manner in which the aboriginal rights of the Métis are defined. At the time when this Court is presented with a Métis claim under s. 35 it will then, with the benefit of the arguments of counsel, a factual context and a specific Métis claim, be able to explore the question of the purposes underlying s. 35's protection of the aboriginal rights of Métis people, and answer the question of the lands of claims which fall within s. 35(1)'s scope when the claimants are Métis. The fact that, for other aboriginal peoples, the protection granted by s. 35 goes to the practices, customs and traditions of aboriginal peoples prior to contact, is not necessarily relevant to the answer which will be given to that question. It may, or it may not, be the case that the claims of the Métis are determined on the basis of the pre-contact practices, customs and traditions of their aboriginal ancestors; whether that is so must await determination in a case in which the issue arises.

Courts must approach the rules of evidence in light of the evidentiary difficulties inherent in adjudicating aboriginal claims

In determining whether an aboriginal claimant has produced evidence sufficient to demonstrate that her activity is an aspect of a practice, custom or tradition integral to a distinctive aboriginal culture, a court should approach the rules of evidence, and interpret the evidence that exists, with a consciousness of the special nature of aboriginal claims, and of the evidentiary difficulties in proving a right which originates in times where there were no written records of the practices, customs and traditions engaged in. The courts must not undervalue the evidence presented by aboriginal claimants simply because that evidence does not conform precisely with the evidentiary standards that would be applied in, for example, a private law torts case.

Claims to aboriginal rights must be adjudicated on a specific rather than general basis

Courts considering a claim to the existence of an aboriginal right must focus specifically on the practices, customs and traditions of the particular aboriginal group claiming the right. In the case of *Kruger*, supra, this Court rejected the notion that claims to aboriginal rights could be determined on a general basis. This position is correct; the existence of an aboriginal right will depend entirely on the practices, customs and traditions of the particular aboriginal community claiming the right. As has already been suggested, aboriginal rights are constitutional rights, but that does not negate the central fact that the interests aboriginal rights are intended to protect relate to the specific history of the group claiming the right. Aboriginal rights are not general and universal; their scope and content must be determined on a case-by-case basis. The fact that one group of aboriginal people has an aboriginal right to do a particular thing will not be, without something more, sufficient to demonstrate that another aboriginal community has the same aboriginal right. The existence of the right will be specific to each aboriginal community.

For a practice, custom or tradition to constitute an aboriginal right it must be of independent significance to the aboriginal culture in which it exists

In identifying those practices, customs and traditions that constitute the aboriginal rights recognized and affirmed by s. 35(1), a court must ensure that the practice, custom or tradition relied upon in a particular case is independently significant to the aboriginal community claiming the right. The practice, custom or tradition cannot exist simply as an incident to another practice, custom or tradition but must rather be itself of integral significance to the aboriginal society. Where two customs exist, but one is merely incidental to the other, the custom which is integral to the aboriginal community in question will qualify as an aboriginal right, but the custom that is merely incidental will not. Incidental practices, customs and traditions cannot qualify as aboriginal rights through a process of piggybacking on integral practices, customs and traditions.

The integral to a distinctive culture test requires that a practice, custom or tradition be distinctive; it does not require that that practice, custom or tradition be distinct

The standard which a practice, custom or tradition must meet in order to be recognized as an aboriginal right is <u>not</u> that it be <u>distinct</u> to the aboriginal culture in question; the aboriginal claimants must simply demonstrate that the practice, custom or tradition is <u>distinctive</u>. A tradition or custom that is <u>distinct</u> is one that is unique -- "different in kind or quality; unlike" (*Concise Oxford Dictionary*, supra). A culture with a distinct tradition must claim that in having such a tradition it is different from other cultures; a claim of distinctness is, by its very nature, a claim relative to other cultures or traditions. By contrast, a culture that claims that a practice, custom or tradition is <u>distinctive</u> — "distinguishing, characteristic" — makes a claim that is not relative; the claim is rather one about the culture's own practices, customs or traditions considered apart from the practices, customs or traditions of any other culture. It is a claim that this tradition or custom makes the culture <u>what it is</u>, not that the practice, custom or tradition is different from the practices, customs or traditions of another culture. The person or community claiming the existence of an aboriginal right protected by s. 35(1) need only show that the particular practice, custom or tradition which it is claiming to be an aboriginal right is distinctive, not that it is distinct. [...]

The influence of European culture will only be relevant to the inquiry if it is demonstrated that the practice, custom or tradition is only integral because of that influence

The fact that Europeans in North America engaged in the same practices, customs or traditions as those under which an aboriginal right is claimed will only be relevant to the aboriginal claim if the practice, custom or tradition in question can only be said to exist because of the influence of European culture. If the practice, custom or tradition was an integral part of the aboriginal community's culture prior to contact with Europeans, the fact that that practice, custom or tradition continued after the arrival of Europeans, and adapted in response to their arrival, is not relevant to determination of the claim; European arrival and influence cannot be used to deprive an aboriginal group of an otherwise valid claim to an aboriginal right. On the other hand, where the practice, custom or tradition arose solely as a response to European influences then that practice, custom or tradition will not meet the standard for recognition of an aboriginal right.

Courts must take into account both the relationship of aboriginal peoples to the land and the distinctive societies and cultures of aboriginal peoples

As was noted in the discussion of the purposes of s. 35(1), aboriginal rights and aboriginal title are related concepts; aboriginal title is a sub-category of aboriginal rights which deals solely with claims of rights to land. The relationship between aboriginal title and aboriginal rights must not, however, confuse the analysis of what constitutes an aboriginal right. Aboriginal rights arise from the prior occupation of land, but they also arise from the prior social organization and distinctive cultures of aboriginal peoples on that land. In considering whether a claim to an aboriginal right has been made out, courts must look at both the relationship of an aboriginal claimant to the land <u>and</u> at the practices, customs and traditions arising from the claimant's distinctive culture and society. Courts must not focus so entirely on the relationship of aboriginal peoples with the land that they lose sight of the other factors relevant to the identification and definition of aboriginal rights. [...]

Application of the Integral to a Distinctive Culture Test to the Appellant's Claim

The first step in the application of the integral to a distinctive culture test requires the court to identify the precise nature of the appellant's claim to have been exercising an aboriginal right. In this case the most accurate characterization of the appellant's position is that she is claiming <u>an aboriginal right to exchange fish for money or for other goods</u>. She is claiming, in other words, that the practices, customs and traditions of the Sto:lo include as an integral part the exchange of fish for money or other goods. [...]

The appellant herself characterizes her claim as based on a right "to sufficient fish to provide for a moderate livelihood". In so doing the appellant relies on the "social" test adopted by Lambert J.A. at the British Columbia Court of Appeal. As has already been noted, however, a claim to an aboriginal right cannot be based on the significance of an aboriginal practice, custom or tradition to the aboriginal community in question. The definition of aboriginal rights is determined through the process of determining whether a particular practice, custom or tradition is integral to the distinctive culture of the aboriginal group. The <u>significance</u> of the practice, custom or tradition is relevant to the determination of whether that practice, custom or tradition is integral, but cannot itself constitute the claim to an aboriginal right. As such, the appellant's claim cannot be characterized as based on an assertion that the Sto:lo's use of the fishery, and the practices, customs and traditions surrounding that use, had the significance of providing the Sto:lo with a moderate livelihood. It must instead be based on the actual practices, customs and traditions related to the fishery, here the custom of exchanging fish for money or other goods.

Having thus identified the nature of the appellant's claim, I turn to the fundamental question of the integral to a distinctive culture test: Was the practice of exchanging fish for money or other goods an integral part of the specific distinctive culture of the Sto:lo prior to contact with Europeans? [...]

In the case at bar, Scarlett Prov. Ct. J., the trial judge, made findings of fact based on the testimony and evidence before him, and then proceeded to make a determination as to whether those findings of fact supported the appellant's claim to the existence of an aboriginal right. [...]

This court was not satisfied upon the evidence that aboriginal trade in salmon took place in any regularized or market sense. Oral evidence demonstrated that trade was incidental to fishing for food purposes. [...]

The findings of fact made by Scarlett Prov. Ct. J. suggest that the exchange of salmon for money or other goods, while certainly taking place in Sto:lo society prior to contact, was not a significant, integral or defining feature of that society. [...]

For these reasons, then, I would conclude that the appellant has failed to demonstrate that the exchange of fish for money or other goods was an integral part of the distinctive Sto:lo society which existed prior to contact. The exchange of fish took place, but was not a central, significant or defining feature of Sto:lo society. The appellant has thus failed to demonstrate that the exchange of salmon for money or other goods by the Sto:lo is an aboriginal right recognized and affirmed under s. 35(1) of the *Constitution Act, 1982*.

The Sparrow Test

Since the appellant has failed to demonstrate that the exchange of fish was an aboriginal right of the Sto:lo, it is unnecessary to consider the tests for extinguishment, infringement and justification laid out by this Court in *Sparrow*, supra.

VI. Disposition

Having concluded that the aboriginal rights of the Sto:lo do not include the right to exchange fish for money or other goods, I would dismiss the appeal and affirm the decision of the Court of Appeal restoring the trial judge's conviction of the appellant for violating s. 61(1) of the *Fisheries Act*. [...]

L'HEUREUX-DUBÉ J. (Dissenting): —

[...] In my view, the definition of aboriginal rights as to their nature and extent must be addressed in the broader context of the historical aboriginal reality in Canada. [...]

Aboriginal people's occupation and use of North American territory was not static, nor, as a general principle, should be the aboriginal rights flowing from it. Natives migrated in response to events such as war, epidemic, famine, dwindling game reserves, etc. Aboriginal practices, traditions and customs also changed and evolved, including the utilization of the land, methods of hunting and fishing, trade of goods between tribes, and so on. The coming of Europeans increased this fluidity and development, bringing novel opportunities, technologies and means to exploit natural resources. [...] Accordingly, the notion of aboriginal rights must be open to fluctuation, change and evolution, not only from one native group to another, but also over time. [...]

The traditional and main component of the doctrine of aboriginal rights relates to aboriginal title, i.e., the *sui generis* proprietary interest which gives native people the right to occupy and use the land at their own discretion, subject to the Crown's ultimate title and exclusive right to purchase the land. [...]

The concept of aboriginal title, however, does not capture the entirety of the doctrine of aboriginal rights. Rather, as its name indicates, the doctrine refers to a broader notion of aboriginal rights arising out of the historic occupation and use of native ancestral lands, which relate not only to aboriginal title, but also to the component elements of this larger right — such as aboriginal rights to hunt, fish or trap, and their accompanying practices, traditions and customs — as well as to other matters, not related to land, that form part of a distinctive aboriginal culture: [...]

Prior to 1982, the doctrine of aboriginal rights was founded only on the common law and aboriginal rights could be extinguished by treaty, conquest and legislation as they were "dependent upon the good will of the Sovereign": [...]

Since then, however, s. 35(1) of the *Constitution Act, 1982* provides constitutional protection to aboriginal interests arising out of the native historic occupation and use of ancestral lands through the recognition and affirmation of "existing aboriginal and treaty rights of the aboriginal peoples of Canada" [...]

[Her Ladyship then reviewed the Sparrow test.]

In the case at bar, the issue relates only to the interpretation of the nature and extent of the Sto:lo's aboriginal right to fish and whether it includes the right to sell, trade and barter fish for livelihood, support and sustenance purposes; i.e., the very first step of the *Sparrow* test, dealing with the assessment and definition of aboriginal rights. [...]

III. Interpretation of Aboriginal Rights

[...] [A]boriginal rights protected under s. 35(1) have to be interpreted in the context of the history and culture of the specific aboriginal society and in a manner that gives the rights meaning to the natives. In that respect, the following remarks of Dickson C.J. and La Forest J. in *Sparrow*, at p. 1112, are particularly apposite:

> While it is impossible to give an easy definition of fishing rights, it is possible, and, indeed, <u>crucial, to be sensitive to the aboriginal perspective itself on the meaning of the rights at stake.</u> (emphasis added.)

Unlike the Chief Justice, I do not think it appropriate to qualify this proposition by saying that the perspective of the common law matters as much as the perspective of the natives when defining aboriginal rights. [...]

Characteristics of aboriginal rights

The issue of the nature and extent of aboriginal rights protected under s. 35(1) is fundamentally about characterization. Which aboriginal practices, traditions and customs warrant constitutional protection? It appears from the jurisprudence developed in the courts below (see the reasons of the British Columbia Court of Appeal and the decision in *Delgamuukw v. British Columbia* (1993), 104 D.L.R. (4th) 470) that two approaches to this difficult question have emerged. The first one, which the Chief Justice endorses, focuses on the particular aboriginal practice, tradition or custom. The second approach, more generic, describes aboriginal rights in a fairly high level of abstraction. For the reasons that follow, I favour the latter approach.

The approach based on aboriginal practices, traditions and customs considers only discrete parts of aboriginal culture, separating them from the general culture in which they are rooted. The analysis turns on the <u>manifestations</u> of the "integral part of [aboriginals'] distinctive culture" introduced in *Sparrow*, supra, at p. 1099. Further, on this view, what makes aboriginal culture distinctive is that which differentiates it from non-aboriginal culture. [...]

Accordingly, if an activity is integral to a culture other than that of aboriginal people, it cannot be part of aboriginal people's distinctive culture. This approach should <u>not</u> be adopted for the following reasons.

First, on the pure terminology angle of the question, this position misconstrues the words "distinctive culture", used in the above excerpt of *Sparrow*, by interpreting it as if it meant "distinct culture". These two expressions connote quite different meanings and must not be confused. The word "distinctive" is defined in *The Concise Oxford Dictionary* (9th ed. 1995) as "distinguishing, characteristic" where the word "distinct" is described as "1. (often foll. by *from*) a) not identical; separate; individual. b) different in kind or quality; unlike". While "distinct" mandates comparison and evaluation from a separate vantage point, "distinctive" requires the object to be observed on its own. While describing an object's "distinctive" qualities may entail describing how the object is different from others (i.e., "distinguishing"), there is nothing in the term that requires it to be plainly different. In fact, all that "distinctive culture" requires is the characterization of aboriginal culture, not its differentiation from non-aboriginal cultures.

While the Chief Justice recognizes the difference between "distinctive" and "distinct", he applies it only as regards the manifestations of the distinctive aboriginal culture, i.e., the individualized practices, traditions and customs of a particular group of aboriginal people. As I will examine in more detail in a moment, the "distinctive" aboriginal culture has, in my view, a generic and much broader application.

Second, holding that what is common to both aboriginal and non-aboriginal cultures must necessarily be non-aboriginal and thus <u>not</u> aboriginal for the purpose of s. 35(1) is, to say the least, an overly majoritarian approach. This is diametrically opposed to the view propounded in *Sparrow*, supra, that the interpretation of aboriginal rights be informed by the fiduciary responsibility of the Crown *vis-à-vis* aboriginal people as well as by the aboriginal perspective on the meaning of the rights. Such considerations command that practices, traditions and customs which characterize aboriginal societies as the original occupiers and users of Canadian lands be protected, despite their common features with non-aboriginal societies.

Finally, an approach based on a dichotomy between aboriginal and non-aboriginal practices, traditions and customs literally amounts to defining aboriginal culture and aboriginal rights as that which is left over after features of non-aboriginal cultures have been taken away. Such a strict construction of constitutionally protected aboriginal rights flies in the face of the generous, large and liberal interpretation of s. 35(1) of the *Constitution Act, 1982* advocated in *Sparrow*.

A better approach, in my view, is to examine the question of the nature and extent of aboriginal rights from a certain level of abstraction and generality.

A generic approach to defining the nature and extent of aboriginal rights starts from the proposition that the notion of "integral part of [aboriginals[a]] distinctive culture" constitutes a general statement regarding the purpose of s. 35(1). Instead of focusing on a particular practice, tradition or custom, this conception refers to a more abstract and profound concept. In fact, similar to the values enshrined in the *Canadian Charter of Rights and Freedoms*, aboriginal rights protected under s. 35(1) should be contemplated on a multi-layered or multi-faceted basis. [...]

Accordingly, s. 35(1) should be viewed as protecting, not a catalogue of individualized practices, traditions or customs, as the Chief Justice does, but the "distinctive culture" of which aboriginal activities are manifestations. Simply put, the emphasis would be on the significance of these activities to natives rather than on the activities themselves.

[...] [T]he aboriginal practices, traditions and customs which form the core of the lives of native people and which provide them with a way and means of living as an organized society will fall within the scope of the constitutional protection under s. 35(1). [...]

Period of time relevant to aboriginal rights

The question of the period of time relevant to the recognition of aboriginal rights relates to whether the practice, tradition or custom has to exist prior to a specific date, and also to the length of time necessary for an aboriginal activity to be recognized as a right under s. 35(1). Here, again, two basic approaches have been advocated in the courts below (see the decisions of the British Columbia Court of Appeal in this case, and in *Delgamuukw v. British Columbia*, supra), namely the "frozen right" approach and the "dynamic right" approach. An examination of each will show that the latter view is to be preferred.

The "frozen right" approach would recognize practices, traditions and customs — forming an integral part of a distinctive aboriginal culture — which have long been in existence at the time of British sovereignty: [...]

This requires the aboriginal right claimant to prove two elements: (1) that the aboriginal activity has continuously existed for "time immemorial", and (2) that it predated the assertion of sovereignty. Defining existing aboriginal rights by referring to pre-contact or pre-sovereignty practices, traditions and customs implies that aboriginal culture was crystallized in some sort of "aboriginal time" prior to the arrival of Europeans. Contrary to the Chief Justice, I do not believe that this approach should be adopted, for the following reasons.

First, relying on the proclamation of sovereignty by the British imperial power as the "cut-off" for the development of aboriginal practices, traditions and customs overstates the impact of European influence on aboriginal communities: [...] From the native people's perspective, the coming of the settlers constitutes one of many factors, though a very significant one, involved in their continuing societal change and evolution. Taking British sovereignty as the turning point in aboriginal culture assumes that everything that the natives did after that date was not sufficiently significant and fundamental to their culture and social organization. This is no doubt contrary to the perspective of aboriginal people as to the significance of European arrival on their rights. [...]

As a third point, in terms of proof, the "frozen right" approach imposes a heavy and unfair burden on the natives: the claimant of an aboriginal right must prove that the aboriginal practice, tradition or custom is not only sufficiently significant and fundamental to the culture and social organization of the aboriginal group, but has also been continuously in existence, but as the Chief Justice stresses, even if interrupted for a certain length of time, for an indeterminate long period of time prior to British sovereignty. This test embodies inappropriate and unprovable assumptions about aboriginal culture and society. It forces the claimant to embark upon a search for a pristine aboriginal society and to prove the continuous existence of the activity for "time immemorial" before the arrival of Europeans. This, to say the least, constitutes a harsh burden of proof, which the relaxation of evidentiary standards suggested by the Chief Justice is insufficient to attenuate. In fact, it is contrary to the interpretative approach propounded by this Court in *Sparrow*, supra, which commands a purposive, liberal and favourable construction of aboriginal rights. [...]

Accordingly, the interpretation of the nature and extent of aboriginal rights must "permit their evolution over time". [...]

The "dynamic right" approach to interpreting the nature and extent of aboriginal rights starts from the proposition that "the phrase 'existing aboriginal rights' must be interpreted flexibly so as to permit their evolution over time" (*Sparrow*, at p. 1093). According to this view, aboriginal rights must be permitted to maintain contemporary relevance in relation to the needs of the natives as their practices, traditions and customs change and evolve with the overall society in which they live. This generous, large and liberal interpretation of aboriginal rights protected under s. 35(1) would ensure their continued vitality. [...]

In short, the substantial continuous period of time necessary to the recognition of aboriginal rights should be assessed based on (1) the type of aboriginal practices, traditions and customs, (2) the particular aboriginal culture and society, and (3) the reference period of 20 to 50 years. Such a time frame does

945

not minimize the fact that in order to benefit from s. 35(1) protection, aboriginal activities must still form the core of the lives of native people. This surely cannot be characterized as an extreme position, as my colleague Justice McLachlin affirms.

[...] I conclude that the Sto:lo Band, of which the appellant is a member, possess an aboriginal right to sell, trade and barter fish for livelihood, support and sustenance purposes. Under s. 35(1) of the *Constitution Act, 1982* this right is protected. [...]

McLACHLIN J. (dissenting): —

[...] My conclusions on this appeal may be summarized as follows. The issue of what constitutes an aboriginal right must, in my view, be answered by looking at what the law has historically accepted as fundamental aboriginal rights. These encompass the right to be sustained from the land or waters upon which an aboriginal people have traditionally relied for sustenance. Trade in the resource to the extent necessary to maintain traditional levels of sustenance is a permitted exercise of this right. The right endures until extinguished by treaty or otherwise. The right is limited to the extent of the aboriginal people's historic reliance on the resource, as well as the power of the Crown to limit or prohibit exploitation of the resource incompatible with its responsible use. Applying these principles, I conclude that the Sto:lo possess an aboriginal right to fish commercially for purposes of basic sustenance, that this right has not been extinguished, that the regulation prohibiting the sale of any fish constitutes a *prima facie* infringement of it, and that this infringement is not justified. Accordingly, I conclude that the appellant's conviction must be set aside.

[...] The first step is to ascertain the aboriginal right which is asserted by Mrs. Van der Peet. Are we concerned with the right to fish, the right to sell fish on a small sustenance-related level, or commercial fishing?

The Chief Justice and Justice L'Heureux-Dubé state that this appeal does not raise the issue of the right of the Sto:lo to engage in commercial fishery. They argue that the sale of one or two fish to a neighbour cannot be considered commerce, and that the British Columbia courts erred in treating it as such.

I agree that this case was defended on the ground that the fish sold by Mrs. Van der Peet were sold for purposes of sustenance. This was not a large corporate money-making activity. In the end, as will be seen, I agree with Justice L'Heureux-Dubé that a large operation geared to producing profits in excess of what the people have historically taken from the river might not be constitutionally protected.

This said, I see little point in labeling Mrs. Van der Peet's sale of fish something other than commerce. When one person sells something to another, that is commerce. Commerce may be large or small, but commerce it remains. On the view I take of the case, the critical question is not whether the sale of the fish is commerce or non-commerce, but whether the sale can be defended as the exercise of a more basic aboriginal right to continue the aboriginal people's historic use of the resource.

Making an artificial distinction between the exchange of fish for money or other goods on the one hand and for commercial purposes on the other, may have serious consequences, if not in this case, in others. If the aboriginal right at issue is defined as the right to trade on a massive, modern scale, few peoples may be expected to establish a commercial right to fish. As the Chief Justice observes in *R. v. N.T.C. Smokehouse Ltd.*, [1996] 2 S.C.R. 672, "[t]he claim to an aboriginal right to exchange fish commercially places a more onerous burden" on the aboriginal claimant "than a claim to an aboriginal right to exchange fish for money or other goods" (para. 20). In the former case, the trade must be shown to have existed pre-contact "on a scale best characterized as commercial" (para. 20). With rare exceptions (see the evidence in R. v. Gladstone, [1996] 2 S.C.R. 723, released concurrently) aboriginal societies historically were not interested in massive sales. Even if they had been, their societies did not afford them mass markets.

(iii) Aboriginal Rights versus the Exercise of Aboriginal Rights

It is necessary to distinguish at the outset between an aboriginal right and the exercise of an aboriginal right. Rights are generally cast in broad, general terms. They remain constant over the centuries. The exercise of rights, on the other hand, may take many forms and vary from place to place and from time to time.

If a specific modern practice is treated as the right at issue, the analysis may be foreclosed before it begins. This is because the modern practice by which the more fundamental right is exercised may not find a counterpart in the aboriginal culture of two or three centuries ago. So if we ask whether there is an aboriginal <u>right</u> to a particular kind of trade in fish, i.e., large-scale commercial trade, the answer in most cases will be negative. On the other hand, if we ask whether there is an aboriginal right to use the fishery resource for the purpose of providing food, clothing or other needs, the answer may be quite different. Having defined the basic underlying right in general terms, the question then becomes whether the modern <u>practice</u> at issue may be characterized as an <u>exercise</u> of the right.

This is how we reconcile the principle that aboriginal rights must be ancestral rights with the uncompromising insistence of this Court that aboriginal rights not be frozen. The rights are ancestral; they are the old rights that have been passed down from previous generations. The <u>exercise</u> of those rights, however, takes modern forms. To fail to recognize the distinction between rights and the contemporary form in which the rights are exercised is to freeze aboriginal societies in their ancient modes and deny to them the right to adapt, as all peoples must, to the changes in the society in which they live.

I share the concern of L'Heureux-Dubé J. that the Chief Justice defines the rights at issue with too much particularity, enabling him to find no aboriginal right where a different analysis might find one. By insisting that Mrs. Van der Peet's modern practice of selling fish be replicated in pre-contact Sto:lo practices, he effectively condemns the Sto:lo to exercise their right precisely as they exercised it hundreds of years ago and precludes a finding that the sale constitutes the exercise of an aboriginal right. [...]

(iv) The Time Frame

The Chief Justice and L'Heureux-Dubé J. differ on the time periods one looks to in identifying aboriginal rights. The Chief Justice stipulates that for a practice to qualify as an aboriginal right it must be traceable to pre-contact times and be identifiable as an "integral" aspect of the group's culture at that early date. Since the barter of fish was not shown to be more than an incidental aspect of Sto:lo society prior to the arrival of the Europeans, the Chief Justice concludes that it does not qualify as an aboriginal right.

L'Heureux-Dubé J., by contrast, minimizes the historic origin of the alleged right. For her, all that is required is that the practice asserted as a right have constituted an integral part of the group's culture and social organization for a period of at least 20 to 50 years, and that it continue to be an integral part of the culture at the time of the assertion of the right.

My own view falls between these extremes. I agree with the Chief Justice that history is important. A recently adopted practice would generally not qualify as being aboriginal. Those things which have in the past been recognized as aboriginal rights have been related to the traditional practices of aboriginal peoples. For this reason, this Court has always been at pains to explore the historical origins of alleged aboriginal rights. [...]

I cannot agree with the Chief Justice, however, that it is essential that a practice be traceable to pre-contact times for it to qualify as a constitutional right. Aboriginal rights find their source not in a magic moment of European contact, but in the traditional laws and customs of the aboriginal people in question. [...]

My concern is that we not substitute an inquiry into the precise moment of first European contact — an inquiry which may prove difficult — for what is really at issue, namely the ancestral customs and laws observed by the indigenous peoples of the territory. [...]

Not only must the proposed aboriginal right be rooted in the historical laws or customs of the people, there must also be continuity between the historic practice and the right asserted. [...]

The continuity requirement does not require the aboriginal people to provide a year-by-year chronicle of how the event has been exercised since time immemorial. Indeed, it is not unusual for the exercise of a right to lapse for a period of time. Failure to exercise it does not demonstrate abandonment of the underlying right. All that is required is that the people establish a link between the modern practice and the historic aboriginal right. [...]

(vii) The Empirical Historic Approach

The tests proposed by my colleagues describe qualities which one would expect to find in aboriginal rights. To this extent they may be informative and helpful. But because they are over inclusive, indeterminate, and ultimately categorical, they fall short, in my respectful opinion, of providing a practically workable principle for identifying what is embraced in the term "existing aboriginal rights" in s. 35(1) of the *Constitution Act, 1982*.

In my view, the better approach to defining aboriginal rights is an empirical approach. Rather than attempting to describe *a priori* what an aboriginal right is, we should look to history to see what sort of practices have been identified as aboriginal rights in the past. From this we may draw inferences as to the sort of things which may qualify as aboriginal rights under s. 35(1). Confronted by a particular claim, we should ask, "Is this <u>like</u> the sort of thing which the law has recognized in the past?". [...]

[Her Ladyship then reviewed the treatment of aboriginal rights in the common law tradition. She found that the right asserted by Ms. Van der Peet was indeed of the kind recognized by the common law in the past. She then went on to consider justifications for the limitations of the right under the second branch of the *Sparrow* test.]

The Chief Justice, while purporting to apply the *Sparrow* test for justification, deviates from its second requirement as well as the first, in my respectful view. Here the stipulations are that the limitation be consistent with the Crown's fiduciary duty to the aboriginal people and that it reflect the priority set out by Dickson J. in *Jack*. The duty of a fiduciary, or trustee, is to protect and conserve the interest of the person whose property is entrusted to him. In the context of aboriginal rights, this requires that the Crown not only preserve the aboriginal people's interest, but also manage it well: *Guerin*. The Chief Justice's test, however, would appear to permit the constitutional aboriginal fishing right to be conveyed by regulation, law or executive act to non-native fishers who have historically fished in the area in the interests of community harmony and reconciliation of aboriginal and non-aboriginal interests. Moreover, the Chief Justice's scheme has the potential to violate the priority scheme for fishing set out in *Jack*. On his test, once conservation is satisfied, a variety of other interests, including the historical participation of non-native fishers, may justify a variety of regulations governing distribution of the resource. The only requirement is that the distribution scheme "take into account" the aboriginal right. Such an approach, I fear, has the potential to violate not only the Crown's fiduciary duty toward native peoples, but also to render meaningless the "limited priority" to the non-commercial fishery endorsed in *Jack* and *Sparrow*. [...]

A second objection to the approach suggested by the Chief Justice is that it is indeterminate and ultimately may speak more to the politically expedient than to legal entitlement. The imprecision of the proposed test is apparent. "In the right circumstances", themselves undefined, governments may abridge aboriginal rights on the basis of an undetermined variety of considerations. While "account" must be taken of the native interest and the Crown's fiduciary obligation, one is left uncertain as to what degree. At the broadest reach, whatever the government of the day deems necessary in order to reconcile aboriginal and non-aboriginal interests might pass muster. In narrower incarnations, the result will depend on doctrine yet to be determined. Upon challenge in the courts, the focus will predictably be on the social justifiability of the measure rather than the rights guaranteed. Courts may properly be expected, the Chief Justice suggests, not to be overly strict in their review; as under s. 1 of the *Charter*, the courts should not negate the government decision, so long as it represents a "reasonable" resolution of conflicting interests. This, with respect, falls short of the "solid constitutional base upon which subsequent negotiations can take place" of which Dickson C.J. and La Forest J. wrote in *Sparrow*, at p. 1105.

My third observation is that the proposed departure from the principle of justification elaborated in Sparrow is unnecessary to provide the "reconciliation" of aboriginal and non-aboriginal interests which is said to require it. The Chief Justice correctly identifies reconciliation between aboriginal and non-aboriginal communities as a goal of fundamental importance. This desire for reconciliation, in many cases long overdue, lay behind the adoption of s. 35(1) of the *Constitution Act, 1982*. [...] The question is how this reconciliation of the different legal cultures of aboriginal and non-aboriginal peoples is to be accomplished. More particularly, does the goal of reconciliation of aboriginal and non-aboriginal interests require that we permit the Crown to require a judicially authorized transfer of the aboriginal right to non-aboriginals without the consent of the aboriginal people, without treaty, and without compensation? I cannot think it does. [...]

[T]he right imposes its own internal limit — equivalence with what by ancestral law and custom the aboriginal people in question took from the resource. The government may impose additional limits under the rubric of justification to ensure that the right is exercised responsibly and in a way that preserves it for future generations. There is no need to impose further limits on it to affect reconciliation between aboriginal and non-aboriginal peoples. [...]

I have argued that the broad approach to justification proposed by the Chief Justice does not conform to the authorities, is indeterminate, and is, in the final analysis unnecessary. Instead, I have proposed that justifiable limitation of aboriginal rights should be confined to regulation to ensure their exercise conserves the resource and ensures responsible use. There remains a final reason why the broader view of justification should not be accepted. It is, in my respectful opinion, unconstitutional. [...]

The relationship between the relative interests in a fishery with respect to which an aboriginal right has been established in the full sense, that is of food, ceremony and articles to meet other needs obtained directly from the fishery or through trade and barter of fish products, may be summarized as follows:

1. The state may limit the exercise of the right of the aboriginal people, for purposes associated with the responsible use of the right, including conservation and prevention of harm to others;

2. Subject to these limitations, the aboriginal people have a priority to fish for food, ceremony, as well as supplementary sustenance defined in terms of the basic needs that the fishery provided to the people in ancestral times;

3. Subject to (1) and (2) non-aboriginal peoples may use the resource.

In times of plentitude, all interests may be satisfied. In times of limited stocks, aboriginal food fishing will have priority, followed by additional aboriginal commercial fishing to satisfy the sustenance the fishery afforded the particular people in ancestral times. The aboriginal priority to commercial fishing is limited to satisfaction of these needs, which typically will be confined to basic amenities. In this sense, the right to fish for commerce is a "limited" priority. If there is insufficient stock to satisfy the entitlement of all aboriginal peoples after required conservation measures, allocations must be made between them. Allocations between aboriginal peoples may also be required to ensure that upstream bands are allowed their fair share of the fishery, whether for food or supplementary sustenance. All this is subject to the overriding power of the state to limit or indeed, prohibit fishing in the interests of conservation.

The consequence of this system of priorities is that the Crown may limit aboriginal fishing by aboriginal people found to possess a right to fish for sustenance on two grounds: (1) on the ground that a limited amount of fish is required to satisfy the basic sustenance requirement of the band, and (2) on the ground of conservation and other limits required to ensure the responsible use of the resource (justification).

Against this background, I return to the question of whether the regulation preventing the Sto:lo from selling any fish is justified. In my view it is not. No compelling purpose such as that proposed in *Sparrow* has been demonstrated. The denial to the Sto:lo of their right to sell fish for basic sustenance has not been shown to be required for conservation or for other purposes related to the continued and responsible exploitation of the resource. The regulation, moreover, violates the priorities set out in *Jack* and *Sparrow* and breaches the fiduciary duty of the Crown to preserve the rights of the aboriginal people to fish in accordance with their ancestral customs and laws by summarily denying an important aspect of the exercise of the right. [...]

R. v. POWLEY
[2003] 2 S.C.R. 207; 230 D.L.R. (4th) 1.

[Ontario charged Steve and Roddy Powley with hunting moose without a licence contrary to the *Game and Fish Act* (Ont.). The Powleys admitted hunting without a licence. They defended against the charge on the basis that as Métis they had an Aboriginal right to hunt for food in the Sault Ste. Marie area.]

THE COURT: —

A. The *Van der Peet* Test

(1) Characterization of the Right

[19] The first step is to characterize the right being claimed: *Van der Peet*, [1996] 2 S.C.R. 507, at para. 76. Aboriginal hunting rights, including Métis rights, are contextual and site-specific. The respondents shot a bull moose near Old Goulais Bay Road, in the environs of Sault Ste. Marie, within the traditional hunting grounds of that Métis community. They made a point of documenting that the moose was intended to provide meat for the winter. The trial judge determined that they were hunting for food, and there is no reason to overturn this finding. The right being claimed can therefore be characterized as the right to hunt for food in the environs of Sault Ste. Marie. [...]

(2) Identification of the Historic Rights-Bearing Community

[21] The trial judge found that a distinctive Métis community emerged in the Upper Great Lakes region in the mid-17th century, and peaked around 1850. We find no reviewable error in the trial judge's findings on this matter, which were confirmed by the Court of Appeal. The record indicates the following: In the mid-17th century, the Jesuits established a mission at Sainte-Marie-du-Sault, in an area characterized by heavy competition among fur traders. In 1750, the French established a fixed trading post on the south bank of the Saint Mary's River. The Sault Ste. Marie post attracted settlement by Métis—the children of unions between European traders and Indian women, and their descendants ... By the early nineteenth century, "[t]he settlement at Sault Ste. Marie was one of the oldest and most important [Métis settlements] in the upper lakes area" ... The Hudson Bay Company operated the St. Mary's post primarily as a depot from 1821 onwards [...]

(3) Identification of the Contemporary Rights-Bearing Community

[24] Aboriginal rights are communal rights: They must be grounded in the existence of a historic and present community, and they may only be exercised by virtue of an individual's ancestrally based membership in the present community. The trial judge found that a Métis community has persisted in and around Sault Ste. Marie despite its decrease in visibility after the signing of the Robinson-Huron Treaty in 1850. While we take note of the trial judge's determination that the Sault Ste. Marie Métis community was to a large extent an "invisible entity" (para. 80) from the mid-19th century to the 1970s, we do not take this to mean that the community ceased to exist or disappeared entirely.

[25] Dr. Lytwyn describes the continued existence of a Métis community in and around Sault Ste. Marie despite the displacement of many of the community's members in the aftermath of the 1850 treaties:

> [T]he Métis continued to live in the Sault Ste. Marie region. Some drifted into the Indian Reserves which had been set apart by the 1850 Treaty. Others lived in areas outside of the town, or in back concessions. The Métis continued to live in much the same manner as they had in the past—fishing, hunting, trapping and harvesting other resources for their livelihood. (Lytwyn Report, p. 31 (emphasis added); see also Morrison, "The Robinson Treaties", at p. 201)

[26] The advent of European control over this area thus interfered with, but did not eliminate, the Sault Ste. Marie Métis community and its traditional practices, as evidenced by census data from the 1860s through the 1890s. Dr. Lytwyn concluded from this census data that "[a]lthough the Métis lost much of their traditional land base at Sault Ste. Marie, they continued to live in the region and gain their livelihood from the resources of the land and waters" (Lytwyn Report, supra, at p. 32). He also noted a tendency for underreporting and lack of

information about the Métis during this period because of their "removal to the peripheries of the town," and "their own disinclination to be identified as Métis" in the wake of the Riel rebellions and the turning of Ontario public opinion against Métis rights through government actions and the media. [...]

[27] We conclude that the evidence supports the trial judge's finding that the community's lack of visibility was explained and does not negate the existence of the contemporary community. There was never a lapse; the Métis community went underground, so to speak, but it continued. Moreover, as indicated below, the "continuity" requirement puts the focus on the continuing practices of members of the community, rather than more generally on the community itself, as indicated below.

[28] The trial judge's finding of a contemporary Métis community in and around Sault Ste. Marie is supported by the evidence and must be upheld.

(4) Verification of the Claimant's Membership in the Relevant Contemporary Community

[29] While determining membership in the Métis community might not be as simple as verifying membership in, for example, an Indian band, this does not detract from the status of Métis people as full-fledged rights-bearers. As Métis communities continue to organize themselves more formally and to assert their constitutional rights, it is imperative that membership requirements become more standardized so that legitimate rights-holders can be identified. In the meantime, courts faced with Métis claims will have to ascertain Métis identity on a case-by-case basis. The inquiry must take into account both the value of community self-definition, and the need for the process of identification to be objectively verifiable. In addition, the criteria for Métis identity under s. 35 must reflect the purpose of this constitutional guarantee: to recognize and affirm the rights of the Métis held by virtue of their direct relationship to this country's original inhabitants and by virtue of the continuity between their customs and traditions and those of their Métis predecessors. This is not an insurmountable task.

[30] We emphasize that we have not been asked, and we do not purport, to set down a comprehensive definition of who is Métis for the purpose of asserting a claim under s. 35. We therefore limit ourselves to indicating the important components of a future definition, while affirming that the creation of appropriate membership tests before disputes arise is an urgent priority. As a general matter, we would endorse the guidelines proposed by Vaillancourt J. and O'Neill J. in the courts below. In particular, we would look to three broad factors as indicia of Métis identity for the purpose of claiming Métis rights under s. 35: self-identification, ancestral connection, and community acceptance.

[31] First, the claimant must self-identify as a member of a Métis community. This self-identification should not be of recent vintage: While an individual's self-identification need not be static or monolithic, claims that are made belatedly in order to benefit from a s. 35 right will not satisfy the self-identification requirement.

[32] Second, the claimant must present evidence of an ancestral connection to a historic Métis community. This objective requirement ensures that he or she has some of the rights have a real link to the historic community whose practices ground the right being claimed. We would not require a minimum "blood quantum", but we would require some proof that the claimant's ancestors belonged to the historic Métis community by birth, adoption, or other means. Like the trial judge, we would abstain from further defining this requirement in the absence of more extensive argument by the parties in a case where this issue is determinative. In this case, the Powleys' Métis ancestry is not disputed.

[33] Third, the claimant must demonstrate that he or she is accepted by the modern community whose continuity with the historic community provides the legal foundation for the right being claimed. Membership in a Métis political organization may be relevant to the question of community acceptance, but it is not sufficient in the absence of a contextual understanding of the membership requirements of the organization and its role in the Métis community. The core of community acceptance is past and ongoing participation in a shared culture, in the customs and traditions that constitute a Métis community's identity and distinguish it from other groups. This is what the community membership criterion is all about. Other indicia of community acceptance might include evidence of participation in community activities and testimony from other members about the claimant's connection to the community and its culture. The range of acceptable forms of evidence does not attenuate the need for an objective demonstration of a solid bond of past and present mutual identification and recognition of common belonging between the claimant and other members of the rights-bearing community. [...]

(5) Identification of the Relevant Time Frame

[36] As indicated above, the pre-contact aspect of the *Van der Peet* test requires adjustment in order to take account of the post-contact ethnogenesis of the Métis and the purpose of s. 35 in protecting the historically important customs and traditions of these distinctive peoples. While the fact of prior occupation grounds aboriginal rights claims for the Inuit and the Indians, the recognition of Métis rights in s. 35 is not reducible to the Métis' Indian ancestry. The unique status of the Métis as an Aboriginal people with post-contact origins requires an adaptation of the pre-contact approach to meet the distinctive historical circumstances surrounding the evolution of Métis communities.

[37] The pre-contact test in *Van der Peet* is based on the constitutional affirmation that aboriginal communities are entitled to continue those practices, customs and traditions that are integral to their distinctive existence or relationship to the land. By analogy, the test for Métis practices should focus on identifying those practices, customs and traditions that are integral to the Métis community's distinctive existence and relationship to the land. This unique history can most appropriately be accommodated by a post contact but pre-control test that identifies the time when Europeans effectively established political and legal control in a particular area. The focus should be on the period after a particular Métis community arose and before it came under the effective control of European laws and customs. This pre-control test enables us to identify those practices, customs and traditions that predate the imposition of European laws and customs on the Métis.

[38] We reject the appellant's argument that Métis rights must find their origin in the pre-contact practices of the Métis' aboriginal ancestors. This theory in effect would deny to Métis their full status as distinctive rights-bearing peoples whose own integral practices are entitled to constitutional protection under s. 35(1). The right claimed here was a practice of both the Ojibway and the Métis. However, as long as the practice grounding the right is distinctive and integral to the pre-control Métis community, it will satisfy this prong of the test. This result flows from the constitutional imperative that we recognize and affirm the aboriginal rights of the Métis, who appeared after the time of first contact. [...]

[40] The historical record indicates that the Sault Ste. Marie Métis community thrived largely unaffected by European laws and customs until colonial policy shifted from one of discouraging settlement to one of negotiating treaties and encouraging settlement in the mid-19th century. The trial judge found, and the parties agreed in their pleadings before the lower courts, that "effective control [of the Upper Great Lakes area] passed from the Aboriginal peoples of the area (Ojibway and Métis) to European control" in the period between 1815 and 1850 (para. 90). The record fully supports the finding that the period just prior to 1850 is the appropriate date for finding effective control in this geographic area, which the Crown agreed was the critical date in its pleadings below.

(6) Determination of Whether the Practice is Integral to the Claimants' Distinctive Culture

[41] The practice of subsistence hunting and fishing was a constant in the Métis community, even though the availability of particular species might have waxed and waned. The evidence indicates that subsistence hunting was an important aspect of Métis life and a defining feature of their special relationship to the land ... A major part of subsistence was the practice at issue here, hunting for food. [...]

[43] Dr. Ray emphasized in his report that a key feature of Métis communities was that "their members earned a substantial part of their livelihood off of the land" (Ray Report, supra, at p. 56). Dr. Lytwyn concurred: "The Métis of Sault Ste. Marie lived off the resources of the land. They obtained their livelihood from hunting, fishing, gathering and cultivating" (Lytwyn Report, at p. 2). He reported that "[w]hile Métis fishing was prominent in the written accounts, hunting was also an important part of their livelihood," and that "[a] traditional winter hunting area for the Sault Métis was the Goulais Bay area" ... He elaborated at p. 6:

> In the mid-19th century, the Métis way of life incorporated many resource harvesting activities. These activities, especially hunting and trapping, were done within traditional territories located within the hinterland of Sault Ste. Marie. The Métis engaged in these activities for generations and, on the eve of the 1850 treaties, hunting, fishing, trapping and gathering were integral activities to the Métis community at Sault Ste. Marie.

[44] This evidence supports the trial judge's finding that hunting for food was integral to the Métis way of life at Sault Ste. Marie in the period just prior to 1850.

(7) Establishment of Continuity Between the Historic Practice and the Contemporary Right Asserted

[45] Although s. 35 protects "existing" rights, it is more than a mere codification of the common law. Section 35 reflects a new promise: a constitutional commitment to protecting practices that were historically important features of particular aboriginal communities. A certain margin of flexibility might be required to ensure that aboriginal practices can evolve and develop over time, but it is not necessary to define or to rely on that margin in this case. Hunting for food was an important feature of the Sault Ste. Marie Métis community, and the practice has been continuous to the present. Steve and Roddy Powley claim a Métis aboriginal right to hunt for food. The right claimed by the Powleys falls squarely within the bounds of the historical practice grounding the right.

(8) Determination of Whether or not the Right was Extinguished

[46] The doctrine of extinguishment applies equally to Métis and to First Nations claims. There is no evidence of extinguishment here, as determined by the trial judge. The Crown's argument for extinguishment is based largely on the Robinson-Huron Treaty of 1850, from which the Métis as a group were explicitly excluded.

(9) If There is a Right, Determination of Whether There is an Infringement

[47] Ontario currently does not recognize any Métis right to hunt for food, or any "special access rights to natural resources" for the Métis whatsoever (appellant's record, at p. 1029). This lack of recognition, and the consequent application of the challenged provisions to the Powleys, infringe their aboriginal right to hunt for food as a continuation of the protected historical practices of the Sault Ste. Marie Métis community.

(10) Determination of Whether the Infringement is Justified

[48] The main justification advanced by the appellant is that of conservation. Although conservation is clearly a very important concern, we agree with the trial judge that the record here does not support this justification. If the moose population in this part of Ontario were under threat, and there was no evidence that it is, the Métis would still be entitled to a priority allocation to satisfy their subsistence needs in accordance with the criteria set out in *R. v. Sparrow*, [1990] 1 S.C.R. 1075. While preventative measures might be required for conservation purposes in the future, we have not been presented with evidence to support such measures here. The Ontario authorities can make out a case for regulation of the aboriginal right to hunt moose for food if and when the need arises. On the available evidence and given the current licensing system, Ontario's blanket denial of any Métis right to hunt for food cannot be justified. [...]

R. v. SAPPIER; R. v. GRAY
2006 S.C.C. 54.

[Sappier and Pochies, Maliseet Indians, and Gray, a Mi'kmaq Indian, were charged under New Brunswick's *Crown Lands and Forests Act* with unlawful possession of Crown timber cut from Crown lands. The logs had been taken from lands traditionally harvested by the respondents' respective First Nations. Those taken by S and P were to be used for the construction of P's house and the residue for community firewood. Those cut by G were to be used to make furniture. None of the accused intended to sell the logs or any product made from them. They defended against the charge by asserting aboriginal and treaty rights to harvest timber for personal use.]

The judgment of McLachlin C.J. and Bastarache, LeBel, Deschamps, Fish, Abella, Charron and Rothstein JJ. was delivered by

BASTARACHE J. — [...]

¶ 20 In order to be an aboriginal right, an activity must be an element of a practice, custom or tradition integral to the distinctive culture of the aboriginal group claiming the right: *R. v. Van der Peet*, at para. 46. The first step is to identify the precise nature of the applicant's claim of having exercised an aboriginal right: *Van der Peet*, at para. 76. In so doing, a court should consider such factors as the nature of the action which the applicant is claiming was done pursuant to an aboriginal right, the nature of the governmental regulation, statute or action being impugned, and the practice, custom or tradition being relied upon to establish the right: *Van der Peet*, at para. 53. In this case, the respondents were charged with the unlawful cutting and possession of Crown timber. They claimed an aboriginal right to harvest timber for personal use so as a defence to those charges. The statute at issue prohibits the unauthorized cutting, damaging, removing and possession of timber from Crown lands. The respondents rely on the pre-contact practice of harvesting timber in order to establish their aboriginal right.

¶ 21 The difficulty in the present cases is that the practice relied upon to found the claims as characterized by the respondents was the object of very little evidence at trial. Instead, the respondents led most of their evidence about the importance of wood in Maliseet and Mi'kmaq cultures and the many uses to which it was put. This is unusual because the jurisprudence of this Court establishes the central importance of the actual practice in founding a claim for an aboriginal right. Aboriginal rights are founded upon practices, customs, or traditions which were integral to the distinctive pre-contact culture of an aboriginal people. They are not generally founded upon the importance of a particular resource. In fact, an aboriginal right cannot be characterized as a right to a particular resource because to do so would be to treat it as akin to a common law property right. In characterizing aboriginal rights as *sui generis*, this Court has rejected the application of traditional common law property concepts to such rights: *Sparrow*, at pp. 1111-12. In my view, the pre-contact practice is central to the *Van der Peet* test for two reasons.

¶ 22 First, in order to grasp the importance of a resource to a particular aboriginal people, the Court seeks to understand how that resource was harvested, extracted and utilized. These practices are the necessary "aboriginal" component in aboriginal rights. As Lamer C.J. explained in *Van der Peet*, at para. 20:

> The task of this Court is to define aboriginal rights in a manner which recognizes that aboriginal rights are *rights* but which does so without losing sight of the fact that they are rights held by aboriginal people because they are *aboriginal*. The Court must neither lose sight of the generalized constitutional status of what s. 35(1) protects, nor can it ignore the necessary specificity which comes from granting special constitutional protection to one part of Canadian society. The Court must define the scope of s. 35(1) in a way which captures both the aboriginal and the rights in aboriginal rights. [Emphasis in original.]

Section 35 of the *Constitution Act, 1982* seeks to provide a constitutional framework for the protection of the distinctive cultures of aboriginal peoples, so that their prior occupation of North America can be recognized and reconciled with the sovereignty of the Crown: see, *Van der Peet*, at para. 31. In an oft-quoted passage, Lamer C.J. acknowledged in *Van der Peet*, at para. 30, that, "the doctrine of aboriginal rights exists, and is recognized and affirmed by s. 35(1), because of one simple fact: when Europeans arrived in North America, aboriginal peoples were already here, living in communities on the land, and participating in distinctive cultures, as they had done for centuries" (emphasis in original deleted). The goal for courts is, therefore, to determine how the claimed right relates to the pre-contact culture or way of life of an aboriginal society. This has been achieved by requiring aboriginal rights claimants to found their claim on a pre-contact practice which was integral to the distinctive culture of the particular aboriginal community. It is critically important that the Court be able to identify a *practice* that helps to define the distinctive way of life of the community as an aboriginal community. The importance of leading evidence about the pre-contact practice upon which the claimed right is based should not be understated. In the absence of such evidence, courts will find it difficult to relate the claimed right to the pre-contact way of life of the specific aboriginal people, so as to trigger s. 35 protection.

¶ 23 Second, it is also necessary to identify the pre-contact practice upon which the claim is founded in order to consider how it might have evolved to its present-day form. This Court has long recognized that aboriginal rights are not frozen in their pre-contact form, and that ancestral rights may find modern expression [...]

¶ 24 In the present cases, the relevant practice for the purposes of the *Van der Peet* test is harvesting wood. It is this practice upon which the respondents opted to found their claims. However, the respondents do not claim a right to harvest wood for any and all purposes — such a right would not provide sufficient specificity to apply the reasoning I have just described. The respondents instead claim the right to harvest timber for personal uses; I find this characterization to be too general as well. As previously explained, it is critical that the Court identify a practice that helps to define the way of life or distinctiveness of the particular aboriginal community. The claimed right should then be delineated in accordance with that practice: see *Van der Peet*, at para. 52. The way of life of the Maliseet and of the Mi'kmaq during the pre-contact period is that of a migratory people who lived from fishing and hunting and who used the rivers and lakes of Eastern Canada for transportation. Thus, the practice should be characterized as the harvesting of wood for certain uses that are directly associated with that particular way of life. The record shows that wood was used to fulfill the communities' domestic needs for such things as shelter, transportation, tools and fuel. I would therefore characterize the respondents' claim as a right to harvest wood for domestic uses as a member of the aboriginal community.

¶ 25 The word "domestic" qualifies the uses to which the harvested timber can be put. The right so characterized has no commercial dimension. The harvested wood cannot be sold, traded or bartered to produce assets or raise money. This is so even if the object of such trade or barter is to finance the building of a dwelling. In other words, although the right would permit the harvesting of timber to be used in the construction of a dwelling, it is not the case that a rightholder can sell the wood in order to raise money to finance the purchase or construction of a dwelling, or any of its components.

¶ 26 The right to harvest wood for domestic uses is a communal one. Section 35 recognizes and affirms existing aboriginal and treaty rights in order to assist in ensuring the continued existence of these particular aboriginal societies. The exercise of the aboriginal right to harvest wood for domestic uses must be tied to this purpose. The right to harvest (which is distinct from the right to make personal use of the harvested product even though they are related) is not one to be exercised by any member of the aboriginal community independently of the aboriginal society it is meant to preserve. It is a right that assists the society in maintaining its distinctive character.

4.2 The Integral to a Distinctive Culture Test

4.2.1 The Evidentiary Problem

¶ 27 The question before the Court at this stage is whether the practice of harvesting wood for domestic uses was integral to the distinctive culture of the Maliseet and Mi'kmaq, pre-contact. As previously explained, very little evidence was led with respect to the actual harvesting practice. Nevertheless, this Court has previously recognized an aboriginal right based on evidence showing the importance of a resource to the pre-contact culture of an aboriginal people. [...]

¶ 28 In the present cases, the evidence established that wood was critically important to the Maliseet and the Mi'kmaq, pre-contact. [...]

¶ 33 I infer from this evidence that the practice of harvesting wood for domestic uses was also significant, though undertaken primarily for survival purposes. Flexibility is important when engaging in the *Van der Peet* analysis because the object is to provide cultural security and continuity for the particular aboriginal society. This object gives context to the analysis. For this reason, courts must be prepared to draw necessary inferences about the existence and integrality of a practice when direct evidence is not available.

¶ 34 Flexibility is also important in the present cases with regard to the relevant time frame during which the practice must be found to have been integral to the distinctive culture of the aboriginal society in question. It is settled law that the time period courts consider in determining whether the *Van der Peet* test has been met is the period prior to contact with the Europeans ... As Lamer C.J. explained in *Van der Peet*, "[b]ecause it is the fact that distinctive aboriginal societies lived on the land prior to the arrival of Europeans that underlies the aboriginal rights protected by s. 35(1), it is to that pre-contact period that the courts must look in identifying aboriginal rights" ... That this is the relevant time should not suggest, however, that the aboriginal group claiming the right must accomplish the next to impossible task of producing conclusive evidence from pre-contact times about the practices, customs and traditions of their community. It would be entirely contrary to the spirit and intent of s. 35(1) to define aboriginal rights in such a fashion so as to preclude in practice any successful claim for the existence of such a right. The evidence relied upon by the applicant and the courts may relate to aboriginal practices, customs and traditions post-contact; it simply needs to be directed at demonstrating which aspects of the aboriginal community and society have their origins pre-contact. It is those practices, customs and traditions that can be rooted in the pre-contact societies of the aboriginal community in question that will constitute aboriginal rights. [...]

4.2.2 <u>Whether a Practice Undertaken for Survival Purposes Can be Considered Integral to an Aboriginal Community's Distinctive Culture</u>

¶ 35 The principal issue on appeal is whether a practice undertaken for survival purposes can meet the integral to a distinctive culture test. The learned trial judge in the *Sappier* and *Polchies* trial concluded that it could not. [...]

¶ 36 Cain Prov. Ct. J. relied on a statement made by Lamer C.J. in *Van der Peet*, at para. 56:

> To recognize and affirm the prior occupation of Canada by distinctive aboriginal societies it is to what makes those societies distinctive that the court must look in identifying aboriginal rights. <u>The court cannot look at those aspects of the aboriginal society that are true of every human society (e.g., eating to survive)</u>, nor can it look at those aspects of the aboriginal society that are only incidental or occasional to that society; the court must look instead to the defining and central attributes of the aboriginal society in question. It is only by focussing on the aspects of the aboriginal society that make that society distinctive that the definition of aboriginal rights will accomplish the purpose underlying s. 35(1). [Emphasis added.]

Relying on this passage, Cain Prov. Ct. J. concluded that harvesting timber to construct a shelter was akin to eating to survive. This statement by Lamer C.J. appears to have resulted in considerable confusion as to whether a practice undertaken strictly for survival purposes can found an aboriginal right claim. However, further in his decision, Lamer C.J. clarifies that the pre-contact practice, custom or tradition relied need not be distinct; it need only be distinctive. In so doing, he confirms that fishing for food can, in certain contexts, meet the integral to a distinctive culture test:

> That the standard an aboriginal community must meet is distinctiveness, not distinctness, arises from the recognition in *Sparrow, supra*, of an aboriginal right to fish for food. Certainly no aboriginal group in Canada could claim that its culture is "distinct" or unique in fishing for food; fishing for food is something done by many different cultures and societies around the world. What the Musqueam claimed in *Sparrow, supra*, was rather that it was fishing for food which, in part, made Musqueam culture what it is; fishing for food was characteristic of Musqueam culture and, therefore, a distinctive part of that culture. Since it was so it constituted an aboriginal right under s. 35(1). [...]

¶ 40 As I have already explained, the purpose of this exercise is to understand the way of life of the particular aboriginal society, pre-contact, and to determine how the claimed right relates to it. This is achieved by founding the claim on a pre-contact practice, and determining whether that practice was integral to the distinctive culture of the aboriginal people in question, pre-contact. Section 35 seeks to protect integral elements of the way of life of these aboriginal societies, including their traditional means of survival. Although this was affirmed in *Sparrow, Adams* and *Côté*, the courts below queried whether a practice undertaken strictly for survival purposes really went to the core of a people's identity. Although intended as a helpful description of the *Van der Peet* test, the reference in *Mitchell* to a "core identity" may have unintentionally resulted in a heightened threshold for establishing an aboriginal right. For this reason, I think it necessary to discard the notion that the pre-contact practice upon which the right is based must go to the core of the society's identity, i.e. its single most important defining character. This has never been the test for establishing an aboriginal right. This Court has clearly held that a claimant need only show that the practice was integral to the aboriginal society's pre-contact distinctive culture.

¶ 41 The notion that the pre-contact practice must be a "defining feature" of the aboriginal society, such that the culture would be "fundamentally altered" without it, has also served in some cases to create artificial barriers to the recognition and affirmation of aboriginal rights. The trial judge in the *Sappier* and *Polchies* prosecution concluded that Maliseet culture would not have been fundamentally altered had wood not been available to it. In his opinion, "[t]he society would in all probability have used some other available material" (p. 13). In response, I would adopt the following comments made by Robertson J.A., on behalf of the Court of Appeal:

> ... I am at a loss to speculate on what other natural resource might have been used had wood not been available. Snow houses would have provided New Brunswick's aboriginal societies with adequate shelter during the winter months only. Whether fish and wildlife by-products would have served as an alternative source of fuel, and an adequate one, is a question on

which I need not speculate. There is also the question as to how the aboriginal societies of New Brunswick would have traversed the lakes and rivers of this Province, in pursuit of fish and wildlife, without the traditional means of transportation: canoes. [para. 91]

I further agree with Robertson J.A. that courts should be cautious in considering whether the particular aboriginal culture would have been fundamentally altered had the gathering activity in question not been pursued. The learned judge correctly notes that "[a] society that fishes for sustenance will survive even if it does not consume meat and the converse is equally true" (para. 92).

4.2.3 Applying the Van der Peet Test: the Meaning of "Distinctive Culture"

¶ 42 This brings us to the question of what is meant by "distinctive culture"? As previously explained, this Court in *Van der Peet* set out to interpret s. 35 of the Constitution in a way which captures both the aboriginal and the rights in aboriginal rights. Lamer C.J. spoke of the "necessary specificity which comes from granting special constitutional protection to one part of Canadian society" (para. 20). It is that aboriginal specificity which the notion of a "distinctive culture" seeks to capture. However, it is clear that "Aboriginality means more than interesting cultural practices and anthropological curiosities worthy only of a museum" [...]

¶ 44 Culture, let alone "distinctive culture", has proven to be a difficult concept to grasp for Canadian courts. Moreover, the term "culture" as it is used in the English language may not find a perfect parallel in certain aboriginal languages. [...] Ultimately, the concept of culture is itself inherently cultural.

¶ 45 The aboriginal rights doctrine, which has been constitutionalized by s. 35, arises from the simple fact of prior occupation of the lands now forming Canada. The "integral to a distinctive culture" test must necessarily be understood in this context. As L'Heureux-Dubé J. explained in dissent in *Van der Peet*, "[t]he 'distinctive aboriginal culture' must be taken to refer to the reality that, despite British sovereignty, aboriginal people were the original organized society occupying and using Canadian lands. [...] The focus of the Court should therefore be on the *nature* of this prior occupation. What is meant by "culture" is really an inquiry into the pre-contact way of life of a particular aboriginal community, including their means of survival, their socialization methods, their legal systems, and, potentially, their trading habits. The use of the word "distinctive" as a qualifier is meant to incorporate an element of aboriginal specificity. However, "distinctive" does not mean "distinct", and the notion of aboriginality must not be reduced to "racialized stereotypes of Aboriginal peoples". [...]

¶ 46 In post-hearing submissions to the Court of Appeal in the *Sappier* and *Polchies* case, the Crown admitted that gathering birch bark for the construction of canoes or hemlock for basket-making were practices likely integral to the distinctive Maliseet culture (para. 94). But it would be a mistake to reduce the entire pre-contact distinctive Maliseet culture to canoe-building and basket-making. To hold otherwise would be to fall in the trap of reducing an entire people's culture to specific anthropological curiosities and, potentially, racialized aboriginal stereotypes. Instead, the Court must first inquire into the way of life of the

Maliseet and Mi'kmaq, pre-contact. As previously explained, these were migratory communities using the rivers and lakes of Eastern Canada for transportation and living essentially from hunting and fishing. The Court must therefore seek to understand how the particular pre-contact practice relied upon relates to that way of life. In the present cases, the practice of harvesting wood for domestic uses including shelter, transportation, fuel and tools is directly related to the way of life I have just described. I have already explained that we must discard the idea that the practice must go to the core of a people's culture. The fact that harvesting wood for domestic uses was undertaken for survival purposes is sufficient, given the evidence adduced at trial, to meet the integral to a distinctive culture threshold.

¶ 47 I therefore conclude that the practice of harvesting wood for domestic uses was integral to the pre-contact distinctive culture of both the Maliseet and Mi'kmaq peoples.

4.3 Continuity of the Claimed Right with the Pre-Contact Practice

¶ 48 Although the nature of the *practice* which founds the aboriginal right claim must be considered in the context of the pre-contact distinctive culture of the particular aboriginal community, the nature of the *right* must be determined in light of present day circumstances. As McLachlin C.J. explained in *R. v. Marshall*, [2005] 2 S.C.R. 220, 2005 SCC 43, at para. 25, "[l]ogical evolution means the same sort of activity, carried on in the modern economy by modern means". It is the practice, along with its associated uses, which must be allowed to evolve. The right to harvest wood for the construction of temporary shelters must be allowed to evolve into a right to harvest wood by modern means to be used in the construction of a modern dwelling. Any other conclusion would freeze the right in its pre-contact form.

¶ 49 Before this Court, the Crown submitted that "[l]arge permanent dwellings, constructed from multi-dimensional wood, obtained by modern methods of forest extraction and milling of lumber, cannot resonate as a Maliseet aboriginal right, or as a proper application of the logical evolution principle", because they are not grounded in traditional Maliseet culture. [...] I find this submission to be contrary to the established jurisprudence of this Court, which has consistently held that ancestral rights may find modern form ... L'Heureux-Dubé J. in dissent in *Van der Peet* emphasized that "aboriginal rights must be permitted to maintain contemporary relevance in relation to the needs of the natives as their practices, traditions and customs change and evolve with the overall society in which they live". [...] If aboriginal rights are not permitted to evolve and take modern forms, then they will become utterly useless. Surely the Crown cannot be suggesting that the respondents, all of whom live on a reserve, would be limited to building wigwams. If such were the case, the doctrine of aboriginal rights would truly be limited to recognizing and affirming a narrow subset of "anthropological curiosities", and our notion of aboriginality would be reduced to a small number of outdated stereotypes. The cultures of the aboriginal peoples who occupied the lands now forming Canada prior to the arrival of the Europeans, and who did so while living in organized societies with their own distinctive ways of life, cannot be reduced to wigwams, baskets and canoes.

4.4   *The Site-Specific Requirement*

¶ 50 This Court has imposed a site-specific requirement on the aboriginal hunting and fishing rights it recognized in *Adams, Côté, Mitchell,* and *Powley.* Lamer C.J. explained in *Adams* at para. 30 that:

> if an aboriginal people demonstrates that hunting on a specific tract of land was an integral part of their distinctive culture then, even if the right exists apart from title to that tract of land, the aboriginal right to hunt is nonetheless defined as, and limited to, the right to hunt on the specific tract of land. A site-specific hunting or fishing right does not, simply because it is independent of aboriginal title to the land on which it took place, become an abstract fishing or hunting right exercisable anywhere; it continues to be a right to hunt or fish on the tract of land in question. [Emphasis in original deleted.]

¶ 51 The characterization of the claimed right in the present cases ... imports a necessary geographical element, and its integrality to the Maliseet and Mi'kmaq cultures should be assessed on this basis [...]

¶ 52 At the trial of Messrs. Sappier and Polchies, the Crown conceded that "the issue of territoriality does not arise in the trial of the defendants on the charges set out herein" [...]

¶ 53 In the *Gray* trial, the trial judge accepted Mr. Sewell's evidence that the Mi'kmaq had traditionally used the Crown lands in question for the purpose of tree harvesting. [...] I would conclude on this basis that Mr. Gray has established an aboriginal right to harvest wood for domestic uses on Crown lands traditionally used for this purpose by members of the Pabineau First Nation.

4.5   *Infringement and Justification*

54 ... the Crown did not attempt to justify the infringement in the present cases [...]

¶ 72 For the above reasons, I conclude that the respondents have made out the defence of aboriginal right. The respondent Mr. Gray possesses an aboriginal right to harvest wood for domestic uses on Crown lands traditionally used for that purpose by members of the Pabineau First Nation. The respondents Messrs. Sappier and Polchies possess an aboriginal right to harvest wood for domestic uses. That right is also site-specific, such that its exercise is necessarily limited to Crown lands traditionally harvested by members of the Woodstock First Nation. [...]

The following are the reasons delivered by

¶ 74 Binnie J. — I agree with my colleague, Bastarache J., about the disposition of this appeal for the reasons he gives except, with respect, for his ruling that:

> [t]he harvested wood cannot be sold, traded or bartered to produce assets or raise money. This is so even if the object of such trade or barter is to finance the building of a shelter. In other words, although the right would permit the harvesting of timber to be used in the construction of a shelter, it is not the case that a rightholder can sell the wood in order to raise money to finance the purchase or construction of a home, or any of its components. [para. 25]

In aboriginal communities pre-contact, as in most societies, there existed a division of labour. This should be reflected in a more flexible concept of the exercise of aboriginal rights *within* modern aboriginal communities, especially considering that the aboriginal right itself is communal in nature. Barter (and, its modern equivalent, sale) within the reserve or other local aboriginal community would reflect a more efficient use of human resources than requiring all members of the reserve or other local aboriginal community to which the right pertains to do everything for themselves. They did not do so historically and they should not have to do so now. On the one hand, it seems to me a Mi'kmaq or Maliseet should be able to sell firewood to his or her aboriginal neighbour or barter it for, say, a side of venison or roofing a house. On the other hand, I agree that trade, barter or sale <u>outside</u> the reserve or other local aboriginal community would represent a commercial activity outside the scope of the aboriginal right established in this case. In other respects I agree with my colleague.

ARTHUR PAPE,[1] "THE S. 35 JUSTIFICATION TEST: THE DEVELOPING JURISPRUDENCE"

Section 35 and Parliamentary Sovereignty

Prior to proclamation of s. 35 of the *Constitution Act, 1982*, legislative power to abridge or extinguish historic aboriginal rights was unchecked. The legal foundation for this power was the doctrine of parliamentary sovereignty, by which governments had virtually unlimited legislative and administrative authority to trump common law rights, including aboriginal rights. In Canada, federal or provincial governments had consistently used that power to ignore or breach the rights of Aboriginal peoples, whenever majoritarian politics made that expedient. Canadian history reveals a pattern by which aboriginal rights were "honoured primarily in the breach". This is a legacy of which the Supreme Court said in *R. v. Sparrow*, [1990] 1 S.C.R. 1025: "We cannot recount with much pride the treatment accorded to the native people of this country;" (¶ 49).

In *Sparrow*, the Supreme Court of Canada explained that section 35 began a new power relationship. Consistent with its analysis of other constitutionally protected rights, the Court based its approach to s. 35 on a purposive analysis. This required the Court to articulate the underlying purposes for the constitutional protection that s. 35 now provides for aboriginal and treaty rights.

---

1   of Pape Salter Teillet, Vancouver and Toronto.

The Court said that a central purpose of s. 35 in 1982 was to change decisively the historic pattern based on parliamentary sovereignty:

> The constitutional recognition afforded by [s. 35] gives a measure of control over governmental conduct and a strong check on legislative power [...] The government is required to bear the burden of justifying any legislation that has some negative effect on any aboriginal right protected under s. 35(1); (¶ 65).

A second purpose of s. 35 was to promote the development of a new, mutually agreed relationship among Canada's governments and the Aboriginal peoples:

> [...] section 35(1), at the least, provides a solid constitutional base upon which subsequent negotiations can take place [...] Section 35 calls for a just settlement for aboriginal peoples [...]

The Court explained this more fully, almost ten years later, when Lamer, C.J. wrote for the majority in *Delgamuukw v. B.C.*, [1997]3 S.C.R. 1010:

> Ultimately, it is through negotiated settlements, with good faith and give and take on all sides, reinforced by the judgments of this Court, that we will achieve [...] the basic purpose of s. 35(1) - the reconciliation of the pre-existence of aboriginal societies with the sovereignty of the Crown. [1123-24]

This second objective reflects a longer term objective, and is consistent with the development of modern treaties in Canada - through land claims and self-government negotiations - which are still under way or completed in many parts of Canada.

The recognition and affirmation of aboriginal and treaty rights in s. 35 of the *Constitution Act, 1982*, set in motion a series of constitutional developments that are unique in the common law world. This renewal of aboriginal rights law gathered significant momentum through the decisions of the Courts during the 1990s. Important additional developments began with decisions in 2004 and 2005, outlining governments' consultation and accommodation obligations when section 35 rights may be at risk. In all, these decisions have profoundly altered the legal relationships among governments, Aboriginal peoples and third parties in Canada.

Constitutional Protection and Legislative Regulation

R. v. Sparrow was the first s. 35 case to reach the Supreme Court of Canada. The *Sparrow* court explained that s. 35 aboriginal and treaty rights will not always prevail over conflicting laws. Aboriginal and treaty rights are constitutionally protected, but are not absolute. Sparrow introduced the idea that governments may "regulate" the exercise of aboriginal and treaty rights, in some circumstances.

Aboriginal and treaty rights now have the same kind of legal status as other constitutionally guaranteed rights in the *Charter of Rights and Freedoms*. Governmental power is constrained by these rights. Still, government may limit constitutionally guaranteed rights if the courts decide that the limit is justified in the circumstances.

For *Charter* rights, the test for determining whether a particular violation of a constitutionally guaranteed right is justified - and therefore lawful - is found in s. 1. But s. 35 is outside the *Charter*, so s. 1 does not apply. Therefore the Supreme Court developed a separate justification test for rights protected by s. 35. This test determines how far governments may go to limit aboriginal and treaty rights.

Apart from s. 35 being outside the *Charter*, there is a second reason why it is appropriate for the Court to depart from s. 1 respecting limits to aboriginal and treaty rights. The *Charter* protects primarily <u>individual</u> rights. This is quite different from the problem of limits to the sorts of <u>collective</u> rights that s. 35 protects.

Regulation Distinguished from Infringement

Sparrow was a prosecution for breach of the statutory regime that regulates the harvesting of fish. In such a case, before reaching the question of whether a law justifiably limits the exercise of an aboriginal right, the Court must determine whether the regulation <u>infringes</u> an existing aboriginal or treaty rights. This involves identifying the right in question, a characterization question of some subtlety discussed at length in *R. v. Van der Peet*, [1996] 2 S.C.R. 507 and subsequent Supreme Court cases. Having identified and proved the right, the challenger must show prima facie infringement. Not all legislative regulation is infringement. To constitute an infringement of aboriginal and treaty rights the challenger must answer three questions:

> First, is the limitation unreasonable? Second, does the regulation impose undue hardship? Third, does the regulation deny to the holders of the right their preferred means of exercising that right? (*Sparrow*, supra., p. 1112, *R. v. Adams*, [1996] 3 S.C.R. 101)

It is only after the challenger has established infringement of a right by leading evidence on these questions that the question of justification arises.

Justifying Limits to Aboriginal and Treaty Rights

The tests for justifying limits to aboriginal and treaty rights have been developed by the courts. How is this judicial power used? The answer is important, for it determines the extent of governmental power over Aboriginal people, and correspondingly, defines the extent of the collective security Aboriginal people enjoy within the Canadian constitutional system.

The tests for justifying limits to aboriginal rights have been developed by the courts' responses to specific disputes. The courts must decide whether existing aboriginal or treaty rights have been infringed, and if so, whether the infringements are lawful. It is within this context that the Court has tried to develop an appropriate approach to justifying limits to s. 35 rights.

The Court has drawn on two separate analytical streams.

First, in explaining why aboriginal and treaty rights are not absolute, but subject to limits, the *Sparrow* Court explored the law of fiduciary relationships. In relying on this body of law for the justification test concerning constitutionally protected aboriginal rights, the Supreme Court of Canada has been very innovative.

The Supreme Court renovated the law of fiduciary relationships in the 1980s: see *Canson Enterprises Ltd. v. Broughton & Co.* (1981) 85 DLR (4th) 129 at 155, *Frame v. Smith*, [1987] 2 SCR 99, and *International Corona Resources Ltd. v. Lac Minerals* [1989] 2 SCR 574 at 598-60. In the course of this development, for the first time in *Guerin v. The Queen*, [1984] 2 S.C.R. 335, the Court applied the law of fiduciary relationships to the relationship between governments and Aboriginal people The core idea of *Guerin* is that government has the responsibility to act in a fiduciary capacity with respect to Aboriginal peoples, and that the relationship between governments and Aboriginal peoples is trust-like rather than adversarial.

In *Sparrow*, this core idea - that government has a duty to act in a fiduciary capacity with respect to Aboriginal peoples - was intertwined with the idea that government had power to limit aboriginal rights:

> We find that the words "recognition and affirmation" incorporate the fiduciary relationship referred to earlier and so import some restraint on the exercise of sovereign power. Rights that are recognized and affirmed are not absolute. Federal legislative powers continue, including, of course, the right to legislate with respect to Indians pursuant to s. 91(24) of the *Constitution Act, 1867*. These powers must, however, now be read together with s. 35(1). In other words, federal power must be reconciled with federal duty and the best way to achieve that reconciliation is to demand the justification of any government regulation that infringes upon or denies aboriginal rights (¶ 62).

The Court relied on the long standing principle that in all governmental dealings with Aboriginal peoples, the honour of the Crown is involved and must be upheld: *Canada v. Cowichan Agricultural Society*, [1950] Ex. C.R. 448; *Nowegijick v. The Queen*, [1983] 1 S.C.R. 29; *Mitchell v. Peguis Indian Band*, [1990] 2 S.C.R. 85. In *Sparrow*, the Supreme Court ruled that limits to aboriginal rights, accordingly, had to be in keeping with "the concept of holding the Crown to a high standard of honourable dealing with respect to the Aboriginal peoples of Canada". This gave the Court control over legislative power to impose limits on the exercise of aboriginal rights.

The way in which a legislative objective is to be attained must uphold the honour of the Crown and must be in keeping with the unique contemporary relationship, grounded in history and policy, between the Crown and Canada's aboriginal peoples. The extent of legislative or regulatory impact on an existing aboriginal right may be scrutinized so as to ensure recognition and affirmation; (¶ 64).

How was the Court's control over legislative power to limit aboriginal rights to be exercised? The Court constructed a three part justification test that governments had to meet when they limited aboriginal and treaty rights. First, no impairment of such rights would be justified unless it was instituted for a "valid legislative objective". Objectives "purporting to prevent harm to the general populace or to aboriginal peoples themselves" would be valid, as would "other objectives found to be compelling and substantial".

Second, the particular infringement must be consistent with the honour of the Crown and the special trust relationship between government and Aboriginal peoples. Third, other contextual factors may be relevant, including whether there has been as little infringement as possible, whether there is compensation for any situation amounting to expropriation of an interest, and whether there has been adequate consultation with the affected Aboriginal people.

The Duty to Consult and Accommodate

In *Sparrow*, the Supreme Court of Canada developed the initial approach for protecting section 35 rights. Cases based on that approach required the proof of an existing right intended for protection by s. 35, and then decided whether a particular infringement was justified. Because that approach required lengthy and expensive trials to prove the existence of all disputed rights, it had the inadvertent effect of limiting the ability of Aboriginal peoples to use the courts to defend their asserted s. 35 rights respecting traditional lands and resources - from the threat of new industrial developments.

In response to that problem, the Supreme Court of Canada developed a second approach for protecting section 35 rights, in two recent cases: *Taku River Tlingit v. B.C.*, [2004] 3 S.C.R. 550 and *Haida Nation v. B.C.*, [2004] 3 S.C.R. 511. In those cases, the Court held that proof of an asserted s. 35 right was not required before the Court could act. Rather, when government was contemplating a decision that might infringe reasonably asserted s. 35 rights, it had a duty to consult with the affected Aboriginal people, with a view to addressing their concerns and accommodating the rights in issue.

In those cases, the First Nations asserted their land and resource rights, but no historic or modern treaties had been concluded. The new duty to consult was developed by the Court in response to government arguments that the Crown had no duty until a s. 35 right had been proved. This was explained in *Haida*:

The jurisprudence of this Court supports the view that the duty to consult and accommodate is part of a process of fair dealing and reconciliation that begins with the assertion of sovereignty and continues beyond formal claims resolution. Reconciliation is not a final legal remedy in the usual sense. Rather, it is a process flowing from rights guaranteed by s. 35(1) of the *Constitution Act, 1982.* This process of reconciliation flows from the Crown's duty of honourable dealing towards Aboriginal peoples, which arise in turn from the Crown's assertion of sovereignty over an Aboriginal people and *de facto* control of land and resources that were formerly in the control of that people [...]

To limit reconciliation to the post-proof sphere risks treating reconciliation as a distant legalistic goal, devoid of the "meaningful content" mandated by the "solemn commitment" made by the Crown in recognizing and affirming Aboriginal rights and title [...] It also risks unfortunate consequences. When the distant goal of proof is finally reached, the Aboriginal people may find their land and resources changes and denuded. This is not reconciliation. Nor is it honourable. [32-33]

This duty is both procedural and substantive. Governments are required to consult in order to learn how asserted rights and interests may be impacted, "with the intention of substantially addressing the concerns of the aboriginal peoples whose lands are at issue."

In *Mikisew Cree v. Canada,* 2005 SCC 69, the Court confirmed that this duty applies to protect treaty rights as well as unextinguished aboriginal rights:

> [...] the principle of consultation in advance of interference with existing treaty rights is a matter of broad general importance to the relations between Aboriginal and non-Aboriginal peoples. It goes to the heart of the relationship and concerns not only the Mikisew but other First Nations and non-Aboriginal governments as well. [3]

Thus there has now been a shift in judicial thinking, away from the original focus on proving rights and considering justification for infringement, and towards the need for the ongoing protection and accommodation of asserted rights, in order to promote fair and just settlements on the path to reconciliation. This shift is giving new empowerment to section 35 rights holders. We will see this new thinking clarified by numerous cases in coming years, as principles are clarified about the nature and scope of the duty, and how it is to be implemented.

In the short time since the enactment of s. 35, the Supreme Court of Canada has been flexible and innovative, and has retained a powerful role for itself in determining the nature and terms of the new constitutionally recognized relationship between the Crown and Aboriginal peoples. That is a significant step forward, since it limits governmental power somewhat, and moves toward a more appropriate balance between the traditional authority of government and the rights and powers of the Aboriginal peoples.

The shift towards consultation as a mechanism to give effect to s. 35 is also consistent with the deepest aspects of the law of aboriginal rights. Aboriginal rights are fundamental human rights, but they are collective rather than individual rights. And it has always been a basic principle of aboriginal rights law, reflected in the *Royal Proclamation* and treaty-making, that the definition, exercise and protection of aboriginal rights - imbedded as they are in the relationship between the indigenous peoples and government - should be determined by negotiated agreements, not by the decisions of the courts or law-making by the legislature. That fundamentally distinguishes s. 35 rights from other rights protected by the *Charter of Rights and Freedoms*.

The development of the s. 35 consultation duty moves Aboriginal peoples, governments and third parties away from either litigation or legislative solutions, and towards negotiated agreements. Although this will not be without its disagreements and difficulties, and litigation will continue to be required to establish principles and standards for implementing the duty, this development of the law will be a substantial assist in promoting the reconciliation objectives which underlie section 35.

(c)   Aboriginal Title

DELGAMUUKW v. BRITISH COLUMBIA
[1997] 3 S.C.R. 1010.

[The appellants, all Gitksan or Wet'suwet'en hereditary chiefs, both individually and on behalf of their "Houses", claimed separate portions of 58,000 square kilometres in British Columbia. For the purpose of the claim, this area was divided into 133 individual territories, claimed by the 71 Houses. This represented all of the Wet'suwet'en people, and all but 12 of the Gitksan Houses. Their claim was originally for "ownership" of the territory and "jurisdiction" over it. (At the Supreme Court, this was transformed into, primarily, a claim for aboriginal title over the land in question.) British Columbia counterclaimed for a declaration that the appellants' have no right or interest in and to the territory or alternatively, that the appellants' cause of action ought to be for compensation from the Government of Canada.

At trial, the appellants' claim was based on their historical use and "ownership" of one or more of the territories. In addition, the Gitksan houses have an "adaawk" which is a collection of sacred oral tradition about their ancestors, histories and territories. The Wet'suwet'en each have a "kungax" which is a spiritual song or dance or performance which ties them to their land. Both of these were entered as evidence on behalf of the appellants. The most significant evidence of spiritual connection between the Houses and their territory was a feast hall where the Gitksan and Wet'suwet'en people tell and re-tell their stories and identify their territories to remind themselves of the sacred connection that they have with their lands. The feast has a ceremonial purpose but is also used for making important decisions.

The trial judge did not accept the appellants' evidence of oral history of attachment to the land. He dismissed the action against Canada, dismissed the plaintiffs' claims for ownership and jurisdiction and for aboriginal rights in the territory, granted a declaration that the plaintiffs were entitled to use unoccupied or vacant land subject to the general law of the province, dismissed the claim for damages and dismissed the province's counterclaim. On appeal, the original claim was altered: the claims for ownership and jurisdiction were replaced with claims for aboriginal title and self-government, respectively. The principal issues on the appeal, some of which raised a number of sub-issues, were as follows: (1) whether the pleadings precluded [the Court from entertaining claims for aboriginal title and self-government; (2) what was the ability of this Court to interfere with the factual findings made by the trial judge; (3) what is the content of aboriginal title, how is it protected by s. 35(1), and what is required for its proof; (4) whether the appellants made out a claim to self-government; and, (5) whether the province had the power to extinguish aboriginal rights after 1871, either under its own jurisdiction or through the operation of s. 88 of the *Indian Act*.]

LAMER C.J. (Cory and Major JJ. Concurring): —

Introduction

This appeal [...] raises a set of interrelated and novel questions which revolve around a single issue — the nature and scope of the constitutional protection afforded by s. 35(1) to common law aboriginal title. [...]

The first [question] is the specific content of aboriginal title, a question which this Court has not yet definitively addressed, either at common law or under s. 35(1). The second is the related question of the test for the proof of title, which, whatever its content, is a right in land, and its relationship to the definition of the aboriginal rights recognized and affirmed by s. 35(1) in *Van der Peet* in terms of activities. The third is whether aboriginal title, as a right in land, mandates a modified approach to the test of justification first laid down in *Sparrow* and elaborated upon in *Gladstone*.

In addition to the relationship between aboriginal title and s. 35(1), this appeal also raises an important practical problem relevant to the proof of aboriginal title which is endemic to aboriginal rights litigation generally — the treatment of the oral histories of Canada's aboriginal peoples by the courts. In *Van der Peet*, I held that the common law rules of evidence should be adapted to take into account the *sui generis* nature of aboriginal rights. In this appeal, the Court must address what specific form those modifications must take.

Finally, given the existence of aboriginal title in British Columbia, this Court must address, on cross-appeal, the question of whether the province of British Columbia, from the time it joined Confederation in 1871, until the entrenchment of s. 35(1) in 1982, had jurisdiction to extinguish the rights of aboriginal peoples, including aboriginal title, in that province. Moreover, if the province was without this jurisdiction, a further question arises — whether provincial laws of general application that would otherwise be inapplicable to Indians and Indian lands could nevertheless extinguish aboriginal rights through the operation of s. 88 of the *Indian Act*, R.S.C., 1985, c. I-5. [...]

V. Analysis

[...] B. *What is the ability of this Court to interfere with the factual findings made by the trial judge?*

[...] *Van der Peet* clarified that deference was owed to findings of fact even when the trial judge misapprehended the law which was applied to those facts, a problem which can arise in quickly evolving areas of law such as the jurisprudence surrounding s. 35(1). [...]

On the other hand, while accepting the general principle of non-interference, this Court has also identified specific situations in which an appeal court can interfere with a finding of fact made at trial. [...] In cases involving the determination of aboriginal rights, appellate intervention is also warranted by the failure of a trial court to appreciate the evidentiary difficulties inherent in adjudicating aboriginal claims when, first, applying the rules of evidence and, second, interpreting the evidence before it. As I said in *Van der Peet*, at para. 68:

> In determining whether an aboriginal claimant has produced evidence sufficient to demonstrate that her activity is an aspect of a practice, custom or tradition integral to a distinctive aboriginal culture, <u>a court should approach the rules of evidence, and interpret the evidence that exists</u>, with a consciousness of the special nature of aboriginal claims, and of the evidentiary difficulties in proving a right which originates in times where there were no written records of the practices, customs and traditions engaged in. <u>The courts must not undervalue the evidence presented by aboriginal claimants simply because that evidence does not conform precisely with the evidentiary standards that would be applied in, for example, a private law torts case</u>. (emphasis added.)

The justification for this special approach can be found in the nature of aboriginal rights themselves. I explained in *Van der Peet* that those rights are aimed at the reconciliation of the prior occupation of North America by distinctive aboriginal societies with the assertion of Crown sovereignty over Canadian territory. They attempt to achieve that reconciliation by "their bridging of aboriginal and non-aboriginal cultures" (at para. 42). Accordingly, "a court must take into account the perspective of the aboriginal people claiming the right. [...] while at the same time taking into account the perspective of the common law" such that "[t]rue reconciliation will, equally, place weight on each" (at paras. 49 and 50).

In other words, although the doctrine of aboriginal rights is a common law doctrine, aboriginal rights are truly *sui generis*, and demand a unique approach to the treatment of evidence which accords due weight to the perspective of aboriginal peoples. However, that accommodation must be done in a manner which does not strain "the Canadian legal and constitutional structure" (at para. 49). Both the principles laid down in *Van der Peet* — first, that trial courts must approach the rules of evidence in light of the evidentiary difficulties inherent in adjudicating aboriginal claims, and second, that trial courts must interpret that evidence in the same spirit — must be understood against this background.

[...] [G]iven that many aboriginal societies did not keep written records at the time of contact or sovereignty, it would be exceedingly difficult for them to produce (at para. 62) "conclusive evidence from pre-contact times about the practices, customs and traditions of their community". Accordingly, I held that (at para. 62):

The evidence relied upon by the applicant and the courts may relate to aboriginal practices, customs and traditions post-contact: it simply needs to be directed at demonstrating which aspects of the aboriginal community and society have their origins <u>pre-contact</u>. (emphasis added.)

The same considerations apply when the time from which title is determined is sovereignty.

This appeal requires us to [...] adapt the laws of evidence so that the aboriginal perspective on their practices, customs and traditions and on their relationship with the land, are given due weight by the courts. In practical terms, this requires the courts to come to terms with the oral histories of aboriginal societies, which, for many aboriginal nations, are the only record of their past. Given that the aboriginal rights recognized and affirmed by s. 35(1) are defined by reference to pre-contact practices or, as I will develop below, in the case of title, pre-sovereignty occupation, those histories play a crucial role in the litigation of aboriginal rights. [...]

(b) Adaawk and Kungax

[...] It is apparent that the adaawk and kungax are of integral importance to the distinctive cultures of the appellant nations. At trial, they were relied on for two distinct purposes. First, the adaawk was relied on as a component of and, therefore, as proof of the existence of a system of land tenure law internal to the Gitksan, which covered the whole territory claimed by that appellant. In other words, it was offered as evidence of the Gitksan's historical use and occupation of that territory. For the Wet'suwet'en, the kungax was offered as proof of the central significance of the claimed lands to their distinctive culture. As I shall explain later in these reasons, both use and occupation, and the central significance of the lands occupied, are relevant to proof of aboriginal title. [...]

[T]he trial judge gave no independent weight to these special oral histories because they did not accurately convey historical truth, because knowledge about those oral histories was confined to the communities whose histories they were and because those oral histories were insufficiently detailed. However, as I mentioned earlier, these are features, to a greater or lesser extent, of all oral histories, not just the adaawk and kungax. The implication of the trial judge's reasoning is that oral histories should never be given any independent weight and are only useful as confirmatory evidence in aboriginal rights litigation. I fear that if this reasoning were followed, the oral histories of aboriginal peoples would be consistently and systematically undervalued by the Canadian legal system, in contradiction of the express instruction to the contrary in *Van der Peet* that trial courts interpret the evidence of aboriginal peoples in light of the difficulties inherent in adjudicating aboriginal claims. [...]

(e) Conclusion

The trial judge's treatment of the various kinds of oral histories did not satisfy the principles I laid down in *Van der Peet*. These errors are particularly worrisome because oral histories were of critical importance to the appellants' case. They used those histories in an attempt to establish their occupation and use of the disputed territory, an essential requirement for aboriginal title. The trial judge, after refusing to admit, or giving no independent weight to these oral histories, reached the conclusion that the appellants had not demonstrated the requisite degree of occupation for "ownership". Had the trial judge assessed the oral histories correctly, his conclusions on these issues of fact might have been very different.

In the circumstances, the factual findings cannot stand. However, given the enormous complexity of the factual issues at hand, it would be impossible for the Court to do justice to the parties by sifting through the record itself and making new factual findings. A new trial is warranted, at which the evidence may be considered in light of the principles laid down in *Van der Peet* and elaborated upon here. In applying these principles, the new trial judge might well share some or all of the findings of fact of McEachern C.J.

C. *What is the content of aboriginal title, how is it protected by s. 35(1), and what is required for its proof?*

(1) Introduction

The parties disagree over whether the appellants have established aboriginal title to the disputed area. [...] I set out these opposing positions by way of illustration and introduction because I believe that all of the parties have characterized the content of aboriginal title incorrectly. The appellants argue that aboriginal title is tantamount to an inalienable fee simple, which confers on aboriginal peoples the rights to use those lands as they choose and which has been constitutionalized by s. 35(1). The respondents offer two alternative formulations: first, that aboriginal title is no more than a bundle of rights to engage in activities which are themselves aboriginal rights recognized and affirmed by s. 35(1), and that the *Constitution Act, 1982*, merely constitutionalizes those individual rights, not the bundle itself, because the latter has no independent content; and second, that aboriginal title, at most, encompasses the right to exclusive use and occupation of land in order to engage in those activities which are aboriginal rights themselves, and that s. 35(1) constitutionalizes this notion of exclusivity.

The content of aboriginal title, in fact, lies somewhere in between these positions. Aboriginal title is a right in land and, as such, is more than the right to engage in specific activities which may be themselves aboriginal rights. Rather, it confers the right to use land for a variety of activities, not all of which need be aspects of practices, customs and traditions which are integral to the distinctive cultures of aboriginal societies. Those activities do not constitute the right *per se*; rather, they are parasitic on the underlying title. However, that range of uses is subject to the limitation that they must not be irreconcilable with the nature of the attachment to the land which forms the basis of the particular group's aboriginal title. This inherent limit, to be explained more fully below, flows from the definition of aboriginal title as a *sui generis* interest in land, and is one way in which aboriginal title is distinct from a fee simple.

(2)   Aboriginal title at common law

[...] Aboriginal title has been described as *sui generis* in order to distinguish it from "normal" proprietary interests, such as fee simple. However, as I will now develop, it is also *sui generis* in the sense that its characteristics cannot be completely explained by reference either to the common law rules of real property or to the rules of property found in aboriginal legal systems. As with other aboriginal rights, it must be understood by reference to both common law and aboriginal perspectives.

The idea that aboriginal title is *sui generis* is the unifying principle underlying the various dimensions of that title. One dimension is its inalienability. Lands held pursuant to aboriginal title cannot be transferred, sold or surrendered to anyone other than the Crown and, as a result, is inalienable to third parties. This Court has taken pains to clarify that aboriginal title is only "personal" in this sense, and does not mean that aboriginal title is a non-proprietary interest which amounts to no more than a licence to use and occupy the land and cannot compete on an equal footing with other proprietary interests: see *Canadian Pacific Ltd. v. Paul*, [1988] 2 S.C.R. 654, at p. 677.

Another dimension of aboriginal title is its source. It had originally been thought that the source of aboriginal title in Canada was the *Royal Proclamation, 1763*: see *St. Catharines Milling*. However, it is now clear that although aboriginal title was recognized by the *Proclamation*, it arises from the prior occupation of Canada by aboriginal peoples. That prior occupation, however, is relevant in two different ways, both of which illustrate the *sui generis* nature of aboriginal title. The first is the physical fact of occupation, which derives from the common law principle that occupation is proof of possession in law. [...] Thus, in *Guerin*, supra, Dickson J. described aboriginal title, at p. 376, as a "legal right derived from the Indians' historic occupation and possession of their tribal lands". What makes aboriginal title *sui generis* is that it arises from possession before the assertion of British sovereignty, whereas normal estates, like fee simple, arise afterward. [...] This idea has been further developed in *Roberts v. Canada*, [1989] 1 S.C.R. 322, where this Court unanimously held at p. 340 that "aboriginal title pre-dated colonization by the British and survived British claims to sovereignty" (also see *Guerin*, supra, at p. 378). What this suggests is a second source for aboriginal title — the relationship between common law and pre-existing systems of aboriginal law.

A further dimension of aboriginal title is the fact that it is held communally. Aboriginal title cannot be held by individual aboriginal persons; it is a collective right to land held by all members of an aboriginal nation. Decisions with respect to that land are also made by that community. This is another feature of aboriginal title which is *sui generis* and distinguishes it from normal property interests.

(b) *The content of aboriginal title*

Although cases involving aboriginal title have come before this Court and Privy Council before, there has never been a definitive statement from either court on the content of aboriginal title. [...]

Although the courts have been less than forthcoming, I have arrived at the conclusion that the content of aboriginal title can be summarized by two propositions: first, that aboriginal title encompasses the right to exclusive use and occupation of the land held pursuant to that title for a variety of purposes, which need not be aspects of those aboriginal practices, customs and traditions which are integral to distinctive aboriginal cultures; and second, that those protected uses must not be irreconcilable with the nature of the group's attachment to that land. For the sake of clarity, I will discuss each of these propositions separately.

Aboriginal title encompasses the right to use the land held pursuant to that title for a variety of purposes, which need not be aspects of those aboriginal practices, cultures and traditions which are integral to <u>distinctive aboriginal cultures</u>.

The respondents argue that aboriginal title merely encompasses the right to engage in activities which are aspects of aboriginal practices, customs and traditions which are integral to distinctive aboriginal cultures of the aboriginal group claiming the right and, at most, adds the notion of exclusivity; i.e., the exclusive right to use the land for those purposes. However, the uses to which lands held pursuant to aboriginal title can be put are not restricted in this way. This conclusion emerges from three sources: (i) the Canadian jurisprudence on aboriginal title, (ii) the relationship between reserve lands and lands held pursuant to aboriginal title, and (iii) the *Indian Oil and Gas Act.*, R.S.C., 1985, c. I-7. As well, although this is not legally determinative, it is supported by the critical literature. [...]

(i) <u>Canadian jurisprudence on aboriginal title</u>

Despite the fact that the jurisprudence on aboriginal title is somewhat underdeveloped, it is clear that the uses to which lands held pursuant to aboriginal title can be put is not restricted to the practices, customs and traditions of aboriginal peoples integral to distinctive aboriginal cultures. In *Guerin*, for example, Dickson J. described aboriginal title as "an interest in land" which encompassed "a legal right to occupy and possess certain lands" (at p. 382). The "right to occupy and possess" is framed in broad terms and, significantly, is not qualified by reference to traditional and customary uses of those lands. Any doubt that the right to occupancy and possession encompasses a broad variety of uses of land was put to rest in *Paul*, where the Court went even further and stated that aboriginal title was "more than the right to enjoyment and occupancy" (at p. 688). Once again, there is no reference to aboriginal practices, customs and traditions as a qualifier on that right. Moreover, I take the reference to "more" as emphasis of the broad notion of use and possession.

(ii) <u>Reserve Land</u>

Another source of support for the conclusion that the uses to which lands held under aboriginal title can be put are not restricted to those grounded in practices, customs and traditions integral to distinctive aboriginal cultures can be found in *Guerin*, where Dickson J. stated at p. 379 that the same legal principles governed the aboriginal interest in reserve lands and lands held pursuant to aboriginal title:

It does not matter, in my opinion, that the present case is concerned with the interest of an Indian Band in a reserve rather than with unrecognised aboriginal title in traditional tribal lands. <u>The Indian interest in the lands is the same in both cases</u>. [...] (emphasis added.)

The nature of the Indian interest in reserve land is very broad, and can found in s. 18 of the *Indian Act*, which I reproduce in full:

18. (1) Subject to this Act, reserves are held by Her Majesty for the <u>use and benefit</u> of the respective bands for which they were set apart, and subject to this Act and to the terms of any treaty or surrender, the Governor in Council may determine whether any purpose for which lands in a reserve are used or are to be used is for the use and benefit of the band.

(2) The Minister may authorize the use of lands in a reserve for the purpose of Indian schools, the administration of Indian affairs, Indian burial grounds, Indian health projects or, with the consent of the council of the band, <u>for any other purpose for the general welfare of the band</u>, and may take any lands in a reserve required for those purposes, but where an individual Indian, immediately prior to the taking, was entitled to the possession of those lands, compensation for that use shall be paid to the Indian, in such amount as may be agreed between the Indian and the Minister, or, failing agreement, as may be determined in such manner as the Minister may direct. (emphasis added.)

The principal provision is s. 18(1), which states that reserve lands are held "for the use and benefit" of the bands which occupy them; those uses and benefits, on the face of the *Indian Act*, do not appear to be restricted to practices, customs and traditions integral to distinctive aboriginal cultures. The breadth of those uses is reinforced by s. 18(2), which states that reserve lands may be used "for any other purpose for the general welfare of the band". The general welfare of the band has not been defined in terms of aboriginal practices, customs and traditions, nor in terms of those activities which have their origin pre-contact; it is a concept, by definition, which incorporates a reference to the present-day needs of aboriginal communities. On the basis of *Guerin*, lands held pursuant to aboriginal title, like reserve lands, are also capable of being used for a broad variety of purposes.

(iii) Indian Oil and Gas Act

The third source for the proposition that the content of aboriginal title is not restricted to practices, customs, and traditions which are integral to distinctive aboriginal cultures is the *Indian Oil and Gas Act*. The overall purpose of the statute is to provide for the exploration of oil and gas on reserve lands through their surrender to the Crown. The statute presumes that the aboriginal interest in reserve land includes mineral rights, a point which this Court unanimously accepted with respect to the *Indian Act* in *Blueberry River Indian Band v. Canada (Department of Indian Affairs and Northern Development)*, [1995] 4 S.C.R. 344. On the basis of *Guerin*, aboriginal title also encompass mineral rights, and lands held pursuant to aboriginal title should be capable of exploitation in the same way, which is certainly not a traditional use for those lands. [...]

In conclusion, the content of aboriginal title is not restricted to those uses which are elements of a practice, custom or tradition integral to the distinctive culture of the aboriginal group claiming the right. However, nor does aboriginal title amount to a form of inalienable fee simple, as I will now explain.

> (c)   *Inherent Limit: Lands held pursuant to aboriginal title cannot be used in a manner that is irreconcilable with the nature of the attachment to the land which forms the basis of the group's claim to aboriginal title.*

The content of aboriginal title contains an inherent limit that lands held pursuant to title cannot be used in a manner that is irreconcilable with the nature of the claimants' attachment to those lands. This limit on the content of aboriginal title is a manifestation of the principle that underlies the various dimensions of that special interest in land — it is a *sui generis* interest that is distinct from "normal" proprietary interests, most notably fee simple.

I arrive at this conclusion by reference to the other dimensions of aboriginal title which are *sui generis* as well. I first consider the source of aboriginal title. As I discussed earlier, aboriginal title arises from the prior occupation of Canada by aboriginal peoples. That prior occupation is relevant in two different ways: first, because of the physical fact of occupation, and second, because aboriginal title originates in part from pre-existing systems of aboriginal law. However, the law of aboriginal title does not only seek to determine the historic rights of aboriginal peoples to land; it also seeks to afford legal protection to prior occupation in the present-day. Implicit in the protection of historic patterns of occupation is a recognition of the importance of the continuity of the relationship of an aboriginal community to its land over time.

I develop this point below with respect to the test for aboriginal title. The relevance of the continuity of the relationship of an aboriginal community with its land here is that it applies not only to the past, but to the future as well. That relationship should not be prevented from continuing into the future. As a result, uses of the lands that would threaten that future relationship are, by their very nature, excluded from the content of aboriginal title.

Accordingly, in my view, lands subject to aboriginal title cannot be put to such uses as may be irreconcilable with the nature of the occupation of that land and the relationship that the particular group has had with the land which together have given rise to aboriginal title in the first place. As discussed below, one of the critical elements in the determination of whether a particular aboriginal group has aboriginal title to certain lands is the matter of the occupancy of those lands. Occupancy is determined by reference to the activities that have taken place on the land and the uses to which the land has been put by the particular group. If lands are so occupied, there will exist a special bond between the group and the land in question such that the land will be part of the definition of the group's distinctive culture. It seems to me that these elements of aboriginal title create an inherent limitation on the uses to which the land, over which such title exists, may be put. For example, if occupation is established with reference to the use of the land as a hunting ground, then the group that successfully claims aboriginal title to that land may not use it in such a fashion as to destroy its value for such a use (*e.g.*, by strip mining it). Similarly, if a group claims a special bond with the land because of its ceremonial or cultural significance, it may not use the land in such a way as to destroy that relationship (e.g., by developing it in such a way that the bond is destroyed, perhaps by turning it into a parking lot).

It is for this reason also that lands held by virtue of aboriginal title may not be alienated. Alienation would bring to an end the entitlement of the aboriginal people to occupy the land and would terminate their relationship with it. I have suggested above that the inalienability of aboriginal lands is, at least in part, a function of the common law principle that settlers in colonies must derive their title from Crown grant and, therefore, cannot acquire title through purchase from aboriginal inhabitants. It is also, again only in part, a function of a general policy "to ensure that Indians are not dispossessed of their entitlements": see *Mitchell v. Peguis Indian Band*, [1990] 2 S.C.R. 85, at p. 133. What the inalienability of lands held pursuant to aboriginal title suggests is that those lands are more than just a fungible commodity. The relationship between an aboriginal community and the lands over which it has aboriginal title has an important non-economic component. The land has an inherent and unique value in itself, which is enjoyed by the community with aboriginal title to it. The community cannot put the land to uses which would destroy that value.

I am cognizant that the *sui generis* nature of aboriginal title precludes the application of "traditional real property rules" to elucidate the content of that title (*St. Mary's Indian Band v. Cranbrook (City)*, [1997] 2 S.C.R. 657, at para. 14). Nevertheless, a useful analogy can be drawn between the limit on aboriginal title and the concept of equitable waste at common law. Under that doctrine, persons who hold a life estate in real property cannot commit "wanton or extravagant acts of destruction" (E. H. Burn, *Cheshire and Burn's Modern Law of Real Property* (14th ed. 1988), at p. 264) or "ruin the property" (Robert E. Megarry and H. W. R. Wade, *The Law of Real Property*, 4th ed. (1975) at p. 105). This description of the limits imposed by the doctrine of equitable waste capture the kind of limit I have in mind here.

Finally, what I have just said regarding the importance of the continuity of the relationship between an aboriginal community and its land, and the non-economic or inherent value of that land, should not be taken to detract from the possibility of surrender to the Crown in exchange for valuable consideration. On the contrary, the idea of surrender reinforces the conclusion that aboriginal title is limited in the way I have described. If aboriginal peoples wish to use their lands in a way that aboriginal title does not permit, then they must surrender those lands and convert them into non-title lands to do so.

The foregoing amounts to a general limitation on the use of lands held by virtue of aboriginal title. It arises from the particular physical and cultural relationship that a group may have with the land and is defined by the source of aboriginal title over it. This is not, I must emphasize, a limitation that restricts the use of the land to those activities that have traditionally been carried out on it. That would amount to a legal straitjacket on aboriginal peoples who have a legitimate legal claim to the land. The approach I have outlined above allows for a full range of uses of the land, subject only to an overarching limit, defined by the special nature of the aboriginal title in that land.

(d) *Aboriginal title under s. 35(1) of the Constitution Act, 1982*

Aboriginal title at common law is protected in its full form by s. 35(1). This conclusion flows from the express language of s. 35(1) itself, which states in full: "[t]he existing aboriginal and treaty rights of the aboriginal peoples of Canada are hereby recognized and affirmed" (emphasis added). On a plain reading of the provision, s. 35(1) did not create aboriginal rights; rather, it accorded constitutional status to those rights which were "existing" in 1982. The provision, at the very least, constitutionalized those rights which aboriginal peoples possessed at common law, since those rights existed at the time s. 35(1) came into force. Since aboriginal title was a common law right whose existence was recognized well before 1982 (e.g., *Calder*, supra), s. 35(1) has constitutionalized it in its full form. [...]

I hasten to add that the constitutionalization of common law aboriginal rights by s. 35(1) does not mean that those rights exhaust the content of s. 35(1). [...]

[T]he existence of a particular aboriginal right at common law is not a *sine qua non* for the proof of an aboriginal right that is recognized and affirmed by s. 35(1). Indeed, none of the decisions of this Court handed down under s. 35(1) in which the existence of an aboriginal right has been demonstrated has relied on the existence of that right at common law. The existence of an aboriginal right at common law is therefore sufficient, but not necessary, for the recognition and affirmation of that right by s. 35(1).

The acknowledgment that s. 35(1) has accorded constitutional status to common law aboriginal title raises a further question — the relationship of aboriginal title to the "aboriginal rights" protected by s. 35(1). [...]

[A]boriginal title is "simply one manifestation of a broader-based conception of aboriginal rights". [...] Thus, although aboriginal title is a species of aboriginal right recognized and affirmed by s. 35(1), it is distinct from other aboriginal rights because it arises where the connection of a group with a piece of land "was of a central significance to their distinctive culture" (at para. 26).

The picture which emerges from *Adams* is that the aboriginal rights which are recognized and affirmed by s. 35(1) fall along a spectrum with respect to their degree of connection with the land. At the one end, there are those aboriginal rights which are practices, customs and traditions that are integral to the distinctive aboriginal culture of the group claiming the right. However, the "occupation and use of the land" where the activity is taking place is not "sufficient to support a claim of title to the land" (at para. 26). Nevertheless, those activities receive constitutional protection. In the middle, there are activities which, out of necessity, take place on land and indeed, might be intimately related to a particular piece of land. Although an aboriginal group may not be able to demonstrate title to the land, it may nevertheless have a site-specific right to engage in a particular activity. [...]

At the other end of the spectrum, there is aboriginal title itself. As *Adams* makes clear, aboriginal title confers more than the right to engage in site-specific activities which are aspects of the practices, customs and traditions of distinctive aboriginal cultures. Site-specific rights can be made out even if title cannot. What aboriginal title confers is the right to the land itself.

Because aboriginal rights can vary with respect to their degree of connection with the land, some aboriginal groups may be unable to make out a claim to title, but will nevertheless possess aboriginal rights that are recognized and affirmed by s. 35(1), including site-specific rights to engage in particular activities. As I explained in *Adams*, this may occur in the case of nomadic peoples who varied "the location of their settlements with the season and changing circumstances" (at para. 27). [...]

(e) *Proof of aboriginal title*

[...] Since the purpose of s. 35(1) is to reconcile the prior presence of aboriginal peoples in North America with the assertion of Crown sovereignty, it is clear from this statement that s. 35(1) must recognize and affirm both aspects of that prior presence — first, the occupation of land, and second, the prior social organization and distinctive cultures of aboriginal peoples on that land. To date the jurisprudence under s. 35(1) has given more emphasis to the second aspect. To a great extent, this has been a function of the types of cases which have come before this Court under s. 35(1) — prosecutions for regulatory offences that, by their very nature, proscribe discrete types of activity.

The adaptation of the test laid down in *Van der Peet* to suit claims to title must be understood as the recognition of the first aspect of that prior presence. However, as will now become apparent, the tests for the identification of aboriginal rights to engage in particular activities and for the identification of aboriginal title share broad similarities. The major distinctions are first, under the test for aboriginal title, the requirement that the land be integral to the distinctive culture of the claimants is subsumed by the requirement of occupancy, and second, whereas the time for the identification of aboriginal rights is the time of first contact, the time for the identification of aboriginal title is the time at which the Crown asserted sovereignty over the land. [...]

<u>The land must have been occupied prior to sovereignty</u>

In order to establish a claim to aboriginal title, the aboriginal group asserting the claim must establish that it occupied the lands in question at the time at <u>which the Crown asserted sovereignty over the land subject to the title</u>. [...]

If present occupation is relied on as proof of occupation pre-sovereignty, <u>there must be a continuity between present and pre-sovereignty occupation.</u> [...]

Needless to say, there is no need to establish "an unbroken chain of continuity" (*Van der Peet*, at para. 65) between present and prior occupation. The occupation and use of lands may have been disrupted for a time, perhaps as a result of the unwillingness of European colonizers to recognize aboriginal title. To impose the requirement of continuity too strictly would risk "undermining the very purposes of s. 35(1) by perpetuating the historical injustice suffered by aboriginal peoples at the hands of colonizers who failed to respect" aboriginal rights to land (*Côté*, supra at para. 53). [...]

At sovereignty, occupation must have been exclusive

Finally, at sovereignty, occupation must have been exclusive. The requirement for exclusivity flows from the definition of aboriginal title itself, because I have defined aboriginal title in terms of the right to exclusive use and occupation of land. Exclusivity, as an aspect of aboriginal title, vests in the aboriginal community which holds the ability to exclude others from the lands held pursuant to that title. The proof of title must, in this respect, mirror the content of the right. Were it possible to prove title without demonstrating exclusive occupation, the result would be absurd, because it would be possible for more than one aboriginal nation to have aboriginal title over the same piece of land, and then for all of them to attempt to assert the right to exclusive use and occupation over it. [...]

    (f) *Infringements of aboriginal title: the test of justification* [...]

    (iii) Justification and Aboriginal Title

The general principles governing justification laid down in *Sparrow*, and embellished by *Gladstone*, operate with respect to infringements of aboriginal title. In the wake of *Gladstone*, the range of legislative objectives that can justify the infringement of aboriginal title is fairly broad. Most of these objectives can be traced to the reconciliation of the prior occupation of North America by aboriginal peoples with the assertion of Crown sovereignty, which entails the recognition that "distinctive aboriginal societies exist within, and are a part of, a broader social, political and economic community" (at para. 73). In my opinion, the development of agriculture, forestry, mining, and hydroelectric power, the general economic development of the interior of British Columbia, protection of the environment or endangered species, the building of infrastructure and the settlement of foreign populations to support those aims, are the kinds of objectives that are consistent with this purpose and, in principle, can justify the infringement of aboriginal title. Whether a particular measure or government act can be explained by reference to one of those objectives, however, is ultimately a question of fact that will have to be examined on a case-by-case basis.

The manner in which the fiduciary duty operates with respect to the second stage of the justification test — both with respect to the standard of scrutiny and the particular form that the fiduciary duty will take — will be a function of the nature of aboriginal title. Three aspects of aboriginal title are relevant here. First, aboriginal title encompasses the right to exclusive use and occupation of land; second, aboriginal title encompasses the right to choose to what uses land can be put, subject to the ultimate limit that those uses cannot destroy the ability of the land to sustain future generations of aboriginal peoples; and third, that lands held pursuant to aboriginal title have an inescapable economic component.

The exclusive nature of aboriginal title is relevant to the degree of scrutiny of the infringing measure or action. For example, if the Crown's fiduciary duty required that aboriginal title be given priority, then it is the altered approach to priority that I laid down in *Gladstone* which should apply. What is required is that the government demonstrate (at para. 62) "both that the process by which it allocated the resource and the actual allocation of the resource which results from that process reflect the prior interest" of the holders of aboriginal title in the land. [...]

Moreover, the other aspects of aboriginal title suggest that the fiduciary duty may be articulated in a manner different than the idea of priority. This point becomes clear from a comparison between aboriginal title and the aboriginal right to fish for food in *Sparrow*. First, aboriginal title encompasses within it a right to choose to what ends a piece of land can be put. The aboriginal right to fish for food, by contrast, does not contain within it the same discretionary component. This aspect of aboriginal title suggests that the fiduciary relationship between the Crown and aboriginal peoples may be satisfied by the involvement of aboriginal peoples in decisions taken with respect to their lands. There is always a duty of consultation. Whether the aboriginal group has been consulted is relevant to determining whether the infringement of aboriginal title is justified, in the same way that the Crown's failure to consult an aboriginal group with respect to the terms by which reserve land is leased may breach its fiduciary duty at common law: *Guerin*. The nature and scope of the duty of consultation will vary with the circumstances. In occasional cases, when the breach is less serious or relatively minor, it will be no more than a duty to discuss important decisions that will be taken with respect to lands held pursuant to aboriginal title. Of course, even in these rare cases when the minimum acceptable standard is consultation, this consultation must be in good faith, and with the intention of substantially addressing the concerns of the aboriginal peoples whose lands are at issue. In most cases, it will be significantly deeper than mere consultation. Some cases may even require the full consent of an aboriginal nation, particularly when provinces enact hunting and fishing regulations in relation to aboriginal lands.

Second, aboriginal title, unlike the aboriginal right to fish for food, has an inescapably economic aspect, particularly when one takes into account the modern uses to which lands held pursuant to aboriginal title can be put. The economic aspect of aboriginal title suggests that compensation is relevant to the question of justification as well, a possibility suggested in *Sparrow* and which I repeated in *Gladstone*. Indeed, compensation for breaches of fiduciary duty are a well-established part of the landscape of aboriginal rights: *Guerin*. In keeping with the duty of honour and good faith on the Crown, fair compensation will ordinarily be required when aboriginal title is infringed. The amount of compensation payable will vary with the nature of the particular aboriginal title affected and with the nature and severity of the infringement and the extent to which aboriginal interests were accommodated. Since the issue of damages was severed from the principal action, we received no submissions on the appropriate legal principles that would be relevant to determining the appropriate level of compensation of infringements of aboriginal title. In the circumstances, it is best that we leave those difficult questions to another day. [...]

E. *Did the province have the power to extinguish aboriginal rights after 1871, either under its own jurisdiction or through the operation of s. 88 of the Indian Act?*

(1) Introduction

For aboriginal rights to be recognized and affirmed by s. 35(1), they must have existed in 1982. Rights which were extinguished by the sovereign before that time are not revived by the provision. In a federal system such as Canada's, the need to determine whether aboriginal rights have been extinguished raises the question of which level of government has jurisdiction to do so. In the context of this appeal, that general question becomes three specific ones. First, there is the question whether the province of British° Columbia, from the time it joined Confederation in 1871, until the entrenchment of s. 35(1) in 1982, had the jurisdiction to extinguish the rights of aboriginal peoples, including aboriginal title, in that province. Second, if the province was without such jurisdiction, another question arises — whether provincial laws which were not in pith and substance aimed at the extinguishment of aboriginal rights could have done so nevertheless if they were laws of general application. The third and final question is whether a provincial law, which could otherwise not extinguish aboriginal rights, be given that effect through referential incorporation by s. 88 of the *Indian Act*. [...]

[The question is whether] provincial laws of general application [...] [can] extinguish aboriginal rights. I have come to the conclusion that a provincial law of general application could not have this effect, for two reasons. First, a law of general application cannot, by definition, meet the standard which has been set by this Court for the extinguishment of aboriginal rights without being *ultra vires* the province. That standard was laid down in *Sparrow*, supra, at p. 1099, as one of "clear and plain" intent. In that decision, the Court drew a distinction between laws which extinguished aboriginal rights, and those which merely regulated them. Although the latter types of laws may have been "necessarily inconsistent" with the continued exercise of aboriginal rights, they could not extinguish those rights. While the requirement of clear and plain intent does not, perhaps, require that the Crown "use language which refers expressly to its extinguishment of aboriginal rights" (*Gladstone*, supra, at para. 34), the standard is still quite high. My concern is that the only laws with the sufficiently clear and plain intention to extinguish aboriginal rights would be laws in relation to Indians and Indian lands. As a result, a provincial law could never, *proprio vigore*, extinguish aboriginal rights, because the intention to do so would take the law outside provincial jurisdiction.

Second, as I mentioned earlier, s. 91(24) protects a core of federal jurisdiction even from provincial laws of general application, through the operation of the doctrine of interjurisdictional immunity. That core has been described as matters touching on "Indianness" or the "core of Indianness" (*Dick*, at pp. 326 and 315 (cites omitted); also see *Four B* at p. 1047 (cites omitted) and *Francis*, at pp. 1028-29 (cites omitted)). The core of Indianness at the heart of s. 91(24) has been defined in both negative and positive terms. Negatively, it has been held to not include labour relations (*Four B*) and the driving of motor vehicles (*Francis*). The only positive formulation of Indianness was offered in *Dick*. Speaking for the Court, Beetz J. assumed, but did not decide, that a provincial hunting law did not apply *proprio vigore* to the members of an Indian band to hunt and because those activities were "at the centre of what they do and who they are" (*supra*, at p. 320). But in *Van der Peet*, I described and defined the aboriginal rights that are recognized and affirmed by s. 35(1) in a similar fashion, as protecting the occupation of land and the activities which are integral to the distinctive aboriginal culture of the group claiming the right. It follows that aboriginal rights are part of the core of Indianness at the heart of s. 91(24). Prior to 1982, as a result, they could not be extinguished by provincial laws of general application.

Section 88 of the *Indian Act*

Provincial laws which would otherwise not apply to Indians *proprio vigore*, however, are allowed to do so by s. 88 of the *Indian Act*, which incorporates by reference provincial laws of general application: *Dick*, at pp. 326-27 (cites omitted); *Derrickson v. Derrickson*, [1986] 1 S.C.R. 285, at p. 297; *Francis*, at pp. 1030-31 (cites omitted). However, it is important to note, in Professor Hogg's words, that s. 88 does not "invigorate" provincial laws which are invalid because they are in relation to Indians and Indian lands (*Constitutional Law of Canada* (3rd ed. 1992), at p. 676; also see *Dick*, at p. 322 (cites omitted)). What this means is that s. 88 extends the effect of provincial laws of general application which cannot apply to Indians and Indian lands because they touch on the Indianness at the core of s. 91(24). For example, a provincial law which regulated hunting may very well touch on this core. Although such a law would not apply to aboriginal people *proprio vigore*, it would still apply through s. 88 of the *Indian Act*, being a law of general application. Such laws are enacted to conserve game and for the safety of all.

The respondent B.C. Crown argues that since such laws are *intra vires* the province, and applicable to aboriginal persons, s. 88 could allow provincial laws to extinguish aboriginal rights. I reject this submission, for the simple reason that s. 88 does not evince the requisite clear and plain intent to extinguish aboriginal rights. The provision states in full:

> 88. Subject to the terms of any treaty and any other Act of Parliament, all laws of general application from time to time in force in any province are applicable to and in respect of Indians in the province, except to the extent that those laws are inconsistent with this Act or any order, rule, regulation, or by-law made thereunder, and except to the extent that those laws make provision for any matter for which provision is made by or under this Act.

I see nothing in the language of the provision which even suggests the intention to extinguish aboriginal rights. Indeed, the explicit reference to treaty rights in s. 88 suggests that the provision was clearly not intended to undermine aboriginal rights.

VI. Conclusion and Disposition

For the reasons I have given above, I would allow the appeal in part, and dismiss the cross-appeal. Reluctantly, I would also order a new trial.

986

I conclude with two observations. The first is that many aboriginal nations with territorial claims that overlap with those of the appellants did not intervene in this appeal, and do not appear to have done so at trial. This is unfortunate, because determinations of aboriginal title for the Gitksan and Wet'suwet'en will undoubtedly affect their claims as well. This is particularly so because aboriginal title encompasses an <u>exclusive</u> right to the use and occupation of land, i.e., to the <u>exclusion</u> of both non-aboriginals and members of other aboriginal nations. It may, therefore, be advisable if those aboriginal nations intervened in any new litigation.

Finally, this litigation has been both long and expensive, not only in economic but in human terms as well. By ordering a new trial, I do not necessarily encourage the parties to proceed to litigation and to settle their dispute through the courts. As was said in *Sparrow*, at p. 1105, s. 35(1) "provides a solid constitutional base upon which subsequent negotiations can take place". Those negotiations should also include other aboriginal nations which have a stake in the territory claimed. Moreover, the Crown is under a moral, if not a legal, duty to enter into and conduct those negotiations in good faith. Ultimately, it is through negotiated settlements, with good faith and give and take on all sides, reinforced by the judgments of this Court, that we will achieve what I stated in *Van der Peet*, supra, at para. 31, to be a basic purpose of s. 35(1) — "the reconciliation of the pre-existence of aboriginal societies with the sovereignty of the Crown". Let us face it, we are all here to stay.

[The concurring reasons of La Forest (L'Heureux-Dubé concurring) and McLachlin JJ. have been omitted. Sopinka J. did not take part in the judgment.]

R. v. MARSHALL; R. v. BERNARD
[2005] 2 S.C.R. 220.

The judgment of McLachlin C.J. and Major, Bastarache, Abella and Charron JJ. was delivered by

THE CHIEF JUSTICE —

¶ 2 ... In the *Marshall* case, Stephen Frederick Marshall and 34 other Mi'kmaq Indians were charged with cutting timber on Crown lands without authorization, contrary to s. 29 of the *Crown Lands Act*, R.S.N.S. 1989, c. 114, between November 1998 and March 1999. [...]

¶ 3 In the *Bernard* case, Joshua Bernard, a Mi'kmaq Indian, was charged with unlawful possession of 23 spruce logs he was hauling from the cutting site to the local saw mill in contravention of s. 67(1)(c) of the *Crown Lands and Forests Act*, S.N.B. 1980, c. C-38.1, as amended [...]

¶ 4 In both cases the trial courts entered convictions. [...]

¶ 37 The respondents claim that they hold aboriginal title to the lands they logged and that therefore they do not need provincial authorization to log [...]

A. *Aboriginal Title at Common Law*

¶ 38 ... Aboriginal peoples used the land in many ways at the time of sovereignty. Some uses, like hunting and fishing, give rights to continue those practices in today's world [cites omitted]. Aboriginal title, based on occupancy at the time of sovereignty, is one of these various aboriginal rights. The respondents ... assert aboriginal title *simpliciter*.

¶ 39 The common law theory underlying recognition of aboriginal title holds that an aboriginal group which occupied land at the time of European sovereignty and never ceded or otherwise lost its right to that land, continues to enjoy title to it. [...]

B. *Standard of Occupation for Title: The Law*

¶ 41 The trial judges in each of *Bernard* and *Marshall* required proof of regular and exclusive use of the cutting sites to establish aboriginal title. The Courts of Appeal held that this test was too strict and applied a less onerous standard of incidental or proximate occupancy. [...]

¶ 46 *Delgamuukw* requires that in analyzing a claim for aboriginal title, the Court must consider both the aboriginal perspective and the common law perspective. [...]

¶ 48 The Court's task in evaluating a claim for an aboriginal right is to examine the pre-sovereignty aboriginal practice and translate that practice, as faithfully and objectively as it can, into a modern legal right. The question is whether the aboriginal practice at the time of assertion of European sovereignty (not, unlike treaties, when a document was signed) translates into a modern legal right, and if so, what right? This exercise involves both aboriginal and European perspectives. The Court must consider the pre-sovereignty practice from the perspective of the aboriginal people. But in translating it to a common law right, the Court must also consider the European perspective; the nature of the right at common law must be examined to determine whether a particular aboriginal practice fits it. This exercise in translating aboriginal practices to modern rights must not be conducted in a formalistic or narrow way. The Court should take a generous view of the aboriginal practice and should not insist on exact conformity to the precise legal parameters of the common law right. The question is whether the practice corresponds to the core concepts of the legal right claimed.

¶ 49 To determine aboriginal entitlement, one looks to aboriginal practices rather than imposing a European template: "In considering whether occupation sufficient to ground title is established, 'one must take into account the group's size, manner of life, material resources, and technological abilities, and the character of the lands claimed'" (*Delgamuukw, per* Lamer C.J., at para. 149). The application of "manner of life" was elaborated by La Forest J. who stated that:

> ... when dealing with a claim of "aboriginal title", the court will focus on the occupation and use of the land as part of the aboriginal society's *traditional way of life*. In pragmatic terms, this means looking at the manner in which the society used the land *to live*, namely to establish villages, to work, to get to work, to hunt, to travel to hunting grounds, to fish, to get to fishing pools, to conduct religious rites, etc. [Emphasis in original; para. 194.]

¶ 50 Thus, to insist that the pre-sovereignty practices correspond in some broad sense to the modern right claimed, is not to ignore the aboriginal perspective. The aboriginal perspective grounds the analysis and imbues its every step. It must be considered in evaluating the practice at issue, and a generous approach must be taken in matching it to the appropriate modern right. Absolute congruity is not required, so long as the practices engage the core idea of the modern right. But as this Court stated in *Marshall 2*, a pre-sovereignty aboriginal practice cannot be transformed into a different modern right.

¶ 51 In summary, the court must examine the pre-sovereignty aboriginal practice and translate that practice into a modern right. The process begins by examining the nature and extent of the pre-sovereignty aboriginal practice in question. It goes on to seek a corresponding common law right. In this way, the process determines the nature and extent of the modern right and reconciles the aboriginal and European perspectives.

¶ 52 The second underlying concept — the range of aboriginal rights — flows from the process of reconciliation just described. Taking the aboriginal perspective into account does not mean that a particular right, like title to the land, is established. The question is what modern right best corresponds to the pre-sovereignty aboriginal practice, examined from the aboriginal perspective.

¶ 53 Different aboriginal practices correspond to different modern rights. This Court has rejected the view of a dominant right to title to the land, from which other rights, like the right to hunt or fish, flow [cites omitted]. It is more accurate to speak of a variety of independent aboriginal rights.

¶ 54 One of these rights is aboriginal title to land. It is established by aboriginal practices that indicate possession similar to that associated with title at common law. In matching common law property rules to aboriginal practice we must be sensitive to the context-specific nature of common law title, as well as the aboriginal perspective. The common law recognizes that possession sufficient to ground title is a matter of fact, depending on all the circumstances, in particular the nature of the land and the manner in which the land is commonly enjoyed [cites omitted]. For example, where marshy land is virtually useless except for shooting, shooting over it may amount to adverse possession: [cites omitted]. The common law also recognizes that a person with adequate possession for title may choose to use it intermittently or sporadically [cites omitted] Finally, the common law recognizes that exclusivity does not preclude consensual arrangements that recognize shared title to the same parcel of land: *Delgamuukw*, at para. 158.

¶ 55 This review of the general principles underlying the issue of aboriginal title to land brings us to the specific requirements for title set out in *Delgamuukw*. To establish title, claimants must prove "exclusive" pre-sovereignty "occupation" of the land by their forebears: *per* Lamer C.J., at para. 143.

¶ 56 "Occupation" means "physical occupation". This "may be established in a variety of ways, ranging from the construction of dwellings through cultivation and enclosure of fields to regular use of definite tracts of land for hunting, fishing or otherwise exploiting its resources": *Delgamuukw, per* Lamer C.J., at para. 149.

¶ 57 "Exclusive" occupation flows from the definition of aboriginal title as "the right to exclusive use and occupation of land". *Delgamuukw*, per Lamer C.J., at para. 155 (emphasis in original). It is consistent with the concept of title to land at common law. Exclusive occupation means "the intention and capacity to retain exclusive control", and is not negated by occasional acts of trespass or the presence of other aboriginal groups with consent (*Delgamuukw*, at para. 156, citing McNeil, at p. 204). Shared exclusivity may result in joint title (para. 158). Non-exclusive occupation may establish aboriginal rights "short of title" (para. 159).

¶ 58 It follows from the requirement of exclusive occupation that exploiting the land, rivers or seaside for hunting, fishing or other resources may translate into aboriginal title to the land if the activity was sufficiently regular and exclusive to comport with title at common law. However, more typically, seasonal hunting and fishing rights exercised in a particular area will translate to a hunting or fishing right. This is plain from this Court's decisions in *Van der Peet, Nikal, Adams* and *Côté*. In those cases, aboriginal peoples asserted and proved ancestral utilization of particular sites for fishing and harvesting the products of the sea. Their forebears had come back to the same place to fish or harvest each year since time immemorial. However, the season over, they left, and the land could be traversed and used by anyone. These facts gave rise not to aboriginal title, but to aboriginal hunting and fishing rights.

¶ 59 The distinction between the requirements for a finding of aboriginal title and the requirements for more restricted rights was affirmed in *Côté*, where the Court held the right to fish was an independent right (para. 38). Similarly in *Adams*, the Court held that rights short of title could exist in the absence of occupation and use of the land sufficient to support a claim of title to the land: see *Adams*, at para. 26; *Côté*, at para. 39; *Delgamuukw*, at para. 159. To say that title flows from occasional entry and use is inconsistent with these cases and the approach to aboriginal title which this Court has consistently maintained. [...]

¶ 62 Aboriginal societies were not strangers to the notions of exclusive physical possession equivalent to common law notions of title: *Delgamuukw*, at para. 156. They often exercised such control over their village sites and larger areas of land which they exploited for agriculture, hunting, fishing or gathering. The question is whether the evidence here establishes this sort of possession.

¶ 63 Having laid out the broad picture, it may be useful to examine more closely three issues that evoked particular discussion here. [...]

¶ 64 The first of these sub-issues is the concept of exclusion. The right to control the land and, if necessary, to exclude others from using it is basic to the notion of title at common law. In European-based systems, this right is assumed by dint of law. Determining whether it was present in a pre-sovereignty aboriginal society, however, can pose difficulties. Often, no right to exclude arises by convention or law. So one must look to evidence. But evidence may be hard to find. The area may have been sparsely populated, with the result that clashes and the need to exclude strangers seldom if ever occurred. Or the people may have been peaceful and have chosen to exercise their control by sharing rather than exclusion. It is therefore critical to view the question of exclusion from the aboriginal perspective. To insist on evidence of overt acts of exclusion in such circumstances may, depending on the circumstances, be unfair. The problem is compounded by the difficulty of producing evidence of what happened hundreds of years ago where no tradition of written history exists.

¶ 65 It follows that evidence of acts of exclusion is not required to establish aboriginal title. All that is required is demonstration of effective control of the land by the group, from which a reasonable inference can be drawn that it could have excluded others had it chosen to do so. The fact that history, insofar as it can be ascertained, discloses no adverse claimants may support this inference. This is what is meant by the requirement of aboriginal title that the lands have been occupied in an exclusive manner.

¶ 66 The second sub-issue is whether nomadic and semi-nomadic peoples can ever claim title to aboriginal land, as distinguished from rights to use the land in traditional ways. The answer is that it depends on the evidence. [...] Whether a nomadic people enjoyed sufficient "physical possession" to give them title to the land, is a question of fact, depending on all the circumstances, in particular the nature of the land and the manner in which it is commonly used. Not every nomadic passage or use will ground title to land ... On the other hand, *Delgamuukw* contemplates that "physical occupation" sufficient to ground title to land may be established by "regular use of definite tracts of land for hunting, fishing or otherwise exploiting its resources" (para. 149). In each case, the question is whether a degree of physical occupation or use equivalent to common law title has been made out.

¶ 67 The third sub-issue is continuity. The requirement of continuity in its most basic sense simply means that claimants must establish they are right holders. Modern-day claimants must establish a connection with the pre-sovereignty group upon whose practices they rely to assert title or claim to a more restricted aboriginal right. The right is based on pre-sovereignty aboriginal practices. To claim it, a modern people must show that the right is the descendant of those practices. Continuity may also be raised in this sense. To claim title, the group's connection with the land must be shown to have been "of a central significance to their distinctive culture": *Adams*, at para. 26. If the group has "maintained a substantial connection" with the land since sovereignty, this establishes the required "central significance": *Delgamuukw, per* Lamer C.J., at paras. 150-51. [...]

¶ 70 In summary, exclusive possession in the sense of intention and capacity to control is required to establish aboriginal title. Typically, this is established by showing regular occupancy or use of definite tracts of land for hunting, fishing or exploiting resources: *Delgamuukw*, at para. 149. Less intensive uses may give rise to different rights. The requirement of physical occupation must be generously interpreted taking into account both the aboriginal perspective and the perspective of the common law: *Delgamuukw*, at para. 156. These principles apply to nomadic and semi-nomadic aboriginal groups; the right in each case depends on what the evidence establishes. Continuity is required, in the sense of showing the group's descent from the pre-sovereignty group whose practices are relied on for the right. On all these matters, evidence of oral history is admissible provided it meets the requisite standards of usefulness and reasonable reliability. The ultimate goal is to translate the pre-sovereignty aboriginal right to a modern common law right. This must be approached with sensitivity to the aboriginal perspective as well as fidelity to the common law concepts involved.

C. *Application of the Legal Test*

¶ 72 ... The trial judge in each case applied the correct test to determine whether the respondents' claim to aboriginal title was established. In each case they required proof of sufficiently regular and exclusive use of the cutting sites by Mi'kmaq people at the time of assertion of sovereignty.

¶ 73 In *Marshall*, Curran Prov. Ct. J. reviewed the authorities and concluded that the line separating sufficient and insufficient occupancy for title is between irregular use of undefined lands on the one hand and regular use of defined lands on the other. "Settlements constitute regular use of defined lands, but they are only one instance of it" (para. 141).

¶ 74 In *Bernard*, Lordon Prov. Ct. J. likewise found that occasional visits to an area did not establish title; there must be "evidence of capacity to retain exclusive control" (para. 110) over the land claimed.

¶ 75 These tests correctly reflect the jurisprudence as discussed above.

¶ 76 Holding otherwise, Cromwell J.A. in *Marshall* held that this test was too strict and that it was sufficient to prove occasional entry and acts from which an intention to occupy the land could be inferred. Similarly, in *Bernard*, Daigle J.A. held that the trial judge erred in requiring proof of specific acts of occupation and regular use in order to ground aboriginal title. It was not in error to state, as Cromwell J.A. did, that acts from which intention to occupy the land could be inferred may ground a claim to common law title. However, as discussed above, this must be coupled with sufficiently regular and exclusive use in order to establish title in the common law sense.

¶ 77 Cromwell J.A. found that this additional requirement is not consistent with the semi-nomadic culture or lifestyle of the Mi'kmaq. With respect, this argument is circular. It starts with the premise that it would be unfair to deny the Mi'kmaq title. In order to avoid this result, it posits that the usual indicia of title at common law — possession of the land in the sense of exclusive right to control — should be diminished because the pre-sovereignty practices proved do not establish title on that test. As discussed, the task of the court is to sensitively assess the evidence and then find the equivalent modern common law right. The common law right to title is commensurate with exclusionary rights of control. That is what it means and has always meant. If the ancient aboriginal practices do not indicate that type of control, then title is not the appropriate right. To confer title in the absence of evidence of sufficiently regular and exclusive pre-sovereignty occupation, would transform the ancient right into a new and different right. It would also obliterate the distinction that this Court has consistently made between lesser aboriginal rights like the right to fish and the highest aboriginal right, the right to title to the land: *Adams* and *Côté*.

D. *Assessment of the Evidence*

¶ 80 ... Curran Prov. Ct. J. "concluded that the Mi'kmaq of the 18th century on mainland Nova Scotia probably had aboriginal title to lands around their local communities, but not to the cutting sites" (para. 143).

¶ 81 In *Bernard*, Lordon Prov. Ct. J. also made a thorough review of the evidence of Mi'kmaq occupation of lands at the time of sovereignty, and concluded that it did not establish title [...]

¶ 83 I conclude that there is no ground to interfere with the trial judges' conclusions on the absence of common law aboriginal title. [...]

¶ 85 The respondents argue that the *Royal Proclamation* of 1763 (see Appendix) reserved to the Mi'kmaq title in all unceded, unpurchased land in the former Nova Scotia, which later was divided into Nova Scotia and New Brunswick. I agree with the courts below that this argument must be rejected. [...] [T]he text, the jurisprudence and historic policy, all support the conclusion that the *Royal Proclamation* did not reserve the former colony of Nova Scotia to the Mi'kmaq. [...]

¶ 109 I would allow the appeals ... and restore the convictions. [...]

The reasons of LeBel and Fish JJ. were delivered by

LeBEL J. —

¶ 110 ... While I am in agreement with the ultimate disposition, I have concerns.... On the issue of aboriginal title, I take the view that ... the majority is too narrowly focused on common law concepts relating to property interests. [...]

¶ 126 Although the test for aboriginal title set out in the Chief Justice's reasons does not foreclose the possibility that semi-nomadic peoples would be able to establish aboriginal title, it may prove to be fundamentally incompatible with a nomadic or semi-nomadic lifestyle. This test might well amount to a denial that any aboriginal title could have been created by such patterns of nomadic or semi-nomadic occupation or use: nomadic life might have given rise to specific rights exercised at specific places or within identifiable territories, but never to a connection with the land itself in the absence of evidence of intensive and regular use of the land.

¶ 127 In my view, aboriginal conceptions of territoriality, land-use and property should be used to modify and adapt the traditional common law concepts of property in order to develop an occupancy standard that incorporates both the aboriginal and common law approaches. Otherwise, we might be implicitly accepting the position that aboriginal peoples had no rights in land prior to the assertion of Crown sovereignty because their views of property or land use do not fit within Euro-centric conceptions of property rights. [...]

¶ 129 As with all aboriginal rights protected by s. 35(1) of the *Constitution Act, 1982*, aboriginal title arises from the prior possession of land and the prior social organization and distinctive cultures of aboriginal peoples on that land [cites omitted]. It originates from "the prior occupation of Canada by aboriginal peoples" and from "the relationship between common law and pre-existing systems of aboriginal law" (*Delgamuukw*, at para. 114). The need to reconcile this prior occupation with the assertion of Crown sovereignty was reinforced in *Delgamuukw* when Lamer C.J. stated that common law aboriginal title "cannot be completely explained by reference either to the common law rules of real property or to the rules of property found in aboriginal legal systems. As with other aboriginal rights, it must be understood by reference to both common law and aboriginal perspectives" (para. 112). [...]

¶ 130 The role of the aboriginal perspective cannot be simply to help in the interpretation of aboriginal practices in order to assess whether they conform to common law concepts of title. The aboriginal perspective shapes the very concept of aboriginal title. "Aboriginal law should not just be received as evidence that Aboriginal peoples did something in the past on a piece of land. It is more than evidence: it is actually law. And so, there should be some way to bring to the decision-making process those laws that arise from the standards of the indigenous people before the court". [...]

¶ 131 At common law, the physical fact of occupation is proof of possession. This explains the common law theory underlying the recognition of aboriginal title that is set out by the Chief Justice at para. 39: "an aboriginal group which occupied land at the time of European sovereignty and never ceded or otherwise lost its right to that land, continues to enjoy title to it". If aboriginal title is a right derived from the historical occupation and possession of land by aboriginal peoples, then notions and principles of ownership cannot be framed exclusively by reference to common law concepts. The patterns and nature of aboriginal occupation of land should inform the standard necessary to prove aboriginal title. The common law notion that "physical occupation is proof of possession" remains, but the nature of the occupation is shaped by the aboriginal perspective, which includes a history of nomadic or semi-nomadic modes of occupation. [...]

European settlement did not terminate the interests of aboriginal peoples arising from their historical occupation and use of the land. To the contrary, aboriginal interests and customary laws were presumed to survive the assertion of sovereignty, and were absorbed into the common law as rights, unless (1) they were incompatible with the Crown's assertion of sovereignty, (2) they were surrendered voluntarily via the treaty process, or (3) the government extinguished them [...]

¶ 134 Nomadic peoples and their modes of occupancy of land cannot be ignored when defining the concept of aboriginal title to land in Canada. [...]

¶ 136 ... the test for proof of aboriginal title cannot simply reflect common law concepts of property and ownership. The nature and patterns of land use that are capable of giving rise to a claim for title are not uniform and are potentially as diverse as the aboriginal peoples that possessed the land prior to the assertion of Crown sovereignty. The fact that a tract of land was used for hunting instead of agriculture does not mean that the group did not possess the land in such a way as to acquire aboriginal title. Taking into account the aboriginal perspective on the occupation of land means that physical occupation as understood by the modern common law is not the governing criterion. The group's relationship with the land is paramount. To impose rigid concepts and criteria is to ignore aboriginal social and cultural practices that may reflect the significance of the land to the group seeking title. The mere fact that the group travelled within its territory and did not cultivate the land should not take away from its title claim.

¶ 137 The standard of proof required to ground a claim must therefore reflect the patterns of occupation of the land prior to the assertion of British sovereignty. [...]

¶ 138 In the context of aboriginal title claims, the physical fact of sedentary and continuous occupation is only one of the sources of title. [...] If the aboriginal perspective is to be taken into account by a court, then the occupancy requirement cannot be equated to the common law notion of possession amounting to a fee simple. On the contrary, proof of aboriginal title relates to the manner in which the aboriginal group used and occupied the land prior to the assertion of Crown sovereignty.

¶ 139 The aboriginal perspective on the occupation of their land can also be gleaned in part, but not exclusively, from pre-sovereignty systems of aboriginal law. The relevant laws consisted of elements of the practices, customs and traditions of aboriginal peoples and might include a land tenure system or laws governing land use.

¶ 140 ... [A]nyone considering the degree of occupation sufficient to establish title must be mindful that aboriginal title is ultimately premised upon the notion that the specific land or territory at issue was of central significance to the aboriginal group's culture. Occupation should therefore be proved by evidence not of regular and intensive use of the land but of the traditions and culture of the group that connect it with the land. Thus, intensity of use is related not only to common law notions of possession but also to the aboriginal perspective.

¶ 141 The record in the courts below lacks the evidentiary foundation necessary to make legal findings on the issue of aboriginal title in respect of the cutting sites in Nova Scotia and New Brunswick and, as a result, the respondents in these cases have failed to sufficiently establish their title claim. In the circumstances, I do not wish to suggest that this decision represents a final determination of the issue of aboriginal title rights in Nova Scotia or New Brunswick. A final determination should be made only where there is an adequate evidentiary foundation that fully examines the relevant legal and historical record. [...]

V. Disposition

¶ 145 For these reasons, I would concur with my colleague, allow the appeals, dismiss the cross-appeal in *Marshall* and restore the convictions.

(d) Treaty Rights

- Research Note -
CANADA'S TREATIES WITH ABORIGINAL PEOPLE

In the period after Confederation, between 1871 and 1921, Canada entered into eleven numbered treaties with the aboriginal peoples. There are other Treaties besides, and many pre-confederation Treaties: see http://www.ainc-inac.gc.ca/pr/trts/hti/site/tri ndex_e.html.

Status of the Treaties

What exactly are these treaties, and what use may courts make of them?

On their face, the treaties seem to contain an exchange of promises. This makes them like a contract. But, unlike a contract

> a treaty represents an exchange of solemn promises between the Crown and the various Indian nations. It is an agreement whose nature is sacred.[1]

This lofty language refers to the juridical novelty by which the treaties establish a special relationship between the First Nations and the Crown. The relationship is special because the obligations created – to cede land masses larger than many countries and to provide reserves and schooling – are unusual, to say the least. The relationship is special also because the concepts underlying the treaties provide an important point of reference for how these communities are to relate to Canada in the future.

Jean Chrétien speaking to Aboriginal delegates concerning the Red Paper brief (Ottawa 1970).

This special nature of Canada's treaties with the aboriginal people has been considered by the commentators and the courts. The Royal Commission on Aboriginal Peoples (RCAP) thought that the treaties allowed Canada to avoid the Indian wars that characterized settlement of the American frontiers, and thus the relationships created undergird the distinctive characteristics of the Canadian polity:

---

[1] *R. v. Badger*, [1996] 1 S.C.R. 771 at paras. 41, 47 [*Badger*]; *R. v. Sioui*, [1990] 1 S.C.R. 1025 at 1063 [*Sioui*].

> The Canada that takes a proud place among the family of
> nations was made possible by the treaties. Our defining
> national characteristics are tolerance, pluralism and democracy.
> Had it not been for the treaties, these defining myths might well
> not have taken hold here. Had it not been for the treaties, wars
> might have replaced the tribal council. Or the territory might
> have been absorbed by the union to the south. Canada would
> have been a very different place if treaty making with the Indian
> nations had been replaced by the waging of war.[1]

In recognition of the fundamental arrangements the treaties established,
RCAP considered that the treaties were properly understood as constitutional in
nature:

> The network of treaties between the Crown and treaty nations is
> described by some as confederal in nature. Treaty rights are
> now recognized and affirmed by s. 35(1) of the Constitution Act,
> 1982. The Commission considers that the treaties do indeed
> form part of the constitution of Canada. When properly
> understood, the treaties set out the terms under which the treaty
> nations agreed to align themselves with the Crown ...The
> Commission concludes that the treaties describe social contracts
> that have enduring significance and that as a result form part of
> the fundamental law of the land. In this sense they are like the
> terms of union whereby former British colonies entered
> Confederation as provinces.[2]

Varieties of these views have been incubating in the courts. The British
Columbia Supreme Court affirmed RCAP's opinion that treaties have always
been constitutional in nature because "long before the 1982 enactment of s. 35,
aboriginal rights formed part of the unwritten principles underlying our Constitution."[3]
This way of putting it – that the treaties inhere in the unwritten architecture of the
constitution and can give rise to constitutional obligations – is the view taken in
the landmark opinion of the Supreme Court in the *Secession Reference*:

> Consistent with this long tradition of respect for minorities,
> which is at least as old as Canada itself, the framers of the
> *Constitution Act, 1982* included in s. 35 explicit protection for existing
> aboriginal and treaty rights, and in s. 25, a non-derogation clause in
> favour of the rights of aboriginal peoples. The "promise" of s. 35, as it

---

1   Canada, Royal Commission on Aboriginal Peoples, *Report of the Royal
     Commission on Aboriginal Peoples*, vol. 2 (Ottawa: Canada Communication
     Group, 1996) at 15 [RCAP].
2   RCAP, *ibid.* at 20.
3   *Campbell v. British Columbia (A.G.)* (2000), 189 D.L.R. (4th) 333 (B.C.S.C.) at
     351.

was termed in *R. v. Sparrow*, [1990] 1 S.C.R. 1075, at p. 1083, recognized not only the ancient occupation of land by aboriginal peoples, but their contribution to the building of Canada, and the special commitments made to them by successive governments. The protection of these rights, so recently and arduously achieved, whether looked at in their own right or as part of the larger concern with minorities, reflects an important underlying constitutional value.[1]

Interpretation of Treaty Texts

Treaty interpretation requires the rules of evidence to be relaxed, and for context to inform the intention of the parties.

> even in the context of a treaty document that purports to contain all of the terms, this Court has made clear in recent cases that extrinsic evidence of the historical and cultural context of a treaty may be received even absent any ambiguity on the face of the treaty.[2]

A principal reason why historical and cultural context is critical to treaty interpretation is that the treaty texts were written by the Crown's representatives. In many cases the Aboriginal people who negotiated the treaties and signed them with a mark were unable to read. Some contemporaneous reports of treaty making show that the written treaty texts differ markedly from the oral promises made by Crown representatives. Treaty 3 is a good example. Treaty 3 was negotiated during an intense three days during which Canada's representatives made many promises in response to Ojibway demands. Some of these were not included in the written treaty text, including promises that the Indians would be exempt from military conscription, that minerals found on reserve would only be sold with the consent of the Indians, that any Indian children who had emigrated to the United States would be admitted to the treaty if they returned within two

---

1   *Reference re : Secession of Quebec*, [1998] 2 S.C.R. 217 at 262-63 (para. 82).
2   *R. v. Marshall*, [1999] 3 S.C.R. 456 at para 11. In *R. v. Taylor and Williams* (1981), 62 C.C.C. (2d) 227 this principle was laid down at p. 236: "... if there is evidence by conduct or otherwise as to how the parties understood the terms of the treaty, then such understanding and practice is of assistance in giving content to the term or terms." This proposition is cited with approval in *Delgamuukw v. British Columbia*, [1997] 3 S.C.R. 1010 at para. 87 and *R. v. Sioui*, [1990] 1 S.C.R. 1025 at 1045. Similarly, Lamer J. stated in *R. v Sioui*, at 1068, that "[t]he historical context, which has been used to demonstrate the existence of the treaty, may equally assist us in interpreting the extent of the rights contained in it".

years, that the Indians would forever have use of their fisheries.[1] The reason why these promises were left out was that the Commissioners had brought with them a text compiled from failed treaty negotiations of the year before. This text did not reflect the many concessions made during the intense three days of negotiations. "In their haste to conclude the agreement, [Canada's treaty commissioners] used as a finalized version the draft treaty from the previous year which would not reflect the new items of agreement in the negotiations just concluded."[2] All of the Chiefs who signed Treaty 3 were unable to read, and 'signed' with a mark. In a *Report* that discussed conflicting Federal and provincial claims in the context of Treaty 3 lands, a Canadian official stated:

> *there were other conditions relating to the reserves not embodied in the treaty, but which should have been so embodied, inasmuch as they were imposed by the Indians during the negotiations for the treaty*, and which are in view of the illiterate condition of the Indians as much conditions of their enjoyment as those actually inserted in the treaty;(emphasis added).[3]

The circumstances surrounding Treaty 3 are not unique.

It is circumstances like these that explain why the courts require that history and surrounding circumstance play important roles in treaty interpretation: it is the only way to really know to what the parties to the treaty agreed. The 'agreement' is to be found in the understandings that the parties to the treaty had, which may be imperfectly reflected by the written text. Courts have been repeatedly warned on this score by the Supreme Court of Canada. Courts have been instructed that history and surrounding circumstance are one of the ways to get at the aboriginal perspective as to what was the content of the agreements: "... if there is evidence by conduct or otherwise as to how the parties understood the terms of the treaty, then such understanding and practice is of assistance in giving content to the term or terms."[4] Courts charged with

---

1   Conscription: see Alexander Morris, *The Treaties of Canada with the Indians of Manitoba and the North-West Territories* (Toronto: Belfords, Clarke & Co., 1880; facsimile edition, Coles Publishing Company, 1979) at 69 [Morris]; minerals: see Morris at 70, returning children: see Morris at 70; fisheries: see S.J. Dawson to L. VanKoughnet (28 May 1888), Ottawa, National Archives of Canada (RG 10, vol. 3800, file 48542).

2   Wayne Daugherty , *Treaty Research Report: Treaty One and Treaty Two* (Ottawa: Treaties and Historical; Research Centre, INAC, 1983), Chapter 3.

3   *Re the Titles of the Dominion and the Province of Ontario Respectively in Indian Lands, Indian Reserves and in the Royal Metals and Other Metals Therein and Timber Thereon* [n.d.], Ottawa, National Archives of Canada (RG 10, vol. 2545, file 111834, pt.1).

4   *R. v. Taylor and Williams* (1982), 34 O.R. (2d) 360 at 367.

interpreting the treaties must consider the Aboriginal perspective, for that is the only way to understand what was agreed. The Supreme Court of Canada requires that

> ... when considering a treaty, a court must take into account the context in which the treaties were negotiated, concluded and committed to writing. The treaties, as written documents, recorded an agreement that had already been reached orally and they did not always record the full extent of the oral agreement. The treaties were drafted in English by representatives of the Canadian government who, it should be assumed, were familiar with common law doctrines. Yet, the treaties were not translated in written form into the languages (here Cree and Dene) of the various Indian nations who were signatories. Even if they had been, it is unlikely that the Indians, who had a history of communicating only orally, would have understood them any differently. As a result, it is well settled that the words in the treaty must not be interpreted in their strict technical sense nor subjected to rigid modern rules of construction.[1]

Historical and cultural context are but one of a set of special rules which apply to the interpretation of Canada's treaties with the aboriginal people. Because the treaties establish a special relationship between peoples, the Courts also require that the treaties be interpreted in a manner that maintains the honour of the Crown.[2] Courts will not countenance any sharp practice or unfair dealing. Courts assume that the Crown intends to comply fully with each promise, obligation or right set out in a treaty, or garnered from reconstruction of the understandings of the parties.[3]

Treaty terms must be assessed with a large, liberal and generous interpretation in favour of the First Nation signatory.[4] Ambiguities, uncertainties

---

[1]   *R. v. Badger*, [1996] 1 S.C.R. 771 at para. 52 [*Badger*]. In *R. v. Marshall*, [1999] 4 S.C.R. 456 at para. 43 the Supreme Court explained:

> If the law is prepared to supply the deficiencies of written contracts prepared by sophisticated parties and their legal advisors in order to produce a sensible result that accords with the intent of both parties, though unexpressed, the law cannot ask less of the honour and dignity of the Crown in its dealings with First Nations.

[2]   *R. v. Badger*, [1996] 1 S.C.R. 771 at para 97.

[3]   See *R. v. Sparrow*, [1990] 1 S.C.R. 1075 at 1107-1108, 1114; *R. v. Taylor and Williams* (1981), 34 O.R. (2d) 360 at 367 (Ont. C.A.).

[4]   *R. v. Simon*, [1985] 2 S.C.R. 387 at 402 [*Simon*]; *R. v. Sioui*, [1990] 1 S.C.R. 1025 at 1035 [*Sioui*].

or doubtful expressions are to be settled in favour of the First Nation signatories.[1] Not only should "treaties and statutes relating to Indians .. be liberally construed,"and doubts "resolved in favour of the Indians"[2] but any limitation which restricts First Nation rights must be narrowly construed.[3]

Remedies for Breach

As we have seen, the exchange of promises that characterizes the treaties makes them seem analogous to contracts, albeit contracts of a very solemn and special public nature. It seems to be this aspect, the exchange of promises meant to bind, that prompts the courts to say that the treaties "create *enforceable* obligations based on the mutual consent of the parties;"[4] (emphasis added), that treaty promises are "binding obligations which would be solemnly respected,"[5] and are "binding obligations" of the Crown.[6] All of this makes it appear that the treaties self-execute in the sense that they are justiciable, and that courts may give remedies for breach of the obligations the treaties create.

It is true that fiduciary obligations and treaty obligations at times overlap in the sense that a breach of treaty can and often does constitute a breach of the Crown's fiduciary obligations to First Nations.[7] It would be wrong to conclude from this overlap that treaty rights depend for enforcement upon the application of fiduciary law. Treaty rights precede fiduciary obligations as independent, *sui generis* entitlements of quasi-constitutional significance. Canada's obligations under the treaties do not arise from the fiduciary relationship between itself and Indian peoples. Canada's obligations have their source in the fact that the people of Canada, as represented by their government, entered into a solemn treaty relationship in which binding promises were made to the aboriginal people in exchange for very substantial consideration given by the Indians in return.

There is not a large amount of litigation which seeks to enforce Canada's treaty promises. What litigation there is uses the treaties as shields against prosecutions or restrictions, not as swords to obtain performance of treaty promises or damages for breach. The explanation for the paucity of litigation probably lies in the fact that in1927, Parliament enacted s.141 of the *Indian Act*, which made it an offence for any legal counsel to receive payment on behalf of any

---

1   *Badger* at 92, 95 (paras. 41, 52); *Nowegijick v. R.*, [1983] 1 S.C.R. 29 at 36 [*Nowegijick*].
2   See *Nowegijick* at 36. See also *Simon* at 402: "Indian treaties should be given a fair, large, liberal construction in favour of the Indians."
3   *Badger; Simon, supra* note 4 at 402, 405-06; *Sioui, supra* note 4 at 1035, 1061; and *Mitchell v. Peguis Indian Band*, [1990] 2 S.C.R. 85 at 142-43.
4   *Badger, supra* note 1 at para. 76.
5   *R. v. Simon*, [1985] 2 S.C.R. 387 at 24.
6   *R. v. Sioui*, [1990] 1 S.C.R. 1025. at 43. See also *Badger, supra* note 1 at 94 (para. 47).
7   *Ontario (Attorney General) v. Bear Island Foundation*, [1991] 2 S.C.R. 570 at 575.

Indian Band for "the prosecution of any claim ... for the benefit of the said tribe or band ,..." This provision remained on the books until 1951.[1] More recently, claims that Canada has violated its treaty promises are funnelled into special dispute resolution fora under Canada's specific claims and treaty land entitlement policies. These policies provide negotiation tables, and funding for negotiations to resolve claims that Canada has breached its lawful obligations under the treaties.[2]

Notwithstanding the absence of treaty litigation, it seems that treaty rights are justiciable and can constitute the basis of a claim for compensatory and equitable remedies, including damages. This is the opinion of the Indian Claims Commission, which holds that treaty rights, "being equitable in nature, can be enforced by the courts, either through an award of specific performance or, in circumstances in which specific performance may not be available, an award of, first, compensatory damages in lieu of the shortfall land, and, second, compensatory damages for late performance."[3] This opinion is also consistent with the court descriptions of the treaties as creating binding and enforceable obligations, previously considered.

Given the independent exchange of promises between the Crown and First Nations recorded by the treaties, the expectations created, the specificity of the promises, and the large consideration provided by the Indians in exchange, it seems that treaty promises are meant to be justiciable. If this proves to be correct, treaty promises are independent sources of legal obligations owed by the Crown. The Indian Claims Commission explained :

> ... it is without question that such treaty covenants are of sufficient importance in modern Canadian society that they stand on their own as sui generis obligations independent of the concept of fiduciary obligation for their legitimacy or enforceability. To suggest that the treaties are reliant on the vehicle of fiduciary duty to make them enforceable would fail to accord them the historical and constitutional importance that they have acquired in Canada.[4]

Extinguishment of Treaty Obligations

Prior to 1982, treaty promises could be extinguished by competent legislative action. Legislation alleged to extinguish a treaty promise must be

---

1   *Indian Act*, S.C. 1926-7, c. 32 and R.S.C. 1927, c. 98, s.141; repealed by S.C. 1950-1, c.29 s.123.
2   For an overview of the specific claims policy see http://www.ainc-inac.gc.ca/ps/clm/scb_e.html.
3   Indian Claims Commission, Long Plain First Nation Inquiry: Loss of Use Claim, March, 2000, at 32. Online: <http://www.indianclaims.ca/download/pdfreports/PDFClaimsReports/English/LongplainEng.pdf>.
4   *Ibid*. at 30.

specific and precise; "if legislation bears on treaty promises, the courts will always strain against adopting an interpretation that has the effect of negating commitments undertaken by the Crown."[1]

Regulatory legislation does not extinguish treaty promises, unless it possesses this specificity. The fact that a right is "controlled in great detail by [a] regulation does not mean that the right is thereby extinguished."[2] Even regulatory legislation that is inconsistent with the continued existence of treaty rights will not extinguish a treaty promise unless it exhibits a "clear and plain intent to extinguish treaty rights,"[3] or the regulation is "wholly incompatible" with the continued exercise of a treaty right.[4] The Crown has the onus to prove extinguishment. To prove a treaty right has been extinguished the Crown must make: "'strict proof of the fact of extinguishment' and evidence of a clear and plain intention on the part of the government to extinguish treaty rights."[5]

R. v. BADGER
[1996] 1 S.C.R. 771.

CORY J. [La Forest, L'Heureux-Dubé, Gonthier, and Iacobucci JJ. Concurring]: —

Three questions must be answered on this appeal. First, do Indians who have status under Treaty No. 8 have the right to hunt for food on privately owned land which lies within the territory surrendered under that Treaty? Secondly, have the hunting rights set out in Treaty No. 8 been extinguished or modified as a result of the provisions of para. 12 of the *Natural Resources Transfer Agreement, 1930* (*Constitution Act, 1930*, Schedule 2)? Thirdly, to what extent, if any, do s. 26(1) and s. 27(1) of the *Wildlife Act*, S.A. 1984, c. W-9.1, apply to the appellants?

Factual Background

[...] The facts are straightforward and undisputed. The appellant Wayne Clarence Badger was charged with shooting a moose outside the permitted hunting season contrary to s. 27(1) of the *Wildlife Act*. The appellants Leroy Steven Kiyawasew and Ernest Clarence Ominayak, who had also shot moose, were charged, under s. 26(1) of the same statute, with hunting without a licence. All three appellants, Cree Indians with status under Treaty No. 8, were hunting for food upon lands falling within the tracts surrendered to Canada by the Treaty.

The lands in question were all privately owned. Mr. Badger shot a moose on brush land with willow regrowth and scrub. There were no fences or signs posted on the land, but a farm house was located a quarter mile from the place where the moose was shot. Mr. Kiyawasew was hunting on a snow-covered field.

---

1   *Mitchell v. Peguis*, [1990] 2 S.C.R. 85 at 119.
2   *R. v. Gladstone*, [1996] 2 S.C.R. 723 at para. 31.
3   *R. v. Sparrow*, [1990] 1 S.C.R. 1075 at 1099.
4   *R. v. Sundown*, [1999] 1 S.C.R. 393 at 414-15 (paras. 41-42).
5   *R. v. Badger*, [1996] 1 S.C.R. 771 at para. 41.

There was no fence, but Mr. Kiyawasew ~~stated~~ that he had passed old run-down barns shortly before he ~~stopped~~ to shoot the moose. He had seen signs which were ~~posted on the land~~ but he was unable to read them from the road. Mr. Ominayak was hunting on uncleared muskeg. There were no fences, signs or buildings in the vicinity.

The appellants were all convicted in the Provincial Court of Alberta. They appealed their summary convictions to the Court of Queen's Bench, challenging the constitutionality of the *Wildlife Act* in so far as it might affect them as Crees with status under Treaty No. 8. The Court of Queen's Bench affirmed the convictions. The appellants' appeals to the Alberta Court of Appeal were also dismissed. [...]

Relevant Treaty and Statutory Provisions

The relevant part of *Treaty No. 8*, made 21 June 1899, provides:

> And Her Majesty the Queen hereby agrees with the said Indians that they shall have right to pursue their usual vocations of hunting, trapping and fishing throughout the tract surrendered as heretofore described, subject to such regulations as may from time to time be made by the Government of the country, acting under the authority of Her Majesty, and saving and excepting such tracts as may be required or taken up from time to time for settlement, mining, lumbering, trading or other purposes.

The *Constitution Act, 1930*, s. 1 provides:

> 1. The agreements set out in the Schedule to this Act are hereby confirmed and shall have the force of law notwithstanding anything in the *Constitution Act, 1867*, or any Act amending the same, or any Act of the Parliament of Canada, or in any Order in Council or terms or conditions of union made or approved under any such Act as aforesaid.

The *Natural Resources Transfer Agreement, 1930* is the Schedule referred to in s. 1. Paragraph 12 of the *NRTA* provides:

> 12. In order to secure to the Indians of the Province the continuance of the supply of game and fish for their support and subsistence, Canada agrees that the laws respecting game in force in the Province from time to time shall apply to the Indians within the boundaries thereof, provided, however, that the said Indians shall have the right, which the Province hereby assures to them, of hunting, trapping and fishing game and fish for food at all seasons of the year on all unoccupied Crown lands and on any other lands to which the said Indians may have a right of access.

Section 35(1) of the *Constitution Act, 1982* provides:

> **35.** (1) The existing aboriginal and treaty rights of the aboriginal peoples of Canada are hereby recognized and affirmed.

Sections 26(1) and 27(1) of the *Wildlife Act* provide:

> **26**(1) A person shall not hunt wildlife unless he holds a licence authorizing him, or is authorized by or under a licence, to hunt wildlife of that kind.

> **27**(1) A person shall not hunt wildlife outside an open season or if there is no open season for that wildlife. [...]

Analysis

On this appeal, the extent of the existing right to hunt for food possessed by Indians who are members of bands which were parties to Treaty No. 8 must be determined. The analysis should proceed through three stages. First, it is necessary to decide what effect para. 12 of the *NRTA* had upon the rights enunciated in Treaty No. 8. After resolving which instrument sets out the right to hunt for food, it is necessary to examine the limitations which are inherent in that right. It must be remembered that, even by the terms of Treaty No. 8, the Indians' right to hunt for food was circumscribed by both geographical limitations and by specific forms of government regulation. Second, consideration must then be given to the question of whether the existing right to hunt for food can be exercised on privately owned land. Third, it is necessary to determine whether the impugned sections of the provincial *Wildlife Act* come within the specific types of regulation which have, since 1899, limited and defined the scope of the right to hunt for food. If they do, those sections do not infringe upon an existing treaty right and will be constitutional. If not, the sections may constitute an infringement of the Treaty rights guaranteed by Treaty No. 8, as modified by the *NRTA*. In this case the impugned provisions should be considered in accordance with the principles set out in *R. v. Sparrow*, [1990] 1 S.C.R. 1075, to determine whether they constitute a *prima facie* infringement of the Treaty rights as modified, and if so, whether the infringement can be justified. [...]

The Existing Right to Hunt for Food

The Hunting Right Provided by Treaty No. 8

Treaty No. 8 is one of eleven numbered treaties concluded between the federal government and various Indian bands between 1871 and 1923. Their objective was to facilitate the settlement of the West. Treaty No. 8, made on June 21, 1899, involved the surrender of vast tracts of land in what is now northern Alberta, northeastern British Columbia, northwestern Saskatchewan and part of the Northwest Territories. In exchange for the land, the Crown made a number of commitments, for example, to provide the bands with reserves, education, annuities, farm equipment, ammunition, and relief in times of famine or pestilence. However, it is clear that for the Indians the guarantee that hunting, fishing and trapping rights would continue was the essential element which led to their signing the treaties. The report of the Commissioners who negotiated Treaty No. 8 on behalf of the government underscored the importance to the Indians of the right to hunt, fish and trap. The Commissioners wrote:

> There was expressed at every point the fear that the making of the treaty would be followed by the curtailment of the hunting and fishing privileges. [...]

> We pointed out [...] that the <u>same means of earning a livelihood would continue after the treaty as existed before it,</u> and that the Indians would be expected to make use of them. [...]

> Our chief difficulty was the apprehension that the hunting and fishing privileges were to be curtailed. The provision in the treaty under which ammunition and twine is to be furnished went far in the direction of quieting the fears of the Indians, for they admitted that it would be unreasonable to furnish the means of hunting and fishing if laws were to be enacted which would make hunting and fishing so restricted as to render it impossible to make a livelihood by such pursuits. But over and above the provision, <u>we had to solemnly assure them that only such laws as to hunting and fishing as were in the interest of the Indians and were found necessary in order to protect the fish and fur-bearing animals would be made, and that they would be as free to hunt and fish after the treaty as they would be if they never entered into it.</u> (emphasis added.)

Treaty No. 8, then, guaranteed that the Indians "shall have the right to pursue their usual vocations of hunting, trapping and fishing". The Treaty, however, imposed two limitations on the right to hunt. First, there was a geographic limitation. The right to hunt could be exercised "throughout the tract surrendered [...] saving and excepting such tracts as may be required or taken up from time to time for settlement, mining, lumbering, trading or other purposes". Second, the right could be limited by government regulations passed for conservation purposes.

Impact of Paragraph 12 of the *NRTA*

Principles of Interpretation

At the outset, it may be helpful to once again set out some of the applicable principles of interpretation. First, it must be remembered that a treaty represents an exchange of solemn promises between the Crown and the various Indian nations. It is an agreement whose nature is sacred. [...] Second, the honour of the Crown is always at stake in its dealing with Indian people. Interpretations of treaties and statutory provisions which have an impact upon treaty or aboriginal rights must be approached in a manner which maintains the integrity of the Crown. It is always assumed that the Crown intends to fulfil its promises. No appearance of "sharp dealing" will be sanctioned. [...] Third, any ambiguities or doubtful expressions in the wording of the treaty or document must be resolved in favour of the Indians. A corollary to this principle is that any limitations which restrict the rights of Indians under treaties must be narrowly construed. [...]

Interpreting the NRTA

The issue at this stage is whether the NRTA extinguished and replaced the Treaty No. 8 right to hunt for food. It is my conclusion that it did not. [...]

It has been held that the NRTA had the clear intention of both limiting and expanding the treaty right to hunt. [...]

This Court most recently considered the effect the NRTA had upon treaty rights in *Horseman* (cites omitted). There, it was held that para. 12 of the NRTA evidenced a clear intention to extinguish the treaty protection of the right to hunt commercially. However, it was emphasized that the right to hunt <u>for food</u> continued to be protected and had in fact been expanded by the NRTA. [...]

Pursuant to s. 1 of the *Constitution Act, 1930*, there can be no doubt that para. 12 of the NRTA is binding law. It is the legal instrument which currently sets out and governs the Indian right to hunt. However, the existence of the NRTA has not deprived Treaty No. 8 of legal significance. Treaties are sacred promises and the Crown's honour requires the Court to assume that the Crown intended to fulfil its promises. Treaty rights can only be amended where it is clear that effect was intended. [...] Unless there is a direct conflict between the NRTA and a treaty, the NRTA will not have modified the treaty rights. Therefore, the NRTA language which outlines the right to hunt for food must be read in light of the fact that this aspect of the treaty right continues in force and effect.

Like Treaty No. 8, the NRTA circumscribes the right to hunt for food with respect to both the geographical area within which this right may be exercised as well as the regulations which may properly be imposed by the government. The geographical limitations must now be considered.

Geographical Limitations on the Right to Hunt for Food

Under the NRTA, Indians may exercise a right to hunt for food "on all unoccupied Crown lands and on any other lands to which the said Indians may have a right of access". In the present appeals, the hunting occurred on lands which had been included in the 1899 surrender but were now privately owned. Therefore, it must be determined whether these privately owned lands were "other lands" to which the Indians had a "right of access" under the Treaty.

At this stage, three preliminary points should be made. First, the "right of access" in the NRTA does not refer to a <u>general</u> right of access but, rather, it is limited to a right of access <u>for the purposes of hunting</u>: [...] For example, everyone can travel on public highways, but this general right of access cannot be read as conferring upon Indians a right to hunt on public highways.

Second, because the various treaties affected by the NRTA contain different wording, the extent of the treaty right to hunt on privately owned land may well differ from one treaty to another. While some treaties contain express provisions with respect to hunting on private land, others, such as Treaty No. 8, do not. Under Treaty No. 8, the right to hunt for food could be exercised throughout the tract surrendered" to the Crown "saving and excepting such tracts as may be required or taken up from time to time for settlement, mining, lumbering, trading or other purposes." Accordingly, if the privately owned land is not "required or taken up" in the manner described in Treaty No. 8, it will be land to which the Indians had a right of access to hunt for food.

Third, the applicable interpretative principles must be borne in mind. Treaties and statutes relating to Indians should be liberally construed and any uncertainties, ambiguities or doubtful expressions should be resolved in favour of the Indians. In addition, when considering a treaty, a court must take into account the context in which the treaties were negotiated, concluded and committed to writing. The treaties, as written documents, recorded an agreement that had already been reached orally and they did not always record the full extent of the oral agreement. [...] The treaties were drafted in English by representatives of the Canadian government who, it should be assumed, were familiar with common law doctrines. Yet, the treaties were not translated in written form into the languages (here Cree and Dene) of the various Indian nations who were signatories. Even if they had been, it is unlikely that the Indians, who had a history of communicating only orally, would have understood them any differently. As a result, it is well settled that the words in the treaty must not be interpreted in their strict technical sense nor subjected to rigid modern rules of construction. Rather, they must be interpreted in the sense that they would naturally have been understood by the Indians at the time of the signing. This applies, as well, to those words in a treaty which impose a limitation on the right which has been granted. [...]

The evidence led at trial indicated that in 1899 the Treaty No. 8 Indians would have understood that land had been "required or taken up" when it was being put to a use which was incompatible with the exercise of the right to hunt. [...]

An interpretation of the Treaty properly founded upon the Indians' understanding of its terms leads to the conclusion that the geographical limitation on the existing hunting right should be based upon a concept of visible, incompatible land use. This approach is consistent with the oral promises made to the Indians at the time the Treaty was signed, with the oral history of the Treaty No. 8 Indians, with earlier case law and with the provisions of the Alberta *Wildlife Act* itself.

The Indian people made their agreements orally and recorded their history orally. Thus, the verbal promises made on behalf of the federal government at the times the treaties were concluded are of great significance in their interpretation. Treaty No. 8 was initially concluded with the Indians at Lesser Slave Lake. The Commissioners then traveled to many other bands in the region and sought their adhesion to the Treaty. Oral promises were made with the Lesser Slave Lake band and with the other Treaty signatories and these promises have been recorded in the Treaty Commissioners' Reports and in contemporary affidavits and diaries of interpreters and other government officials who participated in the negotiations. See in particular: Richard Daniel, "The Spirit and Terms of Treaty Eight", in Richard Price, ed., *The Spirit of the Alberta Indian Treaties*

(1979), at pp. 47-100; and René Fumoleau, O.M.I., *As Long as this Land Shall Last: A History of Treaty 8 and Treaty 11, 1870-1939* (1973), at pp. 73-100. The Indians' primary fear was that the treaty would curtail their ability to pursue their livelihood as hunters, trappers and fishers. Commissioner David Laird, as cited in Daniel, "The Spirit and Terms of Treaty Eight", at p. 76, told the Lesser Slave Lake Indians in 1899:

> Indians have been told that if they make a treaty they will not be allowed to hunt and fish as they do now. This is not true. <u>Indians who take treaty will be just as free to hunt and fish all over as they now are.</u>
>
> <u>In return for this the Government expects that the Indians will not interfere with or molest any miner, traveler or settler.</u> (emphasis added.)

Since the Treaty No. 8 lands were not well suited to agriculture, the government expected little settlement in the area. The Commissioners, cited in Daniel, at p. 81, indicated that "it is safe to say that so long as the fur-bearing animals remain, the great bulk of the Indians will continue to hunt and to trap". The promise that this livelihood would not be affected was repeated to all the bands who signed the Treaty. Although it was expected that some white prospectors might stake claims in the north, this was not expected to have an impact on the Indians' hunting rights. [...]

[T]he oral promises made by the Crown's representatives and the Indians' own oral history indicate that it was understood that land would be taken up and occupied in a way which precluded hunting when it was put to a visible use that was incompatible with hunting. Turning to the case law, it is clear that the courts have also accepted this interpretation and have concluded that whether or not land has been taken up or occupied is a question of fact that must be resolved on a case-by-case basis. [...]

The "visible, incompatible use" approach, which focuses upon the use being made of the land, is appropriate and correct. Although it requires that the particular land use be considered in each case, this standard is neither unduly vague nor unworkable.

In summary, then, the geographical limitation on the right to hunt for food is derived from the terms of the particular treaty if they have not been modified or altered by the provisions of para. 12 of the *NRTA*. In this case, the geographical limitation on the right to hunt for food provided by Treaty No. 8 has not been modified by para. 12 of the *NRTA*. Where lands are privately owned, it must be determined on a case-by-case basis whether they are "other lands" to which Indians had a "right of access" under the Treaty. If the lands are occupied, that is, put to visible use which is incompatible with hunting, Indians will not have a right of access. Conversely, if privately owned land is unoccupied and not put to visible use, Indians, pursuant to Treaty No. 8, will have a right of access in order to hunt for food. The facts presented in each of these appeals must now be considered.

The first is Mr. Badger He was hunting on land covered with second growth willow and scrub. Although there were no fences or signs posted on the land, a farm house was located only one quarter of a mile from the place the moose was killed. The residence did not appear to have been abandoned. Second, Mr. Kiyawasew was hunting on a snow-covered field. Although there was no fence, there were run-down barns nearby and signs were posted on the land. Most importantly, the evidence indicated that in the fall, a crop had been harvested from the field. In the situations presented in both cases, it seems clear that the land was visibly being used. Since the appellants did not have a right of access to these particular tracts of land, their treaty right to hunt for food did not extend to hunting there. As a result, the limitations on hunting set out in the *Wildlife Act* did not infringe upon their existing right and were properly applied to these two appellants. The appeals of Mr. Badger and Mr. Kiyawasew must, therefore, be dismissed.

However, Mr. Ominayak's appeal presents a different situation. He was hunting on uncleared muskeg. No fences or signs were present. Nor were there any buildings located near the site of the kill. Although it was privately owned, it is apparent that this land was not being put to any visible use which would be incompatible with the Indian right to hunt for food. Accordingly, the geographical limitations upon the Treaty right to hunt for food did not preclude Mr. Ominayak from hunting upon this parcel of land. This, however, does not dispose of his appeal. It remains to be seen whether the existing right to hunt was in any other manner circumscribed by a form of government regulation which is permitted under the Treaty.

Permissible Regulatory Limitations on the Right to Hunt for Food

Pursuant to the provisions of s. 88 of the *Indian Act*, provincial laws of general application will apply to Indians. This is so except where they conflict with aboriginal or treaty rights, in which case the latter must prevail. [...] In any event, the regulation of Indian hunting rights would ordinarily come within the jurisdiction of the Federal government and not the Province. However, the issue does not arise in this case since we are dealing with the right to hunt provided by Treaty No. 8 as modified by the *NRTA*. Both the Treaty and the *NRTA* specifically provided that the right would be subject to regulation pertaining to conservation.

Treaty No. 8 provided that the right to hunt would be "subject to such regulations as may from time to time be made by the Government of the country". In the West, a wide range of legislation aimed at conserving game had been enacted by the government beginning as early as the 1880s. Acts and regulations pertaining to conservation measures continued to be passed throughout the entire period during which the numbered treaties were concluded. In *Horseman* (cites omitted), the aim and intent of the regulations was recognized. At page 935, I noted:

> Before the turn of the century the federal game laws of the Unorganized Territories provided for a total ban on hunting certain species (bison and musk oxen) in order to preserve both the species and the supply of game for Indians in the future. See *The Unorganized Territories' Game Preservation Act, 1894*, S.C.

1894, c. 31, ss. 2, 4 to 8 and 26. Even then the advances in firearms and the more efficient techniques of hunting and trapping, coupled with the habitat loss and the over-exploitation of game, (undoubtedly by Europeans more than by Indians), had made it essential to impose conservation measures to preserve species and to provide for hunting for future generations. Moreover, beginning in 1890, provision was made in the federal *Indian Act* for the Superintendent General to make the game laws of Manitoba and the Unorganized Territories applicable to Indians. See *An Act further to amend "The Indian Act" chapter forty-three of the Revised Statutes*, S.C. 1890, c. 29, s. 10. A similar provision was in force in 1930. See *Indian Act*, R.S.C. 1927, c. 98, s. 69.

In light of the existence of these conservation laws prior to signing the Treaty, the Indians would have understood that, by the terms of the Treaty, the government would be permitted to pass regulations with respect to conservation. This concept was explicitly incorporated into the *NRTA* in a modified form providing for Provincial regulatory authority in the field of conservation. Paragraph 12 of the *NRTA* begins by stating its purpose:

> 12.   In order to secure to the Indians of the Province the continuance of the supply of game and fish for their support and subsistence, Canada agrees <u>that the laws respecting game in force in the Province from time to time shall apply to the Indians</u>. [...] (emphasis added.)

It follows that by the terms of both the Treaty and the *NRTA*, provincial game laws would be applicable to Indians so long as they were aimed at conserving the supply of game. However, the provincial government's regulatory authority under the Treaty and the *NRTA* did not extend beyond the realm of conservation. It is the constitutional provisions of para. 12 of the *NRTA* authorizing provincial regulations which make it unnecessary to consider s. 88 of the *Indian Act* and the general application of provincial regulations to Indians.

The licensing provisions contained in the *Wildlife Act* are in part, but not wholly, directed towards questions of conservation. At first blush, then, they may seem to form part of the permissible government regulation which can establish the boundaries of the existing right to hunt for food. However, the partial concern with conservation does not automatically lead to the conclusion that s. 26(1) is permissible regulation. It must still be determined whether the manner in which the licensing scheme is administered conflicts with the hunting right provided under Treaty No. 8 as modified by the *NRTA*.

This analysis should take into account the wording of the treaty and the *NRTA*. I believe this to be appropriate since the object will be to determine first whether there has been a *prima facie* infringement of the Treaty No. 8 right to hunt as modified by the *NRTA* and secondly if there is such an infringement whether it can be justified. In essence, we are dealing with a modified treaty right. This, I believe, follows from the principle referred to earlier that treaty rights should only be considered to be modified if a clear intention to do so has been manifested, in this case, by the *NRTA*. Further, the solemn promises made in the treaty should be altered or modified as little as possible. The *NRTA* clearly intended to modify the right to hunt. It did so by eliminating the right to hunt commercially and by preserving and extending the right to hunt for food. The Treaty right thus modified pertains to the right to hunt for food which prior to the Treaty was an aboriginal right.

For reasons that I will amplify later, it seems logical and appropriate to apply the recently formulated *Sparrow* test in these circumstances. I would add that it can properly be inferred that the concept of reasonableness forms an integral part of the *Sparrow* test. It follows that this concept should be taken into account in the consideration of the justification of an infringement. As a general rule the criteria set out in *Sparrow*, supra, should be applied. However, the reasons in *Sparrow*, supra, make it clear that the suggested criteria are neither exclusive nor exhaustive. It follows that additional criteria may be helpful and applicable in the particular situation presented.

Conflict Between the Wildlife Act and Rights Under Treaty No. 8

It has been recognized that aboriginal and treaty rights are not absolute. The reasons in *Sparrow*, supra, made it clear that aboriginal rights may be overridden if the government is able to justify the infringement. [...]

There is no doubt that aboriginal and treaty rights differ in both origin and structure. Aboriginal rights flow from the customs and traditions of the native peoples. To paraphrase the words of Judson J. in *Calder*, supra, at p. 328, they embody the right of native people to continue living as their forefathers lived. Treaty rights, on the other hand, are those contained in official agreements between the Crown and the native peoples. Treaties are analogous to contracts, albeit of a very solemn and special, public nature. They create enforceable obligations based on the mutual consent of the parties. It follows that the scope of treaty rights will be determined by their wording, which must be interpreted in accordance with the principles enunciated by this Court.

This said, there are also significant aspects of similarity between aboriginal and treaty rights. Although treaty rights are the result of mutual agreement, they, like aboriginal rights, may be unilaterally abridged. [...] It follows that limitations on treaty rights, like breaches of aboriginal rights, should be justified.

In addition, both aboriginal and treaty rights possess in common a unique, *sui generis* nature. [...] In each case, the honour of the Crown is engaged through its relationship with the native people. [...]

The wording of s. 35(1) of the *Constitution Act, 1982* supports a common approach to infringements of aboriginal and treaty rights. It provides that "[t]he existing aboriginal and treaty rights of the aboriginal peoples of Canada are hereby recognized and affirmed". In *Sparrow*, supra, Dickson C.J. and La Forest J. appeared to acknowledge the need for justification in the treaty context. They said this at pp. 1118-19 in relation to *R. v. Eninew* (1984), 12 C.C.C. (3d) 365 (Sask. C.A.), a case which considered the effect of the *Migratory Birds Convention Act* on rights guaranteed under Treaty No. 10:

As we have pointed out, management and conservation of resources is indeed an important and valid legislative objective. Yet, the fact that the objective is of a "reasonable" nature cannot suffice as constitutional recognition and affirmation of aboriginal rights. <u>Rather, the regulations enforced pursuant to a conservation or management objective may be scrutinized according to the justificatory standard outlined above</u>. (emphasis added.)

This standard of scrutiny requires that the Crown demonstrate that the legislation in question advances important general public objectives in such a manner that it ought to prevail. [...]

[A]ny *prima facie* infringement of the rights guaranteed under Treaty No. 8 or the *NRTA* must be justified. How should the infringement of a treaty right be justified? Obviously, the challenged limitation must be considered within the context of the treaty itself. Yet, the recognized principles to be considered and applied in justification should generally be those set out in *Sparrow*, supra. There may well be other factors that should influence the result. The *Sparrow* decision itself recognized that it was not setting a complete catalogue of factors. Nevertheless, these factors may serve as a rough guide when considering the infringement of treaty rights.

Prima Facie Infringement of the Treaty Right to hunt as modified by the *NRTA*

The licensing provisions of the *Wildlife Act* address two objectives: public safety and conservation. These objectives, in and of themselves, are not unconstitutional. However, it is evident from the wording of the Act and its regulations that the manner in which the licensing scheme is set up results in a *prima facie* infringement of the Treaty No.8 right to hunt as modified by the *NRTA*. The statutory scheme establishes a two-step licensing process. The public safety component is the first one that is engaged. [...]

Standing on its own, the requirement that all hunters take gun safety courses and pass hunting competency tests makes eminently good sense. This protects the safety of everyone who hunts, including Indians. [...]

While the general safety component of the licensing provisions may not constitute a *prima facie* infringement, the conservation component appears to present just such an infringement. Provincial regulations for conservation purposes are authorized pursuant to the provisions of the *NRTA*. However, the routine imposition upon Indians of the specific limitations that appear on the face of the hunting licence may not be permissible if they erode an important aspect of the Indian hunting rights. This Court has held on numerous occasions that there can be no limitation on the method, timing and extent of Indian hunting under a Treaty. I would add that a Treaty as amended by the *NRTA* should be considered in the same manner. [...]

Under the present licensing scheme, an Indian who has successfully passed the approved gun safety and hunting competency courses would not be able to exercise the right to hunt without being in breach of the conservation restrictions imposed with respect to the hunting method, the kind and numbers of game, the season and the permissible hunting area, all of which appear on the face of the licence. Moreover, while the Minister may determine how many licences will be made available and what class of licence these will be, no provisions currently exist for "hunting for food" licences.

At present, only sport and commercial hunting are licensed. It is true that the regulations do provide for a subsistence hunting licence. See Alta. Reg. 50/87, s. 25; Alta. Reg. 95/87, s. 7. However, its provisions are so minimal and so restricted that it could never be considered a licence to hunt for food as that term is used in Treaty No. 8 and as it is understood by the Indians. Accordingly, there is no provision for a licence which does not contain the facial restrictions set out earlier. Finally, there is no provision which would guarantee to Indians preferential access to the limited number of licences, nor is there a provision that would exempt them from the licence fee. As a result, Indians, like all other Albertans, would have to apply for a hunting licence from the same limited pool of licences. Further, if they were fortunate enough to be issued a licence, they would have to pay a licensing fee, effectively paying for the privilege of exercising a treaty right. This is clearly in conflict with both the Treaty and *NRTA* provisions.

The present licensing system denies to holders of treaty rights as modified by the *NRTA* the very means of exercising those rights. Limitations of this nature are in direct conflict with the treaty right. Therefore, it must be concluded that s. 26(1) of the *Wildlife Act* conflicts with the hunting right set out in Treaty No. 8 as modified by the *NRTA*.

Accordingly, it is my conclusion that the appellant, Mr. Ominayak, has established the existence of a *prima facie* breach of his treaty right. It now falls to the government to justify that infringement.

<u>Justification</u>

In my view justification of provincial regulations enacted pursuant to the *NRTA* should meet the same test for justification of treaty rights that was set out in *Sparrow*. The reason for this is obvious. The effect of para. 12 of the *NRTA* is to place the Provincial government in exactly the same position which the Federal Crown formerly occupied. Thus the Provincial government has the same duty not to infringe unjustifiably the hunting right provided by Treaty No. 8 as modified by the *NRTA*. Paragraph 12 of the *NRTA* provides that the province may make laws for a conservation purpose, subject to the Indian right to hunt and fish for food. Accordingly, there is a need for a means to assess which conservation laws will if they infringe that right, nevertheless be justifiable. [...]

In the present case, the government has not led any evidence with respect to justification. In the absence of such evidence, it is not open to this Court to supply its own justification. Section 26(1) of the *Wildlife Act* constitutes a *prima facie* infringement of the appellant Mr. Ominayak's treaty right to hunt. Yet, the issue of conservation is of such importance that a new trial must be ordered so that the question of justification may be addressed. [...]

[Sopinka J. [Lamer C.J. concurring] agreed with the reasons and disposition of Cory J. He found, however, that Treaty No. 8 had merged with the *NRTA*, making the latter the sole source of the rights asserted.]

MARSHALL v. THE QUEEN
[1999] 3 S.C.R. 456.

[Marshall caught 463 pounds of eels which he sold for $787.10. He was prosecuted for selling eels without a licence, fishing without a licence and fishing during the close season with illegal nets. He rested his defense entirely on an alleged treaty right arising under the Treaty of Peace and Friendship concluded by Charles Lawrence, Govr and Comr. in Chief of Nova Scotia and Paul Laurent, Chief of the tribe of LaHave Indians on March 10, 1760.]

The judgment of Lamer C.J. and L'Heureux-Dubé, Cory, Iacobucci and Binnie JJ. was delivered by

BINNIE J. — [...]

¶ 5 The starting point for the analysis of the alleged treaty right must be an examination of the specific words used in any written memorandum of its terms. In this case, the task is complicated by the fact the British signed a series of agreements with individual Mi'kmaq communities in 1760 and 1761 intending to have them consolidated into a comprehensive Mi'kmaq treaty that was never in fact brought into existence. The trial judge, Embree Prov. Ct. J., found that by the end of 1761 all of the Mi'kmaq villages in Nova Scotia had entered into separate but similar treaties. Some of these documents are missing. Despite some variations among some of the documents, Embree Prov. Ct. J. was satisfied that the written terms applicable to this dispute were contained in a Treaty of Peace and Friendship entered into by Governor Charles Lawrence on March 10, 1760, which in its entirety provides as follows:

[Chief Laurent promised that the tribe would "not molest any of His Majesty's subjects or their dependents;" would not entice any British soldiers to desert; would settle disputes according to British law, not private revenge; that English prisoners would be freed; that the tribe would not assist the Kings enemies "nor hold any manner of Commerce traffick nor intercourse with them;" and that "we will not traffick, barter or Exchange any Commodities in any manner but with such persons or the managers of such Truck houses as shall be appointed or Established by His Majesty's Governor at Lunenbourg or Elsewhere in Nova Scotia or Accadia."]

¶ 6 The underlined portion of the document, the so-called "trade clause", is framed in negative terms as a restraint on the ability of the Mi'kmaq to trade with non-government individuals. A "truckhouse" was a type of trading post. The evidence showed that the promised government truckhouses disappeared from Nova Scotia within a few years and by 1780 a replacement regime of government licensed traders had also fallen into disuse while the British Crown was attending to the American Revolution. [...]

¶ 7 The appellant's position is that the truckhouse provision not only incorporated the alleged right to trade, but also the right to pursue traditional hunting, fishing and gathering activities in support of that trade. It seems clear that the words of the March 10, 1760 document, standing in isolation, do not support the appellant's argument. The question is whether the underlying negotiations produced a broader agreement between the British and the Mi'kmaq, memorialized only in part by the Treaty of Peace and Friendship, that would protect the appellant's activities that are the subject of the prosecution. I should say at the outset that [...] in my view, the treaty rights are limited to securing "necessaries" (which I construe in the modern context, as equivalent to a moderate livelihood), and do not extend to the open-ended accumulation of wealth. The rights thus construed, however, are in my opinion, treaty rights within the meaning of s. 35 of the *Constitution Act, 1982*, and are subject to regulations that can be justified under the *Badger* test (*R. v. Badger*, [1996] 1 S.C.R 771). [...]

<u>Evidentiary Sources</u>

¶ 9 The Court of Appeal took a strict approach to the use of extrinsic evidence when interpreting the Treaties of 1760-61. Roscoe and Bateman JJ.A. stated at p.194: "While treaties must be interpreted in their historical context, extrinsic evidence cannot be used as an aid to interpretation, in the absence of ambiguity". I think this approach should be rejected for at least three reasons.

¶ 10 Firstly, even in a modern commercial context, extrinsic evidence is available to show that a written document does not include all of the terms of an agreement. [...]

¶ 11 Secondly, even in the context of a treaty document that purports to contain all of the terms, this Court has made clear in recent cases that extrinsic evidence of the historical and cultural context of a treaty may be received even absent any ambiguity on the face of the treaty. [...]

¶ 12 Thirdly, where a treaty was concluded verbally and afterwards written up by representatives of the Crown, it would be unconscionable for the Crown to ignore the oral terms while relying on the written terms, *per* Dickson J. (as he then was) in *Guerin v. The Queen*, [1984] 2 S.C.R. 335. Dickson J. stated for the majority, at p. 388:

> Nonetheless, the Crown, in my view, was not empowered by the surrender document to ignore the oral terms which the Band understood would be embodied in the lease. The oral representations form the backdrop against which the Crown's conduct in discharging its fiduciary obligation must be measured. They inform and confine the field of discretion within which the Crown was free to act. After the Crown's agents had induced the Band to surrender its land on the understanding that the land would be leased on certain terms, it would be unconscionable to permit the Crown simply to ignore those terms.

The *Guerin* case is a strong authority in this respect because the surrender there could only be accepted by the Governor in Council, who was not made aware of any oral terms. The surrender could *not* have been accepted by the departmental officials who were present when the Musqueam made known their conditions. Nevertheless, the Governor in Council was held bound by the oral terms which "the Band understood would be embodied in the lease" (p. 388). In this case, unlike *Guerin*, the Governor did have authority to bind the Crown and was present when the aboriginal leaders made known their terms.

¶ 13 The narrow approach applied by the Court of Appeal to the use of extrinsic evidence apparently derives from the comments of Estey J. in *R. v. Horse*, [1988] 1 S.C.R. 187 [...]

¶ 14 Subsequent cases have distanced themselves from a "strict" rule of treaty interpretation, as more recently discussed by Cory J., in *Badger, supra,* at para. 52:

> [...] when considering a treaty, a court must take into account the context in which the treaties were negotiated, concluded and committed to writing. The treaties, as written documents, recorded an agreement that had already been reached orally and they did not always record the full extent of the oral agreement:(cites omitted). The treaties were drafted in English by representatives of the Canadian government who, it should be assumed, were familiar with common law doctrines. Yet, the treaties were not translated in written form into the languages (here Cree and Dene) of the various Indian nations who were signatories. Even if they had been, it is unlikely that the Indians, who had a history of communicating only orally, would have understood them any differently. As a result, it is well settled that the words in the treaty must not be interpreted in their strict technical sense nor subjected to rigid modern rules of construction. (emphasis added.)

"Generous" rules of interpretation should not be confused with a vague sense of after-the-fact largesse. The special rules are dictated by the special difficulties of ascertaining what in fact was agreed to. The Indian parties did not, for all practical purposes, have the opportunity to create their own written record of the negotiations. Certain assumptions are therefore made about the Crown's approach to treaty making (honourable) which the Court acts upon in its approach to treaty interpretation (flexible) as to the existence of a treaty (*Sioui*, at p. 1049 (cites omitted)), the completeness of any written record (the use, e.g., of context and implied terms to make honourable sense of the treaty arrangement: *Simon v. The Queen*, [1985] 2 S.C.R. 387, and *R. v. Sundown*, [1999] 1 S.C.R. 393), and the interpretation of treaty terms once found to exist (*Badger*). The bottom line is the Court's obligation is to "choose from among the various possible interpretations of the common intention [at the time the treaty was made] the one which best reconciles" the Mi'kmaq interests and those of the British Crown (*Sioui, per* Lamer J., at p. 1069 (emphasis added)). [...]

[His Lordship reviewed the documentary record and expert evidence before concluding that "The written text is incomplete" (para 41). His Lordship then turned to ascertaining the terms of the treaty.]

¶ 41 Having concluded that the written text is incomplete, it is necessary to ascertain the treaty terms not only by reference to the fragmentary historical record, as interpreted by the expert historians, but also in light of the stated objectives of the British and Mi'kmaq in 1760 and the political and economic context in which those objectives were reconciled.

¶ 42 [...] The right to fish is not mentioned in the March 10, 1760 document, nor is it expressly noted elsewhere in the records of the negotiation put in evidence. This is not surprising. As Dickson J. mentioned with reference to the west coast in *Jack,* supra, at p. 311, in colonial times the perception of the fishery resource was one of "limitless proportions".

¶ 43 The law has long recognized that parties make assumptions when they enter into agreements about certain things that give their arrangements efficacy. Courts will imply a contractual term on the basis of presumed intentions of the parties where it is necessary to assure the efficacy of the contract, e.g., where it meets the "officious bystander test". [...] Here, if the ubiquitous officious bystander had said, "This talk about truckhouses is all very well, but if the Mi'kmaq are to make these promises, will they have the right to hunt and fish to catch something to trade at the truckhouses?", the answer would have to be, having regard to the honour of the Crown, "of course". If the law is prepared to supply the deficiencies of written contracts prepared by sophisticated parties and their legal advisors in order to produce a sensible result that accords with the intent of both parties, though unexpressed, the law cannot ask less of the honour and dignity of the Crown in its dealings with First Nations. [...]

[The *Sioui* and *Sundown*] cases employed the concept of implied rights to support the meaningful exercise of express rights granted to the first nations in circumstances where no such implication might necessarily have been made absent the *sui generis* nature of the Crown's relationship to aboriginal people. While I do not believe that in ordinary commercial situations a right to trade implies any right of access to things to trade, I think the honour of the Crown requires nothing less in attempting to make sense of the result of these 1760 negotiations. [...]

¶ 47 The Crown objects strongly to any suggestion that the treaty conferred "*preferential* trading rights". I do not think the appellant needs to show *preferential* trading rights. He only has to show *treaty* trading rights. The settlers and the military undoubtedly hunted and fished for sport or necessaries as well, and traded goods with each other. The issue here is not so much the content of the rights or liberties as the level of legal protection thrown around them. [...]

¶ 49 This appeal puts to the test the principle, emphasized by this Court on several occasions, that the honour of the Crown is always at stake in its dealings with aboriginal people. This is one of the principles of interpretation set forth in *Badger*, supra, by Cory J., at para. 41:

> [...] the honour of the Crown is always at stake in its dealings with Indian people. Interpretations of treaties and statutory provisions which have an impact upon treaty or aboriginal rights must be approached in a manner which maintains the integrity of the Crown. It is always assumed that the Crown intends to fulfil its promises. No appearance of "sharp dealing" will be sanctioned. [...]

¶ 52 I do not think an interpretation of events that turns a positive Mi'kmaq trade demand into a negative Mi'kmaq covenant is consistent with the honour and integrity of the Crown. Nor is it consistent to conclude that the Lieutenant Governor, seeking in good faith to address the trade demands of the Mi'kmaq, accepted the Mi'kmaq suggestion of a trading facility while denying any treaty protection to Mi'kmaq access to the things that were to be traded, even though these things were identified and priced in the treaty negotiations. This was not a commercial contract. The trade arrangement must be interpreted in a manner which gives meaning and substance to the promises made by the Crown. In my view, with respect, the interpretation adopted by the courts below left the Mi'kmaq with an empty shell of a treaty promise. [...]

¶ 53 The appellant argues that the Crown has been in breach of the treaty since 1762, when the truckhouses were terminated, or at least since the 1780s when the replacement system of licensed traders was abandoned. This argument suffers from the same quality of unreasonableness as does the Crown's argument that the treaty left the Mi'kmaq with nothing more than a negative covenant. It was established in *Simon*, supra, at p. 402, that treaty provisions should be interpreted "in a flexible way that is sensitive to the evolution of changes in normal" practice, and *Sundown*, supra, at para. 32, confirms that courts should not use a "frozen-in-time" approach to treaty rights. The appellant cannot, with any show of logic, claim to exercise his treaty rights using an outboard motor while at the same time insist on restoration of the peculiar 18th century institution known as truckhouses.

¶ 54 The Crown, on the other hand, argues that the truckhouse was a time-limited response to a temporary problem. As my colleague McLachlin J. sets out at para. 96, the "core" of the treaty was said to be that "[t]he Mi'kmaq agreed to forgo their trading autonomy and the general trading rights they possessed as British subjects, and to abide by the treaty trade regime. The British, in exchange, undertook to provide the Mi'kmaq with stable trading outlets where European goods were provided at favourable terms while the exclusive trade regime existed". My disagreement with that view, with respect, is that the aboriginal people, as found by the trial judge, relied on European powder, shot and other goods and pushed a trade agenda with the British because their alternative sources of supply had dried up; the real inhibition on trade with the French was not the treaty but the absence of the French, whose military had retreated up the St. Lawrence and whose settlers had been expelled; there is no suggestion in the negotiating records that the truckhouse system was a sort of transitional arrangement expected to be temporary, it only became temporary because the King unexpectedly disallowed the enabling legislation passed by the Nova Scotia House of Assembly; and the notion that the truckhouse was merely a response to a trade restriction overlooks the fact the truckhouse system offered very considerable financial benefits to the Mi'kmaq which they would have wanted to exploit, restriction or no restriction. The promise of access to "necessaries" through trade in wildlife was the key point, and where a right has been granted, there must be more than a mere disappearance of the mechanism created to facilitate the exercise of the right to warrant the conclusion that the right itself is spent or extinguished.

¶ 55 The Crown further argues that the treaty rights, if they exist at all, were "subject to regulation, *ab initio*". The effect, it is argued, is that no *Badger* justification would be required. The Crown's attempt to distinguish *Badger* is not persuasive. *Badger* dealt with treaty rights which were specifically expressed in the treaty (at para. 31) to be "subject to such regulations as may from time to time be made by the Government of the country". Yet the Court concluded that a *Sparrow*-type justification was required.

¶ 56 My view is that the surviving substance of the treaty is not the literal promise of a truckhouse, but a treaty right to continue to obtain necessaries through hunting and fishing by trading the products of those traditional activities subject to restrictions that can be justified under the *Badger* test.

The Limited Scope of the Treaty Right

¶ 57 The Crown expresses the concern that recognition of the existence of a constitutionally entrenched right with, as here, a trading aspect, would open the floodgates to uncontrollable and excessive exploitation of the natural resources. Whereas hunting and fishing for food naturally restricts quantities to the needs and appetites of those entitled to share in the harvest, it is argued that there is no comparable, built-in restriction associated with a trading right, short of the paramount need to conserve the resource. The Court has already addressed this issue in [previous cases]. The ultimate fear is that the appellant, who in this case fished for eels from a small boat using a fyke net, could lever the treaty right into a factory trawler in Pomquet Harbour gathering the available harvest in preference to all non-aboriginal commercial or recreational fishermen. (This is indeed the position advanced by the intervener the Union of New Brunswick Indians.) This fear (or hope) is based on a misunderstanding of the narrow ambit and extent of the treaty right.

¶ 58 The recorded note of February 11, 1760 was that "there might be a Truckhouse established, for the furnishing them with <u>necessaries</u>" (emphasis added). What is contemplated therefore is not a right to trade generally for economic gain, but rather a right to trade for necessaries. The treaty right is a regulated right and can be contained by regulation within its proper limits.

¶ 59 The concept of "necessaries" is today equivalent to the concept of what Lambert J.A., in *R. v. Van der Peet* (1993), 80 B.C.L.R. (2d) 75, at p. 126, described as a "moderate livelihood". Bare subsistence has thankfully receded over the last couple of centuries as an appropriate standard of life for aboriginals and non-aboriginals alike. A moderate livelihood includes such basics as "food, clothing and housing, supplemented by a few amenities", but not the accumulation of wealth (*Gladstone*, supra, at para. 165). It addresses day-to-day needs. This was the common intention in 1760. It is fair that it be given this interpretation today.

¶ 60 [...] In this case, equally, it is not suggested that Mi'kmaq trade historically generated "wealth which would exceed a sustenance lifestyle". Nor would anything more have been contemplated by the parties in 1760.

¶ 61 Catch limits that could reasonably be expected to produce a moderate livelihood for individual Mi'kmaq families at present-day standards can be established by regulation and enforced without violating the treaty right. In that case, the regulations would accommodate the treaty right. Such regulations would *not* constitute an infringement that would have to be justified under the *Badger* standard.

Application to the Facts of this Case

¶ 62 The appellant is charged with three offences: the selling of eels without a licence, fishing without a licence and fishing during the close season with illegal nets. These acts took place at Pomquet Harbour, Antigonish County. For Marshall to have satisfied the regulations, he was required to secure a licence under [the Regulations].

¶ 63 [The Regulations] place the issuance of licences within the absolute discretion of the Minister. [...]

¶ 64 [T]here is nothing in these regulations which gives direction to the Minister to explain how she or he should exercise this discretionary authority in a manner which would respect the appellant's treaty rights. This Court has had the opportunity to review the effect of discretionary licensing schemes on aboriginal and treaty rights: (cites omitted). The test for infringement under s. 35(1) of the *Constitution Act, 1982* was set out in *Sparrow*, supra, at p. 1112:

> To determine whether the fishing rights have been interfered with such as to constitute a *prima facie* infringement of s. 35(1), certain questions must be asked. First, is the limitation unreasonable? Second, does the regulation impose undue hardship? Third, does the regulation deny to the holders of the right their preferred means of exercising that right? The onus of proving a *prima facie* infringement lies on the individual or group challenging the legislation.

Lamer C.J. in *Adams*, supra, applied this test to licensing schemes and stated as follows at para. 54:

> In light of the Crown's unique fiduciary obligations towards aboriginal peoples, <u>Parliament may not simply adopt an unstructured discretionary administrative regime which risks infringing aboriginal rights in a substantial number of applications in the absence of some explicit guidance</u>. If a statute confers an administrative discretion which may carry significant consequences for the exercise of an aboriginal right, the statute or its delegate regulations must outline specific criteria for the granting or refusal of that discretion which seek to accommodate the existence of aboriginal rights. In the absence of such specific guidance, the statute will fail to provide representatives of the Crown with sufficient directives to fulfil their fiduciary duties, and the statute will be found to represent an infringement of aboriginal rights under the *Sparrow* test. (emphasis added.)

Cory J. in *Badger*, supra, at para. 79, found that the test for infringement under s. 35(1) of the *Constitution Act, 1982* was the same for both aboriginal and treaty rights, and thus the words of Lamer C.J. in *Adams*, although in relation to the infringement of aboriginal rights, are equally applicable here. There was nothing at that time which provided the Crown officials with the "sufficient directives" necessary to ensure that the appellant's treaty rights would be respected. To paraphrase *Adams*, at para. 51, under the applicable regulatory regime, the appellant's exercise of his treaty right to fish and trade for sustenance was exercisable only at the absolute discretion of the Minister. Mi'kmaq treaty rights were not accommodated in the Regulations because, presumably, the Crown's position was, and continues to be, that no such treaty rights existed. In the circumstances, the purported regulatory prohibitions against fishing without a licence [...] and of selling eels without a licence [...] do *prima facie* infringe the appellant's treaty rights under the Treaties of 1760-61 and are inoperative against the appellant unless justified under the *Badger* test.

¶ 65 Further, the appellant was charged with fishing during the close season with improper nets, contrary to s. 20 of the *Maritime Provinces Fishery Regulations*. Such a regulation is also a *prima facie* infringement, as noted by Cory J. in *Badger*, supra, at para. 90: "This Court has held on numerous occasions that there can be no limitation on the method, timing and extent of Indian hunting under a Treaty", apart, I would add, from a treaty limitation to that effect.

¶ 66 The appellant caught and sold the eels to support himself and his wife. Accordingly, the close season and the imposition of a discretionary licensing system would, if enforced, interfere with the appellant's treaty right to fish for trading purposes, and the ban on sales would, if enforced, infringe his right to trade for sustenance. In the absence of any justification of the regulatory prohibitions, the appellant is entitled to an acquittal. [...]

The reasons of Gonthier and McLachlin JJ. were delivered by

McLACHLIN J. (dissenting) — [...]

¶ 70 I conclude that the Treaties of 1760-61 created an exclusive trade and truckhouse regime which implicitly gave rise to a limited Mi'kmaq right to bring goods to British trade outlets so long as this regime was extant. The Treaties of 1760-61 granted neither a freestanding right to truckhouses nor a general underlying right to trade outside of the exclusive trade and truckhouse regime. The system of trade exclusivity and correlative British trading outlets died out in the 1780s and with it, the incidental right to bring goods to trade. There is therefore no existing right to trade in the Treaties of 1760-61 that exempts the appellant from the federal fisheries legislation. The charges against him stand. [...]

MARSHALL v. THE QUEEN [MARSHALL II]
[1999] 3 S.C.R. 533.

¶ 1 **THE COURT** — The intervener, the West Nova Fishermen's Coalition (the "Coalition"), applies for a rehearing to have the Court address the regulatory authority of the Government of Canada over the east coast fisheries together with a new trial to allow the Crown to justify for conservation or other purposes the licensing and closed season restriction on the exercise of the appellant's treaty right, and for an order that the Court's judgment, dated September 17, 1999, [1999] 3 S.C.R. 456, be stayed in the meantime. The application is opposed by the Crown, the appellant Marshall and the other interveners. [...]

¶ 4 In its majority judgment, the Court acquitted the appellant of charges arising out of catching 463 pounds of eel and selling them for $787.10. The acquittal was based on a treaty made with the British in 1760, and more particularly, on the oral terms reflected in documents made by the British at the time of the negotiations but recorded incompletely in the "truckhouse" clause of the written treaty. The treaty right permits the Mi'kmaq community to work for a living through continuing access to fish and wildlife to trade for "necessaries", which a majority of the Court interpreted as "food, clothing and housing, supplemented by a few amenities". [...]

¶ 14 As stated in para. 56 of the September 17, 1999 majority judgment, the treaty right was "to continue to obtain necessaries through hunting and fishing by trading the products of those traditional activities <u>subject to restrictions that can be justified under the *Badger* test</u>" (emphasis added). [...] The Crown, as stated, did not offer any evidence or argument justifying the licensing and closed season restrictions. [...] The issue of justification was not before the Court and no judgment was made about whether or not such restrictions could have been justified in relation to the eel fishery had the Crown led evidence and argument to support their applicability. [...]

¶ 19 At the end of the day, it is always open to the Minister (as it was here) to seek to justify the limitation on the treaty right because of the need to conserve the resource in question or for other compelling and substantial public objectives, as discussed below. Equally, it will be open to an accused in future cases to try to show that the treaty right was intended in 1760 by *both* sides to include access to resources other than fish, wildlife and traditionally gathered things such as fruits and berries. The word "gathering" in the September 17, 1999 majority judgment was used in connection with the types of the resources traditionally "gathered" in an aboriginal economy and which were thus reasonably in the contemplation of the parties to the 1760-61 treaties. While treaty rights are capable of evolution within limits, as discussed below, their subject matter (absent a new agreement) cannot be wholly transformed. Certain unjustified assumptions are made in this regard by the Native Council of Nova Scotia on this motion about "the effect of the economic treaty right on forestry, minerals and natural gas deposits offshore". The Union of New Brunswick Indians also suggested on this motion a need to "negotiate an integrated approach dealing with all resources coming within the purview of fishing, hunting and gathering which includes harvesting from the sea, the forests and the land". This extended interpretation of "gathering" is not dealt with in the September 17, 1999 majority judgment, and negotiations with respect to such resources as logging, minerals or offshore natural gas deposits would go beyond the subject matter of this appeal.

¶ 20 The September 17, 1999 majority judgment did not rule that the appellant had established a treaty right "to gather" anything and everything physically capable of being gathered. The issues were much narrower and the ruling was much narrower. No evidence was drawn to our attention, nor was any argument made in the course of this appeal, that trade in logging or minerals, or the exploitation of off-shore natural gas deposits, was in the contemplation of either or both parties to the 1760 treaty; nor was the argument made that exploitation of such resources could be considered a logical evolution of treaty rights to fish and wildlife or to the type of things traditionally "gathered" by the Mi'kmaq in a 1760 aboriginal lifestyle. It is of course open to native communities to assert broader treaty rights in that regard, but if so, the basis for such a claim will have to be established in proceedings where the issue is squarely raised on proper historical evidence, as was done in this case in relation to fish and wildlife. [...]

¶ 21 The fact the Crown elected not to try to justify a closed season on the eel fishery at issue in this case cannot be generalized, as the Coalition's question implies, to a conclusion that closed seasons can never be imposed as part of the government's regulation of the Mi'kmaq limited commercial "right to fish". A "closed season" is clearly a potentially available management tool, but its application to treaty rights will have to be justified for conservation or other purposes. In the absence of such justification, an accused who establishes a treaty right is ordinarily allowed to exercise it. [...]

¶ 25 With all due respect to the Coalition, the government's general regulatory power is clearly affirmed. It is difficult to believe that further repetition of this fundamental point after a rehearing would add anything of significance to what is already stated in the September 17, 1999 majority judgment.

¶ 26 As for the specific matter of licences, the conclusion of the majority judgment was *not* that licensing schemes as such are invalid, but that the imposition of a licensing restriction on the appellant's exercise of the treaty right had not been justified for conservation or other public purposes. [...]

¶ 27 Although no evidence or argument was put forward to justify the licensing requirement in this case, a majority of the Court nevertheless referred at para. 64 of its September 17, 1999 decision to *R. v. Nikal*, [1996] 1 S.C.R. 1013, where Cory J., for the Court, dealt with a licensing issue as follows, at paras. 91 and 92:

> With respect to licensing, the appellant [aboriginal accused] takes the position that once his rights have been established, anything which affects or interferes with the exercise of those rights, no matter how insignificant, constitutes a *prima facie* infringement. It is said that a licence by its very existence is an infringement of the aboriginal right since it infers that government permission is needed to exercise the right and that the appellant is not free to follow his own or his band's discretion in exercising that right.

> This position cannot be correct. It has frequently been said that rights do not exist in a vacuum, and that the rights of one individual or group are necessarily limited by the rights of another. The ability to exercise personal or group rights is necessarily limited by the rights of others. The government must ultimately be able to determine and direct the way in which these rights should interact. [...] Absolute freedom without any restriction necessarily infers a freedom to live without any laws. Such a concept is not acceptable in our society.

¶ 28 The justification for a licensing requirement depends on facts. The Crown in this case declined to offer evidence or argument to support the imposition of a licensing requirement in relation to the small-scale commercial eel fishery in which the appellant participated. [...]

¶ 30 In this case, the prosecution of the appellant was directed to a "closed season" in the eel fishery which the Crown did not try to justify, and that is the precise context in which the majority decision of September 17, 1999 is to be understood. No useful purpose would be served for those like the Coalition who are interested in justifying a closed season in the lobster fishery if a rehearing or a new trial were ordered in this case, which related only to the closed season in the eel fishery. [...]

¶ 32 Mention has already been made of "the *Badger* test" by which governments may justify restrictions on the exercise of treaty rights. The Court in *Badger* extended to treaties the justificatory standard developed for aboriginal rights in *Sparrow*, supra. Cory J. set out the test, in *Badger*, supra, at para. 97 as follows:

> In *Sparrow*, at p. 1113, it was held that in considering whether an infringement of aboriginal or treaty rights could be justified, the following questions should be addressed sequentially:

> First, is there a valid legislative objective? Here the court would inquire into whether the objective of Parliament in authorizing the department to enact regulations regarding fisheries is valid. The objective of the department in setting out the particular regulations would also be scrutinized. [...]

At page 1114, the next step was set out in this way:

> If a valid legislative objective is found, the analysis proceeds to the second part of the justification issue. Here, we refer back to the guiding interpretive principle derived from *Taylor and Williams* and *Guerin*, supra. That is, the honour of the Crown is at stake in dealings with aboriginal peoples. The special trust relationship and the responsibility of the government vis-à-vis aboriginals must be the first consideration in determining whether the legislation or action in question can be justified. [...]

Finally, at p. 1119, it was noted that further questions might also arise depending on the circumstances of the inquiry:

> These include the questions of whether there has been as little infringement as possible in order to effect the desired result; whether, in a situation of expropriation, fair compensation is available; and, whether the aboriginal group in question has been consulted with respect to the conservation measures being implemented. The aboriginal peoples, with their history of conservation-consciousness and interdependence with natural resources, would surely be expected, at the least, to be informed regarding the determination of an appropriate scheme for the regulation of the fisheries.

> We would not wish to set out an exhaustive list of the factors to be considered in the assessment of justification. Suffice it to say that recognition and affirmation requires sensitivity to and respect for the rights of aboriginal peoples on behalf of the government, courts and indeed all Canadians. (emphasis in original.)

¶ 33 The majority judgment of September 17, 1999 did not put in doubt the validity of the *Fisheries Act* or any of its provisions. What it said, in para. 66, was that, "the close season and the imposition of a discretionary licensing system would, if enforced, interfere with the appellant's treaty right to fish for trading purposes, and the ban on sales would, if enforced, infringe his right to trade for sustenance. In the absence of any justification of the regulatory prohibitions, the appellant is entitled to an acquittal" (emphasis added). Section 43 of the Act sets out the basis of a very broad regulatory authority over the fisheries which may extend to the native fishery where justification is shown. [...]

> (Pursuant to this regulatory power, the Governor in Council had, in fact, adopted the *Aboriginal Communal Fishing Licences Regulations*, discussed below.) Although s. 7(1) of the *Fisheries Act* purports to grant the Minister an "absolute discretion" to issue or not to issue leases and licences, this discretion must be read together with the authority of the Governor in Council under s. 43(*f*) to make regulations "respecting the issue, suspension and cancellation of licences and leases". Specific criteria must be established for the exercise by the Minister of his or her discretion to grant or refuse licences in a manner that recognizes and accommodates the existence of an aboriginal or treaty right.[cite to *R. v. Adams*, [1996] 3 S.C.R. 101, at para. 54 omitted]

> While *Adams* dealt with an aboriginal right, the same principle applies to treaty rights.

¶ 34 The *Aboriginal Communal Fishing Licences Regulations*, SOR/93-332, referred to in the September 17, 1999 majority judgment, deal with the food fishery. These regulations provide specific authority to impose conditions where justified respecting the species and quantities of fish that are permitted to be taken or transported; the locations and times at which landing of fish is permitted; the method to be used for the landing of fish and the methods by which the quantity of the fish is to be determined; the information that a designated person or the master of a designated vessel is to report to the Minister or a person specified by the licence holder, prior to commencement of fishing; the locations and times of inspections of the contents of the hold and the procedure to be used in conducting those inspections; the maximum number of persons or vessels that may be designated to carry on fishing and related activities; the maximum number of designated persons who may fish at any one time; the type, size and quantity of fishing gear that may be used by a designated person; and the disposition of fish caught under the authority of the licence. The Governor in Council has the power to amend the *Aboriginal Communal Fishing Licences Regulations* to accommodate a limited commercial fishery as described in the September 17, 1999 majority judgment in addition to the food fishery.

¶ 35 Despite the limitations on the Court's ability in a prosecution to address broader issues not at issue between the Crown and the defence, the majority judgment of September 17, 1999 nevertheless referred to the Court's principal pronouncements on the various grounds on which the exercise of treaty rights may be regulated. These include the following grounds:

¶ 36 (a) *The treaty right itself is a limited right.* The September 17, 1999 majority judgment referred to the "narrow ambit and extent of the treaty right" (para. 57). In its written argument, the Coalition says that the only regulatory method specified in that judgment was a limit on the quantities of fish required to satisfy the Mi'kmaq need for necessaries. This is not so. What the majority judgment said is that the Mi'kmaq treaty right does not extend *beyond* the quantities required to satisfy the need for necessaries. The Court stated at para. 61 of the September 17, 1999 majority judgment:

> Catch limits that could reasonably be expected to produce a moderate livelihood for individual Mi'kmaq families at present-day standards can be established by regulation and enforced <u>without violating the treaty right</u>. In that case, the regulations would accommodate the treaty right. Such regulations would <u>*not*</u> constitute an infringement that would have to be justified under the *Badger* standard. [Underlining added; italics in original.]

¶ 37 In other words, regulations that do no more than reasonably <u>define</u> the Mi'kmaq treaty right in terms that can be administered by the regulator and understood by the Mi'kmaq community that holds the treaty rights do not impair the exercise of the treaty right and therefore do not have to meet the *Badger* standard of justification.

¶ 38 Other limitations apparent in the September 17, 1999 majority judgment include the local nature of the treaties, the communal nature of a treaty right, and the fact it was only hunting and fishing resources to which access was affirmed, together with traditionally gathered things like wild fruit and berries. With regard to the Coalition's concern about the fishing rights of its members, para. 38 of the September 17, 1999 majority judgment noted the trial judge's finding that the Mi'kmaq had been fishing to trade with non-natives for over 200 years prior to the 1760-61 treaties. The 1760-61 treaty rights were thus from their inception enjoyed alongside the commercial and recreational fishery of non-natives. Paragraph 42 of the September 17, 1999 majority judgment recognized that, unlike the scarce fisheries resources of today, the view in 1760 was that the fisheries were of "limitless proportions". On this point, it was noted in para. 53 of the September 17, 1999 majority judgment:

> It was established in *Simon* [*Simon v. The Queen*, [1985] 2 S.C.R. 387], at p. 402, that treaty provisions should be interpreted "in a flexible way that is sensitive to the evolution of changes in normal" practice, and *Sundown* [*R. v. Sundown*, [1999] 1 S.C.R. 393], at para. 32, confirms that courts should not use a "frozen-in-time" approach to treaty rights.

The Mi'kmaq treaty right to participate in the largely unregulated commercial fishery of 1760 has evolved into a treaty right to participate in the largely regulated commercial fishery of the 1990s. [...] Equally, the Mi'kmaq treaty right to hunt and trade in game is not now, any more than it was in 1760, a *commercial* hunt that must be satisfied before non-natives have access to the same resources for recreational or commercial purposes. The emphasis in 1999, as it was in 1760, is on assuring the Mi'kmaq equitable access to identified resources for the purpose of earning a moderate living. In this respect, a treaty right differs from an aboriginal right which in its origin, by definition, was exclusively exercised by aboriginal people prior to contact with Europeans.

¶ 39 Only those regulatory limits that take the Mi'kmaq catch *below* the quantities reasonably expected to produce a moderate livelihood or other limitations that are not inherent in the limited nature of the treaty right itself have to be justified according to the *Badger* test.

¶ 40 (b) *The paramount regulatory objective is the conservation of the resource. This responsibility is placed squarely on the Minister and not on the aboriginal or non-aboriginal users of the resource.* The September 17, 1999 majority decision referred to *Sparrow, supra,* which affirmed the government's paramount authority to act in the interests of conservation. This principle was repeated in *R. v. Gladstone,* [1996] 2 S.C.R. 723, *Nikal, supra, Adams, supra, R. v. Côté,* [1996] 3 S.C.R. 139, and *Delgamuukw, supra,* all of which were referred to in the September 17, 1999 majority judgment.

¶ 41 (c)*The Minister's authority extends to other compelling and substantial public objectives which may include economic and regional fairness, and recognition of the historical reliance upon, and participation in, the fishery by non-aboriginal groups.* The Minister's regulatory authority is not limited to conservation. This was recognized in the submission of the appellant Marshall in opposition to the Coalition's motion. He acknowledges that "it is clear that limits may be imposed to conserve the species/stock being exploited and to protect public safety". Counsel for the appellant Marshall goes on to say: "Likewise, Aboriginal harvesting preferences, <u>together with non-Aboriginal regional/community dependencies</u>, may be taken into account in devising regulatory schemes" (emphasis added). In *Sparrow, supra,* at p. 1119, the Court said "We would not wish to set out an exhaustive list of the factors to be considered in the assessment of justification." It is for the Crown to propose what controls are justified for the management of the resource, and why they are justified. In *Gladstone, supra* (cited at para. 57 of the September 17, 1999 majority judgment), the Chief Justice commented on the differences between a native *food* fishery and a native *commercial* fishery, and stated at para. 75 as follows:

> Although by no means making a definitive statement on this issue, I would suggest that with regards to the distribution of the fisheries resource after conservation goals have been met, objectives such as the pursuit of economic and regional fairness, and the recognition of the historical reliance upon, and participation in, the fishery by non-aboriginal groups, are the type of objectives which can (at least in the right circumstances)

satisfy this standard. In the right circumstances, such objectives are in the interest of all Canadians and, more importantly, the reconciliation of aboriginal societies with the rest of Canadian society may well depend on their successful attainment. (emphasis in original.)

This observation applies with particular force to a treaty right. The aboriginal right at issue in *Gladstone*, supra, was by definition exercised exclusively by aboriginal people prior to contact with Europeans. As stated, no such exclusivity ever attached to the treaty right at issue in this case. Although we note the acknowledgment of the appellant Marshall that "non-Aboriginal regional/community dependencies [...] may be taken into account in devising regulatory schemes", and the statements in *Gladstone*, supra, which support this view, the Court again emphasizes that the specifics of any particular regulatory regime were not and are not before us for decision.

¶ 42 In the case of any treaty right which may be exercised on a commercial scale, the natives constitute only one group of participants, and regard for the interest of the non-natives, as stated in *Gladstone*, supra, may be shown in the right circumstances to be entirely legitimate. Proportionality is an important factor. In asking for a rehearing, the Coalition stated that it is the lobster fishery "in which the Applicant's members are principally engaged and in which, since release of the Reasons for Judgment, controversy as to exercise of the treaty right has most seriously arisen". In response, the affidavit evidence of Dr. Gerard Hare, a fisheries biologist of some 30 years' experience, was filed. The correctness of Dr. Hare's evidence was not contested in reply by the Coalition. Dr. Hare estimated that the non-native lobster fishery in Atlantic Canada, excluding Newfoundland, sets about 1,885,000 traps in inshore waters each year and "[t]o put the situation in perspective, the recent Aboriginal commercial fisheries appear to be minuscule in comparison". It would be significant if it were established that the combined aboriginal food and limited commercial fishery constitute only a "minuscule" percentage of the non-aboriginal commercial catch of a particular species, such as lobster, bearing in mind, however, that a fishery that is "minuscule" on a provincial or regional basis could nevertheless raise conservation issues on a local level if it were concentrated in vulnerable fishing grounds.

¶ 43 (d) *Aboriginal people are entitled to be consulted about limitations on the exercise of treaty and aboriginal rights.* The Court has emphasized the importance in the justification context of consultations with aboriginal peoples. Reference has already been made to the rule in *Sparrow*, supra, at p. 1114, repeated in *Badger*, supra, at para. 97, that:

> The special trust relationship and the responsibility of the government vis-à-vis aboriginals must be the first consideration in determining whether the legislation or action in question can be justified.

The special trust relationship includes the right of the treaty beneficiaries to be consulted about restrictions on their rights, although, as stated in *Delgamuukw*, supra, at para. 168:

> The nature and scope of the duty of consultation will vary with the circumstances.

This variation may reflect such factors as the seriousness and duration of the proposed restriction, and whether or not the Minister is required to act in response to unforeseen or urgent circumstances. As stated, if the consultation does not produce an agreement, the adequacy of the justification of the government's initiative will have to be litigated in the courts.

¶ 44 (e) *The Minister has available for regulatory purposes the full range of resource management tools and techniques, provided their use to limit the exercise of a treaty right can be justified.* If the Crown establishes that the limitations on the treaty right are imposed for a pressing and substantial public purpose, after appropriate consultation with the aboriginal community, and go no further than is required, the same techniques of resource conservation and management as are used to control the non-native fishery may be held to be justified. Equally, however, the concerns and proposals of the native communities must be taken into account, and this might lead to different techniques of conservation and management in respect of the exercise of the treaty right.

¶ 45 In its written argument on this appeal, the Coalition also argued that no treaty right should "operate to involuntarily displace any non-aboriginal existing participant in any commercial fishery", [...] According to this submission, if a treaty right would be disruptive, its existence should be denied or the treaty right should be declared inoperative. This is not a legal principle. It is a political argument. What is more, it is a political argument that was expressly rejected by the political leadership when it decided to include s. 35 in the *Constitution Act, 1982*. [...] It is the obligation of the courts to give effect to that national commitment. No useful purpose would be served by a rehearing of this appeal to revisit such fundamental and incontrovertible principles. [...]

¶ 46 At no stage of this appeal, either before or after September 17, 1999, has any government requested a stay or suspension of judgment. The Coalition asks for the stay based on its theory that the ruling created broad gaps in the regulatory scheme, but for the reasons already explained, its contention appears to be based on a misconception of what was decided on September 17, 1999. The appellant should not have his acquittal kept in jeopardy while issues which are much broader than the specifics of his prosecution are litigated. The request for a stay of the acquittal directed on September 17, 1999, is therefore denied. [...]

PART V

SOME PROBLEMS OF CONSTITUTIONAL REMEDIES

1.   Reading Down

- Research Note -
THE PRESUMPTION OF CONSTITUTIONALITY

Prior to proclamation of the *Canadian Charter of Rights and Freedoms*, Canadian courts had established a modest doctrine of the presumption of constitutionality as part of their responsibilities to hear cases concerning the division of powers. The doctrine had three separate branches: (1) a canon of construction, (2) a presumption of regularity and (3) a true evidentiary presumption of fact. See generally, J.E. Magnet, "The Presumption of Constitutionality" (1980), 18 *Osgoode Hall L.J.* 87. These uses of the doctrine addressed specific problems in court supervision of legal federalism. As will be seen, the transposition of the doctrine to a *Charter of Rights* context poses difficulties.

CONSTRUCTION OF THE CHALLENGED ACT

It is well established in Canadian federalism jurisprudence that if a challenged act is susceptible of two constructions, one of which is constitutionally defective, it will be construed so as to render it *intra vires*. Counsel regularly makes two submissions: (1) the act is *ultra vires* and (2) as a matter of construction the challenged act cannot apply to the attacker's circumstances. The rule flows from the presumption of constitutionality, as Fauteux J. explained in *Reference Re Farm Products Marketing Act (Ontario)*, [1957] S.C.R. 198:

There is a *presumptia juris* as to the existence of the *bona fide* intention of a legislative body to confine itself to its own sphere and a presumption of similar nature that general words in a statute are not intended to extend its operation beyond the territorial authority of the Legislature.

Academic commentators term the phenomenon "reading down"; the wide reach of the statute is narrowed so as to avoid offending constitutional prohibitions. Similarly, the courts will not invalidate a wide grant of power because it might lead to abuse; legislative or administrative misconduct is never assumed. More than speculation or conjecture is needed to sustain a conclusion of constitutional incompetence. As Mr. Justice Ritchie explained in *McNeil v. Nova Scotia Board of Censors*, [1976] 2 S.C.R. 265:

> It is true that no limitations on the authority of the Board are spelled out in the *Act* and that it might be inferred that it *could* possibly effect some of the rights listed by Macdonald, J.A., but having regard to the presumption of constitutional validity to which I have already referred, it appears to me that this does not afford justification for concluding that the purpose of the *Act* was directed to the infringement of one or more of those rights. With the greatest respect, this conclusion appears to me to involve speculation as to the intention of the Legislature and the placing of a construction on the statute which is nowhere made manifest by the language employed in enacting it.

All of this is settled law in federalism cases, but it has become problematic with respect to use of the doctrine in *Charter* cases. The Supreme Court is badly split as to the propriety of adopting this principle in *Charter* cases. At issue is whether the *Charter* should be used as the interpretive tool of choice to renovate the areas of law where the *Charter* does not apply directly in light of *Charter* values. A majority of the Supreme Court has seen the role of the presumption of constitutionality as limited to cases where there is a textual ambiguity to be resolved. A minority of the Court has aimed for a wider scope of the *Charter* as an interpretive tool which could be used to renovate statutory and common law rules in light of *Charter* values. For a discussion of the differing points of view within the Court and the relative merits of the positions regarding indirect *Charter* application see Research Note: Indirect *Charter* Application, infra in Vol. II, Section 2(c) - Indirect Application of the *Charter*.

THE PRESUMPTION OF REGULARITY

The presumption of regularity precedes from the Latin maxim, "omnia praesumuntur rite et solemniter esse acta" – all things are presumed to have been done rightly. This maxim, which was adapted from administrative law, proved to be of some limited use in federalism cases.

In *Charter* cases, the presumption of regularity accords with the general principle that he who alleges violation of a *Charter* right has the *onus* to prove facts in support of that claim. Although the "onus" language is now more familiar to *Charter* jurisprudence, in the sense that attacking counsel must prove facts to demonstrate the *Charter* breach, there may be situations where the homely pre-*Charter* maxim "all things are presumed to have been done rightly" will be more appropriate. Could courts not assume, under this doctrine, that police gave a s. 10(b) warning of the right to counsel, if the attacker offers no contrary evidence?

THE EVIDENTIARY PRESUMPTION OF FACTS

In federalism cases, Canadian courts have been prepared to presume to some degree that all constitutional facts necessary to support a challenged exercise of power exist, to presume that certain legislatively declared facts are true, or even to lighten the standard of proof required for certain constitutional facts.

Courts sitting under the *Charter* have yet to make significant use of the "evidentiary presumption of facts" branch of the doctrine. It is easy to see how they will be tempted to do so. Following invalidation of the rape shield (*Criminal Code*, s. 276) by the Supreme Court, the Minister of Justice introduced into Parliament a revised rape shield in December, 1991 (*An Act to Amend the Criminal Code* (sexual assault)). In the preamble to the Bill, Parliament declares certain facts to be true. This is a familiar form of preemptive justification from the pre-*Charter* era when courts were prepared to accord such legislative declarations considerable weight. As the rape shield amendments make clear, Parliament has now expanded the legislative declaration technique in an attempt to protect its enactments from the *Charter*. Parliament will declare facts in order to buttress the Government's attempt to justify its legislation when faced with the inevitable *Charter* challenge.

Out of respect for a coordinate branch of government, the Courts will certainly be tempted to accord Parliament's declaration of fact some weight, as was previously done in federalism cases. Nevertheless, since many *Charter* cases are almost wholly fact dependant, especially as concerns the section 1 justification, it is hard to see how legislative declarations of fact could significantly influence the courts in such circumstances. Parliament's declaration says, in effect, "facts exist to justify the legislation". Yet in many section 1 cases, Parliament has an affirmative onus to prove such facts, see *R. v. Oakes*, [1986] 1 S.C.R. 103. In these fact dependant cases, legislative declarations would pale in the clearer light of the evidentiary standards demanded by *Oakes* and its progeny.

2.   Severability

REFERENCE RE ALTA. BILL OF RIGHTS ACT; A.G. ALTA. v. A.G. CAN.; A.G. CAN. v. A.G. ALTA.
[1947] A.C. 503 at 509 et seq., [1947] 4 D.L.R. I (P.C.).

VISCOUNT SIMON: —

In this matter consolidated appeals by the Attorney-General for Alberta and the Attorney-General for Canada respectively are brought before the Board from a judgment of the Supreme Court of Alberta (Appellate Division) to which, by the order of the Lieutenant-Governor in Council of Alberta, the question of the validity of "The *Alberta Bill of Rights Act* (c. II of 1946) had been referred. The Supreme Court decided that Part II of the Act was invalid inasmuch as the Alberta legislature had no power to make a law in relation to the subject of "banking," which is part of head 15 of the enumerated classes of subjects which s. 91 of the *British North America Act* exclusively assigned to the Parliament of Canada. The Supreme Court also held that Part I of the Act was *intra vires* of the Alberta legislature and did not pronounce that the Act was invalid as a whole. [...]

The Attorney-General for Alberta contended before the Board that Part II was not legislation relating to "banking" within the meaning of head 15 of s. 91, but was in pith and substance legislation relating to "Property and civil rights in the Province" (head 13 of s. 92). The Attorney-General for Canada contended that the decision of the Supreme Court of Alberta that Part II of the Act was invalid was correct and should be upheld, while in the cross-appeal he urged that the rest of the Act was not severable from Part II with the result that the whole Act was invalid. The Canadian Bankers' Association, which was the second respondent in the appeal of the Attorney-General for Alberta, appeared before their Lordships to assist in upholding the decision of the Supreme Court as to Part II of the Act.

Their Lordships have therefore two questions before them, first, as to the validity of Part II of the Act, and secondly, if Part II is held to be invalid, whether Part I of the Act none the less survives as severable and effective legislation.

[Their Lordships concluded that Part II of the Act was legislation in relation to banking, and was therefore beyond the legislative capacity of the Province.]

[...] There remains the second question, whether when Part II has been struck out from the Act as invalid what is left should be regarded as surviving, or whether, on the contrary, the operation of cutting out Part II involves the consequence that the whole Act is a dead letter. This sort of question arises not infrequently and is often raised (as in the present instance) by asking whether the legislation is *intra vires* "either in whole or in part," but this does not mean that when Part II is declared invalid what remains of the Act is to be examined bit by bit in order to determine whether the legislature would be acting within its powers if it passed what remains. The real question is whether what remains is so inextricably bound up with the part declared invalid that what remains cannot independently survive or, as it has sometimes been put, whether on a fair review of the whole matter it can be assumed that the legislature would have enacted what survives without enacting the part that is *ultra vires* at all. Harvey C.J. dealt with the second question very briefly and answered it by merely saying that Part I is *intra vires*. Their Lordships, as just explained, think that notwithstanding the form of the question put, the matter cannot be disposed of so summarily.

Looking at the Act as a whole, it is clear that its intent and purpose is to establish machinery sufficiently complete in itself to secure that, in accordance with the economic concept of social credit, it will severely restrict chartered banks from continuing to carry on a legitimate part of their present operations. When Part II is cut out, what is left? In the first place, there is left the preamble, some of the later paragraphs of which would have little or no application to Part I standing alone. The sixth paragraph, as already pointed out, when reciting that the discharge of the Province's responsibilities necessitates an achievement of two results, is, as to the second suggested result, plainly pointing to Part II. Again, the definition of "social security pension," as meaning the payment to individuals "as herein provided," of claims on goods and services, etc, within the limitations there indicated, is anticipating and pointing to provisions in Part II, such as s. 15(e) and s. 18, sub-s. 1. Their Lordships have already indicated that they cannot suppose that ss. 3 to 8 in Part I are other than preliminaries to what follows, and while it is true that ss. 9 to 12 include a declaration that citizens of Alberta in certain circumstances are entitled to social security pensions, these declarations remain mere aspirations unless Part II operates to provide how this is to be done. The Attorney-General for Alberta ingeniously argued that Part II was only one method of securing these results, and that Part I standing alone left it in the power of the Lieutenant-Governor in Council to make the necessary provisions "by order" in some other undefined and unascertained form; but, in their Lordships' opinion, this is not the scheme of the Act, nor do the words in s. 14 empower the Lieutenant-Governor in Council to make new machinery which will take the place of Part II. The whole thing hangs together, and if Part II goes there is nothing left to be added to the statute law of Alberta which would have any effective operation. The view which their Lordships have formed is confirmed by the language of s. 28, which shows that the Act cannot come into force unless "it is certified [...] that this Act is valid," etc. Since Part II is invalid, there cannot be a certificate that "this Act" is valid, and thus by the terms of the Act itself, the Act cannot ever come into force. For these reasons their Lordships do not find it possible to agree with the Supreme Court of Alberta that, when Part II has gone, there is yet some part of the Act which survives.

Their Lordships will humbly advise His Majesty that Part II of the Act is *ultra vires* and that, having regard to the relation between Part II and the rest of the Act, the Act as a whole cannot be regarded as valid.

- Research Note -
SEVERABILITY

The approach taken in *Reference Re Alta. Bill of Rights Act*, above, reflects a view consistently expressed by the Privy Council and the Supreme Court of Canada. In *A.G. B.C. v. A.G. Can.*, [1937] A.C. 377 (P.C.), the issue was the validity of the *Natural Products Marketing Act*, 1934 (Can.), c. 57. The Act consisted of two parts. Part I established a Dominion Marketing Board. This was empowered to approve marketing schemes and to regulate the manner of distribution of various products. Part II made provision for the appointment of a committee with the power to investigate all matters relating to the production or marketing of regulated products. The purpose of the investigation was to ascertain charges made on the distribution of products. Receipt of excess charges was made an indictable offence.

Affirming the view of the Supreme Court of Canada that the Act was *ultra vires* the Parliament of Canada, the Privy Council struck down the legislation on the ground that it purported to affect property and civil rights in the province. The Board then went on to consider the severability of Part II of the Act which, it was argued, *was* within the competence of Parliament. Speaking for the Board, Lord Atkin addressed this issue:

It was, however, urged before us that provisions of the Act, notably s. 9 in the first Part, and the whole of Part II., are within the competence of Parliament, Sect. 9 because it only purports to deal with inter-Provincial or export trade; and Part II. because it goes no further than the similar provisions in the *Combines Investigation Act*, and is a genuine exercise of the Dominion legislative authority over criminal law. Reference was made to s. 26 of the Act, which is in these terms: "If it be found that Parliament has exceeded its powers in the enactment of one or more of the provisions of this Act, none of the other or remaining provisions of the Act shall therefore be held to be inoperative or *ultra vires*, but the latter provisions shall stand as if they had been originally enacted as separate and independent enactments and as the only provisions of the Act; the intention of Parliament being to give independent effect to the extent of its powers to every enactment and provision in this Act contained."

It is said that this is a plain indication of the intention of the Legislature to pass any portion of the Act which might be valid in itself, in however truncated form the whole Act is left after rejecting the other portions. Moreover, counsel for British Columbia urged the Board to make a declaration that it was only so far as authority was conferred on the Board to deal with local matters not necessarily ancillary to the main power that the Act was *ultra vires*, and that the validity of each scheme must be determined as matters arise under it. No such declaration was asked for from the Supreme Court. British Columbia did not even appear at the hearing in Canada: and there is no claim for such a declaration in the case filed before this Board. It is of special importance in constitutional questions that this Board should, if possible, have the assistance of the opinion of the members of the Supreme Court: and as a general rule the Board will not be prepared in such cases to entertain claims for relief which have never been formulated in the Dominion Court. In no event, therefore, would they have acceded to the request for such a declaration as mentioned above. It does appear that the question of severability was raised in the factums of the Dominion and Ontario, and their Lordships were told, and of course accept the statement, that this point was mentioned to the Supreme Court. It cannot, they think, have been emphasized, for the very careful judgment of the Court makes no mention of it. There appear to be two answers. In the first place, it appears to their Lordships that the whole texture of the Act is inextricably interwoven, and that neither s. 9 nor Part II. can be contemplated as existing independently of the provisions as to the creation of a Board and the regulation of products. There are no separate and independent enactments to which s. 26 could give a real existence. In the second place, both the Dominion and British Columbia in their Cases filed on this appeal assert that the sections now said to be severable are incidental and ancillary to the main legislation. Their Lordships are of opinion that this is true: and as the main legislation is invalid as being in pith and substance an encroachment upon the Provincial rights the sections referred to must fall with it as being in part merely ancillary to it.

3. Reading In and Delayed Remedies

SCHACHTER v. CANADA
[1992] 2 S.C.R. 679, 93 D.L.R. (4th) 1.

[Schachter applied for paternity benefits under section 32 of the *Unemployment Insurance Act*, 1971, S.C. 1970-71-72, c. 48. Section 32 provided for 15 weeks of "parental benefits] in the case of adoptive parents, but made no provision for parental benefits in the case of natural parents. Schachter's application was denied because he was a natural parent.

The lower court found a violation of s. 15 of the *Charter* because s. 32 of the Act discriminated between natural parents and adoptive parents wanting to take parental leave. On appeal to the Supreme Court of Canada, Canada conceded that s. 32 was an equality violation. The court considered the appropriate remedy and whether the remedy properly fell under s. 52(1) or s. 24(1) of the *Charter*. Under s. 52(1), the question was whether a s. 15 violation required that the impugned legislation be declared of no force and effect. Under s. 24(1), the question was whether the court had power to extend legislative benefits.

Section 24(1) of the *Charter* provides: "Anyone whose rights or freedoms, as guaranteed by this *Charter*, have been infringed or denied may apply to a court of competent jurisdiction to obtain such remedy as the Court considers appropriate and just in the circumstances." Section 52(1) of the *Constitution Act, 1982* provides: "The Constitution of Canada is the supreme law of Canada, and any law that is inconsistent with the provisions of the Constitution is, to the extent of the inconsistency, of no force or effect."]

LAMER C.J. (Sopinka, Gonthier, Cory and McLachlin JJ concurring): —

[...] I.   *Reading in as a Remedial Option under Section 52*

A court has flexibility in determining what course of action to take following a violation of the *Charter* which does not survive s. 1 scrutiny. Section 52 of the *Constitution Act, 1982* mandates the striking down of any law that is inconsistent with the provisions of the Constitution, but only "to the extent of the inconsistency". Depending upon the circumstances, a court may simply strike down, it may strike down and temporarily suspend the declaration of invalidity, or it may resort to the techniques of reading down or reading in. In addition, s. 24 of the *Charter* extends to any court of competent jurisdiction the power to grant an "appropriate and just" remedy to "[a]nyone whose [*Charter*] rights and freedoms [...] have been infringed or denied". In choosing how to apply s. 52 or s. 24 a court will determine its course of action with reference to the nature of the violation and the context of the specific legislation under consideration.

A. The Doctrine of Severance

The flexibility of the language of s. 52 is not a new development in Canadian constitutional law. The courts have always struck down laws only to the extent of the inconsistency using the doctrine of severance or "reading down". Severance is used by the courts so as to interfere with the laws adopted by the legislature as little as possible. Generally speaking, when only a part of a statute or provision violates the Constitution, it is common sense that only the offending portion should be declared to be of no force or effect, and the rest should be spared.

Far from being an unusual technique, severance is an ordinary and everyday part of constitutional adjudication. For instance if a single section of a statute violates the Constitution, normally that section may be severed from the rest of the statute so that the whole statute need not be struck down. To refuse to sever the offending part, and therefore declare inoperative parts of a legislative enactment which do not themselves violate the Constitution, is surely the more difficult course to justify. [...]

Where the offending portion of a statute can be defined in a limited manner it is consistent with legal principles to declare inoperative only that limited portion. In that way, as much of the legislative purpose as possible may be realized. However, there are some cases in which to sever the offending portion would actually be more intrusive to the legislative purpose than the alternate course of striking down provisions which are not themselves offensive but which are closely connected with those that are. This concern is reflected in the classic statement of the test for severance in *Attorney-General for Alberta v. Attorney-General for Canada*, [1947] A.C. 503, at p. 518:

> The real question is whether what remains is so inextricably bound up with the part declared invalid that what remains cannot independently survive or, as it has sometimes been put, whether on a fair review of the whole matter it can be assumed that the legislature would have enacted what survives without enacting the part that is *ultra vires* at all.

This test recognizes that the seemingly laudable purpose of retaining the parts of the legislative scheme which do not offend the Constitution rests on an assumption that the legislature would have passed the constitutionally sound part of the scheme without the unsound part. In some cases this assumption will not be a safe one. In those cases it will be necessary to go further and declare inoperative portions of the legislation which are not themselves unsound.

Therefore, the doctrine of severance requires that a court define carefully the extent of the inconsistency between the statute in question and the requirements of the Constitution, and then declare inoperative (a) the inconsistent portion, and (b) such part of the remainder of which it cannot be safely assumed that the legislature would have enacted it without the inconsistent portion.

B. *Reading In as Akin to Severance*

This same approach should be applied to the question of reading in since extension by way of reading in is closely akin to the practice of severance. The difference is the manner in which the extent of the inconsistency is defined. In the usual case of severance the inconsistency is defined as something improperly included in the statute which can be severed and struck down. In the case of reading in the inconsistency is defined as what the statute wrongly excludes rather than what it wrongly includes. Where the inconsistency is defined as what the statute excludes, the logical result of declaring inoperative that inconsistency may be to include the excluded group within the statutory scheme. This has the effect of extending the reach of the statute by way of reading in rather than reading down.

A statute may be worded in such a way that it gives a benefit or right to one group (inclusive wording) or it may be worded to give a right or benefit to everyone except a certain group (exclusive wording). It would be an arbitrary distinction to treat inclusively and exclusively worded statutes differently. To do so would create a situation where the style of drafting would be the single critical factor in the determination of a remedy. This is entirely inappropriate. [...]

There is nothing in s. 52 of the *Constitution Act, 1982* to suggest that the court should be restricted to the verbal formula employed by the legislature in defining the inconsistency between a statute and the Constitution. Section 52 does not say that the words expressing a law are of no force or effect to the extent that they are inconsistent with the Constitution. It says that a law is of no force or effect to the extent of the inconsistency. Therefore, the inconsistency can be defined as what is left out of the verbal formula as well as what is wrongly included. [...]

C. *The Purposes of Reading In and Severance*

(i) *Respect for the Role of the Legislature*

The logical parallels between reading in and severance are mirrored by their parallel purposes. Reading in is as important a tool as severance in avoiding undue intrusion into the legislative sphere. As with severance, the purpose of reading in is to be as faithful as possible within the requirements of the Constitution to the scheme enacted by the Legislature. [...]

Of course, reading in will not always constitute the lesser intrusion for the same reason that severance sometimes does not. In some cases, it will not be a safe assumption that the legislature would have enacted the constitutionally permissible part of its enactment without the impermissible part. For example, in a benefits case, it may not be a safe assumption that the legislature would have enacted a benefits scheme if it were impermissible to exclude particular parties from entitlement under that scheme. [...]

Reading in should therefore be recognized as a legitimate remedy akin to severance and should be available under s. 52 in cases where it is an appropriate technique to fulfil the purposes of the *Charter* and at the same time minimize the interference of the court with the parts of legislation that do not themselves violate the *Charter*.

II. Choice of Remedial Options under Section 52

A. Defining the Extent of the Inconsistency

The first step in choosing a remedial course under s. 52 is defining the extent of the inconsistency which must be struck down. Usually, the manner in which the law violates the *Charter* and the manner in which it fails to be justified under s. 1 will be critical to this determination. [...]

In some circumstances, s. 52(1) mandates defining the inconsistent portion which must be struck down very broadly. This will almost always be the case where the legislation or legislative provision does not meet the first part of the *Oakes* test, in that the purpose is not sufficiently pressing or substantial to warrant overriding a *Charter* right. Although it predates *Oakes*, supra, *R. v. Big M Drug Mart Ltd.*, [1985] 1 S.C.R. 295, provides a clear example. There Dickson C.J. found that the purpose of the *Lord's Day Act*, R.S.C. 1970, c. L-13, was itself inimical to the values of a free and democratic society. The case stands as authority for the proposition that where the purpose of the legislation is itself unconstitutional, the legislation should be struck down in its entirety. Indeed, it is difficult to imagine anything less being appropriate where the purpose of the legislation is deemed unconstitutional; however, I do not wish to foreclose that possibility prematurely.

(ii) The Rational Connection Test

Where the purpose of the legislation or legislative provision is deemed to be pressing and substantial, but the means used to achieve this objective are found not to be rationally connected to it, the inconsistency to be struck down will generally be the whole of the portion of the legislation which fails the rational connection test. [...]

(iii) The Minimal Impairment/Effects Test

Where the second and/or third elements of the proportionality test are not met, there is more flexibility in defining the extent of the inconsistency. For instance, if the legislative provision fails because it is not carefully tailored to be a minimal intrusion, or because it has effects disproportionate to its purpose, the inconsistency could be defined as being the provisions left out of the legislation which would carefully tailor it, or would avoid a disproportionate effect. According to the logic outlined above, such an inconsistency could be declared inoperative with the result that the statute was extended by way of reading in.

Striking down, severing or reading in may be appropriate in cases where the second and/or third elements of the proportionality test are not met. The choice of remedy will be guided by the following considerations.

B. Deciding whether Severance or Reading In is Appropriate

Having determined what the extent of the inconsistency is, the next question is whether that inconsistency may be dealt with by way of severance, or in some cases reading in, or whether an impugned provision must be struck down in its entirety.

(i) Remedial Precision

While reading in is the logical counterpart of severance, and serves the same purposes, there is one important distinction between the two practices which must be kept in mind. In the case of severance, the inconsistent part of the statutory provision can be defined with some precision on the basis of the requirements of the Constitution. This will not always be so in the case of reading in. In some cases, the question of how the statute ought to be extended in order to comply with the Constitution cannot be answered with a sufficient degree of precision on the basis of constitutional analysis. In such a case, it is the legislature's role to fill in the gaps, not the court's.

[T]he Court should not read in in cases where there is no manner of extension which flows with sufficient precision from the requirements of the Constitution. In such cases, to read in would amount to making ad hoc choices from a variety of options, none of which was pointed to with sufficient precision by the interaction between the statute in question and the requirements of the Constitution. This is the task of the legislature, not the courts.

(ii) Interference With The Legislative Objective

The primary importance of legislative objective quickly emerges from decisions of this Court wherein the possibility of reading down or in has been considered and determined inappropriate.

In *Osborne v. Canada (Treasury Board)*, [1991] 2 S.C.R. 69, at p. 104, Sopinka J. emphasized that it is necessary in fashioning a remedy for a *Charter* violation to both "apply the measures which will best vindicate the values expressed in the *Charter*" and "refrain from intruding into the legislative sphere beyond what is necessary". He determined that reading down was not appropriate in that case but concluded, at p. 104: "Reading down may in some cases be the remedy that achieves the objectives to which I have alluded while at the same time constituting the lesser intrusion into the role of the legislature."

The degree to which a particular remedy intrudes into the legislative sphere can only be determined by giving careful attention to the objective embodied in the legislation in question. This objective may, as suggested above, be obvious from the very text of the provision. In other cases, it may only be illuminated through the evidence put forward under the s. 1 analysis, the failure of which would precede this inquiry. A second level of legislative intention may be manifest in the means chosen to pursue that objective. [...]

Even where extension by way of reading in can be used to further the legislative objective through the very means the legislature has chosen, to do so may, in some cases, involve an intrusion into budgetary decisions which cannot be supported. This Court has held, and rightly so, that budgetary considerations cannot be used to justify a violation under s. 1. However, such considerations are clearly relevant once a violation which does not survive s. 1 has been established, s. 52 is determined to have been engaged and the Court turns its attention to what action should be taken thereunder.

Any remedy granted by a court will have some budgetary repercussions whether it be a saving of money or an expenditure of money. Striking down or severance may well lead to an expenditure of money. [...]

In determining whether reading in is appropriate then, the question is not whether courts can make decisions that impact on budgetary policy, it is to what degree they can appropriately do so. A remedy which entails an intrusion into this sphere so substantial as to change the nature of the legislative scheme in question is clearly inappropriate.

(iii) The Change in Significance of the Remaining Portion

Another way of asking whether to read in or sever would be an illegitimate intrusion into the legislative sphere is to ask whether the significance of the part which would remain is substantially changed when the offending part is excised. [...]

The problem with striking down only the inconsistent portion is that the significance of the remaining portion changes so markedly without the inconsistent portion that the assumption that the legislature would have enacted it is unsafe.

In cases where the issue is whether to extend benefits to a group not included in the statute, the question of the change in significance of the remaining portion sometimes focuses on the relative size of the two relevant groups. [...]

Where the group to be added is smaller than the group originally benefitted, this is an indication that the assumption that the legislature would have enacted the benefit in any case is a sound one. When the group to be added is much larger than the group originally benefitted, this could indicate that the assumption is not safe. This is not because of the numbers per se. Rather, the numbers may indicate that for budgetary reasons, or simply because it constitutes a marked change in the thrust of the original program, it cannot be assumed that the legislature would have passed the benefit without the exclusion. In some contexts, the fact that the group to be added is much larger that the original group will not lead to these conclusions. [...]

Other cases have focused on the significance or longstanding nature of the remaining portion. [...]

It is sensible to consider the significance of the remaining portion when asking whether the assumption that the legislature would have enacted the remaining portion is a safe one. If the remaining portion is very significant, or of a long standing nature, it strengthens the assumption that it would have been enacted without the impermissible portion. [...]

It is important that the courts not unjustifiably invade the domain which is properly that of the legislature. In following either of the alternatives above, the court will be interfering to some extent with the efforts of the legislators of the enactment. Where the result is the removing of a protection that is constitutionally encouraged " that is, judicial consideration before incarceration" as opposed to the enlarging of such a protection, it is submitted that the court should favour a result that would expand the group of persons protected rather than remove that protection completely. [...]

(v) Conclusion

It should be apparent from this analysis that there is no easy formula by which a court may decide whether severance or reading in is appropriate in a given case. While respect for the role of the legislature and the purposes of the *Charter* are the twin guiding principles, these principles can only be fulfilled with respect to the variety of considerations set out above which require careful attention in each case.

C. Whether to Temporarily Suspend the Declaration of Invalidity [...]

A court may strike down legislation of a legislative provision but suspend the effect of that declaration until Parliament or the provincial legislature has had an opportunity to fill the void. This approach is clearly appropriate where the striking down of a provision poses a potential danger to the public (*R. v. Swain*, supra) or otherwise threatens the rule of law (*Reference Re Manitoba Language Rights*), [1985] 1 S.C.R. 721). It may also be appropriate in cases of under inclusiveness as opposed to over breadth. For example, in this case some of the interveners argued that in cases where a denial of equal benefit of the law is alleged, the legislation in question is not usually problematic in and of itself. It is its under inclusiveness that is problematic so striking down the law immediately would deprive deserving persons of benefits without providing them to the applicant. At the same time, if there is no obligation on the government to provide the benefits in the first place, it may be inappropriate to go ahead and extend them. The logical remedy is to strike down but suspend the declaration of invalidity to allow the government to determine whether to cancel or extend the benefits.

I would emphasize that the question of whether to delay the effect of a declaration is an entirely separate question from whether reading in or nullification is the appropriate route under s. 52. While delayed declarations are appropriate in some cases, they are not a panacea for the problem of interference with the institution of the legislature under s. 52 of the *Constitution Act, 1982*.

A delayed declaration is a serious matter from the point of view of the enforcement of the *Charter*. A delayed declaration allows a state of affairs which has been found to violate standards embodied in the *Charter* to persist for a time despite the violation. There may be good pragmatic reasons to allow this in particular cases. However, reading in is much preferable where it is appropriate, since it immediately reconciles the legislation in question with the requirements of the *Charter*.

Furthermore, the fact that the court's declaration is delayed is not really relevant to the question of which course of action, reading in or nullification, is less intrusive upon the institution of the legislature. By deciding upon nullification or reading in, the court has already chosen the less intrusive path. If reading in is less intrusive than nullification in a particular case, then there is no reason to think that a delayed nullification would be any better. To delay nullification forces the matter back onto the legislative agenda at a time not of the choosing of the legislature, and within time limits under which the legislature would not normally be forced to act. This is a serious interference in itself with the institution of the legislature. Where reading in is appropriate, the legislature may consider the issue in its own good time and take whatever action it wishes. Thus delayed declarations of nullity should not be seen as preferable to reading in in cases where reading in is appropriate.

The question whether to delay the application of a declaration of nullity should therefore turn not on considerations of the role of the courts and the legislature, but rather on considerations listed earlier relating to the effect of an immediate declaration on the public.

D. Summary

It is valuable to summarize the above propositions with respect to the operation of s. 52 of the *Constitution Act, 1982* before turning to the question of the independent availability of remedies pursuant to s. 24(1) of the *Charter*. Section 52 is engaged when a law is itself held to be unconstitutional, as opposed to simply a particular action taken under it. Once s. 52 is engaged, three questions must be answered. First, what is the extent of the inconsistency? Second, can that inconsistency be dealt with alone, by way of severance or reading in, or are other parts of the legislation inextricably linked to it? Third, should the declaration of invalidity be temporarily suspended? The factors to be considered can be summarized as follows:

(i) The Extent of the Inconsistency

The extent of the inconsistency should be defined:

A.   broadly where the legislation in question fails the first branch of the *Oakes* test in that its purpose is held not to be sufficiently pressing or substantial to justify infringing a *Charter* right or, indeed, if the purpose is itself held to be unconstitutional – perhaps the legislation in its entirety;

B.   more narrowly where the purpose is held to be sufficiently pressing and substantial, but the legislation fails the first element of the proportionality branch of the *Oakes* test in that the means used to achieve that purpose are held not to be rationally connected to it – generally limited to the particular portion which fails the rational connection test; or,

C.   flexibly where the legislation fails the second or third element of the proportionality branch of the *Oakes* test.

(ii) Severance /Reading In

Severance or reading in will be warranted only in the clearest of cases, that is, where each of the following criteria is met:

A. the legislative objective is obvious, or it is revealed through the evidence offered pursuant to the failed s. 1 argument, and severance or reading in would further that objective, or constitute a lesser interference with that objective than would striking down;

B. the choice of means used by the legislature to further that objective is not so unequivocal that severance/reading in would constitute an unacceptable intrusion into the legislative domain; and,

C. severance or reading in would not involve an intrusion into legislative budgetary decisions so substantial as to change the nature of the legislative scheme in question.

(iii) Temporarily Suspending the Declaration of Invalidity

Temporarily suspending the declaration of invalidity to give Parliament or the provincial legislature in question an opportunity to bring the impugned legislation or legislative provision into line with its constitutional obligations will be warranted even where striking down has been deemed the most appropriate option on the basis of one of the above criteria if:

A. striking down the legislation without enacting something in its place would pose a danger to the public;

B. striking down the legislation without enacting something in its place would threaten the rule of law; or,

C. the legislation was deemed unconstitutional because of under inclusiveness rather than over breadth, and therefore striking down the legislation would result in the deprivation of benefits from deserving persons without thereby benefitting the individual whose rights have been violated.

I should emphasize before I move on that the above propositions are intended as guidelines to assist courts in determining what action under s. 52 is most appropriate in a given case, not as hard and fast rules to be applied regardless of factual context.

Section 24(1)

(i) Section 24(1) Alone

Where s. 52 of the *Constitution Act, 1982* is not engaged, a remedy under s. 24(1) of the *Charter* may nonetheless be available. This will be the case where the statute or provision in question is not in and of itself unconstitutional, but some action taken under it infringes a person's *Charter* rights. Section 24(1) would there provide for an individual remedy for the person whose rights have been so infringed.

This course of action has been described as "reading down as an interpretive technique", but it is not reading down in any real sense and ought not to be confused with the practice of reading down as referred to above. It is, rather, founded upon a presumption of constitutionality. It comes into play when the text of the provision in question supports a constitutional interpretation and the violative action taken under it thereby falls outside the jurisdiction conferred by the provision.

(ii) Section 24(1) in Conjunction with Section 52

An individual remedy under s. 24(1) of the *Charter* will rarely be available in conjunction with action under s. 52 of the *Constitution Act, 1982*. Ordinarily, where a provision is declared unconstitutional and immediately struck down pursuant to s. 52, that will be the end of the matter. No retroactive s. 24 remedy will be available. It follows that where the declaration of invalidity is temporarily suspended, a s. 24 remedy will not often be available either. To allow for s. 24 remedies during the period of suspension would be tantamount to giving the declaration of invalidity retroactive effect. Finally, if a court takes the course of reading down or in, a s. 24 remedy would probably only duplicate the relief flowing from the action that court has already taken.

IV. Remedial Options Appropriate to this Case

A. The Nature of the Right Involved

The right which was determined to be violated here is a positive right: the right to equal benefit of the law. Positive rights by their very nature tend to carry with them special considerations in the remedial context. It will be a rare occasion when a benefit conferring scheme is found to have an unconstitutional purpose. Cases involving positive rights are more likely to fall into the remedial classifications of reading down/reading in or striking down and suspending the operation of the declaration of invalidity than to mandate an immediate striking down. Indeed, if the benefit which is being conferred is itself constitutionally guaranteed (for example, the right to vote), reading in may be mandatory. For a court to deprive persons of a constitutionally guaranteed right by striking down under inclusive legislation would be absurd. Certainly the intrusion into the legislative sphere of extending a constitutionally guaranteed benefit is warranted when the benefit was itself guaranteed by the legislature through constitutional amendment.

Other rights will be more in the nature of "negative" rights, which merely restrict the government. However, even in those cases, the rights may have certain positive aspects. For instance, the right to life, liberty and security of the person is in one sense a negative right, but the requirement that the government respect the "fundamental principles of justice" may provide a basis for characterizing s. 7 as a positive right in some circumstances. Similarly, the equality right is a hybrid of sorts since it is neither purely positive nor purely negative. In some contexts it will be proper to characterize s. 15 as providing positive rights.

The benefit with which we are concerned here is a monetary benefit for parents under the *Unemployment Insurance Act, 1971*, not one which Parliament is constitutionally obliged to provide to the included group or the excluded group. What Parliament is obliged to do, by virtue of the conceded s. 15 violation, is equalize the provision of that benefit. The benefit itself is not constitutionally prohibited; it is simply under inclusive. Thus striking down the provision immediately would be inappropriate as such a course of action would deprive eligible persons of a benefit without providing any relief to the respondent. Such a situation demands, at the very least, that the operation of any declaration of invalidity be suspended to allow Parliament time to bring the provision into line with constitutional requirements. [...]

I think it significant and worthy of mention that in the case Parliament did amend the impugned provision following the launching of this action, and that that amendment was not the one that reading in would have imposed. Parliament equalized the benefits given to adoptive parents and natural parents but not on the same terms as they were originally conferred by s. 32. The two groups now receive equal benefits for ten weeks rather than the original fifteen. This situation provides a valuable illustration of the dangers associated with reading in when legislative intention with respect to budgetary issues is not clear. In this case, reading in would not necessarily further the legislative objective and it would definitely interfere with budgetary decisions in that it would mandate the expenditure of a greater sum of money than Parliament is willing or able to allocate to the program in question.

The Constitutional Questions

Following from the above analysis, I would answer the constitutional questions as follows:

1. Is the Federal Court Trial Division, having found that s. 32 of the *Unemployment Insurance Act, 1971* (subsequently s. 20 of the *Unemployment Insurance Act*, R.S.C., 1985, c. U-1) creates unequal benefit contrary to s. 15(1) of the *Canadian Charter of Rights and Freedoms*, by making a distinction between the benefits available to natural and adoptive parents, required by s. 52(1) of the *Constitution Act, 1982* to declare that s. 32 is of no force and effect?

The answer to question one is, in the present circumstances, yes, leaving open the option of suspending the declaration of invalidity for a period of time to allow Parliament to amend the legislation in a way which meets its constitutional obligations. This is not to say that s. 52 does not provide the flexibility to stop short of striking out an unconstitutional provision in its entirety. Given the appropriate circumstances, a court may choose the options of severance or reading in by which to bring the provision in line with the *Charter*. These options should be exercised only in the clearest of cases, keeping in mind the principles articulated above relating to the nature of the right and the specific context of the legislation.

2.   Does s. 24(1) of the *Charter* confer on the Federal Court Trial Division the power to order that natural parents are entitled to benefits on the same terms as benefits are available to adoptive parents under s. 32 (subsequently s. 20) of that Act?

The answer to question two is no. Section 24(1) provides an individual remedy for actions taken under a law which violate an individual's *Charter* rights. Again, however, a limited power to extend legislation is available to courts in appropriate circumstances by way of the power to read in derived from s. 52 of the *Constitution Act, 1982*.

Disposition

In the result, the appeal is allowed and the judgment of the trial judge set aside. Normally, I would order that s. 32 of the *Unemployment Insurance Act, 1971* (subsequently s. 20 of the *Unemployment Insurance Act, 1982*) be struck down pursuant to s. 52 and be declared to be of no force or effect, and I would further suspend the operation of this declaration to allow Parliament to amend the legislation to bring it into line with its constitutional obligations. There is, however, no need for a declaration of invalidity or a suspension thereof at this stage of this matter given the November 1990 repeal and replacement of the impugned provision.

Further, this is not a case in which extending a remedy, for example damages, under s. 24(1) to the respondent would be appropriate. The classic doctrine of damages is that the plaintiff is to be put in the position he or she would have occupied had there been no wrong. In the present case, there are two possible positions the plaintiff could have been in had there been no wrong. The plaintiff could have received the benefit equally with the original beneficiaries, or there could have been no benefit at all, for the plaintiff or the original beneficiaries. The remedial choice under s. 24 thus rests on an assumption about which position the plaintiff would have been in. However, I have already determined which assumption should be made in the analysis under s. 52, and have determined that it cannot be assumed that the legislature would have enacted the benefit to include the plaintiff. Therefore, the plaintiff is in no worse position now than had there been no wrong. [...]

Ls FOREST J. (L'Heureux-Dubé J. concurring): —

I have had the benefit of reading the reasons of the Chief Justice and I agree with his proposed disposition and answers to the constitutional questions. I take this approach on the simple basis that the legislation concerned concededly violates the *Canadian Charter of Rights and Freedoms* and that it does not fall within the very narrow type of cases where only a portion of the legislation may be read down or corrected by reading in material as being obviously intended by the legislature in any event. As the Chief Justice points out, there is a long tradition of reading down legislation, and I see no reason, where it substantially amounts to the same thing, why reading in should not also be done. I note that the Chief Justice states, and I agree, that these devices should only be employed in the clearest of cases. The courts are not in the business of rewriting legislation. I also agree that there is little point in light of Parliament's subsequent action to declare the impugned legislation invalid and then suspend that declaration

That is sufficient to dispose of the case, and I find it unnecessary to elaborate further. In limiting my reasons in this way, however, I would not wish it to be thought that I fundamentally disagree with what the Chief Justice has to say regarding the means for assessing when the techniques of reading down or reading in should be adopted. Indeed, I find his reasons very helpful in this regard. [...]

Where I am most doubtful about the Chief Justice's reasons is in closely tying the process of reading down or reading in with the checklist set forth in *R. v. Oakes*, [1986] 1 S.C.R. 103. Though this may be useful at times, it may, I fear, encourage a mechanistic approach to the process, rather than encourage examination of more fundamental issues, such as those to which I have referred above, issues that go well beyond the factual context.

VRIEND v. ALBERTA
[1998] I S.C.R. 493.

[For a complete summary of the facts and legal issues in *Vriend*, see infra in Vol. II, Section 3(b)(ii). The Supreme Court found that Alberta's *Individual Rights Protection Act* violated s.15(1) of the *Charter* to the extent it did not protect against discrimination based on sexual orientation. A question arose as to the correct remedy.]

[...]

¶ 144 The leading case on constitutional remedies is *Schachter*, supra. Writing on behalf of the majority in *Schachter*, Lamer C.J. stated that the first step in selecting a remedial course under s. 52 is to define the extent of the *Charter* inconsistency which must be struck down. In the present case, that inconsistency is the exclusion of sexual orientation from the protected grounds of the IRPA. As I have concluded above, this exclusion is an unjustifiable infringement upon the equality rights guaranteed in s. 15 of the *Charter*.

¶ 145 Once the *Charter* inconsistency has been identified, the next step is to determine which remedy is appropriate. In *Schachter*, this Court noted that, depending upon the circumstances, there are several remedial options available to a court in dealing with a *Charter* violation that was not saved by s. 1. These include striking down the legislation, severance of the offending sections, striking down or severance with a temporary suspension of the declaration of invalidity, reading down, and reading provisions into the legislation.

¶ 146 Because the *Charter* violation in the instant case stems from an omission, the remedy of reading down is simply not available. Further, I note that given the considerable number of sections at issue in this case and the important roles they play in the scheme of the IRPA as a whole, severance of these sections from the remainder of the Act would be akin to striking down the entire Act.

¶ 147 The appellants suggest that the circumstances of this case warrant the reading in of sexual orientation into the offending sections of the IRPA. However, in the Alberta Court of Appeal, O'Leary J.A. and Hunt J.A. agreed that the appropriate remedy would be to declare the relevant provisions of the IRPA unconstitutional and to suspend that declaration for a period of time to allow the Legislature to address the matter. McClung J.A. would have gone further and declared the IRPA invalid in its entirety. With respect, for the reasons that follow, I cannot agree with either remedy chosen by the Court of Appeal.

¶ 148 In *Schachter*, Lamer C.J. noted that when determining whether the remedy of reading in is appropriate, courts must have regard to the "twin guiding principles", namely, respect for the role of the legislature and respect for the purposes of the *Charter*, which I have discussed generally above. Turning first to the role of the legislature, Lamer C.J. stated at p. 700 that reading in is an important tool in "avoiding undue intrusion into the legislative sphere. [...] [T]he purpose of reading in is to be as faithful as possible within the requirements of the Constitution to the scheme enacted by the Legislature."

¶ 149 He went on to quote the following passage from Carol Rogerson in "The Judicial Search for Appropriate Remedies Under the *Charter*: The Examples of Overbreadth and Vagueness", in R. J. Sharpe, ed., *Charter* Litigation (1987), 233, at p. 288:

> Courts should certainly go as far as required to protect rights, but no further. Interference with legitimate legislative purposes should be minimized and laws serving such purposes should be allowed to remain operative to the extent that rights are not violated. Legislation which serves desirable social purposes may give rise to entitlements which themselves deserve some protection.

¶ 150 As I discussed above, the purpose of the IRPA is the recognition and protection of the inherent dignity and inalienable rights of Albertans through the elimination of discriminatory practices. It seems to me that the remedy of reading in would minimize interference with this clearly legitimate legislative purpose and thereby avoid excessive intrusion into the legislative sphere whereas striking down the IRPA would deprive all Albertans of human rights protection and thereby unduly interfere with the scheme enacted by the Legislature.

¶ 151 I find support for my position in Haig, supra, where the Ontario Court of Appeal read the words "sexual orientation" into s. 3(1) of the *Canadian Human Rights Act*, R.S.C., 1985, c. H-6. At p. 508, Krever J.A., writing for a unanimous court, stated that it was

> inconceivable [...] that Parliament would have preferred no human rights Act over one that included sexual orientation as a prohibited ground of discrimination. To believe otherwise would be a gratuitous insult to Parliament.

¶ 152 Turning to the second of the twin guiding principles, the respondents suggest that the facts of this case are illustrative of a conflict between two grounds, namely, religion and sexual orientation. If sexual orientation were simply read into the IRPA, the respondents contend that this would undermine the ability of the IRPA to provide protection against discrimination based on religion, one of the fundamental goals of that legislation. This result is alleged to be "inconsistent with the deeper social purposes of the *Charter*."

¶ 153 I concluded above that the internal balancing mechanisms of the IRPA were an adequate means of disposing of any conflict that might arise between religion and sexual orientation. Thus, I cannot accept the respondents' assertion that the reading in approach does not respect the purposes of the *Charter*. In fact, as I see the matter, reading sexual orientation into the IRPA as a further ground of prohibited discrimination can only enhance those purposes. The *Charter*, like the IRPA, is concerned with the promotion and protection of inherent dignity and inalienable rights. Thus, expanding the list of prohibited grounds of discrimination in the IRPA allows this Court to act in a manner which, consistent with the purposes of the *Charter*, would augment the scope of the IRPA's protections. In contrast, striking down or severing parts of the IRPA would deny all Albertans protection from marketplace discrimination. In my view, this result is clearly antithetical to the purposes of the *Charter*.

¶ 154 In *Schachter*, supra, Lamer C.J. noted that the twin guiding principles can only be fulfilled if due consideration is given to several additional criteria which further inform the determination as to whether the remedy of reading in is appropriate. These include remedial precision, budgetary implications, effects on the thrust of the legislation, and interference with legislative objectives.

¶ 155 As to the first of the above listed criteria, the court must be able to define with a "sufficient degree of precision" how the statute ought to be extended in order to comply with the Constitution. I do not believe that the present case is one in which this Court has been improperly called upon to fill in large gaps in the legislation. Rather, in my view, there is remedial precision insofar as the insertion of the words "sexual orientation" into the prohibited grounds of discrimination listed in the preamble and ss. 2(1), 3, 4, 7(1), 8(1), 10 and 16(1) of the IRPA will, without more, ensure the validity of the legislation and remedy the constitutional wrong.

[...]

¶ 160 Turning to budgetary repercussions, in the circumstances of the present appeal, such considerations are not sufficiently significant to warrant avoiding the reading in approach. On this issue, the trial judge stated (at p. 18):

> There will undoubtedly be some budgetary impact on the Human Rights Commission as a result of the addition of sexual orientation as a prohibited ground of discrimination. But, unlike *Schachter* [supra], it would not be substantial enough to change the nature of the scheme of the legislation.

Although the scope of this Court's review of the IRPA is considerably broader than that which the trial judge was asked to undertake, as I noted above, having not heard anything persuasive to the contrary, I am not prepared to interfere with the trial judge's findings on this matter.

¶ 161 As to the effects on the thrust of the legislation, it is difficult to see any deleterious impact. All persons covered under the current scope of the IRPA would continue to benefit from the protection provided by the Act in the same manner as they had before the reading in of sexual orientation. Thus, I conclude that it is reasonable to assume that, if the Legislature had been faced with the choice of having no human rights statute or having one that offered protection on the ground of sexual orientation, the latter option would have been chosen. As the inclusion of sexual orientation in the IRPA does not alter the legislation to any significant degree, it is reasonable to assume that the Legislature would have enacted it in any event.

¶ 162 In addition, in *Schachter*, supra, Lamer C.J. noted that, in cases where the issue is whether to extend benefits to a group excluded from the legislation, the question of the effects on the thrust of the legislation will sometimes focus on the size of the group to be added as compared to the group originally benefitted. He quoted with approval from Knodel, supra, where Rowles J. extended the provision of benefits to spouses to include same-sex spouses. In her view, the remedy of reading in was far less intrusive to the intention of the legislature than striking down the benefits scheme because the group to be added was much smaller than the group already receiving the benefits.

¶ 163 Lamer C.J. went on to note that, "[w]here the group to be added is smaller than the group originally benefitted, this is an indication that the assumption that the legislature would have enacted the benefit in any case is a sound one" (p. 712). In the present case, gay men and lesbians are clearly a smaller group than those already benefitted by the IRPA. Thus, in my view, reading in remains the less intrusive option.

¶ 164 The final criterion to examine is interference with the legislative objective. In *Schachter*, Lamer C.J. commented upon this factor as follows (at pp. 707-8):

> The degree to which a particular remedy intrudes into the legislative sphere can only be determined by giving careful attention to the objective embodied in the legislation in question. [...] A second level of legislative intention may be manifest in the means chosen to pursue that objective.

¶ 165 With regard to the first level of legislative intention, as I discussed above, it is clear that reading sexual orientation into the IRPA would not interfere with the objective of the legislation. Rather, in my view, it can only enhance that objective. However, at first blush, it appears that reading in might interfere with the second level of legislative intention identified by Lamer C.J.

¶ 166 As the Alberta Legislature has expressly chosen to exclude sexual orientation from the list of prohibited grounds of discrimination in the IRPA, the respondents argue that reading in would unduly interfere with the will of the

Government. McClung, J.A. shares this view. In his opinion, the remedy of reading in will never be appropriate where a legislative omission reflects a deliberate choice of the legislating body. He states that if a statute is unconstitutional, "the preferred consequence should be its return to the sponsoring legislature for representative, constitutional overhaul" (p. 35). However, as I see the matter, by definition, *Charter* scrutiny will always involve some interference with the legislative will.

¶ 167 Where a statute has been found to be unconstitutional, whether the court chooses to read provisions into the legislation or to strike it down, legislative intent is necessarily interfered with to some extent. Therefore, the closest a court can come to respecting the legislative intention is to determine what the legislature would likely have done if it had known that its chosen measures would be found unconstitutional. As I see the matter, a deliberate choice of means will not act as a bar to reading in save for those circumstances in which the means chosen can be shown to be of such centrality to the aims of the legislature and so integral to the scheme of the legislation, that the legislature would not have enacted the statute without them.

¶ 168 Indeed, as noted by the intervener Canadian Jewish Congress, if reading in is always deemed an inappropriate remedy where a government has expressly chosen a course of action, this amounts to the suggestion that whenever a government violates a *Charter* right, it ought to do so in a deliberate manner so as to avoid the remedy of reading in. In my view, this is a wholly unacceptable result.

¶ 169 In the case at bar, the means chosen by the legislature, namely, the exclusion of sexual orientation from the IRPA, can hardly be described as integral to the scheme of that Act. Nor can I accept that this choice was of such centrality to the aims of the legislature that it would prefer to sacrifice the entire IRPA rather than include sexual orientation as a prohibited ground of discrimination. [...]

¶ 178 When a court remedies an unconstitutional statute by reading in provisions, no doubt this constrains the legislative process and therefore should not be done needlessly, but only after considered examination. However, in my view, the "parliamentary safeguards" remain. Governments are free to modify the amended legislation by passing exceptions and defences which they feel can be justified under s. 1 of the *Charter*. Thus, when a court reads in, this is not the end of the legislative process because the legislature can pass new legislation in response, as I outlined above (see also Hogg and Bushell, supra). Moreover, the legislators can always turn to s. 33 of the *Charter*, the override provision, which in my view is the ultimate "parliamentary safeguard".

¶ 179 On the basis of the foregoing analysis, I conclude that reading sexual orientation into the impugned provisions of the IRPA is the most appropriate way of remedying this under inclusive legislation. The appellants suggest that this remedy should have immediate effect. I agree. There is no risk in the present case of harmful unintended consequences upon private parties or public funds. [...] Further, the mechanisms to deal with complaints of discrimination on the basis of sexual orientation are already in place and require no significant adjustment. [...]

CORBIERE v. CANADA (MINISTER OF INDIAN AND NORTHERN AFFAIRS)
[1999] 2 S.C.R. 203.

[Subsection 77(1) of the *Indian Act*, RSC 1985, c. I-5 established requirements for persons to be eligible to vote in elections for Indian band councils, including that the voter be "ordinarily resident on the reserve". Non-resident members of the Batchewana Indian Band sought a declaration that s. 77(1) violated s. 15(1) of the *Charter*. The trial judge ruled that s.77(1) infringed s. 15(1) rights and could not be justified under s. 1. The Federal Court of Appeal and the Supreme Court agreed. Each court, however, granted a different constitutional remedy. The trial judge declared s. 77(1) invalid in its entirety and suspended the declaration for a period of 10 months for the Batchewana Band alone. The Court of Appeal did not suspend the invalidity of s.77(1), but granted the Batchewana Band a permanent constitutional exemption from the "ordinarily resident on the reserve" provision.

For a full summary of the facts and issues see infra in Vol. II, Section 9(c)(ii)].

L'HEUREUX-DUBÉ J. (Gonthier, Iacobucci and Binnie JJ concurring): —

[...]

¶ 110 In determining the appropriate remedy, the Court must be guided by the principles of respect for the purposes and values of the *Charter*, and respect for the role of the legislature: *Schachter v. Canada*, [1992] 2 S.C.R. 679, at pp. 700-701; *Vriend*, supra, at para. 148. The first principle was well expressed by Sopinka J. in *Osborne v. Canada (Treasury Board)*, [1991] 2 S.C.R. 69, at p. 104:

> In selecting an appropriate remedy under the *Charter* the primary concern of the court must be to apply the measures that will best vindicate the values expressed in the *Charter* and to provide the form of remedy to those whose rights have been violated that best achieves that objective. This flows from the court's role as guardian of the rights and freedoms which are entrenched as part of the supreme law of Canada.

¶ 111 The first question is whether the appropriate remedy is a constitutional exemption, or one that applies in general. The finding of invalidity above relates not only to the Batchewana Band, but to the legislation in general as it applies to all bands. Therefore, in principle there is no reason that the remedy should be confined to the circumstances of the Batchewana Band. A remedy should normally be as extensive as the violation of equality rights which has been found. The constitutional exemption may apply when it has not been proven that legislation is unconstitutional in general, but that it is unconstitutional in its application to a small subsection of those to whom the legislation applies (cites omitted). This is not the case here.

¶ 112 However, the Court of Appeal held that it would be appropriate to grant a constitutional exemption, since other bands may be able to demonstrate an Aboriginal right to exclude non-residents from decision making, which would affect the analysis of the constitutionality of this provision. With all due respect, a constitutional exemption is not an appropriate remedy in this case. If certain bands can demonstrate an Aboriginal or treaty right to restrict non-residents from voting, this in no way affects the constitutionality of the impugned section of the

Indian Act. It is the order in council made pursuant to s 74(1), bringing the band within the application of the *Indian Act's* electoral rules, which would have to be challenged under such a claim. In analysing such a case, it would have to be determined whether an Aboriginal right had been proven, whether the legislation as it then stands infringes that right, and whether that infringement is justified (cites omitted). A court would also be required to examine how s. 25 of the *Charter* functions when Aboriginal rights are challenged, and how it interacts with other interpretive provisions of the *Charter*.

¶ 113 Nor would such a remedy be the order most respectful of the equality rights of off-reserve band members. If a constitutional exemption were granted, this would place a heavy burden on off-reserve band members, since it would require those in each band to take legal action to put forward their claim. Equality within bands does not require such a heavy burden on claimants. In addition, establishing as a principle that where s. 35 Aboriginal rights might be involved, equality rights must be determined on a band-by-band basis would make the equality rights of Aboriginal people much harder to uphold than those of others, in certain cases. For these reasons, the appropriate remedy is one that applies to the legislation in general, under s. 52(1) of the *Constitution Act, 1982*, and not one confined to the Batchewana Band.

¶ 114 The next issue is what form the general remedy will take. The nature of the violation of equality rights that has been found in this case is different than any that this Court has addressed before. It has been found that, though it would be legitimate for Parliament to create different voting rights for reserve residents and people living off-reserve, in a manner that recognizes non-residents' place in the community, it is not legitimate for Parliament to completely exclude them from voting rights. This is also a situation where the primary effects of this decision will not be felt by the government, but by the bands themselves. In respecting the role of Parliament, these factors should be critical.

¶ 115 In my opinion, it would be inappropriate for this Court to "read in" to the *Indian Act* voting rights for non-residents so that they would be voters for certain purposes but not others. This would involve considerable detailed changes to the legislative scheme. Designing such a detailed scheme, and choosing among various possible options, is not an appropriate role for the Court in this case (see *M. v. H.*, supra, at para. 142, per Iacobucci J.).

¶ 116 There are a number of ways this legislation may be changed so that it respects the equality rights of non-resident band members. Because the regime affects band members most directly, the best remedy is one that will encourage and allow Parliament to consult with and listen to the opinions of Aboriginal people affected by it. The link between public discussion and consultation and the principles of democracy was recently reiterated by this Court in *Reference Re Secession of Quebec*, [1998] 2 S.C.R. 217, at para. 68: "a functioning democracy requires a continuous process of discussion". The principle of democracy underlies the Constitution and the *Charter*, and is one of the important factors guiding the exercise of a court's remedial discretion. It encourages remedies that allow the democratic process of consultation and dialogue to occur. [...] The remedies granted under the *Charter* should, in appropriate cases, encourage and facilitate the inclusion in that dialogue of groups particularly affected by legislation. In determining the appropriate remedy, a court should consider the effect of its order on the democratic process, understood in a broad way, and encourage that process. As Iacobucci J. observed in *Vriend*, supra, at para. 176:

> [T]he concept of democracy means more than majority rule as Dickson C.J. so ably reminded us in *Oakes*, supra. In my view, a democracy requires that legislators take into account the interests of majorities and minorities alike, all of whom will be affected by the decisions they make.

¶ 117 Constitutional remedies should encourage the government to take into account the interests, and views, of minorities. In this way, the principle of democracy that was recognized as an underlying principle of the Constitution in *Reference Re Secession of Quebec*, supra, and was emphasized as an important remedial consideration in *Schachter*, supra, and *Vriend*, supra, will best be given expression.

¶ 118 The above principles suggest, in my view, that the appropriate remedy is a declaration that the words "and is ordinarily resident on the reserve" in s. 77(1) are invalid, and that the effect of this declaration of invalidity be suspended for 18 months. The suspension is longer than the period that would normally be allotted in order to give legislators the time necessary to carry out extensive consultations and respond to the needs of the different groups affected. It will also allow Parliament, if it wishes, to modify s. 77(2) at the same time, which contains the same residency requirement for bands whose councillors are elected in electoral sections, and which, given the values espoused in this decision, will also require revision to conform with s. 15(1). Severing the offending words from the rest of the statute will ensure that, should Parliament choose not to act, all non-residents will be included as voters under s. 77(1), but the nature of band governance and the requirements for voting will otherwise remain the same.

¶ 119 I recognize that suspending the effect of the declaration, combined with the extension of the suspension for such a long period is, in the words of the Chief Justice in *Schachter*, supra, at p. 716, "a serious matter from the point of view of the *Charter*. A delayed declaration allows a state of affairs which has been found to violate standards embodied in the *Charter* to persist for a time despite the violation". However, this best embodies the principles of respect for *Charter* rights and respect for democracy that should guide remedial considerations. Should Parliament decide to change the scheme, it will have an extended period of time in which to consult with those affected by the legislation and balance the affected interests in a manner that respects Aboriginal rights and all band members' equality interests. Should Parliament not change the scheme, off-reserve band members will gain voting rights within the existing scheme.

¶ 120 I also recognize that some may see the section, with the words "and is ordinarily residence on the reserve" no longer included, as possibly giving rise to other constitutional issues. In ordering this remedy, the Court does not foreclose the possibility that, if Parliament does not act to change the legislation, s. 77(1) or related sections of the *Indian Act* may be the subject of a constitutional challenge by on-reserve band members or others.

¶ 121 This suspension of the effect of the declaration, along with the extended period of suspension, is ordered to enable Parliament to consult with the affected groups, and to redesign the voting provisions of the *Indian Act* in a nuanced way that respects equality rights and all affected interests, should it so choose. However, should decisions be made during that period without non-residents' involvement that directly affect their interests and which directly prejudice them, it may be that the decisions themselves could be challenged as violations of non-residents' equality rights. The suspension of the effect of the declaration, in other words, is not a suspension of non-residents' equality rights. Decisions must still be made with respect for those rights.

¶ 122 The final determination is whether the Batchewana Band will be exempted from the suspension of the effect of the declaration. In general, litigants who have brought forward a *Charter* challenge should receive the immediate benefits of the ruling, even if the effect of the declaration is suspended [...]. In my opinion, however, this is one of the exceptional cases where immediate relief should not be given to those who brought the action.

¶ 123 Professor Roach in Constitutional Remedies in Canada (loose-leaf), at pp. 14-85 and 14-86, has identified two possible reasons for which, in general, the claimant in a particular case may have the right to an exemption from the suspension of the effect of the declaration of invalidity, and therefore an immediate remedy:

> Corrective justice would suggest that the successful applicant has a right to remedy while regulatory or public law approaches would only be concerned with giving the applicants enough incentive to bring their case to court.

However, I do not believe that either of these considerations applies in the case at bar. What is at issue in this Court is not a remedy affecting band councils elected under the previous regime, but rather a declaration that will have the effect of changing future election rules. If Parliament chooses either not to act, or to change the legislation to conform with this ruling, the respondents will receive a remedy after the period of suspension expires or when the new legislation comes into effect. This both gives them a personal remedy, and gives applicants in analogous situations an incentive to bring their case forward.

¶ 124 Unlike in other cases where this Court has granted an exemption from the suspension, there are strong administrative reasons not to grant immediate relief to the members of the Batchewana Band. If an exemption from the suspension is given, the Batchewana Band will have to adapt to the inclusion of all non-residents as voters within the existing scheme in the short term. This will require some administrative adjustment. If Parliament then decides to amend the legislation, the Batchewana Band and its members will be required to adapt to a third voting system in a short period of time. This would be inappropriate, and inconsistent with the principles underlying constitutional remedies.

[*The concurring opinion of Mclachlin and Bastarache JJ. (Lamer CJ, Cory and Major JJ concurring) is omitted*. These judges agreed with the remedy proposed by L'Heureux-Dubé J.]

M. v. H.
[1999] 2 S.C.R. 3.

[M and H were a cohabiting same-sex couple. Upon dissolution of the relationship M applied for support under s. 29 of the *Family Law Act*. The support was denied since the definition of "spouse" in this section did not include same-sex couples. The Court of Appeal ruled that s.29 of the *FLA* offended s.15 of the *Charter*. As a remedy the Court of Appeal "read out" the words "a man and woman" from the definition of "spouse" in s. 29 of the *FLA*, and replaced them with the words "two persons". The application of this order was suspended for one year, to give the Ontario legislature time to act. Although M and H settled their differences, the Attorney General was given permission to appeal.]

[...]

¶ 136 Having found that the exclusion of same-sex couples from s. 29 of the *FLA* is unconstitutional and cannot be saved under s. 1 of the *Charter*, I must now consider the issue of remedy under s. 52 of the *Constitution Act, 1982*. In the court below, the words "a man and woman" were read out of the definition of "spouse" in s. 29 of the *FLA* and replaced with the words "two persons". The application of the order was suspended for a period of one year. With respect, I am not convinced that that is a suitable remedy in the circumstances of the present case.

¶ 137 In the leading case on constitutional remedies, *Schachter v. Canada*, [1992] 2 S.C.R. 679, and more recently in *Vriend*, supra, this Court stated that the first step in selecting the appropriate remedial course is to determine the extent of the inconsistency between the impugned legislation and the *Charter*. In the case at bar, the inconsistency emanates from the under inclusive definition of "spouse" in s. 29 of the *FLA*. As I have concluded above, the exclusion of same-sex partners from this definition violates the equality rights guaranteed in s. 15 of the *Charter* and cannot survive any of the stages of review that comprise the s. 1 analysis.

¶ 138 Having identified the extent of the inconsistency, the Court must determine the appropriate remedy. [...]

¶ 139 In determining whether the reading in/reading down option is more appropriate than either striking down or severance, the Court must consider how precisely the remedy can be stated, budgetary implications, the effect the remedy would have on the remaining portion of the legislation, the significance or long-standing nature of the remaining portion and the extent to which a remedy would interfere with legislative objectives (see *Schachter*, supra; *Vriend*, supra). As to the first of these criteria, the remedy of reading in is only available where the court can direct with a sufficient degree of precision what is to be read in to comply with the Constitution. Remedial precision requires that the insertion of a handful of words will, without more, ensure the validity of the legislation and remedy the constitutional wrong (citations omitted).

¶ 140 In the present case, the defect in the definition of "spouse" can be precisely traced to the use of the phrase "a man and woman", which has the effect of excluding same-sex partners from the spousal support scheme under the *FLA*. I recognize that there is remedial precision in so far as reading down this phrase and reading in the words "two persons" will, without more "remedy the constitutional wrong". However, I am not persuaded that reading in will also "ensure the validity of the legislation".

¶ 141 If the remedy adopted by the court below is allowed to stand, s. 29 of the *FLA* will entitle members of same-sex couples who otherwise qualify under the definition of "spouse" to apply for spousal support. However, any attempt to opt out of this regime by means of a cohabitation agreement provided for in s. 53 or a separation agreement set out in s. 54 would not be recognized under the Act. Both ss. 53 and 54 extend to common-law cohabitants but apply only to agreements entered into between "a man and woman". Any extension of s. 29 of the Act would have no effect upon these Part IV domestic contract provisions of the *FLA*, which do not rely upon the Part III definition of "spouse". Thus, same-sex partners would find themselves in the anomalous position of having no means of opting out of the default system of support rights. As this option is available to opposite-sex couples, and protects the ability of couples to choose to order their own affairs in a manner reflecting their own expectations, reading in would in effect remedy one constitutional wrong only to create another, and thereby fail to ensure the validity of the legislation.

¶ 142 In addition, reading into the definition of "spouse" in s. 29 of the Act will have the effect of including same-sex couples in Part V of the *FLA* (Dependants' Claim for Damages), as that part of the Act relies upon the definition of "spouse" as it is defined in Part III. In my opinion, where reading in to one part of a statute will have significant repercussions for a separate and distinct scheme under that Act, it is not safe to assume that the legislature would have enacted the statute in its altered form. In such cases, reading in amounts to the making of ad hoc choices, which Lamer C.J. in *Schachter*, supra, at p. 707, warned is properly the task of the legislatures, not the courts.

¶ 143 In cases where reading in is inappropriate, the court must choose between striking down the legislation in its entirety and severing only the offending portions of the statute. As noted by Lamer C.J. in *Schachter*, at p. 697, "[w]here the offending portion of a statute can be defined in a limited manner it is consistent with legal principles to declare inoperative only that limited portion. In that way, as much of the legislative purpose as possible may be realized."

¶ 144 In the case at bar, striking down the whole of the *FLA* would be excessive as only the definition of "spouse" in Part III of the Act has been found to violate the *Charter*. This is not a case where the parts of the legislative scheme which do offend the *Charter* are so inextricably bound up with the non-offending portions of the statute that what remains cannot independently survive. As a result, it would be safe to assume that the legislature would have passed the constitutionally sound parts of the statute without the unsound parts. [...]

¶ 145 On the basis of the foregoing, I conclude that severing s. 29 of the Act such that it alone is declared of no force or effect is the most appropriate remedy in the present case. This remedy should be temporarily suspended for a period of six months. Although we have been advised against the imposition of a suspension by both the appellant and the respondent, for the reasons which follow, I find that a suspension is necessary.

¶ 146 In *Egan*, at para. 226 (cites omitted), writing in dissent on behalf of myself and Cory J, I would have granted a suspension of the remedy on the basis that "the extension of the spousal allowance, while certainly a legal issue, is also a concern of public policy". In this respect, I noted that "some latitude ought to be given to Parliament to address the issue and devise its own approach to ensuring that the spousal allowance be distributed in a manner that conforms with the equality guarantees of the *Charter*". These same concerns arise in the case at bar with respect to the spousal support scheme under the *FLA*.

¶ 147 In addition, I note that declaring s. 29 of the *FLA* to be of no force or effect may well affect numerous other statutes that rely upon a similar definition of the term "spouse". The legislature may wish to address the validity of these statutes in light of the unconstitutionality of s. 29 of the *FLA*. On this point, I agree with the majority of the Court of Appeal which noted that if left up to the courts, these issues could only be resolved on a case-by-case basis at great cost to private litigants and the public purse. Thus, I believe the legislature ought to be given some latitude in order to address these issues in a more comprehensive fashion.

APPENDIX 1

THE CONSTITUTION ACT, 1867

30 & 31 Victoria, c. 3. (U.K.)

(Consolidated with amendments)

An Act for the Union of Canada, Nova Scotia, and New Brunswick, and the Government thereof; and for Purposes connected therewith

[*29th March 1867.*]

Whereas the Provinces of Canada, Nova Scotia, and New Brunswick have expressed their Desire to be federally united into One Dominion under the Crown of the United Kingdom of Great Britain and Ireland, with a Constitution similar in Principle to that of the United Kingdom:

And whereas such a Union would conduce to the Welfare of the Provinces and promote the Interests of the British Empire:

And whereas on the Establishment of the Union by Authority of Parliament it is expedient, not only that the Constitution of the Legislative Authority in the Dominion be provided for, but also that the Nature of the Executive Government therein be declared:

And whereas it is expedient that Provision be made for the eventual Admission into the Union of other Parts of British North America:

I. PRELIMINARY

Short title 1. This Act may be cited as the *Constitution Act, 1867.*

[Repealed] 2. Repealed.

II. UNION

Declaration of Union 3. It shall be lawful for the Queen, by and with the Advice of Her Majesty's Most Honourable Privy Council, to declare by Proclamation that, on and after a Day therein appointed, not being more than Six Months after the passing of this Act, the Provinces of Canada, Nova Scotia, and New Brunswick shall form and be One Dominion under the Name of Canada; and on and after that Day those Three Provinces shall form and be One Dominion under that Name accordingly.

Construction of subsequent Provisions of Act	4.	Unless it is otherwise expressed or implied, the Name Canada shall be taken to mean Canada as constituted under this Act.
Four Provinces	5.	Canada shall be divided into Four Provinces, named Ontario, Quebec, Nova Scotia, and New Brunswick.
Provinces of Ontario and Quebec	6.	The Parts of the Province of Canada (as it exists at the passing of this Act) which formerly constituted respectively the Provinces of Upper Canada and Lower Canada shall be deemed to be severed, and shall form Two separate Provinces. The Part which formerly constituted the Province of Upper Canada shall constitute the Province of Ontario; and the Part which formerly constituted the Province of Lower Canada shall constitute the Province of Quebec.
Provinces of Nova Scotia and New Brunswick	7.	The Provinces of Nova Scotia and New Brunswick shall have the same Limits as at the passing of this Act.
Decennial Census	8.	In the general Census of the Population of Canada which is hereby required to be taken in the Year One thousand eight hundred and seventy-one, and in every Tenth Year thereafter, the respective Populations of the Four Provinces shall be distinguished.

III. EXECUTIVE POWER

Declaration of Executive Power in the Queen	9.	The Executive Government and Authority of and over Canada is hereby declared to continue and be vested in the Queen.
Application of Provisions referring to Governor General	10.	The Provisions of this Act referring to the Governor General extend and apply to the Governor General for the Time being of Canada, or other the Chief Executive Officer or Administrator for the Time being carrying on the Government of Canada on behalf and in the Name of the Queen, by whatever Title he is designated.

Constitution of Privy Council for Canada	**11.**	There shall be a Council to aid and advise in the Government of Canada, to be styled the Queen's Privy Council for Canada; and the Persons who are to be Members of that Council shall be from Time to Time chosen and summoned by the Governor General and sworn in as Privy Councillors, and Members thereof may be from Time to Time removed by the Governor General.
All Powers under Acts to be exercised by Governor General with Advice of Privy Council, or alone	**12.**	All Powers, Authorities, and Functions which under any Act of the Parliament of Great Britain, or of the Parliament of the United Kingdom of Great Britain and Ireland, or of the Legislature of Upper Canada, Lower Canada, Canada, Nova Scotia, or New Brunswick, are at the Union vested in or exerciseable by the respective Governors or Lieutenant Governors of those Provinces, with the Advice, or with the Advice and Consent, of the respective Executive Councils thereof, or in conjunction with those Councils, or with any Number of Members thereof, or by those Governors or Lieutenant Governors individually, shall, as far as the same continue in existence and capable of being exercised after the Union in relation to the Government of Canada, be vested in and exerciseable by the Governor General, with the Advice or with the Advice and Consent of or in conjunction with the Queen's Privy Council for Canada, or any Members thereof, or by the Governor General individually, as the Case requires, subject nevertheless (except with respect to such as exist under Acts of the Parliament of Great Britain or of the Parliament of the United Kingdom of Great Britain and Ireland) to be abolished or altered by the Parliament of Canada.
Application of Provisions referring to Governor General in Council	**13.**	The Provisions of this Act referring to the Governor General in Council shall be construed as referring to the Governor General acting by and with the Advice of the Queen's Privy Council for Canada.

Power to Her Majesty to authorize Governor General to appoint Deputies

14. It shall be lawful for the Queen, if Her Majesty thinks fit, to authorize the Governor General from Time to Time to appoint any Person or any Persons jointly or severally to be his Deputy or Deputies within any Part or Parts of Canada, and in that Capacity to exercise during the Pleasure of the Governor General such of the Powers, Authorities, and Functions of the Governor General as the Governor General deems it necessary or expedient to assign to him or them, subject to any Limitations or Directions expressed or given by the Queen; but the Appointment of such a Deputy or Deputies shall not affect the Exercise by the Governor General himself of any Power, Authority, or Function.

Command of Armed Forces to continue to be vested in the Queen

15. The Command-in-Chief of the Land and Naval Militia, and of all Naval and Military Forces, of and in Canada, is hereby declared to continue and be vested in the Queen.

Seat of Government of Canada

16. Until the Queen otherwise directs, the Seat of Government of Canada shall be Ottawa.

IV. LEGISLATIVE POWER

Constitution of Parliament of Canada

17. There shall be One Parliament for Canada, consisting of the Queen, an Upper House styled the Senate, and the House of Commons.

Privileges, etc., of Houses

18. The privileges, immunities, and powers to be held, enjoyed, and exercised by the Senate and by the House of Commons, and by the members thereof respectively, shall be such as are from time to time defined by Act of the Parliament of Canada, but so that any Act of the Parliament of Canada defining such privileges, immunities, and powers shall not confer any privileges, immunities, or powers exceeding those at the passing of such Act held, enjoyed, and exercised by the Commons House of Parliament of the United Kingdom of Great Britain and Ireland, and by the members thereof.

First Session of the Parliament of Canada

19. The Parliament of Canada shall be called together not later than Six Months after the Union.

[Repealed]

20. Repealed.

THE SENATE

Number of Senators	**21.**	The Senate shall, subject to the Provisions of this Act, consist of One Hundred and five Members, who shall be styled Senators.
Representation of Provinces in Senate	**22.**	In relation to the Constitution of the Senate Canada shall be deemed to consist of *Four* Divisions:

1. Ontario;

2. Quebec;

3. The Maritime Provinces, Nova Scotia and New Brunswick, and Prince Edward Island;

4. The Western Provinces of Manitoba, British Columbia, Saskatchewan, and Alberta;

which Four Divisions shall (subject to the Provisions of this Act) be equally represented in the Senate as follows: Ontario by twenty-four senators; Quebec by twenty-four senators; the Maritime Provinces and Prince Edward Island by twenty-four senators, ten thereof representing Nova Scotia, ten thereof representing New Brunswick, and four thereof representing Prince Edward Island; the Western Provinces by twenty-four senators, six thereof representing Manitoba, six thereof representing British Columbia, six thereof representing Saskatchewan, and six thereof representing Alberta; Newfoundland shall be entitled to be represented in the Senate by six members; the Yukon Territory and the Northwest Territories shall be entitled to be represented in the Senate by one member each.

In the Case of Quebec each of the Twenty-four Senators representing that Province shall be appointed for One of the Twenty-four Electoral Divisions of Lower Canada specified in Schedule A. to Chapter One of the Consolidated Statutes of Canada.

Qualifications of Senator	**23.**	The Qualifications of a Senator shall be as follows:
	(1)	He shall be of the full age of Thirty Years:

(2)   He shall be either a natural-born Subject of the Queen, or a Subject of the Queen naturalized by an Act of the Parliament of Great Britain, or of the Parliament of the United Kingdom of Great Britain and Ireland, or of the Legislature of One of the Provinces of Upper Canada, Lower Canada, Canada, Nova Scotia, or New Brunswick, before the Union, or of the Parliament of Canada after the Union:

(3)   He shall be legally or equitably seised as of Freehold for his own Use and Benefit of Lands or Tenements held in Free and Common Socage, or seised or possessed for his own Use and Benefit of Lands or Tenements held in Franc-alleu or in Roture, within the Province for which he is appointed, of the Value of Four thousand Dollars, over and above all Rents, Dues, Debts, Charges, Mortgages, and Incumbrances due or payable out of or charged on or affecting the same:

(4)   His Real and Personal Property shall be together worth Four thousand Dollars over and above his Debts and Liabilities:

(5)   He shall be resident in the Province for which he is appointed:

(6)   In the Case of Quebec he shall have his Real Property Qualification in the Electoral Division for which he is appointed, or shall be resident in that Division.

Summons of Senator 24.   The Governor General shall from Time to Time, in the Queen's Name, by Instrument under the Great Seal of Canada, summon qualified Persons to the Senate; and, subject to the Provisions of this Act, every Person so summoned shall become and be a Member of the Senate and a Senator.

[Repealed] 25.   Repealed.

Addition of Senators in certain cases 26.   If at any Time on the Recommendation of the Governor General the Queen thinks fit to direct that Four or Eight Members be added to the Senate, the Governor General may by Summons to Four or Eight qualified Persons (as the Case may be), representing equally the Four Divisions of Canada, add to the Senate accordingly.

Reduction of Senate to normal Number	27.	In case of such Addition being at any Time made, the Governor General shall not summon any Person to the Senate, except on a further like Direction by the Queen on the like Recommendation, to represent one of the Four Divisions until such Division is represented by Twenty-four Senators and no more.
Maximum Number of Senators	28.	The Number of Senators shall not at any Time exceed One Hundred and thirteen.
Tenure of Place in Senate	29.	(1) Subject to subsection (2), a Senator shall, subject to the provisions of this Act, hold his place in the Senate for life.
Retirement upon attaining age of seventy-five years		(2) A Senator who is summoned to the Senate after the coming into force of this subsection shall, subject to this Act, hold his place in the Senate until he attains the age of seventy-five years.
Resignation of Place in Senate	30.	A Senator may by Writing under his Hand addressed to the Governor General resign his Place in the Senate, and thereupon the same shall be vacant.
Disqualification of Senators	31.	The Place of a Senator shall become vacant in any of the following Cases:
	(1)	If for Two consecutive Sessions of the Parliament he fails to give his Attendance in the Senate:
	(2)	If he takes an Oath or makes a Declaration or Acknowledgment of Allegiance, Obedience, or Adherence to a Foreign Power, or does an Act whereby he becomes a Subject or Citizen, or entitled to the Rights or Privileges of a Subject or Citizen, of a Foreign Power:
	(3)	If he is adjudged Bankrupt or Insolvent, or applies for the Benefit of any Law relating to Insolvent Debtors, or becomes a public Defaulter:
	(4)	If he is attainted of Treason or convicted of Felony or of any infamous Crime:

(5) If he ceases to be qualified in respect of Property or of Residence; provided, that a Senator shall not be deemed to have ceased to be qualified in respect of Residence by reason only of his residing at the Seat of the Government of Canada while holding an Office under that Government requiring his Presence there.

Summons on Vacancy in Senate

32. When a Vacancy happens in the Senate by Resignation, Death, or otherwise, the Governor General shall by Summons to a fit and qualified Person fill the Vacancy.

Questions as to Qualifications and Vacancies in Senate

33. If any Question arises respecting the Qualification of a Senator or a Vacancy in the Senate the same shall be heard and determined by the Senate.

Appointment of Speaker of Senate

34. The Governor General may from Time to Time, by Instrument under the Great Seal of Canada, appoint a Senator to be Speaker of the Senate, and may remove him and appoint another in his Stead.

Quorum of Senate

35. Until the Parliament of Canada otherwise provides, the Presence of at least Fifteen Senators, including the Speaker, shall be necessary to constitute a Meeting of the Senate for the Exercise of its Powers.

Voting in Senate

36. Questions arising in the Senate shall be decided by a Majority of Voices, and the Speaker shall in all Cases have a Vote, and when the Voices are equal the Decision shall be deemed to be in the Negative.

THE HOUSE OF COMMONS

Constitution of House of Commons in Canada

37. The House of Commons shall, subject to the Provisions of this Act, consist of two hundred and ninety-five members of whom ninety-nine shall be elected for Ontario, seventy-five for Quebec, eleven for Nova Scotia, ten for New Brunswick, fourteen for Manitoba, thirty-two for British Columbia, four for Prince Edward Island, twenty-six for Alberta, fourteen for Saskatchewan, seven for Newfoundland, one for the Yukon Territory and two for the Northwest Territories.

Summoning of House of Commons   **38.**   The Governor General shall from Time to Time, in the Queen's Name, by Instrument under the Great Seal of Canada, summon and call together the House of Commons.

Senators not to sit in House of Commons   **39.**   A Senator shall not be capable of being elected or of sitting or voting as a Member of the House of Commons.

Electoral districts of the four Provinces   **40.**   Until the Parliament of Canada otherwise provides, Ontario, Quebec, Nova Scotia, and New Brunswick shall, for the Purposes of the Election of Members to serve in the House of Commons, be divided into Electoral Districts as follows:

1. Ontario

Ontario shall be divided into the Counties, Ridings of Counties, Cities, Parts of Cities, and Towns enumerated in the First Schedule to this Act, each whereof shall be an Electoral District, each such District as numbered in that Schedule being entitled to return One Member.

2. Quebec

Quebec shall be divided into Sixty-five Electoral Districts, composed of the Sixty-five Electoral Divisions into which Lower Canada is at the passing of this Act divided under Chapter Two of the Consolidated Statutes of Canada, Chapter Seventy-five of the Consolidated Statutes for Lower Canada, and the Act of the Province of Canada of the Twenty-third Year of the Queen, Chapter One, or any other Act amending the same in force at the Union, so that each such Electoral Division shall be for the Purposes of this Act an Electoral District entitled to return One Member.

3. Nova Scotia

Each of the Eighteen Counties of Nova Scotia shall be an Electoral District. The County of Halifax shall be entitled to return Two Members, and each of the other Counties One Member.

4. New Brunswick

Each of the Fourteen Counties into which New Brunswick is divided, including the City and County of St. John, shall be an Electoral District. The City of St. John shall also be a separate Electoral District. Each of those Fifteen Electoral Districts shall be entitled to return One Member.

Continuance of existing Election Laws until Parliament of Canada otherwise provides	**41.**	Until the Parliament of Canada otherwise provides, all Laws in force in the several Provinces at the Union relative to the following Matters or any of them, namely, — — the Qualifications and Disqualifications of Persons to be elected or to sit or vote as Members of the House of Assembly or Legislative Assembly in the several Provinces, the Voters at Elections of such Members, the Oaths to be taken by Voters, the Returning Officers, their Powers and Duties, the Proceedings at Elections, the Periods during which Elections may be continued, the Trial of controverted Elections, and Proceedings incident thereto, the vacating of Seats of Members, and the Execution of new Writs in case of Seats vacated otherwise than by Dissolution, — — shall respectively apply to Elections of Members to serve in the House of Commons for the same several Provinces.
		Provided that, until the Parliament of Canada otherwise provides, at any Election for a Member of the House of Commons for the District of Algoma, in addition to Persons qualified by the Law of the Province of Canada to vote, every Male British Subject, aged Twenty-one Years or upwards, being a Householder, shall have a Vote.
[Repealed]	**42.**	Repealed.
[Repealed]	**43.**	Repealed.
As to Election of Speaker of House of Commons	**44.**	The House of Commons on its first assembling after a General Election shall proceed with all practicable Speed to elect One of its Members to be Speaker.
As to filling up Vacancy in Office of Speaker	**45.**	In case of a Vacancy happening in the Office of Speaker by Death, Resignation, or otherwise, the House of Commons shall with all practicable Speed proceed to elect another of its Members to be Speaker.

Speaker to preside	**46.**	The Speaker shall preside at all Meetings of the House of Commons.
Provision in case of Absence of Speaker	**47.**	Until the Parliament of Canada otherwise provides, in case of the Absence for any Reason of the Speaker from the Chair of the House of Commons for a Period of Forty-eight consecutive Hours, the House may elect another of its Members to act as Speaker, and the Member so elected shall during the Continuance of such Absence of the Speaker have and execute all the Powers, Privileges, and Duties of Speaker.
Quorum of House of Commons	**48.**	The Presence of at least Twenty Members of the House of Commons shall be necessary to constitute a Meeting of the House for the Exercise of its Powers, and for that Purpose the Speaker shall be reckoned as a Member.
Voting in House of Commons	**49.**	Questions arising in the House of Commons shall be decided by a Majority of Voices other than that of the Speaker, and when the Voices are equal, but not otherwise, the Speaker shall have a Vote.
Duration of House of Commons	**50.**	Every House of Commons shall continue for Five Years from the Day of the Return of the Writs for choosing the House (subject to be sooner dissolved by the Governor General), and no longer.
Readjustment of representation in Commons	**51.**	(1) The number of members of the House of Commons and the representation of the provinces therein shall, on the coming into force of this subsection and thereafter on the completion of each decennial census, be readjusted by such authority, in such manner, and from such time as the Parliament of Canada from time to time provides, subject and according to the following rules:
	1.	There shall be assigned to each of the provinces a number of members equal to the number obtained by dividing the total population of the provinces by two hundred and seventy-nine and by dividing the population of each province by the quotient so obtained, counting any remainder in excess of 0.50 as one after the said process of division.

2.   If the total number of members that would be assigned to a province by the application of rule 1 is less than the total number assigned to that province on the date of coming into force of this subsection, there shall be added to the number of members so assigned such number of members as will result in the province having the same number of members as were assigned on that date.

Yukon Territory, Northwest Territories and Nunavut

(2) The Yukon Territory as bounded and described in the schedule to chapter Y-2 of the Revised Statutes of Canada, 1985, shall be entitled to one member, the Northwest Territories as bounded and described in section 2 of chapter N-27 of the Revised Statutes of Canada, 1985, as amended by section 77 of chapter 28 of the Statutes of Canada, 1993, shall be entitled to one member, and Nunavut as bounded and described in section 3 of chapter 28 of the Statutes of Canada, 1993, shall be entitled to one member.

Constitution of House of Commons

51A.   Notwithstanding anything in this Act a province shall always be entitled to a number of members in the House of Commons not less than the number of senators representing such province.

Increase of Number of House of Commons

52.   The Number of Members of the House of Commons may be from Time to Time increased by the Parliament of Canada, provided the proportionate Representation of the Provinces prescribed by this Act is not thereby disturbed.

MONEY VOTES; ROYAL ASSENT

Appropriation and Tax Bills

53.   Bills for appropriating any Part of the Public Revenue, or for imposing any Tax or Impost, shall originate in the House of Commons.

Recommendation of Money Votes

54.   It shall not be lawful for the House of Commons to adopt or pass any Vote, Resolution, Address, or Bill for the Appropriation of any Part of the Public Revenue, or of any Tax or Impost, to any Purpose that has not been first recommended to that House by Message of the Governor General in the Session in which such Vote, Resolution, Address, or Bill is proposed.

Royal Assent to Bills, etc.

55. Where a Bill passed by the Houses of the Parliament is presented to the Governor General for the Queen's Assent, he shall declare, according to his Discretion, but subject to the Provisions of this Act and to Her Majesty's Instructions, either that he assents thereto in the Queen's Name, or that he withholds the Queen's Assent, or that he reserves the Bill for the Signification of the Queen's Pleasure.

Disallowance by Order in Council of Act assented to by Governor General

56. Where the Governor General assents to a Bill in the Queen's Name, he shall by the first convenient Opportunity send an authentic Copy of the Act to One of Her Majesty's Principal Secretaries of State, and if the Queen in Council within Two Years after Receipt thereof by the Secretary of State thinks fit to disallow the Act, such Disallowance (with a Certificate of the Secretary of State of the Day on which the Act was received by him) being signified by the Governor General, by Speech or Message to each of the Houses of the Parliament or by Proclamation, shall annul the Act from and after the Day of such Signification.

Signification of Queen's Pleasure on Bill reserved

57. A Bill reserved for the Signification of the Queen's Pleasure shall not have any Force unless and until, within Two Years from the Day on which it was presented to the Governor General for the Queen's Assent, the Governor General signifies, by Speech or Message to each of the Houses of the Parliament or by Proclamation, that it has received the Assent of the Queen in Council.

An Entry of every such Speech, Message, or Proclamation shall be made in the Journal of each House, and a Duplicate thereof duly attested shall be delivered to the proper Officer to be kept among the Records of Canada.

V. PROVINCIAL CONSTITUTIONS

EXECUTIVE POWER

Appointment of Lieutenant Governors of Provinces

58. For each Province there shall be an Officer, styled the Lieutenant Governor, appointed by the Governor General in Council by Instrument under the Great Seal of Canada.

Tenure of Office of Lieutenant Governor	59.	A Lieutenant Governor shall hold Office during the Pleasure of the Governor General; but any Lieutenant Governor appointed after the Commencement of the First Session of the Parliament of Canada shall not be removeable within Five Years from his Appointment, except for Cause assigned, which shall be communicated to him in Writing within One Month after the Order for his Removal is made, and shall be communicated by Message to the Senate and to the House of Commons within One Week thereafter if the Parliament is then sitting, and if not then within One Week after the Commencement of the next Session of the Parliament.
Salaries of Lieutenant Governors	60.	The Salaries of the Lieutenant Governors shall be fixed and provided by the Parliament of Canada.
Oaths, etc., of Lieutenant Governor	61.	Every Lieutenant Governor shall, before assuming the Duties of his Office, make and subscribe before the Governor General or some Person authorized by him Oaths of Allegiance and Office similar to those taken by the Governor General.
Application of Provisions referring to Lieutenant Governor	62.	The Provisions of this Act referring to the Lieutenant Governor extend and apply to the Lieutenant Governor for the Time being of each Province, or other the Chief Executive Officer or Administrator for the Time being carrying on the Government of the Province, by whatever Title he is designated.
Appointment of Executive Officers for Ontario and Quebec	63.	The Executive Council of Ontario and of Quebec shall be composed of such Persons as the Lieutenant Governor from Time to Time thinks fit, and in the first instance of the following Officers, namely, — — the Attorney General, the Secretary and Registrar of the Province, the Treasurer of the Province, the Commissioner of Crown Lands, and the Commissioner of Agriculture and Public Works, with in Quebec the Speaker of the Legislative Council and the Solicitor General.
Executive Government of Nova Scotia and New Brunswick	64.	The Constitution of the Executive Authority in each of the Provinces of Nova Scotia and New Brunswick shall, subject to the Provisions of this Act, continue as it exists at the Union until altered under the Authority of this Act.

Powers to be exercised by Lieutenant Governor of Ontario or Quebec with Advice, or alone

65. All Powers, Authorities, and Functions which under any Act of the Parliament of Great Britain, or of the Parliament of the United Kingdom of Great Britain and Ireland, or of the Legislature of Upper Canada, Lower Canada, or Canada, were or are before or at the Union vested in or exerciseable by the respective Governors or Lieutenant Governors of those Provinces, with the Advice or with the Advice and Consent of the respective Executive Councils thereof, or in conjunction with those Councils, or with any Number of Members thereof, or by those Governors or Lieutenant Governors individually, shall, as far as the same are capable of being exercised after the Union in relation to the Government of Ontario and Quebec respectively, be vested in and shall or may be exercised by the Lieutenant Governor of Ontario and Quebec respectively, with the Advice or with the Advice and Consent of or in conjunction with the respective Executive Councils, or any Members thereof, or by the Lieutenant Governor individually, as the Case requires, subject nevertheless (except with respect to such as exist under Acts of the Parliament of Great Britain, or of the Parliament of the United Kingdom of Great Britain and Ireland,) to be abolished or altered by the respective Legislatures of Ontario and Quebec.

Application of Provisions referring to Lieutenant Governor in Council

66. The Provisions of this Act referring to the Lieutenant Governor in Council shall be construed as referring to the Lieutenant Governor of the Province acting by and with the Advice of the Executive Council thereof.

Administration in Absence, etc., of Lieutenant Governor

67. The Governor General in Council may from Time to Time appoint an Administrator to execute the Office and Functions of Lieutenant Governor during his Absence, Illness, or other Inability.

Seats of Provincial Governments

68. Unless and until the Executive Government of any Province otherwise directs with respect to that Province, the Seats of Government of the Provinces shall be as follows, namely, — — of Ontario, the City of Toronto; of Quebec, the City of Quebec; of Nova Scotia, the City of Halifax; and of New Brunswick, the City of Fredericton.

LEGISLATIVE POWER

1. ONTARIO

Legislature for Ontario	69.	There shall be a Legislature for Ontario consisting of the Lieutenant Governor and of One House, styled the Legislative Assembly of Ontario.
Electoral districts	70.	The Legislative Assembly of Ontario shall be composed of Eighty-two Members, to be elected to represent the Eighty-two Electoral Districts set forth in the First Schedule to this Act.

2. QUEBEC

Legislature for Quebec	71.	There shall be a Legislature for Quebec consisting of the Lieutenant Governor and of Two Houses, styled the Legislative Council of Quebec and the Legislative Assembly of Quebec.
Constitution of Legislative Council	72.	The Legislative Council of Quebec shall be composed of Twenty-four Members, to be appointed by the Lieutenant Governor, in the Queen's Name, by Instrument under the Great Seal of Quebec, one being appointed to represent each of the Twenty-four Electoral Divisions of Lower Canada in this Act referred to, and each holding Office for the Term of his Life, unless the Legislature of Quebec otherwise provides under the Provisions of this Act.
Qualification of Legislative Councillors	73.	The Qualifications of the Legislative Councillors of Quebec shall be the same as those of the Senators for Quebec.
Resignation, Disqualification, etc.	74.	The Place of a Legislative Councillor of Quebec shall become vacant in the Cases, *mutatis mutandis*, in which the Place of Senator becomes vacant.
Vacancies	75.	When a Vacancy happens in the Legislative Council of Quebec by Resignation, Death, or otherwise, the Lieutenant Governor, in the Queen's Name, by Instrument under the Great Seal of Quebec, shall appoint a fit and qualified Person to fill the Vacancy.

Questions as to Vacancies, etc.	76.	If any Question arises respecting the Qualification of a Legislative Councillor of Quebec, or a Vacancy in the Legislative Council of Quebec, the same shall be heard and determined by the Legislative Council.
Speaker of Legislative Council	77.	The Lieutenant Governor may from Time to Time, by Instrument under the Great Seal of Quebec, appoint a Member of the Legislative Council of Quebec to be Speaker thereof, and may remove him and appoint another in his Stead.
Quorum of Legislative Council	78.	Until the Legislature of Quebec otherwise provides, the Presence of at least Ten Members of the Legislative Council, including the Speaker, shall be necessary to constitute a Meeting for the Exercise of its Powers.
Voting in Legislative Council	79.	Questions arising in the Legislative Council of Quebec shall be decided by a Majority of Voices, and the Speaker shall in all Cases have a Vote, and when the Voices are equal the Decision shall be deemed to be in the Negative.
Constitution of Legislative Assembly of Quebec	80.	The Legislative Assembly of Quebec shall be composed of Sixty-five Members, to be elected to represent the Sixty-five Electoral Divisions or Districts of Lower Canada in this Act referred to, subject to Alteration thereof by the Legislature of Quebec: Provided that it shall not be lawful to present to the Lieutenant Governor of Quebec for Assent any Bill for altering the Limits of any of the Electoral Divisions or Districts mentioned in the Second Schedule to this Act, unless the Second and Third Readings of such Bill have been passed in the Legislative Assembly with the Concurrence of the Majority of the Members representing all those Electoral Divisions or Districts, and the Assent shall not be given to such Bill unless an Address has been presented by the Legislative Assembly to the Lieutenant Governor stating that it has been so passed.

3. ONTARIO AND QUEBEC

[Repealed]	81.	Repealed.

Summoning of Legislative Assemblies

82.

The Lieutenant Governor of Ontario and of Quebec shall from Time to Time, in the Queen's Name, by Instrument under the Great Seal of the Province, summon and call together the Legislative Assembly of the Province.

Restriction on election of Holders of offices

83.

Until the Legislature of Ontario or of Quebec otherwise provides, a Person accepting or holding in Ontario or in Quebec any Office, Commission, or Employment, permanent or temporary, at the Nomination of the Lieutenant Governor, to which an annual Salary, or any Fee, Allowance, Emolument, or Profit of any Kind or Amount whatever from the Province is attached, shall not be eligible as a Member of the Legislative Assembly of the respective Province, nor shall he sit or vote as such; but nothing in this Section shall make ineligible any Person being a Member of the Executive Council of the respective Province, or holding any of the following Offices, that is to say, the Offices of Attorney General, Secretary and Registrar of the Province, Treasurer of the Province, Commissioner of Crown Lands, and Commissioner of Agriculture and Public Works, and in Quebec Solicitor General, or shall disqualify him to sit or vote in the House for which he is elected, provided he is elected while holding such Office.

Continuance of existing Election Laws

84.

Until the legislatures of Ontario and Quebec respectively otherwise provide, all Laws which at the Union are in force in those Provinces respectively, relative to the following Matters, or any of them, namely, — — the Qualifications and Disqualifications of Persons to be elected or to sit or vote as Members of the Assembly of Canada, the Qualifications or Disqualifications of Voters, the Oaths to be taken by Voters, the Returning Officers, their Powers and Duties, the Proceedings at Elections, the Periods during which such Elections may be continued, and the Trial of controverted Elections and the Proceedings incident thereto, the vacating of the Seats of Members and the issuing and execution of new Writs in case of Seats vacated otherwise than by Dissolution, — — shall respectively apply to Elections of Members to serve in the respective Legislative Assemblies of Ontario and Quebec.

Provided that, until the Legislature of Ontario otherwise provides, at any Election for a Member of the Legislative Assembly of Ontario for the District of Algoma, in addition to Persons qualified by the Law of the Province of Canada to vote, every Male British Subject, aged Twenty-one Years or upwards, being a Householder, shall have a Vote.

Duration of Legislative Assemblies

85. Every Legislative Assembly of Ontario and every Legislative Assembly of Quebec shall continue for Four Years from the Day of the Return of the Writs for choosing the same (subject nevertheless to either the Legislative Assembly of Ontario or the Legislative Assembly of Quebec being sooner dissolved by the Lieutenant Governor of the Province), and no longer.

Yearly Session of Legislature

86. There shall be a Session of the Legislature of Ontario and of that of Quebec once at least in every Year, so that Twelve Months shall not intervene between the last Sitting of the Legislature in each Province in one Session and its first Sitting in the next Session.

Speaker, Quorum, etc.

87. The following Provisions of this Act respecting the House of Commons of Canada shall extend and apply to the Legislative Assemblies of Ontario and Quebec, that is to say, — — the Provisions relating to the Election of a Speaker originally and on Vacancies, the Duties of the Speaker, the Absence of the Speaker, the Quorum, and the Mode of voting, as if those Provisions were here re-enacted and made applicable in Terms to each such Legislative Assembly.

4. NOVA SCOTIA AND NEW BRUNSWICK

Constitutions of Legislatures of Nova Scotia and New Brunswick

88. The Constitution of the Legislature of each of the Provinces of Nova Scotia and New Brunswick shall, subject to the Provisions of this Act, continue as it exists at the Union until altered under the Authority of this Act.

5. ONTARIO, QUEBEC, AND NOVA SCOTIA

[Repealed]

89. Repealed.

6. THE FOUR PROVINCES

Application to Legislatures of Provisions respecting Money Votes, etc.

90. The following Provisions of this Act respecting the Parliament of Canada, namely, — — the Provisions relating to Appropriation and Tax Bills, the Recommendation of Money Votes, the Assent to Bills, the Disallowance of Acts, and the Signification of Pleasure on Bills reserved, — — shall extend and apply to the Legislatures of the several Provinces as if those Provisions were here re-enacted and made applicable in Terms to the respective Provinces and the Legislatures thereof, with the Substitution of the Lieutenant Governor of the Province for the Governor General, of the Governor General for the Queen and for a Secretary of State, of One Year for Two Years, and of the Province for Canada.

VI. DISTRIBUTION OF LEGISLATIVE POWERS

POWERS OF THE PARLIAMENT

Legislative Authority of Parliament of Canada

91. It shall be lawful for the Queen, by and with the Advice and Consent of the Senate and House of Commons, to make Laws for the Peace, Order, and good Government of Canada, in relation to all Matters not coming within the Classes of Subjects by this Act assigned exclusively to the Legislatures of the Provinces; and for greater Certainty, but not so as to restrict the Generality of the foregoing Terms of this Section, it is hereby declared that (notwithstanding anything in this Act) the exclusive Legislative Authority of the Parliament of Canada extends to all Matters coming within the Classes of Subjects next hereinafter enumerated; that is to say,

1. Repealed.

1A. The Public Debt and Property.

2. The Regulation of Trade and Commerce.

2A. Unemployment insurance.

3. The raising of Money by any Mode or System of Taxation.

4. The borrowing of Money on the Public Credit.

5. Postal Service.

6.   The Census and Statistics.

7.   Militia, Military and Naval Service, and Defence.

8.   The fixing of and providing for the Salaries and Allowances of Civil and other Officers of the Government of Canada.

9.   Beacons, Buoys, Lighthouses, and Sable Island.

10.   Navigation and Shipping.

11.   Quarantine and the Establishment and Maintenance of Marine Hospitals.

12.   Sea Coast and Inland Fisheries.

13.   Ferries between a Province and any British or Foreign Country or between Two Provinces.

14.   Currency and Coinage.

15.   Banking, Incorporation of Banks, and the Issue of Paper Money.

16.   Savings Banks.

17.   Weights and Measures.

18.   Bills of Exchange and Promissory Notes.

19.   Interest.

20.   Legal Tender.

21.   Bankruptcy and Insolvency.

22.   Patents of Invention and Discovery.

23.   Copyrights.

24.   Indians, and Lands reserved for the Indians.

25.   Naturalization and Aliens.

26.   Marriage and Divorce.

27.   The Criminal Law, except the Constitution of Courts of Criminal Jurisdiction, but including the Procedure in Criminal Matters.

28.   The Establishment, Maintenance, and Management of Penitentiaries.

29.   Such Classes of Subjects as are expressly excepted in the Enumeration of the Classes of Subjects by this Act assigned exclusively to the Legislatures of the Provinces.

And any Matter coming within any of the Classes of Subjects enumerated in this Section shall not be deemed to come within the Class of Matters of a local or private Nature comprised in the Enumeration of the Classes of Subjects by this Act assigned exclusively to the Legislatures of the Provinces.

EXCLUSIVE POWERS OF PROVINCIAL LEGISLATURES

Subjects of exclusive Provincial Legislation

92. In each Province the Legislature may exclusively make Laws in relation to Matters coming within the Classes of Subjects next hereinafter enumerated; that is to say,

1. Repealed

2. Direct Taxation within the Province in order to the raising of a Revenue for Provincial Purposes.

3. The borrowing of Money on the sole Credit of the Province

4. The Establishment and Tenure of Provincial Offices and the Appointment and Payment of Provincial Officers.

5. The Management and Sale of the Public Lands belonging to the Province and of the Timber and Wood thereon.

6. The Establishment, Maintenance, and Management of Public and Reformatory Prisons in and for the Province.

7. The Establishment, Maintenance, and Management of Hospitals, Asylums, Charities, and Eleemosynary Institutions in and for the Province, other than Marine Hospitals.

8. Municipal Institutions in the Province.

9. Shop, Saloon, Tavern, Auctioneer, and other Licences in order to the raising of a Revenue for Provincial, Local, or Municipal Purposes.

10. Local Works and Undertakings other than such as are of the following Classes:

    (a) Lines of Steam or other Ships, Railways, Canals, Telegraphs, and other Works and Undertakings connecting the Province with any other or others of the Provinces, or extending beyond the Limits of the Province:

(b)   Lines of Steam Ships between the Province and any British or Foreign Country:

(c)   Such Works as, although wholly situate within the Province, are before or after their Execution declared by the Parliament of Canada to be for the general Advantage of Canada or for the Advantage of Two or more of the Provinces.

11.   The Incorporation of Companies with Provincial Objects.

12.   The Solemnization of Marriage in the Province.

13.   Property and Civil Rights in the Province.

14.   The Administration of Justice in the Province, including the Constitution, Maintenance, and Organization of Provincial Courts, both of Civil and of Criminal Jurisdiction, and including Procedure in Civil Matters in those Courts.

15.   The Imposition of Punishment by Fine, Penalty, or Imprisonment for enforcing any Law of the Province made in relation to any Matter coming within any of the Classes of Subjects enumerated in this Section.

16.   Generally all Matters of a merely local or private Nature in the Province.

NON-RENEWABLE NATURAL RESOURCES, FORESTRY RESOURCES AND ELECTRICAL ENERGY

Laws respecting non-renewable Natural resources, Forestry resoruces and electrical energy

92A.   (1) In each province, the legislature may exclusively make laws in relation to

(a)   exploration for non-renewable natural resources in the province;

(b)   development, conservation and management of non-renewable natural resources and forestry resources in the province, including laws in relation to the rate of primary production therefrom; and

(c)   development, conservation and management of sites and facilities in the province for the generation and production of electrical energy.

Export from provinces of resources

(2) In each province, the legislature may make laws in relation to the export from the province to another part of Canada of the primary production from non-renewable natural resources and forestry resources in the province and the production from facilities in the province for the generation of electrical energy, but such laws may not authorize or provide for discrimination in prices or in supplies exported to another part of Canada.

Authority of Parliament

(3) Nothing in subsection (2) derogates from the authority of Parliament to enact laws in relation to the matters referred to in that subsection and, where such a law of Parliament and a law of a province conflict, the law of Parliament prevails to the extent of the conflict.

Taxation of resources

(4) In each province, the legislature may make laws in relation to the raising of money by any mode or system of taxation in respect of

(a) non-renewable natural resources and forestry resources in the province and the primary production therefrom, and

(b) sites and facilities in the province for the generation of electrical energy and the production therefrom,

whether or not such production is exported in whole or in part from the province, but such laws may not authorize or provide for taxation that differentiates between production exported to another part of Canada and production not exported from the province.

"Primary production"

(5) The expression "primary production" has the meaning assigned by the Sixth Schedule.

Existing powers or rights

(6) Nothing in subsections (1) to (5) derogates from any powers or rights that a legislature or government of a province had immediately before the coming into force of this section.

EDUCATION

Legislation respecting Education

93. In and for each Province the Legislature may exclusively make Laws in relation to Education, subject and according to the following Provisions:

(1)   Nothing in any such Law shall prejudicially affect any Right or Privilege with respect to Denominational Schools which any Class of Persons have by Law in the Province at the Union:

(2)   All the Powers, Privileges, and Duties at the Union by Law conferred and imposed in Upper Canada on the Separate Schools and School Trustees of the Queen's Roman Catholic Subjects shall be and the same are hereby extended to the Dissentient Schools of the Queen's Protestant and Roman Catholic Subjects in Quebec:

(3)   Where in any Province a System of Separate or Dissentient Schools exists by Law at the Union or is thereafter established by the Legislature of the Province, an Appeal shall lie to the Governor General in Council from any Act or Decision of any Provincial Authority affecting any Right or Privilege of the Protestant or Roman Catholic Minority of the Queen's Subjects in relation to Education:

(4)   In case any such Provincial Law as from Time to Time seems to the Governor General in Council requisite for the due Execution of the Provisions of this Section is not made, or in case any Decision of the Governor General in Council on any Appeal under this Section is not duly executed by the proper Provincial Authority in that Behalf, then and in every such Case, and as far only as the Circumstances of each Case require, the Parliament of Canada may make remedial Laws for the due Execution of the Provisions of this Section and of any Decision of the Governor General in Council under this Section.

Quebec   **93A.**   Paragraphs (1) to (4) of section 93 do not apply to Quebec.

UNIFORMITY OF LAWS IN ONTARIO, NOVA SCOTIA, AND NEW BRUNSWICK

Legislation for Uniformity of Laws in Three Provinces	94.	Notwithstanding anything in this Act, the Parliament of Canada may make Provision for the Uniformity of all or any of the Laws relative to Property and Civil Rights in Ontario, Nova Scotia, and New Brunswick, and of the Procedure of all or any of the Courts in those Three Provinces, and from and after the passing of any Act in that Behalf the Power of the Parliament of Canada to make Laws in relation to any Matter comprised in any such Act shall, notwithstanding anything in this Act, be unrestricted; but any Act of the Parliament of Canada making Provision for such Uniformity shall not have effect in any Province unless and until it is adopted and enacted as Law by the Legislature thereof.

OLD AGE PENSIONS

Legislation respecting old age pensions and supplementary benefits	94A.	The Parliament of Canada may make laws in relation to old age pensions and supplementary benefits, including survivors' and disability benefits irrespective of age, but no such law shall affect the operation of any law present or future of a provincial legislature in relation to any such matter.

AGRICULTURE AND IMMIGRATION

Concurrent Powers of Legislation respecting Agriculture, etc.	95.	In each Province the Legislature may make Laws in relation to Agriculture in the Province, and to Immigration into the Province; and it is hereby declared that the Parliament of Canada may from Time to Time make Laws in relation to Agriculture in all or any of the Provinces, and to Immigration into all or any of the Provinces; and any Law of the Legislature of a Province relative to Agriculture or to Immigration shall have effect in and for the Province as long and as far only as it is not repugnant to any Act of the Parliament of Canada.

VII. JUDICATURE

Appointment of Judges	96.	The Governor General shall appoint the Judges of the Superior, District, and County Courts in each Province, except those of the Courts of Probate in Nova Scotia and New Brunswick.

Selection of Judges in Ontario, etc.	**97.**	Until the Laws relative to Property and Civil Rights in Ontario, Nova Scotia, and New Brunswick, and the Procedure of the Courts in those Provinces, are made uniform, the Judges of the Courts of those Provinces appointed by the Governor General shall be selected from the respective Bars of those Provinces.
Selection of Judges in Quebec	**98.**	The Judges of the Courts of Quebec shall be selected from the Bar of that Province.
Tenure of office of Judges	**99.**	(1) Subject to subsection two of this section, the Judges of the Superior Courts shall hold office during good behaviour, but shall be removable by the Governor General on Address of the Senate and House of Commons.
Termination at age 75		(2) A Judge of a Superior Court, whether appointed before or after the coming into force of this section, shall cease to hold office upon attaining the age of seventy-five years, or upon the coming into force of this section if at that time he has already attained that age.
Salaries, etc., of Judges	**100.**	The Salaries, Allowances, and Pensions of the Judges of the Superior, District, and County Courts (except the Courts of Probate in Nova Scotia and New Brunswick), and of the Admiralty Courts in Cases where the Judges thereof are for the Time being paid by Salary, shall be fixed and provided by the Parliament of Canada.
General Court of Appeal, etc.	**101.**	The Parliament of Canada may, notwithstanding anything in this Act, from Time to Time provide for the Constitution, Maintenance, and Organization of a General Court of Appeal for Canada, and for the Establishment of any additional Courts for the better Administration of the Laws of Canada.

VIII. REVENUES, DEBTS, ASSETS, TAXATION

Creation of Consolidated Revenue Fund

102. All Duties and Revenues over which the respective Legislatures of Canada, Nova Scotia, and New Brunswick before and at the Union had and have Power of Appropriation, except such Portions thereof as are by this Act reserved to the respective Legislatures of the Provinces, or are raised by them in accordance with the special Powers conferred on them by this Act, shall form One Consolidated Revenue Fund, to be appropriated for the Public Service of Canada in the Manner and subject to the Charges in this Act provided.

Expenses of Collection, etc.

103. The Consolidated Revenue Fund of Canada shall be permanently charged with the Costs, Charges, and Expenses incident to the Collection, Management, and Receipt thereof, and the same shall form the First Charge thereon, subject to be reviewed and audited in such Manner as shall be ordered by the Governor General in Council until the Parliament otherwise provides.

Interest of Provincial Public Debts

104. The annual Interest of the Public Debts of the several Provinces of Canada, Nova Scotia, and New Brunswick at the Union shall form the Second Charge on the Consolidated Revenue Fund of Canada.

Salary of Governor General

105. Unless altered by the Parliament of Canada, the Salary of the Governor General shall be Ten thousand Pounds Sterling Money of the United Kingdom of Great Britain and Ireland, payable out of the Consolidated Revenue Fund of Canada, and the same shall form the Third Charge thereon.

Appropriation from Time to Time

106. Subject to the several Payments by this Act charged on the Consolidated Revenue Fund of Canada, the same shall be appropriated by the Parliament of Canada for the Public Service.

Transfer of Stocks, etc.

107. All Stocks, Cash, Banker's Balances, and Securities for Money belonging to each Province at the Time of the Union, except as in this Act mentioned, shall be the Property of Canada, and shall be taken in Reduction of the Amount of the respective Debts of the Provinces at the Union.

Transfer of Property in Schedule	**108.**	The Public Works and Property of each Province, enumerated in the Third Schedule to this Act, shall be the Property of Canada.
Property in Lands, Mines, etc.	**109.**	All Lands, Mines, Minerals, and Royalties belonging to the several Provinces of Canada, Nova Scotia, and New Brunswick at the Union, and all Sums then due or payable for such Lands, Mines, Minerals, or Royalties, shall belong to the several Provinces of Ontario, Quebec, Nova Scotia, and New Brunswick in which the same are situate or arise, subject to any Trusts existing in respect thereof, and to any Interest other than that of the Province in the same.
Assets connected with Provincial Debts	**110.**	All Assets connected with such Portions of the Public Debt of each Province as are assumed by that Province shall belong to that Province.
Canada to be liable for Provincial Debts	**111.**	Canada shall be liable for the Debts and Liabilities of each Province existing at the Union.
Debts of Ontario and Quebec	**112.**	Ontario and Quebec conjointly shall be liable to Canada for the Amount (if any) by which the Debt of the Province of Canada exceeds at the Union Sixty-two million five hundred thousand Dollars, and shall be charged with Interest at the Rate of Five per Centum per Annum thereon.
Assets of Ontario and Quebec	**113.**	The Assets enumerated in the Fourth Schedule to this Act belonging at the Union to the Province of Canada shall be the Property of Ontario and Quebec conjointly.
Debt of Nova Scotia	**114.**	Nova Scotia shall be liable to Canada for the Amount (if any) by which its Public Debt exceeds at the Union Eight million Dollars, and shall be charged with Interest at the Rate of Five per Centum per Annum thereon.
Debt of New Brunswick	**115.**	New Brunswick shall be liable to Canada for the Amount (if any) by which its Public Debt exceeds at the Union Seven million Dollars, and shall be charged with Interest at the Rate of Five per Centum per Annum thereon.

Payment of interest to Nova Scotia and New Brunswick — 116. In case the Public Debts of Nova Scotia and New Brunswick do not at the Union amount to Eight million and Seven million Dollars respectively, they shall respectively receive by half-yearly Payments in advance from the Government of Canada Interest at Five per Centum per Annum on the Difference between the actual Amounts of their respective Debts and such stipulated Amounts.

Provincial Public Property — 117. The several Provinces shall retain all their respective Public Property not otherwise disposed of in this Act, subject to the Right of Canada to assume any Lands or Public Property required for Fortifications or for the Defence of the Country.

[Repealed] — 118. Repealed.

Further Grant to New Brunswick — 119. New Brunswick shall receive by half-yearly Payments in advance from Canada for the Period of Ten Years from the Union an additional Allowance of Sixty-three thousand Dollars per Annum; but as long as the Public Debt of that Province remains under Seven million Dollars, a Deduction equal to the Interest at Five per Centum per Annum on such Deficiency shall be made from that Allowance of Sixty-three thousand Dollars.

Form of Payments — 120. All Payments to be made under this Act, or in discharge of Liabilities created under any Act of the Provinces of Canada, Nova Scotia, and New Brunswick respectively, and assumed by Canada, shall, until the Parliament of Canada otherwise directs, be made in such Form and Manner as may from Time to Time be ordered by the Governor General in Council.

Canadian Manufactures, etc. — 121. All Articles of the Growth, Produce, or Manufacture of any one of the Provinces shall, from and after the Union, be admitted free into each of the other Provinces.

Continuance of Customs and Excise Laws — 122. The Customs and Excise Laws of each Province shall, subject to the Provisions of this Act, continue in force until altered by the Parliament of Canada.

Exportation and Importation as between Two Provinces	123.	Where Customs Duties are, at the Union, leviable on any Goods, Wares, or Merchandises in any Two Provinces, those Goods, Wares, and Merchandises may, from and after the Union, be imported from one of those Provinces into the other of them on Proof of Payment of the Customs Duty leviable thereon in the Province of Exportation, and on Payment of such further Amount (if any) of Customs Duty as is leviable thereon in the Province of Importation.
Lumber Dues in New Brunswick	124.	Nothing in this Act shall affect the Right of New Brunswick to levy the Lumber Dues provided in Chapter Fifteen of Title Three of the Revised Statutes of New Brunswick, or in any Act amending that Act before or after the Union, and not increasing the Amount of such Dues; but the Lumber of any of the Provinces other than New Brunswick shall not be subject to such Dues.
Exemption of Public Lands, etc.	125.	No Lands or Property belonging to Canada or any Province shall be liable to Taxation.
Provincial Consolidated Revenue Fund	126.	Such Portions of the Duties and Revenues over which the respective Legislatures of Canada, Nova Scotia, and New Brunswick had before the Union Power of Appropriation as are by this Act reserved to the respective Governments or Legislatures of the Provinces, and all Duties and Revenues raised by them in accordance with the special Powers conferred upon them by this Act, shall in each Province form One Consolidated Revenue Fund to be appropriated for the Public Service of the Province.

IX. MISCELLANEOUS PROVISIONS

GENERAL

[Repealed]	127.	Repealed.

Oath of Allegiance, etc.

128.

Every Member of the Senate or House of Commons of Canada shall before taking his Seat therein take and subscribe before the Governor General or some Person authorized by him, and every Member of a Legislative Council or Legislative Assembly of any Province shall before taking his Seat therein take and subscribe before the Lieutenant Governor of the Province or some Person authorized by him, the Oath of Allegiance contained in the Fifth Schedule to this Act; and every Member of the Senate of Canada and every Member of the Legislative Council of Quebec shall also, before taking his Seat therein, take and subscribe before the Governor General, or some Person authorized by him, the Declaration of Qualification contained in the same Schedule.

Continuance of existing Laws, Courts, Officers, etc.

129.

Except as otherwise provided by this Act, all Laws in force in Canada, Nova Scotia, or New Brunswick at the Union, and all Courts of Civil and Criminal Jurisdiction, and all legal Commissions, Powers, and Authorities, and all Officers, Judicial, Administrative, and Ministerial, existing therein at the Union, shall continue in Ontario, Quebec, Nova Scotia, and New Brunswick respectively, as if the Union had not been made; subject nevertheless (except with respect to such as are enacted by or exist under Acts of the Parliament of Great Britain or of the Parliament of the United Kingdom of Great Britain and Ireland), to be repealed, abolished, or altered by the Parliament of Canada, or by the Legislature of the respective Province, according to the Authority of the Parliament or of that Legislature under this Act.

Transfer of Officers to Canada

130.

Until the Parliament of Canada otherwise provides, all Officers of the several Provinces having Duties to discharge in relation to Matters other than those coming within the Classes of Subjects by this Act assigned exclusively to the Legislatures of the Provinces shall be Officers of Canada, and shall continue to discharge the Duties of their respective Offices under the same Liabilities, Responsibilities, and Penalties as if the Union had not been made.

Appointment of new Officers	131.	Until the Parliament of Canada otherwise provides, the Governor General in Council may from Time to Time appoint such Officers as the Governor General in Council deems necessary or proper for the effectual Execution of this Act.
Treaty Obligations	132.	The Parliament and Government of Canada shall have all Powers necessary or proper for performing the Obligations of Canada or of any Province thereof, as Part of the British Empire, towards Foreign Countries, arising under Treaties between the Empire and such Foreign Countries.
Use of English and French Languages	133.	Either the English or the French Language may be used by any Person in the Debates of the Houses of the Parliament of Canada and of the Houses of the Legislature of Quebec; and both those Languages shall be used in the respective Records and Journals of those Houses; and either of those Languages may be used by any Person or in any Pleading or Process in or issuing from any Court of Canada established under this Act, and in or from all or any of the Courts of Quebec.

The Acts of the Parliament of Canada and of the Legislature of Quebec shall be printed and published in both those Languages.

ONTARIO AND QUEBEC

Appointment of Executive Officers for Ontario and Quebec	134.	Until the Legislature of Ontario or of Quebec otherwise provides, the Lieutenant Governors of Ontario and Quebec may each appoint under the Great Seal of the Province the following Officers, to hold Office during Pleasure, that is to say, — — the Attorney General, the Secretary and Registrar of the Province, the Treasurer of the Province, the Commissioner of Crown Lands, and the Commissioner of Agriculture and Public Works, and in the Case of Quebec the Solicitor General, and may, by Order of the Lieutenant Governor in Council, from Time to Time prescribe the Duties of those Officers, and of the several Departments over which they shall preside or to which they shall belong, and of the Officers and Clerks thereof, and may also appoint other and additional Officers to hold Office during Pleasure, and may from Time to

Time prescribe the Dominion of those Officers, and of the several Departments over which they shall preside or to which they shall belong, and of the Officers and Clerks thereof.

Powers, Duties, etc. of Executive Officers	135.	Until the Legislature of Ontario or Quebec otherwise provides, all Rights, Powers, Duties, Functions, Responsibilities, or Authorities at the passing of this Act vested in or imposed on the Attorney General, Solicitor General, Secretary and Registrar of the Province of Canada, Minister of Finance, Commissioner of Crown Lands, Commissioner of Public Works, and Minister of Agriculture and Receiver General, by any Law, Statute, or Ordinance of Upper Canada, Lower Canada, or Canada, and not repugnant to this Act, shall be vested in or imposed on any Officer to be appointed by the Lieutenant Governor for the Discharge of the same or any of them; and the Commissioner of Agriculture and Public Works shall perform the Duties and Functions of the Office of Minister of Agriculture at the passing of this Act imposed by the Law of the Province of Canada, as well as those of the Commissioner of Public Works.
Great Seals	136.	Until altered by the Lieutenant Governor in Council, the Great Seals of Ontario and Quebec respectively shall be the same, or of the same Design, as those used in the Provinces of Upper Canada and Lower Canada respectively before their Union as the Province of Canada.
Construction of temporary Acts	137.	The words "and from thence to the End of the then next ensuing Session of the Legislature," or Words to the same Effect, used in any temporary Act of the Province of Canada not expired before the Union, shall be construed to extend and apply to the next Session of the Parliament of Canada if the Subject Matter of the Act is within the Powers of the same as defined by this Act, or to the next Sessions of the Legislatures of Ontario and Quebec respectively if the Subject Matter of the Act is within the Powers of the same as defined by this Act.

As to Errors in Names	**138.**	From and after the Union the Use of the Words "Upper Canada" instead of "Ontario," or "Lower Canada" instead of "Quebec," in any Deed, Writ, Process, Pleading, Document, Matter, or Thing shall not invalidate the same.
As to issue of Proclamations before Union, to commence after Union	**139.**	Any Proclamation under the Great Seal of the Province of Canada issued before the Union to take effect at a Time which is subsequent to the Union, whether relating to that Province, or to Upper Canada, or to Lower Canada, and the several Matters and Things therein proclaimed, shall be and continue of like Force and Effect as if the Union had not been made.
As to issue of Proclamations after Union	**140.**	Any Proclamation which is authorized by any Act of the Legislature of the Province of Canada to be issued under the Great Seal of the Province of Canada, whether relating to that Province, or to Upper Canada, or to Lower Canada, and which is not issued before the Union, may be issued by the Lieutenant Governor of Ontario or of Quebec, as its Subject Matter requires, under the Great Seal thereof; and from and after the Issue of such Proclamation the same and the several Matters and Things therein proclaimed shall be and continue of the like Force and Effect in Ontario or Quebec as if the Union had not been made.
Penitentiary	**141.**	The Penitentiary of the Province of Canada shall, until the Parliament of Canada otherwise provides, be and continue the Penitentiary of Ontario and of Quebec.
Arbitration respecting Debts, etc.	**142.**	The Division and Adjustment of the Debts, Credits, Liabilities, Properties, and Assets of Upper Canada and Lower Canada shall be referred to the Arbitrament of Three Arbitrators, One chosen by the Government of Ontario, One by the Government of Quebec, and One by the Government of Canada; and the Selection of the Arbitrators shall not be made until the Parliament of Canada and the Legislatures of Ontario and Quebec have met; and the Arbitrator chosen by the Government of Canada shall not be a Resident either in Ontario or in Quebec.

Division of Records	143.	The Governor General in Council may from Time to Time order that such and so many of the Records, Books, and Documents of the Province of Canada as he thinks fit shall be appropriated and delivered either to Ontario or to Quebec, and the same shall thenceforth be the Property of that Province; and any Copy thereof or Extract therefrom, duly certified by the Officer having charge of the Original thereof, shall be admitted as Evidence.
Constitution of Townships in Quebec	144.	The Lieutenant Governor of Quebec may from Time to Time, by Proclamation under the Great Seal of the Province, to take effect from a Day to be appointed therein, constitute Townships in those Parts of the Province of Quebec in which Townships are not then already constituted, and fix the Metes and Bounds thereof.

X. INTERCOLONIAL RAILWAY

[Repealed]	145.	Repealed.

XI. ADMISSION OF OTHER COLONIES

Power to admit Newfoundland, etc., into the Union	146.	It shall be lawful for the Queen, by and with the Advice of Her Majesty's Most Honourable Privy Council, on Addresses from the Houses of the Parliament of Canada, and from the Houses of the respective Legislatures of the Colonies or Provinces of Newfoundland, Prince Edward Island, and British Columbia, to admit those Colonies or Provinces, or any of them, into the Union, and on Address from the Houses of the Parliament of Canada to admit Rupert's Land and the North-western Territory, or either of them, into the Union, on such Terms and Conditions in each Case as are in the Addresses expressed and as the Queen thinks fit to approve, subject to the Provisions of this Act; and the Provisions of any Order in Council in that Behalf shall have effect as if they had been enacted by the Parliament of the United Kingdom of Great Britain and Ireland.

As to Representation of Newfoundland and Prince Edward Island in Senate

147.

In case of the Admission of Newfoundland and Prince Edward Island, or either of them, each shall be entitled to a Representation in the Senate of Canada of Four Members, and (notwithstanding anything in this Act) in case of the Admission of Newfoundland the normal Number of Senators shall be Seventy-six and their maximum Number shall be Eighty-two; but Prince Edward Island when admitted shall be deemed to be comprised in the third of the Three Divisions into which Canada is, in relation to the Constitution of the Senate, divided by this Act, and accordingly, after the Admission of Prince Edward Island, whether Newfoundland is admitted or not, the Representation of Nova Scotia and New Brunswick in the Senate shall, as Vacancies occur, be reduced from Twelve to Ten Members respectively, and the Representation of each of those Provinces shall not be increased at any Time beyond Ten, except under the Provisions of this Act for the Appointment of Three or Six additional Senators under the Direction of the Queen.

APPENDIX 2

THE CONSTITUTION ACT, 1982

PART III
EQUALIZATION AND REGIONAL DISPARITIES

36. (1) Without altering the legislative authority of Parliament or of the provincial legislatures, or the rights of any of them with respect to the exercise of their legislative authority, Parliament and the legislatures, together with the government of Canada and the provincial governments, are committed to

(*a*) promoting equal opportunities for the well-being of Canadians;

(*b*) furthering economic development to reduce disparity in opportunities; and

(*c*) providing essential public services of reasonable quality to all Canadians.

PART V
PROCEDURE FOR AMENDING CONSTITUTION OF CANADA

38. (1) An amendment to the Constitution of Canada may be made by proclamation issued by the Governor General under the Great Seal of Canada where so authorized by

(*a*) resolutions of the Senate and House of Commons; and

(*b*) resolutions of the legislative assemblies of at least two-thirds of the provinces that have, in the aggregate, according to the then latest general census, at least fifty per cent of the population of all the provinces.

(2) An amendment made under subsection (1) that derogates from the legislative powers, the proprietary rights or any other rights or privileges of the legislature or government of a province shall require a resolution supported by a majority of the members of each of the Senate, the House of Commons and the legislative assemblies required under subsection (1).

(3) An amendment referred to in subsection (2) shall not have effect in a province the legislative assembly of which has expressed its dissent thereto by resolution supported by a majority of its members prior to the issue of the proclamation to which the amendment relates unless that legislative assembly, subsequently, by resolution supported by a majority of its members, revokes its dissent and authorizes the amendment.

(4) A resolution of dissent made for the purposes of subsection (3) may be revoked at any time before or after the issue of the proclamation to which it relates.

39. (1) A proclamation shall not be issued under subsection 38(1) before the expiration of one year from the adoption of the resolution initiating the amendment procedure thereunder, unless the legislative assembly of each province has previously adopted a resolution of assent or dissent.

(2) A proclamation shall not be issued under subsection 38(1) after the expiration of three years from the adoption of the resolution initiating the amendment procedure thereunder.

40. Where an amendment is made under subsection 38(1) that transfers provincial legislative powers relating to education or other cultural matters from provincial legislatures to Parliament, Canada shall provide reasonable compensation to any province to which the amendment does not apply.

41. An amendment to the Constitution of Canada in relation to the following matters may be made by proclamation issued by the Governor General under the Great Seal of Canada only where authorized by resolutions of the Senate and House of Commons and of the legislative assembly of each province:

  (*a*) the office of the Queen, the Governor General and the Lieutenant Governor of a province;

  (*b*) the right of a province to a number of members in the House of Commons not less than the number of Senators by which the province is entitled to be represented at the time this Part comes into force;

  (*c*) subject to section 43, the use of the English or the French language;

  (*d*) the composition of the Supreme Court of Canada; and

  (*e*) an amendment to this Part.

42. (1) An amendment to the Constitution of Canada in relation to the following matters may be made only in accordance with subsection 38(1):

  (*a*) the principle of proportionate representation of the provinces in the House of Commons prescribed by the Constitution of Canada;

  (*b*) the powers of the Senate and the method of selecting Senators;

  (*c*) the number of members by which a province is entitled to be represented in the Senate and the residence qualifications of Senators;

  (*d*) subject to paragraph 41(*d*), the Supreme Court of Canada;

  (*e*) the extension of existing provinces into the territories; and

  (*f*) notwithstanding any other law or practice, the establishment of new provinces.

(2) Subsections 38(2) to (4) do not apply in respect of amendments in relation to matters referred to in subsection (1).

43. An amendment to the Constitution of Canada in relation to any provision that applies to one or more, but not all, provinces, including

(a) any alteration to boundaries between provinces, and

(b) any amendment to any provision that relates to the use of the English or the French language within a province,

may be made by proclamation issued by the Governor General under the Great Seal of Canada only where so authorized by resolutions of the Senate and House of Commons and of the legislative assembly of each province to which the amendment applies.

44. Subject to sections 41 and 42, Parliament may exclusively make laws amending the Constitution of Canada in relation to the executive government of Canada or the Senate and House of Commons.

45. Subject to section 41, the legislature of each province may exclusively make laws amending the constitution of the province.

46. (1) The procedures for amendment under sections 38, 41, 42 and 43 may be initiated either by the Senate or the House of Commons or by the legislative assembly of a province.

(2) A resolution of assent made for the purposes of this Part may be revoked at any time before the issue of a proclamation authorized by it.

47. (1) An amendment to the Constitution of Canada made by proclamation under section 38, 41, 42 or 43 may be made without a resolution of the Senate authorizing the issue of the proclamation if, within one hundred and eighty days after the adoption by the House of Commons of a resolution authorizing its issue, the Senate has not adopted such a resolution and if, at any time after the expiration of that period, the House of Commons again adopts the resolution.

(2) Any period when Parliament is prorogued or dissolved shall not be counted in computing the one hundred and eighty day period referred to in subsection (1).

48. The Queen's Privy Council for Canada shall advise the Governor General to issue a proclamation under this Part forthwith on the adoption of the resolutions required for an amendment made by proclamation under this Part.

49. A constitutional conference composed of the Prime Minister of Canada and the first ministers of the provinces shall be convened by the Prime Minister of Canada within fifteen years after this Part comes into force to review the provisions of this Part.

PART VII
GENERAL

52. (1) The Constitution of Canada is the supreme law of Canada, and any law that is inconsistent with the provisions of the Constitution is, to the extent of the inconsistency, of no force or effect.

(2) The Constitution of Canada includes

(a) the *Canada Act 1982*, including this Act;

(b) the Acts and orders referred to in the schedule; and

(c) any amendment to any Act or order referred to in paragraph (a) or (b).

(3) Amendments to the Constitution of Canada shall be made only in accordance with the authority contained in the Constitution of Canada.

53. (1) The enactments referred to in Column I of the schedule are hereby repealed or amended to the extent indicated in Column II thereof and, unless repealed, shall continue as law in Canada under the names set out in Column III thereof.

(2) Every enactment, except the *Canada Act 1982*, that refers to an enactment referred to in the schedule by the name in Column I thereof is hereby amended by substituting for that name the corresponding name in Column III thereof, and any British North America Act not referred to in the schedule may be cited as the *Constitution Act* followed by the year and number, if any, of its enactment.

54. Part IV is repealed on the day that is one year after this Part comes into force and this section may be repealed and this Act renumbered, consequentially upon the repeal of Part IV and this section, by proclamation issued by the Governor General under the Great Seal of Canada.

54.1

55. A French version of the portions of the Constitution of Canada referred to in the schedule shall be prepared by the Minister of Justice of Canada as expeditiously as possible and, when any portion thereof sufficient to warrant action being taken has been so prepared, it shall be put forward for enactment by proclamation issued by the Governor General under the Great Seal of Canada pursuant to the procedure then applicable to an amendment of the same provisions of the Constitution of Canada.

56. Where any portion of the Constitution of Canada has been or is enacted in English and French or where a French version of any portion of the Constitution is enacted pursuant to section 55, the English and French versions of that portion of the Constitution are equally authoritative.

57. The English and French versions of this Act are equally authoritative.

58. Subject to section 59, this Act shall come into force on a day to be fixed by proclamation issued by the Queen or the Governor General under the Great Seal of Canada.

59. (1) Paragraph 23(1)(a) shall come into force in respect of Quebec on a day to be fixed by proclamation issued by the Queen or the Governor General under the Great Seal of Canada.

(2) A proclamation under subsection (1) shall be issued only where authorized by the legislative assembly or government of Quebec.

(3) This section may be repealed on the day paragraph 23(1)(*a*) comes into force in respect of Quebec and this Act amended and renumbered, consequentially upon the repeal of this section, by proclamation issued by the Queen or the Governor General under the Great Seal of Canada.

60. This Act may be cited as the *Constitution Act, 1982,* and the Constitution Acts 1867 to 1975 (No. 2) and this Act may be cited together as the *Constitution Acts, 1867 to 1982.*

61. A reference to the "*Constitution Acts, 1867 to 1982*" shall be deemed to include a reference to the "*Constitution Amendment Proclamation, 1983*".